A COMPANION
TO THE
ROMAN REPUBLIC

BLACKWELL COMPANIONS TO THE ANCIENT WORLD

This series provides sophisticated and authoritative overviews of periods of ancient history, genres of classical literature, and the most important themes in ancient culture. Each volume comprises between twenty-five and forty concise essays written by individual scholars within their area of specialization. The essays are written in a clear, provocative, and lively manner, designed for an international audience of scholars, students, and general readers.

ANCIENT HISTORY

Published

A Companion to the Roman Army
Edited by Paul Erdkamp

A Companion to the Roman Republic
Edited by Nathan Rosenstein and Robert Morstein-Marx

A Companion to the Roman Empire
Edited by David S. Potter

A Companion to the Classical Greek World
Edited by Konrad H. Kinzl

A Companion to the Ancient Near East
Edited by Daniel C. Snell

A Companion to the Hellenistic World
Edited by Andrew Erskine

A Companion to Late Antiquity
Edited by Philip Rousseau

A Companion to Ancient History
Edited by Andrew Erskine

A Companion to Archaic Greece
Edited by Kurt A. Raaflaub and Hans van Wees

A Companion to Julius Caesar
Edited by Miriam Griffin

A Companion to Byzantium
Edited by Liz James

A Companion to Ancient Egypt
Edited by Alan B. Lloyd

In preparation

A Companion to Ancient Macedonia
Edited by Ian Worthington and Joseph Roisman

A Companion to the Punic Wars
Edited by Dexter Hoyos

A Companion to Sparta
Edited by Anton Powell

LITERATURE AND CULTURE

Published

A Companion to Classical Receptions
Edited by Lorna Hardwick and Christopher Stray

A Companion to Greek and Roman Historiography
Edited by John Marincola

A Companion to Catullus
Edited by Marilyn B. Skinner

A Companion to Roman Religion
Edited by Jörg Rüpke

A Companion to Greek Religion
Edited by Daniel Ogden

A Companion to the Classical Tradition
Edited by Craig W. Kallendorf

A Companion to Roman Rhetoric
Edited by William Dominik and Jon Hall

A Companion to Greek Rhetoric
Edited by Ian Worthington

A Companion to Ancient Epic
Edited by John Miles Foley

A Companion to Greek Tragedy
Edited by Justina Gregory

A Companion to Latin Literature
Edited by Stephen Harrison

A Companion to Greek and Roman Political Thought
Edited by Ryan K. Balot

A Companion to Ovid
Edited by Peter E. Knox

A Companion to the Ancient Greek Language
Edited by Egbert Bakker

A Companion to Hellenistic Literature
Edited by Martine Cuypers and James J. Clauss

A Companion to Vergil's *Aeneid* and its Tradition
Edited by Joseph Farrell and Michael C. J. Putnam

A Companion to Horace
Edited by Gregson Davis

In preparation

A Companion to Food in the Ancient World
Edited by John Wilkins

A Companion to the Latin Language
Edited by James Clackson

A Companion to Classical Mythology
Edited by Ken Dowden and Niall Livingstone

A Companion to Sophocles
Edited by Kirk Ormand

A Companion to Aeschylus
Edited by Peter Burian

A Companion to Greek Art
Edited by Tyler Jo Smith and Dimitris Plantzos

A Companion to Families in the Greek and Roman World
Edited by Beryl Rawson

A Companion to Tacitus
Edited by Victoria Pagán

A Companion to the Archaeology of the Ancient Near East
Edited by Daniel Potts

A COMPANION TO THE ROMAN REPUBLIC

Edited by

Nathan Rosenstein and
Robert Morstein-Marx

A John Wiley & Sons, Ltd., Publication

This paperback edition first published 2010
© 2010 Blackwell Publishing Ltd

Edition history: Blackwell Publishing Ltd (hardback, 2007)

Blackwell Publishing was acquired by John Wiley & Sons in February 2007. Blackwell's publishing program
has been merged with Wiley's global Scientific, Technical, and Medical business to form Wiley-Blackwell.

Registered Office
John Wiley & Sons Ltd, The Atrium, Southern Gate, Chichester, West Sussex, PO19 8SQ,
United Kingdom

Editorial Offices
350 Main Street, Malden, MA 02148-5020, USA
9600 Garsington Road, Oxford, OX4 2DQ, UK
The Atrium, Southern Gate, Chichester, West Sussex, PO19 8SQ, UK

For details of our global editorial offices, for customer services, and for information about how to apply for
permission to reuse the copyright material in this book please see our website at www.wiley.com/wiley-
blackwell.

The right of Nathan Rosenstein and Robert Morstein-Marx to be identified as the author of the editorial
material in this work has been asserted in accordance with the UK Copyright, Designs and Patents Act 1988.

Library of Congress Cataloging-in-Publication Data

A companion to the Roman Republic / edited by Nathan Rosenstein and Robert Morstein–Marx.
    p. cm. — (Blackwell companions to the ancient world. Ancient history)
  Includes bibliographical references and index.
  ISBN: 978-1-4051-0217-9 (hardcover : alk. paper) ISBN: 978-1-4443-3413-5 (pbk.: alk. paper)
1. Rome–History–Republic, 510–30 B.C. 2. Rome–Civilization.
I. Rosenstein, Nathan Stewart. II. Morstein–Marx, Robert. III. Series.
DG235.C65 2006
937′.02—dc22

                                  2005021926

A catalogue record for this book is available from the British Library.

Set in 10/12pt Galliard by SPi Publisher Services, Pondicherry, India.

1 2010

For Erich Gruen, in honor of his 70th birthday,
and for Joan Gruen, *in memoriam*

Contents

Maps

Illustrations

Notes on Contributors

Michael C. Alexander is Professor in the Department of History at the University of Illinois at Chicago. His research has focused on the history of the late Roman Republic, particularly the criminal trials of the period. He is the author of *Trials in the Late Roman Republic, 149 BC to 50 BC* (1990) and *The Case for the Prosecution in the Ciceronian Era* (2002).

William W. Batstone is currently Associate Professor of Classics at the Ohio State University. His research interests are primarily in the literature of the Republic and the ways in which modern theoretical perspectives can help us to understand how it bears value and meaning for us. He is the organizer of the Three Year Colloquium of the APA, "Interrogating Theory – Critiquing Practice." His many publications include forthcoming articles on "The Point of Reception Theory" (in R. Thomas and C. Martindale (eds.), *The Uses of Reception*) and "Plautine Farce, Plautine Freedom: An Essay on the Value of Metatheatre" (in his *Defining Gender and Genre in Latin Literature*).

Edward Bispham teaches Ancient History at Brasenose and St. Anne's Colleges, Oxford. He has published on Roman legislation, colonization, politics, and religion. His research interests lie in the history and archaeology of Italy, and his current projects include a (multiauthor) revision of Hermann Peter's *Historicorum Romanorum Reliquiae* and a history of the late Republic.

Anthony Corbeill is Professor of Classics at the University of Kansas and author of two books, *Controlling Laughter: Political Humor in the Late Roman Republic* (1996) and *Nature Embodied: Gesture in Ancient Rome* (2004). His current research explores the kinds of distinctions that the Romans made between the categories of sex and gender, and includes treatment of grammatical gender, bisexual gods, and hermaphrodites.

Jean-Michel David is Professor of Roman History at the University of Paris I Panthéon-Sorbonne. His research focuses on the social, political, and cultural history of the Roman Republic. His works include *Le Patronat judiciaire au dernier siècle de la République romaine* (1992), *La Romanisation de l'Italie* (1994) (translated as *The Roman Conquest of Italy*, 1997), and *La République romaine* (2000).

Luuk de Ligt is Professor of Ancient History at the University of Leiden. His research interests include the social and economic history, demography, legal history, and epigraphy of the Roman Republic and Empire. He is author of *Fairs and Markets in the Roman Empire* (1993) and numerous articles, most recently "Poverty and Demography: The Case of the Gracchan Land Reforms," *Mnemosyne* 57 (2004): 725–57. He is also the editor (along with E. A. Hemelrijk and H. W. Singor) of *Roman Rule and Civic Life: Local and Regional Perspectives* (2004).

Elizabeth Deniaux is Professor of Roman History at the University of Paris X Nanterre. Her research focuses on Roman society and political life in the late Republic. She published an introduction to the French edition of Lily Ross Taylor, *Party Politics in the Age of Caesar* (1977) and compiled a bibliographic addendum for its republication in 2001. She is the author of *Clientèles et pouvoir à l'époque de Cicéron* (1993), *Rome, de la cité-Etat à l'Empire, institutions et vie politique* (2001), and editor of *Rome, pouvoir des images, images du pouvoir* (2000). She is a member of the Franco-Albanian mission and the organizer of the colloquium, "Le canal d'Otrante et la Méditérranée antique et médiévale" (publication forthcoming).

Arthur M. Eckstein is Professor of History at the University of Maryland at College Park. His principal research interests lie in Roman imperial expansion under the Republic, and in the Greek and Roman historiographical response

to that expansion. He is the author of numerous articles and three books: *Senate and General: Individual Decision Making and Roman Foreign Relations, 264–194 B.C.* (1987), *Moral Vision in the Histories of Polybius* (1995), and *The Mediterranean Interstate Anarchy and the Rise of Rome* (forthcoming), and coeditor of *"The Searchers": Essays and Reflections on John Ford's Classic Western* (with Peter Lehman, 2004).

Paul Erdkamp is Research Fellow at the Department of History, University of Leiden. His research interests include Roman warfare, rural society, ancient economy, and demography. He is the author of *Hunger and the Sword. Warfare and Food Supply in Roman Republican Wars, 264–30 BC* (1998) and *The Grain Market in the Roman Empire* (forthcoming).

Daniel J. Gargola is Associate Professor of History at the University of Kentucky. His research focuses on the intersections between politics, religion, and law in republican Rome. He is the author of *Lands, Laws, and Gods: Magistrates and Ceremony in the Regulation of Public Lands in Republican Rome* (1995).

Erich S. Gruen is Gladys Rehard Professor of History and Classics and Chair of the Graduate Program in Ancient History and Mediterranean Archaeology at the University of California, Berkeley. His works on Roman republican history include *The Last Generation of the Roman Republic* (1974), *The Hellenistic World and the Coming of Rome* (1984), and *Culture and Identity in Republican Rome* (1992). His most recent book is *Diaspora: Jews amidst Greeks and Romans* (2002). He is currently working on a long-range project tentatively entitled *Cultural Appropriations and Collective Identity in Antiquity*.

Karl-J. Hölkeskamp is Professor of Ancient History at the Institute of Classical Studies, University of Cologne. He is especially interested in the history of republican Rome, its political culture and society on the one hand, and in the history of archaic Greece, the emergence of the *polis* and of written law on the other. Recent publications include *Sinn (in) der Antike. Orientierungssysteme, Leitbilder und Wertkonzepte im Altertum* (coedited with J. Rüsen, E. Stein-Hölkeskamp, and H. Th. Grütter, 2003); *SENATVS POPVLVSQVE ROMANVS. Die politische Kultur der Republik – Dimensionen und Deutungen* (2004), and *Rekonstruktionen einer Republik. Die politische Kultur des antiken Rom und die Forschung der letzten Jahrzehnte* (2004).

Martin Jehne is Professor of Ancient History at the Institute of History, University of Dresden. His main topic of research for some years now has been the history of the Roman Republic, especially its political system and social structure, but he is also interested in the establishment of monarchy in early imperial times and in Classical Greece, especially its international relations. His publications include *Der Staat des Dictators Caesar* (1987), *Koine Eirene. Untersuchungen zu den Befriedungs- und Stabilisierungsbemühungen in der griechischen Poliswelt des 4. Jahrhunderts v. Chr.* (1994), and *Caesar* (3rd edn, 2004), and, as editor, *Demokratie in Rom? Die Rolle des Volkes in der Politik der römischen Republik* (1995).

C. F. Konrad teaches Classical Studies at Texas A&M University, and conducts research in Roman government, religion, and law, and in Greco-Roman historiography. He is the author of *Plutarch's Sertorius: A Historical Commentary* (1994) and editor of *Augusto augurio: Rerum humanarum et divinarum commenta-* *tiones in honorem Jerzy Linderski* (2004), and is currently working on a study of Roman dictators.

Neville Morley is Senior Lecturer in Ancient History at the University of Bristol. His interests encompass ancient economic and social history, historical theory, and the place of antiquity in nineteenth-century debates on modernity. His recent publications include *Theories, Models and Concepts in Ancient History* (2004) and articles on demography, decadence, and migration, and he is currently completing a book on ancient trade.

Robert Morstein-Marx is Professor of Classics at the University of California, Santa Barbara. His research currently focuses on the intellectual, ideological, and communicative dimensions of late republican politics. He is the author of *Hegemony to Empire: The Development of the Roman Imperium in the East from 148 to 62 BC* (1995) and *Mass Oratory and Political Power in the Late Roman Republic* (2004).

John A. North taught some Greek and more Roman history in University College London from 1963 until 2003. Having been Head of the Department of History for much of the 1990s, he is now Emeritus Professor of History. Most of his published research has concerned the religious history of the Romans and of the Roman Empire, including *Religions of Rome* (with Mary Beard and Simon Price, 1998). Currently, he is working as a member (and co-director) of a funded project, based in University College London, to provide text, translation, and commentary on the *Lexicon of Festus*.

John R. Patterson is University Senior Lecturer in the Faculty of Classics, University of Cambridge, and Director of

Studies in Classics at Magdalene College. His publications include *Political Life in the City of Rome* (2000) and survey articles: "The City of Rome: From Republic to Empire," *JRS* 82 (1992) and (with Emma Dench and Emmanuele Curti) "The Archaeology of Central and Southern Roman Italy: Recent Trends and Approaches," *JRS* 86 (1996).

Mark Pobjoy is Senior Tutor at Magdalen College, Oxford, having formerly been Fellow and Tutor in Ancient History at the College. His interests range from Latin epigraphy and classical historiography to the poetry of Virgil, while his principal speciality is the political history of Roman Italy. His publications include articles on Latin inscriptions and the coinage of the Social War, while his major current project is a work on the history of Capua under Roman rule.

Kurt A. Raaflaub is David Herlihy University Professor and Professor of Classics and History as well as Director of the Program in Ancient Studies at Brown University. His special interests focus on the social, political, and intellectual history of archaic and classical Greece and republican Rome, and more recently on the interaction between Egypt and Ancient West Asia on the one hand; Greece and Rome on the other. Recent publications include *Origins of Democracy in Ancient Greece* (coauthored, 2005), *The Discovery of Freedom in Ancient Greece* (2004), and *War and Society in the Ancient and Medieval Worlds* (coedited with Nathan Rosenstein, 1999).

Beryl Rawson is Professor Emerita and Visiting Fellow in Classics at the Australian National University. She has written on the social, cultural, and political history of Rome (late republican and imperial), and has particular interest in the

family and in children and childhood. Her publications include *The Politics of Friendship. Pompey and Cicero* (1978), *The Family in Ancient Rome: New Perspectives* (1986), *Marriage, Divorce, and Children in Ancient Rome* (1991), *The Roman Family in Italy* (with Paul Weaver, 1997), and *Children and Childhood in Roman Italy* (2003).

Nathan Rosenstein is Professor of History at the Ohio State University. His research focuses on the political culture, economy, demography, and military history of the middle and late Republic. He is the author of *Imperatores Victi: Military Defeat and Aristocratic Competition in the Middle and Late Republic* (1990), *Rome At War: Farms, Families, and Death in the Middle Republic* (2004), and various articles, and the editor (along with Kurt Raaflaub) of *War and Society in the Ancient and Medieval Worlds: Asia, The Mediterranean, Europe, and Mesoamerica* (1999).

Jörg Rüpke is Professor for Comparative Religion (European Polytheistisms) in the Department of Religious Studies of the University of Erfurt and Dean of the Faculty of Philosophy. He is also coordinator of the German Science Foundation's Priority Research Programme 1080: "Roman Imperial and Provincial Religion." His special interests are in the history of religion in the ancient Mediterranean and the sociology of religion. Recently, he coedited *Rituals in Ink* (2004) and published a three-volume prosopography of Roman priests (*Fasti Sacerdotum*, 2005). An English translation of his *Die Religion der Römer: eine Einführung* (2001; Italian edition 2004) is forthcoming.

Simon Stoddart has held posts in Cambridge (Junior Research Fellow, Magdalene College; University Lecturer and

University Senior Lecturer), Oxford (Charter Fellow, Wolfson College), Bristol (Lecturer and Senior Lecturer), and York (Lecturer) and has recently retired as editor of *Antiquity*. He has directed several fieldwork projects in Central Italy (Casentino, Gubbio and Nepi) and has written or edited books on Etruscan Italy, the Mediterranean Bronze Age, the Gubbio fieldwork, landscapes, and the Celts.

W. Jeffrey Tatum is the Olivia Nelson Dorman Professor of Classics at the Florida State University. He is the author of *The Patrician Tribune: Publius Clodius Pulcher* (1999) and numerous articles on Roman history and Latin literature. He is currently finishing a commentary on the *Commentariolum Petitionis* and working on a biography of Julius Caesar.

Mario Torelli is Professor of Archaeology and the History of Greek and Roman Art at the University of Perugia. His many publications include, most recently in English, *Tota Italia: Essays in the Cultural Formation of Roman Italy* (1999), and, as editor, *The Etruscans* (2001).

Katherine E. Welch is Associate Professor at New York University's Institute of Fine Arts. Her interests focus on Roman Italy and Roman Asia Minor, and they include architecture, sculpture, and painting. She has worked at numerous excavations around the Mediterranean and is currently on the staff of the excavations at Aphrodisias in Turkey. She is the author of *The Roman Theater from its Origins to the Colosseum* (2004), coeditor of *Representations of War in Ancient Rome* (with Sheila Dillon, 2005), and has written articles on topics such as Roman theatres and stadia, the basilica, Roman topography, portrait and votive sculpture, and the sculptural and painting decoration of Roman houses.

Alexander Yakobson is senior lecturer in the Department of History at the Hebrew University of Jerusalem. His research interests focus primarily on late republican politics and elections and the early principate. He is the author of a number of articles on the late Republic and early principate and of *Elections and Electioneering in Rome: a Study in the Political System of the Late Republic* (1999).

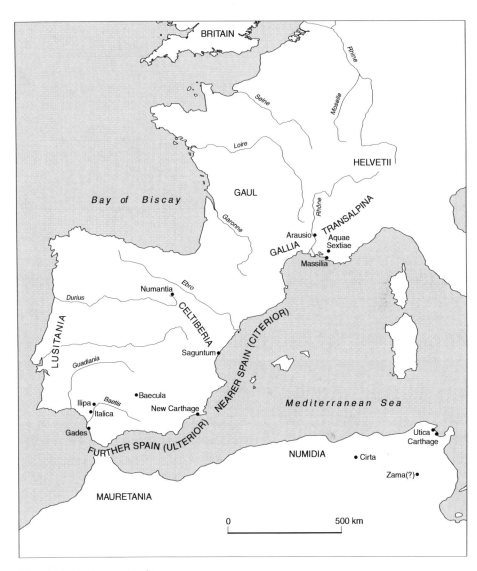

Map 1   The Western Mediterranean

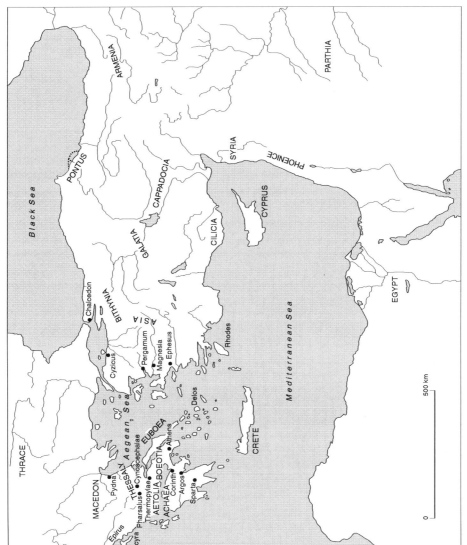

Map 2 The Eastern Mediterranean

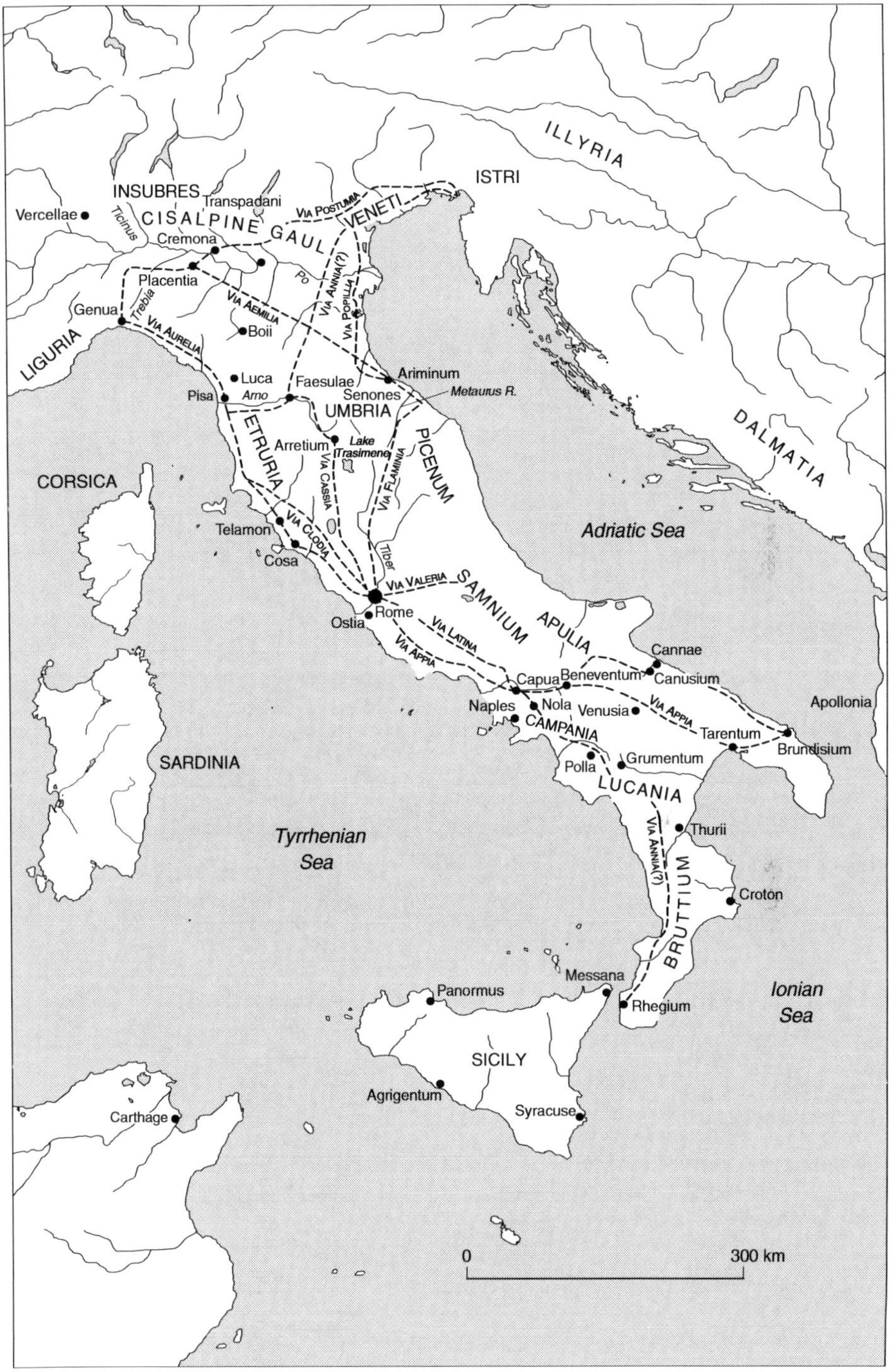

Map 3 Italy and the islands

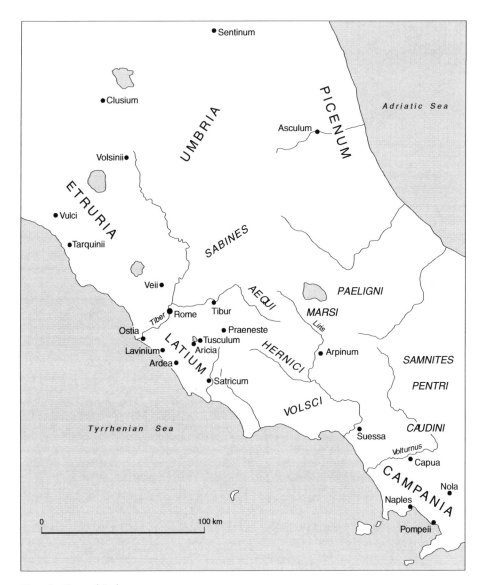

Map 4 Central Italy

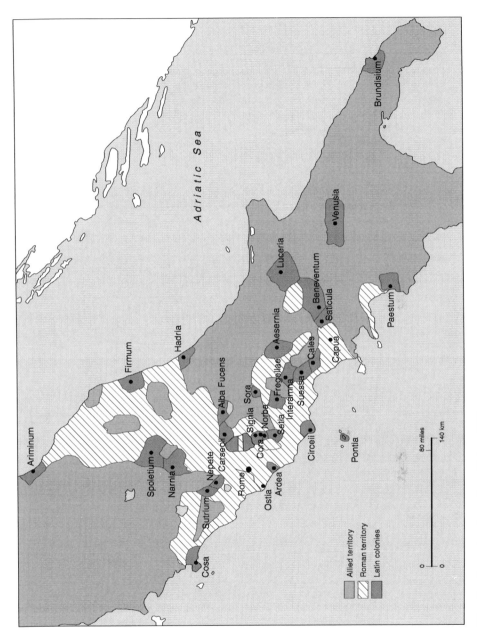

Map 5 Central and southern Italy, c.218

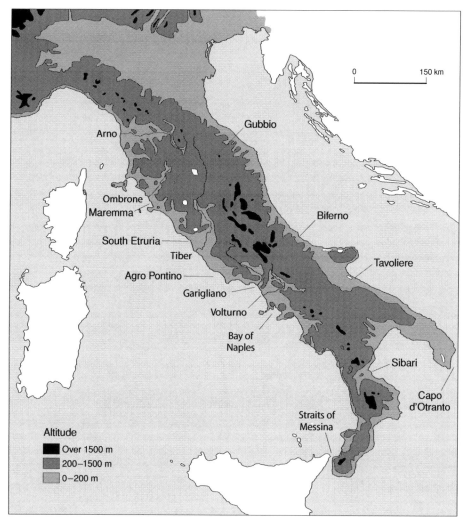

Map 6 The physical landscape of republican Italy

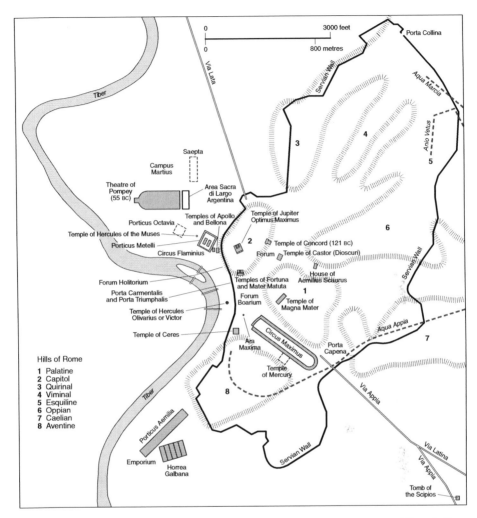

Map 7 The city of Rome from the mid-2nd to the mid-1st century. Dotted lines indicate approximate locations. See Maps 8 and 9 for greater detail in the city center.

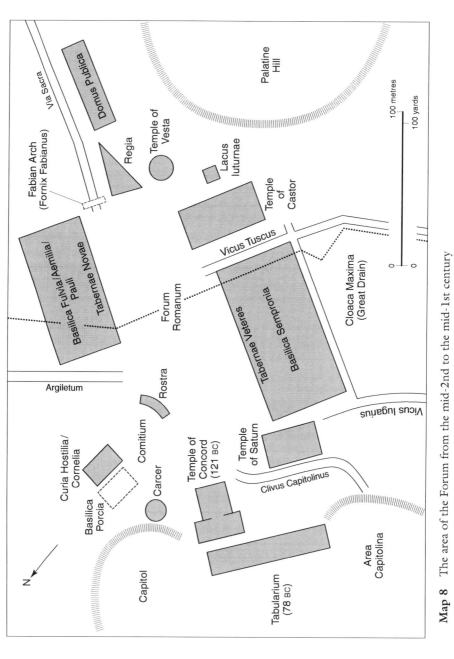

Map 8 The area of the Forum from the mid-2nd to the mid-1st century

Abbreviations

The abbreviations used in this volume for ancient authors and their works as well as for collections of inscriptions are as given in *The Oxford Classical Dictionary*, 3rd edition. Abbreviations of journals may be found in *L'Année philologique* or, in some cases, *The American Journal of Archaeology* 104 (2000), pp. 10–24. Additional abbreviations of which readers should be aware are: *DNP* for *Der kleine Pauly: Enzyklopädie der Antike*, edited by H. Cancik and H. Schneider (16 vols., Stuttgart 1996–2003); *LTUR* for the *Lexicon Topographicum Urbis Romae*, edited by E. M. Steinby (6 vols., Rome 1993–2000); and *ROL* for E. H. Warmington, *The Remains of Old Latin* (4 vols., Cambridge, Mass 1935–40), cited by volume, page number, and, in some cases, item number.

All dates are BC unless otherwise specified.

Preface

When Al Bertrand first approached us about undertaking this volume in the Blackwell Companions to the Ancient World series, in the spring of 2000, the need for it seemed self-evident. Older works like the venerable surveys of H. H. Scullard were very dated both in their overall approach to the subject and their presentation of major controversies. Meanwhile, the continuing archaeological exploration of Italy had vastly enriched our picture of early Rome as well as the Republic. Increasingly sophisticated analysis of the literary aims and research methods of the Latin historiographical tradition had heightened the challenge of confronting the great evidentiary problems of republican history. A sociological approach and a reorientation of perspective from Rome to the imperial periphery had combined to revitalize our understanding of Roman imperialism. Even the study of politics had moved well beyond prosopography and the play of factions; "political culture" had moved to the front and center, and types of evidence formerly neglected were being scrutinized with methods relatively new to the Roman historian. We felt that the time was ripe for a book that could provide students, scholars, and general readers with an up-to-date, one-volume companion to the history of republican Rome, comprising a series of essays on central themes and debates by a number of leading scholars in the field. Although we expected its primary readership to be undergraduate and graduate students, we also hoped that the volume would highlight some of the best recent work in various areas of specialization and thus be of interest to scholars both inside and outside this particular area of study. In the meantime the *Cambridge Companion to the Roman Republic* edited by Harriet Flower has appeared, boasting excellent contributions by a number of distinguished scholars, a few of whom have also contributed to our volume. That admirable work went far to meet the need just described, yet we hope readers will agree that there is still room for another book of this nature. In keeping with the generous parameters laid down for the series, the Blackwell *Companion to the Roman Republic* is considerably larger, which should allow for more exposition, analysis, and narrative over a wider variety of topics in greater depth and detail.

Our broad goal has been to present a variety of important themes in republican history as it is currently practiced while still retaining the narrative force and drama of the Republic's rise and fall. Our introductory section emphasizes the raw material of ancient history – not simply the evidence of texts and physical remains, but broader questions of the models and assumptions that scholars have brought to these artifacts, whether consciously or not, and that continue to shape their interpretations of them. The section opens with a broad historiographical survey of scholarship on the Republic from the early twentieth century up to the present. Chapters 2 and 3 on literary sources, and epigraphy and numismatics introduce readers to crucial types of evidence for the Roman Republican historian, while Chapter 4 surveys the development of the archaeological "face" of the Roman city from the beginning of the Republic to its end. Scholars are also now more than ever aware of the role that the physical environment and landscape have played in shaping the human actions that have taken place within them: hence Chapter 5, "The Physical Geography and Environment of Italy." Part II consists of four chapters of compact but relatively detailed narrative of military and political developments from the city's origins to the death of Julius Caesar. The central goal of this part of the book is to delineate clearly the diachronic framework for the distinct thematic chapters to follow, where analysis and problems of interpretation can be more fully treated. The remainder of the volume is organized under several broad rubrics intended to highlight recent research and current debates in the field. Part III, "Civic Structures," examines the fundamental underpinnings of the Republic (religion, law, the constitution, and the army) while Part IV (social structure, demography, and Roman women) surveys the wealth of studies that have enriched these topics in recent years. Part V, "Political Culture," examines the city of Rome, aristocratic values, popular power, patronage, rhetoric and public life, and reflects the important, new research on these subjects that has energized and enlarged the study of the Republic's political history. Included here is Chapter 21, "The Republican Body," which exemplifies how contemporary studies of republican cultural history are opening important new perspectives on the ways in which power and authority were constructed and wielded in the political arena at Rome. The contemporary focus on the process by which a collective sense of "Romanness" was forged out of the rich diversity of Italy (Romans and "others," history and collective memory, art, literature) is examined in "The Creation of a Roman Identity" (Part VI). The final, seventh part treats a selection of perennial "controversies" (imperialism, agrarian change, Rome's relations with Italy, and the Republic's "fall").

While the seven parts of the book group obviously related themes or types of study, readers should not allow this structure to obscure the many connections that exist between chapters that appear in different sections. We have attempted to mark the more direct interconnections by cross-referencing, but it may also be helpful to highlight in advance a few such points of contact that may not be immediately obvious from a mere perusal of the list of contents. The physical remains, topography, and monuments of the city of Rome during the Republic are discussed in some detail in various parts of the volume: not only Chapters 4 and 16, those most explicitly focused on the urban environment, but 23 (on Roman "collective memory") and 24 (art and architecture) as well. A reader exploring "political culture" or the current debate about Roman "democracy" would do well to start with Chapter 1, which contains an extensive critical review of recent work in this area, before moving on to Part V; and Chapter 23 relates just as closely with this group as it does with those in its immediate proximity. Similarly, readers particularly interested in Part IV's exploration of society should look also to Chapters 13 (on the army), 16 (city of Rome), 19 (patronage) and 27 (economy). Chapters 4 (archaeology) and 20 (rhetoric and public life) contribute notably in their own right to the topic of Part VI, "The Creation of a Roman Identity." Finally, the special problems posed by the literary sources for the early Republic are discussed extensively in the relevant narrative chapter (6) as well as, rather more briefly, the introduction to literary sources in Chapter 2.

Inevitably, some topics and issues are more fully explored than others. Certain omissions proved impossible to remedy within the limitations of time and space under which we were working: so, for example, we regret the lack of an introduction to archaeological methods and approaches to Republican history, and also of a study of the provinces as such. Yet we hope that in sum these chapters will convey the wide interest of much of the work currently being done in Roman Republican history, broadly defined. We are particularly pleased to present here the work of a number of leading international scholars who normally write in languages other than English, and we hope that one of the chief merits of this volume will be to introduce Anglophone students (and perhaps some scholars) to this important body of work.

We warmly thank all of our contributors for their good humor, mostly good timing, and tolerant submission to our occasional editorial hectoring. Those who submitted contributions in foreign languages were very generous with their time in responding to our many queries. We also wish to thank the many others who lightened the burden of bringing this project to fruition. The series editor, Al Bertrand, was responsible for the inception of this book and has remained a constant source of help and encouragement throughout its long and at times difficult gestation. We also thank Angela Cohen and the production staff at Blackwell for their responsiveness and patience. Translations of Chapter 1 by Benjamin Wolkow and of Chapters 19 and 29 by Robert Martz served as the basis for the final versions, and Denice Fett ably shouldered much of the enormous burden of compiling the bibliography. Mark Pobjoy assisted us enormously by correcting a number of potentially confusing slips in the bibliography. Finally, and most importantly, we would like to thank our families, Sara, Eric, and Matthew, Anne and Zoë, for their understanding and support through this project which consumed so much of our time and attention.

Robert Morstein-Marx
Santa Barbara, California
Nathan Rosenstein
Columbus, Ohio

PART I

Introductory

CHAPTER 1

Methods, Models, and Historiography

Martin Jehne

Translated by Robert Morstein-Marx and Benjamin Wolkow

Posterity has always been fascinated with the Roman Republic. The main reason is doubtless the enormous expansion by which the small city-state gradually created a great empire which – at least in its longevity – remains unsurpassed in the Western world to this day among large-scale political organizations that attracted quite broad allegiance. But the complex internal organization of the Roman community has also drawn the attention of later generations. Among the senatorial elite of the Roman Empire the Republic was looked upon as the good old days in which freedom still ruled (see, e.g., Tac. *Agr.* 2.2–3, *Hist.* 1.1.1, *Ann.* 1.1.1); even to the Christian world of Late Antiquity and the Middle Ages it appeared as a period of exemplary accomplishments;[1] to the political thinkers of the Renaissance and early modern age it offered inspiration for the development of models of moderate participatory government;[2] in the nineteenth century Theodor Mommsen reconstructed it as a political system based on immutable principles of law;[3] in the first half of the twentieth century Matthias Gelzer and Ronald Syme emphasized personal relationships as the central structural characteristic of Republican politics;[4] in the second half of the twentieth century the interest in social conflict intensified[5] and a "crisis without alternative" was diagnosed for its last phase;[6] at the end of the twentieth century the Roman Republic was even portrayed as an ancestor of modern democracy.[7] It is in the nature of historiography that such differing approaches and interpretations are all an expression of issues and interests specific to the eras in which they arose, for historical study necessarily draws its questions and concepts from its own time. Nevertheless, this colorful spectrum of reception demonstrates how rich a source of intellectual stimulation the Roman Republic can be, and will certainly remain.

In order to benefit fully from these perspectives and indeed merely to understand the Republic itself, it is absolutely necessary to develop models. In broad terms, a model is the ordering of a series of specific pieces of information by means of a hypothesis about their relationship, ignoring details that may be seen as irrelevant from a given perspective.[8] Such assumptions about relationships are unavoidable if one wishes to give an account that does not consist simply of isolated details. This means that every account is based on models of this type; yet even the author is not always aware of them, and even less often does an interpreter make them explicit for the reader. In the sketch that follows of the major interpretations in modern historiography of the political system of the Roman Republic (for this will be my focus, for the most part) I shall particularly emphasize the analytical models that underlie these interpretations, for only by means of models of this kind can scholars' claims to an understanding of the fundamental characteristics of the Roman Republic take shape. At the same time, models may be judged by their capacity to integrate as comprehensively as possible the basic data that can be gleaned from the sources for the Republic. Finally, one should keep in mind that a model is always selective, since it is based on decisions regarding the importance or unimportance of data that will be seen differently from differing perspectives, or indeed often also from differing historical experiences, with the result that new models will be developed. It is in the nature of the matter that no model is permanent.

The Heroes of the Past: Mommsen, Gelzer, Syme

Any attempt to come to grips with the concepts employed in describing and analyzing the Roman Republic must begin with the great nineteenth-century scholar Theodor Mommsen, who described the rise and fall of the Roman Republic in three substantial volumes of his *History of Rome*.[9] Mommsen's history of the Republic is written in a gripping style, interspersed with colorful character-descriptions of the protagonists such as Cato, Cicero, and Pompey, and driven by the firm conviction that there are historical missions before which nations and individuals can fail or prove their mettle, and necessary historical processes which it is the job of the historian to discover. The work was a worldwide literary triumph, to such an extent that the author was awarded the Nobel Prize for Literature in 1902. This was naturally due to the stylistic and intellectual brilliance of the account, but also to a considerable degree to Mommsen's relentlessly modernizing judgments adduced with great self-confidence, which made for exciting reading among the educated public to whom the work was directed (and still does among readers of today). For Mommsen, politics in the Roman Republic was the concern and creation of a dominant aristocracy based on office holding rather than blood which devoted itself for many years entirely to the service of the community and presided over its rise to empire, but then in the late Republic foundered in chaos and egoism as well as mediocrity. Thus came the historical moment for the genius of Caesar to found a popularly oriented monarchy and thereby to lead the empire to the only form of government that remained viable.

For many decades the study of the Roman Republic as a whole remained under the spell of Mommsen's *History of Rome*, but even more of his *Römisches Staatsrecht* ("Roman Constitutional Law"), in which he systematically laid out the institutions of the Roman state along with their rules and competences as well as their coordination, supported by a careful marshalling and assessment of all available sources.[10] Mommsen's extraordinary achievement of systematization makes this work an enormously impressive juridical edifice that has put its stamp on our conceptions of the Roman state to this day. However, at the root of the success of *Römisches Staatsrecht* lay an appeal not unlike the way in which the *History of Rome* had drawn its narrative pace and its cogency from the compelling premises that the author had made the foundations of his work. The nineteenth-century study of legal concepts was dominated by the idea that a state's legal system was founded on inborn and timeless principles of law whose discovery was the noblest task of the legal historian; and Mommsen, a jurist by training, proceeded from this basic conviction which he then applied to the Roman state. Core elements of Mommsen's construction, such as the all-embracing power to command (*imperium*) possessed by the king which was supposed never to have been substantially limited in the Republic, the idea that the citizen's right to appeal against the penal authority of the magistrates (*provocatio*) was a basic law of the newly founded Republic, and in general the concept of the sovereignty of the People, are consequences of the fiction of immutability with which he approached the subject. All of these ideas have since been thrown into doubt or proven to be improbable by scholars without, however, abandoning Mommsen's edifice completely.[11] This is indeed probably quite unnecessary, for, even if hardly anyone today still accepts Mommsen's conception of an underlying, immutable legal system,[12] nevertheless his immensely learned and intelligent reconstructions of the antiquarian details are indispensable for scholars as well as for students interested in how the Roman Republic functioned.

Against this strong emphasis on legal structure, which in Mommsen's construction seemed to determine the nature of Roman politics, a contrary interpretation was published already in 1912 whose influence is likewise still felt in the present: the sociohistorical account of Matthias Gelzer.[13] The basis of his argument was a new definition of the political governing class, the nobility, to which, according to Gelzer, only the descendants of a consul could belong, while in Mommsen's view some lower offices – specifically the curule aedileship and the praetorship – also sufficed. Building on this premise, in the second part of his work Gelzer identified relationships based on personal ties and reciprocal obligation as a defining element of politics and of the pursuit and exercise of power. Gelzer was Swiss, and his experience with the political conditions of small communities certainly helped him to develop a new perspective, as did also his outsider's stance with regard to the thought of the great Mommsen, a perspective he could more easily adopt than his German colleagues. But the core of his new approach, which was more widely accepted only some years later, lay in a clear emphasis upon the idea that the content of politics as well as the effectiveness of political action was essentially dependant on personal connections within upper-class families and between these and their clients – that is, citizens lower down in the social hierarchy who were tied to them by patronage. Gelzer, who described himself as a social historian and thus explicitly distanced himself from Mommsen's legal-historical perspective,[14] thereby made it possible to recognize the primacy of personal relations over policy in Roman politics. This was seen as a place in which alliances based on the direct exchange of services dominated the struggles for power in the public sphere, which were almost exclusively about personal advancement and prestige. Friedrich Münzer, starting from Gelzer's new conception of Roman politics, later exaggerated the principle of personal alliance and developed his theory of enduring family "parties" forged by means of marriage connections; in so doing he surely gave too much weight to kinship.[15]

Building on the views of Gelzer and Münzer, but with a wholly distinct stamp, Ronald Syme then investigated the transition from Republic to Empire.[16] Clearly inspired by Hitler's rise in Germany and even more by that of Mussolini in Italy, as well as by the establishment of a formally liberal constitution by the despot Stalin, Syme adopted the style of Tacitus to describe the path to sole rule taken by Octavian, the young adopted son and heir of Caesar, and simultaneously practiced the prosopographic method with unsurpassed virtuosity. Prosopography (from the Greek *prosopon*: "person") refers to the scholarly method whereby as much biographical data as possible are gathered about people of a given social class in order to glean evidence primarily about social mobility, but also regional mobility. Prosopographic research, if it is to be taken seriously as a scholarly approach, is therefore social history and not biography for its own sake. In any case, Syme was able to make use of Münzer's research and described in great depth the complex web of personal relationships connecting the members of the narrower ruling groups and also the wider upper class. In this research the central theme, which he presented with great force, was the connection between Octavian's rise to power with the entry of the leading men of the Italian cities into the senatorial aristocracy. Syme summarized the political credo that underlay all his research in the famous dictum: "In all ages, whatever the form and name of government, be it monarchy, republic, or democracy, an oligarchy lurks behind the façade; and Roman history, Republican or Imperial, is the history of the governing class."[17] Accordingly, whoever wishes to comprehend a form of government or its transformation should not concentrate too exclusively on the personalities of the leading men but must analyze the party that is grouped about its figurehead.

Prosopographical Method and the Importance of Personal Relations in Roman Politics

Only with Syme did the view laid out in Gelzer's work of 1912 – that the core of the organizational and power structure of the Roman Republic was to be found in the institution of patronage and in the friendships and enmities of the nobles (*nobiles*) – reach its triumphant culmination, from which it was to dominate scholarship after World War II. Personal relationships were now seen as Rome's fundamental social glue and the essential basis of power in the Republic to which martial success, wealth, rhetoric, communicative skill, and public representation certainly contributed, but essentially as means of broadening and consolidating bands of personal adherents. Prosopographic works collected evidence about the Republican elites and examined their relationships.[18] Penetrating case studies illuminated the background of political machinations by relating the ties and obligations of the agents and bringing into focus what was at stake for them at any one time in the relentless pursuit of power. Against a background so dominated by personal ambition and so little shaped by political substance, scholars were inclined to see in popular initiatives – that is, the policies of certain tribunes of the People since the time of Tiberius Gracchus in 133, who pushed laws through the popular assemblies contrary to the will of the senatorial majority – only a method of increasing one's personal prominence, and no deeper sociopolitical concerns.[19]

Among those who advanced the prosopographic study of personal associations, Ernst Badian merits special distinction for his numerous important contributions since the 1950s, which unfortunately have not yet been assembled in a single volume.[20] A further high point of this line of research is Erich Gruen's copious investigation of *The Last Generation of the Roman Republic*.[21] Gruen comprehensively reevaluated the unusually rich source material of the post-Sullan Republic in order to reconstruct the conflicts and struggles for power of that crucial period. His emphasis falls clearly on the political class, whose personal ties and machinations he meticulously laid open to view without, however, neglecting the broader upper class and the *plebs*. The eruption of civil war in 49 is the culmination of this multifaceted study; the central thesis is that the Roman Republic was intact at its core, or at any rate not at all at the point of collapse, but that it was brought to ruin by the historical accident that an individual by the name of Caesar, as talented as he was unscrupulous, began and won a civil war. Even if the main thesis has not won general acceptance, Gruen's book nevertheless remains indubitably a standard work on Roman politics in the last decades of the Republic (see also Chapter 29).[22]

To Badian also goes the credit for fully applying to Roman foreign policy the idea that personal connections were the main determinant of action. In his classic *Foreign Clientelae* he traced the development of obligations of loyalty which bound Rome with other communities, and which generally began asymmetrically as a result of Roman victories but at any rate increasingly manifested a clear imbalance of power in the course of Rome's rise to empire.[23] These relationships were based on the reciprocity of services rendered and consequent obligations of gratitude that were similar to the connections between patrons and clients at the heart of Roman society. In addition Badian also worked out the connections between Roman politicians and communities and individuals in the empire, which could also be described following the patron – client model. Badian thereby placed emphasis on an enormous network of personal relations which partially replaced governmental administration.

New Concepts: "Crisis" and "Historical Process"

Much of what I have outlined, necessarily sketchily and very selectively, still counts today as part of our basic fund of historical knowledge about the Roman Republic. The works mentioned above mark unmistakable advances; nobody would wish to return to the state of the subject before the investigation of the Roman elite launched by Gelzer and Syme and carried forward to such a high level by Badian, Gruen, and others. Building on this solid foundation of knowledge about the political class, Christian Meier – in his attempt to improve our understanding of why and how the Republic broke down – focused on the practice of politics and its deficiencies.[24] He was able to establish that the limited substance of politics and the great concentration on persons encouraged rather than hindered the mutability of coalitions, and therefore that the scholarly approach that concerned itself with long-standing family alliances and explained decisions as the successes of one or another party was inconsistent with the evidence of our sources, which furnished evidence for swiftly changing relationships.[25] Yet if politics was not characterized by stable factions, this does not mean that the study of personal connections was pointless; rather (according to Meier) such connections were so multifarious and overlapping already in the middle Republic that the capacity to mobilize them in any specific case was not to be taken for granted, nor in any case could they suffice to attain the intended goal: specifically, to win an election.

For the period of upheaval in the late Republic Meier substituted the concept of "crisis" for the term "revolution," which had been widely employed since Mommsen and Syme but was first given precision and theoretical depth by Alfred Heuss.[26] Yet since in the late Republic there was no new social class seeking to drive out the old elite – and therefore no class struggle – and since the civil wars were not conducted even with the pretence of bringing a different type of political structure into existence, the concept of revolution can only be used in a diluted sense, as a process of fundamental change brought about by the considerable use of violence.[27] Meier makes use of a conception of crisis as a stage in which massive problems that are also perceived by contemporaries force either the decisive restoration or collapse of a system; this is considerably better suited than "revolution" to illuminating the conditions of the late Republic.[28]

For the fall of the Republic, Meier coined the phrase "crisis without alternative" (see also Chapter 29).[29] He meant by this that at this time many political actors, if not necessarily all, were conscious that some things were not working as they should in the Republic, but that nobody knew how to repair the damage, and those who might have wielded political power in the system still felt sufficiently secure that no one had the idea of forming an entirely new political structure. Contemporaries were therefore aware of a crisis and also sensed that the crisis was fundamental and could not be made to go away with a few small reforms, but there was neither a plan nor even a kind of vague longing for the removal of the system.

As Meier made clear in his introduction to the new (1980) edition of *Res publica amissa*, his analysis of how politics functioned amounted to a new theory of political association based on the idea of extreme flexibility in forging alliances, and therefore that all remaining assumptions of similarity to modern political parties had finally to be abandoned.[30] Moreover, Meier enriched the understanding of political developments in the Roman Republic by means of his conceptualization of "historical process."[31] This refers to a model of historical change in which a definite direction of change can be recognized which is produced by the actions of individuals and groups, the stimuli ("impulses") of the "historical process." The concept of historical process involves differentiating between primary and secondary effects of actions: primary effects are the intended consequences of actions; secondary effects, the unintended results. Processual developments are marked by the predominance of secondary over primary effects, that is to say that the results of agents' actions slip out of their control. Meier argued that this was the case in the late Republic, the last phase of which indeed he characterized as an "autonomous process," that is, a development in a distinct course that could no longer be changed by the actions of any of the participants.[32] Every attempt to halt or turn back this development only promoted its further advance through its secondary effects. The direction of the historical process had become fully independent of agency.

New Methods: Comparative Studies of the Lower Class and Demographic Modeling

With Meier's reconceptualization of the Roman Republic's tendency to endure our understanding of politics and the rules by which it functioned was substantially deepened. But Meier had concentrated on the political dimension, where the senators played a special role. Although Meier had indeed thoroughly discussed the *equites* ("knights," essentially the vast majority of the wealthy who were *not* senators) and the *plebs*, he had done so to demonstrate that any fundamental reconstruction or reform of the Republic could not have originated with these classes. Indeed, according to Meier the Republic fell into the "crisis without alternative" precisely because the potentially powerful group of the *equites* could safeguard their vital interests without changing the system and the ordinary people could not really attain power despite – or because of – their partial integration into the state by means of the popular assemblies. It was partly only a natural reaction that after long years of the dominance of the political aspect as well as of research into the upper class, interest grew in the 1960s in social history, and particularly in the lower classes. But this was also favored by the general political climate in the West, where the reduction of social inequality had moved higher on the agenda.

Several works now elucidated the harsh living conditions of the Roman *plebs* and described the sometimes violent ways in which they responded;[33] others emphasized the deep fracturing of Roman society owing to social conflicts.[34] That the broad mass of the rural citizen population, which had been largely deprived of their rights, played a decisive role as soldiers in dissolving the aristocratic Republic was seen as an ironic consequence of the relative indifference of the upper class toward the interests of the poor.[35] But in order to understand better the situation of the lower classes it was necessary to investigate issues such as life expectancy, family size, the division between city and hinterland, migration, the burdens of military service and taxes, and the threat of plagues and failed harvests. Karl Julius Beloch's early interest in demographic questions had, however, initially not been taken up by others,[36] and so it was an epochal innovation when Keith Hopkins in the 1960s introduced the methods of historical demography into ancient history.[37] Scholarship at this time became generally somewhat more open to the theoretical stimulus of the social sciences, a change that I cannot pursue here in detail.[38] However, a particular appeal of Hopkins's approach was that quantitative methods of social analysis, which had been considered inapplicable to antiquity because of the very limited and unrepresentative nature of the sources, were now applied to Roman history.

The central problem, however, was a methodological one from the start. As everyone was aware, the usual documentary basis for demographic statistics did not exist for Rome, and even today debate continues as to whether the observations in our sources – for example, concerning population decline – reveal some aspect of actual developments or only about the perceptual patterns and obsessions of the educated classes from whom these statements originate. Statistics based on inscriptions are largely a dead end. Analyses of bones from individual graveyards do not permit as exact a determination of age as one would like, and do not yield precise dates of the time of burial; furthermore, there is always the question of whether or not they are representative. So there was some basis for Hopkins's radical skepticism in excluding all data that were not entirely reliable, attributing no significance to consistency with data from other sources, and essentially relying on comparison with better known pre-modern demographic developments as represented in the Model Life Tables of life expectancy, which are extrapolated by computer modeling from censuses and other quantitative data from pre-industrial societies of the recent past. By this method it is possible to generate different types of demographic development and to see very clearly the consequences of slight changes in some basic parameters like fertility rates or marriage ages. However, it is not easy to prove that Roman demography should be modeled on one type of development rather than another, and the variations are not irrelevant. In the meantime less pessimistic approaches have been advocated that do attribute some validity to the ancient evidence, at least to the extent that clues may be gleaned from it as to which pre-modern type of demographic development the Roman Empire seems to resemble most closely. Now there seems to be some preference for the employment of Model West Level 3.[39] Since in this approach the papyrological evidence from Roman Egypt takes a particularly important place, these simulations and models are oriented to the Imperial period and their details are therefore not central for the purposes of this volume.[40]

While Hopkins's use of the Model Life Tables to formulate hypotheses about Roman demography was focused on the Imperial period, his approach always had significance for the Republic since there is no reason to suppose that the relevant parameters of demographic development had fundamentally changed. This was accepted by Peter Brunt in his monumental study *Italian Manpower*, published already in 1971, in which he had gathered and carefully interpreted all of the data relevant to demographic development from 225 BC to AD 14.[41] In this work Brunt largely wanted to update Beloch's work, but he was also able to make use of Hopkins's first articles. Brunt's book long dominated this area of research; it was the standard work to consult for information on matters such as the scale of mobilization for military service, the nature of population shifts and migrations during the Republic, what was known about the age at which Romans customarily married, and the like. However, in recent years the basis of Beloch and Brunt's analyses, namely their calculation of the citizen population, has been thrown into question above all by Elio Lo Cascio, who roughly triples their figures for the citizen population of the Augustan period. The basis of his reconstruction is the assumption that the Augustan census-figures give the number of male citizens, as was quite traditional.[42] Neville Morley has recently worked out the repercussions that such a population increase since the second century, if accepted, would have on our ideas of the developments of the middle and late Republic.[43] Second-century Italy would then hardly have been marked by a drop in the rural free population but on the contrary by an increase; and this, according to Morley, makes the hunger for land and the Gracchan program of agrarian distribution much more understandable than Beloch's and Brunt's model, according to which sufficient land should actually have been available. But as interesting and promising as these consequences of the "high count" of citizen numbers seem to be, Walter Scheidel has now convincingly demonstrated that the implications of such a densely populated Roman Italy do not fit our knowledge of demographic development and, moreover, contradict some of the other evidence we have.[44] So the better solution seems to be to accept that Augustus changed the meaning of census figures by including not only adult males as before, but also women and children, in accordance with the principle we know to have been followed in the provincial censuses he established for the first time.

Stimulated by this demographic research, and also by the increasingly refined findings of landscape archeology as well as by the search for a better understanding of the conflicts of the Gracchan age and their effects down to the fall of the Republic, scholars have turned increasing attention in recent years to the distribution of property and to the modes of agricultural production and thus embarked upon a closer investigation of the concrete facts of lower-class existence. Much is in flux, and I cannot trace here the wealth of suggestions, hypotheses, and rebuttals. I might single out one new approach: according to Willem Jongman, the great estates that have traditionally bulked so large in accounts of social and economic change in the Middle and Late Republic were not the dominant feature of the Italian countryside, a massive slave population was perhaps more an urban than a rural phenomenon, and the displacement of grain cultivation by the vine and olive may instead have been a marginal development.[45] For land tenure an unusual body of sources is available in the writings of the Roman land surveyors,[46] which had already prompted Max Weber to undertake a seminal investigation. Important studies have now been published of the forms of land division and their symbolic and social significance,[47] and the rituals that attended the foundation of a colony have been made the subject of a stimulating investigation.[48] Nathan Rosenstein shows in his newly published book how the disposition of farmland, family structure, and demographic development interact, and how our reconstructions of specific agricultural forms directly determine our picture of the potential for social and political conflict. Building upon the conclusion that the average age of marriage for men was quite late, he demonstrates that for average Romans the demands of peasant small-farming were more consistent with frequent and long-term military service than had previously been thought.[49] He notes that the high military death rate also brought relief in the competition for ever-scarce farmland, and points out that the survival of soldiers also increased the risk of poverty for their families if they did not succeed in acquiring additional land.[50]

These highly controversial investigations into the size and development of the population have established an important branch of research into the history of the Republic. There is potential here to make a very considerable contribution to social history. For this purpose the most important sources are the Model Life Tables for pre-industrial societies, which alone make a quantitative approach possible; and demographic assertions without a quantitative basis remain impressionistic and of limited validity. That the application of the Model Life Tables has been accepted in general despite some criticism is also connected with a clear adjustment of goals found already in Hopkins's work. That is, the goal is not to find one uniquely valid model with which to portray exactly the structure of the Roman population. Rather, it is to assign the Roman world to a group of such model statistics in a well-reasoned manner, not in order to calculate the Roman numbers precisely but rather to produce a probable range within which Roman circumstances fell. Above all, in this way one can prove that various ancient opinions or modern reconstructions and models are unrealistic – and that is no small thing.

The Decline of Patronage as a Comprehensive Explanation and the "Communicative Turn"

Building on a better understanding of the *plebs* and the *equites* and their political significance in the capital, we were able to see the power networks and competitive struggles of the ruling class in a new light. The criteria for membership in the nobility were now newly reinvestigated, and in so doing the question of the openness of the elite was posed afresh; the scope and practical consequences of the patronage system were also subjected to critical reexamination. Peter Brunt attacked Gelzer's rigid view that only the office of the consul (also the consular tribune and dictator) ennobled a family and returned to Mommsen's position that the curule aedileship and the praetorship would also have been sufficient.[51] Shortly before, Jochen Bleicken had already made clear that the nobility for the Romans was a category of people, not a fixed group held together by regular cooperation, and certainly not a legal category.[52] This means, however, that one cannot count at all on the use of a precisely fixed terminology in our sources, particularly since social groups always have blurred boundaries. Therefore Gelzer's definition cannot be absolutely refuted by the appearance of some contrary examples in the sources' language as long as in the overwhelming majority of cases the members of consular families were counted among the *nobiles*.[53] Furthermore, Karl-Joachim Hölkeskamp has emphasized the meritocratic character of the nobility, that is that individual accomplishment, above all in political office, always played an essential role, so that descent alone was never enough, and inertia was incongruous with this status.[54]

More fundamental criticism of Gelzer's understanding of how Roman politics functioned came from research into the nature of political association or the client system. Here Peter Brunt drew from earlier studies the radical conclusion that personal connections between unequals with reciprocal expectation of benefits, which is often understood under the concept of clientage, normally did not establish exclusive obligations nor were even close to universal to the degree that would in some way have integrated each citizen into the system.[55] Erich Gruen challenged the theory that relations between Rome and the communities and states both within and without the empire were to be seen as patron – client relationships; as for the networks of "foreign *clientelae*" that on an earlier view had held the empire together, Claude Eilers has recently refuted the idea that this type of relationship was generally pervasive and dominant.[56]

No one disputes that the patronage system of the Roman Republic was important, since many resources were allocated through the operation of patronage with complete legality and in full conformity with custom.[57] But the view that political decisions both in the popular assemblies and in the Senate would have been largely determined by patronage relations should now be abandoned at last. This would clear the horizon for studying the remarkable intensity and multifarious forms of communication between upper and lower classes in Rome.

The fact that the focus upon ordinary people was now sharper inspired Claude Nicolet to undertake his impressive portrayal of the Roman Republic from the perspective of the citizen.[58] Nicolet deals with the sharp contrast between the ability of the citizens of the capital to exercise their rights and the diminished capacity of those citizens scattered throughout Italy to do so; he examines in addition the ideology of freedom and its practical consequences for the individual, and above all the areas in which the citizen was directly involved in the affairs of the community, such as the review of the lists of citizens (*census*), military service, taxation, and the popular assemblies. In this sphere, personal presence and communication always played a large role. The citizen had to position himself with regard to the demands of the polity in differing and carefully regulated contexts of communication, and in this very concrete way was integrated into the community.

In 1976, the same year in which the original edition of Nicolet's important book was published, Paul Veyne produced his monumental investigation into ancient "euergetism," the generosity of the wealthy for the benefit of the general public.[59] He impressively documented the great material and even greater communicative investment that the Roman upper classes made on behalf of the *plebs* at Rome, and showed that this behavior cannot simply be put down to social policy or bribery. Our modern inclination to interpret the motives of political agents essentially in terms of the calculation of material interests falls short here. The liberality of Roman senators was an unquestioned part of their self-representation and an essential factor in the integration of the citizenry (see also Chapters 17 and 18).

The books of Nicolet and Veyne granted central importance to communication in the analysis of the Roman Republic, and although some time passed before this perspective won broader acceptance, still today, in hindsight, we can discern a paradigm shift among models of the Republican political system.[60] So the year 1976 brought the "communicative turn" under whose influence scholarship remains to this day.

The Struggle for Democracy

The communicative turn and the shaking of the certainty that an all-embracing system of clientage made Rome into an oligarchy of patrons gathered in the Senate whose innermost circle, the nobility, largely dominated politics, gave considerable impetus for the radically new position taken by Fergus Millar. In a series of articles and books published since 1984 Millar has fought against underestimating the role of the People and the popular assemblies, and has increasingly attributed democratic features to the political system.[61] According to Millar, past research had greatly exaggerated the role of the Senate; the Senate was after all not a parliamentary body with legislative powers; in his view, the idea that the Senate played a governing role in the Republic was a fiction, and the nobility had never formed a dominant group.[62] Millar emphasized the basic facts that the Roman popular assemblies chose the magistrates and above all legislated, which was the accepted manner of validating the fundamental modifications and decisions of the community, at least from the second century. If then the assembled People were not bound by clientage to the members of the ruling class in such a way that they mechanically voted as their patrons commanded, other criteria must have predominated. Millar regarded the great scope of public communication, especially the countless speeches before the assembled People, as proof that the People and their opinions were important, and indeed that orators had to devote a great deal of effort to persuading this People, if they wished to make their mark as politicians and to pursue a successful career despite heavy competition (see also Chapter 20).

Fergus Millar's view that the Roman Republic possessed conspicuously democratic features (and perhaps should even be classified as a democracy) met with a mixed reception, but it is indisputable that Millar's model has, since the mid-1980s, provided the strongest stimulus to the debate about the political system of the Roman Republic.[63] Discussion revolves principally around three points: about the influence of senators and the Senate, the relative openness or exclusiveness of the political elite, and its collective character; about the importance of the popular assemblies and their votes in the political system; and more generally, about the significance of publicity in Roman politics.

Elite Continuity and Senatorial Influence

In criticizing the theory that the Roman Republic was controlled by a narrow elite, Millar was able to build upon the investigation by Hopkins and Burton into the rate at which successive generations of the same family reached the consulship. They had established that the number of consuls with consular ancestors was considerable (around 65 percent), but for the first time they had also clearly stressed that a series of families did not succeed in repeating electoral success in the next generation.[64] Then, in a painstaking prosopographical study, Ernst Badian presented more exact data on the consuls' lineage and found that the proportion of consuls who came from families that had already produced at least one consul never fell below 70 percent in all his periods between 179 and 49.[65] However, it is possible to draw differing conclusions from the finding (which in principle had long been known already) that many consuls of the Republic, but not all, originated from the nobility (however defined) – that is, that there was obvious continuity of the elite but no complete closure of the office-holding aristocracy, and there were certainly chances of entry for outsiders. Should we, with Hopkins and Burton, give central importance to the concept of social mobility, or, following Burckhardt, the oligarchical tendency?[66] The question to what extent noble descent gave increased prospects for success is in no way secondary; the structural determinants of unequal chances for political success inherent in any political system call for examination, all the more so those of a system with marked democratic features, which after all, according to Millar, the Roman Republic was supposed to have been. Since our fragmentary factual evidence leaves us quite in the dark about a number of important questions – for example, the number of candidates in individual elections, the subsequent paths taken by nobles unsuccessful in their political career, the integration of those climbing the ranks into political networks, and the resources of successful and less successful families – we have no other recourse than to undertake a precise examination of the consular lists marked off in periods defined by external criteria, as Hans Beck has now done anew for the middle Republic.[67] If we examine and compare discrete phases, we do not hide the changes that naturally affected entry to the consulate in the course of history behind a single, averaged figure.[68] And the conception of "symbolic capital" borrowed from Pierre Bourdieu may actually convey quite well the significance of family distinction in the political system of the Republic: a solid fund of prestige, which, however, could dissipate if the successes of a man's ancestors lay too far in the past, and which did not determine his own success even if it was fresh and impressive, but instead influenced the competition more or less strongly in relation to other factors.[69]

Millar attacked the widely held views that the Roman Republic was a kind of aristocracy or oligarchy, that it had been governed in some unusual way by a small elite, and that there had been something like a political group of nobles.[70] In fact, however, it is far from self-evident that there would be solidarity among noble families directed against ambitious outsiders, or in pursuit of collective dominance and the preservation or expansion of their competitive advantages, since after all the *nobiles* were engaged in intense competition with each other. Hölkeskamp has now made use of the theory of nobility proposed by the sociologist Georg Simmel to show how competition for office on one hand, and a consensus upon rules for that competition and against rule-breakers on the other, might be reconciled with each other.[71] Furthermore, some years ago Nathan Rosenstein persuasively elucidated an element of the collective ethos of the leadership class that had not been clearly discerned. Rosenstein observed that many Roman magistrates who had suffered military defeat while in command during their period of office afterwards continued their careers without a setback. This seemed an astonishing phenomenon in a society so fixated on war and victory as Rome's. To explain it Rosenstein formulated the illuminating hypothesis that since all the members of the political class were exposed to the risk of military defeat, they cultivated a code of conduct that forbade using such defeats as a political weapon against unsuccessful generals – as long as these had conducted themselves bravely, in accordance with the rule.[72] Rosenstein went on in another study to show that this was not a manifestation of solidarity solely limited to or focused on the nobility, but rather that it encompassed all defeated commanders even if they were "new men" from outside the circle of distinguished families.[73] The group in which this solidarity operated, that is, was that of all magistrates, who were of course senators. The essential point however is that here we come upon a restriction upon competition that was self-regulating and evidently functioned well – which proves that senators and young politicians striving to enter the Senate were in a position to establish and respect such rules.

Ultimately it is not of great importance whether one describes the nobility, the most esteemed families of the senatorial political class, as an aristocracy. Millar's objection that it was not a hereditary aristocracy is not especially consequential,[74] since on the one hand this is evident and undisputed, but on the other, the conception of aristocracy as a prominent and privileged group is not in fact tied to formal heritability. But above all the element of achievement, which is often seen as a central distinction between the modern meritocracy and the class-based concept of aristocracy, is of course not in itself a decisive criterion, since at the root of every aristocracy lies a claim to achievement, as the name "rule of the best" itself shows, except that one did not give evidence of one's capacity for achievement as one does today – by such feeble means as grades on examinations at the top universities for aspiring leaders in the economic realm, or among scientists, by the size of their grants, and so on – but by one's ancestry and the accomplishments of one's ancestors. The fact therefore that Roman politicians regularly needed to be successful in popular elections and that "new men" could also succeed in them, although the members of the ancient noble families statistically (that is, not unconditionally in every actual individual case) had considerably better chances, justifies completely our continued use of the term "aristocracy" for the core of the leadership class, without thereby necessarily making the claim that the entire political system was aristocratic through and through.

In the end one can make the idea of rule by the nobility concrete only through a two-step investigation of the Senate, first by demonstrating that it was predominant in the Republic, then by making a persuasive case that within the Senate the nobility – represented perhaps by the cadre of ex-consuls, although this was not identical with the nobility – determined policy. It is now generally recognized that neither of these propositions held true in uninterrupted and absolute fashion.[75] However it is undeniable that often it was the Senate that set the political course, and that if a threat arose to the system that gave them a privileged position the leading senators might close ranks against it.[76]

On the whole, therefore, it is beyond dispute that the continuity of the elite was considerable and that senators and Senate exerted wide-ranging influence over political decisions and the form that politics took; on the other hand, however, it is equally clear that members of the elite were obliged regularly to communicate with the People and needed to win popular votes for the advancement of their own career and their other objectives.[77] To assess the significance of the democratic features of the Roman Republic the essential questions are therefore those concerning political representation of the People and the scope of decision-making in the popular assemblies.

Assemblies

The ability of the Senate to pursue its goals and to put into practical effect its ability to make recommendations based on its authority (*auctoritas*) was essentially dependent on the degree of solidarity that it was able to develop. As is well known, however, in the last decades of the Republic there was a series of conflicts which could not be resolved within the Senate, with the result that the opportunities for popular action necessarily became correspondingly larger. John North sees here a stimulus for the democratization of the Republic.[78] However, even if the phenomenon as such is undisputed, it is still not at all clear how extensive this democratization was.[79] That substantially depends on our reconstruction and evaluation of the Roman popular assemblies, which have been the subject of vigorous discussion in recent years. In Rome there were various types of popular voting assemblies, all of which were divided into voting units. The relevant ones for our purposes are the "Centuriate" assembly (*comitia centuriata*), which was articulated according to wealth and was responsible above all for the election of the higher offices, and the "Tribal" assembly (*comitia tributa*) and Plebeian assembly (*concilium plebis*) – in both cases divided according to "tribes" (*tribus*), that is, according to regional districts – in which the remaining officials were chosen and almost all laws passed (see Chapter 12).[80]

The openly timocratic structure of the Centuriate assembly in which the consuls were elected has furnished the obvious counter-argument against accepting the idea that the democratic elements were wide-ranging; but this has now been moderated by Alexander Yakobson, who argues that the first class of voters, which was given special weight by the structure of the Centuriate assembly, did not at all consist of the wealthy, but rather of people of quite modest means; and that elections were frequently decided only in the "lower" centuries – that is, that although ordinary people did not possess a vote of equal weight to that of the wealthy they nevertheless were important and correspondingly courted, and also profited from bribery as a result.[81] Even if there are objections against some parts of this astute construction,[82] one can still hardly deny that candidates fought electoral campaigns intensively and committed all their resources, especially their financial means; that the vote of the People was ultimately decisive; and that the result of the elections at least during the Ciceronian era was regarded as highly unpredictable.[83] The question however is: to what sort of disposition among the voting population did the candidates direct this intensive commitment of resources?

For adherents of the thesis that the Roman Republic had pronounced democratic features it is precisely the enormous expenditure with which Roman candidates pursued their campaigns and in general conducted themselves in public that proves the decisive importance of ordinary people in politics and thereby the democratic character of the system.[84] However, an alternative model has been proposed in opposition to this which softens the force of this inference. Research into political culture has developed the distinction between content and expression in politics, with the help of which we are able to adopt an approach that takes better account of the symbolic dimensions of communicative and material exchange.[85] Many activities of the political class in Rome can be understood as acts of euergetism (see above) and of public self-representation. They naturally promoted an individual's prestige and helped him in the elections, and an extraordinary monetary outlay was also more or less standard in campaigns; yet such investments were made not only in pursuit of an thoroughly pragmatic end, as, for example, the election to a particular office, but they were also part of the ethos of Roman politicians. They were a necessary aspect of his role as a member of the political class, who in specific communicative contexts had to show respect to the People as formally the final arbiters, and who in addition had to demonstrate his generosity and concern for their welfare.[86]

Millar dismissed the overt, thoroughly conscious and fully intended inequality of votes in the Centuriate assembly (cf. Cic. *Rep.* 2.39ff.), which hardly manifests a democratic element, with this comment: "The significance of the graduated voting, in descending sequence by groups belonging to different property levels, as found in the 'assembly of centuries' has been absurdly exaggerated."[87] Despite his stated agreement with Yakobson's conclusions,[88] he nevertheless did not wish to concern himself closely with the elections but instead went on in his search for democratic features to the votes on legislation, that is in particular to the popular assemblies organized by "tribes," which had become in practice the chief legislative organ, and to the preparatory and informational meetings called *contiones* whose audience was not formally organized into groups. Millar's repeated emphasis upon the fact that all legislative proposals required popular approval and his derivation of the influence of the popular assembly directly from this principle show that in his model the formal rights of political institutions play an essential role; thus, to a certain degree, he stands in the legal-historical tradition represented above all by Mommsen's *Staatsrecht* (see above).[89] However, the development of historical anthropology has long since drawn the attention of scholars to the social norms of human behavior that are not based on formal law, and from this perspective we have come to recognize that if formal rights are regularly not pursued to their full limit, this customary restraint is a part of the system and not an epiphenomenon irrelevant to the system.[90] So Egon Flaig subsequently drew attention to the fact that the popular assemblies almost always agreed with the bill proposed before it, on the basis of which he went so far as to deny that the popular assemblies were decision-making bodies, defining them instead as "consensus-producing bodies," i.e., as institutions in which upper and lower classes essentially announce their consensus publicly and thereby consolidate it.[91] Scholarly discussion thus shifted to the *contiones*, the non-voting assemblies, which were comprehensively studied by Francisco Pina Polo.[92] Flaig also accepted that in the *contiones* there was a possibility for discussion of competing alternatives and thus conceded to them the power to influence decisions to a relevant degree,[93] while Millar saw in the *contiones* the place where ambitious politicians employed persuasion to prepare the ground for the later voting.[94]

Among the advances brought by Millar's reinterpretation of republican politics was certainly an emphasis upon speech as a medium in which political content was communicated. But here the fact that Roman politicians gave speeches in the popular assemblies before legislative decisions also admits of various interpretations. As Hölkeskamp has emphasized, these speeches do not necessarily imply a situation of open decision-making; rather, there are more or less fixed roles to which orators, who – as Pina Polo has documented – belong almost completely to the upper classes, and the assembled people must accommodate themselves: senators spoke and asserted what needed to be done, the People listened and followed their advice.[95] Senators in the popular assemblies adopted a fairly standardized mode of behavior, emphasizing the competence of the People to make decisions and their own dedication to the interests of the general public. This mode can be described as "joviality," that is, as a specific attitude of interaction among associates of different social status in a well-defined communicative situation, in which the higher-status agents ritually level the differences in status between them and those below them, without awareness of those differences being thereby forgotten.[96]

The symbolic dimension of political communication in Rome has meanwhile been explored in a variety of ways – for example in representational art or as an aspect of the maintenance of order in a city without appreciable policing.[97] It is therefore not absurd to suppose that in the popular assemblies the symbolic reinforcement of social solidarity may have been considerably more important than the specific content of the matter to be decided. Indeed a few years ago Henrik Mouritsen undertook a critical reevaluation of Millar's basic assumptions about those who actually gathered in Roman assemblies and partly cut the ground out from under them. Although Millar had repeatedly acknowledged that personal presence as the basic principle of Roman participation made participation practically impossible for an increasing number of citizens during the course of the Republic, he left it at that.[98] Mouritsen, however, attempted to determine the actual level of participation, at least in broad outline. By calculating the available space for the assembly and the duration of voting he came to the conclusion that at most 3 percent of registered male citizens could be physically present at elections in the late Republic, and he collected strong evidence for substantially lower actual participation in the *contiones* in particular.[99] The mere fact that in an age without microphones the distance over which a speaker could project his voice was limited sets limits upon the size of the group.[100] Furthermore, Mouritsen points out that for this reason alone orators may have been less likely to be able to express themselves successfully – or even to wish to speak – before a hostile audience, for the crowd by its noise could very easily make it impossible for a speaker to be heard. Consequently, he argues, an orator would normally have gathered about himself a group of men who were already committed, which would also explain why we occasionally hear that both a popular tribune and his senatorial opponents were each fully supported by the audiences of two consecutive *contiones*: different audiences were actually present. Mouritsen concludes that "in general the character of a *contio* appears to have been closer to a partisan political manifestation than to a public debate."[101] As Mouritsen rightly observes, Meier's idea that participants in *contiones* and especially in legislative votes would more or less have represented the spectrum of the Roman population is also a groundless hope.[102] Moreover, Mouritsen argues that the ordinary city population, which is often supposed to have been the chief constituent of *contiones*, would have lacked the free time to attend these meetings, since after all they would have needed to work hard for their livelihood and their families, and besides (on his view), it is hard to imagine that such people had any real interest in listening to long speeches on matters that for the most part did not affect them at all while neglecting their own daily necessities. Consequently Mouritsen believes that the audiences of *contiones* would have been members of the leisured class who could afford to spend their time in the assemblies and who readily supported their allies in the senatorial order.[103] Only in the last decades of the Republic, according to Mouritsen, did popular tribunes partly succeed in drawing broader segments of the population into their *contiones* by distinct appeals to their interests; but this also meant that henceforth the *contiones* were increasingly orchestrated partisan rallies.[104]

Mouritsen's arguments, taken as a whole, have considerable weight, even if he is unpersuasive in his claim that economic pressures and a lack of interest in the issues under discussion would as a rule have kept the poorer plebeians away from the assemblies.[105] His criticism of Millar's thesis that the *contiones* and legislative assemblies embodied a democratic element, and that this element was central, has however itself been scrutinized in turn and modified in part by Robert Morstein-Marx in a nuanced analysis of the *contiones*. This study focuses on public speeches, above all those of the *contiones*, a form of political publicity that Morstein-Marx considers to be an essential mark of the system. On his analysis, orators were obliged to appeal continually to the *plebs* and to respond to their feelings and reactions, so that in practice only in exceptional cases could a magistrate make full use of the formal right to impose a tribunician veto or to lay before the voters a contested bill if this was against the clearly expressed will of the People.[106] With judicious argumentation Morstein-Marx substantiates some fundamental elements of Millar's model, above all with his stress upon regular interaction between elite and mass, seen as the central buttress of the political system, and with his recognition that the expression of the popular will in *contiones* was normally decisive. But Morstein-Marx is skeptical about how far one can describe these characteristics of the system as democratic, since he considers too weakly developed a central factor that for him is essential for democracy: debate between alternative views of a problem and more fundamentally the dissemination of information to the general public.[107] On this view, the content of communication was overall so one-sidedly dominated by the members of the upper class that the interests of wider sectors of the population were addressed in politics only in a rudimentary fashion.[108]

Public Politics

Despite their differences, Mouritsen's and Morstein-Marx's reflections upon the structures of Republican politics give a sobering picture of the chances ordinary people had to shape the issues and outcomes of Roman politics in a way that reflected their own interests. Thereby they raise the fundamental question: What, then, does the indisputable intensity and frequency of public action and communication by Roman politicians actually mean for the system? If, as appears probable, the specific content of politics was often less important in the forms of public communication than the expressive aspect – if, that is, the view of an assembly was normally not formed in open discussion but laid forth in splendid rhetoric – then the ritual dimension inherent in these assemblies gains a special significance. Keith Hopkins has argued that the numerous rituals in which citizens participated were an important aspect of public life in Rome.[109] Rituals can be defined as standardized sequences of action, designed for repetition and heavy with symbolism, by means of which participants become integrated as members of a group.[110] If one views the Roman popular assemblies as rituals, then differing integrative functions may be attributed to their different organizational principles: meetings of the Centuriate assembly would then be considered rituals of hierarchy, those of the "Tribal" assembly as rituals of equality.[111] The integrative experience may have given the essential impetus to attend the assemblies even when one's own interests were not at issue in the vote. In addition, the popular assemblies may have attracted a number of ordinary citizens because they could feel important there and enjoy being treated respectfully by the great magnates.[112]

In his latest book, Egon Flaig, building upon his previous research, thoroughly analyzes the ritual dimension of public communication in the Roman Republic and seeks to illuminate its cultural significance.[113] He discusses triumphs, funeral processions, popular assemblies, and games as well as the peculiar gestures of exhibiting scars or tearful pleading. What emerges is a great array of rituals that hold society together by defining roles and by their integrative power, and which as a whole demand an enormous communicative effort from the political class. As Flaig impressively shows, the Roman aristocracy won the *plebs'* wide-ranging obedience by constant hard effort.

The modern concepts to which we should relate the individual elements of the political system of the Roman Republic take into account therefore the ritual dimension of public life, and especially need to account for the great communicative engagement of the political class as well as the simultaneously deep-rooted tendency of the People to comply. One can develop a model that will make these phenomena clearly understandable from a broad conception of institutions.[114] By this definition, institutions are not restricted to what we for the most part understand by the term in ordinary usage, namely formalized organizations like a Department of Inland Revenue or Parliament, but instead patterns of social organization are characterized quite broadly as institutional when they are made enduring by means of symbolic expression of their basic principles and claims to validity. In practice this means that romantic relationships, informal fishing groups, and television dramas are just as institutional as the Marines or Harvard University. The great advantage of such a widened concept of institutions is that it does not unduly privilege legal rules over traditional social norms: both forms are equally effective for the perpetuation and stabilization of behavior and expectations and are more or less symbolically laden, so that so far as their character as institutions is concerned it is impossible to rank one above the other. In the case of the Roman popular assemblies this means, therefore, that rules of procedure are not given more importance than the behavioral pattern that induces citizens to comply with the recommendations of the presiding magistrate. It would be inconsistent with this conception to accept any argument based on the premise that the formally secured rights of the People are a more relevant expression of the system than the fact that regularly these rights are not claimed.

Every ritual that can also be described as an institution in the sense sketched above has an instrumental and a symbolic dimension. To illustrate this, let us have another look at the legislative assemblies: on the one hand laws are passed there and on the other, community is emphasized, status dramatized, and significance experienced in carefully choreographed procedures. A model oriented in this way toward "institutionality" always keeps in view the effects of symbolic action that go along with the production of decisions about issues – effects that are for the most part much more important for the community, its longevity, and continuity (which is always something constructed) than the decisions as such. In my opinion, this approach is able to do justice to the Roman Republic precisely because it avoids the short-circuit caused by supposing that rituals that are performed frequently and at great cost (material and otherwise) ultimately demonstrate the importance of the immediate end (that is, the instrumental dimensions of ritual). An institutional analysis permits us to discern behind many speeches and fine phrases about the People's freedom and its decision-making competence a process of allocating status and binding citizens into a hierarchical community that has nothing to do with democracy.

The publicity of Roman politics has been the focus of research into the Republican political system in recent years, and will probably remain so for some time. In this approach the modes and occasions of communication are an essential issue, but also its locations and their exact appearance, for all these subtly staged forms of public representation played out in specific spaces that by their shape and their symbolic content were multiply interwoven into the event. Senators produced their self-representation (as did members of the other orders) not only with words and gestures but also with images, and modern archaeology has begun to analyze these images and their location from the communicative point of view. (See also chapters 23 and 24.) In general, the media of communication are an important field of this kind of investigation, which can be guided by the approaches taken by research into political culture, ritual, or cultural semantics.[115] Among such matters the presence of the past in the Romans' immediate physical environment is of particular interest.[116]

Even if this research moves in part in other directions and partly leads to other interpretations of Roman politics, nevertheless it remains among Fergus Millar's lasting contributions to have pushed the publicity of politics into the center of analysis of the Roman Republic. That a Roman politician had to deliver speeches on political issues before citizens, that all important decisions had to be made binding in the form of a decree of the People, that every legislative proposal had to be published in a timely manner and made available[117] – all of this had been insufficiently appreciated in earlier research. But Mouritsen hits the mark with his formulation that "the fact that political proceedings are public does not in itself make them 'democratic.'"[118] In my view, the decisive reason why it is impossible to classify the Roman Republic as a democracy, or even to attribute wide-reaching democratic features to it, is the small opportunity for political participation. The fixation upon personal participation in the popular assemblies in Rome as the sole possibility for exercising one's right to vote excluded at least three-quarters of eligible citizens even during the late Republic, when, according to Millar, the balance had shifted to the advantage of the People.[119] The decisive point here is not that only a few actively participated, which is also a constant problem in modern democracies (even if not one so acute). But the spirit of the political system is revealed by the fact that the vast majority could not participate at all, and that those empowered to make decisions never gave so much as a thought to discovering a remedy by means of a representative system: no one in Rome was interested in creating fairness of participatory opportunity for ordinary citizens who lived outside of Rome. It seems to me that this kind of regard for citizens' opportunity of participation at a rudimentary level at least is a necessary (but certainly not sufficient) condition for every democracy.

Looking at the Roman Republic from the Present

At the beginning of this chapter I briefly indicated that the questions and problems that prompt ever-changing ways of conceptualizing the past are stimulated by the particular time in which they arise. When one considers that the model of a Republic that was democratic to a non-negligible degree arose in the 1980s and then quickly enjoyed a certain popularity, one is immediately tempted to think that frustration over developments in contemporary Western democracies favored this turn. The small opportunity in practice for outsiders to ascend into the political class while on the other hand the elite enjoyed great continuity, the dominance of "jovial" rhetoric toward the citizenry while simultaneously the heavily privileged position of the elites was preserved, the superiority of image over political content, not to mention the manipulation of public opinion through the use of the media of communication (which have naturally in the meantime changed fundamentally and become all-pervasive) – all of this could bring a detached observer of our own time straight to the conclusion that conditions in the Roman Republic were really not so very alien, and that one could therefore also confer upon that constitution the honorable – if from this perspective admittedly devalued – title of democracy. Yet Fergus Millar is no resigned witness of his own time, developing a negative idea of democracy and drawing his interpretation from this standpoint; on the contrary, his view of democracy is sober but positive. For him the fundamental questions of sovereignty and participation were stimulated by the consolidation of the European Union and still more by the effects of specifically British parliamentarianism, in which a majority can make extraordinarily wide-reaching and even retroactive decisions. Millar's commitment to present-day participatory models inspired his reflections on the Roman Republic.[120]

In addition, as Millar suggests in his last book and John North confirms,[121] his reflections were for obvious reasons stimulated especially by developments within the state subsystem in which he is professionally situated: that is, the university system. In Great Britain processes have unfolded that reduce the level of participation (against vigorous resistance at first), consolidate hierarchical decision-making, and promote participatory rhetoric under simultaneously ever-tightening administrative control.[122] There certainly are parallels here to the Roman Republic, yet it seems to me that the establishment of the imperial monarchy offers an even better analogy.

Present political conditions give the attentive observer no small stimulus for consideration of the past; and indeed, the distance from ancient Rome to the modern world is sometimes not so very great. Anyone acquainted with the Roman Centuriate assembly knows well that when a vote is taken by groups rather than individual ballots slight majorities are changed to clear ones and, indeed, from time to time – as in the case of the American presidential election of 2000 – a minority in absolute number of votes may prevail over the majority. The fact that the rhetorical drama of expressing devotion to the People need not have anything to do with actual policy can be admirably observed among the orators of the Roman Republic; likewise how special-interest politics for the benefit of narrow groups can be folded into the rhetoric of public welfare. The Roman political class shows us how oligarchy can be justified behind the trumpeting of achievements and the widely acknowledged claim to their recognition, but also for how long a time bitter competition for power and influence did not exclude building consensus on fundamental questions. These examples could be multiplied, but as we regard such parallels we should not forget that the Roman world is interesting not only because on an abstract level some things were similar to today, but also, and at least as much, because many things were very different, which meaningfully broaden our spectrum of the variations of social organization precisely because they are so completely foreign to us. In the following chapters there is a wealth of material for both perspectives.

Guide to Further Reading

Since this chapter is itself in part a bibliographical survey, it will be sufficient here to emphasize a few classics and important recent work. Mommsen 1996 (originally published 1854–6), Gelzer 1969 (originally published 1912), and Syme 1939 are still worth reading for their undiminished intellectual brilliance, even if the models of Roman Republican politics that underlie their reconstructions have since been shown to be deficient in certain aspects. The books by Mommsen and Syme are also examples of great history writing of high literary quality. Scheidel 2001a provides an expert survey of research in Roman demography. Nicolet 1980 vividly portrays how the Republic appeared from a citizen's perspective. Millar 1998 offers a good introduction to public communication in the period 78–50, with exposition and interpretations based closely upon the sources. Yakobson 1999 gives a compellingly written account of Roman elections and canvassing that is full of intelligent and realistic analyses. Mouritsen 2001 is a provocative book about the Roman plebs that presents a great number of novel perspectives and arguments and stimulates thought over a wide area. Morstein-Marx 2004 takes an original approach in investigating the core question of communication between upper and lower classes in Rome; in the process he contests some of Mouritsen's findings and suggests new ways of characterizing the Republic against the background of the democracy – aristocracy dichotomy. Those undaunted by the German language may consult Hölkeskamp 2004a for a recent summary of the debate on the political system of the Roman Republic, with some interesting reflections on possible directions for further research.

Notes

1 Felmy 2001; Millar 2002a: 54–64.
2 Millar 2002a: 64–134.
3 Mommsen 1887–8.
4 Gelzer 1969; Syme 1939.
5 Cf., e.g., Brunt 1971b, 1988c.
6 Cf. Meier 1980.
7 Millar 2002a: 6.
8 Cf., e.g., Finley 1985b: 56–66 for the role of models in historiography.
9 Mommsen 1996 (originally published 1854–6).
10 Mommsen 1887–8. For Mommsen's life and work, cf. now Rebenich 2002.
11 Cf. Heuss 1944 (for *imperium*); Lintott 1972b (for *provocatio*, which he derives from the early self-help of the plebeians and believes to have been formally encoded in legislation only in 300; there are, however, some authors who hold that *provocatio* was introduced by statute in the first year of the Republic).
12 Cf. the critique of Bleicken 1975: 16–51.
13 Gelzer 1969: 1–139.
14 Gelzer 1969: 1. For the different concepts of Mommsen and Gelzer cf. above all Linke and Stemmler 2000a: 1–6.
15 Münzer 1999 (originally published 1920). Münzer's numerous articles on political figures in *Paulys Realencyclopädie der classischen Altertumswissenschaft* remain indispensable for the study of the Republican ruling elite.
16 Syme 1939.
17 Syme 1939: 7.
18 Scullard 1973; Cassola 1962; Lippold 1963; Gruen 1968, 1974; Wiseman 1971; Nicolet 1966, 1974.
19 Cf. Earl 1963; Meier 1965; Martin 1965.
20 Some early papers are collected in Badian 1964.
21 Gruen 1974.
22 Cf., e.g., Deininger 1980: esp. 86–8.
23 Badian 1958a.
24 Meier 1966, 1980.
25 Meier 1980: 174–7; 182–90. Against overestimating family alliances cf. Brunt 1988c: 36–45; also Beard and Crawford 1985: 67–8, who however mistakenly list Meier among the proponents of the faction thesis (67 n.5).
26 Heuss 1956, 1973; cf. also Wallace-Hadrill 1997: 3–6.
27 As in Brunt 1988c: 9–10.

28 On this cf. also Rilinger 1982.
29 Meier 1980: xliii–liii, 149–50, 201–5, 305–6. Cf. Rilinger 1982: 288–92.
30 Meier 1980: xxxii–xliii.
31 Meier 1978: 11–66; 1980: xlvi–xlvii.
32 Meier 1978: 34–41. Cf. Wallace-Hadrill 1997: 22 for a similar analysis with different terminology.
33 Brunt 1966; Yavetz 1958, 1969: 9–37; Lintott 1968.
34 Brunt 1971b.
35 Cf. Brunt 1988c: 275.
36 Beloch 1886.
37 Esp. Hopkins 1966/7; also Hopkins 1978, 1983a.
38 Moses Finley had done much to bring about this broadening of the conceptual framework and expansion of methodologies and use of models: as an example; see his classic work on the ancient economy (Finley 1985a).
39 Scheidel 2001a: 20–1.
40 For the state of the discussion see the highly informative and comprehensive survey of scholarship in Scheidel 2001a.
41 Brunt 1971a.
42 Lo Cascio 1994; 1999a; 2001. See the review of the controversy and arguments in Scheidel 2001a: 52–7.
43 Morley 2001.
44 Scheidel 2004: 5–9.
45 Jongman 2003.
46 Cf. now Campbell 2000.
47 Moatti 1993; Hermon 2001.
48 Gargola 1995.
49 Cf. already Rosenstein 2002.
50 Rosenstein 2004.
51 Brunt 1982.
52 Bleicken 1981: 237–42.
53 For the debate about the concept of *nobilitas* cf. the overview of Goldmann 2002: 50–7.
54 Hölkeskamp 1987: esp. 241–58; 1993.
55 Brunt 1988a; cf. Millar 2002b: 137, 145–6, 1998: 7–9; Yakobson 1999: 112–23; Mouritsen 2001: 68–79.
56 Eilers 2002: esp. 182–90. Cf. Burton 2003.
57 Cf. the judicious analysis of Wallace-Hadrill 1989a and Chapter 19 in this volume.
58 Nicolet 1980 (originally published 1976).
59 Veyne 1990 (originally published 1976).
60 Cf. Flaig 2003: 194.
61 Millar 2002b: 132–142, 165–6 (originally published 1984 and 1995); 1998: 11, 208, 209, 225; 2002a: 6, 180, 181–2. Millar's view became more extreme over time: see Morstein-Marx 2004: 7 n. 32. Cf. also for a sensible discussion of democratic features in Rome Chapter 18.
62 Millar 2002b: 86–7, 90–92, 111, 126–7, 134–6, 149–50; 1998: 4–9, 209.
63 Marcone 2002, a small volume produced for a broad audience, gives a measure of how widely accepted the interpretation of the Roman Republic as democratic at least in its essential elements has become: under the title of "Ancient Democracies" the Roman Republic receives a place beside the Athenian democracy.

64 Hopkins and Burton 1983: 32, 56–7, 64–6, 111–14.

65 Badian 1990a.

66 Burckhardt 1990: 84–8.

67 Beck 2005: 62–113.

68 The division into phases is common (cf. Hopkins and Burton 1983; Badian 1990a).

69 Cf. David 2000: 23, 33–8; Flaig 2003: 61; Hölkeskamp 2004a: 93–105; Beck 2005: 114–54, 395–407.

70 Millar (cf. n. 62). On Millar's sharpening of his objections and their recent, perceptible softening (Millar 2002a: 170–1) Morstein-Marx 2004: 8 n. 38.

71 Hölkeskamp 2004a: 85–92; cf. Gruen 1991; Rosenstein 1993; Flaig 2003: 27–31.

72 Rosenstein 1990.

73 Rosenstein 1992.

74 Millar 1998: 4; cf. 2002b: 104–5, 141. Cf. most recently Hölkeskamp 2004a: 73–84.

75 Cf. the observations of Bleckmann 2002: 231–43 on the dominance of personal ambition even against the line taken by the senate in the age of the First Punic War; cf. also Ryan 1998 on the internal hierarchy of the senate, which according to his findings was not at all wholly dominated by the ex-consuls.

76 Cf., e.g., Meier 1980: 168–9.

77 On the forms of senatorial competition and communication with the people, cf. Yakobson 1999: 184–225; Morstein-Marx 1998.

78 North 1990b: 18; 1990c: 285; 2002: 5; cf. Bleckmann 2002: 227–30.

79 Cf. also Morstein-Marx 2004: esp. 282–3, who points out that the availability of the popular assemblies might also provide a motive for members of the elite to turn against their peers, and that conflict and tension were in any case normal in the late Republic. Even so, in Morstein-Marx's view, this does not at all mean that the actual interests of the wider population thereby determined the substance of politics (281–7).

80 On the various popular assemblies see Chapter 12.

81 Yakobson 1992; 1999: 20–64.

82 Cf. Ryan 2001; 2002–3.

83 Cf. Yakobson 1999: 92–3, 214–15; Mouritsen 2001: 98–9.

84 Cf. especially Yakobson 1999: 22–6.

85 Cf. Jehne 1995a: 7–9; Hölkeskamp 1995: 48 and 2004a: 58–65.

86 Veyne 1976: 401–45 (abridged English version in Veyne 1990: 214–36); Jehne 1995b: 75–6; 2000a: 213–18, 226–30; Flaig 2003: 165–6.

87 Millar 2002a: 178–9.

88 Millar 1998: 6, 18, 203–4. Cf. also Morstein-Marx 1998: 261–2.

89 Cf. Linke and Stemmler 2000a: 7; Hölkeskamp 2004a: 19–20.

90 Briefly treated by Linke and Stemmler 2000a: 7–11.

91 Flaig 1995: 77–91; 2003: 155–74, 184–93.

92 Pina Polo 1989; 1996.

93 Flaig 1995: 93–96, 124–6 and 2003: 195–9. Cf. Morstein-Marx 2004: 124–8, 185–6.

94 Millar 2002b: 123, 136, 142, 158–61, 181–2; 1998: 219–20, 224–5; 2002a: 6.

95 Pina Polo 1996: 178–85; Hölkeskamp 1995: 27–49; 2004a: 88–9.

96 Jehne 2000a: 214–17. For the obligation of candidates from the upper class to show their closeness to the people and to beg the people for support, cf. Morstein-Marx 1998: 265–74.

97 E.g., Hölscher 1978; Nippel 1995; Goltz 2000. Cf. Hölkeskamp 2004a: 70–2.

98 E.g., Millar 2002b: 138, 161, 177–8; 1998: 33–4, 211–12; 2002a: 3, 163, 176.

99   Mouritsen 2001: 18–32.
100   Mouritsen 2001: 25, 47. Cf. also Millar 1998: 223–4, who stresses the possibility that the content of speeches was further disseminated by participants at the assemblies who were able to hear.
101   Mouritsen 2001: 52. Cf. Morstein-Marx 2004: 185 n. 108.
102   Meier 1980: 115; Mouritsen 2001: 45.
103   Mouritsen 2001: 39–45, 60–2.
104   Mouritsen 2001: 38–9, 67, 79–89.
105   After all, their only chance to experience status will have been to participate in a *contio*, in which the presiding magistrate communicated to members of the audience their own importance by means of "jovial" gestures (perhaps also at the games, although it is unclear whether citizens and non-citizens were distinguished by the seating arrangements only from the time of Augustus). See also Morstein-Marx 2004: 126–8.
106   Morstein-Marx 2004: 124–6. Flaig 1995: 93–4; 2003: 201–12 too had already argued that unpopular bills were normally withdrawn. Mouritsen 2001: 54–5; 65–7 believes on the contrary that the standard means of putting an end to popular initiatives was the tribunician veto.
107   Morstein-Marx 2004: 160–203.
108   Morstein-Marx 2004: 285–6.
109   Hopkins 1991.
110   Jehne 2003: 279.
111   Jehne 2003: 284–8; cf. Flaig 2003: 168–74.
112   Jehne 2000b: 676; 2003: 285–8.
113   Flaig 2003.
114   Cf. Linke and Stemmler 2000a: 11–16; Jehne and Mutschler 2000: 552, 554–6; Hölkeskamp 2004a: 67–70.
115   On these approaches see the brief survey by Hölkeskamp 2004a: 57–72.
116   See, e.g., Hölscher 2001; Hölkeskamp 2001a; Morstein-Marx 2004: 92–117; Walter 2004.
117   Also now rightly stressed by North 2002: 5–6.
118   Mouritsen 2001: 46.
119   Millar 2002a: 164.
120   Millar 2002a: 9–10.
121   Millar 2002a: 10; North 2002: 1–3, 12.
122   See North 2002: 4–12, who in his introductory article to a volume presented in honor of Fergus Millar offers a witty appreciation of the dedicatee's work by citing parallels between the Roman Republic and the development of the British university.

CHAPTER 2

Literary Sources

Edward Bispham

All written texts can be seen as forming a single class; to exclude, for example, inscriptions or papyri is problematic. In this chapter I shall, nevertheless, focus on texts which belong to one of the literary genres, texts which were published, copied, lodged in libraries, and put on sale during antiquity. Some, still circulating at the end of the Roman Empire, were preserved and copied in medieval monasteries, to emerge finally from the gloomy *scriptoria* (copying rooms) into the daylight of the Renaissance. Many more had perished during the Middle Ages, if not before; and others remained only as shadows of their former selves: of Livy's 142-book history, 35 books survive.

A standard sourcebook (Greenidge and Clay 1986) collects, over 292 pages, most of the sources for the period 133–70. Such a volume of material for a short period obscures, however, the nugatory survival rate of ancient literature from, and on, the Republic. Complete survivals, like Caesar's accounts of the Gallic and Civil Wars, are exceptional. Of Sallust's major work, the *Histories*, some 530 short snippets survive, mainly quoted by later grammarians interested in his archaizing language. Of Varro's approximately seventy-five works, *On Agriculture* (*De re rustica*) and five books from *On the Latin Language* (*De lingua Latina*) survive as continuous text. The histories of Diodorus, Dionysius, and Dio Cassius, although preserved fully at some points, are at their most abbreviated (by late-antique excerptors) where they cover the Republic; Polybius' history is complete for Books 1–5, a continuous series of extracts for Books 6–16, and more randomly excerpted thereafter, with a few books wholly missing. Much of what survives of the later books is what interested Byzantine readers, hence the preponderance of embassies. This is to say nothing of the dozens of authors now represented by a few fragments, or a bare name, and whom we can only know in the most indirect and capricious way, reading them as we must at the mercy of the later writers who cited them for any number of purposes which are not our own.

Literary texts are studied by, on the one hand, those who attempt to reconstruct past societies across time; and, on the other, those who examine style, diction, techniques of composition, and issues of genre. These two approaches cannot exist in isolation. A literary source is not useless to the historian just because it does not tell stories about the past: plays and poems (and history too) tell us about the times in which they were written.

My main theme, however, will be prose texts about events or individuals, past or present: that is, *historiography*. This term has three, related, meanings, in which the concerns of historians and literary experts come together: (1) the study of how history is written; (2) the study of the written sources available to us as works of literature in cognate genres (prose history, biography, antiquarian writing), and their interrelationships; and (3) the study of how modern scholars have shaped their areas of study: why the history of the late Roman Republic, say, has been written as one of "decline."

Ideological Histories

It is worth asking what (and whom) Roman history was *for*, other than Roman posterity. Whatever the answer is, we may be sure that it was not written specifically for us. Yet *our* interests and agendas, conscious or unconscious, and not those of Romans, shape the way in which we conceive of, and approach, Roman history. Consequently, we need to reflect responsibly on what we are doing and why. And this is bound up with ideological questions.

The first Roman historian, Q. Fabius Pictor, a senator, wrote in Greek, in the late third century (the previous generation had seen a Latin verse epic: Naevius' *Punic War* [*Bellum Punicum*]; see also Chapter 25). It seems highly probable, since he was criticized for his partiality (Polyb. 1.14.1–3, 3.8.1–8), that Fabius' version of the struggle with Carthage defended Rome's record, and sought to justify her imperialism. To this his decision to write in Greek may be in part owed; Greek was *the* language of historical prose at this time, in any case. His bias was a characteristic which Fabius bequeathed to his successors; it is connected to the Roman conception of the "just war" (*bellum iustum*), the insistence that Rome fought only to avenge wrongs done to her or her allies.

Roman history was, then, chauvinistic. This is partly a function of the fact that, even down to the end of the Republic, it was *local* (rather than universal) history, concerned with *Roman* deeds and identity, both at home and abroad. Indeed, it had a practical didactic value, praising virtuous conduct, and discouraging vice; Romans often understood in moral terms changes for which we would today seek a long-term social or economic explanation.[1] This reflects another fundamental characteristic of ancient histories: interest in individuals, in character.[2] The message of much Roman history was that *particular* qualities, manifested in *particular* Romans, explained success. The favor of the gods guiding Rome to her destiny was also important. Roman history was committed and political from the start. Those who wrote it were overwhelmingly representatives of the great aristocratic houses, who had taken the lead in political disputes and wars of conquest. Most were as interested in the preservation of the sociopolitical status quo within Rome as with justifying her external wars. They also introduced gentilician, or family, biases: favorable portraits of the moderate Valerii, or of the Fabii, often derive indirectly from, respectively, Valerius Antias or Fabius Pictor, filtered through successive rewriting.

Beside narrative histories there were *antiquarian* works, encyclopedic treatments of the customs, institutions, rites, and place-names of the Roman People. The scope of their work can be gauged from a remarkable compliment paid by Cicero to Varro, whose *Antiquities* had just been published. Before Varro's researches on "the age of our fatherland, its chronology, the rules governing its sacred rites and its priests, its civic and its military practices, the location of its regions and its sites, the names, natures, functions and causes of all things human and divine," Romans had been so ignorant, says Cicero, that they were like strangers in their own city (*Acad. Post.* 1.3.9).[3] Flattery, of course; but testimony nevertheless to the fragility of certain types of knowledge, and of the gaps which could open up between oral tradition and informed interpretation. Antiquarian writing might seem dry, but it was also political, and highly conservative, written to preserve the past in the face of radical political and social change.[4] As with narrative history, it sought to inculcate the values and cultural choices of the ruling aristocratic elite of the Republic.

All forms of creation of the past had ideological value; what was preserved was significant, and was meant to create matrices within which the *res publica* (the commonwealth) could be expressed by future generations. As writers disagreed about the (ideal) nature of the *res publica*, so their works took different slants. Tim Cornell puts it excellently when he writes: "[Roman historical writing] was an ideological construct designed to control, to justify and to inspire."[5] The account of Rome's political institutions by Polybius concluded with some observations on customs, designed to illustrate Roman character. One is the Roman funeral (6.53–4; see also Chapters 17 and 23), which in his opinion could not fail to inspire the onlooking youth to emulation; it is no accident that he appends a summary of the story of Horatius and the bridge (6.55), which he sees as typical of stories designed to fire the ambition of young Romans.

Polybius advocated political history (*pragmatikē historiē*, 12.25e, "political" in the broadest sense) as an aid to statesmen seeking guidance in particular circumstances. Roman writers, too, were well aware that writing and reading history could have serious practical consequences, and that thus it had to be written responsibly. Sallust (*Iug.* 4.5–6) tells us:

> I have often heard [note the importance of oral tradition] that Q. [Fabius] Maximus, P. Scipio [Africanus], and other eminent men of our community besides, were in the habit of saying this, that when they gazed upon the *imagines* (wax death masks) of their ancestors, their spirit was most powerfully kindled toward virtue. It is obvious that neither that wax nor its shape has in itself such great power, but that because of the recollection of their deeds that flame grows in the breasts of outstanding men, and does not subside before their virtue has equaled the renown and glory of those men. (cf. Polyb. 9.9)

Sallust's presentation of great deeds not only illustrates *exemplarity* as a function of history, but in a sense also sets him on a level with Fabius Maximus and Scipio: both use the contemplation of the past as an incentive to virtue. Half a century before Sallust, the senator Sempronius Asellio wrote criticizing the bare lists of events which seem to have lain at heart of much earlier history: "books of *annales* [as opposed to proper history, see below] are completely unable to move men to be quicker to defend the *res publica* or to be slower off the mark when it comes to acting wrongly" (frag. 2 Peter = Gell. *NA* 5.18. 9).

A Late Bloom . . .

From at least the fourth century annual records of important events were kept by the chief priests; *narrative history* begins only with Fabius Pictor in c.200. Rome was already more than half a millennium old by the time Pictor picked up his stylus. This gap between early events and their first record poses very important questions about the nature of our sources, and the basis on which the gap was filled.

One has little sense that Roman writers were aware of this problem. Working from the (now lost) texts of their predecessors, Livy and Dionysius, hardly uncritical copyists, were shielded from the worst effects of the epistemic gap; for them the problem was no longer finding something to say, but how best to say it. At times, however, they register divergences in the material before them, and display uncertainty about the route forward. Faced with one such discrepancy, Livy (8.40.4–5) not only shows himself aware of the unreliability of information about both individuals and public affairs deriving from self-aggrandizing gentilician sources, such as *laudationes* (funeral eulogies), but significantly adds: "Nor is there extant any writer contemporary with those times on whom reliance may be placed as a sure enough authority" (see also Cic. *Brut.* 61 on *laudationes*). Dionysius (*Ant. Rom.* 1.6.2) saw the first Roman historians as treating "summarily" the period between the foundation of the city and their own times – for the latter he conceded that they were accurate witnesses.

A number of sources for early events may have been available to the first Roman historians (and their successors; see also Chapter 23). Some were exploited: now lost Greek writers like Timaeus of Tauromenion contributed to Roman tradition from at least the fourth century onward; their accounts were not always full or well informed, and their influence is hard to measure.

Turning to domestic sources, we have alluded to the *annales maximi*, annual records on whitened boards kept by the *pontifex maximus* (chief priest): these certainly recorded natural disasters and prodigies, and very probably the important events of the year.[6] Individual boards were probably headed by the names of the eponymous magistrates; perhaps it was this which allowed Polybius to calculate the foundation date of Rome from them (Dion. Hal. *Ant. Rom.* 1.74.3). Cato implies that it was common for historians to reproduce the kind of material found in the *annales maximi* (which he calls the "tablet kept with the *pontifex*"), but rejects this type of writing himself (so, too, Sempronius Asellio (frag. 1 Peter = Gell. *NA* 5.18.7), criticizing its lack of explanatory power; and Cicero (*loc. cit.*) on stylistic grounds). Cicero (*loc. cit.*) tells us that the record ceased to be kept up in the later second century; moreover, he writes about the *annales maximi* in terms which suggest that already by the late 90s they were poorly known.

Nevertheless, both Cato and Cicero suggest that the *annales maximi* influenced Roman historiography. Indeed, a number of authors purport to cite them; and Livy reports prodigies, corn shortages, and pestilences which seem to fit Cato's characterization of them. Yet strong cases have been made that (a) almost all the "fragments" of the *annales maximi* quoted in later writers are from a published *Augustan* edition and have nothing to do with the republican *annales maximi* (which no ancient source claims were published); and (b) that Livy's prodigy notices often do *not* seem to derive from the *annales maximi*.[7] Their influence seems in fact to be limited to the uneven persistence of a bare, unadorned style (it is impossible to say whether this was an epiphenomenon or a defining characteristic of the genre); and the sense that Roman history was properly told on a year-by-year basis, *annalistically* (see below). Beyond this everything is conjecture; modern reconstructions should all be treated with caution.[8]

As for other documentary evidence, inscriptions seem to have been little used. Polybius got Roman experts to translate for him an early treaty between Rome and Carthage (3.22.4–13, 3.33.18, 3.56.4); Licinius Macer used inscribed treaties and "archival" material (the "linen books," Livy 4.17.1–12); both were unusual. Many early inscriptions were probably unrewardingly brief, yet there was one extensive fifth-century document, which would have provided material on institutions and society, although there is little sign that attempts were made to exploit it until the late Republic. This is the Twelve Tables, a series of legal regulations now known only as a series of disembodied quotations in later writers (see also Chapter 11). The disengagement of original elements from the contexts in which, and purposes for which, later writers quote them, is highly problematic.[9] However, we do begin to get a sense of archaic attitudes to matters like inheritance, family structures, property and funerals, as well as the how trials and penalties operated. By the late Republic the Tables were already obscure: Cicero (*Leg.* 2.59) records uncertainty already in the second century as to whether *lessum* meant lamentation or a mourning garment.

In Livy's day lists of all consuls since the start of the Republic and of all generals since Romulus who had celebrated a triumph (the *fasti*) were displayed in the Forum Romanum. Similar consular lists provided the skeleton on which Livy and other writers built their annalistic narratives. Each year was designated by the names of the consuls (e.g., Livy 2.1.1); beginning with their entry into office, military and political events (in which the consuls necessarily took the lead) were recorded for each year.[10] Of course, especially in later books, events were not always so obliging as to limit themselves to a single year, and Livy often has to break off campaign narratives, for example, and resume them under new management. A structural division between internal and external affairs (*domi militiaeque*) characteristic of annalistic writing further complicated matters. Yet Livy exploits this chopping and changing to achieve *variatio* (variety) in the shifting of scene and tone, enlivening the narrative. Indeed, he displays great skill in passing smoothly from one episode to another, often in contrast to more abrupt transitions in Polybius.[11]

Was this how it worked earlier? Livy's fragmentary predecessors are usually referred to as "annalists"; this ought to be a verdict on the structure of their works, but the term has become pejorative, evoking their supposed faults. But did they write annalistically? Cassius Hemina and Calpurnius Piso in the late second century almost certainly did. They were not the first: Ennius in his epic poem (suggestively called *Annales*), published before the middle of the second century, seems to have introduced at least some years with reference to the new consuls (340 Skutsch; cf. 290 Skutsch), and probably did so systematically. What of the first historians? The first three books of Cato's *Origines*, which covered the earliest history of Rome and of Italy, were ill suited to such a structure (see also Chapter 25). As for Pictor, even if he had *fasti* available, and drew on them, we still do not know whether they were in any sense official, or preserved (and probably doctored) by individual families. Nor is it certain how far back such a list would be accurate; some scholars accept entries in Augustan lists only from the late fourth, or even the early third, century onward. For the fifth and fourth centuries, both the disagreements of surviving writers (Diodorus, Livy, e.g., 2.21.4, 4.23.1–3, and 4.17.1–12, Dionysius), and references to rival consular lists (from Calpurnius Piso onwards, e.g., frag. 26 Peter), show that the early *fasti* were already disputed in antiquity. In short, it is not certain whether the narratives of the early historians were shaped by *fasti*, or instead shaped the *fasti* themselves (see also Chapter 6).

Beside these various documentary sources ran a multiplicity of oral traditions: versions of myths; family stories and *laudationes*; plays at religious festivals (the *ludi scaenici*); and Greek techniques of aetiology and etymology. These latter explained, respectively, how, for example, a ritual had come to be the way it was; and what old institutions meant, based on the supposed derivation of their names. Such ways of thinking, ostensibly explaining the present with reference to the past, also offered, in the conservative cultural climate of republican Rome, a means of using the present "logically" to construct the past.

Scholars have long debated the possible influence on early Roman historians of historical "lays" performed at banquets, mentioned by Cato: "and would that there survived those songs, which, in the many centuries before his time were regularly sung at banquets by individual diners in praise of famous men, as Cato recorded in the *Origines*."[12] Cato probably means that the practice did not continue into his own time. Its existence must have been something to which oral tradition itself alerted him, although such songs may have still been sung in the time of Fabius Pictor.

Early Roman history was built on slender foundations. Attempts to write narrative history involved, from the beginning, considerable willingness to invent and to embroider. Our sources are very interested in the foundation of the city and the regal period. After all, the city's origins might be thought to encode much crucial to her identity and her success; yet the interpretation of these strands of tradition is controversial and difficult (see also Chapter 6). The end of the monarchy and the foundation of the Republic are no less problematic. The very character of the Republic was epitomized in the story of the expulsion of the kings; yet variant traditions (Pliny *HN* 34.139; Tac. *Hist.* 3.72) attesting to a *capture* of the city by Lars Porsenna after the expulsion of Tarquinius Superbus (contradicting stories like Horatius and the bridge) at least make it probable that the transition from monarchy to Republic was much more messy than the canonical account suggests.

For the fifth century, and much of the fourth, successive generations of Roman historians must have embellished a scrappy outline of events, by elaborating, inventing, retrojecting, and reproducing individual episodes. We can glimpse the thinness of what the first historians had to go on for this period. Livy (2.16.1) begins a year with the names of the consuls: "Marcus Valerius and P. Postumius were the consuls. In this year war was successfully waged with the Sabines. The consuls triumphed"; this represents half of the entry for this year; such bald entries were later seen as characteristic of the early *annales*. Yet Livy managed to find four books' worth of material between the expulsion of the kings and the fourth century (he used a whole decade (ten books) to relate the Hannibalic War, which lasted 16 years). His contemporary Dionysius was able to write up a much fuller account. His account of the year (503), so briefly described by Livy, is some forty times longer; and he took eight books to get from the start of the Republic to the late fourth century. Yet this represented something of a crash-diet when compared to some late Republican excesses: in the last decades of the second century Cn. Gellius took 15 books for the same period!

Ernst Badian coined the phrase "expansion of the past" for this phenomenon.[13] It is important to remember also that, as time went on, information was also being lost: Plutarch (*Num.* 1) mentions a "Klodios," who claimed that the destruction of Rome by the Gauls in 386 had destroyed all records, making firm pronouncements about the preceding period impossible. Klodios is probably the Sullan historian Claudius Quadrigarius: no fragments of his work refer to this disputed period, and in Book 1 he had already reached the Samnite Wars (fourth to third century). Roman history could also suffer from hemorrhages. Yet despite all these uncertainties and distortions, many historians would accept the existence in some form of a "hard core" of "facts," the skeleton onto which oral tradition, and writers from Fabius onwards, put flesh.[14]

Later historians could also *omit* or *alter* material in earlier writers, in order to make a point. A good example is the duel of Manlius Torquatus with the Gaul in 361 (Livy 7.10.2–14); we can compare Livy's version with that of Claudius Quadrigarius (frag. 10b Peter = Gell. *NA* 9.13). In Livy, Manlius will not fight without his commander's permission, highlighting his dutiful obedience (*disciplina*) – a favorite Livian virtue; where Claudius had the Gaul naked, Livy has him brightly clad; before the engagement Claudius has the Gaul stick his tongue out to taunt Manlius, something Livy can barely bring himself to report; afterwards, Claudius had the victorious Manlius cut off the Gaul's head, but in Livy only the necklace or torque is removed (giving Manlius his *cognomen* [surname)] Torquatus) – and no other damage is done to the body.

Making a Roman Past

What sources exist for which events, and how should they be assessed? Let us answer this question by taking three not entirely arbitrary time slices through the Roman Republic.

Beginnings: c.510–264

Our picture of this period is defined by two Augustan sources, Livy and Dionysius of Halicarnassus. Livy's account is preserved complete until 292, after which we have to rely on late, brief, sometimes garbled, summaries (*Periochae*). Dionysius' 20-book history covered the period until 264, and its value increases for the period after Livy's narrative breaks off; but the last nine books, covering the years 447 onward, are highly fragmentary. From these writers an almost seamless narrative is often synthesized.

Livy (64 BC–AD 12) came from Patavium, a rich town in northern Italy. His work became an instant classic, with the result that his predecessors became little read. Livy was well aware of the poetic or saga-like quality of much of his first five books (1. pref. 6, 3.10.8), and he took the opportunity of Rome's recovery after the Gallic sack to write a second preface, signaling a transition to "more famous and more certain matters" (6.1.3). Yet even the hero of this part of the narrative, Furius Camillus, has long been suspected as more myth than reality. Livy's portrayal of Camillus' role in the refoundation of Rome after the Gallic sack is structured and placed in the narrative in such a way as to make it anticipate an Augustus "refoundation" of Rome.[15] Livy can be read as Augustan as much as he can as the culmination of a Republican historical tradition. Yet it would be simplistic to present Livy as a mouthpiece for Augustus' propaganda.[16] The values which he advocates (chastity, austerity, piety) were republican, and his support for political moderation, restraint, and consensus owes something to the ideas of Cicero as well as to the political climate of Augustan Rome.

Dionysius, a Greek rhetorician active at Rome and a contemporary of Livy, wrote on literary and rhetorical topics as well as history. He contended in the latter that Rome was a Greek *polis*, in terms of its foundation and its original customs and institutions. The thesis is absurd, but it is based on an impressive knowledge of history, ritual, and custom in early Rome, deriving from critical reading of a wide selection of Greek and Roman writers (from whom he provides some extensive citations) and his own observations. He is a valuable source; his evidence is not lightly to be rejected. Yet, as we have seen, even more so than Livy he expands a very bare record, leaving no rhetorician's trick neglected in the search for plausible padding.

These two accounts do not differ much in essentials. Not so Diodorus Siculus, who published his universal history in Greek, probably in the 30s. The first 20 books (to 302) are virtually complete, but his preference for Greek affairs leaves little room for Roman material. His reputation is mixed: he seems to have followed a single source for long stretches, and his quality varies with that of the source. Yet he is not perhaps as trifling a literary figure as often portrayed: much of the emphasis on morality may be his own.[17] Many later writers like Diodorus are now being taken seriously by scholars, and given credit for their own historical visions, instead of being seen as professional manglers of earlier "serious" writers. His chronology is uncertain in places, partly a result of combining Athenian and Roman dates (their respective years began in different months), and then trying to fit the whole into the standard Hellenistic chronological framework, the four-yearly Olympiad cycle. No book is preserved in full after book 20; here it seems he used a Roman source for Roman affairs, perhaps one of the older Roman historians, before turning to Polybius, and this possibility gives added value to his notices on Roman wars, and his heterodox early consular *fasti*.

For the fifth century, and much of the fourth, a healthy skepticism about all but the essentials of the narratives is warranted. From Book 8 Livy's account becomes richer in plausible-looking detail. It can be supplemented, and indeed – for matters like the development of Roman society and religious and political institutions – corrected, from antiquarian material; and from authors like Plutarch, a Greek philosopher active under Trajan and Hadrian, and Pliny the Elder, whose encyclopedic, if not always photographic, memory of much Roman literature informs his *Natural History*, dedicated to the future emperor Titus.

Expansion, 264–146

The start of the First Punic War probably lay only a decade before the birth of Fabius Pictor, who could question men of his father's and grandfather's generations about it. More recent events he had lived through, and as we have seen, Dionysius was satisfied with his accuracy here (which does not allow us to take anything on trust!). Reliable information could in theory have been transmitted to surviving writers like Polybius.

Polybius (c.200–c.118) was a leading statesman in the Achaean League, a major Greek power, in the second quarter of the third century. He wrote to explain to Greeks the meteoric rise to hegemony of Rome between the outbreak of the Hannibalic War and the battle of Pydna (168), which brought together regions which had hitherto only sporadically interacted into a new imperial world (*oikoumenê*) – a control of space and time mirrored in Polybius' work itself. Beginning with the First Punic War, he continued his narrative to the obliteration of Corinth and Carthage in 146.

Polybius was not only contemporary with much of what he records; he was also befriended by some of the leading men in Rome, like Scipio Aemilianus, and witnessed Roman imperialism in action, as at Carthage (he did not like everything he saw). He was a conscientious writer who operated according to serious criteria (12.25e–g, 28.3) for historical research, stressing truthfulness and impartiality (although he displays notable bias, for example, against the Aetolian League), and on causation (e.g., 36.17.1–15, not undermined by his interest in Chance as an agent in human affairs).[18] Abstract analysis of power, its acquisition and effects, on states and individuals, interested him. His work seems to react against much Hellenistic historiography, particularly that branch which sought by vivid description (*enargeia*) to shock and frighten readers. He was nevertheless a major figure in the penetration of Hellenistic intellectual ideas into Roman elite circles.

Polybius' accounts of Roman politics, wars, and diplomacy, are high-grade material, and should be preferred unless they can be shown from other sources to present a biased version. A striking example is found in Appian: his version of the outbreak of the First Illyrian War in the late third century (*Ill.* 7) differs from Polybius' (2.8.1–13): it contains not only very plausible detail on the local situation, but is less hysterical.[19] Polybius' is clearly a pro-Roman, exculpatory account, recounted by Roman aristocrats and/or written by the first Roman historians (themselves contemporaries of this war), stressing Illyrian provocation.

The other major source for this period is books 21–45 of Livy, covering the period 219–167. Livy took a less synoptic view of Rome's expansion (see 23.20.13, 39.48.6, and 41.25.8 for an affected contempt for Greek affairs). Despite this he often evokes sympathy for Rome's enemies in striking description of battles and sieges, designed to arouse readers' emotions (e.g., 31.34.1–5; 33.7.2; cf. Polyb. 18.20.7).

Livy records the traditions which made Rome great, and the virtues and deeds of the Roman leaders *and* People (26.22.14) of the past. The ability to solve internal disputes and unite against enemies provided one basis for the growth of Roman power. The other was divine guidance of Rome from the foundation (note the words of Romulus at 1.9.4); equally, impiety led to setbacks. Of his own day Livy wrote in his preface that Romans could neither endure their vices nor the cures for them: his history is a didactic exercise for the benefit of the present reader and the commonwealth.[20]

Livy glosses over or ignores much that might make Rome look bad, as a comparison with Polybius shows;[21] the altruistic side of Roman imperialism is stressed (e.g., 33.33.5; cf. Polyb. 18.46.4). Again, Scipio Africanus in Livy is the personification of dignified Roman virtues. The portrait is not a whitewash, and Livy (like Polybius) distances himself from Scipio's claims of a miraculous birth or special relationships with the gods (26.19.3–5, 9); Scipio is nevertheless presented as a leader of destiny (*fatalis dux*, 22.53.6). Livy has suppressed much in this portrait: Scipio it was who gave the order for indiscriminate slaughter at New Carthage (contrast Livy 26.46.10 with Polyb. 10.15.4); in Livy he is a model of sexual restraint, which would have surprised Polybius, who called him *philogunḗs*, "fond of women."[22] Scipio illustrates how Livian characterization produces rather wooden moral stereotypes. There are no jokes in Livy: his account (24.24.16) excises Marcellus' jest about Archimedes' defenses at Syracuse, present in Polybius (8.6.6).

Livy has been criticized as a "scissors and paste" historian, uncritically combining material from a variety of sources with little thought for the plausibility or chronological rigor.[23] Yet (especially in books 30–45) there is valuable detail on administration and politics, suggesting that Livy has reproduced his sources with some care: for example, part of Livy's account of the Senate's repression of new forms of the worship of Bacchus in Italy in 186 (39.18.8–9) can be compared (to Livy's credit, in general) with extracts from the contemporary senatorial decree (*ILS* 18 = *ROL* 4: 255–9; see also Chapters 10, 22, and 28). Without this material, our knowledge of early second-century politics would be threadbare. Furthermore, since he follows Polybius at points where the latter's text is lacunose or lost (the Second and Third Macedonian Wars, the Syrian War), his account is invaluable.

Despite all this, our knowledge of parts of this period is defective: we would like to know more about the First Punic War, and its aftermath. For the period after Livy's narrative breaks off, for which Polybius is very fragmentary, our knowledge of both Roman politics and international relations is thin. Yet for economic, social, and cultural history there are other literary sources of some importance. Cato the Elder's *On Agriculture* (*De agricultura*) is the earliest example of extended Latin prose, and is revealing about élite attitudes to farming and moneymaking in a time of rapid change. Slightly earlier are the plays of Plautus and Terence, for which we can assume a wider audience than that for much élite-generated literature (see also Chapter 25). Each offers a different perspective on attitudes to Greek culture in late third- and early second-century Rome. Plautus, although his setting, characters, and plot are all taken directly from Greek models, repeatedly drops in places and institutions which are thoroughly Roman (e.g., *Curc.* 462–86 – the Forum Romanum, *Bacch.* 1068– 75 – the triumph); he plays with ideas of Romans as "barbarians" and of "acting the Greek" (see also Chapter 22). Terence, by contrast, lacks these sudden Roman insertions.[24] Finally, second-century political and forensic (courtroom) speeches were available to first-century writers (Livy 38.54.11, 39.42.6–7, 45.25.3); it is clear, however, that even the speeches of Cato were not systematically published (Cic. *Brut.* 65; see also Chapter 25). All that *we* have are quotations (collected in Malcovati 1976), yet at last Roman politicians begin to speak in their own persons (see also Chapters 20 and 25).

As for later writers, some drew heavily on Livy for universal histories: the Trajanic rhetorician and historian Florus; the fifth-century Christian Orosius, who painstakingly cataloged the disasters which befell Rome under paganism; and the collection of prodigies (warnings sent by gods to men) of Julius Obsequens. A wide range of material comes in Plutarch (e.g., *Aem.*, *Marc.*) and Appian, who wrote in the time of Antoninus Pius a survey of Rome's wars. Not all have survived, but the focus on *res externae* is valuable: Appian treated, for example, wars in Illyria, Spain, Syria, and Africa. Other sources are fragmentary, such as the great imperial history of Dio Cassius, written in the third century AD, preserved for the Republic in two heavily abbreviated Byzantine epitomes, of which that of Zonaras ends in 146.

None of the above should be given preference to Polybius or Livy, unless comparison of their accounts suggests that they offer less distorted information. The use of later writers is fraught with problems. As Edward Gibbon wrote in *The History of the Decline & Fall of the Roman Empire* on the disputed fate of Crispus, son of the emperor Constantine: "If we consult the succeeding writers, . . . their knowledge will appear gradually to encrease as their means of information must have diminished; a circumstance which frequently occurs in historical disquisition."[25] The problem is not just one of knowledge, but of empathy: the institutions and rituals, the political and ideological landscapes of the Republic had either vanished, or been heavily transformed by the end of the Julio-Claudian era (some were already vanishing in the late Republic, hence the upsurge in antiquarian writing). Later writers also had the double-edged weapon of hindsight, which led them to see the collapse of the

Republic as inevitable. Nevertheless, the later sources often drew upon traditions otherwise lost, and some, like Plutarch and Aulus Gellius, were very well read, and even quote directly from lost writers. This does not make them right, but their limited preservation of historical "biodiversity" enriches our approaches to republican history very considerably.

Later sources inevitably alter what they preserve under the influence of their own times and agendas; sometimes they also preserve original discourse: approval and prejudice can be transmitted, albeit with subtle mutations, from writer to writer. This is particularly true of the contempt expressed about radical politics or lowly social origins, where similar views, making the jump from contemporary political rhetoric to history, are expressed in similar language from Polybius to Plutarch.

Crisis, 146–31

The first half of this period is covered by only one narrative source of any detail, namely Appian's *Civil Wars* book 1, which charts the rise of violence in Roman politics, from the tribunate of Ti. Gracchus to the collapse of the post-Sullan oligarchy. After 70, however, we have Cicero and in such volume and detail that the contrast with what went before is like stepping out from a dark interior into a bright summer's morning.

For the earlier part of this period we have quite a lot of information, but it is, paradoxically, very hard to use. Much of it comes in brief remarks made *en passant* by authors whose audiences understood the allusions; and narrative accounts for this period, which ought to provide our contexts, are inadequate. Appian is valuable mainly because we have nothing better. He has an often hazy grasp of republican institutions and legal differences. For example, he writes of the involvement of *Italiôtai* in agrarian issues, but it is unclear whether he means non-Roman Italian allies, or Roman peasants settled in the Italian countryside. By contrast, Diodorus' account of the slave revolts of the late second century in his native Sicily is of great importance.

We have a number of Plutarch's *Parallel Lives* (from the Gracchi to Antony). The Greek cultural revival known as the Second Sophistic led Plutarch to compare Romans and Greeks, and the *Lives* need to be read in pairs, as they were written. They illustrate character, virtue, and vice: Plutarch thought that anecdote could be more revealing than political or military narrative (*Alex.* 1). They were not meant to be comprehensive historical accounts, and often relate incidents with no real clue as to when or why they took place. Nevertheless, modern historians often pressgang Plutarch into a more historical role than that which he envisaged for himself.

The *Iugurtha* of Sallust (c.86–c.35; see also Chapter 25) is an extended account of Rome's war with the Numidian prince, who bribed and murdered his way to sole power in the late second century and was defeated by C. Marius. The real focus of the work is Roman decline, the corruption of the nobility, and the devastating consequences of political ambition. The reader does not get a clear military narrative, and learns little about Numidia despite an ethnographic digression: as Kraus has argued, the ethnography is really one of Rome.[26] Sallust argued that Rome tore herself apart in the absence of an external threat (*metus hostilis*) of the type until recently represented by Carthage (*Cat.* 10, *Iug.* 41). For him the real importance of the war was popular opposition to the pride of the nobility (*Iug.* 5), and its disastrous consequences. Sallust disliked any monopoly of power by "the few," and approaches with fairly even-handed contempt both optimate and *popularis* positions, believing that both ultimately acted as fronts for the long-term ambitions of disingenuous leaders.[27] Likewise, each of two opposing speakers – Lepidus and Philippus – in the *Histories* argues that his advice will guarantee *libertas* (freedom).

Two rhetorical treatises, the anonymous *Art of Rhetoric Dedicated to Herennius* (*Rhetorica ad Herrenium*), and *On Invention* (*De inuentione*) by the young Cicero, offer contemporary views (from different ideological standpoints) of political rhetoric in theory and practice (see also Chapter 20). Both contain incidental material of value for reconstructing recent politics, but often without context; snippet must be combined with potentially irrelevant snippet. Two other Ciceronian works, the political dialog *On the Commonwealth* (*De re publica*) and the rhetorical treatise *On the Orator* (*De oratore*), were set in this period (in 129 and the late 90s, respectively). It is clear that Cicero sought "period" authenticity in these works (which also explored topics of contemporary importance). He wrote to Atticus (*Att.* 13.30.2), asking about the legates of Mummius in 146: the relevant information was not in Polybius, and Cicero was working with a combination of oral tradition (what he remembered Hortensius saying) and written evidence.

Otherwise we must turn to imperial writers. Of Velleius Paterculus' history Book 1 is largely lost; Book 2 began after the sack of Carthage (showing the influence of Sallust). The narrative is continuous, but (until the Civil War between Caesar and Pompey) brief often to the point of obscurity; he often sacrifices detail for pithy rhetorical comment. His Tiberian contemporary Valerius Maximus' *Memorable Doings and Sayings* (*Factorum et dictorum memorabilium*) was probably meant to provide raw material from which orators might draw *exempla* (examples) for their speeches. The moralizing treatment of some subjects (moderation, constancy, mercy, friendship, gratitude) is aided by the sententious style; other concerns are antiquarian (Roman religion and institutions). Valerius drew on a wide range of sources, some of which we have in full, allowing (a sometimes unfavorable) comparison; in other cases he provides much or all of what is known of a particular incident, but again we often lack its context.

Pliny's *Natural History* is saturated with snippets of information on the Republic, especially in the later books (33–6), on metals and minerals and their uses in building and art, where important information on artistic culture, Hellenization and luxury in late republican Rome emerges (see also Chapter 24). Pliny was scholarly by ancient standards (he always read in his litter), but his writing shows signs of haste. He boasted (*praef.* 17) of his 20,000 "facts," and for these his text is ransacked by scholars searching for raw data (the same is true of the early imperial geographer Strabo from Pontus).[28]

We are somewhat better off for the dictatorship of Sulla and the ensuing decade of reactionary politics in Rome and intense fighting overseas. We have fragments of Sallust's *Histories*, covering the period 78–67; six speeches and letters are fully preserved, but reflect Sallustian concerns as much as the original arguments. Appian's *Mithridatic Wars* (*Mithridatica*) and Plutarch's *Sertorius* illuminate foreign wars. Plutarch's drew on Sulla's now lost memoirs for his biographies of Marius and Sulla, making these of extreme interest as well as unreliability; his biographies are thinner hereafter. Finally, Cicero's career as an advocate in the criminal courts began in 80 with the *In Defense of Roscius of Ameria* (*Pro Roscio Amerino*). (See also Chapter 20.)

Until his death in 43 we see late republican history through Cicero's eyes: through his huge output of forensic and political speeches, treatises on rhetoric, ethics, natural philosophy, and political theory, and an enormous body of private correspondence. This contemporary material, above all the letters, makes possible a study of politics and society which is simply not possible for any other period. Cicero was often an eyewitness, and what he did not see, he subjected to the analysis of a powerful mind, albeit one often clouded by vanity. In a sense this is better than a history: it is the raw material from which history is made, and much richer than any history could afford to be.

It is also a curse: Cicero's omnipresent writings create a one-sided picture. Although the *Letters to his Friends* (*Epistulae ad Familiares*) and the *Letters to M. Brutus* (*Epistulae ad M. Brutum*) include letters to Cicero, these tell us little about any of his contemporaries. Sixteen books of correspondence from Cicero to his friend and confidant Atticus (*Epistulae ad Atticum*) survive (with a few gaps) from the mid-60s until a few months before Cicero's death: Atticus' views can sometimes be inferred, but the conversation could hardly be more one-sided. Some letters, for example, *Fam.* 1.9 (to Lentulus Spinther) and *Letters to His Brother Quintus* (*Epistulae ad Q. Fratrem*) 1.1, were clearly meant for wider diffusion as manifestos on, respectively, Cicero's political stance after 56 and the duties of the provincial governor. We must beware of reading the letters as outpourings of the "real" Cicero.

Equally, the law-court speeches present narratives, political assessments, and arguments, which given their length, frequency, and plausibility seem authoritative. Yet we must remember that advocates had an agenda (to get a man convicted or to get him off), and would use every persuasive strategy available to win their case (see also Chapters 20 and 25). Thus Cicero in 70 uses self-interest to persuade senatorial jurors to convict the governor Verres: by convicting they can undo their own reputation for corruption, which he claims is of more concern to the Roman People than the restoration of the powers of the tribunes, and retain their control of the juries. It must, however, have been obvious that reform of the senatorial monopoly was inevitable, and that the People cared much more about tribunician powers than the courts.

Seven years later, Cicero at a *contio* (assembly) convinced the *plebs* that an agrarian bill by the tribune Servilius Rullus, proposing resettlement programs for the urban poor, was not in their interests; and that he, the consul, and not the tribune, was the true *popularis*. The defense of property was a key conservative tenet (Cic. *Att.* 1.19.4, *Off.* 2.73), and one seen to be implicitly threatened by any agrarian reform. Cicero, remarkably, managed to sell to the masses the reactionary aristocratic ideal of *otium cum dignitate* (peace and position); he did so by stealing his opponent's political clothes, and reforging *popularis* language to suit his needs (*Leg. agr.* 2.1–11; cf. 70).

Orators not only manipulate the truth; they also lie. In 66 Cicero claimed to have "thrown dust in the eyes" of the jury before whom which he defended Aulus Cluentius Habitus on a murder charge (Quint. *Inst.* 2.21); but in 70 he had called Cluentius' victory in a similar case a "most disgraceful event" (*Verr.* 1.29). In 52 he defended his political ally Milo, on trial for murdering his (and Cicero's) archenemy, the radical tribune P. Clodius Pulcher, at an inn on the Appian Way. Cicero's argument was that Milo acted in self-defense, and in any case, killing Clodius was a useful act of patriotism. Yet it was widely known that Milo was the aggressor: Asconius Pedianus, an important Neronian commentator on Cicero's speeches, gives us a detailed narrative of the brutal encounter (30–5 C). In fact, Milo's murder of Clodius can have come as no surprise to Cicero, nor to contemporaries: in late 57 Cicero told Atticus (*Att.* 4.5.3) that he was sure Milo would kill Clodius given the chance, indeed Milo had said as much.

The *In Defense of Milo* (*Pro Milone*) illustrates another important issue about Cicero's speeches: the version we read is not always that delivered. In this case Cicero was intimidated by soldiers drafted in by Pompey to surround the court, and spoke briefly and in a subdued fashion – a change from his usual role, brought on as the last of three defense counsel, not to discuss the facts of the case, but to work on the emotions of the jury, either through humor, as in the *pro Caelio*, or indignation, or, most often, by eliciting pity for the defendant. Milo went into exile in Massilia (Marseilles); Cicero rewrote the speech, sending him a copy; Milo, with biting irony, thanked Cicero for not delivering the second version, since he might then have been acquitted, and missed the opportunity to sample the local seafood.

Finally, we must note the moralizing language framing much of Cicero's political discourse. "Seditious" and "turbulent," for example, are descriptions applied to many *populares* (except in speeches in front of the People, where Cicero, as we have seen, adopted different tactics). This is the language of conservative prejudice, not an uncomplicated neutral description. Equally, Cicero calls those who think like him "good men" (*boni*) or "the best men" (*optimates*); far from having moral force, these terms are value-judgments reflecting Cicero's political sympathies: "right-thinking men," i.e., "men like us."[29]

Overall Cicero's value is exceptional, and not just for the historian of politics and political discourse; he exemplifies, and comments on, the importance of rhetoric in politics; revolutionizes Latin philosophy (part of a larger reordering of knowledge which characterized this period); and illustrates social *mores* in a time of acute change. A narrowness of view, which inevitably characterizes any literary product from a male élite *milieu* aimed at the writer's peers, is tempered by relative humanity and considerable intelligence. Yet, these remarkable lenses which allow us to focus on the late Republic also constitute a pair of blinkers, and some scholars have tried to write "non-Ciceronian" versions of, for example, late Republic politics and thought.[30] We need to see the shortcomings as well as the benefits, and to be able to apply a corrective to the Ciceronian picture, although the game is not simply "catch Cicero out."

There is a lot Cicero doesn't tell us: we know about his wavering over whether or not to join Pompey in 49; we need to turn to Plutarch's biography to find out what happened once he made up his mind. Equally, Cicero's speeches do not constitute autonomous chunks of the truth; they belong in a historical context, and sources like Asconius allow us to reconstruct some of that. Additionally, Asconius comments on two speeches now lost, the *In Defense of Cornelius* (*Pro Cornelio*) of 66, and the *In Toga Candida*, which fiercely rebutted the smear campaign mounted by Cicero's rival candidates. Asconius not only reveals that Catilina came a close third in 64, but quotes some of the speech. Asconius can be simplistic, or mistaken, but he is still of considerable value.

For the Gallic campaigns of the 50s and the Civil War, we have Caesar's *Commentarii* (and inferior continuations by his officers). *Commentarii* are technically notebooks, and Caesar's style (writing of himself in the third person) suggests not rhetorical polish but impartiality. His clarity, linguistic purity, and directness combine to create the impression that he tells it as it was, and why it was.[31] Yet Asinius Pollio claimed that Caesar had meant to write the *commentarii* up, correcting certain errors of fact (Suet. *Iul.* 56.4; contrast the flattery of Cic. *Brut.* 262: their brevity and clarity are so striking as to put off serious historians from working them up).

Caesar used them to maintain his profile in Rome, during lengthy absences between 58 and 46, to justify his actions in response to his critics, who wanted to replace him as proconsul of Gaul and bring him to trial, and later sought to blame him for the Civil War (see, for example, *B. Civ.* 1.7: Caesar as the advocate of peace). Behind the Caesarian agenda, we have important data on Rome's early encounters with many Gallic tribes (ethnography offered Romans a way of marking the advance of Roman conquests, and Caesar is no exception), and on Roman warfare, as well as politics.

Like the *Iugurtha*, Sallust's *Catiline* was a monograph, devoted to a specific a theme (Coelius Antipater's focused treatment of the Hannibalic war, and Luccieus' monographs on the Social and first Civil Wars constitute the literary precedents, cf. Cic. *Fam.* 5.12). The almost complete abandonment of the annalistic structure leads in the *Iugurtha* to hazy chronology; and in the *Catiline* to the elision of the gap between the conspiracy and the Sullan dictatorship almost two decades earlier.

In one sense Sallust does not help us to correct the Ciceronian viewpoint: by writing on Catiline he suggests that the conspiracy was as important as Cicero repeatedly claimed; some scholars, however, have suspected Cicero of exaggerating the threat for his own ends. Yet Sallust differs from Cicero at a number of important points, not least on the latter's role: contrast the supporting role he accords Cicero (mentioning his first Catilinarian speech only in passing and ignoring the fourth) with Cicero's own boasting about his achievements.[32] Sallust's acquaintance with key players, and his own recollections, are important, for example, *Cat.* 48.9: he heard Crassus blame Cicero for the damage caused to his reputation when an informant in the Senate implicated him. Further, his style, pointed and uneven (despite his fondness for the rhetorical device of antithesis, or employment of opposites), and his archaizing vocabulary, are the opposite of Cicero, whose full, almost predictably rounded, sentences in the florid Asianic style were already being eclipsed by the terser Atticist mode in Cicero's lifetime.[33]

Sallust shares with many Roman historians his preoccupation with moral decline (and conversely with *uirtus* ("virtue," "courage") – two variant types of which are illustrated in Caesar and Cato (*Cat.* 50.3–53.6; see also Chapters 17 and 25). He also attempted to locate the *causes* of moral decline in the events of recent Roman history, both with his theory of the *metus hostilis,* and his insistence on the interaction between society and individual: after sketching the decline of the traditional Roman character (*Cat.* 10–13), Sallust says (14.1) "*as was very easy to do in such a great and such a corrupted state,* Catilina had around him bands of supporters for every type of scandal and crime." Despite emphasis on character and the individual, it would be wrong to claim that Sallust was interested only in moral dysfunction; he was aware of social and economic crises: see the letter of Cn. Manlius to Marcius Rex (*Cat.* 33, to be read with Catilina's own letter to Catulus at 35).[34]

Sallust was interested in how societal dysfunction is reflected in the ways in which language breaks down, as the concepts which it expresses become just empty names, and human nature (in its worst manifestations) prevails over constructed social formations; similarly he uses antithesis to point up the hidden complexities of individuals.[35] Thus, his characters display mixtures of good and bad qualities, e.g., the antihero Catilina with his heroic death.

Other contemporary writings offer perspectives on other areas of Roman life: élite attitudes to farming in Varro's *On Agriculture,* for example; and the surviving books of his *On the Latin Language,* like Lucretius' hexameter poem on Epicurean philosophy, testify to the same intellectual ferment which we have already noticed in Cicero's treatises. Also interesting, for example, are the poems of Catullus, giving an enthralling view of the late republican élite, its social behavior, and its sexual *mores* (see also Chapter 25). Catullus also mentions the financially unrewarding experience of being on part of a governor's staff (*cohors,* 10, 38) in Bithynia – the expectation clearly was that such postings in the provinces carried the prospect of personal enrichment.

Of later writers, we have considered some already. Besides fragments of lost texts (for a famous fragment of Livy on Cicero's death, see Sen. *Suas.* 6. 17), extended accounts survive. The life of Caesar by the Hadrianic biographer Suetonius, often dismissed as scandalmongering, is full of rich detail and echoes of contemporary ideology. From 69 we have Xiphilinus' epitome of Cassius Dio. Dio's republican material is interesting but understudied. The quality is very patchy, acute and rich in detail in some places (37.49.3: L. Afranius was a better dancer than he was a consul; 40.54: the anecdote about Milo in exile), and thin in others, with errors of chronology and institutional detail. Dio's sources are unknown; the frequently made case for his use of Livy for the first century remains unproven. It is, however, clear that he applied his own judgment in the shaping of his narrative. For example, the familiar picture of moral decline in the late Republic seems absent. Dio's history also represents the most marked instance of the effects of hindsight in later writing: he saw the conflicts of the late Republic very much in terms of the conflict of military strongmen, reminiscent perhaps of the emperors of his own day, like Septimius Severus. He had little sense of the nature of aristocratic competition, or the value system of the Roman élite, whose members are for him either demagogues or creatures of the dynasts.[36]

"Making a Roman Past"

Having looked at how ancient historians set about writing accounts of the Republic, it is worth examining how we attempt the same task. Our view of what the Romans did affects what we think we are doing, whatever sort of exercise we see them as engaged in.

Ancient accounts need to be compared, and collated, combined to produce a coherent account, or sorted into a hierarchy in order to provide the basis for a narrative. Discrepancies need to be ironed out, errors detected and corrected, bias identified and accounted for, and obscurity illuminated. Examination of a writer's agenda, and those of his sources, and his use of them, allow for the detection and neutralization of bias: distortions can be recognized and eliminated, rather like remastering a 1920s jazz session from a badly scratched wax-cylinder recording. This is a day in the office for most ancient historians today.

Underlying this approach, however, is the assumption that there is a truth to be exposed by following rules, ones shared by ancient writers: Cicero asks Lucceius to concede more to their friendship than the laws of history allow (*Fam.* 5.12). Truth is assumed to be empirically or logically demonstrable. A related idea is that history is "mimetic"; that is, it reproduces faithfully the course of events. Not all is absolute: the search for truth often depends on *probabilistic* assumptions of, for example, a hierarchy of sources: "Livy is preferable to Appian," and therefore generally likely to be correct when the two are compared. Another common metaphor is that of *reconstruction*. Where our evidence is either late or consists of heterogeneous passing references, if "the truth is out there," it is out there in lots of very small bits; some of these can be made to fit together, and the historian's craft is the glue. This approach is a *positivist* one; it is related to *foundationalism*, the belief that there are immutable metaphysical and moral truths on which our value-system is founded. Positivism is seen as related to straightforward Anglo-Saxon common sense. The problem with common sense is that it is very hard to measure, not terribly rigorous, and thus a weak basis for historical methodology.

I think there is a lot to be said for positivism (now under heavy challenge from postmodern historians); it has after all produced a consensus about *what happened* which forms the backbone of our discipline. Nevertheless, it is also an approach which can discourage reflection. It is worth examining briefly its claims to truth.

"The truth should be the whole truth." Yet on any definition, Roman writers reproduce the perspectives and the prejudices of a tiny literate élite within Roman society. Roman comedy aimed at a broad audience; political speeches were made to the people, and those of Cicero give us a taste of the oratorical complexity to which the *plebs* was routinely exposed (see also Chapters 20 and 25). Nevertheless, literary sources tell us very little about the ordinary man – and less about women, ordinary or otherwise, except as they fitted into the traditional worldview of the male elite (see also Chapter 15). The world of the sources is one where the urban *plebs* is greedy, sordid and fickle; women lack rationality, and are prone to superstition; and slaves, at best, are cunning tricksters; at worst, the proverb applies: *quot serui tot hostes* – "all slaves are our enemies." The peoples of Italy have hardly any voice in literature, although in the case of inscriptions from our period, Etruscan texts outnumber Latin by a ratio of more than 2:1. The inhabitants of the provinces are virtually ignored. Our literary sources thus offer a partial truth for a privileged few.

Writers inevitably reflect the preoccupations of their age; or, in the words of the Italian historian Benedetto Croce, "all history is contemporary history." Thus, Sir Ronald Syme's *Roman Revolution* (1939) reflects the contemporary rise of fascism in Europe (note the chapter titles "Dux" and the "March on Rome," applicable to Mussolini as much as to Octavian; see also Chapter 1). Are historians' truths true forever, or only true (or truer) for the time of writing? If we agree in large measure about what *happened* in the Roman Republic, each generation keeps reinterpreting *why*, and *what sort of society* it was.

The question of viewpoint is important, because much historical writing today defends one viewpoint against others (e.g., why Caesar *actually* crossed the Rubicon), yet also denies having any viewpoint as a matter of principle: it is *objective*. A belief in historical objectivity presupposes that facts can be empirically determined, and uncomplicatedly accessed, and entails that any personal involvement by the historian will "contaminate" the history being written. Some works use the image of history as *scientific*. Yet history cannot be the subject of repeatable identical experiments under laboratory conditions, with controls; it cannot be scientific. A more common metaphor (cf. Cic. *De or.* 2.36, history as the "*witness* of ages") is that of a courtroom, where rival advocates use evidence to convince a jury. We allow the evidence to "speak for itself"; we let readers judge our arguments against the "facts" presented. Objectivity and impartiality belong in court, but do these metaphors apply to history?

They are often spoken of as if they were timeless, but they are ideologically charged constructs. The idea of impartiality is not new (cf. Sall. *Cat.* 4.2). On the other hand, the analysis of the sources, weighing them against each other, and using ancient evidence to support arguments, these trends we owe to the rationalist thinkers of the Enlightenment, and the new professional historians of the modern period. The German historian Leopold von Ranke (born 1795) has been seen as influential in the development of the idea of a dispassionate facts-only, stripped-down history.[37] In such scenarios the past is "dead," neutral; a defused bomb, which can, indeed, should, be studied for its own sake, without the risk of political explosions. We "do" history in a particular way not necessarily because that is the "right" way, but because that is the way in which our dominant cultural traditions have shaped the discipline, the same traditions which boxed it off and made it an autonomous area of study.

More recent studies on historiography, especially those of Hayden White, have stressed *narrativity*. Texts are just that, texts, narratives; they are *not the same* as past events, and should not be treated as if they were. Instead of a straightforward and dispassionate history, White has argued for *invention* as an important component of all historical writing, and for the historian's need to "write" historical contexts for individual elements of data.[38] This view is echoed in approaches to ancient literary sources.

Those who prize objectivity as the keynote of their own working practices have also assumed that ancient historians, and antiquarians, grammarians, and jurists, operated as they do: impartially, within a "research culture" which allows all available evidence to be brought forward and rigorously assessed.[39] That ancient historians (e.g., Polyb. 12.3–28a) do criticize predecessors (for missing items of evidence, for exaggeration and invention, or for writing in a sensationalist fashion) might encourage such a belief. Yet our objective, empirical historiography is an Enlightenment/Modern mode; it would be wrong to assume that our values applied in antiquity. In fact, scholars have noted how ancient practices of history writing are very different from our own. Importantly, ancient historical writing shared ground with poetry, rhetoric, and drama. Scholars have also pointed to the development of what has been called "unhistorical" thinking, a way of seeing the past fundamentally different from our own.[40] These scholars characterize ancient history as creative and inventive. Woodman, among others, has argued that when ancient writers and theorists talk about "truth," they really refer to an ideal that history should be written without bias, not that it should not be made up; on this view, like orators, historians could be about the business of invention.[41]

Yet it will not do to efface entirely the difference between rhetoric and historiography. The position that the ancients effectively did not have an idea of truth, or that if they did, ancient historians had quite one quite distinct from our own, is unconvincing. As for *inventio*, stressed by Woodman, it is not so much invention in our sense, as the search for materials; Cicero's *On Invention* is about finding material for court speeches, not about making up alibis or other material; this is not disproved by the fact that orators lie. Nevertheless we need to be alert to the many differences between ancient history writing and our own, including the fact that the political cannot be written out of any aspect of the text, as we saw at the start of this chapter: "style reflects ideology."[42]

Guide to Further Reading

Reading the ancient sources is the essential, and the most enjoyable, start. Overviews of Roman literature, not always from a historical point of view: Kenney 1982; Gabba 1983; Potter 1999, Harrison 2005. *OCD*[3] is fundamental. Dramatic and poetic texts: Gratwick 1982a–d; Gruen 1992: 6–83, 183–317; papers in Taplin 2000: 1–74, Wiseman 1998: 1–59, 64–74. Fragmentary Roman historians: Peter (1906–14) and Jacoby (*FGrH* IIIC) are still fundamental; more recently Chassignet (1996, 1999, 2004), Beck and Walter (2001, 2004); see also Badian 1968b; Frier 1999; Brunt 1980c. Priestly records: Beard, North, and Price 1998: ch. 1. On antiquarians: Rawson 1985; Cornell 1995: 18–26; Kaster 1995.

On literary theory see Martindale 1993; de Jong and Sullivan 1994; Fowler 2000; and Heath 2002. On rhetoric and invention in Roman historiography: Wiseman 1979; Woodman 1988; Pelling 1990b; papers in Wiseman and Gill 1993; Wiseman 1994c; Kraus and Woodman 1997; versus Cornell 1986b; Northwood forthcoming. On ancient historiography see papers in Luce 1982; Marincola 1997; Kraus and Woodman 1997; Mellor 1999. On Polybius: Walbank 1972 and 2002: 1–27;

Marincola 2001: 105–49. On Cicero: Habicht 1990; Mitchell 1991; Fuhrmann 1992; Rawson 1994a; his oratory: Vasaly 1993; Gotoff 1993; the letters: Hutchinson 1998. For Caesar: Welch and Powell 1998, and for Sallust: Syme 1964 is still essential; commentaries: McGushin 1977, 1992–4; Paul 1984; Scanlon 1987; Levene 1992; Sallust's ethnography: Scanlon 1988. For Livy, Oakley's introduction (1997) is now standard; other excellent commentaries: Ogilvie 1965; Briscoe 1973, 1981; Kraus 1994. Standard discussions: Walsh 1961; Stadter 1972; Luce 1977; Levene 1993; Moles 1993; Miles 1995; Jaeger 1997. Discussions of other authors include, for Velleius Paterculus: Sumner 1970a, Woodman 1975, 1977, 1983; Asconius, Marshall 1985, Squires 1990; Valerius Maximus, Bloomer 1993 and Wardle 1998 (Introduction); Appian: Gowing 1992, Richardson 2000; Cassius Dio: Millar 1964, Lintott 1997; Dionysius: Gabba 1991.

Acknowledgments

I am grateful to the editors for many helpful comments and a very gentlemanly display of patience; also to Llewelyn Morgan, and Peter Ghosh. All mistakes are my own.

Notes

1 Kraus and Woodman 1997: 7–8.
2 Pelling 1990a.
3 Edwards 1996: 4–6.
4 Millar 2002b: 192–7.
5 Cornell 1986b: 58.
6 See Cato *Orig.* frag. 77 Peter = Gell. *NA* 2.28.6; Cic. *De or.* 2.52–4; Serv. Dan. on Virg. *Aen.* 1.373.
7 Frier 1999; Rawson 1971a.
8 E.g., Bucher 1987.
9 Crawford 1996b: 555–726.
10 Rich 1997; Kraus and Woodman 1997: 61–2.
11 Walsh 1961: 180–1.
12 Cic. *Brut.* 75; cf. *Tusc.* 1.3; and note the "ancestral hymns" about the Twins mentioned by Dion. Hal. *Ant. Rom.* 1.79.10.
13 Badian 1968b: 11; cf. Wiseman 1979: 9–26.
14 Woodman 1988: 77–8, 90–3.
15 Miles 1986; cf .1988; Edwards 1996: 45–52.
16 Galinsky 1996: 280–7; Kraus and Woodman 1997: 70–4.
17 Sacks 1990.
18 Walbank 1972; Eckstein 1995; Davidson 1991.
19 Derow 1973.

20   Kraus and Woodman 1997: 54–6.
21   Walsh 1961: 151–63.
22   Walsh 1961: 93–100.
23   Walsh 1961: 146 for battle "doublets."
24   Leigh 2004.
25   Chapter 18, n.16.
26   Kraus and Woodman 1997: 29.
27   *Iug.* 41–2., *Cat.* 4.2; 36.4–39.6 with Syme 1964: 68; *Hist.* 1.7 McGushin.
28   Beagon 1992; Carey 2003; Murphy 2004; Clarke 1997, 1999.
29   Lacey 1970.
30   Gruen 1974; Rawson 1985.
31   See Morgan 1997 for the political implications of Caesar's interest in language.
32   Syme 1964: 105–11.
33   Sallust's style: Kraus and Woodman 1997: 12.
34   Brunt 1963: 74–5.
35   Scanlon 1980.
36   Lintott 1997: 2251–3.
37   Fornara 1983:194–201.
38   White 1973, 1987.
39   Brunt 1979.
40   Wiseman 1979; Woodman 1988.
41   Woodman 1988.
42   Kraus and Woodman 1997: 12.

CHAPTER 3

Epigraphy and Numismatics

Mark Pobjoy

Epigraphy and numismatics concern material objects surviving from antiquity which challenge our understanding of ancient society in various ways and fuel many current debates. Epigraphy is the study of inscriptions, found on buildings, plaques or tablets of various kinds of stone or metal, altars, stelae, bricks, tiles, and wall plaster, in floor and wall mosaics, on wooden or wax writing-tablets, vessels of pottery, metal, or glass, and on many other things. Clearly the term "inscription" is here given a broad definition, including texts cut into surfaces and texts formed in other ways, such as by painting or by arranging the individual pieces ("tesserae") of a mosaic. However, texts on papyri and texts on coins are usually treated in the first instance as the province of the papyrologist and the numismatist respectively. Numismatics, principally concerned with the study of coins made of precious or base metal, embraces related material also, such as metal "currency bars."

The inscriptions and coins which concern students of the Roman Republic are not merely those produced by the Romans themselves: important evidence about the Republican period comes also from those produced by (or for) other Latin-speaking communities and communities in which another language – particularly Greek, Oscan, or Etruscan – was predominant (see also Chapter 28). But for reasons of space I shall here devote most attention to Roman inscriptions in Latin and Roman coins. In the cases of both epigraphy and numismatics, fresh discoveries mean that the quantity of material available for study increases substantially every year, and reinterpretation of already familiar items is constantly sharpening our picture of central aspects of Republican history.

Epigraphy

The Latin alphabet is derived from the Etruscan alphabet, which in turn derives from the Greek alphabet brought to Italy by Euboean Greek settlers in the eighth century BC. The earliest Latin inscriptions appear to date from the regal period of Rome's history, most famously the "Forum cippus," an inscription on a block of tufa from the heart of Rome itself, datable to the sixth century. It was discovered in 1899 beneath the black marble paving in the Roman Forum, plausibly identified with the "black stone in the *comitium*" referred to by Festus (p.184 L 19–21).[1] This was the place where, according to differing versions, Romulus, Faustulus, or Hostus Hostilius was supposed to have met his death. With the inscription were found the remains of a sanctuary which has been identified with the Volcanal, the shrine of Vulcan.[2] The inscription may well be the one referred to by Dionysius of Halicarnassus as having been set up by Romulus when he erected a statue of himself next to a statue he dedicated to Hephaestus (= Vulcan), and was probably already concealed under the black marble paving when Dionysius wrote (2.54.2).[3] The damaged text, written in archaic Latin script and extremely difficult to interpret, appears to contain imperatives and may in fact have been a sacred law.

Since comparatively few inscriptions survive from the first three centuries of the Republic, it is impossible to say how usual it was in that period for texts to be inscribed in public or private contexts, although we may suspect that only a very small proportion of what was inscribed actually survives, and indeed ancient literature refers to a number of inscriptions which are no longer extant.[4] But many more survive from the widening Roman domain of the second and first centuries BC, when an impressive variety of texts emerges into view. Some texts communicated the rules of a community or decisions taken by an official body. These include laws passed by a popular assembly in Rome (*leges* or *plebiscita*), decrees of the Roman Senate (*senatus consulta*), colonial and municipal charters, and the decrees of local senates. Calendars recorded the dates of markets and festivals and for each day indicated whether assemblies could be held and whether other public business could or could not be conducted.[5] Other inscriptions recorded the acts or pronouncements of one or more officials, particularly magistrates (officers of the state or local community). These might be generous benefactions (examples of "euergetism": see also Chapter 1) or records of the fulfillment of a duty, and included such activities as the construction or repair of buildings.[6] Honorary inscriptions were set up to benefactors and other prominent individuals. Many inscriptions recorded offerings to one or more divinities, often in the form of the fulfillment of a vow ("votive" inscriptions). There are huge numbers of very varied funerary inscriptions. We also find contracts, shop-signs, and electoral slogans. Other texts are found on such diverse items as boundary-markers, milestones, sling-bullets (recording the name of either the target or the sender), lots (used in divination), and tags which accompanied bags of coins.

The surviving inscriptions exhibit great variety in the quality of their lettering, which will have corresponded to some extent with the expertise and expense which went into them. Many survive only in a fragmentary condition. Each requires careful description and illustration when first published, with accurate details about its dimensions, the size and forms of its letters, the material on or in which the text is inscribed, and, where possible, its origin. This information is important in various ways. For example, the letter-forms can often act as a rough guide to the dating of an inscription, since we have a number of texts which are dated to a particular consular year (very occasionally to a specific day within a year) against which we can compare those texts that lack an explicit date. Applied cautiously, this is a useful technique where there is a sufficiently large sample of comparable inscriptions, which can lead to striking conclusions. For example, our text of the contract for the construction of a wall near the temple of Serapis at the Roman colony of Puteoli in Campania, containing the consular date 105, was clearly inscribed during the Principate. It is thus an example of the phenomenon of the reinscribing of older texts, which raises interesting questions about the context of the later inscribing of the text, beyond the questions in any case raised by the original document (*ILLRP* 518 = *ROL* 4:274–9).

Considering an inscription in its full context – textual and physical – is essential for understanding the motives behind the decision to set it up and to word it in a particular way, and this exploration of motives raises key questions about Roman society and politics. One of the earliest Roman funerary inscriptions, that of L. Cornelius Scipio Barbatus, who died c.270, provides a good example (*ILLRP* 309 = *ROL* 4:2–3 no. 2). It is cut on the side of his sarcophagus, which originally resided in "the tomb of the Scipios," their own cemetery on the much-frequented Via Appia, a short distance outside the walls of Rome. Accompanied by an earlier or contemporary inscription painted on the lid ("L. Cornelius Scipio, son of Gnaeus"), the incised text, a verse-inscription, enumerates his qualities – bravery, prudence, good looks, and valor, then his career and achievements (see also Chapter 17). Particularly noteworthy is the description of his offices: "he was consul, censor, and aedile among you." This inscription has been associated with the ascendancy of the elder Scipio Africanus and dated to the end of the third century.[7] The direct address to the readers of the text suggests a political purpose, an address to potential supporters and voters, and the use of the success of Barbatus for the social and political benefit of future generations of his family. Funerary inscriptions, then as now, have at least as much to do with the living as with the dead. In this respect, the funerary inscription of a great man can be seen as the permanent counterpart to the Roman aristocratic funeral described by Polybius (6.53–4).

Like these Scipionic inscriptions, the considerable number of inscriptions from the Greek East dating from the period of the Roman conquest in the second century are contextualized by relatively plentiful information from literary sources. The conquest is a remarkable feat, particularly in that Roman diplomatic skills have managed to persuade no shortage of people, in ancient and modern times, that early Roman interest in Greek lands was noble in character, rather than calculated and grasping. One illustration of the diplomatic effort involved is the inscribed letter of the proconsul T. Quinctius Flamininus, whose defeat of Philip V of Macedon at Cynoscephalae in 197 marked a significant step on the road to Roman control over mainland Greece. His letter to the people of Chyretiae in Thessaly (some time between 197 and 194) concerns a restoration of property to the city, and explicitly states that the Romans wish to be seen as champions of what is noble, "in order that in these matters too men may not be able to slander us," "and because we have in no way wished to be greedy, regarding goodwill and concern for reputation as of the highest importance" (*RDGE* no. 33 = Sherk 1984: no. 4). The word translated as "slander," *katalalein*, matches exactly the term used by Polybius (18.45.1) to convey how the Aetolians, alone of the Greeks at this time, were disparaging the senatorial decree which settled the affairs of Greece in 196. The inscription thus probably records one of the counter-moves to the diplomatic problem which we learn about from our principal literary source. Numerous inscriptions in honor of Flamininus attest to the effectiveness of his work in Greece.[8]

Epigraphic discoveries can deepen our understanding of an apparently familiar phenomenon. The victory of the consul L. Mummius in 146 against the Achaean League and his destruction of Corinth are well known as pivotal events in the history of Roman imperialism, coming in the same year as the younger Scipio Africanus' defeat and destruction of Carthage. Also well known is his plundering of works of art from Corinth and other cities, and his distribution of these to friends, to the city of Rome, and to various other cities in Italy and the provinces (see also Chapter 24). Latin inscriptions are known from a number of Italian cities which were the beneficiaries of Mummius' gifts (Parma, Nursia, Trebula Mutuesca, Cures, and Fregellae), and there are several Greek inscriptions from cities in Greece. But in 2002 a text on a tufa statue base within the colonnade around the temple of Apollo in Pompeii, which had previously only partially been revealed from beneath its covering of plaster, was fully uncovered to reveal a record of Mummius' beneficence in a different language. The retrograde Oscan text, shown in Figure 3.1, reads **l.mummis.l.kúsúl**, "L. Mummius, son of Lucius, consul."[9] This is the only attestation so far of the Oscan term for the Roman office of consul (other terms borrowed from Latin are known, such as **kvaísstur** for quaestor). The highly probable date for the inscription – shortly after Mummius' return from Greece late in 145 – helps to date a building phase of the temple of Apollo and to contextualize part of the history of the cultural Hellenization of Oscan Pompeii as a Roman ally. Mummius was elected censor for

Fig. 3.1 Oscan inscription of L. Mummius at Pompeii (70 cm wide, the inscription itself 58 cm). By permission of the Soprintendenza Archeologica di Pompei. Photo by the author

142–1, and his beneficence has to some extent been connected with this ambition and his election campaign. But there were no direct votes to be won from the inhabitants of the allied community of Pompeii, who will have been neither Roman citizens nor (for the most part) Latin speakers, and there do appear to be broader issues at play here. Leading figures in Roman society cultivated relationships with leading figures in many non-Roman communities, and there was mutual social and political benefit from this interaction. It may be in this context that we should think about Mummius' benefaction to the city (see also Chapter 19). But there may also be a reflection here of a view about the relationship between Rome and her Italian allies, that allied communities should share in the spoils won through the spread of Roman power, which depended to a large extent on their help. The theme of Rome's treatment of her Italian allies and the mismatch between this treatment and their aspirations is of enormous significance in understanding the last century of the Republic.

The impact of the public careers, legislative activity, and violent fate of the Gracchi on the political life of Rome in the late Republic was dramatic, and clearly their experience reflects major economic and social problems in Italy, although there are significant difficulties in gaining a detailed understanding of what happened from our literary sources and from archaeological material. We shall see below how epigraphy benefits our understanding of the legislation of Ti. Sempronius Gracchus' younger brother Gaius, but it also helps us to gain a clearer picture of his activity as a member of the land commission set up under his elder brother's legislation of 133. No fewer than 14 of the boundary stones (*termini*) set in place by the commission have been found in Italy, with a concentration in the south, particularly in Lucania.[10] One of these stones (*ILLRP* 470 = *ROL* 4: 168–9), from ancient Atina in the Vallo di Diano in Lucania, is illustrated in Figure 3.2 (a–c). On its side (a) it has the names of the three commissioners, C. Sempronius Ti.f. (i.e., Gaius Gracchus), Ap. Claudius C.f. (misspelt), and P. Licinius P.f., who are described as "Triumvirs for the adjudication and assignment of lands"; on the top (b) is marked a cross with a circle at its center, and with a letter D formed by using one of the arms of the cross as the upright; and again on the side (c), further along from the names of the commissioners, is marked "K. VII" along a line apparently formed by the extension of the opposite arm of the cross down onto the side of the stone.

The task assigned to the commissioners by Ti. Gracchus' law was to survey current holdings of Roman public land (*ager publicus*) in order to reimpose the legal maximum limit of 500 *iugera* (approximately 310 acres, or 125 ha.) on any one holding, with an extra allowance for up to two sons. They were then to assign the land thereby released to new settlers in relatively small plots. Our epigraphic testimony shows some of the results of their work. This particular *terminus* was clearly one of those placed at a crossroads in the local centuriation scheme, the rectilinear network of roads (*limites*) which was often laid down in a fertile plain which had come under Roman control. The east – west roads were labeled as *decumani*, and the north – south roads as *kardines*. This stone apparently marks the junction of the central *decumanus* and the seventh *kardo*.[11] It thus functions as a road sign as well as an authoritative boundary-marker, and it raises the question of what range of activities was undertaken by the commissioners.[12] It is not impossible that the commissioners themselves laid down

Fig. 3.2a–c *Terminus* set up by Gracchan commissioners near Atina in Lucania (diameter at the top 47 cm). By permission of the Soprintendenza Archeologica delle Province di Napoli e Caserta. Photos by the author

road networks such as this one, in which case their activity was on a very grand scale indeed, since this would have involved the obliteration of many preexisting boundaries and disruption to agricultural life over a considerable period of time. But it is perhaps more likely that they simply used a preexisting centuriation as the basis for their work of measuring the size of current holdings of *ager publicus*, then by a process of exchange (*commutatio*) released a consolidated area of the centuriation scheme for allotment to settlers (cf. App. *B Civ.* 1.18). The stone would then probably have been placed at a crossroads in the area of new settlement. If so, it functioned also as a permanent public reminder to the Roman citizen inhabitants of the area about who was to be thanked for their acquisition of land and consequent livelihood.

The findspot of the Gracchan *terminus* is a few miles along the Vallo di Diano from that of a contemporary or near-contemporary inscription of great interest, which merits more detailed attention. The inscription (Figure 3.3, *ILLRP* 454 = *ROL* 4:150–1), which is sometimes referred to as "the Polla stone" from the name of the town where it was found, is of relevance for several important themes of the period. Its text is as follows:

uiam fecei ab Regio ad Capuam et	I built the road from Rhegium to Capua and

Fig. 3.3 The Polla stone (70 cm wide). Photo by the author

in ea uia ponteis omneis, miliarios

on that road I put all the bridges, milestones,

tabelariosque posciuei. hince sunt
Nouceriam meilia LI, Capuam XXCII[II],
Muranum LXXIIII, Cosentiam CXXIII,
Valentiam CLXXX, ad fretum ad
statuam CCXXXI, Regium CCXXXVII.
suma af Capua Regium meilia CCCXXI.

and mileage-tablets. From here it is
51 miles to Nuceria, 84 to Capua,
74 to Muranum, 123 to Cosentia,
180 to Valentia, 231 to the statue
on the strait, and 237 to Rhegium.
Total from Capua to Rhegium: 321 miles.

et eidem praetor in
Sicilia fugiteiuos Italicorum
conquaeisiuei redideique
homines DCCCCXVII. eidemque
primus fecei ut de agro poplico
aratoribus cederent paastores.
forum aedisque poplicas heic fece[i].

And when I was praetor in
Sicily, I hunted down and returned 917
runaway slaves belonging to *Italici*.
And I was
the first to see to it that on public land
shepherds gave way to plowmen.
I built the forum and public buildings
here.

From the lettering (for example, the form of "P" as a "Π" without the lower part of the right-hand upright, as in the nearby *terminus*), one would date the inscription to the latter decades of the second century. Also of interest in the engraving are the four rectangles cut out of the stone (line 6, line 7 (twice), and line 9), presumably to correct mistakes in the mileage calculations.

The text is an enumeration of the achievements of a prominent individual, but also acts as a mileage-tablet, giving the distances in miles from the forum where it resided along the road that he constructed, first northwards (to Nuceria and beyond that to Capua), then southwards (to Muranum, Cosentia, Valentia, the statue on the strait, and finally Rhegium). The name of the forum in question is likely to depend on the name of the individual who is proclaiming his achievements, which unfortunately is lost: both a "Forum Popili" and a "Forum Anni" are attested as being in the area, and among the suggested candidates are P. Popillius Laenas (consul in 132), T. Annius Luscus (consul in 153), and T. Annius Rufus (consul in 128). Appius Claudius (consul in 143), who is named on our Gracchan *terminus* above, has also been suggested. The personal achievement of the subject of the inscription is the principal focus of its text. Even the overall length of the road and the distances between the towns it connected can be seen as testimony to the scale of his accomplishment, just as the figure of 917 recaptured slaves is intended to arouse admiration and wonder in the reader. And the statue referred to is very likely to be a statue of the road-builder himself. But the value of this inscription for the historian of the Roman Republic does not depend on our being able to decide between these various candidates.[13]

The construction of the road from Rhegium to Capua may well have been connected with the need to transport and supply troops fighting the slaves in revolt in Sicily from c.135. The expense involved in building the road would have been huge, and it is unlikely that the contribution of the author of the inscription was financial as well as supervisory, but he may have been at least partly responsible for the financial outlay required for the construction of the forum and the public buildings where this inscription was displayed. His hunting down of runaway slaves will have been part of Roman operations in suppressing the slave revolt, in which he would have played a prominent part as a praetor.[14] The audience he is addressing is clearly envisaged as being made up of property-owners. His boast of being the first to see to it that "on public land shepherds gave way to plowmen" is particularly striking. Shepherds were often of servile status, and so this claim is probably associated in his thinking with his recapturing of the runaways. We are given no means to date these agrarian activities, whose location is also unclear. Since he has just mentioned Sicily, it is possible that that is where he is claiming to have brought about this change. Another possibility is that he has in mind Italian public land at some distance from the forum. But he may well be referring to activity somewhere along the course of the road, and perhaps specifically in the vicinity of the forum and public buildings. In the light of the well-attested activity of the Gracchan commissioners in the area, it is tempting to make a connection between their work and the activity described here, particularly as Ti. Gracchus is reported to have been inspired to devise his scheme by a journey (through Etruria) where he saw that the land was sparsely populated and that those who were tilling the soil or pasturing the flocks were imported foreign slaves (Plut. *Ti. Gracch.* 8.9). There would thus be an intriguing ideological component to the description of the agrarian work in this inscription, involving a change both in land use and in land users.[15] "I was the first..." implies that others followed, and that being the first to have done this is worthy of particular attention and praise. If the work he did was not associated with the commission (and he would not have had to be a Gracchan commissioner to have contributed to their work), then it would have to have been very similar in nature.

The political and social standing of the author were obviously a concern in his decision to set up this inscription, so can we say more about his political stance? If his work was associated with that of the Gracchan commission (see Chapter 8), it is tempting to associate his political outlook with that of Ti. Gracchus, especially given the repeated references to what belongs to "the People" (the *populus*) – public land (*agro poplico*) and public buildings (*aedis poplicas*). This is not sufficient to allow us to label his stance as politically akin to those later figures who referred to themselves, or were referred to, as "populares" (see also Chapters 12 and 18). But it is at least suggestive of leanings in that direction. The road-builder's reference to the owners of the runaway slaves specifically as *Italici* complicates this question. Why was that something for a prominent Roman to proclaim? It chimes with Diodorus' description of the owners of the runaways in the Sicilian revolt as *Italikoi* or *Italiōtai* (Diod. Sic. 34/5.2.27, 32, 34). Again we find ourselves turning to questions about the political thinking of the Gracchi. It has often been considered that Ti. Gracchus' agrarian legislation was to the advantage of Romans rather than Italian or Latin allies. This is supported by evidence that in 129 there were complaints from Italians and Latins about the work of the commission.[16] But both Plutarch and Appian say that Tiberius suggested something rather different. Plutarch claims that he would repeatedly say to the People from the rostra that while the wild animals that roam over Italy have a cave or resting-place, those "who fight and die for Italy" lack homes and roam about with their wives and children (*Ti. Gracch.* 9.4–5). Appian claims that "during his tribunate he spoke reverentially about the Italic race, as excellent in warfare and from the same stock as the Romans, but gradually declining into poverty and scarcity and having no hope of recovery" (*B Civ.* 1.9). And Velleius Paterculus speaks of him as promising citizenship to the whole of Italy (2.2). So could this inscription be taken as further testimony that Ti. Gracchus, with whose measures its author apparently associates himself, claimed to be working to the advantage of Italians?

An alternative view is possible. Some of the measures of the younger Gracchus are claimed to have been devised originally by his elder brother: so Plutarch talks of Tiberius' proposing a reduction in the length of military service, giving a right of appeal to the People against the verdicts of jurors, and adding to the senatorial jurors an equal number of *equites* (*Ti. Gracch.* 16.1), while Cassius Dio refers to his taking the courts from the Senate and giving them to the *equites* (fr. 83.7). But when we note that the story of Tiberius' journey through Etruria derives from a pamphlet published by his younger brother (Plut. *Ti. Gracch.* 8.9), a suspicion arises that the later measures are being backdated in order to serve Gaius' political goals – in particular the attempt to draw support from those who regarded Tiberius as a hero – rather than merely being wrongly attributed through a confusion of the two brothers by later authors. If that suspicion is correct, one motive for Gaius' attribution of his own measures to his brother may have been to gain support for one in particular which he was going to find very difficult to sell to the Roman People, namely the granting of citizen rights to the Latins and of improved status to the Italians. And so the claims that Tiberius spoke in such terms of Italy and of the Italians may similarly be false, reflecting rather his younger brother's agenda. In that case, the author of our inscription, in emphasizing that he worked to the advantage of Italians, may be reflecting a political stance which was actually quite different from Tiberius' own. Whatever the answers to these difficult questions, many of those who used this road and stopped at the forum will have been Italian allies, and, as in the earlier case of the Pompeian inscription of L. Mummius, such people are here seen to be very much in the minds of prominent Romans.

Legal texts too can help reveal something of the complexity of political thinking in late Republican Rome, as for example in the case of an inscribed law for the recovery of extorted property (*res repetundae*) from northeastern Italy, which has been identified as the *repetundae* law of 123 or 122 attributed to C. Gracchus.[17] No Republican law survives complete, and the fragmentary nature of such texts poses considerable difficulties of reconstruction and interpretation. Following the confirmation of a brilliant analysis of the relationship between the fragments by Harold Mattingly, the *repetundae* law has been shown to be rather less fragmentary than had been thought.[18] It contains remarkably detailed provisions about how Italians, Latins, provincials, and others could receive restitution for property inappropriately taken by any Roman magistrate (whether a senator or not).[19] These included careful procedures for the selection of jurors from an advertised list, and regulations about the dimensions of the ballots with which they voted and about the manner of voting. The ballots were to be marked with A on one side (for "APSOLVO," "I acquit") and C on the other (for "CONDEMNO," "I condemn"). The juror was to scratch out the letter which did not apply, and then, with his arm bare, he was to hold the ballot and place it in the voting-urn in such a way that onlookers could see that a single valid ballot was being used, but not which verdict it indicated.[20] All of the provisions give the impression, at least, of a deep concern for just treatment of non-Romans by Roman officials, which accords very neatly with the tone of anecdotes about the behavior of Roman magistrates in C. Gracchus' published oratory (Gell. *NA* 10.3.3). But alternatively they may be seen as in part an exercise in projecting to non-Romans an image, however false, of Roman decency and honor, and therefore as continuing many years later the work of Flamininus in encouraging a high opinion of the Romans abroad. At all events, such inscriptions reveal something of the intricate history which lies behind the brief and often confused accounts of our literary sources, and give some idea of the labor that went into the drafting of Republican legislation.

On occasion a very famous name turns up in an unexpected epigraphic context, such as when we find the young patrician Catiline along with Pompey as members of the advisory body of Pompey's father at the time of the latter's granting citizenship to a troop of Spanish cavalry during the Social War,[21] or when Cicero appears as a member of the advisory body which confirmed in 73 that the land of the divinity Amphiaraus at Oropus in Boeotia was exempt from tax collection by Roman *publicani* (*RDGE* no. 23; Sherk 1984: no. 70). But the vast majority of names revealed

Fig. 3.4 *Magistri* inscription of 99 BC from northern Campania. By permission of the Soprintendenza Archeologica delle Province di Napoli e Caserta. *Source*: photo by author

by epigraphy, male and female, are those of people whose identity would otherwise be entirely lost. Similarly, epigraphy has greatly increased our awareness of the political life of local communities. The surviving fragments of the charters of the *municipium* of Tarentum in Italy and the colony of Urso in Spain cast much light on local administration, but epigraphy also improves our understanding of areas where Roman control took a different form. In the *ager Campanus*, in the first century the largest remaining stretch of Roman *ager publicus* in Italy, we find that a significant quantity of building work was supervised by boards of local officials (*magistri*) attached to sanctuaries. Some or all of these boards came under the supervision of local districts, which could direct their activity. In important respects the administrative structures revealed by these "*magistri* inscriptions" show that this area bore a firm Roman imprint.[22] One of these texts is illustrated in Figure 3.4. It records that in 99 the listed individuals used the funds of Diana (their sanctuary being the temple of Diana Tifatina) to build a wall, a chamber or porch, and a portico, and to purchase marble statues of Castor and Pollux and a private estate.[23] In this particular example, the apparent erasure of the names of the *magistri* and the position of the names of the consuls show that the inscription has a curious history, which is yet to be satisfactorily explained.[24] In non-Roman communities, also, epigraphy can cast an interesting light on local government. A fragment of the Lex Osca Tabulae Bantinae (a "law" in Oscan on one side of a bronze tablet from ancient Bantia which contains on the other a Roman law dating to the late second century), published in 1969, added an important dimension to studies of this inscription in suggesting that the Latin side, which has a fixing-hole placed beneath the text, predates the Oscan side, where the text has had to be fitted round the fixing-hole.[25] If, then, the Oscan text, which

contains legal rules and rules about the census, and which may therefore be constitutional in character, was inscribed on a reused bronze tablet which had on it a
Roman law dating to the late second century, there are limited possibilities for it
chronologically, since Oscan died out in public epigraphy in the first century. It is
perfectly possible that the Oscan text was actually set up and inscribed during the
Social War rebellion, which saw the neighboring Latin colony of Venusia side with the
rebels. This is sometimes doubted on practical grounds,[26] but it is worth remember-
ing that since the rebels actually set up their own state with a capital at Corfinium and
minted an extensive coinage, there is a natural context for the establishment, or
reestablishment, of a local constitution in Oscan at a community like Bantia.[27] At
all events, in the absence of Oscan literature, Oscan epigraphy is an important
reminder for the historian of the complexity and variety of political life in Italy during
the Republican period (see also Chapter 28).

The enfranchisement of Italy which occurred during and after the Social War
signaled the end not just of the Oscan language in Italy, but also of Etruscan and
other languages. With the predominance of Latin in the expanding Roman realm,
there was a huge increase in its use and in the spread of Latin inscriptions, and vastly
more survive from the Principate than from the Republican period. There is thus also
a direct epigraphic reflection of the expansion of Roman power. By engaging with the
complex dialog between epigraphic and other sorts of evidence, and exploring the
otherwise invisible aspects of ancient life revealed by inscriptions, we can come to a
deeper appreciation of just how far-reaching a process it was.

Numismatics

As is the case with inscriptions, the quantity of coinage which survives from the Republican period is far smaller than that which survives from the Principate, and it constitutes
only a very small fraction of what was minted. But it forms nevertheless a substantial body
of material which offers the historian both a valuable source of evidence and considerable
challenges of interpretation. Coins were mass-produced and were in use over a very wide
area, sometimes well beyond the area for which they were originally intended: Roman
Republican coins are in fact found in some numbers as far afield as India. They are also
very durable items. The surviving coins provide important evidence on many economic,
political, and cultural issues, which sometimes supplements the information provided by
literary texts, sometimes contradicts it, and sometimes reveals things about which the
ancient authors are silent. Very often there is no indication of the archaeological context
in which the coins were discovered, partly because they are such collectable and market-
able items, and it is often not in the interests of those who sell them to reveal the context
of discovery. But where the context is accurately recorded (as in the case of many coin
hoards), this too can contribute valuable evidence. Besides Roman coinage, there are
numerous other contemporary coinages which have a bearing on Roman Republican
history. However, the bulk of our attention here is naturally focused on what was
produced by (or for) the Romans themselves.

Fig. 3.5 Cast bronze bar, Crawford 1974: no. 9/1. © Copyright The Trustees of The British Museum

Within a century of the invention of coinage in Asia Minor in c.600 BC, coins were being minted in most of the major Greek settlements of Italy and Sicily. But it was a long time before the Romans introduced a recognizable monetary system of their own. The outline history of Roman Republican coinage can be summarized as follows. The fifth-century Twelve Tables imply the use of bronze by weight as a measure of value.[28] In the third century, the Romans were using cast bronze bars and coins, the latter based initially on a unit of one Roman pound, termed an "as" (plural: "asses"), which subsequently underwent a series of weight reductions.[29] The bars show various images, the most striking being of an elephant on one side and a sow on the other (Figure 3.5), which has plausibly been associated with a story in Aelian about Pyrrhus' elephants during the Pyrrhic War being frightened away, in part, by the noise made by pigs (*NA* 1.38). This would give a date for this issue of bars of about 275 onwards. The Romans appear to have ceased to produce cast bars in the latter part of the First Punic War (264–41);[30] however, the cast coins (e.g., Figure 3.6) were produced

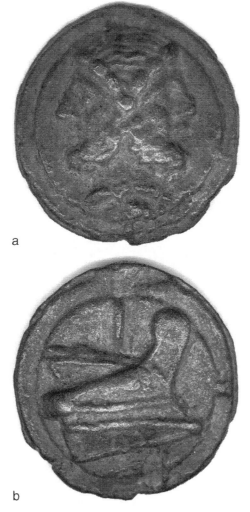

a

b

Fig. 3.6 Cast bronze as Janus/prow, Crawford 1974: no. 35/1 (diameter 6.6 cm). © Copyright The Trustees of The British Museum

until the middle of the Second Punic War (218–01). While the use of cast metal reflects Italian practice, the Romans' adoption of struck coinage reflects Greek influence.[31] The first coins struck for the Romans were minted in the late fourth century, probably at Naples (their types match contemporary Neapolitan issues and their legend, "of the Romans," is in Greek). This was the first token (or "fiduciary") bronze issue,[32] followed soon after by another token bronze issue (with legend in Latin, "ROMANO," probably = "Romanorum," "of the Romans") and the first silver issue, which was probably minted at Rome, featuring images of Mars and a horse's head (also with legend "ROMANO").[33] These early issues may predate the creation of the cast bars and coins, but they do not seem to have established the use of struck coinage as standard, since there is a gap before a continuous sequence of Roman struck coinage, silver and bronze, begins in the late 270s or early 260s, with the legend "ROMANO" giving way to "ROMA" from about 240 onwards. It is not clear what the relationship is between the early bronze and silver struck coinage, and they may indeed have been quite separate: there is no clear relationship of weight between them (the silver coins are based on the Greek didrachm, a two-drachma piece, with occasional silver fractions thereof), and to judge from the recorded findspots they circulated in different areas (the bronze in central Italy, like the cast bars and coins, and the silver further south).[34] The initial relationship between cast and struck bronze coinage is also unclear, but by a certain point in the mid-third century cast bronze coins and struck silver and bronze coins were being produced in parallel, all at Rome, and were clearly related in type and value. In the Republic, the Roman mint was located on the Capitol, near the temple of Juno Moneta,[35] although Roman coins were sometimes minted elsewhere.

The Second Punic War represents a turning-point in the history of Roman coinage, as in Roman history as a whole. Besides witnessing the disappearance of cast bronze coinage, following several reductions in weight standard, it saw first the reduction in weight standard and the debasement of the silver didrachm coinage, and then its replacement by a new coin, the denarius, which became the standard Roman silver coin. It also marked a watershed in the history of numerous other coinages around the Mediterranean world, which in the course of time all came to be replaced or dominated by Roman coinage, but initially reacted to it in strikingly different ways.[36] Following the war, little coinage other than Roman was minted in Italy. The Romans issued more than one gold coinage in the Second Punic War, itself sometimes an indication of severe financial difficulty, but thereafter, apart from an issue under Sulla's dictatorship, gold was not used again until the establishment of a regular gold coinage in 47–6 under Caesar's dictatorship, whereafter the issue of gold coins was standard. The denarius, from its inception in c.211, remained the most important Roman silver coin until well into the third century AD. As its name implies, it was originally tariffed at 10 asses, an as by this time having a weight standard of two ounces (one-sixth of the original weight of 1 lb). There were lower denominations in both silver and bronze. The silver quinarius and sestertius were tariffed at 5 and 2½ asses, respectively, and the bronze had denominations as low as a semuncia (half an uncia, or one twenty-fourth of an as). A bronze as weighed about two ounces at the time of the creation of the denarius, but in time the bronze coinage, now all struck, became entirely fiduciary, like the earlier struck bronze. Roman bronze coinage gradually declined in importance during the course of the second century, and very little bronze coinage was minted in Rome or Italy during the first century. In c.141 the denarius was retariffed at 16 asses, and the quinarius and sestertius accordingly at eight and four asses, respectively. The sestertius, although not commonly issued as an actual coin, became the unit in which very large amounts were reckoned. When tariffed at 2½ asses, it had been represented in texts by the symbol "IIS" ("sestertius" deriving from "semis-tertius," "a half in third place"); after the retariffing, a horizontal line was struck through the symbol, which is therefore usually printed "HS."

It is worth looking briefly at the production, denominational structures, dating, and circulation of Republican coinage, before considering its value as evidence for economic history and for political, social, and cultural history.

The cast coins and currency bars were produced by pouring molten metal into a mold. The struck coins were produced by striking hot coin blanks (metal discs) on an anvil with a punch. One (reverse) die was set into the punch, and another (obverse) die was set into the anvil, so that the images were struck onto the front and back of the coin simultaneously (Figure 3.7).[37] Dies wore out (reverse dies usually somewhat sooner than obverse),[38] and large numbers of reverse and obverse dies might be needed for a single issue of coins. By the time that the denarius was first struck, the regular production of coins was in the hands of junior magistrates known as Tresviri Monetales (referred to here as "moneyers"), who at some point made up three of the *uigintisex-uiri* ("26 men") each year and were probably annually elected officials.[39] Occasionally other magistrates were involved in producing coinage. Although the coins were mass-produced, the dies appear to have been individually cut. There may be only one genuine surviving example of a Roman Republican die,[40] but the study of dies (as deduced from the coins they produced) is an important element in Republican numis-matics, as will become clear below. Along with images and inscriptions, dies often had carved into them denomination marks and control marks, the latter consisting of letters, numerals, or symbols, whose function is on the whole not well understood. Forgeries of Roman coins in the ancient as in the modern world were common.

The weight standards of ancient coins are deduced from the weights of surviving coins. These weights are obviously in the vast majority of cases somewhat less than the original weight of the coins through the wear experienced since minting, but with a

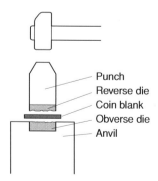

Fig. 3.7 Production of coinage by striking

sufficient number of well-preserved specimens it is possible to come to a close approximation to the original weight standard. Weight standards were correlated to the denominations of coins that were issued, but were subject to change from time to time, and subsequent to the establishment of the denarius there was also one major change in denominational structure (in c.141, noted above). The basic denominational structure of the Roman coinage after the invention of the denarius is as follows:

Silver:		c.211 until c.141	after c.141
	Denarius	10 asses	16 asses
	Quinarius	5 asses	8 asses
	Sestertius	2½ asses	4 asses
Bronze:			
	As	12 unciae	→
	Semis	6 unciae	→
	Triens	4 unciae	→
	Quadrans	3 unciae	→
	Sextans	2 unciae	→
	Uncia	24 scripula	→
	Semuncia	12 scripula	→

There was great variety in the choice of denominations employed in any particular coin issue. Occasionally other denominations besides those listed above were produced.[41]

It is generally much easier to date Roman Republican coins closely than Greek coins, particularly because of the annual turnover of named officials who were responsible for issuing them. Here the evidence of the numerous surviving Republican coin hoards is crucial. The survival of a hoard to the present day means that it was not recovered in antiquity, and therefore to some extent the number of Republican hoards available for study may be a reflection of the political and military disturbance of the Republican period: as far as Italy is concerned, it is noteworthy that there are far fewer coin hoards surviving from the more tranquil period of the early Principate.[42] The survival of so many hoards and the occasional possibility of dating certain coin issues exactly because of their reference to a particular person or event, or of dating them by reference to the non-Roman coins with which they circulated,[43] mean that detailed comparison of the contents of overlapping hoards, taking into account such questions as the degree of wear exhibited by the coins, allows many elements of the long sequence of Republican issues to be securely dated, and many others to be placed within fairly narrow limits.[44] The overstriking of a new coin type onto a preexisting type, with the result that faint traces of the original type may survive, is also sometimes of help in dating.[45] Stylistic analysis of the types employed can help to some extent, although this is far less significant for dating than the hoard evidence. It is very interesting that the evidence of the coins themselves and of their archaeological contexts shows certain of the claims found about Roman coinage in ancient literature to be well off the mark. For example, the dating of the creation of the denarius to c.211 is assured by a combination of hoard evidence, overstriking, and archaeological evidence,[46] but Pliny the Elder dates the introduction of silver coinage and of the denarius to 269–8, both of which claims are clearly false (*HN* 33.44). Much labor has gone into trying to rescue his account, but it is probably better to accept that Romans in the Principate did not understand much about the early history of their coinage.[47] Detailed work on the coinage is constantly allowing refinements and corrections to arguments about the dating of one or more coin issues. A good example is the case of the denarius of Sulla illustrated in Figure 3.8, dated by some to 84–3, during Sulla's return from his eastern campaigns, but argued by others to be a later issue, minted at Rome.[48] The attraction of the later date is principally that while this issue, consisting of the denarius here illustrated and a higher denomination in gold, calls Sulla "IMPER(ATOR) ITERVM," "saluted as commander for the second time," other coinage issued by Sulla which can be dated to 82 calls him simply "IMPE(RATOR)," with no reference to a second salutation.[49] However, Hollstein has demonstrated that consideration of the "die-axes" of this issue shows the earlier date to be correct. The die-axis of a coin is the spatial relationship between the obverse and reverse dies which produced it: if the top is at the same point for both dies, the die-axis is "12 o'clock"; if one is exactly inverted in respect of the other, it is "6 o'clock," and so on. Roman Republican coinage has in general no consistency in respect of its die-axes, but the situation was different in certain parts of the Greek world. The "IMPER(ATOR) ITERVM" coinage turns out to have a regular "12 o'clock" die-axis, which, taken together with other evidence, strongly suggests minting in Greece or Asia Minor, most probably at Athens in 84–3 in preparation for Sulla's invasion of Italy. This is a demonstration of how precise scholarly work can show that what appears to be the natural conclusion to draw about the sequence of two coin issues from their legends is actually a false one, and there are important consequences for the interpretation of this issue's types.[50]

For understanding the circulation of Republican coins, surviving hoards are again crucial, since they provide evidence about the distribution of coinage, the length of time for which coins remained in circulation, and which coins circulated together. Thus we learn that the denarii produced by the Social War rebels circulated with Roman denarii, but ceased to circulate very soon after the war ended,[51] and that, later on, coins of Juba I, king of Numidia, a partisan of Pompey who died in 46, circulated freely with Roman denarii: they are found in no fewer than 26 hoards of the latter half of the first century BC, and continued to circulate until about the end of the first century AD.[52] Coin hoards demonstrate the circulation of coins in rural as well as urban contexts, though there is much disagreement over the extent of this.[53] There appears to have been no Roman equivalent of negotiable paper, and Roman banking is generally held to have been rather unsophisticated,[54] but it appears that in certain contexts it was possible in the late Republic for a large sum to be transferred from one place to another without the actual movement of any coins. This is attested in the case of the companies of tax contractors in Sicily, where the governor of the province could draw on the funds that they held for the sum allotted him by the Senate for his governorship (Cic. *Verr.* 2.3.163–70).[55] However, it was often necessary for large quantities of coinage to be transported over long distances, and in particular coinage,

a

b

Fig. 3.8 Denarius of Sulla, Crawford 1974: no. 359/2 (diameter 1.8 cm). © Copyright The Trustees of The British Museum

and sometimes mints, moved around with armies. For example, Scipio Africanus apparently had been provided with 2,400,000 denarii (or their equivalent) at Rome in 210 to take with him to Spain (Polyb. 10.19.1–2).[56]

In several respects it is more difficult to understand the use of coinage in the Roman world, and more broadly its role in the Roman economy, than we might wish. There is some textual and archaeological evidence about the range of goods and services for which coinage was used in the Roman empire, but much of this comes from the period of the Principate or later and concerns specific provinces (particularly Egypt), making it difficult to be confident about the relevance of this evidence for other times and places. Nevertheless, enough survives to suggest that coinage was in regular use in cities as a means of exchange for goods, and was used also in rural areas, being entirely absent perhaps only in the most remote places. However, there is some evidence for the use of barter as a means of exchange. Coinage was also used for the payment of taxes, rents, and wages, and for credit, but there is evidence too of the use of agricultural produce for all these purposes.[57] We learn from Cicero's *Verrine Orations* that in the late Republic the tax on land in the province of Sicily was paid not in cash but in grain (Cic. *Verr.* 2.3.11–15); the pasture tax, however, and customs dues in Sicily were paid in cash. There may have been considerable variation in the form of tax payment required, whether cash or kind, from place to place, and likewise in the case of rents, wages, and credit.

It appears that coinage was not the only form of money in the late Republic (or in later periods of Roman history). Although the evidence is limited, bullion probably did not function merely as a store of wealth, but was also used directly in monetary transactions. Gold and silver bars have turned up in hoards of Roman coins of the Republican period from regions as widely separated as Spain, Italy, and Romania.[58] Cicero refers in the *Defense of Cluentius* (*pro Cluentio*) of 66 to a theft three years earlier of a quantity of coins and "five pounds of gold" from a safe in the house of one Sassia at Larinum (*Clu.* 179). And in a letter to Atticus of August 45 he refers to "a large weight of silver" in the house of M. Cluvius at Puteoli (*Att.* 13.45.3).[59] This needs to be borne in mind when one moves from questions about the use of coinage to questions about the use of money and about the degree to which the Roman economy was monetized. Bullion may have been a convenient way to make very large payments for a variety of purposes, but it is not clear how often it was used in monetary transactions. So although the cumulative evidence of the widespread use of coins suggests a high, though perhaps varying, degree of monetization in the economy of the late Republic, it is impossible to tell how much large-scale as well as small-scale monetary activity is hidden from our view.

The question arises of how the quantitative study of Republican coinage can improve our understanding of the Roman economy. It is generally recognized that it is unwise to try to assign an economic purpose to a particular coin issue without considering its size. One approach is to attempt to calculate the number of dies that were used for producing specific coin issues. Another is to attempt to calculate the actual number of coins produced. Neither is without its own difficulties, and it is not a straightforward matter to move from one to the other.

Ascertaining the number of dies used to produce particular coin issues can give some idea of the relative scale of production, although it does not neatly reveal how many coins were actually produced (as explained below). In the case of Republican coinage, we are fortunate that one of the moneyers of 82, P. Crepusius, used reverse dies which exhibit a continuous sequence of control-numerals from 1 to approximately 525, with no numeral having more than one die.[60] This has provided a useful test for statistical methods of estimating how many dies were used on the basis of the number represented in given samples of coinage, since we can be confident about the actual number of dies used in this case (give or take a very few).[61] Alternatively, a number of sufficiently large hoards containing datable coins can give a good idea of the relative mint output over the period of production of the coins.[62] Crawford used the evidence of a long sequence of overlapping hoards for quantitative work of a similar sort: here the issues whose dies have been studied and differentiated are used to provide estimates of the number of dies employed to produce the issues for which no die studies have been undertaken.[63] Matters become more difficult when one attempts to calculate the actual number of coins produced in a particular issue. The problem is that there is very considerable margin for error in the estimates of how many coins would be produced by each die, with proposed estimates for Republican silver ranging between 4,500 and 30,000 coins per die, and such comparative evidence as there is does little to encourage optimism about what may be achieved in this sort of work for the Republican period.[64] So even a good estimate of the number of dies employed to produce a given body of coinage does not lead to a simple calculation of the number of coins minted.

As already noted, such information about the size of a coin issue as is available should be taken into account when approaching the question of its economic purpose. It is often suggested that a particular issue, especially a large one, was minted in order to make one or more specific payments, such as those associated with military activity or with building projects (for example, road building or temple construction). There are in fact occasions when a specific purpose is attested in the inscription on a coin, as in the case of Piso and Caepio in 100 (quaestors rather than the more usual Tresviri Monetales), whose coins announce themselves as having been issued "AD FRV(MENTVM) EMV(NDVM)," "for the purchase of grain": this is likely to be associated with the grain law of the tribune Saturninus in that year.[65] In other cases, a purpose is not so directly attested, but can nevertheless plausibly be suggested. So it is with the huge Roman coinage of 90, with dies estimated to number in the thousands. Here the outbreak of the Social War late in the previous year, with the consequent need for making large military payments, is more than likely to be a factor. State expenditure of this sort will probably have been the principal, though not necessarily the only, means by which new coin entered the Roman economy.[66] But while it is likely that such particular purposes were at least partly responsible for the scale of certain coin issues, it is important to remember that a new issue was a contribution to the money supply, not the money supply itself. The supply of money was affected by various factors, such as the use of credit, the availability of usable metal, and the number of old coins ceasing to circulate through casual loss, hoarding, or export, and decisions about how many coins of which denominations should be minted at a particular time will probably have taken into consideration a variety of issues of this kind.[67] The details of the decision-making process are unfortunately obscure to us, but it is likely that the quantity of coinage to be minted was authorized by the Senate early in the year,[68] with occasional decrees to mint more coins later in the year, leading to "special" issues (such as the issue of Piso and Caepio above) which were marked with the legend "EX S(ENATVS) C(ONSVLTO)," "in accordance with a decree of the Senate."[69] We have not infrequent reference in the literary sources to shortages of money in the late Republic,[70] and it is clear that specific economic information will have been taken into account when detailed decisions were made about the minting of coinage. Unfortunately, we are in the dark about how such information was gathered and used, so in the search for specific economic purposes behind a coin issue the conclusions that one could reasonably draw from quantitative analyses of coin output, themselves problematic, are somewhat limited. Nevertheless, the available numismatic evidence does at the very least put certain restraints on economic hypotheses about the late Republic, and it must be taken into account in any attempt to explain the workings of the Roman economy in this period.

It is natural that Roman Republican coins, which exhibit an extraordinary variety of types and are in general so closely datable, have often been exploited as a source of evidence for political, social, and cultural history. Considerable variety, much more than in the case of Greek coinages, is apparent already in the third century,[71] but with the institution of the denarius in c.211 there was further evolution of types, and from c.137 there is a remarkable increase in the variety employed. It is clear in this latter period that the types were usually chosen by the moneyers whose names appear on the coins, because they sometimes contain a specific reference to the family of one of them. It is not clear if this freedom to choose coin types required particular authorization, whether from a decree of the Senate or from legislation, but however it came about, there was a movement toward types which had at least as much to do with a specific family or individual as with Rome as a whole, which can be seen as symbolized by the increasing rarity of the appearance of the legend "ROMA" on the coins (although the dominance of Roman coinage was such that the legend may simply have been felt to be no longer necessary). There are representations of works of art, buildings, mythological scenes, and references to historical and contemporary events and themes. The term "propaganda" is widely used to describe the function of some of these images, but it is often not a helpful notion in this context. Although the coins were indeed mass-produced items, their types can rarely be seen as having the specific purpose of driving people to one side or the other in a conflict or argument. The vast majority of types are better seen as functioning in a more subtle way, as resonating with the preoccupations of contemporary society and reflecting Roman historical consciousness (see also Chapter 23), politics, and culture in a broader sense, rather than as having any such specific agenda.[72] But it is obvious that the future electoral success of a moneyer who advertised his family's history on his coins will have been a significant element in his thinking.

The denarius illustrated in Figure 3.9 was issued by the moneyer P. Nerva in 113 or 112. On the obverse is a bust of Roma, helmeted. On the reverse a figure on the right, standing on a platform (a *pons*), places a ballot into a voting-urn, while on the left the next man to vote receives a ballot from a figure standing behind the platform. The two parallel lines and the line just above the moneyer's name, which appears to carry a tablet with a letter on it (indicating the voting tribe?), probably mark off the voting-area. We think back to the voting regulations in C. Gracchus' extortion law approximately a decade earlier, where the juror's arm had to be bare when the ballot was placed in the urn: here the voter's arm goes slightly upwards, which would help keep the toga clear of it. We can perhaps see here also a reflection of the consequence of the law which Marius passed during his tribunate in 119, by which the *pontes* (voting-platforms) were narrowed (Cic. *Leg.* 3.38; Plut. *Mar.* 4.2): voters could only approach the urn one at a time, having just received their ballot

a

b

Fig. 3.9 Denarius of P. Nerva, Crawford 1974: no. 292/1 (diameter 1.8 cm). © Copyright
The Trustees of The British Museum

from the voting-officer (*custos*), thus making intimidation, bribery, or the use of
false ballots more difficult. Looked at in this light, Marius' law comes across as an
anti-corruption measure, whatever other political purposes it may have served.[73]

The moneyers Kalenus and Cordus issued the denarius illustrated in Figure 3.10
probably in 70. On the obverse are depicted heads identified as HO(NOS) and
VIRT(VS), with KALENI ("of Kalenus"). A temple to Honos and Virtus
("Honor" and "Virtue") had been dedicated by Marius after his defeat of the Cimbri
and Teutoni, and the image on this coin can be seen as a reference to that temple and
the personified virtues it celebrated, virtues associated with military and political
excellence. On the reverse, the right-hand figure identified as RO(MA), shown

Fig. 3.10 Denarius of Kalenus and Cordus, Crawford 1974: no. 403/1 (diameter 2 cm).
© Copyright The Trustees of The British Museum

standing in military attire with her right foot resting on a globe, is exchanging a
greeting with a figure identified as ITAL(IA), who holds a cornucopia; in the exergue
is the legend CORDI ("of Cordus"). This remarkable image of cooperation between
Italy and Rome strongly suggests Roman world conquest, or at least control, assisted
by Italian resources – a striking reflection of Roman self-perception at this time, and
an important reminder not just that the Romans realized that the earth was a globe,
but also that the idea of Rome as having a boundless empire predates by some decades
at least the famous appearance of the idea of empire without end in the poetry of
Virgil (*Aen.* 1.279), who was born in the year in which this coin was probably minted.
On one reading, then, this coin issue is a proud and confident proclamation of
Roman power and of productive cordiality between Rome and Italy. But there may
be more behind its images than appears at first sight. Reflection on the historical
context of its production can suggest a different reading. In the 90s and 80s the

Social War and the Civil Wars had seen Italy in turmoil, with tens of thousands killed, and with repercussions felt across the empire. In the 70s, Rome was faced with more conflicts in Italy – the insurrection supported by the consul Lepidus in 78–7, and, most recently, the slave revolt of Spartacus and his associates, which lasted from 73 to 71 and saw a series of high-ranking Roman commanders suffer humiliating defeats. Rome feared civil war in the difficult climate of 70, with the consuls accepting the need to undertake a public reconciliation in order to ease the tension. Rome's failure to control the seas was a source of great danger until Pompey's success against the pirates in 67, but social and economic turmoil persisted in Italy in the 60s, bursting out in the Catilinarian affair of 63–2. Did Romans in 70 really feel confident in their position of dominance over all other peoples? Did the implied relationship between Rome and Italy of peaceful coexistence and cooperation truly reflect Roman belief at this time? Some may have believed in these things. But an alternative interpretation of these images is that, rather than demonstrating Roman confidence about the present, they in fact reflect Roman aspirations for a more secure future in the wake of the violent upheavals of recent years, and show a desire to instill confidence against a background of insecurity and fear.

We close with an example from the troubled period of the ("Second") Triumvirate (Figure 3.11). It is a denarius issued by L. Plaetorius Cestianus for M. Brutus in 43–2, which depicts on the reverse two daggers, one on either side of a cap, with the words EID(VS) MAR(TIAE) ("the Ides of March," i.e., March 15) beneath. On the obverse is a head of Brutus, with the legend, BRVT(VS) IMP(ERATOR), and the name of the issuer. This famous coin (Dio Cass. 47.25.3) is unique among Roman Republican issues in bearing a particular calendar date, the Ides of March, which leaves no doubt that the symbols are referring to the assassination of Caesar in 44. It belongs to the period between late 43 and the battle of Philippi in the following year, during which time Brutus and Cassius were preparing for the coming conflict with the Caesarians.[74] The daggers which effected the killing and the cap (a *pileus*, worn by freed slaves) symbolize liberty, but why does the coin focus so precisely on the date of the killing? As often, there is probably more to this than is at first apparent.

The date is one of considerable significance in Roman political history, as it is the date on which the new consuls had entered office in the late third century and the first half of the second, until the change brought about in 154 whereby the consuls of the following year and subsequent years entered office on the first day (the Kalends) of January.[75] The period following the successes of the Hannibalic War was often looked back upon by later writers as a golden period in Roman history, which ended, or started to go wrong, at some point in the 150s or 140s, depending on the individual author's point of view. So the Ides of March was the date on which the two consuls had taken up office in this idealized Republic of successful expansion overseas and domestic tranquility, the power of each consul balancing the other's, just as was intended after Brutus' distant ancestor had led the expulsion of the last kings of Rome. Caesar's devaluation of the consulship by having suffect consuls appointed for three months at a time is well known, and his appointment of C. Caninius Rebilus for the latter part of the last day of 45, following the announcement that morning of the death of the suffect consul Q. Fabius Maximus, caused Cicero to joke that this man's vigilance was

a

b

Fig. 3.11 Denarius of M. Brutus and L. Plaetorius Cestianus, Crawford 1974: no. 508/3 (diameter 1.7 cm). © Copyright The Trustees of The British Museum

astounding, since he did not experience a moment's sleep in his entire consulship (*Fam.* 7.30.1–2). However, Cicero and others in fact took the matter very seriously. It is intriguing in this regard to consider the testimony of Suetonius, who tells us that the conspirators wavered between different assassination plans, but when Caesar called a meeting of the Senate for the Ides of March in Pompey's Senate-house, they "had no hesitation in choosing that time and place" (*Iul.* 80.4). The imminence of Caesar's eastern campaigns will have been a factor in the timing, so it is not clear that the meaning of the date actually played a part in the decision about when to kill him. But whether its significance was contemplated before or after the event, the symbolism of the date was a potent emblem in the violent struggles which followed Caesar's death, as the rivals for power competed to persuade the Roman People that it was they who would liberate them. The wealth of such symbols in Roman coinage, in the Republic's political collapse as in its growth, offers endless possibilities for fresh interpretation and new discoveries.

Guide to Further Reading

Epigraphy

The most useful introductions in English to the study of Roman Republican inscriptions in the context of Roman epigraphy as a whole are Gordon 1983 and Keppie 1991. Both have plentiful illustrations, introductions to the complex bibliography on Roman inscriptions, and helpful guidance on the resolution of abbreviations and various technical matters. The best edition of Republican Latin texts is A. Degrassi, *Inscriptiones Latinae Liberae Rei Publicae* (*ILLRP*) (with illustrations in Degrassi, *ILLRP, Imagines*); the fullest collection is volume one of the *Corpus Inscriptionum Latinarum* (second edition). Particularly useful are Cagnat 1914; Bérard 2000 (with annual supplements available over the internet); Calabi Limentani 1991; and Meyer 1973. Important recent studies include Gasperini 1999 and Solin 1999. *L'Année Épigraphique* details each year's new work in Roman epigraphy. For Greek inscriptions relevant to Roman affairs in this period, see *Roman Documents from the Greek East (RDGE)* (Sherk 1969) and Sherk 1984. The forthcoming "Imagines Italicae," supervised by Michael Crawford, should set the study of Italian inscriptions in languages other than Latin, Greek, and Etruscan on a new footing. In *The Journal of Roman Studies* approximately every five years a survey has been published of recent work in Roman epigraphy, the latest being Gordon 2003.

Numismatics

Crawford 1974 is the standard reference work on Roman Republican numismatics, with a full catalog and illustrations, and his books of 1969 and 1985 are essential complements to this, but perhaps the best introductions to the subject are the Republican sections of Burnett 1987 and Howgego 1995. Note also Crawford 1983a. Rutter 2001 is a very useful account of the non-Roman coinages of Italy, and the various papers in Burnett and Crawford 1987 are essential starting-points for the question of the impact of Roman coinage on the rest of the Mediterranean world. Five-yearly surveys of work on Roman Republican numismatics are published in "A Survey of Numismatic Research," the most recent being Alfaro Asíns and Burnett 2003.

Acknowledgments

I am grateful to the editors and, as so often, to Peter Derow, Michael Crawford, and Jonathan Williams for their help. They should not be thought responsible for any shortcomings of this chapter.

Notes

1 *ILLRP* 3, with addenda on pp. 315–16 = *ROL* 4: 242–5; *ILLRP, Imagines*: 378a–d.
2 Coarelli on the Volcanal in Steinby 1993–2000: 5.209–11.
3 Cornell 1995: 94–5.
4 E.g., the treaties with Carthage referred to by Polybius (3.22–7), the first of which he dates to the beginning of the Republic (see Cornell 1995: 210–14), and the laws of the Twelve Tables (Crawford 1996b: no. 40).
5 Fragments of calendars of Republican date survive from Antium (*Inscr. Ital.* 13.2: 8–9) and Rome (Coarelli 1998b: 26–30).
6 Pobjoy 2000a on "euergetism" in such contexts (adjective "euergetic" or "euergetistic" – the latter not my coinage, *pace* Gordon (2003: 228 n.90): e.g., Rajak and Noy 1993: 87).
7 Alternative view in Flower 1996: 170–7.
8 Collected in Sherk 1984: no. 6.
9 Martelli 2002.
10 Useful map in Cornell and Matthews 1982: 57; full list in Campbell 2000: 452–3.
11 Other *termini* have more complex markings on the top (see nos. 4 and 5 in Campbell's list: photographs in Solin and Kajava 1997: 316–18).
12 Gargola 1995: 155–63.
13 The most plausible identification (as T. Annius, consul in 128) is that of Wiseman (1987b: 99–156; 377–9; and 1989).
14 Brennan 2000: 151–3.
15 Purcell 1990: 7–29, esp. 14–20.
16 Cic. *Rep.* 1.31, 3.41 (Italians and Latins); App. *B Civ.* 1.19 (Italians).
17 Crawford 1996b: no. 1.
18 Mattingly 1969. Illustrations in Crawford 1996b: pl. 1, figs 1–2.
19 Sherwin-White 1982: 19.
20 Skillful analysis in Sherwin-White 1982: 19–28.
21 *ILLRP* 515; Gordon 1983: no. 15.
22 Pobjoy 1998.
23 Pobjoy 1997: 86.
24 A *damnatio memoriae*? Or is there a more innocent explanation?
25 Crawford 1996b: no. 7 (Latin), no. 13 (Oscan).
26 Crawford 1996b: 1.274.
27 Pobjoy 2000b.
28 Crawford 1996b: no. 40.
29 The bars are often referred to now as "aes signatum" and the cast coins as "aes grave," although this does not correspond to the ancient use of these terms. The bars appear to have had a weight standard of about five Roman pounds (Burnett 1987: 3).
30 For the explanation, Burnett 1987: 6.
31 Note, however, that the designs on the cast coinage were Greek in inspiration (Burnett 1987: 16).
32 In other words, the metal of the coin was itself worth practically nothing (by contrast with the cast bronze coins): such a coin had value because of its acceptability for exchange, which depended essentially on the strength of the authority which issued it.

33 Crawford 1974: no. 1 (Neapolitan bronze), no. 2 (second bronze issue), no. 13 (first silver). The first silver used to be dated somewhat later (hence the later number in Crawford): see Burnett 1978, 1989; Crawford 1985: 29.

34 Map in Burnett 1987: 2.

35 Meadows and Williams 2001.

36 Burnett and Crawford 1987.

37 In general, Crawford 1974: 2.569–89. References to "obverse" and "reverse" dies therefore pertain to the position of the dies during striking, not to the notional "heads" or "tails" of a coin. It is not always a straightforward matter to identify which was the obverse and which the reverse die, and it is quite possible that these are mislabeled from time to time.

38 Crawford 1974: 2.672.

39 Alternative view in Burnett 1977: 37–44.

40 Crawford 1974: 1.562 n.3. Most surviving dies are probably forgers' dies.

41 These were the decussis, quincussis, tressis, and dupondius (10, 5, 3, and 2 asses, respectively); and the dextans, dodrans, bes, and quincunx (10, 9, 8, and 5 unciae, respectively). For the victoriatus, Crawford 1974: 628–30.

42 Duncan-Jones 1994: 77–8.

43 Burnett 1987: 8–10.

44 Crawford 1969: 1–6.

45 Crawford 1974: 1.105–17, 1985: 336–7.

46 Crawford 1974: 1.28–35.

47 On such errors, Burnett 1987: 10–11.

48 Crawford 1974: no. 359/2 (84–3): contrary view in Martin 1989; Mackay 2000.

49 Crawford 1974: nos. 367–8.

50 Hollstein 2000a: 489–90, 2000b: 136. Metal analysis confirms the argument. The study of die-axes also shows that another issue of Sulla (Crawford 1974: no. 375) was probably minted outside Italy, before 81.

51 Burnett 1998: 168; Pobjoy 2000b: 198 with n.37.

52 Burnett and Crawford 1987: 176–7.

53 Howgego 1992: 16–22; Crawford 1970.

54 Howgego 1992: 28–9.

55 Badian 1972a: 76–7.

56 Equating one talent with 6,000 denarii (Crawford 1974: 1.33). See further Howgego 1994 on coin circulation in the empire as a whole in this and later periods.

57 Howgego 1992: 22–8.

58 Crawford 1969: no. 193 (Spain, a silver bar), no. 259 (Spain, gold bars), no. 331 (Romania, silver bars), no. 357 (Italy, gold bars). Howgego 1990: 13–14, 1992: 9–10.

59 This could refer to silver plate, but the use of "weight" (*pondus*) suggests bullion.

60 Crawford 1974: no. 361.

61 Duncan-Jones 1994: 149–50 for the relative strengths of his own method and that of Carter (1981a, 1981b, 1983). In respect of practical difficulties, note that Carter's original sample of 865 coins more than doubled following further searches (Duncan-Jones 1994: 144, 170).

62 Impressive correlation of the size of datable issues in hoards from the period of the Principate in Duncan-Jones 1994: 113–15.

63 Crawford 1974: 2.640–94.

64 Howgego 1992: 2–4; Duncan-Jones 1994: 163–5 (however, calculations of the ratio of gold to silver coins and dies in the Principate offer further possibilities for estimating die output in that period).

65 Crawford 1974: no. 330.

66 For the possibility of minting for individuals in the late Republic, Howgego 1990: 19–20.

67 On the significance of the velocity of circulation of coinage for the money supply, Howgego 1992: 12–16; for the importance of credit, 13–15.

68 Crawford 1974: 2.616–18.

69 Crawford 1974: 2.606–9.

70 Crawford 1974: 2.634–40.

71 Burnett 1986.

72 Meadows and Williams 2001; Morstein-Marx 2004: 81–91.

73 Marshall 1997: 61, 67–8.

74 Another issue with regular die-axes (Hollstein 2000a: 489, 2000b: 135).

75 Broughton 1951–86: 2.637–9.

CHAPTER 4

The Topography and Archaeology of Republican Rome

Mario Torelli

Translated by Helena Fracchia

The Beginnings of the Republic

Tradition records the dedication of the Temple of Jupiter Optimus Maximus on the Capitol among the most conspicuous and important signs of the birth of the Republic. The colossal building – the largest Etrusco-Italic type temple of all time – was consecrated by the first consul in republican history, although the temple was started by the royal dynasty of the Tarquins in the first half of the sixth century, a date confirmed by the most recent excavations on the temple plateau.[1] Much archaeological evidence of building and town development concurs to delineate the beginnings of a republican political structure, at Rome as in the rest of Latium and in Etruria. The most important of this evidence is the disappearance of the customary seventh- and sixth-century habit of decorating large aristocratic residences with architectural terracottas that glorified the military achievements of the leading men of the state and their rituals – both familial, such as weddings and symposia, and political, such as triumphal departures and returns (these last being the true origin of future republican and imperial ceremonies and related representations). Instead, from the end of the sixth century, decorated terracotta roof-revetments were reserved exclusively for the residences of the gods.[2] Of primary importance for our comprehension of the political climate at the time is the abandonment of the Temple of Fortuna (known later as Fortuna Redux, i.e., "Returning"), a foundation of King Servius connected with the assumption of power and with the notion of triumph.[3]

In the first two decades of the fifth century, the urban expansion of Rome continued briskly, as did the construction of imposing buildings that had carried on through the entire last century of the monarchy: at the end of the seventh century the first Tarquin is credited with the completion of the Circus Maximus (the chariot-racing stadium) and the Cloaca Maxima or "Great Drain" (which emptied the swamp on the site of the later Forum), in addition to the foundation of the temple of Jupiter on the Capitol. This evidence allows us to reconstruct an initial phase in the life of the young Republic, in which not only Rome but also the cities of Latium and southern Etruria continued to enjoy the extraordinary development that had begun in the preceding century.[4] In turn, the consular lists of the first 20 years of the Republic and the beginnings of the conflict between patricians and plebeians only confirm the other types of evidence. Tradition records that among the consuls of the time there were men either of plebeian *gentes* (clans) or of the *nomina Tusca*, respectively, people who did not belong to patrician families or were of Etruscan origin. Immediately after the disappearance of these *gentes* from the consular lists, a discernible "closure" of the patrician class occurred, evident in the exclusive presence of only patrician *gentes* in those same registers after 486 (following Varro's chronology): the beginning of the social unrest of the plebeians is documented by the first mass secessions to the Aventine, one dated to 494, and the other to 471, which is perhaps the more authentic date of the two.

In Rome, and in all the other major Latin cities, from Praeneste to Lavinium, as in the great cities of central and southern Etruria, the first decades of the fifth century are characterized by intensive public building, mainly sacred as far as we know, and no doubt associated with the lively competition between the aristocratic *gentes* that took place at the end of the monarchy in order to ensure preeminence on the new political stage. Even the figural decoration of the roofs of the temples changed: the myth of Hercules, often used by tyrants to represent ideological expectations connected to their social and political role, was abandoned in favor of other Greek mythological subjects that instead illustrated the punishment for the typical vice of the king-tyrant, *hubris*, as well as myths that celebrated virtues more appropriate to the new constitutional situation. This sustained building activity was focused not only on the large state temples, but also concerned minor, or in any event unofficial cult places, where we would expect to see the involvement of those outside the dominant aristocracy. An illuminating example of the life and fortunes of these minor, unofficial cult places is provided by the sanctuary at the Greek emporium in the port of Tarquinia, Gravisca, whose worshipers, Greek and Etruscan merchants and commercial intermediaries, show a number of affinities with the plebeian class in Rome which was forming at that time.[5] In Gravisca during the first two or three decades of the Etruscan and Latin republics we observe a substantial continuity in frequentation and cult: despite the evident drop between 550 and 520, Attic pottery continued to arrive until the beginning of the fifth century, and indeed in the years around 480 the sanctuary was ambitiously reconstructed. The reconstruction, however, lacked the architectural characteristics of contemporary official sacred buildings, which should not be surprising in view of the social and cultural marginality of the visitors to the sanctuary.

Even artisanal production appears to be sustained by the new building activity, and, in general, by the elevated lifestyle of the dominant classes. Plastic and pictorial decoration for the temples represented an important source of commissions for a high-quality artisan who, as in the past, was guided or at least influenced by specialized craftsmen from the Greek areas, now more clearly identifiable as Magna Graecia (the Greek coastal regions of southern Italy) and Sicily. The traditionally favored Ionian models were abandoned when, by the end of the sixth century, systems of terracotta roofing over a wooden superstructure were adopted that were undeniably of Sicilian origin. Pliny (*HN* 35.154) tells us that the cella of the temple of Ceres, Liber, and Libera in Rome, dedicated in 493, was painted by two Greek artists, Damophilus and Gorgasus, the former perhaps grandfather of the homonymous teacher of the painter Zeuxis, born at Heraclea Minoa in the territory of Agrigentum.[6] On the other hand, the presence of painters of Greek origin is well documented in the painted tombs at Tarquinia in the first quarter of the fifth century, with the beginning of a new style and decorative scheme characterized by the placement of a symposium scene at the end and depictions of games along the side walls of the tomb.[7] On the whole, the artisans in Rome who undertook the most demanding projects remained in the shadow of Etruria. This is true not just for architectural terracotta decoration: the only important sculptural work in Rome during these years, the Capitoline she-wolf, is attributable to late-archaic Etruscan foundries (see also Chapter 6). Pottery production, the best attested craft of the time, seems to be located in the principal Latin cities: although local pottery painters, firmly established in Etruria, were absent from Latin cities, production continued of bucchero, the principal fine tableware for all of the archaic period, maintaining a reasonably high quality for the entire time.[8]

The majority of our evidence pertains to architecture. Through the first years of the Republic tradition records a series of temple foundations that documents the coexistence of two different trends in urban development. The first of these trends, following the will of the dominant class, was concentrated in the part of Rome that the monarchy had designated in the formative phase of the city as the area for political activity and an important collective sacred space, i.e., the area of the Forum and the Capitoline Hill behind it, dominated by the temple of Jupiter Optimus Maximus which both emulated and rivaled the temple of Jupiter Latiaris, the collective focus of the Latin People (see Maps 7 and 8). On the one hand, the Regia (or "King's House"), and on the other, the Senate building (Curia) and the Comitium or "Meeting Place," with their numerous associated sanctuaries – all of small dimensions but with considerable significance for the collective social values of the archaic city starting with the heroic tomb of Romulus, the mythic founder of Rome – constituted the natural location for the development of the new Republican religious and political institutions, thus creating an ideal space similar to the agora in Greek cities, indubitably the model for the Roman Forum. The space now took on a definite form: the north side of the open space coincided with monuments of the monarchy, to the west, the Curia and the Comitium, and to the east, the Regia. (Figure 24.2.) The extension of the square was fixed permanently on the southern side by two large temples: one, the temple of Saturn built in 499, was on the same axis as the Curia and the Comitium, placed to the west of the open space that would become the Forum, while the other, the temple of the Dioscuri (Castor and Pollux), was built to the southeast of it in 484. Although the temple of Saturn, which was constructed in relation to an adjacent ancient altar and to the *mundus* ("pit," considered to be the *umbilicus*, "navel," or center of the city), is known only in its Augustan phase, recent excavations at the temple of the Dioscuri have brought to light the original podium and recovered some of the beautiful architectural terracotta decoration, probably originating from Caere and datable to the years between 490 and 470.[9] The two temples exhibit all-too-obvious propagandistic messages, directed at reaffirming the preeminence of Rome in the Latin world and celebrating the new Republican order. Just as the Capitoline temple represented the rival to the ethnic sanctuary of the Latin peoples, so too the temple of Saturn established at Rome the primitive god who was the founder of Latin civilization with a new and formidable synoecistic symbol based on the relationship on one side with the Altar of Saturn and the *mundus*, the "center of the city," and on the other, with the political buildings of the Curia and the Comitium. The other temple, dedicated to the Dioscuri, was intended to celebrate the victory over the Latin peoples and the conclusion of the *foedus Cassianum* (Treaty of Cassius), embracing other political and institutional aspects of the new Republican order with a clear reference (for the Dioscuri too were youthful horsemen) that was destined to last for centuries to the military role of the patrician youth, the *equites*, or "knights."

The other important trend also followed in its own way a path already delineated in the period of kingship under Servius Tullius with his establishment of the temple of Diana, a duplication of the pan-Latin cult at Aricia. This building activity concentrated on the Aventine Hill and well expressed the culture as well as the political and social aspirations of the rising plebeian class, which in this phase was not yet an openly subject and marginalized group. Like the contemporary Forum temples, the new Aventine foundations constituted an opposition, placed at the two extremities of the hill's northeastern slope facing the valley of the Circus Maximus where there existed already an extremely ancient sanctuary to Murcia, one of the archaic manifestations of Venus, with a very strong popular character that is evident in the festivals celebrated there. Of the two new sanctuaries, the first, dedicated in 495 at the southeastern edge of the hill, paid homage to the god of commerce, Mercury, and expressed clearly the economic and ideological formation of a merchant class with a strong Greek element active in the nearby Tiber port. Two years later, in 493, at the opposite, northern extremity of the Aventine slopes – and thus in even closer contact with the river port to the north – the other sanctuary was dedicated to Ceres, Liber, and Libera – the Roman version of a group of Greek divinities, Demeter, Kore, and Dionysus-Iacchus, whose cult was enormously popular, especially in the Greek colonies of Sicily and Magna Graecia. Thanks to its priests and administrators, the sanctuary soon became the political and religious center for plebeians, maintaining a distinctly and palpably Greek character that derived from the mercantile nature of many of its visitors and survived until the imperial period, when the cult was, by law, still administered by a Greek priestess from Velia or from Naples. As we have seen, the cella of the temple was painted by Greek artists, perhaps from Sicily, whose presence is to be connected to either the cult origins or to the commercial traffic of the nearby port.

The Patrician Republic

The archaeological evidence of the next hundred years contrasts strongly with the intensity of building activity and artisanal production from the period between the seventh century and the first decades of the fifth. Already at the beginning of the sixth

century the cemeteries of Rome and Latium, in contrast with their Etruscan counterparts, no longer contain grave goods: almost certainly this phenomenon reflects an
ideological choice, with parallels from the Italiote Greek world. The reason may have
been the adoption of sumptuary laws that restricted opulent funerals, but the result is
that one of the richest sources of the most useful archaeological documentation for
the reconstruction of ancient society is missing. Silence also fell upon public building
that, after the great exploits of the early Republic, would only start again at the
beginning of the fourth century. All of this has caused many archaeologists to talk
about a "crisis of the fifth century," the proof of political, economic, and social
difficulties that the young Republic encountered, steering between wars with neighboring peoples and social conflict that pitted patricians against plebeians. It is evident
that serious social and military problems persisted throughout the century. From the
very beginning of the fifth century, in fact, Italy seems to have been subjected to the
uncontainable pressure of the Italic mountain tribes moving toward the more hos-
pitable areas of Italy, the countryside of Latium and Campania. Latium attracted the
interest of several Umbrian tribes, the Aequi, the Marsi, and especially the Volsci, who
conquered the Pontine swamps, one of the breadbaskets of Rome and of Latium.
Thus there was undoubtedly a crisis, but not entirely as it has traditionally been
understood. At the heart of all the political, social, and economic disarray of the fifth
century unquestionably lies the closing of the patrician order which is recorded in
Rome under the year 486, but very probably was part of a general phenomenon
in Latium and in Etruria. This was an oligarchic decision that took the form of
an absolute rejection of every type of social mobility, both horizontal – which until
that time had been sustained by the entry of foreign clans into the local aristocracies –
as well as vertical, which consequently excluded the citizens of the lower classes from
political life. The great difficulties outlined above began to multiply. Plebeian political
liberty was limited, and aristocratic social groups from outside of the city were barred
from the civic community and political integration; these actions in turn unleashed
conflicts of a varied nature that pitted Romans against the threatening Italic tribes on
the one hand, and on the other, pitted the Senate and the magistrates of the Republic
against the plebeian assembly and tribunes entrenched in their sanctuary on the
Aventine (see also Chapter 6).

The political and social closure imposed by the patrician oligarchy banished from
the civic stage any opportunity to transgress the rigid rules demanded by the need to
bring about an absolute equality among patricians. The sharp change further manifested itself on the public level with the complete cessation of every type of building
activity. In the near-century between the initial phases of the Republic with the
construction of numerous monumental temples through the dedication of the temple
of the Dioscuri in 484 until the vigorous recovery initiated by Camillus after the
conquest of Veii in 393, the sources mention the building of only two temples. One,
dedicated in 466 to Semo Sancus (an obscure deity associated with sowing), was a
minor building, as Livy's description of it as a shrine (*sacellum*) (7.20.8) indicates,
and may actually have been only a restoration of a preexisting building from the
monarchy. The second, dedicated to Apollo in 433 in the context of the plague that
struck Athens in 429, was built on the same place as a shrine or an altar (*Apollinar*)

originally belonging to the monarchic period. Other building activity, such as the site "paved in white stone" near the Circus Maximus in 487 that commemorated the death, possibly by a lightning bolt, of the nine military tribunes with consular power, or the *lacus Curtius* ("Curtius' Pool") fenced off in the center of the Forum in 445 allegedly to celebrate the self-sacrifice of the *eques* Mettius Curtius, does not rise above the level of modest acts of expiation. The Villa Publica in the Campus Martius, erected to meet the requirements of the censors carrying out the census and dedicated in 435, is more closely connected to minor, private architecture than to public building intended for display.

In conformity with the lacuna in temple dedications during these hundred years is the total lack of evidence of architectural terracotta decoration. Bucchero pottery, poorly produced almost everywhere in very few forms until the middle of the fourth century, was by now a pale shadow of the high standard of the archaic period. Fine pottery consisted almost exclusively of unpainted simple ware, while imported pottery, either Greek or Etruscan, became so rare as to be virtually nonexistent. Since we possess hardly any contemporary archaeological data for Rome, it is difficult even to form a precise notion of the archaeological assemblages representative of this period. So faint are the characteristic traces of this "austere" period, which are barely discernible also in the thin and elusive levels of the Latin and Roman colonies of the fifth century, including Ostia.[10]

The Middle Republican Phase

The end of the period of "patrician austerity" came about in 367 with the Licinian-Sextian laws, both the more famous law granting the consulship to the plebeians and the agrarian law, much debated today, but certainly consistent with the new political framework. As in the archaic period, renewed building and artisanal activity at Rome took place in perfect synchrony with what was happening in the rest of Latium, in Etruria, and in Campania, by now under Italic control – that is, all the areas with which Rome once again starts to share cultural forms and artistic trends. We can observe a true rebirth of the culture of archaism and its triumphal rituals, but with a new impetus and innovative forms. This new culture, despite the inevitable differences between its various areas, can be considered substantially homogeneous on the Tyrrhenian side of the peninsula, from the gulf of Salerno to the mouth of the Arno, and is therefore usually defined as a *koiné* or distinct cultural community. At Rome this cultural *koiné* is now more than in the late archaic period clearly influenced by Magna Graecia and Sicily.[11] It is visibly conservative, the concrete expression of the victory obtained over the patrician oligarchy by the plebeian leadership, a social group that, as often happens when subordinate classes rise to power, showed itself to be tenaciously linked to more archaic cultural forms used in preceding periods. It is no surprise that the culture of this middle-Republican *koiné*, constituting the backbone of the Romanization of Italy, should happen in turn to be preserved by the dominant

Romano-Italic classes until the great change brought about by the Mediterranean expansion of Rome in the second century: even after the triumph of late Hellenism at the end of the Republic and the subsequent classicizing conformity under the Julio-Claudian emperors, the formal artistic language of the middle-Republican tradition, preserved at length by the marginal social classes, would undergo a revival in the culture of the ambitious freedmen in the early imperial period.[12] Fundamental to our knowledge of middle-Republican culture in Rome is the discovery and archaeological exploration of the most important Latin colonies, which were responsible for the exportation of the culture of the *koiné* to the entire peninsula well beyond the historical boundaries of its formation and development:[13] Fregellae, Alba Fucens, Cosa and Paestum, founded respectively in 324, 303, and 273, retained in broad outlines the physical aspect Rome had assumed in the second half of the fourth century, an aspect that the continuous building history of the *urbs* has destroyed, leaving behind only a few traces in the literary sources (see Figure 4.1).

In a first phase that covers the first half of the fourth century, the recovery is led by Etruria, still the motor of major economic and cultural phenomena in Italy. However, from c.338 on, following the dissolution of the Latin League and the grant of rights of citizenship without the vote (*civitas sine suffragio*) to the powerful Capuan elite, leadership in the developmental processes of the architectural and visual arts would pass to Rome, which had by now become a formidable power that in the eyes of the Greek world extended well beyond the confines of the Italian peninsula itself. In this sense the Cista Ficoroni is instructive. This unquestioned masterpiece among a class of large bronze containers for feminine cosmetics found exclusively at Praeneste between the end of the fifth and the first half of the third century is finely decorated with incision and appliqués of mythical and genre scenes derived from Italiote

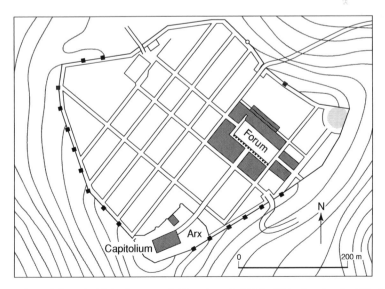

Fig 4.1 Plan of Cosa (mid-2nd century) (Stambaugh 1988: 256; drawing by Elizabeth H. Riorden). Used with permission of The Johns Hopkins University Press

prototypes.[14] The inscription (*ROL* 4: 198–9, no. 2b = *ILS* 8562 = *ILLRP* 1197) tells us that the Cista was made at Rome by one Novius Plautius, whose name identifies him as a Campanian client of an important *gens* from Praeneste that by 358 had entered the Senate of Rome.

The ruling class of the mid-Republic was then eager to reestablish many traditions belonging to the monarchical past, beginning with solemn triumphal celebrations and the building activity that accompanied those triumphs and, more generally, the political competition for magistracies. In consequence, the general character of the new architectural and artisanal culture that spread across Etruria, Latium, and Campania in the middle of the fourth century was one of a true revival of decorative traditions and artistic practices that had flourished until the first decades of the preceding century and then was silenced by a narrowly oligarchical patriciate. Temple decoration used once again the ancient syntax that had been introduced at the end of the sixth century under western Greek influences. Until the second century, the pedimental space would carry only the large mythological scenes applied to the plaques covering the roof's ridge pole (*columen*) and side-beams (*mutuli*);[15] after an initially blatant propagandistic phase referring to the victories of Rome and her allied cities, these scenes somewhat later (around the mid-third century), and in particular among the Italian allies, would fall back on representations that celebrated the mythical origins of the Roman People or the city.

From the beginning of the fourth century, with the end of Attic imported pottery, Falerii, along with the majority of the Etruscan cities and with several Campanian centers, started local pottery production both of red-figure, chiefly for funerary usage, and of black-glaze pottery, which instead became the standard fine tableware. In the beginning Rome, and the rest of the Latin world that was tied to her, did not participate in what was a lively competition between Etruscan and Campanian production centers; by the end of the century, however, Rome would take control of the pottery industry in the allied territories of Falerii and Caere (and perhaps also in the Latin colonies), producing a very particular class of small red-figure plates decorated with female heads of visible Italiote influence, the so-called "Genucilia plates." The wide exportation of these plates makes them an actual "ceramic flag" of Roman expansion during the last decades of the fourth century. Alongside the Genucilia plates, the mass production of black-glaze pottery known as APE (shorthand for "Atelier des Petites Estampilles," coined by J.-P. Morel),[16] with workshops in Rome and her dependent territories for most of the third century and also distributed across the entire peninsula and the western Mediterranean, became another "ceramic flag" of the military conquest of Italy and also of Roman commercial enterprise between 280 and 200, the first period of imperialistic Roman expansionism. Just as the conjunction between the Genucilia plates and the APE pottery distinguishes the oldest period of the Roman conquest of the peninsula, so too the apex of that period is mirrored in the association between APE and "Greco-Italic" type amphorae, the Romano-Campanian development of an originally Campanian amphora.[17]

Another seemingly typical product of the specifically Romano-Campanian and South Etruscan contexts of the *koiné* is the anatomic votive material, a third "archaeological flag" of Roman peninsular expansion, spread in an often surprising quantity through the devotional practices of masses of colonists even in areas where the tradition was not known (see also Chapters 10 and 21).[18] The oldest production, rare enough, but qualitatively excellent, is dated between the end of the fifth and mid-third century, and includes – in addition to sporadic heads – actual statues, found in Latium in the sanctuaries of Madonnella and the Eastern Hill near Lavinium, in the Latin colony of Cales and in the Campanian cities of Capua and Teanum Sidicinum. Starting in the mid-fourth century, a mass production of hands, feet, legs, intestines, and in particular heads began and would continue until the end of the second century, when these votive dedications would be replaced by monetary offerings, a practice that actually started in the mid-third century. The votive heads, which are of great importance archaeologically and for religious history, also have an art-historical significance, and document the origins of the portrait in the Romano-Italic sphere, once again in the wake of both Italiote and Sicilian influences. Written sources mention as early as 338 honorary statues of the great Republican generals, such as an equestrian statue of the consul L. Furius Camillus (grandson of the more famous M. Camillus), and of his colleague, C. Maenius, or the bronze posthumous statue of the great Camillus on the *rostra*: then, one by one, other commemorative dedications followed, signaling the beginning of the practice of dedicating individual portraits as an exceptional sign of distinction permitted by law (*ius imaginum*) only to those who had held the magistracy, a use connected with the exhibition of individual funerary masks in the solemn aristocratic funerals described by Polybius (6.53; see also Chapters 17, 23, and 24).[19] A precious example of the masterpieces produced by mid-Republican bronze sculptors is the head of the so-called Capitoline Brutus (dated to the second half of the fourth century) that finds parallels in some other bronze heads discovered in various places throughout the peninsula. Together with the votive heads, especially the not uncommon examples produced freehand and not in molds, these bronzes exemplify the diffusion of portraiture over the entire third century, characterized by stylistic similarities and a lively sense of formal artistic synthesis (see also Chapter 24).

Among these honorary and votive statues, particularly important was the bronze image of Marsyas, perhaps dated to 295, known to us through coins and through replicas from the Latin colonies of Alba Fucens and Paestum. Such statues were generally dedicated in the Forum to celebrate the glory of the new nobility (*nobilitas*) especially in the decades of the conquest of the peninsula, and were influenced considerably by Italiote and Sicilian Greek art. The close relationship to Italiote and Sicilian Greek art was productive also within the sphere of painting, as one can deduce from the "compendiary" style used in the decoration of the so-called "pocola," a typically Roman production consisting of black-glazed votive cups with overpainted figures and inscribed dedications to various divinities. The "compendiary" style is characterized by spots of color to indicate light, a technique derived from the great painting of the early Hellenistic period. But the same style was also used in the extraordinary painted tomb on the Esquiline, to be identified most likely with the tomb built at public expense for Q. Fabius Rullianus, "First Senator" (*princeps senatus*) and five times consul as well as victorious over the Samnites in 322 and 295 (Figures 24.19a and b; see also Chapter 24). The scenes of military events are perhaps copied from the paintings by C. Fabius Pictor, a relative of Rullianus (and an ancestor of the first Roman historian), in the temple dedicated by Rullianus in 302 to Salus on the Quirinal Hill. All of this demonstrates that the great tradition of Greek painting, obviously adapted to suit the particular needs of the given genre, was also seminal in the creation of the so-called triumphal paintings. These are an artistic expression long understood to be emblematic of the mentality and figurative tradition of Rome, and are also the source of the so-called historical reliefs which are well known from the late Republic to the Imperial age.[20] Such paintings, commissioned by generals in order to be shown first to the Senate and then to the People on the occasion of a triumph, originate exactly in this period in the context of a revival of archaic triumphal ceremonies: with the exception of the paintings by Fabius Pictor, the first securely dated example of triumphal painting, soon followed by a series of other analogous works, is the *Tabula Valeria* dedicated by M. Valerius Messalla either inside or outside of the Curia to commemorate the naval victory of 263 over the Carthaginians and King Hiero of Syracuse (see also Chapter 24).[21]

At the root of the revival of building activity and artistic production in the middle Republican period is the public celebration of the *gens* generated by the military and political successes of members of the nobility: the most important public monuments erected by various magistrates of the *gens* become, in effect, symbols of the fortunes of the family, which continues to see to the repairs, restoration, and reconstruction of these buildings – sometimes for centuries, as the case of the Basilica Aemilia illustrates (Tac. *Ann.* 3.72). On the other hand, in the private sphere, the scarcity of existing data proves that the old regulation of luxury in order to ensure equilibrium among the elite continued to function in some form. Although they remained severe and unadorned, only the aristocratic chamber tombs received attention as central sites for preservation of the memory of the group, as is shown by the first phase of the famous tomb of the Scipios whose progenitor, L. Cornelius Scipio Barbatus (consul in 298), is the only one to have had special treatment: a burial within a sarcophagus similar to a monumental altar of the Greek type (Figure 24.7; see also Chapter 24).[22] As far as we know, houses continued to have modest dimensions and façades: nevertheless, by this period the typical Roman atrium house was well established and, according to some scholars, had an archaic origin, as did the villa type demonstrated by the example found near Rome at the Auditorium site (see also Chapters 16 and 24).[23]

Evidence for public building is abundant and allows us to sketch a rather detailed picture of this crucial phase in the development of Roman art and architecture. For the fourth century, the sources are concentrated almost exclusively on the activity of M. Camillus, "father of his country and second founder of the city" (Livy 7.1.10). Camillus is responsible for the revived emphasis on triumphal ideology (recall that he is said to have celebrated an exceptional triumph by riding in a four-horse chariot: Plut. *Cam.* 7.1): he reconstructed the old sanctuary of Fortuna built by Servius Tullius at the Triumphal Gate (*porta Triumphalis*) and joined to it (or perhaps only restored) the temple of Mater Matuta. Of the complex there survives an impressive platform that supported two twin shrines. For the dedication of a temple to Concord, a personification embodying the harmonious relationship between patricians and plebeians that he had reinforced, Camillus chose the western end of the Forum, at the time still without any important temple buildings: that temple was situated at the center of a rational system of ideological and functional harmony between the Curia and the Comitium on the one side and the temple of Saturn on the other. The other significant moment is the year 318, when the plebeian C. Maenius, who after his victory at Antium in 338 had initiated considerable building activity in the Comitium, held the office of censor. He may have restored the Comitium with a circular set of steps, following a model inspired by Greek *ekklesiasteria* and then reproduced in all the Latin colonies of the fourth and third centuries from Fregellae to Cosa. In the same area he also restored ancient sanctuaries such as the Volcanal, adding the Maenian Column crowned by a statue of Minerva, which probably served as the center of celebrations for the important civic festival, the *Quinquatrus*.[24] In the following decades, the Comitium would become the privileged seat of important monumental dedications, from Marsyas to the she-wolf and the Ficus Ruminalis (a fig tree commemorating the arrival of the semi-divine twins on the Roman riverbank), all offered by plebeian magistrates (see also Chapter 6). Patrician opposition can perhaps be detected only in the consecration, possibly in the years 292–90, of the statues of Alcibiades and of Pythagoras, "the strongest and the wisest of the Greeks," a formula echoed in the famous epitaph inscribed on the sarcophagus of the patrician Scipio Barbatus (*ROL* 4:2–3, nos. 1–2 = *ILS* 1 = *ILLRP* 309; see also Chapters 3, 17, and 22). With this and other contemporary modifications, the Forum lost its former, haphazardly defined character and assumed instead the aspect of completely regular rectangular square, thanks to the completion in 310 of the *tabernae argentariae*, the "moneychangers' district," which replaced the older and perhaps irregularly shaped *tabernae lanienae*, the "butchers' shops." These were moved in turn to the north of the Forum, thus opening up public spaces on the north and south sides of the square to the definitive and official arrival of trade in the Forum area. At the same time, together with the shops that we know were organized on two floors (*maeniana*), private complexes made their appearance around the square built on the model of contemporary houses, i.e., a central atrium and other side rooms, but without a tablinum at the end of the atrium (cf. Figure 24.13). These buildings were thus called *atria*, often named after their owners (e.g., *atrium Titium*, *atrium Maenium*), and were used for various purposes – for auctions (*atria Licinia*) as well as religious ceremonies (*atrium Sutorium*).[25] The perimeter of Cosa's forum provides an idea of this building type, which was at that time very popular at Rome before it was replaced in the second century by other architectural forms such as basilicas and *chalcidica* (porticoed halls with sacred overtones). But the space for the hectic forum life so well described in the first years of the second century in the *Curculio* of Plautus (lines 287–94) was no longer sufficient. Here then, already in the course of the third century, to the northeast of the Forum, a market building (*macellum*) was opened in place of the old fish market (*forum piscarium*), built according to the Carthaginian prototype (from which the name was borrowed) of a colonnaded square with circular buildings in the center.[26] The new fish market appears to be ideally associated with the ancient market spaces to the west of the Forum, along the Tiber and close to the port. These were dedicated to the sale of specific goods, such as the Forum Boarium for cattle and the Forum Holitorium for vegetables, and which illustrate clearly by their very names that an important portion of the city center was destined for mercantile activity.

Public building at the time was dominated by the exceptional censorship of Appius Claudius in the years 312–10. In addition to placing under state control (*publicatio*) the popular cult of the "Great Altar of Hercules" (*ara Maxima Herculis*), which was formerly under the control of the Pinarian *gens*, Appius also completed the via Appia to the allied city of Capua and built the first aqueduct (see Map 7). The *aqua Appia* also had a "public pool" (*piscina publica*), the first communal space in the city for water distribution and for sports from swimming to gymnastics – the forerunner of an institution that Rome would know only at the end of the Republic in the baths of Agrippa. Appius' example was quickly followed by one of the leaders of the nobility who were closest to the plebeians: in 272 M. Curius Dentatus brought to Rome the copious waters of the Anio with an aqueduct later called *Anio Vetus* ("Old Anio"), in order to distinguish it from the *Anio Novus* built by the emperor Claudius in AD 52. If we set aside a few other constructions, such as (in 329) the starting-gates for the chariot races in the Circus Maximus (*carceres*, or "cages"), the city seems to be engaged above all in erecting temples, the results of votive dedications made by victorious magistrates during campaigns or of the ancient custom of *evocatio*, the magical practice by which a Roman general was able to *evocare* – "call over to his side" – the enemy's own divinities in order to leave him without protection. Generals found the money for such constructions from booty stripped from the enemy (see also Chapters 10 and 24); the aediles used the profits from fines; the censors recovered the necessary funds from debtors who owed money to the public Treasury.

These buildings were erected in various parts of the city, often chosen in advance for ideological reasons in order to emphasize by the location certain religious or political values and messages. The southern area of the Campus Martius, flanked by a small tributary of the Tiber, the Stream of Petronius (*amnis Petronia*), became a new focus of development and would be splendidly built up by triumphant generals of the second and first centuries.[27] Major public building in this zone was begun by M'. Curius Dentatus, in the context of his program of improving Rome's water supply: in ca. 290, right beside the *amnis Petronia*, he built the temple of Feronia, a goddess associated with water who had been "called over" (*evocata*) from the conquered Sabines. Good arguments have been made for identifying this building as Temple C in the Area Sacra di Largo Argentina, which is in turn to be identified as the *porticus Minucia* built at the end of the second century by M. Minucius Rufus to surround this and three other sacred buildings (Figure 4.2).[28] This very temple and two others of the remaining temples built between the third and second centuries – Temple A of Iuturna, dedicated c.242 by C. Lutatius Catulus after the victory in the sea battle near the Aegates islands and Temple D dedicated to the *Lares Permarini* (tutelary gods of sea-voyages) built by M. Aemilius Lepidus in 179, the year of his censorship, to commemorate the naval victory of his relative, L. Aemilius Regillus, over Antiochus of Syria in 190 – all serve to characterize the area as the seat of cults linked to waters or to naval victories, which indicates why the area was in the first century AD transformed into a "Water Office" (*statio aquarum*), the office governing Rome's water supply under the Empire. The titular divinity of the fourth temple (B: Figure

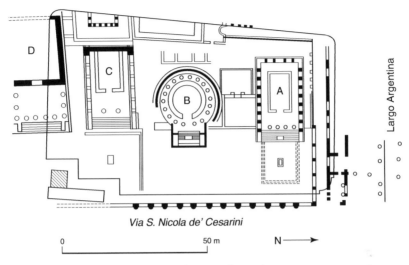

Fig. 4.2 The temples of the Area Sacra di Largo Argentina

24.6), Fortune of This Day (*Fortuna huiusce diei*), built there by reason of family tradition in so far as it was dedicated by another Lutatius Catulus in 101, explains the use of the portico for corn distributions, which were handed out to their recipients on a specific day of the year.[29] They were later housed in the contiguous extension named the Minucian Portico for Corn Distribution (*porticus Minucia frumentaria*).

Other areas built up by the victorious generals are the traditional sites of temples, sometimes vested with specific connotations. The Palatine, the Velia, and the Carinae remained the seats of early cults or of traditional Olympian gods; the plebeian spirit is obvious in the Aventine, while the Quirinal, dear to the Fabii, was the "Sabine" Hill par excellence. With these dedications, triumphant generals of the period outlined their own programs, their future aspirations, and declared their affiliation to political groups.[30] Of great importance for building policies were also the collective tensions arising from military or political events, which could create new cult places. In this specific period we have a number of serious plagues, like that of 293 which was the precipitating event behind the dramatic arrival of the cult of Asclepius on the Tiber Island, but also an atmosphere of popular distress created by the events of the Second Punic War, when, after the consultation of the Sibylline books, two important dedications were made in highly significant areas of the city: first, the unusual dedication of twin temples on the Capitoline to Mens ("Mind") and Venus Erycina ("of Eryx" in Sicily), possibly as an expiation for the emergency enlistment of slaves; then, perhaps prompted by the Attalids, the introduction to the Palatine of *Megale Thea* (Greek "Great Goddess"), the *Magna Mater* ("Great Mother"), one of the Trojan goddesses venerated with bloody rituals and the popular games called the *Ludi Megalenses* (see also Chapter 22).

But the dedication of sanctuaries, temples, and shrines does not give a complete picture of the enormous building activity that followed the end of the patrician – plebeian conflict, a contest not only about political rights but also about Rome's very survival as a city after the Gallic fire. The building effort included also the restoration of the city walls originally built by Servius Tullius, carried out inter-mittently between 377 and 353 (Livy 6.32.1; 7.20.9), possibly with the help of Syracusan engineers. Thereafter, the wall would be repaired only sporadically and partially.[31] More than half a millennium would pass before Rome had to face again the problem of creating a defensive wall.

Luxuria Asiatica

In 182, in the eyes of members of the Macedonian court, Rome still had "the aspect of a city not yet made beautiful either in its public or private spaces" (Livy 40.5.7). The ponderous and archaic character of mid-Republican public architecture, which was nothing more than an updating of sixth-century models, the absence of marble monuments, the urbanistic system lacking unifying porticoes, were the principal elements that must have struck a second-century Greek accustomed to new and glittering Hellenistic capitals with a sophisticated level of urban architecture that was light-years distant from the Etrusco-Italic city made of tufa, wood, and garishly colored terracotta decoration.

At the beginning of the second century, starting with T. Flamininus, the victor over King Philip V of Macedon, the more open-minded members of the nobility developed close contacts with Greece. This, together with an enormous flood of money and slaves – further increased by the rising volume of Italian agricultural exports in the East as well as the West – provided opportunities to the more enterprising sectors of the Roman ruling class and the Italian allies to transform radically the appearance of their cities. Simultaneously, these groups were able to adopt the most elaborate and sophisticated forms of Hellenistic figurative culture, which were considered by many to be an indispensable tool with which to construct a new political image for themselves and for their social class. And there began a flood, with ever increasing intensity, of architects, sculptors, and painters, no longer just from Magna Graecia, as had been the case previously, but now directly emanating from the great Hellenistic capitals. Archaeological research has brought to light several artists who disseminated a Hel-lenistic figurative culture, sometimes in a baroque style, at other times clearly classi-cizing, including sculptors of large cult statues such as Timarchides or Scopas Minor and architects, the creators of important temples such as Hermodorus of Salamis, who created a real Romano-Italic variant of Hellenistic architecture, strongly influenced by the classicizing canon of Hermogenes.[32] The taste for luxury then moved on to private dwellings, even the less opulent ones; workshops producing metal vases multiplied, the production of silver vases being concentrated perhaps in Rome while that of bronze was in Campania.[33] In the age of Caesar, at Arezzo (Arretium), a long-standing production center for black-glazed pottery, the production of elegant "Arretine ware" began which was modeled on the famous Pergamene pottery that imitated metal vases and would become the "ceramic flag" of the early empire.

All of these circumstances quickly set in motion a process of which the ancients themselves were aware, expressed in the famous aphorism, "conquered Greece conquered her brutish victor," a claim that has generated much debate and led many modern scholars to identify this moment as the first Hellenization of Rome. In reality, while sources, materials, and figurative culture tell us that the city had consciously chosen Greek cultural models in one form or another as early as the eighth century,[34] the phrase derives instead from a conservative stereotype of the city of the past as a simple community untouched by the corruption associated with *luxuria*, the unrestrained opulence of the late Republic that in the name of very precise political goals had abandoned the old "national" middle Republican culture.[35] The gradual abandonment of the "national" culture occurred slowly at times and at others with surprising speed, steering between the fierce resistance of the more conservative elite that, like Cato, did not have an aversion to Greek culture but rather a deep fear of the destructive character of many Hellenistic models born within the courts of Alexander's successors and standing in obvious contradiction with the old aristocratic equilibrium that was the basis of Republican institutions. In order to illustrate the contradictory nature of the process, it will suffice to note that in the 70s of the first century Pompey, a figure indubitably given to behavior of an eastern dynastic type, dedicated a building to Hercules "in the Etruscan style" (*tuscanico more*: Vitr. *De arch.* 3.3.5), that is, of a middle Republican type. This was to propose a monumental "national" architecture that obviously contrasted with that of late Hellenism, which had now been well established in Rome since the middle of the previous century.

For the entire second century only a few individuals such as Scipio Africanus and Scipio Aemilianus seem to have adapted themselves to a political style and private life that followed the new models of Hellenistic sophistication. In any event, beginning with the last decades of the second century, the entire governing class in Rome and in Italy started to accelerate its adoption of forms of public building and monument construction that were characterized by display and types of political behavior as well as lifestyle that were now fully informed by what the sources refer as *luxuria* without qualification, labeling it *Asiatica* with obvious reference to its Hellenistic sources. After the well-known socioeconomic and political conflicts between the various classes of the capital and with the other Italic allies, from the war of Fregellae (125) to the Gracchan episodes (133, 123–21), these models with strong Hellenistic dynastic overtones became the property of all, perhaps more emphatically among the Italian allies than at Rome itself, where a residual social control kept dangerous excesses at bay at least until the Social War. Typical of this phase is the behavior of a rich oil merchant of Tibur, M. Octavius Herrenus (or Hersenus). In the closing years of the second century, in the great sanctuary of the Great Altar of Hercules (*ara maxima*) in Rome, he dedicated a temple that is certainly to be identified with the so-called "Temple of Vesta" in the Forum Boarium (Figure 24.5; see also Chapter 24). This was a Hellenistic round temple (*tholos*) made of Greek marble without the typical national podium (which is found instead in the contemporary Temple B [Figure 24.6] in the Area Sacra di Largo Argentina), vying with a second *tholos* also offered to Hercules a few meters away dedicated by Scipio Aemilianus during his censorship of 142. On the other hand, between the end of the second and the beginning of the first century, not only all generals who had celebrated a triumph, whether or not they belonged to the nobility, but also the governing classes of the allied cities became involved in grandiose construction of a political nature. Especially in the Italian cities these buildings give the impression of making a kind of display capable of rivaling the capital city; yet at the same time they give the sense of a need to embrace the traditions and cults of their cities' past in the midst of the ideological storms of those years. All of this is the basis for an impressive building frenzy of extraordinary sanctuaries across all of Tyrrhenian Italy from Latium and Campania, such as that of Fortuna Primigenia at Praeneste (Figures 24.1a and 24.1b), of Jupiter Anxur at Terracina, of Hercules at Tibur (Tivoli) (see also Chapters 24 and 28).[36]

With the progressive destruction of national values and thus also of the traditions of the *gentes*, a style of strong self-representation by individuals ultimately prevailed, often involving people of more modest rank as well. During the second century houses began to manifest ever more evident luxurious elements, such as stuccoes and mosaics, but above all painted decorations imitating precious marbles following Hellenistic models well known at Delos, a style that would be surpassed in the last century of the Republic by a new fashion defined as the "Second Style" according to the traditional classification of Pompeian painting (see also Chapter 24 and Figures 24.22–24.25).[37] The Second Style employed internal decorative schemes that were directly inspired by the palaces of the Hellenistic rulers, embellished with the façades of theatrical stage-buildings (*scaenae frons*) and overflowing with glass, silver, and gold objects. Some exceptional residences, like the House of the Faun at Pompeii and the Pompeian villas of Boscoreale and that of the Mysteries (Figure 24.16) offer painted or mosaic replicas of famous Hellenistic paintings with a significant political or ideological content (cf. Figure 24.26).[38] Luxury villas appear now also, combining the traditional atrium house model with large Hellenistic peristyle courts; they aspire to create an atmosphere of illusion, with idyllic landscapes and ever larger gardens, crowded with copies of Greek statues inspiring meditation and cultured debate as the appropriate setting for the literary dialogues of the age such as those of Cicero (see also Chapter 24). At the end of the second century at Rome monumental individual tombs appeared which were imitations of Hellenistic dynastic mausoleums; throughout the first century the fashion was picked up by local elites across all of Italy (24.7–24.10). The traditional legal restrictions being long forgotten, the practice of erecting portrait statues became widespread among the *nouveaux riches* – so extensively that during his attempt to restore the Republic Sulla was forced to dust off the old regulations of the law (but, as we know, with ephemeral results). The deep tension of the moment is well expressed by the very style of both sculpture and painting, split between replicas of late-Hellenistic baroque models from Asia Minor and respect for the classicizing canons. The dense moralizing pages of Sallust illustrate perfectly the climate created by *luxuria* between the end of the second and the mid-first century, the age of the Social War and of civil conflict, the tragic backdrop to the height of late Republican luxury.

The new Hellenistic culture in Rome and in Italy was able to benefit from some very important technological innovations. Already in the third century it seems that *opus signinum* had been discovered, an impermeable type of plaster (and pavement) derived from Carthaginian models; the material was of extraordinary importance for bath buildings, cisterns, and so forth. At the beginning of the second century a new era began thanks to the discovery of *opus caementicium* (i.e., cement), a mixture of lime and *lapis puteolanus*, the "Puteoli stone" or "pozzolana," a construction technique that supplied late Republican and Imperial engineers and architects with a practical and economic tool allowing the creation of walls of great strength and especially arches and vaulted roofs – the source of the most important innovations in Roman architecture from this moment on.[39] Between 60 and 50, first at Rome and then in Central Italy, *opus reticulatum* was used for luxurious buildings, a refinement of *opus caementicium* in which the surfaces of the concrete walls were faced with a netlike pattern of small blocks.[40]

Temples dedicated by victorious generals would continue to be built in ever-greater numbers and splendor, using the same ideological messages and standing in the same places as in the preceding centuries, but the most favored spot was the Campus Martius.[41] Once the space of the Area Sacra di Largo Argentina was quickly filled, this expanse destined for the grandiose constructions of the Imperial period began to be taken over, with a special emphasis on the area around the Circus inaugurated by C. Flaminius in 221. At the end of the Republic the entire area would be surrounded by sanctuaries, with a sequence of temple buildings flanking the triumphal route intended, here as in other areas such as the Forum Holitorium, to create a solemn effect for the processional route. (See Map 9 and Chapter 23.) The majority of these temples were still of the traditional type; nonetheless a few, like the unique temple of Hercules *Musarum* ("of the Muses") of 187 (Figure 24.4), took unusual forms derived from Greek prototypes, with porticoes, fountains, and exedras while others lacked the characteristic "national" podium, like the temple of Mars in the Circus Flaminius built in 138 completely of marble. Nine years earlier, within the context of his portico (the porticus Metelli), Q. Metellus Macedonicus had dedicated to Jupiter Stator and to Juno Regina the first temples in Rome to show the typical building material of Hellenistic sacred architecture. In 197, L. Stertinius, an unlucky general who had not won a triumph, inaugurated in compensation a new type of monument destined to enjoy great success in future centuries: the triumphal arch (see also Chapters 16 and 24). Not coincidentally, six years later his example was imitated by Scipio Africanus along the ascent to the Capitol (*clivus Capitolinus*), the traditional triumphal route. Very rarely, victors dedicated monuments without a specific sacred building. An isolated example is provided by the case of Cn. Octavius, who in 168 dedicated in the Campus Martius a portico with bronze capitals (the Porticus Octavia: Pliny *HN* 34.13). His example was imitated only after the end of the Republic, with the construction in the Imperial period of many porticoes containing no specific cult places as had been customary. On the other hand, the need for large porticoes to house the increasingly complex activities demanded by public life found a new start with the "invention" of the basilica in 184, when during his censorship M. Porcius Cato built the Basilica Porcia. His example was immediately followed by other members of the aristocracy and created a fashion imitated in the following centuries by all the cities of the Roman Empire.

The real novelty was generated by the urgent demands of the urban population of Rome which depended on corn distribution and by the new building techniques, which together served to open up a new chapter in the development of the city. Starting in 193, the censors set to work on the old Tiber port, rebuilding jetties, adding barriers and access ramps to the river. The most spectacular enterprise of this movement was the colossal Porticus Aemilia: inspired by the third-century "Hypostyle Hall" of Delos, the building had fifty naves roofed by barrel vaults and measured 487 m. long and 90 m deep, serving in its turn as the prototype of all the great mercantile warehouses (*horrea*) which became more and more numerous at Rome and at Ostia in the late Republican period. The radical social and economic transformations of the age brought about major changes in the form of the city: starting from 102, corn distribution took place in the Minucian Portico, near the archive located by the censors in the temple of the Nymphs, where the lists of those entitled to the subsidy were kept. In 123 C. Gracchus changed the direction in which orators delivered speeches to the People (*contiones*) so that they no longer faced the Comitium but the center of the Forum (Plut. *C. Gracch.* 5.3), where the multiplication of law courts scattered about the entire area had already created congestion in the third century.[42]

This congestion was the cause of certain urban changes brought about by Pompey and Caesar whose political purposes very clearly anticipate the building programs of the Empire (see also Chapter 16). His booty-laden eastern triumph permitted Pompey in 55 to carry out a grandiose series of buildings in the Campus Martius, the first real dynastic complex in the Hellenistic mold to be seen at Rome (Figure 24.12).[43] The center of the project was the theater crowned by the formal justification for the construction of the Theater of Pompey: a temple of Venus, the ancestor of Romulus, and thus, in a sense, of all Romans (Lucr. 1.1; see also Chapter 24). Although this was not the first theater of the city (the temples of Apollo and Magna Mater both had steps for spectators of the dramas that attended their festivals, as did a number of sanctuaries in Latium), Pompey's theater was the first to have a permanent stage. Behind the stage sumptuous porticoes were created that, like the theater, were decorated with statues organized according to an ambitious iconological program with a literary background.[44] These porticoes were linked to the Porticus Minucia in order to associate the theater-complex with the area of corn distribution, a fundamental source of electoral consensus. Yet in the portico Pompey also set up the new Curia for meetings of the Senate (where Caesar would be assassinated), linked to the porticoes *ad Nationes* ("By the Nations") or *Lentulorum* ("of the Lentuli"), built by Pompey's supporters to host foreign embassies. The ultimate aim of the project was to move the city's political center from the Forum to the area where grain was distributed and to the Saepta (Voting Enclosure), the location of electoral assemblies. The real model at the heart of this project can be found in the world of the Hellenistic kings and in particular of the Ptolemies, as is shown by the linkage (over a small stream) of the Pompeian complex to the urban villa of the great general on the Pincian Hill. Thanks to the booty from the Gallic wars and with the help of Cicero himself (*Att.* 4.16.8), Caesar was able in 54 to start an ambitious program, but one not coincidentally in a vein contrary to Pompey's projects: Caesar preserved for the

Forum area its historical centrality, enlarging the square to include land bought by Caesar for 60 million sesterces to create a new forum dominated by a temple of Venus, whom he claimed as the ancestor not only of the Roman People but of his *gens* as well. After his victory in the civil war, the dictator conceived of other projects for the monumental complex which were only partially completed owing to his assassination. Still within the square of the Forum, which Caesar repaved, he dedicated in 46 the Basilica Iulia, constructed on the site of the old Basilica Sempronia which had been built in 170 against the "old shops" (*tabernae veteres*) (Liv. 44.16), and in 44 he rebuilt the Curia (also named Iulia) and the Rostra, the speaker's platform. Other equally ambitious projects remained in the planning stages, and were taken up only in part by Augustus: for example, the diversion of the Tiber in the area of the Vatican, which in his plans would take on the role of the Campus Martius and where he intended to reconstruct the Saepta, which was at that time still fenced only in wood; or the transformation of the *cavea* in front of the temple of Apollo into a fixed theater, at a spot where later the theater of Marcellus would be built; or the construction of an artificial lake for naval battles (*naumachia*) and a library, to be organized by Varro – a plan realized instead by his officer, C. Asinius Pollio. These were projects that called for a dynasty. A few years later Rome would have one, although with an urban policy of a somewhat different sort in the person of Caesar's adopted son, Augustus.

Guide to Further Reading

The innovative books by Coarelli 1983–5, 1988c, 1997 have changed our ideas about the topographical development of Republican Rome; detailed entries concerning all public and private buildings known through literary sources and/or archaeological evidence are in Steinby 1993–2000, where the reader will find a careful description of each monument and discussion concerning the most controversial points, supported by the essential bibliographical references. In English, see Richardson 1992, Nash 1968, and Platner and Ashby 1929 for individual monuments; see also the works cited in the Guide to Further Reading of Chapter 16. Chapters 16 and 24 below have many points of contact with this one and offer further bibliographical guidance.

Roman architecture from the Middle Republic is treated by Gros 1996–2001, a new, exhaustive handbook with up-to-date bibliographies; Gros's earlier book (Gros 1978) illustrates his preference for the Late Republic, while for the earliest phases (fifth and fourth centuries) the reader should consult Donati 2000 and Prayon 2000. One will find detailed discussion of temples of the Middle Republic in Ziolkowski 1992, who often disagrees from Coarelli, but rarely with strong arguments; the standard work on Italian monumental sanctuaries of the Late Republic is Coarelli 1987. The story of the general development of urban forms in Italy and Rome is reconstructed in Gros and Torelli 1991 (a third revised edition is in preparation); archaeological reconstructions of urban form and significant public buildings of Latin colonies, specifically Cosa and Paestum, have been offered by Brown 1980 and Torelli 1999.

Even for beginners it is important to consult general books on new types of buildings which, for the Middle Republic, include basilicas (Nünnerich-Asmus 1994) and *macella* (De Ruyt 1983), and for the Late Republic, theater-temples (Hanson 1959), *odeia* (Meinel 1980), *villae* (Carandini and Ricci 1985), and funerary monuments (Hesberg 1992). However, the mentality of the Late Republic is fairly well illustrated by the almost pathological *luxuria* of domestic architecture, which is the subject of an influential book (Wallace-Hadrill 1994); the dwellings of the elite of the Italian towns of the second and early first centuries – often even more affluent than their Roman counterparts – are extensively discussed by Pesando (1997). Finally, the standard work on Roman gardens, Cima and La Rocca 1998, is too sketchy for the Late Republic.

Notes

1   Mura Sommella 1997–8.
2   Torelli 1997: 87–121.
3   Coarelli 1988c: 204–437.
4   Torelli in Gros and Torelli 1991: 69–92.
5   See Torelli 1986.
6   See Torelli 1985.
7   Torelli 1997: 122–51.
8   Rasmussen 1979.
9   Nielsen and Poulsen 1992.
10   Torelli 1999: 19–20.
11   Coarelli 1973.
12   Bianchi Bandinelli 1978.
13   Torelli 1999: 43–88.
14   Menichetti 1995. Note that here and elsewhere "Italiote" refers to the Greek cities of Italy, "Italic" to the indigenous non-Roman Italian peoples, "Italian" to those of the peninsula as a whole.
15   Torelli 1999: 119–49.
16   Morel 1981, 1983.
17   Van der Mersch 2001.
18   Comella 1981.
19   Flower 1996 (who at 53–9 rejects the view that the use of *imagines* was regulated by law); Torelli 1997: 122–51.
20   Cf. Torelli 1982.
21   Pliny *HN* 35.22 (cf. Coarelli 1983–5: 2.53–4); Torelli 1997: 175–99.
22   Coarelli 1972: 36–106.
23   D'Alessio, Ricci, and Carandini 1997.
24   Torelli 2004.
25   Cf. the "atrium for auctions" at Superaequum in *CIL* IX, 3307 = *ILS* 5599.
26   De Ruyt 1983. Compare the second-century market of Morgantina in Sicily: Torelli in Coarelli and Torelli 1991: 193–4.
27   On the Campus Martius, see Coarelli 1997.

28 Later it would be called *Vetus* in order to distinguish it from the colossal portico added by Claudius, which by reason of its specific function carried the name *porticus Minucia frumentaria*.

29 Coarelli 1997: 275–92.

30 Torelli in Gros and Torelli 1991: 99–101.

31 On the problem, see Säflund 1932.

32 Cult statues: Martin 1987. Scopas Minor: Coarelli 1996a. Hermodorus: Gros 1973. Influence of Hermogenes: Hoepfner and Schwandner 1990.

33 Tassinari 1993.

34 For the Greek material of the eighth century at Rome and in Latium, see La Rocca 1977.

35 On the Hellenization of Roman culture, see Gallini 1973.

36 Coarelli 1987.

37 Barbet 1985; Ling 1991.

38 Boscoreale: Torelli 2003. Villa of the Mysteries: Sauron 1998.

39 Coarelli 1977.

40 Torelli 1980.

41 Coarelli 1997.

42 Coarelli 1983–5: 2.157–66. Others date the innovation two decades earlier: cf. Morstein-Marx 2004: 45–6, with n.48.

43 Torelli in Gros and Torelli 1991: 69–92.

44 Sauron 1987.

CHAPTER 5

The Physical Geography and Environment of Republican Italy

Simon Stoddart

Introduction

Republican Italy is defined for the purposes of this chapter as peninsular Italy south of the Po valley (see Map 6). This is a self-contained geomorphological zone by most definitions.[1] The very nature of the peninsula means that it projects into the Mediterranean Sea, creating a central strategic position within the Mediterranean. The eastern flank of the peninsula is covered by the Adriatic, whose access is potentially blocked by the control of the narrows from the Capo d'Otranto across to the Balkan peninsula. The western Tyrrhenian flank is more accessible. The straits of Messina, between Calabria and Sicily, form one point of control, but the whole Tyrrhenian seaboard can also be approached from the west. In these western approaches, the Bay of Naples and the delta of the Tiber form two important nodal zones of communication from the sea and into the hinterland through major rivers. The first was the most northerly point on the peninsula where Greeks placed their colonies. The second was the core area of indigenous state formation. In the area north of the Tiber, the Etruscans first developed the most powerful states of Italy in the central Mediterranean in the course of the early first millennium. In the area immediately south of the Tiber and beyond, the Latins replaced them by the time of the republican period as the leading force.

The climate of republican Italy was essentially the Mediterranean climate of today: a wet winter and an extremely dry summer; although some authors (e.g., Burroughs 2001) suggest that the climate may have been warmer and drier, which would have had implications both for agriculture and health (particularly malaria – see below).[2] Sea level (in areas not subject to tectonic instability) was also relatively stable and has not altered more than half a meter in the last 2000 years, although particular local circumstances along the Tyrrhenian coast may have led to some apparent sea level rise.[3] The altitudinal relief emphasized below was more important in determining variation in the nature of rainfall, temperature, and vegetational cover. The changes in environment were highly regional, generally precipitated by human action working on the potential fragility of the Mediterranean landscape, especially at times of seasonally low vegetation cover between September and November, leading to erosion and alluviation.

The Broad Structural Outlines

The key structural feature of peninsular Italy is the presence of the Apennines, which run from continental Italy through a length of some 1,000 km, covering a breadth of some 50–100 km across, down to Sicily.[4] The peninsula is thus disproportionately mountainous (less than 20 percent is lowland), where substantial changes in altitude can be encountered over a short horizontal distance. Consequently mountain relief has often contributed to the character and definition of political territories and to the essential regionality of Italy. This mountain chain has also had a profound effect on communications within the country, defining the major routes of access between regions and splitting the two sides of the peninsula. In total, this presence of the mountains provides a *longue durée* (that is, long-term) setting for human action in the way defined by Braudel and developed by a number of archaeologists for the Mediterranean region.[5]

This mountain chain forms a continuous and prominent relief from north to south, but is formed of a series of different blocks which have different characteristics. This variability has produced a range of different weathered products that have contributed additionally to the regionality of the peninsula. The same area is also very active geologically, leading to an instability that ranges from the dramatic processes of earthquakes and vulcanism to the more drawn-out but equally imposing processes of erosion and alluviation, which many authors stress took place episodically and thus quite dramatically to the living populations.[6] In this fragile environment, humans must be ready to respond rapidly to perceptible local environmental change.[7]

Neotectonics, that is, the relative youth of mountain building, have led to a considerable verticality of the landscape. Transitions from valleys to mountain summits (between 500 and 1500 m) take place over relatively short horizontal distances and often reach quite substantial heights of 1000–2000 m, and even 2500 m. The relative youth of the landscape has also led to steeper gradients and more constrained width of valleys.[8] These constraints have led to pronounced alternation of aggradation and erosion, leading to a cut-and-fill stratigraphy which has both a general pattern (perhaps a result of climatic change) and local variations (perhaps a result of human land use).

The Northern Apennines

The northern Apennines curve gently from west – northwest towards the east – southeast. Between the Giovi Pass (472 m) near Genova and the upper valleys of the Tiber and the Metauro, the Apennines show an asymmetrical profile. The northern slope running down to the Po valley is relatively gradual, composed of ridges running at right angles to the line of the chain. The southern ("internal") slope is relatively abrupt, marked by broad valleys and basins, running in parallel to the mountain chain itself. The underlying geological structure here has a profound effect on the landscape. On this southern side of the Apennines, there is a series of intermontane basins, well sunk, by Pliocene tectonic action, between parallel ridges running with the main Apennine chain from the northwest to the southeast or from north to south. These basins are drained by the Magra, Serchio, Arno (Sieve, Chiana), and Tiber rivers. All were once lake basins, now turned into river valleys, leading to a broadly similar sequence of often heavy clay sediments. Lake Trasimene, the largest lake of the peninsula (128 sq km), is formed in a shallow (6 m) depression within the alluvial sediments at one end of the Chiana valley.

Much of the relief has been shaped by fluvial action, but given variation by the type of parent rock. The narrow V-shaped valleys of the Ligurian Apennines are cut out of the local marly limestones, sandstones, and shales. The broad alluvial valleys of Emilia to the north are formed from clays and marls. The sharper, narrower Romagna valleys to the northeast are cut from marly sandstones.

The internal area of Tuscany is composed of two zones. The northern area immediately to the south of the Arno has geological formations similar to the Apennines themselves (including limestones and conglomerates). The southern zone around Volterra and beyond has a high presence of marine Pliocene deposits (clays, sands, and gravels). This zone is much affected by dissection and erosion, particularly under the impact of modern agriculture, but this degradation is almost certainly a longer-standing problem. At the southernmost limit of this area lies Monte Amiata (1738 m), the most northerly and some of the most distantly active (9 million to 1 million years ago) evidence of vulcanism in the peninsula. The southern coastal part of this zone comprises the distinctive Maremma region (see below).

The Central Apennines

The central Apennines, which cover the area from the Metauro to the Sangro and Volturno valleys, are younger, more calcareous and dolomitic than the Apennines further south. On the Adriatic flank, the whole zone is characterized by a hilly belt of Pliocene marine deposits. The mountains themselves can be divided into a northern Umbria – Marche section and a southern Abruzzo section.

The northern Umbria – Marche section is made up of deep sea and marly formations, starting in a northwest to southeast direction and ending by running almost north – south toward the south. The peaks of this section vary between 1000–1200 m and 1500–400 m and are often rounded or flat-topped. The geology is composed of various types of limestone: compact and homogeneous, cherty, marly, and thin bedded (*scaglia*). The same asymmetry applies to this area of the Apennines as further north. On the inner Umbrian side of the mountains there are rather longer mountain basins than in Tuscany filled with broadly similar sequences of lake and river deposits (the Tiber valleys, the valleys of Gubbio, Gualdo Tadino, and Norcia). On the Adriatic side, the shorter traverse of rivers cuts across the geological folds before entering Pliocene deposits nearer the coast.

The Gubbio valley is one example of the intermontane lake basins of the western side of the Apennines, which is of interest to republican Italy as the location of the city of Iguvium.[9] The valley nestles in one of the depressions that formed in the Apennines. The key local topographical feature is a prominent limestone escarpment, in part the watershed of the peninsula, that runs the length of the northeastern edge of the valley, reaching an apex of nearly 1,000 m at its central point behind the city of Gubbio. This escarpment dominates a valley at between 300 and 500 m, filled with heavy Pleistocene terraces, later alluvial fans, and colluvial infill. A large proportion of the alluviation and colluviation was probably a consequence of human activity dated in part to the republican period, when rural settlement increased considerably. As a consequence of the central infill of the valley, drainage takes place both to the southeast and the northwest, ultimately reaching the Tiber from two tributaries. To the southwest lie the lower sandstone hills between Gubbio and the neighboring city of Perugia. The whole valley forms a self-contained territory flanking the higher Apennines and the major communication route through to the Adriatic followed by the Flaminia to the east.

The southern Abruzzo section is generally greater in height, rising from the lower mountains of 500–700 m to the upper peaks of some 1,500 m. The mountains are also distributed in three bands of heights forming an even more considerable barrier. From the Adriatic coast one reaches first the Monti della Laga (2,455 m), the Gran Sasso complex, and the Maiella massif (2,795 m). In the middle, there is a broader complex centered on the Velino massif (2,487 m). On the far side, there is lower range of mountains including the Monti Ernici, reaching only 2,000 m in height. Some important rivers arise in these mountains (e.g., the Tronto and the Aterno) and one, the Sagittario, runs through the large intermontane basins of L'Aquila and Sulmona, which are similar in character to those of Umbria and Tuscany further north and west. On the Adriatic flank of these mountains, the coast is bordered by a belt of clays, sands, and conglomerates.

The Pre-Apennines of Latium and Campania

In the regions of Latium and Campania contained by the Apennines there is a heterogeneous zone of geology, dominated by volcanic activity and lower limestone relief. The most prominent (1,000–1,500 m) of this limestone relief, formed by the

Lepini, Aurunci, and Ausoni mountains, separates a northern (Latium) from a southern (Campanian) province of volcanic activity.

The northern volcanic province of Latium has generally an older history which started in Pliocene times, as in the case of the Tolfa mountains, and ceased activity in the Pleistocene. Some of the recent dates of this activity are in the order of 95,000 to 90,000 years ago, although some lake deposits dated to about 40,000 years ago have been overlain by the most recent volcanic material (Tufo Giallo di Sacrofano).[10] By the republican period, volcanic activity would have been long distant, and the distinctive byproducts of the landscape would have been more important. For instance, the Tolfa mountains were an important source of metal ores. The morphology of the landscape is dominated by truncated, flat cones of low height, but wide diameter (up to 30 km). To the north of the Tiber, some of the original calderas are occupied by deep lakes (e.g., Bolsena, 146 m deep, and Vico and Bracciano, 160 m deep). Two of these lakes, Bolsena (114.5 sq km) and Bracciano (67.5 sq km), are the second and fourth largest lakes of the peninsula. A further volcanic lake, Baccano, was drained in Roman times. Four of these lakes have produced pollen sequences which show clearance of vegetation from their often steep, internal slopes during the last 2,500 years, at least in part coinciding with the republican period.[11] In particular, the Monterosi sequence has been tied into the construction of the Via Cassia and contemporary villa construction.

South Etruria (or more exactly southeast Etruria) provides an important and well-studied region both from an archaeological and a landscape perspective. Studies of the geology show how the stratigraphy of a volcanic landscape can support the procurement of a wide range of resources.[12] The harder volcanic rocks provide selci for road surfaces which can be sourced to particular deposits. The softer tuffs provided ready building material, easily cut into blocks for house foundations. Travertines, which precipitated out on the flanks of the Apennines, provided an alternative source of building material (see also Chapter 16). The Plio-Pleistocene clays below these volcanic deposits, revealed by the downcutting of the river systems, offered ready access to material for pottery production. The early work on sources and supply of raw materials is now being taken much further. Different geological zones supplied different building materials.[13] Leucitic balsalts from the Lake Bolsena region were suitable for millstones. On the east side of the Tiber volcanic materials predominated. On the west side of the Tiber, the limestone of the Apennine ranges provided the key local materials. Economic efficiency determined that heavy local materials were frequently employed for construction unless water transport was readily available.

Studies of erosion and sedimentation in this region have shown dramatic changes to the local environment.[14] Initially these were interpreted as a product of climatic change.[15] More recent studies have demonstrated quite clearly at least a contribution of human impact. More specifically, Roman activity contributed greatly to these human-induced changes. Roman rivers and floodplains were very different to those of today.[16] They were distinguished by a regime of shallow, actively migrating channels which were depositing bars of gravel. These conditions may in turn have necessitated some of the Roman engineering schemes to control and traverse the changing environment.

To the south of the Tiber, the Alban hills comprise both secondary volcanoes within older calderas and smaller crater lakes (e.g., Albano, Nemi) formed by explosive events. The peak of volcanic activity in the Alban hills was between 700,000 and 350,000 years ago. Much of the intervening area is filled with plateaux formed by tuff generated by ignimbrite extrusions, ash, and mud flows. These have often been dissected by rivers, cutting down to underlying Pliocene clays.

The southern volcanic province of Campania has remained active into very recent times, most notoriously in AD 79. The morphology is broadly similar to that of the northern Latium province, but still in an earlier stage of evolution, given its continuing activity. For this reason, Vesuvius is today the highest peak, reaching some 1,277m, and has a better-defined cone shape. Other areas, such as the Phlegrean fields, retain a diversity of cones and craters and the plains north of Naples contain extensive plains of tuff. The properties of this region are more extensively discussed below.

The Southern Apennines

The southern Apennines cover the rest of the peninsula from the Sangro and Volturno rivers down to the straits of Messina, although the Calabrian Apennines form a distinct unit. The most prominent feature of the section north of Calabria is the presence of three longitudinal belts.

The first belt, on the Tyrrhenian side of the peninsula, combines large blocks of limestone (continuing south from the Abruzzo) and depressions filled with sandstone and marly flysch. Movement in the Pleistocene created a range of altitudes of these mountains which are generally in the order of 1,300–1,800 m in height. Only three areas reach above 2,000 m: to the north the Matese (2,050 m), to the south Monte Pollino (2,248 m), and to the west Monte Sirino (2,005 m). This is a rugged landscape with zones of prominent karstic activity. These karstic zones are where is there is a prominence of readily dissolved rock (usually limestone) and predominantly underground drainage, marked by numerous abrupt ridges, fissures, sink-holes, and caverns. The Alburni plateau (1,400–1,700 m) is one such karstic zone, characteristically filled with sink-holes. The same activity in the plateau has produced underground drainage and prominent springs.

The central belt consists of a wide depression filled with a confused range of geology, much affected by tectonic activity: flysch, clays, and siliceous and sandstone rocks. This is a zone of moderate relief, only rarely exceeding 1,500m above sea level (asl), and characterized by monotonous ridges formed from easily eroded flysch and thin clay-derived deposits. Landslides are common today. Another distinctive feature is the presence of extinct Monte Vulture volcano protruding from an otherwise sedimentary landscape.

The eastern belt is a continuation of the Plio-Pleistocene deposits found further north along the Adriatic coast, concentrated in the Bradano trough, and separated in part from the coast by the limestone plateaux of Apulia. The main deposits are based on clays, sands, conglomerates, and some soft limestones. The altitude of this area is modest, rarely exceeding 1,000 m, separated by broad valleys. Erosion, leading to landslides, mud flows, and gulleying, is frequent. There are some coastal terraces and sand dunes near the coast.

The Biferno valley provides a good study of one of the river systems running down into the Adriatic.[17] It is not in the top dozen river systems of peninsular Italy, but dominates its local modern region of the Molise and has been the subject of one of the most important regional archaeological surveys in Italy (see Chapter 28). The Biferno rises in the Matese region of the Apennines and runs 83 km to the sea near the modern port of Termoli (Roman Buca?) covering a catchment of 1,311 sq km. The geology reflects in microcosm the broader trends of this local region of the Apennines: Pliocene marine sands in the lowlands, a mixture of conglomerates, sandstones, and clays in the middle valley, and limestone in the mountains. The upper reaches of the valley are dominated by steep ridges (at approaching 2,000 m) enclosing five upland karstic flat-floored basins, themselves at some 1,000 m. The Biferno River itself gathers in a somewhat lower mountain basin at 500 m asl, which included the Roman Bovianum. This basin has a covering of alluvial and colluvial sediments, the most prominent of which is a large alluvial fan at the eastern end. The basin clearly forms one distinct region of the valley, illustrating the effect of topography on political organization, where communication was perhaps easier to the west. The river leaves this basin and enters its middle course, dominated in Roman times by Larinum, through a landscape of soft clays and sands, broken by limestone outcrops. This involves a drop of some 350 m through steep unstable geology. Twenty kilometers from the sea, the river passes through a narrow gap, and meanders through a flood plain, surrounded by dissected plateaux of alluvial sediments.

The Biferno River thus crosses significant ecological boundaries, strongly determined by difference in relief. The first key factor is rainfall. The 800-mm rainfall isohyet differentiates a wetter colder mountainous interior from a coastal region with lower rainfall and very dry summers. Another factor is temperature. Spring temperatures on the coast are comparable with those inland three months later. All these differences are reflected in the limits of cultivation and vegetation: for instance, the limit of olive cultivation occurs approximately half-way up the horizontal length of the valley. This pattern is repeated at a broader scale in each broadly east – west profile of the peninsula.

Recent studies of the Biferno valley have pointed out the significant impact of Samnite and early Roman agricultural activity on the stability of landforms.[18] The depth of alluvial deposits dated by black-glazed and Italian sigillata pottery is greater than at any period until modern times. In the lower parts of the valley and the area of the gorge these deposits reach as much as 3 m, and in the Boiano basin as much as 2 m in depth. In other words, the expansion of agricultural activity in this period (leading to clearance of vegetation which controls runoff) had a profoundly deleterious effect on the landscape, but requiring very probably an ameliorative human response from the first century AD onwards. This detailed instance of human-caused damage and response was most probably repeated at slightly different times throughout the peninsula.

The Apulian Plateaux

The "heel" of Italy, extending northwest into the Murge and the Gargano peninsula, is formed from a very distinct geology, separated from the main Apennines by the Bradano trough. To the north, Monte Gargano is a rugged karstic plateau (600–1,000 m) projecting into the Adriatic sea. This upland is separated from the broader Murge plateau by a wide depression engulfed by the sea in Pleistocene times, and now forming the Tavoliere plain. The Murge plateau is a low, gently undulating tableland of 400–600 m high at its center, broken by abrupt scarps. On the southern slope toward the Gulf of Taranto these plateaux have been profoundly incised to form ravines (locally named *gravine*). In all these karstic areas, there is considerable underground drainage, reducing the surface runoff. The "heel" proper of Italy, the Salentino peninsula, comprises an even lower soft limestone, nonkarstic plateau of 50–200 m in height, with prominent cliffs on the Adriatic coast.

The Calabrian Apennines

In the southern portion of the Apennines (beyond the Pollino area), the chain changes its geological structure and becomes much narrower. This section is composed of raised blocks of crystalline rocks (granites, granodiorites, gneisses, and metamorphosed schists). With the zone there are four main blocks. There is a narrow high coastal chain of 1,000–1,800 m in height. There is the Sila plateau of 1,000–1,400 m (locally beyond 1,900 m), covered by slow-moving streams that drop off the uplands at their edges. South of Catanzaro there are the Serre uplands, with a rugged surface at 1,000–1,400 m asl. Finally, the Aspromonte forms the southern limit of the Italian peninsula. Terraces (*pianalti*) at c.1400 m asl of uncertain origin and incised by mountain streams are a characteristic feature of this mountain range clustered around the central mountain uplands. All these Calabrian mountains are typified by short and violent seasonal streams which carry considerable debris during flood phases. Pliocene marine deposits flank the uplands both to the east and west and penetrate up some of the valleys.

The Sibari embayment is a rare example on this coastline where the narrow coastal strip suddenly widens into a more ample open area.[19] The bay is very well defined by prominent coastal capes to the north (Capo Spulico) and to the south (Capo Trionto). Two principal watercourses, the Coscile and the Crati, unite just before the Ionian coast; to the north and south of these small rivers are other smaller streams which have contributed to the considerable buildup of sediment in the area. All these streams are typically violent, seasonal, and erosive in their force. They also divide the landscape into a series of small territories. A series of elevated Pleistocene terraces surround the embayment at between 80 and 200 m asl. Behind these terraces lie the low hill country of between 400 and 500 m asl, in the inner part made of degraded flysch, in the outer part made of sandy conglomerates. Towering over this zone further behind are the high massifs of the Apennines, cut by gorges which carry the major rivers. These are made up of the characteristic very hard, metamorphic, and igneous rocks of the region: schists, gneiss, granites. Today the local soils in the uplands are very thin and degraded, as a result of extensive clearance; only the hill country of sandy conglomerates and the plain itself offer a better quality of soil for agriculture.

Plains and Coasts

The Italian peninsula is dominated by its upland regions, leaving only a small area for flatter ground. A number of these regions were significantly fertile (well-watered and low-altitude), but also according to recent research potentially unhealthy, since they were probably highly susceptible to malaria.[20] The most prominent wider expanses within the area of republican Italy are the plains of the Tavoliere and Campania. Alluvial plains are more numerous on the Tyrrhenian coast, but usually hemmed in by hills and mountains. The most prominent are the Maremma and the Pontine plain. Most plains are simple strips, bordered by a beach of about 20–25 m asl. There is a major contrast between the two coasts. The Adriatic coast is composed principally of long, straight beaches, occasionally interrupted by headlands. The Gargano promontory and the cliffs of the Salentine peninsula are more dramatic. The Tyrrhenian coast is generally characterized by alternating headlands, smaller or larger embayments, and prominent lagoonal formations.[21] To the north and the south, the coastline is more rocky.

  The Tavoliere, the largest plain of peninsular Italy, covering some 7,000 sq km, is of interest for republican Italy because of the preservation of extensive settlement systems of the period and the connecting road systems based on centers such as Arpi and Lucera.[22] The plain is formed out of a trough in the Apennine system, sitting astride the Bradano trench which runs parallel to the main Apennine range. Its area is defined by two rivers (the Fortore to the north and the Ofanto to the south) and surrounded on three sides by uplands (the Gargano and the Murge to the north and the south, the main Apennine range to the west), and on the fourth side by the sea. The basal limestone of the plain is covered by deposits of fine marine blue clay, followed by yellow clay. Erosion deposits are generally found on these basal levels. At first glance, the area is extremely flat, but as so often in such areas, more detailed examination reveals variations, in this case a series of terraces from 400 m asl down to 3–7 m asl near the sea itself. Within these areas, subtle differences in level can be extremely important for drainage; the river system has generally become more sluggish during the Holocene and in some areas a *crosta* or calcareous deposit has formed as a calcrete beneath the surface, which has helped preserve the form of any structures which cut through this level. The Tavoliere is thus an area where environmental change can be appreciated, principally the product of upland erosion and coastal aggradation, processes which were particularly prominent from the end of the first millennium BC. Through a study of the location of Roman settlement and the examination of sections (e.g., at Marana di Lupara), it can be established that the coastal regions would have been much more lagoonal, open, indeed in part navigable, in Roman times. Sallares suggests that the Alpi area, a lagoonal area to the south would have been highly susceptible to malaria by late republican times.[23]

The Campanian plain is set within the characteristic "great limestone framework" encountered elsewhere in peninsular Italy.[24] The originality lies in its contents, which are frequently derived from volcanic action; a substantial part of the plain is based on volcanic ash; the Campi Flegrei are composed of small hills and craters, the product of volcanic activity close to the surface; the Baiae coastline has a lunar aspect; and the whole is, of course, dominated by deep-seated volcano of Vesuvius itself. The republican populations would have lived some 1,600 years after an eruption of similar scale (technically defined as "Plinian" after the Roman writer Pliny the Younger, who described the eruption) to the one that later engulfed Pompeii in AD 79.[25] This major explosion 1,600 years before AD 79 was probably from a different summit (*Somma antico*), which is of recent formation. However, there were at least nine eruptions in the intervening years, of which three would have been of considerable proportions (defined by vulcanologists as sub-Plinian), and thus the resident populations should have been very aware of the presence and, to some extent, the danger of volcanic action. The last sub-Plinian explosion is dated to about 1000 BC and was followed by four smaller events which laid down thin, dark layers of ash, lapilli, and fine scoria. Study of the erosion of these deposits suggests that as much as 700 years may have elapsed since the last threatening volcanic activity by the time of AD 79, and thus the republican period lay in a period of quiescence, allowing considerable regrowth of vegetation.[26] The Campi Flegrei and the associated promontory (Misenum) and islands (Prochyta [Procida], Vivara, and Pithecusae [Ischia]) represented a more constantly unstable landscape of changing land and sea levels, fumaroles, and springs, associated with classical myth. On Pithecusae there is evidence of the eighth-century BC settlement being engulfed by volcanic ash. Recent studies have shown the instability of the area by establishing the sequence of changes in land-surface level and earthquakes.[27]

The Maremma is one of the larger coastal plains of central Italy which is of interest to republican Italy because of the presence of colonies such as Cosa.[28] It is another area chosen by Sallares to illustrate the potential ecology of malaria and, for him, provides a reason for the hesitant development of the colony.[29] The northern part of the region is bounded by the Colline Metalifere, as the name suggests, an important metal ore zone, which projects into the sea, with Elba at its maritime limits. The whole region is composed of four river basins: the largest, the Ombrone, the fourth largest of the peninsula, is accompanied by three smaller rivers, the Albegna and the Fiora to the south and the Bruna to north. The Albegna (67 km long in a catchment of 737 sq km) forms an important physiographic divide between northern and southern Etruria and is the most studied valley of the region.[30] The valley was thus an important feature of the pre-republican political geography, providing a self-contained buffer zone and a means of communication into the interior. A prominent characteristic feature of the coastal margin of this river valley is the lagoon that runs from Ansedonia to Pescia Romana and the poor drainage promoted by sediment transport from up the valley which blocks the exit to the sea. The Romans attempted to solve these difficulties by means of an artificial cut. Another prominent feature is the high promontory of Monte Argentario, which protects the lagoon from the sea approaches. Behind the lagoons there are also some low, isolated hills which stand above the surrounding alluvial plain; together with a hill zone backing onto the high mountains, these complete the key ecological zones of the valley.[31]

The Agro Pontino is a typical microregion circumscribed by the structural framework of the upland geology of the Italian peninsula.[32] It is of interest to republican Italy, because this geographical region was encircled by the *coloniae* of Circeii (to the south), Satricum (to the north west), and Cora and Setia (to the northeast). It also provides Sallares with his principal study of the potential ecology of malaria in republican Italy.[33] He even suggests that attempts to improve the ecology by Cornelius Cethegus in 160 BC actually improved the breeding conditions for the species of mosquito that carry the disease. To the northeast are the abrupt limestone mountains of the Monte Lepini and the Monti Ausoni. To the northwest are the volcanic deposits of the Latium complex. On the coast to the southeast are the sand and clay marine terraces headed by the limestone outcrop of Monte Circeo. In the middle is a depression filled with peat and clay, which the Romans tried to drain. Recent research has uncovered a complex sequence across the microregion of marine terraces covered locally by windblown material. The upper (25 m) Latina terrace consists of poorly drained lagoonal deposits and well-drained sandy beach deposits from the Middle Pleistocene. The Minturno terrace (16 m), dating to the last interglacial of the Late Pleistocene, comprises a fossil beach and a clayey lagoonal deposit. The Borgo Ermada terrace (6 m), dating to the last glacial of the Late Pleistocene, comprises well-drained sand beach deposits along side poorly drained clayey lagoonal deposits. The youngest Terracina terrace dating to the Holocene (the last 10,000 years) is placed just above modern sea level and combines coastal dunes with lagoonal deposits. Parts of this lower landscape were only reclaimed by Mussolini in his emulation of the ancestral Romans who made various attempts at reclamation. This is the location of extensive peat and clay peat deposits cut off from the sea by coastal terraces. Springs running down from the mountains have also produced travertine deposits. Detailed studies of different parts of the Pontine region have shown different rates of alluviation and colluviation related both to the location in the landscape and the socioeconomic context of the sample zone.[34] In the neighborhood of the republican town of Sezze, the pre-Roman landscape is separated from the republican by a sheet of colluvial sediment.

The Implications of Landscape Relief

The structure of relief profoundly affected communications. For instance, the line of the Via Flaminia, after leaving the volcanic landscape of South Etruria, followed the natural tectonic valleys of Umbria, seeking out a pass in the Apennines to find an exit to the Adriatic Sea. The larger rivers could also have been effectively employed, particularly downstream, to carry mountain resources of wood and stone into the alluvial zones relatively poor in such resources and generally the location of the major cities.

The modern rainfall of the Italian peninsula is profoundly determined by relief and season and there is every reason to think that this would have been broadly the same in the republican period. Annual rainfall exceeds 1,000 mm above 1,000 m and drops to lower levels in the hill and coastal regions, ranging from 800–900 mm in the Arno valley to 600–700 mm in Apulia. Certain zones such as the Tavoliere have particularly low rainfall.

The drainage of the peninsula is also determined by the nature of the structural relief. When coupled with seasonal patterns of rainfall and the porosity of some of the parent rocks, there is a profound seasonality to the flow of many of the rivers. The western side of the Apennines is dominated by five long rivers with large catchments, draining into the Tyrrhenian Sea. These are followed in rank by seven shorter rivers with smaller catchments on the eastern side of the Apennines draining into the Adriatic or the Gulf of Taranto. This effect is particularly marked in central Italy where the two largest rivers, the Arno and the Tiber, dominate their landscapes with sizeable catchments. The longest river is the Tiber, which rises on Monte Fumaiolo in the northern part of the central Apennines and runs some 405 km, draining a catchment of some 17,169 sq km. Its course is first directed south in a route determined by tectonic valleys, and then southeast in its lower reaches, redirected by Pleistocene volcanic action, toward its delta near Ostia. In the course of this flow it changed from a more seasonal river in its upper reaches to the perennial and substantial flow once joined by tributaries such as the Aniene and Nera. This river was an important line of communication since it was navigable up into the higher reaches, although more reliably from Orte south, as supported by the archaeological presence of port installations at Ocriculum, Horta, and Lucus Feroniae.[35] The Arno rises in the Apennines at Monte Falterona (1,654 m) and runs some 241 km in a route also determined by the tectonic basins, covering a catchment of some 8,247 sq km, until it reaches the sea at the modern Marina di Pisa. The next three largest rivers all drain the western flank of the Apennines and are placed in central (Ombrone – 161 km, 3,480 sq km) or southern central Italy (Volturno – 175 km, 5,455 sq km; Liri-Garigliano – 158 km, 5,020 sq km). The next seven largest rivers drain the eastern flank of the Apennines, ranging in size between 149 and 101 km in length and 3,188 and 1,192 sq km in catchment.

These differences in scale provide an important constraint on the scale of political process. Smaller-scale river systems (such as in Calabria) provide a limit to the scale of urban development. The Greek colonies in this region tended to have small hinterlands. Larger-scale river systems (such as the Tiber and the Arno) offered greater potential for the development of an agricultural and industrial infrastructure, as well as larger territorial limits. These river systems permitted the development of the great civilizations of the Etruscans and Latins. Intermediate to these scales are intermontane basins of Gubbio and the upper reaches of the Biferno around Bovianum, which formed natural territories for small urban systems.

Altitude also had an effect on health. Many of the coastal areas below 500 m when combined with specific lagoonal conditions with stagnant water of the right salinity could have provided the right conditions for malaria. Erosion from the uplands, perhaps a consequence of more intensive land-use in the republican period, would have provided extra sediment that contributed to the ponding of lagoonal water along the coast. These changed conditions may have favored an extension of mosquito-breeding conditions. If these conditions existed in specific locations (most particularly in summer and autumn), altitude would have been a way of escaping the lazy mosquito, which is reluctant to engage in long altitudinal flights. However, extreme altitude would have provided its own risks of cold, ruggedness, and low productivity.

Altitude also affected economic potential. Studies of traditional land use, although not directly transferable to the Roman past, point out the major differences which can be tied into literary and archaeological evidence.[36] Mediterranean types of cultivation (olives, vines, fruits, wheat, and maize) were restricted to the lower hillslopes, valleys, and basins. The traditional method of cultivation was *coltura promiscua*, that is, the polyculture or growing together of olives, vines, and cereals to provide temperature and water control. The rearing of animals (chiefly sheep, but also cattle and pigs on the central Apennines and goats in the south) was concentrated on the less fertile ground. An important issue is that of transhumance, an agricultural practice which exploits the contrasts between upland and lowland to move flocks between lowland winter and upland summer pastures. A number of scholars have emphasized the long-standing presence of these economic practices as one potential strategy, facilitated by the mountain-plain structure of the Italian peninsula, requiring political networks as well as ecological complementarity for their effective execution.[37] Modern practices suggest that there were two alternative strategies for sheep and goat rearing.[38] One was transhumance, involving in the most elaborate instances large numbers of animals driven over large distances. The other was to hold the smaller numbers of animals in stalls at night (providing manure for arable cultivation) and then allow them to graze locally. The implications of these issues are discussed in Chapter 27.

The Maritime Approaches

With the greater facility of the modern road network it is easy to take a landlocked attitude to the Italian peninsula. In fact, it is important to offer a complementary maritime survey of the peninsula, an approach to the peninsula that is given credence by the distribution of shipwrecks around the coast.[39] Although it is difficult to interrogate the statistics of shipwrecks, affected as they are by the vagaries of research and depth of water, some indication will be given to the zones of high density below.[40] The sea was not only key to communication but an important source of resources ranging from fish to salt.

Our survey starts with the Gulf of La Spezia in the northwest, an embayment with a small coastal plain, flanked by the points of Portovenere (a narrow, cliffed headland)

and S. Pietro. The Magra delta forms the regional context of the Roman city of Luni, where geomorphological studies have shown considerable buildup of sediment since Roman times.[41] The Apennines behind this city provided an important source of (Carrara) marble from at least classical times. From this point onward the Apennines leave the sea, and the coast of modern Tuscany and Latium sweeps southeast for about 550 km, in a series of broad bays separated by rocky headlands and promontories. Studies of the coastal strip through a combination of archaeological and geomorphological evidence have shown a considerable aggradation of this coastline from at least the republican period onward.[42] The distribution of wrecks containing Dressel 1 amphorae (ceramic containers of republican date) suggests that this was one of the two most important stretches of coastline of the peninsula.[43] A series of islands (Gorgona, Capraia, Pianosa, Elba, Giglio) lie off the coast, providing both important landmarks and, to judge from the number of shipwrecks, problems for shipping (although republican shipwrecks have only been found off Elba, most notably at Capo Sant'Andrea, and off Giglio and Giannutri).

At first there is a beach-fringed plain which widens to accommodate the mouth of the Arno River. This is succeeded by a rocky section which is, in its turn, interrupted by the mouth of the smaller Cecina River (a Dressel 1 shipwreck site). To the south of here, after entering the Maremma, there is the striking promontory of Piombino, which is a projection of the Colline metalifere, with the island of Elba beyond. The bay of Baratti, which served the city of Populonia, was important, as indicated by the quantity of shipwrecks (especially that of Pozzino). Once the landmark of the Piombino promontory has been passed, one enters the major embayment of Follonica drained by the Cornia River. This is followed in turn by another promontory (Punta Ala), the site of at least one shipwreck, and the more ample plain of Grosseto which, in Roman times, would have been lagoonal in character behind sandbars; this is, in part, the delta of the one of the major rivers of Tyrrhenian Italy, the Ombrone. At this point the hills again project into the sea at Talamone, before opening once more into the Albegna valley. At the southern edge of the valley, mariners would see from some distance the promontory of Monte Argentario attached to the mainland by two tombolos (sand bars), containing a lagoon behind. The southern flank of this promontory is the site of at least two republican wrecks. To south there is a 50-km broader plain of beach backed by sandhills, up to 10 km inland, down to the mouth of the Mignone River, containing the mouth of the Fiora River, as well as smaller streams, lagoons, and salt pans. At the site of the Roman and modern Civitavecchia, the mineral-bearing Tolfa mountains come down to the sea, fringed by cliffs and pebble beaches. After this important promontory landmark, the coastal plain again widens for some 60 km, often behind sand dunes and marshland which shield the tuff volcanic plains from the sea. The coastline at Santa Severa not far from the archaic sanctuary port of Pyrgi has yielded at least one prominent republican shipwreck, with finds suggestive of an important route down to Campania. To the south, the delta of the Tiber has extended quite considerably seaward from Ostia since Roman times (in this instance most prominently since AD 1500), and volcanic tuffs behind have also become more eroded. The Capo of Anzio and Monte Circeo, straddling the Pontine plains (see above for more detail) are, however, more stable landmarks (and in case of Circeo a considerable danger) for mariners through the ages.

The next stretch of coast, some 270 km in length, runs down from promontory and port of Gaeta, through the spectacular gulfs of Gaeta, Naples, and Salerno dominated by the volcano of Vesuvius. Rugged and often cliffed peninsulas, headed by the distinctive islands of Ponza, Venotene, Ischia, and Capri, fringe wide, fertile plains. The islands of Ponza and Ventotene and the Secca dei Mattoni reef between the Ponza and Palmarola islands caused the shipwreck of several republican ships. Another reef at Le Grotticelle between the small islands of Ventocene and Santo Stefano (in the Pontine islands) was also destructive to republican shipping.

The promontory of Gaeta is approached from the north from Terracina along a steep, rocky coast rising rapidly to the limestone mountains beyond. The Fondi basin forms a small interruption to this rocky scenery, filled by marshland and lagoons. The Gaeta promontory protects two natural ports. After another headland, a sandy beach, backed by extensive dunes and marsh, sweeps some 60 km round toward Cumae, broken by the mouths of the Garigliano and Volturno, two of the largest rivers of central Italy. An arena of mountains rises behind the extensive plain. At Cape Misenum the coast enters the highly spectacular Bay of Naples. Every place-name one reaches, as one travels around the bay, has a significance for classical history: the well-protected port of Misenum, Baiae, Pozzuoli, and Naples itself. Beaches alternate with rocky coastland in front of Campi Flegrei, all visibly modeled by volcanic action as well as by the sea. Shipwrecks from areas such as the island of Procida show republican activity along the coast. From Naples the bay runs below Vesuvius, remodeled by post Roman activity, before widening into the Sarno plain. The Sorrentine peninsula, composed of limestone and some volcanic tuff much affected by faulting, projects beyond, with Capri to the seaward. At least one point, that of Punta Licosa, proved dangerous to republican shipping. This is largely a coastline of spectacular rocky cliffs, until just beyond Salerno, where there is once again a sizeable plain which widens to some 10 km in the area of the ancient city of Paestum to the south, and provides drainage for the Sele River, dropping from the higher relief of the Eboli that itself backs onto the higher Apennines behind.

To the south from here, before entering northern Calabria, major mountain blocks project into the sea, with Monte Stella (Punto Licosa) to the northeast and Monte Bulgheria (Torre Iscolelli) to the southeast. Only the plain around the ancient Greek city of Velia provides a major break in the rocky coastline, although there are occasionally more fertile coastal strips all the way down the Calabrian coastline. As one enters northern Calabria, the mountains rise almost directly from the sea, with very few coastal plains or river valleys. The coastline swings southwest in the Gulf of S. Eufemia, around the wider valley of the Amato River and toward Capo Vaticano. To the other side of Capo Vaticano, there is another prominent embayment, the Gulf of Gioia, turning south toward Scilla and the modern Villa di S. Giovanni, in close proximity to Sicily.

Turning south around the "toe" of the peninsula, there are some slightly larger coastal plains, and modern Reggio di Calabria takes advantage of one of them. There is generally a narrow beach-fringed plain, backed by highly dissected ridges, that rise rapidly to the Calabrian mountains beyond. Every so often a cape (e.g., Cape Bruzzano) or a more fertile plain interrupts this pattern. Beyond Punto Stilo, one enters the Gulf of Squillace. The character of the coastline only changes markedly on the other side of the Gulf where a series of capes, Castella, Rizzuto, and Colonne, mark a rugged and indented coastline, with, in part, major cliffs rising from the sea.

The Gulf of Taranto, extending almost 500 km between Capo Colonne and Capo S. Maria di Leuca, forms the instep of peninsular Italy. A narrow strip broadens into the wider plains of Neto, Sibari (see above) and, above all, Metapontum. In the region of Metapontum, the coastline rises gradually to a series of terraces. At the eastern edge is the bay of Taranto with its important port and beyond, the limestone cliffs and narrow coastal plain of the Salentine peninsula. Between Taranto and the Cape of S. Maria di Leuca, the promontory of Gallipoli forms one of the major landmarks projecting from the coastline. The bay of Saturo some 12 km to the east of Taranto appears to have provided some danger to shipping, particularly a reef running parallel to the shore. Survey of the Secche di Ugento near Capo Santa Maria di Leuca has also shown that this underwater landmark led to casualties in the republican period.

The more than 500-km stretch from Capo S. Maria di Leuca to Torre Mileto encompasses the heel of the Italian peninsula to a point north of the projecting Gargano peninsula, the spur of peninsular Italy. This is a stretch with few interruptions or indentations until the massive landmark of the Gargano peninsula itself to the north of the wide Tavoliere plain (see above) at the head of the Gulf of Manfredonia. The first part of this stretch is a largely made up of limestone plateaux emerging either directly from the sea or from a coastal plain no more than a few kilometers wide. In the course of this coastline there are occasional inlets and or ports such as Badisco, Otranto, or Brindisi. One republican ship appears to have hit the coast near Porto Badisco and sunk to a depth of nearly 40 m, and there appears to be another concentration of shipwrecks around Brindisi.

The final maritime stretch of republican Italy runs some 400 km up the Adriatic coast from Torre Mileto to Rimini. It is generally a long beach with few breaks, rising from a narrow coastal strip to low hills, subject to erosion, to the high Apennines. Occasionally a major delta (such as that of the Biferno valley – see above) interrupts this progress. Relatively few opportunities for harbor exist along the coast, although shelter is sufficiently frequent to provide reasonable communication at locations such as Pescara, Senigallia, Pesaro, Rimini, and Ancona. It is the promontory of Ancona that provides the most prominent landmark of this coastline.

Geography and History

These diverse geographical features shaped the economic and political development of peninsular Italy. What are the implications of this diversity? The Romans, when developing their empire, would have had to develop a flexible strategy not only to deal with the various political configurations of peninsular Italy (as visible through some of the literary as well as archaeological sources), but also a flexible strategy to deal with the varied geographical features of the peninsula. The varied geographical fabric of peninsular Italy meant that there was no one demographic pattern, no one agriculture, no one industry, but a mosaic of patterns, illustrating an essential element of the *longue durée* of Italy.[44]

The complexity of the interrelationship between humans and environment is illustrated by a series of cycles of interaction. One is a cycle of metallurgical production, forest clearance, and agricultural intensification. The later part of the first millennium BC was a period of intensified metallurgical production, both of iron and more precious metals such as silver. Increased availability of iron for agricultural production (as well as many other uses) would have facilitated more intensive agriculture and vegetational clearance through wide availability of cutting tools. This very clearance would have necessitated more metallurgical production to maintain the agricultural fields, and further clearance to maintain the large supplies of wood to produce the charcoal to produce the iron. A separate cycle may have involved the intensified silver production for coinage (a response in itself perhaps to intensified economic activity in the republican period, including the need even to pay for the military in times of political unrest; see also Chapter 3). This specialized activity also requires wood and has been claimed to be the cause of the first global pollution since lead levels (a byproduct of silver production) have been found in the ice of Greenland.[45] The republican period is also a time of intensified ceramic production, which would have had similar resource requirements.

Another related cycle is that of agricultural expansion and changed ecological conditions with implications for health, particularly in the form of malaria.[46] The regionally specific economic intensification of the Hellenistic/republican period may easily have led to increased erosion through increased runoff of water. It should, however, be pointed out that more local regional research needs to be undertaken to date precisely (by archaeological means) the episodes of alluviation. In these local conditions of erosion, the coastal conditions of specific parts of the peninsula may have been radically changed to have produced lagoonal conditions that promoted malaria. The high presence of disease not only would have affected age expectancy in those very specific regions affected, but also adversely affected the conditions of agricultural intensification, and without either the development of malarial immunity or the input of fresh manpower (by expendable slaves?) the very agricultural intensification, which initiated the cycle, would have been adversely affected. Similarly, urban centers would probably have needed to have been replenished constantly by an influx of population from more healthy, often rural, and usually upland areas.

Ecological collapse should not, however, be overstressed. In explanations of the later collapse of the Roman Empire, some authors have been tempted to overemphasize this explanation.[47] Simplistic relationships must be avoided.[48] Buffering and human response are the normal route. Problems encountered in the republican period may have had a response in terms of better land-use practice in the full imperial period. This makes collapse in the later Empire simply as a response to erosion and degradation less likely as a primary cause.

Some authors envisage a *longue durée* contrast between regions; Walker draws a contrast between the centrality of Tuscany ("in the turbulent midstream of history") compared with the Marche ("destined to remain in the backwaters").[49] It must be recalled that impressions of southern Italy taken from modern land use and distribution of resources are profoundly affected by the events of post-Roman history.[50] Southern Italy was the locus of prosperous Magna Graecia at the time of republican Italy. Today it is a landscape exhausted by overexploitation. There is a complex interplay between geography, economics, and politics, of which this chapter provides merely the geographical foundations.

Guide to Further Reading

There are few comprehensive accounts of the geography and environment of peninsular (republican) Italy as a whole since Italians tend to approach the subject regionally. The best overview of the geology and geomorphology is in an edited volume on Europe (Sestini 1984). The best overall geographies are now rather old in date (Delano-Smith 1979; Walker 1958) – and one of the best introduced British troops to the peninsula during World War II (Mason 1944). The more laborious approach to assembling an understanding of the geography of Italy is to approach the question regionally through the good offices of the *Comunità montane* (the government bodies appointed to develop the upland regions – Di Bartolomeo 1976) or the regional monographs accompanying the National Soil Use maps (e.g., Colamonico 1960; Losacco 1944; Rossi Doria 1963; Ruocco 1970). Greater detail on the structural geology of individual map sheets is provided by illustrative notes for each 1:100,000 mapsheet (e.g., Merla, Ercoli, and Torre 1969). A more unusual (at least for most of us today) approach to the geography is to address the issue from the sea and consult the Mediterranean Pilot guides which point out the key landmarks for sailors (Great Britain, Hydrographic Department 1978). The complexity of the interrelationship between the physical environment and humanity is best explored by reading Sallares (2002) on malaria and the edited volume of Bell and Boardman (1992) on erosion (which includes some Mediterranean papers), while bearing in mind the inherent complexity in such evidence (Endfield 1997). The regionality of peninsular Italy can be best approached by detailed reading of the archaeological projects which take a regional approach conscious of the environmental background. These are now many in number, but three from central Italy can be recommended that present a detailed environmental record as well as some detail of the Roman period (Barker 1995; Carandini and Cambi 2002; Malone and Stoddart 1994). Two southern Italian projects are more focused on the prehistoric period, but give a good sense of their local environment (D'Angelo and Oräzie Vallino 1994; Delano-Smith 1979). The Campanian region deserves special mention because of its volcanic landscapes and the focal importance of Vesuvius, which is more apparent perhaps to us today than to the republican populations (Frederiksen 1984; Sigurdsson 2002).

Notes

1 Sestini 1984.
2 Ortolani and Pagliuca 2003; Burroughs 2001.
3 Flemming 1969; Schmiedt and Caputo 1972.
4 Sestini 1984.
5 Braudel 1972; Barker 1995.
6 Bintliff 1992.
7 Van der Leeuw 2000.
8 Brown 1997.
9 Malone and Stoddart 1994.
10 Bonadonna and Bigazzi 1970; Evernden and Curtis 1965; Alessio et al. 1968.
11 Bonatti 1963; Frank 1969; Kelly and Huntley 1991.
12 Alvarez 1972.
13 Jones 1963; Williams-Thorpe 1988; Laurence 2004.
14 Cherkauer 1976; Judson 1963, 1968.
15 Potter 1976.
16 Brown and Ellis 1995.
17 Barker 1995.
18 Hunt 1995.
19 D'Angelo and Oräzie Vallino 1994.
20 Sallares 2002.
21 Spivey and Stoddart 1990: 24–5.
22 Delano-Smith 1979; Alvisi 1970.
23 Sallares 2002: 262–8.
24 Frederiksen 1984.
25 Vecchio, Albore Livadie, and Castaldo 2002.
26 Sigurdsson 2002.
27 Di Vito and Luongo 2003; Guidoboni 2003.
28 Ciacci 1981.
29 Sallares 2002: 192–200.
30 Cambi 2002.
31 Caravaggi 2002.
32 Kamermans 1991.
33 Sallares 2002: 168–91.
34 Attema, Delvigne, and Haagsma 1999.
35 Patterson 2004.
36 Differences: Mason 1944; literary evidence, e.g., Spurr 1986.
37 E.g., Barker 1989, 1995.
38 Barker and Grant 1991.
39 Mason 1944.
40 Celuzza and Rendini 1991; Parker 1992.
41 Ward-Perkins et al. 1986.
42 Mazzanti and Pasquinucci 1983.
43 Parker 1992: Fig. 8.
44 Sallares 2002.
45 Hong et al. 1994.

46 Sallares 2002.
47 Hughes 1975; Hughes and Thirgood 1982.
48 Tainter 2000: 335–6.
49 Walker 1958: 153.
50 Potter 1987.

PART II

Narrative

CHAPTER 6

Between Myth and History: Rome's Rise from Village to Empire (the Eighth Century to 264)

Kurt A. Raaflaub

The Wolf and the Twins

The Capitoline she-wolf, one of the best-known Etruscan bronze sculptures, probably dates to the first half of the fifth century. Enveloped in famous myths, she served as a symbol for Roman qualities, both positive and negative.[1] Her origin and location in Rome is much debated. She is a mother, depicted in a moment of high alertness, ready to protect her young. Unlike in other representations, she is not shown with the twins, Romulus and Remus; they were added in the Renaissance to adapt the statue to the myth. This raises several questions: why did a wolf become the symbol of Rome? How did Romans and non-Romans interpret this symbol? And why were the twins missing in antiquity?

In republican Rome a statue of a she-wolf stood in two places: one near the "wolf or Mars cave" at the Lupercal on the slope of the Palatine (Dion. Hal. 1.79.8) or (perhaps more probably) near the assembly place (*comitium*) in the Forum, the other on the Capitol where Cicero saw a she-wolf with little Romulus before they were damaged by lightning in 65 (*Div.* 1.20; *Cat.* 3.19). The former presumably was identical with the sculpture the aediles Gnaeus and Quintus Ogulnius set up in 296 at the Ficus Ruminalis (Livy 10.23). An early Roman silver didrachm, coined around the time of Q. Ogulnius' consulship in 269, probably represents this sculpture.[2]

The twins were therefore firmly linked with the wolf from at least the late fourth century. No extant evidence suggests that this myth was generally known much earlier. What explains its emergence at precisely that time? And why did this myth provide Rome with two founders? More importantly, what is the relationship of myth and history in this story – and in other stories about early Rome? The present chapter tries to offer answers to this broader question and to establish what we do know with reasonable certainty about the beginnings and the early history of Rome down to the end of Rome's conquest of Italy and the beginning of its expansion into the western Mediterranean in 264.

Myths

Livy wrote the first five books of his history at the beginning of Augustus' principate (c.29–27). He was the last of a long series of historians who, in dealing with the same issues, had established a firm pattern. Livy thus began with Rome's origins, covering in the first book the period of the kings to the expulsion of Tarquin "the Proud" in 507. From the second book, he described the history of the Republic in annual segments (hence "annalist," writer of annals [*annales*]). His work, impressive in length, dramatic elaboration, and stylistic brilliance, quickly became the vulgate, never repeated and unsurpassed, even if knowledge of alternative traditions and variations remained alive for a long time.

Livy tells the following story (1.1–7). After his flight from burning Troy, Aeneas eventually landed in Italy. The local king, Latinus, offered him his daughter Lavinia in marriage. Hence Aeneas' first city was called Lavinium. His son Ascanius (also called Iulus, claimed as their ancestor by the Julian family) founded Alba Longa, where his descendants, the dynasty of the Silvii, ruled for many generations. Centuries later Amulius usurped the kingship from his older brother, killed his sons, and made his daughter one of the Vestal virgins (who tended the communal hearth, symbol of the community's reproductive power, and were thus sworn to chastity). Yet she caught the eye of Mars, the war god, and gave birth to twins; she was thrown into prison and her sons were exposed in the flood lands of the Tiber. Their basket washed up near a fig tree (the Ficus Ruminalis), a she-wolf suckled them, and one of the king's herdsmen took them home and raised them as his own. As leaders of a band of shepherds, they punished Amulius, freed their mother, and returned their grandfather to his legitimate position. Romulus and Remus then planned to found a settlement at the location where they had been exposed. Since they were twins, they needed a divine sign indicating who would enjoy primacy, rule, and give the city his name. Remus received the first sign, Romulus soon a more impressive one; a fight resulted, and Remus, perhaps provoking Romulus, was killed. Romulus became king and the city was called Rome.

This story apparently was already part of the first Roman historical work, written by Fabius Pictor at the end of the third century to explain to the Greek world how Rome had become a Mediterranean power. A catalog inscription in an ancient library summarizes his first book: "Quintus Fabius, called Pictor,... who wrote about the arrival of Heracles in Italy and of Lanoios and his allies, Aeneas and Ascanius. Much later were Romulus and Remus and the foundation of Rome by Romulus, the first king."[3] Much later: this means after the long dynasty of the Silvii in Alba Longa, about whom there was little to say; Livy too offers only a list of names (1.3.6–9), and for good reasons. The Roman historians and antiquarians (below) dated the foundation of Rome to about the middle of the eighth century (Fabius Pictor to 747,

Varro, a great scholar in Caesar's time, to 753). In Greece also the eighth century (featuring, for example, the inception of the Olympic Games or Sparta's conquest of Messenia) was the earliest period reached by later memory (however patchy and unreliable it may have been). By the late fifth century, Greek scholars knew that the "heroic age" with important events such as the Trojan War (which they considered historical) was even much older. Herodotus dated the Trojan War to around 1300, the third-century Alexandrian scholar Eratosthenes to 1183 (remarkably close to modern dates for the wave of destructions that marked the end of the Bronze Age). This gap between the twelfth and eighth centuries needed to be closed, especially since many Greek aristocratic families claimed descent from the heroes of the Trojan War and other myths. Greek specialists, most famously Hellanicus of Lesbos, (re)constructed king-lists and genealogies that served this very purpose.[4]

When was this chronological gap integrated into Roman perceptions of the city's prehistory? Certainly before Fabius Pictor but apparently not much earlier. Echoes in extant remains of Greek literature permit us to trace the evolution of Rome's foundation myth. Sixth-century authors were aware of Latins and Etruscans and knew that Aeneas had reached Sicily or even Italy. Hellanicus wrote that Aeneas called his foundation Rome because, after their landing in Italy, Rhome, one of the Trojan women, incited the others to burn the ships to prevent further travels. In the fourth century, Roman elite families began to trace their descent to Trojan immigrants. Romulus appeared only in the second half of that century, first as one of several eponymous (name-giving) heroes (like Rhomus or Rhome) who all were believed to be sons or daughters of Aeneas or Ascanius, then as founder. Western Greek authors who in that period mention Romulus do not know Remus yet, and they all date the foundation of Rome in the time of Aeneas or his immediate descendants.

It follows that Rome, like most Greek cities, initially had only one founder. The myth apparently reached its fully developed form in the last decades of the fourth century, shortly before the Ogulnii set up the first statue of the wolf and twins. Exposed children are miraculously saved by wild animals in tales attested in many cultures. But why twins? The formation or evolution of myths is usually based on experiences that are highly important to the community involved. As T. P. Wiseman observes, twin founders may well have been suggested by the double magistracy of the consulship that was firmly established (perhaps after serious conflicts) in 367–6, and by subsequent legal provisions that made plebeian participation in this magistracy (and soon other offices) mandatory, that is, by the rise to political equality of the plebeians and the formation of a patrician – plebeian aristocracy (below). Several specific traits of the myth, including name and character of Remus, point to the same period.[5]

Tradition and Distortion

Clearly, then, the stories connected with Rome's foundation are all late and belong in the realm of myth. The same is most likely true also of the first four kings and most of the stories told about the last three kings, Brutus, Lucretia, and the fall of monarchy, and much that Roman historical tradition reports about the early Republic. This tradition was elaborated continually by Fabius Pictor and many generations of his successors. Most of these works are lost, except for fragments (usually in form of quotations by later authors),[6] but the tradition is preserved in the works of authors of Augustus' time (Livy, Dionysius of Halicarnassus, and Virgil) and the Empire (especially Plutarch). It forms a tangled mix of many different elements, most of which unfortunately are entirely unreliable. In this respect, moreover, "early Roman history" lasts until the late fourth century, when Rome reached the threshold of living memory that was directly accessible to Fabius Pictor and other pioneers of Roman historiography (below). Although distortion is not lacking even later, from the time of the Great Samnite War in the late fourth century the foundation of sources, upon which a critical reconstruction of Roman history could and can be built, gradually became much broader and stronger (here and below, see also Chapter 2).[7]

Still, we should not despair of forming concrete and somewhat reliable views about Rome's development in the previous period. But we need to proceed cautiously, to apply a broad range of critical interpretive methods, and to scale our expectations down. Most of all we need to understand the methods the Roman historians used to fill the thin framework of memories and accepted "facts" available to them with dramatic content and to shape a continuous, interesting and instructive story.

All three aspects are important: the story needed to be continuous because gaps were intellectually and aesthetically annoying; unless it was interesting, the intended readership would desert it; and it had to be instructive for history also served a didactic purpose. The first two points are obvious (even if modern historians find it easier to admit lack of knowledge). The third definitely contradicts modern standards, even if we are aware of the ubiquitous influence of ruling ideologies on the historian's choices and judgments. In antiquity, it was largely self-evident. Thucydides intended his history of the Peloponnesian War to be a "possession for ever" because knowledge of the political patterns he observed, heavily determined by an unchangeable factor (human nature), made it possible to anticipate future developments and to react appropriately to the vicissitudes of politics and war (1.22.4). Polybius considered history the best school for aspiring politicians (1.1, 3.12, 3.31–2, 12.25a). The Romans, whose thinking was rooted in a canon of aristocratic values, found moral aspects more important. Livy perceived great benefit in Rome's earliest history, despite its legendary nature, because it offered positive and negative models (*exempla*), helping each new generation to orient itself (*praef.* 6–13). All these approaches shared a firm belief in the importance of history not only for illuminating the past but also for offering guidance to the present and future. History therefore was both timely (insofar as its interpretation served the specific needs of the author's time) and timeless (insofar as it focused on the basic problems of human and communal, social, and political relations). This is why Polybius, Livy, Sallust, and Plutarch were still among the favorite readings of the American Founders, and Thucydides even today has lost none of his immediacy and relevance.[8]

Not surprisingly, therefore, topicality is one of the most frequent factors distorting the Roman historians' "reconstruction" of early Roman history. Yet there were many others. Apart from the pervasive intrusion of myths and legends, many dramatic episodes probably derived from early plays and heroicizing poetry; others from tales that originally were unrelated to history and invented for different purposes (for example, to illustrate legal issues). Family traditions and funeral orations preserved memories of ancestors and famous deeds but were often exaggerated and enhanced by fiction. When antiquarian interests emerged in the late second century, ancient words, institutions, and customs, and names of places and buildings in and around Rome offered a plethora of material; their origins or causes were explained by etiological stories connected with specific events in Rome's early history. Greek historiography, older and richly developed, yielded models of dramatic events, explanation, and interpretation. Patriotic motives prompted positive reinterpretation of episodes that were considered unflattering or incompatible with Roman decorum. Rhetorical elaboration offered unlimited possibilities of expansion: Livy and especially Dionysius of Halicarnassus abound in long and artful speeches.

If everything else failed, considerations of probability and retrojection of later conditions and patterns proved helpful. Many historians (though not all: Dionysius is a sad exception) were vaguely aware that early Rome had been smaller and simpler than its successor in the middle and late Republic, but they had no idea of how deep and comprehensive these differences really were. They knew, for instance, that Rome's early wars had been confined to feuds with neighboring towns and tribes in the city's close proximity, but they had no compunction in applying to these wars the template of the much longer, larger, and more complex wars against the Samnites and other Italian peoples in the late fourth and early third centuries.

In addition, once a specific story had been integrated into the tradition, it usually remained there. The annalists' primary goal, as Livy confirms (*praef.* 2), was not to engage in thorough research in order to arrive at new insights, better interpretations, or even an independent reconstruction of historical events. It was rather to improve on what others had written before, by enhancing scope, style, drama, and human appeal. This tendency favored stability in the structural canon: the sequence of facts and events could not easily be changed. Evidence preserved in authors independent of the annalist tradition indicates that numerous variations and elements not contained in this canon survived outside of it.[9]

Let us look at a few examples. The selection of Romulus' successor (Numa Pompilius) combines several etiologies transformed into historical narrative (1.17.1–21.5). These focus on specific constitutional issues that (as was suggested, for instance, by the term *interrex*, "in-between king") must have originated in Rome's earliest period. Such issues include the complex modalities to be observed when direct transmission of the leader's political – religious power (*imperium*) was interrupted by his death, and the participation of three authorities in "making" the leader: the gods (through *auspicia*, the observation of the sky and bird-signs), the Senate (through selection), and the People (through confirmation in assembly). The legend of the Horatii and Curiatii (Livy 1.24.1–26.14), embedded in Rome's conquest of Alba Longa and perhaps celebrated in heroicizing songs (see also Chapter 2),[10] explains several topographical and legal oddities, including the location and

arrangement of six ancient tombs between Rome and Alba Longa, the name of the
"Sister's Beam," an obsolete legal procedure (*perduellio*, "treason") that was revived
in a sensational trial in 63, and certain purification rituals that kept being observed in
the family of the Horatii.

In 443, Livy reports (4.9–10), a conflict erupted in the Latin town of Ardea, allied
with Rome, that soon escalated into a regional war. A young orphan woman of lowly
origin was wooed by two suitors: a wealthy aristocrat favored by her mother, and a
commoner (plebeian) preferred by her guardians. In an age of social conflict (below),
this rivalry became part of a factional strife that escalated beyond control. Resolution
within the family proved impossible, a court decided in favor of the mother, the
guardians and a band of plebeians abducted the bride, the aristocrat mobilized his
followers who defeated the plebeians in a battle, the plebeians occupied a hill outside
of Ardea and ravaged the estates of their elite opponents, both parties called for
outside help, in the ensuing war the Romans defeated the Volscians, and the consul
Geganius led the Volscian general Cluilius in triumph to the Capitol. The beautiful
bride was long forgotten. The only historical element in this unlikely tale is perhaps
Geganius' triumph in a Volscian war, listed (like the first election of censors in the
same year) in the annual records of the pontiffs (below). Like many such tales, this
one was probably invented, without specific historical connection or date, by a mid-
or late republican jurist to illustrate with a concrete but fictitious case specific legal
problems resulting from certain rules in the *Twelve Tables* (here concerning the
marriage of an orphaned and therefore legally independent woman). The story was
integrated into the historical tradition because it helped fill a gap (the cause of
Geganius' war), added human drama to a dry historical fact, and offered an opportunity to celebrate early Roman virtues (loyalty to allies and ability, in contrast to the
Ardeans, to resolve civic differences without bloodshed).[11]

Among patriotically motivated distortions, Rome's heroic defense, after the last
Tarquin's expulsion, against his ally, Porsenna of Clusium, easily takes first place.
The deeds of Horatius Cocles, Mucius Scaevola, and Cloelia supposedly impressed
Porsenna so deeply that he preferred to be Rome's friend (Livy 2.9.1–13.11).
An alternative tradition suggests that the Romans capitulated, yielded to Porsenna
territory across the Tiber, hostages, and the insignia of power, and were prohibited
from using iron for other than agrarian purposes. According to this tradition,
Porsenna not only conquered Rome but also ruled over it at least for a short time.[12]

The influence of Greek narrative and interpretive patterns is no less obvious, even if
in some cases they may have been grafted onto a historical core. The legend of the
abduction of the Sabine women (Livy 1.9.1–13.8) explains how Romulus and his
motley crowd of settlers in early Rome provided themselves with the women needed
to complete and perpetuate their community. It preserves the memory of the merging
of two originally separate communities (one Latin, the other Sabine), but may also
reflect the experience of Greek colonists who often left home without women and
acquired them later, peacefully or violently, from native tribes. Greek influence is even
clearer in the last Tarquin's characterization as a tyrant and in the famous tale that
explains his expulsion: the rape of the virtuous Lucretia by the tyrant's son (Livy
1.49–59).[13]

The canonical list of seven kings illustrates the tendency to cling to an orthodox version of events. Whatever the historicity of names and persons, evidence survives outside this tradition suggesting that conditions were more unstable and Rome may have had more "kings." Servius Tullius, wedged in between the two Tarquins (Livy 1.39.1–48.9), supposedly was the son of a prisoner of war (and thus a slave) of royal descent, whom a miracle marked early for future greatness. This legend may derive from his name, Servius (*servus*, slave), while Tullius may rather link him to the third king, Tullus Hostilius. The Etruscans apparently knew Servius as Mastarna, the loyal follower of an Etruscan warlord, Caelius Vibenna. After a defeat, Mastarna settled with the remains of Caelius' army on the hill in Rome that henceforth bore Caelius' name, and, as Servius Tullius, became king. Scholars interpret Mastarna as *magister-na*, that is, a name derived from the function of *magister* (master, leader), in Rome the title of the commander of army and cavalry (*magister populi, magister equitum*) and perhaps initially of the overall leader. Accordingly, unless two persons were here merged into one, a follower of Vibenna named Servius Tullius became *magister* in Rome and remained famous in Etruria as Mastarna.

There were in fact two Vibenna brothers. They are represented in one of the fourth-century frescoes in the François tomb in Vulci: among others, Mastarna liberates Caele Vipinas, while Aule Vipinas stabs his opponent and Marce Camitlnas (Marcus Camillus) is about to kill Cneve Tarchunies Rumach (Gnaeus Tarquinius of Rome; the Roman kings' first name was Lucius). This seems to reflect an episode from an aristocratic feud, in which captives, liberated and equipped with arms by their supporters, take revenge on their captors. Presumably these men were leaders of aristocratic warrior bands that were a common feature at the time. According to a mid-fifth-century inscription, the companions (*sodales*) of Publius Valerius (a name very familiar in Rome) set up a dedication in Mars' sanctuary in Satricum. Porsenna too may have been such a "condottiere." After his victory over Rome, his son Arruns tried to gain control over a neighboring town (Aricia) but was defeated by Latins and allied Greeks. The fleeing remains of his army were sheltered by the Romans (which again reflects Porsenna's influence in Rome). More "kings" thus perhaps "ruled" in Rome than the annalistic tradition indicates, and some of these were little more than aristocratic adventurers who used their warrior bands to seize power over another town. Moreover, the transition from monarchy to Republic may have been more complicated also. The last Tarquin was perhaps expelled not by the Romans themselves but by Porsenna, who was overthrown in turn when his son's defeat at Aricia weakened his resources and authority.[14]

The most important and frequent cause of distortion, however, lies in political concerns. A century of crisis, violence, and civil war began with Tiberius Gracchus' failed attempt in 133 to realize an ambitious program of agrarian reform, and ended with Augustus' victory. Among those involved in intense contentions between "populist" and "conservative" factions (*populares* and *optimates*) we find several senators who wrote historical works. Licinius Macer, whose *annales* were among Livy's primary sources, most likely was tribune of the plebs in 73 and a fierce opponent of the conservative senatorial government that Sulla established after civil war and proscriptions in the late eighties. In describing social conflicts in the early

Republic, he decidedly took the side of the plebeians, introducing new interpretations and precedents, based on contemporary experiences, and emphasizing the role of his ancestors, the Licinii (while his predecessor, Valerius Antias, notoriously exaggerated that of the Valerii). In the crucial year 133, another annalist, L. Calpurnius Piso Frugi, was consul and one of Tiberius Gracchus' leading opponents.[15]

To Piso we owe a telling example of political reinterpretation. In 440–39 Rome was struck by food shortages. All efforts of the grain commissioner, Lucius Minucius, to import food remained unsuccessful. A wealthy citizen, Spurius Maelius, had bought grain abroad and distributed it gratis to the suffering population. This made him popular and overly ambitious; he aimed at sole rule (tyranny, *regnum*). Minucius discovered the plot and informed the Senate. Cincinnatus, famous but by now very old, was made dictator and selected Servilius Ahala as his adjutant (*magister equitum*). When Maelius tried to escape and stirred up the people to avoid arrest, Ahala cut him down. Cincinnatus praised him as savior of the state, Maelius' house was destroyed (the lot, henceforth called Aequimaelium, was left empty forever), and Minucius was honored outside the Porta Trigemina. Three tribunes demanded that Ahala and Minucius be tried for illegally killing a citizen, but they were not heard (Livy 4.12–16; cf. Dion. Hal. 12.1–4).

A few years later, Livy says (4.21.3–4), a plebeian tribune, Spurius Maelius, demanded, again unsuccessfully, that legal action be taken against Minucius and Ahala because of their role in the death of the corn dealer Maelius. Despite the clumsy attempt to explain it, the appearance of Spurius Maelius in different roles in different years suggests that neither role nor year were initially fixed. Moreover, the tale combines three etiologies: of the Aequimaelium, of the column in front of the Porta Trigemina that honored Minucius, and of the byname (*cognomen*) of Servilius (Ahala refers to the armpit where he hid his dagger).[16] Dionysius points out (12.4) that, according to Calpurnius Piso and an even earlier annalist, Cincius Alimentus, Cincinnatus was not made dictator nor Servilius *magister equitum*. Rather, after hearing the compelling accusation of Minucius, the Senate considered a trial unnecessary. Servilius was charged with killing the conspirator and executed the deed immediately.

Events of the year 133 help explain the contradiction between these two versions. Tiberius Gracchus had violated customary rules (*mos maiorum*), set dangerous precedents, and created an explosive situation that the Senate as guardian of tradition, law, and order could not tolerate (see Chapter 8). Because the consul in charge refused to act as long as Gracchus did not openly break the law, some senators seized the initiative and killed Gracchus and many of his supporters. This act of violence prompted a vehement debate. Both sides tried to bolster their positions through trials, new political measures and laws, and, apparently, historical precedents. The Maelius incident was ideal for this purpose. An older tradition, attested by Cincius Alimentus, must have contained not only the etiological elements but also the fact that Ahala had killed Maelius as a potential tyrant. Tiberius' opponents, who had accused him of aiming at *regnum*, needed to emphasize only that in the early Republic senators had killed a would-be tyrant without authorization by office or court, simply because as leading citizens they were responsible for the state's freedom and safety. This is Piso's version. In that of Tiberius' supporters, preserved in Livy and Dionysius, the Senate had strictly followed the law; unlike Gracchus, Maelius had been killed by an official who had been empowered for this very purpose, and only because (again unlike Gracchus) he tried to evade justice and stir up a revolt.[17]

Overall, then, in assessing the value of the Roman tradition great caution is due especially in accepting the sources' interpretation and dramatic elaboration of events. Apart from Dionysius, for almost the entire period covered in the present chapter, Livy (whose first decade ends in 293/2) offers the only fully preserved historical narrative. This does not mean, of course, that Livy was himself responsible for the distortions we discover in his text; most of them he probably found in his sources. Although the basic outline of facts and events probably was largely fixed already at the time of Fabius Pictor, the history he wrote down for the first time underwent comprehensive transformation in the following 200 years or so. Livy often made an effort to deal with flaws he perceived in his sources, but the elegant and dramatic elaboration that was his primary purpose also solidified or worsened earlier distortions. Like many of his predecessors, Livy too reinterpreted Rome's early history from the perspective of his own time. Many instances reflect his concerns with problems that agitated his contemporaries in the critical period when he began his work. In Livy's first ten books early Rome and Augustan Rome, history of the distant past and experiences of the present interact with each other in a fruitful dialectic that is difficult to disentangle but illuminating in both respects.[18]

Consequences and Principles

In dealing with the early period, all Roman historians worked under an overwhelming handicap. Even the pioneers in the late third century wrote centuries after most of the events they described. As a basic rule, living memory reaches back over about three generations or a century (whatever grandchildren hear from their grandparents). Memories about sensational events or eminent personalities may survive longer (what grandparents had heard from their grandparents or what family tradition "remembers"), but these are usually anecdotal and reliable at most in their basic core. They project like islands out of a sea of oblivion that scholars call the "floating gap" because it moves in time, keeping the same chronological distance from each new generation (see also Chapter 23). Ancient scholars tried to bridge this gap and connect the remembered with the "heroic" past (above). Across the floating gap, indeed, lies the mythical past with events and persons (like the Trojan War and Aeneas' arrival in Italy) that mythical memory often organizes in three generations (such as those of the Trojan War heroes, their fathers, and their sons: Anchises, Aeneas, and Ascanius). Such myths may well contain a historical core. Yet, because of an ongoing process of transformation and adaptation that is typical of oral traditions, this core cannot be identified reliably without confirmation by independent evidence that is at least near contemporaneous. Where such evidence survives (as in the case of medieval epics such as the *Chanson de Roland* or the *Nibelungenlied*), we witness a rapid and profound distortion and reorganization of traditions about events, persons, and social conditions, even in tales encapsulated in metrical song.

All this is easily demonstrable with Greek examples but no less true for Rome. In writing about events at the very end of the fourth century and later, the earliest historians could probably rely on living memories of their contemporaries and their immediate ancestors. Only anecdotal memories survived from the previous two centuries. The period of the kings (structured in twice three generations, separated by a transitional one) was essentially mythical. Of this the Romans were unaware, although Livy realizes it for the period before Rome's foundation (*praef.* 6–8). The fifth century and large parts of the fourth were a dark period. Logically, the early historians dwelled on the legendary tales of foundation and kings, rushed through the early Republic, and expanded their narrative once they reached the Samnite and later Italian wars. The late fourth century, like a screen or curtain, barred their view into the more distant past: holes and tears offered tantalizing glimpses; obviously much lay behind it but precise information was unavailable. Naturally, then, to the earliest historians issues and developments known from the late fourth and early third centuries (both in Rome's domestic politics and its relations to the outside world in peace and war) offered patterns and suggestions that they generalized and applied as templates to the entire history of the early Republic. Nor do we need to wonder that they (and their successors) used all kinds of extraneous evidence and all available means to fill the pervasive gaps and construct at least a somewhat continuous, interesting, and accessible narrative, and that later experiences so deeply shaped their interpretation of the early periods.[19]

Yet there were items that proved helpful in historical reconstruction. Songs and early plays were mentioned before; although heroicizing, they often focused on historical events and persons. Family traditions did not consist only of exaggerated accomplishments and fictitious consulships and triumphs. Writing was used from at least the sixth century, even if not for historical purposes. Polybius (3.22) and other historians refer to texts of early treaties and other documents one could still find and read (although with difficulty). Some temples and monuments dated as far back as the sixth century. The calendar and events with religious significance (such as the foundation of sanctuaries, famines, triumphs, omens, prodigies, and the consultation of oracles and the Sibylline books) were recorded by the pontiffs (although it is unclear when such records began), apparently preserved over centuries, and eventually integrated into the "greatest annals" (*annales maximi*); the latter's form, date, publication, and use by historians, however, are shrouded in uncertainty. These records listed also the supreme (eponymous) magistrates who served to date years and records. Although the authenticity of the lists of such magistrates (*fasti*), assembled in the late Republic and Augustus' time, is much debated especially for the early Republic, these types of information provided at least a rough framework of facts and events. Even Livy's report shows that there were still some years in which these basic elements constituted all that could be said.[20]

The modern historian is thus faced with the difficult task of sorting out authentic components from the wild growth of legends and elaboration that evolved over centuries, and of assembling reliable information that survived outside the annalistic tradition. Scholars have suggested a distinction between (authentic) "basic facts" and (unreliable) "narrative superstructure," but the distortions described above unfortunately are no less frequent on the level of basic facts. All we can do, therefore, is to decide from case to case, whenever possible using criteria and testimonia that are independent of the Roman vulgate. Some scholars deride this principle as "hypercritical," insisting that the Roman historians, despite all their shortcomings, were better informed than we are, having at their disposal much information that now is irretrievably lost, and were able to judge from an inside perspective that we cannot possibly acquire. This may be true to some extent, but they were also much less critical, captives of a tradition that in its outlines was considered largely unchangeable, and unable to use methods of modern disciplines (such as archaeology, anthropology, and comparative history) that permit us to deal with the same problems they faced in more sophisticated ways and to gain insights barred to them. Not least, we now understand their methods, preferences, and limitations much better than earlier generations of scholars did. Persistent criticism based on serious skepticism has to remain our principle until we can demonstrate that ancient information is credible. All else would be irresponsible. We thereby sacrifice the possibility of writing a continuous narrative of Rome's early history, but we gain rough outlines of a reliable reconstruction; we can still get from the little village on the Palatine to the city that began to rule an empire, but to do so we have to cross the river, so to speak, not on a broad and elegant bridge but by jumping from stone to stone.[21]

Outlines of a History

Period of the kings

The oldest calendar, dating to the sixth century, before the temple of Jupiter, Juno, and Minerva was built on the Capitol, and extant fragments of the *Law of the Twelve Tables*, dating to the mid-fifth century, are good examples of early Roman documents that are independent of historical traditions. Both reflect an agrarian society, in which trade and crafts were relatively insignificant, that was mostly concerned with harvest, reproduction, and security, and that tried to contain domestic conflicts.[22]

Rome's location was ideal: hills and valleys close to the Tiber, well defensible and at the edge of a large coastal plain, where the river became navigable and an island facilitated its crossing, at the intersection of two important routes of communication (the north – south axis from Etruria through Latium to Campania and the west – east axis from the salt-pans near the Tiber's mouth along the Tiber to inland Italy that was important for the salt trade [*via salaria*]). Rome's site therefore was settled early. In the eighth century it comprised two villages (one of Latins on the Palatine, another of Sabines on the Quirinal) and perhaps other hamlets on hills and in valleys. Rome was not founded; it grew together from this group of small settlements. This is a common pattern in the formation of the community type the Greeks called *polis*: not a "city-state" (because the evolution of the city followed upon that of the *polis*, not every polis contained a city, and, unlike in medieval city-states, the city did not rule over its territory) but a "citizen-state," a community defined by common laws, customs, and religion, in which citizens living in the city and the surrounding territory shared privileges and obligations.

Apart from consultation of the gods, three elements participated in communal decisions: the paramount leader (at least initially more a "chief" than a king, the first among peers), the council of experienced leaders (called "elders," *senes* like *gerontes* in Greece, thus *senatus* like *gerousia* in Sparta), who were the heads of elite families (thus "fathers," *patres*, collectively called *patricii*, "patricians"), and the assembly of landowning farmers who also fought in the communal army. Family and neighborhood groups, perhaps also forming warrior bands led by elite leaders (*curia* from *coviria*, "group of men," perhaps comparable to the Greek *phratria*, "brotherhood"), eventually crystallized into *gentes* ("clans") that, typically, claimed descent from a common ancestor. The great importance they played in the Roman social structure helps explain why the assembly voted in groups (*curiae*, later *centuriae*, "hundreds," and *tribus*, "tribes, districts"), not individually. The emergence of an elite can be observed in early cemeteries in Latium, where among initially undifferentiated tombs gradually groups of graves were marked out by little stone walls and distinguished by precious objects, often imported from afar, marking the dead person as an owner of prestige goods and thus an important personality.[23]

Legendary, religious, and other evidence suggests that Rome combined (ethnically closely related) Latin and Sabine elements. More specifically, ancient religious rituals reflect the emergence of a Latin village out of scattered hamlets (*septimontium* from *saepti montes*, "palisaded hills," rather than *septem montes*, "seven hills") and the merging of this Latin with a Sabine village to form the "twin town" (*urbs geminata*). Sacrifices at boundary stones on roads leading out of Rome even indicate the size of Rome's early territory (*ager Romanus*).[24]

Archaeological evidence indicates that a unified city emerged toward the end of the seventh century with its center in the Forum area that was now paved, comprising an assembly place (*comitium*), a meeting house for the Senate (*curia*), sanctuaries and shrines, and the seat of the *rex* (*regia*). These innovations, and further expansion of public spaces with sanctuaries at the "cattle market" (*forum boarium*) near the Tiber crossing and eventually on the Capitol (the temple of the Capitoline Triad, begun in the late sixth century), were realized under the leadership of Etruscan families that had settled in Rome. Such horizontal mobility is well documented by contemporaneous evidence. Etruscan influence (often concerning issues originating in Greece) is generally believed to have been pervasive at the time; we need think only of the insignia of power (the ivory folding chair [*sella curulis*] or the richly decorated coat of the leader, still worn much later by the *triumphator*), the crucial role of divination (through hepatoscopy, the inspection of the liver of sacrificial animals, and auspices, the observation of the sky and flight of birds), and cultural (sculpture, architecture), technological (road and bridge building, sewer lines [such as the *cloaca maxima* in Rome]), and military aspects (the hoplite phalanx). All this, however, does not mean that Rome at the time was an Etruscan city or a city ruled by Etruscans.[25]

Tradition assigns to Servius Tullius important institutional reforms connected with the hoplite phalanx. This form of fighting had evolved in Greece by the late seventh century. It required a large number of equally equipped, heavily armed infantry soldiers (hoplites from *hoplon*, the large round shield, or *hopla*, the entire set of arms and armor [panoply]), who fought in a close-ranked formation (the phalanx). In Greece the hoplites were independent farmers who could afford the panoply (equivalent to 30 sheep in a late-sixth-century inscription) and had a stake in defending their farms and communal territory against outside enemies. Given the topography of Rome's surroundings, the phalanx was probably effective mostly in formal wars against neighboring communities (such as Etruscan Veii), while raiding and counter-raiding continued to be conducted by warrior bands. At any rate, from the mid-sixth century Rome's army consisted of some units of horsemen and 40 centuries ("hundreds") of infantry that formed "the class" (*classis*), while those who could not afford the panoply counted among those "beneath the class" (*infra classem*, Gell. *NA* 6.13) and as such were secondary citizens. Demographic calculations suggest for that period on a territory of 822 sq km (less than a third of Attica) a total population of 20,000–30,000 (much smaller than what the Romans themselves believed), of whom 6,600–9,900 would have been adult male citizens, 2,700–4,000 hoplites, and 400–600 adult members of the elite (see also Chapter 13).

Accordingly, a hoplite class of 40 centuries would indeed have been the maximum the Romans could muster, and this class most likely was much larger than the patrician elite, even including their clients. Non-elite farmers were thus part of the *classis* (below). The adoption of the hoplite phalanx was an event of great communal significance. The citizen assembly was adjusted to its organization by adding the same number of centuries for older citizens (*seniores*), and the citizen body was restructured into territorial units (districts, *tribus*) that were apparently needed to register the citizens who were not part of aristocratic *gentes*. A few decades later (in 443: Livy 4.8), the office of censor was introduced for the main purpose of maintaining the citizen lists. Much later, perhaps in the late fifth and fourth centuries, in the context of territorial expansion and changes in the army's organization (culminating in the replacement of the phalanx by the more flexible manipular system), other classes were added with inferior equipment and defined by a lower census requirement. The resulting complex system eventually was attributed in its entirety to Servius Tullius (Livy 1.42–3; see also Chapter 13).[26]

The size of territory, city, and population, the number, size, and decoration of public buildings, and the impressive size of private elite houses suggest that Rome by the late sixth century was by far the largest, wealthiest, and most powerful community in Latium, comparable to some of its Etruscan neighbors in the north. A treaty with Carthage, quoted by Polybius (3.22) and dated to the very beginning of the Republic, confirms Rome's leading position in Latium.[27] However we reconstruct the transition from monarchy to Republic, it apparently was a traumatic event, soon enveloped in legends and patriotic aggrandizement (above). Sole rule (*regnum*) henceforth was anathema.

Early Republic: crisis and expansion

In the end, the aristocracy ruled collectively in and through the Senate from among whose members the annual officials were elected. Their power initially remained comprehensive, as that of the king had been, but it was limited by the principles of annual tenure and collegiality (although the double consulship may have been firmly established only in 367/6 and several possibilities tried out before then). To meet new tasks and challenges, in the course of time new offices were introduced (aediles to supervise markets, censors to register citizens and soldiers, praetors to oversee jurisdiction and serve as secondary army commanders, and quaestors to administer public properties and treasuries). Responsibilities were thus gradually distributed among several offices, and the supreme magistrates henceforth focused on political and military leadership. Typically, though, a Roman senator would in the course of his career hold most of these offices; they remained unpaid and were thus considered an honor (hence *honor* for office and *cursus honorum* for the career scheme). This development was completed by the end of the fourth century, even if details (such as minimal age requirements and intervals between consulships) were regulated much later (see also Chapter 12).[28]

By about the second quarter of the fifth century Rome's situation changed profoundly. Tribal migrations had continued or resumed. Celtic tribes (whom the Romans called Gauls) had crossed the Alps and settled in the valley of the Po (hence "Cisalpine Gaul" = "Gaul on the near side of the Alps"), expelling the Etruscans, and farther south along the Adriatic. Mountain tribes in the interior of the Italian peninsula increased their pressure on the fertile coastal plains. Etruscan and Greek communities in Campania, and the Latins in southern Latium, fought for their survival; many were taken over, fully or partially, by Samnites, Volscians and Aequians. Information contained in the annalistic tradition about the frequency and location of Roman battles with neighboring peoples probably derives from the priestly annals; unlike numbers involved, duration of such wars, and dramatic details, it offers a plausible picture and thus is probably authentic – and highly alarming. Almost every year the Romans were fighting with Sabines, Aequians, and Volscians; feuds with Etruscan Veii (only 17 miles away) were frequent; territories that had perhaps been Roman in the sixth century apparently were lost again (by the mid-fifth century, as the *Twelve Tables* indicate, the Tiber was still or again the northern frontier of Rome's territory); even the Latin allies supposedly refused to accept Rome's predominance and in a battle achieved a compromise and collective parity with Rome (the *foedus Cassianum*, "Treaty of Cassius," of 493). In addition, Rome suffered food shortages (apparently recorded in the priestly annals as well) and a general economic decline, attested by a dramatic reduction of imported pottery in tombs and the end of an impressive series of temple constructions (not to be resumed before the late fourth century; see also Chapter 4).[29]

Conditions improved toward the end of the fifth century, and with the conquest of Veii in 396 (which soon assumed legendary fame) Rome at once doubled the size of its territory. But only a few years later (in 390 or 387) it suffered a disastrous defeat against an invading band of Gauls (the "black day of the Allia"). Even if Rome was not, as tradition claimed, largely destroyed (no corresponding destruction layer has yet been found) and perhaps was able to buy off the Gauls (Polyb. 2.18.1–3), this was a traumatic setback with serious consequences that provoked panic reactions even centuries later and burdened Rome with a veritable "security complex." Fights with neighboring tribes resumed. It was only by the mid-fourth century that Rome seemed to have things fully under control. But then the Latin allies revolted and it took a full-scale war to overcome them (340–38).

The previous multilateral alliance system was now replaced by a series of bilateral and "unequal" treaties, in which Rome as the stronger partner dictated the conditions. These conditions, applied also during the conquest of Italy, were, with few exceptions, generous, especially in view of ancient customs of war that gave the victor power to deal at will with the defeated. Some of Rome's former enemies were absorbed; others forced to yield part of their territory (used to settle Roman and allied citizens in *coloniae*, "colonies"); they lost their independent foreign policy, and had to furnish contingents of soldiers for Rome's wars, but they preserved their communal integrity and domestic autonomy. Furthermore, participation in Rome's wars yielded booty, everybody profited from the peace Rome maintained within its sphere of influence, and local elites had the possibility of joining the Roman aristocracy that was no longer able to maintain its previous exclusiveness. With all this, Rome's own territory, cultivated by Roman citizens, its citizen body, manpower reserves, system of alliances, and sphere of influence began to grow, first slowly, then rapidly and exponentially, providing indispensable conditions for further expansion.[30]

Early Republic: domestic conflicts

Along with the changes in Rome's relations to the outside world, its society too was transformed profoundly. Roman tradition believed that the early history of the Republic was dominated by a long and constantly renewed series of social conflicts between the patricians and plebeians, often called the "Struggle of the Orders." Although the definition especially of "plebeians" continues to be debated, most likely they comprised all citizens who did not belong to the patrician *gentes*. They acquired a specific identity when the latter around 487 closed their ranks to newcomers and upstarts and established themselves as an exclusive aristocracy (see also Chapter 4). Conflicts between the classes were motivated by dissatisfaction about the exploitation of traditional relationships of dependence that were defined by debt and obligation and in extreme cases resulted in bondage or enslavement, by the concentration of land in fewer hands and the corresponding demand for the distribution of land, by aristocratic abuses that prompted a demand for codification of laws, and, on the part of an emerging plebeian elite, by the wish to gain access to offices monopolized by the patricians. Acute conflicts supposedly broke out in 495–93, when tensions about the mistreatment of debtors caused the plebeians to leave the city in a collective "secession" (*secessio plebis*) and refuse service in the army until their demands were met (Livy 2.23.1–24.8). These focused on the recognition of specifically plebeian institutions (a plebeian assembly, *concilium plebis*, and plebeian officers, the tribunes of the plebs, who assisted and protected plebeians threatened by patricians and their magistrates [hence later the rights of assistance, *auxilium*, and appeal, *provocatio*]). The Struggle of the Orders ended only in the early third century, when most plebeian demands had been met.

The idea of a class struggle that lasted for 200 years and was fed over that entire period by essentially the same causes is historically implausible. Its final phase, accessible to the earliest historians through living memory, brought the resolution of several important issues. Measures to relieve debt and restrict interest recurred from the second third of the fourth century. In 326 or 313, facilitated by the massive influx of enslaved war captives, debt bondage was virtually abolished. Distribution of land to Roman citizens and Latin allies had taken place already in the fifth century, whenever a new colony was founded; the conquest of Veii allegedly made it possible to settle 4,000 citizens, and colonization continued throughout the conquest of Italy. In 367 the plebeian elite gained access to the consulship; a law of 342 mandated that one consul be plebeian. The censorship was opened to plebeians in 339; the praetorship in 337; important religious offices by 300. In the same time period, a law required the *patres* to sanction bills before rather than after the assembly's vote; a similar law about elections followed in 290. In 300 another law granted the right of appeal (*provocatio*) against physical coercion or execution by a magistrate. In 287, after a crisis brought about by war and debt, and after a plebeian secession from the city, a law, proposed by the dictator Hortensius (*lex Hortensia*), determined that decisions by the plebeian assembly bound the entire citizen body.

By then the plebeian organization was fully integrated into the state's political structures, and a new mixed aristocracy (called *nobilitas*) had been formed from patrician and plebeian elite families. The issues dominating the Struggle of the Order's last phase (debt relief, distribution of land, integration of plebeian institutions, and plebeian access to political and religious offices) clearly shaped the historians' perception of the earlier phases as well. These very issues, various laws that are well attested in this last phase, and the plebeian strategy of seceding from the city in 287 were apparently retrojected into earlier periods and repeated several times. In addition, late republican social conflicts provided the annalists with a wealth of material that was useful for the dramatic elaboration and political interpretation of these conflicts, and the need for historical precedents (above) prompted historians to retroject specific measures or disputes from their own into early republican times. It would seem justified, therefore, to reduce the range of credible information to the Struggle's final phase and, with very few exceptions, to confess ignorance for the previous 150 years.

On current understanding, however, this solution would be too radical and pessimistic. Enough independent evidence survives to suggest that from the early fifth century Rome could indeed have been shaken at least intermittently by serious social conflicts and that these might have focused, among others, on problems that remained important for a long time. Such evidence includes the harsh law of debt fixed in the *Twelve Tables*, the crisis symptoms described earlier that caused economic hardships for many, the highly unusual plebeian institutions that initially must have formed a veritable "state within the state," the patrician aristocracy's exclusiveness, and illuminating analogies in archaic Greece. That it was impossible to overcome these problems with quick and lasting solutions in turn explains the specific character of the plebeian organization that initially focused on protection and self-help.[31]

All this poses several questions. Why, in contrast, for example, with Solonian Athens, were quick and incisive solutions impossible? Why was the patrician aristocracy able for such a long time to resist plebeian demands? Why did such conflicts not escalate into civil war and why was the community not weakened by them so as to succumb to long-lasting external pressure? Answers to these questions help us understand Rome's unique development and its rise to power in the Mediterranean.

The need, constantly repeated over 150 years, to overcome massive outside pressure (above) profoundly shaped Roman society. The elite, on whose qualities of leadership the community depended, developed a specific system of values that focused entirely on these qualities and on service for the community, and exceptional cohesion that helped control constant fierce competition for the highest ranks and offices (see also Chapter 17). The commoners learned to value discipline and solidarity too; despite intense social disagreements, and despite their indispensable and powerful role in army and assembly, they did not seek to overthrow existing structures and hierarchies. The community as a whole developed a remarkable ability to forge compromises and to emerge from serious conflict stronger and more unified.

For these reasons alone, under early republican conditions extreme forms of protest (such as military strike and secession) that the plebeians supposedly employed repeatedly, seem implausible. In a world of constant fights with neighboring tribes and cities, the plebeian farmer-soldiers must have been as interested as the patricians in defending their fields and saving their community. In fact, not only the aristocratic value system but also the plebeians' horizon of expectations adjusted to the necessities, among which war played a crucial role. The soldier-citizens who were called to arms in unprecedented frequency over centuries were conditioned to consider war normal and necessary. The elite needed ever-new wars to prove themselves and gain honor and higher office. Moreover, when the worst period of pressure was over, such wars were profitable in many ways. They yielded booty (precious objects and slaves) and land, filled the public treasury, permitted the erection of monuments, sanctuaries, and public buildings, increased communal power, and even made it possible to diffuse internal conflicts by focusing on external ones (an aspect invoked ad nauseam by later historians), to satisfy plebeian demands at the expense of the defeated rather than the aristocracy, or to intimidate allies and the outside world by constant demonstrations of Rome's superiority. War thus developed its own dynamics, to an extent rarely paralleled in history (see also Chapter 26).[32]

The conquest of Italy

All these mechanisms seem to have been in place by the time of the Samnite Wars in the last third of the fourth century. Apart from the absorption of buffer states that earlier prevented direct conflicts, and an unusual concern for security and tendency toward preventive action, they help explain why the Romans got involved in new wars almost immediately after they had fully overcome their traditional regional enemies (Aequians, Volscians) and assumed full control over their Latin allies (in 338). In a remarkable coincidence, in this very year Philip II of Macedon defeated an alliance of Greek poleis led by Athens. In both Italy and Greece, therefore, the year 338 marks the end of independent city-state systems that were absorbed by expanding territorial states.

It is the collision between two expanding states, too, that caused the outbreak of the Second (Great) Samnite War (327–304) – a war between states, moreover, that, separated by Latins and Campanians, had previously been allied (the so-called First Samnite War [343–341] probably is mostly fictitious). In 321 the Romans suffered a humiliating defeat at the Caudine Forks that compelled them, by replacing the solid phalanx with a more flexible system of smaller units (maniples), to adjust the organization, equipment, and fighting tactics of their army to the challenges of warfare in difficult terrain (see also Chapter 13). After several victories and setbacks the Romans prevailed, aided by a system of colonies that divided their enemies, and the construction of the first "highway" from Rome to Capua (the Via Appia, named after its initiator, Appius Claudius Caecus ["the Blind"], censor in 312). The Samnites and other mountain tribes allied with them, far from broken, were fully defeated only in the Third Samnite War (298–290), but their spirit of independence was a major factor even centuries later in the Italian War (90–88). Etruscans and Gauls were subdued a few years later. Meanwhile, extending their sphere of control to southern Italy, Rome got involved in conflicts between Greek cities. Tarentum enlisted the help of a Greek condottiere, king Pyrrhus of Epirus, who landed in Italy in 280, won two victories over Roman armies while suffering heavy losses himself (thus "Pyrrhic victories"), dissipated his forces in a campaign in Sicily, was defeated decisively in 275, and returned to Greece. Tarentum was taken in 272. Military campaigns continued for a few years, and even in 264, the year of the outbreak of the First Punic War, the Romans needed to set an example by destroying the rebellious Etruscan city of Volsinii.

In a domino effect that, despite serious setbacks, seemed almost unstoppable, these new wars resulted, in only 70 years, in the conquest of all of Italy south of Cisalpine Gaul. And these wars almost seamlessly led into a sequel on an even larger scale: wars against Carthage, the conquest of the western Mediterranean, then wars against the Hellenistic kingdoms in the East, until by the middle of the second century Rome had expanded its rule over almost the entire Mediterranean.

It is debated to what extent the structures Rome created to control Italy reflect not only a hegemonial alliance but the beginnings of imperial rule. At any rate, the foundations of those later successes were laid in the early Republic. Strong leadership by a cohesive aristocracy, solid ties between elite and non-elite, the resolution of domestic conflicts, a massive expansion of Rome's own territory, and a sound strategy of alliance building: these were the main principles that made it possible, despite often almost insurmountable difficulties, to increase communal power steadily and to meet every enemy in a spirit of united resolve and with superior resources.[33]

It goes without saying that this was not possible without harsh determination and cruelty. The armies of prisoners of war, who enabled the Romans eventually to replace dependent labor among their citizens with "chattel slavery," are only one obvious example. Under the new conditions of an ever growing empire that offered vast opportunities for personal enrichment and individual power, the constitution of a polis-state, anachronistic already when Polybius celebrated it in an idealizing analysis (see also Chapter 12), and the elite's value system soon proved inadequate. Early symptoms of the crisis that erupted in the second half of the second century were visible much earlier.[34] Relations with the allies, too, changed rapidly. Increasing tensions eventually resulted, in the early first century, in a monumental revolt. This brings us back to the Roman wolf.

The Wolf as a Symbol

Originally, the wolf probably was a totem animal. Even in historical times, the mountain tribes in Italy knew a ritual they called "sacred spring" (*ver sacrum*; Dion. Hal. 1.16). In times of famine or overpopulation they sent out bands of young people, led by a totem animal, to find a new place to live. According to legend, a mother sow showed Aeneas the place where his Trojans were destined to settle (*Aen.* 8.42–8). A wolf supposedly led the Hirpini, Rome's neighbors, to their territory (Strabo 5.2.50). Wolves were connected with the war god Mars; hence the legend that a she-wolf saved Mars' twin sons. Because the sphere of war and violence (*militiae*) was separated by a sacred boundary (*pomerium*) from that of peace within the city (*domi*), the army (centuriate) assembly met outside the walls on the field of Mars, and the sanctuary of Mars was situated outside the Porta Capena along the Via Appia. Livy says that he was represented there surrounded by wolves (22.1.12). In 296, in a period of grave military danger, the road from the gate to the temple was paved and Mars was honored within the city by a statue of a she-wolf with the twins (above). In the following year, in the battle of Sentinum, a wolf offered the Romans a favorable omen (Livy 10.27.8–9).

By that time, the Romans saw the wolf as a symbol of their descent from Mars and of their military prowess. As such she was represented again on a coin minted in 77. In posture and details this one differs greatly from the Capitoline wolf. She might have been a late response to the war propaganda of the allies who, during their revolt, depicted on some of their coins the Roman wolf gored by the Italian bull (*vitellus > Italia*).[35] In the early first century, a negative interpretation of the wolf was common among Rome's enemies. Mithridates of Pontus, who at the time fought several wars against the Romans in the east, supposedly pronounced, "They themselves say that their founders were brought up by the milk of a she-wolf; just so that entire race has hearts of wolves, insatiable of blood, and ever greedy and lusting after power and riches" (Justin 38.6.7–8). Sallust attributes to Mithridates similar words (*Hist.* 4, frag. 69.5 M), and Livy retrojects this argument too into an early republican context (3.66.4).[36]

Guide to Further Reading

Almost every aspect of the subject matter covered in this chapter is much debated. The methodological difficulties are clearly articulated in Cornell 1995 and Forsythe 2005, representing two starkly opposed approaches (see also, for the early Republic, Chapters 1–2 in Raaflaub 2005). Together with vol. 7.2 of the new *Cambridge Ancient History* (Walbank et al. 1989), these offer excellent surveys and discussions of all relevant issues. Eder 1990 (several chapters written in English) contains important essays on many aspects. On the archaeological evidence, Holloway 1994, Grandazzi 1997, Smith 2000, and Scott 2005 are much preferable to Carandini 1997, whose reconstructions, although offering much valuable information, are vitiated by uncritical acceptance of ancient traditions.

The main sources on Rome's early history (Livy, Dionysius of Halicarnassus, Plutarch) are available in modern translations and bilingual editions (e.g., in the Penguin and Loeb Classical Library series). Even the fragments of the early Roman historians are now easily accessible (n. 6). Kraus and Woodman 1997: 51–81 offer a brief introduction to Livy, the first volume of Oakley's monumental commentary on Livy's second pentad (1997–2004) a detailed one, while Forsythe 1999 analyzes the historian's narrative of early Rome, and Miles 1995, Fox 1996 (also Haehling 1989) emphasize his critical interaction with his own troubled time. Gabba 1991 is excellent on Dionysius of Halicarnassus, but scholarship on other authors dealing with early Rome remains inadequate. On Rome's conquest of Italy, see the bibliography cited in n. 30; on domestic conflicts in the early Republic Raaflaub 1986 (new ed. 2005). Rome's military development in this period still awaits a detailed modern analysis in English; for the fourth century, see Harris, in Eder 1990: 494–510. On economic aspects, see Drummond 1989: 118—43, Cornell 1989: 323–34, and Ampolo 1990. On the *Twelve Tables*, Crawford 1996b (n. 22) is masterful and indispensable.

Notes

1 Kleiner 1992: 23–4 with fig.1. Wiseman 1995; Evans 1992: 59–108; Bremmer 1987. A shorter version of this chapter will be published in German (Raaflaub forthcoming a). I thank both publishers for generously granted permissions, and E. Bispham for sharing with me an early version of his chapter.

2 Crawford 1974: no. 20/1 and p. 714; Kent 1978: pl. 5, no. 8R. A coin of 137 (Crawford, no. 235/1 with pp. 267–8; Kent, pl. 11, no. 31R) more likely depicts the scene described by Livy 1.34.6. Neither corresponds to the Capitoline wolf or another featured on a coin of Publius Satrienus of 77 (n.34 below). Lupercal: Wiseman 1995: 77–88. Comitium: see bibliography in Morstein-Marx 2004: 94 n.115.

3 Frag. 1 in Beck and Walter 2001–4: 1.62–4 (my trans).

4 Trojan War: Burkert 1995. Genealogies (e.g., Hdt. 2.143) and lists: Fornara 1983: 4–12; Meister 1998a. Hellanicus: Meister 1998b.

5 On these and related issues: Wiseman 1995. On Aeneas: *Enea nel Lazio* 1981; Evans 1992: 35–57.

6 Collected by Peter 1914 (P); new editions with trans. and commentary: Beck and Walter 2001–4 (German); Chassignet 1996–9 (French); T. Cornell et al. (English, in preparation; see Cornell in Raaflaub 2005: 63-4).

7 On the scarceness of evidence for the early period, see, e.g., Livy 6.1; Plut. *Numa* 1.2; Cic. *Acad.* 1.3.9 with Edwards 1996: 4–6 (on the increase of knowledge provided by Varro's *Human and Divine Antiquities*; see also chapter 2).

8 Founders: Reinhold 1984; Richard 1994. See Sempronius Asellio, frag. 2 P (Beck and Walter 2001–4: 2.87–90; Gell. *NA* 5.18.9) on the late emergence of emphasis on *exempla*; Sall. *Iug.* 4.5–6 on the powerful influence of the memory of great men's accomplishments.

9 Poetry and drama: Wiseman 1994c: 1–22, 1995: 129–50, 1998. Family traditions: Cic. *Brut.* 62 (cf. Livy 40.3–5). Antiquarians: Rawson 1985: 233–49. Closeness of rhetoric and history: Cic. *Brut.* 42 (cf. *Leg.* 1.2.5). Dionysius: Gabba 1991. Annalists: n.15 below.

10 Cornell 1995: 120 with n.4.

11 Ogilvie 1965: 546–8.

12 Tac. *Hist.* 3.72; Dion. Hal. 5.31–5.; Pliny *HN* 34.39.139; Cornell 1995: 216–18.

13 Sabines: Ogilvie 1965: 64–70; Cornell 1995: 75–7. Colonies: Murray 1993: 115–16. Tyranny: Cornell 1995: 145–50; Forsythe 2005: 147–8.

14 Alföldi 1965: 47–100; Momigliano 1989: 93–103; Cornell 1995: 130–41; Forsythe 2005: 93–108. Mastarna: *CIL* 13.1668; cf. Festus p. 486.12 L; Satricum: Stibbe et al. 1980.

15 Macer: Walt 1997; Beck and Walter 2001–4: 2.314-45; Piso: Forsythe 1994; Beck and Walter 2001–4: 1. 282–329. Livy's sources and predecessors: Wiseman 1979; Cornell 1995: 1–18; Oakley 1997–2004: 1.13–108; Eigler et al. 2003; Forsythe 2005: 60-4. Livy: n.18.

16 Pliny *HN* 18.15; Minucius' column: Crawford 1974: no. 242/1; cf. 243/1 and pp. 273–5; Kent 1978: pl. 12 no. 33R.

17 Cincius frag. 6 P; Beck and Walter 2001–4: 1.137–8 and frag. 8. Piso frag. 24 P; Beck and Walter, ibid. 282–5 and frag. 26; Forsythe 1994: 301–10; Maelius: Ogilvie 1965: 550–7; Cornell 1986b: 58–61. Gracchan crisis: Chapter 8 in this volume.

18 Livy: Walsh 1961; Luce 1977; Kraus and Woodman 1997: 51–81; Forsythe 1999. Livy and his time: Miles 1995; Fox 1996.

19 Raaflaub 1986: 1–2, 201–8 (=2005: 1–2, 187–91). Oral tradition: Vansina 1985; Ungern-Sternberg 1988; Raaflaub 1988, forthcoming b.

20 Writing: Harris 1989: 149–59. Documents: Ampolo 1983; Cornell 1991b, 1995: 12–16; Forsythe 2005: 69–74. Tablets and *annales maximi*: Cato frag. 77 P = 4.3 in Beck and Walter 2001–4: 1.196–7 with 32–7; Cic. *De or.* 2.52; Serv. auct. at Virg. *Aen.* 1.373; Cornell 1995: 13–15; Frier 1999. *Fasti*: Wiseman 1995: 103–7; Rüpke 1995a; Forsythe 2005: 155–66.

21 Methodology: Cornell 1986b: 52–76 vs. Raaflaub 1986: 1–51 (=Raaflaub 2005: 47–74, 1–46); Cornell 1995 vs. Forsythe 2005; see also Saller 1991. Archaeology: Holloway 1994; Smith 2000; Scott 2005. Wiseman 2004 offers an unconventional reconstruction of early Rome.

22 Calendar: *ROL*: 4.450–65; Scullard 1981; Rüpke 1995b. *Twelve Tables*: *ROL*: 3.424–515; Watson 1975; Cornell 1995: 272–92, and esp. Crawford 1996b: 2.555–721; see also Chapter 11 in this volume.

23 Comparison of Rome with the Greek *polis*: Raaflaub 1986: 29–35; 1990; 2005: 15-17. For this entire section, see detailed discussions in relevant chapters of Heurgon 1973; Poucet 1985; Momigliano and Schiavone 1988–; Walbank et al. 1989; Pallottino 1991; Cornell 1995; Flower 2004b; Forsythe 2005.

24 Momigliano 1963: 99–101.

25 Cornell 1995: 151–72; see also Torelli 1989; Momigliano 1989; Cristofani 1988; Ampolo 1988b (including social mobility; e.g., Livy 1.34; 2.16).

26 Servius' reforms: Thomsen 1980; Ampolo 1988a; Cornell 1995: 173–97. Demography: Raaflaub 1986: 41–5 (=2005: 21–2) with bibliography. "Hoplites": Lazenby and White-head 1996; in Greece: Hanson 1991 (229 on cost of panoply), 2000; Raaflaub and Rosenstein 1999: 132–41; military development in Rome: Saulnier 1980; see also Chapter 13 in this volume.

27 Rome's power: Cornell 1989: 243–57. Rome under the Tarquins: Cristofani 1990; private houses: Cristofani 1990: 97–9; see also Coarelli 1988b: 318–39.

28 Drummond 1989: 172–212; Cornell 1995: 226–41; Stewart 1998; Lintott 1999a; see also Chapter 12 in this volume.

29 Raaflaub 1993: 137–41. Latins: Cornell 1989: 264–75. Wars: Cornell 1989: 281–308. Food shortages: Cornell 1995: 267–8. Crisis: Cornell 1995: 225–6, 265–71; Ampolo 1990. See also Scott 2005.

30 Conquest of Italy (in addition to bibliography listed in n.23): Humbert 1978; Harris 1979, 1984c; Cornell 1989: 351–419; Oakley 1993; Rich 1993; Raaflaub 1996; Lomas 2004. Date(s) of the Gallic disaster: Cornell 1995: 314.

31 Raaflaub 1986: 198–243; 1993; 2005: 185–222. All this is much debated; see (with often different views) other chapters in Raaflaub 1986 (=2005); Drummond 1989: 212–42; Cornell 1989: 323–50; Linderski 1990; Mitchell 1990; Ungern-Sternberg 1990, and relevant sections in Cornell 1995; Forsythe 2005. Nobility: Hölkeskamp 1987. Colonization: Salmon 1969.

32 Raaflaub 1996. On public art and architecture: Hölscher 1978; Ziolkowski 1992.

33 Bibliography in n. 30.

34 Polyb. 6.11–18 with Cornell 1991a. Symptoms: Ungern-Sternberg 1986 (=Raaflaub 2005: 312–32). Crisis: see Chapters 8 and 9 in this volume. Slaves: Cornell 1989: 389.

35 Wolf and Mars: Hünemörder 2002: 569 with examples. Coin of 77: Crawford 1974: no. 388 with comm. on p. 404. Bull: Burnett 1998 with pl. 25 nos. 6–7; Kent 1978: pl. 14 no. 46R.

36 See also Vell. Pat. 2.27.2; Fuchs 1938: 15–19.

CHAPTER 7

The Mediterranean Empire
(264–134)

Daniel J. Gargola

By the end of the 270s, Rome had become the dominant power in peninsular Italy and over the next 130 years, its power would penetrate almost every region of the Mediterranean world. Narratives of Rome's emergence as the most powerful state in the Mediterranean world can be written from a number of perspectives. One might consist of an account of the campaigns of its commanders, fleets, and armies, of the Roman state's steadily expanding geographical horizons, and of its dealings, either as a friend, ally, benefactor, enemy, or competitor, with a steadily increasing number of states and polities. To this, one might append an account of the ways that this expanding sphere of interactions influenced the Roman elite's ambitions for themselves and for their state. Other communities, however, possessed their own histories, institutions, and cultures. Thus, there were many histories in the Mediterranean world of the third and second centuries BC, many of which would come to involve Rome in some manner.

The First Punic War (264–241)

The First Punic War broke out on the island of Sicily where the Carthaginians had long had imperial ambitions. After the death in 289 of the Syracusan ruler Agathocles, who had built a powerful state, some of his mercenaries, known as Mamertines, had seized control of Messana, dominating the straits between Italy and Sicily. For years, the Mamertines successfully maintained their position and even extended it through raids that ranged widely over the island. When pressed by Syracusan armies – the victory gave Hiero, the Syracusan general, the opportunity to proclaim himself king – the Mamertines quickly found themselves in need of friends. Here, matters become less certain. Factions among the Mamertines appealed to Carthage and to Rome for aid, but the chronology is uncertain: the appeal to Carthage certainly took place during Hiero's siege of the city, but the plea for Roman assistance may have come somewhat later. In any case, the Carthaginians moved first, installing a garrison in the city and effectively ending Hiero's siege. The Roman response was slower: According to Polybius (1.11.1–3), the Senate feared that Carthaginian control over the island would represent a threat to their leadership in Italy but it did not act decisively. Instead, the consuls of 264, potential leaders in any expedition, persuaded a popular assembly to vote to dispatch an army, encouraging the citizenry with promises of plunder. Senate and magistrates, it should be noted, may have viewed Syracuse as the intended enemy rather than Carthage.[1]

Here, Roman intervention began with a request for assistance, and this same process will frequently reappear in the following decades. Greek and Roman authors often presented the Senate and magistrates as passive, waging war in response to the pleas of others for protection against aggressive neighbors or in defense of Rome and its interests against the assaults of competitors. This form of self-representation presents certain persistent problems in historical interpretation, for the reality behind responses to appeals can be difficult to discern. After all, states, even aggressive ones, can sometimes wage war for just these reasons. But responding favorably to pleas for assistance can also be an aggressive act: states can actively seek new communities to protect, especially in spheres where their perceived competitors are active, and they can decide to give assistance when it is convenient or useful. But still, eager benefactors do require willing beneficiaries (see also Chapter 26).

On Sicily, what began as a conflict between Syracusans and Mamertines spread to engulf the entire island. Some Mamertines, unwilling to accept Carthaginian leadership over their city, expelled their garrison, possibly with Roman assistance. At about the same time, Ap. Claudius Caudex (cos. 264) brought his army across the straits separating Sicily from Italy, despite the presence of a Carthaginian fleet. Hiero and the Carthaginian commander then decided to cooperate. In 263, both consuls led their armies into Sicily, and a number of Sicilian cities sought Rome's friendship. Hiero, the consuls' immediate target, made peace with Rome, formed an alliance, and paid a large indemnity. With the removal of the weakest of the three contending states, the war became a contest between the Romans and the Carthaginians. The consuls of 262 attacked Agrigentum, the Carthaginians' base of operations, and, after a lengthy siege, their armies sacked the city. Polybius (1.20.1–2) maintained that the fall of Agrigentum encouraged the Senate to attempt to drive the Carthaginians entirely from the island. During the war, the Carthaginians were also engaged in wars of expansion in Africa.[2]

The bulk of the war consisted of small-scale land operations on Sicily and naval operations around the island. In 256, however, both consuls attempted to bring the war to a swift conclusion by attacking Carthage itself, perhaps in imitation of a similar assault by Agathocles. After some initial successes, one of the consuls, M. Atilius Regulus, who had remained in Africa, was defeated severely and his army largely destroyed. Except for raids on Italy or Africa, the remainder of the war was fought on Sicily. There, Carthaginian forces steadily lost ground. In 254, two consuls captured

Panormus, the modern Palermo, the largest city on the island that still followed Carthage. Combat in the later stages of the war concentrated around Lilybaeum, the chief Carthaginian fortress in western Sicily, and Drepana, the base for the Punic fleet. Early in 241, C. Lutatius Catulus (cos. 242) defeated a Punic fleet off the Aegates Islands, and the Carthaginian position in Sicily became untenable. In the ensuing negotiations, the Carthaginians agreed to evacuate Sicily, return all prisoners, pay a large indemnity, and refrain from sending warships into Italian waters; Carthage and Rome both agreed not to attack the other's allies.

The treaty did not end hostilities. At the close of the war, the Carthaginians brought their army back to Africa. There, this force – like all Punic armies, an uneasy mixture of Greek, Iberian, Gallic, and Ligurian mercenaries and soldiers provided by allies and dependant Libyan communities – revolted as a result of a pay dispute. After failed negotiations, the revolt spread to dependent communities in Africa. Polybius (1.65.6) described the so-called Mercenary War as "inexpiable" because of its savagery. The Carthaginians won the war, but the Romans took advantage of Carthaginian weakness to impose a further indemnity and to require that Carthaginian forces evacuate Sardinia, where the revolt had spread.

The First Punic War and its aftermath marked a turning point in Roman practice, although the Roman elite may not have realized this at first or intended it. In the long wars that gave Rome leadership over Italy, the Senate had not felt the need to send governors or maintain garrisons after the conclusion of successful wars. For seven years after Rome had forced Carthage to abandon the islands, consuls campaigned in Sardinia and Corsica, defending Rome's position and the communities that had sought its friendship against the inhabitants of the islands' interiors. With the resurgence of Carthaginian power in the 220 s (see below), the Senate may have also feared that its position in Sicily was threatened. Beginning with the elections for 227, Roman assemblies chose two additional praetors (for a total of four), providing more commanders to maintain and assert Roman interests, and from this time, the Senate regularly dispatched two commanders, usually praetors, to guard Rome's position on Sicily and Sardinia. This change, it should be noted, marked the beginning of regular praetorian assignments away from Rome.

Italy and Illyria, 241–219

After the First Punic War and the campaigns of the 230s on Sardinia, the Roman Senate and assemblies also sent magistrates and military forces to northern Italy and across the Adriatic Sea. The wars with Gauls were more persistent and the initiative usually rested with the Senate. By the end of the fourth century, northern Italy contained a complex ethnic mosaic of Gallic tribes, some surviving Etruscan and Umbrian communities, Picentes, and Veneti. Roman authors often divided the Gauls into a few major groupings, such as the Boii, the Insubres, and the Senones, but these larger units themselves were often divided into a number of even smaller units under their own leaders. The Gauls had a long history of enmity with Rome. Early in the fourth century, a large force of Gauls succeeded in sacking Rome, while later Gauls fought with Etruscans, Umbrians, and Samnites against Rome either as allies or as mercenaries. At least in part, Roman operations in Cisalpine and Cispadane Gaul may have grown out of the Roman assertion of leadership over Etruria and Umbria and a desire to deny restive allies there any support.

During the First Punic War, Gauls and Romans fought no major campaigns, possibly a sign of how heavily Roman commanders and forces were committed to the wars in Sicily. Tensions rose again after the end of the war. In 238, the Boii unsuccessfully attacked Ariminum, a colony that Roman officials had established over a generation earlier after Roman armies had virtually destroyed the Senones. In 232, Gaius Flaminius, a tribune of the plebs, proposed and carried an agrarian law instructing that grants of land be made to individual Roman citizens on other land taken from the Senones, an action that Polybius (2.21.7–9) held convinced the Boii and other Gauls that the Romans desired their extermination. In later periods, colleges of special magistrates, chosen for the task according to provisions in the authorizing law itself, implemented land laws such as this.[3] L. Caecilius Metellus (cos. 251, 247), one of the leading senators of the time, served on such a commission, possibly the one established to implement Flaminius' law.

Large-scale war broke out less than a decade after the law's passage. The Roman elite must have viewed hostilities as imminent: in 226, officials buried alive in the Forum Boarium two Gauls and two Greeks to avert a prophecy that Rome would fall again to Gauls. In the following year, a large Gallic force crossed the Apennines into Etruria and defeated a Roman force near Faesulae. Later in the year, however, two consular armies defeated the Gauls at Telamon near Cosa in Etruria. For the next five years, both consuls led their armies into the Po valley, fighting against the Boii, the Insubres, and the Istrii. In 219, a Roman colonial commission founded two large colonies on confiscated land at Placentia and Cremona, bringing the Roman practice of colonization into the Po valley.

Before and after these Gallic wars, Roman commanders also fought two brief Illyrian wars. During the First Punic War, Agron had established a powerful kingdom in Illyria, which he began to expand in alliance with Demetrius II, king of Macedon. His widow and successor Teuta succeeded in overrunning Epirus by land, while pressing the cities of the Dalmatian coast by sea. Pleas for Roman assistance provided the occasion for the Senate to dispatch an embassy demanding redress (Polyb. 2.12.1–4; App. *Ill.* 1.7; see also Chapter 2). According to Polybius, Teuta promised not to intervene in Italy, but the *legati*, and presumably the Senate too, expected complete submission to their demands.[4] After the embassy's failure, the Senate assigned both consuls of 229 Illyria as their province. One broke the Illyrian siege of Corcyra; the other crossed to Apollonia in Epirus. Joining forces, both commanders then moved north, winning over cities on their way, until they forced Teuta to capitulate early in 228. To end the war, Teuta agreed to pay an indemnity and to set limits beyond which Illyrian ships would not sail; Rome formed ties with coastal cities such as Corcyra, Apollonia, and Epidamnus. War broke out again in 220, marking a temporary end to consular campaigns against the Gauls. With the support of Antigonus Doson, who was restoring the power of the Macedonian monarchy,

Demetrius of Pharos replaced Teuta as ruler and began to ignore the limits set by the treaty with Rome. Both consuls of 219 campaigned against him, driving him from his kingdom, but, because of the impending war with Carthage, they brought the war to a swift conclusion. These wars, it should be noted, not only provided Rome with new dependants and a new sphere in which to exercise influence, but also introduced Roman power into an area in which the Macedonian monarchy, one of the strongest states in the Hellenistic east, had long sought dominance.

The Second Punic War (218–201)

Rome's second war with Carthage marked a further escalation in the scale and scope of its campaigns. After the end of the Mercenary War, Carthage began to strengthen its position in Spain, a potential recruiting ground for its armies and a source of timber and metal for ships and other equipment of war, and dispatched Hamilcar Barca, its most successful general in Sicily, as its chief commander. Over the next decade, Hamilcar built an empire that included the valley of the Baetis River, the richest region in the peninsula, and the south coast from Gades to the east. His successors – first, his son-in-law Hasdrubal and then his son Hannibal – maintained this position of power and even campaigned on the central plateau. The formation of this Spanish empire, and the Roman elite's reactions to it, formed the background to the war.

The events that led to the war's outbreak are reasonably clear, although the chronology and the motivations behind them have long been controversial. Polybius, our chief source, placed the war's roots in Hamilcar's hatred of Rome, which he allegedly shared with his son Hannibal, the enmity that members of the Carthaginian elite felt toward the city as a result of the Sardinian episode, and the great success of Carthaginian forces in Spain which increased Carthaginian power.[5] The Roman elite, on the other hand, had come to regard the revival of Carthaginian power with suspicion. In 226 or 225, the Senate dispatched ambassadors to Spain, where they concluded an agreement with Hasdrubal in which the Carthaginian commander promised that his forces would not cross the Ebro River. Massilia, a Greek city in southern Gaul that had ties of friendship with Rome, may have had a hand in the matter: small Greek settlements, colonies of Massilia and under its protection, dotted the Iberian coast north of the Ebro.[6] At some uncertain date, the Senate also established some form of relationship with Saguntum, a town well to the south of the Ebro River. The Saguntines, now under Roman protection, then attacked a neighboring community that either had Carthaginian protection or soon would have it. The Senate sent ambassadors warning Hannibal against attacking Saguntum, but he ignored their demands and attacked the city, which his soldiers sacked. The Senate then dispatched envoys to Carthage demanding that the Carthaginians surrender their commander or face war. This ultimatum, given without the possibility of discussion, shows that the Senate had resolved on war.

The assignments that the Senate gave to the consuls of 218 reveal senators' hopes for the war: Ti. Sempronius Longus received Sicily and Africa with the expectation that, like Regulus, he would attack Carthage; P. Cornelius Scipio obtained Spain. Hannibal's own plans, however, disrupted Roman intentions to carry the war to the centers of Carthaginian power. Leaving his brother Hasdrubal in charge in Spain, Hannibal led the bulk of his army in a long march across the Pyrenees and Alps and into Italy. Scipio sent his army on to Spain under the command of his brother Cn. Scipio and returned to take command himself in northern Italy. Hannibal entered northern Italy late in 218, where he encountered a region in turmoil, disrupted by wars between Romans and Gauls. Earlier in the year, the Boii and Insubres had attacked the colony of Placentia, forced its temporary abandonment, and ambushed a Roman force that was marching to the colonists' assistance. Scipio took command in the north, but his army suffered a defeat near the Ticinus River. Retreating from the battlefield, Scipio took up position at the Trebia River near Placentia, where Longus joined him. Late in December, Hannibal defeated their combined armies.

The Romans and the Carthaginians fought the remainder of the war in a number of distinct theaters with their own rosters of allies and enemies. In Italy, Hannibal moved south in the spring of 217. In Etruria, he ambushed the army of C. Flaminius (cos. 217) on the shores of Lake Trasimene, killing the consul and virtually destroying his force. In 216, Hannibal won another major victory, defeating both consuls near Cannae in Apulia. After Cannae, Capua and portions of the Samnites, Lucanians, and Brutii came over to Hannibal, a sign that their absorption into Rome's network of alliances and of shared citizenship had not eliminated their local identities or their ambitions. And in 212 Hannibal captured Tarentum, aided by a faction in the city, although a Roman garrison continued to hold a fortress controlling the harbor. For the remainder of the war, the Senate, fearing further defections, sometimes kept suspect towns under surveillance. Slowly but steadily, Roman forces prevailed. Capua fell in 211 and Tarentum two years later. The decisive battle took place in 207. Forced to abandon Spain (see below), Hannibal's brother, Hasdrubal, led his army into Italy to join his brother, but he was intercepted by two consular armies and defeated at the Metaurus River. Two years later, Mago, another of Hannibal's brothers, landed in Liguria in an apparent effort to keep the war between Romans and Gauls alive in the north; he too was defeated and killed in 203. Soon after, Hannibal was recalled to defend Carthage, leaving the bulk of his army behind.

In the aftermath of Cannae, the war also spread to Sicily. After the death of Hiero in 216 or 215, Syracuse entered a period of political turmoil, and some factions began to negotiate with the Carthaginians. Ap. Claudius Pulcher (pr. 215), who had crossed to Sicily after Cannae, blocked Carthaginian landings on the island and sought unsuccessfully a settlement with Syracuse. M. Claudius Marcellus (cos. 214) began to besiege the city in 213, while a large Carthaginian force landed in Sicily and soon captured the major city of Agrigentum, which may have come over to the Punic side voluntarily. Other Sicilian cities soon followed. In 212, a new Carthaginian commander failed in an attempt to land reinforcements on the island. Syracuse fell in 211 and Agrigentum in 210. With these victories, fighting on the island ended, but the Roman position on the island had proven vulnerable.

The First Macedonian War (214–205) was another consequence of Hannibal's presence in Italy. Philip V, the young king of Macedon, attempted to reassert

Macedonian power in Illyria and Epirus, where Rome had formed friendships and dependencies after the two Illyrian wars, perhaps intending to profit from the Senate's distraction. After Cannae, Philip dispatched an envoy to Hannibal in Italy, where he concluded an alliance in which the king and the general agreed to regard Rome as their common enemy and arranged that the Romans, upon their expected defeat, be forced to abandon their position in Illyria and Epirus, the likely source of Philip's displeasure (Polyb. 7.9). The Senate, however, learned of the treaty when Philip's envoy was captured during his return journey, and in 215, they dispatched a praetor to Brundisium to guard against any incursions into Italy. The Macedonian monarchy had its own allies and enemies in the Greek world, so that Roman commanders made war along with a number of anti-Macedonian states – among them, the Aetolian League and Attalus, king of Pergamum – which provided the bulk of the forces. When the Aetolians withdrew from the war in 206, negotiations began. The ensuing Peace of Phoinike largely preserved the status quo.

Spain proved to be the decisive theater. For several years after the outbreak of war, P. Scipio (cos. 218), who had rejoined his army, and his brother Gnaeus campaigned in the peninsula, primarily along the coastal plain south of the Ebro River. Then, in 212 or 211, they led their armies into the Baetis valley, one of the centers of Carthaginian power, but, in the face of three Punic armies, they were abandoned by many of their local allies, defeated, and both were killed. The battle virtually destroyed the Roman position in Spain. The next commander, P. Cornelius Scipio, son of the consul of 218, began the recovery. Scipio launched a successful attack in 209 against the city of New Carthage, the main Carthaginian base in the peninsula. In the next year, Scipio and his army, now dominant on the eastern coast of Spain, pushed into the Baetis valley and defeated Hannibal's brother Hasdrubal at Baecula. Soon after, Hasdrubal withdrew to the north, beginning his long march into Italy. In 206, Scipio won another victory at Ilipa, virtually ending Carthaginian power in Spain.

After his victories, Scipio, who had been elected consul for 205, received Sicily as his command in order to prepare for an invasion of Africa. As part of his preparation, he confirmed an alliance with Masinissa, son of a ruler of the Massyles of eastern Numidia, whom the Carthaginians had offended by preferring Syphax, ruler of the rival Masaesyles. Early in 204, Scipio landed at Utica, where Masinissa joined him with the cavalry so essential to warfare in the region, and the two laid siege to the city. In the following year, Scipio and Masinissa won two major victories over the Carthaginians and their allies. In this crisis, the Carthaginians recalled Hannibal from Italy. At Zama in 202, Scipio defeated Hannibal, the bulk of whose soldiers were new recruits. In the peace, Carthage retained its civic existence and a restricted territory in Africa and paid a large indemnity, but it was no longer a major power. Masinissa, on the other hand, became the ruler of a much-enlarged kingdom and the chief prop of Rome's position in the area. Scipio returned to Rome, where he triumphed, assuming the triumphal name of Africanus.

In addition to this narrative of battles and campaigns, other histories can also be written that emphasize the strains that the war placed on Roman institutions. Throughout the war, Senate and magistrates expended great efforts to secure the goodwill of the gods, adjusting older practices and introducing new ones.[7] Livy's Books 21–30, our chief source for the matter, reveal a heightened interest in prodigies and the ritual means for their expiation, public vows on a larger scale, and new festivals and games. Some innovations and ritual performances can be connected with specific events in the war. After the defeat at Lake Trasimene in 217, officials introduced to Rome the worship of the goddess Venus from Eryx on Sicily, and after Cannae, officials again buried alive two Greeks and two Gauls in the Forum Boarium, a rite seemingly performed only when the existence of the state was thought to be endangered. And toward the end of the war, officials vowed to introduce the cult of the *Magna Mater* from Asia Minor.

The war also placed significant pressures on Roman civic institutions. The need for effective commanders placed burdens on traditional patterns of office holding. Iteration or reelection to the consulship became far more frequent, while former consuls sometimes held office as praetor. The extension of terms of command through promagistracies became more common, and individuals sometimes were elected directly to serve as proconsuls rather than as regular magistrates. Some successful commanders, moreover, held continuous commands for relatively long periods – the Scipios in Spain are the clearest example – another departure from past practice. During the war, moreover, Senate and commanders continually pressed allies and citizenry for recruits, taking some whose social status earlier would have excluded them: freedmen, the poor, and slaves.

And then, maintaining large armies and fleets at widely dispersed locations required extraordinary means for their support.[8] Before the war, citizens sometimes were required to make extraordinary contributions, *tributum*, at a rate determined by their census class, in order to finance major wars. In the opening years of the war, payments of *tributum* were imposed, at least once at a double rate, but the burdens of the war quickly overwhelmed the traditional arrangements for public finance. Straitened circumstances led to innovations. Because of the difficulties in supplying Roman forces in Spain, a praetor in 215 sought public contractors, *publicani*, to bid for supply contracts with payment to be made later, but the *publicani* would only bid if they were given exemption from military service and if the state insured all shipments.[9] In 214, the Senate imposed an apparently unprecedented liturgy on wealthier citizens, requiring them to support sailors in the fleet. From around 211, Roman officials began to mint new silver coins, *denarii*, in large numbers, making the currency more suitable for large-scale finance (see also Chapter 3).

Rome and the Mediterranean World, 201–134

The Second Punic War drastically changed Rome's position in the broader Mediterranean world. In the war's many theaters, the Senate and commanders had made Rome part, if sometimes only tenuously and fortuitously, of different regional networks of friendship and enmity. In the first two-thirds of the second century, Roman magistrates and Senate would exercise power and influence over increasingly diverse subjects, allies, and friends. Indeed, to the extent that events can be encompassed in a narrative written from a single perspective or focus, this narrative necessarily must be centered on Rome, its Senate, magistrates, and ruling elite, for the reality of Roman power gave some unity to events in these disparate regions.

The spatial aspects of Roman power should be made clear at the start. In Rome itself, assemblies passed laws and elected magistrates; the Senate issued its edicts, assigned tasks for magistrates, and received foreign embassies seeking Rome's friendship or protection or attempting to avoid its wrath. The city and its institutions, then, were the chief locus of Roman power. Away from the city, the exercise of Roman power and influence rested on commanders – consuls, praetors, or promagistrates – their armies and their entourages, and on occasional delegations of senatorial ambassadors, or *legati*. On the scene, commanders, in practice, had considerable freedom of action, providing yet another locus of decision making.[10]

Consuls and praetors, however, exercised their *imperium*, the power to command that formed the essential basis of their military and judicial functions, only in tasks or *provinciae* to which they had been specifically assigned. In one of the clearest signs of its leading position in the state, each year the Senate defined the *provinciae* that the incoming consuls and praetors would divide by lot among themselves, and it determined which assignments held by the previous year's magistrates would be allowed to continue as promagistracies. Away from Rome, consular and praetorian *provinciae* were military in nature, rather than administrative, so that when the Senate defined such a *provincia*, it was, in effect, announcing its intention to wage war there or to assert or defend claims by armed force.[11] Books 31–45 of Livy's history provide a very nearly complete list of each year's consuls, praetors, promagistrates, legates, and special magisterial commissions, so that the range of official activity can be traced, if only broadly, with some confidence from the end of the Carthaginian War through 167. After 167, however, because of the loss of Livy's history, the record becomes more lacunose.

The considerations that led the Senate to define *provinciae* remain highly controversial – they form one of the central issues in the study of Roman imperial expansion – and these concerns almost certainly varied from time to time and from place to place. The Roman elite of the second century did not view their city's power in terms of territories to be governed or exploited: plundering formed an important element in Roman conceptions of successful warfare, but in Sicily, Spain, and the Greek East, Roman commanders only began the systematic exploitation of local resources slowly and in stages.[12] Instead, Rome's ruling elite saw their city's supremacy as resting on the power of its magistrates to issue orders that must be obeyed, which in turn rested on the military superiority that Roman commanders had established in the field of their operations.[13] In such a political order, the dominant power preserved its position at least in part by responding favorably to the requests of others, especially for protection, and it expanded its influence by granting additional benefactions and by seeking willing beneficiaries. Indeed, embassies from large numbers of states and polities regularly came to Rome seeking audiences with the Senate about just these matters. *Provinciae*, therefore, provide the clearest evidence for the Senate's assessment of opportunities, threats, and risks.

For long, the bulk of consular and praetorian *provinciae* were in Italy, Spain, Sicily, and Sardinia. During the war with Hannibal and for two decades after its end, the Senate occasionally defined *provinciae* in Italy to search out and punish disloyalty or threats against good order. In 186, Roman officials began to investigate and suppress the cult of the god Bacchus, which often involved groups without official sanction practicing rites that included frenzied dancing, the use of cymbals and drums, drinking, and sexual license.[14] The Senate then issued a decree ordering a search for the cult's priests and for the performers of immoral acts, forbidding initiates to gather for their rites, requiring that shrines be dismantled, prohibiting men from serving as priests, and forbidding men and women from mixing on ritual occasions (Livy 39.8–19; *ILS* 18 = *ROL* 4.255–9; see also Chapters 2, 10, 22, and 28). Sp. Postumius Albinus (cos. 186) spent his entire year as consul implementing the decree, and Livy believed that his investigations resulted in many executions. Over the next three years, the Senate twice assigned Apulia to praetors and ordered them to look into the cult. Between 184 and 179, moreover, the Senate three times assigned to praetors the task of investigating the many poisonings said to be taking place, a category of activity that including doing harm through drugs and through the casting of spells.

Large-scale settlement projects throughout the first third of the century were another way of punishing the disloyal and ensuring control, a practice that goes back to the earliest days of Roman expansion in Italy.[15] Immediately after the Hannibalic War, a college of ten special magistrates, *decemviri*, settled veterans of campaigns in Spain, Sicily, and North Africa on some of the land confiscated from rebellious allies. Over the next three decades, the Senate and assemblies ordered the creation of 11 colleges of colonial commissioners, or *triumviri*, in which former consuls and praetors were heavily represented, to reinforce old colonies worn down by the war or to found new ones on territories that had been seized from erstwhile allies.[16] In 173, the Senate assigned to one of the consuls the task of recovering public land in Campania, confiscated from Capua after its defeat, which private individuals had taken as their own, a task that a praetor would complete in 165. Censors would lease the land.

Wars against Gauls, Ligurians, and other inhabitants of the Po valley and adjacent portions of the Alps and Apennines continued without a break. Indeed, the Senate defined more consular *provinciae* here than in any other portion of Rome's sphere of operations. In northern Italy, the initiative clearly lay with the Senate, and eliminating or drastically reducing the Gallic population may well have been among its goals. Between 190 and 167, *triumviri* established eight new colonies to accompany campaigns in northern Italy, and, in 173, *decemviri* distributed small plots of land, primarily along the *via Aemilia* in more scattered settlements. These colonization projects may have settled as many as 50,000 colonists and their families. In 180, moreover, Roman officials deported perhaps as many as 50,000 Ligures from their homes and settled them on confiscated land in the south.

In Spain, just as in Italy, the Senate continued to make magisterial assignments without any apparent break after the Hannibalic War. Roman armies had entered Spain as part of the war against Carthage. By the end of the war, Roman commanders had formed relationships of one kind or another with a number of polities from the Massiliot colonies of the northeastern coast to the Phoenician city of Gades. In the last stages of the war, moreover, Scipio Africanus had settled veterans at Italica, near the modern Seville. Thus, by the end of the war, Rome had acquired a position of leadership in parts of the peninsula, and it faced at least some of the demands that went with it. Maintaining this position, however, proved not to be an easy matter. Spain possessed no large states and few stable polities, and, away from the southern and eastern coasts and the Baetis valley, the inhabitants lived in scattered settlements often without firm structures of authority. In these circumstances, finding ways to defend friends and dependants and preserve Roman authority without the presence of a commander and his soldiers proved impossible. For a few years, commanders chosen by plebiscite specifically to be promagistrates, a carryover from the war, maintained Rome's position. The elections for 198 marked a turning point: Roman assemblies selected six praetors, rather than four, providing two additional commanders, and the Senate sent two praetors to Spain, one in a *provincia* usually identified as Nearer Spain (*Hispania Citerior*) that was centered on the lower Ebro valley and the other, Farther Spain (*Hispania Ulterior*), in the Baetis valley. Whatever the Senate's original expectations, these arrangements would prove long lasting.

In Spain, wars persisted for generations. Commanders usually conducted small-scale campaigns with armies formed from a mixture of soldiers brought from Italy and local levies, and they seemingly had great freedom of action. Behind these conflicts, historians have detected a variety of causes and motives. Some were Roman in origin: commanders searching for plunder and victories; their desire to protect communities who sought Roman protection; their inability to make more stable arrangements. Others derived more specifically from the Iberian communities themselves: the instability of their political arrangements (partly, no doubt, due to the actions of the Roman magistrates themselves) and frequent warfare among communities. As commanders expanded Rome's network of dependent polities and waged war in ever more distant parts of the peninsula, some portions of the peninsula began to experience more settled conditions. While commanding in Nearer Spain, Ti. Sempronius Gracchus (pr. 180) established displaced persons in larger settlements where they were easier to control and attempted to distribute in a more equitable manner the burdens of supporting Roman armies, which had earlier fallen primarily on those communities that were closest to operations. Although later commanders sometimes ignored his fiscal arrangements, sporadic efforts to achieve greater regularity would persist. From the end of the Second Punic War, moreover, Roman authorities had slowly begun to exploit mines in territories that they dominated, usually through the efforts of public contractors or *publicani* from Italy. Operations near New Carthage were on an especially large scale, employing as many as 40,000 slaves, who worked under horrific conditions (Polyb. 34.9.8; Diod. Sic. 5.36–8).[17]

From the mid-150s, consuls often were dispatched as commanders. In some instances, the replacement of a lower-ranking commander by a higher-ranking one may have been due to a lack of suitable consular commands elsewhere.[18] Some wars, however, certainly were larger in scale. Now, campaigns centered on the Lusitanians of the far west and on the Celtiberians of Numantia, a town that occupied a strong position in the upper reaches of the Durius River. The historian Florus (1.33) claimed that these groups proved so difficult to defeat because they were the only ones to produce competent leaders. The Lusitanian wars ended in 138, as a result of the assassination, at Roman instigation, of their leader, Viriathus. The Numantine wars lasted a little longer. From the 150s to the 130s, five Roman consuls made unsuccessful attacks on the town. P. Cornelius Scipio Aemilianus (cos. 134), the victor over Carthage in the Third Punic War (see below), captured Numantia after an eight-month siege.

Campaigns, and thus the definition of *provinciae*, across the Adriatic among the settled states and established empires of the Hellenistic world were less frequent, but larger in scale and much more dramatic, attracting more attention from Greek and Roman historians than the other wars of the time. The Second Macedonian War (200–196) followed almost immediately the end of the war with Hannibal. The historian Livy (31.1.6–2.6) later would claim that the Senate decided to wage war against the Macedonian king, Philip V, partly because senators wished to take revenge for his intervention on the side of Hannibal and partly because they had formed relationships with states and rulers, especially the Aetolian League and the king of Pergamum, who sought their assistance. At first, Roman commanders campaigned in Epirus, protecting friendly states and seeking to force a route over the mountains to the east. The situation changed in Rome's favor with the arrival of T. Quinctius Flamininus (cos. 198), who forced Philip to withdraw from Epirus into Thessaly, where he then defeated Philip's army at Cynoscephalae in 197.

In the settlement, Flamininus, with the assistance of ten senatorial *legati*, reduced the power and influence of Macedon while increasing the sphere of Roman benefactions. Philip was forced to withdraw his garrisons from Greek cities, surrender the bulk of his fleet, and pay Rome a large indemnity. Before his return to Italy, Flamininus proclaimed the freedom of the Greek cities at the Isthmian games, where large crowds customarily gathered. Over the following months, he attempted to settle disputes among a number of Greek cities and leagues. In 194, he returned to Italy with the remainder of his army. Proclamations of freedom such as Flamininus' had long had a prominent place in Hellenistic diplomacy, but they certainly did not mean that the states making these declarations were abandoning a preeminent position, merely that they were promising to impose no garrisons, tribute, or formal signs of submission.[19] After Flamininus' return, the Senate ceased to send new commanders for a time.

In the Greek east, Rome's position played out in a sequence of settlements, more or less long-lasting, interspersed with brief wars against a major power, disaffected dependants, or disruptive communities that only solidified Roman power and illustrated Rome's predominance in force. Throughout, the Senate, at least in form, acted as a leader, protector, and arbiter, rather than as a ruler. Flamininus' settlement did not prove durable. Antiochus III, king of Syria, a monarch who had done much to revive the glories of the Seleucid kingdom, had taken advantage of the war between Rome and Macedon to expand his power in Asia Minor, where his predecessors had long possessed territories and harbored ambitions. Polybius (3.7.1–4) claimed that the machinations of the Aetolians, who felt slighted in the peace that ended the

Second Macedonian War, brought on the Syrian War (192–189), for they invited Antiochus into Greece. As a result of his diplomatic successes, Antiochus dispatched a small force across the Aegean. Early in 191, the consul M'. Acilius Glabrio crossed from Italy, entered Thessaly, and defeated Antiochus' general at Thermopylae. Glabrio then turned on the Aetolians, driving their army from the field, and besieging Naupactus, one of their chief centers. L. Cornelius Scipio (cos. 190), the brother of Africanus, crossed into Asia Minor and defeated Antiochus himself at Magnesia in 109. The next commander, Cn. Manlius Vulso (cos. 189), campaigned against the Galatians in the interior of Asia Minor, perhaps in part to protect the Greeks of Asia from their incursions, and pushed as far east as the Taurus Mountains.

The new settlement emerged in two stages. In the first, L. Scipio dictated that Antiochus withdraw from Asia Minor, pay an indemnity of 15,000 talents, and settle an old debt with Eumenes, king of Pergamum. Vulso, with the assistance of ten *legati*, produced the second set of terms: Antiochus was not to wage war in Europe or in the Aegean and, instead, was to accept the Senate as arbitrator in any future dispute with the states of the area. In this way, Vulso and his advisors made the Senate central to the interrelations among a number of states in a way that did not require it to initiate any actions. In Asia Minor, the Roman commander did not proclaim any general freedom of cities or peoples; instead, he strengthened the position of Eumenes and of the Rhodians, dividing Antiochus' former possessions among them. Soon after, the Senate again ceased to define *provinciae* in the region.

The Aetolian League also suffered severe penalties. After the Roman victory at Thermopylae and the subsequent campaign against them, the Aetolian League sought to negotiate a peace. The Roman terms, however, were quite harsh, and the Aetolians refused to accept them. Eventually, through the mediation of others, the Aetolians were able to secure more favorable terms, but they still lost territory and much of their freedom of action. Magistrates and senators clearly saw the alliance between the Aetolian League and Antiochus III as a betrayal, and Roman conceptions of their relationship with the League proved dominant; the Senate was not very tolerant of the normal maneuvers of Greek diplomatic life.

The next major war eliminated the Macedonian monarchy. Polybius (22.18) placed the blame for the war clearly on Perseus, the new king of Macedon, claiming that he had followed an alleged plan of his father, Philip V, to renew the struggle with Rome. Perseus, who became king in 179, had strengthened his position, waging wars along his northern frontiers, sending embassies, acting as mediator or arbitrator, and performing benefactions. The Senate had long received embassies complaining about the actions of father and son, but for long it had not acted on these complaints, which may indicate that it did not view Perseus as threatening or even that they did not take much notice at all.[20] By 173 and 172, however, the Senate seemingly viewed hostilities as likely, and the complaints of Eumenes, king of Pergamum, may have had a central role in bringing about the shift. In 172, the Senate dispatched *legati* who traveled through Greece and the Aegean renewing relations and observing how states were responding to Perseus' efforts. In the process, they broke up the old Boeotian League, placing friendly factions in charge in individual cities, and persuaded a number of polities to join against Perseus. In 171, a consul arrived in the region with his army, while *legati* sought contributions of troops from as far afield as Numidia and Carthage. Again, a single major battle decided the war's outcome: in 168, L. Aemilius Paullus (cos. 168) defeated Perseus at Pydna.

The peace was severe. Paullus and the *legati* who advised him ended the Macedonian monarchy, which they replaced with four republics, each with its own magistrates and assemblies, and they made Macedonian royal lands and mines the public property of the Roman People, the first clear and permanent Roman possessions in the region. Some Greek cities and leagues – most notably the Achaean and Aetolian Leagues – faced heavy penalties either for showing too much enthusiasm for Perseus or not enough for Rome. The Achaean League had to supply hostages, one of whom was the historian Polybius. Paullus himself led a punitive expedition into Epirus, where he reportedly enslaved 150,000 people.[21]

Paullus marked his victory with ceremonial displays of wealth and power of the kind that had been typical of Hellenistic monarchies. After summoning kings and cities to send delegates to Amphipolis as witnesses, he put on elaborate processions, some military in nature, a range of musical, dramatic, and athletic contests, banquets and symposia, and he arranged for captured weapons to be burned in a giant bonfire as offerings to Mars, Minerva, and Lua Mater. Throughout, Paullus exhibited the Macedonian royal treasury and gave gifts to cities and individuals. Displays of power such as these had long had an important role in the competition among leading states. In response to these celebrations, the Seleucid king, Antiochus IV, put on a similar display of wealth and power, clearly intended to rival Paullus'.[22]

After the war, senatorial ambassadors ranged widely, inspecting local attitudes and imposing settlements to disputes, while various states in the east sent embassies to Rome proclaiming their support, complaining about neighbors, or seeking various favors. In 168, while the war with Perseus was still underway, one embassy headed by C. Popillius Laenas went to Egypt where they forced the Syrian king Antiochus IV to end his successful invasion. After the war, a series of embassies toured the kingdoms of Pergamum, Cappodocia, Syria, and the city of Rhodes. Other embassies settled the civil war between Ptolemy VI and Ptolemy VII in Egypt and intervened in the succession to the Seleucid kingship after the death of Antiochus IV.

In the three decades that separated the First and Third Macedonian Wars, Rome and its power came to be ever more present as a reality, and some Greeks began to assign to the Roman state the traditional trappings of power in the Greek world. For long, Greek cities had established cults of Hellenistic kings, using the language and practices of religion at least in part as a means of seeking benefactions and signaling subordination. After the Roman victory over Philip V, some cities began to institute cults of the goddess Roma, complete with temples, priests, and sacrifices, a practice that accelerated after the defeat of Philip's son Perseus. Here, then, these communities began to treat the Roman state much as they had done its regal predecessors.[23] Indeed, in the aftermath of Perseus' defeat, Prusias, king of Bithynia, who had come to Rome to congratulate the Senate on its victory, prostrated himself before the Senate in a gesture of adoration and addressed them collectively as "Savior Gods," a title long associated with royalty (Polyb. 30.18).

Less than 20 years after the end of the Third Macedonian War, Roman commanders again fought in Macedon and in the Greece. In 150, Andriscus, who claimed to be the son of Perseus, invaded Macedon with Thracian support, and, in the following year, he had taken control of much of the country. Q. Caecilius Metellus (pr. 148) ended his reign. A separate war emerged to the south. The Achaean League, whose relations with the Senate had become increasingly precarious, attempted to force Sparta back into the league. The Spartans, however, appealed to Rome, and the Senate ordered the Achaean League to restore independence to Sparta and to Corinth and Argos as well. When the League continued its war against Sparta, Metellus, now serving as a promagistrate, defeated the League's army in the field. His successor L. Mummius (cos. 146) ended the Achaean War, dissolving the League, if only for a time, and destroying the city of Corinth, emblematic of an increasingly dominant Rome. One long-lasting result of these two conflicts, it should be noted, was that the Senate soon began to assign Macedonia as a *provincia* with regularity, in large part, to defend Macedon and the Greeks to the south from threats from across Macedon's northern frontiers.

One further war put the seal on the wars of the age. After the Second Punic War, Carthage had remained a wealthy and populous city, although a markedly less powerful one; Polybius (18.35.9) thought it to be the richest city in the world. In the half-century between Rome's second and third wars with Carthage, Masinissa had pressed forcefully on Carthaginian frontiers, resulting in a number of Carthaginian and Numidian embassies to Rome and occasional senatorial embassies to Africa. Appian (*Pun.* 67–9) claimed that Masinissa was the aggressor and that the Senate always supported him. In 150, the Carthaginians responded by waging war without Roman permission in violation of their treaty, providing the more militant senators with a pretext for war. Indeed, Polybius (36.2.1) wrote that the Senate had decided to go to war with Carthage long before the formal declaration of war in 149. The realization that Rome was about to declare war prompted at least two delegations to make the journey to Rome. The city of Utica, near to Carthage, sent ambassadors to make their formal surrender, and not much later, Carthaginian ambassadors also arrived in Rome and offered to surrender their city. They received a somewhat deceptive answer: that the Carthaginians could recover their freedom if they surrendered hostages and if they obeyed the commands of the consuls who were preparing their forces. The Carthaginians complied with these conditions, but the consuls continued on their way to Africa with their army and fleet.

The remainder of the drama played out in Africa. L. Marcius Censorinus and M'. Manilius, consuls in 149, received Carthaginian ambassadors at their headquarters in Utica and instructed the Carthaginians to turn over all their armor and military machinery. When the Carthaginians had complied, the consuls then demanded that Carthage be abandoned and its residents move at least ten miles inland. The Livian epitomator (*Per.* 49) held that by this action, the consuls, under the Senate's orders, drove the Carthaginians to fight. Despite Rome's great preponderance of force, Censorinus and Manilius were not successful in their war against Carthage, nor was their successor, L. Calpurnius Piso (cos. 148). The next commander, P. Cornelius

Scipio Aemilianus (cos. 147), the son of L. Aemilius Paullus, victor at Pydna, and by adoption the grandson of Scipio Africanus, was much more successful. In the spring of 146, his soldiers forced their way into the centers of the city with much destruction and slaughter. Scipio then supervised the physical destruction of the city and cursed its site, and, with the assistance of ten *legati*, imposed a settlement rewarding the rulers of Numidia, governed since the death of Masinissa in 148 by Micipsa and his brothers, with grants of territory, ordering the destruction of towns that had remained loyal to Carthage, granting land to towns that had sided with Rome, and imposing on the remaining territory and the surviving population a tribute on land and on persons, an indication of the increasing regularity of Roman financial impositions. Then, Scipio celebrated games and performed sacrifices for his victory and returned to Rome, where he, too, took the triumphal name of Africanus.

Rome, 201–134

In Rome itself, the decades following the Second Punic War marked the high point of the power and influence of the Senate and of the leading families of the ruling elite. Roman government rested on a relatively small number of men who filled Rome's elective offices each year and on assemblies of citizens that, by their votes, authorized laws and filled offices. In assemblies, it should be noted, officeholders had a central role, for assemblies met and voted under the presidency of a consul, praetor, or tribune of the plebs, and they only voted on measures or candidates that the presiding official had put before them. Without a magistrate or a candidate to give voice to their grievances, in other words, the citizenry was left with primarily symbolic forms with which they could express their desires and their grievances (see also Chapters 1 and 18).[24] Yet the Senate, if only informally, occupied a central position in the state: as a body, it gave advice in the form of a decree or *senatus consultum* when consulted by an officeholder, identified magisterial *provinciae*, chose the magistrates who would continue to serve as promagistrates, set the funds that magistrates would receive for their operations, ruled on the acceptability of treaties that magistrates had negotiated, dispatched teams of senatorial *legati*, and determined the validity of rulings by various priestly colleges on matters of ritual and of sacred law.

   The Senate's leadership depended on the willingness of officeholders to submit in important matters to the senatorial consensus and on the readiness of more junior senators to follow those who were more senior. Here, there were significant and continuous sources of tension. Individuals competed, sometimes intensely, for office, and the most successful members of the senatorial elite strove to stand out above their peers. In the competition for office, members of prominent families had a pronounced advantage. Indeed, Roman elite culture provided numerous opportunities for the fortunate to proclaim their ancestry and their connections, perhaps most notably in the display of ancestral masks, or *imagines,* in funerals and in the *atria* of their houses and also in the ceremonial circuits of the Forum, their *ambitiones,* in which candidates were accompanied by prominent senators.[25] There were long-standing efforts to keep competition for popularity, honors, and offices within bounds and to prevent the highly successful from standing out too much above their ostensible equals. From the late fourth century, laws had attempted to limit or prevent iteration of offices. In the first half of the second century, a series of laws attempted to force senatorial careers into more regular patterns, either by requiring candidates for the office of consul to have earlier served as praetors, or by fixing minimum ages at which the offices of consul or praetor could be held, or by requiring a ten-year interval before holding the same office again, or by placing restrictions on the ways in which candidates were permitted to seek office, *leges de ambitu* (see also Chapter 12).[26]

Despite the Senate's preeminence, ambitious individuals did sometimes challenge a senatorial consensus, and here warfare sometimes provided opportunities for individual advancement in ways that could prove disruptive of the established order. Some commanders, unwilling to let slip their opportunity for fame, glory, or profit, ignored senatorial advice or restraints in their *provinciae*. For example, C. Cassius Longinus (cos. 171) left his province against the Gauls in northern Italy on his own authority and tried to attack Macedon through Illyria, an act that reportedly outraged the Senate (Livy 43.1.4–12). By the middle of the century, the distribution of land in colonies and viritane assignments had largely ceased and some wars, especially those in Spain, had proven to be unprofitable for the participants, possibly weakening the willingness to serve that had long bound citizens to magistrates and Senate.[27] Perhaps in an attempt to increase their own popularity, some tribunes of the plebs attempted to block officials from conducting the levy in unpopular wars.

Prosecutions of individuals after they had left office provided one of the few formal restraints on magisterial activity. During the war against Perseus, the Senate rebuked L. Hortensius (pr. 170) for sacking Abdera and selling its people into slavery, while a tribune of the plebs successfully prosecuted C. Lucretius Gallus (pr. 171) before a popular assembly for plundering friendly states. At about the same time, envoys from a number of Iberian communities complained to the Senate about the rapacious conduct of Roman officials, and the Senate instructed a praetor to choose judges, or *recuperatores*, to hear the case. In 149, a permanent court, or *quaestio*, with senatorial judges was established specifically to hear disputes *de rebus repetundis* – suits for recovery of property stolen by officials in their *provinciae*.[28]

The career of Scipio Africanus may illustrate some of the dangers that awaited any individual who did stand out too much. Africanus had emerged from the Second Punic War as the most successful Roman commander and he soon went on to hold further offices: censor and *princeps senatus*, first on the roster of senators, in 199 and consul for the second time in 194. He may have sought to establish his position on grounds that went beyond magistracies and successful commands. Roman authors later claimed that he imitated Alexander the Great or that he was a regular visitor to the temple of Jupiter Optimus Maximus on the Capitol, where the god gave signs of special favor, and similar claims were made in the second century, where they clearly derived from his family and quite possibly ultimately from Scipio himself.[29] Polybius (10.2.12;, 10.4.6), who had close connections with the family, claimed that Africanus wished that his soldiers believe that his efforts were divinely inspired and that he encouraged the belief that he communed with the gods in dreams and while awake. Other senators, however, clearly did not accept the preeminence that Scipio or his family claimed. In the 180s, he came under steady attack, especially in the form of the political prosecutions that were coming to be a pronounced feature of Roman political life. With his influence undermined, he withdrew from the city, and he soon died.[30]

Two generations later, the conduct of wars again provided the opportunity for ambitious individuals to acquire an especially prominent place in the city. An unsuccessful campaign against the Celtiberians in Nearer Spain may have resulted in M. Claudius Marcellus' (cos. 166, 155, 152) third consulship, without recent precedent and against laws requiring a ten-year interval between terms in the same office. A few years, later Scipio Aemilianus took advantage of popular discontent over the course of the war against Carthage to switch his candidacy from the aedilician elections to the consular. Scipio was younger than the minimum age for the office and he had not yet served as praetor, another requirement for the post, but he had the reputation for valor, gained in service in Spain and in Africa, and he was highly popular, perhaps as a result of this. Attempts to bar his candidacy failed in the face of popular protests and the threat of a tribune of the plebs to block any vote unless Aemilianus was permitted to seek the office. After the election, a tribune again intervened, placing before an assembly the motion to give Aemilianus the command against Carthage, instead of distributing consular assignments by lot, the more usual practice.

In the years that followed his victory, Aemilianus continued to press his position among senators outside the customary limits and procedures. In 142, he successfully sought election as censor against a rival who had the support of the Senate. Again, Aemilianus proved to be more popular. In his formal walks through the Forum, his *ambitiones*, Aemilianus was accompanied, not by senators as was customary, but allegedly by men of low birth, some of them freedmen, who were able to gather a crowd and force issues by shouting and stirring up passions (Plut. *Aem.* 38). In 135, Aemilianus again was elected consul for the following year, this time to command against Numantia in Spain, where a series of Roman commanders had earlier failed. Once again, he was chosen in defiance of the law: after M. Claudius Marcellus had held the office of consul for the third time in 152, a new law prohibited holding the office of consul more than once. His campaign against Numantia was successful, increasing still more his prestige.

Aemilianus' career reveals weaknesses in the senatorial regime that would have great import in the following decades. Restrictions on eligibility for office, one of the means by which senators had sought to protect themselves against their more popular peers, worked only when no one mobilized crowds and no plebeian tribune asserted citizens' right to vote as they wished. Aemilianus' career provoked sharp responses among senators, but in the more turbulent years that would follow, Aemilianus came to be seen as a more conventional figure than he may have appeared to many of his contemporaries.

Guide to Further Reading

Roman imperialism and warfare outside of Italy has generated, and continues to generate, a vast scholarly literature. Harris 1979, Gruen 1984a, Linderski 1984, Sherwin-White 1984, Richardson 1986, Eckstein 1987, Rich 1993, and Kallet-Marx 1995 all present overviews of the nature of Roman imperialism. Hoyos 1998 sets out in detail events leading up to the First and Second Punic Wars. Lancel 1995 supplies the Carthaginian background, while Palmer 1997 examines aspects of the relationship between Rome and Carthage outside the framework of the Punic Wars. Goldsworthy 2000b sets out detailed narratives of the three Punic Wars; Lazenby 1996 provides a more detailed account of the campaigns of the First Punic War, as does Lazenby 1978 for the Second. Warrior 1996 scrutinizes the outbreak of the Second Macedonian War, while Gruen 1984a, Sherwin-White 1984, Kallet-Marx 1995, and Bernhardt 1998 provide broad views of Roman intervention in the East. Richardson 1986 provides an overview of the Roman wars in Spain. For the importance of the kings of Pergamum and Numidia in Roman policies, see Braund 1984 and Cimma 1976. Lintott 1993 sets out the institutional basis of Roman power outside of Italy.

The scholarly literature addressing the political, social, and cultural history of Rome and Italy in this period also is very large and growing. Dyson 1985 recounts in detail the wars in Cispadane Gaul, Transpadane Gaul, and Liguria, while Broadhead 2000 examines the demographic consequences of Roman expansion in these regions. Gabba 1989 and Salmon 1969 study the aims and consequences of Roman colonization in Italy, while Gargola 1995 sets out the official practices around it. Erdkamp 1998 and Rosenstein 2004 examine the economic and demographic aspects of Roman warfare. The political order of Rome in this period has been the subject of intense debate. For an overview, see Astin 1989. Millar 1984 and 1989 – now collected in Millar 2002b – emphasizes the democratic features of the Roman political order. Feig Vishnia 1996 gives an in-depth study of popular leadership in its political and social contexts. For the career of Scipio Aemilianus, see Astin 1967.

Notes

1 Hoyos 1998: 53–7.
2 Lancel 1995: 259, 372.
3 Gargola 1995.
4 Linderski 1984: 141.
5 Rich 1996.
6 For Massilia: Hoyos 1998: 169–71.
7 Beard, North, and Price 1998: 79–87.
8 See Erdkamp 1998.
9 For the *publicani*: Badian 1972a.
10 Eckstein 1987.

11 Richardson 1986: 5–10; Lintott 1993: 22–4.
12 On plunder: Gruen 1984b; Ziolkowski 1993; exploitation of local resources: Richardson 1976.
13 Thus, Derow 1979; Kallet-Marx 1995: 18–29. For a different view: Richardson 1979.
14 For differing views: Gruen 1990a; Beard, North, and Price 1998: 92–8.
15 Gabba 1989.
16 Gargola 1995.
17 Richardson 1976.
18 Richardson 1986: 134–7.
19 Gruen 1984a: 132–57.
20 Gruen 1984a: 404.
21 Ziolkowski 1986.
22 Hesberg 1999; Edmondson 1999.
23 Thus, Mellor 1975.
24 For symbolic protests, see Marshall 1984.
25 Flower 1996: 60–70; see also Chapter 17.
26 Astin 1958; Lintott 1990; see also Chapter 12.
27 For ties between resistance to service and the profitability of wars, see Rosenstein 2004: 14.
28 Trials: Gruen 1968; Alexander 1990. It is uncertain whether the laws applied to the property of provincials or only to the property of Roman citizens in the provinces; see Lintott 1993: 97–107; Richardson 1987.
29 Beard, North, and Price 1998: 84–7.
30 For the "fall" of the Scipios, see Gruen 1995.

CHAPTER 8

From the Gracchi to the First Civil War (133–70)

C. F. Konrad

In 137, the consul C. Hostilius Mancinus with his army faced annihilation near Numantia in Spain. The Numantines, however, offered mercy, if terms were vouched for by his quaestor, Ti. Sempronius Gracchus. Tiberius' father (consul 177, 163; censor 169), as governor in Spain (180–178), had gained the trust of that unhappy and exploited province; his mother, Cornelia, was the daughter of Scipio Africanus. Tiberius now negotiated a peace that sent the Romans away under the yoke. The Senate, however, disavowed the treaty, and ordered the hapless consul handed over to the enemy, on the motion of Scipio Aemilianus – Tiberius' brother-in-law. It dealt a stunning blow to Tiberius' *dignitas* ("public reputation, prestige"). To a Roman noble, a slight such as this called for retaliation (Cic. *Har. resp.* 43; Plut. *Ti. Gracch.* 5–7).[1]

The Ghost of Tarquinius, 133

For centuries, the *ager publicus* ("public land") of the Roman People had been available to private users, whether Roman citizens or allies, for a fee payable to the state. Marginal farmers relied on it to make ends meet (their own plots often being insufficient); large-scale operators used it to round out scattered possessions or increase grazing pasture, often buying – or pushing – small neighbors off the public land they occupied (App. *B Civ.* 1.7–8; Plut. *Ti. Gracch.* 8.1–4).[2]

On December 10, 134, Tiberius Gracchus, barely 30, took office as tribune of the plebs. By the first days of 133, he introduced a *lex agraria* ("land law") reestablishing an earlier limit, long ignored, of 500 *iugera* (about 310 acres or 125 ha.) of *ager publicus* that could be occupied and farmed by any one person. Up to those limits, the law granted permanent possession (though not ownership), free of rent, to all current holders of *ager publicus*. The Roman state would reclaim all public land in excess of the legal limit, to distribute it in family-size plots among the landless poor. These plots, however, remained public land; their holders were barred from selling them, becoming thus permanent tenants of the state, secure from being bought out or displaced (App. *B Civ.* 9–11).[3] Nothing in the law affected private property.

The immediate beneficiaries would be the rural (*plebs rustica*) as well as some of the urban poor (*plebs urbana*) – those willing to take up farming. But in turn, the *res publica* would benefit. The only realistic shield from destitution was secure possession of land sufficient for subsistence farming.[4] The unchecked growth of a landless proletariat, both in the country and the City, was bound to create unrest, and dissatisfaction with established government. The nobles could ill afford that. Here was no revolutionary proposal: in boosting the numbers of small farmers (a conservative lot in virtually any society), the law would forestall social, hence eventually, political instability. The winner would be the ruling elite, the nobles – as a group. But individually, they would also be the losers; for the law required sacrifice of them. Most senators, whatever the size of their privately owned land, held *ager publicus* beyond the limit set in Tiberius' bill, and the bulk of what was to be redistributed would have to come from them. If that caused pain to those who had presided over Tiberius' disgrace in the Numantine affair, so much the better.

With Scipio Aemilianus gone to Spain to crush Numantia, Tiberius seized the opportunity. He had substantial backing in the Senate: his father-in-law, the current Appius Claudius, consul in 143 and *princeps senatus* (the man to speak first in the Senate) – a bitter rival of Scipio Aemilianus; also P. Mucius Scaevola, consul now, and his brother, P. Licinius Crassus Dives Mucianus, the leading jurists of their time: both were involved in drafting the bill.[5] Yet he could not count on a majority, and an outright rejection in the Senate would doom his proposal. Hence he brought it directly before the plebeian assembly (Plut. *Ti. Gracch.* 9–20; App. *B Civ.* 9–17).[6] Bypassing the Senate was neither illegal nor, for a tribune, against custom (*mos*); but it entailed the risk of alienating senators who otherwise might show support.

A fellow tribune, M. Octavius, now twice blocked the bill, by veto, from being voted on, prompting Tiberius to present it to the Senate after all. There his opponents had the better of his supporters, yet it appears that no formal recommendation issued as to which tribune ought to yield. Tiberius reintroduced the bill; again, Octavius vetoed it. Past custom did not sanction the veto's repeated use to kill a tribune's bill outright: it might persuade him to withdraw the measure, seeing how it lacked consensus; but failing that, there was no precedent for preventing the People's vote indefinitely. Octavius was departing from *mos*, and in so doing, raised a political dispute to the level of a constitutional crisis: for both he and Tiberius had now reached a point where neither could stand down without damage to his *dignitas*.

Tiberius broke the deadlock with a bill that stripped Octavius of his office, as having abused his veto powers, and the People voted to remove him; no other tribune came to his aid. To argue that Octavius' deposition was "illegal" or "unconstitutional" is to misunderstand the problem. No laws had been violated. Tiberius' move was without precedent – in response to Octavius' unprecedented use of the veto.

Innovation was as much a part of Roman life as clinging to *mos maiorum*, which could give no guidance in situations not experienced before.[7] The danger lay elsewhere. In creating the precedent that an uncooperative colleague could be removed from office, Tiberius knocked away one of the unwritten principles of republican government, as the nobles understood it – the limitation of official power inherent in the presence of colleagues with exactly equal power.[8]

The agrarian law now passed. For its implementation, it authorized a commission of "triumvirs to adjudicate and assign lands"; the People elected Tiberius himself, his father-in-law, Ap. Claudius, and his younger brother Gaius. Yet in making the land reform a Gracchan family project and monopolizing all the goodwill accruing from its beneficiaries, Tiberius escalated, needlessly, his feud with his fellow nobles. Their reaction came with devastating effect. The commission required substantial funds: to survey Italy so as to determine the precise extent of *ager publicus*, and to furnish start-up money and equipment to new settlers (App. *B Civ.* 18). Appropriation was the Senate's prerogative, and it allocated the triumvirs six sesterces per day. Without money, Tiberius' reform was stalled before it had begun.

Chance, unforeseeable, now supervened. King Attalus III of Pergamum died and bequeathed his entire realm to the Roman People. Tiberius immediately, by plebiscite, seized the Pergamene treasure to finance the land reform, and barred the Senate from freeing the cities of the new province ("Asia") in accordance with the royal will: he would recommend better arrangements to the People. It was a stunning lesson in what a single man could do with popular support. It also knocked away a second pillar of republican government, the principle of deciding foreign and fiscal policy in the Senate, collectively and by consensus. The *res publica* of the nobles relied on restraint, mutual as well as self-imposed, on the part of those who managed it: Tiberius was no longer subject to either. He virtually had become the government of Rome. Only now did senators publicly attack him, with charges of despotic behavior, of recruiting a bodyguard from street toughs, of aiming to be sole ruler.[9] Some announced that they would prosecute him as soon as he became a private citizen again.

Tiberius understood. The issue had moved far beyond his land reform (for which he need not fear; no one threatened to repeal it): his future in the state was now at stake. He decided to run for reelection. No law forbade that, either; but it had not happened in 200 years. Combined with all his other acts, it confirmed the worst of fears: he aimed to escape accountability and make his one-man government permanent – enough to cause most nobles sleepless nights as they beheld the specter, rising from the grave, of Tarquin the Proud.

Having sought, and failed, to manipulate in his favor the choice of tribune to preside at the elections, Tiberius had his supporters occupy the Capitol during the night; when the assembly met next morning, they attempted to keep opposing voters from entering. A bloody riot ensued: Tiberius no longer enjoyed overwhelming popular support. At a Senate meeting in the nearby temple of Fides, the consul P. Scaevola refused to intervene: Tiberius had not – yet – broken any laws. Upon which P. Scipio Nasica (consul 138), *pontifex maximus* and Tiberius' cousin, called on everyone to take the safety of the *res publica* into their own hands; arming themselves with debris at hand, he and other senators rushed forth and clubbed Tiberius to death, along with scores of followers.

An even more fundamental element of self-restraint – the unspoken agreement not to take political disputes to the point of lethal violence – was thus swept away. Nasica might believe that he had saved the *res publica*, but at that very moment, Tiberius was already reduced to desperate measures in his bid for reelection: had cooler heads prevailed that day, he might have failed. Worse, in 132 the Senate resolved to apprehend and try those who had "conspired" with Ti. Gracchus: many were put to death (Cic. *Amic.* 37; Val. Max. 4.7.1; Plut. *Ti. Gracch.* 20.3–7). The killings more deeply split the ruling class than anything in memory.

The Allied Question, 132–124

For 15 years, until 118, the agrarian commission carried out Tiberius Gracchus' land reform.[10] Yet it stirred up an issue that had been simmering for a generation: Rome's relations with her Italian allies.

Although allies were not eligible for land assignments under the Gracchan law, allied-held *ager publicus* was subject to redistribution; by 129, large-scale allied occupiers mounted protests against this threat to "their" holdings. Recognizing the problem, Scipio Aemilianus persuaded the Senate to declare allied-held *ager publicus* exempt from the triumvirs' judgment and, consequently, from legal limits and redistribution. Apparently, he intended to go further; but he died on the day he was to give a speech concerning the allies' condition vis-à-vis Rome (App. *B Civ.* 19–20). His friends failed to proceed with his initiative, thus allowing the opposition to seize the issue. In 125, the consul M. Fulvius Flaccus, a land commissioner and since the recent death of Appius Claudius the leader of the Gracchan group, put forward a proposal to grant Roman citizenship to certain allies who desired it, and *provocatio* (the right of appeal to the People against a Roman magistrate's coercive actions) to others who did not (App. *B Civ.* 21; Val. Max. 9.5.1).[11] Foreign affairs intervened before a decision could be reached: Rome's ally Massilia called for help against the Gauls, and the Senate voted the command to Flaccus. His bill died with his departure for the war.

The Great Reformer, 123–121

The initiative, however, remained on Flaccus' side of the political divide. For 123, C. Sempronius Gracchus was elected tribune of the plebs. His brother had focused on a single issue; Gaius' measures (all but one enacted during his first tribunate) point to a comprehensive vision of reform, touching society, economy, financial and provincial administration, and the law (Plut. *C. Gracch.* 4–12; App. *B Civ.* 21–6; cf. Cic. *Rab. Post.* 12).[12]

A new *lex agraria* introduced a rent on land allotted under Tiberius' law and exempted substantial tracts of *ager publicus* from distribution – probably those occupied by allies, thus laying to rest some of their concerns. Regarding new allocations, Gaius shifted the focus of land reform from individual farms in the country toward the founding of new colonies. The most ambitious of these was Iunonia, on the very site of Carthage, with up to 200 *iugera* per settler family, and the first colony to be founded outside Italy.

Yet many proletarians born and raised in Rome were impervious to the joys of tilling the soil, and could not be expected to take up farming anywhere. That rapidly growing segment of the urban population needed to be fed, and most of the grain consumed in Rome – not Italy, which remained self-sufficient – arrived from overseas. Interruptions of that supply often drove the price beyond the purchasing ability of the poor. Gaius' grain law (*lex frumentaria*) required the state to buy and store large quantities of grain, and once every month sell it at a rate below the average market price. Attacked immediately as a demagogue's mass bribe allowing the urban poor to live in idle luxury, the measure was nothing of the sort. It did not give grain away gratis (Cic. *Sest.* 103; Livy *Per.* 60).[13] Unlike his critics, Gaius understood that it was in the self-interest of the ruling elite to ensure access to basic necessities of life; food riots do not promote political stability, and discontent, left unaddressed, will in time produce upheaval.

All this cost money, and was accompanied by measures to increase revenue from taxes and tolls. The most important changed the bidding for contracts to collect the tithe (*decuma*, an annual 10 percent levy on agricultural products) of Asia. Instead of being conducted locally district by district, it henceforth took place in Rome before the censors, as a single contract for the entire province. This reduced the influence, often corrupting, of the provincial governor and enabled Roman public service providers (*publicani*) to bid, while maximizing the revenue thus derived; but it effectively shut out any provincial bidders and all but the largest corporations.

Another law allowed Roman citizens to be tried on capital charges only by the People in assembly or in a court set up by law: henceforth, no criminal court (*quaestio*) could be established merely by Senate decree. A magistrate who, without granting *provocatio*, executed or forced into exile any citizen in contravention of this law became himself subject to prosecution, as did any magistrate or senator who conspired to have anyone falsely convicted on a capital charge.

The most far-reaching of all his laws, however, ended senators' monopoly on acting as single judges in most civil cases and as jurors in the permanently established criminal courts. The *lex iudiciaria* (judiciary law) set up a panel (*album*) of one-third senators and two-thirds equestrians, from which henceforth all civil judges and – in the same 1:2 proportion – jurors in criminal trials were to be drawn (Plut. *C. Gracch.* 5.2–6.1; Livy *Per.* 60).[14] A second law, sponsored by the tribune M'. Acilius Glabrio in 123 or 122,[15] replaced the jurors on the extortion court (*quaestio de repetundis*) with equestrians only, keeping senators thus completely from sitting in judgment on a crime that, in effect, only they could be charged with. Far from trying to undermine it, the *lex repetundarum* aimed at stabilizing the rule of the senatorial elite by enforcing certain restraints that its members were less and less willing to observe on their own.

Both laws had yet another effect, not entirely unintended. They deepened a developing division of the Roman upper class into two distinct groups: a political elite of senatorial families (with the nobles at their center) defined by the holding of elective public office, and an economic elite of landowners and businessmen (soon known as the equestrian order) defined, essentially, by wealth. By effectively pitting equestrians against senators, especially in the extortion court, a new and separate identity was created for each group.[16]

Gaius' legislation – the judiciary and grain laws in particular – generated strong opposition and resentment in the Senate, but no attempts were made to veto any of these bills. He was reelected to a second tribunate without being a declared candidate.[17] Also elected for 122 was an old friend, M. Fulvius Flaccus, recently returned from Gaul: the only instance of a former consul becoming tribune of the plebs.

Gaius now focused on two projects: settling Iunonia and improving the status of Rome's Italian allies. During the first half of 122, he spent over two months in Africa, establishing its initial settlers – 6,000 families drawn from all over Italy. During his absence, persistent reports of negative omens traveled to Rome, and when Gaius returned he found that the popular mood had changed.

A fellow tribune, the noble M. Livius Drusus, had begun to organize the opposition, and with the Senate's backing announced a proposal to found no less than 12 new colonies, with 3,000 families each, all within Italy. Nothing indicates that these colonies ever materialized or were put to a vote, but it proved a major public relations success. Having shamelessly outbid Gaius on colonies, Drusus took a different approach to the allies. Before going to Africa, Gaius had drafted legislation granting full citizenship to the Latin allies, and voting rights to (all?) others (Cic. *Brut.* 99; Plut. *C. Gracch.* 12).[18] Meanwhile Drusus revealed a counterproposal – again, nothing ever came of it, despite ostensibly having the Senate's backing – that no Latin ally should be subject to flogging, and proceeded to attack Gaius for irresponsibly giving away Roman citizenship. In this he was joined by the consul C. Fannius, who had been elected with Gaius' support, but now turned against him, painting a horrifying picture of Roman festivals and assemblies overrun by new citizens. When after his return from Africa Gaius finally scheduled a vote on his proposal, it failed.

Gaius was not elected to a third tribunate, despite an apparent attempt at candidacy. In 121, the consul L. Opimius (an old enemy) moved to cancel the colony at Carthage, Iunonia: a severe blow to Gracchus' and Flaccus' *dignitas*. They mobilized their followers, and during a *contio* on the Capitol, an attendant of the consul was killed in a scuffle with pro-Gracchan toughs. Following demonstrations in the Forum the next day, the Senate, in an unprecedented move, voted to back whatever action the consul took to protect the state, be it in accordance with the law or not (known today as the "last decree," *senatus consultum ultimum*; see also Chapter 12). Opimius ordered all senators and equestrians to present themselves, fully armed, on the Capitol at dawn. Flaccus now gathered supporters at his house; Gaius returned to his own home, despondent and sensing that events were slipping out of control, but unable to overcome aristocratic pride and disavow Flaccus' preparing for armed insurrection. At daybreak, he joined Flaccus in seizing the Aventine. Negotiations failed when Opimius insisted that they disarm and appear before the Senate, and a frontal assault on the Aventine quickly put an end to all resistance. Flaccus was put to death; Gaius Gracchus had his throat cut by a faithful slave. Some 3,000 of their followers perished, either on the Aventine or in summary roundups and executions carried out by Opimius (Cic. *De or.* 2.132–4; Plut. *C. Gracch.* 13.1–18.1; App. *B Civ.* 25–6).[19] Again, a political dispute had flared into bloody violence, yet not spontaneously as in 133: this time it carried a whiff of civil war.

Personal catastrophe notwithstanding, we must not think of the Gracchi as having failed: their legislation endured remarkably. In 111, a new law converted much of the *ager publicus* currently occupied in Italy – up to the Gracchan limit – and all land assigned by the commission into private property, without payment of rent, and fully alienable; but the state still retained plenty of land, especially in allied occupation. Far from dooming Tiberius' land reform, the law of 111 simply meant that after 22 years the process had run its course:[20] Italy was still a land of small and middling farms in the first century BC (see further Chapters 27 and 28).

Although Gaius' colony at Carthage was dismantled, the settlers in North Africa retained their land. Virtually all his other laws remained in force, some beyond the end of the Republic. For a legislative program often accused of undermining the *res publica*, such longevity must astonish: unless one accepts that it was the legislator's personal power, not the substance of his measures, wherein so many nobles perceived the threat.

The Confidence Gap, 121–105

King Micipsa of Numidia died about 118, leaving his sons Adherbal and Hiempsal to be joint kings, together with his nephew Iugurtha (Sall. *Iug.*; Plut. *Mar.* 7–10; cf. Cic. *Brut.* 127–8).[21] Older than his cousins, Iugurtha held the advantage of experience, a ruthless disposition, and close contacts with Roman nobles: he had commanded the Numidian cavalry at Numantia, and impressed Scipio Aemilianus. Taking his own measure of the Roman elite, he returned home convinced that, properly managed, Rome could be kept out of Africa.

Once king, Iugurtha wasted little time in having Hiempsal assassinated and Adherbal expelled (c.116). A senatorial commission under L. Opimius (consul 121) was dispatched to settle things; allegedly bribed by Iugurtha, they granted him the kingdom's western half, less developed than the east (which went to Adherbal) but home to most of Numidia's warrior tribes. In 112, Iugurtha renewed his attack and drove Adherbal into the city of Cirta, tenaciously defended by a large number of resident Roman and Italian merchants. In the Senate, some demanded an immediate military intervention, but Iugurtha's many influential friends insisted on a diplomatic solution; another delegation, headed by M. Aemilius Scaurus (consul 115, censor 109, and *princeps senatus*), went to reason with the king, and achieved nothing. The Italians defending Cirta, weary of the siege and confident in the protection afforded by their being Roman citizens or allies, now urged Adherbal to surrender, on Iugurtha's assurance to spare his life. Thus Cirta was handed over, and sacked; Adherbal tortured to death; the inhabitants, Italians or not, indiscriminately slaughtered.

Even so, Iugurtha's friends in Rome kept stalling; but the butchered merchants of Cirta had friends and relatives, too, and popular pressure managed by the tribune C. Memmius shamed the Senate into action: in 111, the consul L. Calpurnius Bestia invaded Numidia. Applying arguments of material value, Iugurtha persuaded the consul – whose staff included Aemilius Scaurus – to make peace in exchange for a nominal penalty. Although the treaty was received in Rome with consternation, Scaurus' influence kept the Senate from rejecting it. Again, Memmius shaped public anger into a constructive response: granted by plebiscite safe conduct (*fides publica*), Iugurtha was summoned to Rome, to give evidence on those who had accepted bribes. Another tribune, overcome by the king's generosity (Iugurtha had arrived with plenty of funds), vetoed the testimony; and Memmius lacked time to try again.

Yet in 110, the new consul Sp. Postumius Albinus moved to replace Iugurtha with another cousin, Massiva, currently in exile in Rome. Sensing that the balance in the Senate was shifting from his friends to his enemies, Iugurtha calmly had Massiva murdered; unfortunately the assassin, caught, revealed his employer. No sum of money could help now: the Senate ordered Iugurtha out of Italy.

Once in Numidia, Albinus made little military progress, and soon returned to Rome to hold elections. Left in command and unequal to the task, his brother Aulus let the king's agents spread his wealth among the troops; a night assault took the Roman camp without resistance. Again, Iugurtha offered peace, and Aulus signed. The Senate, now past temporizing, repudiated the treaty; but the consul, back to Africa, found the army too demoralized to resume the campaign.

In 109, the tribune C. Mamilius Limetanus by plebiscite set up a special court to try anyone who had given advice and comfort to Iugurtha, or taken his bribe; Opimius, Bestia, Sp. Albinus, and two other senators were convicted and exiled. Meanwhile the new commander, Q. Caecilius Metellus (consul 109), secured significant portions of Numidia; but Iugurtha eluded capture. An emerging sense in Rome that the war had bogged down produced another change in command.

Gaius Marius (157–86) had entered politics as a protégé of the Metelli, and promptly alienated them when tribune (119); unremarkable as praetor (115) and as governor in Spain (114), he had risen as high as a "new man" (*homo novus*, a senator without senatorial ancestors) could reasonably hope. Metellus, however, appreciating his military skill, reconciled and appointed him to his staff in Numidia, where he performed with distinction. In fall 108, Marius decided to run for consul; his (oblique) request for Metellus' support met with the incomparable scorn of a noble looking back on 11 consulships in the family tree (see also Chapter 19). But a flood of letters from merchants and soldiers in Africa, endorsing Marius' candidacy and his charge that Metellus was deliberately prolonging the war, persuaded the business community in Rome, and Marius won. The Senate had already renewed Metellus' command and chosen different provinces for the consuls of 107 (as prescribed by a law of Gaius Gracchus): now a friendly tribune had the Numidian command transferred to Marius by vote of the People.

When recruiting his reinforcements for Africa, Marius dropped the time-honored property qualification and accepted anyone who volunteered – mostly proletarians. (This had been done before, though only in emergencies.) Nothing indicates that he intended to institute a permanent change in policy; he simply sought to disappoint expectations in the Senate that a traditional draft would dent his popularity (Sall. *Iug.* 84–6; Plut. *Mar.* 9.1).[22] The enthusiastic response, however, opened eyes: subsequent commanders simply followed Marius' lead, without, of course, limiting recruitment to volunteers (or proletarians; see also Chapters 13 and 29).

Metellus, thus recalled, was awarded a triumph and the victory name "Numidicus." By 105, Marius had established Roman control in Numidia, installed another nephew of Micipsa as king, and forced Iugurtha to seek refuge with his father-in-law, King Bocchus of Mauretania. Unwilling to embroil himself in a war with Rome, Bocchus opened negotiations; and Marius' quaestor, L. Cornelius Sulla, persuaded him to hand over Iugurtha. Marius returned home in triumph, and learned that he had been elected to a second consulship, for 104.

The Savior of Italy, 104–98

During the last quarter of the century, Germanic peoples – chiefly the Cimbri, Teutoni, and Ambrones – had been migrating south and west to Gaul. In eight years (113–105), they encountered six Roman forces and annihilated each, most resoundingly two armies under the consul Cn. Mallius Maximus and the proconsul Q. Servilius Caepio in 105 near Arausio in the Rhône valley. Panic spread in Italy, and made the conqueror of Iugurtha the man of the hour. Yet for the next two years, the Germans tried their luck in Spain, until in 102 they resolved to visit Italy. In an unprecedented move, Marius was reelected consul year after year. He used this time to reorganize the Roman army (see also Chapter 13).

For their attack on Italy, the Cimbri chose to march across the Alps; the Teutoni and Ambrones down the Rhône and along the coast. At Aquae Sextiae (Aix-en-Provence) in fall 102, Marius destroyed the latter two; his colleague, Q. Lutatius Catulus, having succeeded to a consulship with Marius' help (after a record three electoral defeats), failed to stop the Cimbri in the Alps, and they proceeded to plunder Cisalpine Gaul. Marius was reelected for 101, Catulus prorogued, and both combined their forces. Negotiations with the Cimbri produced nothing but an agreement to fight a battle at Vercellae in the lower Po valley on July 30; the Romans won. Hailed as the savior of Italy, Marius insisted that Catulus be allowed to share his triumph. Soon afterwards, he was elected to a sixth consulship – equaling a record set in 299; yet no man had ever held the office five times in a row (Plut. *Mar.* 11–28; Livy *Per.* 65–7; Val. Max. 2.3.2).[23]

The convictions under the Mamilian *quaestio*, by all-equestrian juries, in 109 had painfully chastised the Senate's handling of the Jugurthine War. In 106, the consul Q.

Servilius Caepio responded with a law requiring jurors of all the courts to be drawn from the extortion court's panel, restructured to comprise both senators and equestrians, in unknown proportion.[24] Yet the following year's disaster at Arausio, largely blamed on Caepio, forced him into exile and opened the doors to a string of attacks on the Senate's hold on government. In (probably) 104 the tribune C. Servilius Glaucia restored the all-equestrian jury to the extortion court, eliminating thus – in consequence of Caepio's general regulation – senators from the law courts altogether, and in 103, the tribune L. Appuleius Saturninus set up a permanent court, all-equestrian, for charges of treason (*quaestio de maiestate*).[25] Saturninus, from a mid-level senatorial family, was closely allied with Marius; by another law he provided land in Africa for the veterans of the Jugurthine War. He and Glaucia shared a personal grudge: during a grain shortage in 105, the Senate had relieved Saturninus from his duties as quaestor at Ostia,[26] and in 102, Metellus Numidicus as censor attempted, unsuccessfully, to expel him and Glaucia from the Senate. For 100, Saturninus was elected to a second tribunate, Glaucia to the praetorship (Plut. *Mar.* 14.11–14, 28.7–29.1; App. *B Civ.* 28).[27]

Again Saturninus took care of Marius' interests (Plut. *Mar.* 29–30; *App. B Civ.* 29–33):[28] his *lex agraria* provided for colonies in Gaul, Corsica, Sicily, Greece, and Macedonia; it authorized Marius to grant Roman citizenship to three persons in each colony, and, significantly, reserved a majority of allocations to Italian allies. Urban proletarians felt much resentment against that last provision (Appian 29–31).[29] When Saturninus ignored a move to force the assembly's dismissal on augural grounds (thunder had been heard[30]), opponents armed with clubs attempted to drive him off; but his supporters – many veterans of Marius – prevailed in the mêlée.

The law produced an unexpected windfall. It required all magistrates and senators to take an oath to uphold it. Confronted in the Senate with charges that it had been enacted by violence and against religious obstacles, Marius took the oath but added the proviso, "insofar as the law is valid." All followed suit – except Metellus Numidicus, who went into exile.

In the fall, Saturninus was reelected to a third tribunate, for 99. Sensing momentum, he and Glaucia resolved to consolidate their influence by having the latter made consul. Yet Glaucia, being praetor, could not legally run for the consulship until 98, for 97 – and Marius disallowed his candidacy. Useful as the two had been to him, he had no intention of handing virtual control of the government to them for all of next year. On election day, the resourceful murder of Glaucia's principal competitor caused elections to be postponed indefinitely. Saturninus now occupied the Capitol, intending to hold an assembly there so as to exempt Glaucia from the laws governing consular candidacies.[31] The Senate voted the "last decree": but this time, unlike Opimius in 121, the consul was instructed to take action not against private citizens engaged in armed insurrection, but against incumbent magistrates, in particular a sacrosanct tribune of the plebs conducting an assembly thereof. No wonder Marius, like most newcomers more deeply attached to the traditional rules and values of the group attained – be it nobility, club, or country – than those born into it, is said to have hesitated; but swayed by Aemilius Scaurus, he called citizens to arms, and they obeyed. Cut off from the Capitol's water supply and unprepared for resistance,

Saturninus and his followers accepted the consul's offer of safe custody until trial; taken to the Senate house, they were soon lynched by a mob that stormed the building. Glaucia, caught hiding in a friend's house, was executed on the spot (Cic. *Brut.* 224; cf. [Aur. Vict.] *De vir. ill.* 73.10; Oros. 5.17.9).

The year 100 thus saw Gaius Marius at the height of his career, the savior both of Italy and the *res publica*. Almost immediately, he squandered much of his political capital when he opposed moves to recall Metellus Numidicus from exile; with Saturninus gone, it was a fight he could not win. The defenders of traditional oligarchic government by the nobility, referring now to themselves as *boni* ("good ones") or *optimates* ("those best qualified"), while dismissing as *populares* ("popularity seekers") those within the ruling elite who would use the assemblies to bypass Senate resistance to their agenda, were in full control. Metellus returned in 98, and Marius had to abandon hopes for a censorship (Plut. *Mar.* 31).[32]

The Unification of Italy, 97–89

Despite the failure of Flaccus' and Gaius Gracchus' proposals to upgrade the status of Rome's Italian allies, discontent among the latter had not grown out of control so far. The agrarian law of 111 left substantial allied-occupied tracts of *ager publicus* untouched, and the censors of 97, M. Antonius (consul 99) and L. Valerius Flaccus (consul 100), friends of Marius both, registered unprecedented numbers of allies as citizens: clearly, mechanisms were developing to extend Roman citizenship, at least among the local elites of Italy.

It thus came as a shock to the Italian allies when legislation by the consuls of 95, L. Licinius Crassus and Q. Mucius Scaevola, set up a special court to investigate and try anyone who claimed citizenship without legally qualifying for it. Large numbers of those recently enrolled suddenly became vulnerable; the penalty upon conviction may have been capital. Worse, the law signaled a sharp turnabout in what had appeared to be an accommodating stance on this issue in recent years; the leaders of allied communities, in particular those not privileged by Latin status, reacted with outrage, and for the first time, their continued loyalty became questionable, should Rome persist in this course (Asc. 67 C; see also Chapter 28).[33]

At last, a group of powerful optimates came to understand that both Italy and the *res publica* might slip from their grip unless they seized the initiative. With the backing of L. Crassus and Aemilius Scaurus, *princeps senatus*, the tribune M. Livius Drusus, son of the man who had derailed Gaius Gracchus, in 91 introduced a legislative package aimed at simultaneously solving the allied question and returning control of the courts to the senatorial oligarchy. All Italian allies were to be granted citizenship. Three hundred equestrians (many of them, conceivably, from Italian local elites, now enfranchised) would be added to the Senate, and juries would henceforth be taken from this enlarged 600-member Senate. The *plebs* was to benefit from a colonization program that relied heavily on *ager publicus* hitherto held by allies (App. *B Civ.* 35).[34]

Some senators objected to the "dilution" of their order and the near tripling of the citizen body virtually overnight. The principal losers, however, would be equestrians, especially those connected with the courts and the *publicani*, who stood to lose what made them a force in the state – control of the courts.[35] Among the allies, the great landholders of Etruria and Umbria in particular resented having to pay (as it were) for citizenship with their excess possessions of *ager publicus*.

Nevertheless, several of these bills passed, endorsed by the Senate. In September, however, Crassus died – and with him, crucial support for Drusus. Marshalling the opposition, the consul L. Marcius Philippus (almost certainly aided by Marius, friend of equestrians and allies, and resenting Drusus for stealing the latter issue from him[36]) within a month swayed the Senate to annul the laws already enacted, on grounds of augural violations. Drusus was assassinated a few days before the scheduled vote on his citizenship bill, which thus became moot (App. *B Civ.* 36).[37]

Convinced that the oligarchy would never grant them, by way of citizenship, a fair share in the empire they had helped build, numerous allied states – chiefly in southern Picenum, central Italy, Samnium, Campania, Lucania, and Apulia – now formed their own confederacy, under the name *Italia*, hoping to break Roman domination of Italy and seize the empire by force. Early in 90, they scored notable victories in what is known as the "Social War" (from *socius*, "ally"); but Etruria and Umbria gave little help to them, and when the Latin colonies (except Venusia) decided to support Rome, the allies no longer stood a chance: Rome's resources, in money and man-power, outweighed theirs.[38]

Within two years, the "Italian" confederacy was defeated. Concerned that the Latins and Etruscans might join the insurrection, in 90 the Senate authorized a law by the consul L. Iulius Caesar that offered citizenship to all allies loyal or willing to lay down arms; in 89, a tribunician law extended the offer to any free inhabitant of Italy presenting himself in Rome within 60 days, while a law of the consul Cn. Pompeius Strabo granted Latin status to the communities north of the Po River: the Roman state now encompassed the peninsula. By 88, only parts of Samnium and Lucania remained at war, with no hope of victory (App. *B Civ.* 37–53).[39]

The March on Rome, 88

The Hellenistic kingdom of Pontus, by the Black Sea, under Mithridates VI Eupator (120–63) had been transformed from a backwater into a leading player in Asia Minor. The king had ancient issues with the neighboring rulers of Bithynia and Cappadocia, who asked Rome to intervene on their behalf. A senatorial commission headed by M'. Aquillius (consul 101) arrived in 90, and ordered Mithridates to withdraw from these kingdoms; which he did. Aquillius now urged Nicomedes IV of Bithynia – unable to repay Rome's generosity from his own pocket – to invade and plunder Pontus; which he did. Mithridates counterattacked, and by the fall of 89, had overrun Bithynia, Cappadocia, and the Roman province of Asia. Aquillius was captured and put to death; Mithridates hailed as liberator in most of the cities. The news arrived in Rome late in 89; war was declared. The king gave his response at Ephesus in 88: some 80,000 Romans and Italians throughout Asia Minor were slaughtered, under happy participation of the local population. Later that year, invited by Athens he invaded Greece (App. *Mith.* 1–29).[40]

The Senate had designated the new war (the First Mithridatic, 89–85) a consular province for 88, and the lot gave it to L. Cornelius Sulla (138–78). A patrician from a family long eclipsed, Sulla had been Marius' quaestor in Africa (107–105), and gained recognition for the extradition of Iugurtha from King Bocchus of Mauretania. In the Cimbrian Wars, Sulla served under Catulus; a praetorship in 97, followed by a command in Cilicia, seemed to mark the limit of his advancement. Soon he and Catulus, with appalling rancor, joined Marius' enemies, the powerful optimate clique (*factio*) once centered around the Metelli. The Social War required military talent; Sulla, with a special grant of *imperium* in south-central Italy, emerged as the most successful commander besides Pompeius Strabo (in Picenum), and finally reached the consulship in 88, having married Caecilia Metella, niece of Numidicus and recent widow of Aemilius Scaurus. His colleague, Q. Pompeius Rufus, when tribune in 100, had worked for Numidicus' recall from exile; his son was married to Sulla's daughter (Plut. *Sull.* 1–6; *Mar.* 26–7, 32; App. *B Civ.* 40, 46, 50–1).[41]

C. Iulius Caesar Strabo also had sought the consulship, despite lacking the legal prerequisites,[42] in evident hope of obtaining the Mithridatic command. The new tribune (since December 10, 89) P. Sulpicius Rufus with armed street gangs forced him to desist, thus securing Sulla's victory – as patricians, he and Caesar could not hold the office the same year. Sulpicius, a noble protégé of L. Crassus and a long-time friend of Livius Drusus and Pompeius Rufus, now attempted to resume Drusus' program of reform: he could be confident in either consul's goodwill. The laws granting the allies citizenship had also limited their enrollment to less than a quarter of the number of tribes, so as to minimize their voting power (Vell. 2.20.2; App. *B Civ.* 49); Sulpicius introduced a bill to distribute them equally among all the tribes. It encountered fierce resistance in the Senate, among the urban crowd, and from both consuls, who imposed a halt (*iustitium*) on public business to prevent a vote. Sulpicius, betrayed by his friends and smarting from damaged *dignitas*, employed his street gangs to create pressure; a riot in the Forum forced Sulla to seek refuge in the house of Marius, who now prevailed on him to lift the *iustitium* in return for safe passage from the City. Thus passed the registration law. Sulla went to Nola (Campania), last stronghold of the insurrection, under siege still by his army (Plut. *Sull.* 7–8; *Mar.* 34–5.4; App. *B Civ.* 55–6).[43]

Marius had helped Sulpicius: the tribune returned the favor, transferring by plebiscite the Mithridatic command to Marius, with a special grant of *imperium*. For Sulla, it meant the full measure of public humiliation, coming on the heels of begging Marius for protection. Marius immediately dispatched his officers to Nola, to take over Sulla's army. Playing on the troops' irrational fears that Marius would raise a new army and leave them behind, cut off from the loot of Greece and Asia – this in the face of officers sent to take them there – the consul reminded them of the affront to his *dignitas* and appealed to their obedience. They promptly stoned Marius' officers to death; next, Sulla marched on Rome, where Pompeius Rufus joined him. The Senate sent envoy after envoy ordering him to stop; Marius and Sulpicius, completely taken by surprise, hastily gathered volunteers to defend the City. In vain: a consul with an army of the Roman People now seized Rome, to settle a personal rivalry over power and prestige (Plut. *Sull.* 8.8–9.14; *Mar.* 35.5–6; App. *B Civ.* 57–9).[44] For the *res publica* of the nobles, it signaled the beginning of the end.

Having occupied Rome, Sulla forced the Senate to declare Marius, Sulpicius, and ten others public enemies (*hostes publici*), to be killed on sight; all but Sulpicius escaped – Marius to Africa. Sulpicius' laws were repealed. To prevent a counterstroke after Sulla left for the East, Pompeius Strabo's army in Picenum was given to Pompeius Rufus; the soldiers killed him on arrival, and Strabo remained in command: Sulla's example was already taking hold. With public sentiment in the City now turning ugly, Sulla held elections; two candidates he favored failed. Early in 87, he took his army to Greece (Plut. *Sull.* 10; *Mar.* 35–40; App. *B Civ.* 59–60).[45]

The First Civil War, 87–82

The new consul L. Cornelius Cinna quickly introduced legislation to enroll the new citizens among all 35 tribes. His colleague, Cn. Octavius, led the resistance; during a bloody riot in the Forum, Octavius' armed gangs drove Cinna from the City. A cowed Senate declared Cinna's consulship forfeit, and Octavius had him replaced with L. Cornelius Merula, the *flamen dialis* – the priest of Iuppiter, so encumbered with religious taboo as to be unable to conduct public business. Cinna proceeded to Nola, where a legion Sulla had left behind accepted him as rightful consul. Conducting levies throughout Italy, he recruited an army from the newly enfranchised and, in summer 87, laid siege to Rome. Hearing the news, Marius returned from Africa, gathered volunteers – many of them serfs and slaves – in Etruria, and systematically cut the City off from all supplies. The Senate summoned Pompeius Strabo from Picenum, only to find that he had secret deals with Cinna in hope of a second consulship. A sought-for alliance with the Samnites failed when the Senate rejected their demand for citizenship; in turn, Cinna and Marius readily agreed. By the fall, famine and disease ravaged Rome, and when Pompeius died, his army disintegrated. Bypassing Octavius, senators arranged terms of surrender with Cinna in November. Merula cooperated by abdicating, thus smoothing Cinna's reinstatement as consul; a vote of the People formally lifted Marius' declaration as a public enemy. Making a last show of defiance while their forces entered Rome, Octavius was cut down (Diod. Sic. 38/39.1–4; App. *B Civ.* 64–70; Gran. Lic. 35.1–50 Criniti).[46]

The two leaders now agreed to eliminate some of their opponents. The most prominent were former friends of Marius who had abandoned him: M. Antonius (consul 99), C. Caesar Strabo, and L. Caesar (consul 90), all killed outright; Catulus committed suicide (as did Merula). The immediate death toll probably did not much exceed the 14 victims known by name, but gangs of marauding slaves spread anarchy over the City, until Cinna had them rounded up and executed: the experience no doubt helped shape later allegations of a "Marian massacre." For 86, Cinna announced himself and Marius as consuls, in an election with no other candidates allowed. Sulla was declared a public enemy, his acts annulled, and his house razed.[47]

Marius died on January 13, 86, in his seventh consulship. Cinna had himself reelected consul for 85 and 84, both times with Cn. Papirius Carbo. Other than measures to stabilize the currency and cancel three-quarters of all debts, we know little of Cinna's policy. Immediate family and some friends joined Sulla in the East, but there was no exodus of respectable senators; loathsome though it was to many, they could live with Cinna's regime and hope for the *res publica* to recover. Nor was Cinna in complete control: the Senate showed considerable independence in dealing with Sulla in those years.[48]

Marius' replacement as consul, L. Valerius Flaccus, arrived in Greece in fall 86 with instructions to fight Mithridates – in cooperation with Sulla, should he prove amenable. Evidently, it was hoped that the past unpleasantries could still be settled peacefully. Sulla meanwhile recaptured Greece from the Pontic armies; with Flaccus he made no contact. The latter crossed to Asia, where one of his officers, C. Flavius Fimbria, murdered him and seized command. Fimbria vigorously campaigned against Mithridates, on one occasion nearly capturing him – but for Sulla's quaestor, L. Licinius Lucullus, who refused to assist. Instead, in fall 85, Sulla concluded peace with Mithridates in the treaty of Dardanus, on spectacularly lenient terms. The king withdrew from Bithynia, Cappadocia, and Roman Asia, but was confirmed in undiminished possession of his ancestral realm; he paid an indemnity of 2,000 talents (48 million sesterces), and was recognized as a Roman ally. Thus Sulla gained freedom of action vis-à-vis the government in Rome. He immediately moved against Fimbria, whose troops chose not to fight; Fimbria committed suicide.

Sulla stayed in Asia until 84, presenting the province with the bill for defecting and cheering the massacre of Romans and Italians in 88: the crushing sum of 20,000 talents, payable at once by those cities that had sided with the king, in addition to housing and paying Sulla's troops during the winter (at 50 times their normal rate). A handful of cities had kept faith with Rome: they were exempt, and rewarded with privileges and territory (Plut. *Sull.* 11–25; *Luc.* 3; App. *Mith.* 30–63).[49]

Still in 85, Sulla wrote to the Senate, announcing his intention to return and punish those who had wronged him; others need not worry. News of the peace of Dardanus had already prompted fears that he might not shrink from full-blown civil war, and Cinna and Carbo were raising money, troops, and political support in Italy. The *princeps senatus*, however, L. Valerius Flaccus (consul 100), prevailed on the Senate to give Sulla a conciliatory response, in effect offering him safe return if he would let bygones be bygones; the consuls meanwhile were instructed to halt their mobilization. They complied; but understanding the need for seasoned troops in case diplomacy should fail, Cinna launched an unpopular campaign in Dalmatia early in 84. Soldiers slew him at Ancona. Carbo tried again to mobilize in Italy, but was recalled to Rome to elect another colleague; prohibitive omens, though, prevented that. His control was slipping.

Sulla responded to the Senate that with his army he could better effect their safety and happiness than they could his; but if he was restored to his rank and property, he would not take matters further. On reaching Brundisium, his own envoys learned of

Cinna's death and Carbo's troubles, and seeing the government in disarray, they immediately returned to alert him to these developments; he promptly prepared to invade Italy (Plut. *Sull.* 11–25; *Luc.* 3; App. *Mith.* 30–63).[50]

Thus the attempt to stave off war by negotiating and not mobilizing – lest it provoke the adversary to strike before he was ready – had its deserved result. Hasty levies now commenced throughout Italy, and by Senate decree, the new citizens were assured of equal registration in all 35 tribes.[51] The consuls of 83, C. Norbanus, a "new man" and old Marian, and L. Cornelius Scipio Asiagenus, noblest of nobles, symbolized how all of Rome, and all of Italy, stood against the invader; but such resolve was brittle – Sulla's army towered above the Senate's levies in experience of combat and of victory, as everybody knew.

Landing at Brundisium in the spring of 83, Sulla defeated Norbanus, then entered peace talks with Scipio while encouraging his troops to fraternize; soon the consul's entire army went over to Sulla.[52] The government never recovered from this opening double blow. Cn. Pompeius, age 23, son of the consul of 89 and biggest landlord in Picenum, raised a private army from his father's veterans and tenants, and offered his services to Sulla, who greeted him as *imperator.* Soon others flocked to Sulla's headquarters – "ruffians and intriguers" for the most part,[53] but also men of substance who lent respectability to the enterprise, like young M. Licinius Crassus, Q. Caecilius Metellus Pius (son of Numidicus), and L. Marcius Philippus, the consul of 91 who had broken Livius Drusus. During the winter, Sulla assured the peoples of Italy (except the Samnites) that he would leave untouched their citizenship and voting rights, thus eliminating a major incentive to fight against him. The election of C. Marius the Son (age 26) as consul for 82, along with Carbo, was a blatant attempt to rally the new citizens; to little avail. He was beaten near Praeneste and bottled up therein, and Sulla now took Rome. When his lieutenants gained victories in the north and in Etruria, desertion grew rampant among the government's forces; soon, Samnite levies provided its most reliable units. (Sulla killed all Samnite prisoners: App. *B Civ.* 87, 93–4.) In a last-ditch effort to relieve Marius in Praeneste, an army of Samnites and Lucanians marched on Rome, and was utterly destroyed on November 1, 82, in the battle at the Colline Gate; Crassus deserves much of the credit. Praeneste soon surrendered; young Marius committed suicide. Pompeius captured Carbo near Sicily and put him to death before year's end. The First Civil War was over – at least in Italy.

Sulla the Fortunate, 82–78

Soon after the Colline Gate, while thousands of prisoners were being slaughtered in the Circus Flaminius, Sulla ordered all who had supported the previous regime (as magistrates or otherwise) "proscribed," i.e., their names advertised on posters throughout Italy, to be killed. Each head drew 50,000 sesterces in reward; their property was sold at auction, their sons and grandsons barred from public office. The lists included some 2,000 names, perhaps 100 of them senators; some escaped, but the majority was hunted down. On land confiscated where the Cinno-Marians had enjoyed particular support (Etruria, Umbria, Campania, Lucania, and Samnium), Sulla settled 23 legions of veterans: together with the proscriptions, the most radical redistribution of property in Roman history – to that point (Plut. *Sull.* 30–1; App. *B Civ.* 95–6, 100, 103).[54]

Late in 82, special legislation authorized the *interrex* (a "caretaker" picked by and from the patrician members of the Senate at a time, known as *interregnum*, when no regular magistrates were left in office) L. Flaccus (consul 100) to name Sulla dictator – the first in 120 years – with extraordinary powers to make laws and reorganize the government (Plut. *Sull.* 32; App. *B Civ.* 97–103).[55] Mostly in 81, he enacted a coherent if questionable program to stabilize the nobles' traditional collective rule, centered in the Senate.

That body, from casualties in civil war, proscription, and even natural attrition, stood now at perhaps half its customary strength of 300; Sulla increased it to 600, handpicking the new members, mostly individuals of equestrian property (not necessarily rank) or less. Juries for the criminal courts were now drawn from this enlarged Senate only.[56] All former magistrates from quaestor upward henceforth became senators automatically, without censorial intervention;[57] the quaestorship itself was made a prerequisite for praetorship and consulate. In view both of the enlarged Senate and increased administrative needs, Sulla raised the number of praetors to eight, and of quaestors to twenty.[58]

The tribunes of the plebs were stripped of their right to introduce bills,[59] and barred from holding any higher magistracy. (Their veto powers remained untouched.) This effectively terminated legislation by plebiscite, and sought to reduce to political irrelevance an ancient office inseparable, in the public mind, from popular rights and freedoms: it was bound to generate resentment, exploitable by ambitious individuals.

Sulla triumphed over Mithridates in January 81, and henceforth went by the official surname "Felix" ("fortunate"; i.e., favored by the gods). Two months later, Cn. Pompeius, having destroyed the remnants of the previous government in Sicily and Africa, celebrated his own triumph: never before had a private citizen with *imperium* done so. The dictator approved, if grudgingly, and called him "Magnus" – "the Great." The name stuck. Later in the year Sulla abdicated his dictatorship at a public gathering,[60] then asked if anyone present wished him to account for any of his actions. No one did.

Following a second consulship, in 80, Sulla retired to Puteoli. Early in 78, while having – as a private citizen! – a local official strangled for embezzling, he suffered a hemorrhage brought on, apparently, by liver failure; he died the next day (Plut. *Sull.* 37).[61] Convinced that his own *dignitas* and the welfare of the *res publica* were inseparable, he had crushed the latter to defend the former; he attempted to restore it in good faith, but having exterminated all those who disagreed with his understanding of a healthy commonwealth, it comes as no surprise that its senatorial rulers, as reorganized by him, should prove ill suited to govern in any manner but the crassest self-interest. The hundreds of – by the nobles' standards – insubstantial "new men" now filling the Senate owed everything to his settlement, without an elitist tradition of public service to guide and restrain their appetites; the nobles who had survived, by abandoning the Republic and joining the usurper, lacked all credibility in professing to uphold collective government by the Senate. The opposing towns and districts of Italy, ravaged by depredation during the Civil War and by reprisals afterward (some 70,000 Sullan veterans settled on their land), had no grounds for loyalty towards the ruling class he put in place. Most of all, "Sulla could not abolish his own example."[62]

The Last, Best Hope? 78–70

Within weeks of Sulla's death, the consul M. Aemilius Lepidus was agitating for restoration of the tribunes' powers and of the dispossessed to their property, and amnesty for the proscribed. In summer 78, expropriated landowners in Etruria forcibly expelled Sullan veterans settled there. Dispatched along with his colleague, Q. Lutatius Catulus, to restore order, Lepidus openly sided with the previous owners; joined by many of the surviving proscribed, notably M. Perperna (praetor by 83), he marched on Rome toward year's end, demanding a second consulship. In January, 77, the Senate, roused from vaccillation by L. Philippus (consul 91), voted the "last decree," instructing Catulus to defend the City; about the same time, Pompeius Magnus was sent with special *imperium* to Cisalpine Gaul, where he quickly crushed and executed its pro-Lepidan commander, M. Iunius Brutus. Meanwhile, in a fight near Rome, Catulus forced Lepidus to withdraw to Sardinia, where he soon died. Perperna then took his army to Spain, which was already slipping from the Sullan Senate's grasp.[63]

Spain's last Cinno-Marian commander, Q. Sertorius (praetor by 83), a "new man" from Nursia, had briefly been forced out by a Sullan army in 81; but with the support of Lusitanian tribes and Marian refugees in Farther Spain, he returned from Mauretania in 80. The next commander in Farther Spain, Q. Metellus Pius (consul 80), pursued the war vigorously and avoided defeat, but proved unable to cope with Sertorius' guerrilla methods; by early 77, the latter controlled large parts of the province of Nearer Spain as well. At this juncture, Perperna arrived and joined forces with Sertorius. Thus in summer 77, both consuls declining the command, Pompeius was sent to Nearer Spain, again with special *imperium* as a private citizen. In 76 Pompeius and Metellus, cooperating closely, destroyed Sertorius' ability to field large armies; by 75, he had lost Lusitania and was reduced to a small area in northern Celtiberia.[64] Yet at the same time, Sertorius moved to take possession of the province of Asia.

For all Sulla's generosity in 85, Mithridates' relations with Rome had remained tense. Besides enduring unprovoked raids (the "Second" Mithridatic War) by the governor of Asia, L. Licinius Murena, in 82, the king had not succeeded in having the treaty of Dardanus ratified. In consequence, he was secure neither in the possession of his kingdom nor in his status as a Roman ally, and by 75 had reached the conclusion that another war was unavoidable. Hoping to keep Roman forces tied down in Spain and to improve the quality of his own, he concluded an alliance with Sertorius: the king gave 3,000 talents (72 million sesterces) and a fleet of 40 ships, while Sertorius sent officers, under one M. Marius, to train the royal army in the Roman manner. Once Mithridates invaded Roman Asia, Marius was to take command as Sertorius' acting governor. (The king received Bithynia and Cappadocia; how long he would have kept to the agreement about Asia is everybody's guess.) The Civil War, outside Italy, thus continued – and merged into the Third Mithridatic War.[65]

Nicomedes IV of Bithynia died in 75, bequeathing his kingdom to the Roman People. Early in 74, the consul M. Aurelius Cotta went to the new province, lest Mithridates attempt to seize it; indeed, the king was mobilizing. Meanwhile the other consul, L. Licinius Lucullus (Sulla's right-hand man during the First Civil War), contrived to have Cilicia assigned to himself, along with Asia and the overall command against Mithridates, war now being virtually certain. Lucullus arrived in Asia in the fall; Mithridates invaded Cappadocia and Bithynia, and defeated Cotta at Calchedon. He next laid siege to Cyzicus, yet unable to provision his forces by sea in winter and cut off on land by Lucullus, Mithridates abandoned the siege with heavy losses in spring 73. An expeditionary force under Marius ran into Lucullus' fleet in the Aegean; Marius was captured and put to death. By autumn 73, the Romans controlled Bithynia, and Mithridates withdrew to Pontus. Lucullus followed and destroyed the king's last army at Cabira in 72; Mithridates narrowly escaped to Armenia, King Tigranes being his son-in-law. In 71, Cotta returned to Rome, and Bithynia was added to Lucullus' command.

To pay Sulla's indemnity in 84, the cities of Asia had to borrow heavily from Roman bankers (the only ones with sufficient capital); with the exorbitant interest charged – 48 percent and up – by 70 the cities' collective debt had risen sixfold. Now Lucullus put an end to this obscene exploitation, canceling interest payments that exceeded principal, and limiting rates; within four years, the province had paid off all debts. This was his finest hour; no other act did as much to buttress Roman rule in Asia Minor. Equestrian men of finance were not amused.[66]

A different crisis arose close to home in 73. A troop of gladiators led by a Thracian named Spartacus broke from its "school" at Capua; the news spread rapidly, and tens of thousands of slaves and impoverished free persons joined the uprising. Rome had fought two fully-fledged Slave Wars in Sicily (135–132, 104–101) within memory; now the Spartacus War engulfed all Italy as far north as Cisalpine Gaul. The slaves routed several Roman armies in 73 and 72; at which point M. Crassus (praetor by 73) was invested with special *imperium* and unlimited resources. In spring, 71 he utterly destroyed the Slave army in Lucania. Spartacus fell in battle; Crassus had 6,000 survivors crucified along the Via Appia, and was awarded an ovation.[67]

In Spain, Sertorius since 75 had been steadily losing control. As Spanish communities kept surrendering to Pompeius, he reacted with savage reprisals, against the natives and against Romans he suspected of secretly trying to strike a deal. Unable to repeat the spectacular feats of his early years and having alienated many of his senior officers, he was assassinated by Perperna late in 73. Perperna now assumed command, but before the end of 72, Pompeius had defeated, captured, and executed him. In spring 71, Metellus and Pompeius returned to Italy.[68]

At age 36, Pompeius had held almost uninterrupted military command for 13 years, without election to a magistracy. Now he sought the consulship, six years short of the legal minimum age, without the prerequisite offices of quaestor and praetor. The Senate voted an exemption: they could not, in good conscience and sound mind, insist that he start at the bottom of the hierarchy. He was elected, together with Crassus, and on December 29, 71 celebrated his second triumph.[69]

Emasculation of the tribunate had not achieved the domestic tranquility Sulla had desired, and grown into a source of popular discontent instead; already in 75, the ban on ex-tribunes' seeking higher office was lifted. Now Pompeius and Crassus – champions of the Sullan takeover – as consuls cooperated in dismantling the remaining restrictions.[70] Sulla's all-senatorial juries had performed discreditably; a law of the praetor L. Aurelius Cotta replaced them with mixed panels: one-third each senators, equestrians, and *tribuni aerarii* (possessing the equestrian property qualification, but socially distinct and inferior). The compromise proved viable, and ended the long struggle over the composition of the courts. For the first time since 86, censors were elected; they expelled 64 members from the Senate. Employing his revived powers, the tribune (A.?) Plautius sponsored a law – without known opposition – that recalled the surviving followers of Lepidus and Sertorius from exile, insofar as they were not among Sulla's proscribed. In a final gesture of self-restraint, Pompeius and Crassus both declined their provinces on stepping down.

The year 70 thus closed on a note of political conciliation and reform. Three grave military threats – to Roman rule in East and West, to established society in Italy, and to the senatorial oligarchy as "restored" by Sulla – had been terminated, some of Sulla's worst excesses rectified; and Pompeius Magnus, now a senator, had to some extent regularized his literally "outstanding" position in the state. To expect him to recede fully into the nominal equality of power and prestige shared by the nobles would be naïve; a reasonable course of action lay in employing his talents in whatever exceptional situations the future might present, in working with him, not against him. More than anything, he craved the recognition and approval of the optimates whose regime he had helped secure by force of arms: to diminish or withhold that recognition would be foolish and irrational. Men, of course, can be both.

Guide to Further Reading

No coherent narrative dedicated to this pivotal epoch in the disintegration of republican government exists, although Badian 1958a and Gruen 1968 often come close, as do the articles collected in Gabba 1976. Bernstein 1978 offers a useful biographical account of Tiberius Gracchus, though Badian 1972b has not been superseded on the political and constitutional issues; Stockton 1979 provides a thoughtful survey of Gaius Gracchus' legislation. Gargola 1995 examines land grants from an unusual perspective, in the context of Roman public ritual, and Badian 1972a furnishes an eminently readable introduction to the world of public contracts and tax collection. Mouritsen's innovative approach to the "allied question" (1998) is a fascinating mix of perspicacity and blindness to the evidence. Pompey (Seager 2002), Sertorius (Spann 1987), Lucullus (Keaveney 1992), and Marius (Evans 1994) all have found extensive treatment in recent biographies. On Sulla, Keaveney 1982c offers thorough documentation and engaging discussion, though bordering on the idolatrous; a diametrically opposite interpretation in Badian 1962b and 1970b. Good treatments of Mithridates and the Slave Wars can be found in McGing 1986 and Bradley 1989. Among commentaries on the principal ancient sources (Sallust, Appian, and Plutarch), Gabba 1958 is indispensable; see also Paul 1984, McGushin 1992–4, and Konrad 1994a. On social history and demography, the great work of Brunt 1971a and 1988c remains fundamental, though important correctives have recently been advanced by Lo Cascio 1994, Morley 2001, and Rosenstein 2002; their findings' implications on the political history of the period still await synthesis. And while the work does not lend itself to easy reading from cover to cover, serious students of the Roman Republic will be well-advised to gain a thorough familiarity with Broughton 1951–86.

Notes

1 Epstein 1987: *passim*.
2 Lintott 1992: 34–43; Gargola 1995: 114–46. Unless indicated otherwise, all references to Appian in this chapter are to Book 1 of the *Civil Wars*.
3 Lintott 1992: 212, 1994c: 62–5.
4 Brunt 1988c: 27–73, 243–5; but see Badian 1972b: 683–4, 717–19.
5 Bernstein 1978: 110–11.
6 Other sources in Broughton 1951–86: 1492–7. Badian 1972b is essential.
7 Badian 1983a: 162; cf. 1972b: 706–12; Cloud 1994: 491–2.
8 Badian 1972b: 715, 722–3.
9 Badian 1972b: 712–16; cf. 1958a: 173–4.
10 Gargola 1997.
11 Badian 1970–1: 391–2; Hands 1967, 1976; *contra*, Brunt 1988c: 94; Mouritsen 1998: 112–13.
12 Broughton 1951–86: 1.513–20; Stockton 1979: 114–75, 226–39.
13 Garnsey and Rathbone 1985.
14 Balsdon 1938 (fundamental); Jones 1960: 39–42; Brunt 1988c: 194–239; Cloud 1994: 505–23; *contra*, Gruen 1968: 86–91; Griffin 1973; Stockton 1979:138–51.
15 Text and commentary in Crawford 1996b: 1.39–112.
16 Brunt 1988c: 144–54.
17 Jones 1960: 35–9.
18 Lintott 1994c: 82; Mouritsen 1998: 120.
19 Lintott 1999a: 88–93.
20 Lintott 1992: 48–55.
21 Broughton 1951–86: 1.531–8; Paul 1984.
22 Brunt 1971a: 82.
23 Keppie 1984: 59–68.
24 Gruen 1968: 158–9; Griffin 1973: 117–18; *contra*, Ferrary 1979: 85–91.

25   Gruen 1968: 165–8; Ferrary 1979: 92–105.
26   Badian 1984: 102 n. 6.
27   Broughton 1951–86: 1.560, 563.
28   Broughton 1951–86: 1.574–8.
29   But see Badian 1984: 108–10, 120.
30   Linderski 1983.
31   Badian 1984: 111–17.
32   Badian 1996a.
33   Badian 1970–1: 390–409; Brunt 1988c: 93–143.
34   Badian 1958a: 216–19; *contra*, Mouritsen 1998: 120–7.
35   Hands 1972.
36   Badian 1963–4: 150–1.
37   Broughton 1951–86: 2.20–5.
38   Gabba 1994a: 113–20.
39   Broughton 1951–86: 2.25–39; Mouritsen 1998: 153–71.
40   McGing 1986: 1–124.
41   Badian 1957; Kallet-Marx 1990: 129–33.
42   Seager 1994a: 165–8.
43   Seager 1994a: 165–9.
44   Keaveney 1983.
45   Broughton 1951–86: 2.39–45.
46   Broughton 1951–86: 2.45–53; Katz 1976a: 523–38; 1976b.
47   Diod. Sic. 38/39.4; Livy *Per.* 70; Plut. *Mar.* 43–5; *Sull.* 22; App. *B Civ.* 71–5; Bulst 1964;
     Seager 1994a: 171–9.
48   Broughton 1951–86: 2.53–62; Badian 1962b: 51–5; *contra*, Keaveney 1984.
49   Badian 1962b: 56–7.
50   Badian 1962b: 57–60; *contra*, Keaveney 1982c: 117–24.
51   Brunt 1988c: 132–6.
52   Plut. *Sull.* 27–32; *Pomp.* 6–12; Livy *Per.* 85–8; App. *B Civ.* 79–94; Broughton 1951–86:
     2.62–74.
53   Badian 1962b: 60. Prime examples are L. Sergius Catilina and C. Verres.
54   Hinard 1985: 104–10.
55   Broughton 1951–86: 2.74–85; Badian 1970b; Keaveney 1982c: 148–203.
56   Brunt 1988c: 218.
57   See, however, Brunt 1988c: 211 n.42.
58   Balsdon 1939; Brennan 2000: 2.388–400.
59   Keaveney 1982c: 169 with n.3; *contra*, Gabba 1958: 273–5.
60   Seager 1994a: 197, 205.
61   Keaveny and Madden 1982: 94–5.
62   Syme 1939: 17; Badian 1970b; 1990b: 26.
63   Sall. *Hist.* 1.54–83; Plut. *Pomp.* 16; App. *B Civ.* 105–7; Gran. Lic. 36.33–48; Broughton
     1951–86: 2. 85–92.
64   Plut. *Sert.* 1–22; App. *B Civ.* 108–12; Broughton 1951–86: 74–100. Spann 1987; Konrad
     1994a; on the chronology, Konrad 1995; *contra*, Brennan 2000: 2.503–15.
65   Plut. *Sert.* 23–4; App. *Mith.* 64–8; McGing 1986: 132–9; Konrad 1994a: 190–202.
66   Plut. *Luc.* 5–23; App. *Mith.* 69–83; Memnon *FGrH* 434 F 1.27–37; Broughton
     1951–86: 2.100–31. Keaveney 1992: 64–98; on the chronology, Konrad 1995: 170–9;
     contra, Brennan 2000: 2.559–62.

67 Plut. *Crass.* 8–11; App. *B Civ.* 116–20; Broughton 1951–86: 2.109–26; Marshall 1976; Ward 1977.
68 Plut. *Sert.* 25–7; App. *B Civ.* 112–15; Konrad 1994a: 202–20.
69 Broughton 1951–86: 2.121–31.
70 But see Seager 1994b: 227.

CHAPTER 9

The Final Crisis (69–44)

W. Jeffrey Tatum

Romans of every order could well believe, in the consulship of Hortensius Hortalus and Quintus Metellus, that stability, so long dissolved in the acid of terror and warfare, was again fixed and hard. The consuls of 69 presided over a year remarkable for its signs of confidence and restored virtue: the censors, elected in 70, completed their work and celebrated the *lustrum*, by means of which ritual the restored and purified state received, after so long an interval, the sanction of the divine order. And yet this was to be the final *lustrum* of the Republic (Aug. *Anc.* 8. 2): in a mere 20 years, Rome would again be plunged into civil war, after which peace would be restored only by way of an enduring autocracy.[1]

A New Beginning

Intensive moralism was not an innovation of the Augustan age. The census concluded in 69 was rigorous: 64 senators were expelled from the body. Plainly the censors agreed with Sulla that moral reform was vital in the aftermath of civil war, a disaster that could only be attributed to depravity on the part of some in the ruling order.[2] It was the regular responsibility of censors to organize the People by classes, thereby enabling each man to exercise his franchise. In the aftermath of the Social War, the citizenry had become expanded, but various disputes, and the civil war, had delayed the actual enfranchisement of Rome's former allies, which was entirely completed only in 84. Finally, in 69, they were enrolled and, thereafter, eligible to vote.[3] The sheer abundance and the geographical range of the new population altered Roman politics drastically. Wealthy Italians possessed regional influence and important votes in the centuriate assembly that aspiring politicians needed to court. At the same time, the expanded citizen body also introduced many new candidates, whose presence exacerbated the already keen competition for offices at every level. Fear of failure amplified the individual noble's sense of *dignitas* and entitlement. It also encouraged all candidates to resort to dishonest means, principally bribery, in order to attract supporters from every order. Illegal electioneering – *ambitus* – became so pervasive a feature of electoral campaigns that most politicians regarded it as indispensable (see also Chapter 1).[4]

Despite this decalescence of political society, the nobility continued to dominate in the consulship and in the Senate.[5] Nor was the aristocracy threatened by the urban poor. Naturally the Senate could not be entirely indifferent to their circumstances. But, outside emergencies, the status quo could be maintained. The constant practice of electioneering enabled the elite regularly to reinforce their superiority in a context that advertised the People's sovereignty, during which exercises the masses displayed their gratitude for the preservation of their meager entitlements. The crowd's volatility was recognized, but the masses were dangerous only when united or organized, conditions that were carefully guarded against by the governing class: hence the Senate's hostility toward demagogues.[6] But it must never be forgotten that the Roman constitution rested on the sovereignty of the People as well as the authority of the Senate. One should not minimize the ideological content of Roman politics: for some (the *optimates*), the prestige of the Senate remained paramount; for others (the *populares*), concern for the sovereignty of the People was not simply a means to personal popularity but a duty and essential to sustaining the Republic. But there existed a great space between these two positions for posturing and maneuver. Historians no longer regard *populares* and *optimates* as collectives resembling political parties.[7] But nor should it be assumed that *popularis* activities ever constituted a movement against the Senate: all senators were aristocrats invested in the continuity of existing institutions of the Republic. Loyalty to these institutions was not in itself controversial. The actualization of that loyalty, however, was a different matter, more contested and vexatious.[8]

It is more difficult for us to assess the economic circumstances of the countryside. The ancient sources lay great stress on the diminution of the peasantry (see Chapters 27 and 28). The evidence of archaeology and the application of reason must alter this view: peasants subsisted and were even necessary to the owners of commercial villas devoted to olive and wine production.[9] Nevertheless, certain regions, such as Etruria, suffered sorely. Like the urban poor, peasants had few possibilities for organizing themselves into influential bodies. Organization and influence are what the peasantry would find, ultimately, in the legions, whose requirements the Senate tended to despise and whose loyalty, in the end, it let slip.[10] That connection, however, was too dimly perceived at this stage. It had been proposed, in 70, that grants of land be made to the veterans of the Sertorian War, but the proposal was dropped on the grounds that its execution was unaffordable.[11] The veterans' supine reaction must have convinced the Senate of its unquestioned supremacy.

Pompey the Great

The restored Republic was active in the early 60s. Numerous reforms were debated and many were passed into law, always contentiously and nearly always raucously.[12] It would be a mistake to make too much of that: Roman politics, simply put, were rough. The story of Rome's final crisis, however, must concentrate on Pompey and must begin with the legislation of A. Gabinius, a tribune of 67, who proposed an extraordinary command to deal with the longstanding problem of piracy in the Mediterranean. Pirates represented a serious threat to the urban plebs: by 67 they had disrupted Rome's vital grain imports.[13] The tribune proposed that one man be assigned the task of eradicating them. His command, the term of which was to be three years, was to be based on a grant of *imperium* empowering him to act over the whole of the sea, over all islands, and along all coasts up to 50 miles inland. The actual commander was to be chosen subsequently to the passage of this law, but popular sentiment made it inevitable that he be Pompey.

The sheer amplitude of the command provoked bitter opposition: so much power and such an opportunity for glory must not be entrusted to one man, and certainly not to a man whose lightning career threatened to rise too high, thereby setting the remainder of the aristocracy in the shade. "Pompey is an illustrious man," his opponent, Q. Lutatius Catulus (cos. 78), conceded in a public speech, "but he is already too illustrious for a free Republic" (Vell. Pat. 2.32.1). Although some smaller fry, like young Julius Caesar, sided with Gabinius, the leading men were united in their opposition.[14] But the People were equally forceful in their support for the measure. The *Lex Gabinia* was passed, and, on the very day of the great man's election to this command, the price of grain in Rome fell. After three months the campaign was successfully concluded, and it was now beyond dispute that Pompey was Rome's greatest military commander.[15]

In 66 one of the tribunes, C. Manilius, proposed a measure whereby Pompey should be assigned the provinces of Cilicia, Bithynia, and Pontus in order for him to assume command of the war against Mithridates, the Pontic king whom Sulla had failed to conquer in the 80s and who was once again at war with Rome (this time since the late 70s). By this one law, three provincial commanders, Lucullus, M'. Acilius Glabrio (cos. 67) and Q. Marcius Rex (cos. 68), would be superseded by Pompey. Their supporters, and Pompey's enemies, combined to resist the measure, but with little hope of success. Although Lucullus had won brilliant successes against Mithridates and Tigranes (the king of Armenia and Mithridates' son-in-law), and had insisted that the war was all but over, the struggle thereafter had become more arduous. But by then Lucullus had put himself in a position to be accused of protracting the war. At the same time, his attempts to regulate the depredations of the *publicani* in Asia had made him hated by the equestrian order, which employed its clout to remove him from authority. Already in 69 the *publicani* had succeeded in arranging for the removal of Asia from Lucullus' command; in 68, after an attempt was made to recall Lucullus, Cilicia was taken from him and assigned to Marcius Rex (cos. 68); and in 67 Bithynia and Pontus were transferred to Glabrio. Neither Glabrio nor Marcius Rex had accomplished anything remarkable during their tenures, and the collapse of Lucullus' stature in Rome was evident in the disintegration of his command.[16] Catulus and Hortensius redeployed the argument that what Manilius proposed deposited too much power in the hands of one man, but this bill enjoyed broad support in the Senate: four distinguished consulars backed it, and proof of its inevitable passage can be observed in the speech delivered by the praetor Cicero (*On the Manilian Law*), himself keen to win Pompey's favor.

Again Pompey triumphed. He drove Mithridates from Asia Minor and quickly dominated the region, reducing Tigranes to dutiful alliance and establishing a wary relationship with the Parthians. Throughout the east Pompey made detailed and lasting administrative arrangements (many lasting until late in the empire) – without the usual and traditional assistance of a senatorial delegation, thereby vindicating the anxieties of his enemies. At last Mithridates simply died, and what remained of his domains Pompey again settled without senatorial advice.[17] By 62, he was ready to return to Rome.

Cicero and the Catilinarian Conspiracy

The politics of the city were far from quiet in Pompey's absence. The elections of 66 were marred by scandal: P. Autronius Paetus and P. Cornelius Sulla were returned as consuls, only to be prosecuted and convicted for *ambitus*. The event was unnerving in its implications for the soundness of Rome's government, a circumstance that helps to explain why the consul who presided over the necessary by-election, L. Volcacius Tullus, refused to accept the candidacy of L. Sergius Catilina: Catiline had recently returned from Africa; his conduct as governor had been deplored in senatorial resolutions and his prosecution for extortion was certain. The new consuls were L. Manlius Torquatus and L. Aurelius Cotta.

Ambitious men were keen to win favor from the absent Pompey. A tribune of 66, C. Memmius (familiar from the poetry of Lucretius and Catullus), prosecuted Lucullus' brother, unsuccessfully, and roused the People in opposition to Lucullus' triumph: similar tactics delayed the triumphs of Q. Metellus Creticus and Marcius Rex. The great man's enemies responded by prosecuting and convicting Manilius (whom Pompey did nothing to assist). In the midst of this sharp practice, it was rumored that Autronius and Sulla were plotting to murder the consuls, for whom a bodyguard was voted by the Senate (Dio 36.44.4).

Few aspiring men had taken more care to cultivate Pompey than Julius Caesar, who had supported the *Lex Gabinia* as well as the *Lex Manilia*. Though his origin was patrician, Caesar enjoyed greater splendor from his maternal lineage (his mother was an Aurelia Cotta). Unfortunately, his family had taken the Marian side in the 80s, a circumstance that Caesar overcame but which rendered him somewhat suspect to the Sullan establishment. Hence his energies in military service and especially in the courts (he was a gifted orator), all devoted to political advancement, an undertaking that required influential friends – like Pompey the Great. But young Caesar never intended to remain one of Pompey's minions. As aedile in 65 Caesar plunged himself into debt in order to produce dazzling games, and he adorned the city with monuments to the victories of Marius, by means of whose popular symbolism he could distinguish himself from his rivals for the People's affections. At the same time, he married a granddaughter of Sulla, Pompeia. He demonstrated similar versatility by securing the friendship, and the financial support, of Crassus, Pompey's rival.

It is an unfortunate reality for the student of the late Republic that we are so poorly informed about Crassus' actions. His importance is undoubted: he possessed wealth and clout enough that few had the courage to cross him. But he preferred to act behind the scenes, so clear sightings are few. Crassus was elected, with Catulus as his colleague, to the censorship in 65. Crassus brought with him an ambitious agenda: he wanted to enfranchise the inhabitants of Transpadana in Cisalpine Gaul and he sought recognition for Ptolemy Alexander's bequest of his kingdom to Rome, a decision that would result in the annexation of Egypt. It was obvious that Crassus would have benefited personally from either scheme, in terms of electoral influence amongst the Transpadani or, in Egypt, owing to the appreciation of *publicani* (and Crassus himself was an active investor in the provinces).[18] Catulus naturally resisted both policies, but the tribunes, and Caesar, supported Crassus' idea of annexing Egypt. Cicero attacked the policy as unjust.[19] And, in the end, both censors resigned in frustration.

Cicero was rapidly rising to prominence in the 60s. Though a "new man" from a municipality, his eloquence and his brilliant intellect, his strong connections within the equestrian order, all in combination with integrity and prudence, rendered him attractive to most segments of Roman society and compensated for his deficient heritage. He challenged corruption, he championed the tribunate and popular rights, he was a loyal friend of Pompey, he recognized the importance of the *publicani*, yet he did not fail to concede the primacy of the Senate and its traditional values.[20] He was elected praetor for 66 at the top of the polls.

For all his talents, Cicero was elevated to the consulship as much by events as by his own industry. Electoral competition, keen and crowded, left losers, whose dignity and personal fortunes became dubious. Debt had become a serious problem. The sheer expense of political life led many senators into debts that could only be discharged by parting with the property on which their status as senators depended. And so they risked ruin. Economic activity in Rome was robust: senators and equestrians were centers of investment and lending; consequently, their difficulties affected other social groups, such as rural tenants and city shopkeepers and even the urban poor. And there was debt in some provinces as well. Romans were unkind and unsympathetic to debtors. The situation, then, was anxious, even potentially danger-ous, but not susceptible to candid or rational analysis – or remedy.[21]

But it was clear to all that sound leadership was necessary. The discontents of the poor must not become a source of disturbance or an invitation to demagogues, nor did straitened senators wish to be discovered for failures or lose their status. In 64 the Senate decreed the suppression of the city's *collegia*, the neighborhood associations, religious and occupational, that organized the urban plebs into societies vital to their personal concerns but, under the circumstances, worrying to the elite. The censors elected in 64, after the abdication of Catulus and Crassus, were prevented from revising the Senate's roster by tribunes fearful of their own expulsion: their success in blocking the revision indicates the extent of their support in the body itself, and the censors had no choice but to resign. Crisis, or even the appearance of crisis, had to be averted, especially from the perspective of Pompey's enemies and rivals: the comple-tion of his eastern assignment would soon make it possible for him to bring his army home to Italy; it was not entirely unreasonable for his opponents to fear a second Sulla in the person of Sulla's hatchet man, and, even for those who were not frightened by that prospect, Pompey's career had given ample evidence of his talent for exploiting public problems for his own advancement. Pompey was a remedy that many in the oligarchy will have wanted to avoid, which meant that the results of the consular elections were especially important.

There were three significant candidates in the consular elections for 63: Cicero, C. Antonius, and Catiline. Antonius, son of the distinguished consul of 99, had been marked by disgrace: evicted from the Senate in the census of 70, he had regained his station and had reached the praetorship in 66. Catiline, denied an opportunity to stand for the consulship in 66, was prevented from standing in the subsequent year by a prosecution for extortion. Cicero's superiority to either of his rivals was as patent in 64 as it is today. Antonius and Catiline combined against the new man, each freighting their campaigns with emphasis on lineage, and Catiline at least enjoyed a reputation for physical courage. But, in the end, Cicero was returned at the top of the polls. Between his rivals there was little to choose, and Antonius defeated Catiline by a narrow margin.

Cicero's leadership was immediately tested. A tribune, P. Servilius Rullus, proposed an agrarian law that would establish colonies and assign public lands both to veterans returning from the Mithridatic War and to the poor. There would be no confiscations; instead, public funds, including the much-anticipated spoil from the east, would guarantee fair purchases of privately held or occupied land. Cicero opposed the bill, in the Senate and in the Forum. His eloquence and his high standing with the populace combined to defeat it. This was, for many amongst the elite, the predictable benefit of sound leadership: the People trusted Cicero and could be persuaded by him, even when he was devoting himself to the most conservative interests of the prosperous classes, in whose debt the orator was well aware that he stood after his triumph over his noble rivals in the consular elections.

But more serious tests awaited. Catiline was again a candidate for the consulship. In this campaign, he postured as the champion of debtors, a category that included farmers, residents of the city, and members of the aristocracy desperate for a new beginning. He also engaged in ample bribery. But Catiline was again defeated. He began to turn to conspiracy as a means of restoring his lost *dignitas*.[22] Other straitened aristocrats recollected Sulla and saw opportunities for themselves in civil disturbance. News of plotting came to Crassus, who informed Cicero. But there were other perturbations. In Etruria ruined peasants, many of them former Sullan troops who had been settled there, were organized by an ex-centurion, C. Manlius, and were preparing to march on the city.

Cicero informed the Senate of the danger posed by Manlius and the emergency decree (the *senatus consultum ultimum*; see also Chapter 12) was passed. Troops were dispatched to deal with the matter. Other deployments were made throughout the peninsula in order to guarantee security. It was only after the Senate had reacted to Manlius that Cicero denounced Catiline by delivering the first of his Catilinarian orations, which drove the bankrupt patrician out of the city. Catiline then took command of Manlius' forces. Soon thereafter Cicero discovered that P. Cornelius

Lentulus Sura, an ex-consul who had been expelled from the Senate in 70 but now held a praetorship, was attempting to rouse into rebellion the Allobroges in Transalpine Gaul – who were themselves overwhelmed by debts and had gained nothing from their appeals to the Senate. An Allobrogian embassy in Rome had been approached; they had in their turn dutifully reported the matter to the consul. Cicero was able to arrest five conspirators, including Lentulus, who admitted the plot. These revelations created panic and inspired multiple accusations of complicity with Catiline.[23]

In December Cicero summoned the Senate to debate the fate of the arrested conspirators. The leading men were for executing them without trial, until Caesar, who was then praetor-elect, put forward an argument for imprisonment. After all, it was a violation of the law to put citizens to death without trial, nor was it clear that, in view of their arrest, such a course could be justified by reference to the *senatus consultum ultimum*.[24] Many were affected by his speech, but the Senate was restored to its previous severity by M. Porcius Cato, who was then merely a tribune-elect. Cato was the great-grandson of Cato the Censor, whose rectitude he self-consciously emulated. Pertinacious and brave, his nobility and his traditional, uncomplicated politics more than compensated, amongst his peers, for his lack of intelligence.[25] His denunciation of the conspirators carried the Senate, and Cicero, who alone was actually responsible for any executive actions, put the conspirators to death immediately. The city had been saved. Thanks were rendered to the gods, and Cicero was hailed as *parens patriae*, father of his country.

The rebellion in Italy was reduced early in 62. Catiline tried to make his way to Transalpine Gaul. He was blocked, however, by Roman troops, and his forces were crushed by an army commanded by Antonius. By the end of 61 the rebellion of the Allobroges was also suppressed.

There was an attempt by Pompey's supporters to capitalize on the danger posed by Catiline. Pompey's former legate, and his relation by marriage, Q. Metellus Nepos, a tribune in 62, proposed two bills, one summoning Pompey to Italy to assume the command against Catiline and another allowing him to stand for the consulship *in absentia*. Nepos' proposals were supported by Caesar, but vetoed by Cato in an assembly marred by violence incited by both tribunes. The *senatus consultum ultimum* was passed, Caesar was suspended from his praetorship, and the Senate urged that Nepos be stripped of his office. Nepos fled to Pompey in what he deemed to be a gesture demonstrating the Senate's violation of the tribunate (it was illegal for tribunes to be away from the city during their tenure of office). Caesar exercised greater prudence. He had already attracted senatorial opprobrium by standing, in the previous year, for the office of pontifex maximus, when it was vacated by the death of Metellus Pius. By doing so, he challenged the claims of two senior *consulares*, Servilius Isauricus (cos. 79) and Catulus. His popularity with the People and his enormous expenditure on bribery secured his election, which astonished – and offended – his seniors. His opposition to the execution of the Catilinarians had not enhanced his reputation for soundness. Now, his career in danger of crashing, Caesar played his part in calming the public and let himself be reconciled with the Senate, which restored him to his office. But the affairs of the city remained unsettled, a circumstance which prompted Cato, bulwark of the *optimates*, to carry a bill extending the benefits of the grain subsidy – with senatorial approval and at enormous public expense.

The Return of Pompey

The Senate had begun to honor Rome's most glorious general even before he had returned: it decreed a public thanksgiving for Pompey's successes, and legislation was passed permitting the great man to assume the garb of a *triumphator* at every public game, an unceasing celebration of his victories. Pompey had established Rome's domination in the east and had imposed his will on its political geography, in consequence of which he had received cult honors on Delos, at Athens, and in other cities, where he was revered as savior, founder, and benefactor; various cities even reckoned time in reference to a Pompeian era. He brought booty to Rome's treasury in enormous quantities, and by virtue of his conquests Rome's public revenues had more than doubled. Pompey himself had become surpassingly rich, in addition to his assets in *gloria*. His return to Italy in 62 was anticipated with excitement – and worry.

But it was far from Pompey's intentions to seize power. Despite his unconventional career, his ambitions were traditional: by dint of his wealth, his military glory, and his unsurpassed popularity with the People, he expected to be welcomed and revered by the Senate as its unquestioned first citizen. He quickly demonstrated that there was no need for alarm: upon his arrival in Italy, near the end of 62, he disbanded his army; his correspondence with fellow senators made clear his devotion to peace; and he displayed his attitude toward Metellus Nepos by divorcing his wife, thus severing his connection. He even sought to establish a relationship with Cato, by proposing to marry one of his nieces (and by proposing to marry his eldest son to her sister). It was an opportunity for Pompey to return to Roman society peacefully and as its foremost citizen, and an opportunity for Cato and his circle to assimilate the great man. But Cato denied Pompey the connection he sought. Pompey had, by demonstrating his desire to join the *optimates*, displayed a weakness that his rivals intended to take advantage of.

Although in 61 Pompey celebrated the grandest triumph in the city's history, the politics of that year were dominated by a scandal and a trial. In December, 62, P. Clodius Pulcher, scion of Rome's most splendid patrician house, the Claudii Pulchri, and a quaestor-elect, had been caught invading the nocturnal rites of the Bona Dea (Good Goddess), celebrated annually and *pro bono publico* (for the welfare of the Roman People). These ceremonies were forbidden to men and therefore irresistible to masculine fantasies, hence their invasion and the subsequent scandal (see also Chapter 15). The matter was far from trifling, but it was inflated by religious anxiety and the Roman penchant for melodramatic moralism. The language of the scandal became the language of political contention: a special tribunal to try Clodius was proposed, the debate over which was couched in terms of optimate oppression and popular license. The contest shunted Pompey's return, and his concerns, away from the center of things: the great man needed to secure land for his veterans and the ratification of his arrangements in the east, but these matters had to wait. In the end, Clodius was acquitted, but not before Cicero (who was a witness for the prosecution) had become Clodius' bitter enemy. A frustrated Pompey then devoted himself to the consular elections for 60: it was now clear that he would need executive support for his agenda. Not long after Clodius' acquittal, Catulus died. The *optimates* began to look to Cato as their spokesman and leader. His attitude toward Pompey could hardly be in doubt.

The First Triumvirate

Pompey's influence outside optimate circles remained strong. L. Afranius, a new man and a close friend of Pompey, was returned as consul, owing to the great man's endorsement and lavish bribes. His colleague, however, was Q. Metellus Celer, the brother of Metellus Nepos, whom Pompey had recently dismissed. Afranius, though a brave soldier and a reliable commander, lacked the resources necessary for subduing the Senate. Pompey arrogantly demanded that his eastern acts be ratified by the Senate *en bloc*. His enemies, however, were mobilized to resist: Celer opposed so summary a review, a line that was fortified by Cato, by Crassus, and by Lucullus, who had come out of retirement to insist that each of Pompey's arrangements be examined in turn and in detail. Afranius was no match for these, and Pompey was forced to accept defeat. He found a more robust representative in the tribune L. Flavius, who proposed an agrarian bill that, like the bill of Plotius in 70 and Rullus in 63, would provide land for Pompey's veterans. The predictable controversies ensued. Celer's resistance was so stiff that, in the end, Pompey once more let the matter drop.

Crassus was in no position to luxuriate in his rival's distress. The *publicani* who had won the normally lucrative contract to collect taxes in the province of Asia had discovered that their bid was too high. In order to avoid losses, they requested a reconsideration of their original arrangement, an action that Cicero deemed dishonorable but which he nevertheless supported for the sake of political harmony. Another influential advocate of the publicans' cause was Crassus, who, it is plausibly asserted, was himself invested in their society.[26] Again there was opposition. Celer rejected the idea of salvaging the *publicani*, as did Cato, whose virulent posture Cicero regarded as impolitic and dangerous.[27]

Enter Caesar, whose first opportunity to stand for the consulship fell in 60. An uprising in Spain, during his tenure as provincial governor, had enabled him to win a victory sufficient to merit a triumph, which meant a glorious homecoming that could only add luster to his candidacy. Caesar had valuable and wealthy friends, the chief of whom were Pompey and Crassus, men whose interests he had long and publicly upheld. It was time to demand reciprocity. In view of such circumstances, Caesar could only be optimistic. But he came to Rome later than he expected, and it was not possible for him to arrange his triumph in time to make the formal announcement obligatory for each candidate for office (the *professio*): in order to celebrate his triumph, Caesar must possess *imperium*, which would lapse if he should transgress the *pomerium*, the religious boundary of the city (distinct from the actual walls of the city or the limits of its habitation); yet it was necessary for a candidate to make his *professio* in person, and this required crossing the *pomerium*.[28] Therefore Caesar wrote to the Senate requesting that he be allowed to present his *professio* in absence.

But he did not reckon with Cato. Cato's son-in-law, M. Calpurnius Bibulus, was also a candidate for the consulship of 59, and he could not have relished Caesar's competition: in 65, when each was aedile, Caesar had completely overshadowed his colleague, and it was known that Caesar now intended to throw his support behind yet another candidate, L. Lucceius, a friend of Pompey. And so Cato now deployed his constitutional rectitude in the hope of improving Bibulus' prospects.[29] It was obvious to Cato that Caesar would choose his triumph over his candidacy, which, after all, he could postpone until the next year. The Senate was persuaded, and no exemption was granted. But Cato misjudged his man: Caesar abandoned his triumph, entered the city, and made his *professio*. Pompey and Crassus backed him – and worked against Bibulus. The *optimates*, however, spent lavishly in winning voters for Bibulus: "even Cato agreed that, in this instance, bribery was done for the sake of the Republic" (Suet. *Iul.* 19.1). In the end, the voters did not share in their partisanship: both Caesar and Bibulus were returned, and many voters will have voted for both men.[30]

For Crassus and for Pompey, this was very much a mixed result. Each could rely on Caesar, but Bibulus was a formidable man who was certain to extend Cato's and the *optimates*' resistance to their interests. But Caesar was ambitious, and indebted, and he was not prepared to see his political career end with his consulship. He succeeded in persuading Pompey and Crassus that, if the three of them should cooperate, they would have the resources necessary to advance their projects even in the teeth of Bibulus and Cato. Consequently, the three cultivated a friendship that has come to be known as the First Triumvirate.[31] The three also sought Cicero's inclusion, but the orator refused. When it became known, the triumvirs' alliance was regarded with suspicion. For Caesar, however, this "three-headed monster," as Varro dubbed it (App. *B Civ.* 2.9), excelled expectations: at once he was the partner, and no longer simply the junior friend, of two magnates.

Caesar began graciously. He displayed deference to the Senate and to his colleague. When he proposed an agrarian law, to meet the needs of Pompey's veterans, it included stipulations and safeguards that ought to have satisfied past opponents of Rullus and of Flavius. Caesar discussed his bill in the Senate, and offered to emend its details. None of this, however, placated Bibulus – or the many in the Senate who simply could not abide the idea of the state's buying and distributing land to veterans and to the poor. Cato obstructed debate by filibuster. Caesar's attempt to silence him was deemed too aggressive and offended the Senate.

Caesar then turned to the People. Bibulus had tribunes enough to veto the measure, but Caesar had a champion in the tribune P. Vatinius, an unattractive but valiant "new man," who, the *optimates* realized, would run roughshod over any colleague who tried to block Caesar's law. Consequently, Bibulus turned to a new tactic: consuls, praetors, and tribunes had the authority to observe the heavens for ill omens (*spectio*), the report of which (*obnuntiatio*) required the postponement of any legislative or electoral assembly. Bibulus announced that on every night preceding an assembly, he would watch the sky. Ordinarily, the mere announcement of an observation was sufficient to cancel an assembly, though technically it was the report that actually enacted the effects of an omen (a distinction that was lost on most Romans and evaded even most members of the Senate).[32] But it was unnatural for a magistrate to employ *spectio* in order to paralyze government for an entire year (Bibulus had declared in public that the People would not have this agrarian law during his consulship). Enormity begat enormity. Ignoring Bibulus, Caesar set a date for a vote on his bill. The Forum was packed with Pompey's veterans, into which company Bibulus and his entourage, which included Cato and three tribunes, forced their way. The consul was heaped with excrement but succeeded in reaching the platform where he intended to announce the omens. This he was prevented from doing by violence: a riot – and injuries – ensued. Bibulus and his followers were ejected, after which Caesar's bill was passed into law. Caesar then demanded that all senators take an oath of obedience to his agrarian law: in the end, even Cato capitulated.

The Senate was shaken. Bibulus, and the three tribunes who supported him, retired from public life. They continued to observe the heavens and to announce unfavorable omens by edict, a practice that put in doubt the legality of all the legislation of the year and certainly emphasized the violent nature of Caesar's consulship. These gestures were not pointless: over the course of the year, the shamelessness of the triumvirs became offensive to the Roman People, who did not hesitate to express themselves with public hissing and booing, and the Senate simmered in its resentment at their outrageous methods. The triumvirs, it could be complained, held the gods and the Senate in contempt.

But for the first months of 59, Caesar was unstoppable. In collaboration with Vatinius, he ignored the Senate and brought directly to the People legislation that satisfied the *publicani* and ratified Pompey's eastern settlement. He sealed his friendship with Pompey by becoming his father-in-law, proof of the permanence of their relationship and of their future cooperation. Vatinius carried a law that created a special command for Caesar in Cisalpine Gaul and Illyria: it extended for five years, and granted him command of three legions. In the Senate, Pompey proposed – and the Senate conceded – that Transalpine Gaul and an additional legion be added to Caesar's command.

As the year passed, however, the People as well as the senatorial rank and file became dissatisfied with the triumvirate's tactics. Pompey, the most distinguished of the three, became the principal target of public disapproval. Consequently, the triumvirs were obliged to take seriously Bibulus' religious challenge to Caesar's and Vatinius' legislation, and they worried over the inevitable reaction when Caesar no longer held the executive power of the consulship.[33] An ominous sign of discontent came when Cicero, while pleading a case, seized the moment to savage the current government. Caesar and Pompey responded immediately. Cicero's enemy, Clodius Pulcher, had, since the disgrace of the Bona Dea scandal, been striving to transfer himself from patrician to plebeian status: by doing so he would become eligible for election as tribune, in which office he hoped to rebound from the setback of his humiliating public trial. The mechanisms for such a transfer were obscure, and Clodius had experienced one setback after another.[34] Now, however, Caesar, as consul, summoned the curiate assembly, which ratified Clodius' adoption by a plebeian. Pompey, who was an augur, was present to guarantee the absence of untoward omens. Suddenly a plebeian, Clodius was eligible for the tribunate in 58, in which office he could harass his enemy (in response to Clodius' adoption Cicero retired to his villas in the country) and could employ his veto to protect the triumvirs from hostile decrees and legislation. One tribune was insufficient for absolute security, but the triumvirs were fortunate in the outcome of the consular elections: Gabinius was elected along with L. Calpurnius Piso, a noble who was also the father-in-law of Caesar.

Clodius, however, had no intention of serving simply as the triumvirate's rear guard. On the first day of his new office, Clodius promulgated, and subsequently carried, four laws. The first established a free monthly ration of grain for Roman citizens. The second restored the *collegia* suppressed by senatorial decree and established new ones. *Collegia* were neighborhood associations, at once religious and occupational: they were attractive to the lower classes and consequently seemed suspicious to many elites. The local prestige of these organizations was enhanced by Clodius' employment of them in the distribution of free grain. These laws made Clodius sensationally popular with the urban plebs for the rest of his life. But the tribune was aware of the danger of appearing too obviously a demagogue. He also passed a law that guaranteed every senator a public hearing before he could be expelled by the censors during their revision of the senate list, which won the appreciation of the Senate's vulnerable membership. And he regulated *obnuntiatio*: the controversy over Bibulus' actions in 59 had made it clear that many senators could no longer distinguish *spectio* from *obnuntiatio*; Clodius' law simply codified in public law what was already definitive in augural law. It was not retroactive and so did nothing to settle the controversy over Caesar's acts. By means of this careful legislative package, which included measures attractive to more than one section of society, Clodius acquired urban clout without sacrificing senatorial respectability.[35] This made him less susceptible to the control of the triumvirs.

At first he was loyal. Clodius rescued Vatinius from his enemies and protected Caesar's acts. But the tribune complicated politics when he put forward a measure banishing anyone who had put a citizen to death without trial: the law was *popularis* — and entirely traditional. But its obvious target was Cicero, owing to his role in the execution of the Catilinarian conspirators. Clodius promulgated his law in conjunction with a measure that awarded the consuls attractive provinces, thereby winning their loyalty. He also proposed an extraordinary command for Cato, who was to be granted *imperium* in order to supervise Rome's annexation of Cyprus, a signal honor. Clodius thus neutralized the *optimates* by implicating their spokesman in his legislative program. For Cicero this was a lethal combination, and he retreated from the city. The orator's property was then plundered, while Clodius passed another law that banished Cicero by name. He erected, over the ruins of Cicero's mansion on the Palatine Hill, a shrine to the goddess Libertas.

The Conference at Luca

Confident that Clodius possessed the energy to protect the triumvirate's interests, Caesar removed himself to his province. But Clodius, buoyed by his unexpectedly easy triumph over Cicero, now directed his hostilities against Pompey. The contest soon led to violence. The tribune intended to raise his stature by challenging Rome's most powerful man and, at the same time, hoped to deploy optimate resentment of Pompey in sustaining his senatorial acceptability. Before the year was out, Clodius had driven Pompey from public life.

Pompey responded to the tribune's attacks by laying the groundwork for the restoration of Cicero, a move that would unambiguously demonstrate his political superiority. In the following year, when Clodius was no longer tribune, Pompey forged a coalition of senators, equestrians, and the prosperous classes throughout Italy. Clodius, however, preserved his hold on the loyalty of the urban plebs, whose violence remained a formidable weapon. Two tribunes, T. Annius Milo and P. Sestius, each a supporter of Pompey's effort to recall Cicero, responded by equipping private guards. The clashes between these rival forces rendered 57 a year of terrible urban violence. Pompey was undaunted, and the centuriate assembly, packed with voters from throughout Italy, overwhelmingly passed into law a measure restoring Cicero from exile.

Pompey's success had been stunning. On Cicero's proposal, he was awarded a special command that put him in charge of Rome's grain supply. Recent shortages had made clear the need for senatorial attention, and Pompey's appointment, it was hoped by Cicero as well as by Pompey, would put Clodius' legislation permanently in the shade.

Yet by his very victory Pompey renewed the resentment against him that Clodius had hoped to exploit. The consular elections for 56 returned Cn. Cornelius Lentulus Marcellinus, an open opponent of the triumvirs, and L. Marcius Philippus, the father-in-law of Cato. Crowds, led by Clodius, chanted denunciations of Pompey, whom they castigated for his failure to resolve the grain shortage. Pompey confided to Cicero that he was certain that Crassus and Clodius were combining against him, and that the *optimates* approved.

Caesar's enemies were also mobilizing themselves: a tribune attempted to recall Caesar for trial, while L. Domitius Ahenobarbus, a candidate for the consulship of 55, declared his intention to terminate Caesar's command as soon as possible.[36] Less bold, Cicero also hoped to exploit Caesar's vulnerability: he suggested that the Senate should once more take up Caesar's agrarian legislation, the modification of which might help to provide funds necessary to assist Pompey in securing grain for the city.

The triumvirate was in danger of fragmentation: the remedy was an expansion of its resources. During the spring of 56 Caesar met with several important senators, the most distinguished of whom was Appius Claudius Pulcher, Clodius' eldest brother. Caesar conferred with Crassus at Ravenna and with Pompey at Luca. The result of these negotiations was not merely the reaffirmation of the triumvirs' friendship, but their alliance with the Claudii Pulchri (one of Pompey's sons now married a daughter of Appius Claudius) and their insistence on the complete loyalty of Cicero.[37] Clodius immediately became a public champion of Pompey's interests, while, in the Senate, Cicero vigorously opposed attempts to truncate Caesar's command.

The principal goal of the new coalition was a second consulship for Crassus and Pompey. But the triumvirs could no longer be certain of election, not least because Domitius Ahenobarbus would be a formidable candidate. Their scheme was to employ popular violence in order to block elections until the following year, when regular elections, conducted under the presidency of a consul, would be replaced, owing to the absence of consuls (their terms expired even if no new consuls had been elected), by an *interregnum*, during which process an *interrex* would be appointed every five days until new consuls were selected. The *interrex* proposed only two candidates to the People, so the triumvirs' goal was to prevent action until Crassus and Pompey were put forward by a friendly *interrex*. Even then, their election was marred by disturbances and by death. Elections for the remaining magistracies were also disrupted: Vatinius and Milo won election to the praetorship; Cato was defeated.

The new consuls oversaw the election of censors, as they had done in 70, and they quickly introduced beneficial legislation: the courts were reformed, and unsavory electioneering practices were curbed. But there were political spoils to be claimed. Caesar's tenure in Gaul was extended for five years; new commands were created for the consuls. Crassus received Syria, from which base he intended an invasion of Parthia, whence (he anticipated) glory and treasure to match his colleague and Caesar. Pompey was assigned the Spanish provinces. Since he continued to be in charge of Rome's grain supply, Pompey decided to manage Spain by means of his legates. In the next year, then, Pompey would possess an accumulation of promagistracies, one of which allowed him to command legions in a distant province while he remained in the vicinity of Rome, a situation that adumbrated the mechanics of the government of the future emperor Augustus. His stature was now quite simply incomparable, and it was dramatically emphasized when Pompey dedicated, with sensational games, his splendid complex on the Campus Martius that included a portico and Rome's first permanent theater.

Caesar in Gaul

When Caesar departed Rome for his Gallic provinces in 58, he could not have imagined that he should only return to the city as an invader. Instead, at that time, he needed something in the way of conspicuous success. Unlike Crassus and Pompey, Caesar had neither great wealth nor great distinction, and he had made many enemies. Even an uneventful command would render him useless to his powerful friends, and consequently vulnerable to those who wanted him ruined. He did not waste time. Caesar attacked the Helvetii in what can only charitably be described as a preemptive strike in defense of his province. By the close of 56 Gaul had been overrun, and Caesar was celebrated in Rome. But he had not genuinely conquered Gaul, and subsequent years were devoted to hard and brutal fighting: recalcitrant tribes were annihilated or enslaved, actions whose ruthlessness was attacked by his enemies in Rome (Cato decried Caesar as a war criminal). However, Caesar's crossing of the Rhine in 55 and his invasions of Britain in the same year and in 54 captured imperialist imaginations in the city, and soon opportunistic politicians were making their way to Gaul to serve with Caesar: they sought friendship with Rome's new military hero, and they sought wealth. The conquest of Gaul made Caesar – and his officers – rich men. It was all nearly undone in 52 by a rebellion led by Vercingetorix. But in the end Roman might was irresistible, and, as the termination of Caesar's command approached, it was clear that he had attained a stature comparable to that of Pompey the Great.[38]

The Outbreak of Civil War

We must now return to 55. The consular elections for the following year returned Appius Claudius Pulcher and Domitius Ahenobarbus. Cato gained the praetorship. Domitius and Cato offered loud protests but could do little to undermine the commands of Caesar or Crassus. The contest for the consulship of 53 was keen, bribery was rampant (the rate of interest doubled during July 54), and the attending controversy led to a postponement of the elections. In September, however, it was revealed that two of the candidates, Cn. Domitius Calvinus (who had opposed the triumvirs in 59) and C. Memmius (whose candidacy was endorsed by Pompey and Caesar), had entered into a disreputable electoral pact with both consuls. As was the case in 65, public confidence was deeply shaken. The elections were further postponed, while prosecutions were prepared. These were matters more pressing than Caesar or Crassus.

It was in the midst of such affairs that Pompey (and Caesar) suffered personal tragedy: Julia, to whom Pompey was devoted, died in childbirth. Yet Pompey could not escape political demands. When the year 53 began without consuls, the Senate called upon him, as proconsul, to help to arrange elections. The new consuls only entered office in July. Then it was learned that Crassus' invasion of Parthia had failed; he and the bulk of his army had been destroyed at Carrhae. There was no danger to the eastern empire: C. Cassius Longinus, Crassus' quaestor (and the future assassin of Caesar), secured Syria's defenses and the Parthians demonstrated no inclination to follow up their victory. But Roman politics were thoroughly altered. Caesar proposed that Pompey marry his great-niece, Octavia (who would be required to divorce her husband, C. Claudius Marcellus, the future consul of 50), while he would divorce Calpurnia to marry Pompey's daughter, herself already married to Faustus Sulla. The complexity of the proposed rearrangements attests to the importance Caesar placed on sustaining his connection with Pompey. But the great man did nothing, for now.

Despite the efforts of the consuls of 53, the elections for 52 were delayed, in what was emerging as a pattern of administrative incompetence. Milo was a candidate for the consulship, endorsed by Cicero and by Cato. His rivals included Q. Caecilius Metellus Pius Scipio Nasica and P. Plautius Hypsaeus, Pompey's friend and former quaestor. Clodius was standing for the praetorship for 52. He also hoped to wreck Milo's chances. The city was plagued by street fighting, as Clodius' and Milo's gangs constantly confronted one another. Once again the new year began without consuls. Another *interregnum* was necessary.

On January 18 Clodius was murdered by Milo. The two men, and their entourages, met accidentally on the via Appia. A scuffle ensued, in which Clodius was wounded and, subsequently and on Milo's instructions, killed.[39] When his body was returned to the city, the urban plebs, outraged, carried Clodius' body into the Senate House, which was set ablaze. The turmoil was compounded by rioting. The People, desperate for reliable government, demanded that Pompey be made dictator or consul. The Senate convened in order to pass the *senatus consultum ultimum*, the phrasing of which made clear the Republic's difficult pass: it called on the *interrex*, the tribunes, and Pompey to preserve the state. But in fact only the proconsul had the means to restore order. It began to appear inevitable that he must be appointed dictator. But Bibulus and Cato devised a novel means of placing Rome in Pompey's hands without resorting to an office so unhappily associated with Sulla. The Senate decreed that the *interrex* should name only one candidate for the consulship and that he should enter office without a colleague. It was done, and Pompey found himself in possession of another unprecedented honor, offered him by a distressed Senate at the urging of his long-standing, and now hard pressed, opponents.

Caesar was not to be overlooked. He enjoyed great influence amongst the tribunes of 52, who combined in a proposal that Caesar should be recalled to Rome to serve as Pompey's colleague. This he rejected, since he had not yet completed his work in Gaul, and in any case the bill would have been too provocative. Instead he persuaded the tribunes to put forward a measure that would allow him to stand in absence for the consulship when his command in Gaul expired. Caesar's purpose was clear. Despite the hostility of his enemies, Caesar remained immune from prosecution so long as he possessed *imperium*. Since his Gallic command was reaching its conclusion, Caesar required either a further extension or a new command in order to preserve his safety. His plan was to settle matters in Gaul and to employ his wealth and glory to win a second consulship, an office he could legally hold in 49. But to campaign in the normal way would leave him vulnerable during the interval between the surrender of his proconsular *imperium* and his assumption of office. This is not to say that condemnation would have become a certainty, but the prospect of a trial, or a series of trials, threatened a reduction in Caesar's prestige whatever their outcome.[40] Hence the usefulness of the Law of the Ten Tribunes, which was carried, with Pompey's backing and despite Cato's inevitable resistance.

Pompey set to his task with characteristic efficiency. He restored public order, and he carried new legislation on bribery and on violence. Under the terms of the latter law, Milo was convicted (Cicero, who defended him, was intimidated by the trial's circumstances and gave a poor performance; see also Chapter 2). Others, including followers of Clodius, were also convicted under this law. Public confidence was rapidly restored. By this time Pompey had married Cornelia, the daughter of Metellus Scipio, who was himself indicted under Pompey's law on bribery – as was Pompey's friend Hypsaeus. Pompey secured his father-in-law's acquittal and arranged for him to be elected his colleague in the consulship. Hypsaeus he dropped, and the man was convicted. It had to be clear to the dimmest that Pompey was repositioning himself.

His posture was made more complicated by his subsequent legislation. Pompey put through a law that required all candidates for office to submit their *professio* in person. The measure was plainly inconsistent with the Law of the Ten Tribunes, which legally it superseded.[41] Pompey insisted that he did not mean to deprive Caesar of his privilege: after the law was passed and engraved, he added to it a codicil stipulating that Caesar was exempt. But this codicil possessed no legal force: its validity depended entirely on Pompey's prestige, which he expected both Caesar and the *optimates* to respect. Before the year was out, the Senate had, for the third time, voted a public thanksgiving for Caesar's victories in Gaul, while Pompey saw to it that his Spanish command was extended for a further five years.

The elections for 51 were free both of violence and corruption, proof of the effectiveness of Pompey's administration. Cato stood for the consulship, promising to recall and to try Caesar if he were elected.[42] The People rejected him. The successful candidates were Ser. Sulpicius Rufus, a learned jurist, and M. Claudius Marcellus, who was Caesar's enemy. But his attacks on Caesar were thwarted by Sulpicius and by Pompey, whose resistance effectively silenced Marcellus. Pompey did, however, acquiesce in a motion brought in by Metellus Scipio that the Gallic provinces should be discussed in the Senate on March 1, 50. By this date, Caesar's command would at least be nearing its conclusion and, consequently, the future of his province was a legitimate issue for discussion.[43] This concession cannot have been welcome to Caesar, since supersession at that time would leave him vulnerable despite Pompey's codicil. But his situation was not yet desperate. The consuls for 50 were to be L. Aemilius Lepidus Paullus, who was indebted to Caesar, and C. Claudius Marcellus, cousin to the consul of 51 but also the husband of Caesar's niece. Still, it was becoming increasingly clear that his position depended on Pompey's continued friendship. Yet Pompey refused to express his views on Caesar's situation until after the Senate had held its debate. When pressed for his reaction if Caesar were to exercise his claim to stand for office in absence while still commanding his army, Pompey replied: "What would I do if my son wanted to take a stick to me?" (Caelius, Cic. *Fam.* 8.8.9). From Pompey's perspective, Caesar's future was secure, so long as he remained subordinate. But his control over Caesar carried weight in the Senate only so long as the *optimates* viewed Caesar as a threat.

In February, 50, Caesar's new friend, the tribune C. Scribonius Curio, who had entered office as the proconsul's enemy, introduced a stunning proposal: it would be best for the Republic if both Caesar and Pompey surrendered their extraordinary commands. At one stroke, the oligarchy would be rid of the threat of Caesar, the elimination of which made Pompey less essential. And Pompey's anomalous preeminence could be undone. In other words, Curio's proposal tended to transform what had appeared a confrontation between Caesar and the senatorial establishment over a matter of procedure into one between Caesar and Pompey over a contest of prestige. Hence the ancient view that Caesar could not endure a superior and Pompey could not abide an equal (Luc. 125–6; Florus 2.13.14). But Curio's proposal had the effect of shifting Pompey toward the position of the *optimates*. He now endorsed the opinion that Caesar should leave his province on the Ides of November, 50. On the likely assumption that Caesar would win election to a consulship for 49 – which assumes that Pompey enforced his codicil in Caesar's behalf – he would still have had to confront a narrow window of vulnerability before entering office. Could Pompey preserve him? And did he want to be preserved by Pompey's prestige? Rumors were current that Caesar was preparing for civil war.

In the summer of 50 Pompey fell seriously ill. The People of Italy united in prayers for his health and in rejoicing at his recovery. This unexpected event deceived Pompey, who confused Italy's affection for him with loyalty that could endure even the extremity of civil war. He soon made his famous boast that, at a stamp of his foot, legions and cavalry would spring forth from the earth (Plut. *Pomp.* 57.5). In his renewed confidence, he now called Curio's bluff. But Curio insisted that Pompey resign first. In December the Senate took a series of votes along the lines of Curio's proposition. The first concerned the question of Caesar's surrendering his command. It passed. Thereafter it voted on Pompey's resignation. This failed to pass. Finally, the body voted on Curio's original proposal – that each should step down – and this passed by a margin of 370 to 22. The senators, this vote makes clear, preferred peace to either Caesar or Pompey. But no action was taken, and Curio soon left Rome to join Caesar. The consul Marcellus, in company with the consuls-elect for 49, L. Cornelius Lentulus Crus and C. Claudius Marcellus (brother of the consul of 51), made a display of placing a sword in Pompey's hands and beseeching him to defend the Republic against Caesar. The gesture was symbolic, but potent, and Pompey accepted the task – if no better solution could be found.

All parties were confident, and each expected the other to give way. On January 1 a letter from Caesar was presented to the Senate, which gave it a hearing only after prodding from the tribunes Marc Antony and Q. Cassius. It was harsh and threatened civil war. A motion was put forward by Metellus Scipio that, unless Caesar dismissed his army before a certain date, he should be judged to be acting against the Republic. The motion was passed, but vetoed by Antony and Q. Cassius. On January 7 the *senatus consultum ultimum* was passed, after which Antony and Q. Cassius were warned not to interfere. They fled to Caesar, as Nepos had to Pompey in 62. Domitius Ahenobarbus was appointed as Caesar's successor. In Rome, the *optimates* and Pompey were alike certain they had won this contest: Caesar's only recourse was civil war. Should Caesar fight, they were sure that he would fail.

Caesar appealed to his army, claiming that Pompey had been corrupted by the *optimates*. He asked his soldiers to defend the rights of the tribunes – and to defend their leader's *dignitas*. Everything hung on their reaction. Caesar's troops proved devoted to their general. And they perceived that they had a stake in the preservation of his *dignitas*, if they hoped for security of their own at the end of their service. Some may have remembered that it was Caesar and not Pompey who had secured land for the great man's veterans – in the teeth of senatorial hostility. Caesar could be counted on. But Pompey had joined with men like Bibulus and Cato in threatening the tribunes: their attitude toward the Roman People was obvious. Not even the legionaries will have wanted civil war, but, from their perspective, it was only by following Caesar that they could fight for *libertas*, which for them was not merely an abstract principle (see also Chapter 29). Pompey and the Senate had no conception of this, and so they were alike shocked when Caesar led his forces into Italy.

Dictator

The civil war was begun by Caesar, and his lightning march through Italy made it impossible for Pompey to prepare any real resistance. The towns of Italy refused to offer opposition: their leading citizens (like the majority in the Senate) desired peace, and they were naturally hesitant to be drawn into a struggle the particulars of which they did not at all appreciate and the repercussions of which they very much hoped to evade (Sulla's brutal treatment of hostile communities had not been forgotten). Pompey lacked any legal authority, except over his own legions and legates, and the *optimates* were loath, or at least very slow, to accept him as their supreme commander (this concession came only in 48). Pompey, who immediately grasped the hopelessness of the Senate's situation, began to plan to evacuate, confident that, like Sulla, he could successfully invade Italy from the east.[44] But the strategic advantages of this move were lost on other senators, who tended to oppose the idea.

The civil war was hard fought. Caesarian successes in Spain were matched by republican victory in Africa. The war waged between Caesar and Pompey should have gone against Caesar, but the republican nobility, envious of their general, goaded him into risky and unnecessary battle at Pharsalus (in 48). Defeated by Caesar, Pompey was soon assassinated in Egypt. Cato, defeated in Africa, committed suicide (in 46). Yet the final battle of the civil war, which took place in 45, was nearly a republican victory (at one stage of the conflict, Caesar believed he had lost and considered suicide: Suet. *Iul.* 36). Caesar's triumph was by no means inevitable, and the ferocity of the struggle must be borne in mind when one contemplates Caesar's dictatorship.

From the very beginning, Caesar trampled on constitutional sensibilities, in matters great and small alike. Nevertheless, he needed respectability and so welcomed the support, or at least the acquiescence, of the aristocracy, even those who had originally supported Pompey. Hence his famous clemency, which pardoned Marcus Brutus – and Cicero. In the course of Caesar's fourth dictatorship – perhaps, at some stage, "for the restoration of the Republic" – he was finally made dictator "for life" (*dictator perpetuo*).[45] This office he often combined with tenure of the consulship. He designated future consuls and praetors, and he deposed office holders at will. With the plunder of the empire at his disposal, he rewarded his soldiers with bounties and he entertained the People. His popularity was unsurpassed. Caesar accumulated an extraordinary list of honors, not a few of which were unprecedented and too many of which suggested that he aimed at regal or even divine status. This too conspicuous monopoly on power and glory made him anathema to the men who felt right in deeming themselves to be his peers. Even Caesar's positive social reforms, of which there were many (e.g., his reform of the calendar, his resolution of the debt crisis, his moral legislation), because they were imposed by order, rankled. And there seemed no limit to his ambition: he planned an eastern campaign against the Parthians; it was believed by some that Caesar aimed at conquering what was left of the world.[46]

But on the Ides of March, only days before he was to leave Rome for the east, great Caesar fell. The conspiracy against him was extensive, and its success, when one considers the aristocracy's almost characteristic incapacity for cooperation during this period, was striking. The leaders of the conspiracy, men like Marcus Brutus, Cassius Longinus, and Decimus Brutus (Cicero had been excluded from the ranks of the tyrannicides), were not Caesar's enemies. In fact, they had benefited from his friendship. But they remained at heart genuine oligarchs, whose ambitions for their own class proved equal to Caesar's ambitions for himself.

It was Cicero's opinion that, in victory, Pompey would not have showed any better than Caesar.[47] And it remains difficult to admire the political and social vision of Caesar's assassins, for whom *libertas* constituted a greedy claim to privileges denied. "They wished it so," was Caesar's judgment on the *optimates* in the aftermath of his victory at the Battle of Pharsalus (Suet. *Iul.* 30. 4). His assessment was not unjust. It was, however, incomplete. He and Pompey, like the *optimates*, bore responsibility. The causes of the civil war were manifold. But the Senate's control of affairs did not collapse owing to foreign invasion or popular rioting in the city or a peasants' revolt in the countryside of Italy. Unrestrained sharp practices by the political elite in their contest for individual domination brought the Republic to a civil war fought, unabashedly, over *dignitas* (see also Chapter 29).

Guide to Further Reading

The last years of the Republic have been intensively studied and only a very few items (all in English) can be adduced here. The narrative of Syme 1939 remains unsurpassed, though its underlying assumptions have become outdated. The clear and concise presentation of Wiseman 1994a and 1994b is excellent and ought to be consulted by anyone interested in this period. The atmosphere, social and political, of the 50s is superbly captured in Wiseman 1985. Taylor 1949 presents a robust and still valuable account of the political dynamics of the late Republic, while Nicolet 1980 and Lintott 1999a provide a constitutional and institutional context. Numerous studies of the period take the form of biography. Gelzer 1968 is the fundamental and standard study of Caesar, though its admiring tone will disturb some readers. Seager 2002 is essential for the career of Pompey and for the political history of the period more generally. Crassus resists satisfactory biographical treatment, but there are useful accounts by Marshall 1976 and Ward 1977. Mitchell 1991 addresses Cicero's career during this period. Tatum 1999 concentrates on Clodius and topics related to his career, including the lower classes and popular violence. These matters are the subjects of several excellent large-scale studies, including Lintott 1999b, MacMullen 1974, Nippel 1995, and Mouritsen 2001. Millar 1998 and Yakobson 1999 argue in favor of a controversial thesis regarding the role of the People, especially the lower orders, in republican politics: although it has won few adherents in the strict sense, this approach has proved to be a useful and beneficial influence on current thinking. Beard and Crawford 1985 offer an intelligent and focused analysis of the problems – political, economic, and institutional – confronting the late Republic. The collapse of the Republic into civil war is explored in detail by Gruen 1974: the thesis of this book, though obscured in its very bulk and frequently criticized, remains plausible and worth considering. The most important treatment of the various matters pertaining to the fall of the Republic is Brunt 1988c.

Notes

1 The ancient evidence for the political history of this period is accumulated and sorted, on a year-by-year basis, in Broughton 1951–86, in consequence of which detailed annotation is unnecessary here.

2 Roman political morality demanded a balance between the ambitious exercise of personal virtue and fealty to the common good: Earl 1967.

3 Brunt 1971a: 91–9.

4 Italians in politics: Wiseman 1971. *Ambitus:* Linderski 1995: 107–14; 638–9; Yakobson 1999.

5 Evidence and further references in Badian 1990a.

6 Vanderbroeck 1987; Mouritsen 2001; Tatum 2004. Cf. Millar 1998.

7 Though it is fair to observe that Cicero's references to the *optimates* very often refer to a narrow combination of nobles. He paints a very different picture, however, in his defense of the senatorial establishment at *Sest.* 98.

8 *Popularis* politics: Tatum 1999: 1–16. The notion of a genuine popular *movement* continues to attract eminent adherents: cf. Wiseman 1994a: (e.g.) 339, 346, 367.

9 Rathbone 1981, but cf. Nicolet 1994: 619. See now Rosenstein 2004.

10 Brunt 1998b.

11 The so-called *Lex Plotia Agraria*: see Marshall 1972.

12 Wiseman 1994a: 329–33.

13 De Souza 1999.

14 Caesar is often (but wrongly) designated the only senator who supported Gabinius' measure: Watkins 1987.

15 Pompey's campaign: Seager 2002: 47–9.

16 Sherwin-White 1984: 159–85. *Contra,* Kallet-Marx 1995: 312–14.

17 Sherwin-White 1984: 186–234.

18 Crassus' investments abroad: Shatzman 1975: 377.

19 In his (fragmentary) speech *De rege Alexandrino.*

20 Challenged corruption: Cic. *Verrines.* Championed tribunate: Cic. *Corn.* Cicero and the equestrian order: Bleicken 1995a; Berry 2003.

21 Frederiksen 1966; Nicolet 1994: 641–2.

22 In a letter to Catulus, Catiline wrote: "I have pursued a course of action that offers hope of preserving what remains of my prestige (*dignitas*)" (Sall. *Cat.* 35.4).

23 The reality of an actual and coherent conspiracy (as opposed to a multiplicity of illicit and dangerous acts given menacing shape by means of Ciceronian rhetoric) is questioned by Seager 1973.

24 Discussion of this complex problem: Drummond 1995.

25 Plut. *Cat. Min.* 1.3: "When he engaged in study, he was slow to comprehend."

26 Badian 1972a: 103–4.

27 Cic. *Att.* 2.1.18: "that man, though he possesses a noble spirit and absolute integrity, none the less is doing the Republic harm, because he speaks in the Senate as if he were in Plato's Republic, not Romulus's cesspool."

28   Regulations affecting *professio*: Linderski 1995: 91–4.

29   Caesar's affair with Servilia, Cato's half-sister, was notorious (Plut. *Brut.* 5) and cannot have improved relations between the two men.

30   In consular elections, Roman voters voted for two candidates.

31   The First Triumvirate was simply a personal agreement. The Second Triumvirate (among Marc Antony, M. Aemilius Lepidus and Octavian) was an entirely different matter: that was a legal entity established by the *Lex Titia* of 43 (sources in Broughton 1951–86: 340). The terminology (which is entirely modern) is unfortunate.

32   Linderski 1995: 425–6; Tatum 1999: 126–30.

33   They were sensible to do so: in 58 two praetors, L. Domitius Ahenobarbus and C. Memmius, insisted on a senatorial debate over the legitimacy of Caesar's acts; the debate lasted three days (Suet. *Iul.* 23). And the controversy continued throughout that year.

34   Transition from patrician to plebeian status: Tatum 1999: 96–102.

35   Tatum 1999: 114–35. It is commonplace, however, for scholars to view the whole of Clodius' legislative package as *popularis* (e.g., Wiseman 1994b: 377–8), but this is an unnatural construction to put on the laws regulating religion and the census and is also to ignore the explicit testimony of Dio 38.12.8.

36   The attempt to try Caesar: Badian 1974.

37   Pompey's connection with Claudii Pulchri: Tatum 1991.

38   The profitability of the Gallic War: Badian 1968a: 89–91.

39   The misleading account of Clodius' death in Cicero's *In Defense of Milo* is corrected by the commentary of Asconius: Asc. 30–2C.

40   Shackleton Bailey 1965–68: 1.38–40 and Gruen 1974: 494–6 argue that there was no realistic possibility of a prosecution and consequently Caesar's motives must be explained otherwise.

41   *Contra*, Gruen 1974: 458–60.

42   Fehrle 1983: 214.

43   The legally appropriate termination of Caesar's command (the *Rechtsfrage* of modern scholarship) was contested at the time (Caes. *B Civ.* 1.9.2; Cic. *Att.* 7.7.6, 7.9.4) and remains uncertain: cf. Seager 2002: 193–5.

44   Cic. *Att.* 9.10.2: "Sulla could; can I not?"

45   Badian 1990b: 34–5.

46   Further particulars and bibliography: Rawson 1994b.

47   Cic. *Att.* 7.7.7, 8.11.2, 9.7.3, 9.10.2, 10.7.1.

PART III

Civic Structures

CHAPTER 10

Communicating with the Gods

Jörg Rüpke

Superhuman Members of Society

Fundamentally, republican religion is not about belief or conduct but action, more specifically, action toward the gods. There was a general consensus among the Romans that besides mortal beings a class of immortal, powerful, caring, and intervening agents existed and had to be dealt with. This chapter focuses on these practices. Methodologically, such an approach allows us to observe the manifold combinations and interactions of religious and nonreligious, political, social, economic, and medical practices. By presupposing the Romans' intention to communicate or at least to take into account the existence of superhuman beings, modern analysis of ancient religious practices can try to identify their internal logic or rationality and can analyze their capacity and problematic aspects when these practices affect processes of political decision-making or the legitimation of power. Analyses of modern religions, which frequently examine institutions with clear-cut organizational boundaries or conscious self-definitions, might profit from a *functional* definition of religion that identifies hidden or "secularized" but nevertheless powerful forms of religion. For the religious practices of the ancient world, which were present in many areas of society that we might consider "secular," that approach would yield less useful results in understanding the particular features of the civic structures of the Roman Republic.

Ancient religious thought did not concentrate on reflecting about the boundaries of "religion." As most of postclassical theological thought did and still does, it reflected about the gods. In republican Rome, however, even for the gods we are dealing with diffuse convictions rather than clearly formulated concepts. *Theologia*, philosophical reasoning about gods (or god), was a trait of Roman religion that was not developed before the second century BC. Roman theology was a result of the intensified cultural contacts with the Hellenistic world from the third century onward. Down to the end of the republican period, writings in Latin about the gods were mostly paraphrases or even translations of Greek texts. This holds true for Ennius' *Euhemerus* (shortly after 200) as well as T. Lucretius Carus' didactic epic *De rerum natura* (*On the Nature of Things*, shortly before 55). M. Tullius Cicero (106–43) intended to provide a comprehensive and critical exposition of Greek theological thought in his works *On the Nature of the Gods* (*De natura deorum*), *On Divination* (*De divinatione*), and *On Fate* (*De fato*).[1] M. Terentius Varro's (116–27) *Antiquitates rerum humanarum et divinarum* (*Human and Divine Antiquities*, preserved only in fragments), integrated and systematized earlier antiquarian accounts of Roman practices and institutions.

The gods whose cultic veneration had been institutionalized by the Roman polity (other gods were irrelevant as long as one did not invade their territory) were part of society. As was true for human members of society, interaction between gods and humans was infrequent outside of a person's large, private space. Wherever it occurred, communication was necessary and regulated, as will be described in the following sections.[2] The gods were addressed in prayer and ritual action. Nonverbal communication intensified oral communication with the invisible addressees and helped to define them. Divinatory elements in ritual checked on the success of the communicatory effort. Such practices underlined the risky character of asymmetric communication with a superior agent. At the same time they provided hints to the god's reaction in the form of the victim's entrails or the shape of the flames on a sacrificial altar.

Some gods were regularly consulted on political decisions (e.g., Jupiter); others were asked for their help and general benevolence, *volens propitius esse/fieri*, "to be/ become willing and benevolent" (e.g., Plaut. *Curc.* 88–9).[3] The aims of this communication and the concepts its words expressed varied. One could seek *venia* (pardon) or to establish *pax* (a pact) with a particular god or all of them. The gods could be asked *sinere* (to allow) or *velle* (to will) something. On the level of the polity, military success was seen as a result of Roman piety, and defeats signaled the wrath of the gods (*ira deorum*). Defeats, however, were occasional; military expansion was continuous. The occasional neglect of *pietas* (piety), if unintentional, as later juridical reasoning specified (Q. Scaev. *iur.* 10), could be healed by *piaculum*, an expiatory sacrifice. Yet *pietas* was not a disposition restricted to the relationship to the gods. Above all it was something that pertained to human interaction, in particular children's behavior toward their parents or clients' behavior toward their patrons. The Romans' dealings with their gods reflected and shaped their social conduct at the same time.

Parting with the Gods

The divine members of Roman society were present in physical space. She or he (a gendered conception was obligatory) had a place of her or his own within the boundaries of Roman territory. The gods' property rights complicated the fundamental difference between public space, that is, territory owned by the community as a whole (a *locus publicus*) and private space owned by a human or corporate (juridical) person (a *locus privatus*). It was easy to give something piously to the gods, but far more problematic to take something piously away from them. Only elaborated rituals enabled the transferral of cultic space from one location to another. Stories about the unmovable god Terminus, who refused to make room for the new Capitoline temple and had to be integrated into the new structure, demonstrated the fact that a god could deny his consent to be moved, to give up his own territory, even if he was given adequate compensation (Livy 1.55.3–4). Thus, the principle of the immobility of the borderlines of private property, marked by *termini* (boundary stones) that were venerated at the festival of the Terminalia (February 23), was secured. Stories of *evocationes*, the "calling out" of deities of besieged cities by promising them a new cult place at Rome, such as the *evocatio* of Juno at the siege of Veii, demonstrated the possibility of such a move and gave prominence to divine decisions: Juno accepted the invitation (Livy. 5.21.3, 22.3–7). These decisions were independent of the worshipers' consent.

Only public space could be made *sacer*, that is, turned into divine property, by the rite of *consecratio* (consecration). The decision to create a public burden entailing expenses of upkeep and rituals was not left to individuals but could only be taken by the Senate and performed by the leading magistrates. At the same time, the change in the status of an area was not supposed to infringe on private property rights. When Cicero was exiled, his enemy Clodius consecrated part of his urban property in order to dispossess him permanently and completely, but on his return Cicero was successful in demonstrating the illegal character of this action and was reinstated (Cic. *Dom.* 51, 62; *Har. resp.*). Not every *locus sacer*, divine property, was transformed into a *templum*, a special type of space for ritual performances. This Latin term did not designate a building; a temple building was called an *aedis*. Instead, an *augur*, a particular type of public priest (see below), established a rectangular space as a *templum* through special rituals of designation and declaration. The choice of the place was a human decision. Only exceptionally would a god directly claim a piece of land. That might happen by a lightning strike leaving a visible mark in the soil. The strip of land would be marked off by a miniature fence or boxlike structure bearing the inscription *fulgur conditum* ("covered lightning-trace").[4] The owner would hardly lose more than a square foot.

Private religious feelings could also lead to designating a larger or smaller place for the veneration of a particular god or group of gods. That would establish a *sacrarium*, something sacred, but not divine property, not a *locus sacer*, in a technical sense. Such a place was easily transferable and convertible back to secular uses. Normally, the problem would not occur. Household shrines were movable altars or cupboards or, frequently, wall paintings. They were only minimally articulated in architecture.[5] The burial of corpses or urns created *loca religiosa* ("places of awe"). Republican Romans were keen to limit burning and burial to places outside the city proper. Exceptions were made only to honor outstanding public figures (Cic. *Leg.* 2.58; Plut. *Quaest. Rom.* 79; Serv. *Aen.* 11.206). Property rights were not to be infringed by a burial, nor were burial places to be violated by using the surrounding area for agriculture or new burials. The concern to formulate effective sanctions or assure property rights resulted in a number of elaborate funerary inscriptions from imperial times spelling out such provisions.

Physical space was not the only form of divine property, as we will see below. The most important form of communication with the gods, the sacrifice, was a form of transfer of property, since it entailed a gift. Depending on what was sacrificed, all of the problems and precautions taken in the case of property transfer were also relevant to the objects involved.

Paying for the Gods

Places owned by gods and dedicated to their veneration could assume different forms. Ideally, a plot of forest or open land (*lucus*) could serve as a place for divine presence. Wherever identifiable, at least minimal structures, an altar, for example, would mark such a place, serve for the cult, and perhaps identify the divine owner. Such places were not restricted to the countryside. The *Volcanal*, a place dedicated to the cult of the god Volcanus (already identified with the Greek Hephaistos by the sixth century), was situated in the *Forum Romanum*, close to the Curia and the Comitium in the very center of an area closely associated with the Romans' identity as a political community. Varro regretted the disappearance of many groves in the growing first-century capital, Rome; they were "objects" of insufficient public interest and sanctions as well as of private greed manifested in houses that occupied ever more space within the city.[6]

Roofed structures for the gods could likewise take different forms. An important cult place of Mars was housed by the Regia and can probably be identified with the trapezoid building on the Via Sacra close to the house of the Vestals (see below). The temple of Vesta, the *aedes Vestae,* was a circular building that did not qualify as a *templum* (see above). The standard form of the rectangular, houselike temple (*aedes*) on a high platform is exemplified by the Capitoline temple of Jupiter overlooking the Forum as well as by many cult buildings in the Forum proper.

Temples were important in Rome's symbolic economy. Large temple buildings were an important means of demonstrating a city's piety, power, and wealth to foreigners. The beginning of the Republic is linked to the dedication of the exceptionally large temple of Jupiter Optimus Maximus on the Capitoline Hill (Livy 2.8.6–8). It is, however, difficult to determine and hotly debated whether and how the exceptional size of the first Capitoline temple, rivaling the religious centers of the contemporary Greek world, relates to the economic and military power of the *grande Roma dei Tarquinii,* the magnificent city of the Etruscan kings whom the Romans had just expelled.[7] The last decades of the second century also saw enormous building projects in the cities surrounding Rome, for example, the monumental façade of the temple of Fortuna at Praeneste or the enormous temple with an area of 91 × 91 m just outside of Tusculum.[8] In this way, the rivals of Rome asserted their independent civic identity and wealth. And the impression of late republican Rome itself on visitors, as expressed in contemporary texts, was not least a product of its magnificent, towering temples. In his first Catilinarian speech, Cicero reminds his fellow citizens of the gods' presence by pointing to the temples around the Forum. Their potential destruction is the embodiment of the imminent danger that Catiline's conspiracy posed to the community as a whole (Cic. *Cat.* 1.33).[9]

And yet, the Rome of gold and marble is an Augustan creation. Despite an impressive series of temples built from the late fourth century onward, many temples seem to have been in need of repair by the time when C. Iulius divi filius Caesar Octavianus (soon to become Augustus) encouraged his generals to rebuild and rededicate urban temples (on dates different from their initial dedications).[10]

Table 10.1 Alphabetical list of republican temples[a] [fo. 370]

Aesculapius (292)	Iuturna (242/1)	Sol Indiges (3rd century)
Bellona (296)	Iuventas (191)	Spes and Fides (258/7)
Bona Dea (2nd century)	Janus (260)	Summanus (276)
Castor and Pollux	Juno Curritis (241)	Tellus (268)
(2nd century?)	Juno Regina (179)	Tempestates (259)
Concordia (216)	Juno Sospita (194)	Tiberinus (3rd century)
Consus (272)	Juppiter Fulgur	Vediovis (194)
Diana (179)	(3rd century)	Vediovis (192)
Faunus (194)	Juppiter Invictus	Venus Erucina (215)
Felicitas (151)	(c. 2nd century)	Venus Erucina (181)
Felicitas Feronia (225)	Juppiter Libertas (246)	Venus Genetrix (46)
Flora (240)	Juppiter Stator (294)	Venus Libitina (status
Flora (3rd century)	Juppiter Stator and	as temple uncertain; 3rd century)
Fons (231)	Juno Regina (146)	Venus Obsequens (295)
Fors Fortuna (293)	Juppiter Victor (295)	Venus Verticordia (114)
Fortuna Equestris (173)	Lares (3rd century)	Venus Victrix Honos and
Fortuna huiusce diei (168)	Lares Permarini (179)	Virtus and Felicitas (55)
Fortuna huiusce diei (101)	Luna (3rd century)	Vica Pota (3rd century)
Fortuna Primigenia (194)	Mars (138)	Victoria Virgo (193)
Fortuna Publica (241)	Mars Invictus	Volcanus (252)
Hercules (3rd century)	(2nd century?)	Vortumnus (264)
Hercules Invictus (292)	Mater Magna (191)	
Hercules Magnus	Mens (215)	
custos (223)	Minerva (263/2)	
Hercules Musarum (189)	Neptunus (257)	
Honos (233)	Ops (3rd century)	
Honos (3rd century)	Ops Opifera (250)	
Honos and Virtus (222)	Pales (267)	
Honos and Virtus	Penates (3rd century)	
(early 1st century)	Pietas (181)	
Hora Quirini (3rd century)	Pietas (91)	
	Portunus (292)	
	Sol and Luna (3rd century)	

[a]   Ziolkowski 1992: 187–8; Wissowa 1912: 594–6.

Between 302, when a temple to Salus vowed in 311 was dedicated on the Quirinal Hill, and 44, when Augustus' father, Julius Caesar, was honored by the decision to build a temple to *Clementia Caesaris*, at least 76 temples were erected at Rome (see Table 10.1). The list (which refutes the idea of a thorough Hellenization of Roman religion from the late third century onward) is restricted to public temples, that is, temples built on public land, dedicated by ordinary magistrates or those appointed especially for this purpose such as *duoviri aedibus dedicandis* (a two-man commission for dedicating a temple) and maintained at public expense. The actual building costs, however, were usually not paid for from the normal budget of the Roman state with its extremely limited administrative machinery (see below).

The money to finance such extraordinary projects came from extraordinary sources and individual initiative. In many cases, temples were vowed by generals on the battlefield. Depending on family traditions, location, situation, perhaps even individual predilections – reasons are normally not given – a military leader facing a difficult situation, or the flight of his own troops, or simply in gratitude for an overwhelming victory named a deity to which he promised a temple and cult at Rome. The booty from his conquest offered the means to finance its construction. However, such building projects were discussed and authorized by the Senate, perhaps modified by priestly interventions, and finally land had to be allotted. In the end, a period of sometimes more than a decade could elapse before the dedication of the finished building could be performed and thereby the religious obligation of the vow discharged, either by the magistrate who vowed it or his son or by someone in public office at the time or specially appointed by the Senate to do so.[11]

A man who founded a temple associated with his own achievement either on the battlefield or in restoring public order by fining somebody acquired prestige thereby. Roman historians, especially the annalists represented by Livy, who is probably the single most important source for the history of republican religion, commemorated a victorious general and his vow. Inscriptions on temple buildings, which are only occasionally preserved from republican times (e.g., *ILS* 20 = *ROL* 4:84 no. 82) would have named the dedicator, e.g., Gnaeus Flavius for the shrine of Concordia (Pliny *HN* 33.19, cf. Livy 9.46.6–7). Public memory, however, stressed the name of the deity and the day of the dedication. The temple known as *Isis Metellina*, which was built for the goddess Isis by a member of the Metellus family, was an exception. There were also other ways to honor a god. Public games, which involved a large portion of the Roman populace, commemorated a victory much more directly and immediately. Such alternatives were often preferred. The long process of decision and construction that temples required and that involved different parties resulted in a symbol of communal coherence and piety much more than of individual achievement and excellence, even if individual initiative provided the starting point (see also Chapter 24).[12] The long-term maintenance of the temple, however, posed problems. Before Augustus, the prestige resulting from restoring temples was minimal and seems to have been sought only in the case of prominent buildings. Public attention was attracted instead by ever larger building complexes, the theatre of Pompey, for instance, or Caesar's *Forum Iulium*.

The Presence of the Gods

The places owned by the gods were privileged places in which to contact them, but they were not the only places for ritual communication, only the preferred ones. Within the framework of a religion that believed in the existence of many different gods – called polytheism only by those who tried to construe their monotheism as a different (and better) form of religion (like the Jewish philosopher Philo of Alexandria) – special places helped to differentiate and to individualize the gods. Even for a triad of gods as closely associated as the Capitoline triad of Jupiter, Juno, and Minerva, the temple on the Capitoline Hill contained not one but three chambers (*cellae*) that housed each of them individually. When M. Claudius Marcellus intended to fulfil his vow of a temple to Honos and Virtus in 208, the priestly college of the pontiffs, experts in law and religious norms, hindered him by arguing that one *cella* could not lawfully be dedicated to two gods. In case of a lightning strike or other prodigy in such a room, expiation would be difficult, they claimed, because it could not be known which god was to be addressed. And again, a single victim could not be sacrificed to two gods. Thus the problem had to be solved by adding a proper temple (*aedes*) for Virtus (Livy 27.25.7–9).

The unique relationship of a specific place to a particular god, however, did not entail a ban on the display of further statues within its chamber. Theological or mythological associations and the arbitrariness of an individual dedicator could add a whole array of images of the same god or others. There would be a central statue to which cult, in particular public cult, would be primarily addressed, but between such a cult statue and others that were merely dedications there was no difference in sacral quality. To draw such a distinction is to introduce an anachronistic concept into ancient Roman thinking, something which is legitimate and possibly helpful in making comparisons with other religions but not helpful in reconstructing the Romans' view of their gods.[13]

The use of images of the gods is probably the precondition for any elaborated polytheistic religion. A differentiated iconography, spread by reproductions in different media, such as statues, paintings, and reliefs on household objects, and furthered by means of literature is the usual way to stabilize a multiplicity of personalized, theriomorphic, or anthropomorphic gods.[14] In contrast to how religion probably developed historically, ancient Greeks and Romans (and much later the first historian of religion, Friedrich Max Müller at Oxford) supposed that the names of the gods existed before their images.[15] Images were thought by late republican theorists like Varro to represent a deterioration from a purer, original religion that began in the late regal period in response to the terracotta images of Jupiter produced for the Capitoline temple (c. 509) by Etruscan artists from Veii (Varro *Ant. rerum. div.* frag. 18 Cardauns). Archaeological findings contradict Varro's theory, however. The early attractiveness of Greek religious imagery and Italian images inspired by the Greek products is impressively attested by the decoration of a pre-republican temple in the Forum Boarium near the church of Sant'Omobono that antedates the Capitoline temple. The archaeological remains of the approximately contemporary cult sites at Pyrgi and Satricum support this conclusion. Just as the Greeks received and employed imagery from the ancient Near East, so Greek and Hellenistic imagery influenced the development of Italian religions. And Roman imagery itself would later be an important factor in modifying the conceptions of the divine in Gaul or among German tribes.[16] The case of Rome does not offer an example of a non-iconic polytheism of faceless spiritual powers.

Researchers interested in Roman primitivism and influenced by late nineteenth-century theories of religious evolution discovered many supposed traces of non-iconic cult.[17] Yet a closer look at examples such as Iuppiter Lapis (Jupiter, the stone), Manalis (a stone manipulated in a rain ritual), or the *spolia opima* (the trophy-like arrangement of the armour of an enemy general slain by a Roman commander) reveals ritual symbols used in front of anthropomorphic deities rather than archaic, pre-iconic cult. Archaic features were honored in religion, however. Terracotta images were still used for deities at a time when bronze or marble had become obligatory for statues of humans, whenever affordable. The same holds true for sacral architecture, which preserved elements of wooden construction and terracotta decoration into the age of limestone and marble. But at Rome, unlike Greece, the cult of unhewn tree trunks was literary fiction.

Images speak only if they are supported by narratives. Just as a non-iconic, pre-anthropomorphic cult is hardly imaginable for an urban center in central Italy on the margins of the Greek, Punic, and Etruscan worlds, so a premythological phase of Roman religion is scarcely detectable. Early vase paintings and figurines of Hephaestus (Vulcan), or of Aeneas carrying his father Anchises, must be related to complex, contemporary narratives that made these images comprehensible (see also Chapters 6 and 23). The dominance of models taken from Greek literary texts have, from the late Republic onwards, induced scholars beginning with the Augustan historian Dionysios of Halicarnassus (in Asia minor), who wrote in Greek, to believe that Roman religion lacked myths.[18] However, the Romans made sense of their world in a particularly distinctive way, by narrating the history of their city, and this trait does not support the claims of Dionysios and other scholars. The Romans memorialized their gods by their appearance in history, by their actions in times of crisis. Also, Roman gods frequently lacked the fully-fledged personalities of Greek deities. Genealogy was less frequently employed to establish relationships among the gods than in Greece. In addition, only second-rank families like the Iulii in the first third of the first century felt the need to increase their prestige by introducing gods among their forebears. Old and dominant families instead legitimated their political positions by the number of consuls they could count among their ancestors.[19] The severing of the leading families' genealogical links to the most important state deity, Jupiter, might have been a self-conscious measure taken during the emergence of the nobility in the middle Republic.[20]

Discussion of the presence of gods in temples and statues must not overlook the fact that many temples were usually closed. They were opened only on the anniversary of their dedication or for a small number of festivals. Alternatively, a custodian (*aedituus*) might be paid to open the temple and supply what was needed for private cult. The opening of all temples constituted a powerful symbolic element within the ritual of *supplicatio*, a festival of supplicatory prayer or thanksgiving involving the whole populace. Thus, even for private worship, time and ritual rhythms as defined by the society and its public priests were important. Hence, the question of time must be addressed before forms of ritual communication can be dealt with.

Sharing Time

Gods could have territorial property. Some of them had temporal property, too. During the Republic, the term *feriae* signaled a god's ownership of a particular day. Jupiter owned all the Ides, the 13th or 15th of each month, and Mars owned the 1st and 23rd of March and other days, too, according to the *Fasti Praenestini* calendar (*Inscr. Ital.* 13.2.123). However, no deity was permitted to own permanently more than one day in succession. In order to avoid conflicts of ownership, at least one free day usually intervened between two *feriae*, replicating the spatial principle of a measurable border between divine territories.[21]

How could divine ownership of time be marked? Just as the usual ritual activity on such a day would be spatially limited, the god's temporal ownership was likewise negatively expressed: *Feriae* were not available for many human activities. On the one hand, there were restrictions on agricultural activities. Cato the Elder discussed in his second-century treatise *On Agriculture* how an intelligent farmer could use such days without breaching religious bans (Cato *Agr.* 2.4, 138; Colum. 2.21; Serv. *Georg.* 1.268–72). But because they lacked a general concept of labor, a general ban of labor did not occur to the religious specialists. Public activities, too, were limited: no popular assemblies could be held, and no juridical activities involving magistrates could be performed. Hence, the occurrence of annual *feriae* or the short-term announcement of extraordinary *feriae* for the expiation of prodigies could severely interrupt or halt processes of decision-making. The legitimate meeting of the Senate, however, was not subject to these bans.

Feriae, however, while an important religious component within the Roman calendar, did not determine its structure. Important elements originated from the period of the lunisolar calendar. Lunisolar calendars were the normal form of calendars in the ancient Mediterranean basin. The months were designed to correspond to the phases of the moon, either through empirical observation and correction or by assigning each month an appropriate and conventional number of days. Twelve lunar cycles, however, equal only 354 days, so this total had to be harmonized with the solar year of 365.24 days by occasional additions (intercalations) of a thirteenth month. At Rome, the first day of the month, the Kalends (*kalendae*) was the day when the size of the waning moon indicated when a new crescent moon would next appear, on a day termed the Nones (*nonae*). The Ides were supposed to correspond to the nights of the full moon. This structure, probably taken over from the Etruscans, was fixed during the early Republic in order to establish a predictable relationship with a recurring week of eight days (without gaps), beginning with a market day (*nundinae*).[22] Although the rituals to determine empirically when months began and ended and the external appearance of a lunisolar calendar were preserved, a calendar based on the solar year was later established, the advantages of which, however, were not fully realized before Caesar. Prior to Caesar's reforms, the calendar contained twelve months of 28, 29, or 31 days each, which resulted in a year of only 355 days. The addition of intercalary months of 22 or 23 days was required to bring the total number of days up to 365, but this task was performed only irregularly by the pontiffs. Consequently, calendar dates could differ significantly from solar dates. Julius Caesar's calendar reform increased the number of days in several months and so reduced the period of intercalation needed to equal 365.24 days per calendar year to a single day every fourth year.[23] Apart from antiquarian sources, to be found particularly in Macrobius' *Saturnalia* (fifth century AD) and Festus' lexicon *De verborum significatu* (*On the Meaning of Words*, second century AD), only one copy of a pre-Julian calendar has survived, the fairly complete fragments of a painted calendar from Antium, the *Fasti Antiates maiores* (*Inscr. Ital.* 13.2.2–27).

Permanently established and annually recurring activities were coordinated with the monthly rhythm. Interest had to be paid on Kalends, loans were drawn on Kalends and repaid on Ides, and birthdays were celebrated on the nearest Kalends or Ides. The Senate met frequently, though far from exclusively, on the Kalends and the Ides. Cicero's long-term planning took place in terms of Kalends, Nones, and Ides. For the meals on these same days the sumptuary laws of the second century permitted greater expenditures than usual.[24] The rituals of these days were addressed to the most important deities of the Roman pantheon – Jupiter, Juno, Mars, and Janus – and performed by the highest priests – pontiffs and the *rex* and *regina sacrorum* (king and queen of the sacrifices). Short-term economic, judicial, and political activities, however, were coordinated with the rhythm of the market days. Prohibiting or permitting popular assemblies led by the tribunes of the *plebs* on these *nundinae* led to serious political conflict and resulted in the Hortensian Law of 287, which precluded holding assemblies on market days. Legislative proposals had to be announced at least three successive market days (*trinundinum*) in advance of the assembly that would vote on them.

The date of its first appearance in the calendar did not necessarily determine the importance of a ritual of communication with the gods. There are no indications that the rituals of many old festivals attracted a large audience. The horse races of the Equirria or the October horse are only known from antiquarian sources. Neither the Saturnalia in mid-December nor the New Year's Day celebration on the *kalendae Ianuariae* involved the great priesthoods, but these festivals were extremely popular and exported to many areas of the Roman Empire. The ancient ritual activities of the *Luperci* and *Salii* were prominent and probably well attended, however. These were groups of (typically) younger priests who performed races or dances in archaic costumes. It was at the Lupercalia of 44 that Antony offered a crown to Caesar.[25] And the Salian priest P. Cornelius Scipio Africanus used the period when the Salian dances were being performed at Rome to demonstrate the seriousness with which he took his religious obligations by interrupting the military campaign he and his brother were conducting in Thrace in 190 (Polyb. 21.13.7–14; Livy 37.33.6–7).

It seems as if some ritual forms developed or imported during the fourth century gained increasing popularity in the third. Such new forms grew out of crisis rituals and remained as such or became annual events. These rituals were characterized by the involvement of numerous gods and numerous men. *Lectisternia* and *sellisternia* displayed special or improvised busts of 12 gods on banquet furniture (couches or chairs, respectively) in public spaces. The supplications (*supplicationes*) or festivals of thanksgiving mentioned above invited the crowd to visit all the temples of the city.[26] The Republic's most spectacular successes were celebrated in the processions (*pompae*) of the circus-games and triumphs (the latter attracting large audiences because of the ever increasing amount of booty displayed; see also Chapters 16 and 23) and the ensuing theatrical games or more old-fashioned races (*ludi*).[27]

The *ludi Romani* (Roman games), also known as *ludi maximi* (greatest games), originated at the beginning of the Republic. They included a procession, sacrifices and races. According to the annalistic tradition (Livy 7.2.1–3; cf. Val. Max. 2.4.4), the expiation of a pestilence caused dramatic performances (*ludi scaenici*) to be added, probably as a fifth day, to the old annual festival.[28] We cannot say much about the form of these musical and dance performances. In 249, on the occasion of the crisis ritual of the *ludi Tarentini*, nocturnal performances of dramatic plays took place that Varro saw as part of the history of Roman drama (in *Cens.* 17.8). Only in 240 did the Romans see translations of Greek plays. In 235 the first dramatic production of Gnaeus Naevius took place (Gell. *NA* 17.21.45). Occasions multiplied. Probably in 220 the *ludi plebeii* (plebeian games) and *ludi Cereris* (games of Ceres) began to be repeated annually. From 217 onwards votive games were a usual expiation measure ordered by the Senate; votive games of victorious magistrates had been given on numerous occasions before this date. In 208 the *ludi Apollinares* (games of Apollo) introduced in 212 became annual; the *ludi Megalenses* for Mater Magna or Cybele were given annually from 191 onwards; and likewise the *ludi Florales* for the goddess Flora from 173. Dramatic productions dominated. That development and the texts produced for the stage are part of the literary history of Rome (see Chapter 25), but primarily these form part of the religious history of the epoch. Dramas were given for the gods.

Communicating with the Gods

The gods could be addressed for many reasons: thanksgiving, asking for favors, exploring the divine will. In general, the Romans were not excessively eager to contact them. The gods were thought of as members of an ordered society who had obligations and rights. They were to receive their share and, for the most part, no more. The astonishing openness of the system that admitted more and more gods on private initiative (see above) does not indicate exaggerated piety but rather corresponds to the openness of the citizen body on the human level. By freeing one's slaves anybody could produce new citizens without a magistrate's permission.

Communicating with the gods by ritual means always had two aspects: the construction of the divine addressee and secondary communication among men. In daily speech, in oratory, or in letters the gods were frequently addressed collectively as *di immortales* (immortal gods). Such a phrase would not do for polytheistic ritual. Among the multitude of gods the right one for the present purpose had to be found and named. The superiority of the addressee and his or her qualities and personality had to be affirmed. Because the addressee was not as visible or tangible in the interaction as human addressees normally were, the speaker's conception of his divine recipient had to be produced and confirmed, one of the most important features of religious ritual. As already mentioned, the choice of the place and the time helped to single out the other pole of the communicative act. As in human relationships between equals or unequals, the choice of the gift was important. It had to be adequate in terms of kind, color, quantity, or value – for example unblemished, white, female cattle for Juno Regina after the birth of a hermaphrodite. The gift could at the same time define the addressee. A deity given a male animal must be male; a deity given a white animal had to be a celestial god. Divination followed, for the success of the actual communication (apart from its later results) was at risk. Every major sacrifice was accompanied by divinatory practices to find out whether the addressee thought the gift was acceptable in that specific situation. The absence of a heart in the victim did not reveal a hidden flaw in the animal chosen. Instead, it constituted a sign sent by the addressee at the very moment of sacrifice. Thus the divinatory practices surrounding the ritual communication were a kind of second-order communication verifying the successful establishment of the first-order communication and stressing that the gods were sovereign with regard to human attempts to contact them.

Indirect human communication is another second-order trait of ritual communication with the gods. Most rituals were prominently and intentionally visible. Secret rituals (mysteries) did not play the same role at Rome they did in Greece.[29] Nocturnal rites were prominent only in the ritual activities of women, for example, the nocturnal prayers of women during the secular games of Augustus or the rites of Bona Dea organized by a leading magistrate's wife.[30] Marginalized social roles and temporal margins reinforced one other, which points up some principles of agency and religious competence. Basically, religious competence, like political position, depended on one's social role. The *pater familias* (the head of the family) led domestic sacrifice, while the magistrate led public sacrifice, supported by noble children and public slaves. The *collegium pontificum*, which included the pontiffs themselves, the *flamines* (priests responsible for individual cults) and the *rex sacrorum*, did have a certain share in public ritual, but typically it participated more in ancient routine rituals and obscure cults than in the great games or spectacular crisis rituals.

The *sacerdotes publici* (public priests) had perhaps in earlier times been more charismatic figures, but in the historic era they were members of the nobility and organized in colleges (see also Chapter 12). Typically, early entry was usual for *flamines* and probably *Luperci* and *Salii* (in their early twenties) as well as for the other priests (in their late twenties or early thirties), and foreshadowed a splendid career. For "new men", on the other hand, membership in a priesthood came after the consulate and crowned a successful career. Hence consular fathers in one priesthood tried to get their sons into another college, if possible one even more prestigious, as early as possible.[31] Cooptation based on friendship and the ban on clan concentration within any one priesthood formed the basic principle of reproduction. It was temporarily modified by elements of popular election – from the second half of the third century onward 17 out of 35 tribes (*tribus*) drawn by lot elected the highest pontiff (*pontifex maximus*) from a list of candidates nominated by the college. For the period after 104 until Sulla and again from 63 onward, the same procedure was at the least also applied to the selection of all augurs and pontiffs. During the late Republic the balance for priests between a lifelong special role and an annual term of office like a magistrate tilted toward the magisterial model, but significant differences between priestly and political roles were maintained.[32]

Socially, the priesthoods formed commissions of the Senate or, from a more anthropological perspective, banqueting circles among the nobility.[33] The size of the colleges, even after this was raised to nine members each by the Ogulnian law in 300, which introduced plebeians into the priesthoods, stayed within the limit seen as optimal for symposia. Only Sulla's policy to secure places in the priesthoods for all his important followers and supporters swelled their ranks to 15. After bloody civil wars, Caesar sought to attain the same goal by adding a sixteenth position to the augurs, pontiffs, and the *quindecimviri sacris faciundis* (15 men for the performance of rituals). The name of the latter college remained the same, however, as did the now ten-member *septemviri epulonum*, the "seven" (previously three) men who cared in particular for the banquets (*epulae*) organized for Jupiter. The *pontifex maximus* (the earliest one to be popularly elected) enjoyed a certain concentration of supervision, but this never supplanted the principle of a broadly and evenly distributed religious competence. Roman priests, the supreme pontiff included, remained part-time – or, better, spare-time – priests.[34] Priestly roles supported social prestige; they did not oppose it. Given these circumstances, the accumulation of religious knowledge or the elaboration of ritual remained meager. The use of writing allowed individuals the possibility of creating additional expertise and elaborating on traditions. Such processes are discernible from the third century onward, for example, in the Commentaries of the Priests (*commentarii sacerdotum*) and in augural monographs composed in the first century, yet these did not gather a momentum that could overrule conflicting views. At least the names of former members could be ascertained beyond doubt.[35] Contrary to widespread opinion, Roman priesthoods had only a limited share in religious communication, and the men who held them did not profit as priests but as members of the nobility in other roles from the enormous intensification of efforts at communication with the gods and their communicatory effects within the society that began in the third century.

Recent interpretations by ancient historians have stressed the intensified communication between the political elite and the Roman People within the ritual framework of the games (see Chapter 1). That contact enforced the mutual relationship of patronage and loyalty and explains the People's willingness to participate in the extensive warfare led by the nobles.[36] Such an interpretation could (and does) gain support from the growing social hierarchization reflected in the seating arrangements at the games and from the People's gestures of greeting, disapproval, or support for individual senators there. It could also point to instances of spontaneous applause for and enforced repetitions of isolated passages in performances that were capable of being taken as comments on the contemporary political scene. Such an interpretation does not, however, succeed in answering or even addressing the question of the relationship of this second-order communication to the primary communication between the People of Rome and the gods that such games represented. Concentrating on the religious framework of political communication does not invalidate the observations referred to in this paragraph, but it does put them into a different and more agent-based perspective.

The gods, whether they were full of anger at the Roman People or had recently been extremely helpful to them, were the addressees of these ritual activities. They were offered the best – cultural innovations recently imported from the Greek world. The ritual agents, the dancers, musicians, and actors (who were undergoing a process of professionalization or who were already professionals at this point) were mere instruments. These performers, who frequently were foreigners themselves, visitors to Rome by force or for profit, put on undeniably Greek performances, culture for ostentation. The gods were spectators, part of the audience, and only participants in a more intensive manner through the sacrifices offered to them. The Roman citizens were spectators, too, watching the gods watching the performances offered to them. The gods' tastes corresponded to those of the elite who were eagerly Hellenizing their villas and lifestyles. The crowd enjoyed participating by observing elite culture. They saw plays performed by the same actors who entertained at aristocratic symposia.[37] Even in their titles, many plays, comedies in particular, stressed their Greek origins, even if they dealt with problems and situations from Roman life (see also Chapter 25). Different genres could address different sorts of problems and values. Historical dramas (*praetexta*) treated the same subjects that the more private and elite forms of epic and historiography did, while comedy dealt with daily life and social structure. The Roman way of life was enhanced by superior foreign cultural products at the same time that Rome demonstrated its dominance by actively and forcefully transporting this culture to Rome. Roman gods enjoyed Greek marble statues, too. It is no accident that the assembly of Roman nobles, the Senate, took care that this form of participation in elite culture was only temporary. The Roman *plebs* would not enjoy a permanent stone theater for watching these performances before the age of Pompey and Caesar, in contrast to circuses, where permanent structures appeared earlier. The Senate's decision might have had another end in view as well. The use of public space in the center of the city for theatrical performances instead of a temple at some random place in the city and the involvement of the magistrates of the year instead of priests who served for life made the dramatic festivals extremely up-to-date, flexible, and central. And they involved many gods and a whole array of public cult, not merely a portion of these dear to a small number of devoted followers and selected by individual decision. The gods were not less but more present. Why?

Legitimizing Men

One should not separate the games from another form of public religion, auspication.[38] Taking the auspices (*auspicia*) was basically the prerogative and activity (*auspicium*) of magistrates. Private auspication existed but did not concern the public, except when it conferred a short-term immunity from the draft (Gell. *NA* 16.4.4).[39] Consuls and praetors had to ask Jupiter for his consent before every major activity, and that consent was valid for that day only. If the activity could not be completed on the same day or consent was not given, the divinatory procedure would have to be repeated another day. At Rome, the normal procedure was for the magistrate to rise before dawn, choose a place for the observation (*spectio*), and wait for a sign. The ritual definition of his field of observation, called a *templum*, while usual for auspication in the daylight, was probably not performed for observations in the dark. Apart from traditional positive or negative signs, which permitted or forbade action, the magistrate himself could define signs that he would consider positive. Once the aural signs had been received (or lightning seen, which conveyed a strong prohibition), the *spectio* was finished, and the action the magistrate intended could be tackled.[40]

This divinatory system produced a piecemeal legitimation of the use of power. Legitimation was given on a daily basis only. A general, who had taken the auspices (after his election as a magistrate) upon entering office, on the day of his departure from Rome, upon crossing rivers, and on many other occasions, also had to repeat the procedure on the morning he proposed to fight a battle. The procedure could be enormously simplified. Generals in the field did not get up after midnight to watch for signs, but had chickens carried around in cages. To take the auspices before battle, generals ordered the chicken keeper (*pullarius*) to feed them and observe how they ate and whether their eating was greedy, which was the best sign (the *tripudium solistimum*, e.g., Livy 10.40.4). The necessity of renewed legitimation remained. Stories about generals' neglect of the auspices resulting in military catastrophes – Flaminius' defeat at Lake Trasimene, for example (Cic. *Div.* 1.77) – drove home the same point. Coins bearing augural symbols, in particular the augural crozier (*lituus*), also stressed the importance of augural legitimation. Furthermore, *obnuntiatio*, the observation and announcement of adverse signs, was possible. Such augural protests were often debated and even neglected, but the system worked and even intensified into the very late Republic.[41]

Claims easily conflicted. Because the rituals and their outcomes were not visible, utterances counted, not verifiable observations. The *augures*, the priestly college that advised and judged in these matters, possessed high prestige. Being in the center of political decisions, special regulations applied to these *augures*. Two members of the same family were not permitted to be members of the *collegium* at the same time, and membership was not cancelled even in cases of exile (a debatable privilege, however). Members were equal in competence, and were not ruled by an *augur maximus* corresponding to the *pontifex maximus*. The term *augur maximus* meant simply the oldest, that is, the longest serving, augur.

Augural legitimation by the gods was not insulated from politics. Religious legitimation went further. Even public votes involved elements of sortition, that is, divine intervention by lot to determine the sequence of the voting units. Other public actions relied on the lot, for example, the assignment of provinces to magistrates and promagistrates.[42] It is obvious to us, and it was obvious to the Romans, that many procedures such as casting lots were open to manipulation, and accusations of manipulation were sure to spark controversy and debate. Thus, their functioning could not be guaranteed by technical procedures but only by the undeniable involvement of the gods, who were even more aware of fictitious signs than contemporary humans. The gods alone were able to ensure effective legitimation by such procedures. To be able to do so, they had to be intensively present, to be talked about, and represented by frequent and lavish cult. *Mos maiorum* (the custom of the ancestors) functioned similarly. Appeal to the forefathers could only be effective if the ancestors were permanently present in statues, rituals, rhetorical *exempla* (exemplary stories), and literature.

Involving All

Involving the gods in public matters was not restricted to magistrates. The gods could send *signa* (signs) to anybody. Private *omina* (omens) were taken seriously even by public institutions, for example, in the context of military conscription (see above). A more difficult problem was presented by the private observation of signs that might be of public importance. Romans were taught how such a conflict ought to be resolved in the Roman way – not by a myth but by an episode from the Republic's early history preserved by Livy (2.36.1–8). The gods warned of a ritual fault in the Roman games by sending a dream to an ordinary citizen, Titus Latinius. His reluctance to risk being held up to ridicule by telling the magistrate about his dream caused the gods to send a massive warning to do so, the death of his son within a few days. However, only after another dream and another warning in form of a sickness that befell Latinius himself did he venture to approach the consul. His message was taken seriously, the message to the Senate was verified by a miracle, and the games were splendidly repeated (Livy 2.37.1). Such a repetition to expiate ritual faults was called *instauratio*.

The Romans dealt with the broad spectrum of obtrusive, oblative signs related to public life under the heading of *prodigia* (prodigies). These could be observed by anyone but had to be reported to a magistrate who would present them to the Senate for discussion. The Senate either made its decision directly or brought the priesthoods in for interpretation and recommendation concerning expiation. Private initiative hence caused senatorial reaction. Within the diffused religious authority of the Roman aristocracy the Senate held a central place and a position of control.

The procedure was frequent and routine. Its importance is demonstrated by the rise of a third college. While the *pontifices* were frequently consulted about prodigies and gave advice on the necessary expiatory rituals (*procuratio prodigiorum*), they seldom performed these. The augurs had no part in the procedures. For very special or new cases, the Sibylline books, a collection of oracles written in Greek, were consulted. For that purpose a small commission of two men was set up, the *duoviri sacris faciundis*, who slowly evolved into a priesthood second only to augurs and pontiffs. The Ogulnian law of 300 initiated this process which created, however, a college with ten members (*decemviri*), a number more appropriate to a political commission than a priesthood (the augurs and pontiffs each had nine members). The assimilation of the *decemviri* to these other priesthoods must have been complete by the end of the third century, and was sealed by the common increase of all three to fifteen and then sixteen members in the first century. The *decemviri* chose a fitting oracle and interpreted it in response to a *prodigium*. Their hallmark was the introduction of new cults, gods, and rituals from the Greek world. Thus, they formed an element of organized innovation within the senatorial system. Occasionally the Senate called upon *haruspices*, Etruscan specialists in divination, particularly extispicy, the examination of the entrails of sacrificial victims. Thus when the Senate ordered it, foreign wisdom could confer legitimacy.

The signs reckoned as prodigies included a wide variety of events. Earthquakes, rains of blood, bleeding statues, temples and statues struck by lightning, hermaph-rodites, two-headed animals, a swarm of bees establishing itself in a temple were all typical signs and brought forth standard expiation, but anything unusual with an ominous quality could be discussed. The system allowed input from everybody, and as Roman territory expanded so, too, did the area regarded as relevant for prodigies and their expiation.[43] Times of crisis encouraged People to involve themselves and the gods even more in Roman life and politics. Auspication as interpreted in the preceding section was but one form of divine presence. It should, however, be stressed that Roman institutions were not prepared to accept communications from the gods without limits. Individual observations of signs could be rejected as not pertaining to society as a whole, and reports of signs could be totally banned.[44]

Prodigies included the misbehavior of priests, especially the priestesses of Vesta, the *virgines Vestales*. These were six girls (from the age of 6 onwards) and women who performed a minimum of 30 years' religious service in the center of Rome, the *aedes Vestae* (see also Chapter 15). The supposedly uniconic cult of the public hearth was (and was regarded by the Romans) as archaic. The concept of their purity made a Vestal's sexual contact with men an offence, *stuprum*, punishable by death. From the perspective of late republican noble families, their daughters, if serving as Vestals, were hostages in the hands of the supreme pontiff, yet the latter's ascendancy was not earlier than the third century. More generally, the Vestals were a female priesthood that symbolized and indicated the purity of the religious system as a whole. Experi-ments attempting to create a comparable role for the priest of Jupiter, the *flamen Dialis*, were restricted to a few instances in the late third century (Val. Max. 1.1.4–5) and were always resisted by the priests subjected to such regulations.[45]

Excluding Others

Recent approaches to the religion of the Roman Republic have stressed its political functions. That might distort reality, but it accords with many contemporary sources. Because religion functioned as an important source of legitimacy for the ruling elite, they fought or avoided the establishment of any independent religious authority. Yet such authorities existed. Their occasional mention in our sources shows that time and again Rome witnessed the appearance of prophetic figures (*vates*). Tradition preserved the memory of the Marcian brothers and their prophecies (*carmina Marciana*) from the era of the Second Punic War. The role of such *vates* seems to have included public criticism of moral misconduct and ethical imperatives. Early Augustan poets revived that role. Horace, for example, uttered his *Epodes* criticizing contemporary politics and society at least partly in the guise of such a warning voice.[46]

Religious competence and hence authority could thus come from outside, and were regarded with suspicion by the political elite. The salvation cult of Dionysus, a classic case of the evolution of an independent religious association in Greek cities beginning in the archaic age, spread throughout central Italy during the fourth and third centuries.[47] At Rome in 186, the Senate prosecuted Dionysiac (or, to use a cultic title, Bacchic) groups according to Livy on charges of political conspiracy and plotting insurrection (Livy 39.8.3–19.7; see Chapters 22 and 28).[48] The resolution of the Senate in response to the discovery of the "Bacchic Conspiracy," known from a southern Italian copy (*Senatus consultum de Bacchanalibus, CIL* 1^2, 581 = *ILLRP* 511 = *ILS* 18 = *ROL* 4:254–59; see also Chapters 2, 22, and 28), refrained from prohibiting the cult as such or infringing the rights of the god Liber/Bacchus. It did, however, severely limit the possibilities of organization by restricting the number of adherents and people who could be present at its rites. The decree also placed formal religious authority in the hands of women only, thus preventing the cult from acquiring any major influence. The copy was found in the territory of a Roman colony and the wording has usually been taken to indicate that Rome intended to put this regulation in force in Italy also.[49] It is difficult to assess, however, how far the Senate was successful or intended to be successful outside Roman territory proper.

Adherents of other cults were present at Rome. The Isiacs, worshipers dedicated to the female deity Isis, followed a cult the origins of which lay in Egypt but had spread throughout the Mediterranean in Hellenistic times. Exotic features made the cult attractive, but they did not hinder far-reaching processes of cultural interchange. During the last century of the Republic (and during the 60s and 50s in particular) the cult was prosecuted, not for the veneration of a foreign deity, however, but on charges of popular unrest and illegal association.[50]

The persecution of these cults did not encourage the survival of favorable sources of information about them, and so an assessment of their impact is difficult. Literary and archaeological evidence attests the spread of Dionysiac as well as Isiac imagery. Thus the situation parallels another important area of personal religion, votive religion.[51] Tens of thousands of votive offerings – miniature objects, symbols of individual status, reproductions of afflicted parts of the body now conveniently published in the series *Corpus delle stipi votive in Italia* – attest to the enormous diffusion and social acceptance of this practice (see also Chapter 4). Religious communication here served very personal ends, such as imploring the help of the gods for healing, childbirth, professional success, or wealth. The granting of divine help was acknowledged by the gift the maker of the vow had promised, thus completing and affirming the extended communication. But a secondary communication among humans was involved, too. The wealth of votive dedications announced to others seeking help the power of the god in whose temple or temple area they were set up. Religious action furthered religious action, action toward the gods.

Conclusion

Powerful, immortal, and invisible, Roman gods could nevertheless be seen as members of Roman society. They were present in spatial, economic, and temporal terms and as images. Yet above all they were present in interaction, in human acts of communication that made use of the temporal and spatial infrastructures of festivals and temples. A diversified system of priesthoods provided expertise for this ritual communication, but the priests did not monopolize contacts between humans and the divine. On the whole, the Romans believed that they owed these communicative efforts to the gods and that they were helpful, effective, and worthy of further elaboration. Ritual communication held an important place in the public life of Roman society. Most Romans were not interested in the private lives of the gods.

Guide to Further Reading

Introductory accounts of Roman religion, not in some cases restricted to the Republic, are given by North 2000, Scheid 2003, and Rüpke 2001c. Liebeschuetz 1979 remains a reliable and thought-provoking history from the late Republic onwards. Beard, North, and Price 1998 combine a volume of historically arranged systematic chapters with a second volume of selections of translated texts and substantial introductions dealing with different topics. The collection of sources in Warrior 2002 is useful, but lacks a coherent critical framework within which to approach these texts. A critical review and comprehensive bibliography on research in Roman religion has been published by Belayche et al. 2000 and 2003 (to be continued). Ando 2003 offers a collection of articles documenting important and divergent approaches to Roman religion. Very valuable, too, is the collection of articles in Bispham and Smith 2000, discussing new evidence as well as interpretative models. Bendlin's criticism of the model of polis religion is deepened in Bendlin 2001. Important rituals are discussed in Bergmann and Kondoleon 1999. Feeney 1998 discusses the relationship between late republican and Augustan literature and religion; his points are taken farther in Barchiesi, Rüpke, and Stevens 2004. Rawson 1985, a monograph on the intellectual history of the Republic, is valuable for republican religion as are many of her articles, collected in Rawson 1991. Linderski 1995 discusses important augural institutions and the literary sources for them. Most of the republican temples are discussed in Ziolkowski 1992, and individual festivals in

Scullard 1981. For a complete prosopography of Roman priests see Rüpke 2005 (English translation forthcoming). For many details on festivals, priesthoods, and rituals, the entries in the *Neue Pauly* (English translation as *Brill's New Pauly*) are useful and supply additional references.

Acknowledgments

I should like to thank Diana Püschel for her help in preparing the English text, Andreas Bendlin for continuing discussion, and the editors for their critical and helpful remarks.

Notes

1   Beard 1986.
2   On communication: Rüpke 2001b.
3   Hickson 1993: 61.
4   Latte 1960: 81.
5   Bakker 1994.
6   Cancik 1985/6.
7   Cornell 1995: 198–214; see Chapters 4 and 6.
8   Coarelli 1987; Quilici and Quilici Gigli 1995.
9   Bendlin 1998.
10 Gros 1976.
11 Orlin 1997.
12 Orlin 1997: 188–90.
13 Scheer 2000: 1–34 for other positions.
14 Gladigow 1983, 1998.
15 Burkert 1985. For Roman religion, a balanced view in Beard, North, and Price 1998: 344–7.
16 For Celtic religion, e.g., Clavel-Lévêque 1972; Van Andringa 2002: 133–204.
17 Wagenvoort 1947.
18 Examples in Scheid 1987; systematic critiques in Graf 1993.
19 Hölkeskamp 1999.
20 Koch 1937, with the introduction of Arcella in Koch 1986.
21 Rüpke 1995b: 492–522, esp. 493.
22 Michels 1967.
23 Rüpke 1995b: 369–91.
24 Rüpke 2001c: 190–7.
25 Cic. *Phil.* 2.87; Nic. Dam. 21; see also *CIL* 6.31200; Val. Max. 2.2.9; and for Augustus' restitution of the Lupercalia: Suet. *Aug.* 31.4.
26 Latte 1960: 242–51; cf. Beard, North, and Price 1998: 63.
27 Bernstein 1998 for *ludi* and for triumphs Rüpke forthcoming; *contra*, Versnel 1970 and Flower 1996.
28 Debate on the reform: Bernstein 1998: 119–29; cf. Rawson 1991: 473.

29 See Kippenberg and Stroumsa 1995.

30 Schnegg-Köhler 2002; Brouwer 1989.

31 North 1990a; Rüpke 2005.

32 *Contra*, Scheid 2001.

33 Banqueting circles: Rüpke 2005: 1419–39.

34 Rüpke 1996.

35 Rawson 1985; Rüpke 2005: 1475–500.

36 Flaig 2003: 232–60.

37 Rüpke 2001a.

38 For all factual information see Linderski 1986.

39 Rüpke 1990: 69.

40 Vaahtera 2001: 115–16 stresses the aural nature of these signs.

41 Linderski 1995: 309–22; Libero 1992.

42 Stewart 1998; cf. Linderski 1995: 467; *contra*, Rosenstein 1995.

43 MacBain 1982; Rosenberger 1998.

44 Scheid 2001.

45 Rüpke 2005: 1571–4.

46 Wiseman 2000.

47 Burkert 1987: 432–51, 1985: 290–5, 1987.

48 Pailler 1988; Beard, North and Price 1998: 91–6.

49 *Contra*, now, however, Mouritsen 1998: 49–58.

50 Mora 1990: 72–87; Malaise 1972.

51 Van Straten 1981; Rüpke 2001c: 154–66.

CHAPTER 11

Law in the Roman Republic

Michael C. Alexander

The Roman Republic witnessed the development of the central concepts, doctrines, and procedures connected with Roman Law. Although most of our sources for Roman Law date from a later period, the authors of these later sources refined what the legal creativity of the Republic had already transmitted to them. "The jurists of the Principate perfected the work of the great originators of the Republic."[1] This chapter describes the institutional framework that created a field of intellectual endeavor that, perhaps more than any other, the Romans created for themselves, rather than borrowing and adapting conceptions from the Greeks.

Evidence

Just as we must view classical Roman Law through the prism of later evidence dating from Late Antiquity, our understanding of Roman Law as it developed during the Republic is based largely on sources from the end of that period or from the early principate, such as Cicero, Dionysius of Halicarnassus, and Livy. Therefore, this chapter will focus primarily on the later Republic, since most of what we know or guess about the early Republican law is based on sources from a much later date. Even if these sources are ostensibly dealing with, e.g., the fifth century BC, their views are often influenced by the legal system that functioned in their own time.

The nature of our literary sources imposes an additional distortion on our understanding of Roman Law. The imperial sources are overwhelmingly juristic, that is, they present views about the law in general, even if to some extent (and modern scholars debate to what extent) these views may reflect opinions about real cases. From the late Republic, on the other hand, we possess over twenty forensic speeches that originated in real trials. Legal historians tend to find these speeches somewhat unsatisfactory as source materials, for a number of reasons: (1) they do not represent precise copies of the speeches as delivered; (2) they were crafted by advocates, not jurists; (3) they were designed to sway citizen jurors, not expert jurists; and (4) they were intended to serve the interests of the advocates' clients, not to present legal doctrine. Nevertheless, even a bewildering speech of Cicero, e.g., his *Pro Cluentio*, tells us more about the details of the trial at which it was delivered than we know for any trial from the imperial period (the one exception being Apuleius' self-defense [*Apology*], a speech delivered at a trial on a charge of magic in the mid-second century AD). This discrepancy in the surviving evidence can easily lead to a misperception that the republican law was practical and based on reality, and imperial law theoretical and based on abstraction. In fact, actual cases and legal science reacted fruitfully with each other during both the Republic and the Empire.

Chronology

The secular law that applied to Roman citizens (*cives Romani*) consists of two parts, *ius civile*, that is, the law for Roman *cives* ("citizens"), which was based on custom, the Twelve Tables, and statutes, and *ius honorarium*, the law developed by the praetors with the authority of their office (*honor*). (Religious law is not covered in this chapter.) The history of Roman Law has been divided into four periods, which, however, do not correspond to the four traditional periods of Roman political and constitutional history (Monarchy, Republic, and Empire [divided into Principate and Dominate]). A typical outline of these periods is:

Archaic (foundation of Rome to 200 BC)
Formative (200 BC to AD 130)
Classical (AD 130–235)
Post-classical (AD 235–534)

This periodization is based on the following turning points. The archaic period presumably began with the foundation of Rome, although it emerges for us only with the Twelve Tables owing to the limitation of our source materials. The formative period begins with the reconstruction of Italy after Rome's victory in the Second Punic War and with Rome's expansion into the Greek East. This chapter will deal primarily with this period, or at least that part of it which fell within the Republic. The formative period can be divided into three sub-periods, according to the engine driving legal change within private law: first, legislation, from about 200; then the praetor's edict,[2] from the Aebutian Law (below) up to the Cornelian Law on the Administration of Justice of 67 (below), and finally the activity of the jurisconsults. The formative period saw the development of four innovative mechanisms in Roman Law: the "statement of issue" (*formula*) as an alternative to the "writ" (*legis actio*), the praetor's annual standing edict (*edictum perpetuum*), the development of the standing criminal court, and the semi-professionalization of the jurisconsult and a concomitant body of juristic literature. Frier argues that the wide powers developed by the praetors and consequent legal instability in the second sub-period were checked by the jurisconsults, who supplied calm and continuity through their legal science.[3] The classical period begins with the fixing of the praetor's *edictum perpetuum* under Hadrian around AD 130.[4] The fall of the Severan emperors marks the beginning of the post-classical era.

Sources of Law

The *ius civile* can be said to be based on four "sources" of law: custom, the Twelve Tables, *legis actiones*, and legislation. The word "source" here is not used to refer to evidence, but to those entities that generated legally authoritative statements.

Custom

Ius civile stems in part from some fundamental concepts and principles of Roman Law, such as paternal power (*patria potestas*).[5] The role of custom, always problematic in jurisprudence, is hard to define. On the one hand, Roman orators frequently held up ancient custom (*mos maiorum*) as a justification for the legal position that they happened to be propounding, or denounced their opponents for contravening the same. Clearly, arguments based on custom had persuasive force. On the other hand, because custom was by definition unwritten, today we are not in a position to evaluate these arguments as readily as we can legal points based on the other legal sources.[6]

Twelve Tables

The Twelve Tables constitute the beginning of Roman Law as we know it. To be sure, the reigns of some of the kings are marked by major acts of legislation according to our (much later) historical accounts, such as the works of Livy and Plutarch; however, these authors are unlikely to have possessed reliable evidence about this legislation. Most likely, proponents of particular legislative programs attempted to garner support for them by linking them to various laws of one king or another (see also Chapter 6). Still, it is entirely reasonable to suppose that Rome had developed a substantial body of law over the course of some three hundred years of history prior to the Twelve Tables (assuming the traditional chronology). According to legend, in 451, as a response to popular pressure, a body of ten legislators (*decemviri*) was elected who produced ten tables of laws, and in the following year a new body of *decemviri* produced two more tables. These last items aroused great resentment, especially by including a ban on marriage between patricians and plebeians. In 449, after a decemvir's attempt to rob a maiden of her virtue was preempted by her father's decision to take her life, the decemvirs were expelled from office (Livy 3.31–59; Dion. Hal. *Ant. Rom.* 10.57–60). Many areas of uncertainty, however, cloud this narrative. For example, the *decemviri*, besides serving as an *ad hoc* commission, are also reported to have performed the quite different role of taking the place of all the ordinary magistrates of Rome. Moreover, some sources attribute Greek influence in the process, claiming that a delegation was sent to Athens in 454 to copy the laws of Solon and to study the laws and customs of the other Greek states (Livy 3.31.8). Scholars agree that this is highly unlikely, though some are willing to posit a Greek influence from southern Italy. Some ancient sources relate that the philosopher Hermodorus of Ephesus, an exile in Italy, assisted the decemvirs (Pompon. *Dig.* 1.2.2.4; Pliny *HN* 34.21; Strabo 14.1.25), and the Tables contain the Greek loan-word *poena* ("punishment").[7] Even though the publication of these laws is presented by our sources as a concession to the common people, almost all of the *decemviri* were patrician. Therefore, the popular movement gave patricians the opportunity to write laws favorable to their own interests. This apparent contradiction can probably be explained by the notion that the publication of law *ipso facto* benefits the less powerful even if the rules are written by the ruling class, in that it forces the members of the ruling class to be consistent, rather than inventing and twisting laws in individual cases to suit their own interests.

The Twelve Tables, while not constituting a systematic legal code, seem to have provided laws in the main areas of Roman life: slavery and freedom, family and property, the economy, and society. Livy describes them as "the source of all public and private law" (3.34.6). We possess only fragments from them, transmitted by later authors in a form of Latin much closer to classical Latin than the archaic form of the language in which they must have been originally written. Each rule is typically expressed as a future imperative clause, with a conditional clause that defines the situation, e.g., on the subject of the repair of roads:

> Ni sam delapidassint, qua volet iumenta agito.
> Unless they laid it with stones, he is to drive carts where he shall wish.

The syntax of the sentence is often quite clumsy, with frequent changes of subject:

> Si in ius vocat, <ito>. Ni it, antestamino.
> If he [i.e., a plaintiff] summons to law, he [the defendant] is to go. If he does not go, he [the plaintiff] is to call [someone else] to witness.[8]

In spite of these limitations, the Twelve Tables provide the starting point for discussion of many (possibly preexisting) areas of Roman Law: for example, trial procedure, debt and debt bondage (*nexum*), the power of the head of the family (*paterfamilias*), marriage, succession, property transfers, delicts (roughly equivalent to torts), theft, homicide, and treason.

Publication of writs

The issue of publication arose again in 304, when the official calendar, with days when legal actions could and could not be brought (see Chapter 11), and the precise wording of previously existing *legis actiones* ("writs"), were made public by Cn. Flavius (Cic. *Mur.* 25; *Att.* 6.1.8; Livy 9.46.5; Pliny *HN* 33.17). The steps whereby this disclosure took place are somewhat clouded. We know that Flavius was the son of a freedman, that he served as a public scribe to Appius Claudius Caecus (cens. 312), that he became curule aedile, and that he disclosed this material previously known only to the *pontifices* (priests). However, the order of these events is unclear, as is the role of his patron Appius, who may have encouraged his protégé to engage in this seditious activity, as well as the identity of the source from whom, according to one account (Pompon. *Dig.* 1.2.2.7), Flavius stole the information. It was important to know the exact wording of the *legis actiones* because the success of a lawsuit could easily hinge on the choice of words; thus, a suit relating to the destruction of vines failed once because the plaintiff, by referring to them as *"vites"* ("vines") rather than the more general *arbores* ("trees"), had failed to create a sufficient link to the Twelve Tables (Gai. *Inst.* 4.11).[9] Publication of the calendar, with the legal characteristic of each date, must have become more important as Roman territory expanded and Roman citizens lived ever farther from the city of Rome. Otherwise people might have journeyed to Rome to attend to legal business, only to find that a series of *dies nefasti* (days unfit for business) rendered the trip useless.[10] Moreover, knowledge of the law, as long as it had been a patrician monopoly, must have enhanced patrician power, because non-patricians would have been dependent on them for assistance in legal matters. The Roman aristocracy's resentment against Flavius suggests that the publication of legal norms chiefly benefited those outside the group of insiders who administered the law.

Legislation

The fourth source of the *ius civile* was legislation, either statutes (*leges*), which were enacted by one of the assemblies of the Roman People, or decisions enacted by the plebeians (*plebiscite*; see also Chapter 12). After 286 BC, *plebiscita* became binding on all citizens, both patrician and plebeian. Decrees of the Senate (*senatus consulta*), on the other hand, did not possess the force of law during the Republic.[11] Once *plebiscita* could be used to legislate for all citizens, they appear to have become the normal medium for legislation on matters relating to private law. Legislation dealt with many different aspects of life, for example, legal procedure, debt, property, and family law.[12] Many statutes were not designed to lead to the outright prohibition of certain actions or to prosecute those who had committed them; their primary effect was to render unenforceable in court certain claims resulting from those actions. For example, if someone who had been promised a gift contrary to the provisions of the Cincian Law of 204 BC went to court to claim his gift, the defense could counter the claim by arguing that the gift violated that statute.[13]

Private Law and the Praetor's Law

By the end of the Republic the *formula* had almost entirely replaced the *legis actio* as the main structural element in private law. The *legis actiones* were ready-made, verbally fixed expressions of the case at issue, whereas the *formula* allowed the parties to a lawsuit and the praetor to negotiate a precise formulation of the legal issue in a case, which could then be decided by a judge or judges (*iudex* or *iudices*).[14] The existence, or the increased importance, of the *formula* was the result of the Aebutian Law, which was enacted probably in the second century. For a long time the *legis actio* and the *formula* coexisted, in spite of the virtues of the latter, since the older procedure might offer some advantage to one of the parties.[15] We know that, by the time of Aulus Gellius (second century AD), the *legis actio* was a dead letter. Gellius relates an anecdote in which an expert in Roman Law lumps the *legis actio* together with a group of legal terms that were rendered obsolete by the passage of the Aebutian Law. Apart from the use of the *legis actio* before the centumviral court, Gellius' expert concludes that the practicing jurisconsult of that day no longer needed to know about this procedure (Gell. *NA* 16.10.8; Gai. *Inst.* 4.30). The formulary procedure in private law created a division of a lawsuit into two parts. The first, in the praetor's court (*in iure*), would occur before a magistrate (generally a praetor), during which the issue in the case would be defined through the *formula*. The second part "before judges" (*apud iudices*) would occur before a juror (*iudex*), a small group of "recoverers" (*recuperatores*), or a large group of jurors (*centumviri*), who were charged with applying the law to the factual and legal situation as he or they were able to discover it. The verdict of the juror or these adjudicators was not subject to appeal.

The *ius honorarium* (magistrate's law) came into being to "assist, supplement, or correct" the *ius civile*, from which it remained separate in Roman jurisprudence (Papin. *Dig.* 1.1.7.1). Two praetors, the urban praetor and the peregrine praetor, ran the law courts dealing with private matters, with the sole exception of the law of sale, which fell within the domain of the aediles.[16] Although praetors did not decide on verdicts in a trial, they did decide whether or not a case would go to trial, and whether to grant any number of requests that were likely to arise. These included injunctions to prevent certain things from taking place, grants of possession, and overturning the results of some deceptive practices. At the beginning of their 12-month term the new praetors announced an edict, called an *edictum perpetuum*, that clarified what kinds of cases they would admit to their dockets, and what other rulings they were willing to grant. Although originally the praetor may have simply been supplying remedies effectively to "shore up" the traditional *ius civile*, the praetor's edict ultimately became one of the main vehicles for the development of Roman Law.[17] Cicero's attack on Verres, who served as urban praetor at Rome in 74, provides our fullest example of the workings of the *ius honorarium* (2 *Verr.* 1.103–58), particularly in matters relating to succession.[18] The power of the *ius honorarium* was somewhat limited in 67 by a statute which required that praetors announce the rules they intended to follow at the beginning of their term of office, and that they adhere to those rules for the duration of their term (Asc. 59C; Dio Cass. 36.40.1).[19] This law, designed to reduce the power of praetors to curry favor through arbitrary or inconsistent rulings, is generally seen to have ushered in a change in the focus of legal innovation, from the heyday of the urban praetor to that of the jurists.

Criminal Law

In the field of criminal law, a major shift has occurred in current thought about its origins. For Mommsen, the key institutions were magisterial *coercitio* ("compulsion") and *provocatio* ("appeal") to the People. He posited three steps in criminal procedure: a decision by a magistrate to execute or flog a Roman citizen, appeal by a citizen to the Roman People against this executive (not judicial) action, and finally an assembly of the Roman People that functioned as a trial court to decide whether to uphold or quash the magistrate's decision.[20] Kunkel has attempted to undermine this reconstruction. He points to the paucity of evidence supporting Mommsen's theory, to the fact that those officials recorded as presiding over the comitial trials never held the magistracies that included *coercitio* among their powers, and finally to the implausibility that ordinary crime (as opposed to political crime) could have been handled by the cumbersome process of a popular vote in the Centuriate Assembly. On the basis of some scraps of evidence, he posits an archaic procedure of private prosecution for ordinary crime.[21] In Kunkel's view the essential limitation on the magistrate's power and protection for the citizen lay in the principle that, in any trial of a Roman citizen, the magistrate was bound by the decision of an advisory council (*consilium*) that in essence functioned as a jury. For example, he maintains that whenever a Roman citizen was brought to trial before the three magistrates who handled ordinary crimes (*tresviri capitales*), a *consilium* sat in judgment and pronounced a verdict.[22] In his view, then, the procedure of the later standing criminal courts (*quaestiones perpetuae*, to use the modern term; below) was a direct descendant of these earlier kinds of courts, whereas Mommsen's model of *coercitio* followed by comitial trial stands in sharp contrast to the subsequent standing criminal court. However, while Kunkel's reconstruction is generally compelling when dealing with the steps in the development of the *quaestio perpetua* during the second and first centuries, it is less so when dealing with the very scanty evidence for the earliest beginnings of Roman criminal law. A fundamental obstacle to any reconstruction of Roman criminal procedure remains that the standing criminal courts allowed for no appeal from their verdicts, this despite the fact that Cicero places great emphasis on *provocatio* as a bulwark of a Roman citizen's freedom (*Rep.* 2.54, *Leg,* 3.6, 27, *De or.* 2.199).

Two generalizations about Roman criminal law may suggest ways to circumvent, if not resolve, the controversy between Mommsen's and Kunkel's points of view. Roman criminal law was hardly a uniform system; rather, it was marked by two basic distinctions, both recognized by Kunkel. First, crimes that threatened the state were viewed in a fundamentally different way from crimes that affected only an individual or perhaps an individual and his or her immediate circle. Second, while all Roman citizens, unlike slaves, had a right not to be dishonored arbitrarily, it was thought natural that upper-class individuals would receive fundamentally different legal treatment than their lower-class contemporaries. In other words, although the formal distinction between "more honorable people" (*honestiores*) and "more humble people" (*humiliores*), with milder punishments for the former, did not achieve official status until the imperial era, already during the Republic differing social status generated a different system of criminal justice for upper- and lower-class citizens. So it is not surprising to find a variety of criminal procedures that do not conform to one principle in any obvious way.

Before the first standing criminal court (*quaestio perpetua*) was introduced in 149, there were five ways of dealing with crime.[23] (1) A *paterfamilias* could punish a family member who broke the law (see also Chapter 15). (2) The *tresviri capitales* provided summary justice for servile or lower-class freeborn malefactors. (3) An aggrieved citizen could prosecute another in a private criminal action that would, if successful, lead to the defendant being bound to the complainant. (4) A magistrate (generally a tribune of the People) could bring a citizen before the Centuriate Assembly for judgment in what is in modern scholarly parlance referred to as a *iudicium populi* ("people's court"). The crime charged was almost always treason, so clearly this unwieldy procedure was set in motion only for the most serious of charges. After Sulla's reform of the judicial system in 81, this procedure almost entirely disappears. (5) A special commission could be established by the Senate to investigate a serious threat to the state, especially from multiple crimes committed by groups. A law passed when Gaius Gracchus was tribune of the People (123 and 122 BC) required that the establishment of such a commission be approved by the People, and this requirement rendered this option less attractive. Different procedures were targeted at different sorts of people. Procedure no. 2 applied solely to lower-class citizens, whereas for the most part only upper-class citizens were in a position to commit the crimes prosecuted under procedure no. 4. Single individuals would rarely find themselves before a special commission (no. 5).

The last century of the Republic saw a major shift to a new form of criminal procedure termed today the *quaestiones perpetuae*, or standing criminal courts; these are also referred to as the *iudicia publica* ("public courts"). This institution was created in 149 to deal with the problem of Roman governors misusing their powers in their provinces. As Rome's empire expanded, promagisterial malfeasance was a rising problem that the Roman Senate first attempted to address by creating special commissions, usually as a direct response to the entreaties of foreign embassies. However, in 149 a permanent court, complete with an assigned magistrate and a cadre of jurors, was established to deal with extortion (*repetundae*).[24] We know that Sulla's legislation created at least half a dozen such standing courts, although several probably had already come into existence between 149 and Sulla's dictatorship. The *quaestiones perpetuae* were the most enduring elements in Sulla's legislation, and indeed one of the most enduring products of the Roman Republic, since they lasted well into the Principate, having ceased by the early third century AD (Paul. *Dig.* 48.1.8). By then they had become the venue for lower-class defendants, while senatorial and imperial courts assumed the business of trying individuals charged with crimes that affected the state.[25] The courts as of 80 were as follows:[26] (1) extortion (*res repetundae*)[27]; (2) embezzlement of state property (*peculatus*); (3) electoral misconduct (*ambitus*); (4) treason (*maiestas*); (5) murder and poisoning (*de sicariis et veneficiis* – this probably joined two previous courts, one for "dagger-men," and one for poisoners); (6) violence (*vis*); (7) forgery (*de falsis*); and possibly (8) injury *(de iniuriis)*. Praetors presided over these courts, with the frequent exception of the court dealing with murder and poisoning, in which it was more normal for a special official, called a *iudex quaestionis*, to preside (see also Chapter 20).[28]

While most of these courts arose out of one legislative program (Sulla's), they varied according to the purpose of each law. For example, the penalties were different. In the case of extortion and embezzlement, the issue was the improper receipt of money, and so a calculation of damages *(litis aestimatio)* was held to determine how much money was owed, and to whom. The penalty was strengthened in successive laws relating to *ambitus*, from a ten-year ban on candidacy to office, to a ten-year banishment from Rome and Italy, and then perhaps exile for life. We do not know what the penalty was for those who were convicted *de iniuriis*. The penalty prescribed in the murder and poisoning court, in the court on "political associations" *(de sodaliciis)*, and in the violence *(vis)* court was capital. By custom – at least for the kind of upper-class defendant who predominated in these *quaestiones* – a capital penalty did not involve actual execution but *de facto* banishment, ratified by a statute or plebiscite interdicting the condemned from fire and water *(interdictio aquae et ignis)*. In other words, the defendant was allowed to flee beyond Roman jurisdiction to avoid death (Polyb. 6.14.7). But condemnation in these courts also brought disgrace *(infamia)* and almost always, in the case of courts with a pecuniary penalty, bankruptcy, so exile was a frequent result of a condemnation. Some statutes setting up these *quaestiones* may have offered rewards *(praemia)* to a successful prosecutor – for example, money, an elevation in status, or forgiveness for past crimes of which he had been convicted. However, these rewards were not uniform under all these statutes. Judicial rewards seem to have particularly generous under those statutes aimed at electoral misconduct, probably because such crimes involved complex operations and required incentives to convince some of the participants to inform on other confederates.[29]

In many ways, trials in these *quaestiones* contained the elements that we today expect of a trial: a defendant, defended by one or more speakers *(patroni)*; a presiding magistrate, although unlike a modern judge he probably had little control over the actual trial once it began; and a jury. As with modern trials, prosecution and defense had some rights to reject jurors whom they found unsuitable; however, the number of jurors varied, and the jury decided its verdict by simple majority vote. Although the issue of whether the jurors should be senators or "knights" *(equites)* wracked the late Republic (Tac. *Ann.* 12.60.4), a consensus prevailed that jurors needed to be drawn from the upper classes rather than from a cross-section of the population, presumably because rich people were thought to be more expensive to bribe. During a trial each side made a set speech, or speeches, prepared in advance but delivered extemporaneously. Presentation of witnesses followed; the prosecution, but not the defense, had the right to compel the testimony of a limited number of witnesses. Then the jurors voted. In the extortion and embezzlement courts, the *litis aestimatio* followed to assess and allocate damages.[30]

Five features stand out in sharp contrast to modern judicial procedure. First, the prosecutor was not a government official, but a private citizen. Very often at least one of the prosecutors was an injured party, with skilled speakers brought in to assist him. Since service as a prosecutor was thought to provide an appropriate beginning to a political career, as long as one did not persist in this vein, the prosecutors tended to be younger, less experienced, and less prestigious than the defense speakers. Second, slave witnesses had to be interrogated under torture (see also Chapter 14). Third, after presentation of evidence the prosecution and defense speakers dueled in a question-and-answer session called an *altercatio*. Fourth, there is a meager amount of evidence to suggest, and a substantial amount of evidence that fails to contradict, the conclusion that prosecutors did not present in advance of the trial itself a bill of indictment containing a list of specific alleged crimes; rather, during the trial prosecutors were free to present any charges that constituted violations of the statute under which the trial was being held.[31] Finally, the magistrate did not control the court proceedings by accepting or overruling objections from the opposing attorneys. The speakers were free to say what they wanted and to present whatever evidence they chose. While to modern observers this freedom might lend the appearance of anarchy to Roman judicial proceedings, ultimately Roman jurors determined what was or was not appropriate for them to consider, according to their understanding of what was relevant to the case.

Law outside Rome

When we think about law in the Roman world of the Republic, it is natural to focus on Roman Law, but in fact most inhabitants who lived under Roman rule could neither avail themselves of the protections of Roman Law, nor were they normally liable under it, except for situations in which they had interacted with a Roman citizen. Only following the conclusion of the Social War in the early first century, when free Italians were enrolled as Roman citizens, did most residents of Italy become subject to Roman Law. Before that most belonged to allied states that maintained autonomy and, therefore, their own legal system and judiciary. However, it is not entirely clear whether after Italian enfranchisement all Roman citizens, many of whom now lived far from Rome, were subject to courts at Rome for acts committed in their own localities. Cloud raises the issue of murder and violence committed within Italy.[32] The jurisdiction of the *quaestio de sicariis*, for example, applied only within one Roman mile of Rome (*Collatio* 1.3.1). Possibly a Roman citizen could be prosecuted in the same trial for murders committed both within Rome and beyond Rome, as perhaps Cluentius was in 66.

Similarly, under normal circumstances most inhabitants of Rome's empire, which by the end of the Republic was far-flung, even if it had not yet reached its greatest extent, were unable to avail themselves of Roman Law. The Roman governor wielded enormous power, whenever he chose to exercise it, over Romans and non-Romans alike, although Roman citizens possessed some due process rights that non-Romans did not, and some cities had special privileges that limited the jurisdiction of Roman officials. Each governor issued an edict analogous to the urban praetor's annual edict, and this edict presumably embodied concepts and principles of Roman Law. Though the governor delegated some judicial activity to subordinates, such as his quaestors, he traveled around his province extensively to hold trials, advised by a *consilium* composed of locally resident Roman citizens and members of his staff. Nevertheless, during his tenure in office, a governor wielded enormous power, checked only by the threat of an indictment for provincial extortion trial that might be launched after his term of office had expired.[33]

The Jurisconsults

The most distinctive aspect of Roman legal institutions was the jurisconsult (variously termed *iurisconsultus, iurisprudens,* or *iurisperitus*), who inherited the prestige of the public priests (*pontifices)* of Rome in the area of law. The role of the jurisconsults was, in Cicero's words (*De or.* 1.212), to *respondere* (provide legal advice in response to questions), *agere* (assist in trials), and *cavere* (draft documents). Our main source for the development of the role of the jurisconsult comes from a selection found in the *Digest* (1.2.2.pr.-53) from the *Enchiridium,* or *Manual,* of Pomponius, a jurist of the second century AD. Although the text is often vexed, and the author's historical sense is weak, it provides a capsule history of Roman jurisprudence – the *locus classicus* on the subject. Pomponius writes that knowledge of the Twelve Tables and of the *legis actiones* lay in the hands of the College of *Pontifices,* and that one of the priests was selected each year to preside over matters of private law (see also Chapter 10). This remained the practice for nearly a hundred years, until Cn. Flavius published the *legis actiones* (Pompon. *Dig.* 1.2.2.6–7). Pomponius mentions 25 jurisconsults from the Republican period, including some very well-known names, such as Ap. Claudius Caecus (cos. 307 and 296), the builder of the *via Appia* (*Dig.* 1.2.2.36), and P. Rutilius Rufus (cos. 105), who despite his exemplary conduct as legate in Asia was condemned in the extortion court (*Dig.* 1.2.2.40).

The jurisconsults became the dominant force in the development of Roman law, particularly private law. Schiller identifies four factors responsible for their remarkable influence: (1) they constituted a specific group of individuals dedicated to the law; (2) they possessed comprehensive expertise in private law; (3) they were closely involved in the administration of law; and (4) they accepted disagreement and debate among themselves as normal.[34] Jurists trained their successors by allowing young men to hear them respond to legal questions in their homes and in the Forum (see also Chapter 20).[35] Ti. Coruncanius (*pontifex maximus* c.254–243) was the first to make public pronouncements (*profiteri*) about the law (Pompon. *Dig.* 1.2.2.38). In this connection Pomponius (*Dig.* 1.2.2.35) makes it clear that he is referring to his willingness to speak publicly about the law, as opposed to restricting his pronouncements to private communication with those who had brought him questions, and Pomponius adds that his *responsa* (answers) have been remembered, although no writings of his survived. The first jurist to leave an extensive written record was Sex. Aelius Paetus Catus (cos. 198), who wrote a work called the *Tripertita,* or three-part work, so titled because it in some manner divided legal knowledge into three parts, namely the Law of the Twelve Tables, then a section that furnished interpretation of them, and a third providing the relevant *legis actio* (Pompon. *Dig.* 1.2.2.38). Pomponius says that the three "founders of the civil law" (*Dig.* 1.2.2.39) were P. Mucius Scaevola (cos. 133, *pontifex maximus* 130–c.115), an ally of Ti. Gracchus, M. Iunius Brutus (pr. c.140), whose *responsa* were contained in a work on the civil law (*de iure civili*), and M'. Manilius (cos. 149).

Q. Mucius Scaevola (cos. 95, *pontifex maximus* c.89–82) "Pontifex," the son of the first of these, and killed in 82, raised the systematic exposition of the law to a new level of sophistication: "He was the first to arrange the civil law in categories" (Pompon. *Dig.* 1.2.2.41).[36] For example, he divided tutorship (*tutela*) into five categories (*genera*) (Gai. *Inst.* 1.188). Although the term *genera* has been argued to have come from Greek dialectic, which was characterized by analysis into the *genos* (genus) and *eidos* (species), the mere use of this term, especially without its companion *species*, does not provide a strong case for direct Greek influence. Of course, Mucius, like any educated Roman, would naturally have been familiar with Greek philosophy. As Wieacker points out, philologists, who typically deal with a Greco-Roman high culture, are inclined to attribute to Greek philosophy an important influence on Roman jurisprudence, whereas specialists in Roman law, according to Wieacker, are more likely to view Roman jurisprudence as a continuous and autonomous discipline.[37] In any event, the issue of influence from Greek philosophy on the jurisconsults has to be addressed both in terms of its likely effect on the substance of Roman Law, that is, decisions in individual cases, and in terms of the jurisconsults' employment of Greek philosophical methods to analyze and present Roman Law (see also Chapter 20).[38]

Of the later Republican jurists, C. Aquillius Gallus (pr. 66) carried high prestige among the people (*Dig.* 1.2.2.42). He served as a legal advisor to Cicero's client Caecina (Cic. *Caecin.* 77–9, 95), and gave "his dominion (*regnum*) in the courts" (Cic. *Att.* 1.1.1) as one reason for declining to stand for election to the consulate of 63.[39] The last great jurist of the republican era was Ser. Sulpicius Rufus (cos. 51).[40] Pomponius (*Dig.* 1.2.2.43) relates the story that Servius, having already achieved high standing as an orator, was unable to understand a response to a legal question that he himself had posed to the great jurisconsult, Q. Mucius Scaevola. Mucius reportedly took him to task for displaying such ignorance of the law, ignorance unbefitting a distinguished patrician, noble, and forensic orator such as himself. Stung by this criticism, Servius went on to become the most distinguished jurist of the last decades of the Republic. He was a prolific author, composing nearly 180 book chapters (*libri*) comprising many works about the law.[41]

Kunkel has produced a theory about the social status of the jurisconsult that has served as the reference point for all subsequent discussion of the subject.[42] He maintains that, whereas in the second century jurisconsults were aristocrats who almost always achieved the consulate, in the first six decades of the first century, jurisconsults were usually of equestrian status and almost never achieved the consulate. Cicero mocked the jurisconsults and their inability to translate juristic eminence into political success through his portrayal of Servius Sulpicius' unsuccessful campaign for the consulate of 62 (the famous "*Juristenkomik*," *pro Murena*; see below); it is worth noting, however, that Servius did reach that office in 51. Kunkel posits two causes of the jurisconsults' decline in status: (1) Late republican political instability, which undercut the rule of law and made oratory a more successful route to power than jurisprudence, and (2) a weakening of the aristocracy, thus opening the way for the knights (*equites*) to take over. Legal historians have questioned some aspects of Kunkel's account, particularly when he employs an expansive definition of "equestrian" that includes many who went on to acquire senatorial status. Frier argues that, in fact, during the post-Sullan period, when Roman citizenship spread throughout the Italian peninsula, jurisprudence exercised a great appeal to recently enfranchised Italian Roman citizens, just as the Roman political arena did. He argues that they wished to make use of law to advance their substantial economic interests, and that they therefore had an interest in strengthening legal stability in order to protect themselves, as new citizens, against the traditionally powerful Roman elite, to insulate their property from political perturbations, and to reduce the risk involved in economic decision-making.[43]

Frier distinguishes between the "external" aspect of jurisprudence – responses to the specific questions of petitioners – and the "internal" aspect – the development of an intellectual discipline of law. He maintains, "during the late Republic the 'internal' aspect of legal science steadily gained strength at the expense of the 'external' aspect, until the communication of law came to be thought of as only an ancillary part of a jurist's duties, while legal science was increasingly looked upon as a study of value in itself."[44] Frier identifies Q. Mucius Scaevola ("Pontifex") as the key figure in this change, arguing that when he came on the scene, the stability of the *ius civile* had been threatened by the formulary procedure and the related changeability of the Praetor's Edict, as well as by the growth of rhetorical advocacy. However, Frier also argues that Mucius' commentary on the *ius civile* was essentially conservative, in that it focused on the Roman Law of the Twelve Tables and early statutes, to the neglect of issues raised by the increasingly sophisticated economy of the first century. By contrast, Servius' writings focused on the Praetor's Edict. Frier stresses the originality of Mucius' "casuistic" method: Mucius presented a series of cases in which a legal rule operated, without attempting to formulate the legal rule in the abstract. This method stands in contrast to Anglo-American case law, which draws on the presentation of real or hypothetical cases to illustrate abstract principles. Such a presentation would have made rough going for the novice, and was really aimed at an audience of other legal experts. According to Frier, the development of legal science during the last decades of the Republic therefore raised the prestige of the *ius civile*, and countered the instability caused by the praetors and the orators. It also allowed jurists to influence legal developments without having to become excessively embroiled in individual cases.[45]

The Advocates

Another kind of participant whom litigating parties brought into their case was the advocate (see also Chapters 19, 20, and 25). Unlike in Athenian legal proceedings, where the parties would generally read speeches written for them by others, in the

Roman courts each side was represented by an orator. While the presence of this professional speaker did not preclude the possibility that a prosecutor or defendant might also speak on his, or possibly her (Val. Max. 8.3.1–3), own behalf, an orator was expected to take the lead. But however great his rhetorical powers, he was not necessarily an expert in the law. Therefore, the two groups, orators and jurisconsults, were viewed as distinct,[46] although some orators did possess extensive legal experience, and some jurisconsults were passably good orators: Cicero describes Scaevola as "the most eloquent among those learned in the law, the most learned in the law among the eloquent" (Cic. *De or.* 1.180), and his speeches were actually published (Cic. *Brut.* 163). Cicero states that Servius Sulpicius had started out in rhetoric (*Brut.* 151), as Pomponius says about Aelius Tubero (*Dig.* 1.2.2.46). A few orators had jurisprudential expertise, notably Crassus (Cic. *De or.* 1.40, 216, *Brut.* 145), not to mention Cicero himself, who had studied law under Mucius the augur (*Brut.* 306), and wrote a work (no longer extant) *On Reducing the Civil Law to a Science* (Gell. *NA* 1.22.7; cf. Cic. *De or.* 2.142, where Cicero has Crassus promise to write such a work).[47]

This role of the orator in Roman litigation introduced an element into Roman forensic oratory not present in the Athenian courts, one that Roman rhetorical manuals had to interject as they translated and adapted their Greek predecessors. Most importantly, the Roman advocates brought their own character (*ethos*) into play in order to strengthen the case that they were representing (*De or.* 2.182–4; see also Chapters 20 and 25).[48] These advocates were technically not allowed to accept fees from their clients (*clientes*), and were supposed to act out of a spirit of *noblesse oblige* (see also Chapter 19). Even Kelly, who is inclined to emphasize the practical obstacles to real legal equity, accepts the idea that the institution of forensic *clientela* helps explain why even a poor man could probably find an advocate if he needed one.[49] It was particularly praiseworthy to speak on behalf of a defendant (Cic. *Off.* 2.51), and prosecution was undertaken generally only by younger aristocrats attempting to launch their political careers.

Jurisconsults and Advocates

The relationship between jurisconsult and advocate caused some friction in ancient Rome. For the views of jurisconsults about the advocates, we have to depend on the anecdotes that Cicero puts in the mouth of the chief interlocutor of his dialogue *On the Orator* (*De Oratore*), L. Licinius Crassus (cos. 95). In addition to his reputation as the leading Roman orator of his generation, he possessed excellent legal knowledge (*De or.* 1.166–200). In *On the Orator*, Cicero has Crassus expound on the theme of the advocate who knew so little about the law that he harmed his client's case. For example, he tells of one trial in which the plaintiff's advocate claimed more compensation than the *legis actio* that formed the basis of the case would allow, thereby potentially dooming the action to failure. The defendant's advocate, meanwhile, protested against the size of the plaintiff's claim, not realizing that it lay to his client's interest not to dispute it, and thus to allow a fatally flawed action to go forward (*De or.* 1.167).

In contrast to Crassus' purported contempt for the legal impairments of orators, the orators themselves sometimes showed little respect for the jurisconsults, even though they depended on them for legal advice to prepare their case. Orators regarded the jurisconsults as failed advocates and, thus, as their inferiors, whose function was to supply them with some of the weapons necessary to win the battle that they themselves controlled (Quint. *Inst.* 12.3.4, 9; Cic. *Top.* 65).[50] Roman orators could portray the work of the jurisconsults in a ridiculous light, as Cicero does in his defense of Murena (*Mur.* 23–9). After Murena had defeated the noted jurisconsult Ser. Sulpicius Rufus in 63 for the consulate of 62, Sulpicius accused him of electoral malpractice (*ambitus*). In such a prosecution it was normal to argue that the defeated candidate had by far the better chance of winning and, thus, that the winning candidate must have used improper means to counteract this natural advantage. Sulpicius pointed to his service as a jurisconsult as a source of popularity, so Cicero, as Murena's advocate, ridicules both jurisconsults and jurisprudence in general for their use of the Latin language in ways that make no sense to normal Romans. As exaggerated as Cicero's treatment of this theme may seem, it clearly resonated in Roman popular consciousness.

Traditionally, the influence of oratory on the law, from actual trials to theoretical jurisprudence, has been viewed as malign; whereas jurisconsults guarded Law as an autonomous and everlasting science, advocates used sophistic tricks in defense of ephemeral causes:

> Faithful to the pontifical tradition they (viz., the jurisconsults) were not mere partisans, ready to forward a client's cause by any and every available means, including falsehood, calumny, and emotional appeals, but guardians and promoters of the law. To this tradition they were resolved to be true, and fortunate it was for Roman legal science that they stood fast and refused to suffer the noisome weed of rhetoric, which choked so much else that was fine and precious, to invade their profession.[51]

In support of this point of view, scholars have pointed to a statement of the jurisconsult Aquillius Gallus quoted by Cicero (*Top.* 51): " 'This has nothing to do with the law; it has to do with Cicero,' said our friend Gallus, if anyone brought him anything involving a question of fact." This statement has been interpreted to mean that the task of the jurisconsult was connected only with the law, while the task of the forensic orator was connected only with non-legal matters. However, Crook argues persuasively that the passage should be translated as "This is not law, (it's a fact): it's for Cicero." According to Crook, therefore, Gallus' remark does imply that jurisconsults should deal only with the law, and not facts, but it does not say that the orators cannot deal with the law. "The facts *were* their territory – facts in the context of the law."[52] But how much attention did Roman forensic orators pay to the facts? Crook attacks the view that Roman advocates strayed into irrelevancy because they misapplied the precepts of Greek rhetorical manuals to the Roman courts, which used a substantially different procedure from their Greek counterparts. Clarke had contrasted Greek and Roman courts. For example, in Athenian courts witnesses were heard before speeches were delivered, and so the Athenian speakers were introducing arguments based on evidence that had already been presented to the court; in Roman courts the order was reversed, and therefore the Roman advocate when presenting his case could not refer to a known body of fact, and might not even be familiar with the facts that would be introduced by the other side.[53] Crook, on the contrary, while he accepts the argument that Roman forensic speeches were full of irrelevancy, maintains that the various digressions were well calculated to serve the clients' interests.[54] Another viewpoint related to the orators' supposed indifference to law, and accepted by many Roman historians in past decades, maintained that Roman trials, particularly criminal trials, were so bound up in the political conflicts of the time that the verdict often depended more on political considerations than on a judicial combination of relevant facts with the law. This viewpoint now finds less acceptance than previously.[55]

A well-attested lawsuit that took place in the late 90s seems at first glance to present an archetypical struggle between jurisprudence and oratory. Coponius left an inheritance to his child or children; however, in the event that the offspring died before reaching the age of majority, he designated M'. Curius as substitute heir. When Coponius died, he had no children, so Curius believed that he was entitled to inherit. However, a relative of Coponius, named M. Coponius, who stood to inherit if Coponius was judged to have died intestate, challenged Curius' claim to the inheritance. He pointed out that the conditions of the will had not been met: Coponius had left no children not because they had died, but because none had ever been born. The jurist Q. Mucius Scaevola "Pontifex" (cos. 95), representing M. Coponius, argued for a literal interpretation of the will; the case of Curius was presented by Crassus (also cos. 95), who maintained that his client ought to inherit according to the intention (*voluntas*) of the testator (Cic. *Inv. rhet.* 2.122, *Caecin.* 53, 69, *De or.* 1.180, 238, 242–4, 2.24, 140–1, 221; *Brut.* 144–6, 194–8, 256; *Top.* 44; Quint. *Inst.* 7.6.9).

Stroux interpreted this trial, which goes by the name of the *causa Curiana*, as a turning point in a development from an archaic literal form of jurisprudence, to a more flexible form that in general was influenced by philosophy and Aristotelian rhetoric, and specifically employed the Aristotelian concept of *to epieikes*, or *aequitas* ("equity").[56] This seemingly plausible interpretation dissolves upon closer scrutiny, and has now generally been rejected. To view Scaevola as the personification of literal-minded jurisprudence and Crassus as the personification of flexible rhetoric is mistaken. Scaevola's brief was as much based on rhetorical commonplaces as that of Crassus, nor did it present an unassailable legal argument. " . . . Scaevola's argument in this case was essentially only a handbook rehash of the rhetorical defense of *scriptum*, and not an exercise in abstract jurisprudence."[57] Crassus, on the other hand, attempted to show that Scaevola's interpretation of the law was not the only one possible, for indeed it raised a fundamental and disputed question in the law of succession. In addition, he adduced analogous legal precedents to support his emphasis on *voluntas* (Cic. *Top.* 44), and relied on the opinions of a jurist (his father-in-law Q. Mucius Scaevola "Augur" [cos. 117]) in making his case (Cic. *Caecin.* 69). Cicero presents the case as a prime example for the need of orators to know some law, if only to avoid the appearance of incompetence (Cic. *De or.* 1.180).[58] Crassus and Scaevola were both acting as advocates and were both making the best possible case for their client. Were Crassus to have been defending Coponius, and Scaevola Curius, rather than the other way around, the rhetorical commonplaces that each employed would most probably have been similarly reversed. In fact, we know that Scaevola was well equipped to argue on the basis of intention (Cic. *Brut.* 145, Pompon. *Dig.* 34.2.33), and Crassus could and did present an argument based on the letter of the law (Cic. *Off.* 3.67).[59] That Crassus and Scaevola were both excellent advocates capable of marshalling legal arguments in an expert manner should hardly cause surprise, for Crassus was reputed the best jurisconsult among the speakers, and Scaevola the best speaker among the jurisconsults (Cic. *Brut.* 145). In short, the *causa Curiana* did not open the door to a more flexible jurisprudence.[60]

Crook, in fact, attacks the previously accepted contention that the growth of advocacy in the second and first centuries caused a divorce between jurisprudence and oratory, and the decline of the latter in the early Principate, by cheapening trials with a rhetorical bag of tricks. If the most productive period of Roman Law coincided with the heyday of the forensic advocates and their rhetoric, he argues, we need to consider the possibility, at least, that rhetoric had a salutary effect on jurisprudence. As Frier argues, the growth of oratory compelled legal science to rest on socially persuasive foundations broader than the law alone.[61]

Guide to Further Reading

Crook's chapter on private law (Crook 1994) and Cloud's on criminal and constitutional law (Cloud 1994) in the *Cambridge Ancient History* provide good starting points for the study of Roman Law. Crook 1967 presents a lively overview of Roman society through its law, and Johnston 1999 attempts to understand Roman Law in light of its society and economy. Jolowicz and Nicholas 1972 gives a chronologically organized description of the development of Roman Law, as does Kunkel 1973. For those trained in modern law, the most accessible introduction may be Wolff 1951. Thomas 1976 presents an outline of classical Roman Law according to the standard scheme (actions, property, obligations, persons, and succession). Schiller 1978 is very helpful in explaining the basics of research in Roman Law. Watson 1974 deals with private law in the last two centuries of the Republic.

Perhaps the best way to get a sense of Roman legal thinking is to work through a book of the *Digest*; this approach has been greatly facilitated by the four-volume translation of the *Digest*, including Latin text, edited by Alan Watson (*Digest of Justinian* 1985); a separate revised version of the translation alone has also been published (*Digest of Justinian* 1998). A less expensive alternative is the Penguin translation of the section of the *Digest* that deals with delicts (*Digest of Roman Law*), and Frier 1989 uses the casebook method as practiced in American law schools to elucidate this material, much of which is based on republican law. Robinson 1997 outlines the sources for the study of Roman Law, and how they can be marshaled in historical research. No ancient work provides a clearer and more authoritative account of ancient oratory and the contexts in which it operated than Cicero's *On the Orator*, written in 55. May and Wisse 2001 provide a useful translation, with introduction and explanatory material.

Many readers of this volume will have been introduced to Roman Law through the medium of Cicero's forensic speeches. Frier 1985 offers a brilliant and profound explication not merely of the trial in which Cicero delivered the *pro Caecina*, but also of the historical and jurisprudential context in which the trial took place. Bauman 1996 gives an overview of Roman criminal law. Riggsby 1999 provides a scholarly yet concise and readable analysis of the criminal courts of Cicero's time. Crook 1995 presents a sensible defense of the role of the advocate in Roman trials, and Alexander 2002 attempts to understand criminal trials of the Late Republic from the point of view of the prosecutor. For the details of court procedure, the venerable Greenidge 1901 is still a very useful manual. Brennan 2000, in his magisterial study of the praetorship, analyzes the praetor's judicial functions.

Acknowledgments

I would like to thank Prof. Nicholas K. Rauh of Purdue University and Joseph O'Neill, a former graduate student in the Department of History at the University of Illinois at Chicago, for their comments and corrections on an earlier draft of this chapter, as well as the editors of this volume.

Notes

1   Schulz 1946: 126. See also Crook 1995: 177.
2   Kelly 1966a: 346–8; Watson 1974: 31–62, "The Development of the Praetor's Edict."
3   Frier 1983: 222, 239–41, contesting Schulz 1946: 50, 53.
4   Schulz 1946: 99, for Augustus' rule as the beginning of this period. See also Schulz 1946: 39 for the term "Hellenistic" instead of "formative"; see also Crook 1994: 549.
5   Crook 1994: 532.
6   Watson 1974: 169–70; see also Schiller 1971: 41–55; Thomas 1976: 27–9; Schiller 1978: 253–6.
7   Crook 1994: 549; Cornell 1995: 275.
8   Cornell 1995: 279.
9   Daube 1961: 4–5; Watson 1973: 390.
10 Michels 1967: 110–11, 117–18.
11 Watson 1974: 21–30. But see also Kunkel 1973: 125–6.
12 Crook 1994: 548, 561–3; Crawford 1996b for an overview of Roman legislation.
13 Jolowicz and Nicholas 1972: 87, 207.
14 Crook 1967: 77.
15 Schulz 1946: 76.

16 Brennan 2000: 2.607–9.
17 Kelly 1966a: 348–51, speculative but plausible.
18 Frier 1983: 233 on changes in the praetorian edict between 81 and 60.
19 Jolowicz and Nicholas 1972: 97–101; Crook 1994: 533.
20 Mommsen 1899: 151–74.
21 Kunkel 1962; Jolowicz and Nicholas 1972: 305–17; Lintott 1999a: 153–7.
22 Kunkel 1962: 74.
23 Cloud 1994: 498–505.
24 Cloud 1994: 507–8.
25 Jones 1972: 96–7.
26 Cloud 1994: 505–30.
27 Lintott 1992: 88–169; Crawford 1996b: 1.65–112, no. 1 for the text of and commentary
    on an epigraphically preserved extortion law.
28 Brennan 2000: 2.420–1.
29 Alexander 1985.
30 Greenidge 1901: 456–504.
31 Alexander 1982.
32 Cloud 1994: 527–8.
33 Greenidge 1901: 410–14; Lintott 1993: 36–40, 54–69; Richardson 1994: 589–91.
34 Schiller 1971: 153–4.
35 Atkinson 1970: 31–43.
36 Schiller 1978: 312–15. Bauman 1983: 340–423; this book and Bauman 1985 connect
    legal and political history.
37 Wieacker 1969: 452.
38 Stein 1966: 33 is more ready to acknowledge Greek influence than most Roman law
    scholars. See Watson 1974: 191–3, challenging Schulz 1946: 94; cf. 62. Watson 1974:
    186–95, refining the distinction between substance and form, argues in general against
    Greek influence on Roman Law. On legal definition, as analyzed by Cicero, see Harries
    2002. On Roman legal writing in the Republic and early Principate, see Bauman 1973b.
39 Frier 1985: 139–49.
40 Schiller 1978: 315–17; Bauman 1985: 4–65.
41 Frier 1985: 153–5.
42 Kunkel 1967, esp. 6–37 for brief descriptions of 56 jurisconsults.
43 Frier 1985: 252–60.
44 Frier 1985: 141.
45 Frier 1985: 155–71.
46 *Contra*, Tellegen 1983; David 1992a: 437 n.93.
47 Crook 1995: 146 n.169, *contra*, Schulz 1946: 69.
48 Kennedy 1968.
49 Kelly 1966b: 84 n.1.
50 Crook 1995: 143.
51 Schulz 1946: 54–5.
52 Crook 1995: 143.
53 Clarke 1996: 62–3.
54 Crook 1995: 140–1.
55 Clarke 1996: 65; Riggsby 1999: 5–20; Alexander 2002: 31–8.
56 Stroux 1926: 29–31 = Stroux 1949: 42–6.

57 Frier 1985: 136, citing Cic. *De or.* 1.244; see also Wieacker 1967, Watson 1974: 129–31, and Bauman 1983: 349–51.

58 Watson 1971: 55, 59; Vaughn 1985: 210–14; Frier 1985: 136 n.131. The victory of Crassus does not prove that the legal doctrine presented by him carried the day already in this era; see Mod. *Dig.* 28.6.4 pr. On *aequitas*: Schiller 1941: 753–8, comparing Roman *interpretatio* and Anglo-American interpretation.

59 Vaughn 1985: 222; Dyck 1996: 579.

60 Vaughn 1985; Watson 1971: 94–6; Bauman 1980: 112–16.

61 Crook 1995: 176; Frier 1985: 137.

CHAPTER 12

The Constitution of the Roman Republic

John A. North

Introduction

Republican Rome never had a written constitution. This was not because the Romans were unaware of the possibility of codifying their constitutional practice, because they could and did produce written constitutions for the cities (*coloniae*) they founded in Italy, certainly by the end of the period and probably from the late fourth century onward.[1] In their own case, however, they believed that their system had developed over generations through the accumulating wisdom of their ancestors, not through a single act of legislation. The constitution was not wholly unwritten either, because they passed many laws that modified preexisting practice, changing the number of magistrates, changing procedure in the assemblies, redefining the role of the Senate, and much else. There were also changes that were not so formally recognized, but simply accepted as the way in which business should be handled; adopting a procedure on a particular occasion might always form a precedent for the future.

The consequence is naturally to make the "Roman Constitution" difficult to define and elusive to locate. Modern accounts have sometimes seemed to give the impression of a unified, legally defined, coherent system. This impression is supported by detailed descriptions of the system in action based on reports of individual transactions. This is one sense in which the word "constitution" may be used; but the "constitution" is also the set of rules and principles, written or not, which defines what is permitted or forbidden within the established framework of sovereignty. This is normally evoked only when there are conflicts and disputes about the powers of different bodies or when changes in practice are needed or proposed. This chapter will first try to see what sources of information we have about the Roman system and its early development; then examine its basic working in the late republican period; thirdly look at what light some instances of conflict between powers can throw on the Roman conception. The main argument will be that change and historical evolution must be recognized in any description of the working of the system and that its character must be assessed at any period in the light of that period's conditions.

The term the Romans used for their own system of government was *res publica*, literally "the public thing," which gave rise eventually to our word "republic." The word was used both for the city or state as opposed to the individual citizen and for the particular constitutional system that they maintained from the end of the sixth century onward. The Romans themselves saw a high degree of continuity between the sixth-century origins of this form of government and its continuation down to the first century, to the lifetimes of Cicero and Caesar; but this long period saw radical changes in all aspects of the city of Rome and its life. In the sixth century, Rome was a small town speaking a language shared only by its immediate neighbors, and controlling only a limited area of central Italy; by the first century, it had become the richest and most powerful state in the Mediterranean area, ruling directly territories from Spain in the West to Anatolia in the East. Even the idea of the Romans themselves had been transformed in the course of this unrelenting expansion: not only was the population of Rome the city perhaps approaching one million, but membership of the Roman community – "the Roman citizenship" – had been extended gradually outside the immediate vicinity of the city until it included all the free citizens of Italy. If there is truth to be found in the claim that the constitution was the same at the end of this process as it had been at the beginning, the element of continuity will need to be carefully defined. In any simple sense, the Roman system changed totally in the course of five centuries, though, as the Romans thought themselves, the underlying principles survived.

Cicero, in his political dialogue the *Republic* (Book 2), written in the 50s, not long before the collapse of the republican order during the 40s and 30s, traces republican institutions further back in time than the foundation of the Republic itself. The tradition he followed was that a succession of kings had ruled and to these the different republican institutions owed their origins, many to Romulus the founder, others to Numa, the founder of religious institutions, or to the later kings. The historian Livy, writing a quarter of a century later, presents this as a process of development: the early Romans needed parental guidance; when the last king turned tyrant and was expelled, they had matured and could take care of themselves (Livy 2.1). It is a paradox that the Romans designed their republican system to avoid kingship as the greatest threat to liberty; but regarded their early kings mostly as benefactors, not villains.[2] If the historical accounts of the earliest Republic are to be trusted, then there must be some truth in this picture: basic institutions such as the Senate, the assemblies of the People, the priestly colleges, are assumed to exist already. Modern accounts, led by the classic works of nineteenth-century scholarship which assembled the data, have often followed this ancient tradition by seeing profound continuities from regal to republican Rome, especially in the nature of the powers exercised by the officials who took over from the kings.

There is a great deal to be said for the attempt to understand any constitutional system by tracing its development over time. There is, however, a major problem when applying this method to Rome: for the later Roman Republic we have good information; the earlier the period to be considered, the weaker is the information and the less reliable the conclusions that can be drawn. For the early Republic, we are almost wholly dependent on accounts written centuries later by historians, such as Livy and Dionysius of Halicarnassus, who, at best, had a limited grip on the historical situation they were describing.[3] For the late republican system, we have strong and at times even contemporary sources of information. First, and most direct, are the texts of laws that were passed by Roman political assemblies, recorded as inscriptions on bronze and still surviving today; there are also texts of decrees of the Senate, preserved in various ways.[4] Secondly, there is evidence to be drawn from historians, from other writers, and above all from Cicero's speeches and correspondence about the actual practice of the assemblies, of the Senate at work, of other political meetings, of magistrates at home and abroad; from all this material we can infer much about the rules by which political life in fact operated. Thirdly, we have an invaluable account, written by the second-century Greek historian Polybius (in *Histories*, Book 6), of the constitution as he saw it – the view of a well-informed outsider.[5] Fourthly, we have Cicero's attempts, in his *Republic* and *Laws*, to write his own version of a Roman constitution, albeit as he would have preferred it rather than as it really was in his day (see also Chapter 2).[6]

The evidence is therefore rich, detailed and written from different viewpoints, but all of it comes from the last century of the Republic and is only fully reliable when dealing with that short and relatively well-documented period. One option therefore is simply to describe the late republican situation and not to attempt to reconstruct its past. Such a description is offered below; but it is not possible to be satisfied with this alone. Any constitutional system mediates between the past and the present: its purpose is to provide means of showing how present or proposed actions conform to an old-established rule. In addition, the Romans placed a high value on tradition and therefore took constitutional decisions on the basis of claimed ancient precedents. They appealed to the conception of the *mos maiorum* (ancestral custom) as a reliable guide to legitimacy, implying that continuity was always desirable.[7] It is therefore necessary to work out how the constitution in fact developed so as to understand their ideas of the past. Historians of the Republic try to make sense of Rome's history from the foundation of the Republic, however thin and inadequate they find the surviving accounts. It would be a counsel of despair to say that we cannot even trace some of the main lines of development.

Early Developments

Some key moments of the early history of the Romans formed an essential part of their awareness of their own past and of the character of their institutions. One such moment was the point (traditionally dated to 509) at which the last of the Roman kings was expelled and the monarchic system replaced by magistrates appointed annually. The standard ancient belief (as expressed, e.g., by Livy 2.1–2) was that from this date onward two consuls were elected to hold office for one year, and in due course hold elections for their successors. So, from the very beginning, principles were established that excluded the possibility of return to monarchy: a fixed term for any office; the sharing of power with a colleague; the need for elections to be held by the current office-holder. These principles certainly existed later on and continued to be valid through the late Republic and even into the Empire, but modern discussion has increasingly tended to see the situation after the expulsion of the kings as only a tentative first step toward this later system; on this view, historians writing in the first century BC simply failed to realize how different was the Rome of 600 from the one they knew 500 years later.[8]

It is at least very plausible that the main features of the late republican state as described below can be traced back with some confidence into the second and third centuries. Rome in 300 was recognizably like Rome in 100 in its basic workings. Earlier than that, certainty is unattainable. One antiquarian source – but only one (Festus 290 L) – mentions incidentally that by an Ovinian law, of uncertain date but probably fourth-century, it was fixed that the Senate should consist of the "best men from every order" chosen by the censor, while previously it had been no disgrace for a leading Roman to be passed over in the list. This account can only imply that before the date of this law, the senators were not a fixed body of ex-magistrates, but that a new list was nominated each year. If so, they cannot conceivably have been playing the central role in the constitution that the later Senate did.[9] The fact that we cannot be certain on such a fundamental point as this illustrates how deep are the problems in the way of reconstructing the situation in the fifth and fourth centuries.

The early history of the Roman Republic gave it in one respect at least a character different from most other constitutional systems: the Romans inherited from this early period two conflicting systems that coexisted within the republican order. One was the system of the *populus*; the other, that of the *plebs*. In the later Republic, it was believed that the early population had been divided into two castes, patricians and plebeians; the *populus* consisted of both castes, but the *plebs* only of plebeians. The great mass of the citizens were plebeians, while the political power lay with the patricians who controlled the offices, priesthoods, and law. It is uncertain whether this latter belief was correct or whether it was a retrojection of the situation in the late Republic, when certain patrician clans (*gentes*) held limited inherited privileges in access to office and priesthoods, while the mass of the citizens were plebeians, though by that time including many of the richest and most powerful of the *gentes*.[10]

The accounts we have attribute one set of institutions to the *populus Romanus*, i.e., the established regime, dominated by the patricians; another set to the *plebs*. The plebeians had their own Assembly and, through it, they elected their own magistrates, made their own decisions, and passed their own laws. It seems almost as if there were two states coexisting within the single city, though with overlapping membership. These ancient plebeian institutions were still in existence in the late Republic and played a key role in political history throughout the Republic. The story goes that in the earliest days of the Republic their status was denied by the established regime; that their powers were accepted and incorporated in the course of the Struggle of the Orders; and that, once patricians and plebeians had settled their historic differences, what had once been revolutionary measures came to coexist peacefully with the traditional ones (see Chapter 6). There must be some truth in this narrative, because plebeian officers retained in the first century powers that could be used as weapons of resistance to the authority of the senatorial elite. The revival and use of these ancient powers played a crucial role in the progressive loss of control by the ruling elite that marked the years of the end of the second century and the first half of the first century.

It is also widely accepted that the last years of the fourth century and the early years of the third saw changes of great importance in the evolution of the Roman state. Militarily, Rome began the process of dominating Italy by the creation of a system of city foundations and alliances; politically, the richest families – both patrician and plebeian – were forging a new ruling class, based on success in reaching the consulship, for which both groups were now eligible, and on control of access to power through election. The resulting oligarchy is often called the *nobiles* (nobles), and although the meaning of the term is disputed and the use of any term suggests a degree of class stability that was never in fact achieved by the great families concerned, it has served as a useful shorthand for the dominant elite at any point (see also Chapter 1).[11]

Constitutional Working in the Late Republic

In some respects, it is misleading to think of ancient political institutions through the same terminology as we use for modern ones. Such words as "democracy," "government," "the state," "religion" suggest parallels between ancient and modern conditions that can easily mislead. One such crucial difference is that nothing in ancient Rome corresponds to our notion of an elected government or administration, a group of people charged with carrying on the business of the state and associated with specific theories or policies. In Rome, there were numbers of elected officials – "the magistrates" – charged with particular duties, but never meeting as a group. They held office for a year and were then replaced by their successors. There could be and often was conflict rather than cooperation between these office holders. Policy was discussed and formulated in various arenas (popular meetings (*contiones*); senate meetings; meetings in private houses), but decision and action depended on collaboration between three groups – the voting assemblies, the magistrates, and the Senate. Only by examining the interaction of the three can a picture emerge of the way the constitution could have worked; but first the character of each of the three must be assessed.

Voting Assemblies in Rome

At least in theory, the sovereign bodies in Rome were the primary assemblies (*comitia*) of the Roman People (whether as *populus Romanus* or *plebs Romana*)[12] (see Table 12.1). Only these bodies could hold elections for magistracies; only they could

Table 12.1 Roman assemblies in the late Republic [fo. 441]

	Curiata	*Centuriata*	*Tributa populi*	*Tributa plebis*
Composition	30 lictors, 1 to represent each *curia*	All citizens	All citizens	All plebeians
Meeting place	*Comitium*	Campus Martius	Forum or Capitol, except for elections (Campus Martius)	As for *tributa populi*
Structure	30 *curiae*, 10 from each of 3 ancient tribes	193 centuries, of which 18 *equites*, 170 *pedites*, 5 unarmed	35 tribes, 4 urban, 31 rural	As for *tributa populi*
Presiding officer	Consul, praetor, *pontifex maximus*	Consul, praetor, dictator, *interrex*	Consul, praetor	Tribune of the plebs or aedile of the plebs
Elections	None	Consuls, praetors, censors	Curule aediles, quaestors	Tribunes, aediles of the plebs
Legislation	(under consul) confirm *imperium*; (under *p.m.*) wills, adoptions, etc.	Not normal after 218, except to declare war	Normal in late Republic	Laws (*plebiscita*) proposed by tribunes
Judicial functions	None	Capital charges, but rare in 1st century	Serious charges, but later replaced by courts	As for *tributa populi*, but involving the tribunes

approve laws and also approve certain decisions for action; they were also traditionally courts of justice, though such trials had largely been taken over by standing courts (*quaestiones perpetuae*) by the first century (see also Chapter 11). Without the approval of the *comitia*, much business could not have been completed. All Roman citizens had the right to vote; originally, this meant only those living in the immediate vicinity, but Romans throughout the republican period both admitted adjacent communities to their citizenship and accepted the descendants of freed slaves as full fellow-citizens.[13] Women were entirely excluded from voting and office holding, as they were from military service. Rich women in the later Republic exercised much influence on politics, but not in any public arena (see also Chapter 15).

The *comitia* did not include debate or discussion: the function of *comitia* was to take decisions by voting, the voters being divided into groups, different for the different *comitia*. Discussion and debate took place at a separate meeting called a *contio*. The *contio* was not informal: it had to be summoned by particular magistrates and concern particular business, but it did serve as a possible arena for the expression of views both by set speeches (some of which survive) and by demonstrations of enthusiasm or hostility toward proposals or individuals (see below, and also Chapters 18 and 20).[14]

The system of voting by groups is a characteristic feature of the Roman system that had a remarkable impact on the nature of their political life and differentiated it sharply from the model of voting, known from, e.g., Athens, in which each adult male had a single vote equal to that of all others. Roman votes were never equal. The three main types of assembly corresponded to three different divisions of the Roman People, by *curiae* (*comitia curiata*), by centuries (*comitia centuriata*), and by tribes (*comitia tributa*). The *comitia curiata* may have been the earliest, as the *curiae* were divisions connected with the regal tribal system, about which we know very little; in the late Republic this still met in the form of 30 representatives from the 30 *curiae*, but mostly for ceremonial or ritual purposes.[15]

The *comitia centuriata* was also thought to have been created in the regal period, but was evidently reformed in the course of the Republican period; the century was originally a military unit and the *comitia* took place outside the city's ritual boundary in the Campus Martius, as though it continued to be in essence a meeting of the Roman army. By the late Republic, the century to which an individual citizen belonged was determined, not by military considerations at all, but by a complicated system of classes based on a man's declared property: thus, if you fell in a particular property class you were placed in a century appropriate to your status; also if you were over 46 years of age, you were placed in a century of older men (*seniores*). Proportionately more centuries were allocated to the richer citizens and the same number of centuries to the older ones as to the younger. The mass of the infantry, traditionally peasant farmer-solders owning their own land, were in the lower and larger property-classes. Those without property at all were all registered together in a single century. When the votes were being counted, the richer citizens voted first and once a majority had been reached, the result was declared. The effect of the system was to ensure that the older, richer citizens carried more effective voting weight, the younger and poorer less. It was a consciously contrived conservative system, insuring that the better-off voters would always determine the business, unless they were deeply divided amongst themselves.[16]

The *comitia tributa* seems to have existed in two forms in the late Republic: the *comitia plebis* was the original assembly of the plebeians, presided over by the tribune; the *comitia populi* was a later formation, presided over by a consul or praetor. Both assemblies were based on the institution of the *tribus* (tribe). Each Roman citizen was by birth or by legal act a member of one of 35 tribes, and the full form of his name included the tribe to which he and his family belonged. The invention of the tribe was attributed to King Servius Tullius, who divided the city into four units for this purpose. As Roman citizenship expanded, the number of city tribes remained, but the number of "rustic tribes," each representing a geographic area, increased progressively to the total of 35, reached in 241. From that point onward, new citizens were enrolled in the existing 35, so the geographic unity was lost and the tribes came to have membership drawn from different areas of Italy.[17] As with the other *comitia*, the system worked by voting within the group so as to determine how the tribe's single vote would be cast, but in this case there was no apparent system of privileging the better-off citizens. However, the fact that the mass of the citizens living in the city of Rome was confined to the four urban tribes does imply that a man's vote was worth more if he was registered in a "rustic" tribe than in an urban one. Presumably, also, since all assemblies were held in Rome, poor voters living far from the city would have been reluctant or unable to travel to vote. So the result might be that richer voters could dominate the 31 rustic tribes and ignore the views of the more populous urban ones. This effect, while real enough, may have been offset by the fact that membership in a tribe was inherited, so that those who migrated from country to city or from other parts of Italy into Rome, as thousands did, would have continued to vote in the tribe where their ancestors had originally been registered. In any case, the outcome seems to be that the *comitia tributa* was far more likely than the *comitia centuriata* to vote in ways of which the ruling elite disapproved. This is indeed what happened in the last years of the Republic.[18]

Magistrates

In the late Republic, there was a sequence of magistracies of increasing seniority, which had to be held in order and which had minimum ages attached to them. The starting point was the office of quaestor, which could be held at the age of 30. The endpoint was the consulship, the senior magistracy of the sequence, which could be held at 42 by a plebeian, two years younger by a patrician. At every stage of this sequence there were competitive elections, and each successive office offered greater opportunities for influence and power, leading to the major commands which were only allocated to the consuls. Each office was only held once, so that opportunities did not recur if the first tenure was not a success; the consulship, however, could be held more than once, but only after a fixed interval of ten years.[19]

At each level, the magistrates had defined duties to perform and defined powers that they were able to exercise (see Table 12.2). The supreme power lay with the consuls (or the *dictator*, in case of emergency) and had two aspects: the power (*imperium*) to command men either at home or in the military field and the power (*auspicium*) to consult the gods on behalf of the state. In the influential account developed by Mommsen,[20] these powers both derived ultimately from the single unlimited power of the kings, which could only be passed on from one holder to another in unbroken sequence. Only the two consuls could hold elections for the senior offices of state. If both consuls died before one of them had held the elections in the *comitia centuriata*, no other magistrate, not even the praetor, could perform this function. If there were no consuls, the *auspicia* were said to revert to the *patres*, a term normally used for the whole Senate; in effect, the Senate acquired the right to appoint one of their number as *interrex* for five days, and this special official could either hand on the auspices to a successor or hold the elections himself. In this way the continuity of the auspices was preserved and a legitimate consul could be

Table 12.2 Roman magistrates in the late Republic [fo. 445]

Magistracy	Powers	Age of tenure	Election	Number	History
Dictator (not more than six months)	Superior to all other offices – 24 lictors		Nominated by consul at the Senate's request	One, with a "master of the horse" below him	From 501. Rare after 3rd century but used by Sulla in 82–1; Caesar in 49–4
Censor (18 months, every five years)	Review of senate list; taking of census; "care of morals"	At least middle 40s, often older	Created by consul, after vote in *comitia centuriata*.	Two	Introduced 443; erratic after 86
Consul (One year)	Holds major *imperium* home and abroad – 12 lictors	After 180, at least 42 (patricians 40)	Created by consul or dictator, after vote in *comitia centuriata*	Two, the *fasces* alternating monthly	From early Republic; plebeians admitted 366
Praetor (One year)	Judicial duties in Rome; command of armies outside Rome.	After 180, at least 39 (patricians 37)	Created by consul, after vote in *comitia centuriata*	1 in 366; 2 in 242; 2 more from c.230; 8 by time of Sulla; later – 10/14/16	Introduced in 366, perhaps first as military office, later legal office
Aedile (One year)	Markets, roads, food supply, archives, annual games	36	Plebeian aediles in *comitia tributa*, presided over by tribune; curule, presided over by consul	2 plebeian, 2 curule later 2 for food-supply (46)	2 plebeian in 496; 2 curule in 366; 2 *cereales* in 46.
Quaestor (1 year from Dec. 5)	Assist magistrates with treasury; archives; Italy and the provinces – esp. financial	30 (after 80)	In *comitia tributa*, presided over by a consul	4 early Republic; 10 by 197; 20 from 80; 40 under Caesar	Had automatic entry to Senate after Sulla
Tribune of the plebs (1 year, from Dec. 10)	Propose bills to *comitia tributa*; right to veto acts of magistrates	Unfixed, but often after quaestorship	In *comitia tributa*, presided by a tribune	10 from 366	Created by plebs alone in 496

appointed. The title *interrex* obviously suggests that this institution derived from the times of the king (the *rex*), and it may be that the word *patres* in this context does not mean the whole Senate, but a special patrician subset of it.[21] The senior magistrates were also confirmed in office by a special *lex* (law) called a *lex curiata*, which was passed in the *comitia curiata*; by the late Republic this law had become more or less a ritual action and its meaning was obscure even to contemporaries. But all these proceedings confirm how highly the Romans rated the idea of maintaining a chain of continuity from the earliest times.[22]

Whatever may have been the character or name of the earliest senior magistracy of Rome, by the late Republic there had developed a hierarchy of offices through which the individual was expected to pass on his way to the senior office. There was no differentiation between civil and military careers, and competence was assumed in both respects, at least at the senior levels. Both quaestor and aedile had defined and relatively junior functions, the quaestor in finance or as the aide to a provincial governor, the aedile in the administration of Rome the city. The praetor's position is far more powerful: he shares in the *imperium* of the two consuls, even though his own is lesser than that of a consul and he must give way in case of a conflict.[23]

The tribunate of the plebs, although held by many plebeians in the course of the sequence of offices and before the praetorship, still carried with it the extraordinary powers that the early plebeians had fought to achieve in earlier centuries. The tribune did not have *imperium* and his powers were held to derive ultimately from oaths sworn by the plebeians, but subsequently accepted by the Roman state. The tribune had the right to intercede to protect the rights of any citizen if he needed protection against abuse by one of the other magistrates; he had the right of veto against any action of another magistrate, or against any decree of the Senate. Only the dictator was secure against a tribune's intervention. The tribune also had the right to convene the Senate; to preside over the *comitia tributa*, and to call and address a *contio*. In other words, the office carried with it enormous potential for political action, but also a great capacity for disrupting the course of business when the tribune was resisting action that he judged not in the Roman People's interest. Whatever the revolutionary origins of their office, by the third and second centuries, many tribunes were members of the same landowning families as were praetors and consuls; they also often, though not invariably, appear in the narrative of events as agents of senatorial policies, using their powers to propose legislation with senatorial backing. They do also on occasion act more independently or become involved in conflict with more senior magistrates, not least when they think the consuls are pursuing the draft more vigorously than they should.[24]

The existence of the ancient rights of the tribune was not apparently a matter of dispute. Inconvenient they may have been, but it was only their use on individual occasions that was resisted. After 133, when Tiberius Gracchus, the son of a distinguished noble used it to pass legislation in the teeth of the Senate's resistance, the office became spectacularly more prominent in political life. The trouble caused by successive reforming tribunes in subsequent years led to a determined attempt by the dictator Sulla in 81–80 to abolish many of their powers, and also to inhibit those who held the office from ever holding the higher magistracies. This ingenious attempt to separate the tribunate from the career ladder was bitterly resisted and had to be reversed in the course of the 70s. One limitation on the tribunate's power was maintained: like other offices, it could only be held for one year and efforts to create the possibility of reelection were resisted.[25]

The magistrates as a group were the main active agents in the Roman system. They held between them, for their year of office, the capacity to take political initiatives. Without their support, nothing could be done in the way of administration, legislation, or the furthering of any policy. It is tempting to think of them as the government; but in fact they acted as individuals, pursuing different objectives and clashing with one another. Only in the last days of the Republic do we find anything resembling a political party, or a conflict of ideologies, when two groups called the *populares* and the *optimates* are found in sporadic conflict; even then, the word *popularis* indicates not a popular party in our sense, but a set of attitudes, ideas, and political techniques adopted by those in any one year who were resisting the domination of the Senate by appealing to the voters for support, while the opposing term (*optimates*) indicates those defending traditional patterns of authority.

In order to work as successfully as it did, this political system made serious demands on its members. They had to accept limits on the fulfillment of their ambitions: the supreme ambition was to achieve high office, military success, the holding of a triumphal procession, and the political authority that these successes brought with them. To those who achieved this came glory, the possibility of higher office and repeated consulships; but they could only hold this power at long intervals, since the whole purpose of the system was to ensure the rotation of office between equals in the competition, so that nobody achieved a concentration of power and success such as to threaten the stability of the *res publica*. Those who failed to achieve glory as consul did not get a second chance. The implication was, for instance, that however talented you might be as a general, you could not achieve the command of an army until you were middle-aged; and even then you would have to give it up again at the end of your term. Secondly, since the magistrates were not in a position to act or think as a group and there was no government to do it for them, the only policy-forming body that existed was the Senate. If any coherent direction was to be maintained, the magistrates had to accept the authority of the Senate and treat its advice as binding.

The Senate

There were close links between magistracies and Senate. In the first place, all members of the Senate were normally ex-magistrates and in the last years of the Republic it was automatic that quaestors became senators, so that election to that office defined the members of the senatorial class year by year. Secondly, the Senate's proceedings were structured by the ranking of the senators according to the level they had reached in their careers; thus the ex-consuls (the *consulares*) were given the first chance to speak in debate and were generally able to dominate. They were followed by the ex-praetors (*praetorii*), and so on. Junior members would rarely influence events. There was also a special magistracy called the censorship, held almost always by ex-consuls, whose duties included the reviewing of the lists of senators: they could expel senators of whom they disapproved and add to the list those they wished to advance. This particular task of the censors became unnecessary in the late Republic, with the new system of the automatic entry of the quaestors.[26]

The Senate then provided a lifetime role of influence for those who had held the prescribed series of one-year offices. The constitutional powers of the Senate were limited, but their informal influence was very great. They could not pass laws, but only have them proposed by a magistrate to an assembly; they did not sit as a court of law; they could not elect any state officials. Their power rested mostly, though not entirely, on the respect that their advice commanded. Whereas an assembly law was expressed in the imperative mood and issued orders that had to be obeyed, a decree of the Senate characteristically conveyed the Senate's opinion to the magistrate that he would be acting rightly if he took a certain step. The effect may be the same, but the implied relationship is quite different.[27] As a matter of fact, in the late republican period, magistrates do quite frequently defy the Senate's advice, and it is far from clear that the Senate could impose its wishes, other than by argument or pressure (see below).

The Senate and the decrees that it passed dealt with a very wide range of Roman public business. They discussed military policy and the conduct of wars; they dealt with virtually all issues of foreign policy and received delegations from all kinds of cities, whether from within or without the established provinces; they handled much religious business, where religious rituals and political business converged; they dealt with financial matters of all kinds; they took responsibility for law and order issues throughout Italy. In many of these areas, they effectively made the decisions: for instance, year by year it was they who decided which legions would be allocated to which provinces and whether the commander should be a consul, a praetor or a promagistrate.[28] The final details of which individual took which command was decided either by drawing lots or (in the case of the consuls) by agreement;[29] but the allocation of resources to imperial purposes was a senatorial matter. It will be clear below that in other areas too they did far more than just offer advice.

The priests

Priesthoods in Rome must be seen as part of the constitutional system, but they have a very special role within it. The four most senior colleges (*pontifices, augures, quindecimviri s.f.,* and *septemviri epulones,* for which, see Table 12.3) consist for the most part of leading members of the ruling elite, including at any point ex-consuls. It was not necessary to be a member of the Senate to become a priest; young men were sometimes chosen, but young priests always came from distinguished families and were unlikely to be non-senators for long. Priests, like senators, were appointed for life. When dealing with religious business, the Senate regularly consulted the relevant college of priests, though the final recommendation for action came from the Senate, not the college itself.[30] The augurs in particular played a crucial constitutional role, as arbiters of the legitimacy of many forms of public action. All important public meetings were preceded by a consultation of the gods; any irregularity (*vitium*) in the conduct of these rituals threatened the legal status of the action that followed. In such matters, the college acted as an advisory body to the

Table 12.3 Priestly roles in Rome [fo. 450]

Priesthood	Membership	Functions	Notes
Augures (Augurs)	3; 9 (from 300); 15 (from 81/80); 16 (under Caesar)	Divined, primarily through birds, to seek deities' consent to action. Defined sacred space	Continued to hold office, even if exiled
Pontifices (Pontiffs)	?; 9 (from 300); 15 (81/80); 16 (under Caesar)	Responsible for rituals, festivals, etc. Advised senate/citizens on religious law	Head of the college was the *Pontifex Maximus*, elected from 3rd century
Virgines Vestales (Vestals) (members of pontifical college)	6	Maintained cult of Vesta, including sacred hearth; ritual duties in many festivals	Full-time obligations, special privileges
Flamines (Flamens) (members of pontifical college)	3 major; 12 minor	Priests of specific gods/goddesses: three major ones of Jupiter, Mars, and Quirinus	*Flamen* of Jupiter had special taboos, restrictions. Major *flamines* restricted in movement
Rex sacrorum (Sacred King) (member of pontifical college)	1	Carried out the King's religious rituals under the Republic	Prohibited from any part in politics
Quindecimviri sacris faciundis (15 men for ritual actions)	2; 10 (from 367); 15 (from 81/80); 16 (Caesar)	Kept and consulted the Sibylline Books	Responsibility for "foreign" cults in Rome
Septemviri epulones (7 men for the ritual meals)	3 (from 196); 7 (from 81/80); 10 (under Caesar)	Organized ritual meals for gods at Games	New college created in 196
Fetiales	20	Ritual conduct of war and peace	Still active in 2nd century
Haruspices	Unknown, but later list of 60	Advise Senate on public prodigies, recommend ritual action	Originally Etruscans invited in to give advice. Organized on Roman lines at uncertain date

Senate on the state of the augural law (*ius augurale*).[31] A similar role was played by the college of *fetiales* in relation to the making of treaties, the declaring of war, and the conduct of diplomatic relations before war with foreign powers. Again, they had their own system of law (*ius fetiale*) and could be asked by the Senate for advice (see also Chapter 10).[32]

Here as elsewhere, we find the Senate playing a crucial intermediary role: they asked the priests for an opinion about procedures, or questions of law; unless asked, the priests could only raise the matter in virtue of their status as senators, but not formally report as a college; when they did report, it was the Senate that issued instructions as to the actions to be taken. The procedure is at root the same as that when dealing with the annual list of prodigies: the priests were consulted about the year's prodigies and their advice regularly heeded; but it was the Senate that decreed what should be done and in general the magistrates who carried out the rituals on the state's behalf.[33]

The functioning of the system

The Senate was, then, the key institution in the making of policy decisions. The power of action lay with the magistrates, but they received and usually respected the Senate's advice. It took courage if not foolhardiness to defy their advice, unless for very special reasons. Meanwhile, the assemblies were needed to confirm senatorial policy in some areas, to pass necessary legislation, and to elect the magistrates for each year. Modern discussion has taken this view of the Senate to considerable lengths. The consensus has been that effective power really lay, at least until the last years of the Republic, with the great noble families of Rome, who were able as a group to control decision making in all spheres of action. They could monopolize the senior magistracies by excluding newcomers in the elections. Consequently their members dominated all the senior positions in the Senate, so virtually keeping control of its business. Voting in the assemblies on laws and other matters could be controlled by use of the influence of the great families over their members and their clients, so that effectively the major families had block votes with which they could negotiate.[34]

It may seem surprising that the best ancient account of how this system functioned gives a radically different picture. It comes from the Greek historian Polybius, writing in the 140s–130s, just before the problems of the later republican years began (6.11–18; 43–58). His view was that Rome was an example of a mixed constitution, by which he meant that the elements of monarchy (the consuls), of oligarchy (the Senate), and of democracy (the assemblies) were in balance, so that none of the three would threaten stability by becoming dominant and therefore extremist. This idea is evidently derived from the tradition of Greek political thought, which had long seen the rule of one, the rule of the few, and the rule of the many as the triad of possibilities for any city-state.

Polybius' emphasis is not just on the three elements of the system; he has much to say also on the interdependence of these three elements and on the checks and balances that kept the whole system, on his view, in a state of long-term stability. He develops this idea in some detail (6.15–18), and it seems to be derived from direct knowledge or local information rather than from any Greek preconception. It is true, for instance, that the distribution of powers forced the Senate to make use of the powers of the magistrates to enact what it wished, or obstruct what it did not wish, and of the assemblies to vote on recommended laws. Polybius is right to say that the need for collaboration between institutions was a characteristic feature of the Roman system. From Polybius' time onward, as he himself predicted (6.57), collaboration came to be less and less common among Roman politicians. How to reconcile

Polybius' ideas with the evidence of actual political practice in Rome has been a crucial issue in recent discussions of the constitution (see also Chapter 1).

Change and Conflict

There is no doubt that the *comitia* had the power to change established constitutional practice in many areas, and frequently did so. Thus the Hortensian Law of c.287 established that the decrees of the plebs had the same force as laws passed through the other *comitia*;[35] the ages at which the magistracies could be held were fixed by the Villian Law of 180;[36] old methods of voting were replaced by secret ballots in the course of the 130s, through the Gabinian Law and the Cassian Law (see also Chapter 18);[37] the method of selecting priests of the major colleges was fixed by the Domitian Law of 104, and so on.[38] Whether there were limits to this capacity is not clear, but legislation never seems to have touched directly on some core areas of the tradition such as *imperium, auspicium*, or the sacred laws of the priestly colleges. The Romans themselves must have been well aware that their constitution depended on a long series of laws, not just on tradition or the *mos maiorum*.

Major modifications were also introduced by evolution rather than legislation, and here there was obviously far more room for confusion as to what was traditional and what was the innovation of earlier generations. Thus, for example, the Roman system of administering provinces outside Italy seems largely to have developed from precedent to precedent. The original sense of the word *provincia* (province) was a job, which might be a legal task, an administrative task, or a military command; in the course of time, without losing the original sense, the word became specially associated with the area of the Empire to which a magistrate was sent. As the number of provinces to be administered grew, the Romans at first increased the number of praetors from the original one to two, four, and then six. But they also had a procedure called *prorogatio*, through which the power of an annual magistrate could be "prorogued" for a second or third year, during which the consul or praetor continued to hold the *imperium* and hence to hold a province or to command in the field if necessary. Originally this step had to be taken by a popular assembly, but it came to be a regular part of the Senate's business to decide which *provinciae* should be consular or praetorian, and which should be held by prorogued magistrates from previous years. As a result of this, by the late second century, the provincial governors came to be not the current magistrates, who mostly stayed in Rome for the year, but the proconsuls and propraetors, who were the immediate ex-consuls or ex-praetors. This whole imperial system grew up, not as a result of legislation, but through the gradual extension of existing powers and procedures.[39]

There is no question, therefore, that the constitution evolved over time, never remaining static for very long, and that the introduction of changes, whether brought about by legislation or by evolution, implied awareness in the reformers both of the existing order and of the possibility of innovation. Adaptability to new conditions was obviously essential in such a dramatically changing society as Rome over the centuries of the Republic, but the combination of belief in an ancient system with constant adjustment to new conditions must have brought risks. What happened when conflict arose, as it often did, between the different elements of the constitution?

A frequent source of conflict was in the charged relationship between the Senate and the individual commander or governor. One famous example was that of one of the consuls of 173, M. Popillius Laenas. Popillius, in command in Liguria, attacked a local people, the Statelliates, destroyed their town, and sold them into slavery, despite the fact that they had not made war on Rome and had surrendered unconditionally. Decrees were passed condemning these actions and instructing Popillius to reverse his "atrocious" actions. Popillius defied the Senate in person, ferociously criticized and fined the praetor who had chaired the Senate meeting that had condemned him and, returning to his province, persisted in his policies. The consuls of 172 were Popillius' brother Gaius and P. Aelius Ligus; Ligus initially put the matter on the Senate's agenda, but was then persuaded to back his colleague so that the two consuls jointly refused to allow the Senate to debate the issue any further. The Senate, by way of retaliation, refused to conduct any further public business until the matter had been resolved. This produced constitutional deadlock, only broken when two tribunes took up the Senate's cause, set up a special procedure to put Popillius on trial, and forced him to come back to Rome by threatening to have the trial conducted in his absence. To some extent at least, the Senate's decrees were thus finally enforced and at least partial reparation paid to the Statelliates (Livy 42.8.1–9.7, 21.1–5). But Popillius himself found yet another ally in the praetor charged with holding the trial, who allowed the proceedings to be unresolved at the end of his year of office, so the special commission lapsed without condemning him (Livy 42.22.1–8).

The Senate's constitutional weakness is very clear here, as on similar if less dramatic occasions. They are unable to act at all unless the presiding magistrate puts the motion to them; it is interesting that Popillius can load blame on the praetor who had chaired the Senate in the consuls' absence. The only way forward is to find other friendly magistrates, the two tribunes who are prepared to take action in the *comitia* and propose legislation that sets the stage for judicial proceedings. Some of the specific weaknesses revealed here are gradually remedied in the legislation of the following decades, so that permanent courts and limitations on the actions of proconsuls are established between 149 and 80.[40] But the weakness of the Senate's capacity to enforce its wishes was not resolved.

A century later, in a very different situation, the same weakness is apparent in what the Senate can achieve. The senators in 62 almost to a man wished, rightly or wrongly, to find some way of condemning P. Clodius for an act of sacrilegious intrusion into the mysteries of the Bona Dea; our informant is Cicero, in letters written at the time, from a point of view totally hostile to Clodius. It becomes clear that the Senate can only act by persuading magistrates to put a bill to the Assembly on its behalf; the consul who carried out this duty did so at best half-heartedly and the proceedings were deferred. The Senate passed a stronger decree and a tribune vetoed it. The Senate next adopted the same tactic as in 171, refusing to conduct any business until the matter of the sacrilege had been resolved. Eventually a compromise was reached and the bill passed, in a weaker form (Cic. *Att.* 1.14.1–5 (= 14.1–5 SB); 1.16.1–2 (=16.1–2 SB)).[41]

One circumstance in which the Senate did have the power of decision is in the cancellation of legislation of which it disapproved. This happened in the specialized case of a law passed in circumstances that violated the proper procedures, particularly the correct taking of the *auspicia*. The Senate could then consult the augurs who gave a ruling as to whether a *vitium* (fault) had occurred; if so, the Senate, receiving this report, had the power to pass a decree that the Roman People were not bound by the law. A similar procedure applied to faulty elections, where the Senate called on the magistrates to abdicate. In these particular cases, the augurs acted as a constitutional advisory committee. Their authority over the sacred law enabled them to give the Senate the basis for effective action, which it often lacked in other circumstances.[42]

Here again, however, there are limits. The issue arose most famously after the legislation passed by Julius Caesar in 59, which was supposedly flawed, since it was only carried in the teeth of religious obstruction by his colleague in the consulate. Caesar's opponents argued that both his own laws and also those proposed by Clodius the following year had been carried against the *auspicia* and were therefore vulnerable to negation in the Senate. Some augurs even stated at a *contio*, in response to Clodius, that they would, if consulted, report that a *vitium* had taken place. The problem was that, if Caesar's wide-ranging legislation had been rescinded, then all actions taken under it would also become invalid and administrative chaos would have resulted. Clodius could safely ask the question, because he knew it could never lead to any effective action (Cic. *Dom.* 40, *Har. resp.* 48).[43]

In many other circumstances of conflict, the evidence gives the strong impression that the search for a solution was not a matter of consistently applying established constitutional principles, but of finding some improvised solution. A series of incidents from the third century onward involved a clash between priests. In each case, the *pontifex maximus* (head of the college of *pontifices*, see Table 12.3) tried to stop a senior *flamen* from leaving Rome to carry out his duties as a magistrate; *flamines* had ritual duties that had to be conducted in Rome, and to prevent their abandoning these the *pontifex* had the power to impose a fine. There was obviously a constitutional point here: did public duty override religious obligation? The priests themselves, the Senate, speeches at *contiones*, all failed to resolve the issue. The resolution came in an appeal to the tribunes of the plebs, who took the issue to the *comitia plebis*, where a vote backed the *pontifex maximus*. The priests in question were the most senior patrician priests; so it seems inconceivable that there could have been any precedent in earlier centuries for patricians to appeal through plebeian magistrates. The procedure was probably invented on the first occasion we hear about it. A vote by the sovereign Roman People was the only way to resolve such an issue; a way to hold the vote had to be found, even at the price of involving the tribunes.[44]

At the end of the Republic, a famous long-running dispute encapsulates the problems. The Senate claimed the right, in the case of a constitutional crisis, to pass a decree (the so-called *senatus consultum ultimum* – their decree of last resort) calling on the magistrates to take any necessary measures to defend the Republic. It did so in its attempts to restrain successive reforming tribunes and to deal with the ensuing violence. It is not clear exactly what effect this decree had on the subsequent position of the magistrates concerned, if they had, for instance, put allegedly rebellious citizens to death. In 121, the consul, L. Opimius, was acquitted on a murder charge in exactly these circumstances; but Cicero, who had put alleged rebels to death in 63, after the passing of this same decree, was nevertheless exiled through a special law passed through the *comitia*. It seems clear that the Senate's claim had grown up, not as a result of any legislation, but on the basis of a supposedly traditional power; there seems to have been no way of testing its legality, except in the trials, but these are themselves indecisive, because the courts only had power to condemn or acquit, not to settle the constitutional issue. In 49, on the eve of civil war, the Senate used the decree again, this time against Caesar, despite the efforts of supportive tribunes to use their vetoes in his support. Caesar (*B Civ.* 1.5) criticizes the overriding of the veto and the abuse of the decree, but he does not challenge its validity.[45]

The implication of this discussion is not that the Romans did not seek to resolve problems in line with established practice, using whatever precedents, traditions, laws, or decrees would provide guidance; but there seems to have been no easy route to achieving such a resolution. The constitutional rules changed as conditions varied; various different means were employed to make these changes; the situation of the Senate remained for the most part advisory in legal terms, while in practice it attempted to guide the Republic and all its policies. Progressively, the actual working of the political system rested less on clear constitutional principles and more on convention and tradition.

Characterizing the Roman System

Recent debate has concentrated very much on the issue of how the system of the Republic should be assessed. Differing views on this have led to the reexamination of many of the basic practices, particularly in the later Republic, where the evidence is so much stronger, but also in earlier periods. On what has in the past proved the dominant view,[46] the constitutional set-up, as described, e.g., by Polybius, had little to do with the realities of power, except as a framework within which the dominant elite operated. Control, on this view, was exercised wholly by a landowning oligarchy of noble families, which succeeded in monopolizing access to the senior magistracies, in manipulating the business of the Senate in its own interest, and in controlling the actual voting by a mixture of persuasion and bribery, but above all through their long-term influence over their dependants, who included many citizens and the descendants of their freed slaves. The picture offered was therefore one in which there was virtually no limit during the middle republican centuries to the dominance of the great patrician and plebeian noble families. These families did indeed compete for office, for commands, and for the profits that could be derived from commands; but they did so to an extent that did not admit outsiders into the circle of power and therefore did not compromise the complete domination exercised by their class. Quite elaborate techniques were devised by scholars to extract from evidence, often consisting of no more than lists of names, theories as to which families worked together in long-term alliances, which were hostile to one another (see also Chapter 1).[47]

The plausibility of these ideas always depended on treating the late republican period as radically different from the preceding centuries. With the revival progressively from 133 onward of tribunician resistance to senatorial control over decision making, political life in the late Republic became competitive and violent in ways inconceivable in earlier centuries. One possible factor in the change was the introduction of the secret ballot in the 130s, which may have destroyed the capacity of the noble families to check how their clients voted (see Chapter 19).

Since the mid-1980s a counter-theory has been developed that seeks to bring out the democratic elements and even to claim that the constitution of the Romans should be seen as democratic in its essential nature.[48] The argument is based on the reversal in two respects of the dominant theory's assumptions: first, it treats Polybius' analysis of the constitution as first-class evidence; secondly, it uses the rich evidence from Cicero's productive years in the 60s and 50s as evidence of Roman political ideas, assumptions, and attitudes. There is no argument that Cicero's speeches and letters reveal his constant concern with the state of public opinion among the People of Rome. To a great extent, he fears it and fears the success of his enemies in manipulating it to suit their own purposes, especially in the case of his archenemy Clodius. There is all the same an assumption behind what he writes that voting in the assemblies is of the highest importance; this is not a culture in which the ruling elite can afford to ignore popular wishes. There is a good deal of evidence to support this basic perception. So far as elections go, a late republican pamphlet – the *Handbook on Electioneering* (*Commentariolum petitionis*) – gives a cynical analysis of how to win votes: persuasion, promises, personal approaches, canvassing in the Forum, using all possible influence, and so on. There is much evidence of, or at least constant allegations of, the massive use of bribery by politicians, and enormous sums were spent putting on entertainments to please the voters: nobody spends money buying votes that do not matter.[49] In the case of legislation, there is repeated evidence that laws were sometimes passed of which the senatorial majority strongly disapproved.

This view has been powerfully argued and attracted support; and few seem currently to wish to defend the old dominant view in its extreme form. But there have also been strong reactions.[50] The democratic view rests very strongly on the evidence of the constitution; but that assumes precisely that descriptions of the constitution can be taken as at least approximating to the political realities at some point in time. As argued above, Roman practice seems to have been far too changeable over time, far too liable to improvisation for this to be at all a reliable guide.[51] Again, the interpretation of late republican rhetoric is itself a highly contentious field: Cicero speaks as if the *comitia* provided satisfactory expressions of the will of the Roman People; but he must have known better than we do the inadequacies of the system as an expression of the popular will. His language may reflect the necessities of political argument rather than the actual conditions of the time. Recent work has emphasized the problems of the voting system itself and generated lower and lower estimates of the percentage of those who had with the right to vote who could actually have voted on a single day.[52] All theories have to reckon with the possibility that the voters were in fact only a slightly wider section of the political elite than the senatorial class, and that the whole political process had little or nothing to do with the poorer classes in Roman society, let alone those living in other parts of Italy (see also Chapter 18).[53]

Much scrutiny is currently focused on the character of public debate at *contiones*, of which we hear a good deal in Cicero's speeches and letters. The truth may well be that such meetings resembled political theatre – or political advertising – rather than an ideal rational debate.[54] Certainly at these debates, as in all political matters, the initiative rested with magistrates all drawn from rich, powerful families, who monopolized the wealth, the patronage, the rhetorical skills, the authority, not least the religious authority, that Roman society had to offer. These considerations lead naturally enough to the suggestion that the activity of politics in the late Republic would be better understood not on the model of modern preoccupations with the discovery and expression of the popular will, but rather as a highly ritualized expression of the relative powers of magistrates, Senate, and People aimed at achieving the consensus needed for common action (see also Chapter 1).[55] Interesting though this approach may be, there are still factors that it has difficulty explaining: actual decisions are taken by vote that the dominant elite deplores; and ideas and policies come to be associated with the two groups of political actors, both *populares* and *optimates*.

Underlying much of this debate is the controversy about how far the picture of Roman political culture that can be drawn from the rich evidence of the 60s and 50s can safely be transferred to earlier periods. It is still arguable that the democratic elements in the constitution became important when and only when the ruling elite were deeply divided on particular issues and the *comitia* became the only place where the disputes could be resolved.[56] If so, then the evident concern with public opinion in Cicero's day can be explained not as a long-term feature of the constitution, but as a function of the progressively more polarized attitudes within the elite as the challenge to the authority of the Senate by tribunes and proconsuls became ever more frequent. A good formulation would be that the constitution from early days carried with it a democratic potential which the dominant oligarchy strove to limit with varying degrees of success in different periods.[57] Their greatest assets were their social and economic power, while the Senate's constitutional position was an abiding vulnerability. In the late Republic, the personal restraints on which the system once depended had given way to an individualism to which there was no quick enough answer.

Guide to Further Reading

The best sources of basic information in English on the Roman constitution are Lintott 1999a and several articles in Hornblower and Spawforth 1996, including those on *comitia*, Senate, consul, praetor, *tribus, tribuni plebis, provincia*, and many others. The activities of Roman magistrates are listed with references year by year in Broughton 1951–86, an essential tool of research. For those who read German, Mommsen 1887–8 remains the fullest discussion as well as providing the intellectual basis on which all subsequent work rests, even when his approach is being contested.

For the problems of early republican Rome, Cornell 1995 is an excellent introduction, taking a positive view of the sources. Constitutional aspects of the work of the college of augurs are discussed with great learning in Linderski 1986. Astin 1989 provides a notably well-balanced account of the position in the middle republican years. Recent debate on the middle and late Republic was sparked by the articles of Millar, collected in Millar 2002b; for reaction to his views, see especially Harris 1990b, Mouritsen 2001, and Hölkeskamp 2000b, as well as the studies collected in Jehne 1995c. The *contio* now has its own penetrating book-length treatment in Morstein-Marx 2004. In dealing with any constitutional issue, it always essential to bear in mind the social, economic, and religious context within which the issue arose and was decided: Nicolet 1980 and Purcell 1994 are most helpful guides into this wider arena.

Notes

1　For the constitution of a colony in Spain, see Crawford 1996b: 393–454, with translation at 421–2.
2　On the tradition as handled by Cicero and Livy, Cornell in Powell and North 2001: 41–56.
3　Cornell 1995: 1–30.
4　Laws collected in Crawford 1996b; a typical Senate decree translated in Sherk 1984: 81–3.
5　Lintott 1999a: 16–26; Millar 2002b: 109–42.
6　Powell in Powell and North 2001: 17–39.
7　Lintott 1999a: 4–6.
8　On early Rome, Cornell 1995; Stewart 1998.
9　Cornell 2000b.
10　For a sceptical view: Mitchell 1986.
11　Gelzer 1969; Hölkeskamp 1987.
12　For assemblies in general: Taylor 1960; Lintott 1999a: 40–64.
13　Citizenship: Sherwin-White 1973; Nicolet 1980.
14　Mouritsen 2001: 38–62; Morstein-Marx 2004.
15　Lintott 1999a: 49–50.
16　Lintott 1999a: 55–63; Yakobson 1999: 20–64.
17　For the tribes: Taylor 1960; Lintott 1999a: 50–5.
18　See Chapters 1 and 18.
19　Astin 1958; Lintott 1999a: 144–6.
20　Mommsen 1887–8: 1.27–75; for discussion, Stewart 1998: 7–9; Brennan 2000: 12–33.
21　Magdelain 1964.
22　Mommsen 1887–8: 608–15; Brennan 2000: 18–20.
23　Lintott 1999a: 107–9; Brennan 2000.
24　Bleicken 1955; Astin 1989: 193–6; Lintott 1999a: 21–8.
25　Lintott 1999a: 208–13.
26　Nicolet 1980: 49–88; Lintott 1999a: 115–20.
27　Magdelain 1978: 23–8.
28　For the republican Senate: Bonnefond-Coudry 1989; Lintott 1999a: 65–86.
29　Stewart 1998; for a different view, Rosenstein 1995.

30 Beard in Beard and North 1990: 30–4.

31 Linderski 1986; Beard, North, and Price 1998: 21–4.

32 Rüpke 1990: 97–117; Beard, North, and Price 1998: 26–7.

33 Beard, North, and Price 1998: 37–9.

34 Scullard 1973; for a moderate view, Meier 1980; North 1990b (=1990c); Wiseman 2002.

35 Broughton 1951–86: 1.185.

36 Astin 1958.

37 Broughton 1951–86: 1.483; 485.

38 Broughton 1951–86: 1.559; North 1990a.

39 Badian 1996b; Brennan 2000: 36–246.

40 Lintott 1999a: 157–62.

41 Millar 1998: 118–21.

42 For augural law: Linderski 1986; Giovannini 1998.

43 Linderski 1986: 2209–15.

44 Bleicken 1957; Beard, North, and Price 1998: 105–8.

45 For the so-called "ultimate" decree: Lintott 1999a: 89–93; for a radical reexamination of the evidence, Drummond 1995, esp. 81–95.

46 Gelzer 1969 (originally published 1912); Scullard 1973, esp. xvii–xxxi; Meier 1980.

47 Münzer 1999 (originally published 1920).

48 Millar 2002b; 109–61, 85–108 (=1984, 1986, 1989), 1998; see also, for a more qualified view, Yakobson 1999, 2004.

49 Lintott 1990.

50 North 1990b (=1990c); Harris 1990b; Jehne 1995c; Flaig 1995; Mouritsen 2001.

51 Hölkeskamp 2000a.

52 Mouritsen 2001: 18–37; for the life of the *plebs* in this period: Purcell 1994.

53 As argued by Mouritsen 2001: 43–62; for firm opposition to his view, Morstein-Marx 2004: 42 n.32; 122–3; Yakobson 2004: 203–4, 206–7, and see Chapter 19.

54 Hölkeskamp 1995; Pina Polo 1996; Mouritsen 2001: 38–62; Morstein-Marx 2004.

55 Hopkins 1991; Flaig 1995.

56 North 1990b (=1990c); for criticism, Morstein-Marx 2004: 283–4.

57 The institution of the voting groups could be interpreted an early effort in this direction.

CHAPTER 13

Army and Society

Paul Erdkamp

Introduction

The Roman army of the Republic – like any other army – was first and foremost a fighting organization. Its prime purpose was to defeat the enemy in battle. To achieve this goal, a body of men was assigned various tasks and structured into units. The instruments that were used to perform their task on the battlefield included not only weapons and military equipment, but also tactical means that were based on training, discipline, and experience. Moreover, no army could stay in the field for long without a supporting organization. Structure, weaponry, tactics, and organization were determined by the need to perform the army's prime function effectively. If not, the army would soon have ceased to exist. However, no army is solely shaped by its primary purpose. Armies function in a landscape and are part of society, which, if they do not exactly determine the army, at least set bounds to its shape and functioning. Ecological factors and the economic, social, and political features of society partly explain the characteristic features of an army. As Roman society changed, so did the army. Moreover, the geography and climate of the lands in which the armies operated shaped the way Roman wars were fought. In his *Histories*, for example, the second-century historian Polybius notes the tenaciousness with which the Romans and their opponents fought during the wars in Spain. Only the approach of winter, he says, could disrupt the continuous fighting (35.1). In short, wars were restrained by the ecological conditions of agriculture and transport, and by the economic, social, and political structures of the society of which the army was a significant part.

However, this is not to argue for some kind of ecological determinism, or for a one-sided emphasis on the "external" influences of politics and economics. Wars were of great importance to Rome, and the army was an integral part of society, if only because its social and political leaders functioned as its commanders and the citizenry of Rome and its allies manned the armies. Warfare was sufficiently important to influence and direct developments in society and politics. For one thing, society created the instruments and means that the army needed to defeat its enemies; the needs of war caused developments that altered the conditions in which the army operated. Developments concerning the army in republican Rome are thus to be understood against the interaction of both army and society. The increase in scale of Roman warfare necessitated the further development of a supporting organization. The ability to defeat the ecological factor remained small, however, because Rome never escaped the limitations of a pre-industrial society, with its very limited sources of energy. Nevertheless, during the course of its Republican wars Rome built up an organization that was at least partly capable of overcoming the limitations offered by agriculture, land, and climate in waging war. This development contributed significantly to Rome's ability and willingness to engage in overseas wars, which ultimately led to expansion on an unprecedented scale. War was thus an important part of state formation during the Republic. At the end of the Republic, Rome was able to bring together and sustain huge numbers of men that fought such famous battles as Philippi (42) and Actium (31). The latter battle left it to Octavian (63 BC–AD 14), the future emperor Augustus, to solve the problems of military deployment on such a vast scale.

Battles and Raids in Early Rome

During the regal period, Rome fought wars with the neighboring towns in Etruria and Latium, but the stories of these wars in our sources are largely fictitious. According to tradition, after the last king was expelled, Rome became involved in wars with its Latin neighbors, who were decisively defeated at Lake Regillus (496). A treaty was signed in 493, which, however, did not end hostilities with the Latins. During the fifth century, several wars were also fought with Etruscan towns, among which neighboring Veii – an Etruscan city-state to the north and equal to Rome in wealth and power – was the most important. Enemies of a different nature appear in the annalistic accounts at about the time of the signing of the treaty with the Latins. For the next century or so, the Volsci, Aequi, and Sabines were to be persistent opponents. The incursions of Volsci and Aequi in central Italy and of the Lucanians and Bruttians into the coastal areas of southern Italy were the result of migratory movements from the mountainous regions of the interior. Several towns in Campania and in southern and eastern Latium were taken over by these peoples. For the next decades, important Latin towns, such as Tibur and Praeneste, disappear from view.[1]

Due to the annalistic nature of our sources, we are told about wars between Rome and the Volsci or Aequi in almost every year. Since events were told year-by-year and later annalists had to work on the basis of very few (if, indeed, any) sources, it was natural to include and repeat for each and every year the same statements about hostilities with one or the other of Rome's opponents (see also Chapter 2). The Roman sources without exception blame hostilities on the opponents, who are depicted as poor, uncultured, and rapacious highland peoples. However, bands of Romans, who acted upon their own private initiative, were undoubtedly also not averse to some plundering. The main aim of such raids was the gathering of booty, consisting of cattle, slaves, and other movable items of wealth. Raids occasionally caused punitive expeditions on a larger scale, sometimes ending in battle. In most years, however, hostilities did not consist of full-blown campaigns of Rome's entire army, but rather of small-scale and short-lived raids into enemy territory. Battles were surely not fought each year. Hence, we should distinguish between two kinds of military action in these years: on the one hand, plundering raids by small groups into hostile territory; on the other hand, campaigns by the men in arms of the Roman community, led by their highest magistrates (see also Chapter 6).[2]

The two kinds of military action demanded different kinds of fighting. It is generally assumed that during the sixth century the peoples of central Italy had taken over the Greek way of waging war, i.e., employed heavy infantry (called hoplites) in a solid formation (the *phalanx*). Hoplite warfare had emerged in Greece during the seventh century, and it is likely that it was introduced soon afterward in central Italy by way of the Greek cities in the south. Hoplite warfare was based on the principle that a heavily armed body of men, who were sufficiently courageous and disciplined to remain in a solid formation, was almost invincible. Hoplite warfare, however, was not suited to many of the hostilities in which Rome was involved during the fifth century. Heavily armed soldiers could not perform swift raids into hostile territory. Moreover, much of the terrain in which the Aequi and Volsci had to be fought was too rugged to suit a *phalanx*. Hence, many actions were not undertaken by the entire armed forces of Rome but by smaller groups who did not fight in solid formation. The defeat of the *gens* of the Fabii at the Cremera River, who in 479 went to war against Veii on their own, may reflect such activities: "And so long as nothing more than plundering was afoot, the Fabii were not only an adequate garrison for the fort, but roaming about in the region where the Tuscan territory bordered on the Roman, they afforded security to their own countrymen and annoyance to the enemy" (Livy 2.49.9).

Livy nicely emphasizes (maybe inadvertently) the small scale and mobile nature of the Fabian activities. However, they were annihilated when they met an opposing force. Although one should remain skeptical regarding the stories told by Livy about fifth-century warfare, the fact that – in marked contrast to previous years – members of the Fabian *gens* disappear from the list of consuls for the next 12 years may offer some support for the veracity of the story. Not all actions, however, were of this kind. Some of the towns in the plains of Latium had been taken over by the highland peoples. Hence, not all actions were raids and not all fights occurred in mountainous areas. Apart from swift and small-scale actions undertaken by lightly armed men, battles were fought between neighboring towns and city-states in which the full force of the heavy infantry was turned against the enemy.

Hoplites and Citizens in the Early and Middle Republic

In comparison to the times when aristocratic warriors fought each other in highly individual actions, hoplite forces had expanded the number of men that were actively involved in fighting and thus had increased the military strength of a community. The change also reflected a shift in political power and social status. Henceforth, the army consisted of men who performed their duty as citizens by fighting their community's enemies. They acquired and maintained their own equipment, which in the case of a heavily armed foot soldier demanded some wealth. In agricultural societies such as early Greece or Rome, the heavy infantry (or hoplites), who formed the core of the army, therefore largely consisted of prosperous farmers. The very rich families – the members of the aristocracy – continued to play a special role: they provided the cavalry, whose status was still large, although its role on the battlefield was secondary to that of the heavy infantry. The rise of the hoplite army thus reflects an increase of the political power of a larger, well-to-do segment of society.

The close relationship between army and politics is clearly revealed in the Roman constitution that is traditionally ascribed to Rome's sixth king, Servius Tullius. Livy and Dionysius of Halicarnassus, who wrote their accounts in the late first century BC, give descriptions of this constitution. According to both authors, Servius Tullius introduced a system in which the citizenry was divided into five property classes. Each class had its own weaponry. Although Livy (1.43) and Dionysius (4.16) disagree in detail, they agree that the equipment of the first class was the heaviest, II and III less heavy, and that the members of classes IV and V were lightly armed. Each class was divided into a number of *centuriae* in the following manner:

I *classis*:	80 *centuriae*
II *classis*:	20 *centuriae*
III *classis*:	20 *centuriae*
IV *classis*:	20 *centuriae*
V *classis*:	30 *centuriae*

However, actually there were seven classes, since there was a "class" of the wealthiest citizens, consisting of the *equites* (horsemen), and also a group called *infra classem*, i.e., "those below the classes," consisting of the poor. The *equites* had 18 *centuriae*, the *infra classem* 5. Moreover, the *centuriae* in each class were equally divided into two groups: the *iuniores* (men aged 18–46) and the *seniores* (over 46). The latter were not normally expected to fight. The *centuriae* formed the basic units of voters in one particular kind of assembly of the Roman People (the *comitia centuriata*). This assembly, in which the majority of *centuriae* was decisive, decided on war and peace and elected the magistrates that served as commanding officers. The division of *centuriae* shows that power in the assembly securely rested with the *equites* and the first *classis*, in other words, with the rich and well-to-do segments of society, and that also greater voting power was placed in the hands of the older citizens. The close relationship between army and assembly is obvious. It is reflected in the fact that the *comitia centuriata* assembled on the *Campus Martius*, which was outside the borders of the city. It was strictly forbidden for Roman citizens to enter the city in arms. Hence, this location shows that the *comitia centuriata* originally had been the assembly of the citizenry in arms under the leadership of the chief magistrates (see also Chapter 12).

However, Livy and Dionysius depict a political structure as it pertained in much later times, when the development of army and assembly had separated. Much of the debate among modern historians centers on the problem of how to reconstruct the origins of the system that the later tradition ascribed to Servius Tullius. There seems to be consensus now that there originally had been just one *classis*. The introduction of the heavy infantry brought with it the need to distinguish only between those who were sufficiently wealthy to serve as hoplites and those who were not. The aristocracy served as horsemen; the rest were *infra classem* and either fought as lightly armed troops or acted as servants. The questions remain when the classes II–V were added to the original *classis*, and how to interpret the variety of equipment between the classes. Some reject the differences of weaponry among the classes and argue that there was no place in a hoplite phalanx for such a diversity of arms.[3]

The close relationship between army and politics continued to play a role in the conflicts of the early Republic. According to the literary sources, the so-called "Struggle of the Orders" centered on the struggle of the wealthy plebeians to gain political influence and of the poor masses against poverty and indebtedness. The dates and events as given by Livy and other authors cannot be taken at face value, but it seems probable that at one point the plebeians seceded from the Roman community (traditionally in 494) and created their own political institutions as instruments in their political fight. The withdrawal of their men was intended to put pressure on their patrician opponents. It has rightly been pointed out that the traditional dichotomy between patricians and plebeians cannot be correct, since the military predominance of the plebeian farmers, who served as hoplites, would have crushed any opposition.[4] At the same time, however, the plebeian cause cannot have been confined to the starving mass of poor farmers, since their *secessio* would have been of little concern to the predominant classes. Hence, a military role seems to have been played by a wider segment of society than a pure hoplite army implies. We have already seen that the nature of Roman fighting and the terrain in which many campaigns had to be fought rules out the idea that warfare was exclusively in the hands of a hoplite phalanx. This hypothesis is supported by the fact that during the fourth century the Roman army was based on a manipular structure that operated markedly different from a "pure" hoplite army. There is little reason to assume a drastic reform of the Roman army in the meantime. Hence, already in the fifth century, men who were not armed or did not fight like hoplites, and who were less wealthy, contributed to Rome's military power (see also Chapter 6).

The Conquest of Italy (c.400–270)

During the approximately 120 years from the capture and destruction of Veii (traditionally 396) to the final defeat of the Hellenistic warlord Pyrrhus in 275, Roman warfare grew in range, duration, and complexity. Because of Rome's successes against the Volsci, Etruscans, and Latins, its military scope and ambitions increased, which ultimately drew it into conflict with the Samnites, who largely lived in the mountainous areas of central and southern Italy. During the wars with the Samnites at the end of the fourth and the beginning of the third century, Rome occasionally confronted coalitions that also included Gauls, Etruscans, and Umbrians. To cope with these threats, the standard army of each of the two consuls was increased to two legions, which meant that Rome raised four legions of 4,500 men each. However, Rome did not fight these wars by itself. The treaty concluded with the Latins in 493 already stipulated that the allies contribute soldiers who would fight under Roman command. The system of allies was restructured in 338, when Rome defeated its Latin allies and enrolled most of them among its own citizens.[5] At the end of the fourth century, a consular army consisted of two infantry legions and two units of allied infantry forces of similar size. The allies contributed large contingents of horsemen, who fought alongside the Roman cavalry. The allies were organized and equipped in a similar manner to the Roman forces. In short, these allied units, which served under Roman command, were assimilated to and incorporated in the Roman army. From a military point of view, there was little distinction between the Roman legions and the allied forces.

When in 281 the city of Tarentum requested help from Pyrrhus (319–272), Rome for the first time confronted a professional, Hellenistic army led by a modern and experienced general. Despite several defeats inflicted by Pyrrhus' Macedonian *phalanx*, Rome emerged victorious from the war. Against the rigid tactics of the *phalanx*, Rome employed the much more flexible system of the maniples. The Roman legions faced battle not in a solid formation but in three lines, each composed of maniples that fought and maneuvered as more or less independent units. The flexibility of the manipular legion had probably been perfected during the wars against the Samnites, which were generally fought in the rough terrain of the mountainous interior of the peninsula.

The increased scale, range, and complexity of Roman warfare imposed new demands upon the recruitment and provisioning of the troops. In response, the Roman state created means in order to cope with the requirements of the Roman armies and to increase their effectiveness. In the fifth and early fourth century, military operations had been short-lived and seasonal affairs. Because the operations of the Roman armies had been limited to neighboring regions, the soldiers simply left their homes with sufficient food to sustain them for a few days. For the remainder, they lived off the land. Most operations did not last long enough to disturb the working of the land, while the short campaigns, if successful, offered an immediate source of income in the form of booty. Living off the land beyond the summer period would have been difficult, because stores of food would be brought into walled towns, out of reach of passing armies. However, the larger scale and complexity of later wars demanded the more continuous deployment of Roman soldiers. When Rome sought the final destruction of Veii at the end of the fourth century, its campaigns against such a powerful state were more prolonged and systematic than in previous wars. Hence, it is not surprising that, according to Livy, military pay was first introduced during the siege of Veii. Although the sources do not say so explicitly, military pay was introduced evidently in order to tide the farmer-soldiers over for the duration of the campaign and to compensate them for the loss of labor on the land. Moreover, protracted operations far afield required some organization of the provisioning of food. The allied communities and *coloniae* probably contributed supplies to the Roman armies, just as they would during the wars that were fought in Italy in the late third century. The *coloniae* that were established by Rome throughout the peninsula not only served as a means to settle loyal citizens and allies in strategically important locations, but they also created a network of secure towns in hostile territory that could be used as military bases. In the year 312, Rome's first paved road, the Via Appia, was built between Rome and Capua. It was later extended to Beneventum. More roads were soon to follow. The purpose of such roads was not so much to ease the travel of the armies but primarily to facilitate military transports. In addition, these roads symbolized Roman control and thus Roman power (see also Chapter 28). Supporting the armies induced other innovations: from about the time of the capture of Veii, the sources first mention the *tributum*, a property tax that was levied to pay for military expenditure, and the imposition of indemnities on defeated enemies. Moreover, the first issues of silver coins by Rome were minted in Campania around the year 310, probably in order to pay for the construction of the Via Appia (see also Chapter 3).[6] The needs of war were thus an important force in the process of state formation in Rome.

Overseas Expansion (264–149)

The hundred years that followed the start of the First Punic War (264) saw the defeat and downfall of all the other great powers in the Mediterranean world. First Carthage, then Macedon and the Seleucid Empire were defeated in a series of overseas wars. Again, the increase in range, scale, and complexity altered the character of the Roman army and of the military apparatus. It was no longer a simple farmer-militia that confronted the Carthaginians in 264. As we have seen, during the conquest of Italy, Rome had begun to develop the necessary means to wage war on a grand scale. Nevertheless, the effort that was needed to emerge victorious from the wars against the major powers of the Mediterranean not only changed the Roman army, but also the Roman state.

While Carthage and the Hellenistic kingdoms relied on professional soldiers and mercenaries, the legions that faced these armies in battle consisted of soldiers who were recruited from among Rome's citizenry. Each male citizen was liable to serve for a maximum of 16 years in the infantry. It should be noted, however, that they did not serve this term in successive years and that many citizens did not serve for the full 16 years. A Roman legion consisted of 3,000 heavy infantry and 1,200 lightly armed troops (*velites*). The heavy infantry was armed with a large shield and two spears that were thrown at short range, but their main weapon was the sword, which was used to thrust and to stab. The Roman heavy infantry faced battle in a formation of three lines: the first line (*hastati*) consisted of the youngest soldiers; the second of the soldiers in their late twenties or early thirties (the *principes*). The older veterans (*triarii*) formed the final line. The Romans did not fight in a closed formation, which made it possible for the first line to withdraw behind the next line.[7] According to Polybius, the Roman lines approached the enemy with much noise and shouting (Polyb. 15.12.8). Within 30 m of the enemy, the spears were thrown in order to create further confusion within the enemy lines.[8] The role of the cavalry during battle was mostly to attack the infantry formation in the flanks or in the back.[9] Battles usually took several hours, but fighting was not intense for the whole duration of the engagement, much of which consisted of the maneuvering of troops. As long as the battle formations remained intact, the number of casualties was usually limited. Most men were killed when the formation dissolved and the soldiers fled, which explains the great disparity in most battles between the number of casualties on the winning and those on the losing side. Success in battle depended partly on the morale and discipline of the soldiers and their ability to hold their place in a situation that was as threatening as it was confusing. Therefore, the Romans placed the most experienced soldiers in the back of the battle formation. An important role in maintaining discipline was also played by the centurions, men of tested worth who had risen from the ranks. Each legion contained six military tribunes, who were often young men from senatorial families beginning their military and political career as officers in the legions (see also Chapter 19). The officers in the allied forces were also drawn from among the wealthiest families of Roman citizens.

Roman success against Carthage and the Hellenistic kingdoms of the East has been explained in various ways. Some have stressed the flexible nature of the Roman battle formation, which was more effective than the rigid *phalanx* that was still employed by the Hellenistic states.[10] Polybius, who came to Rome as a hostage but soon befriended members of the leading families, was inspired by the city's rise to write a Roman history in which he tried to explain to his fellow-Greeks the causes of Rome's invincibility. Part of the explanation he sought in the Roman Constitution, which in his eyes ensured a stable government, part in the nature of Roman society, which he describes as obsessed by war. In his description of the Roman military system, Polybius emphasizes the Roman methods of encouraging soldiers to face danger. Those who fled or threw away their weapons were punished by death, but those who had shown exceptional courage in battle were praised by the commander in front of the entire army. Various crowns and other decorations were awarded to soldiers who had exposed themselves to danger beyond the call of duty (see also Chapter 17).

> The men who receive these trophies not only enjoy great prestige in the army and soon afterwards in their homes, but they are also singled out for precedence in religious processions when they return. On these occasions nobody is allowed to wear decorations save those who have been honoured for their bravery by the consuls, and it is the custom to hang up the trophies, and to regard them as proofs and visible symbols of their valour. So when we consider this people's almost obsessive concern with military rewards and punishments, and the immense importance which they attach to both, it is not surprising that they emerge with brilliant success from every war in which they engage. (Polyb. 6.39 [trans. I. Scott-Kilvert])

Some have explained the militaristic nature of Roman society by the advantages that successful wars brought to each segment of society: the upper classes needed war to win fame and increase or uphold their status, while both upper and lower classes reaped the material rewards of war in the form of booty, slaves, and land.[11] The military nature of Roman society is also shown by the fact that down to around 100 young Romans of prominent families served in the army for ten years before they could start a career in public office. Political and military careers were not separated: praetors and consuls not only took care of civic matters in Rome, they also commanded the Roman armies. The political system did not always elect the most talented commanders to high political offices, which not rarely resulted in disastrous defeats against more cunning generals. The idea seems to have been that members of the leading families were capable of commanding Roman armies simply because of their upbringing and virtue. Defeat was not even a serious obstacle in one's further career: many Romans who met defeat in battle went on to hold the most prestigious posts in Rome's political system.[12] Nevertheless, victory in battle and success in war brought enormous prestige in Rome.

Winning battles was not the same, however, as winning wars. Rome lost battles against many opponents, the most famous of whom is the Carthaginian Hannibal (247/6–183), who started the Second Punic War (218–201) with an army that was better trained, more experienced, and better led than their Roman adversaries. Rome gained the upper hand in the wars with Carthage, Macedon, and the Seleucid Empire because it developed the necessary means to exploit the vast and ever increasing resources and manpower of its empire. This enabled Rome to raise and support large armies and to focus the military force of the entire Empire on its overseas adversaries.

Managing Military Manpower during the Mid-Republic

A first element of Rome's success consisted of its vast manpower, which was a decisive advantage in the wars against the great Mediterranean powers. However, the political system that enabled Rome to use the manpower resources of the Italian peninsula was already created during the conquest of Italy – as Pyrrhus discovered, whose relatively small forces defeated their Roman opponents on several occasions only to find new armies raised against him. His own army of professional soldiers could not be so easily replenished, making his losses – despite his victories – much harder to bear.

Rome's manpower turned out to be crucial in the struggle against Hannibal during the Second Punic War. According to Polybius (2.24), the list of men capable of bearing arms among Roman citizens and allies that was presented to the Roman authorities on the eve of the Second Punic War numbered about 700,000 infantry soldiers and 70,000 horsemen. Although Polybius' numbers cannot be taken at face value, they indicate the vast pool of potential recruits that Rome could fall back upon.[13] The manpower available to Rome explains how Rome could survive a war that started so disastrously and even continue to wage war on several fronts simultaneously. However, Roman resources during the Second Punic War were stretched to the limit. Roman armies were defeated and almost annihilated at Lake Trasimene in 217 and at Cannae in 216. At Cannae, at least 40,000 Romans and allies are said to have lost their lives. The number of legions raised during the war also illustrates the strain on Roman manpower. While a total force of four legions each year had been normal in previous decades, the number of legions was raised to more than twenty annually from 214 until 206. These figures do not reflect the actual number of men under arms, since casualties and problems of recruitment in the end resulted in seriously undermanned legions. Nevertheless, it has been estimated that at the height of the war, 29 percent of adult male citizens were serving in the legions. After the war, these numbers were reduced to 10–15 percent.[14] In addition, the war against Hannibal required some legions to remain under arms for many successive years.

Rome could sustain such an effort because it recruited its soldiers from among its entire citizenry. According to Polybius (6.19–21), all men of military age (between 18 and 46) who owned property worth at least 400 drachmas (probably equal to 4,000 asses) had to present themselves annually at the Capitol, where Roman officers selected the recruits from those present. The selection of recruits was called the *dilectus* ("the choosing"). In practice, in Polybius' time soldiers were not only mustered in Rome but also on other locations because Roman citizens were increasingly spread across the peninsula.[15] The recruiting system ensured a vast pool of experienced soldiers since, apart from the youngest recruits, most men had already served on one or more campaigns. Hence Rome was able to bear disastrous losses and still manage to raise armies that were ready to fight. Only during the severest crises, such as the early years of the Second Punic War, are we told that Rome was forced to enroll slaves and freedmen in its armies.

In contrast to Greek cities, Rome readily accepted foreigners amongst its citizenry and even incorporated defeated communities into the Roman state. Consequently, the available manpower steadily increased, thereby contributing to Rome's military power. From 338 onward, partial citizenship was forced upon some of the subjected peoples. Rome had no desire to incorporate all its defeated enemies, since that would have been impossible in a state that still perceived itself as essentially a city. A system of alliances was created that tied the independent tribes and communities in Italy to Rome (see also Chapter 28). The allies remained autonomous and had various rights and privileges, but all the Italic allies were obliged to offer support in times of war. Rome devised a system that made good use of the manpower and resources of allies and subjected peoples while maintaining their character as independent communities. Rome annexed part of the land of defeated communities in order to establish colonies. The settlers of some of these colonies became Roman citizens, but most received Latin citizenship, which meant that their citizens served in the allied forces.

The Food Supply of the Roman Armies in the Middle Republic

A second cornerstone of Roman military success was the ability to feed large armies. At the start of the campaigning season in Spain in 195, Cato the Elder (234–149) said "the war will sustain itself" (Livy 34.9.12), on the basis of which it has often been suggested that Roman troops in general sustained themselves through foraging and plundering. In reality, Roman armies could not rely on living off the land since this would have posed too many restrictions on the army and thus would have reduced its effectiveness. In order to put pressure on an enemy one needed the ability to concentrate many troops in one area and to retain their presence there as long as necessary. This was impossible, however, while living off the land, because most regions were not productive enough to sustain large armies and because the available resources were inadequate during winter. The Roman armies that fought against the Hellenistic kingdoms in the early second century not uncommonly numbered some 40,000 men (including servants and muleteers), and in addition about 4,000 horses and some 3,000 or 4,000 pack animals. The daily consumption of corn of such an army amounted to 60 tonnes. Because wagons hampered the mobility of the army too much, the primary means available to transport equipment and supplies in the army train was the pack animal, each carrying a load of at most 100 kg. Hence an army could not carry much food in its baggage train. In order to feed the armies on campaign, the Romans created a supply system that ensured a stable and secure food supply but at the same time least hampered its operational flexibility. This system consisted of the long-distance supply of provisions by sea or navigable rivers to strategic bases in or near the war-zone, from where a shuttle-system of wagons and pack animals supplied the troops.[16]

The period of the overseas wars saw a shift from ad hoc to structural means to satisfy the armies' needs for corn. The First Punic War (264–241) was the first that engaged Roman troops for consecutive years in a distant war-zone. Polybius' account of this war shows that the provisions for the troops stationed on Sicily were acquired by means of requisitions, contributions, and purchases from allied and subject communities as the need arose. The Second Punic War provided the impulse to create more structural means for the acquisition of corn on behalf of the armies. Rome needed to raise and support several armies simultaneously in order to fight the Carthaginians and their allies in Italy, Spain, and Cisalpine Gaul. The productive capacity of Italy was much reduced by the devastation caused by the Second Punic War, though it still had to furnish most of the provisions required. The sheer survival of Rome depended on whether Rome succeeded in managing the food supply of its armies. Hence during the later years of the Second Punic War an annual grain-tax, the *decuma* ("tithe"), was introduced in both Sicily and Sardinia, consisting of one-tenth of the harvest. In some years an additional tenth of the harvest was requisitioned. Rome relied heavily on existing mechanisms, as is indicated by the fact that Roman taxation on the island was governed by a law, the *lex Hieronica*, named after the former king of Syracuse, Hiero II (269?–215). A similar system was later introduced in Spain, where a grain-tax of one-twentieth of the harvest was levied. Roman levies in kind arose directly from the need to supply the armies.[17]

The system of acquisition and supply was put to good use during the wars in the East, which followed closely on the end of the Second Punic War. During the wars against Macedon (200–197; 171–168) and Antiochus (191–188), the Roman armies were largely fed from taxes levied in Sicily and Sardinia and from gifts of corn arriving from Carthage and Numidia. The corn supply of its armies enabled Rome to ship its legions to overseas war-zones and to maintain their presence as long as needed, regardless of the fertility of the region, the approach of winter, or the devastation that was the result of war. Having a secure food supply, the commanders were less often forced to engage the enemy at an unsuitable time, thus increasing their strategic flexibility. Roman troops could maneuver or just wait until the enemy was forced to fight under adverse conditions. However, operations were still restricted by the limitations imposed by climate and landscape. While Roman soldiers could march anywhere, it remained impossible to transport thousands of tonnes of foodstuffs into inland regions, which seriously undermined the war effort in the interior of the Mediterranean peninsulas. For example, because Rome could not concentrate large armies in inland Spain, logistical problems severely hampered Rome's effort to defeat the relatively weak Spanish tribes.

In short, Rome created a political system in Italy that was determined by the needs of war and ensured that former enemies contributed to the Roman war-effort. The creation of provinces and the imposition of taxes, which were important steps in the process of state formation, were both a direct consequence of war. In general, we may conclude that the manpower of Italy and the material resources of the provinces, in particular grain, enabled Rome to raise and support the armies that defeated Carthage and the kingdoms of the East.

The Aftermath of Success: Crisis or Change?

The idea long prevailed among modern historians that during the second century Rome suffered a shortage of military manpower. Appian started his books on the civil wars of the late Republic – written centuries after the events – with an account of the hardships of the common people in Italy in the late second century: as a result of Roman expansion the rich became richer, gathering large landholdings at the cost of the smallholder and replacing the free population with the slaves that had been captured during the wars. Part of the blame was put on military service: "The Italian people dwindled in numbers and strength, being oppressed by penury, taxes, and military service" (App. *B Civ.* 1.7). Similarly, the first-century historian Sallust wrote: "The people were burdened with military service and poverty. The generals divided the spoils of war with a few friends. Meanwhile the parents or little children of the soldiers, if they had a powerful neighbour, were driven from their homes" (*Iug.* 41.7–8). Ti. Gracchus' scheme to distribute public land among poor citizens (during his year as tribune of the plebs in 133) has often been interpreted as a means to restore the dwindling number of potential recruits. Similarly, a shortage of manpower explained the gradual reduction of the property qualifications for Roman recruits in this period.

In recent decades, however, opinions have significantly changed.[18] Scholars realize that the decline of the peasantry has been much overstated. Indeed, it is true that the Second Punic War had a disastrous impact on the population size of Italy due to casualties of war, famine, and epidemics. However, the demographic impact of the

Second Punic War was only short term. Signs of recovery can be seen already before the mid-century.[19] Moreover, the growth in the ownership of large estates in Italy was a gradual and uneven process. In some regions, the growth of commercial farming already started during the third century, while other regions remained untouched until the first. Peasant farms continued to thrive alongside wealthy estates and even predominated in those regions that were of little interest to rich landowners (see Chapters 27 and 28).

What about the disastrous effects of military service? It is true that in the second century most soldiers served for many years in succession. However, the traditional view that such soldiers returned to barren fields and to farms that were deserted by their wives and children has to be rejected. The regular but temporary withdrawal of a part of their adult males need not automatically have had a negative impact on peasant communities. For one thing, many recruits were young and unmarried, and they did not have families to support, although they contributed their labor to the cultivation of the family plots.[20] One has to keep in mind, too, that peasant farming in pre-industrial societies was generally characterized by underemployment. In other words, peasant households tended to have a surplus of labor that could not be fruitfully used on their small plots of land. Hence, the withdrawal of part of the labor was not disastrous. Moreover, family relations helped to spread the burden of recruitment. In each society, household formation is determined by social, economic, and demographic circumstances, and in second-century Italy, recruitment was – and had been for centuries – an important fact of life. Many rural households probably consisted of various married and unmarried adults, their offspring and/or parents. The co-residence of relatives and their sharing of land and other resources diminished the impact of the withdrawal of part of adult laborers from peasant farms. If adult men were recruited into the army, others within the household were left. Those men whose families had too little land to support all their members may actually have perceived recruitment as a temporary subsistence strategy.[21] Most campaigns lasted for some years and, if successful, offered the veterans wealth in the form of booty. This is not to say that all conscripts were happy with their fate, but there is no indication that enlistment in general was rejected. Much depended on the war for which soldiers were enlisted, since some wars offered more booty and less hardship than others. Service in the armies that fought against the Spanish tribes or against the hostile peoples in northern Italy was, for instance, unpopular, while soldiers were ready to fight in the Greek East. In short, Rome's armies did not suffer from a shortage of manpower.

The negative undertone in many of our sources on the second century should be seen in light of the moralistic tendency of such ancient historians as Sallust and Livy, who emphasized the negative side of Rome's rise to empire. It was a part of the political rhetoric in late republican Rome to blame the leading political families for having established their wealth and power on the backs of the common people. In the introduction to his *Civil Wars*, Appian's objective was to emphasize that Rome's successes in its overseas wars caused the Italian farmers who manned its armies to suffer and forced them to abandon their land, their places taken by their enslaved former foes. Whatever the sources say, the changes during the second century do not reflect a shortage of military manpower but rather a gradual change in the nature of recruitment and military service.

The Army of the Late Republic

Changes in the army during the Late Republic caused and reflect changes in the relationship between soldiers and civilians and in the role of the army in society and politics. Although the older literature used to blame Marius (156–86) – a successful general, but not so successful a statesman – for creating this situation, his role may be more adequately explained as a response to changing circumstances.

The Roman army experienced serious problems in the second half of the second century: many campaigns in Spain were unsuccessful and the war against the Numidian king Iugurtha (112–105) at first showed little success, causing dissatisfaction among Roman voters. Disaster arose during the war against the Cimbri and Teutones – Germanic peoples who had left their northern homes and threatened Roman Gaul and Italy. In the battle at Arausio (105) in southern Gaul, tens of thousands of Roman soldiers are said to have lost their lives. One of the causes may have been the lack of great wars in previous decades, owing to which the expertise among soldiers and commanders declined. Military troubles in Numidia brought Marius – a military man who was not of noble birth – to power. During his bid for the consulship, Marius (156–86) contrasted his own professionalism with the amateurism of his aristocratic opponents. Consequently, the voters elected Marius consul six times during the years 107–100, which reflects their distrust in the leading families in a time of crisis.

In preparation for his campaign against Iugurtha, Marius called for volunteers among the veterans and among the poorest Roman citizens (*capite censi*) (Sall. *Iug.* 86.2). In other words, he enlisted men from the proletariat in his army who did not qualify for infantry service, and he paid for their equipment from the public treasury. This was not as great an innovation as it might seem: the property qualifications had been reduced regularly during the past century. According to Livy, under the "Servian constitution" the property qualification for service in the legions had been 11,000 asses. Polybius mentions a figure of 400 drachmas (probably representing 4,000 asses), while Cicero informs us that the property qualification was only 1,500 asses. Scholars disagree on the interpretation of these figures. However, it seems clear that, even before Marius enlisted the proletariat in the army, the threshold was so low that the owners of even the smallest farms qualified. Nevertheless, Marius took an important step when in practical terms he abolished the property qualification.

The legions also became more homogeneous, but at the same time their link with the city of Rome became weaker. Marius is probably to be credited with reorganizing the legions, as a result of which all distinctions of property or age were abolished. The entire legion came to consist of heavy infantry equipped with sword and throwing spear (*pilum*). One of Marius' innovations was that he introduced a single standard for the entire legion: the silver eagle became the symbol of the legion's collective pride. In the coming decades, many armies developed a corporate identity that was missing in previous centuries. This is most clearly reflected in the names that some armies derived from their commanders: the *Sullani* or the *Fimbriani*. The legion was divided into ten uniform cohorts of approximately 500 men each. Under Caesar (100–44), the cohort operated quite independently, which improved the tactical flexibility of the Roman army in battle. The professionalization of the army is also shown by the fact that Caesar's armies included men who were able to perform great engineering feats, such as building a bridge that spanned the Rhine.

Important changes stemmed from the Social War (91–88), during which many amongst Rome's former allies fought either to destroy Rome or at least to improve their own position. Rome gained the upper hand but not without offering Roman citizenship at first to those allies that had remained loyal, and later also to those it defeated. This meant not only that the allied contingents from Italy ceased to exist but also that in future recruiting officers enlisted men into the legions throughout the peninsula. During his war in Gaul (58–50), Caesar even went a step further when he enlisted men from Gallia Transpadana (the region between the Po and the Alps) who did not have full Roman citizenship. Two components of the former legion had disappeared by the early first century: the lightly armed *velites* and the cavalry of Roman citizens. Their role was taken over by non-Italic peoples who fought alongside the legions. Rome had occasionally used Spanish or Numidian cavalry or Cretan archers at the time of the Second Punic War, but during the first century, non-Italic contingents of light troops and horsemen came to play a large and structural role in the Roman army.[22]

Masters of the State

The changes in the social composition of the armies had important consequences for Roman society and the political events of the last decades of the Republic – an age that was plagued by civil war. Already during the second century, many conscripts had reenlisted after their discharge, but now volunteers from the lower classes who had chosen military service as a means of subsistence increasingly manned the legions. More than in the second century, armies of the late Republic included professional officers and experienced soldiers, whose presence often turned the scale in the battles between political opponents at the end of the Republic. Although recruits were still levied from among the citizenry, military expertise was increasingly concentrated in fewer hands. Three aspects of the role of the army will be discussed here: veteran settlement, professionalism in the army, and the soldiers' willingness to engage in civil war.

As in the previous century, the troops were discharged after a campaign had ended. Most of the first-century legionaries, however, came from a segment of society that had been poor to begin with, and few had any property to return to. Successful campaigns offered wealth in the form of booty and bonuses, but most soldiers desired a more substantial property after their discharge. They wanted land. However, the majority of the Senate, who would never be in a position to command an army, persistently resisted any plans to distribute land among veterans. They feared that the collective distribution of land to veterans would serve to increase the power base of those few senators who commanded armies. The majority may, in fact, have been right, but their stubborn resistance only helped to bring about what they were trying to prevent, since soldiers now depended on the political influence of their former commanders.

The first Roman forces to attack Rome itself were the soldiers of Sulla (138–78), who had been assigned the war against Mithradates (c.132–63). When Marius succeeded by dubious means in taking away the command in this war from Sulla, the latter responded by marching on Rome (88). After Sulla's army had successfully fought king Mithradates in the East (88–84) and, on their return to Italy, had defeated his political opponents (83–82), who had taken possession of Rome in his absence, his soldiers were the first veterans to receive land on a large scale. They received the land that was taken from those Italian communities that had supported Sulla's enemies. For years to come, these veteran colonies continued to play a role in Rome's internal struggles. Veteran settlement became an even greater problem during the 40s and 30s, when the civil wars were fought by ever increasing armies. On the eve of the final struggle between Octavian and Marc Antony (82–30), which ended with the defeat of Antony at Actium in the year 31, an estimated 250,000 Roman men were under arms; many of them received land after the war had ended. In order to keep the troops satisfied, Octavian had to requisition land from communities in Italy and elsewhere on a large scale, thereby causing widespread hardship and poverty.[23]

The degree of professionalism of the late republican armies is still a matter of some debate.[24] Many scholars agree that the abolition of the minimum census qualification for military service opened up the armies for men from the poorer masses who sought a living in the legions. The armies came largely to consist of volunteers whose long terms of service turned them into professionals. Soldiers generally served for eight or ten years successively before their discharge; many troops even remained under arms for much longer periods. Some of the soldiers in Caesar's legions served not only during his Gallic War (58–50 BC) and the campaigns against his political opponents (49–45 BC), but continued to fight under his political heirs after he was murdered in 44 BC. Admittedly, some troops served for much shorter periods and not all recruits volunteered. In particular, in times of civil war recruits were enlisted from among those liable for service, and some units only served for relatively short periods. Not all soldiers remained in the army for many years, but many veterans reenlisted after discharge. Furthermore, the military power of men like Caesar, Pompey, Octavian, and Antony was based on the fact that the core of their armies consisted of seasoned troops. In the end, no statesman could play a role in the political conflicts during the final decades of the Republic without commanding an army of experienced and hardened soldiers. Contemporary authors were well aware of this fact. When Caesar led his legions into civil war after crossing the Rubicon in 49, Cicero realized that the troops that Pompey and his aristocratic allies mustered in Italy were no match for the soldiers that had conquered Gaul under Caesar's command. All commanders of the time tried to enlist and retain as many veterans as possible. However, the legions turned out to be an unwieldy instrument, the more so when the soldiers came to realize their value during the endless civil wars that followed after the murder of Caesar in 44 BC:

> The soldiers thought that they were not so much serving in the army as lending assistance, by their own favour and judgement, to leaders who needed them for their own personal ends. Desertion, which had formerly been unpardonable, was actually rewarded with gifts, and whole armies resorted to it, including some illustrious men, who did not consider it desertion to change to a like cause, for all parties were alike ... Understanding these facts the generals tolerated this behaviour, for they knew that their authority over their armies depended on gifts rather than on law. (App. *B Civ.* 5.17 [trans. H. White])

Roman soldiers were willing to fight other Roman soldiers and even to attack Rome itself. This may partly be explained by the soldiers' background: recruits increasingly came from remote regions and from communities that had resisted Rome during the Social War. Recruitment in Rome itself was rare. Only in times of crisis, such as 90, 49, and 43, were troops levied in the city. By the time of the late Republic, the populace of the capital was deemed unfit for military service. Loyalty to Rome may have been further weakened by the poverty and hardship (much of it resulting from the Social War and subsequent civil wars) that had forced many to seek a means of subsistence in the armies.[25] In the case of Caesar, an additional role may have been played by the fact that most soldiers in his legions came from the same area, Cisalpine Gaul, which increased the internal consistency of his forces. Moreover, successful generals were held in high esteem by their soldiers, the more so as their general's glory was felt to increase their own.

Because of their military value, much attention was paid to the officers and centurions. Two instances may illustrate the changes in this regard. When Sulla marched toward Rome in 88, almost all of his officers left him. Early in the first century, many officers were young nobles or members of families that were aligned to the leading oligarchy. Things had changed by mid-century. When Caesar crossed the Rubicon, all but one of his officers followed him. During his years in Gaul, Caesar had created a middle cadre that largely consisted of young men of fairly humble origins who had no ties to the leading families of Rome. They were professional soldiers, whose career depended on Caesar and his fate alone. Commanders like Caesar realized the worth of an experienced and loyal middle cadre. Hence, they offered wealth and social status to their officers and centurions. However, although the political conflicts of the late Republic were decided on the battlefield, the role of the armies as willing instruments of a commander's ambitions should not be exaggerated. Most soldiers still had respect for law and order, and were more eager to fight for their commander if they reckoned that his case was just. The generals were wise to emphasize their legitimacy and to stress that they fought for the People's sovereignty. An example of this can be seen at the crossing of the Rubicon. According to our sources, the soldiers went to war not only for Caesar's honor, but also to defend the tribunes of the plebs (see also Chapter 29). Many years later, the troops of Antony and Octavian did not accept the continuous conflicts between Caesar's two political heirs, and for a while they refused to fight each other. Despite the changes in the social structure of the Roman armies, late republican troops were not automatically eager to follow their commanders into civil war.[26] Nevertheless, it was Octavian's army that won the empire for him and decided the fate of the Republic.

Epilog

Some of the late republican veterans appear on inscriptions, such as Marcus Billienus, who had fought at Actium, and whose funerary inscription informs us that he had been settled in Ateste, where he later became a member of the town council. The example of Marcus Billienus shows that many veterans became well-to-do members of the local elite. We may be sure that in the early years of Augustus' reign, during which he gradually shaped the principate, people like Marcus Billienus were contented citizens and loyal supporters of the new order.[27]

The army of Augustus became an important pillar and source of stability for the emerging principate. However, we should not forget that Augustus' army was shaped by the experiences during the disastrous decades of civil war between Sulla's march on Rome in 88 and the battle of Actium in 31. The armies of the Republic had been raised for each particular conflict and been disbanded afterward. This had resulted in occasional mass levies. The discharge of such troops constituted one of the main problems of the late Republic. Therefore, Augustus reshaped the legions and the auxiliary forces into permanent units. Concomitantly, he reorganized the recruitment of soldiers for the army. From now on, soldiers were to serve for the largest part of their adult life, but they could count on a bonus upon discharge – either a piece of land or a substantial sum of money – to support them after their retirement. However, recruits came less and less from Italy itself. In the long run, civil society and the Roman army became disconnected entities in Italy and the Mediterranean heart of the Empire.

Guide to Further Reading

In contrast to the vast literature on the imperial army, recent publications on the army of the Republic are sparse. The last extensive coverage of the republican army is Keppie 1984, which is good on strictly military affairs. A very good and excellently illustrated introduction to Roman warfare in general can be found in the first chapters of Goldsworthy 2000a. Sabin 2000 offers a detailed analysis of the experience of battle. A modern study of the development of the army in the context of Republican society, economy, and demography, however, remains a desideratum. Rosenstein 1999 offers a brief, but stimulating view on these matters. Similar discussions concerning the fourth and early third centuries are Harris 1990a and Oakley 1993. On army and warfare in early Rome, Cornell 1995 is essential (though sometimes controversial) reading. On warfare in archaic Italy, see Rawlings 1999. Regarding the age of overseas expansion, see Lazenby 1996 on the First Punic War; Cornell

1996; Daly 2002 on the Second Punic War. Harris 1979 emphasizes the militaristic nature of Roman society, but see also Rich 1993 (and elsewhere in this volume). Rosenstein 1990 discusses the role of military success in the career of the aristocracy. A basic quantitative study of manpower still is Brunt 1971a. Rich 1983, Rathbone 1993a, Lo Cascio 2001, and Rosenstein 2004 review the evidence on recruitment and manpower, but without reaching consensus on many issues. Erdkamp 1998 offers an investigation of how republican society and economy functioned in times of war, focusing on military provisioning as well as civilian food supply. The first part of Roth 1999 is an excellent study of military logistics during the Middle and Late Republic. Few publications deal with the late republican army in general; see on warfare in this period Goldsworthy 1996. On the Roman cavalry in the Middle and Late Republic: McCall 2002. On the role of the army in society and politics, see Brunt 1988a, Patterson 1993, and de Blois 2000.

Notes

1   Cornell 1995: 293–309.
2   Oakley 1993: 14–18; Rich 1998: 5–6.
3   Sumner 1970b; Kienast 1975; E. Rawson 1991: 51–7; Cornell 1995: 173–97.
4   Rich 1998: 6.
5   Cornell 1995: 347–52.
6   Crawford 1985: 25–9.
7   Wheeler 1979; Goldsworthy 2000a: 49–55; Daly 2002.
8   *Contra*, Zhmodikov 2000.
9   McCall 2002.
10 Goldsworthy 2000a: 49–75.
11 Harris 1979; Oakley 1993: 22–8; see, however, Rich 1993.
12 Rosenstein 1990.
13 Brunt 1971a: 44–60; Baronowski 1993: 181–202; less skeptical: Lo Cascio 2001.
14 Brunt 1971a; Hopkins 1978: 31.
15 Brunt 1971a: 625–34; Nicolet 1980: 96–102; E. Rawson 1991: 36–40.
16 Erdkamp 1998: 46–83; Roth 1999: 156–222.
17 Erdkamp 1995; 1998: 84–121.
18 Rich 1983; Rathbone 1993a; Lo Cascio 2001.
19 Erdkamp 1998: 270–96. Cf. Cornell 1996: 97–113; Rosenstein 2002.
20 Rosenstein 2004.
21 Erdkamp 1998: 249–68.
22 Keppie 1984: 63–77. On the cavalry: McCall 2002: 100–13.
23 Keppie 1983.
24 Nicolet 1980: 129–37; Rich 1983; Keppie 1984: 61–2; Brunt 1988a; Rathbone 1993a; Patterson 1993: 97–9.
25 Patterson 1993: 107.
26 de Blois 2000. Cf. Nicolet 1980: 137–48; Brunt 1988a.
27 Keppie 1983: 104–12.

PART IV

Society

CHAPTER 14

Social Structure and Demography

Neville Morley

Cicero's Rome

In the fourth of his orations against Catiline, delivered before the Senate in 63, Cicero asserts once again that the whole of Rome is united behind him. "All men are here, of every order, of all origins and indeed of all ages. The Forum is full, the temples about the Forum are full, all the approaches to this temple and place are full. For this case is the only one known since the founding of the city in which all think as one" (*Cat.* 4.14). To reinforce his argument, he lists the different groups that have now joined together in their hope that the Senate will come to the correct decision. First come the *equites*, the group of wealthy Romans from which the Senate drew its members, "who concede supremacy to you in rank and decision-making as they compete with you in their love of the *res publica*" (*Cat.* 4.15). Secondly, the tribunes of the treasury and the clerks. Thirdly, the mass of the citizens: "the whole multitude of free-born citizens (*ingenui*) is here, even the poorest. For is there anyone to whom these temples, the sight of the city, the possession of liberty and even the light itself and the common soil of the fatherland are not precious and sweet and delightful?" (*Cat.* 4.16). Fourthly, the *liberti*, the former slaves who received citizenship when they were manumitted: "it is worth the effort, Conscript Fathers, to take note of the eagerness of the freedmen, who, having gained the benefit of citizenship by their own virtue, truly judge this to be their native land" (*Cat.* 4.16). That completes the roll-call of respectable members of society, but Catiline is such a threat to Rome that "there is no slave, as long as his condition of servitude is not too severe, who does not give his support, as much as he dares and is able, to the common cause" (*Cat.* 4.16).

The force of Cicero's argument comes from the assumption that Roman society was not completely homogeneous, but consisted of a number of distinct groups whose interests were often opposed; only when the state was in real danger would these groups set aside their differences. The study of social structure rests on a similar assumption; societies are seen to be made up of interdependent social groups that shape the behavior of their individual members. The members of a particular group will tend to have common interests and to share a way of life; where power and resources are distributed unevenly across the society, there is likely to be a strong correlation between an individual's social group and his or her prospects, occupation, access to resources, and even life expectancy. Social interaction between members of the same group is likely to be very different in nature from that between members of different groups, if the latter interact at all; sometimes, indeed, the interests shared by members of the same group may lead them to act in concert, and in opposition to other groups. Social conflict can be one of the main determinants of historical events, but at the same time any society, in order to survive, will have means of mediating between the interests of different groups and building consensus – if only, as Cicero tries to do, by uniting them against a common enemy.

Any complex society will contain a wide range of different sorts of social groups and associations, both formal and informal; any individual is likely to belong to a number of different ones. The crucial analytical problem is therefore to identify which of these groups are the most important, both from the point of view of their influence on the behavior of individuals and as regards the overall workings of society. This is a matter of some contention in the study of modern society; there are a number of competing theories, some of which will be discussed below, that claim to have uncovered the basic structures of social relations. In considering a historical society, however, there is the initial question of whether we should employ actors' or observers' categories in our analysis: that is to say, whether we should analyze Roman society purely in the terms that the Romans themselves used to describe it, or whether it is legitimate and productive to employ concepts developed by modern sociological theory.

Roman writers, like their Greek predecessors, did not distinguish conceptually between the spheres of "society" and "politics" in the way that modern studies do; the phrase *res publica* can reasonably be translated as "state" in some contexts and "society" (in the broadest sense) in others. Cicero's list of the different groups that, for him, made up Roman society is driven by his political concerns, but it goes beyond the narrowly political: he emphasizes the freeborn – freedman distinction, although this made little difference in strictly political terms (freedmen could not stand for office, but in practice neither could most citizens); he includes slaves, despite their complete exclusion from the sphere of political activity; and he completely ignores both census groups and tribes, the formal divisions of the Roman citizen body. In other words, he favors broader categories of analysis over the clearly defined (but, by implication, arbitrary) units of the political system, emphasizing "social" and "ideological" distinctions as much as the divisions established by the Roman census. Thus it could be argued that Cicero provides the historian with a ready-made set of social categories that reflect the way in which the Romans actually thought, avoiding any need to distort the ancient evidence to fit anachronistic modern categories such as "class" or "status groups."

There is no denying the importance of Cicero's view of Roman society in so far as it must at times have influenced his decisions and actions; since this passage of the speech would work only if its basic assumptions were shared by its audience, we might cautiously take it as evidence also for the prevailing attitude of the rest of the Senate. As a means of understanding Roman social structure, however, it has certain limitations. In the first place, Cicero does not actually offer a consistent picture. The groups he describes are distinguished from one another in different ways, rather than being based on a single principle of social differentiation: senators are distinguished from *equites* by the fact that they had held a magistracy, whereas the *equites* had chosen not to pursue political careers (or had failed to get themselves elected); *equites* in turn were distinguished from the rest of the population by their wealth, a division established by the census; tribunes of the treasury were distinguished from the mass of the population by their office, freeborn and freedmen were distinguished by birth, and slaves and the free were divided by legal status.

More significantly, on other occasions Cicero offers different accounts of Roman society. In his second oration against Catiline, once again enumerating the components of a united Rome, he lists the consuls and the generals, the *coloniae* and the *municipia* (different categories of Italian towns; see also Chapter 28), the Senate, the *equites*, and the People of Rome, as well as the city, the treasury, and the taxes, all Italy, the provinces, and foreign nations (*Cat.* 2.25); perhaps the fact that this speech was delivered before the People led him to play down differences between freeborn and freedmen. In the first book of his work *On Duties* (*De Officiis*), he distinguishes between the different duties of magistrates, private citizens, and resident foreigners, having previously also mentioned slaves as a distinct group (*Off.* 1.124, 1.41). In his more philosophical work *The Republic* (*De republica*) he identifies three key groups – the magistrates, the leading citizens, and the People (*Rep.* 2.57) – and divides the People on the basis of wealth: the taxpayers (*assidui*) who contribute money to the state, and the poor (*proletarii*) who can contribute only their offspring (*Rep.* 2.40). In the fourth oration against Catiline, after the passages quoted, he focuses on a particular section (*genus*) of the People – not now differentiating between freeborn and freedman – defined by occupation: the "poor and inexperienced" who worked in shops and workshops, *tabernae*, and who were considered as likely adherents of Catiline (*Cat.* 4.17). In another speech he distinguishes (without explaining the distinction) between the *populus* (a word which normally refers to the whole body of the citizens) and the mass of the poor, the *plebs* (*Mur.* 1). Cicero acknowledges, but generally dismisses, differences within the Senate and the *equites* based on lineage and background: patrician and plebeian, the man of "noble" lineage (*nobilis*) and the "new man" (*novus homo*) who was the first in his family to enter the Senate (*Mur.* 15–16). He consistently distinguishes between Senate and *equites*, while noting that, in most leading families, different generations could be found in either category.

Overall, then, Cicero identifies and employs a wide range of different means of dividing up Roman society: legal status, political status, wealth, lineage, occupation, place of origin, moral standing. He does not indicate which of these are to his mind most significant, apart from the clearly polemical assertion that none of them matter compared with dedication to the best interests of Rome (compare *Sest.* 96 on the different groups that make up the "optimates," the group who favored the policies of those whom Cicero refers to as "the best citizens"). If we want to make use of Cicero's categories of social analysis, which ones do we choose? All the groups identified – with the exception of the tribunes of the treasury and the clerks – can be considered significant social groupings with common interests and with which individuals might identify; but it is left entirely unclear how important the free/ freedman/slave distinction was in shaping social action compared with the citizen/ non-citizen divide or the Roman/Italian split. Perhaps Roman society was indeed fragmented in this way, with a confusing array of different groups and no clear organizing principle; but perhaps that impression is simply a consequence of the fact that Cicero develops different accounts of the composition of the Roman People for different purposes.

This leads to the second limitation of his account, namely that these images of Roman society are hardly objective. Arguably, no account of society can ever be wholly neutral – the various modern theories of social organization have definite political overtones – but we should certainly be suspicious of the version offered by an interested party, a direct participant in political activity. In many cases, Cicero's description is expressly designed to achieve a particular end; thus he creates the image of a stable, united society in order to cast Catiline and followers not merely as an opposing group within society but as outsiders, bandits, enemies of the state – and therefore to be treated with no mercy. At times he aims to legitimize the domination of his own group, offering a justification as much as a description of the status quo. Society is to be organized according to the principle of aristocracy, giving power to the "best men" (*optimi*), "for there is no occasion for revolution when each person is firmly placed in his own rank" (*Rep.* 1.69); on the other hand, "when equal honour is had by the highest and the lowest, who are of necessity in every population, this very evenness is most uneven" (*Rep.* 1.53). The magistrates and leading citizens are to have power and influence, the People are to have "enough" liberty (*Rep.* 2.57): "do we not see that dominion has been given to the best by nature itself, with the greatest benefit to the weak?" (*Rep.* 3.37). It scarcely needs to be said that the best judges of virtue and ability are the *optimi* themselves; following philosophical convention, he notes that the "mob (*volgus* – scarcely a neutral, objective category of analysis) does not fully understand how far it is from perfection; in so far as it understands anything, however, it considers that nothing is missing; the same thing happens in poems, pictures and many other such things, that the inexperienced are entertained by and praise things that are not worthy of praise" (*Off.* 3.15). Naturally, such people need to recognize their place and accept guidance.

This account of Roman society is not wholly self-serving; it is simply that society can look different from different locations within the structure, and that Cicero, a senator, interprets it according to the prejudices and obsessions of his own social group. Social relationships, for example, are considered entirely from the perspective of the elite political class. He focuses above all on the workings of friendship between equals, *amicitia* (here involving both senators and *equites*, without clear distinction; note Cicero's intimate friendship with Atticus, an *eques*). Social life at this level is all about complex networks of kinship, affection, and obligation, a constant traffic in gifts, favors, influence, and information. Cicero's interest in other sorts of social relationships is confined to those which are relevant to political ambitions. Thus he has a certain amount to say about patron – client relations, in which members of the lower orders provided votes, voices, and their presence in the retinue of the elite in the hope of receiving support, protection, or the benefits of influence in return (see also Chapter 19). Every aspiring politician needs a crowd of supporters, and so some contact with the masses is beneficial; "if you defend a needy man, who is however honest and temperate, all the respectable common folk, of whom there is a great multitude among the People, see you as a protector provided for them" (*Off.* 2.70; see generally the *Election Manual* [*Commentariolum Petitionis*] sometimes ascribed to Cicero's brother). Cicero notices the ways that the masses organize their own social relationships, for example, the "associations" (*collegia*), only in so far as they offer an opportunity of recruiting support, or represent a threat as a source of support for a rival like Clodius. This is a particular problem for history of the associations, which appear under the Republic as armed gangs involved in street brawls and under the Principate as respectable gatherings of merchants and craftsmen, holding dinners and conducting religious rites; but in general our knowledge of the social organization of the mass of the population is at the mercy of the very limited perspective of sources like Cicero.

The third limitation of Cicero's account is that it is largely static, referring to one particular period. He comments on changes in relations within groups (the old patrician – plebeian conflict is now seen to be irrelevant: *Mur.* 17) and between groups (the Senate and the *equites* are supposedly no longer at variance: *Cat.* 4.15), and on the breakdown of social consensus since the time of Sulla, observing that Rome is now governed by fear rather than respect (e.g., *Off.* 2.26–9). However, he does not apparently consider that the different parts of Roman society might themselves change; on the contrary, the Roman social order was established back in the time of Servius, the sixth king of Rome (*Rep.* 2.39). This is a problem for all accounts of social structure, trying to balance synchronic description and diachronic narrative, and such structures do generally remain more or less the same over many generations. However, there is reason to think that the last two centuries of the Republic were times of significant social change, with the growth in the numbers of slaves and freedmen and the extension of the Roman citizenship – in most ancient societies, a narrowly defined, jealously guarded privilege – to the rest of Italy. Cicero shows some awareness that his world is changing, but lacks the long view and the benefit of hindsight to make proper sense of it.

For these reasons, therefore, we cannot take Cicero to offer a complete, or wholly reliable, account of Roman society. It should also be noted that the concern about the "anachronism" of modern sociological concepts compared with ancient terminology is a red herring: some measure of anachronism is inevitable whenever we translate Roman terms into English. Consider Cicero's statement that "all men are here, of every order (*ordo*), of all origins (*genus*) and indeed of all ages." *Ordo* can be translated as, among other things, rank, order, class, and station; *genus* as birth, origin, race, descent, kind, sort, or class; each of these choices has different implications. The decision as to whether *genus* should be translated as "origin" or "class," or indeed "kind," is made on the basis of the translator's understanding of Roman society, mapping Cicero's categories onto modern categories. This being the case, it seems better to make sense of Roman terminology explicitly in terms of precisely defined sociological categories, where the modern overtones and implications are made explicit, rather than the "fuzzy" categories of everyday language. Even if we choose to leave terms in the original, to emphasize the lack of an exact equivalent in English and the fact that any translation is potentially misleading, we still need to consider what sorts of groups these are in modern terms.

There is a more positive case for drawing on modern terminology. First, it can, sometimes, offer greater precision, if only because we have to be more conscious about the status of our concepts. Secondly, it can offer the possibility of understanding ancient society as a system better than the Romans could themselves, drawing on the benefits of hindsight and the specialized study of social structures – above all, the use of models that aim to simplify a complex reality in order to make it more intelligible. Thirdly, it offers the possibility of making useful comparisons with other, similar societies – especially those whose social structures are rather better documented than those of classical antiquity – and makes it easier for others to draw on Roman evidence. Ancient history can only benefit from greater communication with other periods of history and other social sciences, but in order to do that it needs to make greater use of a common language, the standard terms of social analysis. However, there is no one universal system for making sense of social structure, but a variety of different theories; in considering what sorts of groups made up Roman society and how they related to one another, we need also to consider which of the various images of society presented by these theories seems most persuasive.

Orders and Status Groups

One model of social structure often applied to pre-industrial European societies is that of estates or orders: such a society is arranged in a hierarchy or pyramid of hereditary groups, with different degrees of honor and power. On the face of it, Rome fits such a model, with a clear social hierarchy from the old consular families at the top to the poor *proletarii* and the slaves at the bottom. However, there are crucial differences, especially as regards those at the top of society. In medieval and early modern societies, birth, wealth, and power commonly went together, but it was birth that conferred noble status and thus membership of the ruling elite; a poor noble was not a contradiction in terms. In Rome, however, membership of the *equites* and thus eligibility to stand for office depended on the possession of a considerable fortune. The greatest power and the highest reputation in the state were obtained not through birth but through success in elections; noble lineage might be an advantage for a candidate, but it was unlikely to be sufficient without money, powerful friends, and a reputation for military, administrative, or legal competence. A number of famous names recur constantly in republican politics, but as members of the same *gens*, or clan, rather than a single family line; senators' sons did not always follow them into the Senate.[1] At the bottom of society, also, the hereditary principle was not dominant. Citizen status was inherited, but it was also granted to slaves who had been properly manumitted and to allies of Rome. People could be born, as well as made, slaves, but some slaves at least – above all those who were most intimate with their master or mistress, like secretaries, maids, or nurses – could hope to gain their freedom in due course. The special status of *libertus*, freedman, which included certain restrictions on citizen rights and a set of obligations toward the former master, lasted for a single generation; children born after the freedman gained his liberty were considered indistinguishable from any other freeborn citizen. In general, the notion of a pyramid of hereditary orders does not do justice to the fluidity and complexity of Roman society.

A related but more flexible concept is that of status groups. The idea of status was elaborated by the pioneering sociologist Max Weber, who developed it on the basis of data gathered from a range of historical societies, including classical antiquity:

> "Status" shall mean an effective claim to social esteem in terms of positive or negative privileges; it is typically founded on (a) style of life, hence (b) formal education, which may be (α) empirical training or (β) rational instruction, and the corresponding forms of behaviour, (c) hereditary or occupational prestige. In practice, status expresses itself through (α) connubium (β) commensality, possibly (γ) monopolistic appropriation of privileged modes of acquisition or the abhorrence of certain kinds of acquisition, (δ) status conventions (traditions) of other kinds.[2]

Status may be defined legally and politically (the status of citizen, or *eques*, or slave), or it may be governed by expectations of a particular way of life (notoriously, ancient writers regarded manual labor as slavish; as Cicero puts it, "no workshop can have anything of the freeborn man about it" [*Off.* 1.150]. In most cases social status involves more than one form of differentiation, which are mutually reinforcing: the rulers of Rome are "good men," *boni*, both morally and materially superior, since their wealth gives them the leisure to cultivate a higher sensibility. A key aspect of Weber's approach is that social esteem, and thus the groups defined by their particular claims to social esteem, does not depend on a single marker but on a range of status indicators, some of which may be necessary but none of which is sufficient on its own. Thus to become a senator it is necessary to be rich, but a rich freedman would not be accepted; noble lineage might be a source of status, but it is not sufficient to guarantee access to power.

In these terms, it makes sense to identify "the Roman elite" as a whole as a distinct status group, rather than focusing on the divisions between senators and *equites*. Clearly there was a hierarchy of honor based on office holding within this group, and fierce competition between some of its members for those offices; but the common ground between the senators and those who either failed or chose not to pursue senatorial careers is more striking than the differences. As noted above, families moved between Senate and *equites* in different generations; any senator might have an equestrian father or brother, let alone other relatives. They were all wealthy; they were similarly marked out from the common People by their costumes (senators had a broad purple stripe on the toga, *equites* a narrow one); they received the same education in language, literature, and rhetoric, and shared in the same culture; they tended to marry within the group (Weber's *connubium*), and regularly entertained one another at dinner (*commensality*), as well as exchanging gifts and favors. Cicero's correspondence with Atticus is clearly a matter of intercourse between equals who have chosen different paths in life but who share a common outlook, rather than a relationship that crosses major social boundaries.

It has been suggested that the *equites* were businessmen, whereas senators were expressly forbidden to own ships for the purposes of trade and so relied on land for their income. In fact, most equestrians were landowners, and even those who wished to take on public contracts (supplying the army or collecting taxes) had to be substantial landowners in order to give the required surety. Their main role in business was as financiers, not as day-to-day operatives; senators could be just as involved in such activities, operating through agents (Plut. *Cat. Mai.* 21.5–6). Nevertheless, occupation was a key marker of elite status, for both groups; direct involvement in retail trade or manual labor was "illiberal" and "sordid." Agriculture was always regarded as the most honorable way of making money – as Cato put it, "from the farmers come the bravest men and the most vigorous soldiers, and this sort of acquisition is the most sacred and the most reliable and the least likely to arouse hatred" (*Agr.* preface) – and the Roman elite were able to convince themselves that owning a farm that was worked and managed by slaves was quite as virtuous as plowing it oneself. Other sources of income, like the maritime loans in which Cato was involved, the construction industry (Crassus owned a gang of slave workmen who were employed on building projects), or rents from urban properties (like the slum housing owned by Cicero), could be equally acceptable, provided that they were on a sufficiently grand scale or, better, left in the hands of slaves and freedmen, with the owner collecting the profits at arm's length. In this, as in much else, Cicero's work *On Duties* offers a handbook of proper behavior for members of the Roman elite – or, to be more exact, for those like himself who sought to join it despite the fact that they did not come from one of the old noble families.

Unlike an estates-based society, status in Rome was not acquired automatically. A certain measure of social esteem could be obtained without excessive effort on the basis of wealth and a decent family name; however, for outsiders, and for those who sought to achieve higher prestige within the elite, status needed to be worked for and paid for, and success could never be guaranteed. Roman society at the highest level was fiercely competitive; given the diminishing number of posts as one moved up the political ladder, it was inevitable that many of those who aspired to a consulship would be disappointed. Office brought status; status did not automatically confer office, since it was necessary to submit to the arbitration of the People, but it was essential to be accepted by those already at the top of society as an equal, and to appear to the masses as a suitable leader (see also Chapters 17 and 20). One recurring theme in Cicero's discussions of Roman politics, and his speeches against or in defense of other members of the elite, is the need to behave in a manner appropriate to one's status, and to treat others according to theirs. In practice, this always involved striking a balance: between conviviality and excess (compare Cicero's denunciation of a hung-over Antony for vomiting in front of an assembly of the Roman People; *Phil.* 2.63), between generosity to one's friends and undue favoritism, and between appropriate public benefactions and demagogic extravagance. Most awkwardly, the would-be politician needed a house, a lifestyle, and a retinue commensurate with the status to which he aspired, without being seen to fall into reprehensible luxuriousness (see also Chapters 4, 16, and 24):

> The Roman people hates private luxury, it esteems public munificence; it does not love lavish banquets, still less sordid behaviour and brutality; it recognises differences in services and circumstances, the interchange of work and pleasure. You assert that nothing should influence the minds of men in raising someone to a magistracy except dignity, but in what is most important you yourself fail to preserve your dignity. (Cic. *Mur.* 76)

Some accounts of status assume that its rules are clear, if complex; that is to say, it should always be possible to assign an individual to his or her correct station, and that the behavior appropriate to a particular station was well known. The Roman evidence suggests that, at least at the highest level, status was always negotiable, even contentious. The Roman elite sought to police the boundaries of their group, to admit only those who met their exacting standards of conduct – without clearly defining, or agreeing on, what those standards were. It was clear who *was* a senator, and who was in theory eligible to become one, but never who *ought* to be one; thus the censors, in theory, scrutinized not only the wealth of individual members of the elite but their conduct, and would expel those whose behavior was unacceptable.[3] Cicero's regular reiteration of the theme that patrician blood was no guarantee of ability and the lack of noble ancestors no bar to the consulship makes it clear that others in the Senate had different views of the necessary qualifications for high office. One of the key changes in the late Republic is a dramatic increase in the resources available to some members of the elite, especially successful generals, to fund their bids for status. This produced an equally dramatic increase in the levels of public munificence, both traditional forms (the ceremonies associated with elite funerals were expanded to include days of gladiatorial combat; the buildings constructed by triumphant generals became ever more lavish, and included theaters as well as temples; see also Chapters 4, 17, and 24) and innovations, as Clodius employed the resources of the state to distribute free grain to the whole plebs. The rules about what was appropriate behavior for a member of the elite became still more uncertain; the traditional restraints on excess and luxury were, at least in the eyes of Cicero, cast aside.

The idea of status offers a productive way of interpreting the social behavior of the Roman elite, as they sought both to distinguish themselves clearly from the mass of society and to improve their standing according to the finer gradations of prestige within the group. Further down the social scale, we can identify several obvious status divisions. Citizenship originally brought with it both rights and duties: the citizen was soldier and taxpayer, voter and recipient of public bounty; the non-citizen, whether slave or foreigner, was excluded not only from political activity but also from the full protection of the law. Citizen status was established by enrollment in the census, and marked by distinctive activities (military service, voting); it is not evident that there were clear distinctions in education, dress, occupation, or lifestyle that would mark citizen from non-citizen, and the differences between, for example, city-dweller and countryman must have been far more noticeable in this respect.

The Romans had long distinguished themselves from other ancient societies in their relative willingness to extend citizenship to allies and even to former slaves, let alone to anyone with some claim to Roman blood; it was therefore not confined to those who could, at least in theory, take an active role in politics. In the course of the late Republic, the idea of citizenship changed further: the property tax was abolished, the practice that military service was gradated according to wealth was abandoned, and citizen status was extended to the whole of Italy after the Social War. It has long been assumed that the Italian allies went to war to gain admission to Roman citizenship, showing its continuing desirability; this view has recently been challenged, but in any event the Social War marks the complete abandonment of the "city-state" model of society, with a small but cohesive citizen body, in favor of an entirely "new and artificial" community in which most individuals identified with their native town as much as with Rome (see also Chapter 28).[4] It was necessary to develop new symbols and myths to try to unite such a heterogeneous body; Cicero's notion of the "two fatherlands" (*patriae*), to which one owes different sorts of duty, is the philosophical expression of this need, while the story of Romulus' use of the Asylum to build up Rome's population, welcoming as a citizen anyone who wished to join, might have been designed expressly to legitimize the idea of a citizen body based not on birth but on the desire to become Roman.[5]

The other great status divide in the mass of the population was between free and slave, with freedmen as a special category of the former. According to our sources, *libertas* (liberty) was the rallying cry of the masses: the right to a proper trial and to appeal to the tribunes of the *plebs*, in order to avoid being reduced to the status of slaves by the dominance of the wealthy elite.[6] The severest condemnation of behavior in Cicero's eyes is that it is unworthy of a freeborn man; to receive a wage for unskilled labor is a mark of slavery (*Off.* 150), and the greatest risk for any Roman is becoming a slave to one's passions or appetites (*Rep.* 3.35–7). Slaves had no status: they were stripped of kinship ties, social esteem, and often even their names when they became slaves, and were then, in theory at least, wholly dependent on their owners. They were property, to be bought and sold at will; their relationships were not formally recognized, so that families could be broken up at any time; they could be used and abused in almost any way their owner chose, physically, psychologically, and sexually. Freedom, enshrined in the political and legal system, provided at least some protection from absolute domination and exploitation by the powerful.

The ideological distinction between freedom and slavery was clear; it is less certain how far it worked in practice. Indeed, it has been argued that the Roman elite developed the "legal fiction" of absolute dominion of masters over slaves in response to the prevalence of slavery and the difficulty in distinguishing free from slave, since there was no clear-cut distinction in dress or occupation.[7] Slaves might at times have an advantage over free men; their value to their owners meant that they would be fed and clothed, whereas the independent freeborn might be left to starve. Slaves could sometimes possess a sort of power, since those who served as personal attendants became so intimate with their owners; certainly the elite had far greater and more regular contact with such slaves than with the poor masses. Slaves were not treated identically; there was a clear hierarchy of status, from the chain gang in the fields to intimate body servants and secretaries. Some slaves were far better educated than the vast majority of the population, and there was even the possibility of intimate and affectionate relationships, such as that between Cicero and Tiro, which were free from constant competitive element of friendships with "equals." Manumission was a reasonable prospect for some categories of slave, who might then rise to prominence amongst the plebs, or in a few cases even higher in society, despite the taint of slavery. In some later sources, such as Juvenal's satires, there is anger and bewilderment that slaves, let alone ex-slaves, might have a higher status than freeborn Romans because of their wealth and influence. Whatever the ideological assumption that "slave" equates with "dependent" and is always inferior to "free," in practice the situation seems sometimes to have been much more complicated.

There is also the fundamental problem of knowing how the mass of the population thought about social status; whether they valued citizenship as highly as the politics-obsessed elite who produced the written sources, and whether they thought in terms of the free – slave divide. We have no useful accounts of social relationships from either the free poor or slaves. The slave characters in the plays of Plautus, like the depiction of the cunning slave in the anonymous *Life of Aesop*, offer insight into the anxieties and curiosity of the elite about the "itchy eye" – annoying but indispensable – of slavery, while Apuleius' powerful fable of the plight of the slave, desperately attempting to prove himself human, is in the end equally limited, a work of imagination rather than experience (see also Chapter 25).[8] Epigraphical evidence gets us closer to the attitudes of the ordinary members of society who commissioned inscriptions, but it is of course a matter of public display rather than private thoughts, with all the limitations that that implies, and is biased towards those with the wealth and motivation to put up inscriptions, not a representative sample of Roman society as a whole.[9] That "epigraphic habit" does constitute evidence of status concerns in its own right; epigraphy shows that many freedmen did wish to emphasize and advertise their achievement of freedom, to the extent that their presence in the population of Rome, and the frequency of manumission, has often been overestimated. It can also be noted that these freedmen, and the others who declined to record their legal status, did not accept the elite valuation of their occupations in status terms; plenty chose to identify themselves as craftsmen and traders, basing their public identity on their profession. We might speculate that wealth and lifestyle – which floor of the apartment block they lived on, variety and security of diet, level of education, office-holding in an association, funeral arrangements (from mass burial pits to a place in a communal mausoleum to an elaborate, self-advertising tomb) – were far more important to most Romans than strict legal or political status.[10]

The most obvious problem with employing the idea of status is that most of our impressions of its operation come from the elite, who were obsessed with the struggle for prestige. It is virtually an "actors' category," and as such subject to the limitations noted earlier for Cicero's view of society. All too easily it supports a view of an ordered, hierarchical society in which everyone knew his or her place and knew the proper way to behave toward those in other status groups; whereas, as has been suggested here, recognition of the status of others and assertion of one's own social standing was always a matter of negotiation and even argument, with disputes over which status criteria (wealth, birth, or lifestyle, for example) should be applied. Other serious objections are that an approach based on status groups tends to be descriptive rather than analytical – the groups remain more or less fixed, even as individuals move between them – and that it focuses attention too much on individuals and their own sense of social identity, ignoring more significant structures that shaped social action without the participants being wholly aware of them. Disputes over lifestyle choices and personal identity offer little basis for collective action or social conflict; in which case one must wonder why conflict nevertheless takes place.

Relations of Production

Social historians who regard the status-based view of society as at best naïve and potentially misleading tend to prefer a different term of analysis: class. This is a problematic term, since it is used in a number of different ways; in everyday usage it is equivalent to "status group," while in sociology it may be used to describe a system of social stratification based on economic criteria (primary industry, white-collar workers, professionals). The concept is most closely associated with Marxism, where it has a more specific and technical definition, and from which it acquires most of its political overtones; however, although Marx himself used the term extensively and insisted on its importance – "the history of all hitherto existing society is the history of class struggle" – he never provided a detailed definition of it. Much effort has therefore been expended in trying to establish exactly how Marx understood the concept; an important question in intellectual history, especially for Marxists who wish to claim the authority of the founder for their particular version, but for the purposes of historical study a "Marx-influenced" definition may be sufficient.[11]

> There are really only two ways of thinking theoretically about class: either as a structural *location* or as a social *relation*. The first and more common of these treats class as a form of "stratification", a layer in a hierarchical structure, differentiated according to "economic" criteria... In contrast to this geological model, there is a socio-historical conception of class as a relation between appropriators and producers, determined by the specific form in which, to use Marx's phrase, "surplus labour is pumped out of the direct producers".[12]

The "stratification" approach falls foul of the same objections raised above about "status," tending to be descriptive rather than analytical, and is certainly not distinctively Marxist. For that reason, it is suggested, the focus should be on the actual social relationships between different groups, rather than simply comparing their income or occupation.

> *Class* (essentially a relationship) is the collective social expression of the fact of exploitation, the way in which exploitation is embodied in a social structure. By *exploitation* I mean the appropriation of part of the product of the labour of others: in a commodity-producing society this is the appropriation of what Marx called "surplus value". *A class*

(a particular class) is a group of persons in a community identified by their position in the whole system of social production, defined above all according to their relationship (primarily in terms of the degree of ownership or control) to the conditions of production (that is to say, the means and labour of production) and to other classes.[13]

As we might expect, the Marxist approach to "class" is essentially materialist and economic. Classes are defined not by their location in a hierarchy of status but by their place in the system of production; the means by which individuals support themselves and their families, and the way in which their labor contributes to the overall economic system. A clear distinction is drawn between those who own the means of production (self-sufficient peasant smallholders, wealthy property-owners) and those who have to make a living by working the property of others (slaves, tenants, wage laborers). Further distinctions may be based on the nature of the individual's productive activity, and above all their relation with those in other classes; for example, the tenant farmer hands over part of the produce of his labor to the landlord in a social or economic contract, while the slave's labor power is wholly owned by his owner; the peasant works his own land whereas the property magnate depends on exploiting the labor of others.

This definition of class, then, has a number of implications for the workings of society. First, there is a strong correlation between an individual's class and his/her level of education, diet, general state of health, living conditions, and so forth; further, access to the opportunities to improve one's social and economic position are not equally distributed throughout society, so that in fact most people remain in the class of their parents. Those with greater economic power are able to convert it into political and social power as well, to reinforce their dominant position; the state acts to enforce property rights and deal with unrest amongst the lower orders; education and culture provide ideological support for the status quo. In other words, class divisions permeate the political, social, and cultural spheres as well as the economic. Of course, evidence for the living conditions or the culture of Rome's lower classes is limited, but it is clear that we cannot simply assume that our elite sources speak for the whole of society.

In all but the simplest of societies, there is a variety of ways of organizing production, and hence there are a number of different classes. At the top, of course, are the great property-owners, who make their living by creaming off the "surplus value" created by those who worked their lands or labored in their workshops, whether free men or slaves. Rome, like most other ancient states, was dominated economically and politically by the interests of rich landowners; the opportunities for making money in trade or industry were much more limited, and even here much of the profits went to the landowners who, directly or indirectly, provided the finance and owned the workshops. Roman society was divided up according to the wealth of individuals, wealth was essential to gain access to political power, and, by the late Republic, political power (to be exact, the provincial governorships exercised by praetors and consuls after their year in office) could bring substantial financial reward. For Cicero, one of the two functions of justice in maintaining society is the defense of private property (*Off.* 1.20–1), and he returns to this theme when denouncing proposals for agrarian laws or the cancellation of debts. Praising the constitution of Servius, he argues that "the man for whom the good fortune of the community was most important carried the greatest weight in voting" – that is to say, the rich man (*Rep.* 2.40). Such attitudes can be seen in the behavior of the Senate, even when the senators disagreed on the best course of action. In the disputes over land reform in the late Republic (see Chapter 27), the majority of senators were always opposed to such proposals, seeing them as attacks on private property in general (if not their own illegally occupied lands in particular); the few who argued for redistribution were arguably motivated by the longer-term but equally self-interested belief that senatorial wealth and security would be better served by making concessions and supporting the peasant class that supplied soldiers to defend the state (and their property).

The identification of classes in the rest of Roman society has, historically, been somewhat confused by the fact that Marx's discussions focused primarily on the conflict between bourgeoisie and proletariat; historians tended to look for ancient equivalents of these two groups, and to reject the concept of class on the grounds that slaves and peasants would be put into the same class.[14] In fact these two classes are specific to modern capitalist society; earlier societies had different classes, reflecting their different ways of organizing production, and generally more than two. This does raise the question of how many different classes should be identified; for example, whether the position of a craftsman working on his own is sufficiently distinct in economic terms from that of a craftsman working alongside his slave that they should be considered as different classes. Opponents of the concept complain that it ignores crucial differences between individuals, while its supporters argue that the basic similarity of individuals' economic position outweighs superficial differences and provides a better explanation of their place in society. It is, arguably, more useful to understand society in terms of a limited number of large classes, even if these do have internal differences and divisions, than fragmented into lots of tiny classes which differ from one another only marginally.

Neither slaves nor free laborers owned their means of production, but they were exploited in quite different ways – the slave was, in theory at least, a thinking tool, part of the means of production – and so they need not be considered to belong to a single class. Indeed, given the wide range of different ways in which slaves were employed, it is arguable whether they should be considered as a single class. Some slaves were exploited for their labor power, on villa estates, in mines, and in workshops. They may perhaps have been more productive than free workers, at least within the highly organized system of villa cultivation; slave labor was certainly much more profitable than leasing the estate to a tenant, albeit at the cost of increased supervision.[15] Some slaves, however, were employed as overseers, *vilici*, given the responsibility of supervising their fellows; some were employed as agents, conducting business on their owner's behalf, and were even allowed a sum of money known as the *peculium* with which to do business on their own account and, one day, purchase their freedom. Some slaves were employed for their mental capacities and education, as tutors and secretaries, while others had no economic role but ministered to personal pleasure and served as status symbols. These different roles determined not only the day-to-day activity of the slaves, and their degree of independence, but their access to privileges such as a partner and family life, and the possibility of manumission.

In Roman ideology, all slaves were utterly dependent and exploitable, lower than any free man; in practice, many of them enjoyed better living conditions, security, and prospects than many of the free. In class terms, the difference between free and slave sometimes seems less significant than the divide between those who had control over some property (even if technically the slave's *peculium* remained the property of the owner) and those who had nothing; those whose occupation lay in supervising the work of others or in conducting business, and those who merely labored. The elite tendency to equate manual labor and slavishness had some truth in it; unskilled laborers had more in common with the slaves on the villa chain gang than with prosperous merchants, the slave mineworker had more in common with a poor citizen than with Cicero's slave secretary.

Unlike status groups, classes are defined in direct opposition to one another. The interests of a group that controls the means of production and relies on the labor of others to exploit them can never be reconciled with the interests of those who have to sell or barter their labor power to gain access to the means of life, let alone those who are compelled to labor for others. Society is therefore understood as an arena of class struggle; not necessarily of open war between self-conscious classes, but certainly of a constant clash of conflicting interests and demands. These conflicts, fought out in the economic, social, political, or cultural spheres, can provide the engine of social and economic change, as property owners seek to maintain the structures of inequality and to increase their profits, and the property-less seek to resist further exploitation. The transformation of Italian society in the late Republic has been interpreted in class terms: military success brought about a shift in the balance of power between landowners and peasants.[16] Where previously economic exploitation of the masses had been limited by the elite's need for soldiers, the influx of wealth and slaves made it possible to break the link; the peasant class was broken, replaced on the land by more profitable slave cultivators, and reduced to a class of landless laborers from which soldiers could be recruited. None of this was planned, or even recognized at the time; it was simply the result of the elite pursuing their own interests at the expense of others. Indeed, they did this even at the expense of society: the expansion of the poor urban masses and the separation of the army from civil society both contributed to the civil wars that brought about the replacement of oligarchy with monarchy, partly, it may be suggested, on the basis that monarchy was better able to maintain peace and protect property rights. It should be noted that this reconstruction is controversial, with fierce disputes over the interpretation of the archaeological evidence for changes in rural settlement patterns, but it offers one powerful interpretation of the events of the late Republic (see Chapters 27 and 28).[17]

The Roman "class struggle," according to this account, was driven primarily by elite acquisitiveness, not by the resistance of the exploited. Historically, elites have always been far readier than the masses to recognize their class interests and to act accordingly. Those who occupy a particular position in the system of production have common interests as a result, and would benefit if they acted collectively; but they do not necessarily recognize this, especially as other forces in society are tending to undermine any nascent "class consciousness" in favor of a panoply of social identities. The Roman elite employed a variety of means to divide the exploited class: selective patronage of the "respectable" *plebs* who might be persuaded to support the interests of property (note Cicero's praise of the shopkeepers, whose livelihood is said to depend on peace (*Cat.* 4.17), although other sources suggest that this group was notoriously restive), the redistribution of state wealth to win over sections of the urban masses, the role of military service in binding some of the poor to members of the elite (if not to the state as a whole) and, above all, the ideology of *libertas*, freedom, that concealed the common interests of the free poor and the lowest slaves in resisting exploitation behind the screen of status difference (see also Chapters 13, 18, and 19).

Domination and Dependence

Class and status are not mutually exclusive ways of understanding society; they emphasize different aspects of multifaceted social behavior, and so offer different perspectives on social structure. It is a matter of the historian's personal and ideological preferences which concept is believed to yield the greatest insight; whether "status" seems to obscure (perhaps intentionally) class divisions and conflict, or "class" is felt to privilege economic factors over individuals' own sense of social identity. When considering slavery, however, both ideas seem somewhat inadequate. To treat slavery merely as a status category seems to play down its often brutal reality, while class analysis suggests that slaves should not be considered as a category at all: the fundamental identity of slaves' experiences is ignored, simply because they did different jobs (see also Chapters 27 and 28).

An alternative approach is to focus not on slaves as a kind of group but on slavery as a particular sort of social relationship; the nature of this relationship shaped the behavior of both masters and slaves. Slavery was an extreme form of dependence, with the slave expected to be absolutely submissive and regarded as absolutely inferior.[18] Slaves had no status; they were stripped of kinship connections, ancestry, reputation, and any other source of an independent social identity when they became slaves, and were left wholly dependent on their owner. They could thus be treated as tools, or objects, with impunity; employed in degrading occupations, beaten to make them work harder, sexually abused, thrown away when worn out or broken. Slaves had no right to companionship, or family life, or food and shelter, let alone security or hope; they might succeed in obtaining these things, but all depended on the whim of the master, and such "privileges" could just as easily be taken away. Every slave, however faithful or industrious, lived under the threat of violence and torture; it was simply assumed that, because of their inferiority, they would require such discipline. In a trial, the evidence of slaves was admissible only if it had been obtained under torture.

The actual practice of slavery was inevitably complicated by the fact that owners could not necessarily count on the absolute submission of their slaves. The stripping of personal identity, the threat of violence, the selective offering and with-holding of privileges, and the hope of manumission can all be seen not just as expressions of the slave owner's power over the slave but also as means for main-taining that power. The slave's spirit had to be broken, the slave had to be persuaded to cooperate, and to focus his or her energies on competing with other slaves for their owner's approval. The slave owners' tactics were not always wholly successful. There were relatively few large-scale slave revolts; those that did occur, in Sicily in 136–132 and 104–101 and in Italy under Spartacus from 73 to 71, seem to have been prompted by a particular combination of excessive brutality, opportunity, and the presence of a charismatic leader.[19] However, there is evidence of constant resistance on an individual basis: shirking, vandalism, petty theft, and running away (Cicero's letters, for example, include a record of his efforts to recover one of his escaped slaves). A constant concern in the manuals of the Roman agronomists is the unreliability and untrustworthiness of slaves, which threatened the landowner's profits; the proposed solution to this problem is the careful selection of a suitable *vilicus*, the slave who would manage the estate and supervise the other slaves, but then the landowner was left worrying about how to supervise the supervisor. The master – slave relationship was asymmetrical but not wholly one-sided; the slave owners' need for the profits and status that could be obtained from slavery left them in a sense dependent on their slaves. A slave's loyalty and faithfulness was taken to reflect the virtue not of the slave but of the master; conversely, however, slaves who misbehaved or absconded could affect their master's reputation.

Slavery, then, involved a struggle for advantage between two unequal but not completely mismatched parties. This does not exclude the possibility that some master – slave relationships could become genuinely affectionate, given that they lived in such close intimacy in the household – though the portrayal of slaves in literature tends to exemplify anxiety that even the loyal attendant is basically motiv-ated by self-interest, and is in a position to manipulate a less cunning master (see also Chapter 25).[20] Equally, the self-interest of master and slave might coincide. The cooperative slave might gain alleviation of some of the harsher conditions of slavery, a measure of security compared with a poor free man, some independence of action and power over other slaves, and eventually manumission. At this point they gained citizenship as well as freedom, and might hope to benefit from continuing association with their former owner, or from a legacy to set themselves up in business – at the expense of continuing, if reduced, dependence, as a freedman was constrained to support and do some work for his former master.[21] It is impossible to say how frequent manumission was in practice – certainly not all slaves were in a position to gain the trust and affection of their master, and Roman law set limits on the proportion of slaves which could be manumitted – but it was always there as a possibility, an incentive to cooperate.

Clearly the owner gained from having a cooperative, industrious slave; and, for all their anxieties about trusting slaves, the Roman elite showed a clear preference for managing business through their slaves and freedmen, rather than employing free men. The wealthy made use of the institution of the *peculium*, the sum of money that might be given to slaves to manage themselves, to set up their dependents as ship owners, traders, bankers, and moneylenders, as well as managers of farms and workshops. They were thus able to spread their investments over a vast geographical area, to reduce their exposure to risk (since the owner was liable only to the value of the sum originally granted to the slave, not for any greater losses) and to avoid contamination of their status by direct involvement in disreputable activities, while still reaping profits.[22] The legal limits on the owner's liability for the actions of his slave made this an economically rational approach to business, especially given the elite's general aversion to risk. However, the reactive nature of Roman lawmaking suggests that the law simply reflected an elite preference for personalized, dependent relationships over impersonal dealings based on money.

Indeed, one might think of Roman society as a whole as being structured around the principles of dependence and dominance. Slavery was the most extreme expression of this, but the relationships between former owner and freedman, patron and client, husband and wife, father and children, and even Rome and her allies and subjects were also based on these principles. Such relationships, it has been suggested, were the prime mechanism for the allocation of scarce resources and the dominant means of legitimizing the social order; they can also be seen as the main influence on the behavior of individuals toward one another.[23] The *Election Manual* assumes that Italy is covered by a network of dependent relationships, so that the aspiring politician in Rome must aim to win the support of the men in the towns who will then mobilize their supporters in his cause. The conventions of elite discourse insisted that relations between members of the elite were to be described in terms of friendship, not dependence; but in many cases the asymmetry of power, influence, and status is obvious, and it is difficult not to think of such "friendship" as another form of patronage (see also Chapter 19).[24] Even the nature of the self was understood in terms of dominance and submission: the mind rules over lust as a master rules slaves, while the master restrains his slaves as reason restrains the evil and weak elements of the mind (Cic. *Rep.* 3.37).

Like slavery, patronage largely but not entirely served the interests of the more powerful party. The elite patron gained support, votes, status, and deference to further his own ambitions, and the acquiescence and cooperation of his clients in the existing political system, enshrining the dominance of the elite as a whole. The client was forced to submit in the hope of gaining access to key resources; sometimes material assistance (food, land, money), sometimes advice and influence in dealing with the law or other authority. The relationship was reinforced by the law – it was an offense to give evidence against one's patron or to vote against him – by the tradition of military discipline and ingrained obedience to the officer class, and by the myths and traditions that emphasized the special qualities of the Roman elite, giving them an aura of authority. But of course the benefits of having a patron could be real; patrons might not in fact be able to assist all their clients, but assistance was unlikely from any other quarter. The law forbade a patron from defrauding his client, and in practice the individual patron could never be wholly dominant or exploit the client's dependence too severely, since the client was generally free to choose another patron (see also Chapter 19).[25]

Vertical relationships between members of different social groups tend to weaken horizontal relationships within those groups; hence, perhaps, the distinct lack of class solidarity or collective action from the poor masses of the Roman Republic. Patronage can be seen as one of the most important forces for cohesion in Roman society, and for ensuring the dominance of the political elite (see Chapter 19). However, by the last century BC this seems increasingly to be an ideal more than a reality; there is a clear sense that many of the discussions of patronage and social relationships in the sources are self-consciously looking back to an earlier time when the system was believed to have worked properly.[26] Just as the enormous expansion of slave numbers had depersonalized relations between masters and most of their slaves, so the city of Rome had grown to such a size that personalized patron – client relationships of the traditional kind can have involved only a small proportion of its population; it was increasingly a city of migrants and their descendants, disconnected from their old social relationships and alienated from the society in which they now lived. Descriptions of urban life in the succeeding century express anxiety about the decline of deference and status distinctions, and the pervasive influence of money in social intercourse; this clearly threatened the dominance of the elite. In the late Republic, the greatest concern for many was the rise of effective but impersonal relationships between mass and elite, as wealthy individuals sought to mobilize the support of the entire *plebs* through mass benefaction and the cultivation of their image as defenders of the People – a practice in due course to be monopolized by the emperors. Personal ties of dependence continued to be the preferred mode of social and economic behavior for the elite under the Principate – a classic later example is the way that the younger Pliny sought to develop such relationships with the wine dealers who had purchased his grape harvest (Pliny *Ep.* 8.2) – but Roman society was now organized around a different relationship of dominance and dependence, between the emperor and his People.

Demography and Decline

The Romans' own perception of the first-century Republic was that a stable society, whose different elements had been established by legendary figures like Romulus and Servius, was now being undermined and transformed by an array of malign forces: corruption, luxury, ambition, faithlessness, violence. As Dionysius of Halicarnassus argued, summarizing the institution of patronage for a Greek audience, "the practices instituted by Romulus established so great a consensus amongst the People of Rome that there was no bloodshed or murder amongst them for six hundred and thirty years" (*Ant. Rom.* 2.11.2). The modern perspective, taking the long view over decades or centuries, is that societies are never static. "Social structure" shapes and influences the behavior of individuals, rather than determining their actions, and the cumulative effect of individual social behavior can transform society over time. Romans' pursuit of their own interests brought about movement between social groups, changes in the ways that the boundaries of those groups were defined (the development of new criteria to identify the elite, for example) and the rise of new groups (slaves, freedmen, and the urban poor). External factors might either change an individual's behavior or give them more power to pursue their interests; thus the influx of wealth and slaves from Rome's conquests prompted far-reaching changes in the Italian countryside, with consequences for society as a whole (see also Chapters 27 and 28).[27] The changes of the final century of the Republic were particularly dramatic, at least in the political sphere, but it would be misleading to assume that Roman society was stable and unchanging until the Gracchi undermined its foundations.

There were, after all, other kinds of structures, besides the framework of social groups and relationships, that influenced and constrained social behavior by setting the "limits of the possible." One such set of limits on human action is established by the environment, the combination of climate, geography, and the distribution of natural resources that favored certain sorts of agriculture (and thus influenced the class structure of antiquity) and encouraged the development of particular patterns of settlement and communication (see Chapter 5).[28] Environmental change in the pre-industrial era was generally slow, so that its effects were scarcely perceptible at the human level; far more significant in the medium term were the limits set by human reproduction. The size of a population in relation to the availability of resources, its rates of mortality and fertility, its age structure and sex ratio, and the average life expectancy, all have far-reaching implications for the fate of individuals and the society in which they live.

> It should be obvious that if we have no conception of the numbers of peoples about whom we write and read we cannot envisage them in their concrete reality. What does a statement about the Romans mean if we do not know roughly how many Romans there were? Without such knowledge even politics and war cannot be understood. For instance, a description of Roman political institutions in the third century B.C. could only be misleading if we did not know that the citizen body was so numerous and scattered that in the absence of the representative principle the democratic features which they seem to manifest were bound to be illusory in practice.[29]

Clearly this affects more than politics; the size of the population has implications for military activity (the size of the pool of potential recruits), economic structures (the availability of labor, the degree of poverty and inequality, the level of malnutrition) and social relations (the relative numbers of slaves and masters, elite and masses). In turn, political, military, economic, and social behavior has unforeseen consequences for the population, as the war effort reduces the pool of men who will produce the next generation, and poverty and malnutrition reduce the fertility of the mass of citizens.

Demography is not only, or even mainly, concerned with population size; such absolute figures can be simplistic and misleading, since populations never remain static. More often, the focus is on demographic structures and processes, the ways in which the population changes over time. Study of rates of mortality and fertility can provide vital insights into the workings of the family: we can see the complex interrelation between the average age at marriage of men and women, the average numbers of children (both in total, and those who survive infancy), and the likelihood of the family reproducing itself in the next generation (see also Chapter 15). Demography affects our view of both the frequency and the motives for infanticide, as well as the traditions of *patria potestas* and adoption.[30] Thinking beyond the family, it raises questions about the age structure of society. Recalling Cicero's stress on men "of every order, of all origins and indeed of all ages" (*Cat.* 4.14), should we think of Rome as divided between age groups with different interests and patterns of social behavior, with the young sent off to fight wars on behalf of the old men who held power (since eligibility for different magistracies depended, at least in theory, on age)? Certainly rates of birth and death might affect relations between different social groups; thus the oldest senatorial families proved unable to reproduce at a rate which would replace their numbers in the next generation, and so always had to draw new recruits from the wider equestrian order.[31]

The importance of demography, with its implications for every aspect of ancient history, has been increasingly acknowledged, especially since the mid-1990s.[32] However, there is a fundamental problem; we do not have adequate evidence for a proper study of ancient demographic structures, either in quantity or quality. There is no ancient equivalent of the parish register of births, marriages, and deaths; under the Republic, the census, because its original purpose was to police the citizen body and to establish Rome's military strength, recorded only absolute numbers, not the age structure of the population, and ignored women, children, slaves, and other noncitizens. Historians have therefore been faced with a choice: to make the best of such "proxy" data as is available – tombstones, for example, and tax registers from Egypt – or to focus on comparative evidence, on the assumption that the Roman population cannot have been too dissimilar in its structure to the populations of other preindustrial societies about which we know rather more.

These two approaches are frequently in direct conflict. Demography suggests questions that might be asked of evidence that was never intended to be used for demographic purposes. For example, Roman epitaphs often include the age of the deceased; given a sufficiently large sample, information about what proportion of the population is dying at different ages can be extrapolated to produce a model of the age structure of society and its average life expectancy. However, if this data is considered in relation to our knowledge of the demography of other societies, it seems clearly flawed. Epitaphs tend to record ages in multiples of five and ten (a phenomenon known as "age-rounding"), and many of the ages recorded seem implausibly high for a pre-industrial society (but perfectly explicable if one recalls that old age was greatly respected in antiquity, and the lack of records meant that many people might be quite uncertain of their real age). Above all, there are far too few infant burials, whereas in a typical premodern society with life expectancy at birth of 25 years ($e_0=25$), mortality in the first year of life might be as high as 30 percent, with 50 percent of a "birth cohort" dying by the age of 10. Either the Romans were much healthier than we thought, or there is a problem with the evidence; most likely another manifestation of the "epigraphic habit," such that inscriptions provide information not about the reality of demographic structures but about the attitudes and assumptions of those who chose to spend money on commemoration – in this case, evidence that many infant deaths were not commemorated in the way that adult deaths were.[33]

Similar objections can be made to other attempts at reconstructing Roman demography from ancient evidence; if it is assumed that the appropriate comparisons for antiquity are underdeveloped societies with high levels of mortality and low life-expectancy, the picture of Roman demographic structures offered by the sources cannot possibly be correct, and so the evidence must be at fault. However, it is clearly a radical step to reject all ancient sources out of hand; it can be argued instead that a different comparison should be made, and that, if the ancient evidence suggests that average life expectancy at birth was 35 rather than 25, Rome should be thought of as having a more modern demographic structure, with lower mortality rates. This fits with the belief of some historians that Rome was a more sophisticated and developed society than the labels "pre-modern" or "pre-industrial" would suggest; others argue that "the burden of proof is firmly on those who wish to assert that the Roman population in general had a lower mortality than other pre-industrial populations with similar technical achievements or towns; they must show that there were present in the Roman Empire factors which could have led to a general diminution of mortality."[34]

It should also be noted that there are problems with the "model life tables" from which historians draw their impressions of pre-industrial population structure.[35] Life tables offer models of the age structures of different populations, showing the complex ways in which life expectancy and rates of mortality and fertility interact; however, they are based not on actual pre-industrial populations but on mathematical extrapolation from modern populations, and they deliberately exclude the distorting effects of diseases such as malaria on age structure. They are idealized models that offer a sense of how the ancient world might have been, not how it must have been; they need to be employed sensitively, reintroducing factors such as the effects of disease and of "culturally specific" behavior like infanticide and the limited reproductive opportunities available to slaves. Above all, the historian has to decide which model to employ, based on prior assumptions about the nature of antiquity. It is generally, but not universally, accepted that Rome is best understood as a "high-pressure" pre-industrial society, with high rates of mortality and fertility and an average expectation of life at birth of 25.

There are still more problems with the reconstruction of absolute population numbers for any period. We have no idea of the number of slaves in Italy, for example, beyond the general impression that it increased significantly over the last two centuries of the Republic (see Chapter 28). It was in no one's interest to attempt to count them; our evidence is limited to occasional impressionistic comments in the literary sources, such as the remark of the medical writer Galen that there was one slave to every two free men in the city of Pergamum (5.49K). It is at best possible to exclude some of the wilder estimates through consideration of the capacity of Italy to support a large population (though that of course depends on the figure assumed for the free population) and by considering the rate of imports necessary to sustain a particular number of slaves, given that not all slaves were able to reproduce and mortality rates were high.[36] We are ignorant of the numbers of freedmen, besides noting that they dominate the body of inscriptions from the city of Rome. Estimates for the urban population are based on the city's grain supply and the figures for recipients of the corn dole; even more speculative estimates for the populations of other towns of Italy are offered on the basis of such evidence as the size of the built-up area, the length of the walls, and the number of citizens who benefited from the generosity of local notables.[37] Estimates of the population of Pompeii, the city for which the most archaeological evidence is available, vary from 10,000–12,000 to 25,000–30,000, depending largely on the historian's prior assumptions about the city's society and economy.[38]

The fiercest debate has been over the size of the total population of Italy, partly because there is some, apparently useable, evidence – the figures produced by the Roman census, especially those collected under Augustus – and partly because demographic change seems to be central to the whole process of the transformation of the rural economy in the late Republic (see Chapters 27 and 28).[39] The Augustan census in 28 recorded a figure of just over 4 million; the census under the Republic had always counted only adult males, and so this figure suggests that the total free population, including women and children, was about 10 million. This can be compared with the population figure of 4.5 million that has been estimated for 225, on the basis of Polybius' account of the military strength of Rome and its allies at that date. Over two centuries, therefore, the free population of Italy more than doubled. However, the idea of a population expansion seems incompatible with historical accounts of the crisis of the Italian peasantry and the depopulation of the countryside in this period, and so this interpretation of the Augustan total has often been rejected. If the Augustan census is interpreted instead as having included all citizens, not just adult males, it indicates a total population of just 4 million, a slight decline since 225 which can be attributed to the effects of constant warfare and the displacement of peasants to make way for slave labor into the countryside.[40] This "low" estimate of the Augustan population, and the "decline" theory of Italian demography, has been dominant since Brunt's 1971 study of the Roman population, and underpins most historical accounts of the period; if the "high" figure were accepted, history – political history, not just economic and social – would have to be rewritten.[41]

Neither interpretation can be proved beyond doubt on the basis of the literary evidence, and so the proponents of each view have turned to comparative arguments. Once again, however, this depends on prior assumptions about the ancient world, which determine what is chosen as the most appropriate comparison. The "high" figure implies that Augustan Italy was more densely populated than nineteenth-century Italy: is this grounds for rejecting it, since pre-industrial technology was inadequate to support so many people, or grounds for taking a more positive view of the efficiency of Italian agriculture? The rate of population increase seems implausibly high, especially taking into account the "population sink" effects of high mortality rates in the city of Rome, if Roman Italy is compared to early modern Europe; but comparable rates of increase are known from nineteenth-century America. In other words, comparative evidence and modern scientific knowledge can suggest what *might* have been possible, but they cannot say how things *must* have been. The latest twist in the debate is the suggestion that the population figure for 225, which all participants have hitherto taken for granted, should be revised downward, giving a better fit with evidence that implies a rising population (such as growing competition for land) without implying that Italy was grossly overpopulated by the time of Augustus (see Chapter 27).

"Scarce source references are interpreted through the lens of conflicting samples of comparative data."[42] This might indeed be said of all approaches to the study of Roman social structure, not just the demographic perspective. Roman social structure looks significantly different depending on one's choice of analytical categories; and the historian's preference for particular concepts and particular historical comparisons often depends on prior assumptions, not just about Rome but about "society" in general. From almost every perspective, the late Republic is a period of major changes (not necessarily to be considered as "decline") in the composition of social groups and the dynamics of social relationships; but the nature of those changes, and the best tools for understanding them, remain matters of fierce debate.

Guide to Further Reading

The best introduction to different aspects of Roman social structure is Garnsey and Saller 1987: chapters 6–8: it focuses on the Principate, but most of its key ideas are applicable to the Republic. On the nature of the Roman elite and the workings of politics see Hopkins and Burton 1983, and, briefly but provocatively, Beard and Crawford 1985. On the Roman citizenship, see Nicolet 1980 and Gardner 1993; on patronage, the important articles in Wallace-Hadrill 1989b; on the social identity of the lower classes, Joshel 1992. Recent ideas on Cicero's orations against Catiline, and on the development of Latin language and literature as a means of social differentiation, in Habinek 1998; on the role of morality in Roman social and political discourse, Edwards 1993. Burke 1980 offers a good general introduction to the use of modern sociological concepts in history; see also Morley 1996: chapter 4. On status, see Finley 1985a: chapter 2; on class, de Ste Croix 1981 and the more general discussion in Wood 1995. Slavery: Bradley 1994 offers an excellent introduction to the subject, with a guide to further reading. Patterson 1982 is a fascinating comparative study of the institution. Fitzgerald 2000 surveys Roman literary representations of slavery; Garnsey 1996 covers intellectual and philosophical attitudes. Demography: Parkin 1992 is a good introduction to the subject in general, especially the evidence and its limitations; Scheidel 2001a offers a still more pessimistic view on how little we really know, while also surveying recent debates. Brunt 1971a remains the basic account of Italian population under the Republic; recent arguments on population decline can be found in Lo Cascio 1994 and Morley 2001.

Notes

1   Hopkins and Burton 1983.
2   Weber 1968: 305–6.
3   Edwards 1993.
4   On the motives for the Social War, Mouritsen 1998; new ideas of citizenship, Wiedemann 1994: 12–13.

5 On myths of Romulus and Remus, Wiseman 1995.
6 Nicolet 1980: 320–4.
7 Patterson 1982: 30.
8 Hopkins 1993; Fitzgerald 2000.
9 MacMullen 1982b on the "epigraphic habit"; generally Joshel 1992.
10 On the way of life of the poor, Whittaker 1993b; Purcell 1994; Patterson 1992a.
11 Cf. de Ste Croix 1981: 30: "I myself believe that there is nothing in this book which Marx himself (after some argument, perhaps!) would not have been willing to accept."
12 Wood 1995: 76.
13 de Ste Croix 1981: 43.
14 E.g., Finley 1985a: 49.
15 On the profitability of slave agriculture, Morley 1996: 108–42.
16 Carandini 1988; Giardina and Schiavone 1981. Cf. Rathbone 1983.
17 For critiques, see Rosenstein 2004 and de Ligt 2003.
18 Bradley 1994: 4–5.
19 Bradley 1989.
20 Fitzgerald 2000: 13–31.
21 Watson 1987: 35–45.
22 Johnston 1999: 99–108.
23 Johnson and Dandeker 1989: 223.
24 Saller 1989; cf. Konstan 1997: 135–7.
25 On the inability of patrons to help everyone, Wallace-Hadrill 1989a: 72–3.
26 Wallace-Hadrill 1989a: 66–7.
27 Hopkins 1978.
28 Braudel 1980, Horden and Purcell 2000.
29 Brunt 1971a: 3.
30 Cf. Saller 1994 (and Chapter 15 in this volume).
31 Hopkins and Burton 1983.
32 Scheidel 2001a.
33 Hopkins 1966/7: 264.
34 Hopkins 1966/7: 264.
35 Scheidel 2001b.
36 Scheidel 1997.
37 Rome: Morley 1996: 33–46; Italian towns, Duncan-Jones 1982: 259–77.
38 Jongman 1988: 108–12.
39 On this topic see, among others, Brunt 1971a; Lo Cascio 1994; Morley 1996: 46–50; Scheidel 2001a: 52–7.
40 As in Hopkins 1978; cf. Rathbone 1981.
41 Cf. the attempt in Morley 2001.
42 Scheidel 2001a: 55.

CHAPTER 15

Finding Roman Women

Beryl Rawson

In 1965 Moses Finley published an article, "The silent women of ancient Rome" (unchanged in 1968 and 1977 reprints), arguing that the sources for Roman women were few, "at cross-purposes" with one another, and included no woman's voice; hence we could form no reliable picture of women in that society. Since then, there has been a flood of books and articles on women of Rome and of many other parts of the ancient world. None of them has been able to find the direct voice of such women, with a few exceptions (the poets Sappho and Sulpicia, a few epitaphs and monuments), but we have become more expert in how to read a wide range of sources to help us see women in the contexts in which they operated. Study of "the Roman family"[1] has developed in many directions since the initial modern studies in the field, helping us better understand women's roles and relationships with husbands, children, the household, and the interface of these with public life. Studies of benefactions ("euergetism") and patronage have revealed more of women's economic and social activities, as have the studies of professions and jobs. Since Crook's 1967 work, studies of the voluminous Roman legal texts have been more interested in societal implications than fine jurisprudential points, and women of various status groups are found to be frequent figures in the case studies examined.

New methodology has led to more subtle understanding of "representations," especially in art and literature. Large bodies of funerary inscriptions have been systematically studied, illuminating personal relationships and revealing the central role of mother – father – child relationships. Other disciplines, especially anthropology and demography, have provided comparative perspectives, for instance on ritual, relationships, health, and death. Modern interest in topics such as sexuality and eroticism has encouraged scholars to look at Roman evidence with a different eye. Our challenge is to try to interpret "representations" and to elicit something of "reality" – or, better, "realities" – for different women.

Much of the new work has focused on the imperial period, where there is a greater quantity and diversity of ancient sources. For the period before the first century BC, the only continuous, near-contemporary historical source which remains is the early part of the history written by the Greek Polybius. There are fragments extant of various Latin annalists, the epic poet and dramatist Ennius, and of Cato the Elder's history. The focus of all these is political and military and not such as to tell us much about women or social and cultural life. There are the Latin plays of Plautus and Terence, but as these were based on Greek originals it is difficult to know to what degree they represent Roman life (see also Chapter 25). Archaeology yields little for our topic in the period before the first century, although Etruscan material provides a useful contrast. The few inscriptions extant for this period mostly record official acts and careers, and although Roman coinage becomes richer toward the end of the second century there is little to be deduced from it for our topic. The Twelve Tables were the earliest codification of Roman law (mid-fifth century), and enough of it has been reconstructed to give us some insight into early Roman values, social relationships, the principles of property, and individuals' rights and duties. Marriage was recognized as a fundamental institution in society. Women could own property in their own right from at least this period. The principle of equal inheritance rights for daughters and sons was recognized.

For the first half of the first century, the contemporary sources we still possess are more numerous and more diverse. The works of Caesar and Sallust are the earliest analytical history in Latin to survive, going beyond the chronological accounts of earlier annalists. Neither of these writers, however, provides much material for our purpose, except for Sallust's thumbnail sketch of Sempronia as a woman of high rank involved in Catiline's conspiracy to seize power in 63, to which we shall return. Cicero's writings, especially his letters and speeches, throw more light on women active in the society of his day, and extracts from some contemporaries' commentaries on Roman law survive in the later compilation, the *Digest*. Cornelius Nepos' surviving biographies and fragments are of some limited use. Catullus' love poetry takes us into the world of sex, marriage, and society, and Lucretius' philosophical epic *On the Nature of the World* (*De rerum natura*) offers the occasional glimpse into human emotions. The inscriptions of the first half of the first century are not the rich source for personal relationships which later ones are, but an epitaph for Aurelia Philematio and her spouse (Fig. 15.1) anticipates the taste for such commemoration which developed quickly in the period following the fall of the Republic. Individual women had been commemorated with public statues as ideals of Roman virtues: Cloelia, a young woman of the late sixth century, for her bravery and patriotism; Cornelia, mother of the Gracchi and daughter of Scipio Africanus, as the ideal mother (but also a symbol in the factional politics of the late second century). It was when a taste for private funerary commemoration developed in the early to mid- first century that humbler people, including women and children (many of them slaves or of slave origin), began to find a place. We shall return to these below.

Later sources, both Latin and Greek, for the republican period will be drawn on below. Those closest in time to our period were the historian Livy (late first century BC into early first century AD) and the moral anecdotalist Valerius Maximus (first half of the first century AD).

Problems involved in using the available sources to reconstruct, or imagine, Rome of the republican period are inherent in every chapter of this book. For this chapter, there is a particular problem which must be faced in trying to discover "real" Roman women and their contexts. That is the strongly moral purpose of much Roman writing (especially history), the use of myth, and the role of women as symbols of past virtues and vices. Interpretations of myths and legends have varied considerably over the years, and there is still work to be done in learning to interpret these aspects. It is an area where it is difficult to free oneself from assumptions and personal ideologies, but a fresh approach and an open mind are needed.

One of the most enduring of Roman legends was the rape of Lucretia. Attributed to the sixth century, the story enshrined the ideal of female chastity and the honor of Roman women determined to die, if necessary, in the cause of that ideal. Rape was also a prime element in the story of the fifth-century Verginia, presented as a more defenseless young girl than the high-ranking married woman of independent character which Lucretia was. Verginia's father took the initiative to protect her from a loss of status and from abduction by killing her himself. Apart from Livy's detailed account (1. 57–9), Cicero was earlier able to refer to Lucretia briefly, as part of a well-known story, when explaining the transition from monarchy to Republic (*Rep.* 2.25.46). A century and a half later, Juvenal could refer in the same breath to Lucretia and Verginia as warnings of the potential curse of beauty, and the folly of humans who pray for such apparent blessings (*Satires* 10. 193–5), and assume that the allusions would be readily understood. Such myths and stories were laid deep in the consciousness of girls and boys in their early years. Both these stories had political purposes, but they also perpetuated the Roman ideal of female chastity and the close identity of this with a Roman man's own identity and honor. When women behaved independently, or, according to more traditional views, improperly, their menfolk were criticized for not exercising the control expected of them.

This kind of criticism is expressed in a speech attributed by Livy (34. 1–8) to Cato the Elder in 195, when women staged a public demonstration in Rome to obtain the repeal of the Oppian Law, a wartime measure which continued to restrict women's wealth and display. The speech excoriated fellow-senators for allowing the women to behave so freely. Although the form of the speech is Livy's creation, source analysis has shown that Livy used many original records. Many earlier speeches, including those of Cato, were still available. Much of Cato's speech criticizes women and men alike for their acquisitive tastes, and recognizes that women often have their own wealth to draw on for display. There is a political as well as moral color to his criticism of women: they were meeting secretly and planning collective action. We can detect the long-standing Roman fear of gatherings which were not officially sanctioned and closely supervised. The same fear surfaces in Livy's account of the "Bacchanalian affair" of 186 (see also Chapters 2, 10, 22, and 28); and it was an important element in criticism of Christian communities later. The meetings for the Oppian Law demonstrations must have been in private homes. It is clear that women of substance were involved. The tribune who replied to Cato's speech referred to the respectable women (*honestae*) in the demonstration, whose presence inhibited Cato from criticism of individual women. References to wives of senators, who wanted finery to match their husbands', indicate women of rank. And there is general admission that there were many precedents for women's collective public action, always for public benefit (*bono publico*). The Sabine women had intervened between the warring camps of their fathers and Roman husbands; Roman women had contributed wealth to the treasury in times of crisis; and they had been prominent in religious rites, such as the introduction of Cybele to Rome. Such roles were recognized by many men. In spite of Cato's opposition the Oppian Law was repealed: men with views more sympathetic to the women's case prevailed.

We find a different analysis of this incident in Valerius Maximus (9.1.3). He too places it in the context of the end of the Second Punic War, in a climate where there was less need of austerity and firm discipline, but this was a general climate, where women shared in the growing luxury and self-expression. For women, however, Valerius' term is "boldness" (*audacia*). Valerius Maximus attributes women's behavior to their lack of intellectual seriousness and the lack of outlets for them to participate in public life, with the implication that the two factors are interrelated. There had been precedents for women playing an important role in public life, but these were in time of crisis and not a regular and accepted part of the fabric of Roman public life. As political crises multiplied near the end of the Republic, some women's names became prominent as active agents: Sempronia, wife of a consul of 77, well-born, with many talents, but in her association with Catiline's conspiracy in 63 portrayed by Sallust as having as many vices as charms, although her intellect was not contemptible (*Cat.* 25); Servilia, mother of Brutus and half-sister of Cato the Younger and prominent in Cicero's letters of the forties; Fulvia, married successively to Clodius, Curio, and Marc Antony. There was clearly active discussion and unease in the late Republic and early Empire about social as well as political conflict. The growing wealth and independence of women was one factor common to most analyses, but it was not the only one. Valerius Maximus perceived that men too had slipped away from earlier standards of self-discipline (*continentia*) and were implicitly more guilty, having more experience and training in matters of public importance. Men's spending practices and needs increased in the last century or so of the Republic, as competition for office and status intensified (see also Chapter 17). The costs of public life for ambitious men were probably behind some moves to restrict women's share of wealthy estates, such as the Voconian Law of 169. Gardner recognizes this, considering the law as "not hostile" to women who, as she says, still had many opportunities to acquire wealth.[2]

Eventually, competition and conflict came to a head in political and military action, and it was only after two rounds of civil wars in the forties and thirties that Octavian/Augustus gained supreme power and set about finding solutions for Rome's perceived problems. His measures were initially political and constitutional; from an early stage they also encompassed urban renewal. It was only in 18 that he directly faced moral issues and their ramifications. Before that year, most aspects of marriage and family life were dealt with within the family, rather than being regulated by legislation. Adultery, for example, was a matter between husband and wife or dealt with by a family council, until Augustus transferred responsibility for it to a public court. Adultery had always been defined as a woman's crime, so Augustus' law (the *lex*

Iulia de adulteriis) provided for the wife to be the primary target of prosecutions, although there were also penalties for the husband and lover of the guilty woman. The wife's sexual propriety was essential to men's confidence in the legitimacy of their children, their primary heirs. This was an economic issue as well as a moral one, but it has been a "gut issue" for men down through the ages.

There had been a long tradition in republican Rome of censors' having moral supervision of the population. This was exercised through the male head of family (the *paterfamilias*), who had responsibility for the women under his authority (*potestas*). One group of women whose behavior was of particular public concern, which went beyond family or censors' responsibility, was the Vestal Virgins. As we have a long series of incidents recorded for these women, and know many of them by name (in spite of Finley's claim of the comparative anonymity of Roman women), they might repay closer examination for their intrinsic importance and for what they might reflect of developments involving women more widely. Until now, discussion of them has largely focused on religion and the Vestals' ambivalent status (for instance, male privileges but female virginity; see also Chapter 10). It might be profitable to consider them in their wider social and political context.

The shrine of the goddess Vesta in the Forum contained an eternal flame whose continued fire protected Rome's security and continuity. Her six priestesses, responsible for this flame, entered service in childhood and served for at least 30 years, under strict terms of celibacy. Their chastity was thus a matter of national security. Led by a Chief Vestal, they were of impeccable birth and had important roles in public ritual. They had special privileges, such as financial autonomy, being legally independent (*sui iuris*). We know nothing of their training or education after entry to the religious order, but either by formal coaching within the college or by the very experience of public privilege they came to understand their potential for real (if indirect) power in politics and public life. Of numerous examples of this, one of the best known is their role in late 63, when they intervened with the consul Cicero, who was agonizing about what to recommend to the Senate about the penalty for the captured high-ranking Catilinarian conspirators. Plutarch tells us (*Cic.* 20.1–2) that on the crucial night the festival of the Bona Dea ("the Good Goddess") was being celebrated, open only to women. The sacrificial fire on the altar blazed up unexpectedly, and the Vestal Virgins interpreted this in political terms, as a sign that in the national interest the consul should hold firm in pursuing punishment for the conspirators. The message, which they sent immediately to Cicero, strengthened him to bring on a debate the next morning, which led to the death penalty for the conspirators. The story reflects extraordinary initiative on the part of the Vestals, conscious of their influence and standing and well-informed on the details of a current political crisis.

In that same year, one of the Vestals (Licinia) was active in supporting the candidacy of her relative L. Licinius Murena for the following year's consulship. One gesture of support was to give Murena her space (*locus*) at the gladiatorial games. Augustus later allocated particular seats to the Vestals at public spectacles, but it is likely that they sat with other women of rank in the Republic. At the gladiatorial games, men and women were not segregated from each other; so whatever space Licinia allocated to Murena (for himself or his connections) was probably in close proximity to the Vestals and thus of high visibility and prestige. Cicero, defending Murena on a charge of bribery, refers to Licinia's gesture as one of a range of benefits which candidates for office might justifiably receive from family and friends (*Mur.* 73). Cicero had a vested interest in justifying benefits which had been criticized by the prosecution as improper influence, but he does not contest the fact of Licinia's gesture. A reference elsewhere to Clodia, wife of the consul of 60, Metellus Celer, reveals that various people of rank had privileged public space to dispose of; her brother Clodius resented her unwillingness to share with him much of her "consular space" at the games and so help his political campaign in that year (Cicero *Att.* 2.1.5).

The mixture of religious and secular life experienced by priests at Rome, including the Vestals, is illustrated by a report of a pontifical banquet put on in 69 to honor the inauguration of L. Cornelius Lentulus Niger as a priest of Mars (*flamen Martialis*), one of the senior religious officials at Rome. The report comes from the fifth-century AD writer Macrobius (*Sat.* 3.13.10–11), but he cites the pontifical records as his authority. It was a lavish banquet, in rooms elaborately decorated and fitted with fine furnishings. Those present were the male priests, four named Vestals, and two other women – these two were Lentulus' wife Publicia, who as wife of the *flamen* became *flaminica* and took on religious duties, and Publicia's mother Sempronia – a select and high-ranking company. (Macrobius' male-oriented viewpoint is reflected in his reference to Sempronia as the mother-in-law of Lentulus. Surely she was there as Publicia's mother? There is no evidence to suggest that a mother-in-law had any special standing.) Macrobius tells the story as an example of the great value once attached to the pleasures of the table, much greater than in his own day. This was a standard of living to which those present in 69 were accustomed. The priests were public officials, not ordained or consecrated in the way priests in our own society are, and all were very much part of the public life of their day (see also Chapters 10 and 12). In August of 69 the conversation at this dinner must have been lively: elections, a serious pirate problem in the Mediterranean, erosion of Lucullus' command in the East, the aftermath of the trial of Verres for corruption as governor of Sicily, and the trial in the same year (also for corruption as a provincial governor) of the brother of one of the Vestals, Fonteia. Fonteia is not named as being present at the banquet. Perhaps it would have been seen as inappropriate for her to attend the grand pontifical celebration. Defendants and their supporters often put on mourning during a trial, and Cicero makes much, in his defense speech, of Fonteia's tearful presence and intercession for her brother (*Font.* 46–9). Those Vestals present, however, and the other two women, will have made the most of their opportunity to keep abreast of social and political issues of the highest importance in Rome.

In 61 the Vestals had a direct role in investigating a scandal which had erupted around Clodius, whose career had made a promising beginning with election in that year to the quaestorship but who was threatened by allegations that he had committed sacrilege by being smuggled into the women-only ritual of Bona Dea. The Vestals, officiating at the ritual, might themselves have witnessed Clodius' intrusion. As we saw above, they socialized with some of the most distinguished women (and men) in Rome, and those women will have been present. Clodius' sisters were surely present – the three women named Clodia – and others with family and political connections with Clodius and the Claudius clan. The Senate required the Vestals, with the relevant priests (the *pontifices*), to pronounce on whether the rites had been vitiated. The Vestals must have been under great pressure and lobbying, but they could hardly avoid concurring that a wrong (a *nefas*) had occurred. Lobbying of them and by them probably continued when Clodius was brought to trial before a specially constituted tribunal for what we would call sacrilege but what was a new interpretation of *incestum*. Clodius' acquittal is usually put down to bribery of the jury, but we can guess that personal and political pressure was also brought to bear on many of the jurors. A particular role for women in this is suggested by Cicero (*Att.* 1.16.5, in the year 61), who as a witness against Clodius had reason to discredit the jurors after the verdict. The majority of them, he alleges, were disreputable and short of money, but the bribes also included assignations with "certain ladies" and introductions to youths of high-ranking families. Might the ladies too have been of elite families, bringing to bear whatever pressure they could on social peers (the jurors were senators and equestrians)? That such pressure included sexual favors is not implausible, but it might well have had other dimensions. From what we have already seen, upper-class women had many opportunities to be familiar with public controversies and many reasons to wish to influence them.

A casualty of the scandal was Caesar's then wife Pompeia, in whose house the ritual was being celebrated, as wife of a magistrate with *imperium* (Caesar was praetor). There was inevitable suspicion that she was the attraction for Clodius' intrusion, and anyway she had responsibility for the good conduct of the evening. Caesar divorced her, not explicitly for sexual misconduct (which would have involved disruption to any public ties with Clodius), but with the famous words attributed to him by Plutarch (*Caes.* 10) that Caesar's wife must be above suspicion.

In the totality and special nature of their powers and status, Vestal Virgins were not like other women and cannot be taken as wholly representative of Roman women. But they were human beings, members of families which carried on with the business of everyday life, and they interacted with these families and with the wider public. Although the Vestals lived in a special house, adjoining Vesta's shrine, this was in the middle of the Forum, the center of Rome's public life and all kinds of comings and goings (see Map 8). They were in no way cloistered, and we have seen some examples of their influence and indeed involvement in various aspects of Roman life. They gossiped, as did many Roman men, and the women who shared in these conversations will have shared many of the Vestals' economic, political, and social interests. Women friends had estates to administer (although, unlike the Vestals, they were supervised by a *tutor*, a kind of financial guardian), their menfolk competed for political office and in business, and women played a role in marriage arrangements and other family alliances. Such shared interests and activities suggest that in the Vestals we can get some reflection of other women of their time (although the context will be largely upper-class). It was not just the Vestals' religious role that made them taken seriously, by both men and women, in wider aspects of Roman life. Priestesses in other societies, such as classical Athens, are not known to have had such influence and involvement. The Vestals were in many ways women of their time.

The requirement for celibacy, however, was absolute, and the traditional penalty for breaking that vow (*incestum*) was to be buried alive (because direct execution of a sacrosanct person would have been sacrilege). The string of prosecutions against Vestals from at least the fourth century reflects the seriousness with which their vows were taken in public life; but other factors may have lain behind the charge of *incestum*. This charge was the most direct way of striking at the central identity and status of a Vestal, and the link with national security took it beyond the sphere of private morals into that of the public interest. There is a series of named Vestal Virgins in the records of Rome.[3] A number of these were convicted of *incestum*. Sometimes the male accomplices were named and also charged; and if convicted they were subject to severe penalties, such as public execution in the Forum or a public flogging which resulted in death; but they were not subject to the traditional penalty reserved for the sacrosanct bodies of the Vestals. Not all of the Vestals charged were convicted. The number of acquittals probably reflects the influence and powerful connections of these women. In 114 and 113, there was much popular discontent with the acquittals of two of the three Vestals who had been prosecuted. The suspicion that tight upper-class loyalties were achieving such verdicts is revealed in the political action which was immediately taken to obtain new trials under a new form of jurisdiction. Attacks were at least as much on the *pontifex maximus* and the *pontifices*, who had presided at the earlier trial in the traditional procedure. The appointment of a special prosecutor for a new trial was carried through by a plebiscite sponsored by a tribune of the plebs. (This is the immediate post-Gracchan period.) This time, convictions were obtained not only of the original three but of several others, and the death penalty was imposed. (The method of death was perhaps not by the traditional method, because the *pontifex maximus* did not preside.)[4] Although the new procedure satisfied the complaints of "the People," the executions brought much criticism for their harshness. One of those charged in 114 was a young Marcus Antonius, the future famous orator and the grandfather of the triumvir Marc Antony. He seized the high moral ground (by not taking advantage of magisterial immunity), and this, with his already gifted oratory and the loyalty of one of his slaves, achieved his acquittal. The charge does not seem to have affected his later career. Crassus' defense, when he was charged with being the lover of a Vestal in 75, was that he was pursuing her to wheedle a desirable property out of her, at a low price. The judges found the motive of avarice more plausible than that of sexual seduction and dismissed the charge. Plutarch tells the story (*Crass.* 1.2) to illustrate one of Crassus' prime characteristics; but it is also for us another illustration of Vestals as women of property and business dealings. The prosecutions of men of rank also suggest possible political motives.

Although the charge of *incestum* probably often had ulterior motives, the charge itself need not lack some credibility. The Vestals moved freely enough in society to have opportunities to form liaisons; there were many adventurous young men in that society, of whom Clodius and the love poet Catullus are examples; and most periods of history have provided examples of "errant" nuns and priests. Nevertheless, we have seen enough of Vestals' activities to understand that prosecutions of them might have been a means to silence their political voice or that of their connections. Prosecutions could also be provoked, in times of national crisis, by the heightened

tensions in society. Toward the end of the third century, when Hannibal was inflicting
defeat on the Romans on Italian soil, popular superstition was aroused by fearsome
prodigies. Before the Battle of Cannae, in 216, two Vestals charged with unchastity
were an easy target and were executed, but after the disastrous battle the unchastity
was seen as a portent (*prodigium*) which required a different expiation. In 114 there
were rumblings of imminent threats to Roman power, from Africa and the eastern
Mediterranean and the northern borders.

There may also have been a growing fear, in conservative quarters, of women of
wealth and influence. We may, in the past, have underestimated the real political
power of upper-class women because the study of "politics" focused on the men who
competed for magistracies and military command and in the law courts. But today we
are well aware of the wider meaning of political power, and can recognize it in the
world of business, law, the media, and entertainment. The old prosopographical
method, previously applied mainly to Roman men (see Chapter 1), might fruitfully
be extended to women: by examining their family connections and traditions, we
might more easily recognize their active roles in networks, patronage, business,
friendships and enmities, and intellectual life.

By the late Republic, Roman women seem seldom to have entered a husband's
legal power (*manus*), or ownership, when they married. They remained subject to the
power (*potestas*) of their *paterfamilias*, usually their father, while he was alive, meaning that, among other things, daughters could not own property or make valid
contracts. After his death they were technically independent (*sui iuris*), but in many
matters, especially the administration of property, they were subject to the supervision of an overseer, or guardian (a *tutor*). Women of initiative, however, do not seem
to have been seriously hampered by this, and the very ownership of wealth and
property gave those whose possessed them great status and influence, both inside
the family and beyond. There was a long tradition of criticism of women who were
domineering because of the size of their dowry or extravagant because of their love of
spending (especially on clothes). In fact, it had been a rhetorical commonplace for
centuries to deplore wealth and luxury; often this was associated with nostalgia for a
supposed earlier period of virtue and simplicity. The criticism of women in particular
indicates a society where a not inconsiderable number of women were used to
handling and displaying wealth. The resources of such women were gratefully
exploited by the state in times of national emergency.

Roman women had never changed their name on marriage. They retained the
name of their natal family, and thus an identity separate from their husband's,
although they might sometimes be identified as "the wife of...", for instance, the
most notorious of the Clodia sisters, married to Q. Caecilius Metellus Celer, might be
referred to as "Clodia Metelli." Cornelia (above) and Caecilia Metella (below) are
each identified as daughter and wife of a noble man.

The extensive powers of the male head of household (the *paterfamilias*) have often
been seen as severely inhibiting the freedom and independence of family members.
Slaves owned by the *paterfamilias* were indeed property, subject entirely to their
master's power (although toward the end of our period public opinion and then
legislation placed limits on the more extreme forms of such power, recognizing some

form of humanity even in slaves; see also Chapter 14). Adult sons and daughters, however, almost always lived in separate, independent households. Young men often did this as they became active in public life, and husbands and wives established their own households on marriage. This separate physical existence, and the demographic forces which left most adults fatherless and often parentless from young adulthood or earlier, contributed to more independent lives than the legal technicalities would suggest.

Republican women of many social levels were left with even more independent responsibilities as Rome extended her power in Italy, the Mediterranean, and beyond, and men were called away to fight wars and administer new provinces. Wives in city and country must have had to make many decisions about the rearing and education of children, household budgets, and family businesses. Women had probably always contributed to agricultural and other labor, but in the absence of men of military age the burden was heavier for women, and children took on more at early ages, especially in households with modest or no assistance from slaves. For the women widowed by these circumstances, such responsibilities were permanent. Remarriage for women was frequent in Roman society but not universal. Because husbands were typically about ten years older than their wives (see below), ordinary mortality ensured that there were always more young women seeking husbands than men looking for wives, and the same difference in numbers will have obtained among widows and widowers. In addition, supplies of men in the prime of life were severely reduced in periods of prolonged warfare. Daughters had fewer prospects of marriage in their hometown.

It is impossible to recover the voice of women affected by these absences and deaths. Did they thrive on new responsibilities? Did these responsibilities contribute to the apparent social unease, discontent, or even revolution which can be detected in Rome from Augustus' time, when husbands were no longer absent for such long periods? In the twentieth century, periods of world wars saw women in the Western world take on responsibilities and positions in the workforce which had previously belonged to men. When returned soldiers began to reclaim their old positions and there were many pressures to put women back into a more restricted domestic role, much social and economic tension resulted. For literate and cultivated upper-class Roman women, the return of absentee husbands might have inhibited some women's social and intellectual freedom. Rome's great love poetry was all written in the late Republic and the very early Principate. It was "probably almost all inspired by adulterous affairs with temporarily deserted upper-class wives. Later, husbands were less fully committed to public affairs, or took their wives to the provinces with them, and love poetry at Rome died."[5] That poetry does not seem to have been addressed to single younger women. Their chaperoning cannot have been foolproof, but there is no real evidence of their love affairs, and accusations of such affairs are absent from political invective at Rome.

How lower-class and rural women fared in wartime is not clear from our sources. Lower-class women must always have needed to have jobs, and inscriptions record a wide variety of working women, in clerical jobs and entertainment, as nurses and midwives, personal attendants, beauticians, and, beyond the household, barmaids and prostitutes. Most of these are from the city of Rome, and slaves and ex-slaves dominate the record from the second century, in a wide range of specialized jobs. The growing number of slaves brought into Rome (mostly from the East), and often reared there, could learn crafts and specialized forms of service in their owners' households, sometimes from early childhood. Ex-slaves were often sponsored in businesses by their former owners. If rural women were forced to migrate to Rome for jobs, they must have found the competition difficult.[6]

Valuable as inscriptions are for jobs and careers, most funerary epitaphs record only a name or a set of names. Until the late Republic, inscriptions tended to be honorific ones attesting public careers, and women did not receive these, being ineligible to hold city magistracies, govern provinces, hold priesthoods (except for Vestals), or serve in the army. The occasional statues for women might have had a brief inscription attached to identify them. It was with funerary inscriptions, which became more numerous from the early or mid-first century, that a wider range of the population began to be represented. What these people commemorated, above all, was family relationships: they often had little else to record. Moreover, the family relationships recorded were overwhelmingly those of close kin (fathers, mothers, sons, daughters, spouses) rather than of more extended links. An exhaustive study of hundreds of thousands of Latin inscriptions by Saller and Shaw, which revealed these patterns of commemoration, opened a new era in the study of Roman social history.[7] It argued the hypothesis that these close-knit relationships (our "nuclear family") were the primary focus of family sentiment, rather than those of extended family or clan; they represented major forms of Roman social structure. The bulk of the inscriptions in that study are imperial in date, but the patterns are similar in the republican ones which exist. It is unlikely that the forms of relationships attested in the new form of commemoration in the late Republic had suddenly emerged. They surely existed for a considerable time before this, but it was only in the first century that lower ranks in society had the means and motivation to leave a public and durable record of them. Leading the new trend were ex-slaves or people of recent slave origin, proclaiming their new freedom and, often, Roman citizenship. There are fewer women and girls attested on these tombstones than men and boys, which is typical of all of the Roman evidence which we have – literature, law, art, inscriptions. But mothers, daughters, and wives are much more prominent than males or females of more distant relationships. Even in the earlier inscriptions, if the few women commemorated have any identifier beyond their name it is a family role, usually *uxor* (wife) or *mater* (mother).

The law defined girls as fit to marry at 12 and boys at 14, but evidence of such young marriages is sparse. Women did tend to marry younger than men: a ten-year age gap between spouses seems to have been common. Some upper-class women, whose arranged marriages had political, economic, and social implications, did marry young. The daughters of Cicero, Pompey, and Caesar (Tullia, Pompeia, Julia) all made their first marriages in their early to mid-teens. These ages are never given to us explicitly: we have to calculate them from a variety of literary references, and often the calculations are only approximate.

At those ages they would have had little say in the choice of partner, although the law required both of the marrying individuals to express understanding and willingness to marry. (This is recorded in the *Digest* 23.1.7.1, 23.2.2 – both passages attributed to Paul – of the early third century AD, but generally taken to codify what had been the practice for many centuries.) Outside these elite families, women's age at marriage tended to be in the late teens. Shaw deduced this by studying the pattern of commemoration for deceased females in funerary inscriptions.[8] The commemorators were overwhelmingly parents and husbands. Shaw was able to identify an age point where the role of parents declined and that of husbands began to take over, and he argued that it was marriage which brought about this change. It was, in general, in the late teens that women outside elite families began to have husbands to commemorate them.

Women who married very young seldom became mothers before their late teens, fecundity being low in very young women. Modern biological studies have made us aware of this, and reasons for it, but some Roman awareness of it is clear from Augustus' marriage legislation: it applied to women only from the age of 20. Moreover, infant mortality was high, so that successful births might come even later. Maternal mortality in childbirth was not as high, but was far higher than in the developed world today, where it is about 0.1 per 1,000. The worst modern rate, in poor, rural societies, is about 17 per 1,000. Estimates of Roman maternal mortality rates are 10 to 15 per 1,000.[9] It was only in Tullia's third marriage that she bore her first child, when she was about 30, and even then the child was premature and did not survive. Her second child, nearly four years later, survived only a month beyond his mother's own death in childbirth in 45. Rome was again embroiled in warfare – this time civil war – and Tullia's husband P. Cornelius Dolabella was away fighting on Caesar's side in 49–48 and again in 45. Tullia's pregnancies and death must have been lonely affairs. What we know of her circumstances comes from her father Cicero, who grieved greatly for this favorite child.

A girl of a different social class who "married" very early was Aurelia Philematium/ Philematio, whose handsome first-century memorial stone is shown in Figure 15.1. This epitaph (*CIL* 1². 1221; 6. 9499 = *ROL* 4:22–5 no. 53) commemorates her as a wife, and was probably put up by her husband, L. Aurelius Hermia, whose details are also given. Records of this kind yield valuable personal information, even to those without much knowledge of Latin: the name structure is informative, the Roman numerals are still in use today, and the terms for family relationships are soon learned: *pater, mater, uir, uxor, filius, filia* (father, mother, husband, wife, son, daughter). The names here reveal that the couple were born slaves and later given freedom: the abbreviation "L(uci) l(ibertus/-a)" = freedperson of Lucius. Slaves legally had no parents, so when freed they took on the family name of their former owner (here, a L. Aurelius). Their nomenclature and their status put them in a kind of filial relationship with their owner, now their patron (*patronus* or *patrona*; see also Chapters 14 and 19). Whereas the daughter of M. Tullius Cicero was Tullia M(arci) f(ilia), "daughter of Marcus Tullius," and his son was M. Tullius M(arci) f(ilius) Cicero, ex-slaves have the title *libertus/-a* in place of *filius/-a*. Hermia and Philematium had been fellow-slaves in the Aurelian household for some time, and were freed by the same owner (*conleibertus* [an archaic spelling] = fellow-freedperson), perhaps with a view to their marriage. Their relationship before their freedom was not a formal Roman marriage but *contubernium* (cohabitation). Philematio's words, in the first person, tell us that

Fig. 15.1 Stone stele of husband and wife, L.Aurelius L.l. Hermia and Aurelia L.l. Philematio, Rome, 1st century BC. British Museum, *Catalogue of Sculpture*, iii, no. 2274; *CIL* 6. 9499.
© Copyright The Trustees of The British Museum

Hermia took her into his care from the time she was 7, so that he was "more than her
fellow-freedman but, over and above that, her parent (*parens*)." Until she died at the
age of 40, she had been a faithful and virtuous wife, knowing no other relationship (ll.
5–6). Here are the slave echoes of the upper-class ideal of *uniuira*, "knowing only
one husband," which remained a desirable quality even in a society of high mortality
and frequent remarriage.

Although slaves could not legally marry, they often formed marital relationships
and produced children. Such children were born slaves and belonged to their
mother's owner, but any children born after her freedom were freeborn. A child
was its mother's child and took her name and status if its father were not eligible to
marry the mother at the time of the child's birth. The lack of a formal marriage
seems to be due to ineligibility rather than unwillingness to marry, as far as we can
judge from evidence available. Even when one or both partners was not a free
citizen, they often used marital vocabulary and ideals. Aurelia Philematio's epitaph
reflects that, and the iconography reinforces the words. So children's "illegitimate"
status was often a function of a parent's status and in these circumstances did not
bear the moral stigma which attached to illegitimacy in later, Christian societies. If
both partners were free by the time of the birth they could legally marry, and their
child would be not only freeborn but could take its father's name and proudly
advertise the filiation (e.g., "M.f.") of citizen status. This social mobility, within
one generation, is clear in the epitaph of P. Seruilius Q. f. Globulus, his father Q.
Seruilius Q. l. Hilarus, and the father's wife Sempronia C. l. Eune (*CIL* 6. 26410),
later in the first century.[10]

Philematio's monument is not as elegant, in lettering or form, as many later ones.
But it must still have involved considerable expense. It is partly a tribute to her
husband's love, which he professes was equal to hers for him (*studio parili*). But it

was also a tribute to how well he had done in his trade of butcher (*lanius*) and in moving out of slavery and being able to make a proper Roman marriage. Many of the lower classes could afford no memorial at all and they remain unrecorded. But those who began to erect such tributes in the last century BC express much more of family relationships, virtues, and affection than do any upper-class monuments of the time (see also Chapter 25). The inscription on one of the few memorials to an upper-class woman, the large, imposing tower for Caecilia Metella on the Via Appia leading south out of Rome (where many tombs clustered, burial within the walls of the city being forbidden), bears only her name (Figures 25.10a–b). The form of the name, Caecilia Q. Cretici f. Metella Crassi, does tell the world that she is the daughter of Q. Caecilius Metellus Creticus, consul in 69, and wife of Crassus, probably a son of the triumvir Crassus (consul in 70). The monument seems to be Augustan in date, so who survived from the late Republic to build and dedicate this tomb for Metella? Upper-class tombs are not as forthcoming as those of slaves and ex-slaves, whose families were not famous, and so their details had to be spelled out to the public to proclaim the existence and success of their members. This difference in commemorative practice need not reflect a difference in affective relationships: different commemorative fashions for different social strata are attested in other societies and have been attributed to various factors, such as changing tastes and motivation. We know that Cicero pondered long and hard about a suitable memorial for Tullia after she died. It was probably going to be on an estate outside of Rome, which may help explain the lack of upper-class family memorials at Rome and the preponderance of those of the lower strata (who had no country estates). The growing interest in family commemoration was notable enough for Augustus to exploit it in his own policies and monuments. The Ara Pacis (the Altar of Peace), dedicated in 9 BC, gave a prominence to the figures of women and children which had been previously unknown in official monuments.

When women remarried, they were of an age to take a more active role in the choice of partner, especially if they were by then *sui iuris*. Can we say that they married "for love"? The sources do not provide enough evidence of motivation to answer this, but there are hints that it could happen. Cicero's letters from Cilicia in 50 show his unease at the plans made by his wife and daughter for Tullia's marriage to Dolabella, but he concurred because the two women were "delighted by the young man's attentiveness and charm" (*Att.* 6.6.1). There is more evidence of the development of love within marriage.[11] We need to guard against any cultural assumptions about loveless arranged marriages, and against misunderstanding the Roman ideal of chastity (*castitas*) in wives. The ideal denoted faithfulness rather than celibacy or frigidity. Sexual pleasure was surely a motive and a reward for marriage, for women as well as for men. That the sexual drive continued in older women is clear from Latin literary references. These references are all pejorative but the image itself suggests that older women did not necessarily lose their sense of sexuality. The hostile references to lascivious older women are all post-republican, and are at odds with the republican image of the mother, often an older woman, as a figure of authority and respect. Catullus is insulting about Lesbia when she ends their affair, but she is still beautiful and desirable, and these are not his most vitriolic and scabrous poems, which are often aimed at men and probably with a political edge. Only a generation later, however, Horace's attack (in *Epodes* 8 and 12) is on the loathsomeness of older women wanting to be lovers. He is on the cusp of republican and imperial periods, so perhaps he reflects not so much a change in attitude as a "bipartite" view of women.[12] And if we consider the different genres in which the references occur, is it not more likely that the brutal, ridiculing tone of satire is due to genre rather than to a real change in attitudes and behavior from republican to imperial period?

The question arises of when women were considered middle-aged or elderly. Although mortality rates were high, elderly people were not especially rare. Those who survived to the age of 50 had good chances of living another 10–15 years. But individuals aged at different rates, depending on lifestyle, resources, and many external circumstances such as climate and location. One result of the age gap between husband and wife was that mothers tended to outlive fathers. This had implications for the position and roles of a widow, and for her relationships with her children and grandchildren.

Augustus' family legislation penalized unmarried or childless women between the ages of 20 and 49, so we can assume that by the late Republic these were considered the normal limits of the childbearing years. Corresponding ages for men were 25 and 59. The actual penalties, economic and political, were of little importance to the mass of Roman women, but they give us an idea of the period of fecundity in women's lives and one aspect of women's identity. Although the primary purpose of marriage was procreation of children (*liberorum quaerundorum causa*), women were free to marry after the age of 50. That they did so is reflected in various pieces of imperial legislation which set out the inheritance implications for such a marriage. Sexual enjoyment and companionship would have been among the motives for older women to marry, or, more often, to remarry. Economic and social security must also have been a concern for many older women who had been widowed or divorced, unless they owned considerable property, especially if there were no children to assist them and share their lives.

Although there is some evidence from the second century AD that there was a predisposition in the law to expect children to support parents,[13] there is no evidence of this for the republican period. The deep-seated and long-standing ideals of *pietas* in Roman society suggest that there were at least moral expectations of such support from an early period, but there were no formal provisions. This is consistent with Roman practice with regard to the family in general. Before Augustus, almost all such practice was private and internal to the family or *familia*. Public concern for children, women, the elderly, the sick, slaves – the normally weaker members of society – surfaces in the second century AD, but there are no references back to republican precedents. It was centuries before public charitable institutions were established, and even then the care of women is not prominent. Perhaps in that later period the convent was seen as an adequate and appropriate place of refuge for lone women.

Women's relationships and roles within the home can be illuminated by a study of domestic space (see also Chapters 4, 16, and 24). In the Roman home, there was not the same concept of privacy, or dichotomy between public and private, which is familiar to most of us today (see Figures 25.14–17). Nor was there segregation of the sexes. When men of standing held open house in their atrium in the mornings to receive the greetings (*salutationes*) of friends and clients, wives and children could be present on at least some occasions. Women joined men at dinner. Slaves were omnipresent. In the overcrowded apartments of the poor, there was enforced inter-mingling and sharing of space, and a heightened role for the local neighborhood. People of all social levels in Rome and other parts of Italy lived much of their lives outdoors, and it is useful to visualize them in the physical context of their activities. We have seen women at theaters and other public spectacles; they frequented the public baths, probably at different times or in different sections from men. They are to be found at other forms of public entertainment and ritual, such as triumphs, religious festivals, and funerals. Some religious rites were open only to women (such as the Bona Dea); in others women played an important part (such as the Bacchanalia festival). They joined men and children on other occasions. For instance, in 63 Cicero invited men to come out onto the streets with their wives and children for thanks-giving at his exposure of the Catilinarian conspiracy (*Cat.* 3.23). Children are visible in both public and private life. Looking for girls in the various spaces should help us understand ways in which they learnt to be Roman women. Some girls went to school, others were taught privately at home. They were an essential part of various religious rites. In these they were not silent ciphers but active participants, often needing physical stamina for long processions and mental effort to memorize and rehearse songs and ritual. Examples range over a long period: girls led such a procession in 207 (Livy 27. 37. 5–15), and Augustus' revival of the Secular Games in 17 had equal choruses of girls and boys singing and processing. On at least some occasions, children dined with adults in the home. And everywhere, at home and in the city, there were visual images which helped shape their perceptions of history, interrelationships, and self-identity. Girls were probably sexually aware from an early age: they participated in marriage celebrations, they socialized often with slaves, there was a general lack of privacy, and the painted walls of houses often had explicit scenes which we might consider erotic.

Even when we have found a series of named women over several centuries, of various classes, ethnicities, and ages, and reconstructed something of their circum-stances, we are far from knowing much of their inner lives. We can deduce something of their family relationships – relationships sometimes of political and economic significance, perhaps often of some commitment and affection. We know from anthropological studies of modern high-mortality societies that the likelihood of losing children at young ages does not preclude grief and grieving. We might speculate on the effects of frequent divorce and remarriage. Did this loosen family bonds and change the concept of "family"? Although children technically "belonged" to the father, and were "his" after divorce, there is evidence of mothers' continuing to show commitment to children, even beyond what was required by law. One example of this is Cicero's wife Terentia, as illustrated in Dixon's study of Terentia's disposition of property.[14] Women were often commemorators on chil-dren's epitaphs.

The thread of rape and condemnation of women in Roman myth and legend has led some to see a strong misogynistic viewpoint in Roman thought and society. But if we look at a broad range of stories, and are not misleadingly selective, is that the overriding impression conveyed? There are indeed "bad" women in Roman legend: strong women, rather than helpless victims. In the very story of Lucretia, Livy provides a flashback to another woman whose actions hastened the fall of the monarchy: Tullia, a royal daughter, who was not a victim but a protagonist in royal arrogance and violence. Tarpeia took the initiative to admit the Sabine enemies to Rome's Capitoline Hill, where the place of her death subsequently symbolized the death of traitors and other criminals (the Tarpeian Rock). But Cloelia (whose statue we referred to above) used her courage and physical prowess in Rome's patriotic interests. A more historical figure was Claudia, whose virtue was vindicated in the late third century by her success in getting up the Tiber the boat carrying the image of the goddess Cybele which was to save Rome from its current problems. There were variant versions of most of these stories, indicating a live tradition, reinterpreted for different generations but not meaningless or irrelevant. Both strong and weak women had a place in such tradition, as did the more numerous strong and weak men.

Females were far from invisible in Roman public and private life. Were they marginalized? Like most women in most societies until recently, they did not have the political rights of standing for office or voting in elections or on legislation. They did have a range of legal and social rights, in accordance with their status as freeborn citizen, freed ex-slave, slave, or free foreigner. It might well have been class, as much as gender, which determined their roles.

To try to make some sense of their roles and relationships, if not of their inner lives, we need to reconsider all the stories which we have, in their full context, put these together with other records of females such as epitaphs and the law, and think further about the physical spaces in which they are found.

Guide to Further Reading

Pomeroy 1975 began a generation of prolific and varied scholarship on women in the ancient Greek and Roman worlds. Dixon 2001 provides a valuable review of such work, and explicitly addresses "readings" in her exploration of "sources, *genres* and real life." The influence of feminist thought is discussed in McManus 1997 and Doherty 2001. The latter provides a succinct comment on gender and myth in the light of modern theory.

A series of Roman Family books began with Rawson 1986 and has continued with B. Rawson 1991, Rawson and Weaver 1997, and George 2005. Other work during this period, on family and related topics, includes Bradley 1991, Dixon 1992, Gardner 1998, Parkin 1992, 2003, Saller 1994, and Treggiari 1991, which contain further references. Excellent studies of Roman law include Gardner 1986, 1998, Champlin 1991 (on inheritance), and Treggiari 1991 (on marriage). McGinn 1998 focuses on legal aspects of prostitution but encompasses many aspects of sexuality and status. Parkin 1992, 2003 draws out many of the implications for women of the new demographic work. See Cokayne 2003 for emotional aspects of old age. On women in jobs, Kampen 1981 provides a valuable insight into the economy and ideology of working women, although all her material (visual and written) is imperial. Evans 1991 provides useful appendices of republican evidence for women in jobs. Most of the work on domestic space and on art (public and private) deals with post-republican material, and there are few visual representations of women in the Republic. But the Etruscan art discussed by Bonfante 1994 must have been known to Romans. And Clarke 1998 points out that Hellenistic art and artifacts depicting various scenes of love-making were in wide use and widely visible. Cf. Clarke 2003. Richlin 1983 remains a significant study of the sexual representation of bodies in Latin literature.

Notes

1 Rawson 1986.
2 Gardner 1986: 170–7.
3 Documented in the annual lists in Broughton 1951–86.
4 The last imposition of the traditional penalty was by Domitian, probably in AD 89, and it was already rare by then.
5 Rawson 1986: 29.
6 Evans 1991 argues this. But Rosenstein 2004 challenges it, and provides a different demographic analysis of rural Italy as affected by war.
7 Saller and Shaw 1984.
8 Shaw 1987.
9 Parkin 1992: 104–5.
10 Illustrated in Rawson 2003: fig. 1.5. Details on "illegitimacy" in Rawson 1989.
11 See Treggiari 1991 and Dixon 2003.
12 A term used by Hallett 1989.
13 Parkin 2003: 213–16.
14 Dixon 1986.

PART V

Political Culture

CHAPTER 16

The City of Rome

John R. Patterson

Introduction

It is possible to write (or, at least, conceive of writing) two histories of the city of Rome under the Republic. One is the history of the Roman elite and the way in which the city formed a privileged stage for their political rivalries, played out both in the formal settings of the Senate and the popular assemblies and in less formal but equally important contexts which included the display of their wealth, influence, and distinction through the construction of houses and public buildings, the entertainments they organized for the Roman populace, and the tombs they set up on the roads which led into the city.

The other is the history of the mass of the People of Rome: how the city's population expanded dramatically during the republican period, and especially in the first century, as large numbers of slaves were brought to the city and individuals migrated to Rome from all over Italy and, increasingly, beyond; the implications of the crowded and unsanitary conditions in which, for the most part, the inhabitants of Rome below the level of the elite had to live; and the strategies devised to supply the growing city's population with food and water.

This chapter sets out not only to outline the histories of "elite Rome" and "Rome of the masses," but also to explore how far these two histories can be seen to interrelate from the political, social, and economic points of view and the extent to which rich, poor, and not-so-poor interacted in various urban contexts. The focus will be predominantly on the period between the late fourth and late first centuries, but with occasional reference back to the early years of the Republic.

The historian of the city of Rome is faced with two main problems: one a more acute version of those characteristic of the history of the Republic in general and the other specifically relating to the reconstruction of urban topography in this period. For the study of competition within the Roman elite, we are of course reliant on the various literary narratives and biographies – Livy, Plutarch, and so on – influenced by the various perspectives which derive from the sources on which their work is based, coupled with those deriving from the context and period in which the individual authors themselves are writing. Also valuable (for the first century) are the contemporary writings of Cicero and Sallust. There are considerable discrepancies in the amount of information available for different periods, most of the third century and the years between 167 and 133 being particularly thinly documented. For traditions relating to particular locations in the city, we can draw on the fragments preserved of Roman antiquarian writers such as Varro and Festus; while Livy's summaries of the events of each year preserve valuable information about the construction and dedication of public buildings in particular.[1]

Writing the history of the poor in a society is in general much more difficult than writing that of the wealthy, and this is particularly true in the case of the Roman Republic. Often we have to extrapolate from evidence relating to the Imperial period, and for both Republic and Empire we frequently need also to draw on comparative material from better-documented pre-industrial societies. Similarly, reconstructing the topography of republican Rome is even more difficult than conducting the same exercise for the Imperial period. There are very few standing monuments of republican date, the temples of the Forum Boarium and Largo Argentina being exceptional in this respect (see Figures 4.2 and 24.5–6). In addition to being covered by the later buildings of modern, renaissance, and mediaeval Rome – especially in areas of dense later habitation like the Campus Martius – the republican levels of the city are largely concealed by the remains of the Imperial city. The preserved fragments of the Marble Plan of Rome once displayed in the Temple of Peace likewise depict Rome as it was in the early third century AD. The interpretation of the excavations of the republican city that took place in the late nineteenth century (those of Boni in the Forum Romanum, for example) were controversial at the time and continue to be a focus of debate and discussion. Some inscriptions, mostly funerary or related to the dedication of buildings or statues, do survive from the city of the mid- and late Republic, as do images of monuments on coins that date from the late second century onward (though the accuracy of the images they display is frequently very dubious). Some stress must therefore be laid on the provisional nature of conclusions derived from the study of the topography of the city, which need continually to be revised as new excavations take place and more information comes to light.

Elite Political Competition at Rome

Recent excavations in Rome have demonstrated that the city created by the Kings and inherited by the Republic was a center of major importance, not only in the context of Italy but in the wider Mediterranean world as well (see also Chapter 4).[2] Massive civil engineering work had created the public space we know as the Forum Romanum, and an impressive series of temples had been built, culminating in that of Jupiter on the Capitol, which is now known to have stood on a podium 72 × 54 m in length, even larger than previously suspected.[3] The surviving so-called "Servian" walls of the city, which have normally been identified with the wall-circuit that, according to Livy (6.32), was begun in 378, are now thought, in part at least, to date to the sixth century.[4] In either case, by the mid-fourth century Rome's walls enclosed an area of over 400 hectares, making it a city on a scale comparable to that of celebrated Greek colonies such as Akragas and Syracuse.[5]

It is at the end of the fourth century, a period of major significance for Rome in many other ways too, that we can see a new phase of building activity taking place. In the years which followed the Latin war of 343–341, the restructured Roman alliance was embarking on a series of long-term wars against their central Italian neighbors – Samnites, Etruscans, Umbrians, Sabines – which in less than a century saw them seize control of the whole of the Italian peninsula to the south of the Po valley.[6] As Rome's armies began to campaign overseas (beginning with the First Punic War in Sicily), the scale of the booty they brought back increased still further and so did the rivalries within the highly competitive Roman elite: funerary epitaphs recorded in literature and on stone from this period record the desire of individuals to be remembered as "first, best, and greatest."[7] The culmination of an aristocrat's military career was a triumph: awarded by the Senate, this was a celebratory ritual procession through the streets of Rome, the victorious commander following the magistrates, Senate, and soldiers: literary accounts describe graphically the display of captives and booty this might involve.[8] The commemoration of victories extended beyond the occasion of the triumph, though: it became common practice from the late fourth century for generals to vow temples to the gods in the hope of achieving a successful outcome of the campaign in which they were involved. When they returned victorious to Rome, the temples would be constructed, the process overseen by the Senate (see also Chapters 4, 10, and 24).[9]

Many of these temples were constructed in the Campus Martius and along the route traditionally followed by the triumphal procession (see Map 9 and also Chapter 23). This assembled in the Circus Flaminius and then passed through the Forum Boarium and the Circus Maximus before skirting the Palatine and following the Via Sacra through the Forum Romanum, finally climbing the Clivus Capitolinus to the temple of Jupiter.[10] The choice of these locations stressed the association of the temples with the triumph, and those on the Campus Martius in particular could also have been visible from the Saepta, where the *comitia centuriata* assembled to elect the senior magistrates.[11] The temples thus served not only to express the gratitude of the city, and of the generals who dedicated them, to the gods for a successful military campaign, but commemorated this success for posterity, in a way which contributed to the distinction of the general's family and might be borne in mind by the voters when his descendants stood for public office.

In the second century, the number of temples built appears to have declined somewhat as other types of commemorative building were increasingly favored by the elite: arches, porticoes, and basilicas in particular. These also had a significant impact on the appearance of the city. Porticoes, such as the Porticus Octavia of 168 and Porticus Metelli of 146, were frequently erected adjacent to temples in places with triumphal associations, as were arches, such as those set up in the Circus Maximus and Forum Boarium by L. Stertinius in 196, even though he did not even request a triumph (Livy 33.27.3–4). By contrast, the basilicas that came to surround the Forum Romanum – the Porcia of 184, the Fulvia of 179, and the Sempronia of 169 – were normally constructed with public funds by the censors, by whose names they came to be known (see also Chapters 4 and 24).[12]

Elite rivalry was not expressed only through officially sanctioned public buildings, however: houses and tombs were likewise used to reinforce the eminence of the aristocratic family. The location, design, and contents of the house all played a part in this (see also Chapter 24).[13] A location close to the Forum itself, in the nearby Subura, or on the Capitol was particularly appropriate for the ambitious politician; but the nearby Palatine Hill was the predominantly favored place of residence for the Roman aristocracy. To own a strikingly grand or unusual house afforded welcome publicity for the aspiring candidate, as Cn. Octavius, a *novus homo*, discovered when his success in achieving the consulship in 165 was ascribed to the impressive appearance of his residence (Cic. *Off.* 1.138). Equally, the *atrium* of an aristocratic house might be filled not only with masks depicting the owner's ancestors but also depictions of their achievements, archives, and family trees.[14] Even the exterior of the house reflected the distinction of its occupant: a general who had celebrated a triumph was entitled to display armor captured from the enemy on the doorposts of the house, visible to passersby, and these spoils could not legally be removed even if the house was sold to someone else (Pliny *HN* 35. 6–7; see also Chapter 18). Archaeological investigations in recent years have helped cast light on the aristocratic houses of Rome in the Republic, which had otherwise largely been known indirectly, by means of the better preserved houses of Pompeii. Excavations on the Palatine have revealed the remains of a series of *domus* on the slope leading down to the Forum: one is identified with that of M. Aemilius Scaurus, aedile in 58, but four earlier *atrium* houses have also been discovered on the site, dating back to the sixth century.[15] Their location on the Via Sacra places these, too, in close relation with the traditional route of the triumph.

The family tombs set up by Roman nobles on the outskirts of the city again contributed to reinforcing the distinguished image of their family, and indeed the whole complex of ceremonies relating to the burial of the dead also constituted a focus of aristocratic rivalry. The funeral ceremony began at the aristocrat's house, where he would be laid out in the *atrium* and then carried in procession to the Forum, accompanied by actors wearing the wax masks depicting his ancestors. His nearest male relative would deliver a funerary oration from the Rostra, the speakers' platform, and afterwards the body would be carried to the family tomb and there buried or cremated.[16] Typically, an aristocratic funeral would conclude with a banquet and (from the mid-third century) with gladiatorial combats, which usually took place in the Forum (see also Chapters 17, 23, and 25). One area of the city particularly notable for aristocratic tombs was the Via Appia, just outside the Porta Capena: here could be found the tombs of the Metelli, Servilii, and Cornelii, including the monument of the Scipiones, which was excavated in the eighteenth century (Figures 24.7 and 24.9a–b).[17] This contained the sarcophagus of L. Cornelius Scipio Barbatus (cos. 298), his son L. Cornelius Scipio (cos. 259), and several other members of the family.[18] Indeed, this area of the city was characterized by aristocratic rivalry in several different respects. Although the location of the temple of the Tempestates (vowed by the last-mentioned during the first Punic war) is not precisely known, it was in this general area of the city and quite possibly close to the family tomb; in the same way, the temple of Virtus dedicated in 205 by the son of

M. Claudius Marcellus, the conqueror of Syracuse, was close to the family mausoleum near the Porta Capena (Livy 27.25.6–10; 29.11.13). Another notable aristocratic tomb, identified by some scholars with that of Q. Fabius Maximus Rullianus, who won several notable victories over the Samnites in the late fourth and early third centuries, has been found on the Esquiline: inside it are depicted images of Roman and Samnite warriors (Figures 25.19a–b; see also Chapter 25).[19]

One particularly striking feature of these manifestations of aristocratic competition is the way in which they presuppose an audience. The triumph was a ceremony which involved not only the victorious general himself but also the army, who marched in the triumphal procession, the Senate and magistrates, and the Roman People as a whole, who watched the spectacle. Polybius described triumphs as occasions on which "the generals display their achievements clearly before the eyes of the citizens" (6.15.8). The aristocrat's house was not a private space, but a quasi-public one, where he would meet his clients and hold meetings with political associates (Vitr. *De arch.* 6.5.2); and even passersby could see the spoils displayed outside houses and tombs located close to main roads. In the same way, the aristocratic funeral was an occasion at which the presence of the Roman public was an important element: Polybius explicitly draws attention to this when he notes that the speech delivered before the crowd: "the masses . . . are affected with such feelings that the occurrence appears to be a loss for the whole state, not just those mourning the dead man" (6.53.3). The banquet and gladiatorial games that followed provided another occasion on which the family's generosity to the People could be manifested. Many of those watching the gladiators from the limited number of spaces available in the temporary stands erected around the Forum are likely to have had particularly close links to the family of the deceased, but their presence was significant nevertheless; likewise the fact that these "family" occasions took place in the public spaces of the city, the Rostra and the Forum.

The quest for glory among the aristocrats was therefore one which was played out before a popular audience in the city – quite appropriately, as they depended on the votes of the People for election to the magistracies which allowed them to achieve distinction within the Roman state. Roman nobles were thought to have a distinct advantage in electoral contests:[20] drawing attention to the victories that their distinguished ancestors and they themselves had won and the offices they had held was something that took place not only in the course of political canvassing but on many other occasions. Victory temples and other public monuments, the display of records in the *atrium*, and commemoration at funerals made the family's achievements visible for all to see.

Although the political and social structures that encouraged this close relationship between individual ambition and public and private building can be traced back to the late fourth century, there are indications that the competitiveness that lay behind it increased to a significant degree in the years after the Hannibalic War and then again in the first century. The early second century saw hitherto unparalleled quantities of wealth coming into Rome, much of it spent on public building – infrastructural works such as warehouses and aqueducts as well as monuments linked with elite display and public life. One symptom of the increase in the level and scale of competition in this period is the way in which temples built in the latter half of the second century – the "aedes Metelli" and "aedes Mariana," for example – tended to be known by the name of their builder rather than by the deity to which they were dedicated;[21] likewise the way in which new materials and architectural styles began to be employed in temple building. For example, the first temple entirely constructed in marble at Rome was the Temple of Jupiter Stator, built in the Circus Flaminius in 146, while the use of the Ionic and Corinthian orders can be seen in the surviving temples of the Forum Boarium. Although the earliest aristocratic tombs appear to have been comparatively modest in terms of public display – the inscribed sarcophagi of the Scipiones were contained within the walls of the tomb – more ostentatious styles of funerary monument can be seen to emerge in the second century.[22] In the middle of that century the exterior of the tomb of the Scipios was refurbished and decorated with paintings and statues; similarly the tomb of the Claudii Marcelli was rebuilt in the same period with statues and a boastful external inscription honoring "three Marcelli, nine times consuls" (Asc. 12C).[23] In the first century, the scale of competition became even more dramatic: Pliny observed that although the house of the consul of 78, Aemilius Lepidus, was the finest in Rome at the time, it was not even in the first hundred just 35 years later (Pliny *HN* 36.109). At the same time, expenditure on funerary banquets and gladiatorial games became gradually more and more lavish, with the number of combatants involved increasing steadily.[24]

The concentration of wealth and power in the hands of a few exceptionally wealthy and ambitious individuals in the first century – Sulla, Crassus, Caesar, Pompey – also had a significant effect on the appearance of the city. Individual temples and other monuments were still being built, but increasingly these were subordinated to large-scale projects that were to transform the cityscape of Rome: the theater and portico of Pompey, and the complex initiated by Julius Caesar, to include the Temple of Venus Genetrix and a new senate-house and Forum (see also Chapters 4 and 24). The monuments of the city were thus both a stage for and a product of the political struggles of the Republic, reflecting the increasing levels of competition within the Roman elite and the central importance of their relationship with the Roman People for the aristocracy (see also Chapter 18). It was only really with the advent of the dynasts that Rome achieved a monumental setting appropriate for its international importance, however, as disparate initiatives by individual members of the aristocracy gave way to a more coherent and centralized approach to Rome's civic space.[25]

The Growth of the Metropolis

By any standards Rome of the late Republic was an extremely populous city. At the time of Augustus, it is estimated that it had a population of nearly a million people (see also Chapter 14). The starting point for reconstructing the city's population are the figures, preserved in the literary and epigraphic record, for those receiving state grain (and other related benefits) at Rome in the late first century. Suetonius tells us that 320,000 people were drawing the grain dole by the time of Caesar, who then reduced the number by more than half to 150,000 (*Iul.* 41.3); between 200,000 and 320,000 received cash handouts or grain on various occasions during Augustus' principate (*RG* 15). These numbers represented a privileged category of male citizens within the urban population: when account is taken of free women and children and in addition ex-slaves of both sexes, foreigners, soldiers, and slaves, the total adds up to 800,000–1,000,000.[26] What is harder to determine is the process by which this population grew. As Scheidel observes: "we can only guess at the growth rates of the republican city of Rome."[27] Attempts to calculate the trajectory of the population of Rome on the basis of the provision of water supply and the building of new aqueducts are not entirely convincing, as these may primarily reflect the influx of wealth into the city from overseas conquest, and only indirectly give an indication of the urban population.[28]

One feature of the demography of ancient Rome that has emerged with particular clarity from recent work is the exceptionally high level of mortality that characterized the city. Study of Christian tomb-inscriptions from the catacombs (which record precisely the deceased's date of death) has demonstrated a strikingly diverse pattern in the distribution of deaths across the seasons at Rome: the peak of mortality was in the late summer. Such a peak would indicate high mortality in the society in general and is consonant with a predominance of deaths caused by pulmonary disease (including tuberculosis) and gastrointestinal problems, but it also suggests that these conditions may have been aggravated by endemic malaria.[29] That malaria was a serious problem at Rome in later periods is clear: the low-lying and marshy regions of the city, frequently affected by the flooding of the Tiber, provided many opportunities for the breeding of the anopheles mosquito, which spreads the disease, while the healthy characteristics of the city's hills were well known (Cic. *Rep.* 2.11; Livy 5.54.4).[30] Rich as well as poor were affected: the *impluvia* characteristic of the *atrium* houses favored by the aristocracy provided an ideal breeding ground for mosquitoes.[31]

The prevalence of these illnesses, aggravated by the cramped and unsanitary conditions in which Rome's inhabitants lived (see below), may have resulted in an average life expectancy at birth of less than 20 years, with serious implications for the demography of the city as a whole.[32] Without continuous migration to Rome, the city's population would have dwindled as a result of the disparity in numbers of births and deaths. Given that between the beginning of the second century and the end of the first, the population of Rome apparently increased (very roughly) from some 200,000 to a million, the extent of migration to the city must have been on a massive scale, since it allowed the population not just to remain steady but to increase dramatically; though views differ on where the migrants came from and what the effects on the population of Italy (and the Empire beyond) would have been.[33] Many of these "migrants" were slaves, brought to Rome in the aftermath of Roman victories; others came (more or less) of their own volition, drawn by the attractions of the capital and/or problematic circumstances at home.[34] There are some reasons to think that both "push" and "pull" factors – in particular, rural upheavals during and in the aftermath of the Social War and the provision of free grain in the city – were particularly felt in the first century (see also Chapter 28), in which case the extent of migration in that period must have been on a staggering scale.[35] Appian saw the grain dole as a factor attracting "the idle, the impoverished and the reckless of all Italy" to the city (App. *B Civ.* 2.120), reflecting Sallust's similar view that "the young men who had endured their poverty by working in the fields were attracted by private and public distributions and came to prefer a life of leisure in the city to their thankless labour" (Sall. *Cat.* 37.7). Dionysius alleges that slaves were freed in order that they might receive the dole (rather than their masters having to support them: Dion. Hal. *Ant. Rom.* 4.24.5). Much of this may be conventional anti-migrant rhetoric, but the expulsion of foreigners attested in 65 (Dio Cass. 37.9.5) and the efforts by Caesar to resettle city dwellers in colonies overseas (80,000 of them, according to Suetonius) together suggest that there was indeed a substantial influx of people in this period.[36] In any case, the migrants would have been among those most liable to infection with the range of life-threatening diseases to which they were exposed: especially if they came from districts where malaria was not prevalent and so had not acquired immunity to it.[37]

Living Conditions in the City

One significant factor behind the low life expectancy in the city of Rome was the living conditions of the urban population (or the vast majority of that population). However, the problem of the availability of source material is particularly acute in this context: very little literary or archaeological data specifically relate to living conditions in the Republic, and instead we need to reconstruct arrangements for the housing and burial of the poor (for example) from a scatter of pieces of evidence which largely date from the Imperial and late antique periods. Poor housing with inadequate sanitary facilities, high levels of contamination of food and drinking water, and overcrowding can be seen to be symptomatic of the Imperial city and inevitably must have characterized the republican city also, especially in the period of greatest growth: there is documentary evidence of a series of fires, floods, plagues, and other disasters which would have made living conditions even more difficult.[38]

It is also clear, however, that there was a wide variation in wealth and status between the Roman political elite and the most impoverished inhabitants of the city. Comparative study of other pre-industrial cities has revealed a hierarchy of poverty ranging from the destitute (some 4–6 percent: typically incapable of manual labor due to age, illness, or disability), the ordinary poor (some 20 percent: able to work, but permanently on the verge of crisis), and the temporary poor (some 30–40 percent: artisans or traders, normally employed, but liable to fall into poverty as a result of illness or other disaster).[39] A range of strategies was available to those who fell between the extremes of wealth and poverty which might (to a greater or lesser extent) help allow them to survive and serve to alleviate the difficulties achieving adequate living conditions.

The grim reality of the life of the poorest at Rome is illustrated by their fate after their deaths: it has been estimated that some 1,500 paupers annually would have been buried in mass graves on the Esquiline even in "normal" years without particularly noteworthy epidemics.[40] During their lives, most of them would have slept rough, living in shanties (*tuguria*) or in tombs on the outskirts of the city. Those of the poor who had a regular, if limited, income were able to rent rooms in taverns (*cauponae*) or on the upper floors of apartment blocks (*insulae*). Though the latter type of building is particularly well known from the imperial period, an account in Livy of how an ox climbed to the top of an *insula* close to the cattle market of the Forum Boarium in 218 suggests that examples could already be found in the third century (21.62.3). By the late Republic *insulae* featured regularly in the property portfolio of the Roman elite: Cicero owned such properties in the Argiletum and on the Aventine (Cic. *Att.* 12.32, 16.1). These provided a regular and substantial return in the form of hard cash, though with significant risks for the owner involved, too, as the buildings were liable to fire, collapse, and other hazards. Slum property might be let out to poorer tenants, with rent paid on a daily basis, while the more affluent occupied the better apartments on a longer-term basis.[41]

The city of Rome could be an anonymous and potentially hostile place, and there were limited sources of support available for the migrant to the city, especially for those who arrived without family ties in the metropolis. One possibility for those below the elite was to seek to exploit the possibilities offered by patronage to find a place to live: the degree to which this was a feasible strategy, however, would depend significantly on the status of the individuals themselves and their degree of closeness to an individual member of the elite (see also Chapter 19). The distinction made by Tacitus between the "filthy plebs" and the "respectable element of the people, attached to the great houses" was as appropriate for the Republic as for the year of Nero's death (*Hist.* 1.4). The latter might be "attached" to the houses of the elite in a physical as well as a metaphorical sense: evidence from Pompeii suggests that ex-slaves, individuals, and families favored by the wealthy owners of *atrium* houses might occupy flats (*cenacula*), balconies, and workshops (*tabernae*) around the house, and a similar model might be suggested for Rome in the mid-Republic too.[42] Aristocratic houses with associated *tabernae* were to be found around the Forum into the second century;[43] while Livy, in his account of the Bacchanalian affair in 186 describes how Hispala, who had provided information about the cult to the authorities, was installed by the consul in a "safe house" in the form of a *cenaculum* above his mother-in-law's home (39.14.2). By the time of the Empire and perhaps already in the late Republic, however, there was a tendency for some areas, like the Palatine, to see a concentration of aristocratic residences, while other districts – the Subura, Transtiberim, and (until the high Empire) the Aventine – were characterized by a predominance of popular housing.

Another strategy available to the migrant was to exploit networks provided by those from one's own town or region who were already installed in the capital: this scenario is slightly better attested for the Empire than for the Republic,[44] but the toponym "Fregellae" at Rome known from Festus (*Gloss. Lat.* 80L) suggests that there was a particular region in the city known for migrants from that town, most likely in the aftermath of its destruction in 125.[45]

A third possibility, and one of particular importance in the late Republic (though not one that helped much with the problems of housing), was to become involved in and seek the support of a *collegium* – a popular association linked with a particular cult, neighborhood in the city, or trade. Comparative evidence suggests that the development of popular associations can be an important means of integrating new inhabitants into a growing city.[46] The development of *collegia* at Rome in the 60s and subsequent decades – which caused the Roman authorities great concern and saw repeated attempts to suppress them because of their involvement in political violence – may thus be symptomatic of the growth of the city population at this time and of the limited scope of traditional patronage to control and order the flow of new-comers. Notoriously, the *collegia* were associated in this period with the political ambitions of Clodius. As Mouritsen has pointed out, migrants from Italy who continued to be registered in the rural voting tribes were highly prized by those involved in political canvassing, given the comparatively limited number of people at Rome able to vote in those tribes, and for this reason would have been welcomed with open arms by the *collegia* and those who cultivated their support.[47]

The Changing Nature of Political Space

Formal political activity in Rome took place according to strict rules (Maps 7 and 8; see also Chapter 12). The Senate had its own designated meeting place, the *curia*, located on a low hill overlooking the Forum, for example, though it might also gather in one of Rome's temples, as it was required to meet in a location religiously designated by the augurs.[48] Meetings of the popular assemblies took place in different locations according to the assembly in question: the *comitia centuriata* had to meet in the Campus Martius, beyond the *pomerium*, for example. Since it constituted the Roman People assembled as for war, it was forbidden to meet within the city limits. The *comitia tributa* (and *concilium plebis*) also gathered in the Campus for elections (at least from the first century), but for legislative purposes they met predominantly either in the Comitium, Forum, or Capitol.[49] Given this tendency to conservatism in the institutions of Roman politics, where practices relating to the formal meetings of assemblies can in fact be seen to change, this can often reflect significant broader trends: notably the advent of "popular politics" under the leadership of radical tribunes from the mid-second century onward and the exceptional predominance in public life of the dynasts of the late Republic (see also Chapter 18).

For example, the building history of the *curia* during the first century can be seen to reflect the institutional history of the Senate itself: we know that the ancient *curia Hostilia* was rebuilt by Sulla, to provide accommodation for the Senate he had expanded from 300 to 600 members. Sulla's Senate House was destroyed in the disturbances which followed the death of Clodius in 52 (see below), and although it was subsequently rebuilt by the dictator's son Faustus Sulla, the new building was soon demolished "so that the name of Sulla should not be preserved on it" (Dio Cass. 44.5.2). Work on a new *curia*, aligned with Caesar's new Forum, was eventually completed in 29 by Octavian.[50] The impact of successive dictators, Sulla and Caesar, on this centrally important monument is very striking.

Just below the *curia* was the *comitium*, an open area traditionally used for meetings of the *comitia tributa* and *concilium plebis* and for *contiones*, at which magistrates would address the Roman People. Together the two monuments reflected the close interrelation of the Senate and People of Rome in the political ideology of the Roman state and were imitated in the layout of the civic monuments of Latin colonies (cf. Figure 4.1). Adjacent was the speaker's platform (*rostra*), the *tribunal* (where legal judgments were made by the praetors), and the prison (*carcer*), where capital sentences were carried out. In the years after the Latin War, this area came to be characterized by a series of statues and monuments which commemorated Rome's past history and was thus also a place of collective memory: the beaks of the Latin ships captured at Antium in 338 were displayed on the *rostra*, the *columna Maenia* commemorated the same victory, and statues of Pythagoras and Alcibiades were set up "at the corners of the *comitium*" at the time of the Samnite Wars (see also Chapters 23 and 24). The trend was reinforced after the First Punic War with the setting up of the sundial removed from Catana in Sicily in 263 by M' Valerius Messalla and the victory monument of Cn. Duilius three years later (see also Chapter 23).[51]

Different reconstructions of the *comitium* in the late Republic have been proposed, either circular (Coarelli) or roughly triangular in shape (Carafa), illustrating, incidentally, the provisionality of our knowledge of even the most central monuments of the Roman Republic. This has made the impact of Sulla's rebuilding of the *curia* on the popular space of the *comitium* difficult to assess, especially since in Carafa's reconstruction that building is at a level some 10 m higher than the *comitium*.[52] Pliny reports that the statues of Pythagoras and Alcibiades were removed at that time (*HN* 34.26), and an equestrian statue of Sulla himself was set up close to the *rostra* (App. *B Civ.* 1.97). What is clear, however, is that Caesar's reorganization of the area, completed by Octavian, was on a major scale: just as the senate-house was rebuilt, the *comitium* was also swept away, and the *rostra* replaced on a completely new alignment.[53]

The *comitium* similarly plays an important part in the history of "popular participation" at Rome. In 145 we hear that the tribune C. Licinius Crassus transferred voting assemblies from the *comitium* to the Forum (Varr. *Rust.* 1.2.9); subsequently C. Gracchus also transferred *contiones* (Plut. *C. Gracch.* 5.3).[54] Views differ as to whether ideological or practical considerations provided the main impetus behind this reform: both may have played a part.[55] The population of Rome was increasing significantly at this time, but the number of voters that the *comitium* would have held has been estimated between 3,000 and 5,000, whereas the Forum could hold considerably more. Estimates of those able to attend and vote there range between 10,000 and 30,000. Equally, as Plutarch notes, the move had a strong symbolic impact, as speakers addressing the People were now in effect turning their backs on the senate-house. The issue of numbers attending assemblies is an important one in the context of the debate about "democracy at Rome": even if the Forum, on a maximum estimate, were completely filled by voters (or the Saepta in the Campus Martius, variously estimated to have held some 30,000–70,000 people), only a small proportion of the overall Roman citizenry would in practice have actually been able to vote.[56] This observation tends to reinforce those analyses which take the view that although public meetings,

voting, and elections played an important part in public life at Rome, those involved
were likely to be a select and unrepresentative body of people and that the role of the
People may thus have been largely a symbolic selection between, and validation of,
individuals from the elite (see also Chapters 1, 12, and 18).[57]

The spread of political violence in the first century may be seen in part as yet
another possible consequence of the increasing growth of the city, together with the
changing nature of politics and the declining importance of patronage (see also
Chapter 19). Whereas second-century episodes of violence – e.g., the episode in
185 when "Claudian force" was successfully used to ensure the election of a member
of that family or the murders of the Gracchi by mobs led by Scipio Nasica and
Opimius, respectively – were to a significant extent, it appears, the result of deployment of supporters and associates by member of the elite,[58] the increasingly frequent
outbreaks of political violence in the first century appear to involve more fragmented
groups, including the *collegia*, though with members of the elite – Clodius and Milo,
for example – often taking the lead. This led on occasion to what we might see as an
appropriation by the mob of the traditional uses of public space by the Roman
aristocracy. The funeral of Clodius is a case in point: it drew on the traditions of the
aristocratic funeral but subverted them, also, as Cicero notes (Cic. *Mil.* 33). Clodius'
battered body was taken by a crowd of his supporters from his *atrium* to the Forum
without the usual accompaniment of busts of his ancestors (of whom Clodius had
many distinguished examples). The body was displayed on the *rostra* as usual, but the
commemorative oration delivered by the tribunes rather than by a family member.
The culmination of the ceremony was the cremation of Clodius in the *curia*, which
was followed by a funerary banquet in the Forum. Dio observes that this sequence of
events was a deliberate choice, "not under the sort of impulse that suddenly seizes
crowds." Afterwards, an attack was made on Milo's house nearby, but the rioters were
driven off by a volley of arrows. An assault on the house of M. Aemilius Lepidus was
more successful, however, as the mob smashed up his *atrium*, masks of ancestors
included (Asc. 32-3C, 43C; Dio Cass. 40.48–9; App. *B Civ.* 2.21).[59] Where traditionally the aristocratic house had been the venue for the peaceful greeting of clients,
houses now acted as garrisons, the targets for violence, or places of refuge, as in 75
when the two consuls of the year had to take refuge from a hungry mob in the house
of one of them on the Via Sacra (Sall. *Hist.* 2.45M = 2.42 McGushin).[60] Even the
Forum itself, for all its ancient traditions, was now regularly the scene of violence.[61]

Supplying Rome's Needs

How did the city of Rome acquire the food, water, and other supplies it needed? Not
only did the city have a rapidly increasing population during the mid- and late
republican periods, it was also the seat of the Roman elite, where their houses and
households were located. Consumption in the city thus included the demand generated by the aristocracy as well as the subsistence requirements of the population as a
whole. As usual, the evidence from the Imperial period is fuller than that for the

Republic, so much about the extent of demand and arrangements for supply in the earlier period must remain hypothetical.

Assuming a total population of about a million at Rome, it has been estimated that a minimum of 237,000 tonnes of wheat, 100,000 tonnes of wine, and 18,000 tonnes of olive oil would have been needed in the city annually; if the weight of the containers for the wine and oil is added to that of the produce itself, the minimum figure grows to more than 400,000 tonnes. Given the demand for other goods and agricultural produce across Roman society, the total quantities actually brought to the city would have been larger still.[62] In particular, there was a large (and increasing) market for luxuries in the city, generated by the senators, members of the equestrian order, and the upper echelons of the *plebs*. Indeed, extravagant dining was a cause of repeated concern to the Roman authorities, during the second century in particular, and numerous pieces of sumptuary legislation were enacted: the Lex Fannia of 161 instituted a maximum expenditure on festive occasions of 100 asses per dinner, and this figure was subsequently raised by Sulla to 300 asses (Gell. *NA* 2.24). The fact that sumptuary legislation had to be reiterated frequently, however, suggests not only that the practical impact was limited and that ostentation in dining continued to flourish, but that ideological considerations were paramount in the promulgation of these laws, which are best seen as a contribution to defining Roman identity.[63] The influx of wealth from Rome's overseas conquests and exposure to foreign luxury were conventionally blamed for this enthusiasm for extravagant living (Polyb. 31.25.2–7; Livy 39.6.7–9). Writing from the point of view of the first-century farmer, Varro draws attention to the wealth to be gained by producing luxury foodstuffs in the periphery of Rome: triumphs, banquets, and *collegia* dinners provided a regular and lucrative market (*Rust.* 3.2.15–17).

In the past, particular attention has been paid to the way in which Rome acts as an example of the ideal type of the "consumer city," a concept derived ultimately from the work of Max Weber and other nineteenth-century social theorists but associated in more recent years primarily with the work of M. I. Finley.[64] The city, by virtue of its political authority, is seen as consuming the resources of its hinterland in the form of rents and taxes rather than generating income by means of production and manufacture. Indeed, Finley sees the city of Rome as the "quintessential consumer-city," conforming most closely to this model.[65] In recent years, however, the focus of debate on the "consumer-city" has tended to shift away from the city itself toward the hinterland, whether seen in terms of the immediate environs of Rome or as the whole of the Empire, and has explored the implications for the economies of these areas of the demand generated by Rome with its large population and high prices.[66] Here I focus primarily on the nature of arrangements made to feed and supply with water Rome's vast population; the consequences for the appearance of the city; and the implications both for Roman politics and for the survival strategies available to those below the elite.

At the beginning of the Republic Rome's extensive territory had been one of its particular strengths, but by the end of the third century the resources available from the city's immediate hinterland had long since been outstripped.[67] From the end of that century, we hear of the exaction of taxes in the form of grain from the provinces of Sicily and Sardinia, to be followed later by that of Africa; grain might also be gifted to Rome by well-disposed foreign rulers. The city population, however, was in competition with Roman armies in the field for such supplies (see also Chapter 13).[68] When, during the early Republic, there were shortages of corn, it was from other areas of Italy that the Romans obtained additional supplies, and the peninsula continued to supply the city with substantial quantities of grain and other types of agricultural produce.[69]

A range of potential problems might have affected the supply of food to the city, however, and in particular that of corn, the chief staple food. Corn yields in antiquity (as in other periods before the use of chemical fertilizers became widespread) were highly variable from year to year and from place to place, given also the risk of damage to crops as a result of bad weather, drought, or vermin.[70] Added to this were natural disasters – epidemics, fires and storms – which affected the cultivation, transport, and storage of the grain; man-made causes of crisis such as slave revolts, warfare, and piracy; and the competing demands of the army. The corn supply of Rome was permanently at risk of disruption and crisis as a result of some or all of these factors; the result would be high prices for some and starvation for others when grain became unavailable in sufficient quantities and was, as a result, priced beyond the financial capabilities of the poor.[71]

The traditional solution to these difficulties adopted by the Roman elite was a range of ad hoc measures: the aediles, whose responsibility the grain supply was, would obtain additional supplies beyond the usual sources either by purchase or gift. An inscription records how additional supplies were obtained from the Thessalians, probably in 129, following a visit by a Roman aedile; the Lex Gabinia of 67, authorizing military operations against the pirates who were disrupting the grain supply, can be seen as an initiative in the same tradition.[72] From 123, however, more systematic arrangements began to be implemented: at the initiative of the tribune C. Gracchus grain was provided at a fixed price ($6\frac{1}{3}$ asses per modius) for a fixed number of beneficiaries.[73] Measures were also taken to build state granaries (Plut. *C. Gracch.* 5.2, 6.3). In subsequent years the provision of fixed-price grain continued to be a contentious issue: the "grain dole" was abolished by Sulla, revived in a modest way in 73, and then amplified in 62 before being made free to recipients during the tribunate of P. Clodius in 58. In general, the traditional aristocracy saw the intervention of the state in the provision of grain as detrimental to their authority over the lower orders in Rome; but there was also an awareness, especially in the first century, of the risks to the stability of the city that food riots could pose. In 62, the traditionalist senator Cato introduced proposals for enhancement of the corn distributions, apparently in response to the social and political tensions revealed by the recent Catilinarian uprising. The initiatives introduced by Pompey, who was given responsibility for improving the corn supply in 57, and subsequently Caesar as dictator, look forward to those of the emperors, for example, in providing incentives for those involved in shipping the grain and seeking to create a new harbor at Ostia so the largest grain ships could berth there rather than having to transship their cargoes at Puteoli.[74]

Although it is not known where the Gracchan warehouses were located, there is considerable evidence of the way in which the increasing demand for goods and produce was reflected in the built environment of the city during the second century. In 193 the aediles M. Aemilius Lepidus and L. Aemilius Paullus built a *porticus* by the Tiber, creating an *emporium* (port) below the Aventine Hill where ships with provisions for the city were unloaded (Livy 35.10.12). Subsequently this facility was extended and developed, with a series of stairways constructed to connect the *porticus* with the wharves (Livy 41.27.8).[75] These public constructions were complemented by other warehouses (*horrea*), a series of which were built below the Aventine from the late second century onward by aristocratic families and evidently formed a part of their property portfolio in the same way their urban residential properties did. Indeed the tomb of Ser. Sulpicius Galba, consul in 108 and probably the builder of the Horrea Galbana ("filled with wine, oil and similar goods," according to a scholiast on Horace: Porphyry on Hor. *Carm.* 4.12.18), was located near his warehouse.[76] Meanwhile, a specialist market building for the sale of luxury foods, the *macellum*, was constructed behind the Forum Romanum following a fire there in 210, and replaced the food shops and earlier market buildings that had previously surrounded the Forum.[77] The public grain distributions, however, appear to have taken place in the Circus Flaminius or the Campus Martius near the Saepta, all locations with strong links to "popular politics," reflecting the populist character of the innovation (see also Chapter 4).[78]

Considerable efforts were also made from the late fourth century onward to provide a more copious and more reliable water supply for the city. The first of these was the construction of the Aqua Appia, built (like the Via Appia) by Ap. Claudius Caecus, the censor of 312, and was followed by the Anio Vetus (272), Aqua Marcia (144), and Aqua Tepula (125), though we also hear of an (abortive) attempt to build an aqueduct by the censors of 179 (Livy 40.51.7). The building of the Marcia had the effect of doubling the water supply to the city, and its construction was associated by Frontinus with the growth of Rome (Frontin. *Aq.* 7). All of these initiatives can also be seen as "triumphal" in a loose sense, as the wealth required to carry out these major projects was derived from the spoils of victory over the Samnites, Pyrrhus, Corinth, and Carthage: the Marcia in particular had a major visual impact on the city, also, as for some 10 km the channel was carried on arcades across the Roman Campagna, which were then apparently reused for the Tepula nearly twenty years later.[79]

The wide range of building projects undertaken at Rome under the mid- and late Republic – temples, porticoes, basilicas, and private housing, as well as the aqueducts[80] – generated a vast demand for building materials. Monumental buildings were traditionally constructed in stone blocks (*opus quadratum*), using tufa, which was derived from volcanic outcrops in Rome's immediate hinterland, and later travertine from around Tibur. With the development of the *opus incertum* (and subsequently *opus quasi-reticulatum*) style of stone-faced concrete in the early second century, however, lime (which came from the limestone foothills of the Apennines) and volcanic pozzolana (an essential ingredient in the concrete mix) were also needed in large quantities (see also Chapter 5).[81] The building industry generated substantial demand for wood, which was in addition needed for heating, cooking, and cremations.[82]

Even when fixed-price (or even free) food distributions had been introduced, by no means were the financial and nutritional needs of the poor satisfied. Eligibility for the distributions was related to citizenship, not need; so many migrants who would have benefited most were ineligible, and those who did receive cheap or free grain would need additional cash to pay for the milling of the grain, buy other sorts of food (typically vegetables, wine, and oil), and also provide for their families.[83] Hence there was a large pool of potential labor in the city, seeking permanent or (more realistically) temporary employment: both the building trade itself and the operations to supply the city with building materials and other goods provided a major source of jobs.[84] Mattingly and Aldrete have calculated that, assuming an average size for ships of 250 tonnes, a minimum of 1,692 shiploads of goods would have had to arrive in Rome annually to provide the city with grain, wine, and oil.[85] Given the repeated loading and unloading required as the goods were transferred first to warehouses and then to customers, it is clear that a large workforce would have been needed, but largely a casual one – the constraints of the sailing season meant that activity was concentrated into a restricted period in spring and summer, so to maintain a force of slaves for this highly seasonal work would have been uneconomic.[86] Indeed, the traditional "popular" associations of the Aventine and Transtiberim regions of the city may in part reflect their proximity to a major source of employment for the urban plebs.

The growth of the city's population, the building industry generated by the construction of public monuments and private housing, and the structures which allowed for the feeding of that population were thus closely interlinked; the megalopolis had a vast population to feed and house but also an abundance of casual labor to help ensure this was done.

Conclusion

Decades of archaeological research in the city of Rome have demonstrated the centrality of buildings and monuments for our understanding of how Roman politics – both formal and informal – worked and illustrated how changes in public space can be seen to reflect the changing nature of politics in the mid- and late Republic. Future topographical work will continue to correct and amplify our knowledge of the public monuments of the city – and provide surprises too, no doubt. At the same time, a comparative approach to the history of the city has highlighted the existence of hierarchies below the political elite: the degree to which "rich" and "poor" interrelated to a great extent tends to reflect these hierarchies. Ideologically, there was a close relationship between Senate and People, and aspiring politicians relied on popular support to gain advancement. In practice, however, it was the upper echelons of the urban plebs with which the elite had the closest links: these were the men who voted in the higher classes of the *comitia centuriata*, were guests when feasts and games were arranged by the elite, and might live in accommodation owned by their patrons. Where those below this privileged category lived under the Republic is less clear;[87] and the role of the *collegia* in the lives of those without direct access to elite support would also repay further investigation. It is likely, however, that the poorest inhabitants of the city, migrants in particular, would have had limited contact with the upper classes except perhaps on the periphery of the city, where beggars accosted affluent passersby and the tombs of the aristocracy and the shacks of the homeless existed in close proximity.[88]

Guide to Further Reading

The study of the city of Rome in antiquity has been placed on an entirely new footing with the completion in 2000 of the *Lexicon Topographicum Urbis Romae* (Steinby 1993–2000), its six volumes providing an exhaustive guide to the topography and monuments of the ancient city. Richardson 1992 provides less detailed coverage, but is more accessible for the English-language reader; see also Platner and Ashby 1929. Stambaugh 1988 provides a synthetic survey of the development of the city and various features of urban life; Claridge 1998 is an up-to-date guidebook to the surviving remains, with much useful information about the layout and history of the city. Since the 1980s there has been an upsurge in archaeological activity at Rome: some of this work is reviewed in Patterson 1992b, and extremely useful synopses of recent work in the city are published in the *Bullettino della Commissione Archeologica Comunale di Roma* (*BCAR*): see vols. 98 (1997): 329–98, 100 (2001): 325–91, and 102 (2001): 365–422 for the most recent of these. Coulston and Dodge 2000 contains a series of useful articles on a range of aspects of the city's archaeology: a sourcebook on the city by the same authors is forthcoming, which will serve to replace Dudley 1967. Chapter 4 above has many points of contact with the present one and offers a narrative of the development of the city from the beginning of the Republic.

On the different topics under consideration in this chapter, the following are recommended. Political competition: Flower 1996 covers a wide range of topics related to the physical manifestations of aristocratic competition; Patterson 2000a (with further bibliography) provides an introduction to the topic. The growth of the metropolis: see in particular Morley 1996, and the essays in Edwards and Woolf 2003, for discussion of the demographic characteristics of the city and their implications. Living conditions: the classic article by Scobie (1986) is now complemented by Purcell 1994. See Whittaker 1993a for a valuable account of "the poor" at Rome. Changing political space: the implications of this for our broader understanding of how Roman politics worked are explored in particular by Millar (1989, 1998) and, reacting to his approach, Mouritsen (2001) and Morstein-Marx (2004). Supplying the city: Rickman (1980) and Garnsey (1988) investigate the mechanisms devised to supply the city with food, and the political implications. For building materials see Meiggs 1982 and DeLaine 1995.

Notes

1   Oakley 1997–2004: 60–1.
2   Cristofani 1990, though note the critique of Gabba 1998, Smith 2000.
3   Mura Sommella 2000, 2001: 263–4.
4   Andreussi 1996; Cifani 2003.
5   Cornell 1995: 198–204.
6   Cornell 1995: 352–63.
7   Wiseman 1985: 3–6.
8   Hopkins 1978: 25–7, with Beard 2003: 25–6.
9   Ziolkowski 1992; Oakley 1993: 27, 33–5; Orlin 1997.
10 Coarelli 1988c: 365.
11 Favro 1994.
12 Cornell 2000a: 47–50.
13 Wiseman 1994c: 98–115; Wallace-Hadrill 1994: 5–16.
14 Flower 1996: 185–222.
15 Carandini 1988; Carandini and Carafa 1995: 215–82.
16 Polyb. 6. 53–4; Hopkins 1983a: 201–2; Flower 1996: 91–127; and see Chapter 18.
17 Cic. *Tusc.* 1.7.13; Patterson 2000b: 98.
18 Flower 1996: 159–80.
19 Coarelli 1973: 200–8.
20 Wiseman 1971: 100–7; Morstein-Marx 1998: 270–83; Yakobson 1999: 184–225.
21 Orlin 1997: 193–4.
22 Hesberg 1992: 22–4.
23 Flower 1996: 163–6. Following Coarelli 1999b, I take the Asconius text to be referring to a family tomb close to the temples of Honos and Virtus, rather than to the temples themselves, as do, e.g., Marshall 1985: 102 and Sehlmeyer 1999: 164.
24 Purcell 1994: 682; Flower 1996: 122–6.
25 Cornell 2000a: 56.
26 Hopkins 1978: 96–8; Morley 1996: 33–9. For an attempt to reduce this estimate on the grounds that it would imply an excessively high population density for the city, see Storey 1997.
27 Scheidel 2001a: 63. See Chapter 27 for some estimates.
28 Dodge 2000: 172.
29 Scheidel 1994c; Shaw 1996; Scheidel 2003.
30 Sallares 2002: 201–34; Scheidel 2003: 165–6.
31 Scheidel 1999; Scheidel 2003: 166.
32 Scheidel 2003: 175.
33 Morley 1996: 44–50; Lo Cascio 2001: 113–19 with Scheidel 2001a: 28.
34 Morley 2003; Noy 2000: 86–90.
35 Purcell 1994: 652.
36 Suet. *Iul.* 42.1; Brunt 1971a: 255–9.
37 Sallares 2002: 223–7; Scheidel 2003: 164–5.
38 Scobie 1986.
39 Whittaker 1993a: 276; Garnsey 1998: 226–7.
40 Bodel 1994: 38–54; Bodel 2000: 128–35.
41 Frier 1980: 34–9; Parkins 1997b: 92–7; Patterson 2000c.

42 Purcell 1994: 675; Pirson 1997.
43 Wallace-Hadrill 1991: 262–3.
44 Noy 2000: 146–9; 151–2.
45 Coarelli and Monti 1998: 42.
46 Patterson 1994: 237.
47 Mouritsen 2001: 84.
48 Bonnefond-Coudry 1989: 25–197.
49 Taylor 1966: 34–58.
50 Coarelli 1983–5: 234–7; Coarelli 1993.
51 Coarelli 1983–5: 11–123; Millar 1989; Purcell 1995; Morstein-Marx 2004: 92–107; see also Chapter 24.
52 Carafa 1998: 155; Morstein-Marx 2004: 47–8.
53 Coarelli 1983–5: 233–57.
54 Coarelli 1983–5: 157–8; Mouritsen 2001: 20–6; Morstein-Marx 2004: 47–8.
55 Mouritsen 2001: 20–4; Morstein-Marx 2004: 45–7.
56 MacMullen 1980; Mouritsen 2001: 18–37; see also Chapter 19.
57 North 1990b; Mouritsen 2001: 1–17; Morstein-Marx 2004: 279–87.
58 Nippel 1995: 56–60, 70–4; Lintott 1999b: 175–203.
59 Sumi 1997; Morstein-Marx 2004: 1–4.
60 Patterson 2000a: 65.
61 Purcell 1995: 335.
62 Mattingly and Aldrete 2000: 154–6.
63 Lintott 1972a: 631–2; de Ligt 2002: 3–12.
64 Finley 1981; Whittaker 1990, 1995; the papers in Parkins 1997a, esp. the concluding essay by Mattingly.
65 Finley 1981: 21.
66 E.g., Morley 1996: 13–21; Hopkins 2002: esp. 229; and, more generally, Erdkamp 2001.
67 Cornell 1995: 204–8.
68 Erdkamp 2000.
69 Rickman 1980: 36–42; Spurr 1986; Garnsey 1988: 182–91.
70 Hopkins 1983b: 90; Garnsey 1988: 8–26.
71 Garnsey 1988: 196; Cherry 1993.
72 Garnsey, Gallant, and Rathbone 1984, with Garnsey and Rathbone 1985: 25; Garnsey 1988: 196–7; Kallet-Marx 1995: 315–16.
73 A *modius* of grain weighed approximately 6.75 kg, while its cost was about half Cicero's estimate of a laborer's daily wage: *Q. Rosc.* 28.
74 Rickman 1980: 48–60; Garnsey 1988: 195–217.
75 Mocchegiani Carpano 1995; Coarelli 1999a.
76 Rickman 1971: 97–104; Coarelli 1996c, 1999c.
77 De Ruyt 1983: 158–60; Pisani Sartorio 1996.
78 Virlouvet 1987; Coarelli 1997: 296–345.
79 Dodge 2000: 170–5.
80 Coarelli 1977.
81 Coarelli 1977: 9–16; DeLaine 1995; 2000: 134–5.
82 Meiggs 1982: 218–59.
83 Cherry 1993; Garnsey 1998: 237–9.
84 DeLaine 2000: 135–6.
85 Mattingly and Aldrete 2000: 154.

86   Brunt 1980a: 93–4.
87   Wallace-Hadrill 2001.
88   Patterson 2000b: 102–3.

CHAPTER 17

Aristocratic Values

Nathan Rosenstein

Honor was everything at Rome, every aristocrat's all-consuming ambition, and the struggle to gain it started early according to Polybius. An Achaean Greek from a leading political family who suffered deportation to Italy in 167, Polybius lived almost two decades among the Romans, and sought in his *Histories* to help his countrymen understand them. To explain what enabled the Romans to recover from the catastrophic defeats they suffered early in the Hannibalic War, Polybius pointed (among other things) to their funeral ceremonies (see also Chapters 16, 23, and 24). These, in his view, produced "men ready to endure anything to win a reputation in their country for valour":

> Whenever one of their illustrious men dies, in the course of his funeral, the body with all of its paraphernalia is carried into the forum to the Rostra, as a raised platform there is called . . . [H]is son . . . or, failing him, one of his relations mounts the Rostra and delivers a speech concerning the virtues of the deceased and the successful exploits performed by him in his lifetime . . . After the burial . . . they place the likeness of the deceased in the most conspicuous spot in his house . . . These likenesses they display at public sacrifices adorned with much care. And when any illustrious member of the family dies, they carry these masks to the funeral, putting them on men . . . as like the originals as possible in height and other personal peculiarities. And these substitutes assume clothes according to the rank of the person represented. If he was a consul or praetor, a toga with purple stripes; if a censor, whole purple; if he had also celebrated a triumph or performed any exploit of that kind, a toga embroidered with gold. These representatives also ride themselves in chariots, while the fasces and axes and all the other customary insignia of the particular offices lead the way . . . On arriving at the Rostra, they all take their seats on ivory chairs in their order. There could not easily be a more inspiring spectacle than this for a young man of noble ambitions and virtuous aspirations . . . Besides, the speaker over the body about to be buried, after having finished the panegyric of this particular person, starts upon the others whose representatives are present, beginning with the most ancient, and recounts the successes and achievements of each. By this means the glorious

memory of brave men is continually renewed; the fame of those who have performed any noble deed is never allowed to die... But the chief benefit of the ceremony is that it inspires young men to shrink from no exertion for the general welfare, in the hope of obtaining the glory which awaits the brave. (Polyb. 6.52. 11–54.3 [trans. Shuckburgh])

No wonder, then, that the Romans could fight their way back from the brink of disaster and ultimately triumph if nothing was more important to them than "a reputation for valor." But Polybius' description also underscores the link at Rome between courage, public office, and honor. Those who displayed exceptional valor were those worthy of holding the Republic's highest magistracies, and it was here that they could win the great military victories that bestowed the truly out-standing glory commemorated in funeral pageantry, in the eulogies pronounced on these occasions, or on the tombs where such men were finally laid to rest, such as in this inscription for L. Cornelius Scipio Barbatus, consul in 298 (although the inscrip-tion dates from the early second century; see Figure 24.7):

Lucius Cornelius Scipio Barbatus, son of his father Gnaeus, a strong man and a wise one, whose courage closely matched his good looks. He was consul, censor, and aedile among you. He captured Taurasia and Cisauna in Samnium, subjugated the whole of Lucania, and brought back hostages. (*CIL* 1.2.7 = *ROL* 4:3 no. 2)

The Latin term for courage or valor is *virtus*, a word whose meaning grows increasingly complex over the course of the second and first centuries, but its primary sense in the middle Republic is martial. Courage was fundamental, the essential foundation to any aristocrat's struggle for eminence, "nearly the most important thing in every state," Polybius reported, "but especially in Rome" (Polyb. 31.29.1). Those whose accomplishments on the battlefield won them renown were recognized as the Republic's natural leaders, a connection made explicit in the aftermath of Cannae. Losses in that disaster and prior reverses had so depleted the ranks of the Senate that a special effort had to be undertaken to replenish its membership. The men selected were, first, those who had held various minor public offices, then "those who had spoils taken from the enemy on display in their homes or who had been decorated for saving the life of a citizen in combat" (Livy 23.23.5–6; see also Chapters 16 and 24). The civic crown, a wreath of oak leaves awarded for saving a citizen's life, was bestowed for an act of exceptional gallantry: one had not only to save another's life but slay the enemy threatening him without giving ground in the fight (Gell. *NA* 5.6.13). Likewise a young aristocrat won spoils by stripping the enemy he killed in individual combat in a duel or in the general mêlée of battle (Gell. *NA* 2.11.3). This principle extended to all the decorations for valor awarded to soldiers; they bespoke courage in circumstances when there was no need to endanger one's life, bravery "above and beyond the call of duty," in other words. Worn in religious processions, they formed an important element in one's public image (Polyb. 6.39.1–10; see also Chapter 13). Renown (*gloria*) seen in the visible tokens of one's courage and heard in others' praise of one's exploits (*laus*) paved the way to public office, at least initially. When around 124 Gaius Marius first sought one of the lower rungs on the political ladder, his reputation as a soldier won him unanimous election (Sall. *Iug.* 63.3–4; cf. Plut. *Marius* 3.2–4.1).

Superior courage in combat thus set some men apart from others and fit them to lead. As such, it served as a central element within the system of values that justified the dominance of the Republic's upper class. Outstanding valor was thought to have accumulated in certain families, so that over time their descendants came to be viewed as having a greater store of it than others and hence a greater claim on public offices and positions of leadership. But the ideological charge of courage ran in both directions, for if certain families' superior *virtus* explained why some men and not others were entitled to wield power, it also set a high standard to which subsequent generations were expected to measure up, as the boasts on the tomb of Gnaius Cornelius Scipio Hispanus, praetor in 139, make clear:

> By my character I increased the valorous deeds (*virtutes*) of my forebears. I have had children and emulated the exploits of my father. I sustained the praise of my ancestors, so that they rejoice that I was born to them. My office has ennobled my descendants. (*CIL* 1.2.15 = *ROL* 4:9 no. 10)

Consequently, the lives of young aristocrats during the third and second centuries were arranged to afford wide scope for the display of courage and the winning of renown. Ten years of military service beginning at age 17 were required before anyone could run for public office, and members of Rome's elite along with other wealthy citizens spent them serving in the cavalry. The nature of cavalry combat and its role as an element in military operations offered many opportunities to display bravery, far more than service as an infantryman. Interestingly, until the Hannibalic War Roman cavalrymen fought without the benefit of effective defensive armor. The reasons probably reflect the value they placed on the greater freedom of movement and comfort that the absence of heavy armor allowed, but one consequence – if not a cause – of this preference was an increased likelihood of sustaining wounds, and honorable scars, those on the front of the body, were a visible symbol of *virtus*. Scars could be displayed to demonstrate personal worth and lay claim to political authority, as Marcus Servilius Pulex Geminus (cos. 202) did in 167, when in seeking to sway an assembly to his point of view he tore off his toga and pointed to his scars, describing where and when he had received each one. His gesture was scarcely unprecedented or unparalleled (Livy 45.39.16–17).

The heavy emphasis on martial courage is hardly surprising in view of the nearly constant warfare Rome was engaged in during these centuries, but its roots go much farther back, to the earliest days of the Republic. Beginning in the fifth century, Rome, along with Latium, came under extraordinary military pressure from migrating peoples moving out of the mountainous areas to the east and south. Concurrently and continuing throughout the fourth and well into the third centuries, powerful Etruscan cities, Gallic tribes, and confederations of Samnite peoples posed equally grave challenges to Rome (see also Chapters 6 and 26). The severity of these threats prompted a complex response at Rome, one crucial element of which was the development of a strong military ethos among the aristocracy along with an intense dedication to the public welfare. Honor was to be sought only within the context of the Republic's public affairs (*res publica*), and in view of Italy's endemic conflicts in these years Rome's most pressing issue was first and foremost war.

Yet as crucial as martial valor was to aristocratic identity in the early and middle Republic and as important as war remained as a source of glory to the very end, courage by no means constituted the sum of aristocratic values. One of the fullest and earliest statements of the ideals that animated the members of Rome's upper class appears in a eulogy delivered in 221 at the funeral of Lucius Caecilius Metellus, consul in 251 and 247, by his son, Quintus Metellus, preserved by the Elder Pliny:

> Lucius had been a priest (*pontifex*), twice consul, dictator, master of the cavalry, and one of a board of fifteen for assigning land. He was the first to lead elephants in a triumphal procession, captured in the first Punic War. His father, Quintus wrote, "had achieved the ten greatest and best things that wise men spend their lives seeking. For he had wished to be a first-class warrior; the best orator; the bravest general; to conduct the greatest affairs under his own authority; to enjoy the greatest honor; to be a man of the highest wisdom; to be considered the top senator; to acquire great wealth honorably; to be survived by many children; and to be the most renowned man in the state. All these things came to pass for him and for no other since the foundation of the city." (Pliny *HN* 7.139–40)

As we might expect, prowess in combat takes pride of place, but it is striking in view of the enormous value placed on military courage that Quintus Metellus listed his father's excellence as an orator second in this catalog of virtues, ahead of his qualities as a general. Ever since Harris' seminal study arguing for the importance of war in aristocratic ideology (1979: 10–41), scholars have largely accepted the Republican elite's bellicose character. But while a reputation for bravery in battle was certainly essential to success in an aristocrat's struggle for honor, more was required than simply this. So in 167 the young Publius Cornelius Scipio Aemilianus, then about 18, complained to his friend Polybius:

> in a quiet and subdued voice, and with the blood mounting to his cheeks ... "I am considered by everybody, I hear, to be a mild, effete person, and far removed from the true Roman character and ways, because I don't care for pleading in the law courts. And they say that the family I come of requires a different kind of representative, and not the sort that I am. That is what annoys me most." (Polyb. 31.23.9–12 [trans. Shuckburgh])

Service as an advocate in the courts (for which no fee was permitted) can from one perspective be seen as a form of ritualized combat and hence just another arena where aristocrats competed against one another for glory and praise. And paradoxically, in a culture that valued military achievement so highly and offered so many opportunities to win it, something quite different might be needed to make a young man stand out. Servilius' opponent in the debate mentioned above was Servius Sulpicius Galba, a youngster who, Servilius charged, knew only how to talk, not fight. Yet Galba reached the consulship in 144; he was hands-down the leading orator of his day (Cic. *Brut.* 82). And skill at public speaking played a vital role in the rise of Marcus

Porcius Cato the Censor, the first of his family to reach high office. He was, to be sure, a valiant warrior, but his biographer Plutarch also underscores the boost Cato's tireless efforts as a pleader in the courts gave him early in his career (Plut. *Cato Mai.* 1.4–6, 3.3).

Skill as a public speaker was unquestionably essential for any public figure (see also Chapter 20). This was how magistrates and others persuaded assemblies of citizens to pass laws or give them their votes in elections. Generals, too, needed to address troops before battles and at other times as well. But beyond being a tool of leadership, public speaking, particularly speaking on behalf of parties to lawsuits, won friends, friends whose gratitude could become the currency that purchased political success. The "Handbook on Electioneering" (*Commentariolum Petitionis*) addressed to Cicero and perhaps written by his brother Quintus, emphasizes the importance of calling on the help of the friends Cicero had won by representing them in court in his campaign for the consulship (*Comm. Pet.* 19–20). Pleading on behalf of a party to a lawsuit or a criminal indictment was an important aspect of patronage, and while recent scholars have dethroned the patron–client relationship from the central role it was once thought to have played in determining the outcomes of political competition (see Chapter 1), the value aristocrats placed on their role as patrons cannot be gainsaid (see Chapter 19). As Plautus, writing in the early second century, has one of his characters say, "Everyone wants a mob of clients" (*Men.* 574), a desire reflected, too, in the architecture of aristocratic houses, with their ample courtyards (*atria*) and other reception rooms geared to receiving morning greetings (*salutationes*) of those who came to pay their respects and, often, to ask advice or seek favors (Vitr. 6.5.1–2; cf. Figures 24.14 and 15a–b and Chapters 19 and 24). Patronage linked individual aristocrats and families to both Romans and non-Romans beneath them in wealth, power, and/or dignity (termed "friends" [*amici*] if social equals or near-equals, "clients" otherwise) who in return for the favors and assistance (*beneficia*) they received were expected to display loyalty (*fides*) to the patrons who dispensed them. The value of "a mob of clients" lay less in their votes (although these were not unimportant) than in the social prestige they conferred upon their patron. In Rome, to seem important was in many ways to be important, and the greater the throng of people who attended a figure the more obvious was his eminence. They represented his "symbolic capital," a resource acquired through services bestowed on individual members of the crowd or on them collectively as citizens of the Republic. Thus Livy could represent Aemilianus' grandfather, the great Africanus, as descending to the Forum to meet his opponents in a political contest accompanied by a great host of friends and clients and then humiliating his enemies by departing to offer sacrifice in thanksgiving for his victory over Carthage accompanied by the entire assembly (Livy 38.51.6, 12–13). Cicero, too, measured his public standing by the size of his morning levee and the group that accompanied him down to the Forum (Cic. *Att.* 1.18.1, 2.22.3). Naturally the endorsement of such commanding figures counted for a great deal in a young aristocrat's climb up the political ladder. This was why Aemilianus' contemporaries spent their time pleading in the law courts and paying morning calls (Polyb. 31.29.8), both offering patronage and seeking it from others, weaving the fabric of social obligations that would support their struggle for office.

Thus some combination of the glory and renown a young aristocrat had won on the battlefield and perhaps in the courtroom, coupled with the support of those he had aided in their suits or in other ways and the backing of powerful patrons combined to form the foundation for his political career, a succession of campaigns for public offices that, if all went well, issued ultimately in tenure of those posts that brought military command – the consulship and, less frequently, the praetorship – wherein enormous glory could be won. Time and again, aristocrats celebrated their accomplishments in command of the Republic's armies, as in the list of cities captured and regions conquered in the inscription of Scipio Barbatus, quoted above, or those celebrated in that of his son (consul in 259, although again the inscription dates to the early second century): "Almost all agree that this man, Lucius Scipio, was the best of the good men at Rome. He was Barbatus' son, a consul, censor, and aedile among you. He took Corsica and the city of Aleria, and gave a temple to the storm gods in recompense for their help" (*CIL* 1.2.9 = *ROL* 4:5 no. 4).

Such achievements received their crowning reward in the triumph, a religious procession by a general and his army to the temple of Jupiter Greatest and Best, Rome's supreme deity, on Capitoline Hill to offer thanks for victory (see also Chapters 16 and 23). Both solemn and boisterous, the procession was also a celebration of the general himself, borne in a chariot and dressed to look like Jupiter. It was "the moment when a Roman knew he was first, best, and greatest," the acknowledgment that a man like Lucius Metellus had proven himself "the bravest general."[1] But while the claim to have conducted "the greatest affairs under his own authority" that follows in his eulogy certainly encompasses the military operations Metellus directed against the Carthaginians in his consulships and that won him his triumph, its scope is broader. Metellus distributed land to colonists and served as dictator to conduct elections in the absence of the consuls. Similarly, Barbatus' funeral inscription and that of his son list their tenures of the offices of aedile and censor as well as consul, and neither entailed military operations. Magistrates laid claim to glory on the basis of a wide variety of achievements. One boasted in an inscription dating to around 132 of building roads and bridges, rounding up fugitive slaves, and recovering public lands illegally occupied (*ILS* 23 = *ROL* 4:151 no. 11; see also Chapter 3). Laws were known by the names of the magistrates who proposed them; public buildings by the names of those who had overseen their construction. Serving as a general was simply one aspect, albeit an enormously important one, of service to the public affairs of the Romans, the *res publica populi Romani*. The latter were the source of glory and renown, warfare only insofar as it constituted the most important element in the city's business.

This strong link at Rome between service to the Republic and personal prestige had two important consequences. First, aristocratic ambition provided the impetus that made the government go. No salaries attached to public office; no professional bureaucracy managed the city's day-to-day affairs. The operation of the government depended entirely upon the voluntary efforts of individual members of the upper class who, in so doing, both sought prestige but at the same time defined themselves as members of the Republic's elite. Managing Rome's public business was simply what aristocrats did. The connection between glory and the *res publica* in turn was vital to the latter's success. Aristocratic ambition accounted for much of Rome's diplomatic and military aggressiveness since war afforded opportunities for the combats and conquests that bestowed glory (although this might be tempered by other factors; see also Chapter 26). Second, the linkage meant that office holding assumed enormous importance in the economy of aristocratic values, for it was tenure of a magistracy that enabled a person to perform the greatest services for Rome, confer the greatest benefits upon his fellow-citizens, and so win the greatest glory (see also Chapter 23). The nexus connecting a man's standing in the eyes of his community and office is evident not only in Polybius' description of aristocratic funerals, but even in the Latin term *honor* itself, which can mean both "honor" and "public office." More importantly, this nexus imparted to aristocratic culture its intense competitiveness, for the numbers of aedileships, praetorships, consulates, and censorships were strictly limited. There were always more aspirants than ambitions that could be accommodated. And by the death of Lucius Metellus at the latest, an informal hierarchy among the offices had developed, later codified in the Villian law of 180 which established minimum ages for magistracies. This "course of offices" (*cursus honorum*; see also Chapter 12) was so arranged that generally the higher one climbed, the fewer the places available on the next rung. Consequently, competition grew more intense the farther one rose until at the very pinnacle, the censorship, whose two holders were elected only once every five years or so, only the most eminent and successful figures – former consuls who often had won triumphs – were able to vie for it. Intense competitive pressures were also an important reason for the aristocracy to insist on strict limits to tenure of public office – usually one year – and to seek to limit opportunities to hold the same office a second time. Even at moments of grave military crisis, the Senate was loath to suspend normal contention for the consulship in favor of consensus candidates whose military experience the emergency might seem to demand.[2]

The intensity of competition for the highest magistracies, however, arose from more than simply the chance these afforded to manage the city's weightiest affairs, as important as that was. For the Republic could be served in other important ways, too, as Quintus Metellus' claim that his father had enjoyed the greatest honor, was a man of the highest wisdom, and was considered the top senator suggests. At some point fairly early in a young aristocrat's progress along the "course of offices" (usually at the next quinquennial review of the Senate after he had held a quaestorship or tribunate), the censors enrolled him in the Senate where the city's public business was identified, debated, and addressed through legislative initiatives, resolutions, and diplomacy. Yet the quality of the service a senator could render here was largely limited by the rank he had achieved. Deliberations proceeded according to *honor*: those who had held consulships (*consulares*) spoke first, beginning (until c.81) with the "First Senator" (*princeps senatus*) appointed by the censors when they drew up the list of senators.[3] Ex-praetors followed and so on down the hierarchy until a consensus had been reached or the senators were ready to vote. All too frequently junior members never got the chance to speak, or spoke only after senior figures had staked out the main positions in the debate.[4] Only those who had reached the highest offices regularly were able to give the Republic the full benefit of their wisdom and so claim to be a "top senator," one of the "first men of the state" (*principes civitatis*). These were men who by virtue of their services to the Republic had acquired the greatest prestige (*dignitas*) and whose advice was backed by great authority (*auctoritas*). Authority was fundamental to power in the Senate and influence within the Republic (see also Chapter 20). It conveyed something like a stamp of approval and so served in a sense to guarantee that the course of action advocated or the advice offered by someone who possessed it (an *auctor*) was right and proper by virtue of his record of achievement and the superior judgment and insight that it attested. As such, authority implicitly demanded trust (*fides*) on the part of those to whom it was directed, a demand difficult to resist except when opposed by the authority of a figure of equal or greater dignity.[5] Its potency in public debate is well illustrated by a famous episode from late in the life of Marcus Aemilius Scaurus, consul in 115, censor in 109, and First Senator. Quintus Varius, a tribune of the plebs and much junior to Scaurus, accused him in 90 of instigating the allies to revolt. Scaurus, old and ill, came into court and in response to the charge simply said, " 'Quintus Varius the Spaniard says that Marcus Scaurus, the First Senator, called the allies to revolt; Marcus Scaurus, the First Senator, denies it. There are no witnesses. Which of the two, Citizens, is it fitting for you to believe?' Scaurus' response so changed the minds of everyone that the charges were dismissed by the tribune himself" (Asc. 22C; see also Chapter 20). Public office was the gateway to authority and so the foundation of influence (*gravitas*) in the *res publica*, raising the stakes in electoral contests all the higher.

Service to the *res publica* and its connection to public office in turn played a vital role in establishing and sustaining the legitimacy of aristocratic rule. Polybius, in his well-known analysis of the Roman constitution, emphasizes the citizens' powers to bestow honor and inflict punishments through their votes in the public assemblies, powers "by which alone oligarchies and states and in sum the whole life of mankind are held together" (6.14.4). The Republic's rulers and those who aspired to join their ranks had to submit themselves repeatedly to popular judgment, not only in the formal contexts of elections, public speeches, or trials but informally, too, in the court of public opinion, as Scipio Aemilianus' acute consciousness of what people were saying about him and his poor reputation reveals. The quality and quantity of a man's services to the people, both individually and collectively, along with those of his ancestors constituted the basis for the people's judgment of his worthiness for high office – ultimately an evaluation of moral worth: "In truth, the people bestow offices on those who are worthy, which very things in a state are the finest prize for excellence of character" (Polyb. 6.14.9). The services one rendered to the *res publica* stemmed then from the kind of person one was, and the intense competition for office among aristocrats drove them individually to form themselves into the kinds of people worthy of such distinctions, men dedicated wholly and utterly to the public's welfare even to the point of the ultimate sacrifice.

> Many Romans have volunteered to decide a whole battle by single combat. Not a few have deliberately accepted certain death, some in time of war to secure the safety of the rest, some in time of peace to preserve the safety of the commonwealth. There have also been instances of men in office putting their own sons to death, in defiance of every custom and law, because they rated the interest of their country higher than those of natural ties even with their nearest and dearest. (Polyb. 6.54.4–5 [trans. Shuckburgh])

But at the same time, the judgments of character that these votes represented also constituted an act of acquiescence on the part of the public in the aristocracy's leadership, validating its right to rule. The collective ascendancy of the Senate, in other words, rested upon the citizens' regular, almost ritual approbation of individual aristocrats' claims to have lived up to the set of elite ideals that both Rome's rulers and the public embraced. With every public judgment that someone had so well served the *res publica* through his courage in battle, his solicitude for clients, and his management of the public's business that he deserved to be elevated to high office, the leadership of those who collectively embodied those ideals was legitimated and strengthened. And from this perspective, the pageantry that advertised the success of individual aristocrats in meeting these ideals – triumphs, funerals, and the like – was just one more way in which the public, by its participation and approval, could voice its acquiescence in and support for the moral economy that underpinned the elite's supremacy at Rome (see also Chapter 1). On the other hand, because aristocratic rule depended so much on aristocrats being seen to embrace the values of their class, the aristocracy was collectively vigilant in policing its moral boundaries, in seeing to it that service to the public remained the focus of aristocratic life and that deviations were repressed. The censors' quinquennial review of the Senate's membership and their expulsion of senators deemed to have fallen below the moral standards appropriate to their station represent only the most obvious example of the aristocracy's self-discipline. Cato the Elder as censor once expelled a senator for kissing his own wife in broad daylight in the presence of his daughter (Plut. *Cat. Mai.* 17.7), only one of the many moral rebukes delivered in a censorship renowned for enforcing rectitude and strict, old-fashioned virtue.

It is not surprising, therefore, that contemporary aristocratic testimony from this era seems to attach little value to much within the private lives of these men (see also Chapter 24). Lucius Metellus' many offspring were a point of pride; so, too, Scipio Hispanus' progeny. But their families' presence in these laudatory contexts seems to bespeak less the pleasure they gave their fathers than the services their sons would render the state and so their contributions to upholding the glory and status of their line. Hispanus' achievements had made his ancestors glad that he had been born, so his inscription claimed. The personal qualities of Marcus Cato, particularly his well-known severity, also derived their primary value in the eyes of his contemporaries from their application in the public sphere. His moral rectitude was celebrated (albeit most often by himself) for the contribution it made to his conduct of the Republic's business, in his censorship, for example, or in prosecuting Rome's war in Spain. In a speech recounting his achievements as consul there he proclaimed that he was generous to his soldiers in the matter of booty but took none for himself, preferring "to contend with the brave about bravery rather than about money with the richest and greed with the greediest" (Plut. *Cato Mai.* 10.4). Cato's rectitude in fiscal matters was hardly unique. Polybius insisted, despite the incredulity he anticipated among his Greek readers, that Roman aristocrats in his experience rarely embezzled public funds entrusted to them and were scrupulous in their private financial dealings (6.56.13–15, 31.26.1–27.16).

Yet wealth posed a troubling dilemma for Rome's rulers. Its potentially corrosive effects on central elements within the system of aristocratic values were obvious. Another of Cato's speeches complained that some people had purchased the enemy spoils they displayed on the walls of their homes rather than won them legitimately (*ORF*[4] Cato no. 8, 97; cf. Pliny *HN* 35.7). And the pursuit of money could easily subvert the ideal of public service. Metellus' son stressed that his father's wealth had been acquired "honorably," perhaps from that portion of the spoils of war that fell to a general as his share. But one cannot rule out the possibility of a canny head for business either. Cato's only surviving work, "On Agriculture" (*De agricultura*) is less a "how-to" manual for the few novice farmers among his aristocratic contemporaries than a celebration of his own hardheaded practicality, shrewdness, and skill in making his farms turn a profit. This exemplar of old-fashioned values could claim that a farmer whose storage facilities enabled him to hold his oil and wine until the market was ripe acquired *virtus* and *gloria* (!) thereby (*Agr.* 3.2). But farming was one thing, trade another. Cato also asserted that farmers produced the bravest, most energetic soldiers, and that farming was a particularly upright and stable way of making a living. Those who pursued it were least likely to be discontented. In other words, they made the best citizens. Trade, on the other hand, although sometimes more profitable than farming, was risky and ignoble (*Agr.* praef. 1–4). Obviously, aristocrats should keep away from it, and to ensure that they did legislation was passed around 219 prohibiting senators or their sons from owning oceangoing ships suitable for long-distance commerce. Yet it is revealing of the senators' ambivalence toward moneymaking that only one of them supported the law (Livy 21.63.3–4). Being rich was good and certainly necessary, although not sufficient, for membership in the Republic's ruling class (see also Chapter 14). Hence senators were loath to preclude the profits that could be gained here; even Cato himself pursued trading ventures, but only decently cloaked behind a front man (Plut. *Cato Mai.* 21.6).

But while wealth was hardly incompatible with the aristocratic ethos, this was so only to the extent that it could be accommodated within the overall framework of elite values. What most troubled Cato and other aristocrats of his generation was the connection of wealth with luxury and the turn toward private indulgence, vice, and foreign ways at the expense of dedication to public duty that luxury could entail. Cato as censor did his best to repress extravagance, and from time to time attempts were made to do so through sumptuary legislation as well. These reactions, coming at a time when some of Rome's conquests had brought great riches to the city and to a few among its elite, all attest to some degree of anxiety among aristocrats over the potentially pernicious effects of this sudden prosperity and its association with an embrace of Hellenistic cultural practices that in the minds of some threatened the very "Roman-ness" of Rome. However, charges of degeneracy and corruption also need to be understood as important tools for enforcing a code of social norms that empowered those who controlled them, men like Cato or, interestingly, the young Scipio Aemilianus. He won a great reputation among his contemporaries simply by leading an upright life and for his magnanimity and cleanhandedness in money matters at a time when the rest of the youth, Polybius assures his readers, were addicted to all manner of extravagance, corruption, and vice (Polyb. 31.25.2–8,

28.10–13), a rectitude on display again in later years when in 129 Aemilianus complained of the degeneracy of well-born young Romans in learning to sing and dance (Macr. *Sat.* 3.14.6–7)!

Yet it is clear that aristocratic norms and the values they reflected were evolving in complex ways even during Aemilianus' lifetime. Consider the "five greatest and chief good things" that his slightly younger contemporary, Publius Licinius Crassus Dives Mucianus (cos. 131), possessed in the judgment of the historian Sempronius Asellio who wrote about a generation later, early in the first century: He was the richest, the most noble, the most eloquent, the most learned in the law, and the chief priest (*pontifex maximus*) (Gell. *NA* 1.13.10). Strikingly absent is any reference to military glory, although Mucianus himself was hardly indifferent to it. He used his position as chief priest to elbow his colleague in the consulship out of the way on a religious technicality to obtain command of a war in Asia Minor. But it ended badly: not only was Mucianus defeated but captured and killed. That Asellio could still consider him a paragon despite his lack of success on the battlefield indicates that for Asellio martial courage was no longer the essential aristocratic virtue that Polybius had claimed only a few decades earlier. Instead, Asellio's emphasis on Mucianus' wealth (without specifying how he had obtained it) testifies to the increasing importance of money in an aristocrat's efforts to construct a favorable public image. Lavish public entertainments – shows, spectacles, feasts – had long been an element of aristocratic competition; what had changed was the scale on which such events were mounted. The first gladiatorial combats were presented in 264 by Marcus and Decimus Iunius Brutus Pera in honor of their late father (see also Chapter 16). Three pairs fought. By 174, the number of fighters had increased to 74 pairs (Livy 41.28.11). Such games could be extraordinarily expensive. Polybius estimated the cost at around 30 talents (one talent was about 26 kg of silver) "if they were done right," yet the entire fortune of Lucius Aemilius Paullus, consul in 182 and 168 and one of the leading senators of his day, amounted to only 60 talents when he died in 160 (Polyb. 31.28.3–7). Along with an increasing expectation of public largess, the cost of an aristocratic lifestyle was growing as well. The censors of 275 had expelled Publius Cornelius Rufinus, twice consul, from the Senate for possessing silver vessels weighing 10 lb, yet the consul of 121, Quintus Fabius Allobrogicus, had a silver service weighing a thousand times that (Val. Max. 2.9.4; Livy *Per.* 14; Pliny *HN* 33.141). In the minds of later authors this growth in private ostentation began in the early second century. Livy, writing under the emperor Augustus, claimed that lavishness and luxury had entered Rome with the elaborate dining room furniture, tableware, and other accoutrements of gracious living that Gnaeus Manlius Vulso brought back from his victory over the Hellenistic king Antiochus the Great and displayed in his triumph in 187 (Livy 39.6.7–9). But the historian Lucius Calpurnius Piso Frugi, consul in 133 and censor in 120, seems already to have fixated on the same event a century before Livy, and Polybius, too, located the beginnings of decadence among the aristocracy in the mid-second century (Pliny *HN* 34.14; Polyb. 31.25.2–8). Increasing expectations of openhandedness and splendor on the part of the political elite in turn led to a growing emphasis on wealth, escalating pressure to acquire it and hence to an increase in their readiness to abuse provincials for gain. Rome passed its first law defining the extortion of money by magistrates from foreigners as a crime in 149, but it did little to curb the problem. Gaius Gracchus, in a speech before the populace in 124, defended his conduct as quaestor in Sicily thus: "I returned to Rome with my money-belts, which I'd taken out full of silver, empty... others took back home amphoras, which they had brought out filled with wine, stuffed with silver" (Gell. *NA* 15.12.4). Money from foreign cities and rulers, too, began to flow into the purses of influential senators in Rome. Such "gifts" were nothing more than bribes, so Gaius charged in a speech on another occasion (Gell. *NA* 11.10.2–6). Similar accusations – accompanied occasionally by public outrage and judicial condemnation – henceforth formed a regular feature of political invective, while the effects of the aristocracy's growing wealth began to be felt in political competition. A series of laws, starting with the *lex Cornelia Baebia* of 181 and extending down to the end of the Republic, sought to stem the tide of electoral corruption and bribery, largely without success.

Oratory remains in Asellio's view supremely important, all the more so in view of the growing need to sway popular assemblies in the intensified political competition over legislation that developed during the last third of the second century. But the stress on eloquence also reflects a rapidly increasing sophistication in its practice through the elaboration of technique under the influence of Hellenistic rhetorical teachers and treatises. It was no longer enough simply to be a forceful speaker like Cato; one needed considerable coaching and practice in order to construct the arguments and command the rhetoric that would persuade. The level of skill and accomplishment required to compete in the public assemblies meant that political success was increasingly open only to those who could afford the necessary education (see also Chapter 20). The importance that Asellio attaches to Mucianus' mastery of the law likewise attests to a growing refinement in its analysis and interpretation during his lifetime with the rise of the *iurisconsulti*, one of the most important of whom was Mucianus' brother by birth, Publius Mucius Scaevola (see also Chapter 11). But again, this development simply represents an elaboration of the traditional importance the aristocratic value system attached to the services a patron offered both as a legal adviser to those who sought his guidance and as an advocate in court. However, as both legal science and rhetoric became more complex and the level of skill requisite to excel in each grew, a bifurcation, termed "structural differentiation," began to develop whereby each discipline ultimately acquired its own institutional structures and personnel.[6] Mucianus stands at its beginning. He still united command of both fields in his own person, yet Asellio could present them as separate and distinct areas of aristocratic achievement.

A similar process of differentiation may lurk behind the prominence Asellio gives to Mucianus' office of chief priest. Religion was another aspect of the public business for which the city's aristocracy had long taken responsibility, both collectively, since the Senate superintended Rome's relations with the gods, and individually, by serving in various individual priesthoods and on the three great boards of priests. The Republic's elected magistrates, too, were charged with conducting the ceremonies and sacrifices through which the city assured itself of divine support in its endeavors. The Romans viewed that support, the product of the peace of the gods (*pax deorum*), as the bedrock of their community's well-being and success (see also Chapter 10) whence arose its vital importance in the eyes of both the citizens and their leaders. Polybius was struck by the prominence accorded to religious rituals at Rome (Polyb. 3.112.6–9, 6.56.6–8). But although Lucius Metellus had been a pontiff, his son elected to pass over his father's religious prominence in his eulogy. Scipio Barbatus, too, had been a pontiff, in fact probably the chief priest in his day, yet this finds no mention on his tomb inscription. Asellio's decision to place this office among the "five greatest and chief goods" therefore may reflect the early first century's increasing perception of religious knowledge as a distinct category of aristocratic attainment, like oratory and legal science, rather than something lumped in among the general, all-purpose service to the Republic's public affairs and the private interests of clients that any aristocrat was expected to render.

Interesting, too, from this perspective is Asellio's emphasis on Mucianus' pedigree: he was "the most noble." The Latin word *nobilitas*, usually translated, as here, "nobility" but perhaps more accurately as "notability" or "celebrity," had acquired by at least the early second century the secondary meaning of "aristocracy." By the age of Cicero, however, it had come to define not the aristocracy as a whole but an elite within it, those whose ancestors had held high public office – generally speaking, the consulship, although this point is debated (see also Chapter 1).[7] The members of the nobility both self-consciously defined themselves as an inner elite and further believed that their ancestry entitled them to those same offices, again the consulship in particular. Modern scholarship usually identifies the period around 300 as the point at which the nobility first developed in consequence of the patricians' gradual accommodation of plebeian leaders' demands for access to the consulship and other high offices. Thereafter both ancestry and accomplishment figured in the electoral calculus. While the former might qualify someone to compete for office and could constitute a strong recommendation, a candidate had to be able to show through his own attainments at war and in other endeavors that he was worthy to hold it. Those who could do so not only led the Republic but bestowed upon their descendants nobility, the lustrous afterglow of their glory that in turn constituted a benchmark against which succeeding generations had to measure themselves. Scions of the nobility had to demonstrate to voters that they could meet the high standards of service set by their ancestors, a burden whose weight Scipio Aemilianus certainly felt, as noted above. And having done so, a man could take a satisfied pride in the accomplishment, as Scipio Hispanus did in the inscription that graced his tomb.

Although scholars debate just how exclusive this inner circle within the aristocracy was during the middle and late Republic, its existence cannot be denied.[8] The proportion of consuls whose fathers or grandfathers had held that same office is very high in the period 179–49, well over half, and if one includes those with a more distant consular ancestor the count rises to about 80 percent (see also Chapter 1). A comparable count back to 300 would undoubtedly yield similar proportions. But when precisely this group developed a self-conscious identity is unclear. Interestingly, Scipio Hispanus not only proclaimed his emulation of his father's exploits but further that "my office has ennobled my descendants." Hispanus' family was among the most eminent and ancient of aristocratic houses, boasting consuls back to the fourth century, yet Hispanus himself never reached the consulship. He was praetor in 139 and apparently died not long thereafter. One would think his insistence on the luster his praetorship bestowed upon his progeny scarcely worth the trouble. But it may in fact reflect the development around this time of a consciousness that descent from earlier officeholders was yet another criterion of aristocratic self-definition, part of the increasing complexity and differentiation that aristocratic identity was then undergoing, reflected also in Asellio's identification of Mucianus' "greatest nobility" as a discrete element among the latter's "five greatest and chief goods."

If this is what was going on, then the absence of any mention of Mucianus' martial qualities may simply reflect another aspect of this process. By Cicero's day a category of experts within the upper class could be identified, the "military men" (*viri militares*). To be sure, ordinary aristocrats still officered the legions and led Rome's armies; the greatest glory still derived from leading Roman arms to victory. But technical skill in military operations was thought to reside in a smaller group of specialists who were then beginning to define themselves and be identified by others primarily by knowledge that once had been assumed to be general among the Republic's elite. Marius famously based his claim to the consulate in 107, in the speech to the people that Sallust gives him, on his first-hand experience of war in contrast to those aristocrats from prominent families who needed to read books to learn generalship upon becoming consuls (Sall. *Iug.* 85.5–12). And around the late second or early first century the requirement of ten years' prior military service for candidates for public office seems to have been abandoned, so that men of Cicero's generation often had little of the direct experience of war that would have enabled them to assert that they were "first-class warriors."

Still, none of these categories was exclusive; as Mucianus' example demonstrates, excellence in more than one could be claimed by a single individual. Rather, an increasingly multifaceted and elaborate aristocratic ethos was evolving out of a more unitary system of values as Roman society and culture evolved along similar lines. And the process continued into the last decades of the Republic. A very great deal of evidence for these developments might be brought forward, particularly from the works of Cicero, but perhaps the most revealing single passage comes not from that author but from his younger contemporary, Sallust, who drew the following well-known comparison between two of the most prominent figures from the Republic's last generation, Cato the Younger and Caesar. Both men, Sallust wrote, possessed outstanding *virtus*, meaning here "personal excellence" rather than the simple "courage" that the term conveyed among earlier generations. But the excellence of each man, in Sallust's view, was manifested in a quite different way.

Each was roughly equal in birth, age, and eloquence; in greatness of mind they were on a par, likewise in renown, but differently in each. Caesar was considered great because of his favors and his lavishness, Cato because of the uprightness of his life. His kindness and compassion made the former famous; sternness increased the dignity of the latter. Caesar gained renown by giving, by supporting, and by forgiving, Cato by overlooking nothing. In the one was a refuge for the wretched, in the other a bane for the evil. The indulgence of the one was praised, the steadfastness of the other. Ultimately, Caesar determined to labor and be vigilant, to focus on his friends' affairs and ignore his own, to deny nothing that was worthy to give. He was hoping for a great command for himself, an army, and a new war where his excellence could shine. But Cato's passion was for self-restraint, propriety, and above all sternness. He did not contend with the rich in riches or with the partisan in partisanship but with the vigorous in excellence, with the decorous in decency, and with the innocent in refraining from wrongdoing. He preferred to be rather than to seem good. So the less he sought renown, the more it followed him. (Sall. *Cat.* 54.1–6)

Caesar's ambitions in Sallust's presentation seem very traditional: the glory and fame derived from military conquest. But the qualities that would propel him to the offices wherein he could win these laurels were those of character rather than prior services to Rome as a warrior. Even Caesar's efforts on behalf of others, which fall squarely within the traditional role of patron, seem less a matter of what he did than of the kind of person he was. In Cato this shift is even more marked. Sallust has very little to say about what Cato accomplished for the Republic or his friends. He focuses instead on those aspects of his character that contributed to Cato's renown. The point to stress here is not that earlier Romans were not compassionate or severe; indeed, Cato's great-grandfather, Cato the Censor, was much celebrated for the latter quality. Nor can one claim that the great-grandson failed to pursue a conventional career of both public service and private benefaction. Rather what demands attention is Sallust's focus not on Cato's or even Caesar's achievements but the character of each man. Personal deportment, moral and ethical qualities, and adherence to principle now count as crucial values for Sallust, alongside of, or even in lieu of, the sorts of attainments that aristocrats had long been accustomed to use as their yardstick of self-worth. To be sure, this emphasis derives in large part from Sallust's preoccupation with *virtus* as the foundation of Roman greatness and the role of moral decline in the Republic's collapse into civil war. But the theme resonated with Sallust's audience and was of course taken up and elaborated by writers during the Augustan age, and it is no coincidence that their embrace of an aristocratic ethos that stressed individual character developed at the very moment when Caesar's victory in the civil wars of 49–45 was changing fundamentally the ground rules of aristocratic competition and ending political liberty (*libertas*) at Rome forever.

Liberty is a complex concept, important aspects of which bear on the relationship of ordinary citizens to the government of Rome, both in terms of the rights and protections they enjoyed and their role in elections and legislation (see also Chapters 14 and 18). But for aristocrats, an essential component was the freedom of the city's public affairs from the control of a tyrant or a small clique (*factio*) and consequently the freedom of individual aristocrats to compete to serve the Republic through office holding, legislation, or participation in other public matters and to serve the interests of friends and clients through patronage. Caesar and subsequently his adoptive son Augustus imposed strict limits on that freedom. Although aristocrats continued to seek prestige from holding public office, playing a prominent role in public affairs, and serving the interests of friends and clients after 44, the extent to which they could do so was entirely at the whim of the emperor. A monarchy precluded the open political competition that was the foundation of aristocratic liberty. Now whatever glory and renown were to be gained from serving the *res publica* would be apportioned as the emperor saw fit. Monarchy also subverted the moral economy that had sustained aristocratic authority in the Republic. Offices and honor came no longer from the people's acknowledgment of individual character and achievement but through imperial favor. Patronage, too, henceforth derived ultimately from the same source. Consequently, their inner lives were all that aristocrats could truly claim to control any more. Virtues like those of Sallust's Cato became in the minds of his contemporaries the only venue for free rivalry and achievement, the only arena of aristocratic endeavor wherein liberty was still possible and true glory and renown might still be won.

The evolution in the aristocracy's value system also bears upon the problem of their cohesion. How an elite whose ethos embraced an intense, lifelong rivalry for prominence could nevertheless find a basis for cooperation has rarely received sustained scholarly attention, but obviously their ability to find commonality amid a welter of competing self-interests facilitated not only the Republic's system of government but also its acquisition of an empire. And the failure of that consensus in turn helped direct those same aristocratic energies against one another in two devastating spasms of civil war. In seeking to account for these phenomena, a relatively narrow range of values – prowess in war, efforts as a patron, service to the general public business, limited ways of gaining and displaying wealth – contributed powerfully to consensus and thus cohesion within a highly competitive system. Merit could be fairly easily defined even as who had more of it was being hotly contested. But the process grew more difficult once the range of values and attainments became wider and more differentiated. Who was to say whether the moral integrity of someone like Cato outweighed Caesar's selfless efforts on behalf of his friends in the struggle for glory and praise? The Republic's changing circumstances simply compounded the problem since values could have quite different weights in the eyes of the public and the aristocrats themselves as perceptions of Rome's situation altered. Being a "first-class warrior" counted for quite a bit more in the dangerous and threatening world of third-century Italy than in the age of Cicero when Roman power was unassailable.

Yet for a long time the consensus held, for the system of aristocratic values also acted in ways to limit competition as well as foster it, and in so doing protected the Republic and its ruling class from some of its detrimental consequences. So for example, a serious threat to liberty lay in the monopolization of offices by one or a few men. Since tenure of public office, particularly the consulship, was crucial to attaining glory and renown, repeated tenure of this office could easily breed resentment and division within the aristocracy's ranks. Therefore law and custom limited the degree of electoral success anyone could attain. Public offices could only be held for one year and reelection to the same office was restricted. A ten-year interval was required between one term as consul and the next, and after c.152 iteration was forbidden altogether. These rules aimed to prevent any single person or small group from so dominating the Republic's highest magistracies that they thereby acquired prestige, glory, and hence authority great enough to dominate the *res publica*. Equally important, the regulations made opportunities to win offices and honor widely available within the aristocracy, which in turn helped foster concord. Many could believe they stood a chance of winning these offices (even though not all of them would), and so were willing to endorse the competition and the system of governance based on it.

But ultimately the aristocracy itself had to make and enforce these regulations, while the citizens of Rome, through their votes at elections or in legislative assemblies, were the arbiters of the rivalry the limits restricted, and circumstances could easily arise to induce senators and voters to violate them. The exigencies of war are a case in point. The Republic recruited its armies from the citizens who elected its consuls; the sons of senators served, too. And any aristocracy has a strong interest in enhancing the military effectiveness of the state it rules. In such circumstances how could the need to share out opportunities for honor widely within the ranks of the ruling class prevail over the demands of war? Why did concern to place experienced generals with a record of success in command not lead the Senate and the voters to elevate the same few men to the consulship time and again, former consuls whose earlier victories might seem to offer the strong likelihood of more to come? The questions are hardly hypothetical. The citizenry on many occasions reelected former consuls, despite laws limiting or forbidding altogether repetition of this office, often with the Senate's blessing.

Yet the overall trend is otherwise: between 300 and 49 the percentage of consulships held by ex-consuls declined markedly. Competition was fostered and cohesion enhanced despite the pressures of war. But occasional illicit reelections attest the frailty of the laws intended to control them and underscore the ineffectiveness of any system of rules in the absence of a strong commitment to abide by them, and a commitment of this sort could only come from a framework of beliefs and values that validated the presumptions upon which such limits rested. So in selecting consuls, aristocrats and the public made their choices acting under the belief that *any* high-ranking senator was capable of leading a Roman army to victory because success sprang far less from technical training and hands-on experience than from a general's personal character, that is, his *virtus*. And *virtus*, which any aristocrat from early on had striven to demonstrate, all aristocrats could claim, especially those whose ancestors' offices and achievements bestowed upon them a greater measure of it than others – even with little direct experience in command, even if prior attempts had been disastrous failures. Values that enabled aristocrats and ordinary citizens alike to agree to evaluate claims to military leadership in this way built support for a system of governance that placed many different members of the ruling class in these positions and so fostered cohesion. Similarly, an ideology that valorized aristocratic dedication to public service and to advancing the interests of clients and friends built consensus around the value system itself while nonetheless permitting a vigorous competition to win honor in pursuit of the myriad endeavors these principles encompassed.

Guide to Further Reading

The ethos of the Republican aristocracy is a vast and complex topic, aspects of which impinge upon the subject matter of several of the contributions to this volume, to which the reader is directed for detailed bibliography and suggestions for further reading. There is currently no good synthetic work in English on the topic. Earl 1961 and 1967 are now very much out of date; for a descriptive catalogue of virtues see Lind 1979 and 1986 and, in French, Hellegouarc'h 1963. On the prominence of war in the aristocratic value system Harris 1979 is fundamental. On cavalry service, wounds, and scars, see Oakley 1985, Leigh 1995, and now McCall 2002. For aristocratic funerals, Flower 1996 is basic. On *virtus* see McDonnell 1990, unfortunately not easily available (but see now McDonnell 2006). Work on the moral economy of Rome has mainly been in German, e.g., Hölkeskamp 1987, Flaig 2003, but see now Morstein-Marx 2004. Shatzman 1975 surveys the evidence for the wealth of senators and their attitudes toward it; Gruen 1992 covers the confrontation of Roman aristocratic values and Greek culture; and on Roman "decadence" see Edwards 1993. On Cato the Censor and Scipio Aemilianus: Astin 1967, 1978. For electoral corruption, see Lintott 1990 and Yakobson 1999. On the nobility, Gelzer 1969 (translating a work that first appeared in 1912) is essential, although Brunt 1982 challenges his definition of *nobilitas*. See also Hölkeskamp 1993. On nobility and the consulship, see Hopkins and Burton 1983 and Badian 1990a. For "structural differentiation" see Hopkins 1978. *Viri Militares*: Smith 1958. On oratory, see now Morstein-Marx 2004. For *libertas*, see Wirszubski 1968, and on the aristocracy's response to its loss of freedom under the emperors, see especially Barton 1993. On the limitation of aristocratic competition, see Rosenstein 1990, 1993.

Notes

1   Wiseman 1985: 4.
2   Rosenstein 1993.
3   After c.81 BC the custom of naming a *princeps senatus* seems to have lapsed; thereafter the two consuls-elect – if elections had taken place – initiated debate.
4   *Contra*, however, Ryan 1998.
5   Galinsky 1996: 12–16.
6   Hopkins 1978: 74–96.
7   Gelzer 1969; Brunt 1982; Hölkeskamp 1993.
8   Hopkins and Burton 1983; Badian 1990a.

CHAPTER 18

Popular Power in the Roman Republic

Alexander Yakobson

The Nature of the Debate

How real was the power of the People in the Roman Republic? The legal powers of the assemblies were wide-ranging. Throughout the history of the Republic, all laws and elections of magistrates depended on a popular vote in these assemblies. Major political (and some other) trials were regularly brought before the People down to the time of Sulla; popular votes often determined issues of war and peace, either directly or indirectly, through tribunician bills conferring "extraordinary commands" (see also Chapter 12). But how real was all this? Wasn't the Roman Republic, after all, an oligarchy run by a narrow ruling class? Were the various forms of popular participation in politics more than a charade, a smokescreen, mere lip service? And even if they were more than that – how much more? How free were the voters when they voted, and did the wishes of the populace, in the final analysis, really matter? How did the enormous economic and social disparities within the citizen body affect the balance of power within the Roman political system? Did this system include a significant democratic element – something that was claimed by Polybius in his famous account of Rome's "mixed constitution" (6.11–18), but denied or doubted by many modern historians?

These questions have for some time been at the heart of a vigorous scholarly debate (see also Chapter 1). Anything approaching a consensus can hardly be expected. This, of course, is not unusual for debates touching on broad questions of interpretation. Perhaps, however, there is a deeper reason for the persistent and rather fierce disagreement in this case. Not uniquely, but still to a greater degree than in many other cases, the debate on the power of the People versus the power of the elite in Rome resounds with echoes of our own views, perceptions, assumptions, and prejudices on some of the most vital and controversial issues of modern society and politics. This inevitable modern "contamination" of the scholarly controversy might as well be acknowledged, so that we may try to contain and control it.

We may, and should, remind ourselves that our business is to analyze Roman society, not to make value judgments about it; that, for the purposes of this analysis, our own views on democracy and oligarchy, populism and elitism are irrelevant; that, moreover, modern political terms sometimes have a very different meaning than ancient ones, even when the same words are employed. Nevertheless, we find it hard to operate with such terms as democracy, popular power, elite control and manipulation, as if these were purely analytical concepts. In our world, "dignifying" a political system with the name of democracy (or, in Rome's case, conceding that it had a significant democratic aspect) amounts, almost inevitably, to a value judgment – sometimes highly controversial, often influenced by ideological preferences. Moreover, we are used to various modern regimes posing as democracies without justification, or pretending to be more democratic than they are; we will not always recognize as genuinely democratic even a political system which (unlike the Roman Republic) has all the trappings of a democracy and officially defines itself as such. Finally, a modern critical observer tends to look beyond constitutional and legal norms and examine whether a given social structure can be described as truly democratic. Do we then wish to use this term (even in a qualified way) when describing the Roman Republic with the immense wealth, power, influence and prestige of its elite, with its powerful Senate, with its proud nobles who, in Sallust's famous metaphor (*Iug.* 63.6–7), passed the highest offices of state from hand to hand?

On the other hand, it may be objected that our reluctance to concede that there were genuinely democratic elements in the Roman political system (i.e., that the formal competence of the assemblies translated itself into real political power) stems largely from an unrealistic, idealized concept of democracy in general, and, in particular, of how a modern democracy actually works. Is not a modern democratic electorate sometimes influenced, manipulated, brainwashed, bribed by the political and social elite – occasionally into betraying what some consider to be its true interests? Do not huge disparities in wealth and social status often go hand in hand with a highly developed political democracy (and sometimes with an officially proclaimed social one)? Is a voter in a modern democracy always free from social and economic constraints? Is not he (or she; here, indeed, there is a radical difference between our world and the ancient one; see also Chapter 15) sometimes influenced by patronage, by deference to social superiors, by family and clan loyalties, by the prestige of a renowned family name, by the power of a dominant ideology? And when the People have voted – are all important questions of public policy invariably settled according to the outcome of their vote? Have modern social elites never monopolized (or nearly monopolized) the higher offices of state? And generally, how far is the life of a modern democratic society really shaped by the wishes of "the populace"?

It can thus be argued that many (though not all) of the "oligarchic" features of Roman society and politics are merely another example of the "iron law of oligarchy" in action. This modern maxim asserts that in every social system, including formally democratic ones, a powerful ruling elite will inevitably emerge. Indeed, it has been argued that the People's power was exercised in Rome (principally through legislation) more directly, and thus, in an important sense, more effectively, than in modern representative democracies.[1] In the Late Republic, the People's power to legislate against the wishes of the majority of the elite was repeatedly exercised by tribunes of the plebs bringing highly controversial measures before the plebeian tribal assembly. From time to time this had also happened in earlier periods. Polybius, in his mid-second-century account, describes legislation against the wishes of the Senate, initiated by tribunes, as a realistic possibility – part of the balance on which the republican system rested (6.16.3). What, it may be asked, would modern democratic politics look like, if every law had to be passed by popular referendum, in a manner comparable to the Roman system allowing each of the ten tribunes to propose laws on issues of highest importance? What, indeed, would modern democracies look like if every year were to be an election year, as in Rome (with the campaign taking up a good part of it, as canvassing for the consulship often did in the Late Republic)? The relative importance of such considerations on the one hand, and of the undemocratic features of Roman politics (including the absence of universal and equal suffrage) on the other, is of course debatable. It is worth noting that in Athens, "one man, one vote" obtained since the days of Solon – long before the emergence of democracy. In a modern democracy, "one person, one vote" is such a fundamental principle that no polity can even pretend to be democratic without applying it. It is, then, highly significant that this principle did not apply in Rome – especially in the centuriate assembly (although the extent of the resulting inequality and disfranchisement is debatable). On the other hand, it is a historical fact that the representative system has been advocated, in preference to direct democracy – for example, by the authors of the "Federalist Papers" – precisely on the grounds that it made it possible to "tame" the dangerous power of the masses. The American "founding fathers" were willing to accept wide (though not universal) popular suffrage, but not a direct power of political decision-making by the People.

These observations may produce in some, instead of openness to the idea that certain features of Roman politics were genuinely democratic, a cynical dismissal of democracy in general. But this need not be so. What the "iron law of oligarchy" asserts is that there is always an oligarchy – not that all oligarchies are alike, that powerful elites are necessarily (or even typically) all-powerful and free to disregard the people's wishes, that constitutional structures are merely a charade, or that public opinion doesn't matter. Thus, while it is obvious that any account of the Roman assemblies' legal powers cannot be regarded as "the whole story," we should not therefore assume that it is not an important – perhaps very important, vitally important – part of it. Or should we? Given the well-known formal and informal constraints and limitations, how important, in the final analysis, could the power of the Roman People be? While I strongly incline to the view that the power accorded to the People was, so far from being mere charade, a vitally important part of the republican political system, it might as well be admitted that there can probably be no clear-cut, "scientifically objective" answer to such a question.

The Senatorial Perspective

How did the Romans themselves see it? The voices that our sources enable us to hear are mainly – almost exclusively – those belonging to the elite: the class of office holders and office seekers, coming chiefly from senatorial, but sometimes from other upper-class families. Did, then, Roman senators regard their class as (nearly) all-powerful, and the popular aspects of politics as merely a sham? When a senator faced, as he had to do quite often, a popular vote that affected him, his family and friends, or the interests of his class – could he usually await its outcome with equanimity? Did Roman aristocrats behave as if public opinion didn't matter, or mattered little?

The answer provided by the sources to these questions is, it seems, generally negative. Indeed, as regards elections, even the most aristocratic reading of republican politics can hardly postulate equanimity on the part of the average aristocratic candidate, since one aristocratic candidate's victory would typically mean another aristocratic candidate's defeat. This gave the voting populace an important leverage in its relations with the elite. As for legislation, the history of the "Struggle of the Orders," as told by our sources, abounds with instances of the assemblies legislating against the wishes of the patrician nobility. The Middle Republic appears to have been a period of relative "harmony" in this respect (not a complete one, as we shall see); in the Late Republic, notoriously, the more democratic tribal assembly was quite capable of legislating against the wishes of the majority of the Senate. Moreover, powerful nobles were certainly not immune to the danger of conviction, and sometimes severe punishment, by a popular assembly (tribal or centuriate) – from the early days of the Republic, according to traditional accounts. Plenty of such cases are attested for the "harmonious" Middle Republic.[2] It is thus hardly surprising that senators did not, in general, speak – or behave – as if the assemblies did not matter.

This conclusion is of obvious significance. The senatorial elite consisted, by definition, of people who depended on repeated popular election to the magistracies; they knew well how the structures of power – formal and informal – operated in their society. Their assessment of the balance of power in it cannot be lightly dismissed. Of course, it might be colored by their own ideological perceptions. A Roman senator was perhaps even less able than a modern historian to assess the extent of the People's power in the state without being influenced by his views on how much – or how little – power should, ideally, be entrusted to the People. So when we hear (as we shortly will) complaints that the power of the multitude is enormous, scandalous, that the good and the great – the *boni* – are left without any influence – all this should not of course be taken at face value.

More telling are the assessments manifested, indirectly but powerfully, in the actual political and social behavior of these people. The sources testify to the persistent efforts of Roman senators to gain and maintain popularity, to ingratiate themselves with the plebs, to outstrip their fellow-"oligarchs" in this respect. Much of Roman public life, and of senators' social life, can be said to have consisted of those efforts. A member of the Roman elite was constantly engaged in a fiercely competitive race with other members of his class (see also Chapters 14 and 17). The results of this race were determined to a large degree (though not exclusively) by popular support – principally through elections, but also in various other ways. Sometimes this quest for popularity, for the power based on popular support, and for the prizes that went with this power, led those people to espouse controversial popular causes. This might bring them into bitter conflict with the majority of the Senate.

In the turbulent last century of the Republic this was an important feature of Roman politics. The fundamental logic of the system – that of aristocratic competition – might tempt ambitious aristocrats, sometimes precisely the most self-confident and daringly ambitious, to act against the collective interests of the elite. This must account, to a large extent, for the phenomenon of "Popular" (*popularis*) politicians – although, of course, there is no need to dismiss the possibility that some of them were genuine reformers and "friends of the People." At any rate, the late-republican *populares* – starting with Tiberius Gracchus and his agrarian law – were not typically enemies of the Senate deliberately seeking to destroy its authority (nor is there any reason to assume that such an objective would have enjoyed wide popular support). They were politicians pursuing a senatorial career and making use (sometimes only at a certain stage of it) of the popular element in the republican political system – above all, of the People's powers of legislation. What set them apart was that – in the opinion of the majority of the Senate – they played this card excessively and irresponsibly. *Popularis* laws might confer material benefits on the plebs – as did the various agrarian laws, or the laws providing the city populace with grain at a lowered price (passed by Gaius Gracchus in 123) and eventually free of charge (passed by Clodius in 58). They might also effect changes (significant, but never truly revolutionary) in the Roman system of government itself – for example, when the senators' control over standing courts was removed (Gaius Gracchus, in 123) or weakened, or when the election of priests was handed over to the People (Domitius Ahenobarbus, in 104), or when the use by the elite of procedural devices to obstruct undesirable popular legislation was curtailed (Clodius, in 58).[3]

Alongside this structural incentive for aristocratic radicalism there existed, naturally, strong disincentives. The resentment of one's peers and seniors was not a thing to be lightly incurred. Most senators used more conventional – less controversial and dangerous – means of competing for the People's favor. They won wars, celebrated triumphs, distributed booty, displayed the masks of their famous ancestors at funeral processions, constructed public buildings. They cultivated the reputation of generous patrons and benefactors; they provided the plebs with "bread and circuses," staged games, spectacles, and gladiatorial contests, they pumped enormous sums of money into the electorate in order to improve, directly or indirectly, legally or illegally, their chances of climbing the ladder of magistracies (see also Chapter 16). Thus they manipulated and bribed the populace into accepting and maintaining the power of the elite; or, seen from another angle, they rendered unto the People that which, under the ground rules of republican politics, was due to the People. The elitist and popular aspects of republican politics are, to a large degree, precisely that – two aspects, two different ways to look at the same interaction between the populace and the elite. Of course, there is no true symmetry here: nobody will argue that the power of the elite was merely an illusion, while many scholars do argue that the power of the common people was, if not wholly illusory, then certainly far too limited to be defined as a genuine and significant democratic element in the system. Which brings us back to the question of how these things looked from the viewpoint of the Roman elite.

Cicero's *Laws* and the People's Power

The third book of Cicero's political dialogue *On the Laws* (*De Legibus*) provides an important testimony. In this sequel to his *On the Commonwealth* (*De re publica*), written in the late 50s and perhaps still under revision until his death, Cicero describes the laws of a well-governed commonwealth as nearly identical to those of the Roman Republic – which seemed to him, in its uncorrupted form, the nearest approximation possible to an ideal state. Cicero, who had adopted in the earlier work Polybius' definition of Rome as a "mixed and balanced polity" combining the royal, aristocratic, and democratic elements (represented by the consuls, the Senate, and the assemblies), now introduces in his code of laws two of the most conspicuously popular features of republican politics: the powers of the tribunes of the plebs, and secret voting in the assemblies. On both these points he is vigorously opposed by his brother Quintus. In the two ensuing debates, Quintus represents an undiluted "optimate" point of view – (i.e., one that favored maintaining the authority of the Senate and the social influence of the elite). Marcus (who had started his career with some moderately "Popular" credentials but later adopted a pragmatic but distinctly optimate stance) defends his proposals and the need to concede those two rights to the People. The two debates touch, directly or indirectly, on almost every point of controversy in the modern argument about the political character of the Republic.

Quintus (*Leg.* 3.19–22) attacks the tribunate as "a pernicious thing, born in sedition [during the so-called Struggle of the Orders] and promoting sedition":

> What damage it caused! First, true to its impious nature, it deprived the senators of every honor, made whatever was base equal to the best, upset and confused everything. Even after it had overthrown the authority of the leading men it never rested. For, to say nothing of Gaius Flaminius and the events of the distant past, what rights did Tiberius Gracchus' tribunate leave good citizens? (*Leg.* 3.19–20)

But the troubles did not start in 133: Quintus relates that five years earlier a "mean and vile" tribune of the plebs had cast two eminent consuls into prison. He then marshals the turbulent "Popular" tribunes of the Late Republic: Gaius Gracchus, who "wholly subverted the constitution"; "Saturninus, Sulpicius and the rest whose assaults the Republic could not repel without resorting to arms" (*Leg.* 3.20); and finally, P. Clodius Pulcher, M. Cicero's nemesis who briefly drove him into exile for unlawfully executing the Catilinarian conspirators, and who carried the law conferring on the Roman plebs a privilege it would retain for centuries – free grain. Concluding his speech, Quintus praises Sulla for curtailing the tribunes' powers during his dictatorship; on Pompey's restoration of them in 70 he will say nothing, being unable to praise and unwilling to criticize.

Quintus' claims that the tribunate robbed the Roman elite of all its influence should naturally be taken with a considerable amount of salt. Nevertheless, the passage clearly portrays the tribunate as more than a minor irritation from the senatorial point of view. Moreover, the tribunate of Tiberius Gracchus was not, according to Quintus, the first "modern" realization of this institution's subversive potential. In his second speech, Quintus deals with the ballot laws. This, again, brings him to the good old days before the Gracchi. These days, it turns out, were not quite so good as to rule out mischievous popular legislation undermining the power of the elite. This time, Marcus Cicero himself professes to be uncertain on the "difficult and much debated question" whether votes should be recorded openly or secretly. In principle, of course, open voting is preferable, but "the question is whether or not this can be obtained" (*Leg.* 3.33). But Quintus refuses to accept his brother's implied assumption that one cannot swim against the tide of public opinion:

> This view... is very frequently injurious to the state: namely, when something that is thought to be right and proper is considered unattainable on the grounds that the people cannot be opposed. But firstly they can be opposed, if one acts with determination; moreover, it is better to be violently overthrown while defending a good cause than to yield to an evil one. For who is unaware that the ballot laws have deprived the champions of the senate of all their influence?... A hiding-place should not have been given to the people where the ballot can conceal a mischievous vote while keeping good citizens in ignorance of each voter's opinions. (*Leg.* 3.34.)

He proceeds with a hostile account of the history of the four ballot laws (that incrementally introduced the secret ballot for all types of popular voting), assailing each of the tribunes who carried them.[4] The first two – the Gabinian Law of 139 and the Cassian Law of 137, regarding electoral and judicial assemblies (except for cases of treason – *perduellio*), respectively – predate the tribunate of Tiberius Gracchus. It has often been claimed that Tiberius revived the long-dormant powers of the tribunate in order to carry his law in the teeth of senatorial opposition. But the possibility of such legislation, mentioned by Polybius (6.16.3), had not been merely theoretical before 133.

Nor was the figure of an aristocratic radical espousing highly controversial "Popular" causes, well known to the students of the Late Republic, wholly absent from Roman politics before 133. L. Cassius Longinus Ravilla, who, as tribune of the plebs, carried the ballot law in 137, was, according to Quintus, "a noble, but – I mean no offence to his family – he broke ranks with the good citizens, and was always hunting for approving chatter in *popularis* fashion" (*Leg.* 3.35). The passage of the Cassian Law appears to have been accompanied by a dramatic confrontation. According to Cicero's testimony elsewhere, "the tribune of the plebs Marcus Antius Briso long resisted the ballot law [of Cassius], supported by the consul Marcus Lepidus, and this was a source of reproach to Publius [Scipio Aemilianus] Africanus because Briso was believed to have relented due to his influence" (*Brut.* 97). Quintus recalls this criticism and warns his brother that he will be similarly blamed for introducing the ballot into his code of laws; Marcus refers to Scipio's defense, which has not survived (*Leg.* 3.37–8). The matter was well remembered, almost a century after the event, as a classic example of a great political controversy.[5] The prevailing senatorial opinion at the time, and the senatorial tradition thereafter, were clearly hostile to the reform and its supporters.

While the author of the Cassian law is described as an aristocrat who played the demagogue, the first ballot law, relating to elections, is said to have been carried by "an unknown man of lowly origin," Aulus Gabinius. How "low" could the origin of a tribune of the plebs have been? An evidently hostile tradition calls him a slave's grandson (Livy *Oxy. Per.* 54.193). Whether true or not, this was probably at least believable. Of course, a slave's grandson could have been a wealthy man. But this example should remind us that when referring to the Roman elite, we are not talking about a few aristocratic clans. The class of office holders and office seekers was much wider. Many of those people, while certainly belonging to the "upper class" from the viewpoint of the poor, must have seemed "low" indeed to true aristocrats. The *nobilitas* itself – an elite within the elite – which maintained a strong hold on the consulship, was not a closed caste. From time to time its ranks were joined by "new men" who made their way to the top – with the help of the electorate of the centuriate assembly (see also Chapters 1 and 17).[6] Aulus Gabinius, allegedly the grandson of a slave, made history as tribune of the plebs. He is not known to have held office thereafter; but it is possible that two of his sons rose to the praetorship, and Aulus Gabinius (the consul of 58) may have been his grandson.[7]

It has been argued that in 133, Marcus Octavius' persistence in sticking to his veto against an obviously popular law was far more unconventional than Tiberius' determination to pass his agrarian law without consultation with the Senate and contrary to its wishes (see Chapter 8).[8] This is possible, though there is no certainty as to the conventions governing the use of the tribunes' powers. In 137, in any case, a tribune acting in the interests of the Senate was persuaded to withdraw his veto (though the fact that Scipio was "blamed" for this implies that such a result was not a foregone conclusion). In this, to be sure, he deferred to the authority of a great noble; a mere M. Antius Briso might well defer to Scipio Aemilianus. We are not told whether considerations of his own popularity – or rather, fear of unpopularity, in case he insisted on obstructing the law – played a part in his decision. Possibly it did – after all, the tribune's earlier stance had been supported by the consul and, presumably, by the majority of the Senate, which might be thought to outweigh the influence even of Scipio Aemilianus.

Marcus Octavius, at all events, does not appear to have held any magistracy after 133 – though the Senate and "the wealthy" in general might have been expected to wish to reward their loyal champion. This was, probably, the real price that Octavius had to pay for his opposition to the agrarian law. His wholly unprecedented and, surely, unexpected deposition by a popular vote could in itself, despite the humiliation involved, have only been considered as a long-term political boon – if not for the power of the People. A tribune wishing to continue his political career after the tribunate might think twice before standing in the way of a highly popular law. On the other hand, when a man had reached the pinnacle of his career and no longer expected to need the People's votes for himself, he might well be thinking about the political career of his son, or perhaps his younger brother; moreover, his power and prestige among his friends and fellow-"oligarchs" depended to a large extent on the efficacy of his public support for other candidates. Family and faction are quite properly described as major sources of the Roman elite's power; but here too, it would be wrong to analyze the elitist and popular aspects of Roman politics as a "zero-sum game." Furthermore, unpopularity (however incurred) might spell disaster at a trial before the People. Whether one chooses to regard those trials primarily as inspired by personal and factional rivalry within the Senate (which engendered prosecutions), or as an exercise of popular control over the elite, in any case it is obvious that an unpopular aristocrat was easy prey for his aristocratic rivals – and a popular one, doubly formidable to them.

Moreover, facing an angry crowd is not a pleasant experience, whether or not it consists of potential voters. And a Roman senator constantly faced crowds (see also Chapter 20). He had to face them not just in the assemblies and in the mass meetings (*contiones*), not seldom unruly and tumultuous, where public affairs were debated but no voting took place.[9] Trials before magistrates or standing courts were conducted not in some well-guarded "Palace of Justice" but in the Forum, with a large popular audience present, visible and often audible.[10] And, of course, a senator met the Roman plebs in the theater and the Circus, not to mention the streets of the city. He did not have to face those crowds alone, to be sure, but accompanied by a respectable number of attendants. Still, it seems that a modern democracy often shields its senior politicians, the people's representatives and servants, from day-to-day contact with the common people, far better than was the case in Rome with proud nobles pursuing a senatorial career. A Roman aristocratic politician was not sped through the city in a convoy of cars with closed curtains. Nor was the Roman elite protected by a police force. Unpopularity was not something that a Roman "oligarch" would incur lightly. It has been suggested that, owing to the various limitations and constraints imposed by the system, "the Roman *populus* exercised influence not through participation in the formal machinery of government . . . but by taking to the streets, by agitation, demonstrations and riots."[11] But formal and informal expressions of popular will were in fact closely connected and largely complementary; the latter might greatly reinforce the efficacy of the former. Members of the elite who acted in flagrant defiance of public opinion might have to pay a heavy price – formally and informally. It is often said that Roman magistrates, though elected by the People, were not conceived of as "people's representatives" and, once elected, were under no obligation to follow the People's wishes. However, the system provided them with plenty of good egoistic reasons to seek popularity and to eschew unpopularity.

It is against this background that we should consider the political significance of the various procedural devices enabling members of the elite to prevent popular assemblies from expressing their will – the veto, the wide powers of the presiding magistrate, religious obstruction (see also Chapter 12). These were powerful weapons, and powerful incentives could exist for using them in the interests of the elite; but there might also be good reasons to refrain from using them. It was far from inevitable that a friendly tribune would be available with his veto at the Senate's call. Marcus Cicero, replying to his brother's attack on the tribunate, and referring to Octavius' veto, implies that at least one of the ten tribunes could always be counted on: "Has there ever been a college of tribunes so desperate that not one of the ten maintained his sanity?" (*Leg.* 3.24). When this is said in light of the experience of the Late Republic, it is, obviously, special pleading. This rhetorical exaggeration (on a par with Quintus' claims that the power of the *boni* was wholly subverted by the tribunate and the ballot) has sometimes been echoed by modern historians who overstate the ease with which the Senate could, especially in the days of pre-Gracchan "harmony," wield this weapon in defense of its interests. Roman assemblies have been described as legally "sovereign" on the grounds that they possessed unfettered powers of legislation. On the other hand, it can be argued that even in the strictly formal sense, these assemblies cannot be properly defined as sovereign, given the various legal possibilities that existed for obstructing their will before a decision could be voted on. But the argument over the precise meaning and applicability of this non-Roman term to Roman politics is somewhat beside the point. The real (as opposed to formal) power, and the real weaknesses, of the Roman assemblies depended, to a large degree, on whether those members of the elite who were in a position to obstruct the popular will thought it expedient (or even safe) to do so. This might depend on a delicate balance of incentives and disincentives – widely varying from occasion to occasion. A similar balance of considerations might encourage or deter an elected official (usually a tribune) to activate the People's power of legislation by proposing a "Popular" bill, or to put his legal authority to other "Popular" uses (see also Chapter 20).

Playing the "Popular" Card

Going now back to the ballot law of 137 – even if we assume that, in withdrawing his veto, Briso simply deferred to Scipio Aemilianus, without being influenced by fear of unpopularity – the question still remains: why would Scipio use his influence to support the ballot law, and why, for that matter, would Cassius propose it? Why, indeed, would a Scipio and a Cassius repeatedly initiate and support highly controversial popular measures? We are often assured that these individuals were, typically, power-hungry aristocratic opportunists rather than genuine reformers who cared for the common People. But this, of course, is precisely what makes their behavior so telling. Why did members of the highest Roman nobility repeatedly choose to play the "Popular" card? Scipio Aemilianus was certainly not, either by conviction or out of opportunism, a rabid democrat. He would eventually justify in public the murder of Tiberius Gracchus, and Cicero would choose him, in his *Republic*, as the chief spokesman for the "balanced" Roman polity as it had supposedly existed before the Gracchi, when a free people voluntarily accepted the guidance of an enlightened aristocracy. And yet there was nothing extraordinary in the stance he took in 137: throughout his career he repeatedly displayed a marked "Popular" tendency – and enjoyed particularly strong popular support, which allowed him to outstrip his aristocratic rivals.[12] For this he was blamed and assailed – but not regarded by the majority of the Senate as an enemy of the established order. Of course, he was never a truly radical *popularis*. But it is also likely that many senators would have admitted, just as M. Cicero argued repeatedly, that a certain degree of pandering to the People's wishes not merely made good political sense, but might sometimes be politically inevitable. It could thus be plausibly presented as a "safety valve" contributing to the overall stability of the system (as M. Cicero insists in the *Laws*), as well as serving the interests of individual members of the elite. Up to a certain point, the use of such tactics by ambitious politicians was part and parcel of the traditional game of republican politics.

The proposer of the law, L. Cassius Longinus Ravilla, went on to become consul in 127 and censor in 125. This, it has been argued, would hardly have happened if he had "deeply offended the aristocracy" by his ballot law; hence, contrary to Cicero's testimony, the law itself need not be considered as truly "Popular"[13] (and thus cannot testify to the power of the People in Roman politics). But this argument hinges on the assumption that the "aristocracy" controlled Roman elections (at least in the centuriate assembly which chose the higher magistrates) to the extent of being able to ensure a defeat of someone who had indeed "deeply offended" it. This alleged control has often been attributed to the power of aristocratic patronage, as well as to the complicated (and imperfectly understood) system of voting by property-classes, in descending order, in the centuriate assembly. But while this assembly certainly gave a weighted vote to the better off, the extent to which it disadvantaged or disfranchised the lower orders is debatable.[14] At least the more extreme versions of the "oligarchic" theory of how this assembly worked cannot be sustained – if only because the powerful first property-class itself cannot be identified with any kind of "oligarchy." Neither "the ruling class" nor "the wealthy" (who can be loosely identified with the *Equites* – a much narrower category than the first class) can be said to have controlled the centuriate assembly directly, even under the most "oligarchic" reconstruction of it. Sulla, at any rate, did not rely on the structure of the centuriate assembly to block the way to the top for those who, as tribunes, had "deeply offended the aristocracy." He made ex-tribunes ineligible to hold further magistracies – obviously estimating that a radical tribunate might actually improve, and certainly could not be counted on to damage, one's chances of being elected to higher office. If one assumes that the centuriate assembly was "oligarchic" enough to damage the chances of someone who had offended the elite to reach higher office, we must conclude that the *popularis* tribunes of the Late Republic systematically and deliberately undermined their chances of pursuing a successful political career after the tribunate. This is highly unlikely.

In fact, however, some of the most famous radical tribunes of the Late Republic would never reach higher office – not because the electorate of the centuriate assembly punished them for their radicalism, but, in Quintus' words, because "the Republic could not protect itself [from them] without resorting to arms" (*Leg.* 3.20). The ability of the Roman ruling class to remove some of its worst enemies by force (and, in most cases, to get away with this) is impressive and telling. But the champions of the elite had no monopoly on violence. Both Saturninus and Sulpicius (Rufus), mentioned by Quintus, as well as Clodius, had resorted to robust and effective violence against the interests of the majority of the Senate before violence was successfully employed against them. The same applies to politically inspired prosecutions that cut short many a promising career: populares as well as optimates might wield this weapon against their opponents, or fall victim to it.

As for the view that the Roman voter was, typically, an obedient client voting for his patron (or according to his instructions) – this view has been largely discredited. It is now widely accepted that modern accounts of patronage portraying it as "the key" to understanding Roman society and politics have been greatly exaggerated – far beyond anything that can be read in (or, reasonably, into) the sources (see also Chapters 1 and 19).[15] At least in its more extreme version, this theory of patronage would make largely incomprehensible not just the political history of the Late Republic, when legislative assemblies repeatedly defied the majority of the Senate, but various mid-republican political events (including the adoption of the first two ballot laws). Indeed, the traditional history of the "Struggle of the Orders" (assuming that it is not wholly fictitious) contradicts this theory, although there are reasons for assuming that ties of patronage were stronger – perhaps much stronger – in these earlier times. This is not to deny the great social and political importance of various unequal personal and quasi-personal ties – whether or not these should be properly defined as patronage (a question to which great, sometimes perhaps excessive, importance has been attached). Moreover, money could buy votes. More or less crude electoral bribery could sometimes be disguised as traditional aristocratic patronage or munificence (while in fact, since it was offered on a competitive basis, it cut across the web of genuinely personal ties). The material resources at the disposal of Roman senators, especially once they could use the wealth of the Empire in order to finance their political careers, were truly enormous. Whether, or how far, genuinely free political choice can be exercised by voters under conditions of glaring economic and social inequality – to this question different people will offer very different answers. But it is obvious that the political and electoral needs of the "oligarchs" translated themselves into considerable material benefits for the Roman populace.

The vote of individuals, groups, and sometimes whole communities was indeed influenced "from above," by powerful senators, patrons, benefactors, and bribery agents; from above, but often in different and conflicting directions.[16] Especially at elections, when different members of the elite competed for the People's votes, the Roman elite was, virtually by definition, divided against itself. It is in legislative assemblies, whenever a "Popular" measure was proposed, and at some politically significant popular trials, that one might expect the elite (and sometimes "the wealthy" in general) to close ranks, pooling their resources. It is all the more significant that such efforts were far from invariably successful – among other things, no doubt, because the need to curry favor with the People encouraged some senators to play the "Popular" card. And, of course, the first three ballot laws (until the introduction of the ballot into legislative assemblies), as well as the agrarian law of Tiberius Gracchus, were adopted by open voting, in defiance of any pressures "from above." In order to define the Roman Republic as a democracy (even if a "flawed" one) it would have had to be shown that the assemblies (putting aside for a moment the question of their composition) were *always*, or nearly always, capable of imposing their will on a (more or less united) Senate, in the face of determined resistance. This can hardly be demonstrated, for any period of republican history. But *sometimes* the popular will did prevail, on important and controversial issues, against senatorial opposition and obstruction. Sometimes this can be attributed to the support of wealthier non-senatorial elements – notably, when it came to laws benefiting the Equites (e.g., on the composition of the courts). But we also have examples of legislation specifically in favor of the lower (not necessarily the lowest) orders – such as the grain laws (or the agrarian reform of 133 – though not necessarily all agrarian laws). This seems to justify treating the popular aspect of republican politics seriously.

But the question of the Roman assemblies' composition cannot of course be put aside. In the Late Republic, the tribal assembly was, as is widely accepted, largely controlled by the urban plebs (no longer confined, as it once had been, to the four urban tribes). Admittedly, the urban plebs itself was only a minority of the citizen body, now extending to the whole free population of Italy. For the great majority of citizens living far from Rome, their right of suffrage was purely theoretical. But the voting power of the urban plebs still made this assembly "popular" in an important sense – certainly more popular than the centuriate assembly and much too popular and independent from the viewpoint of the elite.

However, it has been rightly pointed out that the limited space available in the various voting locations meant that in practice, only a small minority of the city populace could participate in any given assembly. For the Roman Forum, where the legislative tribal assemblies took place after 145, the theoretical maximum has been assessed at 15,000–20,000 voters. Various technical considerations (weighty but less than iron-clad, given the paucity of the available evidence) suggest that the usual number of voters was much smaller.[17] In a city whose free-citizen population numbered hundreds of thousands, such numbers may well seem unimpressive. The assumption that it was relatively easier to control and manipulate a smaller number of voters seems reasonable. Nevertheless, it is an undeniable fact, accepted by scholars with very divergent views of republican politics, that in the Late Republic several thousand men gathered in the Forum could quite realistically be expected to defy the power and influence of the Roman elite on issues of great importance.[18]

It has been suggested that "this cosy arrangement [whereby the elite had controlled the legislative assemblies] broke down in the later second century...[as] a consequence of members of the lower classes now turning up for assemblies they had not previously attended. That happened at the initiative of magistrates who sought popular support to press through legislation against the opposition of the Senate and the upper classes."[19] But it was the fundamental logic of Rome's competitive politics, not confined to any particular period, which might sometimes impel a magistrate to seek popular support in order to press through legislation opposed by the Senate – or perhaps to oppose the Senate in order to gain popular support. From the time of the Gracchi on, this mechanism, indeed, worked more powerfully than before. The preceding decades are known as a period of "harmony" – basically, senatorial predominance with the People's acquiescence; but they are also a poorly documented period (with Livy's narrative lost). The little that we hear about the first two ballot laws may well be just a faint echo of a fierce political controversy (especially in the case of the Cassian law). There may have been examples of this mechanism in action, during this period, that left no traces in the surviving sources.[20] Gaius Flaminius, having carried his agrarian law as tribune in 232 against strong senatorial opposition, went on to become consul and censor. In 218, according to Livy, he was the only senator (though this has been doubted by some historians) who supported the Claudian law forbidding senators and their sons to possess large seagoing ships. "The law, which was vehemently opposed, was a cause of great resentment against Flaminius on the part of the nobles, but brought him the favor of the plebs and hence a second consulship" (Livy 21.63.3–4).

Popular Legitimacy and the Stability of the System

When, toward the end of his speech, Quintus urges Marcus Cicero to remove the ballot laws from his code, it turns out that in practice, this staunch optimate was just as aware as his "soft" brother that the elite was far from all-powerful in its dealings with the People: "Therefore, since we are now not simply reviewing the laws of the Roman people, but reviving old laws that have vanished, or else establishing new ones, I think you should propose, not what can be obtained from the Roman People in its present state, but what is best" (3.37). Quintus realizes that full-fledged senatorial domination is unattainable in practice, but refuses to give it up, as a matter of principle, in a treatise on the best laws. But Marcus Cicero the unabashed pragmatist had little time for purely theoretical considerations divorced from political reality.[21] The People's power was, to him, a "fact of life"; any head-on attack on it was futile. It had to be accepted, integrated into the system, and manipulated, as far as possible, in the interests of the system's overall stability. The popular element of the constitution was there – it was a wise statesman's part to make it function as a safety valve. But there was no question of removing it, no use to speculate about such things even theoretically. A form of government aristocratic enough to allow the state to be governed rationally, but popular enough to enjoy the necessary broad legitimacy, would preserve, as it did in the good old days (at least as a rule – he was well aware of the exceptions), the Senate's leading role in shaping public policy. This, for Cicero, was the best of all possible political worlds. When he insists, repeatedly,[22] that the authority of the *boni* is best preserved by conceding a moderate degree of political liberty (and hence, power) to the plebs he is, to a large extent, making a virtue of necessity.

On the ballot, Cicero suggests a compromise: preserving the written ballot, but allowing voters to show it to any of the "best citizens" upon request, repealing all the laws that forbade one to accost a voter and question him as to his vote. This would "give the appearance of liberty (*libertatis species*), preserve the authority of the good citizens, and remove a cause of dissension" (*Leg.* 3.39). *Libertatis species* has been taken to mean that for Cicero, "the liberty conceded to the people . . . was tolerable only in so far as it was specious"; he "wish[ed it] to be a mere sham."[23] In and of itself, this phrase does lend itself to such an interpretation – but it is dangerous to rely wholly on a single phrase from Cicero's complicated and dialectical argument. In defending the tribunate, Cicero chooses to present the glass of popular liberty (and power) as half-full rather than half-empty: "Thus either the kings should never have been expelled, or else real liberty, not a nominal one, had to be given to the plebs" (*Leg.* 3.25).[24]

But the difference between the two passages is not just in rhetorical emphasis. As regards the ballot, Cicero proposes a change that would limit popular freedom by exposing voters to greater pressures from above – contrary to his usual policy of maintaining the broad lines of the constitutional status quo in his "code of laws." This, while exposing him as a rather lukewarm defender of popular rights, also shows that in his estimation, the ballot, as it actually functioned in his time, gave the humbler sort of voters much more than just an "appearance of liberty." The tribunate, on the other hand, was evidently too rooted in the system to be tampered with. Therefore it had to be adopted "as it is in our state" (*Leg.* 3.19) and eloquently defended:

> You say that the tribunes of the plebs have excessive power. Who denies that? But the unrestrained force of the people is much more savage, much more violent; however, it is sometimes milder because it has a leader than if it did not . . . "But," you say, "sometimes the tribunes inflame the people." "Yes, but they often soothe them too.

This is followed by a piece of special pleading already mentioned – a misleading rhetorical question which implies that not a single college of tribunes is so "desperate" as to lack a "sane" tribune willing to defend the state against his colleagues.

In his concluding remarks Cicero defends the restoration of the tribunes' powers by Pompey in 70:

> You say you cannot praise Pompey in this one matter; but you do not seem to have sufficiently considered this point – that he had not only to look to what was best but also what was inevitable. He understood that this power could not be withheld from our state; for how could our people go without it once they had experienced it when they had demanded it so vehemently before they knew what it was? It was incumbent on a wise citizen not to leave to some dangerous demagogue a cause that was not vicious in itself and so popular that it could not be opposed. (*Leg.* 3.26)

At the outset of this chapter we asked how real was the people's power in the Republic; this passage seems to indicate that it was real enough. The context does not suggest a rhetorical overstatement of the people's power (such as might be advisable when addressing the People in a *contio*). The people's role in Roman politics is often portrayed as essentially passive, on the grounds that any legislative initiative had to come from an office holder – a member of the elite, rather than from the "floor of the assembly" (as in Athens).[25] This was, indeed, a significant limitation. But it was in the nature of things, as Cicero's passage shows, that a sufficiently strong and persistent popular demand would eventually be taken up by an ambitious politician[26] (not necessarily by a tribune – which is why Sulla's emasculation of the tribunate could not stand). Of course, Cicero's apologetic account ignores the part played in the events by Pompey's own ambitions. Pompey did not just "rescue" the cause of restoring the tribune's powers from being taken up by some reckless *popularis*. He greatly benefited from being identified with this cause – possibly already as candidate for the consulship of 70, and certainly in the 60s, when "Popular" tribunes carried the laws conferring on Pompey his extraordinary commands, with the enthusiastic support of the People (against strong senatorial opposition). Here again we see the interconnection and interplay between popular and aristocratic politics – or, to take a less sanguine view of things (since we are approaching the end of the Republic), between popular support and the rise of the "dynasts" who would pave the way to autocracy.

Even the most charitable modern reader will react to the idyllic picture drawn by Cicero – popular liberty in harmony with senatorial authority – with a fair dose of skepticism. The stability of the "balanced" constitution (as envisaged by Cicero and in actual practice, assuming that his vision is not wholly divorced from Roman, particularly mid-republican, realities) depended heavily on various forms of elite control and manipulation. In the final analysis, it depended on the People's acquiescence. It appears to have been a widely shared feeling that the Roman state was, generally, in good hands when it was governed by scions of the noble families that had made it great, and guided by the collective wisdom and experience of the Senate. This basic acceptance of the aristocratic ethos did not rule out an occasional outburst of popular resentment and dissatisfaction with the elite – even in the most "harmonious" of times. On the other hand, it was far from wholly shattered even in the last century of the Republic. However achieved, popular legitimacy and acceptance of the system were its main bulwarks; though, of course, this "however" reintroduces, by the back door, some of the traditional explanations for the system's stability and longevity having to do with the elite's economic resources, social influence, prestige, and authority. Whether "consent of the governed" obtained under such conditions should count as genuinely "democratic" – on this question no general agreement should be expected. But, at any rate, this consent could not be taken for granted; the "oligarchs" had to work hard in order to obtain it.

"The ideology of the ruling class" was accepted by the People of Rome "to an extraordinary degree."[27] To be sure, the ruling class possessed powerful tools for shaping public opinion and fostering what some will define as "false consciousness" among the People. But it must always be borne in mind that this class lacked an effective mechanism of state coercion, and its individual members had to compete with each other for popular support. The People's acquiescence and support could not be commanded – it had to be earned. A Roman senator was constantly concerned to gain and retain it; senatorial politics cannot be properly understood without taking this fact into consideration (see also Chapters 17, 19, and 20). In presenting a realistic picture of republican politics and society, it is necessary to go beyond the traditional dichotomy between "democracy" and "oligarchy," between the power of the People and the power of the elite. The actual content of Roman public life was shaped by a complicated interplay between these powerful forces.

Guide to Further Reading

The debate on the People's role in the republican political system was largely sparked by F. Millar's attack, in a series of articles in the 1980s, on the traditional oligarchic interpretation which minimized the power of the People in the "senatorial Republic." See Millar 1984, 1986, 1989 (now incorporated in Millar 2002b). See also Millar 1998, 2002a. Over time, Millar "radicalized" his thesis, now stressing not just the importance of the popular element (in line with Polybius' theory of "mixed constitution"), but its centrality in the republican system. His arguments have proved as controversial as they were stimulating. The ongoing debate has contributed greatly to our understanding of republican politics and society. Despite widely divergent views (on the general assessment of the republican system of government as well as on numerous specific issues), few will dismiss today the importance of Roman popular politics altogether; the purely oligarchic model is widely felt to be unsatisfactory. For some recent contributions to the debate (with extensive bibliographies) see Jehne 1995c, Yakobson 1999, Hölkeskamp 2000a, Mouritsen 2001, Flaig 2003, Hölkeskamp 2004a, Morstein-Marx 2004. See also, e.g., Vanderbroeck 1987, Brunt 1988c, Astin 1989, Thommen 1989, Burckhardt 1990, North 1990b, Rosenstein 1990, Harris 1990b, Gruen 1991, Eder 1991, Mackie 1992, Jehne 1993, Rosenstein 1993, Purcell 1994, Gruen 1995: vii–xxi; Badian 1996c, Pina Polo 1996, Gabba 1997, Pani 1997, Lintott 1999a: 191–213. On the ballot laws specifically, see Harris 1989, Gruen 1991, Jehne 1993, Marshall 1997, Hall 1998, Salerno 1999, Yakobson 1999: 126–33. Worthy of note also is Dyck 2004, a new and important commentary on Cicero's *On the Laws*.

Notes

1   Millar 2002a: 144–5, 181–2.
2   Cf. Cic. *Leg.* 3.34 ("most powerful men" condemned by open voting).
3   See Mouritsen 2001: 68–9 – a catalog of late-republican *popularis* laws.
4   It has been suggested that Cicero's account exaggerates the "Popular" significance of the ballot laws. Nevertheless, all the evidence indicates that it was quite considerable. See on this Yakobson 1999: 126–33. See Morstein-Marx 2004: 84–9, on the early numismatic link between the Cassian Law and popular liberty (in a coin minted in 126).
5   See also Cic. *Sest.* 103; *Amic.* 41; Asc. 78 C; cf. Pliny *Epist.* 3.20.1.
6   See on this Hopkins and Burton 1983 (arguing against the more extreme view of the exclusive and closed nature of the nobility).
7   See Münzer 1910; von der Mühll 1910.
8   Badian 1972b.
9   For *contiones* and their importance see now Morstein-Marx 2004.
10 See Millar 1998: *passim*, stressing the "open-air" character of Roman public life.
11 Finley 1983: 91; cf. Mouritsen 2001: 147.
12 See Astin 1967: esp. 26–34.

13 Harris 1989: 170.

14 See on this Yakobson 1999: 20–64; *contra*, Ryan 2001.

15 See on this esp. Brunt 1988c: 382–442; cf. Mouritsen 2001: 3.

16 Cf. Millar 2002b: 112. According to North 1990b: 18, "the popular will of the Roman people found expression in the context, and only in the context, of divisions within the oligarchy." Taking "oligarchy" in a broad and flexible (though still meaningful) sense, this definition can be accepted – but bearing in mind that "divisions within the oligarchy" were intrinsic to the system.

17 Mouritsen 2001: 20–3.

18 Cf. Mouritsen 2001: 131.

19 Mouritsen 2001: 79. Mouritsen mentions Flaminius' agrarian law in 232 as "an early example of lower-class mobilization" (cf. Polyb. 2.21.7–8); the first two ballot laws "may be signs of the growing disunity within the elite, which fully erupted in 133."

20 For several known examples, during the first decades of the second century, of legislation that "benefited the common people to some degree" (possibly, though not necessarily, implying that they were opposed by the Senate), see Vishnia 1996: 192–3. Cf. Badian 1996c: 187–8, 201, 211 (unattested legislation); 213 n.44 (tribunes representing the interests of the "People" in the Middle Republic).

21 Cf. Cic. *Rep.* 2.57, 2.21 (on Plato's Republic).

22 In both the *Laws* and the *Republic*; see, e.g., *Rep.* 2.55.

23 Brunt 1988c: 325–6, 281 (referring to this and similar passages in both treatises).

24 He adds that it was granted "in such a manner that the plebs was induced by many excellent provisions to yield to the authority of the leading citizens." This probably refers to senatorial authorization for laws passed by the plebeian assembly (thus Brunt 1988c: 324), required until the Hortensian law (c.287), but may have a wider application, as part of Cicero's "safety valve" argument. In the *Republic*, Cicero similarly insists that it was essential to give the People not just a modicum of political liberty but sufficient liberty in order to ensure the proper balance and stability of the "mixed constitution" – as well as the salutary influence of the *principes*; see *Rep.* 2.55–9.

25 "[T]he assemblies were deprived of any independent political initiative" – Mouritsen 2001: 128.

26 Cf. North 1990b: 18. See Plut. *Ti. Gracch.* 8 (graffiti calling for an agrarian law).

27 Finley 1983: 141. On the People accepting the aristocratic ethos see Hölkeskamp 1993: 33; Hölkeskamp 2000a: 220–3; Lintott 1999a: 198; Morstein-Marx 2004.

CHAPTER 19

Patronage

Elizabeth Deniaux

Translated by Robert Morstein-Marx and Robert Martz

Patronage, the Exchange of Favors, and Social Harmony

From Rome's earliest days a code of values had been established that within the hierarchy of social obligations privileged those linked to the fundamental space of the home and family by blood ties and patronage under various forms. The Roman citizen was not only subject to the law but was also a member of a network of personal relations that the law recognized. The patron–client relationship was central to the Roman cultural experience. According to tradition, its origin went back to Romulus himself, who had made it hereditary. Dionysius of Halicarnassus says of Romulus, "He gave the plebeians over to the patricians as a sacred trust, and permitted each of the common People to cultivate as patron whomever he wished . . . In this way he made the connection between them one both humane and worthy of citizens" (*Ant. Rom.* 2.9.2–3).[1] Cicero underscores the attribution to Romulus as well, noting that "he had the common people enrolled as clients of the leading men" (*Rep.* 2.16).

The Romans formalized these relationships but passed on to us few precise accounts of them, which makes them difficult to study even though they have a significant place among their stock of cultural symbols. When Virgil in the *Aeneid* describes those awaiting their punishment in Tartarus (6.609), he allots a place right next to parricides to persons who had not respected their obligations toward their clients. Fustel de Coulanges, who was the first to use the terms "patronage" and "voluntary clientship" to describe these relationships of mutual obligation, noted that the expression "to be in the trust (*fides*) of another" was undoubtedly the most common formulation. It is in fact the word *fides*, sworn faith, which underlies these obligations. Both favors (*beneficia*) and services, or marks of gratitude (*officia*), necessarily implied an ethic of reciprocity that influenced the persons involved and also their reputation, which was measured according to their respect for their private obligations and their ability to preserve the patronal networks passed down by their families.[2]

The exchange of services and benefits pertained not only to private morality but also to Roman public morality. Election to a Roman magistracy was perceived as a unanimous expression of the People who offered their vote as a favor, a collective *beneficium*, to the politician who sought it. It was the People's *beneficium* that permitted one to attain the summit of glory by virtue of the honor of election (see also Chapters 17 and 18). The relationship of exchange between the People and the future magistrate is attested in our texts, which assert that the People were won over by the past *beneficia* of the candidate and the hope of more to come. Every electoral campaign illustrated the personal aspect of the relationship with the candidate, since anyone pursuing a campaign had to solicit the voters individually by emphasizing his past services, his previous actions that remained in the collective memory (see also Chapter 23). The relationship thus established was a form of community patronage.[3]

Dionysius of Halicarnassus' view of Roman clientship was inspired by an idealized past, evoking concord and social cohesion. Writing in the Augustan period, he describes the relationship between patrons and clients in the Roman constitution's earliest phase and portrays them as in a perfect form: there was such benevolence between the two parties that each did its best not to be surpassed by the other in this domain. Patrons explained the law to their clients, sought to protect them and not to impose any burden upon them. They were entitled to bring suits on behalf of their clients. Clients rendered services of all kinds to their patrons and assured them of their financial assistance: they contributed to the dowry of the patron's daughter, they participated in collecting ransom for a patron who had been captured or a fine levied on a patron who had lost a suit, and they shared his expenses of public office. Patrons and clients could not vote against each other, nor could they bring a charge or testify in court against the other (Dion. Hal. *Rom. Ant.* 2.10). This picture was inspired by a social and political ideal of concord worked out later in accordance with aristocratic ideals favored in Rome in the first century BC. When Dionysius claims that it was impious and illegal for a client and patron to bring charges or give testimony against each other he takes up a formula expressed in the archaic law of the Twelve Tables asserting that a patron who harmed his client should become *sacer*, that is, devoted to the gods and therefore able to be killed with impunity (Crawford 1996b: 689–90, Tab. VIII.10 = Riccobono, *FIRA* XII Tab. 8.21). Assistance at law (or at least neutrality in the courts) was always a patron's most important duty. Republican legislation also allowed for the exclusion of persons connected not only by blood but also by relations of *fides* from participation in legal proceedings against each other.

A specific example of this kind of exemption is well known to us because it involves the career of C. Marius. In 115, when Marius was on trial for electoral bribery and the prosecution called C. Herennius to testify, he refused, declaring that it was contrary to custom for a patron to give testimony against a client, adding that Marius' parents and Marius himself had long been clients of the Herennii. According to Plutarch (*Mar.* 5.4.), Marius rejected the argument, declaring that once he had been elected to his first magistracy he had ceased to be a client – a claim that Plutarch corrects for his Greek readers, adding that not all magistracies freed one from obligations toward a patron, only the higher, so-called "curule" ones.[4] This episode has been discussed at length by those interested in the archaic institution of clientship and its formal restrictions, in particular Theodor Mommsen.[5] We see from this example that even at the end of the Republic respect for traditional patronal duties toward clients was supported by such a strong social consensus that they could constitute a valid excuse for a refusal to testify. On the other hand, a client's inferior status disappeared when he had been elected to a high magistracy.

During this period, the word "client" was never attributed to a magistrate who held a magistracy with the power to command (*imperium*) – that is, consuls and praetors in the main – since attainment of this kind of office freed one from the traditional obligations of a client. On the other hand, it was not unknown for an eminent person who had held one of these offices to present himself as a client in order to obtain assistance. Such was the nature of a letter to Cicero written in 45 in which the proconsul P. Vatinius (consul in 47) pleads with the great orator to continue exercising his patronage over himself as his client: "If you maintain your customary care for your clientele, here I am, P. Vatinius, your client" (Cic. *Fam.* 5.9.1). Cicero had earlier defended him in court at the request of Caesar and Crassus in 54. He had become his patron in this trial. Legally Vatinius could no longer be Cicero's client after his election to high office, but Vatinius insisted upon his dependence because he hoped thereby to gain Cicero's protection. In 45 Vatinius was governor of Illyricum and seeking a triumph; he was canvassing the support of Cicero, a powerful senator of consular rank, in the hope of winning the Senate's authorization.

This letter highlights the contradiction between formal rules and actual usage because it shows that it was permissible to suggest rather ostentatiously that a state of dependence persisted in order to continue receiving favors and services. It therefore demonstrates the impossibility of holding to the strict, formal usage of words in the study of Roman patronage and clientship.[6] When we examine such terms as *cliens*, *clientela*, and *patronus* at the end of the Republic we are quickly checked by their infrequent occurrence: in Cicero, our main source, *cliens* is very rarely associated with the name of a person, and *patronus* typically denotes a person's advocate in court, that is, the *patronus causae*.[7] It is exceedingly uncommon for a man to refer to himself as someone's client, and it was rare for Cicero to designate someone else as his own client. The language of social subordination could seem arrogant if it was used by a patron to express his superiority and the weakness of his client. The term *amicus* ("friend") was much more honorable for the client than the literal term *cliens*. The very word *necessarius* ("close connection"), which was frequently used to denote a friend, placed emphasis on an exchange of services and on the duties that arose from a relationship of *necessitudo* ("obligation" or "bond"). The rarity of the words "patron" and "client" outside of the judicial context is no evidence of the weakening of the interpersonal ties that structured Roman society, but a sign rather that they had lost the strict, exclusionary character that they had once had in the archaic age. In the imperial period Romans were still discussing the relative ranking of ties of kinship and clientship in the hierarchy of obligations that were imposed upon a Roman (Gell. *NA* 5.13). To define patronage I shall adopt a broad definition, one more sociological than judicial, borrowed from scholars who describe modes of behavior observable in contemporary Mediterranean societies in which a code of honor and loyalty is likewise apparent: "an asymmetrical, quasi-moral relation between a person (the patron) who directly provides protection and assistance (patronage), and/or who influences persons (clients) who depend on him for such assistance. Clients, in turn, provide loyalty and support when called on to do so."[8]

At Rome, the institution of patronage (*patrocinium*) appeared in many forms and involved different types of relationships. Some involved those who had been citizens for a long time, others new citizens. *Fides* was hereditary, but it was also possible to enter into someone's *fides* by statute, or voluntarily by a sort of personal contract. With the Roman conquest, military defeats were followed by a *deditio* (unconditional surrender) by the vanquished, who then entered the *fides* of the conqueror.

The example of Marius attests to the hereditary nature of the private ties between the Herennii and his family. At the end of the Republic it is difficult to trace the transmission of these personal attachments from one generation to another. However, Cicero's letters of recommendation sometimes supply information about the long-standing nature of the relationship between Cicero and his correspondent, an antiquity asserted all the more strongly when services were being demanded from the one being solicited. Thus, the family of the Munatii Planci, local magnates from Tibur, were for a long time among the clients of Cicero; regarding two of its members he uses the expression "ancestral connection" (*paterna necessitudo*), and even invokes a bond to the entire household in a letter addressed to L. Munatius Plancus (*Fam.* 10.3.2, 13.29). He cites this "ancestral connection" also in letters sent to L. Plotius Plancus, Munatius' brother (*Att.* 16.16A, 16B). These two magistrates of the Caesarian age had a brother, T. Munatius Plancus Bursa, whom Cicero had defended in court. But this man gravely violated the pact of loyalty that linked his family to the orator. As tribune of the plebs in 52, he took the side of Clodius and accused a friend of Cicero's. That is why, at a period when Cicero was pleading almost solely for the defense, he took the trouble to prosecute the man himself in a criminal trial.[9]

A relationship of patronage was also created between former master and ex-slave when, by the voluntary act of the owner, a slave was emancipated and thereby given liberty and citizenship. The master changed from the slave's *dominus* ("lord") into the new freedman's *patronus*. The freedman, as recipient of the priceless gift of liberty, remained subject to the *fides* of his patron; he had at all times to behave in accordance with his obligation toward the one whose name he had adopted upon receiving Roman citizenship. Proof of this was his respect (*obsequium*) and the required services he owed his patron (*operae*) – the concrete marks of his devotion.[10] This kind of patronage was imposed by another. But a free man could also request someone's *fides* and freely enter into their clientele. The young jurist C. Trebatius Testa entrusted himself from his youth to the *fides* of Cicero, who saw to his education (*Fam.* 7.5.3, 7.17). Cicero subsequently recommended his client and student to Caesar, commander of the army in Gaul, so that he in turn might advance his protégé's career. In his letter to Caesar, in order to add solemnity to the recommendation, he evokes the symbolic transfer of clientage in the ancient manner, from his own hand to Caesar's (*Fam.* 7.5). Originally, in fact, the custom of personal recommendation, which perpetuated itself to the end of the Republic in a less rigid form, formed a moral obligation and created a duty of *fides*. Traditionally, the request to enter a state of clientship voluntarily was called *applicatio* ("attachment"). But the expression is very rarely used, in contrast to *commendatio* ("act of entrusting").[11] The etymology of the word *commendare*, "to entrust into the hand (*manus*)," or *se commendare*, "to entrust oneself into the hand," indeed refers to the gesture (joining of right hands [*data dextera*]) by which a request for assistance and protection was symbolized. This kind of commitment of one person to the care of another was often alluded to in critical moments in which the very life of the person who entrusted himself was in danger.[12]

Commitment into the *fides* of a patron by means of a symbolic gesture can also be seen in the pacts of hospitality that linked Romans and foreigners. A picture of this is given by the mythical example of the king of Latium, Latinus, who holds out his right hand as he welcomes Aeneas and the Trojans: "Latinus gave his right hand as a pledge of future friendship" (Livy 1.1.8). Ties of hospitality were often associated with the duties of a client. The guest-friends of senators and Roman magistrates were the most significant persons in the cities of Italy or of the provinces. In Greece as at Rome, a guest-friend was a person to whom one offered shelter and guaranteed security. For this welcome and protection reciprocity was expected. With characteristic attention to the concrete, the Roman would exchange with his guest-friend a token of this agreement, the *tessera hospitalis*, a small bronze object divided into two parts, one of which was retained by each of the parties.

When Rome extended its citizenship and became an empire, the patron–client relationship often made it possible to maintain the links that Rome had established with individuals and communities in Italy and the provinces. According to tradition, a Roman conqueror became the patron of the People he had conquered and this patronage passed on to his descendants. This is affirmed by Cicero: "among our people . . . those who had received states and peoples conquered in war into their power became, according to ancestral custom, their protectors" (*Off.* 1.35). Historians claim that "surrender into the trust" (*deditio in fidem*) of the conqueror was among the privileged means of entering into the clientele of a conqueror. However, there are controversies about the precise form of this arrangement.[13] Conquest was the work of an individual who acted in the name of the People and Senate of Rome and who took certain actions toward an adversary whom he had defeated. The most conspicuous example is that of Sicily. After the Syracusans' defeat in 212 they officially surrendered to their conqueror, M. Claudius Marcellus; but the affair is more complex, for it was at Rome, after Marcellus' military victory over Syracuse, that a delegation from the city proposed to Marcellus that he become their patron.[14] The clan of the Claudii had exercised a permanent patronage over Sicily that could still be seen in operation at the time of the prosecution of its governor Verres (70). The patrician Claudii Pulchri had intervened in Sicily during the First Punic War and the plebeian Claudii Marcelli later became the most reliable supporters of the Sicilians. Festivals were organized in honor of these "ancient patrons." Statues representing M. Claudius Marcellus decorated public places of the cities. The Syracusans had decreed that the People should sacrifice to the gods every time Marcellus or a member of his family entered the city.

After administering a province an ex-governor could multiply benefits for his former province. Often he had the opportunity to create new groups of clients for his own profit. The island of Cyprus, included in the province of Cilicia which Cicero had governed, continued to receive his protection. A letter of Cicero's in which he entrusts the island to his quaestor, C. Sextilius Rufus, tells us that Cicero also exercised his patronage over the city of Paphos (*Fam.* 13.48). However, Cyprus was also in the clientele of M. Porcius Cato, who had imposed provincial government there in 58 (Cic. *Fam.* 15.4.15). A Roman of status inferior to the governor could use his presence in the province to draw new patronal connections to himself. It was because he had been quaestor of Lilybeaum that Cicero was asked to take up the case of the Sicilian victims of Verres' corruption. P. Clodius was also quaestor of Sicily when he asked Cicero whether it his custom to supply seats at the Roman games to his Sicilian clients.[15]

Foundation of colonies was a means of expanding the clientele of those who were in charge of the settlement, who then became the colonists' patrons; so P. Cornelius Sulla, nephew of Sulla the dictator, was chosen as the patron of the colony of Pompeii founded by his uncle.[16] Moreover, those who established the colony had at their disposal reserves of land that they could use to benefit their friends, whom they also had the right to enroll among the colonists. In this way Marius gave Roman citizenship to some Italians before the Social War, and Caesar did likewise for certain Greek aristocrats who were among his clients.[17] Colonists also remained attached to the families of those who had allocated land to them. Caesar's veterans, as beneficiaries of his colonial foundations, were easily mobilized by Octavian after Caesar's death. A law from the end of the Republic attests to the hereditary character of this form of patronage in the colony of Urso in Spain.[18]

Patronage established by conquest gave way to other realities at the end of the Republic. Today, when historians describe the relationship between Romans and the cities or peoples of the empire during this period, they emphasize the voluntary forms, personal and collective, by which persons were entrusted to another's protection. Civic communities appear to have been protected by patrons, whom they honor in inscriptions, but these were patrons whom they had solicited ("patronage by request").[19] Exiles also became patrons of the cities in which they resided. For example, the city of Dyrrachium across the Adriatic, which had received him well during his voyage into exile, remained in Cicero's *fides*.[20] During or after the exercise of an official function, Romans might become patrons of cities in nearby provinces. The point is underscored by recent epigraphic discoveries, especially in the Greek East. At the end of the second century and especially in the first, the names of Roman protectors appeared in Greek inscriptions of the cities, who designated them by the term *pátrōn*, a loan-word from the Latin. The procedure for voluntary entry into a clientele has been thoroughly analyzed thanks to an extraordinary document from Aphrodisias in Caria, a letter honoring Q. Oppius, patron of the city, who had been proconsul of Cilicia when Mithridates invaded the western part of Asia Minor (89 and early 88). The study of this document reveals many levels of decision making in seeking a patron, of which the first was a constitutional decision of the city in favor of choosing a protector, followed by solicitation of the future patron. An embassy was accordingly sent to him, bringing not only the official request from his future clients but arguments in its favor. The city hoped that by entering into Oppius' patronage it would be rewarded for its previous actions and earn future benefits. The agreement of the patron was generally commemorated by the inscription of the official text on bronze tablets, "patronal tablets" (*tabulae patronatus*) placed in a public area. The case of Q. Oppius is complex. In order to resist Mithridates, Q. Oppius had made an appeal to the allies of Rome and, despite Aphrodisias' location outside the province, it sent him some troops. At the end of the war, Q. Oppius, while visiting the island of Cos, was approached by an embassy from Aphrodisias, which transmitted the request to become his client, citing its loyalty to Rome and its past services in favor of Q. Oppius. He accepted, and the text of his favorable response was engraved for posterity.[21] Voluntary entry into clientship was thus one approach to patronage for individuals as well as communities.[22] Patronage of a man chosen in this way operated over very large domains and its study offers insight into one of the essential mechanisms of Roman power.

The Duty of Assistance

The most important duty of the patron was legal assistance. This was linked to the archaic tradition of the institution of patronage. A patron was a powerful person who had to keep his door open and receive those who came to greet him and request his assistance. The framework of Roman aristocratic life is clear testimony to the importance of patronage in the Roman cultural experience. The morning levee (*salutatio*) is the cliental ritual par excellence, the practice of greeting the patron at his house at daybreak. Lines of clients queued up each morning at the door of a powerful man. To this ritual was added the *aditus*, literally "access," an audience with the master of the house, who had to leave his door open to be accessible to all sorts of requests. As Cicero says, "in those days people used to approach such men... sitting in their formal seat at home, not only in order to consult them about the law but even about the marriage of a daughter, purchase of land, cultivating their fields, in sum about every duty or business" (Cic. *De Orat.* 3.133). The layout of the Roman house was, moreover, designed for the reception of clients. Vitruvius, the theorist of Roman architecture, held that

> for nobles..., who must receive the public during their tenure of offices and magistracies, one must build magnificent vestibules, spacious atria and peristyles, groves and wide walkways conducive to a proper image of dignity. Moreover let them have libraries, art-galleries and reception rooms... since in their houses frequently public business will be transacted and private lawsuits and appeals settled. (Vitr. *De arch.* 6.5.2; see also Chapter 24)

Legal protection and the provision of legal advice in a society where private suits and public trials were very frequent were imposed by familial tradition on members of the nobility, who could thus attach a great number of individuals to themselves in return. Knowledge of the law, eloquence, and constant accessibility permitted them to strengthen these ties, to recruit new clients, and to encourage new exchanges of services. At Rome it was forbidden to pay for legal assistance according to the Cincian Law passed in 204. However, legal competence and the ability to plead a case increased an individual's prestige as well as the number of those loyal to him by placing them in his debt. The obligation to return the service in the short or long term is tied to a strategy of accumulating a sort of "symbolic capital" that was the product of trust and loyalty, of an honorable reputation and of influence (*gratia*), and could be mobilized in all the various circumstances of social and political life.

It was by speaking in the courts that Cato the Elder, a new man who possessed no inherited connections in Rome, initially created a network of people indebted to him. Plutarch recounts how the future censor, originally from Tusculum and without famous ancestors, had begun his career by training himself in oratory and in assisting in court those in the surrounding small towns and municipalities who asked him for such help (Plut. *Cat. Mai.* 1.3). It is true that he also possessed an eminent supporter. The patrician L. Valerius Flaccus, who was his neighbor, supported his career in Rome. This man would even go on to hold the consulship with him in 195. Cicero created a large body of clients for himself by virtue of his ability as an advocate both for the prosecution and defense. He mobilized this "surplus of gratitude" at the time of his election to the consulship in 63. His brother, Quintus, who wrote a short manual on electoral campaigning for him, had strongly urged him to do so: "You will compensate handsomely for the newness of your name by means of your fame as an orator. One who is thought to be a worthy advocate for ex-consuls can hardly be thought unworthy of the consulship" (Cic. *Comment. Pet.* 2.)

Assistance in court was one of the most important services a Roman could render his guest-friends and his foreign clients. Compliance with this duty could lead one to intervention in the political arena. Cicero illustrates the point, stating that "At a time when our affairs were flourishing, the most illustrious men of our city believed that it was their greatest and finest service to protect from all injustice and defend the well-being of all their guest-friends, clients, and foreign peoples that were in the friendship and power of the Roman People" (Cic. *Div. Caec.* 66). The most important trials involved extortion by former magistrates in the province that they had governed (the charge *de repetundis*). The Calpurnian Law of 149 established a special tribunal for these cases, which were heard in the Forum. More laws establishing further permanent courts followed (see also Chapters 11 and 20). Ties of solidarity imposed on Roman patrons the duty to bring accusations against corrupt former governors in order to defend their own provincial clients who were victims of these men's crimes. M. Aemilius Scaurus, the governor of Sardinia, was accused of extortion by the Sardinians in 54. P. Valerius Triarius brought the accusation and became the Sardinians' prosecuting counsel (*patronus causae*) in the trial. His father had been the governor of Sardinia in 77. Cicero, a former quaestor of the island of Sicily, claimed that he had been asked by all the Sicilians to prosecute Verres, and especially by his guest-friends. He was chosen as the Sicilians' advocate to bring the charge that increased his renown and the gratitude of the Sicilians.

In the history of the great public trials, the bonds of solidarity which led to bringing an accusation also were conducive to organizing the defense. The authority of powerful friends who demonstrated their support to a defendant could strongly influence the court in his favor. However, patronage operated in the judicial realm also in an indirect manner. A powerful friend or a patron sometimes interceded in favor of his protégé even before the trial began by approaching the person who would be the judge. The morning levee provided an occasion to transmit the request through the access it gave to the private home of the judge or president of the tribunal. The vulnerability of Roman justice to power and influence has long been noted. Inequality was manifest in the weight accorded to prestige, authority, and favor, indeed to all the accompanying marks of power.

Cicero's letters of recommendation illustrate the important role that private intercession played during these trials. Such letters were a written substitute for oral requests. They permitted one who was outside of Rome, especially one who was governing a province, to remain available to his friends and thus to compensate for the effects of a temporary absence. When his proconsulship in Cilicia in 51–50 separated Cicero from the center of political decision-making, he wrote numerous letters of recommendation, some of which were for friends who faced possible prosecution. Three letters intended to support his friend M. Fabius Gallus suggest the different types of aid that could be given by a powerful figure. The first is a letter of advice to a powerful friend urging him to use his influence, his *gratia,* to prevent the brother of M. Fabius Gallus from taking legal action against him. The second is a request directed to another friend, M. Caelius Rufus, that he become the advocate (*patronus*) of M. Fabius Gallus in case a trial was unavoidable. The third is addressed to the magistrate who would preside over the trial, one of the praetors of the year 50. On behalf of his friend Cicero asks the praetor to give him easy access to explain himself and later, when the case is judged, to grant him justice willingly. Unfortunately we have no idea whether, or how far, these successive interventions were effective.[23]

Governing a province consisted almost entirely of the administration of justice, according to a letter of Cicero to his brother Quintus (*Q. fr.* 1.1.20; see also Chapter 11). Cicero's letters of recommendation give us a view of the main areas of a governor's competence: criminal trials, but especially financial matters, communal debts, inheritances. Urgent appeals for trials involving financial affairs and interests in the province do not always convey the details of the cases, inasmuch as letters of recommendation intentionally employ an abstract vocabulary, focusing on praise for the governor's indulgence and magnanimity. The governor's freedom of action might well lead to abuses of his judicial power in order to show favor to friends supported by powerful patrons. The attitude a governor took toward the private contractors of state revenues and business (*publicani*) might be adapted according to circumstances, but also in accordance with the strength of their support. In Rome Cicero had always supported the state contractors. They performed important services for him during his proconsulship, and Cicero himself, during his passage through Asia Minor to and from Cilicia, attempted by means of his recommendation to facilitate the negotiations of his friends among the contractors even with towns that did not belong to his province.[24]

Patronage and the Networks of Power

A patron was a person who facilitated personal access to those who exercised power. Patronage can thus be considered as a structure of political communication. The interplay between private relationships and political behavior also made respect of cliental obligations into an important element in decision making. In the mechanisms of Roman power and in particular of political decision-making at the highest level, the role of personal relations can sometimes be discerned, as well as the influence exerted by respect for a private obligation upon the motivation for a political act. The ties that connected the leading men of the cities of Italy or the provinces with the members of the Roman ruling class provided the Romans with multiple sources of information and various means of action. At Rome, in contrast to our modern societies, there did not exist a bureaucracy that ensured contact between the citizens or subjects of Rome, in Italy and in the provinces, and the apparatus of government. Patronage could furnish this kind of mediation. Italian and provincial clients gave their patrons the means to obtain information quickly, despite long distances.

Patrons gave their Italian and provincial clients the opportunity to approach indirectly the men who wielded power at Rome, to communicate with those who exercised public duties as equals or even as friends, and to set in motion the most powerful parts of the Roman body politic. In the time of Sulla, one of the most notorious crimes of his freedman Chrysogonus was perpetrated upon Sextus Roscius, a local magnate of Ameria in Umbria, who was accused of parricide in order to appropriate his property. Roscius enjoyed an extraordinary network of guest-friends, since he had established relationships of hospitality with the Metelli, the Servilii, and the Scipios. However, in the particularly hostile political circumstances of the time, it fell to Cicero, a young, still little-known orator, to undertake his defense at the request of Roscius' patrons, delivering a speech that still survives. Again, when the leading men of the province of Sicily were wronged by Verres they informed their patrons. Some even fled to Rome, where they were received in the homes of their guest-friends. A notable instance is the case of Sthenius of Thermae; his patrons were able to induce the tribunes of the plebs to intervene in his behalf, and indeed even the Senate, before whom the consuls spoke in his favor.[25]

The support of patrons could also have financial effects, in particular the securing of tax exemptions. For example, the names of the individuals mentioned as patrons on the honorific inscriptions at Oropus in Greece are those of senators who had reached the summit of their political career at the time of the dispute between the priests of the sanctuary of Amphiaraus at Oropus and the state contractors (*publicani*), a financial dispute that was resolved in 73 by a senatorial decree in favor of the sanctuary. On the basis of this fact F. Canali de Rossi argues plausibly that the three Roman senators honored at Oropus (C. Scribonius Curio, Cn. Cornelius Lentulus, Cn. Calpurnius Piso) had used their power in Rome to intervene on behalf of the sanctuary of Amphiaraus.[26] Clients and patrons also generally made use of patronage as a medium of information. As was noted above, the city of Dyrrachium was a long-standing client of Cicero. Its residents were his main source of information on the actions of L. Calpurnius Piso Caesoninus as governor of Macedon between 57 and 55 (unpaid soldiers and financial irregularities) that Cicero reported to the Senate.[27] The case of the Allobroges is also famous due to its implications for the successful suppression of Catiline's conspiracy. In 63 the ambassadors of this tribe of Trans-alpine Gaul had come to Rome to complain about their governors. They were solicited by the friends of Catiline to foment disturbances in Gaul, but instead alerted their patron, Q. Fabius Sanga, who informed Cicero. Compromising letters then permitted the consul to uncover the threat facing the city and to act against it (Sall. *Cat.* 41.4, 46, 47). The usual view is that Fabius Sanga was the Allobroges' patron because he was a descendant of Q. Fabius Maximus Allobrogicus, consul in 121, who had conquered the Allobroges in 120.[28]

The assistance given by clients was valued in all aspects of a patron's public life. Clients even saw to the physical security of their patron in the absence of a permanent police force. The young men of the town of Reate constituted a bodyguard for Cicero during his consulship in 63 at the time of the Catilinarian conspiracy (Cic. *Scaur.* 27). During their tenure of the aedileship, patrons who needed to obtain the gratitude of the Roman People to lay the groundwork for future elections demanded a great deal from their clients. Thus the residents of Messina in Sicily lent statues to C. Claudius Pulcher, notably one of Cupid sculpted by Praxiteles, in order to give more pomp to the games that he organized during his aedileship in 99 (Cic. *Verr.* 2.4.3, 6). An extraordinarily munificent aedileship might be supported by clients' gifts of grain for the city of Rome and wild animals for the games. In 196, during his aedileship, C. Flaminius distributed grain that the Sicilians had offered him in memory of his father, who had been praetor of Sicily in 227 (Livy 33.42.8). The Sicilians showed their gratitude also to Cicero after his success over Verres in 70. In his aedileship in 69 they sent him enough grain to lower the price in Rome during a time of great scarcity and high prices (Plut. *Cic.* 8.2).[29] A recently discovered inscription has given evidence of an earlier example of such generosity. A decree from Larissa in Thessaly (Greece) tells us that the Thessalian League had made a contribution to Rome's food supply in the form of a grant of wheat to an aedile, Q. Caecilius Metellus, in gratitude for his family's actions in their behalf.[30]

When the Romans authorized the importation of African wild animals by a law passed in 170, a member of the family of the Scipios, P. Cornelius Scipio Nasica Corculum, aedile in 169, provided African animals (63 panthers, 40 elephants, 40 bears) for a public wild-beast hunt (*venatio*). He had indirectly inherited the patron-age that his kinsman Scipio Africanus, the conqueror of Hannibal, had established over Massinissa, the king of Numidia (Livy 44.18. 8), and he subsequently had a brilliant career, becoming consul twice (in 162 and 155) and censor (159). Patronal relationships were typically such an important resource for the organization of the wild-beast spectacles that when Cicero became governor of Cilicia, he was forced to confront a remarkable request by his friend and protégé, M. Caelius Rufus, aedile in 50, to organize hunts throughout the cities of his province in order to obtain panthers for the games Caelius was responsible for presenting.[31]

The patronage of a Roman magistrate and his family over a region of Italy could open up access to other types of services. The patronage that the family of Pompey exercised over Picenum is well known. Pompey's father, Cn. Pompeius Strabo, had invited officers of Picenum to join his staff at the time of the Social War (*ILLRP* 515). Some years later, the young Pompey raised three legions there which he put at Sulla's disposal as he returned from the East to take back power in Rome. Again, in 56 Pompey was able to gather a large force from Picenum against Clodius. Finally, in 49, he recruited a large number of troops there for use against Caesar. Also in 49 L. Domitius Ahenobarbus recruited slaves, freedmen, and tenants in the region of Cosa where he held land in order to supply crews for the fleet he had created to support the Pompeians in Marseilles (Caes. *B Civ.* 1.34.2).

Toward the end of the Republic some cities had established multiple patron–client relationships with the generals or politicians who were their intermediaries with Roman power. It was at times difficult for them to make a choice between their multiple loyalties to patrons, the nature of whose protection varied depending on circumstances. The people of Marseilles, who owed loyalty to Pompey as much as to Caesar,[32] finally decided to side with Pompey, who had exercised his patronage over them before Caesar. When they were defeated by Caesar he punished them harshly.

The times of Caesar's consulship (59) and later of his dictatorship (46–44) were also marked by other conflicts of patronage. The settlement of thousands of veterans, clients of Caesar, on lands that had been allotted to them posed a threat to landownership in Italy and the communities of the provinces. Thus Caesar's land-allotments prompted in response patronal intercessions, as attested by Cicero's letters of recommendation. When, for example, the residents of Volaterrae (Volterra) in Italy (Cic. *Fam.* 13.4) and Buthrotum in Epirus (northwest Greece) were threatened with expropriation, Cicero's intervention gave them the wherewithal to resist arbitrary confiscations (Cic. *Att.* 15.14; 16.16 A–F). Patronage allowed political decisions to be manipulated in favor of clients and clienteles. Cicero's recommendations were moreover accompanied by new requests for patronage: he entrusted the people of Volaterrae to the *fides* of a legate of Caesar for their protection and those of Buthrotum to that of the consul, Dolabella.[33]

Patronage and Careers

At Rome access to political office, and thus to the Senate, was the principal criterion of social differentiation. The wealthiest men and those who had the good fortune to belong to a family that had already supplied magistrates to the state enjoyed advantages, in particular that of supporting numerous inherited clients who could be mobilized at election time. A "new man" without famous ancestors who pursued a high magistracy could hope that by exploiting cliental connections acquired by his patron he would receive indispensable support. This possibility is demonstrated by the story of C. Cicereius, which was passed on as a model of exemplary behavior. Cicereius was praetor in 173, a member of a Campanian family that was in the clientele of the Scipios. In 175, as a candidate for praetor at the same time as L. Scipio, he had stepped aside to allow Scipio to be elected when he saw that he was ahead in the balloting. However, he was elected praetor the following year, in recognition of this gesture and thanks to the support of his patrons' family.[34] On the other hand, the election to the consulship of C. Marius, legate in Africa in the war against Jugurtha, seemed revolutionary. He was hastening to canvass in Rome for the consulship when Q. Caecilius Metellus, who was both his commander in chief and his patron, advised him to wait to pursue his candidacy together with Metellus' own son, who was at that time only 20 years old. Perhaps this was in effect an offer of his own clients' aid in the election, but if so Marius rejected this promise of support, left Africa precipitately, and was elected consul for 107 (see also Chapter 8). The circumstances were exceptional. Other forms of association had come into play. His officers, Roman knights (*equites*), had written from Africa to their families that the war against Jugurtha could not be won unless Marius were elected consul and chosen as commander-in-chief. Marius' friends "in the end inflamed the plebs to the point that all the laborers and peasants, who had no property or credit but what was in their hands, dropped their work and escorted Marius about, sacrificing their own needs in favor of his election."[35] True, the introduction of the secret ballot in elections by a law of 139 made voting less dependant on traditional clienteles by weakening the dominance of patronal obligations (see also Chapter 18).[36] The voters' decision now seemed more dependent on a man's personality, on the strong advocacy of his friends, and on the choice of good intermediaries to serve as relays in the large undertaking that a political campaign inevitably constituted, particularly once all the Italians had become eligible to participate in Roman political life. Having become citizens on account of the Social War, the Italians had to wait a generation to be placed on the voting rolls and be counted in the census in Rome. Sulla had in fact suppressed the census, which was resumed in the consulship of Pompey and Crassus in 70. Undoubtedly numerous Italians participated in the election of Cicero in 64 to the consulship of 63. Being of Italian origin and not belonging to the Roman senatorial aristocracy, the orator made a reputation for himself in the Forum through trials such as the prosecution of Verres. He had had to develop for his use alternative networks among the Roman aristocracy, the Roman People, and also throughout the Italian peninsula. The advice given to him by his brother Quintus, who wrote for him the *Handbook of Electioneering*, called for dividing all Italy into sectors, searching for supporters in all the cities as well as power-brokers who could intervene on his behalf with the citizens of their tribes.[37] We can indeed trace the groups of clients attached to Cicero across the Italian peninsula, just as we can those of other leading politicians. His birthplace Arpinum and the neighboring towns were in his clientele, but also important cities and towns in Campania, like Capua,[38] Atella, Cales, and cities in the south of Italy (all the towns from Vibo to Brundisium),[39] Etruscan cities like Arretium (Arezzo) and especially Volaterrae, and finally the town of Reate in the Sabine country.[40]

At Rome, crowds of attendants marked the rhythms of citizens' official life. Linked by the obligations of private clientship and of communal appreciation, friends and clients accompanied politicians to whom they wished to show their attachment, particularly at the time of the elections. Escorting processions invaded the streets of the city just as crowds who wished to greet powerful men besieged the doors of their houses. The retinue that surrounded a candidate before an election was a sign in a kind of parallel language that allowed observers to appreciate a politician's popularity and made it possible to assess the strength of his patronage as well as his capacity to mobilize all the elements of the electorate.[41] While the size of the retinue was important, it had to show great diversity in order to convey an impression of the breadth of the candidate's social connections. This service was requested from friends and clients as well as from all those who had received a benefit from him and thus owed him gratitude. Quintus Cicero refers to the practice in the *Handbook on Electioneering*, advising his brother to "see to it that both the number of your friends and their social diversity are made visible; for you have," adds Quintus,

> what few "new men" have had: all the state contractors (*publicani*), nearly the entire order of knights (*equites*), many towns that are wholly in your camp, many men of every order whom you have defended, a number of associations (*collegia*), and also that large group of young men whom the study of oratory has brought over to you, a daily crowd of friends in constant attendance. (Cic. *Comment. Pet.* 3)

Gratitude for services rendered was made manifest in a sort of collective ritual that united all those who had received even a rather modest favor from the candidate. "Men of small resources have no other opportunity to put us in their debt or to pay back a favor than by performing this service of attending us in our campaigns" (Cic. *Mur.* 70). This mark of respect consecrated by ancient custom was evidently demanded to some extent from other social groups as well, but "constant attendance of this kind is only for friends of humble status who are otherwise unoccupied" (Cic. *Mur.* 70). Regular presence in the entourage could not be expected of anyone but such lower-class "friends," "since to attend candidates connected to them for whole days continuously is a service that cannot be performed or even requested from senators or from Roman knights (*equites*); if men like that frequent our house, if sometimes they accompany us down to the Forum . . . this passes for a mark of great respect and attention" (Cic. *Mur.* 70). It was moreover customary for friends to perform a type of public solicitation in favor of the future magistrate at the same time that he himself solicited votes from his fellow-citizens. Those thus publicly endorsing the candidate, called *suffragatores*, explained to future voters the reasons for their support.[42] The extraordinary breadth of Cicero's organization and his mobilization of a large clientele created by himself made it possible in 64 for a "new man," exceptionally, to be elected to the consulship for 63.

Success in a career was first and foremost a product of election, but it also drew upon a complex network of patronage before a man pursued his first political offices. This is how a man aspiring to undertake a career could make himself known. An apprenticeship in politics owed much to the methods of instruction used by teachers of oratory and of law, in particular to the practice of participating in debates among a circle of disciples (see also Chapter 20). Military service was also an essential pre-requisite for the right to canvass for political office. The state authorized the Roman magistrate who commanded an army or who governed a province to choose his staff; he was free to recruit his subordinates, from the legates to the prefects, and to choose a certain number of the military tribunes (those that were not elected by the assemblies). By resorting to his friends and clients to carry out these duties the commander could widen the pool of candidates, be confident of the loyalty of those who would accompany him, and strengthen his ties with those who had recommended men to him. The texts that give evidence of governors' entourages only rarely attest to specific names of the intermediaries who had facilitated their selection. The persons who were recruited into the personal advisory councils (*consilia*) of Quintus and Marcus Cicero, however, yield useful information about the presence of local families from Arpinum. Cicero's letters of recommendation also sometimes make reference to patronal requests for military posts in the army of Gaul, especially during 54; they were addressed to Caesar, one of whose legates was Quintus, Cicero's brother. Among these was also C. Trebatius Testa, mentioned above. It is possible that at this time service in the military tribunate or prefectures gave these officers entry into the order of knights (*equites*). Indeed, the procedures of the census by which *equites* were recruited were carried out very irregularly toward the end of the Republic. Among the wealthy local leaders of the Italian cities, there was a very strong desire to enter the equestrian order, a necessary step for advancement in Roman society.

Officers hoped for their commander's continuing support in their subsequent career. "New men" obtained magistracies after having served Scipio Africanus well. At the end of the Republic, the prestige of the great generals contributed greatly to their officers' careers. L. Afranius, Pompey's legate in Spain and the East, became praetor in 71; his election to the consulship in 60 was notorious for the bribery and machinations employed by Pompey to ensure his old subordinate's victory at the polls. A. Hirtius, L. Munatius Plancus, and C. Asinius Pollio began their military careers with Caesar and, after his death, reached the higher magistracies. At the time of the Civil Wars, however, officers of high social rank had to make choices with dramatic consequences, since their preexisting cliental obligations drew them to one or the other side of the conflict. So, for example, T. Labienus, one of Caesar's great generals, who was originally from Picenum, where the family of Pompey had a large clientele, had to abandon Caesar in order to stay loyal to Pompey, who earlier, while he was still on friendly terms with Caesar, had arranged for Labienus' appointment to Caesar's army.[43] We also know that the centurions who had been appointed to Caesar's army on Pompey's recommendation were left free, when the two old allies took up arms against each other, to pass over to the army of their old patron, Pompey (Suet. *Iul.* 75.1).

A grant of Roman citizenship, which gave a person a privileged status in the empire and eventually to undertake a career in Roman service, could also be the subject of patronal intervention. Local aristocrats of Italy, and after the Social War, those of Cisalpine Gaul, Sicily, and other provinces aspired to be integrated into the Roman community. The game of patronage that made individual access to this privileged status possible under the Republic can sometimes be reconstructed based on the name a new citizen received. This was testimony to a person's appreciation of the one who had intervened in his behalf, and it was passed on to his descendants as a permanent sign of gratitude toward the patron responsible for conferring this benefit (*beneficium*). Pompey gave his name to many foreigners, in Gaul as well as in Sicily and the East. The Augustan historian Trogus was a Gaul of the Vocontii named Cn. Pompeius Trogus; Theophanes of Mitylene, Pompey's officer and historian of his deeds, became Cn. Pompeius Theophanes after having received the citizenship in a military assembly during his patron's eastern campaigns (Cic. *Arch.* 24). Caesar's grants of Roman citizenship were certainly much more numerous and more complex than those of other commanders. To secure this benefit, men who enjoyed a close relationship with Caesar could be used as intermediaries. So, in 45, we see Cicero appealing to P. Cornelius Dolabella, then probably one of Caesar's legates, to request citizenship in his own name for one of Cicero's Sicilian guest-friends. Upon receiving the grant his protégé took the name P. Cornelius Megas in memory of Dolabella's request before Caesar (Cic. *Fam.* 13.36.1).

Cicero's patronage of guest-friends in the years 47–45 manifested itself as well in another way. Their social rank alone could not protect them from entanglement in Roman power struggles. Very important people, sometimes described as the "leading men" (*principes*) of their cities, were forced to take sides in the civil wars. Mainten-ance of their freedom, their rights, and their preeminence in their city after they had chosen Pompey's side depended on the attitude of the governor whom Caesar had sent to govern their province. The patronage of Cicero, one who could approach the Caesarian governor to recommend them as to a friend, served to protect them.[44] Caesar had treated Cicero magnanimously after his victory over Pompey at Pharsalus. Cicero's power of mediation, which was linked to his personal credit with the dictator, was made possible also by Caesar's own friends. Many of Caesar's closest associates belonged to families tied to Cicero in a long-standing relationship re-inforced by reciprocal exchanges of services. Some had been his students in rhetoric and responded to his requests with a benevolence that attested to their gratitude. Cicero's patronage went into operation again as soon as the conflicts became sharply personal and there was a corresponding intensification of the search for individual and collective protection. But Caesar alone exercised the power of decision and his will was dominant.

Conclusion

Italy's entry into Roman citizenship and the growth of the empire transformed the traditional equilibriums. Large groups of clients still constituted an important elem-ent of political power. The glory of traditional patrons was amplified when it was joined by a reputation for preserving those clients passed down by their ancestors, as is demonstrated by the example of the young Tiberius Claudius Nero, father of the emperor Tiberius, who traveled to Asia in 50 to support his family's "enormous clienteles" (Cic. *Fam.* 13.64). But a great debate among historians has recently arisen over the actual role of cliental networks in Roman political life, particularly in winning elections (see also Chapters 1, 12, and 18). Some, such as Claude Nicolet, have argued that clients formed "an electoral army, each man at his post, dedicated to promoting their patron's career,"[45] while others, on the contrary, place the emphasis on popular participation and tend to minimize the direct role of cliental groups in affecting electoral outcomes.[46] It is true that the secret vote, demanded as a privilege due to the People of the greatest nation on earth, was a right whose consequences were unpredictable, a privilege that inspired fear. Politicians expended considerable effort to create a good public image for themselves in the hope of giving an impression that the community was unanimously in their favor even before the assembly voted. Networks of clients then served to mobilize all categories of voters in their patron's favor.

From this perspective, patronage emerges as an indispensable form of mediation. In a society in which vertical connections are preeminent, patronage is an essential element of social relations. Today's historians are interested in the patrons' power of mediation, just as they are also in clientship as a structure of social and political communication. The success of intercession and the importance of favors granted confirm the power of the networks possessed by the oldest families and, toward the end of the Republic especially, the power of the great generals. In Italy and throughout the empire Caesar and Pompey were able, through their patronal networks, to mobilize the resources of men and cash that they needed for their wars. Later, Caesar became the sole arbiter of patronal conflicts between those who sought by means of their own networks to make requests of him. He took control of the ties of patronage in his own interest at the moment when, by means of his acts of generosity and his "popular" program, he secured the loyalty of the greater part of the People who had already, in a sense, become his clients.

Guide to Further Reading

Good starting points for further reading include Saller 1982, Brunt 1988a; Wallace-Hadrill 1989b, and if the French language is no hindrance, Rouland 1979 and Deniaux 1993. For the "sociological" rather than "lexicographic" definition of patronage as a hierarchical but reciprocal relationship, see also Boissevain 1974, Gellner and Waterbury 1977, Johnson and Dandeker 1989; for other important sociological work on modern patronage, see Eisenstadt and Roninger 1980, 1984; Boissevain 1966; and for the link between clientship and politics, Médard 1976. Patronage's role as an expression of *fides* or a system of gift-exchange is emphasized by Gelzer 1969, Freyburger 1986, Veyne 1990; judicial patronage is analyzed by David 1992a, 1997. On *fides* see also Hellegouarc'h 1963: 23–35. For divergent views on the importance of patronage as a model for control and administration of the empire, see Harmand 1957, Badian 1958a, Gruen 1984a, Rich 1989, Eilers 2002, Burton 2003. For varying judgments on the electoral importance of clients, see Nicolet 1980, Brunt 1988a, Millar 1998, Yakobson 1999. The idea of a sort of "communal patronage" exercised by popular politicians over the Roman plebs as a whole can be explored in Nicolet and Ferrary 1983; Deniaux and Schmitt-Pantel 1987–9, Millar 1998. For the conception of Caesar as ultimate, sole patron, see Syme 1939; Yavetz 1969, 1983.

Notes

1 On the constitution of Romulus, see Gabba 1960, 1982, 1991.

2 Fustel de Coulanges 1890: esp. 205–47, "Voluntary clientship in the last centuries of the Republic."

3 On the collective favor conferred by the People, see Cic. *Planc.* 12. On the role of the People, see Millar 1998. Finley 1983 brings this into the discussion of patronage in a chapter entitled "Authority and Patronage." Cf. Deniaux and Schmitt-Pantel 1987–9.

4 Weynand 1935: coll. 1368–9; Deniaux 1973.

5 Mommsen 1864: 326, 365. According to his theory, the plebeians were originally classified as clients. Clients were non-patricians who were placed under the patronage of the patrician clans (*gentes*). However, after having held a curule magistracy a plebeian would have been released from his cliental obligations and became a fully independent Roman citizen. On this theory and the subject of clientage in German historiography, see David 1997.

6 Not all historians agree on this point. In opposition to the general view that patronage remained important to the end of the Republic Brunt 1988a argues that we can observe at this point a weakening of the bonds of clientship. Brunt is, however, critical of the work of Rouland, who held that the absence of the words *patronus* and *cliens* showed that these bonds were in decline.

7 Neuhauser 1958; David 1992a.

8 Boissevain 1977: 81.

9 Asc. *Mil.* 31 C; Plut. *Cic.* 25.1; Cic. *Fam.* 7.2.3 (the accusation for political violence). On this trial, see Gruen 1974: 346–7.

10 On emancipation and the obligations of freedmen, see Treggiari 1969; Fabre 1981.

11 On *applicatio*, see von Premerstein 1900. It is difficult to investigate its origins (cf. Badian 1958a: 7–8), since the expression "law of attachment" is used only in an obscure Ciceronian passage (*De Or.* 1.177) which concerns the property and inheritance of a foreigner in exile in Rome who was attached to a patron by this method and had died without an heir.

12 This might be used as a courtroom rhetorical device to win sympathy for the accused: cf. Cic. *Inv.* 1.109. Cicero himself symbolically adapted this kind of request for protection when he commended himself to the *fides* of Atticus before departing into exile (*Att.* 3.20.2).

13 See, e.g., Lintott 1993; Eilers 2002: 38–60; cf. Nörr 1991; Hölkeskamp 2000b.

14 Conquest of Syracuse: Polyb. 8.37; Livy 25.23–32; Plut. *Marc.* 18–19. Entry into Marcellus' clientele: Livy 26.32; Plut. *Marc.* 23.9. On the patrons of Sicily, see Brunt 1980b.

15 P. Clodius had been quaestor in Sicily in 61–60. When Cicero replied that this was not his practice, P. Clodius retorted that as a new patron of Sicily he would adopt it (Cic. *Att.* 2.1.5).

16 Cicero defended him in 62. See Cic. *Sull.* 62 on his role in the colony's foundation.

17 For Marius, see Cic. *Balb.* 50, Val. Max. 5.2.8, Plut. *Mar.* 28.2; for Caesar, see Strabo 5.1.6 and Deniaux 1993: 315–25.

18 For the text, see Crawford 1996b: no. 25, line 97. On Caesar's social policy, see Yavetz 1983.

19 Cf. the analysis by Eilers 2002, esp. ch. 2, "Becoming a Client."

20 Cic. *Planc.* 97; also *Fam.* 14.3.4, which attests to Cicero's permanent protection.

21 Published by Reynolds 1982: no. 3. Cf. also the study of this document by Eilers 2002: 23–7.

22 On patronage over communities, cf. Ferrary 1997; Canali de Rossi 2001.

23 Cic. *Fam.* 9.25.3, 2.14, 13.59. On the role of letters of recommendation and the Roman judicial practices, see Cotton 1986b.

24 Cic. *Fam.* 13.9, 65: recommendation of the "Bithynian company" and of P. Terentius Hispo. The interpretation of these letters and the definition of the precise area in which these contractors operated pose numerous problems: cf. Nicolet 1975, Cotton 1986a, Deniaux 1993: 242–8. On the relationship between governors and the contractors of state revenues, see Badian 1972a.

25 Cic. *Verr.* 2.2.100–3, on which see Deniaux 1987.

26 *RDGE* 23; Canali de Rossi 2001: 65–6, 140–1.

27 See Cicero's *Against Piso*, which he delivered before the Senate in 55.

28 On the difficulty of tracing this Fabius Sanga to the conqueror's family, however, see Eilers 2002: 46–50.

29 Deniaux 1994.

30 Cf. also Deniaux 1994: 250, and the comments of A. Gara on this subject, in Deniaux 1994: 252. There is uncertainty over the date of the inscription (text in *SEG* 34.558): cf. the comments of Garnsey, Gallant, and Rathbone 1984 and Kallet-Marx 1995: 55–6, n.44.

31 Cic. *Fam.* 2.12.2, 8.2.2, 8.4.5, 8.8.10, 8.9.3.

32 Caes. *B Civ.* 1.34, 35, a very interesting text regarding the debates that arose from these tragic conflicts of patronage.

33 Cic. *Fam.* 13.4; *Att.* 15.14. On this form of patronage see Deniaux 1993: 352–66.

34 Val. Max. 3.5.1, 4.5.3, with Broughton 1951–86: 1.408.

35 Sall. *Iug.* 73.6. On the election of C. Marius to the consulship of 107, cf. Plut. *Mar.* 7–9.

36 On Roman elections, see Taylor 1966a; Nicolet 1980; Yakobson 1999.

37 Cic. *Comment. Pet.* 30–2. On the great value of this work see David et al. 1973; Laser 1999; and especially the rich synthesis of Morstein-Marx 1998.

38 Cicero had been chosen as the sole patron of the community (*conventus*) of Capuans after the Catilinarian conspiracy (Cic. *Sest.* 9). He seems to have remained one of the patrons of the colony founded subsequently: Antony addressed him as a patron of Capua before sending new colonists to its territory (Cic. *Phil.* 2.102).

39 Cic. *Planc.* 97. On Cicero's clientele, see Deniaux 1993: 373–7.

40 Cic. *Fam.* 13.4, *Caec.* 97, *Scaur.* 27.

41 Deniaux 1997.

42 So, for example, Q. Caecilius Metellus Pius, consul in 80, a scion of the highest nobility, supplicated the People in support of Q. Calidius' campaign for the praetorship because as tribune in 98 the latter had introduced a law supporting the restoration from exile of his father, Q. Caecilius Metellus Numidicus. Cicero was already a famous orator when he supplicated the People in Cn. Plancius' favor, reminding them that the young man, as quaestor in Thessalonica, had saved his life by taking him in during his flight from Rome as an exile.

43 Syme 1938. On recommendation to a post of military command, see Saller 1980: 44–59; Cotton 1981; Deniaux 1993: 297–310.

44 Twelve guest-friends recommended by Cicero were subjects of requests for protection during the years 47–45. See, for example, the brief recommendation of Hagesaretus of

Larissa to Servius Sulpicius Rufus (Cic. *Fam.* 13.25). The role of this important person during the civil war may be explained by a text that suggests that he was the leader of the Pompeian party in Larissa in 48 (Caes. *B Civ.* 3.35.2). His name also appears on an inscription from Larissa (*IG* 2.549, line 7). On this person, see Deniaux 1993: 350–2, 505–6 (nr. 54).

45 Nicolet 1977: 233.
46 Cf. Brunt 1988a; Millar 1998; Yakobson 1999.

CHAPTER 20

Rhetoric and Public Life

Jean-Michel David

Translated by Robert Morstein-Marx and Robert Martz

As in all ancient cities, Roman politics in the age of the Republic were characterized by the form of interaction that linked together all its political agents and, for the most part, took the form of public, verbal debate. Consequently every politician was necessarily defined as an orator – one capable of making speeches before large audiences and of persuading them (Figure. 21.1).

Yet as obvious as this simple necessity may appear, it was hardly available to just anyone. Indeed, one who ventured to address the Senate or the Roman People already had to enjoy a recognized position within the community. Contrary to the practice in democratic cities, an ordinary citizen had no opportunity to take the floor and participate in a political debate. Only members of the aristocracy were able to do so, and more precisely, those who had already held a magistracy. These were men who possessed powerful social influence as a result of their wealth or their network of clients, or had the prior benefit of prestige conferred by the splendor of their achievements or the antiquity of their family. They therefore enjoyed what was called *auctoritas* ("authority," "credibility"), which gave them the right to speak publicly and to persuade their fellow-citizens that their proposals were best.

This crucial quality, however, was not enough. One also had to be able to deliver a coherent and well-argued speech. This long presented little difficulty, since the public expected nothing more than a firm and clear statement that conformed to a set of principles shared by the community. But a change came when philosophy and rhetoric, brought in the train of Hellenism, became fully integrated into the cultural universe of the Roman aristocracy. Henceforth orators had to raise themselves to the higher intellectual standards that now prevailed. Neither personal authority nor appeals to ancestral tradition (*mos maiorum*) were enough. It was necessary to justify one's decisions by accommodating one's arguments to general principles of truth and justice. Above all, one had to perfect the techniques of argumentation and ornamentation that gave speeches their power. Not everyone was equally capable of this.

This change had a number of consequences. First of all it imposed on members of the aristocracy the need to acquire the principles and methods on which this new art of oratory rested. This was not the greatest difficulty: for this purpose study would suffice, with Greek teachers of rhetoric and philosophers and subsequently with those Romans who had become skilled in these disciplines. But the rise of oratorical standards also had the effect of adding a new dimension to the field of aristocratic competition. To be heard and to convince, it was no longer enough to have a strong record of accomplishment or to belong to a famous family; one also had to prevail in rhetorical duels that were fought out at the level of the general principles on which the city rested. Now that eloquence had become a technical discipline it was transformed into an instrument of power that opened new avenues to the ambitious. It therefore posed a threat that called for control. Politicians at the end of the Republic had only two ways to do this: to be great orators themselves, or to secure the assistance of better ones among their networks of patronage and *amicitia* ("friendship," including the political and instrumental as well as affective senses of our word). And since these two methods were hardly contradictory, they were both employed.

The history of the relationship between rhetoric and public life in the Roman Republic is an aspect as much of social history as cultural history. To the extent that oratorical ability was primarily a means of political action, it was one of the qualities that defined membership in the Roman aristocracy (see also Chapter 17). A Roman politician possessed no other means of communication by which to make himself known and appreciated by his fellow-citizens than the speeches he made, the arguments he used, and the self-image that he created in this way. Rhetoric was as much an art of aristocratic behavior and of the ethos of leadership as it was an art of speaking. The following study will focus sharply on the relationship between these two aspects of oratory, the cultural and the political, since it was through their intersection that public action took on its specific character.

Circumstances and Conditions of Civic Oratory

Throughout the history of the Republic, two kinds of political proceedings regularly called for speeches on the part of those involved: the assemblies of the People and meetings of the Senate. Then, from the middle of the second century, a third appeared: trials before the standing criminal courts (*quaestiones perpetuae*), which took on increasing importance as their number grew and they played a progressively more political role. As these trials were chiefly intended to judge crimes committed by members of the aristocracy, they often led to the condemnation and ruin of important men. They therefore gave rise to a decisive change in the history of political oratory. Indeed, in contrast to the first two types of assemblies where speaking was restricted to well-known civic figures, judicial proceedings were in principle open to any citizen and permitted those who risked them to deliver a speech that could exert an influence on politics. In all three cases, material and institutional circumstances determined the context in which the speakers had to express themselves and imposed a corresponding variety of rules for working up their speeches.

All the decisions of the Roman People were preceded by speeches, whether they were elections, legislative votes, or popular trials. Orators delivered their speeches during the public meetings (*contiones*) held at the very place where the voting assemblies were to gather: on the Campus Martius near the "enclosure" (*Saepta*) when the decision involved the centuriate assembly; when it involved the tribal assembly, at the same place on the Campus Martius, at the Circus Flaminius, in the open space on the Capitol (the *Area Capitolina*) or in the Forum. Whenever the sources allow us to envision the arrangement of the space we find the same situation. Speakers addressed the People from the height of a platform: the *rostra* in the Forum, the podium of the temple of Castor in the Forum, that of the temple of Jupiter on the Capitol or still others on the Campus Martius. These structures gave those who stood on them the ability to project their voices to a considerable distance. But this was only a consequence of a more general function: due to their elevation they gave the magistrate who held the assembly the necessary distance to exercise his power. They set between the speaker and the People that same magisterial distance that the lictors or other attendants (*viatores*) imposed on passers-by. And, since the decisions taken there often demanded the approval of the gods, the tribunals themselves, including the *rostra*, were *templa*, inaugurated places (see also Chapter 10).[1]

It is evident therefore that not just anyone could mount the podium and address the People. Only those whom the magistrate presiding over the meeting had invited could do so. We accordingly discover, when we read the lists that we have compiled of those attested by our sources as speakers in such meetings, that most were leading figures: priests, magistrates, or former magistrates.

In order to make a speech in a *contio*, one therefore had to possess sufficient authority. Cicero expresses this very well in speaking of himself when, after being elected praetor, he dared for the first time to make a speech before a popular assembly. Until then, he says, he had only pleaded in the law courts, and it was only at the rank he had at last reached that the *auctoritas* his magistracy conferred upon him and the oratorical competence he had gained through numerous courtroom speeches finally permitted him to hope to persuade the Roman citizenry.[2] Conversely, he was indignant when, in 59, the tribune of the plebs Vatinius allowed Lucius Vettius to speak – a sort of "agent provocateur" who sought to implicate the opponents of the triumvirate in a plot to murder Pompey: "when... you brought L. Vettius before the assembly, when you set an informer on the *rostra* – that place consecrated by the augurs, where other tribunes regularly brought forth the leaders of the city to ascertain their opinion."[3] Membership among the elite who governed the city was thus a necessary condition for addressing the People, inasmuch as the decisions taken here shaped the future.[4] Thus it seemed improper for anyone other than those whose calling was to lead the People to be given the opportunity to enlighten them with their advice.

The form of interaction that emerged was not one of debate (see also Chapters 12 and 18). The magistrate who summoned the assembly and presided over it had responsibility for determining the order of speeches. He might choose to invite certain speakers to mount the platform, or on the contrary might constrain others to express their views below the *rostra* and thus in a completely ineffectual way (Cic. *Att.* 2.24.3). He gave the right to speak, took it away, and put an end to discussion by dissolving the meeting. In conducting the assembly, the presiding magistrate put himself on stage and thus sought to win approval for his own political stance. More often than not he succeeded.[5] The People, for their part, had to be content to listen. If they approved or disapproved of the views presented to them, they could do so only with their silence, shouts, or other collective demonstrations. In the *contio*, the relationship established between orators and audience preserved the same unequal quality as the one that linked the magistrate possessing *imperium* or tribunician power to the Roman People whom he had to inform and convince, but who in principle remained under the authority of their leaders.

This gave a particular form to speeches delivered before the People. First, the physical setting, its symbolic meaning, and the very distance that the voice had to cover necessitated a powerful oratorical performance. Orators tended to adopt a style that gave the greater weight to emotion[6] and to emphasize in their choice of arguments their personal connection with their audience.[7] They stressed their status in the city, their devotion, and their zeal in defending its interests. And they had to recognize as well the role and majesty of the Roman People, in whom they acknowledged the power to decide. The exchange imposed a necessity on the part of the orator on one hand to emphasize his legitimacy and thus to rely on his *auctoritas*, and on the other to win the confidence of his audience and thus to find the arguments that would win its support. Consequently the oratorical styles available to him oscillated between affirmation of his own authority, of his competence, and of his devotion to the citizenry, and recognition of the rights and aspirations of his fellow-citizens.

In the first case, he would give himself an air of authority that corresponded well to the position of leadership that he occupied. The best example of this stance is doubtless the remark that the consul P. Scipio Nasica directed one day at the People after they had interrupted his speech with a shout of disapproval: "Be silent, please, citizens, for I understand better than you what is best for the Republic." If we are to believe our source, this produced a respectful silence among his audience.[8] An oratorical ethos of this kind therefore corresponded to a traditional type: the image of the magistrate possessing *imperium*, whose function was to give orders.[9] This answered to an expectation on the part of the citizenry and earned the trust of his fellow-citizens for one who knew how to show himself worthy of it.

The second, and opposite, style – the one most frequently employed at the end of the Republic – led the orator to underscore his dedication to the cause of the People, to take account of their difficulties and to make proposals that pleased them. This kind of oratorical posture is sometimes called "popular eloquence" (*eloquentia popularis*). One could take as an example this passage that Cicero quotes from a speech given by L. Licinius Crassus in 106 to support the proposed law of Servilius Caepio, which sought to reduce the power of the prosecutors in the criminal courts: "Rescue us from our troubles, rescue us from the jaws of men whose savagery cannot be sated with our blood! Don't allow us to be slaves to anyone but all of you together, whose slaves we can and should be" (Cic. *De. Or.* 1.225). This type of oratory had been extensively developed by certain politicians – the Gracchi in particular – who made use of the tribunate of the plebs to promote a policy of reform that won them popular support. This contributed to the definition of another type of political leader, one attentive to the needs of the People and capable of braving conservative interests, but whose oratorical stance rested more on a style exploiting pathos and emotion.

In the Senate the atmosphere was different. Meetings of the Senate brought together a relatively small number of people in an enclosed space. True, the senators numbered 300 until Sulla and 600 afterward. But this roster never represented the real number of those in attendance, and the figure of 400 senators actually in attendance seems to have been reached only on the most important occasions. We can therefore presume that most meetings must have brought together no more than half of this potential audience. The places where they assembled also had to be "inaugurated," i.e., consecrated by an augur. Most of the time senators met in the Curia, located in the Forum, or in one of the temples situated on the Campus Martius (Apollo or Bellona), on the Capitol (Jupiter Optimus Maximus) or in the Forum (Concord or Castor).[10] There they took their seats on benches and spoke from where they sat.[11] The speeches they delivered did not therefore involve the same unequal relationship that connected the magistrates to the Roman People. Here, debates were joined between men who were peers.

An exception to this rule, however, was that the magistrate who presided over the meeting followed a precise order of speaking when decisions were being made. Until the early first century, the presiding magistrate gave the opportunity to speak first to the one whom the last censors, when establishing the senatorial roster, had designated "First Senator" (*princeps senatus*), that is to say the oldest or (from 209) the most distinguished of the patrician former censors (see also Chapter 17). Thereafter, the first speaker was the former consul whom the presider particularly wished to honor (preceded by the two consuls-elect if the annual election had taken place). Once this eminent person had delivered his views the magistrate would then pass to the rest of the senators present, following a descending hierarchy of rank defined by the highest office each had held. Each gave his opinion (*sententia*), sometimes in the form of a lengthy argument, sometimes briefly expressing agreement with an opinion already set forth. Thus only the most important figures of the city had the opportunity to make an extended speech; certainly, the names that our sources have preserved of senators who spoke on one occasion or another demonstrate a clear prevalence of former dictators, censors, and consuls. This does not indicate that the younger senators were excluded from debates, but their turn to speak did not come until after the more esteemed senators had spoken, so that they could more often adhere to an opinion already expressed than dare to articulate a new one.[12]

This connection between the order of speaking and a senator's rank, that is, his *dignitas*, had great influence on the mode of communication and the style of oratory adopted in the Senate. Speeches in the Senate did not involve addressing a group of ordinary citizens from on high but involved speaking in an enclosed space, on the same level, to equals or superiors. Each senator therefore had to choose the words and arguments that corresponded to his position, striking a balance among assurance, audacity, and conformity to adapt his proposal precisely to the *auctoritas* that he was acknowledged to hold. Pliny the Younger, under the Empire, recalled the distant past when the education of a young senator passed in an apprenticeship in senatorial convention:

> This is why those who would later be candidates for office used to stand by the doors of the Curia and be observers of public deliberation of the city before taking part in them...What powers those consulting the body, what rights those delivering their opinions had; how forceful magistrates could be, how free the rest; when one should yield, when stand firm; when to be silent and how long to speak; when to separate contradictory motions and how to add a rider to an earlier one; in short, senatorial procedure in its entirety was taught by the most reliable method of instruction: by example. (Pliny *Ep.* 8.14.5–6)

Political debate between aristocrats thus depended upon an acute awareness of the status that each held – status that set the conditions for challenges and tests of relative strength. It was not so much by grand flourishes of gesture and speech as by proposals aptly harmonized with the orator's circumstances that he was able to maintain or acquire the necessary political influence.

The creation and development of the standing courts (*quaestiones perpetuae*) from the middle of the second century opened up a new field for political oratory. These new procedures were added to, and then in practice substituted for, the trials which up to this point members of the aristocracy had conducted before the assemblies (*iudicia populi*). The main courts that appeared or gained importance during this period were: the *quaestio de repetundis*, which concerned extortion of funds at the expense of provincials; the *quaestio de peculatu*, concerning embezzlement of the property of the city; the *quaestio de ambitu*, for electoral fraud; the *quaestio de maiestate*, which concerned crimes against the majesty of the Roman People; the *quaestio de sicariis et veneficiis*, which involved armed gangs and poisonings; and the *quaestio de vi* for public violence. These courts essentially involved members of the senatorial order and obliged them to defend themselves before juries composed (depending on the period) of senators, *equites*, or a combination of the two (see also Chapter 11). The penalty could be a fine, or it could be capital, resulting in exile and confiscation of property. The stakes were thus very high and weighed heavily on the careers and the lives of members of the aristocracy who had always to fear prosecution by their adversaries.

The conditions that governed speakers' participation and delivery in the law courts were, however, notably distinct from those that prevailed in meetings of the People and of the Senate. Pleaders fell into two categories: those appearing for the prosecution and those for the defense. They addressed a jury of 50 to 75 members seated on a platform and presided over by a magistrate. These orators were surrounded by the principals, their witnesses, and their supporters who occupied benches that faced the jury on the pavement of the Forum. The 250 to 350 people who participated in the trial in this way roughly constituted a circle which was itself surrounded by a numerous and attentive crowd ready to express itself noisily (see also Chapter 18).[13]

This, then, was the orators' situation: they had to convince an audience composed of important members of the aristocracy regarding the guilt or innocence of a senator. They thereby assumed certain weighty responsibilities which placed them at the heart of the friendly and hostile relations that spread across the upper strata of society. But at the same time, they called upon all the spectators to witness not only the facts of the case, but also the courage and eloquence that they demonstrated in pursuit of their task (see also Chapter 17). The *quaestiones* thus became a crucial part of Roman civic life toward the end of the Republic. They opened a space for political expression to orators who were not senators and who without this opportunity would not have been able to give their opinion in a public forum. They also gave the Roman People the opportunity to reach their own conclusions and to express their emotions in less solemn circumstances than in *contiones* (see also Chapter 18).

But the situation of prosecutors differed from that of defense counsel. The prosecuting speakers had to prove their charges. They were thus encouraged to develop an offensive oratorical strategy that in the name of the superior interests of the city led them to attack well-known figures such as former magistrates, rich in connections and sometimes in prestige. Since the process gave any citizen the right to haul a senator before a court, those who ventured to undertake this role were most often "new men" or young nobles seeking to start their careers. In each case, they found themselves in a position of inferior status relative to their opponent. They therefore often followed the path of "popular eloquence" and took up on their own account that rhetorical ethos of the defender of the People's interests which deployed an aggressive, violent, and emotional kind of oratory against the conservatives' arguments.

On the other side, speakers for the defense were most often senators who had reached the highest echelon of society. The main reason for this was that a defendant of senatorial rank would find it difficult to abase himself by appealing to a person of inferior status for protection and thus risk putting himself in this person's debt for a service as important as acquittal on a capital charge (see also Chapter 19). Furthermore, the defense had to be reinforced by persons with the greatest authority possible. These men played the role of protectors (*patroni*) and adopted oratorical styles that conformed to their position: defending with dignity and sobriety when possible, but at the same time not hesitating to resort to emotion and appeals to pity if the situation warranted it. The stakes were so high that they had to make use of every resource offered by oratorical art; so in this way the most talented forensic speakers achieved disproportionate influence and reputation in Rome.

All the orators who pleaded before the courts acted therefore according to their place in the hierarchy of status and position. Those who were best known took advantage of their past and the confidence their fellow-citizens had accorded them. Those who could hardly boast this kind of background sought to be judged on their skill and their devotion to the city or to their friends. They thus anticipated the role of defender and leader of the civic community to which they aspired, and whose image they assumed.

Whatever opportunities were presented to Roman orators for speaking on the three main stages of Roman political life, they all had to take up attitudes, choose arguments, and construct an image adapted to the status they held in the city. Oratory could not be separated either from prestige (*dignitas*) or *auctoritas*. It expressed the first while deriving from and reinforcing the second. Each specific status induced a corresponding mode of behavior and an oratorical ethos founded in fact on the ethos of governance that defined the leader of the city, which the orator was or sought to be.

The Development of the Art of Oratory and Efforts to Control its Power

At the end of the second century and the beginning of the first, an important change took place. Rhetoric and philosophy made their appearance as methods of thought and verbal composition, and became established in the cultural universe of the Roman aristocracy. Before this time, even if philosophical theories of Greek origin, especially Pythagorism, were of course present in Italian society, it seems that they had not produced a specific teaching method and a means to acquire skills, nor had they permitted development of the atmosphere of competition and technical evaluation that accompanied this introduction of the intellectual disciplines of thought and speech. The art of oratory was still simply one of the abilities expected of all aristocrats, just as were military skill, knowledge of law and a concern for the preservation of one's patrimony. It was one of the virtues that funeral eulogies celebrated and inscriptions or historical tradition commemorated (see also Chapter 17).[14] Like the others, it required no additional prior training beyond that which consisted in following the example and counsel of one's father or other relative, or perhaps of attaching oneself to a senator who was a friend of the family in accordance with the practice called *tirocinium* (a kind of apprenticeship).[15] The only rules of oratorical instruction were those that enjoined clarity of exposition. Cato the Elder, who championed this method of education, summed it up with these simple words: "grasp the matter; the words will follow" (*rem tene verba sequentur*).[16] The knowledge that a young man acquired in this kind of context in practice largely involved reproducing and continuing the gestures and bearing of his father and thereby the aristocratic ethos that showed the legitimacy of his membership among the elite and assured the manifestation of *auctoritas*.

Brevity and *gravitas* therefore characterized the oratorical style of the earliest orators. The latter term encapsulated the authority of proposals delivered with seriousness and reserve and filled with the assurance and the spirit of command bestowed by the tenure of office past or present.[17] One of the best examples one can give of this is the defense that Aemilius Scaurus, censor in 109, presented on his own behalf when Q. Varius, tribune of the plebs in 90, launched a prosecution against him: "Quintus Varius the Spaniard says that Marcus Scaurus, the First Senator, called the allies to revolt; Marcus Scaurus, the First Senator, denies it. There are no witnesses. Which of the two, Citizens, is it fitting for you to believe?" (Asc. 22 C; see also Chapter 17). Cicero also noted in connection with this man that his oratory possessed a commanding gravity and a kind of natural authority, and added that such a style was more suited to the Senate than to the courts, for it inspired confidence through its unadorned compression.[18]

This old style of oratory that accorded the central role to *dignitas* had, however, to yield to a more elaborate art of speaking when rhetoric and philosophical modes of thought finally took hold in Roman society (cf. Cic. *De Or.* 1.14–15). The process occupied the latter half of the second century. The two landmark dates are supplied by the lectures of Carneades in Rome in 155[19] and the appearance of the first Latin rhetorical works and teachers of rhetoric toward the end of the 90s and start of the 80s. The first episode shows how unacquainted the Roman educated public was with dialectical reasoning and the second marked the moment at which certain Romans undertook in their turn to teach and write rhetorical treatises.

In 155, then, the Athenians aimed to convince their Roman judges by choosing as ambassadors the three heads of the main philosophical schools: Carneades, Diogenes of Seleucia, and Critolaus. The first of them, the Skeptic Carneades, made use of his time in Rome lecturing on philosophical themes, notably on justice; he would develop a thesis one day and then argue against it the next. He was only employing dialectic reasoning to bring out the truth. This Socratic method, which was called *disputatio in utramque partem* ("two-sided argument"), was common to both the Peripatetic and Skeptic schools. Its objective was to work out all the arguments in favor of a thesis and then to work out all those in favor of the opposite thesis. The confrontation between the two positions allowed one to approach the truth (for the Peripatetics) or to show that in fact it was inaccessible (for the Skeptics).[20] But in both cases this approach defined truth as a thing to be known through reflection and debate, and not by virtue of the speaker's authority.

Carneades' initiative provoked strong emotions among the Roman public; there was great interest, which showed that this method of reasoning was unfamiliar, but also concern.[21] Its effect was to diminish the emphasis upon ethos as a basis for credibility and to weaken the traditional foundations of Roman oratory. It provoked in response the displeasure of conservatives who saw to it that the ambassadors departed. Among these men, Cato the Elder was the one who played the decisive role in this affair. He was undoubtedly well versed in Greek philosophy and literature, but he recognized the danger posed by the shift from the intellectual authority of the Roman aristocrat, a personal quality derived from his position as father, magistrate, or senator, to that of the philosopher, who claimed to discover truth and to determine the justice of actions through reflection on the nature of the world and of men. Throughout this period he maintained the same position, and sought through his writings and own personal example to strengthen the principle that morality conforming to ancestral tradition (*mos maiorum*) and a type of knowledge based on memorization and observation of paternal instruction were best.

Yet this struggle was nothing more than a rearguard action. Rhetorical art and philosophical method penetrated Roman society nonetheless. But the issues that arose from this process were extremely important.

At the beginning of the first century, the point at which our sources allow us an accurate appreciation of its organization, the art of rhetoric rested upon a certain number of rules and precepts that were arranged in a comprehensive classification.[22] It comprised five parts: *inventio*, or the art of discovering arguments; *dispositio*, the organization of the speech; *elocutio*, which dealt with style; *memoria*, which laid down the rules of memorization; and *pronuntiatio*, which set out those of delivery. The orators distinguished in addition three types of oratory: epideictic (i.e., generally ceremonial), deliberative, and judicial, as well as three kinds of style: simple, middle, or grand. All this led up to a precise classification of situations and roles. The rules of *inventio* in particular supplied the method by which an orator could determine what was called the *status* of the case: whether one had, for example, to deny the criminal nature of the act that had been committed, to invoke an overriding necessity, or instead to plead that the action was involuntary. Those of *dispositio* and *elocutio* furnished precepts regarding stylistic figures. Those of *pronuntiatio* indicated above all the bodily posture, gestures, and even the style of dress that one ought to adopt (cf. Quint. *Inst.* 11.3.163; see also Chapter 21). So when we consider that giving a speech was not just a matter of stating a proposal but a way of providing the public with an image of oneself as the politician that one was or wished to be, of demonstrating one's intelligence and one's capacity to find convincing arguments, of adopting in a general way the expected manner of a magistrate and leader of the city and making oneself known as such, we can understand how the introduction and development of this discipline could have been a source of instability in Roman society (see also Chapter 25).

All the more so because the techniques of acquiring these skills were relatively simple. They of course included the acquisition of rules, and exercises in translation and in imitation of models. But above all they involved practice in pleading or speaking on a set question or fictitious case (*declamatio*). There one encountered again the method of *disputatio in utramque partem*, now applied to a particular situation. This method permitted the student to examine all the aspects of a case and to bring out the most pertinent arguments.

These elementary techniques, however, could seem insufficient to the most demanding students. Cicero insisted that it was possible to depart from the particular matter at hand and turn attention to general considerations of principles of utility, justice, or honor which enriched the speech and elevated the debate. Those who were able to do this found the means to produce amplitude of expression (*copia*) in a proven technique nourished by political and philosophical reflection.[23] They seduced and convinced their audiences with the power of their thought. They also moved them, inspiring anger or enthusiasm once they were able to induce their audiences to share their own feelings by finding the right words and reinforcing them with appropriate gestures. The first to reach this level, if we follow Cicero, were M. Antonius, censor in 97, and L. Licinius Crassus, censor in 92.[24] Once such methods were in use, how was anything to survive of the old sententious oratory that rested above all on the affirmation of *auctoritas*? And how could those who mastered them fail to prevail over their rivals?

Since from now on the entire training of a Roman politician was based on these new techniques both with respect to its characteristic modes of thought and the models that were held up for imitation, it was absolutely necessary for aristocratic families to acquire and somehow to control them. The richest, the most powerful and, to begin with, those who were most open to the Greek East fairly easily found a way to do this. Their houses were inhabited by literate slaves and freedmen, and especially by Greek teachers of rhetoric, philosophers, or intellectuals who were their guests. The young men who belonged to this social milieu could receive training from them. Scipio Aemilianus and the Gracchi were among the first to benefit from their learning.[25] As their mastery of rhetoric increased, the most eloquent Roman senators became teachers in their turn and drew to themselves audiences and students hoping to receive the means of acquiring these new tools for the exercise of power.[26] The Greek discipline of rhetoric thus put itself at the service of Roman political thought and action. This type of training also continued to adhere to the tradition of the *tirocinium* and of aristocratic social relations. Even if it had left the narrow circle of the family, it respected the hierarchies of *dignitas* and the rules of the cliental relationship by placing the younger men under the authority of their elders and thus allowed the transmission of this knowledge to remain an exclusive domain of the political elite.

At the beginning of the first century, however, other methods appeared which were not inconsequential for the place of rhetoric in public life and the position in the city of those who mastered it. The possibilities of access to oratorical knowledge expanded to the point where the process could seem for a time to threaten the effective monopoly exercised by the senatorial aristocracy. The custom arose of going straight to the source for one's training. Young Romans visited Greece or Asia Minor and attended there the lectures of the heads of the oratorical schools and the best-known orators. The first to do this were leading members of the equestrian order or the young sons of senators. One might cite the cases of Cicero and his cousin Lucius, or later on, Caesar or Antony. But the phenomenon seems not to have become widespread until the first century, and not to have been more than a kind of advanced training that complemented the education one had already acquired.[27]

Manuals in Latin were written and published. We know of the existence of four, of which two survive. The oldest was probably that composed by M. Antonius, censor of 97, which carried the title of *On Oratorical Technique* (*De ratione dicendi*).[28] The second concerned bodily attitude and gesture (*De gestu*). This was the work of L. Plotius Gallus, a rhetorician (Quint. *Inst.* 11.3.143). The other two whose text comes down to us were the *Art of Rhetoric Dedicated to Herennius*, whose author is unknown but which dates certainly to 86–82,[29] and *On Invention*, which the young Cicero composed at around the same time, in 84 or 83.[30] Though Cicero's small book demonstrated a certain interest in philosophical arguments, the two works were above all collections of precepts that in fact only summarized the major elements of rhetoric. And the first two manuals, whose titles refer to *inventio* (discovery of arguments) and *dispositio* (arrangement) in the first case and to *pronuntiatio* (delivery) in the second, are not likely to have been different in this respect.

These works, however, constituted only a part of the training in the art of oratory, whose core was constituted by *declamatio*, the composition and delivery of mock speeches on traditional "school" topics. So at the end of the 90s the "Latin rhetoricians" (*rhetores latini*), of whom we know only L. Plotius Gallus by name, opened schools in Rome. They offered a curriculum that was doubtless rather superficial, consisting of precepts and exercises of declamation. This kind of institution responded to a strong demand. It undoubtedly addressed itself to young men of the lower senatorial, equestrian, or municipal aristocracy who did not necessarily find a place readily in the institution of the *tirocinium* and who were acquiring here the means of political action. Their objective was certainly not to make speeches in public meetings or the Senate, to which they did not have access, but to gain the capacity to plead in the criminal courts and possibly by this means to launch a career successfully (see also Chapter 28).

In fact, they presented a threat. At the end of the second century and the beginning of the first a number of prosecutors who came before the criminal courts were newcomers to the Roman political scene. They did not enjoy the legitimacy bestowed by belonging to an aristocratic family, nor the integration within a network of personal relationships that would render them at least somewhat controllable. Some of them were not even Roman citizens and attempted to win that status by means of a successful prosecution. The prosecutorial rhetoric that they were led to adopt drove them to assume the pose of the *popularis* orator, the defender of the interests of the People in the face of a corrupt nobility. Ready to exploit pathos and to stoke their listeners' anger, they set themselves in a confrontational relationship with an elite sure of its own legitimacy.

The aristocracy that governed the city could not accept the establishment of such a system of instruction in competition with the traditional one given within the framework of the *tirocinium*, one that would ultimately produce these uncontrollable orators of a somewhat lower social rank and, in some cases, with Marian sympathies. Their reaction was very hostile. Teachers and students were mocked and denounced as shrill and ill-educated charlatans. Finally, in 92 their activities were condemned by the censors of the year, Cn. Domitius Ahenobarbus and L. Licinius Crassus (the great orator praised by Cicero). The reason they cited was that the schools were places where one learned insolence and effrontery (*impudentia*).[31] This was a reference to the idea that those who benefited from this teaching could, with its help, rise above their station by daring to give speeches in public, and it reaffirmed that eloquence could do no more than make manifest the excellence that a man had already acquired through his exercise of civic authority.

The affair of the Latin rhetoricians was highly significant. This episode demonstrated simultaneously the culmination of the process by which rhetoric penetrated the Roman world and the importance that oratorical competence had gained in the civic equilibrium. No doubt the censors' edict had a limited effect. Private instruction continued or reappeared (cf. Suet. *Rhet.* 2–6). But the essential principles had been reaffirmed, which amounted to the claim that mastery of oratory could not be separated from that of authority.

The case of Cicero reveals all these issues with great clarity. He was doubtless the greatest orator of the Late Republic and his successes as well as the setbacks that he would encounter give us a clear picture of the importance of the art of oratory in public life. Born in 106 to a very distinguished family within the equestrian order and already well known to the highest ranks of the senatorial aristocracy, he was received toward the end of the 90s into the circles of L. Licinius Crassus and the jurist Q. Mucius Scaevola (called "the augur" to distinguish him from his homonymous cousin, "the pontiff"). He had therefore benefited from the process of integration characteristic of the *tirocinium*. He was educated in rhetoric and philosophy among his friends and the Greek teachers who then resided in Rome, and he himself wrote a manual on oratory in the late 80s. He then received instruction in Greece and Asia Minor by the most renowned specialists.[32] He had thus equipped himself with the most dependable tools for taking part effectively in Roman public life.

He built the first part of his career on mastering the oratorical art and pleading before the criminal courts. Two successful cases in particular allowed him to enlarge his support within the senatorial order and to win public esteem and confidence. The first was his defense in 81 or 80 of Sex. Roscius of Ameria, falsely accused of parricide by relatives who wished thereby to cover up a murder committed during the Sullan proscriptions. The young Cicero demonstrated some courage here, since in attacking the agents of the dictator he could not avoid being seen as opposing Sulla himself. The second was the accusation he brought in 70 against C. Verres, the governor of Sicily, who had subjected those he had governed to severe and systematic extortion. Beyond the gratitude of the cities of Sicily, this case won him a reputation for firmness and justice that commended and advanced his further career. He followed this up by continuing to defend clients in the courts and administering a succession of public offices, and by these means he raised himself to the summit of political life.

Throughout his life, his mastery of rhetoric brought him two principal benefits. Since eloquence gave him the capability to triumph in oratorical contests and to convince his audience, it was to him that the other members of the aristocracy appealed when a difficult case had to be pleaded, or one in which the stakes were high. Since his speeches before the Senate or the People were effective, it was important to gain his support or at least avoid his hostility. His talent made him powerful and he was able to capitalize on it. In the system of reciprocal gift-exchange that structured relationships between Romans, his speeches, and above all his forensic speeches, permitted him to create deep debts of gratitude not only among those he defended but also among their relatives and friends who had undertaken obligations on their behalf (see Cic. *Comment. Pet.* 19). Cicero thus created his own network of clients and friends among powerful figures – sometimes even of a rank superior to his own – as well as among cities whose interests he had undertaken to defend (see also Chapter 19). His influence came into play in decisions that were taken in Rome and extended to Italy, Sicily, and the other regions of the Mediterranean world.

But oratory was not just an instrument of political action; there was in addition another, more important effect. It was the means by which the orator constructed a public image for himself. The causes he took up and the arguments he developed, even the style of oratory he adopted – more or less reserved, more or less passionate – defined his place in the political arena. The image that he projected of himself was not distinct from that of the politician he was. It was reinforced by his audience's commitment to him, if he knew how to arouse their support for his arguments and how to provoke anger or enthusiasm. Eloquence thus became a source of charisma, and brought the orator who demonstrated it to the peak of the city's hierarchy.

Beyond the power, influence, and authority that gave the orator the opportunity to carry weight in political decisions, rhetorical eminence gave him the power to act as a model toward his fellow-citizens in two ways. The first derived from the fact that he attracted students who would be trained under his tutelage in oratory and philosophical and political thought. The institution of the *tirocinium* remained very much alive to the end of the Republic. Cicero was surrounded by a circle of students or admirers which included men who would become the principal politicians of the 50s and 40s.[33] This kind of attachment could have very concrete effects. When, for example, Cicero was driven into exile, more than 20,000 young men, according to Plutarch, took up mourning on his behalf and sought to prevent his expulsion (Plut. *Cic.* 31.1). The number may perhaps be exaggerated, but it well testifies to the palpable social influence that Cicero had gained though his fame and teaching.

More precisely still, it was the method of rhetorical training itself, declamation, that created the conditions of intellectual and political influence. Cicero, like all the best orators, drew the power of his oratory from elevating the particular to the general, and thus from enriching debate through philosophical reflection. The *disputatio in utramque partem* was not merely the tool by which one devised arguments. It was also the means to define moral and civic principles. Thus when, in 46 or 44, Cicero practiced declamation with his Caesarian friends P. Cornelius Dolabella, A. Hirtius, and C. Vibius Pansa, the subjects that they chose together were precisely those that corresponded to the immediate political situation, such as this theme at the moment of Caesar's victory: "Whether the wise man ought to remain in a city that had fallen into the hands of a tyrant"(see also Chapter 25).[34] Such fictitious speeches were no longer simply students' exercises; they were becoming instruments of an intellectual and political debate in which depth and richness of thought created the conditions of influence. Rhetoric and philosophical debate had become the general framework that structured the creation and presentation of concepts, and thus the forms taken by reasoning. In this way those who had, like Cicero, made themselves masters of the subject possessed considerable intellectual influence.

Moreover, the eminence that they enjoyed was not limited to their circle of friends nor to the audience of Romans that could be present to hear their speeches. Beginning especially around the middle of the second century the speeches of leading politicians were published, either on their own initiative or that of their friends and admirers.[35] But it was not only the text of the speeches that was disseminated. Students and admirers also drew upon the memory of gestures and bodily stances that had accompanied some argument or some phrase of the discourse that they were seeking to imitate (see also Chapter 21). Training proceeded by reproducing a model. And this model, far from constituting merely a discursive utterance, encompassed on the contrary an orator's entire public deportment, reflecting a particular form of the ethos that defined a leader of the city.[36] The intellectual and political primacy of the great orators thus extended beyond the bounds of Rome. It followed the paths of imitation and contributed to making them public figures of the first rank.

Rhetoric therefore played a decisive role in Roman political life at the end of the Republic because it made powerful and influential politicians of those, like Cicero, who mastered it. But it was not enough to elevate them to the front rank. Those who in fact truly made Rome's history – Marius, Sulla, Pompey, or Caesar – did not owe their position to oratory. Although they were excellent orators (with the apparent exception of Marius), they essentially drew their glory and power from their military commands. The proper relationship to maintain with oratory, however, presented a quandary for them. They could not scorn it, since it remained a necessary instrument for them or a possible menace in the hands of their opponents. But they could not stake much on rhetorical contests, since from their superior position they simply had too much to lose.[37] They therefore held back and remained silent rather than joining in these conflicts where they risked losing the authority that had set them at the pinnacle of the city. Since they were unwilling to engage personally to protect their position, their only recourse was to induce their friends and partisans to intervene. Thus, depending on circumstances, the most powerful made use of ambitious young men to bring accusations against an opponent, a renowned consular to defend a friend, a loyal tribune of the plebs to promulgate a law or impose a veto. Lacking the ability to control oratory, their power and social influence allowed them at least to control the orators. Consequently, if the art of oratory was henceforth available to all, the laws of *amicitia* and cliental dependence continued to regulate public speech (see also Chapter 19). Cicero was duly obliged to understand this in 54 when Pompey forced him to defend Gabinius, his great enemy. From this point on rhetoric, like all other instruments of civic action, was subject to the hard laws of a kind of power that could no longer be shared.

Throughout the history of the Roman Republic, oratory remained a decisive instrument of political debate and action. Debates unfolded and decisions were taken essentially by means of speeches. But in contrast to the practice of democratic cities, only the most renowned members of the senatorial aristocracy enjoyed the capacity to address their peers or their fellow-citizens. One had to have reached a certain rank, and to possess a certain authority, to be heard and to convince. From the middle of the second century, however, two series of events modified this situation. The first was institutional in nature. The creation and development of the criminal courts allowed individuals who did not belong to the elite of the city to speak before tribunals whose penalties directly touched members of the Senate. Even if the context was judicial, the effects of these procedures were political. The second was a product of cultural history. The spread of rhetorical knowledge and philosophical thought to the heart of Roman society had the effect of providing stronger instruments of persuasion, of intellectual prominence, and thus of power to those who mastered them. The stakes were considerable because the art of rhetoric not only allowed one to construct convincing speeches; it also offered a means of defining a mode of public conduct that reflected the ethos expected of a leader of the city. Once such instruments were at the disposal of those who knew how to use them, the consequences could be formidable.

If these men were individuals who did not belong to the political elite of the city, the opportunities they thus acquired for personal advancement and political action free from effective social control were a source of disequilibrium. The reaction against them could not fail to be rather sharp, as the injunction against the Latin rhetoricians indicates. If, conversely, they were men who possessed all the marks of legitimacy, then the social, political, and intellectual influence that they were able to draw from their art gave them the strength to prevail over their rivals. Mastery of the oratorical art had become indispensable to every member of the aristocracy. Moreover, the rules of rhetoric and teachings of philosophy henceforward supplied the methods and framework of political thought and debate. Cicero, who was no doubt the greatest master of these arts, derived all his prestige and political influence from this source. He was not the only one to do so. But it was elsewhere, on the battlefields of civil war, that the destiny of the Republic was decisively determined; and the consequences of the process that had set such a high value on public speech soon disappeared in the arena of monarchic oratory.

Guide to Further Reading

A proper understanding of the connections between rhetoric and political life demands a prior grasp of how the city functioned, which may be gained from other contributions to this volume, especially Chapter 12, but also 1, 11, and 18.

Regarding the circumstances of political debate in the popular assemblies, see Taylor 1966a, which still offers an excellent picture of the concrete conditions under which they proceeded, and recently Morstein-Marx 2004, which analyzes the modes of interaction between the orator and his audience. (On the recent debate about the actual role of the People in decision making and therefore on the arguably "democratic" nature of political debate, see Chapters 1, 12, and 18 in this volume.) For senatorial debate, see Bonnefond-Coudry 1989 and Ryan 1998; for forensic debate, David 1992a. The political importance of the great trials of the end of the Republic emerges clearly from Gruen 1968 and 1974.

The history of rhetoric should be set in the general context of the cultural history of the Republic: see Rawson 1985. All the information on the period before Sulla has now been assembled in Suerbaum 2002. The question of Hellenism is clearly central. Gruen 1992 has shown that there are no grounds for invoking the idea of a battle of cultures. (See also Chapter 22.) Yet one should still not underestimate the depth of the opposition between the intellectual and "ethical" (i.e., based on rhetorical ethos: n.17 above) models since they constituted at once tools of persuasion, legitimation, and therefore of power. (See especially the affair of the Latin rhetoricians.)

Clarke 1951 and especially Kennedy 1972 offer a good approach to the history of rhetoric specifically. The issues of the pre-Ciceronian period are well presented by Calboli 1982. A useful introduction to Ciceronian rhetorical theory is J. May and J. Wisse's translation of *On the Orator*: May and Wisse 2001. Finally, Bonner 1977 offers a history of education, including methods of training.

Reading Cicero remains the best way to approach him: the speeches (e.g., the *Defense of Roscius of Ameria*; the *Against Verres*, Second Phase, Book 4 or 5; the *Defense of Murena*, *Catilinarian Orations*, the *Defense of Sestius*, *Defense of Milo*, the *Philippics*), the dialogues (e. g., *On the Orator*, *On Duties*, *On Supreme Good and Evil*, *Discussions at Tusculum*), and the letters (one might select one or two years of the correspondence). The bibliography on Cicero is immense: on the rhetorical writings and speeches, one might start with May 2002. The two-volume biography by Mitchell (1979 and 1991) is a good introduction to Cicero's life and political career.

Notes

1 On these points, see, e.g., Asc. 40 C.; Cic. *Leg. Man.* 70; Livy 8.14.12, 23.10.5; Varr. *Ling.* 6.91; Tac. *Ann.* 4.36.

2 Cic. *Leg. Man.* 2. The normal moment was, however, the aedileship.

3 Cic. *Vat.* 24. Cf. Cic. *Att.* 2.24.2–4, *Sest.* 132; Suet. *Iul.* 20.8; Plut. *Luc.* 42.7; Dio Cass. 38.9.4.

4 We should also remember that funerals for members of the aristocracy afforded the opportunity for speeches from the rostra: the eulogy (*laudatio*) of the deceased was an occasion to recall his deeds and to impress upon the collective mind the legitimacy of his son's succession, or that of another close relative who was addressing the People. See esp. Flower 1996: 128–58; Flaig 2003: 49–68.

5 Morstein-Marx 2004: esp. 160–203.

6 Mack 1937: 80–124.

7 Hölkeskamp 1995: 11–49 and esp. Morstein-Marx 2004: 203–40.

8 Val. Max. 3.7.3. The episode dates to 138.

9 See esp. Cic. *De Or.* 2.333–9, 1.31; *Mur.* 24.

10 Bonnefond-Coudry 1989: 25–160.

11 On the arrangement of these places see Taylor and Scott 1969: 529–82.

12 On these questions see Bonnefond-Coudry 1989: 452–554, 683–711, Ryan 1998.

13 David 1992a: 463–87.

14 See, e.g., the eulogy of L. Caecilius Metellus (consul 251 and 247) by his son (consul 206), preserved by Pliny *HN* 7.139–40; or again the praises of Cato in Nep. *Cat.* 3.1, Livy 39.40.3–8, and Quint. *Inst.* 12.11.23. Cf. Flower 1996: 136–45, Flaig 2003: 49–98.

15 See esp. Tac. *Dial.* 34.1–2, Cic. *Off.* 2.46. I have discussed the most important aspects in David 1992a: 336–41.

16 Cato *Fil.* fr. 15 Jordan. On Cato and his oratory, see especially Kennedy 1972: 38–60; Calboli 1978: 11–35.

17 On *gravitas*, see Hellegouarc'h 1963: 279–90. *Gravitas* in oratory is an aspect of rhetorical *ethos*, i.e., persuasiveness through the projection of character.

18 Cic. *Brut.* 111–12; cf. 116. Cicero stresses that what Scaurus lacked was the technical skill of rhetoric (*doctrina*); cf. also Cic. *De. Or.* 1.38 on the father of the Gracchi, and the example of Q. Fabius Cunctator in Plut. *Fab.* 1.7–9.

19 Already in 161 the Senate had passed a decree expelling foreign teachers of rhetoric and philosophers from the city of Rome (Suet. *Rhet.* 1.1; Gell. *NA* 15.11.1). We know very little of this measure, but it is probable that it corresponds to the same anxiety that was provoked by Carneades' lectures.

20 Granatelli 1990: 165–81.

21 Plut. *Cat. Mai.* 22.2. Carneades' audience understood Greek, but the philosophical method was new to them.

22   For what follows, cf. *Rhet. Her. passim*, esp. 1.2–3, 4.11, and Cic. *Inv. Rhet. passim*, esp. 1.7, 1.9.

23   This was Cicero's definition of the accomplished orator. On all these points, see esp. Cic. *De Or.* 1.16–20, 48–73, 93–5, 202; 2.133–41; 3.54, 76, 80, 107, 120–5, 142–3; *Orat.* 13–17, 45–7, 113–20; *Part. or.* 79 and in general Barwick 1963.

24   Cic. *Brut.* 138–65. On all these points, see Narducci 1997: esp. 19–76.

25   Suerbaum 2002: 482, 498–9.

26   The first person explicitly mentioned is M. Aemilius Lepidus Porcina (cos. 137) (Cic. *Brut.* 95–6), and one might add C. Papirius Carbo (cos. 120), who practiced declamation and was certainly not alone in doing so (Cic. *Brut.* 105).

27   Rawson 1985: 9–13; Ferrary 1988: 602–7.

28   Suerbaum 2002: 509–10.

29   Kennedy 1972: 111–13, 118–26, 130–5; Achard 1989: v–liii; Calboli 1993: 1–74.

30   Kennedy 1972: 106–11, 135–8; Achard 1994: 5–29.

31   Cf. Suet. *Rhet.* 1.1; Gell. *NA.* 15.11.2. and esp. Cic. *De. Or.* 3.93–5.

32   He had also been tempted by the instruction of Plotius Gallus (Suet. *Rhet.* 2.1.) On Cicero's education, see Cic. *Brut.* 303–16; Plut. *Cic.* 3–4.

33   We can count among the first group M. Caelius Rufus (praetor 48), P. Licinius Crassus, the son of the triumvir, or P. Cornelius Spinther (son of the consul of 57) and among the second, figures as important as L. Aemilius Lepidus Paullus (consul 50), C. Scribonius Curio (tribune of the plebs 50), M. Antonius the triumvir, and C. Cassius Longinus and M. Junius Brutus (Q. Servilius Caepio Brutus), the assassins of Caesar. See David 1992a: 397–9.

34   Cic. *Fam.* 9.16.6–7, 18.1; 7.33.1–2; *Fat.* 2–3. Cf. *Att.* 9.4; Sen. *Controv.* 1, praef. 11; Suet. *Rhet.* 1.3; Quint. *Inst.* 12.11.6.

35   Pina Polo 1996: 26–33; Narducci 1997: 157–73.

36   "Quotations" of gesture thus accompanied textual allusions; see David 1992b.

37   See, e.g., Pompey's difficulties before certain *contiones* (Cic. *Q. Fr.* 2.3.2; Plut. *Pomp.* 51.6–8), or Cicero's remarks (*Att.* 1.18.6) and those of Plutarch concerning his speeches in the court (*Pomp.* 23.3–6).

CHAPTER 21

The Republican Body

Anthony Corbeill

A Body Politic with Two Political Bodies

In republican society, viewers of the movements and appearance of male bodies were trained to discern clues to the moral and political consciousness that lay beneath physique. My overview of the two principal ways in which the Roman elite wished for these bodies to be represented begins with a pair of passages from ancient authors that bracket the period under consideration. The first occurs in the historian Livy's version of events that were alleged to have occurred in 494 BC. In reaction to the practice at Rome of debt slavery (*nexum*), by which a wealthy creditor gained mastery over a debtor's physical well-being, the plebeian members of the army literally withdraw their bodies from participation in society, settling upon a hill outside the city to protest the conditions of the poor. The Senate sends to speak on its behalf a member of plebeian descent, the former consul, Menenius Agrippa, who offers the crowd a parable that Shakespeare was to use to open *Coriolanus*.[1] The human body, he relates, was once in a state of internal revolution, since the limbs perceived that the stomach alone enjoyed the fruits of their constant labor. As a result, the extremities withdrew their usual services – hands no longer providing food, mouth refusing to accept what was offered, teeth disdaining their own work – until eventually the body as a whole began to waste away. The political moral of Agrippa's fable is clear: the senatorial stomach may seem at rest (*quietum*), but its unnoticed workings are essential to the survival of the community. Within the dramatic context of Livy's own narrative, subsequent events soon prove the validity of the parable. Like the restful stomach, it is Menenius at the center of the angry masses that allows the opposing factions of the early Republic to cohere.[2] At the same time, however, Menenius' analogy calls attention to the very political tension that it is designed to alleviate. Despite the tale's emphasis on the mutual benefits that cooperation can offer to society, the dichotomy of Senate versus non-elite ultimately obtrudes, reasserting the paradox that union is in fact possible only through the imposition and enforcement of hierarchies. The Senate's privileged role, like the stomach's, is a function of the natural order. It is perhaps, then, not so ironic that the terms reached by the opposing parties – the creation of the office of tribune of the plebs and, eventually, of its independent Tribal Assembly – underscores the potentially fragmentary condition of the Roman citizen body. Furthermore, as we shall see, these newly created tribunes will themselves be included in the subsequent centuries of the Republic among those parts of the state that function analogously to the rebel limbs of Menenius' parable. In the dichotomy of bodily representation that I intend to trace in this chapter, the active bodies of both these tribunes and other members of the non-elite will continue to contrast in the political arena with the calm physical appearance of the elite.

A comparison employed in the mid-second century AD provides my second starting point: a rare and vivid snapshot of a scene that must have taken place daily throughout Rome's empire and during the late Republic. The orator Apuleius has been relating to his audience at Carthage the dilemma of the public speaker – the greater respect he demands from his audience, the more exposed he becomes to the possibility for public embarrassment. "Being low class provides plenty of excuses, having status (*dignitas*) plenty of difficulties" (Apul. *Flor.* 9.8). Apuleius then compares his own predicament with the particular behaviors of the elite and non-elite as each performs, side by side, their respective public duties. The proconsul, he notes, speaks infrequently and with moderation from a seated position, since his words can quite literally become law, while his personal attendant (*praeco*), unrestrained by the same considerations for status (*dignitas*), can either be stationary or wander about as he shouts contentedly at those in attendance. Contrasting public functions produce contrasting physical behavior.

These anecdotes – one a parable, the other an analogy – are two of only a handful of textual descriptions that allow us to perceive how the non-elite, the majority of Roman citizens, were meant to view their leaders as they performed affairs of state. What is particularly intriguing about these passages is the awareness that the elite participants betray concerning the potential for their calm façades to fail at persuading. The calm stomach in Menenius' parable hardly matches the anxious Senate back in Rome's Curia, and the composure of Apuleius' magistrate hides a continual fear of misprision. Nevertheless, despite these glimpses behind the calm, both passages succeed in reaffirming the dichotomy promoted in elite-authored texts between the willfulness of unchecked physical activity – inevitably performed by either the non-elite or a malfunctioning member of the elite – and the authority conveyed by the stable body.

In the following pages, I wish to summarize the many manifestations that this dichotomy has taken in recent scholarship on the role of gesture and the body in ancient Rome. The two contrasting forms of elite or non-elite representation appear as readable in the physique of every Roman citizen and allow the educated – or prompted – viewer to read properly their meanings. I do not wish, however, to try to re-create what political activity at Rome may literally have looked like, a scholarly pursuit that in the end must prove elusive,[3] but rather to analyze why our elite-based texts place so much emphasis on specific types of physical action. My discussion throughout is informed by Pierre Bourdieu's notion of the *habitus*, by which a given culture's political activity becomes "*em-bodied*, turned into a permanent disposition, a durable way of standing, speaking, walking, and thereby of feeling and thinking."[4] As in the traditional society of the Kabyle of North Africa that Bourdieu studies, our ancient textual evidence depicts Romans of the Republic as displaying two *habitus* around which other aspects of society organize themselves. The elements that inform the division at Rome are, however, never strictly defined since each *habitus* engages in a constant process of revising itself in contradistinction with its counterpart. I will be showing some of the various opposing categories that lie on each side of this ideological divide and conclude by offering suggestions for further research on the ways in which, and the reasons why, these oppositions continued (and, indeed, still continue) to survive.

Body and Soul

The notion that the physical appearance of a person, while both at rest and in motion, reflects the status of the internal soul had great currency in the Greek and Roman worlds. For our period this is succinctly expressed in a passage from *On the Laws* in which Cicero recounts the origins of human appearance: "Then Nature shaped the facial features in such a way as to represent the character hidden deep within" (*Leg.* 1.27). As a corollary to Cicero's assertion, morally suspect persons were represented as exhibiting physical ugliness throughout classical art and literature, a bias from whose exploitation we have scarcely escaped.[5] It is common to find the physically deformed or their representations used as apotropaic devices, arousing laughter to ward off the evil eye, or as a means of expiating a community's anxieties.[6] Philosophical speculation such as we read in *On the Laws* concerning how nature endowed humans with an external appearance that reflected internal morality and intention was to grow into the science of physiognomics. Basing their writings on empirical observation of the visible world and often using the corresponding features of animals to elucidate human qualities that their bearers may be striving to keep hidden, these writers on physiognomy categorize the physical features of the human body according to how they help a viewer determine moral character. Eyes that glisten like marble, for example, will betray a lack of chastity, and a truly masculine body, while walking, will be longer from the top of the head to the navel than from the navel to the soles of the feet. Physiognomic principles such as these were consistently applied by writers, and understood by readers, throughout the entire range of Greek and Roman literature.[7]

Consideration of the role that the physique could play in philosophical enquiry raises important questions about the possibility that physical appearance was exploited as a means of social control. As early as Homer's *Iliad*, the ugly and malformed Thersites is publicly ridiculed and beaten for holding an opinion contrary to that of the ruling elite. In a politically competitive society such as republican Rome, public figures also can be found openly criticizing opponents for physical features that are depicted as deviating from some unstated norm of perfection.[8] In a speech from 142, Scipio Aemilianus inveighs against Publius Sulpicius Gallus:

If someone, drenched daily in perfumes, adorns himself before a mirror, shaves his eyebrows, walks about with his beard plucked and thigh hairs pulled out; who, as a young boy with his lover, wearing a long-sleeved tunic, was accustomed to lie in the low spot at banquets, who is not only fond of wine, but fond of men also, then would anyone doubt that this man has done the same thing that pathics usually do? (Gell. *NA* 6.12.5 = *ORF*[4]Scipio Aemilianus no. 21, 17)

It is hardly surprising that Aemilianus would rebuke his opponent for the willful manipulation of physical appearance – shaving his brows and depilating his legs – especially since it allows him to imply that this care is designed to attract men in the context of the luxurious banquet. Indications of effeminate behavior, as revealed in over-elaborate attention to the body, constituted stock charges in Roman invective. What may occasion surprise, however, is that public speakers also did not feel constrained from impugning a physique over which an opponent had no apparent control. A revealing example of this practice is preserved in Cicero's discussion of rhetorical humor in *On the Orator*, where the interlocutor Julius Caesar Strabo cites the mockery of a deformed person as an example of a successful type of joke. The great orator Lucius Licinius Crassus addresses a certain Lamia, about whom we otherwise know nothing. Strabo is careful to inform us, however, that Lamia has deviated from normal standards of physical appearance; he is "malformed" (*deformis*). After sharing this important detail, Strabo continues: "Since this Lamia kept interrupting him in an offensive manner, Crassus remarked, 'Let's hear the pretty little boy;' when there was a peal of approving laughter Lamia replied, 'I wasn't responsible for molding my beauty, but I was for my talent (*ingenium*).' At this Crassus responded, 'Let's hear the skillful speaker!' and was met with a much stronger burst of approving laughter" (*De or.* 2.262). It is significant that this exchange does not work in Crassus' favor simply because he mocked Lamia's physical appearance. Lamia has attempted, quite naturally by modern standards, to dissociate the quality of inborn beauty from that of acquired talent. Yet this attempt rebels against the etymology of the Latin word for "talent" that he uses, *ingenium* – literally, "the thing one is born with." Crassus in response sides with etymology in insisting upon the coherence of beauty and talent, a coherence he reinforces by the repetitious jingle of his two punch lines (*"audiamus...pulchellum puerum"*; *"audiamus...disertum"*). The fact that the second witticism meets with greater approval from the crowd would indicate that physical peculiarities implied a lack in other areas; the idea of a deformed person being a good speaker occasions public ridicule. As occurs throughout Roman oratory, external malformations are portrayed as making manifest internal moral and intellectual deficiencies.

I should stress at this point that the bias against physical appearance normally relied upon a trained speaker for it to wield persuasive power over an audience. There do of course exist some passages from the Republic (although rarely in oratorical contexts) in which authors argue that physical appearance has no connection with moral character. In fact, Lamia's objection to Crassus' first gibe – "I wasn't responsible for molding my beauty, but I was for my talent" – attests to just such a perspective, and to the possibility that this counterpoint would find sympathy with an audience.

An anecdote preserved by Pliny the Elder provides another example of how the category of physical peculiarities was under contention on a broader level, outside the arena of political debate. A number of texts indicate that during the Republic physical deformities could prevent a person from holding magistracies and participating in public religious ceremonies.[9] Pliny relates how during the Second Punic War Marcus Sergius suffered multiple wounds but nevertheless, by relying upon the use of a prosthetic right hand, accomplished an impressive series of military victories. (Impressive indeed, as Pliny somberly remarks, despite the fact that Sergius' great-grandson was to be the notorious Catiline.) In 197, opponents of Sergius wished to prevent him from conducting sacrifices while praetor on the grounds of his being "infirm" (*debilis*, Pliny *HN* 7.104–5). Although the success or failure of Sergius' subsequent appeal is not known, the anecdote remains revealing. The very existence of episodes such as this attests that the equation of external and internal states of being represented a constant source of contention. In conducting the state properly, bodies mattered.

In light of the value placed upon normative physical appearance, the peculiar phenomenon of the Roman cognomen occasions surprise. In Rome, male citizens had a minimum of two names, a praenomen and nomen ("Marcus Tullius"). Among some individuals – and in our period this would include principally members of the senatorial class – a third name, or cognomen, was added to these two ("Marcus Tullius Cicero").[10] The reasons behind the rise of the cognomen and the means by which these names were distributed remain shrouded in uncertainty. Yet it is undisputed that, by the early first century BC, citizens began to be designated on laws and senatorial decrees by cognomen rather than by tribal designation.[11] What is unusual about this phenomenon, and unique among other ancient Mediterranean societies, is that approximately 40 percent of the names extant from the Republic describe peculiarities of the body, and the majority of these seem likely to be pejorative. As a result, a citizen would daily encounter on the streets of Rome men with cognomina such as "Bowlegs" (*Varus*), "Warty" (*Verrucosus*), and "Cross-eyed" (*Strabo*). The fact that these names were originally bestowed in adulthood indicates that they were unlikely to have had an apotropaic function (a suggestion rendered further unlikely by the fact that the older names, praenomen and nomen, both have positive connotations for the person named). In light of the phenomena I have mentioned above, it is peculiar that the elite would have chosen as a mark of distinction from the rest of the population an additional name that would have highlighted a physical peculiarity, and have done so pejoratively. The conjecture that these were originally playful nicknames that an individual willingly adopted for himself[12] neglects the abundant evidence that Romans treated physical defects as an element of the unnatural, and that these cognomina became an official marker not only of the original bearer but also of his descendants. Since this practice of pejorative naming structurally resembles the forms of abuse regularly found in aristocratic invective – including the mockery of an opponent's name – it has been suggested that the application of a cognomen may have served as a means of exercising social control over families that had grown to become potentially too powerful.[13] Another suggestion is that this traded abuse derives from a native Roman competitive ethos that highly values the willingness to endure shame.[14] Whatever the explanation, the elite politicians of our period exhibit a mysterious relationship with one another's physical bodies, ridiculing in public political contexts an adversary's physical blemishes while at the same time adopting descriptions of them (or being compelled to adopt these descriptions?) as personal designations.

Creating Us and Them

The Delphic oracle's famous pronouncement to Socrates to "know yourself" receives a telling gloss in one of Cicero's moral treatises: "The only knowledge of our selves is to have learned the power of body and mind (*corporis animique*) and to follow the life that makes full use of them" (*Fin.* 5.44). Although spoken by a proponent of the Old Academy, Marcus Pupius Piso Calpurnianus, this formulation is in keeping with the perception of the body offered by Cicero in the passage from *On the Laws* cited above. When transferred into a Roman context, in other words, knowledge of one's self does not concentrate solely on the metaphysical abstractions of how the soul exists outside the phenomenological world. Rather, the serious pursuit of self-mastery at Rome engages actively and equally with the physical body, and does so in a world containing other such bodies. This conception of the mind and body acting in tandem informs aspects of Roman society that extend beyond how to interpret an oracle from Delphi.

Exploitation of the interconnectedness between the body and the world within which it moves occurs in numerous spheres of Roman daily life, including religious ceremony, legal procedure, medical practice, and political gatherings. At the most straightforward level, as early as the fourth century Italian ritual included the offering of votive objects to the gods that consist primarily of terracotta models of human body parts. By offering a representation of one's foot, for example, the worshiper bids the god to cure an ailment in the corresponding part of his or her body (see also Chapters 4 and 10).[15] On less specific occasions, the prayer gestures employed by the Romans involved the body of the worshiper in even more active participation with its surroundings. Arms were not simply stretched to the sky, as is commonly portrayed, but in the direction of wherever the desired deity was thought to reside, be it toward the sky, the earth, a temple, or a statue.[16] Another form of worship that involves the active participation of the body finds the Roman spinning clockwise in a complete circle before a temple or other sacred object.[17] This physical movement, for which Plutarch would later offer a series of rationalizing explanations (*Vit. Num.* 14), seems to have signaled the end of a prayer by placing either the worshiper or the object worshiped in a protective circle. Many parallels survive for encircling an object in order to protect it, such as the regular lustration of city walls and farmers' fields. Perhaps the closest parallel for this sort of movement occurs in what we would designate as the legal sphere, in a procedure that would have been a familiar sight in the city of Rome. Upon freeing a slave through the procedure involving the rod that symbolized ownership (*festuca*), the master grasped the slave and spun him or her in a complete circle in the praetor's presence.[18] The spin not only symbolized the passage of the slave from servitude to freedom, but it also appears to have effected that passage. The encirclement of bodies played a role in medical practice as well. Numerous texts attest that pregnant women avoided any kind of bonds as the time for delivery drew near. One passage in particular indicates that a possible way of inducing labor involved the prospective father symbolically binding and unbinding the woman in turn while saying, "The same man who has bound you will also release you" (Plin. *HN* 28.42). Indeed, it would seem difficult to exaggerate the presence of encirclement, binding, and their avoidance in Roman society.[19] An offhand remark of Pliny the Elder provides an especially telling indication that the practice was ubiquitous, time-honored, and inherently Roman: "Our ancestors forbade gestures such as the clasping or crossing of knees in meetings of generals and magistrates since they hinder all action. They also forbade them for similar reasons whenever sacred rites and vows were being performed" (*HN* 28.59). It is the elite character of the extant textual evidence that tends to obscure the phenomena that the above texts describe as common. Could discussions in the Senate have included sentiments such as the following: "As we deliberate these issues, my fellow senators, please refrain from crossing your fingers"? We cannot know. It is demonstrable, nevertheless, that the human body's perceived ability to affect and alter the natural world informed every significant aspect of Roman public life.

These examples show how Roman bodies either directly intervened, or refrained from interaction, with their nonhuman surroundings in order to ensure the proper results of an action; a timely birth, for example, or an auspicious war council. When the principal interaction occurs not between the body and nature but among human beings, a third element is introduced into the dynamic: the eyes of fellow-citizens, who make observations and evaluations of the physical activity unfolding before them. Cicero's moral treatises again provide important indications of how different bodily attitudes would have been read. In a section of *On Moral Duties* that treats the social and moral etiquette of the body, he writes that appropriate standards of public display (*decorum*) govern what an individual should do and say. This *decorum* can also be revealed in the ways that one moves the body and holds it still.[20] Proper embodiment, whether at rest or in motion, projects a person in complete control, in a state that Cicero designates *constantia* – as, literally, a "standing-together-ness." It is clear that the term *constantia* should not be read as a dead metaphor, but that this Latin word has been deliberately chosen to describe the concrete stance of public *decorum*. As often in Latin, the ethical vocabulary that Cicero employs describes moral notions through terms that are both visible and physical; e.g., *rectus* ("upright" but also "right"), *aequus* ("level" and "just").

Later in the same treatise Cicero remarks on appropriate gait. Walking too slowly can convey signs of effeminacy, he writes, but at the same time excessive haste should be avoided since it causes "quick breathing, a changed facial expression, a misshapen mouth – all features that make perfectly clear a lack of *constantia*" (*Off.* 1.131). The ever-present viewer is conceived of as an ever-present judge. As one of Cicero's interlocutors notes elsewhere, it is Nature that governs the semiotics of the body: "Is there any type of bodily movement or posture that Nature does not judge worthy of notice? And as for how someone walks and sits, or the type of facial features and expression each person has – is there nothing in these matters that we consider either worthy or unworthy of a freeborn person? Isn't it true that we consider many people worthy of our contempt who, through a certain kind of movement or posture, seem to have scorned the law and limit of Nature?" (*Fin.* 5.47). As we shall see, this passage does not simply show Cicero passing on to his reader Greek notions that have no relevance to the Roman context. The public figure striding and gesticulating before his fellow-citizens acts either naturally or unnaturally. The properly informed viewer has the means to decide.

Roman texts assign a number of other traits and affectations to one side or the other of the dichotomy natural/unnatural. Before turning to how this dichotomy is played out in the public sphere in particular, I would like to cite one final passage from *On Moral Duties* that typifies the constant process of redefinition that occurs in these texts to guarantee that the divide will always remain distinct. The passage treats the issue of how beauty (*pulchritudo*) plays a role in the projection of public decorum (*Off.* 1.130). There are – no surprise here – two forms of beauty, the female and the male (*muliebris, virilis*). Each type of beauty Cicero describes with terms that reson- ate outside the limits of his moral treatise; in female beauty *venustas* predominates, while *dignitas* distinguishes male beauty. *Dignitas*, etymologically related to the Latin words that describe "appropriate" moral behavior (e.g., *decet, decorum*), is most commonly attested in describing the desirable qualities of the Roman elite. "It is the aristocratic notion *par excellence*," and can designate by metonymy both the Senate itself and the entire class of the Roman elite.[21] A "man" who exhibits the appropriate physical beauty, therefore, will also possess the less apparent "dignity" of a man of high political stature. Cicero's use of *venustas* to describe the feminine form of beauty is equally suggestive. In the political arena of Ciceronian oratory, where women play no active role, this noun and its corresponding adjective (*venustus*) participate instead in an ongoing debate in Roman society concerning the value of Greek-style aestheticism to Roman political life.[22] When applied in a political context, in other words, a male exhibiting "feminine beauty" (*venustas*) threatens to overlook native sensibilities in favor of a foreign aestheticism and thereby becomes exposed as a potential object of hostile invective. In political discourse, as is well attested, Greek preciosity and physical effeminacy are natural and constant companions.[23]

Close definitions of natural types of movement inevitably create the category of the unnatural. We have just seen one way in which this divide allows Romans to distin- guish in their public speech between Roman and Greek notions of propriety. The dichotomy could also be structured along the divide between urban Romans – that is, Romans from the capital city itself – and Roman citizens from the rest of Italy and the provinces. Beginning in the late second century, forms of oratory that are meant to appeal to the People as a broad category (as opposed to the elite) become identified with an active and overemotional form of oratorical delivery. Even though this identification seems to be inaccurate from an historical standpoint, its usefulness for promoting an ideology of political bodies caused it to be enshrined among the *topoi* found in rhetorical handbooks.[24] This association also came to have an effect upon daily oratorical practice, resulting in the creation of an identifiable popular *habitus*.

Fledgling orators from outside the capital who attempt to make their mark in Rome came to be identified with a particular style of delivery, attracting to themselves opprobrious terms such as "bitter" (*acerbus*), "sharp" (*acer*), "reckless" (*asper*), and "violent" (*vehemens*). These adjectives appeal strongly to the senses of hearing and viewing, with the result that this class of public speaker came to embody in the eyes of the Roman audience corresponding traits, and particular body types came to be equated with particular political practices.[25] Circumstances outside the strictly political – a nexus of circumstances that Bourdieu would see as contributing to the formation of a *habitus* for these popular politicians – assist in maintaining and reinforcing this contrast between the calm and controlled elite speaker and our excitable upstart. Since the commonest path for the unestablished orator to obtain wide recognition involved his undertaking the prosecution of a prominent member of the elite, this avenue further identifies the new orator with an ethos of confrontation. Those orators with no connections among the urban elite would also have had less access to the closed circles of elite education, which by the second century will have required as preliminary background a thorough knowledge of the Greek language and of Hellenic rhetorical precepts.[26] Following this Greek training, the elite path to eloquence culminated in the purely Roman practice of the *tirocinium fori*, an apprentice-style period during which the aspiring orator accompanies an already established member of Rome's elite as he goes about his daily duties. These differences in how oratorical practice was inculcated served to separate further the elite from the non-elite. Extant texts provide clear evidence for the success of this separation, depicting non-elites as regularly mocked for their non-urban pronunciation, vocabulary, body language, and humor.[27] Attempts were made to alleviate this gap by leveling the differences in how orators received their training. As often, the normally hostile tone of our extant sources makes it difficult to evaluate the precise nature of these attempts at reforming the elite model. In the 90s, a group of teachers who called themselves "Latin Rhetors" founded a school in which rhetorical education was made accessible in the Latin, and not the Greek, language. The impetus driving these educators and the precise form of instruction that they offered remain mysterious. The sources do not equivocate, however, about two salient facts: the schools were very popular among the young and correspondingly unpopular among certain members of the elite. The "Latin rhetors" prompted a disapproving edict from the Roman censors of 92: these new schools violate established and venerable tradition (*mos maiorum*) since "our ancestors have decided what they wanted their children to learn and what schools they should attend."[28] Apparently, accessible education in the native tongue, a significant part of what these teachers offered, did not match the ideal of the "ancestors" (see also Chapter 20).

Of the two opposing *habitus* that developed during this period – the elite and the popular – one particular aspect seems to have had strong political connotations. An individual's gait, singled out in contemporary philosophical treatises as providing a marker for distinguishing natural from unnatural movements, also had currency in invective texts from the late Republic. Already in ancient Greece, observers could identify ways of walking as manifesting aspects of an individual's social status and gender.[29] In the Republic, this type of observation provided an additional means for marking out the popular politician as somehow unnatural vis-à-vis his elite counterpart. Elite invective portrayed the gait of popular politicians as matching their alleged delivery: whether out of control or excessively languid, the walk betrayed a state of mind with insecure access to reason and truth. Gaius Gracchus, the tribune of the People in the late second century who was literally to become the embodiment of popular rhetoric for later politicians, is described by Plutarch as "intense and vehement,...the first Roman to walk around on the rostra and to pull the toga from his shoulders while speaking."[30] That this demeanor came to signify a brand of politics is clear from an oration of Cicero over half a century later, when he marks the gait of Gracchus and two other tribunes as distinct from that of a serious politician (*Sest.* 105). Another tribune, Lucius Appuleius Saturninus, is described as capturing the People's attention not through reason and eloquence, but "by his appearance, his way of moving, and his very clothing" (Cic. *Brut.* 224). Distracting movement also characterizes the tribune Sextus Titius, who was "so languid and soft in his gestures that a dance was created called the 'Titius'" (Cic. *Brut.* 225). It is no accident that dancing joins the list of movements that distinguish the popular politician. The term *cinaedus*, used at Rome to describe a male who plays the passive role in a homoerotic relationship, derives from a Greek word meaning "dancer."[31] From the point of view of our dichotomous model, conjoined with the characterization of the non-elite as overemotional, unnatural, and potentially deceptive is the implication that their bodily movement betrays an inherent effeminacy.[32] With the identification of the unnatural walk, the Roman populace acquired another means of visually detecting political deviance.

The elite identifies an opposing politician as exhibiting an emotional style of delivery and an uncontrolled, non-masculine walk. Since these features stand in contrast with the physically composed, and hence morally stable, member of the elite, the corresponding insincerity of the popular rhetoric becomes apparent to those possessing an elite viewpoint. This stigma attached to allegedly insincere body movement informs another cultural prejudice: the oft-found anxiety that writers on Roman rhetoric record about orators studying under stage actors.[33] In comparison with the actor, the orator must be constantly careful that his gestures not be perceived as inconsistent with his emotions, thereby suggesting to his audience that his words are untrue.[34] And in addition to the potential that histrionic movement possesses for giving the orator's performance an air of unreality, association with actors carries with it connotations of suspect morals and civic liabilities, since the Roman actor receives payment for offering his body to public observation.[35] As with the popular politician, the actor's unwillingness to maintain bodily *decorum* exposes him as unnatural and deceptive, as a failed male and citizen.

The category of the natural is also contested among the elite themselves. A dichotomy analogous to the one I have sketched out may be traced in the rhetorical controversies that prevailed during the late republican period regarding "Asianist" and "Attic" forms of oratory.[36] According to this debate, Asianist oratory was characterized by florid and ornate styles of expression and delivery; Atticists, by contrast, self-consciously employed a simplicity of language and expression that was thought to resemble the prose style of fifth- and fourth-century Athens. The vocabulary used in Roman debates over the relative virtues and faults of the two styles often involves terms that describe the body, and in ways that align with a division between masculine and feminine. The more florid manifestations of the Asianist style attract adjectives that describe enervation and effeminacy – "loose," "emasculated," "loinless," and "softer than a man" – while opponents characterize Atticists as "bloodless" and "without juice."[37] As with the other types of invective that I have been mentioning, these terms also have associations that indicate that more is at stake than simply name-calling. The slander seems to find its origins in each school's particular beliefs in the regimen that the orator's body was expected to follow.[38] "Our way of speaking mirrors our way of life" (*talis oratio qualis vita*) – this ancient adage applies not simply to words and rhetorical flourishes, but to the very ways in which the body strode, gestured, and spoke, and to the training that one underwent to learn how to control these bodily movements.

Roman costume conspires with these stereotyped movements to reinforce elite ideologies. Roman *matronae*, the female heads of household, were expected to wear as outer garments heavy and restrictive clothing such as the long, white *stola*; this style of dress was understood to signal the sexual inviolability of the wearer and, by inference, that of her household.[39] For men, also, style of dress played an active role in conveying internal intentions and morality. The way that the toga falls over the body with its heavy folds determines the elite movement outlined in the rhetorical treatises: the restricted use of the left hand, the right arm never raised above the shoulder, limited speed. Accordingly, Quintilian spends several sections of his excursus on oratorical delivery advising proper wear and use of the toga, since improper use can betray the unskilled speaker (Quint. *Inst.* 11.3.137–49). Quintilian's awareness of the importance of dress to status carries over into Roman art, where the toga becomes an important symbol of the elite virtues of *constantia* and *gravitas*. The values that this item of clothing represents inform the particular feature of Roman sculpture that Brilliant has termed the "appendage aesthetic," by which the gestures of head and arms give individuality to the contrasting stability and uniformity of the clothed torso (see Figure 21.1).[40] In fact, the toga itself becomes a stable signifier of the orator from as early as the period of *tirocinium fori*, when youths of the elite observed the political business carried out by their elders (see also Chapter 20). A passage from Cicero states that during this period young men wore a style of the toga that severely limited their gestures.[41] Since this *tirocinium* marked a liminal period between adoption of the "toga of a man" (*toga virilis*) and the actual ability to become an adult orator, it would seem that mastery of the toga represents the final step in attaining manhood.[42] As I mentioned earlier, this type of training would have been largely restricted to children of the elite. The ability to practice oratorical gestures while wearing the toga projects the qualities of a true *vir*, a manliness once again associated most closely with elite urban politicians.

Modern scholars have most fully explored the dichotomy between masculine and non-masculine demeanors in the context of what is now commonly referred to as the "penetration model." According to this model, a man's sexual role is defined not by the sex of his object of desire but by the manner in which sexual contact takes place. In such a scenario, the "penetrator," regardless of whether he be engaging with a man or a woman, is in the active role. In contrast with the penetrator, the passive

FIRENZE - Museo Archeologico : Sezione Etrusca - L'Oratore : statua in bronzo. *Edizioni Brogi*

Fig. 21.1 The "Arringatore" (Aulus Metellus); bronze sculpture from the early 1st century BCE. Museo Archeologico, Florence. Photo Alinari, Florence

recipient of sexual activity, if a man, is demeaned and regarded as having lower social value.[43] This is not the place to enter into the debate about actual versus represented sexual preferences and practices, but this model does have an undeniable effect on the ways in which the public male body was viewed and constructed in Roman oratory. If one is successful in portraying an opponent as adopting the effeminate role in sexual relations, the charge carries with it a whole cathexis of unmanly activity, so that male effeminacy becomes perceived as a "political, social and moral weakness."[44] The personal again becomes the political, as an individual's sexual activity determines on what side of the masculine/feminine divide he rightly belongs.

Questioning the Truth of Nature

Just because you're better than me
Doesn't mean I'm lazy.
Just because you're going forwards
Doesn't mean I'm going backwards . . .
Just because I dress like this
Doesn't mean I'm a communist.
– Billy Bragg, "To Have and To Have Not" (1983)

This lyric from the rock musician Billy Bragg succinctly supplies from the popular side of the divide a possible counter-argument that our elite sources from ancient Rome have effectively silenced. In these lines, Bragg ironizes a number of traits that modern capitalist society identifies with success. Had their voices survived, we could perhaps hear the popular politicians of the late Republic echo these sentiments – a certain style of dress need not betoken a specific political stance, and resistance to achieving the elite definition of success need not be equated with failure. The dichotomy of "us" and "them" (or indeed of "to have" and "to have not") that I have tried to trace in our written sources on the body in republican Rome could very well have been – and, I suspect, was in fact – anathema to the Catulli, Clodii, and Catilines of Cicero's day. While our sources repeatedly attest to Bourdieu's assertion that "to bring order is to bring division, to divide the universe into opposing entities," we must also be aware that in establishing order the process of division simplifies, inevitably in the service of oppression.[45] Had we the available sources, it would perhaps be possible to write another version of the republican body, one that shows Roman society in all its complexities.[46] The omnipresent slaves, the recently freed, the elite relocated from the provinces, the wealthy *publicani*, the new bride, the retired soldier, each of these segments of the population surely saw his or her own body differently from the ways in which Cicero saw his own (and, of course, theirs). I would like, then, to close by suggesting ways in which the simplicity of my previous analysis can be proven incorrect.

The Roman soldier, by turns boastful yet revered, lumbering yet heroic, occupies a peculiar situation in Roman society.[47] By joining the military, the new soldier passes from the status of a free Roman citizen to that of a member of the army, a transition marked by an oath of obedience (*sacramentum*) that signals a new relationship with his own body. Through his sworn obedience to the state or to his commander, the soldier represents a significant challenge to the paradigm that equates maleness with physical impenetrability. In the valiant fighting of wars he is the epitome of manly courage (*virtus*), despite the fact that he may regularly subject himself to the penetration of his body's boundaries, not only by the receipt of wounds, but also by disciplinary beatings at the hands of his commanding officers.[48] In addition to these two forms of physical violation, famous stories narrating the soldier's willingness to sacrifice himself helped Romans identify the traits that characterize honor.[49] Scaevola, who burned his right hand in defiance of the threat of torture, and Regulus, who vehemently argued to the Roman Senate that his inevitable torture at the hands of the Carthaginians was in the state's best interest, are only two of the many Romans whose virtue in wartime provided exemplary tales for teachers, rhetoricians, and moralists.[50] And indeed in the oratorical realm there is evidence that members of the military recognized the unique relationship that they had with their bodies. Former soldiers, by dramatically displaying their battle scars, offer a model by which penetrability could be construed as a marker of status (see also Chapter 17).[51] In opposition to the inviolate and unviolated elite body, the damaged veteran, it has been claimed, attempted to construct a competing category.

The *cinaedus*, the man who enjoys being sexually penetrated by other men, either in the mouth or the anus, would seem diametrically opposed to the soldier. Even here, however, non-elite texts encourage us to consider the possibility of slippage, such as the humorous story of the soldier of Pompey the Great, whose allegedly indisputable status as a *cinaedus* allowed him to commit crimes without raising suspicions of his complicity (Phaed. app. 8). It is likely that the *cinaedus* who often appears in invective texts and who falls, in the model offered here, squarely on the non-male/unnatural/non-elite side of the divide, is far more complicated than the penetration model offered by elite texts asserts. Passages from non-elite texts make it clear that the term *cinaedi* could also be applied to men who are known to be active penetrators of women (e.g., Catull. 57). Suggestive arguments have been made that these individuals identified as a group and may have constituted a subculture that has left only scant traces in our extant textual and material evidence.[52]

As we have seen, the sources expend a great deal of energy devising ways in which non-elite men belong to the feminine side of our dichotomy. Yet they devote little space, especially in public contexts, to describing the bodies of women themselves. As a result, I will restrict my remarks here to the ways in which the public contesting of gender categories among men has been used to reveal ways in which elite Roman society constructed women. Women can be represented as exhibiting the same qualities that their male elders would consider valuable; for example Porcia, the wife of Brutus, emulates the virtue of her father Marcus Cato in the very act of committing suicide.[53] And yet to show that a woman possesses qualities that are similar to men does not make her a moral equal. Public invective, for example, portrays women as wielding masculine power only as a means of demeaning the men who are associated with and therefore, by the logic of these texts, subservient to them. In the case of Ciceronian oratory one may cite, for example, the prostitute Chelidon, whom Cicero portrays as controlling Verres' praetorship in Rome, or Clodia, the "true" mastermind behind the prosecution of Caelius.[54] The representation of female homoerotic behavior also does not deviate from the dichotomy of masculine/non-masculine: our texts concur that in these sexual relations one partner must fill the role of "penetrator" and the other that of "penetrated."[55] In both these cases, a woman's similarity with men tells us much about male representations of women but far less, if anything, about a woman's real lived experience. For a woman to have power, as our model has led us to expect, she must emulate the qualities of a man (see also Chapter 15).

Another fruitful avenue of approach could consider evidence that elite individuals consciously constructed for themselves a *habitus* that is intended to compete with the elite paradigm. Scholars of ancient sexuality frequently mention an anecdote preserved about the distinguished orator Quintus Hortensius, Cicero's great rival in the Forum. Accused on one occasion by an opposing speaker, Torquatus, for his effeminate dress and demeanor, and compared with a female dancer named Dionysia, Hortensius responded "in a soft and gentle voice" by unexpectedly embracing the charges made against him and by even doing so partly in Greek: "I much prefer to be a Dionysia than what you are Torquatus – without a Muse, without Aphrodite, without Dionysus."[56] Is this to be construed as evidence for a subculture of males in Rome who willingly wish to be viewed as effeminate, or does it simply represent an unpredictable retort that is intended primarily to highlight an opponent's boorishness and lack of refinement? A similar riposte made by Julius Caesar, again in a public context, supports the notion that there may have existed during the Republic a competing elite *habitus*. After Caesar boasted in a crowded senate house that he wished to force all his opponents to fellate him – a remark placing him firmly on the masculine side of the penetration model – a senator replied tauntingly that such a request would be difficult to grant to a woman. At this point, Suetonius tells us, Caesar commented that "in Syria, Semiramis had been a queen too, and the Amazons once possessed a great portion of Asia" (Suet. *Iul.* 22.2). As with Hortensius, whose enthusiastic embrace of Greek aestheticism before Torquatus can be paralleled from other areas of his life, so too does Caesar's apparently surprising remark align with other ways in which tradition describes him as identifying with a decidedly nonmasculine lifestyle. Sure signs of this underlying effeminacy, the sources say, were Caesar's style of wearing the toga, his elaborate hairstyle, and the habit of scratching his head with one finger – a signal in ancient Rome that advertised one man's willingness to submit sexually to other men.[57] These physical manifestations correspond with the verbal abuse heaped upon Caesar by opponents: "a man for all women, and a woman for all men" (Suet. *Iul.* 52.3) and "the queen of Bithynia" (referring to Caesar's youthful service under King Nicomedes; Suet. *Iul.* 49.1–4). It is tempting to see in these charges not random abuse, but a political appeal by Caesar to non-elite beliefs and opinions that have been obscured by our hostile sources.[58]

Reading against and through our sources, in other words, can help reconstruct ways of life that are all but lost to us. This kind of investigation is familiar to critics of literature. In the case of Catullus, for example, close semantic analysis demonstrates the ways in which this poet transforms the aesthetic vocabulary created by the elite into a new definition of what is socially valuable;[59] his conflation of sexual and social systems of domination has also been read as a critique of elite values (see also Chapter 25).[60] Such an analysis can also be applied to individuals who may seem far outside the political and public life of Rome.[61] Each of these studies shares a willingness to read through well-known texts. Invective, in particular, whether composed in verse or for the Forum, offers the possibility of being interpreted not from the point of view of the elite class that has constructed the alleged violations but from the point of view of the very persons attacked. Could they in fact be offering resistance, or refinements, to the dominant cultural and moral paradigm? Pursuing such questions offers one way of resurrecting their long-dead bodies.

Guide to Further Reading

Much interesting work remains to be done in defining what constitutes Roman bodies and the ways in which they interrelate with one another. The best single resource for examining the uses of the body in Rome remains Sittl 1890. Although limited in its analysis, and tending to view Greek and Roman understandings of gesture from all periods as monolithic, this work remains an impressive achievement and an indispensable starting point for examining both the textual and visual evidence. De Jorio [1832] 2000, a pathbreaking study that employs comparative evidence to analyze ancient gesture, is still worth consulting on specific issues. For art, Brilliant 1963 provides the most complete discussion of the particularly Roman ways that the body could be represented visually, covering a much wider range of material and subject matter than its subtitle would suggest. Barton 2001 quotes extensively from the ancient sources suggestive remarks that illuminate the peculiar relationship that Romans had with their bodies; for the head in particular, see Richlin 1999. Corbeill 2004 uses case studies of selected gestural phenomena to explore the links that Romans perceived between their bodies and the external world. For physiognomic writers, Evans 1969 provides the best overview and Gleason 1995, although covering the Second Sophistic, offers an innovative approach to these texts that has been fruitfully applied by scholars to texts from the Republic.

By exploiting remarks on oratorical delivery found in rhetorical handbooks (especially Quint. *Inst.* 11.3, for which see Maier-Eichhorn 1989 [commentary]; Graf 1991), several recent studies have examined the role of gesture in public oratory of the late Republic and early Empire. Aldrete 1999 analyzes how the speaker used body and voice in interacting with his audience, while Gunderson 2000 explores the interrelationship between rhetoric and masculinity. Hall and Bond 2002 (with an accompanying video) use primary sources to reconstruct how Cicero may have delivered specific passages of his oratory. Of special interest in determining the social and political significance of oratorical gesture is a series of articles by David (in particular 1980 and 1983a), who speculates on how historical conditions determined specific styles of oratorical deportment, in particular that of the non-elite public speaker at Rome.

The abundant recent scholarship on ancient sexuality has had a major impact on approaches to the Roman body. I restrict mention to those works in English that have the most relevance to my own limited discussion. The work of Amy Richlin (see especially 1983 and 1993) is always provocative and especially sensitive to issues of gender. Edwards 1993: 63–97 discusses reasons why discourses on sex are consistently intertwined with other forms of public discourse. Hallett and Skinner 1997 contains a useful collection of material covering many aspects of Roman sexuality; see also Fredrick 2002b. Williams 1999 is the most convenient resource for assessing the meanings of Roman masculinity, male homoeroticism, and the ways in which these behaviors are marked in the human body. Visual material illustrating attitudes toward sexuality and sexual behavior is amply documented in Clarke 1998.

Acknowledgments

I would like to thank my colleague, Tara Silvestri Welch, for improvements to this chapter, and I am grateful for the many astute observations from the editors. All translations from Latin and Greek are my own.

Notes

1 Livy 2.32; Dyck 1996: 526–7. On the historicity of the anecdote, see the bibliography cited by Ogilvie 1965: 312–13.
2 Other ancient accounts, by stressing the unrest of Menenius' auditors, point up even more the contrast implied in Livy's narrative (Dion. Hal. *Ant. Rom.* 6.87.1; Dio Cass. 4.10, 4.13).
3 Gunderson 2000: 1–6.
4 Bourdieu 1990: 70; original emphasis.
5 Garland 1995: 87–104.
6 Barton 1993: 167–72.
7 Evans 1969.
8 Corbeill 1996: 14–56.
9 Corbeill 1996: 25.
10 Freed slaves also often had three names during this period, but since their cognomen would normally have been easily recognizable as their former slave name, there would have been little confusion with elite practice; see further A. Mau *RE* 4: 228.6–12; Treggiari 1969: 7 n.1.
11 Mommsen 1864: 62–3.
12 Kajanto 1965: 20; Kajanto's monograph is the essential starting point on the subject.
13 Corbeill 1996: 57–98.
14 Barton 2001: 236–9 with n.189.
15 Beard, North, and Price 1998: 12–13, 69.
16 Appel 1889: 194–7.
17 Appel 1889: 213–14.

18 Sittl 1890: 132 and n.7, Corbeill 2005.
19 Heckenbach 1911 offers a full collection.
20 *Off.* 1.125–6: *in corporis… motu et statu*; Narducci 1989: 156–88.
21 Hellegouarc'h 1963: 408.
22 Krostenko 2001: 154–201, esp. 185–93.
23 MacMullen 1982a.
24 David 1979.
25 David 1980.
26 The urban education of the young Cicero, born outside Rome, provides an unusual exception; see Corbeill 2002: 25–9.
27 David 1983a.
28 Suet. *Rhet.* 25.2; Gruen 1990b: 179–91.
29 Bremmer 1991.
30 Plut. *Ti. Gracch.* 2.2; David 1983b.
31 Williams 1999: 175–8.
32 Corbeill 2004: 107–37.
33 Graf 1991: 48–51.
34 Morstein-Marx 2004: 242–6.
35 Edwards 1997.
36 Leeman 1963: 1.136–67.
37 Richlin 1997: 106–7.
38 Dugan 2001.
39 Sebesta 1998.
40 Brilliant 1963: 10, 26–31. The three statues depicted in Brilliant 1963: 69 (figs. 2.48–2.50) also illustrate this point nicely.
41 Cic. *Cael.* 11, with Richardson and Richardson 1966: esp. 266–8.
42 Richlin 1993: 547–8.
43 Richlin 1993; Parker 1997; Williams 1999: 160–224.
44 Edwards 1993: 65; Corbeill 1996: 99–173.
45 Bourdieu 1990: 210.
46 Fredrick 2002a: esp. 240–3.
47 Horsfall 2003: 103–15.
48 Walters 1997.
49 Barton 2001: 38–56.
50 E.g., Val. Max. 3.3.1; Cic. *Off.* 3.99–115, with Dyck 1996.
51 Leigh 1995.
52 Richlin 1993; *contra*, Williams 1999: 218–24.
53 Hallett 1989.
54 Hillard 1989.
55 Hallett 1997.
56 Gell. *NA* 1.5.2–3; Williams 1999: 155–7.
57 Toga: Suet. *Iul.* 45.3, Dio Cass. 43.43.4, Macrob. *Sat.* 2.3.9; hairstyle: Plut. *Vit. Caes.* 4.9; Dio Cass. 43.43.5; Macrob. *Sat.* 2.3.9; finger gesture: Plut. *Vit. Caes.* 4.9, with Corbeill 1996: 164–5.
58 Corbeill 2004: 133–7.
59 Krostenko 2001: 233–90.
60 Skinner 1997.
61 See Gordon 2002, on Lucretius.

PART VI

The Creation of a Roman Identity

CHAPTER 22

Romans and Others

Erich S. Gruen

Romans had a penchant for stressing their special values, qualities, and character. The assertions of leaders and the writings of intellectuals regularly affirmed their distinctiveness. A contrast with other peoples loomed large in the development of a self-perception. The history of Rome had, after all, taken shape in a setting that involved confrontations with other cultures right from the start. Etruscans and Greeks had a significant presence in the Italian peninsula in the formative years of the young city. Territorial expansion within Italy brought encounters with Sabines, Samnites, Oscans, and others even before Romans moved abroad. Exposure to Phoenician culture in North Africa, to Gauls in northern Italy, to mixed ethnic groups in Sicily, Sardinia, and Spain, preceded (and overlapped with) the great era of engagement with the Greek world of the east. The importance of differentiating Roman features took on greater urgency.

Cato the Elder gave voice to a celebrated antithesis: "the words of the Greeks issue from their lips; those of the Romans come from the heart" (Plut. *Cat. Mai.* 12.5). Cicero later sharpened the contrast, juxtaposing Greek *levitas* with Roman *gravitas* (Cic. *Sest.* 141). In assessing those who dwelled further east, the Roman orator could become progressively more caustic. He ascribed to the Greeks themselves slurs against Asians that he gleefully transmitted (or invented). Stereotypes, so Cicero alleged, reached the status of proverbs: the best way to improve a Phrygian was to whip him; the ultimate insult was to label an individual the worst of the Mysians; as for Carians, they are so worthless as to be fit only for human experiments (Cic. *Flac.* 65). Cappadocians became emblematic for stupidity, tastelessness, and a low form of humanity (Cic. *Red. Sen.* 14). Syrians and Jews are peoples born for servitude (Cic. *Prov. Cons.* 10). Livy delivers the same denunciation of the servile character of Syrians, and even lumps Asiatic Greeks into that category (Livy 35.49.8, 36.17.4–5). And Cicero targets Jews directly as addicted to a "barbarian superstition" (Cic. *Flac.* 67).

Phoenicians, of course, fared no better. Craft and deception were their hallmarks, a perception widespread among Greeks, and perpetuated by some Romans. *Punica fides* became proverbial (cf. Livy 21.4.9, 22.6.12). For Cicero, Phoenicians were acknowledged by written and material testimony alike as the most treacherous of all peoples. And Sardinians suffered from an even worse taint, for they were of Phoenician stock but they had been rejected by the Phoenicians themselves and abandoned on that disagreeable island (Cic. *Scaur.* 42). Egyptians were beyond the pale. No eastern people drew greater derision among Romans. The worship of animals especially prompted the scorn of Cicero, who denounced the depraved superstition that would lead Egyptians to prefer any form of torture than to do harm to an ibis, an asp, a cat, a dog, or a crocodile (e.g. Cic. *Tusc.* 5.78, *Nat. D.* 1.16.43).

When looking west Romans tended to see barbarism. Cicero brands the Gauls as practicing the savage and barbaric custom of human sacrifice (Cic. *Font.* 31). Cruelty and ferocity mark their character (Cic. *Font.* 33, 41, 43–4). Elsewhere he lumps Gauls, Spaniards, and Africans together: they are all monstrous and barbarian nations (Cic. *Q Fr.* 1.1.27). Spaniards even brushed their teeth in urine, according to Catullus (Catull. 37.20, 39.17–21). Blending of east and west brought still greater degeneracy, so Livy would have it. The Gauls at least used to be fierce fighters, terrifying their foes, though Roman virtue always surpassed Gallic ravings. But once Gauls moved east and mingled with Hellenic folk, they became infected with Greek decadence, a mixed bag of "Gallo-Grecians," just like the Macedonians, who came as conquerors of the Near East and then deteriorated into Syrians, Parthians, and Egyptians (Livy 38.17.5–11).

Stereotypes abound. Harsh judgments by Roman writers on alien peoples seem common and characteristic.[1] How best to interpret them? One might infer a Roman inferiority complex, particularly with regard to Greeks, conscious of their own late arrival amid the cultures of the Mediterranean and concerned to establish their credentials by asserting the superiority of their values and principles. And the debunking of other peoples, both east and west, allowed Romans to sharpen and articulate the qualities that could help to define their own identity.

The explanation seems reasonable enough. On closer scrutiny, however, it is inadequate and simplistic – indeed, may point in exactly the wrong direction. Roman traditions did not claim purity of lineage. Distinctiveness of blood or heritage never took hold as part of the Roman self-conception. Indeed, the Romans had no term for non-Roman. They had to borrow the Greek notion of "barbarian," a particular irony since it signified in origin non-Greek speakers – a category into which the Romans themselves fell. Mixed ancestry, in fact, was part of the Roman image from its inception. Instead of an embarrassment, it served as a source of pride.

Hellenic Traditions and Roman Origins

As is well known, Greek writers imposed a Hellenic genealogy upon Rome. Stories circulated in diverse and entangled forms, connecting Rome's ancestry with celebrated legends of the Trojan War and its aftermath. Various versions traced Roman origins to Achaeans returning after the fall of Troy, to Odysseus or his sons (see also

Chapter 25), to descendants of Heracles, to the Arcadian hero Evander, son of Hermes, or to a fictitious Trojan captive named Rhome who gave her name to the city. As early as the 4th century, some writers labeled Rome simply as a Greek city (Plut. *Cam.* 22.2). The stories became enmeshed in comparable tales that made Aeneas, the Trojan prince who survived the destruction of his city, become the founder of Rome or, at least, of Alba Longa, Rome's putative mother city. Permutations and combinations multiplied. Ingenious Greek writers blended or mixed traditions, including even a version that had both Odysseus and Aeneas, once great antagonists, collaborate in bringing the legacy of Greece's most illustrious era to the founding of Rome. Of course, indigenous traditions also existed, most notably that of the twins Romulus and Remus who were adjudged responsible for the creation of the city. Hellenic intellectuals, however, managed to weave the web of their tales to encompass and appropriate those stories, rendering the twins, in diverse tales, as distant descendants of Aeneas (see also Chapter 6).[2]

Most or all of this stemmed from the Greek imagination. Greeks were especially inventive and adroit at linking the origins of great cities and peoples to Hellenic forebears.[3] That will raise no eyebrows. Far more interesting is the Roman reaction. The stories came in many varieties. But no hint surfaces of a Roman effort to spurn foreign roots and insist on indigenous beginnings. Quite the contrary. Historians and poets welcomed that association with the eastern Mediterranean, reshaped and perpetuated it (see also Chapter 25).

The first Roman historian wrote in Greek. Fabius Pictor composed his work near the end of the third century. He embraced the tale of Aeneas as forefather of Rome, or at least a version of that tale that has Aeneas' son Ascanius found Alba Longa, the mother city of Rome (Diod. Sic.7.5.4–5; Dion. Hal. 1.74.1; Plut. *Rom.* 3.1–3). Even more interesting, Pictor conveyed stories of still earlier migrations from the Greek world: Heracles himself landed in Italy, and the Arcadian hero Evander who planted a colony on the Palatine Hill introduced the alphabet, an invention that the Greeks had actually borrowed from the Phoenicians (Pictor, F 1–2, Beck and Walter). The Roman historian, in short, did not hesitate to endorse legends that linked Roman origins to Hellenic ancestors, indeed to acknowledge that cultural underpinnings went back to the Phoenicians. Far from shunning alien associations, he proudly proclaimed them.

Cato the Elder gained the reputation of a nativist spokesman. Numerous accounts have him inveigh against Hellenic influence in Roman society. Among other things, he made a point of composing his history in Latin, breaking with the traditions of Greek historiography. The significance of his posturing can be debated.[4] But the myths of Hellenic figures at the dawn of Roman history found their way into Cato's work as well. The surviving fragments of his *Origines* report an intricate tangle of legends involving Aeneas, Ascanius, Alba Longa, and a link between Trojans and Latins cemented by the wedding of Aeneas and Lavinia, daughter of the indigenous king Latinus (Cato, F 1.4–15, Beck and Walter). And Cato, like Fabius, traces Roman roots back further still into Hellenic mists. He accepted the notion that Aborigines in Italy from whom the Romans descended, were, in fact, Greek (Dion. Hal. 1.11.1, 1.13.2). And he perpetuated a tradition in which Arcadians under

Evander disseminated the Aeolic dialect among Italians, a tongue adopted by none other than Romulus himself (Cato, F 1.19; cf. 2.26, Beck and Walter).

Early Roman poets followed suit. Naevius in the late third century and Ennius not long thereafter accepted the lore and even telescoped the tradition. They discarded intermediaries and the long generations between Aeneas and Romulus, making Romulus a grandson of Aeneas on his mother's side (Serv. *Ad Aen.* 1.273). The Trojan origins of Rome were firmly established in the middle Republic, but variants in detail abounded. Roman writers felt no allegiance to a putative canonical story later associated with Virgil. They felt free to fiddle with the fictions.

A noteworthy fact needs to be underscored. Although Troy as ultimate progenitor of Rome prevailed in the tradition, this was a Troy enmeshed with Greece. One version at least gave Aeneas' ancestors a foothold in Arcadia. The tale had Atlas as first king of the land, his illustrious descendants including the Arcadian Dardanus, son of Zeus. Dardanus then moved his family and followers to the Troad to escape the devastation of a flood. In this narrative, Aeneas, the quintessential Trojan, actually possessed Arcadian lineage (Dion. Hal. 1.60–1). Greek intellectuals, particularly Arcadians, had responsibility for the tale and proceeded to embellish it (Dion. Hal. 1.49.1–2; Strabo 13.1.53).[5] More striking, however, Roman intellectuals bought it. The most erudite man of the late Republic, Varro, subscribed to the tradition that Aeneas stemmed from Arcadia (Serv. *Ad Aen.* 3.167, 7.207).

Cato further acknowledged foreign origins for other cities and peoples of Italy. Multiple legends lurk behind the fragments of that author. In a telling example, Cato – followed by a later second-century Roman historian Cn. Gellius – reported that the Sabines stemmed from a Spartan founder named, naturally, Sabus. And there is more to this than mere etymological fiction. Sabines came to embody the austerity and moral virtue Romans held dear.[6] The Romans, according to Cato, developed their hardy traits from imitation of the Sabines, and the latter derived that admirable toughness from the toughest of peoples, the Spartans (Cato F 2.22, Beck and Walter 2001–4; cf. Ov. *Fast.* 1.260–1). Hence, Cato, the apostle of Roman ruggedness, traced its genesis to the Lacedaemonians as embodiment of Hellenic hardiness. Cato found foreign connections elsewhere among Italian communities. And he was not shy about incorporating those traditions in his *Origines.* So, Argos was the mother city of Falerii in southern Etruria; Greek-speaking peoples founded Pisa; the community of Politorium, just south of Rome, took its name from Polites, son of the Trojan king Priam; a town called Thebes existed among the Lucanians; and Tibur (Tivoli) was planted by an Arcadian who headed the fleet of Evander (Cato F 2.15, 2.24, 2.26, 3.2; Beck and Walter 2001–4). Just how these stories were fleshed out eludes our grasp. But the acceptance of legends that linked Italian cities to forebears from abroad held sway even with Cato the Censor, the self-professed champion of Roman chauvinism.

All of this affords a valuable window on Roman mentality. The fashioning of a national image did not require disassociation or distance from others. Quite the contrary. The emperor Claudius looked back on the early history of the city and observed that Roman kings came from elsewhere than Rome. Tarquinius Priscus in fact, so Claudius declared in a public inscription, was born of an Etruscan mother and a Corinthian father (*ILS* 212). Greek blood therefore flowed in the veins of Roman monarchs. And the lineage was openly embraced by the emperor. The idea of autochthony or indigenous origins never made much headway in Rome. Legends and fables, bewildering in their variety though they be, consistently portrayed the nation as deriving from the cultures of the east. The concocted Trojans held pride of place, but Roman writers did not eradicate Hellenic beginnings and even paid homage to Phoenician contributions. Roman identity was from the start deeply entangled with others. The sense of a composite people who belonged intimately to the broader Mediterranean world held a central place in Roman self-perception (see also Chapter 25).

Pythagoras and Rome

The appeal of external cultures manifested itself in manifold ways. A striking example exists in the Roman fascination for Pythagoreanism. Not that this went deep. Nor will many have immersed themselves in the philosophic teachings of the sect. But a popular tale had it that the second king of Rome, Numa Pompilius, had studied with Pythagoras himself at Croton in southern Italy, whence he came to take up the throne in Rome. Pythagoras had instructed him in the proper manner of worshiping the gods, and much else besides, lessons that Numa transferred to Rome where he laid the foundation of its religious institutions (Dion. Hal. 2.59.1; Diod. Sic. 8.14). The king, himself from the Sabine country, gained his intellectual training from a Greek sage, and brought the combination of austerity, abstinence, and learning to Rome. The link between these two figures was, of course, a fiction. Chronology alone ruled it out, as many ancient writers themselves observed. Numa, according to conventional calculations, died a century and a half before Pythagoras moved from his native Samos to southern Italy. And the idea that a Sabine had ever heard of him, let alone imbibed philosophy from him, struck some as preposterous. The refutation of this purported contact held importance for certain Roman intellectuals who sought to affirm that the virtues and moral qualities of Numa Pompilius were home-grown, a product of Sabine upbringing rather than alien teachings (Cic. *Rep.* 2.28–9; Livy 1.18.1–3; Dion. Hal. 2.59). All the more surprising and significant, then, that the story persisted. Discrepancy in the dates did not derail it. Ovid retails the legend as uncontested fact (Ov. *Fast.* 3.151–4; *Met.* 15.1–8, 15.60–72; *Pont.* 3.341–4). And other writers addressed the incongruity by devising dodges or reaching for parallels that would keep the Pythagoras/Numa bond alive (Plut. *Num.* 1.3–4, 8.2–8, 11.1–2, 22.3–4). That itself tells us much.[7]

The story doubtless had its roots in Hellenic speculation. Biographers of Pythagoras, like Aristoxenus of Tarentum in the early third century, made him teacher or counselor to a host of Italic peoples from Lucanians to Romans (Diog. Laert. 8.14; Porph. *Pyth.* 22). It seemed suitable enough to have him as mentor to Numa, the father of Roman religious law. Pythagoras took central place in this form of the legend. What carries special interest, however, is the Roman adoption of that legend.

Willingness to appropriate and convey a story that conceived the revered lawgiver from the Sabine country as pupil of the Hellenic sage has revealing implications for the Roman self-image. Cicero, who disbelieved the tale, nevertheless recognized its force and significance. He saw it as consequence of Roman engagement in Magna Graecia, acquaintance with Pythagoras' repute, and readiness to find in the sound judgment and sagacity of Numa a counterpart to the Greek wise man (Cic. *Tusc.* 4.2–3).

Pythagoras' high esteem in Rome can be viewed from a different angle. The oracle at Delphi, so we are told, advised the Romans, in the course of the Samnite wars, to erect statues to the wisest and bravest of the Greeks. The Senate chose to install an image of Pythagoras in the first category, Alcibiades in the second (Pliny *HN*, 34.26; Plut. *Num.* 8.10). That Rome should be taking counsel with the oracular shrine of Apollo as early as the Samnite wars can be questioned. And the Romans may have embraced the philosopher as a means of appeal to the Greeks of southern Italy who would be useful in a contest against Samnites. But the statue of Pythagoras in the *comitium* stood until the time of Sulla, who needed the space for his expanded senate house. The story itself attests to the reputation that Pythagoras continued to enjoy among Romans. Cato the Elder, so it was said, found the sect appealing enough to gain instruction from a Pythagorean philosopher in Tarentum (Plut. *Cat. Mai.* 2.3; cf. Cic *Sen.* 41). One report even had it that Pythagoras received an award of Roman citizenship (Plut. *Num.* 8.9). Here again the tale counts for more than the truth. Legitimate doubts can be raised about the proposition that Pythagoras became a Roman citizen. The concept perhaps reflects Hellenic and Hellenistic practices of granting honorary citizen privileges to distinguished individuals. But the story, whatever its origins, would have found favor among the Romans. It had the added dimension of reference to Rome's liberality in expansion of the franchise to "aliens."

Manumission and Incorporation

A Roman institution, unique in antiquity, affirms this attitude quite decisively: the admission of freed slaves to the citizenship. The Greeks observed the practice with some astonishment. We learn of it first through the eyes of a Hellenistic monarch. Philip V, ruler of Macedon, in a letter to the Greek city of Larissa in Thessaly, noted the Roman custom of according citizenship to freedmen and commended it to the Larissans (*Syll.* 3, 543: 29–34). The Greeks may have been surprised. For the Romans this was routine. Liberality with the franchise speaks volumes. Extension of citizen privileges to communities and peoples within Italy was generous but not startling. A similar generosity toward slaves stood in a different category. The large majority of slaves acquired in this period came from abroad, prisoners of war reduced to servitude or captives purchased on the slave mart. Homegrown slaves existed too, but they will have been the children or descendants of those brought to Italy in servile status.[8] Manumission came more readily in the city than in the countryside, a reward for loyalty and industry, an incentive for obedience, a means of perpetuating the system while liberating the individual. And masters had motives that were not always altruistic. Slaves might purchase freedom with their savings; they would still owe informal allegiance to an ex-master and form part of his clientage, a source of social prestige and political authority (see also Chapter 14).[9]

Whatever the motives, however, the fact of frequent manumission is notable and meaningful. The ready entrance of freedmen into the citizen body signified a level of comfort with foreigners that was unmatched elsewhere in the classical world. What counts here is not liberality or generosity, but the presumption that citizenship could be shared by those of alien birth. Assimilation to Roman ways sufficed to authorize the award of full civic privileges. Romans evidently did not worry about diluting the purity of the stock. Nor did they balk at the exercise of political rights by those whose roots lay in Spain, Cilicia, or Syria. Numbers cannot be ascertained. But the citizenry plainly swelled substantially through the absorption of former slaves. Augustus eventually put on the brake – but not on racial grounds.[10] The attitude of the Roman Republic is clear enough: its populace could only benefit from the admixture of people from everywhere in the Mediterranean.

Alien Cults and Institutions

The sphere of religion underscores this point. Roman religious consciousness from an early stage acknowledged ingredients that were ostensibly non-Roman. Legend dated the arrival in Rome of the Sibylline Books, a collection of Greek oracles in verse, to the time of Tarquinius Superbus. The Books, supervised by a Roman college of priests, were frequently consulted on matters of religion affecting state interest and were treated *Graeco ritu*, in Greek mode of ritual (Dion. Hal. 4.62; Aul. Gell. 1.19.1; Varro *Ling.* 7.8).[11] The temple of Ceres, Liber, and Libera received authorization from the Sibylline Books in the early fifth century, according to tradition, its rites eventually governed by Greek priestesses from southern Italy, another indication of official welcome to Hellenic elements in Roman practice (Dion. Hal. 6.17.2; Cic. *Balb.* 55).[12] In comparable fashion, Rome embraced Etruscan diviners, the *haruspices*. They claimed (or were conceived as having) access to ancient Etruscan skill in interpreting prodigies. At least from the time of the early third century they were consulted frequently by Rome to disclose the meaning of bizarre prodigies and to examine the entrails of sacrificial animals. *Haruspices* eventually became an organized body of diviners fitted into the structure of Rome's religious establishment, while retaining their character or image as Etruscans steeped in native lore (see also Chapter 10).[13]

State action could take more direct form. Romans reached out explicitly to the Greek world in 293, in the wake of an epidemic. On the recommendation of the Sibylline Books, an official delegation went to Epidaurus, there to summon the healing god Aesculapius for assistance. As the tale goes, the god, in the form of a snake, slithered voluntarily onto the Roman vessel and then slithered off again at the Tiber Island. That would mark the spot for a new temple to Aesculapius whose powers had terminated the plague (Livy 10.47.6–7; Val. Max. 1.8.2).[14] Whatever

the truth of the story, the shrine is a fact. And concoction of the tale itself demonstrates the readiness of Roman writers to ascribe religious institutions to Hellenic
authority. In 217, during the dark days of the Hannibalic War, Rome turned again to
foreign divinities. The goddess Venus Erycina moved from Sicily to a new shrine on
the Capitoline Hill in Rome. The deity blended Hellenic and Punic elements, a
combination evidently acceptable to Rome (Livy 22.9–10, 23.30–1).[15] In the next
decade a still more dramatic transfer took place. On the advice of the Sibylline Books
Roman authorities had the Magna Mater shipped from Asia Minor to Rome in the
form of a black stone that emblematized her cult. This Hellenized Anatolian divinity
received a new temple on the Palatine Hill, with annual games to be celebrated in her
honor. Magna Mater or Cybele had the great advantage not only of reinforcing
Rome's links with the Hellenistic kingdom of Pergamum but of symbolizing the
nation's roots in Troy (Livy 29.10.4–1.8; Ov. *Fast.* 4.247–348).[16] The gyrating
castrated priests who serviced the cult with wild dancing and clashing cymbals, to
be sure, needed to be controlled. And regulations banned citizens from the cult's
priesthood, for Roman sensitivities found the behavior unbecoming (Dion. Hal.
2.19). But the temple occupied a prominent place on the Palatine, and the annual
festivals continued to be central events on the Roman calendar (see also Chapter 4).[17]

A notorious episode seems, on the face of it, to contradict Roman openness to alien
cults. In 186 the Senate came down with thunderous fury against the rites of Bacchus,
dissolving its associations, persecuting its leaders, hunting down its adherents, and
firmly suppressing its worship (Livy 39.8–19; *ILS* 18 = *ROL* 4:255–9; see also
Chapters 2, 10, and 28). The reasons for this explosion of state power targeting
the Bacchic sect remain obscure. A concern for the highly organized structure of the
cells that cut across conventional social groups, representing a powerful religious
community outside the control of the state, may have played a role.[18] Or else Roman
leaders exaggerated the threat presented by the Bacchants and utilized the opportunity to make public demonstration of their own authority and the collective ascendancy
of the Senate.[19] Whatever the explanation, it needs to be stressed that this episode is
quite extraordinary, lacked real precursors, and set no precedents. The Bacchic cult
had long been familiar to Romans prior to this period. And it did not disappear
thereafter. The actions of 186 in no way signaled a crackdown on alien cults generally.

Occasional demonstrations of state authority over alternative forms of religious
expression did occur periodically. Jews were expelled from Rome in 139, together
with astrologers. And the Senate took action against the shrines of Isis several times in
the 50s and 40s (Val. Max. 1.3.3–4; Tert. *Ad Nat.* 1.10; Dio Cass. 40.47.3, 42.26).[20]
The actions, however, had no lasting effects, and very likely intended none. Jews were
back in Rome (if they ever left) in substantial numbers before the late Republic. And
the continued existence of the Isis cult in the city holds greater significance than
temporary state hostility. The exhibit of Roman authority had its uses from time to
time, when ad hoc circumstances called for it. But there was no enduring repression
of foreign rites.

How then to characterize a Roman outlook on external religions and national
identity? "Tolerance" of other sects is a term often applied. But that misconceives the
essential disposition. The very notion of tolerance (no Latin word exists for it in this

sense) implies a central and uniform religious structure that indulged in lenience toward deviant sects or practices. The concept simply does not apply to the fundamentally pluralist and polytheist society of Rome. Romans were neither tolerant nor intolerant.[21] The embrace of ostensibly alien cults was part and parcel of Roman identity, not a matter of broadmindedness or liberality. The Romans, as a celebrated tale has it, defeated their bitter foe, the Etruscan city of Veii, in 396 by calling out (*evocatio*) its patron deity Juno and installing her in a temple on the Aventine Hill (Livy 5.21.1–7; see also Chapters 4 and 10). The Etruscan divinity thus became a Roman one, not a defeat of the other's god but an appropriation of it. The Sibylline Books may have been inscribed in Greek as a repository of Greek oracular wisdom but they were integrated seamlessly into a Roman system. And when senators summoned the Magna Mater from the Troad, the act signified that this purportedly foreign cult was, in fact, fundamentally Roman. The Great Mother had her home on Mount Ida, where Aeneas had repaired after the fall of Troy and from which he set forth to lay the foundations of Roman identity.

The acquisition of the Magna Mater, not coincidentally, had the sanction of the Delphic oracle. Roman envoys visited that most sacred and venerable of Greek shrines and operated in part under its instructions (Livy 29.10.6, 29.11.5–7). Recognition of the power and prestige of Delphi may have had multiple motives in the Mediterranean world of the late third century. But it is vital to note that this was far from the first time that Rome had resort to Pythian Apollo. Various tales record consultations of the oracle that go back to the era of the Roman kings. Tarquin the Proud purportedly sent to Delphi for interpretation of an ominous portent – and got a fuller response than he had bargained for (Livy 1.56.4–13; Ov. *Fast.* 2.711–20). At the siege of Veii a miraculous rise in the waters of the Alban lake prompted another embassy to Apollo to solicit a rendering of its meaning (Livy 5.15–17; Val. Max. 1.6.3). And after the fall of Veii, Rome redeemed the vow of its victorious commander to Apollo by purchasing gold for a splendid offering to Delphi (Livy 5.21.1–2, 5.23.8–11, 5.25.4–10, 5.28.1–5). The Samnite War provided a further occasion: Delphi advised Rome to erect statues of the most valorous Greek and the wisest. The Roman Senate duly complied (Pliny *HN* 34.26; Plut. *Num.* 8.10). The historicity of these visits is questionable.[22] But no matter. They held a firm place in the tradition. More reliable is the notice that Rome's great victory over the Gauls at Clastidium in 222, a turning point in the contest for northern Italy, prompted the dispatch of a golden bowl to Delphi to commemorate the triumph (Plut. *Marc.* 8.6). That gesture implies an open acknowledgment of the Hellenic shrine's authority and of Roman deference to it.

A still more pointed declaration of this relationship came a few years later. The Hannibalic War threatened to bring Rome to its knees, and frightful omens followed the calamity at Cannae in 216. The Romans forthwith sent an embassy to the Delphic oracle, headed by the formidable statesman and historian Q. Fabius Pictor. Whatever he may have heard at Delphi, Fabius returned with a list of prescriptions detailing the proper means to propitiate the gods and the specific deities to whom entreaties should be made. Promises of success accompanied the advice, and a request that gifts be sent to Apollo from the spoils that were to come. Fabius returned home, conspicuously displaying the laurel crown that he had worn to Delphi, which he deposited on Apollo's altar in Rome (Livy 22.57.4–5, 23.11.1–6). The act emblematized an identification of Pythian Apollo with the divinity worshiped in Rome. All fell out as predicted. Rome emerged victorious against Hannibal, and a new embassy returned to Delphi with a handsome gift fashioned out of the spoils of war. A reciprocal gesture from the oracle forecast still greater successes for the future (Livy 28.45.12, 29.10.6).[23] The interchanges carried notable significance. Rome had proclaimed, through one of its most distinguished representatives, a close and fruitful association with Greece's holiest shrine – from which the western power had been a signal beneficiary.

Rome benefited too, as a famous story recounts, from Greek stimulus in the fashioning of the Twelve Tables, the very foundation of Roman law (see also Chapters 6 and 11). According to the narrative, internal strife in the mid-fifth century led to the appointment of a commission to draw up a legal code. The Senate therefore assigned three men as envoys to Athens, there to transcribe the laws of Solon and employ them as models for Rome's legislation. The task was appropriately discharged. The envoys returned with a copy of the Solonian measures in hand, and employed it in framing the Roman counterpart (Livy 3.31.8, 3.32.6, 3.33.3–5; Dion. Hal. 10.51.5, 10.52.4, 10.55.5). Rome thus owed the origin of its law code to Athenian inspiration. An alternative tradition had it that the Greek philosopher Hermodorus of Ephesus conveniently happened to be in Rome, in exile from his native city, and acted as adviser to the Romans in drafting the Twelve Tables, for which service he received a statue set up in the *comitium* at public expense (Pliny *HN*, 34.21; cf. Strabo 14.1.25; *Dig.* 1.2.2.4).

The tales have no claim on historicity. Indeed, they are hardly compatible with one another. The similarity of at least parts of the Twelve Tables to certain Solonian laws was recognized by Cicero who saw even a near-verbatim translation in one instance – though he knows nothing of a mission to Athens (Cic. *Leg.* 2.59, 2.64). That legend may have been made up in the late Republic when writers embellished on the parallels to invent an actual trip resulting in an Athenian pattern for Roman legislators.[24] The similarities more likely came from interaction with the Greeks of southern Italy. But creation of the tales carries the real significance. The idea that Rome's most venerable laws, the basis for its whole legal system, derived inspiration, influence, or intellectual input from Greeks offers important insight. Roman mythmakers constructed or enhanced the narratives without embarrassment, even had their leaders actively seek and take advice from Hellenic sources. The debt was more than acknowledged here; it was fantasized.

Phoenicians and Carthaginians

Carthage represented the most formidable and fearsome foe of the Roman Republic. The nation fought Romans in three Punic wars, and its great general Hannibal almost put a premature end to the history of Rome. It causes no surprise that Romans demonized the Carthaginians or their forebears the Phoenicians. Hannibal himself served as a bogeyman for many generations of misbehaving Roman children. The portrait surfaces already with Cato the Elder, who characterized Carthaginians as treaty-breakers and savage in war (*Rhet. Her.* 4.20). A century later Cicero delivered comparably harsh judgments. He reckoned the Phoenician penchant for the sea as mere brigandage and piracy (Cic. *Rep.* 2.9). It was not so much innate character as the location of the Carthaginians that fired them with enthusiasm for acquisitiveness: harbors and ready communication with other peoples induced them to lead the life of fraudulence and mendacity (Cic. *Leg. Agr.* 2.95). Even more pointedly, Cicero branded the Phoenicians as the most duplicitous of nations, and then added that their descendants the Carthaginians, by repeated violations of treaties, proved themselves fully up to the standards of their forefathers (Cic. *Scaur.* 42). *Punica fides* (Carthaginian perfidy) became proverbial in the Roman vocabulary, as both Sallust and Livy attest (Sall. *Iug.* 108.3; Livy 21.4.9, 22.6.12, 30.30.27, 42.47.7). Matters only got worse when later writers looked back on Carthaginian history and labeled that people as cruel, ferocious, and despotic, while their chief trait remained that of deceit, best exhibited in flagrant breaking of treaties (Val. Max. 7.4.2, 7.4.4; Plut. *Prae. Ger. Reip.* 6; App. *Pun.* 62–4; Sil. *Pun.* 3.231–4).[25]

Yet it will not do to leave matters at that. The stereotypes retailed by Roman writers were little more than conventional slurs that stemmed from long-standing ancient attitudes quite independent of Rome. Phoenicians were great seafarers and merchantmen, an occupation that lent itself to the presumption of craftiness and duplicity in the interests of gain. The reputation appears already in Homer's *Odyssey* (13.271–86, 14.287–300, 15.415–18) and recurs in Plato (*Resp.* 414c, 435c–436a; *Leg.* 747c). Romans simply repeated the clichés – but with perhaps less conviction than is often assumed.

An important text deserves notice here. The comic dramatist Plautus produced a play entitled *Poenulus* ("The Little Carthaginian") within a decade or so after the end of the Hannibalic War (see also Chapter 25).[26] One might anticipate animus and malevolence toward the foe that had ravaged Italy and had inflicted such grievous pain upon Rome. Yet the play leaves a very different and surprising impression. To be sure, Plautus worked, as so often, with a Greek comedy, now lost, as model, and none can say how closely he may or may not have reproduced that model (see also Chapter 25). Nonetheless, the fact of the drama's production at a time when Roman memories of Carthaginian terror and devastation were still fresh must speak to the expectations of Plautus' audience. And it is striking that the Carthaginian for whom the play is named does not come off badly at all. Quite the contrary.

Poenulus is stocked with stock characters: the lovesick youth, the tricky slave, the despicable pimp, the admirable courtesan, the swaggering soldier. But the Carthaginian Hanno stands apart from the conventions. He is, of course, an alien to the society he enters. Plautus underscores the Phoenician traits that are mocked and held in contempt by other characters. The prologue itself introduces Hanno as one who knows all languages – and is thus a master at dissimulation. "He is a Carthaginian indeed; what need to say more?" (Plaut. *Poen.* 111–12). The standard stereotype of the deceitful Phoenician thus surfaces from the start. Hanno's clothing, style, and demeanor then come in for ridicule. The slave Milphio compares his attire to that of some bizarre bird, adding slurs in slang appropriate to Carthaginians, and noting that Hanno's attendants, while showing no fingers, have rings in their ears (Plaut. *Poen.* 975–81).[27] Milphio fails to understand Hanno's Punic, but his ludicrous mistranslations only reinforce the conventional conceptions that the Carthaginian must be a merchant out to trick his interlocutors, like a fork-tongued serpent (Plaut. *Poen.* 1009–22, 1032–4). The boastful general heaps further scorn on Hanno, deriding his long tunic as sign of a shopkeeper's attendant and his garb generally as indicative of effeminacy and male prostitution (Plaut. *Poen.* 1298, 1303, 1317–18; see also Chapter 21). Multiple slanders greet Hanno's appearance and behavior.

The caricatures, however, correspond not at all to the character of the Carthaginian. Hanno is a thoroughly sympathetic figure, searching the Mediterranean for his kidnapped daughters, and exhibiting a generous spirit to all parties when they are found. A penchant for playfulness induces him to engage in some subterfuge before the denouement, but he plainly deserves his happy ending. The discrepancy between the humaneness of the man and the snide comments leveled at him must be deliberate. Plautus does not here endorse the stereotypes but subverts them. They are put in the mouths of the conniving slave and the puffed-up warrior. Hanno emerges with full credit, an embodied refutation of traditional travesties. Production of the *Poenulus* in the aftermath of the Carthaginian war – and presumably to a receptive audience – puts putative prejudice in an altogether different and more positive light.

We have testimony also to Roman respect for Punic learning. The Carthaginian agricultural writer Mago composed a massive treatise on farming in 28 volumes. The work came into Roman hands in the middle of the second century, and the Roman Senate itself commissioned a full-scale translation of it into Latin – even though Cato's manual on the subject was already available. The *patres* entrusted this task to a member of the senatorial nobility who also happened to be fluent in Punic and headed a team of experts to accomplish the mission. The decision plainly came at the highest level. Of course, works on agriculture had pragmatic, not just (if at all) literary, value. But Mago's contribution, subsequently rendered in an abbreviated version into Greek, had important impact upon the Roman specialists in this field, Varro and Columella (Pliny *HN* 18.5.22; Varro *Rust.* 1.1.1.10; Col. *Rust.* 1.1.13).[28] And Roman intellectuals made good use of other Punic works. Sallust, for instance, had the geographic books of Hiempsal translated from the Punic for him, and drew on them for his history of the Jugurthine War (Sall. *Iug.* 17.7). The reputation of Phoenicia does not resolve itself into stereotypes. A century after Sallust, the geographer Pomponius Mela, from Roman Spain and writing in Latin, heaped praise upon Phoenicians as accomplished in both war and peace, skilled in literature and the arts, no mere sailors but rulers over nations (Mela 1.65).[29]

Roman regard for Phoenicians eclipsed the caricatures. As long ago as the third century BC, Fabius Pictor had traced the coming of the alphabet to Italy from Arcadian settlers who derived their knowledge from the Phoenicians. And a host of other respectful references set the stage for Virgil's moving depiction of Dido, the Carthaginian queen, a rich, complex, and ultimately appealing figure.

The Gallic Impression

The Gauls or Celts represent inveterate adversaries of Rome. The Gallic sack of Rome in the early fourth century remained a blot on the city's history. Repeated battles engaged Romans with Celts in northern Italy during the third and early second centuries. The Achaean historian Polybius, who wrote his work in Rome under Roman patronage, recorded those wars, reflecting attitudes of ambivalence that mingled contempt with fear and respect. Gauls struck terror into foes, and harbored special hostility against Rome (Polyb. 2.18.1–2, 2.31.7, 3.34.2, 3.78.5).[30] Polybius probes their faults, perhaps a reassurance to Roman readers: Gauls are greedy, fickle, and untrustworthy, internally divided, addicted to drinking, frightening in their initial assault but incapable of keeping it up (Polyb. 2.7.5–6, 2.19.3–4, 2.32.7–8, 2.33.2–3, 2.35.6, 3.78.2). The historian, however, acknowledges commendable traits that made the Gauls worthy rivals. He introduces them as men of size and beauty, boldly courageous in war, a boldness to which he reverts on a number of occasions (Polyb. 2.15.7, 2.18.1–2, 2.35.2, 3.34.2). He admired the good order of their military formation (Polyb. 2.29.5). And, most tellingly, he ascribes their rallying against Rome to a fierce resistance against what would otherwise be wholesale expulsion and destruction (Polyb. 2.21.9). These are no mere clichés and stereotypes.

Greeks interested themselves in Gallic ethnography. Posidonius wrote on the subject in the early first century BC. Comments on Gauls, whether from Posidonius or elsewhere, surface in Diodorus and Strabo, reflecting what may indeed have become commonplaces: Gauls were tall and muscular, immoderate drinkers, occasionally drinking themselves into a stupor, greedy and acquisitive, terrifying in appearance and fearless in war (Diod. Sic. 5.26.3, 5.27.4, 5.28.1, 5.29.1–3, 5.31.1; Strabo 4.4.2–6).[31] And Cicero, when it suited his purpose at a court of law, denounced Gauls as untrustworthy witnesses. They pay no attention to oaths for they pay no respect to religion or the gods. Even the most admirable of Gauls does not belong on a plane with the lowest citizen of Rome (Cic. *Font.* 27, 29–31).[32] These are rhetorical ploys, not sober assessments.

Serious Romans took Gauls seriously. A fragment of Cato the Elder takes us by surprise on this score. He had observed Celts at first hand in the Hannibalic War and in Spain. Cato reports that most of Gaul pursues two things most assiduously: the art of war and speaking with wit (Cato F 2.3, Beck and Walter 2001–4; cf. Diod. Sic. 5.31.1; Strabo 4.1.5).[33] We would not have expected the latter.

The Roman best in a position to speak knowledgeably about Gauls was Julius Caesar who fought them for nearly a decade. His observations are complex and considered. To be sure, Caesar conveys some clichés. He too probably read Posidonius or other ethnographic treatments of the Gauls. So, his *Gallic Wars* includes allusions to them as a capricious and unstable people (Caes. *B Gall.* 2.1.3, 3.8.3, 4.5.1, 4.13.3). And the label of a nation that is quick to go to war but unable to sustain it reappears in Caesar's account as well (Caes. *B Gall.* 3.19.6). He delivered other negative verdicts when it suited the purposes of his narrative. He deems recklessness as a national trait and ties it to foolishness and weakness of mind (Caes. *B Gall.* 7.42.2, 7.77.9). He even accused some Gauls of treachery – though not as a national trait (Caes. *B Gall.* 7.5.5–6, 7.17.7, 7.54.2).[34]

Caesar could also draw attention to characteristics of the Celts in a literary device to reflect upon the deficiencies of his own society. His treatise opens with praise of the Belgae as bravest of all Gallic tribes precisely because they dwelled at the greatest distance from the Roman province (Caes. *B Gall.* 1.1.3; cf. 2.4). He makes a comparable comment about the Gauls as a whole: they used to exceed the Germans in valor, but those days have passed; proximity of Roman provinces acquainted them with luxury goods, and they have gone soft (Caes. *B Gall.* 6.24.1, 6.24.5–6).[35]

But Caesar did not rely on artificial concoctions or literary stereotypes. He fought Gallic tribes and he delivered thoughtful judgments – many of them quite positive. The Nervii, for instance, gained renown as the fiercest of Gallic fighters, deliberately prohibiting import of wine and other goods that might enervate their spirits, scorning other tribes that had surrendered to Rome and abandoned ancestral virtue (Caes. *B Gall.* 2.15.3–5, 2.27.5). Caesar frequently ascribed courage (*virtus*) to Gallic warriors.[36] And, like Polybius before him, Caesar presented Gauls as fighting to preserve the liberty that they had inherited from their ancestors rather than suffer servitude under the Romans (Caes. *B Gall.* 1.17.4, 3.8.4, 3.10.3, 5.27.6, 7.1.5, 7.1.8, 7.4.4, 7.37.4, 7.77.13–16).

Perhaps most noteworthy is Caesar's evaluation of Celtic religious practices. The Druids, the priestly establishment among the Gauls, later branded as dangerous and suppressed by Augustus, religious leaders who condoned and supervised human sacrifice, received no strictures from Caesar. He described their rituals in straightforward and detached fashion, passing no negative verdict even upon the sacrificial rites, approving their educational endeavors, and noting their doctrine of metempsychosis that encouraged valor among their people (Caes. *B Gall.* 6.13.3, 6.14.1–6, 6.16.1–2). And his description of Celtic gods makes them equivalent to Roman divinities, both in name and in function, without suggesting any distinction or peculiarities (Caes. *B Gall.* 6.17.1–3).[37] Far from distancing Roman characteristics from the alien, Caesar practically turned the Gauls into good (or better than) Romans.

A century later the emperor Claudius argued for the introduction of Gallic provincials into the Roman Senate. The speech that Tacitus puts into his mouth, a faithful one at least in spirit, as we know from a contemporary inscription, accurately epitomizes Roman sentiments. Claudius affirmed that what ultimately caused the failure of Sparta and Athens, despite their military predominance, was the practice of shunning conquered peoples as aliens. Rome's success, by contrast, came precisely because the nation, from Romulus on, translated former foes into new citizens (Tac. *Ann.* 11.23–5; cf. *ILS* 212). The Gauls can serve on this score as prime example of the Roman disposition toward foreigners, even ancient enemies.

People of Color

Bias and bigotry do not prevail even in an area where one might most readily expect to find them: Roman attitudes toward blacks. Evidence is slim from the Republic. Acquaintance with the peoples south of Egypt expanded notably only with the advent of the Empire. But the later testimony allows for some extrapolation. And it makes clear that even the most conspicuous "otherness" did not issue in hostility and alienation.

Aithiops or "Ethiopian," a Greek concoction meaning "sunburnt face," became the conventional designation for a black man, adopted by Romans in the Latinized form of *Aethiops*. The description itself carried no negative connotation. Indeed Ethiopians enjoyed a favorable reputation in Greek literature. Homer famously has Zeus, accompanied by the rest of the gods, sup with the "blameless Ethiopians" on a 12-day holiday (Hom. *Il.* 1.423–4; cf. 23.205–7). Herodotus holds the Ethiopians and their ancient rulers in high regard as people of piety and integrity (Hdt. 2.137, 2.139, 3.20–2). More striking still, the Greek historian reported that Ethiopians were said to be the tallest and most attractive of all men (Hdt. 3.20). Not that the Greeks were color blind. The Danaids of Aeschylus' *Suppliant Maidens* are "black and burnt by the sun" and the Ethiopians of his *Prometheus Bound* are a nation of black men living by the fountain of the sun (Aesch. *Supp.* 154–5; *PV* 807–12). Herodotus indeed notes that the Ethiopians of Libya have the curliest hair in the world (Hdt. 7.70). These and other Greek allusions were accompanied by no negative judgment.[38] The high repute of the Ethiopians emerges with clarity in the work of Diodorus, the Sicilian historian writing in the age of Augustus. For Diodorus their piety was proverbial, the first of men who learned to honor the gods with sacrifices, festivals, and processions, and were blessed in turn by the gods who granted them an enduring state of freedom and internal peace, as well as protection from foreign domination. Indeed, so Diodorus reports, the Ethiopians have a history that antedates the Egyptians themselves and are responsible for most of Egypt's social and religious institutions, even the use of hieroglyphics (Diod. Sic. 3.2–4). This idealized image of Ethiopians, particularly those from the capital at Meroe, as pious, generous, and righteous was picked up and perpetuated by numerous writers of the Roman Empire (e.g., Sen. *Ira* 3.20.2; Paus. 1.33.4; Lucian *Iupp. Trag.* 37; Philostr. *VA* 6.4.21).[39]

Romans, of course, were not oblivious to the physical characteristics of the Ethiopians. The black skin, woolly hair, flat noses, and thick lips were frequently commented upon (*Moretum* 31–5; Vitr. 6.1.3–4; Petron. 102; Pliny *HN* 2.189). Nor did they regard those characteristics as especially desirable. A white/black contrast, then as now, gave advantage to the former in popular imagination and conventional language.[40] Moreover, a strong strain in ancient thinking traced physical features to environmental circumstances. Northern peoples, braced by cold, were stereotyped as blond, white-skinned, fierce, and bold, but also reckless and stupid. Southerners, by contrast, in warm climes, swarthy of complexion, with curly hair, were more intelligent and quick-witted, but cowardly, fickle, unreliable, greedy, and mendacious. The classic contrast held between Scythians in the north and Egyptians and Ethiopians in the south (e.g., Strabo 1.1.13, 1.2.27). On this scale, Greeks and Romans, of course, had the advantage of dwelling in the Mediterranean environment, a moderate middle way, that not only combined intelligence with courage but produced the pale brown complexion and hair that struck just the right balance.[41] That outlook had a broad following but had more to do with establishing the superiority of Mediterranean peoples than with excoriating others. It contained no overtones of anti-black sentiment.

The degree to which blacks were assimilated into Roman society cannot be determined. Most entered Italy as slaves, whether through war or the mart. But it is essential to note that slavery and blackness had no connection _per se_. The vast majority of slaves in Italy were white. And the practice of manumission, with concomitant Roman citizenship, applied to all races and ethnicities alike. Nothing suggests that black freedmen suffered any liability by virtue of their skin. To be sure, most will have entered the ranks of laborers and joined the less privileged members of society. But their complexion did not put them at the bottom of the ladder. Literary texts, in addition to the material evidence of statuettes and ceramic representations, disclose blacks in a wide range of occupations as soldiers, cooks, construction workers, actors, entertainers, assistants in the baths, and personal attendants. None of these, of course, were high-status positions, but blackness itself carried no handicap to further mobility. Some of the entertainers could capture considerable acclaim and renown, and soldiers might attain officer rank.[42]

Miscegenation occurred without stigma. Growing familiarity with blacks who served in the same households with whites or labored side by side with them in the workplace must have increased the number of cross-racial unions. Adultery, of course, was frowned on. And sexual liaisons that involved persons of quite different social stations would naturally draw scorn. But race mixture as such did not engender opprobrium, a fact of notable significance for the Roman mentality.

In at least one area, blacks held positions of some importance. The cult of Isis spread around the Mediterranean, with Meroe as one of its principal centers, and made considerable headway in Rome itself. There, Ethiopians played a major role as ministers to the cult, their expertise in the ritual in demand and respected.[43]

In exceptional cases, a rise to prominence could be quite notable. The ancient biography of the celebrated comic dramatist Terence, ascribed to Suetonius, claims that he was born in Carthage of African stock and dark color, brought to Rome as a slave, and freed because of his talent and good looks (Suet. _Vita Ter._ 1, 5; see also Chapter 25). That Terence, in fact, was black, cannot be confirmed. The biographer may simply have made an inference, erroneous or guesswork, from his _cognomen_, P. Terentius Afer. But, even if it lacks foundation, the inference implies that such a career was open to talented slaves of dark complexion from Africa. The existence of bronze and marble heads of personages with Negroid features indicates clearly enough that these were men who had reached positions of some stature and wealth.[44] Notions of innate inferiority make no appearance here. Blacks had access to integration in Roman society.

The Jewish Presence

In some ways, the most alien presence in Rome during the Republic was that of the Jews. Their customs, practices, and beliefs had little in common with the traditional values espoused by Romans. And Jews, notoriously, kept to themselves, maintaining a separate identity that set them apart from conventional political and social relationships in Rome. As Tacitus later remarked, Jews show intense loyalty to one another but hostility to everyone else. They hold all things profane that Romans regard as sacred, and allow everything that Romans forbid (Tac. *Hist.* 5.4.1, 5.5.1).[45]

Were Jews then excluded from polite society, marginalized or oppressed?[46] Cicero rails against them in a speech, defending his client against charges of infractions committed in the province of Asia. He refers to the "barbaric superstition" of the Jews and speaks with contempt of that nation whose institutions differ so sharply from those of Rome's ancestors and whose inferiority was established by the gods themselves in authorizing the recent Roman conquest of their land (Cic. *Flacc.* 67, 69). But rhetoric plays a larger role here than prejudice. Cicero, in building a case for the defendant, spews equal vitriol (and at greater length) against Asian Greeks, against Lydians, Phrygians, and Mysians (Cic. *Flac.* 3, 6–26, 60–6). More importantly, his remarks on the Jews inadvertently disclose a place in society quite at variance with the objectives of his speech. The orator complains of Jewish demonstrations at Roman political gatherings, demonstrations that were not uncommon, indeed often influential, and in no way illegitimate (Cic. *Flac.* 66–7). When their interests called for it, Jews could freely press their views on the public scene. The Jewish crowds that gathered consisted primarily of Roman citizens, not slaves, freedmen or outsiders. An established community of Jews existed in Rome by the early first century, and probably had for some time before.[47] They had access to civic privileges and carried weight in public deliberations. They kept a clear sense of their own identity and solidarity, but gained no small measure of integration within Roman society.

The great scholar Varro, who could eschew Ciceronian rhetoric, paid the Jews a signal compliment. He held that the ancient Romans for more than a century and a half had followed the admirable practice of worshiping the gods without the use of images. Things had gone downhill since then, and respect for the gods had diminished. For the practice of true piety, he observed, Romans should look to the Jews (August. *De civ. D.* 4.31).

Conclusion

Romans, of course, indulged in slurs and stereotypes, conventions and clichés, in describing the characteristics of others. They never doubted their superiority over the peoples they had absorbed and the nations they had subdued. But their self-image did not require disparagement, let alone exclusion, of the alien. Once one departs from the commonplaces and conducts a deeper probe, a very different picture emerges. Romans embraced legends that traced their origins to Greeks and Trojans, appropriated (and acknowledged) cults, traditions, and honored figures from abroad, freely bestowed franchise upon foreigners, held even former enemies in high regard, and shared civic privileges with immigrants of altogether different appearance, demeanor, and history.

Guide to Further Reading

The subject is a complex and ambiguous one. Only a selection of topics could be covered in a short chapter. A valuable and very wide assemblage of testimony on Roman attitudes toward foreign peoples may be found in Balsdon 1979, although the organization is somewhat erratic and the analysis minimal. Momigliano 1975 remains a classic, engagingly written and provocative, but short on the Roman side. Reactions and relations between Romans and other Italian clans are given only passing notice here. But the incisive book of Dench 1995 merits recommendation. A multitude of works treat Roman responses to Greeks and appropriation of Greek culture. The relation of Hellenic traditions to Rome's sense of its own origins and identity is discussed in Gruen 1992 and Erskine 2001. There is much to be learned about religious institutions and their implications for Roman openness to alien cults and practices in North 1979, Orlin 1997, and Beard, North, and Price 1998. The ambivalent portrayals of Phoenicians and Carthaginians need considerably more work in the scholarship. Prandi 1979 and Mazza 1988 are only a beginning. The extensive study by Kremer 1994 is the most useful compendium on the depiction of Gauls and Celts in Roman writings during the Republic, but there is room for a more analytical probe of that topic. The sensibilities of Romans toward blacks and their characterizations of peoples labeled "Ethiopians" have been better served in scholarship, especially by Snowden 1970, 1983 and Thompson 1989. Roman perceptions of Jews have gained widespread scrutiny, but most of the evidence is Imperial rather than Republican, and much of the discussion has been devoted to assessing the extent of Roman "anti-semitism." The scholarship more recently has moved in other directions, as for example in Schäfer 1997 and Gruen 2002 (with different slants). Finally, two forthcoming works merit notice. A parallel piece on "Romans and Others" by Y. Syed has appeared in Harrison 2005. And the substantial volume by B. Isaac 2004, a wide-ranging and very important study of "proto-racism" in antiquity, offers a considerably darker picture than is presented in this chapter.

Notes

1 Balsdon 1979: 30–4, 59–70; Dauge 1981: 57–131. Cf. most recently Burns 2003: 7–8, 12–24; Isaac 2004: 381–405.
2 Cornell 1975: 1–32; Gruen 1992: 8–21; Erskine 2001: 15–43.
3 Bickermann 1952: 65–81.
4 Gruen 1992: 52–83; Henrichs 1995: 244–50.
5 Erskine 2001: 119–21.
6 Dench 1995: 86–93.
7 Garbarino 1973: 2.223–44; Gruen 1990b: 158–62.
8 Treggiari 1969: 1–11.
9 Treggiari 1969: 11–20; Bradley 1984: 81–5; Gardner 1993: 7–38; Bradley 1994: 158–65.
10 Cogrossi 1979: 158–77; Bradley 1984: 87–95; Gardner 1993: 39–41.

11 Gruen 1990b: 7–8; Scheid 1995: 25–6; Orlin 1997: 76–97; Beard, North, and Price 1998: 62–3.
12 Beard, North, and Price 1998: 64–6.
13 MacBain 1982: 43–59; Beard, North, and Price 1998: 19–20.
14 Orlin 1997: 106–8.
15 Schilling 1954: 233–66.
16 Gruen 1990b: 5–33; Erskine 2001: 205–24.
17 Goldberg 1998: 1–20.
18 North 1979: 92–7.
19 Gruen 1990b: 34–78.
20 Takács 1995: 57–63.
21 Beard, North, and Price 1998: 212.
22 Fontenrose 1978: 65, 314, 334, 342–3.
23 Gruen 1990b: 10.
24 Siewert 1978: 331–44; Cornell 1995: 274–5; Isaac 2004: 324–5.
25 Prandi 1979: 90–7; Mazza 1988: 562–4.
26 Maurach 1988: 32–3.
27 Maurach 1988: 145–6; Syed 2005: 363–70.
28 Heurgon 1976: 441–56.
29 Batty 2000: 70–94.
30 Williams 2001: 79–88.
31 Malitz 1983: 169–98; Kremer 1994: 266–72, 304–15; Isaac 2004: 416–18.
32 Kremer 1994: 94–104.
33 Momigliano 1975: 65; Williams 2001: 79–80.
34 Barlow 1998: 139–70.
35 Kremer 1994: 202–18.
36 Rawlings 1998: 179–80; Isaac 2004: 415–16.
37 Burns 2003: 131–3.
38 Snowden 1970: 144–5; 1983: 46–9.
39 Snowden 1970: 147–55; Thompson 1989: 88–93.
40 Snowden 1983: 82–5.
41 Snowden 1983: 85–7; Thompson 1989: 101–6.
42 Snowden 1970: 161–8, 187–8; 1983: 88–91.
43 Snowden 1970: 189–90; 1983: 97–9.
44 Snowden 1970: 187–8; 1983: 90, 93.
45 Bloch 2002: 91–7; Isaac 2004: 450–65.
46 Schäfer 1997: 180–95.
47 Gruen 2002: 19–23.

CHAPTER 23

History and Collective Memory in the Middle Republic

Karl-J. Hölkeskamp

Legends of the origins of the Roman People and their rise to imperial greatness, full-blooded stories about feats of courage in war and peace of the great heroes of the glorious past, and exemplary anecdotes about their staunch steadfastness in the face of adversity: in the eyes of mid- and late-republican Romans – this was the stuff that history was made of. Polybius – the Greek historian who tried to explain how the Romans succeeded in subjecting nearly the whole inhabited world under their sole dominion in less than 53 years – also knew of many stories about many men that were already part and parcel of Roman history in his day.[1] This kind of (hi-)story and the concomitant conception of Rome's past, which every reasonably well-educated Roman used to have at the tips of his fingers, had been the main subject matter and, indeed, the backbone of historiography ever since its beginnings in the final decades of the third century.

From this decisive initial stage onward, the practice of writing history – that is, by definition, Roman history – was, and would remain at least until the end of the following century, a prestigious task for members of the sociopolitical elite:[2] Q. Fabius Pictor – according to the unanimous conviction of later Romans, the founder of this typically Roman-style historiography, who nevertheless wrote in Greek – was a senator, perhaps of praetorian rank, a diplomat, and above all a scion of one of the oldest and most renowned houses of the patrician aristocracy, the Fabian clan[3] – we shall have to return to their particular place in the storehouse of foundation myths. Quite a few of his successors in the second century – from A. Postumius Albinus, another patrician, to the plebeians L. Calpurnius Piso, C. Sempronius Tuditanus, and C. Fannius[4] – even reached the consulship and thus belonged to the exclusive innermost circle of the senatorial class. And M. Porcius Cato – a "new man" (*homo novus*), Consul 195 and Censor 184, later surnamed "Censorius" and himself an "example" (*exemplum*) of censorious strictness in every sense of the concept – was also known for his original work on the origins of the Roman (and other Italian) People(s): his *Origines* were the first history in Latin prose (see also Chapter 2).[5] All of these men wrote not only the glorious history of the Roman People but also what they quite naturally believed to be, first and foremost, the history of their own class: the common threads of this history were the achievements of the *populus Romanus* at home and abroad and the exemplary deeds of true Romans, many (not all) of them nobles like themselves, their achievements on the battlefield, their feats as orators, patrons, and senior statesmen in the Senate, the courts, and assemblies, which in one way or another all contributed to Rome's rise to her prestige and position in the world of their own day. At the same time, this kind of history reflected and reformulated the framework of values and norms of the elite, thus affirming their common code of behavior and binding rules, which were also enshrined in the *exempla*. This special historiography "alla Romana" thus served to strengthen the collective identity and legitimacy of a ruling class or meritocracy, based on an ideology of permanent, unfailing, and unerring service to the *populus Romanus* and the greatness of their Empire.

The fully developed vision of Rome's glorious past as we find it in Livy's grand history "from the foundation of the city" (*ab urbe condita*) features several typical characteristics. There is the emphasis on the humble beginnings of the city on the banks of the Tiber, founded by Romulus according to the time-honored rules and divinely sanctioned rituals of augury and sacrifice.[6] His hut on the Palatine, the cradle of the imperial city, may as such have been a fiction, but as a symbol of a legendary past it was a sacred place.[7] There is the notion of a pristine innocence combined with moral firmness, piety, and the virtues of frugality and simplicity which were believed to be the basis of a particular strength, self-confidence, vigor, fortitude, and equanimity in the face of adversity – a notion inseparably combined with an unshakeable belief in Rome's superiority over all other nations, friend and foe.

This particular conglomerate of values and convictions was epitomized in stories illustrating the most central and exemplary Roman virtues like the famous anecdote about the dictator L. Quinctius Cincinnatus. This legendary figure – the only "hope of the empire of the Roman People" in deadly peril, according to Livy – was, according to the tradition, literally called from the plow to save the Republic: Cincinnatus was working in the fields of his modest farm on the right bank of the Tiber when the envoys of the Senate met him to inform him of his appointment and to urge him to assume supreme command immediately.[8] Although reluctant to leave his home, this true Roman followed the call of Senate and People, discharged his duties with exemplary devotion, saved the army and the Republic, returned to the city in triumph, resigned the dictatorship after only 16 days and resumed his simple life as a farmer content to cultivate his land with his own hands.

There was another idea that was part and parcel of the Romans' view of the early stages of their glorious history. The city's humble origins were thought to have already contained in embryo the future greatness of the Empire, a vision that has found its classic articulation in Virgil's *Aeneid* (1.257–96). Here Jupiter prophesizes that the descendants of the small group of Trojans under their leader Aeneas, who at this point have not even reached Italy, will become the "lords of the world," to whom he, Jupiter, will grant an *imperium sine fine*, an empire without limit or end in space or time (1.278–9). Here we find Rome's arduous ascent to universal rule explicitly prefigured: it is the will of the gods – as Livy has the immortalized founder-hero Romulus declare (1.16.6–7) – that the city on the Tiber will become "the head of the world" (*caput orbis terrarum*).

The certainty that informs Virgil's vision has strong precursors in the Republic. Already then, the military conquest of other peoples appeared as the fulfillment of a special relationship between the Romans and their divine supporters: it was indeed Fabius Pictor who already mentioned a miraculous portent on the Capitol, foretelling Rome's rise to the dominion of the world.[9] The individual stages of military expansion coincided with the long series of great men like Cincinnatus, whose names only needed to be mentioned in order to bring to mind their feats of heroism, which in effect meant their contributions to the extension of Roman power. This "honor roll" of Rome's "collective memory" included, first of all, Romulus, the founder of the city; the other kings, like Numa Pompilius and Servius Tullius, who paved the way for the republican heroes; and the heroes of the Republic themselves. Their long line begins with L. Iunius Brutus – avenger, founder of the Republic, and its first consul.[10] Other prominent figures in the republican Hall of Fame were M. Furius Camillus – conqueror of the Gauls and the "second founder of Rome" after Romulus;[11] M'. Curius Dentatus – victor over half a dozen Italian peoples and above all over the king Pyrrhus, a "new man" (*homo novus*) without aristocratic ancestors and yet another epitome of frugality and incorruptibility;[12] and, last but not least, Q. Fabius Maximus – the great "Delayer" (*Cunctator*), who became the savior of the Republic through his circumspect caution and steadfastness in Rome's life-and-death struggle with Hannibal.[13]

In Virgil, to be sure, center stage is taken by "Augustus Caesar, who has so often been promised, the son of a god, who shall again set up the Golden Age" (*Aen.* 6.791–4). But already 150 years earlier, Virgil's epic predecessor Ennius (239–169) had traced Rome's series of heroes from the beginning down to his own time in his *Annales*. The poem celebrated Aeneas and above all Romulus, "father," "creator," "guardian of the fatherland," living "in heaven with his divine ancestors,"[14] as well as Curius Dentatus, "whom nobody could ever overcome, with iron or with gold,"[15] and the great *Cunctator* – "the man who by delaying saved our cause."[16] Ennius also praised the "invincible" Scipio Africanus, whose deeds needed a Homer to praise them,[17] and the Elder Cato, who personified, like no one else, the traditional simplicity of the Roman character – the perfect illustration of Ennius' famous line: "On customs of old as well as men rests the Roman cause" (*moribus antiquis res stat Romana virisque*).[18]

In Ennius and Virgil – and, for that matter, in the received version of Roman history in Livy – we capture in a relatively late, literary format the kind of material that already in the Middle Republic formed the core of Rome's "cultural memory." Remembrance of things past – Roman style – revolved around the great figures who invariably enhanced Roman power in a seemingly endless series of wars that the "nation in the toga" (Virg. *Aen.* 1.282) underwent in the course of its history: a glorious record of heroes and their deeds, towering figures or awe-inspiring "ancestors" (*maiores*) all, who acted out their particular part in Rome's predestined mission relentlessly to wage war on her enemies and unyieldingly pursue the ultimate goal of universal rule. Roman history crystallized around these figures in the form of personalized stories, including many *exempla*, i.e., precedents with a normative-exemplary force that could be called upon in all situations and at any time.[19] As a corollary, this view of Rome's glorious past was imbued with a particular "theology of victory" that endowed the rise of the city with a religious aura.[20]

These stories illustrate several aspects of the specifically Roman manifestation of what we might call "collective" or, following Jan Assmann and others, "cultural memory."[21] Generally speaking, the concept refers to the collectively shared knowledge of a society, the peculiar set of certainties and convictions it has about itself and, in particular, about its historical roots. The collective memory helps a group or a society as a whole to articulate an awareness of its defining characteristics and its unity, and therefore forms an essential basis for its self-image and identity. More specifically, this means that the cultural memory is the main source for patterns of perception, for conceptions of order, right and wrong, and for the framework in which to interpret one's own contemporary social environment and world of experience. This implies that the stored body of cultural knowledge can never be arbitrary, is never selected in a haphazard fashion. For on the one hand, it has an educational function, disciplining and integrating the members of a society and thereby reinforcing its cohesion, and, on the other, a society's shared cultural knowledge possesses a normative dimension as it contains binding "instructions" about how to act in the present and the future.

In order to fulfill these functions of founding and reinforcing collective identity in practice, cultural memory does not depend on the antiquarian storage of its contents in archives or, for that matter, in the writings of learned specialists such as professional historians. Rather, it needs entirely different forms of cultivation, a broad spectrum of ways and media of preservation, regeneration, and transmission. Fixing cultural knowledge in writing – in the shape of canonical texts or, as in the Roman case, in the form of historiographical narratives written by retired senatorial amateurs addressing themselves to a narrow circle of educated peers in the know – is by no means the only or even the most obvious medium.[22] As in many (premodern) societies, other media are equally or even more important: oral transmission and memorial days, festivals, ceremonies, and other rituals of all sorts, preserved for generations, as well as the topographical and social spaces in which they take place, including the buildings and monuments that mark such "memorable" locations, as well as the locations themselves. The spectrum of forms, institutions, and places through which a cultural memory may find its articulation and permanence, the relative importance of these forms and, above all, the specific, synergetic connections of media and locations that result in "systems" or "landscapes" of memory are characteristic of a specific society. In fact, they are themselves integral components of its cultural memory.

These general definitions lead to another central aspect of the topic: memory, in particular cultural memory, needs spaces and places. According to Pierre Nora, these places include not just memorials and other locations of memory fixed in physical space: his "realms of memory" comprehend rituals and festivals, anniversaries, images, and texts – after all, the range of meanings and connotations of Nora's concept of *lieux de mémoire* covers the literal as well as metaphorical sense.[23] His notion of "memory domains" here overlaps with our conception of a cultural memory. In concrete terms, what needs to be explored in this chapter is precisely the nexus between forms and media of Roman memory on the one hand, and its culturally and socially conditioned contents, which address Roman needs for meaning, order, and orientation, on the other. In ancient city-states in particular, well-defined "public spaces" take on particular importance: they form the concrete venues in which the processes of political decision-making, religious festivals, and everyday communication among the citizens (in the strict sense of the term) take place. The political culture of classical city-states is therefore on a structural level shaped by a specific logic of space and spatiality, directness and density.[24]

In short, we have to assume that every group which has an image of itself as a group aims to take permanent possession of and, as it were, "colonize" specific, meaningful locations, which are symbols of its identity and fixed points of reference for its memory; that, in other words, memory tends toward spatiality and that we therefore have to reckon with a special significance and function of such memory domains. Against this backdrop, we may view the city of Rome in the Middle Republic as a "stage of history" in a double sense of the term, that is, as an urban space where important events took place and the space where remembrance of such events was visibly staged in ephemeral rituals as well as in a permanent "scenery" or "landscape" of memory.[25] This evolving relationship between history and its transformation into memory finds material articulation in monuments of all types, such as temples and other public buildings, equestrian and other honorary statues, as well as the texts that can be found *in situ*: dedicatory inscriptions on buildings that evoke the memory of the dedicant, specific events and their concomitant stories, or the explanatory inscriptions (*tituli*) on statues of different types.[26]

A fundamental feature of the Roman republican cultural memory, then, is the "monumental memory" developed in the third and second centuries, the arrangement and evolution of this core area of cultural memory, i.e., the public spaces in the center of the city, the temples and altars, statues, and other images of all kinds, as well as the semantics of their symbolism and the messages and stories contained therein. In the cityscape of *memoria* in stone and (some) marble that was Rome, the heroes mentioned above, who had made its history, were permanently on display and thus, in the full sense of the word, omnipresent. They and their memorable deeds and achievements were the core and kernel of Rome's monumental memory; they colonized the public spaces of the city through all kinds of memorials, such as buildings and victory monuments, dedications of spoils and statues, in particular on the Capitol, in the Comitium and the Forum.[27]

There is an interplay, then, between the locations and the stories attached to them, between their public functions in any period of Roman history and the ways of recalling past events. Roman society, of course, is not exclusively a community of memory, but also a religious, and, not least, a political community. Although these dimensions are closely related, they are never fully identical: their interrelation and their complex web of references among each other presuppose that the individual aspects retain their distinctiveness and contrasts. As a result of this nexus, temples, states, and other monuments, their respective (hi-)stories and messages, their location and spaces form a physical as well as mental landscape fraught with political, historical, sacral, and mythical meanings and messages. Not only can such a landscape be "read" like a text, since it stores the full spectrum of myths, historical, etiological, and other stories – it can also be experienced directly, by Roman citizens as viewers, in the concrete sense of walking through it and looking around.[28]

This experience is heightened during the time of a procession, which moved from one meaningful location to the next, thereby galvanizing memories and reinvigorating the nexus of associations that attached Rome's contemporary urban topography to her past. For example, the well-known ritual of the specific Roman variant of a public funeral procession must have been "read" by the viewers in this way. It was the Greek Polybius who described this very Roman practice (6.53.1–54.3 and see also Chapters 16, 17, and 24): the procession of predeceased members of a great family – each represented by a person wearing the robes of curule offices each had held, or even triumphal attire and the wax mask (*imago*) of the respective ancestor – symbolically accompanied their recently deceased descendant on his last way through the city. In its chronological order the procession mirrored the clan's history and continuity and, at the same time, it represented its accumulation of *honores*, political offices, priesthoods, and other marks of distinction. And last but not least it asserted, as it were, its visibility and presence in the present. The procession ended at one of the most prominent public spaces in the city – the *rostra*: it was here that these visible representatives of the glorious past of their family (as well as, again at the same time, of the Republic as a whole) settled down – on curule chairs, and right next to the Comitium with its particularly dense politico-memorial topography of statues and other monuments (to be discussed below). And it was here that their services to the *res publica* in war and peace were commemorated together with the achievements and virtues of the deceased in a highly stylized kind of funeral oration. Such a eulogy delivered by a scion of the clan symbolically present here, was the best medium to affirm the identity of this particular group of "the ancestors" as historical figures of the *populus Romanus* at large, and at the same time, it served to renew the inseparable link between past and present.[29]

The most spectacular procession, however, was of course the triumph – the venerable entry of the victorious general and his army into the city.[30] At first, the triumph appears as a magnificent spectacle. At its center stood, on the one hand, the victorious magistrate and general himself, who could personally lay claim to the victory as the holder of *imperium* and the power to take the auspices (see also Chapter 10), and, on the other, the deed itself – a deed for the *res publica*, its greatness (*maiestas*) and imperial power. The decision of the Senate to award a triumph signaled that the political-military elite of the Republic recognized this achievement and decided to allow it to be staged in front of the *populus Romanus*.

The temple of Jupiter on the Capitol was the final destination of the procession, and its ultimate point of reference. But the route to the Capitol was itself already embedded in the sacral and political topography of the city of Rome (see Map 9). The assembly point of the procession was, appropriately for an event dominated by soldiers, the *campus Martius* ("Field of Mars").[31] Here, at the outskirts of the city

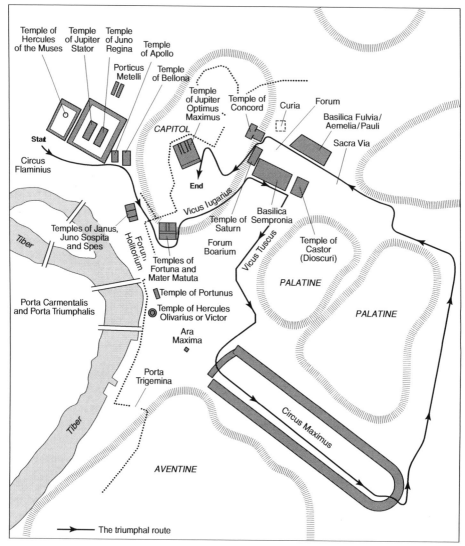

Map 9   The triumphal route

– and outside the sacred boundary of the city (the *pomerium*) – the returning holder
of *imperium* awaited the Senate's decision on whether he was allowed to celebrate a
triumph. The procession proper began with a march through the "Triumphal Gate"
(*porta triumphalis*) – a sort of virtual gate at the south side of the *campus Martius*,
which had a symbolic significance: it was opened only for this very purpose, i.e., the
entry of a *triumphator* into the city. The procession then proceeded along the Forum
Holitorium and the Forum Boarium toward the Circus Maximus, around the Palatine, and then turned left toward the Forum.[32] On the *Sacra via*, it traversed the full
length of the Forum and stopped at the crossroads of *Sacra via* and *clivus Capitolinus*

at the foot of the hill.[33] At this point, the *triumphator* dismounted from his chariot and ascended to the temple on foot. There he laid down the laurel-twigs and garlands of the *fasces* at the statue of Jupiter, dedicated spoils of arms, and sacrificed a white bull. These ritual acts completed the cycle of war, which had begun in this very place – with the departing general taking auspices, performing sacrifices, and uttering vows before joining his army.

The procession and its route staged the felicitous and victorious return after a departure into the unknown, a ritual homecoming from a hostile outside world into the space of the city, from the realm *militiae* back into the sphere *domi*, from war to peace. The route circled the ancient core of the city, the aforementioned residence of Romulus on the Palatine. Sacrifices marked decisive stages on the way – as at the *porta triumphalis* and on the altar on the Capitol, where both circles, the actual and the symbolic, found their final closure. The sacral landscape of the city thus dominated the triumph as an urban ritual through its fixed and immovable signposts. Conversely, each celebrated triumph renewed and indeed regenerated the symbolic significance of the urban landscape in general, as well as of the particular central space of memory that included the Capitol, the Comitium, and the Forum.

Let us take a look at the development of this hallowed ground in the two centuries between the establishment of Rome as a hegemonial power in central Italy in 338 down to the annihilation of Carthage in 146, when Rome's pan-Mediterranean empire took shape. Within this period, acting or former holders of *imperium* vowed and dedicated more than thirty temples to a variety of divinities on this route as well as in adjacent areas.[34] These temples often recalled military victories and were frequently built from the profits of war in the shape of booty. Such buildings were a religious as well as expensive way forever to inscribe the ephemeral ceremony of the triumphal procession in the monumental memory of the city (see also Chapters 4, 10, and 24).

However, temples were not the only means to achieve such visible permanence. Conspicuously, in the course of these two centuries, other kinds of monuments virtually began to clutter the area of Capitol, Comitium, and Forum. To begin with, there were dedications of spoils, which were regularly and obviously fraught with historical associations.[35] The most famous example is also the earliest of which we have certain evidence: in 338, after his triumph over the city of Antium at the end of the Romano-Latin war, the consul C. Maenius had the rams – the so-called "beaks" or *rostra* – of the vanquished vessels affixed at the speaker's platform on the Forum, called the *rostra* from then onward (Livy 8.14.12; see also Chapters 4, 16, and 24).[36] Such a striking display of spoils soon found imitators. The consul Duilius – victor over the fleet of the Carthaginians at Mylae in 260 and the first to celebrate a "naval triumph" – was possibly honored with two columns decorated with such beaks.[37] The columns were strategically placed at important points of the triumphal route: one in the Forum, according to several of our sources, most likely in the vicinity of the speaker's platform; the other perhaps at the Circus Maximus (Serv. *ad Georg.* 3.29). Other *columnae rostratae* were to follow – such as the column that Octavian had put up after his victory over Sextus Pompeius in the Forum Romanum in 36, resorting as he did to what was by then a traditional medium of commemoration in order to immortalize his military success.[38]

From early on, we find monuments that combined the display of spoils with honorific statues, thereby establishing an inseparable and conspicuous link between the general in command and his victory. A famous *triumphator* – already a highly symbolic figure at the beginning of the second century – achieved this in a particularly sophisticated and suggestive fashion: Fabius Maximus, the great Cunctator, consul for the fifth time in 209 and conqueror of Tarentum, ordered the bronze statue of Hercules by the famous sculptor Lysippus to be removed from that city as spoils and had it erected on the Capitol. Next to it, he had an equestrian statue of himself put up, made of the same material. The colossal Hercules did not just refer to the other Hercules monuments along the triumphal route, such as the venerable *Ara Maxima* ("Greatest Altar") on the Forum Boarium, the temple of Hercules, and the statue of Hercules Triumphalis, which at such occasions was dressed up in triumphal garb and received a sacrifice (Pliny *HN* 34.33).[39] The Cunctator will also not have minded that some of the more educated visitors to the Capitol would have had further associations when viewing the two statues, such as the mythic origins of the *gens Fabia*, one of the oldest patrician clans: its founder was supposed to have sprung from an encounter between Hercules and a nymph.[40]

Less than a century later, the *gens Fabia* had established its monumental presence at the other end of that central space between Forum and Capitol, at precisely the point where the *Sacra via* enters the Forum at the *Regia*, one of the places which every triumphal procession passed on its way to the Capitol. Here a latter-day Fabius Maximus erected an arch that anticipated the triumphal monuments of later periods, the so-called *fornix Fabianus* (see also Chapter 24).[41] This arch was decorated with portraits and statues, which sported inscriptions that recalled the deeds and the triumphs (in the technical as well as the non-technical sense of the concept) of those represented. Such *tituli* and, on occasions, somewhat more extensive *elogia* were also attached to dedications and monuments made up of spoils, such as the *columna rostrata* of Duilius, which seems to have carried a lengthy honorary inscription enumerating the exploits and achievements of the victor of the battle of Mylae: monument and statue, image and text, hero and heroic deed refer to, and mutually explain, each other, thus reinforcing their common message.[42]

At the same time, the *fornix Fabianus* referred to its model, which stood in demonstrative fashion at the end and climax of each triumphal procession, on the Capitol. There, Scipio Africanus, the conqueror of Hannibal, had put up the *fornix Scipionis*, a widely visible monumental arch with seven gilded statues and two equestrian figures (Livy 37.3.7).[43] Given the man, his achievements and ambitions, and his status, one has to ask: where else?

A special chain of associations was connected with a similar monument, another equestrian statue of a *triumphator*, which the consul Q. Marcius Tremulus had erected toward the end of the fourth century, after his victory over the rebellious Hernici in southeast Latium. Tellingly, the statue stood in front of the ancient temple of Castor.[44] According to a venerable legend, Castor and Pollux, the divine Dioscuri and patron-heroes of the cavalry, appeared to the Romans during the legendary battle at Lake

Regillus in 499 and ensured a Roman victory; marvelously the twins were seen that same evening in Rome as messengers of the success on the battlefield, while watering their horses in the *lacus Iuturnae*, the spring-fed "pool of Juturna" in the Forum. This remained a numinous location, and right next to it stood the temple which the Romans are said to have dedicated to the divine twins only a few years after the battle.[45] Even centuries later this story and its individual elements circulated in Rome: the battle and the treaty with the Latins (and Hernici), the famous Treaty of Cassius (*foedus Cassianum*), the hotly contested Roman hegemony in Latium,[46] and – last but not least – the myth of the intervention of the Dioscuri on the side of the Romans. In the second century in particular, the divine twins were very much alive in the Roman imagination. Some said that they appeared after the Battle of Pydna in 168 and then again in the war against the Cimbri.[47] Shortly afterward, in the 90s of the first century, a certain A. Postumius Albinus had coins minted that featured the Dioscuri. Every Roman was perfectly able to decode the image of two horsemen watering their horses at a lake, and they would also recall that, once upon a time, the Roman dictator, general, and *triumphator* over the Latins had been another A. Postumius – the one who had received the honorable name "Regillensis."[48]

This example illustrates the specifically Roman way of connecting in visible and invisible, explicit and implicit, spatial and conceptual ways the broad spectrum of different media – monuments, images, and texts – and their contents and messages, such as legendary origins and exemplary milestones in the ascent to imperial greatness. Through the communal use and administration of numinous places, temples, and altars of Rome's sacral topography on the one hand, and the locations of memory and monuments of victorious wars on the other, a particular topography of accumulated as well as accumulative memory came into being.[49] Each triumph did not just proceed into, and through the midst of, this landscape, passing by many monumental reminders of previous triumphs. Each and every triumphal celebration also added something new and thereby enriched Rome's memorial landscape: a statue here, a temple there, or, perhaps, a dedication of enemy weapons or other spoils. New monuments, together with their attending stories, were thus constantly added to those already in place. The larger urban context of Rome's monumental memory in general on the one hand and the concrete messages of the older monuments in this landscape on the other assigned a special place and meaning to every new element in the rich texture of the whole.[50]

Rome's urban landscape of memory thus acquired more and more texture, plurality, and, with the emergence of new media, polysemy. Yet the basic message for the spectator, whether Roman or foreigner, friend or foe, remained the same and even became ever more powerful over time: each new war, each city sacked, each people conquered, each triumph was an expression of Roman might, supported by the gods, and therefore morally legitimate, a quasi-necessary step in the irresistible spread of Roman power across the globe. But this is not yet the full story. Beyond the concrete location of individual monuments and their use and administration, we need to consider how precisely they were spread across the city, and how their relative positions affected their impact and significance. On closer inspection, privileged "clusters" of memorable objects and places emerge within the city – there were hierarchies, zones of particular prominence, and subtle distinctions.

The heavy concentration of monuments on the Capitol is unsurprising. After all, the Capitol with its temple of Jupiter Optimus Maximus was not just the towering finish of each triumph; this hill was inextricably linked to the origins of Roman greatness and the foundation of the *libera res publica* – both through its history and the stories affiliated with the building and dedication of the temple.[51] The core and kernel of the ideology of the Capitoline Hill was the confidence it inspired that the Romans would overcome each and every danger, owing to an overriding invincibility guaranteed through divine support. This, after all, was the location where the sacred geese of Juno had cackled, waking up the exhausted defenders just in time to reject the hordes of greedy Gauls who, under the cover of darkness, had tried to storm the last bulwark of the city.[52] And this was also the location where the same man who had held the last line of defense against the Gauls, M. Manlius Capitolinus, was thrown off the cliff because of his purported ambition for kingship (see also Chapter 24).[53] Legends over legends – all of which also figured prominently in the mainstream historiographical tradition – were attached to this place as a symbol of the free Republic and its defense against external and internal enemies, endowing the Capitol with a unique *genius loci*.

As we have seen, it was here, on the most famous and sacred of the seven hills of the city, that great men such as Fabius Cunctator and Scipio Africanus strove to display their fame in striking, monumental visual form, and they were not alone. Toward the end of our period, that is, about the middle of the second century, it seems to have been almost an unwritten rule that every *triumphator* left his mark on the Capitol. But the Capitol was not the only place for aristocratic display, and apparently, not even the most exclusive. The second space, in which a conspicuous number of monuments of all kinds accumulated over time, was the area on the north side of the Forum below the Arx around the Comitium between the Senate House – the *curia Hostilia* – and the *rostra*. At least in the late Republic, this relatively small area was considered a particularly pronounced and venerable location of memory.

To begin with, Comitium and Capitol share important characteristics. Both possess a sacral aura. The Comitium (or part of it) was possibly a reserved and inaugurated space, a *templum*. Certainly, it contained several numinous places, such as the "grave of Romulus" under what later became known as the *Lapis Niger* or "Black Stone."[54] Several monuments stood here which recalled the legendary beginnings when the Romans still struggled for freedom and survival, such as a statue of Horatius Cocles who had single-handedly opposed the troops of the Etruscan king Porsenna and successfully denied the enemy entry into the city by destroying the bridge that led across the Tiber – yet another story about the heroism and exemplary virtue of a true Roman that was told and retold, in quite a few variants, in historiography since its beginnings in the mid-Republic. Already for Polybius, this famous legend was only an example of the many stories about Romans engaging in single combat to decide a battle and facing certain death in order to save the lives of fellow-citizens.[55]

Once again, the statue of Cocles was not an isolated item.[56] Around and on the Comitium, there was a veritable cluster of monuments made up of spoils, columns, and equestrian statues representing icons of Roman virtue such as Duilius, mentioned above, and other republican heroes which stood in the immediate vicinity (Pliny *HN* 34, 20–3). This cluster included the Maenian Column, a monument in honor of that same Maenius who had originally adorned the speaker's platform with the *rostra* (see also Chapter 4). It was again this Maenius who – together with his colleague as consul in 338, L. Furius Camillus – had been awarded equestrian statues after the final conquest of the Latins who had revolted and the ensuing triumphs. These monuments also stood at the Comitium, perhaps even right next to the newly adorned speaker's platform – which was in turn later considered the "most conspicuous place" (Pliny *HN* 34.24). On the opposite side, the boundary of the Comitium was a building that possessed a particularly venerable aura of sanctity and majesty and radiated, as Cicero put it, a particular "power of admonition," by reminding everyone of the performances of a Scipio or a Cato: the *Curia Hostilia*, the main venue of the Senate, a "haven for all peoples," a "shrine," a "sanctuary" and, indeed, "the head of the city."[57] On its wall, a famous painting recalled the victory and triumph of Valerius Messala at the beginning of the First Punic War (Pliny *HN* 35.22).

Above all, however, the space between Curia and *rostra* was one of the two locations where (probably until the middle of the second century) the assembly of the People met. In the Comitium and the *campus Martius* the *populus Romanus* took on its institutional form in the *comitia*. Most of the laws were passed here, and it was here that the voting for the numerous minor magistrates and the tribunate took place. It was the place, or space, for the regular, ongoing communication between magistrates, senators, and citizens, between the political elite and the People (see also Chapters 18 and 20). The area of the Comitium and, later on, the somewhat larger Forum, were the most important civic and symbolic spaces within Rome's dense political topography. For despite imperial expansion, the *res publica* retained a political set-up in which the passing of laws, elections, the law courts of the People, and the most important religious ceremonies maintained their particular city-state character and remained, as it were, entrenched in the urban landscape within the city, with the Capitol, Comitium, and Curia, Forum, and *campus Martius* as foci.

Rome's landscape of memory was thus in fact identical with the arena in which a member of the political elite had to appear in various functions, as orator in debates in political controversies, as defense counsel or prosecutor in lawsuits or, for that matter, as a young man and next of kin required to deliver the eulogy over a senior member of his family who had just died (see also Chapters 17 and 20). To perform well in these public settings was as important for a political career as fulfilling one's duties as senator and patron, magistrate or general – for without the kind of recognition that one achieved through strenuous efforts in the urban arena of political and/or ceremonial oratory, it was impossible to attain these offices and functions (and the concomitant reputation and rank in one's peer group) in the first place.[58] All members of the political class were keen on advancing their political career and inevitably had to make their mark in the public spaces of the city – from the young senator who belonged to an old, established family to the ambitious "new man" who had to do without well-known, that is (literally) "noble" ancestors, from the middling magistrate eager to reach higher office to the former consul bent on further enhancing his authority, reputation, and prestige.

Unlike the venerable Capitol, which was somewhat removed from daily political negotiations, the Forum and the Comitium were spaces of aristocratic competition. It was down there that members of the political class vied for offices, rank, and influence, that is, in typically Roman terms, for *honos* and *honores*, *dignitas*, and *auctoritas*. The Forum and the Comitium, or rather the *rostra*, which were right in between the two, were the places where the ruling elite met the People. The same People, at another point of Rome's political topography, the *campus Martius*, constituted itself in the Centuriate Assembly as the *populus Romanus*, to award the aforementioned *honores*. Membership and rank within Rome's meritocracy depended entirely on these public elections, and only the greatest "honor," the consulship, offered its incumbent as holder of *imperium* a realistic chance to scale the last and highest level of Roman *gloria*: the triumph, an achievement that in turn allowed the *triumphator* to inscribe himself permanently in Rome's memorial topography and public memory.

In the code of norms and values of the republican aristocracy these honors, as other honors in the concrete shape of *honores*, were regarded as the rightful recognition of services rendered to the *res publica*, in politics and, above all, in war (see also Chapter 17). Civic and military duties were the only source of such rewards and formed the sole basis of prominence and prestige, of the *dignitas* and *auctoritas* of the successful *nobilis* and, in general, of aristocratic status.[59] Without *honores*, a Roman could not enter into the glorious history of the *res publica* and her monumental memory. Only *honores* and deeds in the service of the Republic became history – and in this case, only "his-story" – in the form of exemplary stories and imposing monuments. These stories in turn added to the "symbolic capital" of the respective *gens* and the political elite as a whole – both accrued triumphs and consulships in an accumulative fashion.[60] Just like the monumental memory of the Republic, this capital needed preservation, transmission, and permanent increase and amplification – both by individual aristocrats who adduced the collective achievements of their *gens* as an argument in inner aristocratic rivalries for magistracies and status, and by the aristocracy as a whole, which defined itself collectively through service for the *res publica* and the glorious history of this service. The ultimate frame of reference for this nexus of identity, memory, and politics was the myth of Rome's divine mission to rule the world, which in turn came to provide the main theme and inspiration of historiography.

By the mid-second century, this myth was already fully developed: from the foundation of the city, war and conquest had always been what Rome or "Romanness" was all about. This was simply taken for granted, like the concomitant moral system of values, norms, and rewards. Unsurprisingly, in Rome's collective mythic imagination, it was Romulus himself who celebrated the first triumph and thereby inaugurated this institution and the long series of victory celebrations that stretched from the legendary past to the present and thus firmly connected them. Romulus, the first king, also initiated – and this is not as paradoxical as it sounds – the impressive roll call of republican heroes.[61]

In this society, history did not just boil down to the series of wars and victories as things of a glorious past. The past was never remote, never turned into a period removed from present concerns, which would only be of interest to historians or antiquarians. In other words, in Rome's "memorial space" the distinction that modern scholars like to draw between "communicative memory," which is in the full sense of the concept "present in the present" as it covers only two or three generations, and the "cultural memory," with its selective and stylized preservation of events of a more remote past, does not apply: in Rome, memories that a given generation shares by having lived through the same events merge imperceptibly with a kind of transgenerational memory that is made up of venerable myths, histories, and the *exempla* of the ancestors (see also Chapter 6). To put it even more pointedly: in the cultural memory of the Republic around 150, Romulus and Brutus, the first triumph and the initial struggles of the young Republic, are as vivid and immediate as Scipio Africanus and the Second Punic War or L. Aemilius Paullus and his spectacular triumph of 167.[62] All these historical figures and past events, remote as well as recent, are present, in all sorts of respects, in the form of signs, symbols, and telling monuments: the entire memorable past, from Romulus to Aemilius Paullus, continues to tower over the present. In Rome, the present never obliterates the past, since none of the memorable events are ever marginalized or fully forgotten. The past is continuously transformed into history (and the symbolic capital which it carries), and in this guise retains its presence in the memory of each new generation.

This specific "presence of the past in the present"[63] was inseparably connected with the basic conviction that each generation was part of a process and a mission that united Romulus and Brutus, Maenius and Duilius, the Cunctator and the Elder Africanus, as well as more recent heroes such as Aemilius Paullus or the Younger Africanus. The past is therefore always a "contemporary past." The permanent presence of Rome's monumental memory, with its constant reminders and its literally omnipresent allusions to specific stories on the one hand, and the importance of this memory for the orientations, values and goals, the code of behavior, the institutions and the political decisions of the present on the other render the distinction between past and present virtually meaningless. To put this conclusion in concepts once again borrowed from Pierre Nora, the *populus Romanus* and its political elite formed a great, collective *milieu de mémoire*: a vibrant, evolving community of memory. In the midst of this community, there was a complex pattern or landscape of *lieux de mémoire*: these concrete traces and marked spaces of remembrance retained, continuously reproduced, and indeed re-enforced their meanings and messages over time.[64]

Only in this special variant of a *milieu de mémoire* could that subtle hierarchy of locations could emerge which defined itself through its proximity to politics, prestige, and warfare: the area around the Comitium and the *rostra* feature a coincidence of sacral landscape, political topography, and space of memory and remembrance. That is why we here find the highest concentration of memorials which enacted a vision of Rome's greatness that linked her origins to the later stages in her historical evolution and further up to each contemporary generation.

Guide to Further Reading

The debate on the "collective" or "cultural memory" of groups, social classes, and whole societies past and present, which features prominently in the vast field of cultural studies, is very much a phenomenon of "Old Europe" – that is why the bulk of the relevant literature is in languages other than English, above all in French (Nora 1984) and German (Assmann and Hölscher 1988; Assmann 1992, 2000). The contributions in English (e.g., Burke 1989; Fentress and Wickham 1992; Crane 1997; Confino 1997), stimulating though they are, do not cover the whole range of issues that have been raised in the continental debate over the last two decades. The text above is mainly based on the work of Hölscher (esp. 1978, 1990, 2001), Walter (2001, 2003, 2004), and my own publications (Hölkeskamp 1993, 1996, 2001a – updated in 2004b – and 2004a) – all but one, alas, in German. The most important recent contributions in English on the typically Roman (republican) ways and practices to (re-)construct the origins and history of the city again deal with a broad range of particular aspects, but only occasionally touch on general theoretical problems concerning the concept of cultural memory: compare especially Dupont 1992 (on memory, time, and space); Edwards 1996 on Rome as the city of memories (a rather subjective, indeed extravagant *tour d'horizon*), Favro 1988 on memory and public space and Favro 1996 on "defining the urban image of (republican) Rome"; see now especially Morstein-Marx 2004: 68–118. Holliday 2002 deals with what he calls the rhetoric of history and the functions of historical commemorations in the republican milieu from the point of view of an art historian (which is somehow too narrow a perspective cf. Hölkeskamp 2005). In this context, a recent study on yet another exemplary Roman deserves a special mention: Flower 2003 (on M. Claudius Marcellus, conqueror of Syracuse). The most detailed analyses of great Romans as "icons of virtue" are, however, in French (and one in German): Coudry and Späth 2001. For an introduction to Roman historiography generally, see Chapter 2 in this volume; but see especially Beck and Walter 2001; Walter 2001, 2004, for its character as a practice of *memoria*. For a brief introduction to republican political life in general, with valuable suggestions for further reading, see Chapter 1 in this volume.

The best surveys of the topography of the *urbs* and its sacral and political landscape in English are Stambaugh 1988 and Cornell 2000a; compare also Patterson 1992b for a discussion of modern research. Kuttner 2004 gives a vivid picture of the intense monumentalization of the republican city (318 and passim). However, the most comprehensive work on the urban texture of Rome and its development from earliest times to the Empire is Kolb 2002. On the urban landscape of (mid-)republican Rome, the development of public space, buildings, and monuments, etc.: Coarelli 1977; Richardson 1991: 392–402; Patterson 1992b: 185–204; Cornell 2000a; Kolb 2002; as well as, for the late Republic, Favro 1996: 24–41, 42–50. For individual monuments, see Richardson 1992; Steinby 1993–2000 (especially the articles by Tagliamonte and Reusser: 1. 226–31, 232–4 (on the Capitol); Coarelli: 1. 309–14 (on the Comitium); and Tagliamonte and Purcell: 2. 313–25, 325–36); Favro 1988 (on the Forum Romanum).

The best modern study on the *pompa funebris* is Flower 1996 – compare also Bodel 1999; Hölkeskamp 1995, 1996; and recently Walter 2003, Flaig 2003. The most stimulating article on the triumph in English is Favro 1994; compare (from a different perspective and somewhat impressionistic) Brilliant 1999 – but see also Hölscher 2001 and again Flaig 2003. Flower 2004a, the best introduction into this culture of spectacles, and Gruen 1996 treat both funerals and triumphs – the latter also touches on other aspects of republican political culture: representative art, the self-image of the *nobilitas* and, in a few pages, gives his view of 400 years of aristocratic ascendancy (Gruen's citation of previous work on these topics is, however, highly selective).

Notes

1   Polyb. 1.1.5–6, 2.7, 3.1.4, 6.2.3, 50.6, 6.54. 6, cf. 54. 2–5; cf. Walbank 1957–79: 1.40 and on "exemplary stories," below n.54.
2   Beck and Walter 2001: 15–50.
3   Beck and Walter 2001: 55–61 and the surviving fragments (62–136); Beck 2003; Walter 2004; Oakley 1997–2004: 1. 72–104.
4   Beck and Walter 2001: 225–31, 282–329, 330–9; Walter 2004.
5   Beck and Walter 2001: 148–224; Walter 2004.
6   Enn. *Ann.* frag. 72–91 Sk(utsch); Livy 1.6.4–8.1; Dion. Hal. *Ant. Rom.* 1.88.1–3, etc. The tradition is very complex; cf. Poucet 1985: 169–300, 315–48; Wiseman 1995; Hillen 2003: 62–196; Ungern-Sternberg 1993.
7   Cf. Richardson 1992: 74; Coarelli in Steinby 1993–2000: 1, 241–2; Edwards 1996: 31–42.
8   Livy 3.26.8–29.7; Dion. Hal. *Ant. Rom.* 10.24.1–25.3; Pliny *HN* 18.20. Cic. *Fin.* 2.12 and *Sen.* 56 show that Cincinnatus was a "household name" by the late Republic. Cf. Ogilvie 1965: 436–45.
9   Frag. 16 in Beck and Walter 2001: 103–5; cf. Livy 1.55.1.5–6, 5.54.7; Dion. Hal. *Ant. Rom.* 4.59.1–61.2; Hölkeskamp 2001a: 97–8; 99–100 (= 2004b, 137–8, 139–40).
10 Cf. Welwei 2001.
11 Livy 5.49.7, 7.1.10, cf. Ogilvie 1965: 739; Oakley 1997–2004: 2.37, and now Edwards 1996: 44–52; Walter 2000; Coudry 2001; Späth 2001.
12 Cic. *Sen.* 55–6; *Parad.* 38, cf. *Rep.* 3.40; *Parad.* 12, 48; Berrendonner 2001; Vigourt 2001.
13 Cf. recently Beck 2000.
14 Frags. 106–8 and 110 Sk (= Cic. *Rep.* 1.64; *Tusc.* 1.28 and *De or.* 3.154); cf. frag. 54, with Skutsch 1985: 258–9, 261–2; Hillen 2003: 150–5.
15 Frag. 456 Sk (= Cic. *Rep.* 3.6), with Skutsch 1985: 612–14.
16 Frags. 363–65 Sk (= Cic. *Off.* 1.84, *Sen.* 10; cf. Cic. *Att.* 2.19.1; Virg. *Aen.* 6.845; Livy 30.26.9), with Skutsch 1985: 528–32.

17   Suda s. v. Ennios; Cic. *Orat.* 152, cf. sed. incert. frag. xxxvi (= Cic. *Arch.* 22), with Skutsch 1985: 642–3.
18   Frag. 156 Sk; cf. sed. incert. frag. xxxvi (= Cic. *Arch.* 22, on Cato) with Skutsch 1985: 528–32; cf. 1–2.
19   Cf. Hölkeskamp 1996: 308–20 (= 2004b: 176–87); Roller 2004: 4–7, 50–3, and *passim*; Feldherr 1998; Chaplin 2000.
20   Fears 1981.
21   Assmann and Hölscher 1988; Assmann 1992, 2000.
22   Beck and Walter 2001: 47–50; Walter 2001, 2004.
23   Nora 1984.
24   Hölscher 1998 is now fundamental.
25   Edwards 1996: 27–43; Hölkeskamp 2001a (= 2004b: 137–68).
26   Hölkeskamp 1996: 305–8 (= 2004b: 173–6); Bergemann 1990: 1–48; Sehlmeyer 1999.
27   Hölscher 1978 (the fundamental study), 1990, 2001; Favro 1988; Gruen 1996: 217–20; Hölkeskamp 1996, 2001 (= 2004b: 169–98, 137–68). See also the Guide to Further Reading above.
28   Favro 1996: 24–41 for a walk through republican Rome in 52, and cf. 252–80 for AD 14; cf. also Edwards 1996.
29   Flower 1996: 16–59, 91–158; Hölkeskamp 1995: 11–12, 30–2, 44–6, 1996: 320–3 (= 2004b: 219–20, 237–8, 250–2, 188–90); Gruen 1996: 222–3; Bodel 1999 and now Flaig 2003; Blösel 2003; Walter 2003, 2004.
30   Favro 1994; Gruen 1996: 220–2; Brilliant 1999 and, above all, Hölscher 2001; cf. also Hölkeskamp 2001a (= 2004b: 137–68).
31   Richardson 1992: 65–7; Wiseman in Steinby 1993–2000: 1. 220–5 and now Coarelli 1997.
32   Coarelli in Steinby 1993–2000: 2. 295–7, 299 and Ciancio Rossetto in Steinby 1993–2000: 2. 272–7.
33   Coarelli in Steinby 1993–2000: 4. 223–8 and Wiseman in Steinby 1993–2000: 1. 280–1.
34   Pietilä-Castrén 1987; cf. Coarelli 1977: 20–3, and, for individual temples, Ziolkowski 1992.
35   Edwards 2003.
36   Coarelli in Steinby 1993–2000: 4. 212–14; see fig. 2.
37   Richardson 1992: 97; Chioffi in Steinby 1993–2000: 1, 309.
38   Richardson 1992: 96–7; Palombi in Steinby 1993–2000: 1. 307–8.
39   Richardson 1992: 186–9; Viscogliosi and Coarelli in Steinby 1993–2000: 3. 13–14, 15–17.
40   Hölkeskamp 1999: 10, 15 (= 2004b: 205, 210–1).
41   Richardson 1992: 154; Chioffi in Steinby 1993–2000: 2. 264–6.
42   Flower 1996: 159–84 and now Witzmann 2000; Sehlmeyer 2000. Cf. *Inscr. It.* 13.3.69 = *CIL* I² 25 = VI 1300 and VI 8.3 1300 Add.
43   Coarelli in Steinby 1993–2000: 2. 266–7.
44   Livy 9.43.22; cf. Cic. *Phil.* 6.13; Pliny *HN* 34.23. Cf. Bergemann 1990: 156.
45   Richardson 1992: 230–1; Steinby in Steinby 1993–2000: 3. 168–70, and Nielsen in Steinby 1993–2000: 1. 242–5.
46   Cornell 1995: 299–301.
47   Cic. *Nat. D.* 2.6, 3.11–12; Dion. Hal. *Ant. Rom.* 6.13.1–5; Val. Max. 1.8.1; Pliny *HN* 7.86.
48   Crawford 1974: 335 (on Nos. 335, 10a–b).
49   Cancik 1985/6.

50 Favro 1994; Hölkeskamp 2001a (= 2004b: 137–68).

51 Richardson 1992: 31–2; Edwards 1996: 69–95.

52 Livy 5.47.1–11 with Ogilvie 1965: 734–5; Dion. Hal. *Ant. Rom.* 13.7.1–8.4 and also Enn. *Ann.* Frag. 227–8 Sk with Skutsch 1985: 405–7. Cf. Horsfall in Bremmer and Horsfall 1987: 63–75.

53 Livy 6.11.1–10, 14.1–17.6, 18.1–20.16 with Oakley 1997: 476–502; 515–68; Dion. Hal. *Ant. Rom.* 14.4. Cf. Wiseman 1987b: 225–43; Jaeger 1997: 57–93.

54 Coarelli 1983–5: 1.161–99; Coarelli in Steinby 1993–2000: 4. 295–6.

55 According to Polybius, Cocles was indeed killed when he plunged into the Tiber in full armor (6.54.4–55.4); cf., however, the variants in Livy 2.10.2–12; Dion. Hal. *Ant. Rom.* 5.23.2–25.3; Plut. *Pobl.* 16.7–8. Cic. *Parad.* 11–12 mentions him in a catalog of "household names" that, among others, includes Romulus and Numa Pompilius, Brutus, Curius Dentatus, Africanus, and Cato; cf. also Cic. *Off.* 1.61, *Leg.* 2.10. Cf. now Roller 2004: 10–28, *passim.*

56 Coarelli 1983–5: 27–53, 87–123.

57 Cic. *Fin.* 5.2, *Mil.* 90; cf. *Cat.* 4.2. Cf. Coarelli in Steinby 1993–2000: 1. 331–2.

58 Hölkeskamp 1995 and now Morstein-Marx 2004; see also Chapter 20.

59 Hölkeskamp 1987: 204–27, 245–50, 1993: 25–31 (= 2004b: 27–33).

60 On Pierre Bourdieu's concept of "symbolic capital," see Hölkeskamp 2004a.

61 Dion. Hal. *Ant. Rom.* 2.34.1–3; *Inscr. Ital.* 13.1.534. Cf. Ungern-Sternberg 1993.

62 Still remembered as particularly splendid in Cicero's day: Cic. *Mur.* 31; *Cat.* 4.21; *Fin.* 5. 70; cf. *Inscr. Ital.* 13.1.556.

63 Bloch 1977.

64 Nora 1984: XVII.

CHAPTER 24

Art and Architecture in the Roman Republic

Katherine E. Welch

Art historians have long searched for what might have been distinctive, or "essential" about Roman art, in contrast to art of the Greeks and other peoples of the ancient Mediterranean. This search was initiated by those who came of age in Europe in the mid-later nineteenth century, when concepts of "national identity" were of paramount concern.[1] The "Romanness" of Roman art proved, however, to be elusive. Certain features, such as realism in portraiture or spatial illusionism, continuous narrative and historicity in relief, were seized upon as distinctive. But it became apparent that all these aspects were present in some form in earlier Greek art. Eventually art historians began moving away from the search for what was specifically Roman, emphasizing instead qualities such as eclecticism, diversity, and flexibility of artistic motifs and styles as the hallmarks of Roman art.[2] The recent trend has been to analyze Roman art in relation to the authoritative Greek prototypes that it drew upon, which were creatively remodeled for purposes of new visual expression.[3]

I would suggest that art historians have perhaps given up too soon in the search for what, in an overarching sense, is "Roman" in Roman art. If it is to be found, however, the search must be carried out in a difficult, sometimes sparsely documented period of Rome's history, namely the Republic, particularly the third to second century when Rome was first arriving on the world stage and defining itself in relation to its subject peoples. It is here that we are likely to discover the ideologies instrumental in the formation of later, better-documented Roman art. I offer two suggestions. First, true artistic innovation occurred when there was a particular Roman agenda for visual expression and no available Greek model or a Greek model that needed adjustment or "improvement." Second, the features of republican art that make it different from that of the Greeks – and therefore distinctive in its own right – can all be traced back to three particularly Roman (usually inextricable) concerns: practical functionality, competition, and warfare.

Because republican art has not survived extensively, an interdisciplinary method must be employed, using all the available evidence, in order to reconstruct the intended meaning and reception of artifacts and monuments. What makes art of this period particularly stimulating is that one needs to combine empirical with theoretical approaches in a more daring way than is required with art of the imperial and later periods.[4]

Most surviving republican art and architecture is from the city of Rome, and it is there that most categories of Roman art originated. This art is notably inventive and diverse because of an ethos of intense competition among members of the Roman elite (usually the art patrons), compared to production there during the principate when the imperial family monopolized art patronage.

Architecture

More than any other category of art production, architecture was the one of which Romans were self-consciously proud. Many surviving signatures – names of the architects inscribed on buildings – are in Latin, while those on sculptures are nearly always Greek.[5] The Roman attitude toward architecture is an interesting mixture of pride and moralism. Pliny (*HN* 36.101), for example, speaks of Rome vanquishing the world with its architecture, emphasizing its scale and grandeur (*maiestas*). Frontinus (*Aq.* 1.16) marvels at the *utilitas* (usefulness, in the size, capacity, and ingenuity of engineering) of Roman aqueducts and compares them, derisively, to the "famous but useless works of the Greeks." Strabo (5.3.8), writing in Greek in Augustan times, marvels at the southern Campus Martius, crowded with its many spectator buildings (three theaters and an amphitheater), and compares the stunning urban ensemble to a *skenographia* ("stage painting"), of which he had never seen the like.

It was in architecture that the Romans seem to have thought that they made their greatest artistic contribution (e.g., Mart. *Spect.* 1), and it was in the Republic that most Roman building types came into being. Republican architecture is characterized not by wholesale invention, but rather creative recombinations of elements from the Greek repertoire. For example, the vault and arch were used in the Greek world, but in "low"-status contexts, such as tunnels, gates, and earthen tombs (for structural reasons). Italy brought it a new aesthetic prominence with the creation of the arch-in-order, or "fornix" motif, comprising an arch or vault framed by a columnar order and entablature, as in the Sanctuary of Fortuna at Praeneste (late second century, Figure 24.1a).[6] Republican architecture is also characterized by a prodigal use of concrete substructures, used in order to recast the landscape by building up – whereas Greeks tended to dig terraces in and down – implying a different attitude toward the landscape. The Sanctuary at Praeneste is ultimately based upon Hellenistic sanctuaries such as the Asklepieion at Kos.[7] But it was an "improvement" on Greek prototypes in its loftiness (made possible by substructures), rigid axiality of plan, and virtuoso use of such original features as concealed, curving barrel vaults (Figure 24.1b).

Fig. 24.1a Sanctuary of Fortuna Primigenia, Praeneste, model, late 2nd century BC. Photo by Marvin Trachtenberg

Rome's celebrated innovation with concrete had a practical genesis. Concrete had been used in a limited way in Greek contexts; indeed Greek architects used mostly cut stone of good quality, which they had in abundance. Central Italy, on the other hand, has plentiful supplies of volcanic tufa and high-quality limestone – the essential ingredients of concrete. After the Second Punic war, unprecedented numbers of slaves poured into Rome. Rome's new wealth attracted people from the

Fig. 24.1b Sanctuary of Fortuna Primigenia, Praeneste. Photo by the author

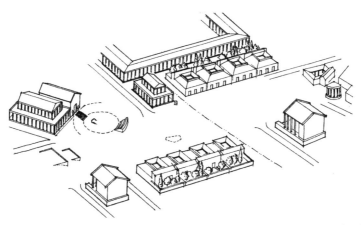

Fig. 24.2 *Forum Romanum*, 5th to 3rd centuries BC, possible reconstruction (Welch 2003: fig. 11; drawing Philip Stinson). Foreground: Temple of Saturn (left); Castor and Pollux (right). Reprinted by permission of K. Welch and the *Journal of Roman Archaeology*

countryside looking for work, and the population grew dramatically. Grain storage facilities had to be exponentially and quickly augmented. Concrete began to be used more and more – because it could be constructed with an unskilled labor force – in the erection of warehouses, for example the so-called *Porticus Aemilia* (early second century), which is over a kilometer in length and made entirely of barrel-vaulted concrete (see also Chapter 4).

The Forum

This public square was where business was conducted, where the People met, listened to political speeches, voted, worshiped, and attended public trials; as well as where aristocratic funeral processions and gladiatorial games were held.[8] Shortly after the fall of the monarchy, two notable state temples were built here, that of Saturn (where public records were kept) and of Castor and Pollux (Figure 24.2). These would have been Etrusco-Italic in plan and elevation: set on high podia, with deep porches, widely spaced Tuscan columns placed frontally, and with steeply angled pediments and ponderous, overhanging eaves. Such (non-Greek) architectural features were connected with inherited Etruscan practices of augury (interpreting the flight of birds; see also Chapter 10). The priest, who watched from the temple porch, needed a good view out to the sky and protection from the elements while he waited – often for a very long time – until things looked exactly right.

The association of Castor and Pollux with the cavalry suggests that the Temple was connected politically with the patrician aristocracy that had created the Republic. Indeed, this was where the *transvectio equitum* (annual parade of the patrician cavalry) made a processional stop on its way to the Capitol. The Temple of Saturn, on the other hand, made a statement about religious ideology. On the spot, there had existed a small pre-Etruscan altar to Saturn. But as Saturn was an old Latin deity, the Etruscan kings had evidently not been interested in monumentalizing the sacred area. The altar was now reconstructed and the accompanying great Temple completed as early as 497, presumably as an assertion of new Latin religious devotion.

After the patrician caste lost its monopoly over public affairs over the course of the fourth century, wealthy plebeians became eligible for public office. There followed a period of fierce political competition, which in turn precipitated great expansion and innovation in the artistic sphere. It has been argued that this period saw the genesis of the first truly Roman (as opposed to Etruscan or Greek) art.[9] One of the first plebeians to publicly advertise himself was C. Maenius, victor in the Latin Wars at Antium. In 338 he attached *rostra* (beaks) of captured ships to the speaker's platform. This was the first overtly self-glorifying monument in Rome's history. Nearby, the Senate honored him with a statue of himself on a column (a Greek statuary convention) and in the vicinity both Maenius and the patrician L. Furius Camillus (co-consuls that year) had equestrian statue portraits set up (Cic. *Sest.* 8.18; Livy 8.13.9). These are earliest known uses in Rome of this elevated portrait format, one that had both military and Greek associations.

The victory monuments of an individual, and a plebeian no less, now dominated the northwest sector of the Forum (not coincidentally, this was the area of Maenius' ancestral *domus*). In 306 Q. Marcius Tremulus (after his victory over the Hernici) placed an equestrian statue of himself in another highly charged location – at the other end of the Forum in front of the Temple of Castor and Pollux. Then C. Duilius improved upon Maenius' column by setting up a column portrait, as Maenius had, in the northwest sector of the Forum but now attaching the *rostra* of captured Carthaginian ships to the shaft, to commemorate his specific military victory.[10] Not to be outdone, M. Aemilius Paullus (also victor in the First Punic War) set up a rostrated column portrait not in the Forum, but in the more prestigious location of the Capitol, high above the others. In the middle Republic, therefore, the Forum and even the Capitol had become places of open, military self-advertisement in a way previously unknown in Greece or Rome (see also Chapters 4, 16, and 23).[11] Such monuments were not merely decorative but political in function: they enhanced military reputation, which in turn brought public acclaim, votes, access to high office and more prestigious (potentially lucrative) military commands (see Chapter 17).

In the case of more junior politicians, military reputation brought access to high public office. Aediles and praetors supplemented state funds to sponsor *ludi*, comprising stage plays and chariot racing (on the Greek model), and wild-beast hunts, using exotic animals brought to Rome, sometimes from military campaigns.[12] These games were held in theaters and in the *Circus Maximus*, respectively. They also sponsored *munera* (privately funded gladiatorial combats, which were held in the Forum itself in honor, usually, of a deceased father) (e.g. Polyb. 31.27.4; see also Chapters 16 and 17). While the *munera* took place in a religious context, they also had military associations (Cic. *Tusc.* 2.41; *SHA Max.* 8). Such combats initially involved prisoners of war wearing their own armor – for example, Samnites and Thracians – thus reenacting for the metropolitan public an individual family's own military successes (hence the genesis of two common types of Roman gladiator: the Samnite and the *Thraex*).[13]

The canonical oval form of the amphitheater (such as the one at Pompeii, c.70) was dictated by the oblong shape of the Roman Forum, where wooden seating was erected for gladiatorial shows on a semi-regular basis from the third to first centuries. The prestigious location of these temporary arenas in the Forum made them the model for the earliest stone amphitheaters in the towns of Italy, where the oval shape and functional appearance were proudly reproduced in the era of the Social and Civil Wars, a time of great cultural change accompanying Italian unification under Rome.[14]

During the third century, the Forum was still surrounded by atrium houses of the nobility, whose façades were decorated with spoils of war: captured weapons and armor won by family members over the course of centuries (see also Chapters 16 and 17).[15] It was once thought that these structures were public in nature, used as offices (*atria publica*). It has been convincingly argued, however, that the houses around Italic *fora* were standard private dwellings (*domus*), whose atria would, at the family's discretion, be open to clients. And the *Forum Romanum* was surely no different.[16] This illustrates an important difference between the Forum and the Greek Agora. Agoras were surrounded by temples and stoas, not by houses. This was because in Greece the line between public and private space was clearly defined, while in Rome it was not. In elite Roman houses, only the back rooms (dining rooms, *cubicula* [bedrooms], garden) were fully private. Moreover, the atrium was partially visible to anyone outside (doors were kept open except when there was a death in the family: Tac. *Ann.* 2.83).[17]

Under Greek influence, the Forum began to change in the third to second centuries. A great fire swept its north side in 210. The few remaining houses were purchased piecemeal and replaced by basilicas, sponsored by censors. Basilicas in the republican period functioned as covered extensions of the Forum; they were places of business and did not yet have a judicial function. The first well-documented one is the Basilica Porcia (184), of an early type, relatively broad in plan and open to the forum by means of external colonnades.[18] Shortly afterward, the Basilicas Aemilia (also called Fulvia) and Sempronia were built. These had internal colonnades defining elongated central naves. This elongated and "improved" type of basilica became canonical. By the mid-second century, therefore, the old Italic Forum had changed to something resembling Greek agoras, surrounded by columns (see Map 8).

The *Forum Romanum* provided the architectural model for the *fora* of Rome's colonies in the West. At Cosa, the forum was surrounded by atrium houses, a small basilica, and a round *comitium* at the foot of the senate house (*curia*), along Roman lines (Figure 4.1). The arrangement is tighter and more regular because Cosa was planned *ex novo* on flat ground, while the Roman Forum was the product of additions over many centuries and was surrounded by hilly terrain. Roman cities in the East were planned with less of a blueprint-like quality, reflecting the amalgamation of two different cultures and politically motivated care in allowing Greek identity to remain relatively intact. Even at the military colony of Corinth, the Caesarian colonists simply added an amphitheater and superimposed a new Roman grid (with major north–south and east–west arteries: *cardo* and *decumanus maximus*, respectively) over the existing city, leaving intact the earlier buildings not destroyed by L. Mummius.[19]

Manubial temples

In addition to state temples, there were – beginning in the fourth century – many temples in Rome dedicated privately by victorious generals *ex manubiis*, that is, from the proceeds of war (see also Chapters 4, 10, 16, and 23).[20] These comprise one of the most diverse architectural genres of any period. The innovation was motivated by the need to advertise military achievement by making individual, distinctive architectural statements. Some early examples are the temples in the *Area Sacra di Sant' Omobono* (site of Rome's port at the time). One of the kings in the Regal period had built a temple there, which is notable for having fine surviving acroterial sculpture in Archaic Style.[21] Shortly after the founding of the Republic, this temple seems to have been intentionally demolished and covered by a massive earthen deposit, presumably as a symbolic gesture commemorating the expulsion of the kings. A platform of tufa was later constructed over this, probably by Furius Camillus, who won Rome's first major victory over the Etruscans at Veii (396). Two temples were built upon the platform: one commissioned by Camillus, the other by Fulvius Flaccus, who defeated Volsinii in 264.[22] Flaccus' temple precinct is notable for its display of scores of looted bronze statues, only three feet high (a common statuary size at the time).[23] These temples, dedicated to Fortuna and Mater Matuta, respectively, continued to adhere to traditional Etrusco-Italic architectural forms.[24]

A change occurred in the later third century under Greek influence, with Greek architectural orders (Doric and Ionic) making their appearance, for example, in the *Forum Holitorium* temples (Figure 24.3).[25] While these used Greek orders and columnar proportions, they still retained high podia in Italic fashion and used travertine and tufa (no doubt stuccoed in white and with architectural details in colored paint). These temples, along with a series of four in the *Area Sacra di Largo Argentina* (Figure 4.2), show that the triumphal route, from its beginnings in the Campus Martius to the *Porta Triumphalis*,[26] was tightly packed with manubial temples, one directly upon the next, each permanently evoking a specific general's victory (Map 9).

As political and financial stakes heightened in the second century (the time of Rome's greatest overseas military expansion), manubial temples became ever more architecturally inventive. M. Fulvius Nobilior built a wholly original temple, dedicated to Hercules of the Muses, after his victory at Ambracia in 189 (Figure 24.4). The Temple is known only from the Severan Marble Plan, and its plan and elevation are controversial. According to one scholar, it was a concrete rotunda with a dome, a columnar pedimented porch, and a flight of steps at the front leading up to it.[27] If indeed the Marble Plan shows the temple in its original state (rather than as renovated later on), the building might have resembled the Pantheon, albeit on a much smaller scale and utilizing local building materials.

Generals in the middle republican period began placing large columnar porticoes around their manubial temples, in imitation of the columnar *temene* that surrounded Greek temples. The first attested one was that of Q. Metellus Macedonicus (the *Porticus Metelli*), which surrounded his Temple of *Jupiter Stator.*[28] The space around

Fig. 24.3 Ionic temple in the *Forum Holitorium*, Rome, early 2nd century BC, view; ruins incorporated into the church of San Nicola in Carcere. Photo by the author

the temple was filled with looted statuary, most famously the equestrian group of Alexander and his companions by Lysippus. Metellus need not have been the first

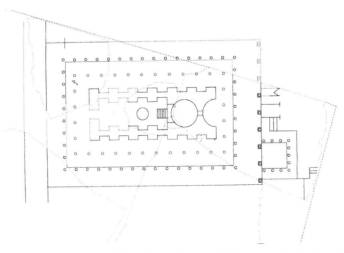

Fig. 24.4 Temple of Hercules of the Muses, Rome, 180s BC, as depicted on the Severan Marble Plan (Coarelli 1997: fig. 112). Reprinted by permission of Edizioni Quasar

general to surround his temple with a large portico, however. In fact, the likeliest candidate for this innovation is M. Claudius Marcellus, by reason of the sheer number of statues and paintings brought back by him from Syracuse in 211 and whose Temple of Honos and Virtus, where many of the works were exhibited, became a great tourist attraction (Livy 26.211–8; 34.4.1–5; Plut. *Marc.* 21.1–2, 30).

Metellus' temple was the first marble one in Rome, designed by Hermodorus of Salamis, and was in every sense Hellenistic: Ionic, peripteral, and sitting upon a low *krepis*.[29] He commissioned the cult statue from contemporary Greek artists, Polykles and Dionysios, sons of Timarchides (Pliny *HN* 36.35). The Temple of Jupiter Stator is an example of the wholesale adoption of a Greek prototype. A later such example is the (still standing) round Temple in the *Forum Boarium* (Figure 24.5). One proposal is that it was erected by an oil merchant to honor Hercules Olivarius.[30] More likely, it was dedicated to Hercules Victor by L. Mummius.[31] The building is a Greek *tholos*, almost entirely of Pentelic marble and sitting on a low *krepis*, comparable, for example, to the Philippeion at Olympia.[32] It would have been strikingly different from the surrounding manubial temples in the neighborhood, Etrusco-Italic or Greco-Italic in form and made of travertine and stuccoed tufa. Note that this is the first known temple in Rome of the Corinthian order. The choice of order would perhaps then have carried a particular poignancy, as Mummius was the destroyer of Corinth.

The next generation of temple builders, those born in the 150s,[33] seems to have been more aware of aesthetic considerations regarding the urban landscape. An example is Temple B (the round temple) in the *Area Sacra di Largo Argentina*, dedicated by Q. Lutatius Catulus (cos. 102) to *Fortuna Huiusce Diei* "Fortune of the Present Day" (Figure 24.6; see also Figure 4.2).[34] The temple was built in an area

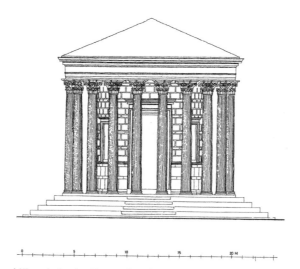

Fig. 24.5 Round Temple in the *Forum Boarium*, Rome mid-2nd century BC, reconstructed elevation (Steinby 1993–2003: 3, fig. 16, after F. Rakob and W. Heilmeyer (1973), *Der Rundtempel am Tiber in Rom*. Mainz. Beil. 23). Reprinted by permission of Edizioni Quasar

packed with traditional Etrusco-Italic tufa temples of the fourth and third centuries.[35] Temple B was built in the latest architectural style: it was a round *tholos*. Yet the Greek model was now pointedly adjusted by placing the temple on a high podium and adding a frontal staircase in the old Italic manner. Catulus also chose to use travertine and tufa, when he could easily have afforded to use marble. The sophistication of the patron is not in doubt, and it may be suggested that his temple made a carefully formulated statement by being modern but remaining in keeping aesthetically with the surrounding traditional temples.[36]

Arches

Another means of military self-commemoration was the honorific arch, an invention of the Republic. Like victory monuments, arches of the republican period all stood alongside of, or spanned, the triumphal route (see also Chapters 4 and 23 and Map 9).[37] The earliest known ones were three set up by one individual with a new representative agenda, L. Stertinius in 196, after his victory in Spain: two in the *Forum Boarium* and one in the *Circus Maximus*. One may suggest that the arches were commissioned in lieu of a formal triumph, which Stertinius did not seek – perhaps the Senate would not have granted him one, or because his looted material from Spain would not compare in splendor and quantity to that coming in from the Greek East. Livy (33.27) tells us that the arches supported *signa aurata*: gilded bronze statues. In 190 P. Cornelius Scipio Africanus erected an arch in a more prestigious location, alongside the Clivus Capitolinus leading up to the Capitoline Hill (Livy 37.3), again in no apparent connection to a triumph. It supported nine gilded bronze statues (*signa*) and a pair of horses.[38] With these early arches it is not

Fig. 24.6 Temple B, *Area Sacra di Largo Argentina*, Rome, late 2nd century BC, view. Photo by the author

clear if they supported statues of deities or portrait statues.[39] By at least the later second century, portrait statues stood atop arches, as suggested by the evidence of the Fornix Fabianus, which spanned the Sacred Way near the Forum (see also Chapter 23). It was set up by Q. Fabius Maximus Allobrogicus in 120 and was restored in 56 by his grandson. We know from inscriptions (dating from the restoration) that at least three portrait statues stood on top: Fabius Allobrogicus, L. Aemilius Paullus, and P. Cornelius Scipio Africanus. Archaeology indicates that these were standing (as opposed to equestrian) statues. Republican arches were not decorated with relief sculpture (this practice evidently began in the Julio-Claudian period), and did not support triumphal chariots (an innovation of the Augustan period).[40] Once the imperial family had monopolized the triumph, it became desirable to employ relief decoration and a new, more elevated statue format in order to differentiate imperial arches from the old republican ones. Not coincidentally, at this time the word *arcus* supplanted the old (less elegant) term *fornix*.[41] Republican arches were simply huge statue bases, used for permanent military commemoration in conjunction with – or in lieu of – a formal triumph, a victory monument, or a manubial temple filled with plundered statues.

Tombs

Like manubial temple architecture, tomb building was quite eclectic and for similar reasons of competitive self-advertisement (see also Chapters 4 and 16). A tomb was the best way to ensure that one's memory would live on, especially since Roman belief in the afterlife does not seem to have been very strong.[42] Wealthy Romans built tombs along the streets leading out of the city in all shapes and sizes,[43] constituting a kind of architectural "free-for-all," which one today can appreciate at the well-preserved *Porta Nocera* cemetery in the southern sector of Pompeii. Tombs were often located in the area of extra-urban properties owned by the families that built them,[44] as may have been the case with the Tomb of the Scipios. Monumental tombs began to be built in the middle Republic, but as with the Scipios' Tomb in its original

Fig. 24.7 Reconstructed elevation of the façade of the Tomb of the Scipios, Rome, 2nd century BC (Steinby 1993–2003: 3, fig. 138, after F. Coarelli). Reprinted by permission of Edizioni Quasar

phase (third century), these were mostly chamber tombs, concealed beneath the earth. In the second century the façade of the Tomb of the Scipios was redesigned to be exposed to the Via Appia, with engaged columns framing niches containing statues – of Scipio Africanus the Elder, his brother Lucius (Asiagenus), and the poet Ennius – in a configuration meant to invoke a Greek princely tomb (Figure 24.7).[45] This is usually interpreted simply as a matter of Hellenization, but as L. Scipio was victorious in Asia and his brother Scipio had acted as legate in Macedon, this kind of decoration may also have been a way of commemorating the family's military victories in the territories of the Hellenistic kings. This would also explain the inclusion of Ennius, who had written a play (called a *praetexta*) about the victories of Scipio Africanus.

In the late Republic, especially in the last generation, tomb architecture became whimsically idiosyncratic. A well-known tomb of the 20s, shaped like a great pyramid, still survives and is located on the *Via Ostiense* in Rome (Figure 24.8). The man who built it was C. Cestius, about whom relatively little is known (he may have been a *praetor* in Cicero's time; Cic. *Phil.* 3.2.6). It is often assumed that his odd choice of tomb type had to do with a contemporary fascination for things Egyptian (after the Battle of Actium and death of Antony and Cleopatra). This is true in part. But given

Fig. 24.8 Drawing of the tomb of C. Cestius, Via Ostiense, Rome, late 1st century BC. Courtesy of Deutsches Archäologisches Institut, Rom; DAI Rome neg. 4296

the fact that Cestius made Agrippa his heir (as the inscription on the tomb states), it is possible that he had served with Agrippa, perhaps as a legate, in Egypt after Actium. Such pyramids were conspicuous in places like Egypt and Ethiopia. Perhaps, then, the tomb also makes a reference to this man's military career.[46] In a more general sense, it could also (like the obelisks in Rome taken from Egypt) be a statement of Rome's victory over Egypt and the tomb occupant's support of the new principate.

Tombs of the highest elite are often notably austere in their exterior decoration. The Tomb of Caecilia Metella (wife of Crassus) on the Via Appia (Figures 24.9a and 24.9b), for example, is an enormous round structure with earthen mound at the top, evidently intended to evoke Etruscan *tumuli*, such as those at Cerveteri. But architectural decoration is quite minimal, being limited to a frieze of garlands, trophies, and bound captives beneath – allusions to her family's military achievements. Members of the elite already had honorific monuments and statues in public places in which their deeds were outlined (by inscription) and their portraits displayed. There was little need for showiness in a funerary context. Individuals lower on the economic and social scale, on the other hand, had no such opportunities for public honorific statues and monuments. Therefore, beginning in the late Republic, they used tombs to display portraits of themselves (either in full statue format evoking public honorific statues or in bust form, evoking ancestor portraits displayed in aristocratic houses; see Figure 15.1).[47] They also used tombs as a means to commemorate their public activities and/or professions in life, for example in the so-called Tomb of the Baker – built by a wealthy freedman who made his money in the bread industry – shaped like a dough-kneading machine and including portrait statues of him and his wife in high relief and a frieze with detailed scenes of bread making (Figure 24.10). Such reliefs often feature proportional distortion of form and perspectival illogicalities (some-

Fig. 24.9a Tomb of Caecilia Metella, Via Appia, Rome, mid-1st century BC, view. Courtesy of Deutsches Archäologisches Institut, Rom; DAI Rome neg. 63.1401

Fig. 24.9b Tomb of Caecilia Metella, Via Appia, Rome, mid-1st century BC, drawing of frieze (R. Paris [ed.] 2000, *La villa dei Quintili*. Milan. Fig. 38) Reprinted by permission of Mondadori Electa

times called "plebeian art,"[48] but which already existed in a less exaggerated manner in Greek grave reliefs and paintings). The reasons for this development were practical. The (mostly *nouveaux riche*) patrons often wished to include as much self-advertising material as possible in the relatively small space available to them (see also Chapter 15). Here we have the genesis of the peculiarly Roman funerary "career relief,"[49] a category of art production stemming from the relatively fluid class structure of Roman society.

Theaters

The Roman theater was created in an atmosphere charged with awareness of an authoritative model: the Greek theater. But in the Roman theatre there are significant departures. Roman theaters had a physically integrated cavea and stage, and the *scaenae frons* was much taller and wider and was filled with elaborate columns, entablatures, and statues (Figure 24.11a), while the Greek theater had a horseshoe-shaped cavea and small, low, physically separated stage, or skene (Figure 24.11b). If one wished to describe, briefly, how the Roman theater differed from the Greek, one might choose the words "closure" and "façadism," the qualities most praised by ancient authors regarding Roman architecture: *utilitas* and *maiestas*.

The earliest known theater of standard Roman type is the Theater of Pompey of 55.[50] Not only was it the first permanent theater in Rome, but also it canonized the Roman theater as an architectural type. Immediate antecedents for the Theater of Pompey existed, not in Hellenistic Greece or South Italy, as is sometimes said, but in lost wooden structures at Rome.[51] Plays such as those of Plautus had been staged on the area in front of the steps of temples (see also Chapter 25).[52] As early as 179, however, M. Aemilius Lepidus built a *cavea et proscaenium* (wooden "auditorium and

Fig. 24.10   So-called Tomb of the Baker, Rome, view. Photo by Marvin Trachtenberg

stage" [Livy 40.51.3], presumably physically separated in Greek fashion) on flat ground near the location of the later Theater of Marcellus. With the multiplication of *ludi* and the increasing competition among the sponsors, ever finer and more inventive theaters began being built. By the mid-second century the stage building

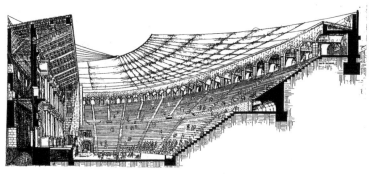

Fig. 24.11a   Roman Theater, reconstructed section. George C. Izenour's drawings of the theater. Reproduced with the permission of Rare Books and Manuscripts. Special Collections Library, the Pennsylvania Libraries

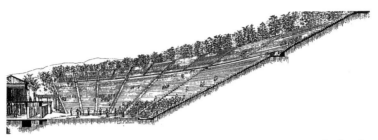

Fig. 24.11b Greek Theater, reconstructed section. George C. Izenour's drawings of the theater. Reproduced with the permission of Rare Books and Manuscripts. Special Collections Library, the Pennsylvania Libraries

seems already to have assumed its characteristically large size (Polyb. 30.22.2). By the first century the wooden theatres, described by the sources, begin to sound like canonical Roman theaters. The proverbial example is the sumptuous wooden theater of M. Aemilius Scaurus built in 58 BC, which had an extravagant three-story *scaenae frons* filled with statues (notwithstanding its extravagance, his theatre was in use for barely a month: Pliny *HN* 34.36; 36. 5; 113–15.). It has recently been argued that Rome's singular adaptation of the Hellenistic skene had its genesis in theaters erected specifically by triumphant generals in the second century and was initially developed to display plundered Greek statuary, perhaps on the occasion of the general's votive games that featured *praetextae* (plays about the general's own military exploits).[53]

When, famously, the censors of 154 were nearly finished building a permanent theater on the Palatine for the *ludi Megalenses*, the Senate decreed not only that the theater should be demolished, but that the Roman People should watch their plays standing, lest they decline into Greek effeminacy (Livy *Per.* 48; Val. Max. 2.4.1–2).[54] This senatorial prohibition, which did not last long, had less to do with moral reservations (if it had, the plays themselves would have been forbidden) than with political concerns. It was caused in part by a collective senatorial agenda of managing the *populus Romanus*. In effect, the prohibition against permanent theaters denied the Roman People a permanent meeting place. The physically integrated cavea and stage building made the Roman theater easier to control (this is also why Roman theaters are generally smaller than Greek theaters), and the extravagant ritual of erecting and dismantling temporary structures every year served as a visual reminder of senatorial power.[55] The Roman stage (*pulpitum*) was positioned low so that the senators could get a good view of the show, whereas in a Hellenistic theater the stage was positioned higher so that the whole audience could see well. Notably, the Roman magistrate who had paid for the show was seated not near the orchestra but above the *tribunalia* at the far end of the stage, that is, in the most conspicuous place in the cavea. The oblique view of the show from there was not good, but in Rome it was evidently more important to be seen by the audience than to have a good view of the drama (here is the historical kernel of seating practices in modern opera houses).

In Greek theaters, the audience had a spectacular view out from the theater of the landscape or the sea. In Roman theaters, on the other hand, the audience had no view of the outside world. The massive Roman stage building with its monumental columnar orders and lavish statuary display was not adaptable to the drama. It functioned to suggest to the audience something greater than themselves. In essence, the architecture of the Roman theater was designed to make the majority of the spectators feel awed – and small.[56]

Pompey's theater, innovatively, combined the cavea with a large quadriporticus (Figure 24.12), a configuration that became common for theaters in the West, e.g., at Ostia.[57] One reason for the quadriporticus was to offer the People a promenade filled with statues, commissioned specifically for the monument (in this case having to do with themes of love and war).[58] The portico would above all, however, have recalled a manubial porticus. Included in it were sculptural representations of the 14 nations vanquished by Pompey, reminding viewers of his status as the first Mediterranean-wide conqueror. The whole complex was built *ex manubiis* and dedicated to *Venus Victrix* (it also included a shrine to Venus, which may have helped to lessen senatorial resistance to a permanent theater). At the time Pompey built his theater he had refused to relinquish his *imperium* and thus could not enter the *pomerium* (sacred boundary of the city). He accordingly constructed a residence for himself adjoining the theater complex, and he included in the quadriporticus the *Curia Pompeii*, so he could attend senate meetings while still keeping soldiers under his command (it was here that Caesar was later assassinated at the foot of Pompey's statue). The developed form of the Theater of Pompey, then, represents an architecture of regulation and hierarchy, which had its genesis in practical Roman needs for popular control and self-advertisement, particularly with regard to military reputation (see also Chapter 4).

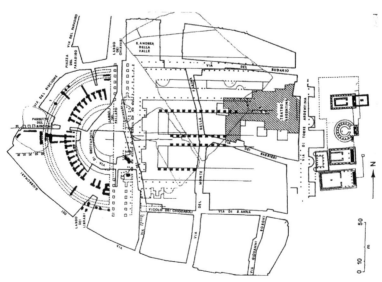

Fig. 24.12 Theater of Pompey, according to the Severan Marble Plan and archaeological remains, showing modern street blocks, 55 BC (Coarelli 1997: 540). Reprinted by permission of Edizioni Quasar

Houses and villas

Before the 1980s aristocratic mansions of the Republic were known largely from second-century examples at Pompeii and Cosa. Excavations on the lower slopes of the Palatine, however, have revealed a series of atrium houses dating to the sixth century, when Rome seems to have been under Etruscan cultural (if not political) hegemony.[59] The discoveries confirmed that the atrium house with all of its component parts – *fauces* (vestibule), *compluvium* (cantilevered, square opening in the roof), *tablinum* (reception room), and *hortus* (vegetable garden at the back) – was a central Italian (probably Etruscan) phenomenon, not something that had originated in multicultural Campania.

Such ancestral atrium houses were inhabited by the Roman aristocracy from the Archaic period all the way down to the Great Fire of Nero of 64 AD, as archaeology and Suet. *Ner.* 38.2 demonstrate (see also Chapters 4 and 16). In the middle republican period houses were remarkably similar in dimension and configuration (Figure 24.13). The sameness of elite mansions in the middle republican period in terms of plan and size was a visual analog of the conservative Roman ideology of equality among the ruling class. Having a large and extravagant dwelling might suggest aspirations to tyranny, punishment for which could include destruction of one's house after erection, as happened to M. Manlius Capitolinus in 384 (Livy 5.47.8; 6.20.13; see also Chapter 23). Houses on the Palatine were tightly packed, and rarely changed hands or were expanded until the later second century, when conservative traditions began to break down.[60] This chronological shift with regard to house alteration is corroborated by archaeology: one particular house, carefully

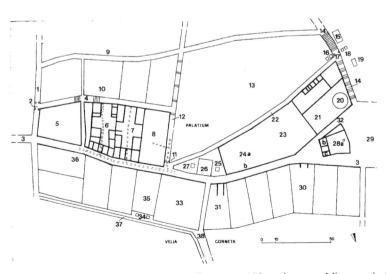

Fig. 24.13 Houses on the lower Palatine Hill, Rome, mid- to late republican periods, plan (Cristofani 1991: 97). Reprinted by permission of Edizioni Quasar

investigated, was much the same from the sixth all the way down to the first century, when it was substantially remodeled.[61]

Eventually, under Greek influence, some of these old atrium houses were modernized to include columns: tetrastyle atria, as reflected in the House of the Silver Wedding and porticoes in the back in place of the *hortus*, as in the House of Sallust (Figures 24.14a and 24.14b), both at Pompeii.[62] Based on literary evidence, several of the surviving houses on the lower Palatine can plausibly be identified as belonging to specific historical personages, such as M. Aemilius Scaurus (aedile 58). People of the middle classes lived in smaller houses of more irregular size and room configuration, as discoveries at Pompeii and Cosa have shown.[63] While the Palatine was largely inhabited by the upper classes, the plebs of Rome lived cheek-by-jowl with the nobility in all of Rome's other neighborhoods, such as the Subura, where *tabernae* fronted the houses and *collegia* and multistory apartment buildings (*insulae*) stood close to traditional aristocratic mansions: atrium houses, sometimes with peristyles at the back, as seen on the Severan marble plan (Figure 24.15) and as reflected in the House of the Faun at Pompeii.[64]

In the second and first centuries, elite Romans began building villas, mostly in Campania, where they could indulge in a Greek-style private life, away from public scrutiny. An important component of this kind of life was to be surrounded by Greek statues. These new villas, therefore, featured roomy peristyles, containing space for statuary displays and evoking the atmosphere of Greek gymnasia, sanctuaries, palaces, etc. Early villas, such as the Villa of the Mysteries (Figure 24.16), included atria and were axial in their arrangement of rooms (Vit. 6.5.3). Others were loose and nonaxial in plan, often overlooking the sea (as with Lucullus' properties in Campania; see below). Some villas included extensive facilities for agricultural production and slave accommodation, for example, the first-century villa at Settefinestre (cf. Varro *RR* 1.13.6).[65]

The origins of the luxury villa are quite controversial.[66] Before the mid-later second century, Romans had large farms and may have had primitive villas with few amenities (e.g., Cato *Agr.* 4; Col. 1.4.8; cf. Sall. *Cat.* 11.12.3). The first indication of anything luxurious comes from one of Cato's very last speeches (*ORF*[4] Cato no. 8, 185: 152 BC), in which he complains of villas decorated with Numidian marble pavements (i.e., *giallo antico*). That Cato focuses on this in a speech as late as the mid-second century suggests that such embellishments were new at the time.[67] P. Scipio Africanus the Elder had a villa at Liternum – a dismal site (Vell. Pat. 1.15.2) – which he built when he went into exile. Livy (38.52.1–3) calls it a "country place" (*prodicta*); Seneca (*Ep.* 86) and Cicero (*de Off.* 3.2) refer to it as a villa, but Seneca says it resembled a fortress. Cicero (*Nat. D.* 2.4.12) mentions "*horti Scipionis*," but these are thought to be agricultural properties (possibly in the vicinity of the Tomb of the Scipios on the Via Appia),[68] nothing comparable to the villas of the first century (indeed, we hear of no further *horti* until those of L. Lucullus in the early first century).[69] Finally, M. Aemilius Lepidus (cos. 187) had properties (*praedia*) at Terracina (Livy 40.51.2), and L. Aemilius Paullus had *paralioi agroi* ("country places by the sea") at Formiae (Plut. *Aem.* 39.1) (see also Chapter 28).

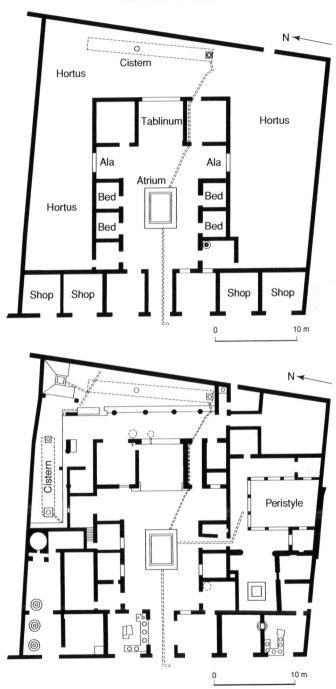

Figs. 24.14a and b House of Sallust, Pompeii, plans of 2nd- and 1st-century BC phases (J. Ward-Perkins and A. Claridge (1978), *Pompeii AD 79. Treasures from the National Archaeological Museum, Naples, and the Pompeii Antiquarium*. New York. Fig. 53) Reprinted by permission of Anne Laidlaw

Fig. 24.15 *Vicus Patricius* as depicted on the Severan Marble Plan (Axel Boëthius and J. B. Ward-Perkins, 1970, *Etruscan and Early Roman Architecture*, Penguin, fig. 53). Copyright © the Estate of Axel Boëthius and JB Ward-Perkins, 1970

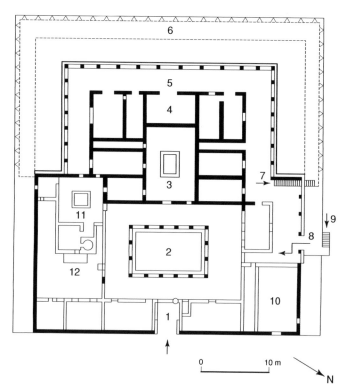

Fig. 24.16 Villa of the Mysteries, Pompeii, plan, first phase, 2nd century BC (Gros 1996–2001: 2, fig. 290)

The first genuine-sounding luxury villas date only to the time of the Gracchi and Marius. Marius had a "villa" near Baiae on the promontory at Misenum (Plut. *Mar.* 34.2, using the phrase *polyteles oikia*, "an impressive dwelling": cf. Pliny *HN* 18.32.). Lucullus' villas at Naples involved elaborate waterworks, earning him the nickname "Xerxes in a Toga" (Plut. *Luc.* 39.1–4; Varro *Rust.* 1.2.10; 3.4.3; 6.5.3. His villas were widely imitated [Cic. *Off.* 1.140] and became the proverbial precedent for later luxury villas, which proliferated in Campania after the Mediterranean was cleared of pirates). At Rome, however, Lucullus tried something even more daring. He was the first to build a luxury villa, located provocatively at the very doorstep of the city, on the Pincian Hill.[70] This villa, euphemistically called a *hortus*, or vegetable garden, featured an innovation: a huge exedra facing west at the edge of the hill toward the sunset (now the site of the Spanish Steps). The effect here would have been very much like that of the terraced sanctuaries of Latium, such as that at Praeneste.[71] The *horti Luculliani*, of course, constituted the model of the later, better-documented *horti* in Rome's suburbs, such as the Gardens of Maecenas (and ultimately resulted in imperial villas such as Hadrian's).

Art

"Ideal" sculpture

A *sine qua non* for successful villa life was to surround oneself with Greek decorative sculpture. This category of art production is often referred to as "ideal," a term from the German *Idealplastik*, and it consists of sculptures of Greek divine, mythological, heroic, or genre subject matter. "Ideal" sculpture constitutes by far the largest category of Roman sculptural production. Much of this sculpture was purely decorative; but some was also cultic and votive. Most of it was manufactured for the Roman villa market, which burgeoned in the early first century. For a long time the study of "ideal" sculpture was dominated by close examination of Roman replicas (*Kopienkritik*) to reconstruct the appearance of lost Greek originals. More recently, interest has shifted to issues of Roman display contexts and the ways that Roman-period sculptors adjusted Greek prototypes.[72] Sometimes the statues are signed by the artists (especially in the case of virtuoso replicas such as those from the late republican villa at Sperlonga[73]). In all cases, the artists' names are Greek.

Because of some discoveries in Rome and environs of high-quality, life-sized statuary of the fourth to third centuries in terracotta (see below), it is probable that early on there were top-grade statues in Rome in that medium, but such first-class statuary in bronze and marble really only began to be brought to Rome on a large scale as war booty by M. Claudius Marcellus in 211. The spoils of Syracuse were proverbially linked with the onset of domestic luxury in Rome.[74] By the time of Mummius' sack of Corinth (146), Rome had become home to great "collections" of Greek art.[75] Much of this looted artwork was put on public display in manubial temples and porticoes.[76] But some was also placed in Roman atrium houses.[77] The

Elder Cato, complaining that images of gods were being treated in the Roman *domus* like household furniture, implies that the selection criteria for such displays were motivated by a wish to have case examples of different statuary forms (*exempla earum facierum*: *ORF*[4] Cato no. 8, 98).

Archaeology, and some famous letters of Cicero, indicate that the installations in republican villas, for example the Villa of the Papyri, were assembled quickly and featured dense, heterogeneous displays of statues without overarching theme or consistency of sculpted subjects (the only clear pattern in this villa's statuary decoration is that it is grouped, to a large extent, by medium, format, and pose).[78] The same diversity is evident in middle-class houses at Pompeii, where statues are displayed in a crowded, "busy" manner, in a way imitative of late republican, elite villas.[79] By contrast, statues in Hellenistic houses were considerably fewer and more austere in installation (they seem to have been carefully chosen over a longer period of time for specific display spots).[80] Statuary installations in Greek sanctuaries would have been dense and eclectic, but this was an agglutinative phenomenon, resulting from votive dedications over time, sometimes many centuries. Roman statuary displays, however, were assembled quickly as an *ad hoc* collection.[81] Their diversity in subject matter, size, and "period-styles," it may be suggested, can be traced back to middle republican practices of divorcing plundered statues from their original Greek

Fig. 24.17   Roman replica of the so-called Discophoros, 5th century BC. Courtesy of the Aphrodisias Excavations, Institute of Fine Arts, New York University

Fig. 24.18 Muse (Melpomene), late 1st century BC. Courtesy of the Aphrodisias Excavations, Institute of Fine Arts, New York University

contexts. Having been seized (and removed from their original inscribed bases) in huge numbers, from all manner of buildings and spaces in the Greek world, they were grouped together anew in a uniquely Roman context – the triumphal procession – where they were arranged not by subject matter or theme, but apparently by medium, size, and pose.[82] Afterwards, a portion of them would be set aside – with an emphasis on variegated form – for domestic display.

When republican generals dedicated plundered statues, they inscribed their own names as dedicators and sometimes the identity of the people from whom they were plundered, never the title of the works or the artists' names (which, for Greeks of the time, would have been interesting information[83]). At his ancestral town of Tusculum, for example, M. Fulvius Nobilior (cos. 189) set up a looted statue with the following, typically republican, inscribed base: *M. Fulvius M.f. Ser. n. co(n)s(ul) Aetolia cepit* ("M. Fulvius, consul, son of Marcus, grandson of Servius, took [it] from Aetolia"),[84] in a way comparable to how generals had traditionally inscribed their names on looted weapons and armor. This and other evidence indicate that looted Greek statues were initially conceived of more as trophies than artworks *per se*.[85] The Roman mentality concerning art during this period was not, as it seems, one of connoisseurship but rather a pragmatic "booty mentality" (getting as many works, and as many different kinds of work, as possible).[86]

Fig. 24.19a "Esquiline Historical Fragment," probably early 3rd century BC, view. Courtesy of Deutsches Archäologisches Institut, Rom; DAI Rome neg. 34.1929

The supply of war booty in the form of Greek statuary sharply declined after Mummius' sack of Corinth in 146. Large numbers of original statues could no longer be looted from the East because wars here had generally ceased and these areas remained mostly at peace with Rome. But the demand for decorative sculpture had already been established. The "copying industry" was then set in motion to satisfy it.[87] By the late second /early first century, Romans who wanted to decorate their homes with statues could purchase them *en masse* from Greece (as did Cicero) or could buy them in a local workshop in Rome (e.g., that of Arcesilaus or Pasiteles).[88] Rome now had unfettered access to the marble quarries in Greece, so statues could be produced that were affordable to a wider group of people, not just the great *triumphatores* and their friends, but to other members of the elite.

Artists now began to produce three categories of "ideal" sculpture: close replicas of Greek originals (Figure 24.17), variants on Greek originals, and "new creations" based on Greek themes (Figure 24.18).[89] (Replication had occurred earlier in Greece but not comparably in scale of production or accuracy of copying.) The "new creations" eventually constituted by far the most numerous (and inventive) category

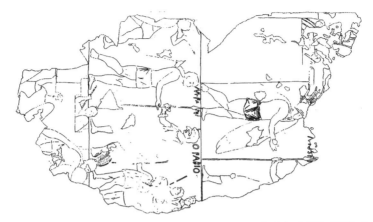

Fig. 24.19b "Esquiline Historical Fragment," line drawing, Steinby 1993–2000: 3, fig. 144. Reprinted by permission of Edizioni Quasar

Fig. 24.20 House of Sallust, Pompeii, view of atrium with First Style Wall Painting, 2nd century BC (*Fototeca Unione* 27231)

of statues for a practical reason. The "copying industry" was market driven: the existing repertory of Greek sculpture had to be exponentially expanded in order to meet the burgeoning Roman demand, once the villa had been established. This need to expand the repertoire also motivated a transformation of the representational traditions inherited from the Greeks, in the combination of different "period-styles" (Classical, Hellenistic, and Archaic) in single statues.[90]

Wall painting

Like decorative sculpture, most Roman wall painting is Greek in subject matter, because both these categories of art were commissioned mostly for private consumption. The earliest extant Roman wall painting, however, depicts Roman scenes (Figures 24.19a and 14.19b). Poorly preserved, the "Esquiline Historical Fragment"[91] has four surviving registers, the first and fourth showing a battle scene between Romans and Samnites, identifiable by armor. The second shows two leaders, one dressed in a republican toga (the so-called *toga exigua*) and carrying a spear, the other wearing a helmet and a short waist-wrapped tunic (perhaps including a cuirass) and outfitted with greaves and shield. The figures, who are inscribed by name – Fabius and Fannius – approach one another in front of a city wall. In the third register the same figures appear to be negotiating (the second figure is now bareheaded). It is not absolutely clear if Fannius is a Samnite commander or a Roman legate (the former seems more probable). But because of the battle scenes between Romans and Samnites, the painting surely depicts episodes from the Samnite Wars. Though its chronology is debated, it is probably third century, and "Fabius" may represent Q. Fabius Rullianus, *triumphator* in the Second Samnite War.

Despite its iconic status in the literature, the "Esquiline Historical Fragment" is not typical of Roman painting. It is an example of the public genre of "triumphal

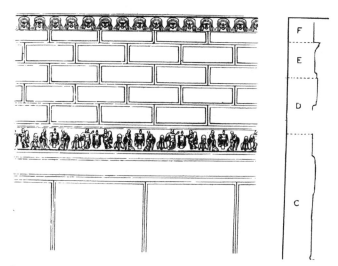

Fig. 24.21   Reconstructed elevation of the interior of a House at Fregellae, early 2nd century BC (Coarelli 1996b, fig. 106). Reprinted by permission of Edizioni Quasar

Fig. 24.22 Early Second Style Wall Painting, House of the Griffins on the Palatine, Rome, late 2nd century BC. Courtesy of Deutsches Archäologisches Institut, Rom; DAI Rome neg. 66.4

painting" (here reproduced inside a general's tomb). A didactic kind of representation, it makes allusions to special moments in, or the topography of, a campaign. The battle scenes seem to have been rendered in typical Hellenistic (dramatic) manner because models were available, while the Fabius and Fannius registers are presented in a matter-of-fact, "style-less" way, without allegory or elevating iconography.[92] These registers seem to be visual analogs of the Latin *commentarii* of later times: flat, matter-of fact narratives, lacking the rhetorical flourishes one finds in Greek battle narratives (such as Xenophon's *Anabasis*).[93]

For wall painting from domestic contexts we have considerably more evidence, from Pompeii and its environs. In the late nineteenth century A. Mau divided the different types of such wall painting into four styles.[94] A shorthand way of conceiving the first two styles – those pertinent to the Republic – is as follows: the Masonry Style and the Architectural Style. In the middle Republic (and perhaps earlier) elite Romans decorated their homes in First Style, which used painted stucco in relief and featured rectangular panels resembling ashlar masonry, in different colors (Figure 24.20).[95] The effect would have been that of "faux" marble revetment. Sometimes it is clear that the painters were attempting to imitate specific exotic marbles, such as translucent onyx or fiery *giallo antico*.

The houses at the Roman colony of Fregellae reveal that First Style decoration could include friezes at eye level (in Fregellae's case, of painted terracotta in relief).[96] While this convention is derived directly from Greek sources,[97] it is notable that at Fregellae the subject matter is historical and military (Figure 24.21). The fragments

Fig. 24.23   Second Style Wall Painting depicting allegory of Macedonia and Asia, villa at Boscoreale, 1st century BC. Courtesy of Deutsches Archäologisches Institut, Rom; DAI Rome neg. 66.1853

Fig. 24.24   Second Style Wall Painting, Villa of the Mysteries, Pompeii, 1st century BC. Courtesy of Deutsches Archäologisches Institut, Rom; DAI Rome neg. 57. 843A

all depicted scenes of trophies, captives, Victories, and scenes of battle between Romans and Macedonians (identifiable by shields). The Greek prototype, then, has been adjusted to serve a Roman agenda of domestic representation. The houses were probably inhabited by veterans of Rome's wars with Antiochus III (in which Fregellae took part), and the friezes were surely imitative of similar ones in the atrium houses of the capital.

We are in a very different world when we move down to the late Republic and the Second Style, which features megalographic scenes from Greek mythology, Hellenistic royal themes, and architectural scenes evoking Greek palaces and sanctuaries. It is distinguished by the rendition, on a flat wall, of the impression of spatial depth by means of painted pilasters, projecting entablatures, porticoes dramatically receding into the distance, and so on. Second Style is associated with "Hellenization," especially with Campanian villa culture of the first century, and there are clear Greek antecedents for the early Second Style.[98] The earliest extant example of Second Style in Italy, however, comes not from Campania but from Rome and not from a villa, but from a *domus* on the Palatine, the so-called House of the Griffins (Figure 24.22), the back parts of which (dining and bedrooms) survive because they were preserved in the foundations for Domitian's palace.[99] The house is now conventionally dated (by its construction technique) to 110–100, suggesting that the Style came into being some time beforehand.

There is no consensus as to exactly when or where "full-blown" or "high" Second Style originated, and its chronology and development are controversial.[100] The most widely accepted view connects it with Hellenistic palace architecture and with luxury building materials that began to arrive in Rome in the second century, providing a new repertoire of motifs for wall painters.[101] Some "high" Second Style ensembles feature clear copies of original Greek paintings, such as a triclinium in the villa at Boscoreale. There, painted pillars divide megalographic scenes, some pertaining to the Macedonian dynasty (Figure 24.23).[102] Others, such as those from the Villa of the Mysteries (Figure 24.24), are contemporary, *ad hoc* creations, featuring sumptuous vistas evoking Greek settings. We hear nothing of the artists and copyists of such

Fig. 24.25 Second Style Wall Painting, Odyssey Landscapes, Rome, 1st century BC: scene at left: Odysseus in Circe's Palace. Photo by Peter von Blanckenhagen, courtesy of the Institute of Fine Arts, New York University

paintings because we lack signatures (the Roman wall-painting profession was held in low esteem: e.g., Pliny *HN* 35.118).

High Second Style first appears in Pompeian houses (e.g., the House of the Silver Wedding) and in nearby villas associated with the settlement of Sulla's veterans in Pompeii and its *ager* (territory). That this type of wall painting may have originated in Rome is suggested not only by the prototypical version of it decorating the House of the Griffins (late 2nd century) on the Palatine but by the fact that the only well-dated example of full-blown Second Style, known as "The Odyssey Landscapes," comes not from Campania but from an atrium-peristyle *domus* in the Subura region of the capital. This painting cycle (Figure 24.25) decorated the back wall of a columnar portico or peristyle, and the presence of a pre-Julian calendar on the same wall probably suggests a date before c.50.[103] The paintings here comprise romantic representations, in continuous narrative, of the wanderings of Odysseus and companions, with small figures in an atmospheric landscape (divided by fictive pilasters), presumably replicas from an uninterrupted original Greek frieze.[104]

The Second Style was considerably more flamboyant than the First and greatly augmented the "busy" effect of the display spaces with their variegated and dense statuary displays. The predilection for decorating houses and villas with sculpture in this manner – each piece conjuring up different associations – may have directly encouraged the development of high Second Style, which is often extremely rich in motifs, sometimes without apparent order and often lacking in logical juxtaposition of iconographic elements, causing the viewer's eye to flicker this way and that, as did statues of widely disparate subject matter. The "opening up" of the wall by means of architectural illusionism in Second Style may have originally been devised by artists to complement the many decorative statues crowded together (by Greek domestic standards). The result was a highly ornate domestic aesthetic unique to Rome.

Fig. 24.26   Mosaic floor with *emblema* showing scene of Theseus and the Minotaur, House of the Labyrinth, Pompeii, 1st century BC, view. Photo by the author

Fig. 24.27 Tetrastyle atrium with *opus sectile* floor, "House of Championett," Pompeii, 1st century BC, view. Photo by the author

Mosaic and opus sectile

Mosaic floors in domestic contexts contributed to the already "busy" effect of room decoration created by the wall painting and statuary displays.[105] Campanian houses of the second century (those decorated in First Style) had mostly monochrome mosaic floors with borders depicting vegetal and other motifs, based on Greek themes (such as theater masks), produced in local workshops.[106] The House of the Faun (late second century) is notable for having an exceptionally fine mosaic depicting the battle between Alexander and the Persian king Darius, positioned in a distyle columnar exedra in the smaller of two peristyles.[107] The tesserae used are miniscule (*"opus vermiculatum"*: Pliny *HN* 36.185), and the effect is like that of a fine, late Classical painting (it is in fact a replica of such a painting). This mosaic and the house's *fauces* (decorated to resemble a Greek tomb or stage façade) indicate that a fully Hellenized Oscan family lived here.

Rooms in Pompeian houses of the first century (those associated with Sulla's veteran colonization and equipped with Second Style wall painting) are often covered in white mosaic tesserae with central *emblemata*, squarish in shape (between 1–1.5 m.), depicting mythological scenes, e.g., Theseus and the Minotaur from a dining room in the House of the Labyrinth (Figure 24.26).[108] Another technique of the time was to cover the entire floor with monochrome mosaic punctuated by relatively primitive *opus sectile* (irregularly cut pieces of imported marble in various colors). Two good examples are a late republican mansion discovered under the Flavian-period *Ludus Magnus* in Rome[109] and the atrium of the "House of Championett" at Pompeii, a terrace house with a tetrastyle atrium, built by Sulla's veteran colonists (Figure 24.27). In the latter (a clear imitation of the very latest metropolitan proto-

Fig. 24.28 Scene of riderless horse from frieze on the pillar monument of L. Aemilius Paullus, Delphi, mid-2nd century BC. Foto Marburg 135132, #55.1615

types), the pieces of cut marble are yellow-red *giallo antico* (from Tunisia), purple-mottled *pavonazetto* (Phrygia), green serpentine (Peloponnesus), multicolored Africano (Teos), and pink-veined *Porta Santa* (Chios). Strikingly, the marble fragments are inset in a "gemlike" fashion into a surrounding "sea" of black mosaic tesserae.

For mosaic from public buildings we have mainly Praeneste, where some exceptionally fine mosaics covered the floors of two rooms (probably official reception and dining rooms) adjoining the Forum. They, like the Sanctuary above, date to the later second century. In one of these rooms was a fish mosaic (locally conceived); in the other was a Nilotic mosaic with multiple scenes rendered in varying degrees of bird's-eye perspective.[110] The latter is quite clearly a copy of a Hellenistic (Ptolemaic) original painting, featuring banqueting scenes, Nile expeditions, Egyptian temples, exotic animals (labeled in Greek), and pygmies in the less civilized, southern part of the Nile (cf. Diod. Sic. 31.18.2).[111] The citizens of Praeneste are known from inscriptions to have had trading relations with Greece. It would make sense, then, for Praeneste to have such sophisticated decoration, presumably a source of awe and envy in surrounding, less well-connected Latin communities.

Architectural sculpture and relief

While little pedimental sculpture from temples survives, one discovery from the Via San Gregorio suggests that work of the best quality was possible already in the middle republican period.[112] The reliefs feature a central figure of Mars, and it is possible that they belonged to an attested temple of that god on the Caelian Hill. What is notable about these sculptures is that, while they are in terracotta, they are comparable to the best such marble carving in contemporary Greece.

Fig. 24.29 Census scene from the so-called Altar of Domitius Ahenobarbus, early 1st century BC. Foto Marburg 163045, #56.682

The battle scenes in the Fregellae friezes (discussed above) are important because, though carved in good Hellenistic style, the subject matter is historical (an actual battle between Romans and Hellenistic Greeks), not allegorical, as was often the case in Greek relief sculpture.[113] Another such "historical" frieze was carved on a pillar at Delphi, commissioned by Aemilius Paullus after his victory over Perseus. The dedicatory inscription is in Latin (no concession to Greek viewers here), baldly stating:

Fig. 24.30 Panel depicting Victories and Shield, Piazza dell Consolazione, Rome, 1st century BC. Courtesy of Deutsches Archäologisches Institut, Rom; DAI Rome neg. 41.2317

L. Aimilius [sic] L.F. inperator [sic] de rege Perse Macdonibusque cepet ("L. Aemilius, son of Lucius, Imperator, took [it] from Perseus, king of the Macedonians": [*ILLRP* no. 323 = *ROL* 4:79 no. 66]). The frieze depicts the Battle of Pydna (168) between Paullus and Perseus.[114] The figures are clearly identifiable by their armor, and there is a representation of a riderless horse (Figure 24.28) that figured anecdotally in the battle (Plut. *Aem.* 18; Livy 44.40.4–10). In style the frieze is Hellenistic (comparable, for example, to that from the Temple of Artemis at Magnesia on the Meander[115]). In its heightened historical specificity, however, it is Roman.

When Greek models were not available styles of relief carving are somehow different and recognizably not Greek. An example is the census scene on the so-called "Altar of Domitius Ahenobarbus" (also referred to as the "Paris–Munich reliefs").[116] The monument, which consists of four relief panels, was not an altar but functioned as cladding for a great statue base. Three of the panels show a marine cortège, including Neptune and Amphitrite. The fourth shows a Roman scene of census (Figure 24.29) and the *lustrum* (sacrifice) that followed it. The reliefs were found near the *Circus Flaminius*, an area crowded with manubial temples, and the identities of the dedicator (presumably a general) and temple with which they may have been associated (e.g., Mars or Neptune?) are controversial. The census includes a representation of Mars (taller than the other figures), next to the togate censor who is sacrificing. The raison d'être of the census in Rome was, of course, to determine who was eligible for military service. The large size of the base suggests that a statue group stood on it, displayed outdoors, near a manubial temple, perhaps one dedicated to Neptune, given the marine cortège (commemorating a victory at sea). It could, for example, have been dedicated as a victory monument by M. Antonius, consul in 99 and victor over Cilician pirates.[117] The marine cortège is in Hellenistic style, because Greek models were available for such scenes. But the census (a peculiarly Roman ritual) lacked such models and is done differently, in a matter-of-fact style, apparently lacking in artifice and neither Hellenistic nor Classical in appearance.

A final series of republican relief sculptures survive: the so-called Sant'Omobono Victory panels (also called the "Reliefs from the *Piazza della Consolazione*"), perhaps commemorating Sulla's victories (Figure 24.30). They were found in the precinct of the *Porta Triumphalis*, and it is likely that they fell from the Capitoline Hill. Again, they functioned as cladding for a very large statue base. It has been argued, partly on the basis of numismatic evidence, that they supported a statue group showing the surrender to Sulla of Jugurtha.[118] This monument seems to have been Sulla's competitive response to the Trophies of Marius, which also stood on the Capitoline and commemorated Marius' victories in Africa and over the Germans (Vel. Pat. 2.43.4; Suet. *Iul.* 11).

The panels depict shields, trophies, captured armor, heads of Roma, and two victories (perhaps alluding to the two trophies Sulla erected after the battle of Chaironea). Between the victories is a shield with two *erotes* (an allusion to Sulla's patron deity, Venus?). The elements are arranged in an "iconic" fashion with no overlapping of the figural decoration (this pattern is also seen in the Fregellae friezes and on republican coins,[119] and – one may hypothesize – was inspired by the way that spoils had been attached to the façades of Roman houses and/or the back walls of Greek stoas; see also Chapters 16 and 17). On the one hand, this seems to be a typical way of depicting captured weapons in the republican period: straightforward and instantly readable.[120] Yet, if the previously mentioned interpretations are correct, the iconography is allusive and symbolic, implying a high level of intellectual conception. This would be in keeping with the late republican period, a time of increased sophistication when generals, at ever-higher stakes, were breaking out of the old mold and therefore needed to distinguish themselves in original ways. New imperatives provided the impetus for novel modes of artistic expression.

It is notable that what little relief sculpture survives mostly concerns war, whether literally (the Paullus frieze), tangentially (census), allegorically (marine cortège), or emblematically (Sant' Omobono reliefs). Most such reliefs constituted cladding for victory monuments positioned along the triumphal route, functioning as an alternative means of military self-commemoration instead of, or in addition to, a manubial temple.

Coins

Like Greek coinage, Roman coinage has much to do with religion. Unlike Greek coinage, however, Roman coinage also has much to do with the commemoration of war and of individual familial achievements.[121] Some of Rome's earliest coins (Second Punic War) depict a ship's prow on the reverse and heads of Mars and of Janus (god of doorways) on the obverse.[122] The meaning of Mars is clear, and the ship's prow is an obvious reference to naval victory. The liminal nature of Janus has been the subject of a major study,[123] but there may also be a more pragmatic reason for this god's prominence on coins. Janus' temple was located at the busiest intersection in Rome, where the Forum adjoined the Argiletum. The doors of this temple were always kept open in times of war. Throughout the entire republican period, the doors were closed on only three occasions.[124] As a result, Janus' cult statue was always visible to the public, unlike most other cult statues that were visible only sometimes, particularly on the feast day of the deity in question. Janus was a constant reminder that Rome was at war, hence the god's ubiquity in middle republican coinage. In the second century heads of a helmeted Roma begin to appear on coins. Heads of Virtus (the personification of aggressive manliness and military courage) then appear in the early first century (presumably representing the old cult statue of Virtus, which had been installed in Marcellus' Temple of Honos and Virtus of 206). Notably, Roma and Virtus are nearly identical in their iconography,[125] a fact that is starkly revealing about how Romans conceived of themselves in this formative period.

An added impetus for the moneyers to regard coin issues as theirs to design personally may have resulted from the Gabinian law (139), which provided for the secret ballot in elections, motivated by a need for self-advertisement when one's clients could no longer always be counted upon to vote in one's favor (see Chapters 1, 18, and 19).[126] Allusions to particular *gentes* on coin obverses had previously been indirect; now they became more obvious. Symbols of public office such as sacrificial jugs and the *lituus* (augural staff) abound, as do trophies, Victoria riding on a chariot,

Fig. 24.31 Portrait head, c. 1st century BC, Osimo, Museo Civico. Photo by R. R. R. Smith

triumphatores in chariots, trophies with kneeling bound captives, captured weapons and armor, soldiers charging into battle,[127] etc. Such scenes alluded to the civic and military achievements of the moneyers' families. Now portraits of (deceased) ancestors of the moneyers begin to appear on coinage. An example is a coin of 96 with a reverse type showing three horsemen charging down a fallen warrior.[128] One of the moneyers was A. Postumius Albinus, and the reverse type presumably shows a scene from the Battle of Lake Regillus in which his ancestor took part (Florus 1.5.2–3). Such an overtly violent iconography, which became standard in Roman imperial coinage, would never appear on a Hellenistic coin. It was in late republican coinage that personification, allegory, symbol, and allusion first developed into a coherent and complex visual language, unique to Rome (see also Chapter 3).[129]

Portrait sculpture

Roman portraiture of the republican era is distinguished in large part by its emphasis on representations of middle-aged, battle-hardened men, with individually shaped heads, wrinkles, pronounced nasal–labial lines, creases on the neck and eyes, sagging under chins, closely shaved or bald heads, receding hairlines, facial scars, warts and, above all, intensely lifelike forward gazes.[130] What distinguishes it from Greek por-

Fig. 24.32 Portrait head, c. 1st century BC ("Marius"), Munich (Saskia, Jic-0647)

traiture is that it conveys the immediate and palpable effect of a powerful individual presence. The emphasis on heightened realism is often referred to as "verism." Within the repertoire of realistic-looking republican portraits there was a spectrum of severity and apparent age. To take two examples of the highest quality, at one end of the spectrum is the portrait of a wizened individual from Osimo in northern Italy (Figure 24.31). At the other end is the so-called "Marius," now in Munich (Figure 24.32).[131] The Munich head is turned slightly to one side; his eyes are exaggeratedly penetrating; and his lips are parted. These are elevating devices derived from the Hellenistic repertoire. Still, one would not identify this person as a Greek; he is clearly Roman. Republican portraits convey not Greek ideals of beauty (youthful, "regular" features) but the qualities of *virtus* (aggressive manliness and military courage), *severitas*, and *auctoritas* (see also Chapters 17 and 21). Female portraiture of the period is somewhat less severe and rather blander, with more of an emphasis on youth, though there are many examples of Roman matrons with realistic, aging faces combined with contemporary hairstyles, such as a head of a Roman woman from a Roman house on Delos, dating probably to the later second century[132]

The relative dearth of republican portrait sculpture has to do with the fact that most of it was bronze (e.g., the famous Capitoline Brutus), which was later melted down. Marble only became available on a wide scale for portraiture after the Carrara (Luna) quarries were opened in the time of Caesar and Augustus. Most of the few

Fig. 24.33 Portrait head of Pompey, Ny Carlsberg Glyptotek, Copenhage. Courtesy of Deutsches Archäologisches Institut, Rom; DAI Rome neg. 31.591

surviving republican portraits are unidentifiable and therefore difficult to date. From the fourth and third centuries we have some terracotta portraits from Rome and around Latium. The quality varies from poor and bland in appearance to exceptionally fine and Hellenizing. Some of the best such portraits are those of women. Two from Aricia are over life-size and idealized to an extent, but mature in appearance.[133] They wear jewelry and appear to be of high rank. For the late republican period we have portraits from the middle classes of Roman Italy (mostly of limestone and terracotta), which exhibit a formulaic severity, some quite realistic-looking but of lower quality than in Rome.[134]

During the middle decades of the first century "veristic" portraits (those of the moneyers' families) begin to appear on Roman coin obverses.[135] The first securely dated Roman republican portrait in the round is an imperial copy of a portrait of Pompey the Great in Copenhagen (Figure 24.33), identifiable by comparison with his posthumous coin portraits.[136] Pompey was unusually young when he came to prominence and therefore his portrait appears younger than what we see in many other republican portraits, and his hair is somewhat longer. He has a cowlick-like quiff of hair above the forehead that some have seen as a reference to Alexander the Great's *anastole*. His portrait is otherwise unqualifiedly mundane. To the modern eye the portrait has an almost comical appearance, but it is an indication that Pompey was not – and did not wish to present himself as – a "good-looking" man in the Greek sense (youthful, "ideal"). The coin portraits of Marc Antony, who, given his persona,

Fig. 24.34 Portrait head of Julius Caesar, Museo Archeologico, Turin. Courtesy of Deutsches Archäologisches Institut, Rom; DAI Rome neg. 74.1565

might have been expected to use an elevating, Hellenistic image, are almost ruthlessly rendered (he is shown with a toothless jaw). Julius Caesar, ironically, has a particularly mundane, "dry" portrait, known from coins and a head in Turin (Figure 24.34).[137] Considering his unprecedented personal power as dictator, Caesar may have chosen to portray himself in as traditional a mode as possible precisely to temper his actual radical position. During the late republican period portrait statues of elite Romans began for the first time to combine realistic-looking, middle-aged heads with naked or semi-nude youthful, heroic bodies – a non-Greek practice and an incongruity to the modern eye.[138] The statue body was a symbolic means of conveying military prowess, one of the most important qualities that a Roman of this period could possess.

What accounts for the visual differences between Greek and Roman portraiture? Greek portraits of generals, orators, politicians, and philosophers of the Classical and Hellenistic period had included realistic elements: e.g., Themistocles (fifth century),[139] Demosthenes (fourth century),[140] and a series of bearded and younger aristocrats, e.g., in the museum at Kos (second century).[141] But all of these have certain elevating features, which most republican portraits lack. There is a debate about where and why the republican portrait style originated (see also Chapter 4). One view holds that realistic portraiture was already a minority option in Greece, and that Romans adopted and heightened it when they needed to differentiate themselves from Greeks; another idea is that the Roman portrait style of heightened realism was adopted – in part – in reaction to the youthful, dynamic portraits of Hellenistic kings.[142] A further supposition is that Roman portraiture of the second century was a realistic one, but under Greek influence certain elevating devices were now included; the exaggeratedly realistic-looking portraiture, which we think of as "veristic," crystallized only in the first century.[143] These interpretations will have to be rethought to an extent because of an article that discusses a series of recently excavated neck pendants (*bullae*) from Delos and a Roman administrative building at Kedesh, in southern Phoenicia, which have "veristic" portrait busts on them and names inscribed in Latin (as yet unpublished).[144] The *bullae* from Kedesh are securely dated to the first half of the second century and therefore suggest that "veristic" portraiture may have already begun to have been used regularly in Rome at least as early.

The Kedesh material would support the traditional view that the heightened style of realism in republican portraiture was connected with the long-standing Roman custom of making painted wax masks, highly realistic in appearance (Pliny *HN* 35.5; Polyb. 6.53.5–8). This practice may have begun during the fourth century, which first saw open competition between aristocrats. The masks were kept in cupboards in the atrium and worn by the men of the household during funeral processions. These were not "death masks" (masks molded on the face of a cadaver) but were crafted during the person's lifetime. It is not clear if they were sculpted by eye or were made by actually molding wax to the face (the former seems more probable). The ancient sources tell us exactly for what these masks were intended. During the funeral procession they advertised the family's illustrious lineage; viewed in the atrium they provided a constant reminder to the younger men of the great military deeds of their ancestors, which needed to be emulated (see Chapters 4, 16, 17, and 23).[145]

Why are republican portraits so minutely differentiated in terms of physiognomic detail? Until the civil wars and chaos of the late second/first centuries, Roman society was characterized by a degree of conformism and checks and balances in government designed to keep any one individual from gaining too much power. The consulship was limited in duration. Victorious generals could celebrate their victories in chariots dressed as kings, but only for one or a few days at most. A law of 180 made it illegal for any man to hold the consulship if he was under 42,[146] and Romans could not hold any office (even the quaestorship) unless they had served ten years in the Roman army (Polyb. 6.19.5).[147]

It is for these reasons that republican portraiture has a formulaic severity and conformist quality to it – because one was expected to look middle-aged and experienced in one's portrait. Within that relatively confined template, however, each portrait needed to compete for the viewer's attention in the context of the closely packed honorific statues in the Forum, and especially the crowded displays of the ancestor portraits in the atrium house.[148] The most practical means to achieve this was to add minutely specific physiognomic details (facial peculiarities and asymmetries, individualized noses, warts, etc.). This can be seen as a direct visual analog to practices of Roman nomenclature. Many Greek names have to do with deities (Demetrios – belonging to Demeter) or virtues (Chrysostomos – golden-tongued).

By contrast, Romans had supplemental names often descriptive in physiognomic terms: *Nasica* (large-nosed), *Barbatus* (bearded), *Pulcher* (handsome), *Strabo* (one who squints; see also Chapter 21).[149] These functioned to differentiate specific individuals from other family members who had exactly the same name, e.g., Q. Fabius Maximus: the most famous member of this large family was *Q. Fabius Maximus Verrucosus* ("Warty") *Cunctator* ("Delayer," a reference to his battle tactics with Hannibal). The best explanation for the heightened realism and eerie effect of immediate presence in republican portraiture is the particularly Roman need to compete for personal and military reputation, which was constrained into collective expectations of equal power-sharing. This portraiture is a singular historical phenomenon and one of the most compelling art forms of any period.

Guide to Further Reading

While several thematically organized and thought-provoking introductions to Roman Republican art do exist in English (D'Ambra 1998; Beard and Henderson 2001; Kuttner 2004), they tend either to be brief, to exclude architecture, or to require prior knowledge of this complicated field of art (for which a solid understanding of chronology is critical). The best survey in English so far is Stewart 2004 (see also his stimulating book of 2003 on Roman statues), which – while pithy and focused more on the imperial period – is solid and theoretically informed.

Some seminal European works on art of the Republic have now been translated into English (Zanker 1988, 1998; Hölscher 2004; Adam 1994). Meanwhile, many important books and articles by scholars active in America and Britain that deal with republican subjects have appeared, e.g., Clarke 2003; Gruen 1992; Kuttner 1993; Smith 1988, 1991; Wiseman 1987a; Wallace-Hadrill 1994; Terrenato 2001b. A number of edited volumes contain important material: Hofter 1988 (in German); De Grummond and Ridgway 1996; Torelli 1999; Gazda 2002 (all in English). Two older but still important works in German should also be mentioned: Zanker 1976b and Hölscher 1978. F. Coarelli's prolific work on republican art, architecture, and topography is regularly groundbreaking and should be read by the advanced Roman student. Note especially Coarelli 1996a (in Italian – a selection of his essays) and (in English) 1977 and 1998, which give an idea of his skillful interdisciplinary method, combining art and archaeology. For some very recent publications on Roman art in general and reflections on the current state of the field, see Elsner 2004; Kampen 2003; and Brilliant 1998 (all in English).

For iconography (figures in statues, painting, etc.) there is the indispensable *Lexicon Iconographicum Mythologiae Classicae* (*LIMC*). For sculpture ("ideal" and portrait) see Hallett 1995, 2005; Rose forthcoming). For the city of Rome see Chapters 4 and 16 above, with their Guides to Further Reading. On the historiography of Roman art, see Brendel 1979 and especially Elsner's introduction in Hölscher 2004. For architecture: Boëthius 1978 and Anderson 1997. For more technical aspects of architectural planning and building technique, see Adam 1994;

Jones 2000; Taylor 2003. The advanced student should read Gros 1978 and Gros 1996–2001 (in French), as well as Vitruvius in Gros, Corso, and Romano 1997. For Roman relief, see Torelli 1982; Holliday 2002; and Ryberg 1955. T. Hölscher is now working on a substantial survey of Roman relief sculpture (in German). On mosaics, see the comprehensive Dunbabin 1999. For painting see Ling 1991 (a basic survey) and various articles by Bergmann (1995, 2001), which are particularly evocative and engaging. On tombs see Toynbee 1971; Hesberg 1992; and Petersen 2003. On current archaeological exploration see Patterson 1992b and Curti, Dench, and Patterson 1996. Finally, for coins (see also Chapter 3), see the exhaustive study of Crawford 1974, who is masterful on historical aspects, less so on art-historical ones; also Hölscher 1982 (in German). For the art historian, much remains to be done on the iconography of republican coins; in fact, that field is a potential gold mine for new ideas.

Readers should also review the Guide to Further Reading for Chapter 4 for further pertinent bibliographical suggestions.

Notes

1   See Brendel 1979; Hölscher 2004 (introduction by J. Elsner).
2   On the interconnectedness of style, subject matter, and display context in Roman art: esp. Hölscher 1984, 2004.
3   E.g., Zanker 1974; Gazda 2002.
4   For the method, e.g., Coarelli 1996a.
5   Anderson 1997: 3–67; Toynbee 1951.
6   Coarelli 1978; Gullini 1973.
7   Pollitt 1986: figs. 245–246.
8   Best recent discussion: N. Purcell in Steinby 1993–2000: 2. 325–6.
9   Hölscher 1978, 1980a.
10 Cf. Zanker 1988: fig. 32.
11 Hölscher 1978: 338–44, 1984: 12–14; Sehlmeyer 1999: 40–60, 117–20.
12 E.g., Sen. *de Brev. Vit.* 13.3; Pliny *HN* 8.16; Welch forthcoming a; *ludi*: Bernstein 1998.
13 For the different types of gladiator, Junkelmann 2000.
14 Welch 1994, forthcoming a.
15 Rawson 1990: 158–73; Wiseman 1987a: 394–5.
16 Fentress and Rabinowitz 1996; Fentress 2000: 18–20; Livy (26.27.3) calls the Forum houses "*privata aedificia.*"
17 Wallace-Hadrill 1994: 5; Flower 1996: 188.
18 For an even earlier basilica in the Forum, Duckworth 1955; Welch 2003.
19 Fentress 2000; Torelli 1999.
20 Ziolkowski 1992; Shatzman 1972. Cf. Orlin 1997, arguing that such temples were state-sponsored. See also chapter 10.
21 Athena presenting Herakles on Olympus: Bertoletti, Cima, and Talamo 1997: fig. 1.1a.
23 Ioppolo 1963–4: figs. 7, 19, 26; cf. Pliny *HN* 34.23–4.
24 Cf. Brown 1980: figs. 60, 68.
25 Coarelli 1988c: 104, Figure 20.

26 Coarelli 1968.
27 Coarelli 1997: 452–84, figs. 112–114.
28 Coarelli 1997: 529–38, fig. 132.
29 Cf. Coarelli 1997: fig. 132 (Temple of Jupiter Stator) to fig. 130 (Asclepieion at Messene).
30 Polykles: Coarelli 1996a: esp. 67–84; Hercules Olivarius: Coarelli 1988c: 98–100, 181–204, fig. 100.
31 Ziolkowski 1992.
32 Seiler 1986: 89–103, fig. 39.
33 The first generation to have been tutored specifically about Greek art: Plut. *Aem.* 6.4–5.
34 Head of colossal cult statue: Cimino and Nota Santi 1998: 84.
35 Catulus may have repaved the whole area in travertine and surrounded it with a portico: Coarelli et al. 1981.
36 See McDonnell 2006. On Catulus as author and translator of Greek poetry: Bardon 1950.
37 Kleiner 1985: 14–19; De Maria 1988: 31–7.
38 Calabi Limentani 1982.
39 Deities: Kähler 1939: 377–8; Spano 1950; Kleiner 1985: 16; De Maria 1988. Portrait statues: Coarelli 1972: 71.
40 E.g., Kleiner 1985: 88, fig. 67.
41 Wallace-Hadrill 1990.
42 E.g., Hopkins 1983a: 230 (common epitaph).
43 Hesberg 1992; Hesberg and Zanker 1987; Toynbee 1971.
44 Purcell 1987.
45 Coarelli 1996a: 179–238, figs. 58, 65; Flower 1996: 160–80.
46 Udell 2004.
47 Bonifacio 1997: 57–80. Zanker 1975, 1992.
48 Bianchi Bandinelli 1970: 51–105. See Petersen 2003.
49 Zimmer 1982.
50 Coarelli 1997: 539–80, figs. 135, 136, 140.
51 Beacham 1991: 56–85; Gruen 1992: 183–222. Cf. earlier Dörpfeld 1896: 386–96; Bieber 1961: 333–45; Lawrence 1983: 372 and n.9.
52 Goldberg 1998.
53 Klar forthcoming. Also Manuwald 2001.
54 Gruen 1992: 206–10; Coleman 2000: 219–21.
55 Gruen, 1992: 209–10.
56 Welch 1997.
57 Ciancio Rossetto and Pisani Sartorio 1994: II, 534–6.
58 Coarelli 1971–2; Kuttner 1999.
59 Carandini 1990a, 1990b. For the general visual milieu: Cristofani 1990; Proietti 1980; Pairault Massa 1992; Torelli 2000.
60 Statistics: Royo 1999: 52–117, esp. 116–17.
61 Gros 1996–2001: 2. 36–8, figs. 21, 22; 74–5, figs. 64, 65.
62 Coarelli 1996a: 344–59; Silver Wedding: Pugliese Carratelli 1990: 4.449–69; Richardson 1988: 154, 159. Sallust: Laidlaw 1993. Recent excavations have suggested that the garden area (*hortus*) of the House of Sallust may have been smaller and more confined to the back of the house than the published plans show, but this is as yet not clear.
63 Nappo 1997; Fentress 2000; Bruno and Scott 1993.
64 Welch 2003: 17 with n.50; Wallace-Hadrill 1991. Faun: Richardson 1988: 115–17.

65   Gros 1996–2001: 2.279–84, figs. 302–307.
66   See, e.g., Terrenato 2001b; Gros 1996–2001: 2.265–75; Lauter 1998; Mielsch 1987: 37–9; D'Arms 1970: 10–11; Grimal 1969: 21–4.
67   *Contra*, Zanker 1998: 136–42, esp. 136, n.4.
68   Steinby 1993–2000: 4.281–5; Bodel 1997: 5–35, esp. 6, n.7.
69   Häuber 1998.
70   Plut. *Luc.* 39.2; Cic. *Sest.* 98; Plut. *Sulla* 31.4; Zanker 1998; 141; Wallace-Hadrill 1998.
71   Lucullus had a family connection in the Sullan colonization of Praeneste, which could in part account for the architectural innovation: Coarelli 1996a: 327–38.
72   See Smith 1991: 14–17, 128, 258–61; Zanker 1974; Wünsche 1972; Preisshofen and Zanker 1970–1; Gazda 2002.
73   Smith 1991: 110–11, figs. 144–147.
74   Polyb. 9.10, 6.10; Livy 25.49.1–2, 26.21.7–9, 34.4.1–5; Plut. *Marc.* 21.1–2, 21.4–5. See McDonnell forthcoming.
75   Strong 1973; Pollitt 1978.
76   Pietilä-Castrén 1987; Aberson 1994; Orlin 1997: 122–7.
77   Polyb. 31.25.6–8, 9.10.12–13; Cic. *Rep.* 1.21. Welch forthcoming b.
78   De Staebler 2004; Neudecker 1988: 105–14.
79   Zanker 1979, 1998: 141–74. Cf. the first-century shipwrecks: Fuchs 1963; Hellenkemper Salies 1994; Bol 1972.
80   Harward 1982.
81   See Cicero's letters: *Att.* 1.1–3; 1.3–4; 1.4–4; 1.5–6; 1.6–7; 1.8; 1.9–10; 1.11–12.
82   Livy 39.5.13–17; Polyb. 21.30.9; Livy 34.52.4–5; Plut. *Aem.* 32–4; esp. Cic. *Verr.* 2.57. Cf. Ath. 5.197C–203B.
83   Herodas *Mime* 4.26–40; Paus. 5.16; Pliny *HN* 34.49–83.
84   *ILLRP* 322 (= *ROL* 4: 79 no. 67), with 218, 295, 321, 326, 326, 328. Bloy 1998–9.
85   Fab. Pict. frg. 18; Rawson 1990: 163. See Livy 38.43.3–10; Hölscher 1980b: 355–6, n.33.
86   Pape 1975: 56–65, 96–9; Künzl 1988: 109–13; Waurick 1975: esp. 36–40; Welch forthcoming b. *Contra*, Gruen 1992: 84–130.
87   Exactly when and why the "copying industry" began is controversial. The earliest known precise replica is the Diadoumenos from a Roman house on Delos (late second century: Stewart 1990: pls. 383–385). See Bieber 1974; Ridgway 1984: esp. 5–30, 2002; Niemeier 1985; Marvin 1989; Smith 1991: 258–61; Hallett 1995; Fullerton 1998; Fuchs 1999; Gazda 2002.
88   References in Stewart 1990: 230, 306–10.
89   Stewart 1990: pls. 847–851, 860–861.
90   Wünsche 1972; Zanker 1974; Pollitt 1986: 169–84.
91   Bertoletti, Cima, and Talamo 1997: 42–3; Hölscher 1978: 346–8, 1980a: 270–1; *Roma Medio Repubblicana* 200–8; Holliday 2002: 83–91.
92   That artists could work in an elevated, Classical style, when Greek models were available, is shown by the Praenestine cists (Bordenache Battaglia 1990) and tomb paintings from Paestum (Pontrandolfo and Rouveret 1992; and from Nola, as yet unpublished).
93   Bömer 1953. Caesar's are the most famous, but there is a fragment of one by Trajan. The "Esquiline Historical Fragment" has been seen as an antecedent for the Column of Trajan, with army scenes arranged in continuous narrative in horizontal registers. Other modes of triumphal painting, providing geographical and topographical detail, are clearly Greek in inspiration: Hölscher 1980b: 352–3, 2004: 38 n.2; Holliday 2002: 80–2.
94   See Strocka 1996: IV, 414–25 *s.v. Pompeiani, Stili*.

95   Laidlaw 1985.

96   Coarelli 1996b.

97   House of the Comedians, Delos: Bruneau 1970: fig. 110.

98   Fittschen 1976: 541; Charatzopoulou 2000: 43–9; Petsas 1966; Bruno 1985: 55–9;
      Lehmann 1979: 223–9.

99   Rizzo 1936; Ling 1991: 23–4. But see Tybout 2001: 55 n.12; Strocka 1996: IV, *sv.*
      Pompeiani, Stili.

100   Tybout 1989, 2001; Bergmann 2001.

101   Fittschen 1976.

102   Smith 1994. The effect in this case is thought to mimic Greek picture galleries, or
      perhaps ones in Rome's manubial temples; e.g., Pliny *HN* 35.49.173. Bergmann
      1995: 90; Isager 1991: 157–67.

103   Coarelli 1998; cf. Biering 1995, who dates the paintings later.

104   Blanckenhagen 1963.

105   Dunbabin 1999.

106   Pollitt 1986: 222–3, fig. 236; Beard and Henderson 2001: 13–23, fig. P. 19.

107   Dunbabin 1999: 40–3, fig. 41; Cohen 1997; Gros 1996–2001: 2, fig. 34.

108   Dunbabin 1999: 39–40, figs. 40, 53.

109   Colini and Cozza 1962, color pl.

110   Pollitt 1986: 205–8, figs. 221, 222; Dunbabin 1999: 49–52, fig. 47.

112   Ferrea 2002; Kleiner 1992: 52–4.

113   E.g., Stewart 1990: pls. 692–711 (Great Altar at Pergamon). In Greek panel painting
      and statuary displays, at least, there may have been more specificity, e.g., in the case of the
      Alexander mosaic, which carefully differentiates Greeks and Persians by dress and armor;
      and the Granikos group by Lysippos depicting Alexander and his companions on
      horseback (Vell. Pat. 1.11.3–4; Pliny *HN* 34.64). See also Smith 1991: 184–5, fig.
      207.2 (Temple of Hekate at Lagina).

114   Pollitt 1986: 155–8, figs. 162–4; Holliday 2002: 91–6.

115   Smith 1991: 184, figs. 205.1–2.

116   Kleiner 1992: 49–51, figs. 130, 131; Torelli 1982: 5–25; Stewart 1990: 843–6; cf.
      Holliday 2002: 161–73.

117   Kuttner 1993: 198–239; Coarelli 1997: 397–446, figs. 109–110.

118   Hölscher 1980b; Schäfer 1979; Kleiner 1992: 51–2.

119   E.g., Crawford 1974: no. 452, 2.

120   Compare the artful jumble of spoils on the frieze in the precinct surrounding the Temple
      of Athena Nike at Pergamon: Lawrence 1983: fig. 241.

121   Hölscher 1982, 1984: 12–16; generally Crawford 1974.

122   Crawford 1974: no. 35.

123   Holland 1961.

124   Beard, North, and Price 1998: 1–2.

125   Cf. Crawford 1974: no. 281 (Roma), no. 401 (Virtus).

126   Crawford 1974: 728; *contra*, Meadows and Williams 2001: 37–49.

127   Crawford 1974: nos. 289, 1; 326, 2; 326, 1 and 2; 427, 1; 295, no 286.

128   Crawford 1974: no. 335:9. Hölscher 1984: 13.

129   Hölscher 1980b: 272–3, 1982, 1984: 12–16, forthcoming; Backendorf 1998.

130   Rose forthcoming collects most of the (vast) bibliography on this subject.

131   Giuliani 1986: 175–89, fig. 48; review Smith, *Gnomon* 60 (1988): 761–3.

132   Smith 1991: fig. 318.

133   *Roma Medio Repubblicana*: pls. 625, 626.
134   See, e.g., Denti 1991; Bonifacio 1997: 57–80, pls. 14, 15.
135   E.g., Toynbee 1978: 21–5, figs 1, 8; Vessberg 1941: 40–6, 71–9, 173–231; Crawford 1974: nos. 749–750; Sehlmeyer 1999: 178–85.
136   Toynbee 1978: 24–8, figs. 16, 17; Smith 1988: generally 128–30, 136–7; cf. Giuliani 1986: 67–93.
137   Toynbee 1978: 41–8.
138   E.g., Smith 1991: figs. 315, 319; Himmelmann 1989: 100–25, figs. 46–50; Hallett forthcoming.
139   Stewart 1990: pls. 232–233.
140   Smith 1991: fig. 39.
141   Kabus-Preisshofen 1989: pls. 16, 44, 46, 47, 54.
142   Zanker 1976a; Smith 1988: 128–30.
143   Giuliani 1986: 239–45.
144   Rose forthcoming.
145   Polyb. 6.53.1–10; Pliny *HN* 35.6–8; Cic. *Phil.* 2.26; Pliny *Ep.* 3.6.
146   Astin 1958.
147   Harris 1979: 12.
148   Pliny *HN* 34.30; Flower 1996: 186–203.
149   Kajanto 1965.

CHAPTER 25

Literature

William W. Batstone

Introduction

In the early years of Augustus' rule, the Roman historian Livy told the following story of Rome's early growth:

> Meanwhile, the city was expanding with its fortifications by adding place after place... Then, Romulus deployed a plan used by the founders of cities for increasing the population: they gather to themselves an obscure and impoverished band and pretend that the earth has produced autochthonous offspring for them. So, he opened a sanctuary in a place enclosed between two groves as you ascend the Capitoline. Rabble from the surrounding peoples fled to this place, all without distinction as to whether they were free or slaves, but eager for a change in circumstances. This was the first source of strength for the greatness that had begun. (Livy 1.8.4–6).

Roman identity even at its origins is not a natural state, but rather a naturalized status. The Romans are not an autochthonous or essentialized people (see also Chapter 22). Their city was named for Romulus, an Alban, a shepherd, and a murderer. In fact, in Livy's story, the early Romans are not even all free men. The story suggests that Roman identity is not to be reduced to the normative claims that the Romans made about themselves. Those claims, like the claim of autochthony, reflect political ambitions, moral posturing, and power plays. They are but the pretense of unity behind which the complex process of identity formation takes place. But Livy's story tells us something else as well. Rome is the place which recognizes its hybridity and pretense, and where the naturalization of foreigners is as close as we get to Roman identity. That process, the process of involving foreigners in the common interests of fellow Roman citizens, is at the root of our notion of "civilizing" someone.

In this chapter I shall look at some of the ways in which Roman literature of the Republic participated in the processes of identity formation. For the most part Roman literary identity entails imitating, appropriating, and assimilating Greek achievements. It is a process of "translation," for which the Roman term, *vertere*, means "to turn, twist, transform." The term suggests that what is translated is both changed and given a new direction. Roman literature turned Greek achievements toward Roman concerns while it turned Greek concepts into Graeco-Latin concepts and turned the Greek forms into the Latin achievements. And the process had surplus benefits. It not only found a language in which to speak about Roman ambitions and desires but required that the Romans come to know themselves through the imitation and understanding of others. It required seeing the Greek achievement as something Roman, or potentially Roman, and behind that intuition lie certain assumptions about common interests and desires. Such an intuition requires both empathy (to understand how someone else sees the world) and duplicity (to place oneself in the other's position without confusing that position with one's own interests). It requires both the ability to represent others and to see all such representations, even the representation of one's self, as a rhetorical ploy in the games for power and position that take place in the Forum. And, perhaps most importantly, it is a process that changes the Roman as much as it changes the culture it appropriates. The Graeco-Roman literary culture that Rome created was formed by the imitation, appropriation, and assimilation of Greek forms into new Graeco-Roman forms.

The process of "turning, twisting, and transforming" which translates literature is central to Roman identity in other ways. It may refer to how one is "turned out" or to the way we turn ourselves into good and moral beings or into false friends. It is also the basic idea behind our literary term, "trope" (from the Greek for "turning"), a figure of speech or of thought, a way of turning language so that it means something more or different than its literal or common meaning. Just as Roman literary identity is deeply involved in the "turning" which constitutes translation, so social, political, and even personal identity is implicated in processes of transformation and troping – ways of negotiating the world through rhetoric and pretense and of understanding the self and others through metaphor and metonymy.

This aggressive, acquisitive project that turns Greek achievements into Roman possessions also keeps turning Romans into some new hybridity that continues to disclose what is Roman. Thus, Romanness in the Republic is not to be confused with the political posturing of its orators. It is not even some compound of influences. It is the process by which the contestants compete simultaneously for personal influence and for their own symbolic and rhetorical definitions of Rome. This process entails the continuous troping of oneself and others in a contest for self-definition and self-aggrandizement. But what makes this process "Roman," other than the vigor, success, and self-consciousness with which it is carried out, is the alignment of self-aggrandizement with the larger aggrandizement of Rome. The cultural project of Rome, like Western civilization itself, is in this way always aligned with power, and its operations may be ameliorative, or violent, or both.

Beginnings

Roman literature began in 240 when Livius Andronicus, a Greek slave from southern Italy, turned a Greek play into Latin for the celebration of Rome's victory over Carthage in the First Punic War.[1] Among the many oddities of this story is the fact that we can put a date on the beginning of Roman literature. Other languages have their earliest poems; Roman literature has a beginning. And this beginning is precisely a multicultural moment of translation and transformation, one that believes in both the value of another national literature and the value of Roman participation in that cultural achievement. It was a transformation, however, that would change Roman festivals and the Latin language as well as the Greek traditions Livius translated.

Livius came to Rome as a prisoner of war. He was an actor who produced tragedies and comedies and wrote hymns; he was a tutor, who translated the *Odyssey* for his students. The fragments we have of this translation show that it was not merely a trot for reading Greek. The meter is the Saturnian – a name that suggests an Italic origin, although the current consensus is that even this meter is the result of the influence of Greek culture on Rome from the sixth century on. Whatever its origin, the adaptation of Greek epic meter into Latin Saturnian meter is an attempt to naturalize the cultural value of Homer. Similarly, the Greek "Muse" that Homer invokes in the first line of his poem becomes the Latin rustic deity, Camena, one of the Roman fountain goddesses. Perhaps an odd choice until one realizes that in the tradition of poets and fountains, poets drank from fountains that defined their inspiration; Livius drinks from Italian fountains. His line replaces the varied elegance of Homer's diction with archaic Latin alliteration. The hero, Odysseus, who in Homer is *polutropos*, "a man of many turns," is in Andronicus *versutus*, likewise "twisty," but with two additional implications: one, moral, which is to say that the Roman translation imports a potentially pejorative perspective on the hero;[2] and the other literary, that is, in Andronicus when Odysseus is "translated" as *versutus*, he is made into *versus*, and so becomes "well-versed or well-turned." In Andronicus' translation, "the well-versed Ulysses" traveling westward across the Mediterranean (a hero who in some legends traveled with Aeneas and helped to found Latin cities; see also Chapter 22) becomes (at least potentially) a trope for translation and cultural acquisition.

Livius Andronicus set in motion a process that was at once appropriative and transformative. He adds patronymics: Kalypso becomes "the nymph, Calypso, daughter of Atlas" and the Muse becomes "the divine daughter of Admonition." "The baneful destiny of death" is reimagined within Roman divination and religion as "the day which Fatality foretold." Andronicus does not just translate Homeric ideas; he Romanizes them. As the Greek slave made the Homeric achievement accessible in Latin and made Latin permeable to Greek ideas, he turned himself into a Roman and invented Roman literature.

Soon, Naevius, an Italian born near Capua, would rework and expand these techniques to create a cultural and literary idiom that was at once Greek and Roman: his *Bellum Poenicum* was both the historical account of the First Punic War and a literary epic with the machinery of Greek mythology. But what is most remarkable about Naevius' world is that Naevius himself took part in this war: Naevius, then, tells a story of himself that takes place in a hybrid world that exists only in his literary imagination. It is rather like the shield he describes: "Upon it were engraved images, like the Titans, /the Giants with double bodies, the great Atlases, /Grubber and Purple, the sons of Earth" (*Pun.* 19) In this world, identity is the process of assimilation and appropriation. Naevius is not the man who fought the Carthaginians in the First Punic War, but the cultural assimilator who could see that war in terms of Homer's *Iliad* and Achilles' shield.

But the assimilation of Greek culture that was taking place during the third and second centuries was not unproblematic.[3] Roman grammarians adopted Greek terms to describe their language and their rhetoric. Roman aristocrats learned Greek and they called those who did not speak Greek or Latin "barbarians" (from *barbaros*, Greek for those who did not speak Greek). But they mocked Greek intellectualism, contemned Greek manners, plundered Greek cities, labeled political enemies "Little Greeks" (*Graeculi*), and felt that it was a political disadvantage even to appear to speak Greek. While they complained about the paucity of their vocabulary, they were consistently eliminating what was inelegant, superfluous, and inefficient from it.[4] In a field of responses as charged and contradictory as this, it is clear that none of the positions taken says anything comprehensive about what was happening to Roman identity. The process was so highly charged precisely because Roman culture was defining itself in terms of Greek culture (see also Chapter 22).

Resistance to this Hellenization is exemplified by Cato, a wealthy farmer born in Tusculum in 234, 15 miles south of Rome, and a vocal anti-Hellene. In 204 as military tribune he met Ennius, an intellectual born in 239 in Calabria – a place where Oscan, Greek, and Latin culture intersected – and serving in the Roman army. He brought Ennius to Rome. Both men found themselves at the center of complex efforts to wrestle with (or deploy for political gain) what it meant to be Roman. Cato, a new man to the Roman political scene, staked his future on a conservative stand toward both politics and literature and became a vocal anti-Hellene. He wrote a prose history of Rome in which the actions of Roman generals were always cast as the actions of the state and its officers, not the achievements of individuals (see also Chapter 2). This emphasis on the Roman state and its offices, however, was not without its rhetorical and literary posturing: Cato called his history the *Origines*, or "The Origins," a title that espoused on its surface a conservative stance, while it translated into Latin the title of one of the most influential of Greek poems, Callimachus' *Aetia*, a clever, learned, and elitist poem on Greek mythology and human psychology. Thus, even Cato's anti-Hellenic posturing was deployed in Hellenic terms. But if Cato was saying to the cultural elite that the true Roman response to the sophisticated learning of Callimachus' *Aetia* was his Roman *Origines*, Ennius took up the challenge. He wrote an epic poem, one that began the long process of adapting the Greek hexameter to Latin norms. He borrowed heavily from both Homer, Callimachus, and the tragedians. Then he titled his Callimachean–Homeric epic *Annales* after the annual records of Roman history kept by priests.

Both the conservative and the innovator are engaged in a contest for what Rome will mean and how its history will be written by appropriating and deploying the cultural cache of both Rome and Greece: Cato writes a radically conservative, moralistic history and gives it a neo-Callimachean title, while Ennius writes a neo-Callimachean epic and gives it a conservative Roman title. Rome was defining itself with and against the cultural prestige of Greece to such an extent that neither Cato nor Ennius could position themselves in the Roman cultural debate without positioning themselves in terms of Greece. And it is, of course, no surprise that Cato himself, despite his staunch opposition to Hellenistic excesses, was well versed in Greek, employed Ennius as a Greek tutor for his children, studied Pythagorean philosophy and wrote on rhetoric.[5]

Ennius' poem became the national epic of Rome, until it was supplanted by Virgil's *Aeneid*. In addition to negotiating a Graeco-Roman identity and extending the tradition that began with Livius Andronicus and Naevius, it took an aggressive stance toward the literature it assimilated. Two examples will show the degree of appropriation and suggest the energies that it required. First, Ennius had to adapt the Greek hexameter to the Latin language. This was no easy task. On the one hand, the Greek language was qualitative, creating metrical effects out of the length (not the accent) of syllables; it had formulaic phrases that, among other things, could bring the hexameter to a close; and it was well furnished with short syllables which kept the verse light and swift. Latin, on the other hand, had (by comparison) too many long syllables, no tradition of formulaic epic verse, and a stress accent that could create tedious sing-song effects when syllabic stress coincided with the long (qualitative) syllable of the verse. To make the Greek hexameter work in Latin, Ennius had to invent (or apply) new aesthetic principles: he changed the pause that divided the line; he created tensions between the pulse of the hexameter and the stress accents of prose pronunciation; he developed patterns of conflict and resolution that moved the verse forward while emphasizing its dactylic rhythm in every cadence.[6] Line after line of Ennius is already applying the principles that will shape the stately measure of Virgil's verse – a verse that is simultaneously Greek and indelibly Latin. After Ennius, the Latin hexameter was the established form, and no one again attempted to write a long poem in Saturnians.

Second, he undertook a work that was simultaneously historiographical and epic. Beginning with the fall of Troy and the regal period, he continued his epic down to his present. This is unique: we have poems that are foundation epics and chronicles of peoples, poems that sing the praises of kings, but we know of no prior poetic history of a nation from its origins to the present. The *Iliad*, by way of contrast, takes place over roughly a two-week period. Ennius' expansion clearly reflects upon his own ambitions. But, when we recall that he was Messapian by birth, Oscan by family connection, Greek by education, and Roman by military service, one cannot ignore the extraordinary global ambitions of this epic and Roman project. Ennius, a Calabrian who became a Roman, continued the cultural acquisition of Greece by joining his ambitions to the aggrandizement of Rome as he turned national history into epic.

Ennius was proud of his assimilation of Greek culture. Near the beginning of his epic, he records that Homer came to him and told him that he was "Homer reborn." The dream is itself an echo of a Hesiodic dream told in Callimachean fashion. And, for his position as poet, he rejected the Roman term, *vates*, and preferred the Greek term, *poeta*. But when he came to write his epitaph, it was resoundingly Roman: "Behold, *my fellow-citizens*, the image that recalls the old man Ennius; /He composed the greatest deeds of *your* fore-fathers" (*Epig.* 1). Here, a citizen addresses fellow-citizens while remaining fully conscious of his naturalized status ("*your* fore-fathers"). One might even say that his status as Roman depends as much upon his naturalization as it does upon his ability to represent for Romans their history as Romans (see also Chapter 28).

Shortly after Cato and Ennius had imagined Romanness as deeply engaged with the assimilation and appropriation of Greek values and culture, Mummius sacked and wasted Corinth, bringing to Rome what he could of those extravagant and luxurious Greek treasures (see also Chapter 24) – a reminder that appropriation is not always generous nor assimilation respectful.

Roman Comedy

The Roman Comedy known as *palliata* consists of "translations" of Greek plays for the Roman audience of the second century. Its most popular playwright was Plautus, an Umbrian born in the mid-third century, who is said to have died in 184. Twice he refers to his art of translation as "a barbarian transformation" (*As.* 11, *Trin.* 19) and here we will be interested in what that ironic self-description means and entails.[7] His drama takes place in a hybrid world of Greek cities, Latin puns, Roman morals, and a mixture of Greek and Roman institutions. Nevertheless, there is little agreement about what makes his plays Roman. At the level of style, it is easy to speak of his exuberant energies: drama marked by wordplay and metrical variety, by song, and farce, and set pieces like the "running slave" and the "overheard plot." Throughout there is a "metatheatrical" awareness on the part of the characters that they are characters in a play. All of these elements, however, except the lyric aria, can be found to some degree in Greek plays he translated. What, then, is Roman about Plautine comedy? And what version of Roman identity does this hybrid genre present?

An early play, *The Swaggering Soldier*, provides some clues. Plautus tells us that it is a translation of a Greek play, *The Braggart*, and we can note that already in the title Plautus has turned the emphasis from social morality to individual character. Furthermore, in the Plautus play braggadocio is hardly a fault in itself, since it characterizes the clever slave who runs the show. Further, the soldier with his pretentious name, Pyrgopolynices ("Victor MultiTowers"), or his opponent, Bumbomachides Clutomistharnikarchides ("McMercenaryFameKing, son of BoomBattle"), may easily remind the audience of both arrogant Greek mercenaries and the self-important Roman aristocracy with names like Publius Cornelius Scipio Aemilianus Africanus Numantinus. What this suggests is that Plautus has turned his attention away from the moral concerns of Greek comedy toward the psychological problem of self-importance. And when in the course of the plot the clever slave convinces the swaggering soldier that he is an "adulterer," we may see that the drama is concerned with how others exploit our self-images. In fact, Plautus offers his own analysis of this concern early in the drama when the slave Palaestrio is about to convince another slave, Sceledrus, that he did not see his master's girl visiting the neighbor. As part of the trick, this girl pretends not to know Sceledrus, which of course confuses the slave. Palaestrio warns: "The trick is, Sceledrus, to discover if we are our own selves or someone else's. Someone of the neighbors may have changed us when we were not looking." And, in fact, this is exactly what happens in the play: Palaestrio turns Sceledrus into a bad slave, Pyrgopolynices into an "adulterer," and himself into a free man. This is the insight of an acquisitive culture with a rhetoricized sense of identity, and in transforming the Greek play Plautus transforms his own audience into characters who know about and laugh at the way the world transforms us whether we are on our guard or not.

Until 1976, we had no means of comparing a Plautine play with its Greek "model." Now, however, we can compare some lines from Plautus' *Bacchides* with the parallel lines from Menander. The comparison reveals much that we already suspected: Plautus invents and expands, disregards the easy ellipses of conventional conversation and replaces them with extended jokes, turns serious melodrama into farce, and so on.[8] But in doing this, Plautus also discovers aspects of interaction that Menander overlooked.

In the scene we have, a young man thinks his friend has betrayed him by taking up with his girlfriend. Menander has the young man speak a few self-absorbed and self-protective strategic lines: the girl's to blame; I'd better return the money to my father; she'll be sorry when I'm broke. Plautus' young man, on the other hand, is confused, filled with hate and love; he tries to develop a strategy, only to collapse in self-contradiction and psychological pratfalls (e.g., "she's not getting the last laugh; I'll go to my father and . . . steal something."). In Menander the young man is strategic and makes a choice; in Plautus, he refuses to choose precisely because he is really pulled between contradictory impulses and desires. Plautus, then, acts as Menander's therapist, revealing and giving expression to the drives and contradictions that Menander suppresses. The young man in Menander represses his anger in his soliloquy, and comes right to the point when the friends meet. Plautus, on the other hand, develops a war-metaphor as the friends circle each other, one thinking the other is his heart's enemy, the other (who has no idea what is going on) merely trying to help a friend in distress. The lover obliquely attacks his friend for the moral decay of the times while the friend sympathizes with the "betrayed lover's" pain and also attacks the moral decay of the times. This is all quite brilliant and funny, but what scholars have missed is that it is not so much a translation, as a strong reading of Menander's social world. Plautus finds in the niceties of that world repressed energies and contradictions as well as opportunities for self-invention and manipulation. Personal pain, commitment, and even morality are deployed in a game for position, a game in which the lover tries to turn his friend into a confessed criminal, while the friend turns himself into the faithful ally. This may be farce, but this farce allows the young men to discover the truth about their friendship (they are both moralists) and the audience to recognize that reality is made from the roles we play, the traps we lay, the tricks we plan.

The Plautine play celebrates the energies and the duplicity required when Rome was possessing and changing the Mediterranean. It celebrates those energies by finding them lurking everywhere: in the psychology of the duped and swindled, in the slippery characters who keep playing out of role, in the outrageous plots and exaggerated arias, but most of all in the way the plays interrupt the action, stop the plot, postpone the final victory just for the chance to play one more time with the psyche and symbolic systems of others. When at the end of *The Swaggering Soldier* Palaestrio can simply walk away to freedom (see also Chapter 14), he prefers to return to the soldier, to flatter him yet again, to run the risk of having the soldier refuse to free him. Why? It seems that the play is not about the nominal freedom of the slave or the recovery of the girlfriend. It is about the pleasure of playing with the symbolic, especially if it changes someone else's world and puts you in control of them. This is real freedom.

The translator, the self-transformer, the betrayer of another are tropes of each other. In Plautus it is only the slave, known as a *versipellis*, or "skin-changer," who can fully manipulate the illusion, but everyone has a stake in it. Everyone eavesdrops on everyone else, becomes the analyst of everyone else's practice – just as Plautus is the analyst of Menander. This requires empathy, the capacity to get within another's psyche, to see how another sees the world, and it requires the capacity to play roles and yet not to confuse oneself with those roles. This is what it meant to be Roman on the Plautine stage, just as it is what it meant to be Roman when Scipio at Utica pretended to an exhausted Syphax that the war had ground to a halt, that it was time for a peace agreement. While the generals met to discuss terms, Scipio's lieutenants dressed shabbily as slaves, scouted the camp, found weaknesses and exits. Then Scipio suddenly and unilaterally broke off negotiations; the camp was torched and few escaped (Polyb. 14.1.1–6.5).

Terence (c.190–159), a comic writer of the next generation, a slave born in Africa, understood the Plautine achievement, but attempted to reinsert the very aspect of Romanness that was always in tension with symbolic manipulation: moral obligation. Thus, his Demea in *The Brothers* is a strict, moralistic, dyspeptic character very much like the grumpy men in Menander. Demea, however, is not finally forced to be sociable – the goal of a comedy of manners. Instead, Terence fashions a Demea who, like the clever slave, knows how to play the role of the "pleasant old man," and to turn the desires and the pretenses of others (including his very pleasant brother Micio's) against them, to make social facility a way to coerce moral rigidity (*severitas*). What is Roman here is not Demea's *severitas* or even the time-honored opposition between "sociability" and "morality." It is rather the distance between character and role which allows Demea to gain the upper hand. For Plautus as well as for Terence, the issue is representation: not who you are so much as how you represent yourself and how others represent you. Plautine comedy celebrates freedom: the freedom of characters from their roles, the freedom of the slave, even the freedom of language to proliferate in figures of speech and thought. Terentian comedy, which in many ways is more like what we know of Greek new comedy, reorients character as the-role-we-play in terms of larger moral issues. In Terence, character becomes part of the rhetoric of virtue.

"Satire is Wholly Roman" – Quintillian

The experience of identity as complicit with but not identical to the roles we adopt is essential to the way Roman identity played out in the late Republic and beyond. This allowed the assimilation and adaptation of Greek forms just as it was encouraged by the various therapeutic philosophies of the Hellenistic period which practiced self-surveillance and self-discipline, and was nourished by the competing demands of self-interest and religious obligation. It is not surprising, then, that *persona* – a term meaning "mask" and the origin of our word "person" – is essential to understanding satire, the one genre that the Romans of the Republic seem to have invented. Nor is it surprising that this genre is both deeply indebted to Greek forms (Stoic and Cynic diatribe, iambic poetry, mock epic, and even Aristophanic comedy) and as hybrid, complex, slippery, and socially adept as the clever slave of comedy. Although the genre includes many moods and *personae* (the angry satirist, the laughing satirist, the self-effacing satirist, the mock-epic satirist), it seems in general to be characterized by the witty attack upon the vices of others, popular moralizing, and autobiography. When characterized in this way, one can see that in many ways it translates the contests of the comic stage into an autobiographical and moralizing mode. To the extent that this mode is directed at others, satire pretends to be part of a moral and social pedagogy; to the extent that it is also directed upon the speaker (upon either his outrage or his foibles), the same genre participates in a kind of ironic self-therapy. In both instances, however, it fixes its aim on the external behaviors and postures by which we invent ourselves and present ourselves to others.

Ennius wrote the first satires, but it was Gaius Lucilius (d. 102), a friend of Scipio Aemilianus, who created the genre we know. We cannot here survey the fragments of the 30 books that he wrote, but we can make two points about his verse. First, he attacked an extraordinary range of targets. Nothing in Roman intellectual, political, or social life seems to be outside his scope: literary bombast, superstition, avarice, hypocrisy, and anger. But the attacks themselves are usually not upon substance, but upon pretensions. Thus, after some stoic moralizing of his own, he makes fun of the pretensions of stoic moralizing. He aims at the masks that others wear:

> Now, in fact, from morning to night, on vacation or at work, the entire population, commons and nobles alike, all of them deploy themselves in the Forum and never cease to give themselves to one and the same pursuit and artifice: to cheat provided that it can be done safely, to fight by duplicitous means, to compete with flattery, to present themselves as "a good man", and to lay traps as if everyone were an enemy to everyone else. (Luc. 1228–34 Marx = *ROL* 3:373, frags. 1145–51)

Satire like this is a diagnosis of Roman society.

The second point to make comes from an observation by Horace, the last satirist of the Republic: He says that Lucilius "would confide his innermost thoughts to his writings, as if they were his trustworthy comrades . . . And so it happens that all of the man's life lies open as if it were painted on a votive tablet" (*Sat.* 2.1.30–4). Horace is here being typically cagey. On the one hand, he describes the scope of Lucilian satire as essentially autobiographical (what he saw, did, and thought) – open, complete, honest. But then he says that it was like the gaudy paintings you find in temples, paintings that tell an exaggerated story of danger, shipwreck, and escape (see also Chapter 24). Horace's analogy points to the potential for self-irony that is implicit in Lucilius' range of personae: preacher, man of the world, buffoon, hurt friend, indignant critic, and philological grammarian. In the hands of Lucilius, then, the satiric tendency of comedy and diatribe begins to move in two directions: both out to the world of fools and pretenders and inward toward the satirist himself, another faker, another "skin-changer."

But it was Horace, born in Venusia in southern Italy in 65, who pulled together the many elements of this skin-changing ironic genre. We will not discuss the range of his satire nor illustrate its many and complex literary virtues, but instead look briefly at how comedic *personae*, social criticism, and autobiographical irony come together in a brilliant version of moral self-improvement. In Satire 1.4 Horace defends himself against charges that as a satirist he is a public nuisance who attacks anyone and whom everyone hates. In his defense, he claims that his habit of criticism is something he learned from his father. Then he describes his father, walking with him through the Forum, encouraging him to live well by pointing out the vices of others. Horace says that his satire is no more than the continuation of this habit, a minor vice that he learned from his father. He practices self-correction by noting the failures of others, and, only when he has time, does he write it up.

This vignette is both touching and literary. The father Horace describes may or may not be like his own father, but he is an explicit imitation of Demea in the Terence comedy, *The Brothers*. Not the Demea of the play's last act who has learned to pretend to have social graces, but the Demea we see in the middle of the play glorying in his success as moral pedagogue for his son while wholly ignorant of the fact that his son has taken up with a prostitute. As he explains his technique of citing others as moral exempla, the slave mocks and parodies him.

When Horace adopts this figure as the model of his own satiric impulse and then stigmatizes his actions as a "minor vice," we are caught in a complex relationship to the problem of moral pedagogy. Horace blurs the line between objectifying the vices of others and objectifying himself, as he presents the objectification of vices – including the self-importance which allows moral objectification – as both a vice and the way to see our own vices. The moral lesson here seems to be that we need to objectify ourselves, to see the roles we play in society, just as we need to objectify others to make moral progress, and part of this progress entails seeing the objectification itself as pretentious and misinformed. Horace imagines the moral life as an unending tension between the self we present to the world and the self that presents, directs, and deploys itself in the world. Between the two there is always a gap. In Horace that gap may be expressed as the contradiction of trying to bring an end to judgmental stigma by stigmatizing the practice of stigmatizing.

In the final analysis, who we are, that is, being a "Roman" or being a "moral person," is a posture of self-surveillance, a "naturalized" status, a claim on the attention of others, but one that does not confuse role with identity or truth-claims with the truth. This, of course, creates a split or gap at the heart of Romanness, but it is one that allowed Roman literature to explore, if not create, an internal difference which will inform Western ethics and Western psychology right on down to the present day. We are not what we are, we are not a thing, but we are a way of being, an open capacity to assume new roles, endlessly troping ourselves.

National History – Satiric History

Roman historiography begins either with Fabius Pictor, who between 215 and 200 wrote a history of Rome in Greek, or with Cato's *Origines*, a work discussed above in the context of Cato's anti-Hellenism and begun sometime after 170 (see also Chapter 2).[9] Before these men wrote, the sources for Roman history existed primarily in the *Annales*, yearly records kept by the priests and in family traditions and public documents. Fabius and Cato were the first to apply Greek standards of investigation to the source material with an eye to discovering the truth about the past, and they composed a narrative that presented Rome both to itself and to the world. It is typical of Roman identity-formation that we are asked to choose between a work about Rome in Greek addressed to Greeks and a work in Latin by one of the period's most vocal opponents of excessive Greek influence.

By the time Fabius wrote, the Greeks had already taught other nations to write history in Greek and in the Greek manner. But the Greeks did not write their own national history. They remained even in the Hellenistic period a fractious collection of kingdoms, leagues, city-states without any unifying political and cultural identity: a Spartan was not an Athenian. When Fabius wrote, however, a Tuscan or a Sabine or a Latin could be a Roman, and Fabius helped establish the myths that Romans claimed as their own (see also Chapter 22). He standardized the foundation myth of Romulus and Remus. He ordered his material in terms of the Roman chronology of the *Annales*. He recorded customs, ceremonies, and cultural history. While it is easy to understand his decision to use Greek, since he was using Greek methods and Greek sources to address a world whose international culture was Greek, it is also important that the first historical version of Roman identity is itself a kind of translation, not of Greek into Latin, but of Latin experience into Greek, a form of self-objectification. He began the task of seeing Roman history in the light of Greek history and of measuring the Roman past in terms of the Greek past.

If Roman historiography begins in Greek with Fabius, it becomes fully Roman when Cato writes his *Origines*. It is, of course, another irony that, while the Roman aristocrat Fabius writes in Greek, it is the "new man" from Tusculum that writes in Latin. But Cato's conception of Rome is as important as his use of Latin: First, Rome is hybrid (the "aborigines" are from Achaia and the Sabines from Sparta; Latin is a Greek dialect). Second, and complicit with its hybridity, Rome is a "Republic," a "public entity," a possession of the People. As a result, "Romanness" has nothing to do with birth and everything to do with service to the Republic. When Cato refused to record the names of leaders in the wars he wrote about and, instead, referred to them by their military titles, he went much further than any other Roman in making an important point about Roman identity. A large part of what makes one Roman is the alignment of one's own personal self-aggrandizement with the larger aggrandizement of Rome (see also Chapters 17 and 23). In Cato's extreme presentation this reflects a tension within Roman identity between self-aggrandizement (which, of course, would characterize Cato's own brilliant career) and the loss of self required when one is reduced or assimilated to one's role as Roman. It would be interesting to know how Cato handled the problem when he quotes from his own speeches, but his unique presentation itself aligns his presentation of Rome with his self-presentation. This alignment is also part of an ideology that would formalize "treason" as the crime of *maiestas*, as putting personal power ahead of the Republic (the word means literally a crime against the "greater-ness" of the state) and sees "exile" as a loss of life: it was thought of as "capital punishment" because a separation from the center (Rome) that gave shape and meaning to one's self-aggrandizing activities was a loss of life.

We turn now to Sallust, a Sabine born in Amiternum in 86 and probably a member of his municipal aristocracy. After a checkered career as a politician, which included expulsion from the Senate in 50, he turned to history writing (see also Chapter 2).[10] He wrote two monographs, one on the Conspiracy of Catiline and another on the African war against Jugurtha, and an annalistic history beginning with the events of 78 and continuing down to at least 67. Among other things, his work continues the record of Roman identity-formation as an alignment of personal aggrandizement with the aggrandizement of Rome.

> I think Athenian history was pretty great and glorious, but still a little less significant than its reputation. Because Athens produced men of great talent, Athenian deeds are known throughout the world. The virtue of those who did the deeds is equated with the talent of those who celebrated them. Rome, on the other hand, never had that advantage because men with the greatest understanding were men of action" (*Cat.* 8.2–5)

It's a complex trick that Sallust performs here: the praise of Athenian historiography simultaneously detracts from the prestige of Athens and adds to the prestige of Sallust's chosen project, one that enhances the prestige of Rome.

Competitive self-aggrandizement put to the service of Rome is even a theme of Sallust's history: "The hardest struggle for glory was between Romans themselves" (*Cat.* 7.5) and "Quarrels, discord, strife was practiced with enemies; citizens competed with citizens for virtue" (*Cat.* 9.2). And who were these citizens? "As I understand the tradition, the city of Rome was founded and inhabited in the beginning by Trojans, who came in exile with their leader Aeneas after wandering about without any fixed home. They were joined by aborigines, an agrarian people without laws, without governmental authority, free and unrestrained" (*Cat.* 6.1). For Sallust this native hybridity was held together by a discourse of virtue: men should work as hard as possible to be remembered for a long time; they should exercise strength of mind and of body, but the body should serve the mind.[11] Ironically, however, Catiline himself is the example that demonstrates and aggravates the ways in which this discourse does not work: he was known for remarkable strength of mind and body;

he could make his body serve his mind with incredible endurance; and, if Sallust the historian is successful in his monograph, Catiline will indeed be remembered for a long time: "This criminal event I consider especially memorable because of the extraordinary nature of the crime and its danger" (*Cat.* 4.4).

The tension between Roman morality and Roman history that Sallust presents is one that makes his history a satirical one and it is one that finds Roman identity to be deeply divided, rhetorically motivated, and aggressively self-destructive.[12] One instance will illustrate. Near the end of the work on Catiline, Sallust compares two men of extraordinary virtue, but different character, Cato the younger and Julius Caesar (see also Chapter 17). In the comparison the virtues of one man cancel out the virtues of the other. "Caesar was considered great for charity and generosity; Cato for integrity." Does this imply that Caesar's generosity is self-serving or that Cato's integrity is mean-spirited? "Caesar achieved glory by giving, helping, forgiving; Cato by not offering bribes." It is as if Cato's virtue attacks Caesar's virtue by turning benevolence into bribery. The problem of virtue has become so rhetoricized that virtue is put in conflict with itself.[13] As Sallust objectifies the disintegration of the Republic, he discovers that identity (here called "nature and character") is even for "virtuous men" a manipulative, competitive capacity to assume a rhetorical position vis-à-vis another. What is missing is the centripetal force of Rome as an understood or agreed upon center, at the same time that it is deployed as the rhetorical center.

Oratory and the Rhetoric of Advocacy

Oratory in the Republic was the place where various versions of Romanness were most publicly performed, practiced, constructed, and contested (see also Chapter 20). The process of making claims and counter-claims about what is just and Roman is ultimately a process of self-interrogation (What does it mean to be a Roman?) and self-representation (How do I represent myself as Roman?), and it is not surprising that these are the same forces that shape Roman comedy and satire.

Roman oratory for us begins with Greek rhetoricians (who were expelled from Rome in 161) and the same Cato who opposed excessive Greek influence. Still, Cato wrote on rhetoric and kept written versions of his own speeches, revised them in his old age, and used them in his *Origines* (see also Chapter 2). They were part of his public record, and they illustrate how oratory at Rome depended upon a deeply rhetorical sense of self and was one place where Romanness, and not just prudence or policy, was contested. In 168, during the fourth year of an inconclusive war with Macedonia, an embassy from Rhodes arrived in the Senate hoping to change the terms of their allegiance. Hitherto they had been allied with Rome, but now they wished to play the role of negotiator between Rome and Macedonia's king Perseus. Unfortunately, they arrived just after news of Perseus' capture had been received. Some Romans were angry and wanted to attack the haughty and arrogant Rhodians. Cato opposed any such action, and addressed the Senate in terms of human psychology: "I know," he said, "that it often happens that most people swell with anger and increase and grow in pride and ferocity when ambitions flourish and prosper and succeed" (*ORF*⁴ Cato no. 8, 163 = Gell. *NA* 6.3.14). Cato makes two brilliant moves here. First, he assigns to the Romans the very characteristics they wanted to punish: pride and arrogance. Second, he exonerates the Roman response as typical and human. While his prudential concern is that the Romans not do anything rash, he argues for restraint by collapsing the difference between the haughty Rhodians and the haughty Romans. At the end he comes back to Roman-ness and, like the satirists, asks his audience to step back a bit from their own impulses and see themselves more clearly:

> They say that the Rhodians are haughty and proud, and in making this objection they point to a flaw that I would not want alleged about me or my children. But let them be haughty and proud! What difference does that make to us? Are you going to get angry just because someone is more haughty and proud than we are? (*ORF*⁴ Cato no. 8, 169 = Gell. *NA* 6.3.50)

For all his alleged moral severity, Cato in this speech exemplifies the tolerant humanity we associate with the best of Roman ethics. His manipulation of argument here entails a complex interchanging of roles: Cato would not like to be a haughty Roman (which gives him credentials to judge others) but provides in himself an example of how haughty Romans can be tolerant, if not indifferent to, Rhodian haughtiness. The speech constructs a place where Romans can accept their Roman responsibilities in terms of what it means to be a Roman – both a haughty, arrogant Roman and a tolerant prudential Roman.

Cato's awareness of the complex negotiations between speaker and audience is given theoretical expression in the Roman revision of Aristotelian rhetoric. Aristotle had analyzed argument in terms of three "proofs": *logos* (logic), *pathos* (emotion), and *ethos* (character). Thus, a speaker might convince a jury by the rigor of his logic, or he might win sympathy for his position by the appeal to and display of emotions, or he might evince a presumption of good faith because of his character and sincerity. The Romans adopted the Greek analysis, but revised its articulation of specific technical elements and focused on the effect that a speech had upon the audience as a dynamic process that bound speaker, speech, and listener together. "Logic" became *probare*, that is, "to win cognitive assent, to get accepted as true." In many of its uses, it has nothing explicitly to do with logic, but only with the belief that something is true. "Emotion" became *movere*, that is, "to move the audience," which emphasizes the active role of the orator in manipulating feelings. And, finally, "character" is reimagined as *conciliare*, "to reconcile the audience to the judgment it is being asked to make," that is, to make the audience feel that the position which the orator takes is one that their character also allows them to take. If he demands justice be done because of a heinous crime, *conciliare* means that the orator uses his character, his measured outrage, his capacity to feel the pain and fear of others, as a way to reconcile a cruel punishment with a healthy state. *Conciliare*, then, refers not just to the recognized status of the orator, but to his display of emotions and capacities to respond. While this confounds the neat Greek division between emotion and character, it recognizes that persuasion is not the result of specific techniques, but a relationship between audience and speaker, one that involves a sense that something is true combined with emotions that are appropriate to the verdict. This is how community is formed, and in nearly all of his performances, Cicero constructs Romanness as a contest for the hearts and minds (*conciliare*) of good citizens to feel (*movere*) certain things in making a judgment (*probare*).

Both the need to revise Greek rhetoric and the representative powers of Roman rhetoric are implicit in a feature of the Roman forensic system that makes it formally different from the Greek system (see also Chapters 11 and 20). In Athens, the rhetor wrote speeches for the client who spoke for himself. In Rome, the orator spoke as a patron on behalf of his client.[14] This difference had enormous consequences: for instance, what a husband could say about finding another man in bed with his wife had to be revised for the public character of the patron. The patron's outrage could not be the naked emotions of betrayal and anger that a husband might, even should, express; he had to show the civic emotions that protect husbands from betrayal and society from acts of unrestrained vengeance. Furthermore, the simplest part of the oration, the narrative statement of facts, could, even must, now become a fiction of community. The orator had to represent to the jury what had been the experience of another. He had to speak as if he had seen what another had seen and felt what another had felt. His own *persona* became the site where the demands of justice and vengeance faced the demands of community. This position between the victim and the law allows Cicero to turn the prosecution of Verres into a defense of both Sicily and the senatorial courts. In fact, what Cicero does is to trope successful and honest prosecution as a defense of law and order (the courts) and a defense of the victim (Sicily). It is a trope the Sicilians, who are demanding recompense for extortion, cannot use without what would appear as self-serving arrogance. They cannot say, "Save yourselves and your system by giving us back our money." But Cicero can say, "Let's save ourselves and our system by returning the money." Similarly, in the *pro Caelio* Cicero's position as the representative of Caelius, who is charged with violence and attempted murder, allows him to portray the entire affair as a silly comedy of unrequited love. To do this, he adopts the *persona* of the pleasant old man of comedy and argues, in essence, "What's the fuss? Boys will be boys." Surely, Caelius, the defendant, cannot defend himself by playing the role of a callow lover!

The advocate, like the clever slave, plays a role and manipulates the symbolic capital of Rome on behalf of his client and himself.[15] This is a representational system in which the orator, while contesting justice and equity, constructed and contested Romanness as well. It is fitting, then, that Cicero's primary claim on behalf of the citizenship of the Greek poet Archias is that he is and should be a Roman citizen because he represents Rome to Romans and to others: "shall we reject this man . . . who is our man by his own desire and according to our laws . . . especially when he, Archias, has devoted all his energy and all his genius to spreading the glory and renown of the Roman People?" (*Arch.* 9.19).

Catullan Lyric and the Individual Voice

The processes of mimesis and alterity that inhere in any form of representation are also at work in the lyrics of the poet Catullus. Like other Romans, Catullus explores and articulates his own experience both by adopting Greek ideas and practices and by positioning himself against them. Lyric, however, like satire, added a new dimension to this dynamic: the distance between self and role that representation requires allowed Catullus to explore his differences from himself and from certain aspects of the Roman world. If we can describe what we find in the Plautine slave as a multiple self, as the ability to take on many roles, we may think of the Catullan self as a divided self, a self uncomfortable within the limits of any one role.[16]

Catullus was born in Verona about 87. One may emphasize his role as a "new poet," bringing a more refined Greek sensibility to lyric, or as an extension of the past, of comedy and epigram. He was, of course, both, and the hybrid literature he created allowed him to trope and interrogate Greek norms and forms while making Roman lyric a place where versions of himself could be represented and contested.[17]

Catullus and his poetic coterie brought the aesthetic ideals of Callimachus (the greatest of the Hellenistic Greek poets and arguably the most influential poet Greece produced) to Rome: these ideals included learned allusion, carefully refined and short forms, and an interest in psychological aberrations. He translates Callimachus' "Lock of Berenice" (65) and claims that he cannot write without his library (68.33). He contrasts Cinna's carefully written *Zmyrna* with the long and muddy bombast of Hortalus and the *Annales* of Volusius (95). And he calls his girlfriend "Lesbia," a pseudonym which refers to the Greek love poet Sappho who was born on the island of Lesbos. But the neo-Callimachaean learning that would change Latin poetry is already rhetoricized in Catullus. In his introductory poem 1 he offers a presentation copy of his lyrics to the prose historian Cornelius Nepos. Nepos' appreciation appears to be based upon shared values: Catullus' book is new and Nepos' work is daring; Catullus' book is small and Nepos' history is brief; Catullus' poetry is exquisitely polished, and Nepos' history has required much labor. But the terms do not quite fit: Nepos' labor recalls the work of the farm; his god is Jupiter, the god of epic and history, not the Apolline god of lyric; and his appreciation of Catullus is given in indefinite pronouns, words that are potentially as dismissive ("whatever") as appreciative ("something"). Thus, as Catullus announces the values that his poetry depends upon, he reaches beyond the particular reader to a Hellenistic tradition of learned and allusive writing, at the same time that he satirizes even the appreciative reader.

The tension between the absolutist standards of a Hellenistic aesthetic and the playful realities of the (Roman) world allows Catullus to portray even his own aesthetic as a ploy. In one of his most famous poems (7), he responds to Lesbia's question, "how many kisses are enough for you?": "as great as the number of Libyan sands which lie in Cyrene, rich in asafoetida, between the oracle of hot Jupiter and the sacred sepulcher of aged Battus." He has embroidered a cliché, "as many as the sands of the desert" with ostentatious learning. Then, he repeats his answer: "as many as the stars that gaze on the furtive love affairs of men in the silence of the night," another cliché, but this time in simple language evoking a scene from popular romantic drama, an art form that Callimachus himself contemned. Part of the point, of course, is that everyone knows passion just as we know its clichés. Callimachean learning is just another way of talking about passion, perhaps it is its own passion, but there is nothing essential in its relationship to love. It is just love wearing, as it were, a professor's mask.

The appropriation of Greek literary styles and mannerisms as a means to understanding, exploring, expanding, and differentiating the Roman experience is central to what is Roman. Catullus 51 translates a famous Sappho poem about erotic passion but ends by adding a political and moral comment. This turn to the moral is one of the most troubling in Catullus' corpus: while pursuing a love affair with another man's wife he makes claims on the language of political allegiance and ethics – "fidelity," "obligation," "good will," "contractual agreement," "family and political friendship," "good words," and "good works." The idea that the claims of personal erotic passions can be analogous to the claims made by contractual negotiations or to the bonds felt by fathers for their sons and sons-in-law is stunning, and it is an insight that comes from the assimilation of Sappho's erotic world to the political world of Rome. In a sense, this form of "turning" and "troping" (translation) finds the world of Sapphic eros within Catullus' world and, at the same time, changes it.

One way Sapphic eros represents and changes Catullus' world is through the very trope that names his lover "Lesbia." Sappho's coterie of young women on Lesbos, for whom she wrote many of her love poems, gives us the modern term "lesbian." As Catullus poetry unpacks what it would mean to be a "Lesbian lover," not only does his beloved Lesbia become his Muse, but he becomes like a woman. He is plowed and deflowered (poem 11). There is a figurative coherence, then, between Catullus' translation of Sappho, his lover's name, Lesbia, and the gender-bending that appears so frequently in Catullan lyric.

Throughout Catullus' corpus there is a sense that the presence of desire and passion, for all its intensity, does not create a full and present person. In fact, it seems to create a divided persona. Poem 16 is a riddle that addresses this issue. Here, Catullus threatens to assault two readers who have taken his poetry literally and concluded that he must be a passive homosexual, a *pathicus* (see also Chapter 21). He asserts that what a poet says and how he lives are two different things, that a poet should be a "good man," *pius*, but that poems require wit and a sexy veneer. Then, he again threatens to assault the readers who thought he was a *pathicus*. It is, of course, witty to prove one's aggressive manliness by threatening to assault readers sexually; but there is a problem with logic: if a poet's life is different from his words, what is the status of either the threat or the claim that he is not passive? If you believe that a poet's words and poet's actions are different, then Catullus is not threatening his readers; he is merely making a sexy claim about his sexual aggressivity. On the other hand, if you take the threat literally, then you have to reject the claim that a poet's words and a poet's actions are different. There is no solution to the contradiction, but that is also the point. One cannot place a neat divide between what poets say and what they do, nor can one merely equate what they say and who they are. It is the mystery of self and representation that every representation tells some truth and some falsehood. And, yet, it is by virtue of these representations that we figure ourselves out as well as cut the figure of who we are.[18]

In Catullus' verse we find many versions of Roman identity. He shows how the appropriation of the property of provincials in an imperialistic international culture is central to the expectations of young men in Rome, and how the inhabitants of distant places can so easily become "native products" (10). He shows us Rome as the place that distributes the power and wealth of empire, and as the place where personal successes and failures in the foreign service have little to do with the security and nonchalance of the Forum, which is protected by larger political and military successes. All of this is part of Roman identity. But the Catullan corpus participates in the construction of identity when it postures and plays, when it finds itself at odds with itself and uses the figures of others for self-interrogation and self-aggrandizement.

"Roman Philosophy"

There was no Roman philosophy as such, at least not before Quintus Sextus created a short-lived sect that joined Stoic ethics to some principles of Pythagoreanism in the early years of the Augustan principate. In fact, the Romans were introduced to philosophy at a time when cynicism and a logical critique of most metaphysical systems were already underway.[19] In 155 Carneades, an adherent of Plato's Academy, gave public lectures in Rome: he would speak in defense of justice on one day and on the next defend injustice (see also Chapter 20). Cato had Carneades and his philosophic embassy hurried out of Rome. The next year two Epicurean teachers were expelled from Rome. Gradually, however, the Roman aristocracy learned philosophy. For the most part, it remained a Greek import, taught by Greeks, often in Athens, until Cicero "taught philosophy to speak Latin and gave it citizenship" (*Fin.* 3.40). By the early empire, Augustus felt it useful to have a court philosopher. Today, a large part of our philosophical terminology is Latin: "virtue," "substance," "essence," "principle," "potential," "accident," "final cause," "efficient cause," etc.

The story of how this happened is complex and, for the most part, takes place after the Republic. But two writers of the Republic, Cicero and Lucretius, played a fundamental role in helping later Romans make Greek philosophy a part of Roman culture and so an expression of Roman identity. Not surprisingly, an important point of entry for philosophical influence was rhetoric: *pro* and *contra* arguments were useful for the budding orator (see also Chapter 20). But the late Republic discovered more than practical forensic value in this style of argument. Cicero made it a part of his urgent and practical philosophical meditations. While the Roman encounter with other Greek cultural achievements often troped their serious pretensions in order to play with how they were rhetorically constructed, the Roman encounter with rhetorical philosophy rediscovered practical, political, and moral value in probing the problems of ethics and justice from all sides.

During the dark days of the civil war (46–44) Cicero wrote over thirty books on philosophy. He explored political, ethical, and metaphysical questions while advocating the therapeutic value of philosophical dialog and debate. His final work, *On Duties*, addressed to his son, turns to Stoic philosophy to understand the practical moral obligations of a Roman, but it is especially typical of the Roman interest in philosophy that Cicero focuses in on the demands of sociopolitical contexts. In the last book of *On Duties*, he even takes up a question omitted by other philosophers: Can morality conflict with expediency (see also Chapter 20)? His allegiances were eclectic, his perspective skeptical, and his writing rhetorical, not technical. But it was his sense that philosophy could not be divorced from rhetoric, that it needed eloquence to persuade, and that it must address the real problems of Romans that gave his writings their significance. His use of Roman examples, Roman themes and values, and Roman history created a body of work that was identifiably Roman in content as well as in its insistence upon testing theory against the world.

Lucretius (c. 94–55), on the other hand, had a different effect. Nothing was less Roman from the perspective of substance and belief than Epicureanism and nothing was less rhetorical than the dry prose of Epicurus. But Lucretius found in the arguments of Epicurus a practical philosophy that he believed could address man's unhappiness and provide a social ethics that would act as a corrective to the self-destructive immorality of the Republic. He turned the prose of Epicurus, who distrusted poetry and rhetoric, into an epic diction with the power to influence Virgil. In content, he was a disciple, but in rhetorical and emotional power and in his passionate insistence on the social relevance of his philosophy he was a Roman innovator.

Although Epicureans believed that the gods were indifferent to man, Lucretius figured the creative power of nature as the goddess Venus, mother of Aeneas and founder of the Roman race; and then he pictured Mars, her husband and god of war, reclining in her lap, seduced away from the destructiveness of civil war. But, perhaps more telling, Lucretius figured Epicurus himself as a Roman father and patron, and in this role he offered a Roman challenge to what most of the aristocracy would have thought of as Roman virtues: war, aggression, political activity, and self-promotion (see also Chapter 17). It is, of course, true that Lucretius himself in doing this enacts many of those same aggressive, acquisitive, self-promoting virtues.

Despite Lucretius' many differences with Cicero, they share the same urgent need for a therapeutic philosophy that can address the problems of Rome. This urgency shapes a rhetoric of conviction and belief which transformed the theoretical emphasis of Greek philosophy just as much as the writers transformed the Latin language and the rhetoric of virtue. For all their differences (and Roman philosophy might be defined by the idiosyncrasy of its practitioners), their practice of philosophy shares several aspects of that project we call Roman identity: the cultural achievements of Greece are transformed so as to serve both the individual competitive needs of Cicero and Lucretius while aligning their personal success with practical and historical success of Rome. As a result, abstract philosophical argument became a personal and therapeutic tool for an urgent self-transformation.

Conclusion

It is remarkable that none of the Latin writers we have discussed above was a native of Rome itself (see also Chapter 28). In fact, of the Latin writers we know, only Julius

Caesar came from the city. (Fabius Pictor was born in Rome, but his literary activity was in Greek.) But each contributed to Roman cultural identity through a process of self-transformation and alignment with Rome that changed Rome and its cultural acquisitions (see also Chapter 22). Roman cultural identity was not a fixed thing or even an agreement among Romans as to who they were, but a competitive and acquisitive process of self-transformation and adjustment. Similarly, the Roman self, as presented, explored, and acquired in the Republic, was an aggressive and competitive project in assimilating, manipulating, and controlling others. It competes with others for standing and self-determination and is changed by the very process of competition. At the core of the Roman identity is a contest to see who gets to say who we are, who gets to mobilize the symbolic value of cultural achievements and public discourse, who gets to turn whom into a Roman or a non-Roman. This process requires both the deployment of rhetoric and a deep belief in the rhetorical nature of human activity. Just as their empire was successful on land and sea by adopting and adapting to the military resources of the enemy, so their cultural empire continually drew within the Roman sphere the successes and accomplishments of Greece by adopting and changing those successes. It all goes back to Plautus' slave: "The trick is to discover if we are our own selves or someone else's self." Someone may have turned us into Romans when we weren't looking. In 212 AD the emperor Caracalla issued an edict that turned all free men of the Empire into Romans. Today, if you look in a modern Greek dictionary under the term that derives from the Latin for "a Roman," *Romaios*, you will find the definition "a modern Greek person." Roman identity, then, like the secular capitalism of Western civilization, is the process that naturalizes you into a Roman citizen, and it makes no difference whether you or someone else civilizes you.

Guide to Further Reading

There are no wholly satisfactory discussions of Roman identity in the Republic, and that is, no doubt, in part because the topic is itself so vast, entailing the details and problems of history, language, literature, culture, and interpretation. Discussion is also hampered by a tendency on the part of scholars to want a definition of identity, to fix it as a specific relationship of "Romans" to "others," or to political power. Whenever this is done, scholars find themselves taking sides within the ongoing Roman debate about Romanness, rather than describing Roman identity. There are two reasons for this: first, the "other" in Roman contests for identity is frequently Roman in its own terms. Second, the assertion of identity is not the same thing as the practice of identity.

A basic introduction to the literature should begin with Kenney 1982. The general historical background and the issues raised by Rome's encounter with Greek culture are addressed by Gruen (1984a, 1990b, 1992). Gruen's emphasis on the appeal of Hellenism should be balanced by studies that emphasize ambivalence and tension: Jocelyn 1977, Astin 1978, and MacMullen 1991. Earl 1967 helps one think about "Roman morality" and what "virtue" meant to the aristocracy, but this dated work should be complemented with Edwards 1993, who is sensitive to the fact that moral rhetoric may not always mean what it says. Recently, the field of "cultural studies" has enriched and complicated our ideas of how literature and politics work together to create a sense of "identity." Habinek 1998 is exemplary, although this study continues into the Empire. In a related study, Farrell 2001 focuses on the Latin language as a place where culture and identity are explored and created.

Against the general background provided by these works, the reader will have to turn to studies of individual authors and genres, when they are available. Bain 1979 demonstrates how an aesthetic reading of Plautus is still shaped by Fraenkel 1960. Anderson 1999, though marred by a narrow historicism, considers how Plautine comedy is specifically Roman. Republican historiography remains the province of experts. Batstone 1990 provides an introduction to Sallust which explores the contradictions that Earl 1961 wants to eliminate. Recent work on Cicero relates oratory to cultural symbolism: Vasaly 1993; Konstan 1993; Batstone 1994. Catullus' poetry is itself a battleground for self-definition among critics. Of the many recent studies, Fitzgerald 1995 is the most explicitly concerned with competitive self-definition. Janan 1994 explores the interplay of desire and identity, while Batstone 1993 sees lyric identity as deeply rhetorical. Roman philosophy remains a field that is rarely studied for what it is – Lucretius is read in terms of Virgil, Cicero for his history of the Academics. Long 2003 provides a good overview of the problem and suggests useful ways to begin thinking about what the Romans did with and to the philosophy they appropriated

Notes

1   Kenney 1982 reviews the facts.
2   Cf. Val. Max. 7.4.1–ext. 2 on "stratagems."
3   Gruen 1984a: 250–72.
4   For a moral reading of the poverty of Latin, see Farrell 2001: 28–51.
5   Cic. *de Sen.* 41, Plut. *Cato* 2.3, *de Vir. Ill.* 471. The authenticity of these stories is not as important as the way they exemplify the cultural dialogue.
6   Skutsch 1985: 46–67.
7   Anderson 1996.
8   See Handley 1968; Bain 1979; Barsby 1986; Batstone 2005.
9   Pictor: Momigliano 1990: 80–108; Cato: Kenney 1982: 149–52.
10   The standard work on Sallust is Syme 1964.
11   Earl 1961, 1967.
12   Batstone 1990.
13   Batstone 1988.
14   On the "rhetoric of advocacy" see Kennedy 1968.
15   Konstan 1993; Batstone 1994.
16   For a psychological interpretation, see Janan 1994.
17   "Lyric" is being used here loosely in the modern sense, not in the rigid generic sense of the ancient world.
18   On the relationship of rhetoric, logic, and poetry, see Batstone 1993.
19   For a survey, see Long 2003.

PART VII

Controversies

CHAPTER 26

Conceptualizing Roman Imperial Expansion under the Republic: An Introduction

Arthur M. Eckstein

The world has long been fascinated by Roman imperial expansion, and rightly so. The reason for fascination was already explained by the Greek historian Polybius (c.150), a contemporary witness: "Who is so indolent a person as not to wish to know by what means and because of what qualities of government and way of life the Romans have succeeded in subjecting almost the entire known world to their rule (*arché*) – and this within a period of 53 years?" (Polyb. 1.1.5). Polybius meant the period between 220 and 167, during which time Rome defeated Carthage in the western Mediterranean, and in the Greek East defeated the great monarchies of the Antigonids (based in Macedon) and the Seleucids (based in Syria and Mesopotamia). The result was Roman dominance from Spain to Syria. This chapter will focus on that crucial period but will also discuss the phenomenon of large-scale Roman expansion in the last stages of the Republic (the first century).

The huge geographical scope of dominance achieved by the Roman Republic already by the 160s was unparalleled for an ancient city-state.[1] Monarchs in antiquity had achieved wide and long-lasting territorial rule, but never city-state republics or democracies. The nearest city-state rival to Rome in domination over others was Athens in the fifth century, but the Athenians' empire had covered a much smaller territory, and lasted only some 70 years before being destroyed by rival powers in the Peloponnesian War. The area covered by Roman domination was not only immensely larger, but it appeared to Polybius in 150 that there were no competitors on the Mediterranean horizon with the military, political, economic, and social resources to challenge the Romans' domination – and he was right.

Yet an ambiguity regarding the nature of "empire" is apparent in Polybius' date for the achievement of universal Roman rule: 168/7. At that time there existed not a single

Roman-ruled province in the Greek East, not a single Roman army – nor was there even any permanent Roman diplomatic representation. Indeed, Polybius' Roman empire, at least in the East, consisted solely of legally independent states.[2] Yet the Roman statesman Cato the Elder in 167 seems to have thought the geographical scope of Rome's dominion was similar to that depicted by Polybius.[3] In what sense, then, was Rome in the mid-second century already an "empire"? The answer here leads into a discussion of why the modern study of Roman imperial expansion under the Republic is fraught both with scholarly controversy, and – unusual for a controversy dealing with events so far in the past – fraught with emotion.

The answer has to do not with institutions, but with the existence and employment of power. As A. P. Thornton has written, at the heart of the concept of "imperialism" is the image of dominance, of power asserted, "and power is neither used nor witnessed without emotion."[4] Power asserted: the Romans had a word for this. It was *imperium*, a word from which our terms "empire," "imperialism," and "emperor" all descend. Originally, *imperium* was the legal power to command obedience that Roman public officials possessed by virtue of election to office by the populace (and by virtue of the favor of the gods; see also Chapters 10 and 12). By extension and metaphor, *imperium* came to denote the power of the polity of the Roman People to command obedience as well, obedience to its orders internationally: the *imperium* of the Roman People (*imperium populi Romani*). Gradually, too, the term came to denote the geographical area where such commands of the Roman People would be obeyed: hence, empire.[5] But the geographical scope of obeyed commands had little to do with the varied institutions through which such commands might be transmitted; the *imperium populi Romani* did not require the existence of provinces, soldiers, and governors. It was enough for the exercise of *imperium*, for its geographical scope, if a Greek state (or Celtic tribe), legally independent, obeyed what it was told to do by Rome or by a representative of Rome – as, for instance, did the powerful King Antiochus IV, in a famous incident in 168 when he was ordered by the Senate to abandon his conquest of Egypt (Polyb. 29.27.1–10; Livy 45.12.3–8).[6] As Derow has pointed out, the habitual stance of the Roman State throughout Polybius' *Histories* is one of giving orders to foreign polities – orders which it firmly expects to be obeyed.[7] This explains why both Cato and Polybius saw the Mediterranean as an *arché* ruled by Rome decades before there were permanent Roman provinces there. Yet the Romans never did develop a word corresponding to the process of "imperialism."[8] Romans were uninterested in abstractions, but no Greek philosopher or historian developed a term directly corresponding to "imperialism" either. "Imperialism," employed by modern scholars to analyze ancient Rome, is actually a modern word – and one with an unusual history.

Originally, "imperialism" denoted the internal political dominance of an all-powerful ruler ("emperor") over his subject population: the classic ancient examples of this "imperialism" were the Roman emperors of the first to fourth centuries AD; the classic modern example was Napoleon Bonaparte. When early and mid-nineteenth-century writers spoke of "imperialism," they meant internal dictatorship, not expansionist foreign policy. "Imperialism" as a term denoting desire for foreign empire only emerged in the 1870s, during the controversy in Britain over the successful attempt by Prime Minister Benjamin Disraeli to have Queen Victoria proclaimed by Parliament not merely Queen of England but Empress of India: to favor such a move was "imperialism." "Imperialism" is still linked here to dictatorial rule (Victoria as "empress"), which was why Disraeli's effort was controversial: opponents claimed that Queen Victoria, a constitutional monarch, should make no claim to dictatorship. But because the term also now denoted rule over a foreign country, indeed a faraway country, "imperialism" after the mid-1870s came to denote the desire to rule over foreigners. This development was accelerated, because in the two decades after the proclamation of Victoria as Empress of India the conquest and imposition of direct political control over Africa (and parts of Asia) by European powers was extraordinary in scale – and the process itself soon came to be called "imperialism."[9] Yet the Earl of Caernarvon could write in 1878 that "imperialism, as such, is a newly coined word to me" – and he was the British Colonial Secretary![10]

"Imperialism" was from the beginning, then, not only a modern word but one caught up in controversy over the warlike and expansionist use of power by modern states, and particularly the intense debate over European and, later, American domination of "the third world." And the controversy over modern empire has had, in turn, a profound and continuing impact upon scholarly writing on the expansion of Rome, because "power is neither used or witnessed without emotion." At first the emotions provoked by European imperialism were positive – at least among Europeans. Empire was thought to be both natural in a Darwinian sense (the rule of the stronger) and morally progressive, in that Europeans were bringing education, enlightenment, economic progress, and good government in the wake of their machine guns.[11] But soon enough there came a rebellion by intellectuals against the brutality and self-confidence of "the imperialists" (the advocates and organizers of European empire). Many intellectuals attributed the extraordinary expansion of European power in the tropics between 1870 and 1900 not to the virtues but to the socio-economic pathologies within modern European society: empire was neither natural nor good; it had unnatural causes and was evil. By extension, all imperial expansion – including in the distant past – was easily thought to derive from similar social pathologies within the imperial state.

The pioneering intellectual analysis of imperialism and empire as moral critique was Hobson's *Imperialism: A Study* (1902). Hobson's goal was to attack Britain's role in the Boer War (1899–1902), but he also gave a critical analysis of the entire expansion of the British Empire since 1870. Arguing that the Empire had brought little benefit either to ordinary Britons or to the subordinated populations, Hobson attributed British expansion to economic and financial distortions within British society. Capitalist overproduction of goods at home led to a search to create new markets for those goods overseas by force; surplus of capital at home led to the investment of capital overseas by the rich – and then to the demand that these risky investments be protected by British military intervention and direct British rule.[12] Lenin based much of his own analysis on Hobson, but in *Imperialism: The Highest Stage of Capitalism* (1920) he added the idea that the domination of the great European and American monopolies, and their (economic) division of the world, did not even require the intervention of governments; the indirect economic empire of the corporations (backed, to be sure, by government force) was just as efficient at extracting wealth from subject populations – which both Hobson and Lenin believed to be the primary goal of empire. Lenin's prestige as a successful revolutionary and the founding father of the Soviet Union ensured that his economic ideas long had wide circulation.[13]

These economic analyses of "imperialism" in the modern world had their impact on modern discussion of the motives of Roman Republican expansion. If the basic goal of empire is financial and economic profit, then we must search for Roman financial, commercial, and economic motives and interest groups in order to explain Roman actions. Commercial interests at Rome certainly sometimes benefited from the creation of empire. Slave-dealers followed Roman armies, as they did most armies in antiquity, and – if those armies were successful – reaped their grim profits (see also Chapters 27 and 28); but there is no evidence that the Roman government ever engaged in wars as slave-hunts.[14] Roman government-contracting companies (*publicani*) gained control over the mines in Spain in the 190s, and the proceeds were huge (Polyb. 34.9.8–11 = Strabo 3.2.10).[15] Again, in 187 the Senate passed a decree allowing the city of Ambracia on the Adriatic coast of Greece to impose whatever harbor dues it wished – yet Romans and Latins (mostly merchants, one would think) were to be exempt (Livy 38.44.4). But the provision in this senatorial decree was unique as far as we know, and the decree as a whole was concerned with restoring the Ambracian economy in response to accusations that the city had been unfairly attacked by a Roman general (Livy 38.43.1–2, 44.3–6).[16] In any case these are the benefits of empire; the question is whether capitalist cabals originated Roman wars.

This claim indeed used to be made.[17] But the evidence is sparse. Probably the best example of the influence of commercial interest-groups is the complaints by Italian merchants to the Senate about piracy in the Adriatic Sea in the 230s; these helped lead to the Roman decision to intervene militarily in Maritime Illyria in 229 – the first time Roman forces had ever gone east of the Adriatic. But the merchants had to complain a long time before getting action from the Senate (Polyb. 2.8.3), and the motives of many senators in 230/229 may have been strategic (the rise of a powerful pirate state in Illyria on the eastern flank of Italy) rather than economic.[18] Other examples are far less clear, and in any case run up against the fact that most senatorial aristocrats were large landowners, not merchants; indeed, senators were forbidden by law after 218 to engage in large-scale trade (Livy 21.632.3; cf. Plaut. *Merc.* 73–78; Cic. *Verr.* 2.5.45). The law was sometimes skirted via senators' use of front men, but the fact remains that senatorial interests were primarily landed interests, and thus are not likely to have taken the interests of merchants (a lower status-group in Roman society) into constant and serious account (Plut. *Cat. Mai* 21.5–6; Cic. *Verr.* 2.5.45). The relationship between the Senate and the *publicani*, for instance, was filled with suspicion, with the senators on watch (after bitter experience) for the defrauding of the Roman State by businessmen.[19]

Repeated victories in war certainly brought wealth to Rome and to individual Romans in the form of loot, and wealth to the State via the large war indemnities that were imposed on defeated polities. But again, there is little evidence that the

Roman Republic ever went to war in order to gain loot and money; these were the beneficial consequences of victory rather than the causes of wars. Indeed, wars were (and are) risky financial investments; Rome owed its citizen-creditors heavily after the Hannibalic War, but new military commitments prevented full monetary repayment (Livy 31.13.2–9).[20] It also appears doubtful that most Roman provinces down through the 130s did more than pay their way financially. Sicily after 210 was exceptional; other provinces – for instance, Macedonia after the 140s, with its long barbarian frontier requiring strenuous defense – ran at a loss. Even Spain, with its great mines, barely covered the cost of constant Roman warfare there.[21] The Senate in 167 rejected pressure from *publicani* favoring direct Roman rule in Macedon in order to gain control over the Macedonian mines – precisely because of perceived strategic costs for the State. It was new and serious military-political problems with a revanchist Macedonian monarchy that ultimately led to the establishment of a permanent province there in the 140s.[22]

Moreover, the idea that modern financial and economic interests regularly manipulated their governments in the age of modern European expansion has itself come under increasing doubt by scholars. Instead it appears that governmental elites in the late nineteenth and early twentieth centuries were primarily concerned with geopolitics and national security issues.[23] How much more likely is that to have been the case with ancient governmental elites, such as that of the Roman Republic, which were made up primarily of large landowners, in societies where the "commercial" element – let alone the "industrial" element – was always small?

This point about the "archaic" nature of Roman society leads us to another major thinker who has greatly influenced modern scholarly approaches to the causes of imperial expansion. Writing in horrified reaction to World War I, Joseph Schumpeter in his *Sociology of Imperialisms* (1919) drew a conclusion opposite to that of Lenin and Hobson. The causes of war and imperial expansion were still to be found in pathologies within the societies of expansionist states, but the pathologies did not arise from capitalism, for capitalists tended to favor peace, since peace encouraged trade. Rather, the problem lay in the control over government policy still exercised by old precapitalist elites who possessed a primitive, warlike ideology. The powerful place in society enjoyed by these premodern elites had originated in their leadership in war and expansion, and was in fact threatened by modernization and capitalism. Consequently, they sought to maintain their status through war and expansion. Imperialism was authored by such governmental elites, not by capitalist cabals, and it had no rational state goal, such as economic or financial profit. Schumpeter famously defined imperialism as "the objectless disposition on the part of a state to unlimited forcible expansion."[24] This unlimited expansion was the work of the archaic elements in society that constituted "a war machine." With the rise of capitalism the social classes constituting the war machine had begun to outlive their usefulness in protecting society, but – in another famous phrase – "created by wars that required it, the machine now created the wars it required."[25]

Schumpeter-like thinking has had a larger impact on modern scholars' concepts of Roman imperial expansion than the economic-financial theories of Hobson and Lenin. This is because the Schumpeterian image of an "archaic" premodern elite imbued with a primitive ethos of war appears to fit much better as a description of the Roman senatorial aristocracy than does the image of calculating capitalist financiers found in Hobson and Lenin.[26]

One starts from the fact that for the first centuries of Rome's existence, it was under constant military pressure from powerful neighbors: the other cities of Latium; the Etruscans to the north; Sabine and other raiders from the hills to the east and south. The situation was compounded after 400 by powerful raids into central Italy from Celtic tribes that had taken up residence in the Po Valley. One of those attacks destroyed the city of Rome itself around 390.[27] Under such external pressures the Romans naturally developed a militarized culture and a militaristic governing elite. It was the only way to survive in – and then prevail over – this harsh environment (see also Chapters 6 and 17).

The Schumpeterian approach, mixed with some Marxist economic analysis, found brilliant expression in the immensely influential book by W. V. Harris, *War and Imperialism in Republican Rome, 327–70 B.C.* (1979). Harris addresses the mystery of why, after two centuries as a rather ordinary city-state barely able to hold its own, Rome from the 330s suddenly began an extraordinary career of expansion which led in 150 years to domination of the entire Mediterranean. Harris's answer is that Rome by the 330s had become an exceptionally militarized, militaristic, bellicose, and aggressive state – exceptional not just in modern terms, but in ancient terms as well. Rome was led by a senatorial aristocracy for whom war-making was the primary life experience. War-making for them was glorious in its essence, the primary road to political power and influence, personally profitable (via loot), and socially salutary, for success in war preserved the status and power of the aristocracy while providing, in the form of the distribution of confiscated enemy land to the poor, a solution to the problem of the maldistribution of wealth and land at Rome itself. The Roman populace, eager for loot and land to ease their difficult lives, participated willingly in the Roman career of bellicosity and aggression. Roman warfare was exceptionally brutal in practice, and Roman weaponry exceptionally savage in design. Romans of all classes idolized victory and fervently worshiped the goddess Victoria. Ideology at Rome, as seen in the quinquennial prayer of the censors for "increase in the things of the Romans," was overtly expansionist.[28]

On such a reconstruction, war at Rome became a sinister Schumpeterian nexus where crucial social, political, and economic interests converged. In fact, many scholars now argue that by the fourth century war for Rome was a social, political, and economic *necessity.* "War was necessary to satisfy the material and ideological needs of the aristocracy... and war became necessary to resolve social and economic problems."[29] Some scholars argue that war in fact was now *so* indispensable to the functioning of Roman society that "the Romans will have looked for war when none was ready at hand."[30] This is Rome the war machine. Hence Rome's extraordinary rise to power in the Mediterranean is easily explained as the result of continual aggression against its neighbors by a state that had become an insatiable Schumpeterian predator.[31] Scholars now regularly assert that Rome devoted itself to an expansionist foreign policy "to an exceptional degree"; that it pursued "a continuous policy of aggression"; that it was "the rotten apple" in the Hellenistic system of states.[32] The majority of studies on Roman expansion under the Middle Republic now take this stance.[33]

But problems exist here also. First, it is difficult to believe that the ordinary Roman farmers continually drafted for strenuous and dangerous service in the army in this period would have accepted such a burden unless they thought it inevitable and necessary for the protection of their families, property, and community. One should not forget that Roman troops were conscripted citizens, and a conscripted citizen-soldier and his family are going to be politically sensitive to wars of choice as opposed to wars of necessity. There *was* occasional reluctance of the populace to serve (see also Chapter 27), and it brought forth from the elite a public rhetoric that emphasized not profit or glory or land grants but – precisely – self-defense.[34] Successful war brought benefits to all levels of Roman society, but the enormous strains which war simultaneously imposed on that society should not be forgotten. It was not only that army service was disruptive of economic life. The fact is that Rome suffered *90* major defeats on the battlefield under the Republic.[35] This is a staggering number, suggesting in itself that the enemies Rome was fighting were not mere victims. Thousands of ordinary Roman farmers died in all these Roman defeats – and, of course, they died in victories as well. This is one reason why charges of warmongering were – as we know – politically damaging to members of the Roman elite.[36] One should not think of the Roman People as either fools or a mass of professional pirates.[37]

Nor should "the Roman senatorial aristocracy" be seen as a single entity pursuing its corporate interests through constant and even unnecessary war. The evidence indicates that factional, family, and personal jealousies within the Senate were intense (see also Chapters 1 and 17), and often acted to block glory-hunting by individuals. Indeed, many aristocrats did not spend their terms of public office in battle and glory (despite the way Livy sometimes reads), but in ordinary administration; such men had strong reasons not to allow excessive opportunities to others.[38] And senators knew that the mortality-rate among young military tribunes – often the sons of senatorial families – could be high in battle.[39] Senators are not likely to have gone to war lightly.

In understanding the assertive Roman stance in the interstate arena, we also need to consider that as a result of two centuries of severe attacks from neighboring states down to 340, Romans may well have been far more sensitive to possible security threats than are modern scholars sitting in their libraries. As Raaflaub says, Rome's difficult early history produced an elite that was "nervous and highly security-conscious, all too willing to take preventive actions whenever they perceived a possible threat, or to accept offers of alliance that to us seem to have entailed more problems than advantages."[40] But Raaflaub also tends to argue that after around 340 the external threats to Roman security were not real.[41] Given all the defeats the Roman suffered (see above), and enemies such as Hannibal, or the conquering Greek monarchs Philip V and Antiochus III, or the periodic invasions of central Italy by Celtic tribal peoples from the Po Valley, this seems doubtful. And it matters to our historical understanding whether the threats *were* real. Here Rich concludes from his study of Roman war-making in the Middle Republic that "The Senate never began a war without reasons, just because it had to have a war somewhere."[42]

To be sure, advocates of an insatiable Roman "war-machine" in the Middle Republic point to the action against the Dalmatians in 156 as an explicit case where Rome went to war because the Senate thought the army needed exercise (Polyb. 32.13.7–9; see also Chapter 28).[43] But even in the Dalmatian case, Polybius indicates that other factors were involved: the damaging raids of the Dalmatians against friends of Rome (which had led to frequent complaints to the Senate), insults to the Roman envoys sent to order the raiding stopped, and hence a desire to terrorize these tribes into obedience in a region where Roman power had long been little in evidence (Polyb. 32.9, 13.6, 8).[44] Moreover, – and this is striking – in Polybius the Dalmatian conflict takes place after a 12-year period of relative peace (32.13.7).[45]

Indeed, such incidents as the Dalmatian conflict must be balanced against the more important general trend: "continuous war, which was the dominant feature of Roman life in the fourth and third centuries, was already beginning to disappear in the first half of the second century."[46] Although the standard textbook dates for the *Pax Romana*, the famous "Roman Peace" in the Mediterranean, are 31 BC to AD 250, the fact is that the Roman Peace was emerging in large regions of the Mediterranean at a much earlier date: Sicily after 210; peninsular Italy after 200; the Po Valley after 190; most of Spain after 133; North Africa after 100; and for ever longer stretches of time in the Greek East.[47] But how can the *Pax Romana* have emerged in so many regions so early if the Roman Republic was a war machine not merely geared for war but dependent upon war in order to prosper? On this, Rich has shown that Republican warfare even during the great age of expansion in the Mediterranean, 264–146, was not at all regular in intensity, i.e., "mechanical" or even "biological." Rather, it varied greatly in intensity according to the real external crises Rome faced, and even in this period we find many consuls (the highest regularly elected officials) and praetors (the second-highest officials) serving as administrators of relatively peaceful provinces rather than as generals commanding large-scale fighting.[48]

This general trend suggests that when serious threats had finally all been dealt with, when control was finally established where the Romans needed it or simply desired it, Roman warfare in the Middle Republic noticeably diminished.[49] To be sure, in the Middle Republic a senatorial aristocrat could not run for public office at Rome without having served ten campaigns in the army (Polyb. 3.19.4) – and since election to public office was the goal of all senatorial aristocrats, the experience of army life and war was thus the primary life-experience of young elite men from about age 17 to 27.[50] Yet even in the period of great overseas expansion Cato the Elder's enormous influence in the Senate and before the People did not rest primarily on his military achievements (though he certainly had achievements to his credit).[51] Again, the most important figure in the Senate around 110 was M. Aemilius Scaurus, whose *auctoritas* was immense, but Scaurus had not reached his exalted status through achievement in war; in succeeding decades the same was true of influential figures such as L. Licinius Crassus or Q. Lutatius Catulus or – most obviously – M. Tullius Cicero. These men became famous and influential as orators, lawyers, and senatorial politicians, not military men. Indeed, it is clear from Cicero's own career that the Polybian requirement for 10 campaigns of army service before running for office had lapsed at Rome by 100 if not earlier.[52] Such evidence, taken in connection with the growing

Pax Romana, suggests that the intense militarism we see in the Middle Republic was a response to a specific set of circumstances and threats, and that as these circumstances became from the Roman point of view more congenial, the aristocracy and society became less militarized (see also Chapters 17 and 20).[53]

This is not at all to deny the militarism and bellicosity of Roman society under the Middle Republic. The Romans were successful after around 340 in expanding their power and influence, and they intended to be. A very significant percentage of male citizens (10–15 percent) were drafted into the army every year, which meant that direct experience of war among the Roman populace in the Middle Republic was from a modern perspective extraordinarily widespread (see also Chapters 13 and 28).[54] Roman culture, religion, and ethics were everywhere informed by militaristic values, and the Roman diplomatic stance toward the outside world was indeed instinctively one of coercion, not persuasion. All this is well established.[55]

Yet beyond the early growth of the Roman Peace under the Republic, believers in an insatiable "Roman war machine" as the explanation for Rome's success must deal with an additional analytical problem: they tend to study Roman "imperialism" in the Middle Republic as if Rome were the only polity of consequence in the world: the sole polity with harshly militaristic characteristics and the sole polity with an impact on historical events. This is an isolationist and introverted historiography. If one raises one's eyes from Rome itself to look at the broader geopolitical field in which Rome existed, the questions become different. What did the conduct of other states contribute to the history of Roman expansion in the Middle Republic? How different was Rome from the other major states with which it competed in Italy and then the Mediterranean for security and power? And if Rome was *not* much different, if the Romans were exceptionally bellicose and warlike in our terms but not in terms of their own environment, then how do we account for their exceptional success?

Here we can employ with profit the newer approaches used in the study of modern imperialisms. Whereas focus on the pathologies of the imperial metropole emerged as an intellectual response to modern European colonialism, conversely the end of European empires after World War II (and especially after 1960) created enough intellectual and political space for analyses that looked for explanation beyond the aggressive characteristics of the imperial state itself. Two such approaches claim to offer a fuller depiction of (complex) historical processes than does the metropole-centered focus.

The first approach underlines the role played in imperial expansion not by the institutions, characteristics, and actions of the imperial center, but by those of the polities that were eventually subordinated: "the periphery" as opposed to the metropole.[56] Situations often exist on the periphery that are conducive to intervention: weak states under local threat asking for help and protection from the outside power; factionalized and divided states where one faction or another asks for help from the outside power; relatively strong states – but not as strong as they think or wish – whose aggressive conduct draws justified geopolitical concern. Such situations and such polities lead naturally to efforts at metropolitan control – and so, to empire. Similarly, "periphery-centered" scholars stress that empires endure (as with Rome) or fail (as with Athens) not only through military force from the center, but in good part though the collaboration in imperial rule which metropoles are able to elicit (or not) from the people and polities of the subordinated periphery. Empire is in that sense from start to finish an interactive and collaborative project.

The virtue of the "periphery-centered" approach is that it gives agency in the historical process to actors other than the imperial center. When one puts explanatory focus on the (pathological) character and actions of the metropole alone, then the agency of these other actors, and the resultant interstate complexity of inter-action, is – ahistorically – denied.[57] Thus an important yet typical diplomatic interaction in the ancient world was a weaker state under local threat asking for the protection of a stronger one; stronger states strongly tended to answer such pleas, even though an affirmative answer meant the risk of transforming a local conflict into something larger. The phenomenon and its dangers had been examined in detail already by Thucydides in the fifth century.[58] Polybius thought that to accept a plea for protection from a weaker state was typical of all great states (24.10.11), and the Romans often faced such pleas. One cannot fully understand the development of Roman hegemony unless this interactive process is taken into account (see also Chapters 7 and 28). In 343, for instance, the town of Teanum Sidicinum in Campa-nia, threatened by attack from highland Samnites, called upon the city of Capua for protection. The Capuans answered affirmatively, but the Samnites defeated them twice and soon were threatening Capua itself. The Capuans in turn asked Rome for protection, and the Romans – after hesitation – answered affirmatively, warning the Samnites away from attacking Capua. The result was soon war between Rome and the Samnites. Livy's comment is that this war between Rome and the Samnites "arose from the quarrels of others" (7.29.3).[59] Political scientists, observing this phenom-enon at work in the modern world, have called it "empire by invitation" – invitation to protective hegemony from polities under local threat.[60] As happened in the case of Rome, Teanum, Capua, and the Samnites, the phenomenon – widespread as it was (and is) – posed obvious dangers for increased conflict between competing great powers.

Again, there are clear instances in antiquity where rulers of states on the periphery of a great power wrongly calculated their own strength, and acted provocatively. An example is Demetrius of Pharos' actions against states friendly to Rome in Illyria around 225–219, which eventually led to Roman military intervention – an inter-vention which would not have occurred without Demetrius' own aggressions.[61] Conversely, Roman diplomatic skill in eliciting widespread and long-lasting collabor-ation from people and polities on its periphery was certainly an important factor in the relatively stable hegemony that Rome was able to establish first in Italy and then in the Mediterranean primarily by force.[62] In the Greek East, furthermore, Roman diplomatic skill in creating hegemony came from an extended learning process in which the Romans themselves adapted significantly to Hellenistic ways of diplomatic interaction.[63]

Placing causal emphasis upon the actions and attitudes of the "peripheral" states and not solely on the metropole rightly emphasizes the complexity of interstate life and the difficulty which even a powerful state has in controlling (or even predicting) those interactions.[64] Yet this approach also runs a danger of gravely underestimating the role played by the great powers themselves. Just as the lesser states were not and are not solely the helpless victims of the aggressions of the great states, so the great powers were not and are not the helpless victims of the manipulations or provocations of peripheral polities. Decisions to intervene are ultimately theirs alone.[65] Similarly, while the eliciting of collaboration is a crucial element especially to the efficiency of imperial rule, one must remember that the use of force by the center is still the basis on which all empire is founded.[66]

Still, in leading us away from an introverted historiography where Rome, its culture, and its society are studied in isolation, and instead toward the character of the interactive geopolitical field in which metropoles such as Rome are situated, the periphery-centered scholars point us in a fruitful direction. This brings us to the final analytical approach: international-systems theory.

Modern international-systems theory is dominated by a family of pessimistic theories about international interaction called "Realism." Contemporary Realist thinking rose to intellectual prominence as a response to the terrible international events of the 1930s, followed by the horrors of World War II and then the onset and long persistence of the Cold War despite many diplomatic efforts at détente.[67] And while taken aback by the peaceful ending of the Cold War in 1989–91 and the alleged relative success and smooth working of international institutions during the 1990s, Realists have returned to their grim element ever since September 11, 2001.

What is grim about the interstate world as Realists portray it? The answer is clear from the major Realist manifesto, Kenneth Waltz's *Theory of International Politics* (1979). Waltz posits, first, that a state always exists in a system of which it is one unit among many; these systems have their own characteristics, which in turn have great impact upon the units within them. Second, much of the behavior of states in the international arena is caused by their self-seeking within a situation of anarchy. "Anarchy" means that the international world consists of sovereign and independent states without international law, and/or the effective means to enforce it. In the absence of international law, states must provide for their own security – which takes power. Hence, third, sternly power-maximizing behavior becomes prevalent among all decision-making elites.[68] Such conduct originates not so much from greed as from the desire for self-preservation in a fiercely competitive world: "States must meet the demands of the political eco-system or court annihilation."[69] The combination of anarchy with ruthless power-maximizing behavior leads to a fourth principle: "The state within states conducts its affairs in the brooding shadow of violence." In systems of interstate anarchy war, or the threat of war, is always present – and every state must be prepared to defend its interests through violence. Hence all states become highly militarized.[70] Indeed, in such an environment, "war is normal," that is, the normative means of resolving the serious conflicts of interest which often arise between and among independent and sovereign states.[71] Under such conditions, to say that a state frequently goes to war is merely to say that it is experiencing intense competition from other units within the anarchic system.[72] In sum, the interstate world is by its nature a tragic one, with states having to adapt their cultures to a very harsh environment. Successful adaptation to that environment leads states in the direction of bellicosity, aggression, and expansion – but that is just part of the tragedy.[73]

This approach is sociological – the sociology of states in interaction without law – as opposed to metropole-centered theories, which correspond, one may say, to the study of individual psychopathology. Any such sociological approach is wary of attributing large systemic effects to the conduct of a single individual, in this case a state – even an important one.[74] International relations theorists term the metropole-centered approach "unit attribute theory," and they are suspicious of it. The work of Harris and his supporters on Rome is, of course, a classic example of it. But if in a system of interstate anarchy warfare is regular and militarism the common behavior of most states, i.e., if war is the "normal" if tragic way by which most states resolve clashes of interest, then unit attribute theory must be used very sparingly. The danger lies in mistaking "normal" if tragic interstate violence for exceptional belligerence, in mistaking general tragedy for individual "evil."[75]

"Realist" international-systems theory has been criticized for offering too pessimistic a view of interstate relations. The interstate world may be (and always has been) an anarchy unregulated by international law, but not every system of anarchy is totally brutal.[76] On the other hand, the grim principles of state behavior proposed by Realism seem to hold up well if not for all systems, then at least for especially competitive (i.e., pathological) ones.[77]

Was the Hellenistic Mediterranean such a pathological system? If so, then any analysis of Roman expansion in the Middle Republic requires us to consider the pressures such a pathological state-system must have exerted on all states. We would also have to take into account not only the agency of weaker states on the periphery of Roman power, but – even more importantly – the agency of the powerful states that lay beyond the Roman periphery, that is, other metropoles or potential metropoles. On such a reconstruction, Rome was an aggressive and expansionist state but it existed and acted in a context it had not created and did not control. And Rome's main targets were other aggressive and expansionist states.[78]

For the ancient world, little work has yet been done on international-systems topics. Preliminary comments will have to suffice here. The Hellenistic Mediterranean indeed seems to have been a brutally competitive state system. It was a structural anarchy: although there were a few informal norms of interstate conduct, such as not murdering ambassadors coming from another state, there was no international law and no means of enforcing even the few informal norms that existed. Thus although many sacred sites and shrines were supposedly protected by decrees from states guaranteeing inviolability, in reality such places were sacked and looted with impunity. No "international" effort was ever mounted to protect them militarily, and no one was ever punished for sacking them.[79] Without mechanisms of enforcement, international law does not exist.[80] Polybius himself stressed to his audience that theirs was world where relations between states were unregulated by anyone with the ability to impose justice (5.67.11–68.2).

The absence of international law in the Hellenistic age, as in the previous Classical age, resulted in a strong trend toward militarism and power-maximizing conduct among states. Hellenistic Greeks, like Classical Greeks, did put significant effort into attempting mediation and arbitration of conflicts, and this did help somewhat to ameliorate the situation.[81] But no great state ever accepted third-party arbitration, turning over its decisions on state interests to another.[82] Thus as Rostovtzeff concluded long ago, on important interstate issues "in the ancient world, the sole deciding force was might."[83] This was a fundamental fact, and it affected the conduct of all polities.

One sometimes still hears talk of a "Hellenistic balance of power" as a conscious effort among the great Greek states to limit their war-making and their ambitions, to create a "consensual community."[84] But such a view is really no longer tenable. Pierre Lévêque and M. M. Austin have shown how much the Hellenistic monarchs were ideologically, politically, and socially focused on war for the security of their realms and their personal positions, how militaristic and expansionist in ethos the decision-making elites of these states were, and how huge were their wars, fought with far larger armies than in the Classical period.[85] Like the Romans, the Greeks fervently worshiped Victory (*Nike* – an important goddess with many temples, like Victoria at Rome). Warfare was endemic: in the 163 years between 323 and 160 just six years were without major wars involving one or more of the great dynasties.[86] What held for the monarchies held also for middle-sized polities such as the Kingdom of Pergamum or the Achaean League – which, like Rome, were at war just about every year. And the same was true even for very small city-states, which pursued their own ferocious "mini-imperialisms" against their small neighbors.[87] In the western Mediterranean, the rivals of Rome for security and power were all highly militaristic, bellicose, and aggressive polities: proceeding chronologically, this was true of the Latin cities, the Etruscan cities, the Aequi and Volsci, the Samnites, Tarentum, Carthage, and of course the Celtic peoples of northern Italy who had already destroyed Rome once.[88] Polybius thought the Romans were courageous – but he thought the Macedonians were fiercer and braver; this gives an idea of the Romans' environment.[89] An additional factor contributing to the Mediterranean chaos was unsophisticated diplomacy: there were no permanent ambassadorial missions between states, which meant that continuous communication – which moderns take for granted and think necessary for smooth relations – was lacking. Meanwhile the basic instinct of *all* ancient governments in interstate crises was to engage in threats and coercion (not persuasion) of others – a habit of diplomacy that contributed its own destabilizing impact to interstate relations.[90]

One should note also the fragility of all these ancient states compared to the robustness of modern nation-states, and the impact this may have had on decision making. City-states in antiquity could often simply be annihilated: 40 were destroyed in the Peloponnesian War alone. And the frailty of even powerful states is stunning. Carthage went from being an imperial power to the point of physical destruction at the hands of its own mercenaries between 245 and 240. Rome in the 230s and 220s might have disappeared under a tidal wave of Celtic attack (Polyb. 2.35) – as almost occurred in 390. The Ptolemaic empire based on Egypt, one of the three pillars of "the Hellenistic balance of power," collapsed between 207 and 200: a child on the throne; a series of unstable regencies in the capital at Alexandria (replaced by coup or riot); massive indigenous rebellion in Upper and Middle Egypt – followed by large-scale assault against the weakened empire from the vigorous rulers Philip V of Macedon and Antiochus III of Syria. In such a world, possible external security threats were bound to be taken with the utmost seriousness by all governing elites.[91] Similarly, to answer requests for help from weaker states affirmatively – dangerous as that could be – was to take steps to increase one's own resources while denying resources to potential competitors.[92] Such actions, if successfully carried through, also increased one's reputation as a powerful polity, and in a world without law, a fearsome reputation is an advantage in terms of security and survival.[93]

If the above depiction of the violent and lawless environment in which the Roman Republic came to maturity is correct, then the thesis that Rome owed its success primarily to exceptionally intense militarism, bellicosity, and aggression ought to be treated with skepticism. The Romans were indeed militaristic, bellicose, expansionist, and aggressive; but so was just about everyone else (in good part as a result of the pressures of the system). But if so, then Roman militarism, bellicosity, and aggressiveness cannot by themselves be the explanation for Rome's exceptional success during the Middle Republic.

What, then, *is* the explanation? When ancient intellectuals considered the rise of states to hegemonic power, they focused not on these states' internal pathologies but on their internal *strengths*, i.e., the strengths that allowed states to prevail over a cruel environment.[94] Hence Polybius in Book 6 of his *Histories* famously sought the explanation of Rome's rise to world power in the virtues of Rome's "mixed constitution," which fostered political stability in the face of crises and military disasters, as well as in the self-restrained and patriotic (self-sacrificing) Roman way of life (see also Chapters 12 and 18).[95] Let us for the moment adopt the ancient approach of looking for strengths and not pathologies.

When one considers the two main types of states with which the Romans competed for survival and power in the Mediterranean – city-states and large territorial monarchies – one sees that each of these types of polity had significant weaknesses. Most ancient city-states were fiercely reluctant to admit outsiders to citizenship. As a result, although they were highly integrated polities capable of mobilizing a high percentage of their people in a crisis, their population resources were strictly limited, and they could be overwhelmed. By contrast, great territorial monarchies had potential resources much larger than any city-state, but their diverse populations of taxpaying subjects were not well integrated into the state or with each other; and since the monarchical regimes depended on military prestige for political stability, they could not, politically, take many defeats on the battlefield. In short, one type of state competing with Rome was well integrated but not large, the other large but not well integrated.

By contrast, the Romans proved capable of producing a polity that was *both* large *and* relatively well integrated. The towns of Latium had long had strong mutual ties, including intermarriage and interchangeable citizenship, and the foundation-legends of Rome stressed that its population had always been multiethnic (Latins, Sabines, Etruscans, and even Greeks and Trojans; see also Chapters 22 and 25). Rome was thus never as fiercely exclusivist as the Greek city-states. After the Latin War of 340–338 the Senate evolved a system whereby Roman citizenship was divorced both from ethnicity and location (see also Chapter 28). Rather, it became purely a legal status that was available to the "deserving," who did not even have to speak Latin.

Combined with a clear willingness to use ferocious violence to keep subordinate polities in line, this relative Roman inclusiveness enabled Rome to create first a quite stable hegemony in west-central Italy in the generation after 340, and then a quite stable confederation throughout the entire Italian peninsula in the two generations that followed. To do this required great Roman skill in alliance management, but it produced a system with far greater potential rewards for loyal allies and far more likely punishments for the recalcitrant or rebellious than, for instance, the allies of Athens confronted in the fifth century. Hence Rome's stability and strength.[96]

And eventually more was involved than skillful alliance-management. There was also skill at managing integration. The Romans – very gradually – forged the peoples of Italy into one people, the Romans (see also Chapters 25 and 28).[97] It was a long and involved process not complete even by the end of the Republic. But the implications for Rome's exceptional success in the cruel Mediterranean competition for security and power were seen long ago by Theodor Mommsen.[98] He exaggerated in asserting that Rome came the closest among ancient Mediterranean polities to creating a nation-state. Rome created something different from a nation-state; otherwise the extension of Roman citizenship beyond Italy itself – a prominent phenomenon of the Empire – would not have occurred. Yet Mommsen was also correct to emphasize Rome's exceptional achievement. The creation of a polity that was simultaneously both large and increasingly well integrated gave Rome the advantage of control over large-scale resources which any large and integrated state would have in competition against large but potentially unstable dynastic empires or against small and limited city-states or loose tribal groupings.[99] I would argue that it was from this achievement, unique in the ancient world – along with intense Roman militarism, bellicosity, and aggressiveness, which must never be forgotten – that Roman hegemony emerged.

But what of the Late Republic, and the huge territorial conquests of Pompey, Caesar, and Augustus? Those conquests resulted in an enormous geographical expansion of direct Roman rule and indirect Roman influence. Pompey's campaigns in the East in the 60s led to the Roman annexation of Syria, previously the center of the Seleucid monarchy, as well as extending Roman power into Judaea and eastern Asia Minor. Caesar, of course, conquered Gaul as far as the Rhine, and even invaded Britain. Augustus annexed Egypt, previously the center of the Ptolemaic monarchy, and took the Roman frontier in the Balkans as far north as the Danube. He wished to go further, including the conquest of Germany as far as the Elbe.[100] Should not the spectacular military achievements of these Romans be seen as simply a continuation of the exceptionally pathological and aggressive militarism which many scholars have posited as characteristic of the Middle Republic?

To a large extent the answer to this complex issue has already been indirectly provided by Cornell, but several points deserve emphasis.[101] First, as the *Pax Romana* gradually emerged in many regions of the Mediterranean after 200/180, the *overall* character of Roman military endeavor changed. The majority of Roman armies and their commanders became engaged in garrison and administration duties, in military control, not in annual large-scale war (see above). This is already the situation that would exist more famously later, under the emperors. The Roman

Peace of the Republic, as during the Empire, usually involved a certain level of "low-intensity" warfare – e.g., bandit-suppression, or policing of the frontier. But this is not large-scale war: major wars against foreign enemies grew intermittent and infrequent after the early second century, and this overall trend continued into the Late Republic. Both periods thus stand together, in sharp contrast to the continual great conflicts in which Rome engaged in the fourth, third, and early second centuries. Similarly, the character of Roman military forces after the mid-second century was also changing. They were ceasing to be the annually conscripted militia of citizens typical of all ancient city-states, representative of and integral to Roman society; instead the army was gradually becoming a corps of often long-service professionals, men removed from general Roman society – a development which, again, would reach full fruition under the emperors.

The combination of these developments in fact suggests that Roman society over the last 130 years or so of the Republic was becoming an increasingly *civilian* one.[102] Strikingly, this development includes a majority of the senatorial aristocracy, whose socioeconomic-political needs have usually been depicted as the dynamic force behind the Middle Republican "war machine." Hence in the *Jugurthine War*, written in the 40s, the Roman historian Sallust could depict Marius in 107 comparing his own extensive military experience with the majority of the Senate, who only read about wars in books. Whether this is an accurate depiction of the situation in 107 is not clear, but Sallust clearly expected his aristocratic audience to accept the contrast as natural (see also Chapters 13 and 17).[103]

Yet the emergence of an increasingly civilian society at Rome is not the impression most people have of the Late Republic, because to see it requires careful scrutiny of scattered sources, and because the growth of the *Pax Romana* under the Republic and the increasingly civilian nature of Roman Republican society are subtle and long-term trends. Moreover, they are masked from us by two more dramatic phenomena of this period. First, the civil wars – hugely disruptive and destructive to Roman society – continue to fascinate modern scholars, with the result that the focus of modern attention is still on Roman warfare – though these were not *foreign* wars. And the towering figures of the great conquerors of the last generation of the Republic themselves mask the more subtle developments. The conquerors were famous men and fascinating men – but we must understand that they were unusual men.

Here Tim Cornell points to a second little noticed continuity between military conditions in the late Republic and later in the age of the emperors. Pompey's conquests in the East, Caesar's conquest of Gaul, Augustus' expansion to the Danube and his attempt to extend Roman control to the Elbe, Claudius' conquest of Britain, and Trajan's conquest of Dacia and attempted conquest of Mesopotamia are all of a piece. That is: from the 60s BC to the AD 110s, the relatively peaceful conditions prevailing in most of the Mediterranean – a situation already emerging a century before Pompey – were dramatically interrupted by territorial conquests at the hands of great Roman dynasts. This is true whether we call these dynasts emperors or not.[104] To this list of conquerors in Cornell one may add two failed large campaigns against the Parthians: Crassus' attempt in 54–53 to equal the conquests of Pompey and Caesar, and Marc Antony's similar effort in 36–34.[105]

If the Roman State after the early second century had already shifted *primarily* to a stance of administrative control, with its primary task the maintenance of military supervision over a now congenial Roman-dominated international environment, why and how did such great conquering figures arise? The answer is probably that the great dynasts were products of what has come to be called "the Roman Revolution." Possession of empire offered enormous opportunities for the acquisition of wealth, influence, and power for certain Roman aristocrats – the provincial governors of the richest provinces (see also Chapter 29).[106] Polybius (31.25.3-5a) already depicts Cato the Elder in the 150s as worried about the social and cultural consequences of the increasing flow of wealth into Rome (see also Chapter 17). But the men who had the opportunity to make the greatest fortunes were few in number. It depended upon which province you got to govern and the task assigned you by the Senate. Cicero did not do well financially as governor of poverty-stricken Cilicia in the late 50s, in part because of the nature of his province, in part because he refused to be involved in monetary corruption. Pompeius stands in stark contrast: after his conquests of 67–62 he "left the East not only its patron but to a considerable extent (and one hard to realize these days) its owner."[107] Pompeius' wealth came both from the vast loot won in his campaigns and from using his political influence on behalf of eastern governments (e.g., to gain official recognition at Rome for King Ariobarzanes II of Cappadocia.)[108] Caesar's loot from Gaul was similar.[109] A good portion of this wealth was then filtered down to Pompeius' and Caesars' officers and soldiers, as gifts and bonuses. These benefactions, in turn, won personal loyalty for the general – from armies that were no longer a citizen militia of small farmers as in the Middle Republic but were now made up of professionals drawn from a rural proletariat (see also Chapters 13 and 28). The result was that some within the Roman aristocracy, which was still a highly competitive society, acquired personal power and prestige on a hitherto unimaginable scale. While most men did not seek such great prizes, a few men did. The way was through foreign conquests.

The effect of these developments can be seen, for instance, in the career of M. Licinius Crassus. He was the conqueror of Spartacus in the 70s, but a slave-war brought little glory. Faced with the competition of Pompey and Caesar for the prestige and wealth necessary to dominate Roman politics, Crassus procured himself a large command against the Parthians. Plutarch indicates that this war was prompted by megalomania, and had no justification in morality or strategic utility (*Crass.* 16). It ended in disaster.[110] What is striking is not merely Plutarch's criticism, but how unpopular Crassus' war was among the Roman populace at the time. The tribune C. Ateius Capito openly accused Crassus of starting an unjust war "against men who had done the city no wrong" (Plut. *Crass.* 16.3) – publicly warning of dire omens from the gods as the army departed the city. Ateius had widespread support.[111] Nor did Caesar escape severe public criticism at Rome for pushing his mandate in Gaul to the point of total conquest, including war with the Germans. Cato the Younger in 55 publicly warned the Senate on religious grounds against Caesar's conduct toward the Germans, and later misfortunes to Caesar's army may have been portrayed as a fulfillment of Cato's prophesy (Plut. *Cat. Min.* 51.1, 3–4, *Caes.* 22.4).[112] Indeed, Caesar's own troops came close to mutiny as they marched against the German tribes, partly on grounds that they were undertaking a war that was neither morally proper (i.e., it was aggressive) nor formally voted at Rome, but undertaken merely on account of Caesar's personal ambition (*philotimia*: Cass. Dio 38.35.2).

What Cassius Dio terms ambition is probably the key. There is telling evidence that Pompey, Caesar, Antony, and for that matter Trajan, all patterned themselves in part not on Roman models but on Alexander the Great, the king of Macedon.[113] From the 60s until the death of Trajan 180 years later, certain men who possessed extraordinary abilities (or at least extraordinary ambitions) attempted to extend the frontiers of Roman control through large-scale war. In the last stages of the Republic, the vast riches, influence, and power that accrued to such men if successful made it difficult for traditional republican institutions to constrain and contain them – and so, in the end, there emerged the emperors. But these aggressive Roman dynasts were simply not the norm of Roman administration during these two centuries – neither in the Late Republic nor in the early Empire. Indeed, sometimes the conquerors acted because of fortuitous constellations of politics. The emperor Tiberius (AD 14–37), a very experienced general, administered a quite peaceful reign for 24 years, but the emperor Claudius' political position was shaky because he had no military or political credentials – and so Claudius from AD 43 began the conquest of Britain. In addition, once the emperors were in control at the center, it became politically dangerous for any provincial governor to engage in large-scale war. Emperors became reluctant even to put members of the senatorial class in charge of provinces with large armies, because of the potential political competition they represented.[114] These latter phenomena certainly helped to limit large-scale Roman war-making. But they are only contributing factors to the basic structural phenomenon we have underlined as developing once the major foreign powers in the Mediterranean, themselves highly aggressive states, had been defeated by Rome: the emerging structure of the *Pax Romana* under the Republic.

Our conclusion is that in conceptualizing the spectacular expansion of Roman power in the Middle Republic, the original and great age of Roman imperial expansion, we are best off not attributing what occurred simply to "unit attribute theory." Rome was not a static society, and its "unit attributes" did not remain constant. Under the pressure of powerful external threats Rome developed a harsh militarism that suffused all aspects of life; the bellicosity and aggressiveness of Rome of the Middle Republic are clear. But this did not make Rome into a war machine. The age of annual large-scale warfare was limited in time, because it was limited by circumstances. When the major threats to Rome's security had been ended or dealt with to Roman satisfaction, so did the age of annual war. During the last 130 years of the Republic an increasingly civilian society gradually emerged, a precursor to the civilian society we are more familiar with under the Empire. Great figures – both in the late Republic and under the Empire – were still motivated by great military ambitions, but these extraordinary men should not be allowed to overshadow the fundamental trend, which was no longer toward conquest and war.

The Romans, then, had proved themselves the most capable of the ferocious states with which they had competed for security and power in the fourth and third centuries in a very harsh and unforgiving anarchical state system. Successful by the early second century in the brutal competition for international power, the Romans then proved themselves capable for several centuries at running a large-scale and integrated state that was relatively peaceful (though never totally so), covering the entire Mediterranean. As Waltz therefore puts it (and he was not talking about Rome), in the grim competition of the international system, "states are alike in the tasks they face though not in their ability to perform them."[115] Roman society turned out to have the ability to perform several successive difficult tasks.

Or do remarks such as Waltz's simply constitute the smug discourse of the victors, "the Realist shrug," as a colleague of mine has said? "That's the way the world is."[116] Waltz is a powerful but particularly American voice: the world, and the past, may look different from Ottawa, or Mexico City – not to mention Paris or Baghdad. What is certain is that the study of Roman imperial expansion, amid all the fine scholarship that it has produced, will remain deeply affected by the interstate politics not of the past alone, but also of the modern world. Therefore, as Thornton indicated of all empires, the study of Rome's rise to world power will always be approached not just with intellect but with emotion.

Guide to Further Reading

The scholarly literature on Roman imperial expansion is vast, and the literature on theories of imperialism in general is even vaster. Compensation can be found in the fact that many studies in these controversial fields are of outstandingly high quality both in terms of content and style – though they rarely agree with each other. For imperialism theory in general, Hobson 1902 remains a fascinating and influential discussion of metropole-centered theory. Robinson and Gallagher 1961 is a wonderfully written reconstruction of British expansion in Africa that strongly emphasizes the independent agency of the polities on the periphery in bringing about British expansion; equally good and broader in scope (including France, Germany, and Italy), but working from the same theoretical foundation, is Robinson and Gallagher in Louis 1976: 73–127. The classic work on international systems theory and anarchy, and their impact upon the prevalence of war and state expansion, is Waltz 1979, but it is a difficult read. Mearsheimer 2001 offers a clear and forceful introduction to the Realist hypotheses; one could profitably begin there. On Roman imperial expansion under the Republic, the most influential work since the 1980s has been Harris 1979: well written and deeply researched, it approaches the issue of Roman expansion from a sternly metropole-centered analysis. Harris is required reading in the graduate study of Roman history, and his approach dominates the field. Raaflaub 1996 is an excellent and sophisticated study along the same lines. The beginning of a critique can be found in Sherwin-White 1980. Gruen 1984a is a monumental work emphasizing that Rome's empire in the Middle Republic was the result of an encounter (in this case, with Hellenistic traditions), not a construct that came out from Rome ready-made and was simply imposed. In that sense, it is in the Robinson and Gallagher tradition. Kallet-Marx 1995 carries this interactive approach down into the late Republic in good fashion. No work yet approaches Roman expansion from an overtly international-systems perspective. But Austin 1986 and Ma 2000 have transformed our understanding of the character of Hellenistic states large and small, emphasizing their intense and ferocious bellicosity; this finding in turn helps provide a broader context for the bellicosity of Roman culture and action. The most judicious and balanced analysis of the entire issue of expansion under the Republic is Rich 1993, who finds that many factors (not all of them on the Roman side) determined the course of Mediterranean events. And Cornell 1993, in a brilliant discussion of why Roman imperial expansion came to an end, offers much insight into its goals. Finally, for the complex and sophisticated response of the Greek intellectual Polybius to the growth of Roman power, see Eckstein 1995.

Notes

1   Raaflaub 1991: 570–1.
2   Richardson 1979: 1–11.
3   See Gell. 6.3.13 = ORF^4 Cato no. 8, 164 (speech for the Rhodians), with Kallet-Marx 1995: 26–7, and cf. Cic. *Mur.* 75. Gruen 1984a: 278–81, 284–5 argues the Romans only recognized their "empire" a century later (based on *Rhet. Her.* 4.9.13).
4   Thornton 1965: 2.
5   Richardson 1991: 1–9; Kallet-Marx 1995: 337–42.
6   Cf. Morgan 1990.
7   Derow 1979.
8   Cf. Lintott 1981.
9   Koebner and Schmidt 1964: 107–65.
10 Koebner and Schmidt 1964: 95.
11 Morris 1968.
12 Hobson 1902: esp. 71–93.
13 Lenin 1920 (written in 1916). Links between Hobson and Lenin: Eckstein 1991.
14 Gruen 1984a: 295–9.
15 Gruen 1984a: 300 n.64.
16 The decree also authorized the recovery of all property looted by Roman troops; cf. Gruen 1984a: 310–11.
17 E.g., Kahn 1986.
18 Marasco 1986.
19 Gruen 1984a: 304–5.
20 Briscoe 1973: 91–3.
21 Richardson 1986: 176–9.
22 Gruen 1982: 262–7; Kallet-Marx 1995: 11–41.
23 Hyam 1999; on the Boer War, see Porter 1980; Smith 1995.
24 Schumpeter 1951: 6.
25 Schumpeter 1951: 25.
26 See Schumpeter's own description of the Roman aristocracy: 1951: 51–3.
27 Cornell 1995: 81–118, 198–271; Williams 2001: 100–84.
28 Harris 1979: 9–130; Hopkins 1978: 25–37.

29   Raaflaub 1996: 278 (the quote), cf. 296–7; see also Harris 1984a: 14; Harris 1990: 505–6; Raaflaub, Richards, and Samons 1992: 27, 29.

30   Oakley 1993: 16; cf. Harris 1979: 161–254, esp. 213, 217.

31   See Harris 1979: 105–17, 161–254 *passim*; Harris 1984a: esp. 13–15, 21–2; Harris 1990a: esp. 495.

32   Raaflaub, Richards, and Samons 1992: 34, cf. 13–15, 49–50; Oakley 1993: 33, cf. 31; Keeley 1996: 128; cf. Veyne 1975: 794–5, 818–19, 823–4, Cornell 1995: 365, 367.

33   E.g., Rowland 1983; Rawson 1986, esp. 423; Mandell 1991; Hölkeskamp 1993; Habicht 1997: 185, cf. 194–5; Rosenstein 1999: 193–205; Campbell 2002: 167–9.

34   E.g., in 342: Hölkeskamp 1993: 12–13, and in 200: Livy 31.6–7.

35   Rosenstein 1990: 179–203.

36   E.g., criticisms of M. Claudius Marcellus' attack on Syracuse in 214: Eckstein 1987: 169–77; Manlius Vulso's attack on the Celts of Asia Minor in 188: Rich 1993: 56–9; Crassus in 54 for war against the Parthians: Ward 1977: 285–7. Certainly, the prospect of booty *may have* occasionally helped incite Roman citizen-soldiers to war – although whether Polyb. 1.11.2 exemplifies this is uncertain, since the meaning of the passage is disputed: see Eckstein 1980; Hoyos 1984.

37   Despite Veyne 1975: 819 and Cornell 1995: 367.

38   Sherwin-White 1980: 178, 1984: 11–15; cf. esp. Rich 1993: 55–60.

39   Harris's 20 percent of military tribunes in any battle (1979: 39–40) is probably too high, but clearly many young officers died. On mortality rates among Roman conscripts during the Middle Republic, see now Rosenstein 2004: 107–40.

40   Raaflaub 1996: 292; contrast Harris 1979: 189 on Rome's cynical alliance making.

41   Raaflaub 1991: 576.

42   Rich 1993: 60.

43   Harris 1979: 10, 233–4.

44   Cf. Wilkes 1969: 30–1; Walbank 1957–79: 3.535. The Dalmatians were not easy to defeat: App. *Illyr.* 11; Strabo 7.5.5.

45   Cf. Cornell 1993: 157.

46   Cornell 1993: 155.

47   Cornell 1993: 157–60.

48   Rich 1993: 139–70.

49   Rich 1993: 144–55.

50   Harris 1979: 10–12.

51   Astin 1978: 288–94.

52   Harris 1979: 12 and n.4.

53   But not unmilitarized: even Cicero had served as a young man during the Social War: Mitchell 1979: 8–9.

54   Hopkins 1978: 32–5.

55   Coercion: Veyne 1975; Derow 1979.

56   Robinson and Gallagher 1961; cf. Robinson and Gallagher 1962; Robinson 1972.

57   E.g., Mandell 1989: 89–94, esp. 92, discusses the outbreak of Rome's war with Antiochus III of Syria without reference to Antiochus' invasion of European Greece.

58   Thuc. 1.24–50, the appeal of Corcyra to Athens for protection against Corinth; cf. Crane 1992.

59   Cf. Messana's appeal in 264; Saguntum's in 220; and that of Egypt, Pergamum, Rhodes, and Athens in 200.

60   Lundestad 1986, 1990.

61   Eckstein 1994.

62   Strauss 1997; Ando 2000.

63   Gruen 1984a.

64   On complexity of interaction within a system, see Jervis 1997: 92–124, 253–95.

65   Louis 1976.

66   Campbell 2002; cf. Atmore 1984 on Britain in India.

67   Kahler 1997.

68   Mearsheimer 2001.

69   Sterling 1974: 336; self-preservation: Waltz 1988: 616.

70   Waltz 1979: 102.

71   Waltz 1959: 160; Waltz 1979: 102; Waltz 1988: 620–1 (quote); Waltz 2000: 8; Wight 1978: 137. Cf. Holsti 1991; Geller and Singer 1998.

72   Keeley 1996: 96.

73   Spirtas 1996: 385–423; Copeland 2000: 2, 17, 145–7, 165–8, 245; Mearsheimer 2001.

74   Abrams 1982: 2–3; Midlarsky 1988: 2–3; Thompson 1988: 12–13.

75   Waltz 1979: esp. 61–5, 68; Morgenthau 1973: 49–50.

76   Baldwin 1993; Kegley 1995; Wendt 1992 – all written in the "sunny" 1990s.

77   Wohlforth 2001.

78   Goldsworthy 2000b: 71.

79   Meyer 1999: 461; de Souza 1999: 69.

80   Badian 1983b: 401–5.

81   Ager 1996; Piccirilli 1973.

82   Badian 1983b: 402.

83   Rostovtzeff 1922: 43, cf. Larsen 1962: 233–4.

84   Klose 1982: esp. 80–8; Will 1984: 61; Bederman 2001: 43 and n.63.

85   Lévêque 1968; Austin 1986.

86   Lévêque 1968: 279 and n. 108, concluding that "la guerre est le recours…normal." Note, too, Polyb. 5.106.1–5, 18.3.2–8.

87   Ma 2000.

88   Early Latium: Giovannini 1999: 45–8; Etruria: Barker and Rasmussen 1998; Samnium: Dench 1995: 68, 100, 141, cf. Oakley 1993: 13; Tarentum: Wuilleumier 1939: 51–75, 185–93; Carthage: Ameling 1993, esp. 180–1; Celts: Williams 2001: 140–84. Note that the "Roman" swords whose cruelty so concerns Harris (1979: 52 and n.5) were in origin Celtiberian: Briscoe 1973: 140–1.

89   Polyb. 5.2.6, Livy (P) 32.18.1, (P) 45.30.7, with Eckstein 1997: 181–2.

90   Coercive diplomacy in Classical and Hellenistic Greece: see, e.g., Plut. *Pyrrh.* 27; Polyb. 4.25–6; Polyb. 4.47, 50; cf. Grant 1965. On its destabilizing impact: Ferrar 1981: 194–200; Stevenson 1997: esp. 134–5.

91   Beston 2000: 318–19 notes how often in Hellenistic literature the leaders of a state are depicted as worried while others enjoy themselves.

92   Glaser 1997.

93   Hoyos 1998: esp. 233–59; cf. Anderson 1999 on conditions in Philadelphia's inner city and its application to interstate relations: Offner 1995; Eckstein 2000: 877–9.

94   De Romilly 1977: 20–41.

95   Walbank 1972: ch. V, and now Walbank 1998.

96   Strauss 1997: 128–29.

97   *Contra*, however, Mouritsen 1998.

98   Mommsen 1907: 340–5.

99 On the advantages in interstate competition enjoyed by large well-integrated states, see Doyle 1986: 34–47.

100 Pompey: Seager 2002: 40–62; Caesar: Gelzer 1968: 102–94; cf. Goldsworthy 1998: 193–212. Augustus: Wells 1972.

101 Cornell 1993: 154–68.

102 Cornell 1993: 164–7.

103 Sall. *Iug.* 85.12 with Cornell 1993: 166.

104 Cornell 1993: 159.

105 Crassus: Ward 1977: 262–88; Antony: Syme 1939: 263–4.

106 Badian 1968a: 60–92. Governors were backed by armed force: 84–5.

107 Badian 1968a: 83–4.

108 Badian 1968a: 82–3. The same sort of political help to indigenous rulers made millionaires of British military leaders in Bengal and Awad in the eighteenth century: James 1997: 45–60.

109 Badian 1968a: 89–90.

110 Ward 1977: 262–88.

111 See Rosenstein 1990: 71 and n.62; cf. Ward 1977: 285–7.

112 Powell 1998: 123–4.

113 Michel 1967.

114 Cornell 1993: 162–3; cf. Birley 1953.

115 Waltz 1979: 96.

116 See Ashby 1984.

CHAPTER 27

The Economy: Agrarian Change During the Second Century

Luuk de Ligt

Sources and Obstacles

In his inaugural lecture on agricultural developments during the second century BC the Dutch ancient historian P. W. De Neeve argued that "the agrarian history of antiquity should, in principle, be treated as agrarian history in the general sense."[1] Few would dispute this assertion, if it is taken to mean that those trying to reconstruct agrarian developments in any period of Graeco-Roman history must acquaint themselves with at least some of the methods and models designed to deal with better documented phases of agrarian history.[2] On the other hand, a structural dearth of evidence, along with the fragmentary and anecdotal character of the extant sources, continues to make it difficult for students of ancient agrarian history to carry out the kind of in-depth analysis commonly undertaken by specialists in early modern agrarian history. In this sense it is certainly more correct to characterize ancient agrarian history as "ancient in the first place and agrarian only secondly."[3] In many cases, in fact, the state of the evidence makes it impossible to assess the relative merits of radically different reconstructions of basic trends in the agrarian economies of ancient societies. This has led one modern scholar to point out certain similarities between the study of ancient agrarian history and Jonathan Swift's satirical description of a scientific project "for extracting sunbeams out of cucumbers, which were to be put into vials hermetically sealed, and let out to warm the air in raw inclement summers."[4]

The prospects of those aspiring to recover the principal outlines of Italy's rural history during the second century may be slightly more favorable than those of the scientist of Swift's Academy of Lagado, but the materials available to them are certainly less than ideal (see also Chapter 28). The only extensive description of agrarian changes between 201 and 133 to have survived is that in the first book of

Appian's *Civil Wars* (*Bella Civilia*), a work of the second century AD. The main points of Appian's account can be summarized as follows. As the Romans conquered their way through Italy, they assigned its cultivated land to Roman colonists, sold it, or leased it out. "After the war" (possibly the Second Punic War) large tracts of land lay uncultivated, so general permission was given for this land to be used, its rent being set at one-tenth of the produce of arable land and one-fifth of that of orchards. According to Appian, the aim of this move was "to increase the numbers of the People of Italy." What actually happened, however, was that the rich gained possession of most of the uncultivated land and turned it into slave-staffed estates and ranches. As the poor were progressively bought out or driven off their holdings, "the powerful were becoming extremely rich . . . while the Italian People were suffering from depopulation and a shortage of men, worn down as they were by poverty and taxes and military service" (*B Civ.* 1.7). In order to deal with this development a tribunician law was passed forbidding any one person to hold more than 500 *iugera* of (public?) land and stating that no more than 100 large or 500 small animals might be pastured on state-owned tracts of uncultivated land. Unfortunately for the rural poor, the effect of this law was nil, partly because the ban on holdings of over 500 *iugera* could easily be evaded by means of bogus transfers to friends and relatives, but mainly because no real attempt was made to enforce the law, with the result that the rich simply ignored it. Although this description poses some serious problems of interpretation, the overall picture is reasonably clear: during the period preceding the Gracchan land reforms the rapid spread of large slave-staffed estates caused Italy's free peasantry to decline.[5]

Essentially the same picture emerges from Plutarch's *Life of Tiberius Gracchus*, which belongs to the early decades of the second century AD. According to Plutarch, Tiberius Gracchus began to worry about the fate of the rural poor when he was traveling through the coastal parts of Etruria, where "barbarian slaves introduced from abroad" had replaced the native Italian population (Plut. *Ti. Gracch.* 8.7). His solution was to propose a law declaring it illegal for anyone to hold more than 500 *iugera* of public land. All holdings in excess of this were to be repossessed by the state and distributed among the poor. Plutarch adds color to his sketch by quoting from a speech in which Tiberius Gracchus is said to have defended his proposal: "The wild beasts that roam over Italy have their dens and holes to lurk in, but the men who fight and die for their country enjoy the common air and light and nothing else . . . They are called the masters of the world, but they do not possess a single clod of earth which is truly their own" (*Ti. Gracch.* 9.4–5). This account is very similar to Appian's, again suggesting that during the second century Italy's free peasantry came under increasing threat from the ever-expanding slave-staffed estates of the rich.

A regrettable dearth of republican sources concerning developments in the Italian countryside makes it difficult to assess either of these impressionistic accounts, but the fact that agricultural slavery expanded during the second century is not in doubt (see also Chapters 14 and 28). Unless such an expansion did take place, it is impossible to account for the three large-scale slave revolts that took place in Italy and Sicily between 136 and 71 (alongside the smaller revolts that are known to have occurred in Campania and Apulia).[6] Confirmation is supplied by Cato's treatise

De Agricultura (written c.160), a rare piece of contemporary evidence that describes modestly sized slave-staffed farms (*villae*) for the commercial production of wine and olive oil. These model estates, one of 25 and one of 60 hectares, are described as being staffed with 16 and 13 slaves, respectively. Since Cato tells his readers how much various pieces of agricultural equipment currently cost in Suessa, Pompeii, Capua, and Nola (chs. 22 and 135), it can be inferred that his estates were somewhere in Campania.

Important though they are, these clues give us no insight into the quantitative expansion of rural slavery, which is why many ancient historians have approached this problem indirectly by examining the numerical decline of the free rural population. This leads us to the surviving literary and epigraphic evidence concerning demographic developments, which consists of a much discussed passage from Polybius (2.23–4), some fifteen census figures reported by Livy (or his epitomator), and three epigraphic references to the number of Roman citizens in the time of Augustus (see also Chapter 14).

Modern reconstructions of the fate of Italy's free rural population in the second century have tended to focus on Livy's figures, since these are the only data to refer directly to the period in question. The overall pattern can be summarized as follows. After a dramatic decline during the Second Punic War, the census figures rise to c.337,000 in 164/163, a figure higher than any of those recorded for the third century. After this peak, however, the figures suggest stabilization or slow decline, only c.318,000 citizens being included in the census of 136/135. Not surprisingly, this has been taken to confirm the theory that the free rural population, pushed off the land and reduced to poverty by the expansion of rural slavery, became less and less capable of physical reproduction.[7]

Apart from this mixed bag of literary data there is little to go on except the results of the extensive fieldwalking campaigns that took place in Italy from the early 1950s onward. As we shall presently see, many of the small sites discovered during these campaigns were initially dated to the last two centuries BC, leading some archaeologists to question the prevailing theory that this period witnessed a decline in the number of free country-dwellers. From the mid-1980s onward, however, there has been a growing awareness that many earlier interpretations were based on questionable methodological assumptions. As a result of this, the view that archaeology is the only reliable gateway to ancient rural society has been abandoned in favor of the view that all the existing "evidence," whether written or unwritten, is "soft" in the sense of being open to widely diverging interpretations.

Slaves and Peasants: Approaches and Problems

One of the most influential attempts so far to make sense of the miscellaneous data referred to above has been Hopkins' analysis of the causes and effects of the growth of a "slave society" in Italy during the last two centuries of the Republic.[8] The starting point of Hopkins' account was the observation that republican Rome was an uncompromisingly militaristic society in which a large proportion of the adult citizen population was recruited for military service. Initially most of the wars involving the Romans and their allies were fought on Italian soil, allowing peasant soldiers to return to their farms at the end of the fighting season. From about 200 onward, however, the theatre of war moved to Greece, Asia Minor, Africa, and Spain, taking over 100,000 Romans and other Italians overseas. The expansion of large estates was thus encouraged by what was effectively a form of peasant emigration.

Another factor propelling this expansion was the enormously increased income (in the form of booty, for example) generated by the acquisition of an empire. Most of this income flowed into the purses of the Roman elite and a significant part of it was used to buy Italian land, partly because there were few alternative opportunities for investment and partly because landowning conferred social status. Since much of the most desirable land in central and southern Italy had previously been cultivated by free peasants, the inevitable outcome of this development was a drastic decline in their numbers. During the second century free peasants who no longer had any land to work had two main options available to them: they could make a fresh start in a newly founded Roman or Latin colony (although few colonies were founded after 177), or they could try their luck in the expanding city of Rome. Here newly arrived peasant migrants became part of the urban proletariat that constituted the most important market for the surpluses produced on the slave-staffed *villae* of the rich. In this way the displacement of free peasants further stimulated the production of cash crops on large estates. When the number of impoverished peasants continued to grow during the first century, the Roman government devised a new solution: mass migration to newly established colonies in southern Gaul, Spain, Africa Proconsularis, and other parts of the Mediterranean. In economic terms the effect of this was to make even more land available for occupation by the elite.

One important merit of Hopkins' account is that it attempts something more than an impressionistic sketch, interpreting the scattered literary data against the background of an overall reconstruction of the history of Italy's population during the last two centuries of the Republic. Two pieces of ancient evidence are central to this reconstruction: Polybius' survey of Roman manpower resources in 225 BC and the Augustan census figures. Following the conclusions reached in Brunt's *Italian Manpower*, Hopkins assumed that central and southern Italy had some 3 million free inhabitants in 225 BC and that the free population of Cisalpine Gaul was of the order of 1.4 million. This gave the whole of Italy some 4.5 million free inhabitants, of whom more than 400,000 were likely to have been urban. His next step was to interpret the Augustan census figures as suggesting that Italy had roughly 4 million free inhabitants in 28 BC; of these he assigned 1.1 million to cities and towns. These figures, if correct, would mean that over the course of 200 years the rural free population declined from c.4.1 to c.2.9 million, a drop of nearly 30 percent. Meanwhile, Hopkins estimated Italy's slave population to have increased from c.500,000 in 225 to about 2 million in 28. Of these 2 million early-imperial slaves he assigned 1.2 million to the countryside. These calculations, of course, support Hopkins' central observation that "Roman peasant soldiers were fighting for their own displacement."[9]

In view of the elegant coherence of this account of the demographic and agrarian history of late republican Italy, it is not perhaps surprising that much research on this subject from the early 1980s onward could fairly be described as a series of attempts to refine and supplement a theory whose main tenets were generally accepted. One example of this approach is De Neeve's attempt to reassess certain aspects of Italian agrarian history in the light of Von Thünen's theory about the location of various types of market-orientated agricultural production.[10] This theory relies upon the observation that transport costs are a crucial factor in choosing sites for market-orientated farms. In practice this means not only that higher transport costs mean lower profits, but also that products "compete" for the use of land close to given market locations. Building on these ideas, Von Thünen was able to establish a broad relationship between location and intensity of production in market-orientated farms producing certain cash crops. The geographical pattern that his analysis showed consisted of a series of concentric belts surrounding the central market. In the belt closest to the center, market-orientated farmers tended to specialize in horticulture and intensive dairy farming. The second belt was characterized by market-orientated forestry and the third by arable farming whose intensity decreased as distance from the market increased. In the outmost ring, market-oriented producers concentrated on extensive stock-breeding.

As De Neeve pointed out, the ancient evidence concerning market-orientated production in the last two centuries of the Republic fits this model remarkably well. Cato and other sources tell us that labor-intensive horticulture and intensive breeding (*pastio villatica*) were practiced near Rome; there is also good evidence for a second belt characterized by slave-staffed "plantations" for the commercial production of wine and olive oil.[11] Furthermore, extensive stock-raising took place in peripheral regions such as Apulia and Lucania, exactly as the model predicts. For De Neeve, all this demonstrated that the market-oriented farms of the elite could properly be called "capitalistic" in that their owners or managers were engaged in cash-crop production that took into account the cost of all three "classical" factors of production (land, labor and capital). While this attempt to reinterpret the ancient evidence in the light of modern economic theory was strikingly novel, its results were of course entirely compatible with Hopkins' theories.

A second new line of inquiry that has enriched our understanding of slave-based agricultural production without altering the overall picture has to do with slave-staffed estates for the commercial production of grain, whose existence is implied by Von Thünen's distinction between "intensive" and "extensive" ways of growing grain. A publication that has had considerable influence in this area is Spurr's book on arable cultivation in Roman Italy, which demonstrates that slave-staffed *villae* cultivating grain could have been profitable.[12] Since there is good evidence to suggest that slaves were used in commercial arable farming (e.g., Col. *Rust.* 2.12.7–9), there can be no doubt that agricultural slavery was not specifically linked to commercial arboriculture. On the other hand, the fact that the three republican and early imperial agronomists do not have much to say about slave-staffed *villae* whose principal commercial product was grain may perhaps be taken as an indication that agricultural slaves were *typically* used on estates whose principal cash crops were grapes and olives.

In any case, the existence of slave-staffed grain-growing estates can easily be fitted into the traditional picture of the rise of the slave-staffed *villa*.

A third interesting development has been the realization that at least some of the features that characterize the agrarian economy of late republican Italy may well have dated back to the third or fourth centuries. Although the literary sources for this period occasionally refer to slave-run estates, the main reason for thinking that their development must have antedated the Second Punic War has to do with the history of debt-bondage. In a penetrating analysis, Finley called attention to the fact that the abolishment of voluntary contracts of debt-bondage in 326 or 313 must have created a demand for an alternative supply of laborers to work the estates of the rich. This demand can only have been met by using slaves.[13] At the same time, the sending out of a large number of impoverished peasants to colonies in various parts of Italy must have enabled the rich to build up larger holdings.[14] It is therefore highly probable that Italian agriculture was partly dependent upon slave labor well before the first decades of the second century. This convincing theory is, of course, entirely compatible with the overall tenor of Hopkins' analysis. The idea that the widespread use of slaves in Italian agriculture antedated the Second Punic War is, indeed, implied by his suggestion that there may have been around 500,000 slaves in Italy in 225.

Alongside these investigations into the history of agricultural slavery, another wave of recent publications has focused on the history of so-called transhumant pastoralism, a system in which herds or flocks of animals are kept in the lowlands during the cold season and taken to mountain pastures during the summer. Although the amount of ancient evidence relating to this type of pastoralism is not exactly overwhelming, it is striking to find that most of the surviving sources refer to the movement of flocks over long distances. Varro, for instance, turns out to have owned flocks that were driven all the way from northern Apulia to Reate, northeast of Rome (*Rust.* 2 praef. 6). Since there is good comparative evidence for flocks being driven over similarly long distances in early modern Italy and Spain, there has been a tendency to assume the existence of an almost timeless, specifically Mediterranean form of pastoralism characterized by the "horizontal" movement of animals between widely separated areas.[15] In recent years, however, considerable doubt has been cast on the idea that this type of pastoralism represents a logical response to the geographical and climatic conditions prevailing in southern Europe. Garnsey, for example, has emphasized the importance of various political and economic factors such as the unification of Italy, the confiscations that followed the Second Punic War, and the enrichment of Roman magnates during the wars of the second century, while others have identified the growth of Rome as a further precondition.[16] It is, in short, becoming increasingly clear that the rise of large-scale "horizontal" transhumance was the product of specific historical circumstances many of which happen to be identical with those behind the rise of slave-staffed *villae*.

While these new approaches have deepened our understanding of the emergence of slave-staffed estates and large-scale transhumant pastoralism, the fate of the free Italian peasantry has also attracted a considerable amount of attention. Here too some interesting new interpretations have been developed. A notable example is Rathbone's attempt to question the existence of any direct causal link between the

rise of slave-staffed *villae* and the numerical decline of the free peasantry of central
Italy. His reanalysis centered on the coastal town of Cosa, founded as a Latin colony
in 273. From a handful of literary data it would appear that Cosa originally had
between 3,500 and 5,000 colonists, with their families. Livy (33.24.8–9) reports that
the colony was permitted to take on a further 1,000 families in 197, which suggests
that by then its original population had declined by about 20 to 30 percent. According to Rathbone, a decline of this order can be accounted for by assuming that on
average around 700 adult men from Cosa would have been doing military service at
any one time, that the annual casualty rate was just over 7 percent and that when a
smallholder was killed on campaign his family would then abandon his allotment in
one out of four cases.[17] Against this theory it has been pointed out that the annual
call-up rate assumed by Rathbone is excessive and that he takes insufficient account of
the Roman census figures.[18] There are also some grounds for thinking that many
rural households were perfectly capable of dealing with the negative consequences of
heavy recruitment and high casualty rates. It has been pointed out, for instance, that
much of the productive work normally carried out by men could equally well have
been done by women, many of whom are likely to have become the *de facto* heads of
their households during the absence of their husbands or sons.[19] Moreover, many
rural households are likely to have contained an extended multigenerational family or
two coresident nuclear families. Such households would have been in a good position
to adjust to temporary or permanent changes in their manpower. We cannot, in fact,
rule out the possibility that in strictly economic terms the effects of conscription may
have been largely positive, since many rural households suffered from a structural
labor overcapacity.[20] Finally, Sallares has recently argued that the free population of
Cosa's rural territory in particular may well have declined not because of military
death rates, but because of malaria (see also Chapter 5).[21]

An alternative version of the theory of population decline stresses the importance
of economic factors. One of those to take this approach has been De Neeve, who
pointed out that even peasant families whose produce was principally used to supply
their own needs must have marketed some of their surpluses.[22] In his view, the
emergence and spread of market-orientated *villae*, most deliberately situated so as
to permit cost-effective transport, meant increased competition, which led to a
further contraction of the free rural population. An important weakness of this line
of reasoning is that most of republican Italy's peasants are likely to have operated their
farms according to the principles of what the Russian agronomist A. V. Chayanov
called a "peasant economy."[23] The kind of agricultural production described by this
term is carried on by a peasant family whose primary aim is to satisfy the consumption
needs of its members. Unlike "capitalist" farmers, the "peasants" within such an
economy do not take into account labor as a separate factor of production. The
practical significance of this is that peasants are willing to expend "irrationally" large
amounts of labor on cultivating their plots in order to secure the family's basic
sustenance. Since the same applies to the effort involved in getting their produce to
market, peasants are normally able to undercut the prices charged by highly efficient
commercial farmers.[24] The lesson to be learned from this is that the free peasants of
republican Italy may well have been more resilient than is often assumed, since they

were already prepared to accept the huge expenditure of labor necessary to survive on seemingly inadequate plots of land.

The theme of resilience leads us to another aspect of Italian agrarian history that has attracted a considerable amount of attention since the early 1980s. As may be gathered from the preceding pages, authors such as Appian and Plutarch are insistent as to the negative effects of the spread of slave-staffed estates, which they describe as pushing the free peasantry off the land. A close reading of the Roman agronomists reveals this picture to be overly pessimistic. As Peter Garnsey and Dominic Rathbone have demonstrated, Cato, Varro, and Columella are unanimous in assuming that slave-run *villae* specializing in wine or olives were structurally dependent on outside labor during the harvesting season, for the simple reason that they had to keep the permanent workforce as small as possible in order to turn a satisfactory profit. The main reason why the *villa* system was more economically efficient than traditional farming was, in fact, "because it carried no surplus labor... because it exploited the underemployment of the neighbouring free peasantry." In other words, the mere existence of a successful *villa* system implies the survival of a large pool of peasant smallholders (see also Chapter 28).[25]

The new approaches that we have discussed have undoubtedly introduced a more realistic view of agrarian change during the second century, but few ancient historians have gone so far as to challenge the prevailing view that the post-Hannibalic period witnessed a rapid growth in the slave population and a corresponding decrease in the number of free country-dwellers.[26] The revisionist conclusions reached by a group of archaeologists during the 1970s, however, did exactly that, as did Lo Cascio's radical reinterpretation of the demographic history of late republican Italy.

The first attempts to use archaeological evidence to investigate the fate of Italy's free peasantry were inspired by the results of the extensive fieldwalking campaigns carried out by the British School at Rome during the 1950s and 1960s. One of the basic assumptions underlying these campaigns was that the occupational history of entire landscapes could be recovered by identifying concentrations of pottery as the remains of ancient farm buildings and dating them to broad chronological periods. Thus sites containing sherds of grey bucchero were assigned to the fifth or fourth centuries BC, while sites with black-glaze or red-gloss pottery sherds were respectively dated to the last three centuries of the Republic (300–30 BC) or to the early Empire.[27] Applying this method to the *ager Veientanus* north of Rome, British archaeologists attributed far fewer sites to the late Etruscan period (127) than to the late republican (242), dating even more sites to the early Empire (327). Since the fieldwalking campaigns carried out in neighboring areas produced similar patterns, the inescapable conclusion seemed to be that, in southern Etruria at least, the last three centuries BC had witnessed not a drastic decline in numbers of free country-dwellers, but an unprecedented "population explosion."[28]

As archaeologists became more aware of methodological problems, however, it rapidly became obvious that this scenario of continuous demographic expansion required revision. A reexamination of 600 sherds collected during the fieldwalking campaigns of the 1950s and 1960s appeared to suggest that some 80 percent of the black-glaze pottery recovered in the south Etruria surveys belonged to the fourth to second centuries BC and a mere 20 percent to the period between 200 and 30 BC.[29] Could this mean that there really had been a "crisis of the second century BC" after all?

Further difficulties appeared when American and Italian teams carried out surveys in the territory of Cosa. Although literary evidence suggests that between 3,500 and 5,000 families were sent out to this Latin colony (cf. above), only a handful of the rural sites discovered during these campaigns could be assigned to the third century.[30] About 100 appeared to belong to the second century, but even this suggested a very poor recovery rate. This has led some scholars to suggest that many peasants may have lived in farms that were too flimsily built to show up as modern plowscatters, and others to venture the hypothesis that many smallholders may have been too poor to afford black-glaze pottery.[31]

Yet another problem has to do with the tendency to interpret the "small" republican sites as representing the farms of subsistence-oriented peasants and the "large" ones as the remains of slave-staffed *villae*. Here the main difficulty is that most of the "large" republican sites seem to date from the first century. Since this finding does not agree with the literary sources, Rathbone has suggested that many of the "small" sites discovered in the Italian countryside may actually represent modestly sized *villae* of the Catonian type. A corollary of this reinterpretation is that really big sites such as the *villa* at Settefinestre are seen as representing new consolidations of property by citizens who gained by the Social War and the Sullan proscriptions.[32] In any case, there are strong indications that the history of the *villa* followed different trajectories in different parts of Italy. It has long been realized, for instance, that the republican *villae* whose remains were discovered in the *ager Cosanus* were much larger than those represented by the "large" sites of southern Etruria.[33] There are also good grounds for believing that *villae* remained a phenomenon of limited importance in many inland districts such as the territories of Saturnia and Volaterra.[34] Finally, archaeologists have now begun to distance themselves from the traditional assumption that "large sites" (i.e., *villae*) should invariably be linked to what Marxist archaeologists used to call "the slave mode of production". It is becoming increasingly clear that *villae* existed in a variety of cultural and chronological contexts within which they had completely different functions. The few *villae* that have been discovered in the territory of Etruscan Volaterra, for example, seem to have functioned mainly as status symbols and as expressions of elite control over the landscape (see also Chapters 24 and 28).[35]

The impressive methodological advances that have been achieved in survey archaeology have thus done much to undermine the credibility of earlier claims concerning the spread of slave-staffed estates and the survival or otherwise of subsistence-oriented smallholders. This loss of innocence cannot be regarded as a negative development. In fact, the realization that both the literary and the archaeological data are open to various interpretations may well prepare the ground for new inquiries that do not privilege one type of evidence over the other (see also Chapter 28).

Perhaps predictably, the abandonment of earlier attempts to use archaeological evidence to undermine the testimony of the literary sources has not ended the debate over the exact nature of the "crisis" that supposedly prompted the Gracchan land reforms. Just as new forms of archaeological "source criticism" were beginning to gain ground in survey archaeology, a new challenge to the prevailing orthodoxy appeared in the form of the theories of the Italian ancient historian Lo Cascio (see Chapter 14). One of the building blocks of Lo Cascio's radical reinterpretation of late republican history is the theory that the Augustan census figures included only adult males. If this is correct, Italy must have had some 12 million free inhabitants in 28 BC, in other words three times as many as has traditionally been believed.[36] If there were only 4.5 million free Italians in 225 (cf. above), however, the theory requires an implausible rate of population growth. According to Lo Cascio, the solution to this problem may well be that the Polybian manpower figures included only those adult males aged between 17 and 45 (the so-called *iuniores*). The population of central and southern Italy would thus have been around 3.5 million and Italy as a whole would have had about 5 million inhabitants.[37] If these figures are accepted, the Augustan figure can be accounted for by assuming that the free Italian population expanded at an annual rate of 0.5 percent during the last two centuries of the Republic.

For the purposes of this chapter, the most interesting aspect of this alternative reconstruction is that it is incompatible with the traditional view that the Gracchan land reforms were prompted by worries concerning the number of Roman citizens eligible for the call-up.[38] This explains why Lo Cascio reinterprets Appian's statement that Tiberius Gracchus was trying to avert the threat of *dysandria* (usually translated as "lack of men") among the Italian population as referring specifically to the numbers of well-fed men who were physically fit for military service.[39] Since a shortage of such men can be interpreted as the inevitable result of population growth without any corresponding increase in the amount of land under cultivation, the Gracchan reforms might be seen as intended to solve a social and military problem rather than to halt a demographic downturn in the free Italian population.[40]

Although this ingenious theory has impressed some ancient historians, it has also met with severe criticism. It has been pointed out that Lo Cascio's estimates imply that the population of central and southern Italy (including slaves) was at least 13 million in 28 BC, even though the peninsula had only about 6.3 million inhabitants in 1600. Furthermore, if only 40 percent of Italy's land surface was cultivated in early imperial times, Lo Cascio's figures imply an average population density equal to that of the famously fertile Nile valley. Finally, the theory can only be maintained by assuming that the Roman censuses of the second and first centuries were utterly unsuccessful, with no more than one third of adult males being registered by the censors in 70/69. This has led one critic to comment that had Lo Cascio's figures been correct, "the census of 70/69 BC would have been a joke rather than a census."[41] For all these reasons, Lo Cascio's theory cannot be regarded as a convincing alternative to earlier theories about the nature of the agrarian "crisis" that gave rise to the *lex Sempronia agraria* of 133 (see also Chapter 14).

Toward a New Interpretation?

As we have seen, Appian and Plutarch describe the second century as a period during which Italy's free population declined as a result of the expansion of rural slavery. Although twentieth-century scholarship has found fault with their accounts in numerous details, their general sketch of the background to the Gracchan land reforms is still very much on the table. Thus Hopkins' contention that Italy's free country-dwelling population declined from c.4.1 million to c.2.9 million between 225 and 28, while the slave population increased from c.500,000 to roughly 2 million, is essentially a sophisticated restatement of the old theory that the expansion of rural slavery pushed large numbers of free peasants off the land. Recent research has embellished this picture with many additional nuances, but every attempt to offer a *radically* new reconstruction has either suffered from serious methodological weaknesses or simply failed to fit the surviving evidence convincingly.

Despite this, even a superficial reexamination of some of the basic assumptions underlying most recent work on this subject is enough to reveal unexplored possibilities, especially with respect to the demographic reconstructions that inform many publications on late republican history. Even if Lo Cascio's "high" theory of demographic development is rejected, the extant data can be used to support a reconstruction of agrarian development during this period that is substantially different from any put forward so far.

One of the assumptions I have in mind concerns the expansion of rural slavery. As we have seen, Hopkins assumes that early imperial Italy had some 2 million slaves, of whom 1.2 million worked in the countryside. One of the reasons why these figures do not inspire much confidence is that the few pieces of relevant information in the ancient sources are compatible with a very wide range of estimates. Even if Appian's assertion that some 120,000 slaves took part in Spartacus' uprising is correct, for example, it does not permit us to infer that there must have been 2 or 3 million slaves in late republican Italy. More generally, the fact that Hopkins' scheme assumes a third of Italy's population in 28 to have been slaves raises the suspicion that the figure of 2 million was inspired by the fact that 33 percent of people in the antebellum South were slaves.[42] Finally and perhaps most importantly, a labor force of 1.2 million rural slaves would have been wildly in excess of that required to work the wine and olive-oil estates of the elite. Jongman has demonstrated that fewer than 200,000 hectares of Italian land could have kept Italy's entire urban population fully supplied with wine and olive oil during the early Empire.[43] Now, according to the Roman agronomists it took one slave to work 7 *iugera* (1.75 ha.) of vineyard, while oleoculture required an even lower labor input per hectare (Col. *Rust.* 3.3.8; Pliny *HN* 17.215).[44] It seems realistic to assume from this that Italian arboriculture in general required one slave for every two hectares. Combining this ratio with Jongman's estimate of the amount of land required to keep the cities and towns of Italy supplied with wine and olive oil suggests that this level of production would have demanded only 100,000 slaves. Even if we assume that it took another 100,000 slaves to assist and/or supervise this force and that 50,000 more were used to grow the cereals consumed by all the estate staff, we will still have a figure of only 250,000. The theory that there were 1.2 million rural slaves in late republican Italy can thus only be maintained by assuming that some 80 percent of the rural slave work force was used to grow grain.[45] Although slaves are known to have been used in grain farming (cf. above), it seems doubtful whether any ancient historian would be prepared to defend this extreme hypothesis. The only other way to push up the number of rural slaves would be to assume that hundreds of thousands of slaves were employed not on slave-staffed *villae* but on small family farms. To the best of my knowledge there is no evidence to support this theory.

For the purposes of this contribution it is important not to lose sight of the fact that the production figures underlying my calculations relate to the early years of the Empire, when Italy's towns and cities probably had about 1.9 million inhabitants.[46] Italy must, however, have been far less extensively urbanized in 133 than in (say) 28 BC and the number of slaves needed to grow grapes and olives for the urban market of that time can only have been correspondingly lower. Moreover, if the early imperial figures may require upward adjustment to take substantial wine exports from Italy into account, the same is unlikely to apply to the period 201–133. It may therefore be suggested that even if slaves were widely employed in grain production during this period, the total number of slaves in Italy is likely to have been far smaller than is usually thought. This finding is entirely compatible with the theory that the development of slave-staffed estates reduced the amount of land cultivated by free peasants *in certain parts of Italy.* It seems, however, far-fetched to suppose that regional developments of this sort brought about a decline in the number of free country-dwellers in Italy as a whole.

If the number of rurally employed slaves has been exaggerated, the question arises whether the data we have on the free Italian population support the traditional view that the free peasantry declined during the second century. As we have seen, Hopkins' reconstruction of Italy's demographic history during the last two centuries of the Republic was based on the idea that Italy (including Cisalpina) had some 4 million free inhabitants in the age of Augustus, having had 4.5 million in 225. Although the proper interpretation of the Augustan census figures is a hotly debated issue (see also Chapter 14), the traditional reading on which the former figure is based is almost certainly correct. What, though, of the theory that Italy had 4.5 million free inhabitants in 225? As I have already explained, this figure has been derived by assuming that central and southern Italy had 3 million free inhabitants and Cisalpine Gaul 1.5 million. Both these estimates are, however, open to challenge. The figure for Cisalpine Gaul is based on Brunt's suggestion that there were probably between 300,000 and 500,000 adult males in this region on the eve of the Second Punic War.[47] Extrapolation from the very highest figure in this range suggests that Cisalpina had 1.5 million free inhabitants in all. If the lowest figure in the range is used instead, however, the free population of Cisalpine Gaul drops to around 1 million and that of Italy as a whole to around 4 million (see also Chapter 14).

The theory that central and southern Italy had about 3 million free inhabitants in 225 is equally dubious, being based on a controversial reading of the Polybian manpower figures. The essence of this reading is that these figures included every adult male Roman citizen regardless of his age, but counted only men aged between 17 and 45 in the case of the Latin and other Italian allies. If, however, we assume that all free adult men were counted whatever their age and origin, the free population of central and southern Italy drops from 3 to 2.5 million.[48] In short, since the significance of the figures for 225 is a matter of interpretation it is entirely possible that Italy had just as many free inhabitants in 28 as it did in 225. We cannot even rule out the possibility that the combined impact of the Second Punic War, the civil wars of the first century, and the emigration of large numbers of Italians to colonies outside the Italian peninsula was insufficient to prevent the free Italian population from *growing* from around 3.5 million in 225 BC to roughly 4 million in 28 BC.

A closely related question concerns the quantitative fate of the Roman citizen body. As is generally known, every reconstruction of the demographic trajectory of this Italian subgroup has to rely upon the surviving census figures, whose correct inter-pretation remains controversial. Even if not all of these figures can be explained, however, there seem to be no good grounds to dispute the widely held view that in principle at least the Roman censors were supposed to register all male citizens age 17 or over, including proletarians and the so-called *cives sine suffragio* ("citizens without the vote").[49] Building on this interpretation, many scholars have observed that the census figure for 164/163, when around 337,000 citizens were registered, is substantially higher than any of the figures relating to the third century. This would seem to indicate that the citizen body recovered quickly from the terrible losses suffered during the Second Punic War.[50]

Interpreting the census figures for the next five decades is far more difficult. The main problem is that the figures for the period 159–130 are slightly lower than that for 164/163 (only around 319,000 citizens being counted in 131/130), but also much lower than the figures for 125/124 and 115/114, when the censors managed to register some 395,000 citizens. Unsurprisingly, the 159–130 figures have been interpreted as illustrating the decline of the free rural population that allegedly lay behind the Gracchan land reforms. A major weakness of this theory is, of course, that it cannot explain the sudden increase reflected in the figures for 125/124 and 115/114. The only way around this problem is to follow Beloch's suggestion that the figures for these years should be amended to around 295,000.[51] In other words, the theory of population decline can only be maintained by manipulating the surviving evidence!

For this reason alone it seems preferable to seek an alternative explanation for the figures for the three decades preceding the Gracchan land reforms. One strong possibility is that Rome's prolonged overseas campaigns (especially the unrewarding wars in Spain) may have made the prospect of military service far less appealing to many adult citizens. Since the most obvious way of dodging the draft would have been to avoid being registered by the censors, such a change in attitude could very well account for the relatively low census figures of the mid-second century.[52] In short, while the high census figures for 125/124 and 115/114 are completely incompatible with any theory of population decline, the low figures for the period preceding the Gracchan land reforms can easily be accommodated within a scenario of continuing demographic expansion.

In order to put some flesh on the bones of this alternative reconstruction we must also take into account the growth of the city of Rome (see also Chapter 16). A dearth of reliable data makes it impossible to follow this process in detail, which is why the few estimates of Rome's population on the eve of the Gracchan land reforms that have been attempted range from around 200,000 to 400,000.[53] Despite the uncertainty surrounding them, even these very approximate figures have interesting implications for the numerical fate of the free country-dwelling population during the second century. Even if we allow pre-Gracchan Rome the largest population ever suggested, it is unlikely to have been inhabited by more than 100,000 adult male citizens. Combining this figure with our earlier finding that Italy had about 400,000 adult male citizens in the late 130s suggests that some 300,000 male citizens age 17 or over must have lived in smaller towns or in the countryside. Interestingly, this rough estimate more or less equals Italy's total number of adult male citizens on the eve of the Hannibalic War.[54] If the census figures for 125/124 and 115/114 are correct, then we must conclude that the theory of a drastic decline in the number of free country-dwellers is completely untenable, at least with regard to the second century. This conclusion fits in quite nicely with our earlier finding that the expansion of rural slavery must have been much less dramatic than is often assumed.

Why, then, do our sources explain the Sempronian Land Law of 133 as an attempt to halt a decline in the rural population caused by the steady expansion of slave-staffed estates? Part of the answer to this question may be that this law was prompted by developments in the coastal districts of Etruria (cf. Plut. *Ti. Gracch.* 8.7) and other parts of central Italy where slave-staffed estates are indeed likely to have pushed a significant number of free peasants off the land (see also Chapter 28). It may, however, also be suggested that Tiberius Gracchus was reacting to an increase in rural poverty without realizing that this was being caused by an ongoing process of demographic growth.[55] The census figures for the 140s and 130s, moreover, may well have led him to believe that the free citizen population had begun to decline: not until 125/124 BC would the figures reveal that the Republic now had more citizens than ever before.

If this interpretation is correct, the period 201–133 witnessed both the expansion of rural slavery and an increase in the number of Italy's country-dwelling citizens. Initially the coexistence of these processes resulted in intense competition for access to public land in Italy.[56] When the Roman elite came out on top, political stability could only be preserved by finding an alternative outlet for the expanding free population of Italy. The sending out of some 265,000 adult male citizens to colonies in other parts of the Mediterranean should be seen as part of the solution to this problem.

Guide to Further Reading

Although agrarian developments in late republican Italy have attracted a great deal of attention over the past few decades, Toynbee 1965 and Hopkins 1978 remain the most recent synthetic accounts. Recent discussions of the *lex Sempronia agraria* of 133 and of the undoing of the Gracchan land reforms include Bringmann 1985, Perelli 1993, and de Ligt 2001. More general discussions of the history of state-owned land during the Republic may be found in Flach 1990, Gargola 1995, Hermon 2001, and Rathbone 2003. A path-breaking new edition of the epigraphic *lex agraria* of 111 (or 106?) is included in the first volume of Crawford 1996b, whose commentary does not, however, entirely supersede that of Lintott 1992. Another interesting topic is the growing importance of tenancy, on which see de Neeve 1984a, Rosafio 1993, Scheidel 1994a, de Ligt 2000, and Rosenstein 2004: 76–7, 181–2. There is also a considerable body of literature on the rise of the *vilicus* and on the legal rules governing the management of slave-staffed *villae*; see Aubert 1994, Carlsen 1995, and de Ligt 1999. The use of wage labor in Italian agriculture and the connotations of the Latin term *mercennarius* are discussed by Bürge 1990, Möller 1993, and Scheidel 1994a. On the habitation patterns of the free rural population Garnsey 1979 (to be consulted with Scheidel's valuable addendum in Garnsey 1998) remains fundamental. For extensive bibliographical information on the recent wave of demographic studies see Chapter 14 of this volume.

Notes

1   De Neeve 1984b: 41.
2   Scheidel 1994a: 1.
3   De Neeve 1990: 398–9.
4   Scheidel 1994a: 1, referring to *Gulliver's Travels* III.5.
5   Richardson 1980; Bleicken 1990; Rathbone 2003.
6   Bradley 1989.
7   Brunt 1971a.
8   Hopkins 1978.
9   Hopkins 1978: 30.
10 De Neeve 1984b; cf. Thünen 1966.
11 Cf. Rinkewitz 1984; Morley 1996.
12 Spurr 1986; cf. Scheidel 1994b.
13 Finley 1980: 83–6; Rosenstein 2004: 77.
14 Cornell 1995: 393–4.
15 Gabba and Pasquinucci 1979.
16 Garnsey 1986; Morley 1996: 157.
17 Rathbone 1981: 18–19.
18 Rich 1983: 296 n.44.
19 Evans 1991; Rosenstein 2004: 93–8.
20 Erdkamp 1998: 266–7.
21 Sallares 2002: 250–1.
22 De Neeve 1984b: 15, 32–3.
23 Chayanov 1966.
24 De Ligt 1993: 214 n.57.
25 Garnsey 1980; Rathbone 1981: quote p.15; cf. Ikeguchi 1999–2000.
26 Cf. Cornell 1996.
27 Potter 1979.
28 Frederiksen 1970–1.
29 Liverani 1984.
30 Dyson 1978; Attolini et al. 1991.
31 Arthur 1991b: 64; Rathbone 1993b: 19.

32   Rathbone 1993b: 19.
33   Potter 1991: 199.
34   Rasmussen 1991; Terrenato 1998.
35   Terrenato 1998.
36   Lo Cascio 1994.
37   Lo Cascio 1999b.
38   Cf. Morley 2001.
39   Lo Cascio 2003.
40   Lo Cascio 1999a: 230–1.
41   Scheidel 1996: 168.
42   Scheidel 1999b.
43   Jongman 2003.
44   Duncan-Jones 1982: 327.
45   De Ligt 2003, 2004.
46   Jongman 2003.
47   Brunt 1971a: 189.
48   De Ligt 2003, 2004.
49   Brunt 1971a.
50   E.g., Erdkamp 1998.
51   Beloch 1886: 351; Toynbee 1965: 471.
52   De Ligt 2003, 2004; Rosenstein 2004: 157.
53   Brunt 1971a: 384; Virlouvet 1994: 20.
54   Brunt 1971a: 61–2.
55   De Ligt 2003, 2004; Rosenstein 2004: 155.
56   Cf. Morley 2001: 58.

CHAPTER 28

Rome and Italy

John R. Patterson

Introduction

Italy was (and is) characterized by the variety of its natural landscapes (see also Chapter 5), and this natural diversity has been reflected in the diverse histories of the different regions of the peninsula – cultural, political, and economic. The multiplicity of languages spoken (and written) in ancient Italy in addition to Latin included Oscan, Umbrian, Etruscan, and Greek, which was used by the settlers who had established cities on the western and southern coasts of Italy during the eighth to sixth centuries. Urban settlement was characteristic also of the Etruscan peoples in the seventh and sixth centuries; by contrast, the Samnites and their Oscan-speaking neighbors in the central Apennines largely lived in scattered communities organized around hillforts, villages, and sanctuaries, and a range of possibilities can be detected between these two extremes. Funerary practices again show great diversity, with different forms of inhumation and cremation being used in the various regions and sometimes a combination of the two: in Daunia, for example, the deceased might be cremated on a pyre within the tomb, which was then sealed up, as in the case of the "Tomb of the Osiers" at Canusium.[1]

Writing the history of Italy in the period of the Roman Republic inevitably involves taking account of these patterns of variation: indeed, it was only with Augustus that a unified entity resembling modern "Italy" came into being. The Transpadani (peoples occupying the territory between the Alps and the river Po) were granted Roman citizenship only under Julius Caesar, and during the Empire Sicily and Sardinia continued to have the status of provinces. A further complication is the nature of the source material available: the literary texts on which we largely rely for the narrative of Rome's conquest of, and subsequent relationships with, the peoples of Italy tend to see the history of Italy from the point of view of the victorious Romans rather than that of the Italians. These texts, frequently written centuries after the events they describe, are also influenced by the political context in which the authors (or the sources on which they themselves rely) were writing, whether the fierce rivalries of high politics in republican Rome or the more peaceful but equally misleading perspective of the imperial provinces (see also Chapter 2), and it is frequently difficult to tell how far the anecdotes they report can be used to construct a more general picture of the economic and social changes of the period. By comparison with the Empire, few Roman inscriptions were set up in the Republican period, though some inscribed texts in languages other than Latin have been preserved which cast light on the traditions of indigenous cultures and the changing political institutions of Rome's allies, for example, the adoption of Roman terminology for magistracies (see also Chapter 3). Archaeology therefore takes on a particular importance in our understanding of republican Italy, helping to demonstrate the degree to which Roman rule impacted on different areas of the peninsula, and in particular the ways in which Italians adopted Roman (or Greek) cultural traditions as well as the social and economic effects of Roman conquest, in terms of the impact on patterns of rural settlement and the development of urban centers. In this period, Rome's relationship with the Italian peoples was central to virtually all aspects of Roman political and economic life: the Italians provided substantial contingents for Rome's armies throughout, the grants of citizenship following the Social War dramatically increased the number of Roman citizens, and the effects of civil war, coupled with more general patterns of agricultural change, led to an instability in the countryside of Italy which was to contribute in a significant way to the eventual collapse of the Roman Republic. All the more reason, then, to seek to understand the nature of Rome's relationships with Italy and its peoples in this period; though the complex picture being revealed by current archaeological work warns against excessively generalizing explanations.

Rome's Conquest of Italy in the Late Fourth and Early Third Centuries

The conquest of Italy allowed the Romans to devise and perfect the techniques with which they were later able to establish and maintain control over an empire that extended beyond the peninsula and, indeed, beyond the Mediterranean region. These ranged from extreme violence to diplomatic initiatives, which often involved co-opting the support of local elites, and were deployed according to the sociopolitical structures the Romans encountered among their enemies and the nature of local reaction to the advent of Roman power. While the Romans normally saw themselves as responding to threats to their own interests, and the military ethos of Roman society and the ambitions of individual generals had an important part to play (see also Chapter 26), recurrent long-term strategies can also be detected, though the ways in which they were implemented reflected local circumstances.[2]

A significant turning point in this respect was the "Latin war" of 341–338. In the aftermath of a revolt by the Latins, the ancient alliance between Rome and the peoples of Latium was dissolved and a new framework of relationships between Rome and the Italian peoples was established in the vicinity of Rome and beyond. Some communities were incorporated into the Roman state and received full citizenship; others were granted *civitas sine suffragio* ("citizenship without voting-rights"), and were liable for the same burdens and responsibilities as full citizens but without the right to participate in Roman politics. Alliances were also established with individual communities or peoples beyond Latium who had not been awarded either form of citizenship. All had to provide manpower for the military forces led by Rome (see also Chapters 13 and 26): by 264 the Romans had over 150 such allies.[3]

Also particularly characteristic of this period, and central to Roman strategy in Italy, was the establishment of new communities known as "Roman" (or "citizen") and Latin colonies. The former tended to be small in scale (perhaps only several hundred men) and consisted of Roman citizens; the latter were rather larger and might include several thousand colonists, comprising Latins and even elements from the existing local populations as well as Romans. Those settled in Roman colonies retained their citizenship, while settlers in Latin colonies became citizens of their new community, which acquired political institutions and structures modeled on those of Rome. Both forms of colony, however, were strategic in aim, establishing strongholds loyal to Rome in areas currently being brought under Roman rule or recently conquered.[4] How this worked in one particular area, the central Apennines, can be seen from the establishment of Latin colonies at Cales (334), Fregellae (328), and Interamna Lirenas (312) in the valley of the Liri, and Luceria (314) in Daunia to the east, which together surrounded the Samnite heartland. After the Samnites rose in support of Pyrrhus' invasion, additional colonies were set up at Beneventum (268) to the south and Aesernia (263) to the north, which further contributed to isolating them. In the same way, Latin colonies were established at Alba Fucens in 303 and (after several years of trying) in 298 at Carsioli, which controlled the territory of the Aequi (Livy 10.3.2, 10.13.1).[5]

Hand in hand with the establishment of colonies went the construction and extension of the Roman road network. Sometimes following preexisting routes and sometimes adopting new ones, the roads had an overtly military purpose – in this case to allow Roman armies to travel swiftly across Italy and to provide links with the colonies. The Via Appia, built to connect Rome and Capua in 312, also linked Rome with Suessa, founded the previous year, and the colonies subsequently established at Sinuessa and Minturnae (296). The Via Appia also provided an alternative to the Via Latina between Rome and Campania, which followed the valleys of the Sangro and the Liri. The Via Latina is persuasively dated by Coarelli to the 330s or 320s and is to be connected with the establishment of Cales, Fregellae, and Interamna. The building of the Via Valeria in 307, extending the Via Tiburtina eastward into the Apennines, likewise appears to be the precursor of the military campaigns against the Aequi in 304 and the foundation of the colonies at Alba Fucens and Carseoli. Road building and the establishment of colonies can be seen as working together to establish Roman military control of potentially hostile territory.[6] There were more general consequences, also, however: the building of new roads created a symbol of the increasing Roman control over Italy, a message reinforced by the milestones recording the names of those who had built or restored the road: the earliest extant example, from the Via Appia, dates from the mid-third century (*CIL* 10. 6838 = *ILS* 5801 = *ILLRP* 448; cf. Figure 3.3 above). Roads had the effect of restructuring the geography of the peninsula, marginalizing areas which they bypassed and contributing to the economic and political advancement of those places through which they ran.[7] Equally, the land-division schemes associated with the establishment of colonies also had a major impact on the rural landscape: this can best be seen from the well-preserved centuria-tion grids of the Po valley, which divided the countryside into square or rectangular units of land, while the colonies themselves can also be seen as models of Roman urbanism for the surrounding peoples (see also Chapter 3 and cf. Figures 3.2a–c).[8]

Where Rome's enemies were not organized in towns, a direct assault was frequently the preferred strategy, and this might be followed up by the establishment of colonies in the ravaged landscape. A case in point is that of the Aequi: Livy reports that 31 of their *oppida* (fortified centers) were destroyed and burnt, and sees this brutality as an *exemplum* which intimidated the neighboring peoples into requesting an alliance with Rome (9.45.17–18): Alba Fucens itself was apparently established on the site of one of these *oppida*.[9] The abandonment of nucleated sites across the Salento peninsula following the Roman conquest in 267–266 likewise suggests a violent and disruptive intervention, and in 244 a Latin colony was established at Brundisium.[10] Where the Romans came into contact with peoples with a strong urban tradition, however, the situation was more complex. In dealing with the Greek communities of south Italy, the Romans needed to involve themselves in intricate relationships of rivalry and enmity between the individual city-states on the coast and between them and the Lucanians and other indigenous populations inland; they frequently had to address councils and assemblies and persuade the communities in open debate. In the 280s, for example, Roman support was deliberately sought by Thurii, Rhegium, and other cities, but this aroused the hostility of Tarentum, and a Roman embassy was humili-ated by the assembly there (App. *Sam.* 7, Dion. Hal. *Ant. Rom.* 19.5).[11] The Romans became adept at exploiting for their own advantage the internal civic strife to which Greek cities were (according to our sources) notoriously prone, typically supporting (and being supported by) the upper classes against the *demos* (the mass of the people): at Naples in 327, we find the *demos* favoring the Samnites and the oligarchs the Romans (Dion. Hal. 15.6). In the same way we find the Romans intervening in internal disputes in the cities of Etruria (Livy 10.5.13): in 296, to the approval of the local upper classes, they suppressed "seditions" in Lucania on the part of "needy plebeian leaders" (Livy 10.18.8), while the consequence of a revolt of serfs at Volsinii in 264 was that the Romans crushed the rebels, restored the traditional elite to their traditional authority in the community, and moved the city to a new site some miles away (Zonar. 8.7).[12]

Livy, describing the events of 320 when the Roman army, which had been defeated and humiliated by the Samnites at the battle of the Caudine Forks in the previous year, won a dramatic victory over the same enemies at Luceria, pauses to speculate what would have been the outcome had Rome come into conflict with Alexander the Great (who had died only three years previously).[13] Livy's conclusion, not surpris-ingly, is that the Romans would have been victorious. He stresses not only the skill of the Roman commanders and the superior tactics and equipment of the Roman soldiery but especially the manpower at Rome's disposal, which enabled them to fight on several fronts at once (Livy 9.16–19). It was the nature of Rome's relationship with the Italian allies that enabled them to mobilize and deploy this manpower so effectively (see also Chapter 13). Italy had become a patchwork of communities of differing status and with a range of formal relationships to Rome: Latin and Roman colonies, those holding citizenship of various types, and allies. This plurality of statuses both reflected the cultural and political diversity of the peninsula but also reduced the likelihood of the Italians joining together in rebellion, as the allied communities were unable to have dealings with each other except through Rome. The Romans were thus in a position of immense power, able to "divide and rule" a population already fragmented by local cultural identities, while at the same time controlling the manpower they needed for further imperial expansion. That the majority of Italians remained loyal to Rome even during the crisis of Hannibal's invasion illustrates the strength of the system they had devised.

The Italians and the Consequences of Imperial Expansion

As Roman rule expanded first into Sicily and then beyond, the Italian contingents in the army were of vital importance: indeed, Rome needed to wage war continually in order to exploit the alliance effectively, as the benefits it derived from it came in the form of manpower rather than income.[14] Although Rome provided food for allied military contingents, the allies themselves were responsible for paying their soldiers; by contrast, Roman citizens no longer had to pay tribute after 167.[15] According to Polybius, indeed, the need to keep the allied forces occupied was one factor which induced the Romans to mount a campaign against the Dalmatians in 157: "they did not wish the men of Italy to become effeminate as a result of the lengthy peace" (Polyb. 32.13.6; see also Chapter 26). Italian troops, allies and colonists alike, took a leading role as armies led by Roman generals advanced into northern Italy, Spain, Greece, Asia Minor, and Africa: indeed, there are indications that allies might be chosen for particularly perilous missions and that losses among them might be treated more lightly than Roman casualties. Livy reports that only about a hundred soldiers among the Roman-led forces at the battle of Pydna died in action, "the great majority of them Paelignians" (44.42.7–8).[16] On the other hand, sculptural reliefs depicting scenes from the battles of Magnesia and Myonnesos in 190 were displayed in a house at Fregellae, quite likely reflecting the householder's own participation in those campaigns, in which we know that a unit of Fregellani was involved (Figure 24.21 above).[17] The displays of these scenes, recalling those in the *atria* of triumphal generals at Rome, indicate a pride in their role on the part of the commanders of the Latin contingents. When the Roman commander L. Mummius destroyed Corinth in 146, the statues and paintings he brought back were displayed in towns across

Italy, and another case is also known from Italica in Spain.[18] Whereas a century before it was the towns of Italy that were being despoiled for the benefit of the Romans – statues removed from Volsinii in 264 were displayed in the temple of Fortuna and Mater Matuta below the Capitol, for example – now the Italians were themselves beneficiaries of Rome's conquest of overseas territories (see also Chapter 24).

The impact of participation in these wars of empire was highly significant for the Italian communities in many different ways, and paradoxically this contributed to consolidating the structure established by the Romans to control Italy as well as laying the seeds of allied unrest which were to lead eventually to the outbreak of the Social War. Individual soldiers in the allied armies received the same quantities of booty as their Roman counterparts. When in 177, exceptionally, the allied troops were only granted half the booty the Roman soldiers received, this led to great ill feeling and a silent protest at the general's triumph (Livy 41.13.8). The allies could benefit also from allocations of land in colonies and the increased availability of slaves. In addition, there were considerable benefits to be derived from commercial activity in the provinces, in which it is clear that Italians had a very significant involvement. Large numbers of Italians are known to have been involved in trade at Delos, which in 166 became a free port and was the main center for the slave trade in the Aegean (Strabo 14.5.2). Many of these traders came from south Italy, and the names of Oscan derivation attested there indicate an origin in Campania or the central Apennines for a substantial proportion of them.[19] The "agora of the Italians" at Delos, a building with a colonnade surrounding an open space, has been variously interpreted as a slave market or an exercise area for the Italian community.[20] Casual finds across central and southern Italy of second-century, small-denomination coins from Greece tend to confirm that contact with the Greek world was not an unusual experience for the local populations.[21] By the end of the second century there were substantial numbers of Italians settled not only on the islands of the Aegean but also in the provinces of Asia and Africa.[22] Many victims of Jugurtha's assaults on the cities of Cirta and Vaga were Italians (Sall. *Iug.* 26, 47, 66–7);[23] when in 88 Mithridates led an uprising in Asia against Rome and called for a massacre of Romans, a high proportion of those killed were Italians (App. *Mith.* 23; Plut. *Sull.* 24.4): evidently the rebels did not differentiate between Romans and Italians, who were collectively termed *Romaioi*.[24]

Italian communities benefited from this influx of wealth collectively, as well. An exceptionally generous benefactor in the late second or early first century at Aletrium, some 70 km southeast of Rome, single-handedly transformed the appearance of his home town:

> By decree of the town's Senate, L. Betilienus L.f. Varus saw to the construction of the buildings listed below: all the pavements in the town; the portico by which one enters the citadel; the exercise-area for sports; the sundial; the market-building; the basilica which was to be plastered (?); public seating; the bathing pool; the reservoir at the city gate; he also brought water up 340 feet into the upper city, constructing aqueduct arches and solid pipes. (*ILS* 5348 = *ROL* 4:146–7 no. 6).[25]

The family's wealth was in part derived from the export of oil amphorae from the region of Brundisium, again exploiting the commercial openings made possible by the Roman conquest of the Aegean.[26] Indeed, the building of monumental sanctuaries seems to have been particularly characteristic of this period in Latium and the adjacent territories: grandiose examples dating to the late second/early first centuries BC have been identified at Fregellae, Praeneste (Figure 24.1a–b), Tibur, Cora, and elsewhere, modeled on Hellenistic sanctuaries such as those at Kos, Lindos, and Delos itself.[27] Even the Samnite sanctuaries of the central Apennines – Pietrabbondante, S. Giovanni in Galdo, Vastogirardi, and others – were rebuilt in Hellenistic style in the same period, with colonnades and (in the case of the late second-century phase at Pietrabbondante) a theater: both the resources needed to build the sanctuaries and the architectural inspiration for their design came from the East.[28] It is worth emphasizing that the cultural influence of the Greek world on these areas of Italy appears to have been direct or transmitted via the agency of Campania rather than mediated through Rome: in general, Rome was rather slower than its Italian allies in adopting cultural innovations such as the theater, the first permanent example of which at Rome (the theater of Pompey) was built in 55 (see also Chapters 4 and 24).

Tensions between Rome and Italy: The "Social War"

Although the material prosperity derived from successful overseas campaigns benefited some sectors of the allied and other Italian populations, as also did the increasing possibility of commercial activity, there were still tensions inherent in the relationship with Rome. During the war against Hannibal several peoples and cities in south Italy, most notoriously Capua, had abandoned the Roman alliance: the Roman victory over the Carthaginians was followed by the extensive confiscation of land in the offending areas, together with other punishments. As a result, in the years after the Hannibalic war the Roman authorities had to balance anxieties about (for example) the malign influence of Greek culture in Italy with the risk of alienating the allies by excessive intrusion into their affairs. The evidence is sketchy, and the literary and epigraphic sources only occasionally illuminate episodes that attracted the attention of the Roman authorities. These are difficult to weave into a coherent narrative.

In 186 the Romans took measures to suppress the secret worship of Bacchus by cult-groups; although the evidence largely relates to Roman territory (including the Ager Teuranus, where a copy of the Senate's decree was found [*ILS* 18 = *ROL* 4: 254–9; see also Chapters 2, 10, and 22]), the measures taken may well also have affected allied territory also.[29] Certainly, when problems relating to the Bacchanalia surfaced again in 181 in Apulia, the praetor to whom the area had been allocated was instructed by the Senate to take drastic action (Livy 40.19). Increasingly the Romans were also to be found resolving local disputes, as between the people of Pisa and their neighbors at the colony of Luca in 168 (Livy 45.13.10–11); in 117 the Romans similarly resolved a boundary dispute between the people of Genua and the Veturii

Langenses, Ligurians who lived in the mountainous hinterland of that city (*ILS* 5946 = *ROL* 4:262–71). The most powerful and influential city in Italy, Rome was a natural – indeed in practical terms the only – potential arbitrator.[30]

At the same time, there are episodes of highhanded and illegal behavior by individual Romans in their dealings with the allies. In 173 the marble roof-tiles from the Temple of Hera Lacinia at Croton were removed by the censor, Q. Fulvius Flaccus, to be reused in the temple of Fortuna Equestris he was building at Rome. There was an outcry in the Senate, and the tiles were restored, but it was found too difficult to restore them to the roof of the temple (Livy 42.3.1–11).

When the pace of overseas conquest slowed following the destruction of Carthage and Corinth in 146, and lucrative campaigning against the wealthy cities of the East was replaced by a sequence of wars of attrition against the impoverished but hostile peoples of Spain, the underlying tensions in the relationship between Rome and Italy were exacerbated. To a great extent the military successes of the early second century and consequent influx of wealth had tended to limit stresses within the alliance, as they had within Roman internal politics; now, however, the prospect of gaining land through colonization had ceased with the end of colonial settlement, while the Romans alone were able to tender for lucrative public contracts, such as the right to collect the taxes of the province of Asia following Gaius Gracchus' reorganization of the system of taxation there (see Chapter 8). According to Velleius there were always twice the number of allies as Romans in the army (2.15), and while the context of the passage – the grievances of the rebels at the time of the Social War – is strongly rhetorical, it does indeed appear that the pressures of military service on the allies, which had declined from a high point after the Hannibalic wars, became (or were felt to have become) much more burdensome in the late second century.[31] Partly this would have been owing to difficulties in recruiting citizens for the campaigns in question, but there are also indications from earlier in the century that individual Latins and allies alike were migrating to Rome, and such a decline in allied manpower would have increased the difficulty of fulfilling the allied states' obligations to Rome (Livy 41.8.6–12). At the same time there was arguably a perception that "the Romans were prepared to fight to the last Italian," as E. T. Salmon memorably put it.[32] Furthermore, efforts to satisfy popular demands for land at Rome, notably by Tiberius Gracchus, tended to be at the expense of the allied elites, as public land they had occupied was threatened with redistribution by the Gracchan land-commissioners; Appian reports that the allies enlisted the help of Scipio Aemilianus to draw attention to their grievances (*B Civ.* 1.18–19). Fragments of speeches by Gaius Gracchus reveal continuing complaints of bad behavior by individual Romans toward the allies and indeed Latin colonies, which conflicted with the increasing affluence and self-confidence of their communities: in particular the case of a magistrate of Teanum in Campania, who was publicly beaten because the town's baths were not clean enough for a visiting consul's wife, and that of a peasant from Venusia, beaten to death for making a joke about a Roman passing in a litter (Gell. *NA* 10.3.3).

In this general climate of tension and hostility, and following a mysterious (but unsuccessful) attempt by the consul of 125, M. Fulvius Flaccus, to resolve the situation by proposing an extension of the citizenship, the Latin colony of Fregellae revolted against Rome, for reasons that remain unclear. The rebellion may in part reflect the changing composition of the population there: Livy reports in 177 the arrival of 4,000 Samnite and Paelignian families in the city (41.8.6–8). However, the city was an affluent one, as its archaeological remains suggest, and given its status as a leader of the Latin colonies, the leaders of the revolt may have envisaged that more general support would have been forthcoming from other colonies.[33]

In spite of, or reinforced by, the brutal suppression of Fregellae, Italian discontent persisted and culminated in the Social War of 91–89, in which significant elements of the alliance revolted against Rome: chiefly the Samnites, Lucanians, and the other peoples of the central Apennines together with Apulians and the Latin colony of Venusia, with some limited involvement by Umbrians and Etruscans.[34] Several different interpretations of this revolt have been offered by modern scholars: the Social War is variously seen as primarily motivated by a desire on the part of the allies to gain the advantages of Roman citizenship;[35] to seek greater involvement in determining Roman foreign policy, to help promote their exploitation of the Empire;[36] or in essence as a rebellion against Roman rule.[37] Recently H. Mouritsen has considerably strengthened the case for the latter view, pointing out that those ancient sources which stress the importance of Roman citizenship as a motivation for the rebels tend to be writing from the perspective of the Imperial period, when the benefits of acquiring citizenship were much more clear-cut than they arguably were in the early first century BC. Within the general context of discontent with Roman hegemony a range of explanations is still possible, given the possible divergence in interests between elite and masses within the Italian communities and between different communities, reflecting their cultural and political diversity; similarly, allied aims and intentions may have changed in the period leading up to and during the course of the war.[38] What is clear is that the brutality and disruption caused by the war itself and by its aftermath had far-reaching consequences.

Italy in the Aftermath of the Social War

Both at Rome and in the towns and the countryside of Italy the impact of the Social War was very severe: indeed, one main consequence was no less than the reorganization of the Roman state. In 90 the Romans granted their citizenship to those Italians who had stayed loyal and the remainder of the former allies were granted it in the following year (except for the Samnites and Lucanians, who were still involved in hostilities). It was some time, however, before the full impact of this was felt at Rome: only in 70–69 were the newly enfranchised Italians enrolled to a significant extent in the voting-tribes. The impact at the local level was twofold. First, former allied towns and Latin colonies now became *municipia populi Romani* ("municipalities of the Roman People"), their inhabitants becoming at the same time citizens both of their local community and of Rome (Cic. *Leg.* 2.5). Secondly, members of local elites could now aspire to political advancement at Rome rather than just in their own community. Though it was only in the time of Caesar (and to a greater extent that of

Augustus) that the impact of the upward mobility of the Italian elites can fully be seen, glimpses of the advancing Italians can be seen in the years which preceded the civil wars (see also Chapter 20). At a trial in 54, Cicero describes how Cn. Plancius, from Atina on the borders of Samnium and Latium, had come to Rome the previous year to campaign for the aedileship, surrounded by supporters not only from his home town, but from the neighboring cities of Arpinum, Sora, Casinum, Aquinum, Venafrum, and Allifae (Cic. *Planc.* 22). Of course Cicero, who was defending his client against a charge of bribery, was trying to show that Plancius was so popular that he had no need to resort to illegal tactics, but the text illustrates the way in which ambitious Italians might potentially have deployed their support. Indeed, the *Commentariolum Petitionis* (a "Handbook of Electioneering" apparently composed for Cicero by his brother Quintus) was addressed to a candidate for whom the Italian vote was potentially of major importance: Quintus advises Cicero "to bear in mind the whole of Italy divided into its tribal divisions" (Cic. *Comment. pet.* 30).

During the first century, the towns of Italy acquired a range of civic amenities and public monuments, either to reflect their new status or (in the case of those communities which already had citizen status) to emulate the activity taking place in the new *municipia*.[39] At Pompeii, for example, which had been a center of rebellion in the Social War and which became a Sullan colony, we see an amphitheater, a covered theater, and the Forum baths being built in the years after the Sullan settlement.[40] Urban centers became the primary focus of elite activity, replacing the previously predominant villages and rural districts in those areas that did not have a long tradition of urban settlement; rural sanctuaries frequently declined in importance also. This urbanization reflected both the civic pride of the elites, and the potential availability of resources that might previously have been spent on the allied contingents in the army.

Against this pattern of elite advancement and urban development, however, can be set a rather gloomier picture of rural instability and disorder. Prominent among the construction projects in this period were wall-circuits, gates, and fortifications: these were not merely symbolic statements about civic status but reflected a general insecurity, and they frequently had to be defended.[41] The Social War was remembered as a conflict of particular horror and brutality, involving as it did armies that had served together and acquired the same high level of training and discipline. Numerous cities were sacked and destroyed in the fighting, including Grumentum, Aesernia, Nuceria, and Asculum.[42] The conflict was fought out entirely in Italy, and according to Florus, "neither the devastation brought about by Hannibal nor by Pyrrhus was more serious"(2.6). After the civil war between Sulla and Marius which followed the Social War, extensive tracts of land were confiscated from cities and individuals which had opposed the victorious Sulla and redistributed to the dictator's veterans: the upheavals caused by these interventions were in themselves considerable (and long-lasting). Distinctive elements continued to be identifiable in the population of Arretium into the first century AD, for example, descended from the original inhabitants and the Sullan settlers.[43]

A series of problems continued to affect the Italian countryside in the years following Sulla's dictatorship: the revolt of M. Aemilius Lepidus in 78, which culminated in a march on Rome; attacks by pirates, who raided the coast of Italy attacking the ports of Ostia and Caieta and even abducted two praetors (Plut. *Pomp.* 24; Cic. *Leg. Man.* 33). In 73 and 72, Spartacus' rebel slaves caused destruction across Italy, especially in the south. Banditry and rural violence were to some extent endemic in Italy, even in periods of apparent calm: in the early second century AD, for example, Pliny describes an episode when an *eques* known to a friend of his set off from Ocriculum in Umbria to travel north along the Via Flaminia but was never seen again (Plin. *Ep.* 6.25). Indeed, Italy in the first century BC, with its displaced peasantry and military veterans, provides a classic illustration of the conditions in which rural banditry typically tends to flourish.[44] In 63, Catiline sought to draw on the support both of those dispossessed by Sullan colonial schemes and the less successful colonists themselves (Cic. *Mur.* 49; Sall. *Cat.* 28). The widespread disturbances across Italy at this time, though only hinted at by the literary sources, can also be seen to reflect Italian anxieties about the consequences of further land-distribution schemes.[45] In 59 Julius Caesar and his colleague M. Bibulus were allocated the province of the *"silvae callesque Italiae"* ("woods and roads of Italy") after the completion of their consular year (Suet. *Iul.* 19.2). Although, as Suetonius notes, this was seen as a ruse to avoid Caesar obtaining an overseas province with greater scope for gaining military glory, there was no doubt that the Italian countryside needed the attention of the Roman authorities.[46]

Peasants, Slaves, and the Changing Face of Italian Agriculture

The economic consequences for the Italian countryside of Rome's imperial expansion in this period have been a particular focus of scholarly discussion in recent years (see also Chapter 27), though debate about many of the interrelated factors involved – the expansion of slavery in Italy, the apparent decline in the free peasantry, difficulties in recruiting soldiers for the Roman army, the development of large estates, mass migration to the city of Rome – can be traced back to ancient sources, and to the second-century AD literary accounts of Appian and Plutarch in particular. "The rich . . . farmed extensive tracts of land, instead of individual estates, using bought slaves as laborers or shepherds, in case free laborers should be drawn away from farming into the army. . . a shortage of population afflicted the Italians, who were suffering from poverty, taxes and military service." (App. *B Civ.* 1.7); "The poor, pushed off their land, no longer presented themselves enthusiastically for military service, and neglected to rear children, so that soon the whole of Italy realized that there was a shortage of free men. Instead it was filled with foreign slave-gangs whom the rich, having expelled the citizens, were using to cultivate their estates" (Plut. *Ti. Gracch.* 8.3). The substantial numbers of slaves and quantities of wealth brought into Rome as a result of the continuous wars waged in the second century led, it has been argued, to investment in Italian land and to the formation of large estates, often on public land, worked by the slaves. This contributed to the impoverishment of the Italian peasantry, already suffering as a result of long-term military service and enforced absence from their estates. Migration to towns, and in particular the city of Rome, itself contributed to a growth in urban markets, which were supplied by the large estates.[47] An additional factor, according to some scholars, was "Hannibal's Legacy": the disastrous impact on the countryside of Hannibal's campaigns in Italy during the course of the Second Punic War.[48]

The different elements of this influential model have come under scrutiny from several perspectives, beginning with the key literary texts themselves. During their lives Tiberius and Gaius Gracchus were controversial figures, and after their deaths they continued to be: their radical policies and violent ends led them to be variously considered as martyrs or villains. Cicero, for example, could refer to "the kind of consul who – like many – thinks it an outrage to praise the Gracchi" (*Leg. Agr.* 2.10). As a result, literary accounts of their views and activities have to be treated with particular care, the more so when (like those of Appian and Plutarch) they date from the second century AD, during which issues relating to Italian agriculture and the population of Italy had again become a preoccupation of the Roman authorities.[49]

It is clear from a range of evidence that the numbers of slaves brought into Italy in the second century was very substantial: according to Livy's figures, over 300,000 people were enslaved as a result of conquest in the period 201–167. However, the most dramatic individual episode of enslavement known to the literary sources, when 150,000 slaves from Epirus were sold into slavery in 167 (many of whom were probably brought to Italy), seems to have been exceptional, as it took place in the aftermath of a plague in 174 which caused the death of many slaves in Italy;[50] indeed, there were several occasions, such as the transferal of 47,000 Ligurians and their families to Samnium in 181–180, when the Romans deliberately avoided enslaving defeated populations (Livy 40.38, 41.3–4). Conversely, there are indications that large numbers of slaves were already being brought into Rome from the late fourth century onward. Again according to Livy, some 69,000 prisoners were enslaved during the Italian wars in the years between 297 and 293, and even if the figures for individual campaigns are regarded as doubtful, the fact that debt-bondage was abolished at Rome in the same period would suggest that the beginnings of an economy relying significantly on chattel-slavery may be detected well before the second century.[51] Similarly, thousands of slaves were recruited into the Roman army following the disaster at Cannae in 216, again implying that there were significant numbers at Rome (Livy 22.57.11).[52] How far these slaves were used on the land, or alternatively in urban contexts (for example, as domestic servants in the increasingly ostentatious houses of the Roman aristocracy) is unclear, however.[53] If, as seems likely, those enslaved in the mid-Republic were predominantly male and the proportion of slaves obtained through breeding was as a result comparatively low, most of those brought to Italy in the second century may (in effect) have simply replaced those slaves who had died (see also Chapters 14 and 27).[54]

Literary accounts describe in graphic terms the quantities of precious metals and art objects brought into Rome and displayed in triumphs in this period (see also Chapter 24).[55] Few realistic alternatives to land existed as a means to invest newly found wealth in second-century Rome, and the confiscation of extensive tracts of property from Italian communities, particularly in the aftermath of the Hannibalic War, meant that as well as the possibility of buying or otherwise acquiring land for private use there was considerable scope for exploiting ager *publicus* ("public land") as well – whether legally (up to 500 iugera of it, about 310 acres or 125 hectares) or illegally. Indeed, as *ager publicus* had very often previously been common land held by the local communities, its loss tended disproportionately to affect the poorer inhabitants who relied upon it to complement their own modest properties. This potentially contributed to the destabilization of the peasantry in affected areas.[56] It has recently been shown that long-term military service is likely to have played a less important role in encouraging this process in the second century than traditionally believed. Expeditions extending from one year to the next can, like the origins of the slave economy, be traced back to the fourth century, and the pattern of recruitment allowed small family farms to coexist with heavy military commitments.[57] Where peasants did leave their farms, this may have been due as much to "pull" factors (the perceived attractions of migration to Rome, to one of the Roman or Latin colonies established in northern Italy in the years leading up to 177, or an independent move to the Po valley) as much as to factors tending to push them off the land.[58] In any case, the supposed incompatibility of slaves and peasants on the land has been exaggerated; in economic terms, it made sense for a core workforce of slaves on a large estate to be reinforced by casual free labor, and while considerations of prestige may have been important to Roman landowners as well as maximizing their income, examples of estates run with mixed labor forces can be illustrated from the literary sources (see also Chapter 27).[59] The agricultural writers recommended the use of casual labor and tenants to complement an otherwise predominantly slave workforce (e.g., Cato *Agr.* 1.4; Col. *Rust.* 1.7), while for the first century Horace implies that his Sabine farm was run by a *vilicus* (estate manager), eight slaves, and five tenant-farmers (*Sat.* 2.7.118, *Epist.* 1.14.1–3). Tenancy in particular had numerous advantages both for the tenants themselves (who had access to the power networks mediated through patronage and support in time of crisis) as well as for landlords (who had a flexible source of labor, demanding little effort on their part, and at the same time a potential source of political support), though its extent and importance before the first century have been queried.[60]

That the city of Rome increased significantly in size during the Republic is clear (see also Chapter 16), and this in itself was sufficient to have a significant impact on the Italian countryside: Rome was not just the largest city in Italy by far in terms of the size of its population but also housed many of its wealthiest inhabitants, resulting in a market not just for grain, wine, and other produce for consumption by the masses but also luxury foods and goods of all kinds. It was the "consumer city" *par excellence*. The nature of the relationship between the growth of large estates, the expansion of the city population, and the migration of the peasantry is not entirely clear, however: although there are already indicators of official concern about levels of migration to Rome in the 170s (see above), it may well be that the period of greatest growth was in the latter part of the second and the following century rather than earlier in the second century, the result of a range of factors including the provision of reduced-price grain by Gaius Gracchus, subsequently made free by P. Clodius Pulcher in 58, together with the dislocation of the countryside caused by the Social War and by the conflicts which followed it.

Given the diverse geographical, climatic, and geological conditions found across the Italian peninsula, we should expect different areas to be affected in different ways by the advent of slavery and the demand generated by the city: indeed, Von Thunen's model of the "isolated city," suggesting that produce for a city is likely to be grown where it is most remunerative to do so, has successfully been used to model the economy of Rome's hinterland with suggestive results (see also Chapter 27).[61] Areas closest to and with good communication links with Rome by road, sea, and river – in particular Central Tyrrhenian Italy, and the valley of the Tiber – are thus potentially likely to have been most affected by the impact of the Roman market, though even districts further away from the capital were still influenced by it insofar as they produced crops or goods capable of being moved to and consumed in the city of Rome (the products of transhumant pastoralism, for example).[62] Literary texts do indeed tend to confirm this pattern: the advice on where to purchase agricultural equipment provided by Cato's *De agricultura*, for example, presupposes a Campanian location for his slave-run farm, and an account reported in Plutarch but apparently drawn from a political pamphlet of Gaius Gracchus describes how Tiberius Gracchus became aware of the problems affecting Italy when traveling through an area of the Tuscan countryside cultivated by slaves. As Gracchus was heading for Numantia in Spain, it is a reasonable supposition that the route he followed was that of the Via Aurelia along the coast (Plut. *Ti Gracch.* 8.7; see also Chapter 27).

Turning to the archaeological record, it should be noted that the growth of large estates (especially those associated with slave labor) is not easy to detect definitively, as what tend to be preserved in the plow soil (and thus retrieved by excavation or surface survey) are the remains of substantial farm buildings (or "villas"), which may reflect a taste for elegant rural living as much as new forms of agricultural exploitation; the relationship between the villas and the changing nature of the economy was potentially a complex one.[63] Likewise, it is difficult clearly to demonstrate the "decline of the peasantry" by means of the archaeological record, as the rural poor must be imagined living in modest and often impermanent structures with limited, if any, access to the finewares normally used to identify and date rural habitations. Frequently, when putative "small farms" identified by survey are selected for excavation, they turn out to be rather more substantial than expected, and in any case excavated sites usually tend not to reveal the social or legal status of the occupants.[64] Nevertheless, the evidence provided by archaeological field survey and villa excavations is clearly of crucial importance to our understanding of the whole problem of the agrarian economy of Italy, as M. Frederiksen emphasized in a pioneering paper delivered at a conference in 1969.[65] Detailed archaeological research carried out in coastal Etruria and northern Campania complements the literary indications that these areas were particularly characterized by the presence of what Carandini has termed the "*villa centrale*," intensively producing crops for the markets reached by road, sea, and river and relying on a predominantly servile workforce.[66] In the Ager Cosanus (in Etruria) and the Ager Falernus (in Campania), such villas are predominantly a phenomenon of the second half of the second century and the first half of the first century; in the second century they tend to belong to the local elites, but by the first many have come into the ownership of the Roman elite. The later first century is marked by the development of lavish villas along the coast in both regions (see also Chapters 24 and 27). Even within those areas most engaged in production for export and the supply of the city of Rome, however, significantly different patterns of settlement can be identified even within a comparatively short distance: in the valley of the Albegna only a few kilometers from the Ager Cosanus, a rather different pattern of settlement has been identified, based on the *"ville periferiche,"* which are seen as exploiting more marginal land for the local market with a more varied workforce, including tenants as well as slaves. In northern Campania, the greater prosperity of Suessa in the Imperial period by comparison with the nearby Ager Falernus is seen as reflecting the greater diversity of agricultural production there.[67] In the same way, many diverse patterns can be identified across different areas of Italy: around Volterra there is a striking continuity in the landscape with very few villas; in the middle Tiber valley the second and first centuries are marked by a striking decline in the number of settlements.[68] In southern Italy, the pattern of settlement revealed by a range of survey and excavation projects again reveals significant diversity across the areas envisaged as having been most severely affected by "Hannibal's legacy."[69]

The evidence of amphorae tends to complement the picture derived from field survey: the replacement of Greco-Italic amphorae with the more robust Dressel 1 amphora type, specifically designed for the long-distance transport of wine, takes place in the second half of the second century, reflecting the increasing importance in the late second and first centuries of the specialist production of wine for export to Rome, Gaul, or beyond.[70] It is worth emphasizing that only a small proportion of the overall territory of Italy could have been devoted to this production, however.[71]

Just as the allegedly disastrous impact of rural slavery on the Italian peasantry in the second century has been queried in recent years, so has the supposed manpower shortage in the Roman army in the same period. The decline of the peasantry, it has been argued, led to a shortage of men to serve in the army, which is indicated by repeated reductions in the level of the property qualification for military service attested during the second century and Marius' recruitment of soldiers from the poorest class at Rome, the *capite censi*, who had previously not been obliged to serve at all, for his campaigns against Jugurtha in 107.[72] However, there are indications that the rural peasantry did continue to be conscripted into the army in significant numbers into the first century, so Marius' initiative, rather than constituting a significant step toward the "professionalization of the Roman army," can perhaps best be seen as an *ad hoc* measure, and the reduction in the property qualification understood more as a response to a general lack of enthusiasm for military service in the latter part of the second century than an indicator of the disappearance of the peasantry (see also Chapters 13 and 27).[73]

There is thus considerable scope for revising the traditional model of the consequences for the Italian countryside of Rome's imperial expansion. Such revision would need to take due account not only of the geographical diversity of Italy and the varying impact of the market of Rome (and other Italian towns), but also the converging indications that it was firstly the late fourth century, and then the later second and (especially) the first centuries which saw the most substantial changes in the rural economy of many areas of Italy.

The years after the Latin war can be seen to be of crucial importance not just as the origin of the political and military structures which enabled the Romans effectively to exploit the military manpower of their allies in long-term campaigns, but also in terms of the development of an economic system in which slaves played a significant part. Unfortunately our knowledge of developments in the third century is hampered by the comparative absence of literary sources for that period.[74] In the first half of the second century some areas of the South were clearly affected by the aftermath of the Pyrrhic and Hannibalic wars and the large-scale confiscation of land that resulted from them. The slowdown in military expansion in the latter half of that century, coupled with the end of colonization, however, led to reluctance on the part of the peasantry, Roman and Italian, to serve in the army and saw an increasing tendency of the country-dwellers to migrate to the city of Rome. The development of the rural villa, and the production of wine for export can be traced in this period to the most economically vibrant areas of Rome's hinterland. It was at the end of the second century and still further in the first century that these trends became most pronounced. The upheavals caused by the Social War and the conflicts which followed it were of major importance: it is in this period that we can trace the increasingly "professional" army of the late Republic, reliant on its generals for land on their demobilization. The same rural dislocation also pushed the uprooted peasantry toward the city of Rome, which retained its existing attractions to migrants, enhanced by the availability of fixed-price, or free, grain. A further source of pressure on traditional forms of agriculture was the possibility, indeed the obligation, for ambitious members of Roman and Italian elites to undertake increasingly high levels of expenditure with a view to their personal advancement and/or the embellishment of their community (see also Chapters 1 and 17): and now virtually all of Italy was likely to be affected. It was in the late second and early first centuries that the lavish sanctuaries and public buildings of the cities of Latium were constructed, followed shortly afterward by the widespread development of urban centers as Italian communities became *municipia*. The advent of the Italian elites in Roman politics was one factor that contributed to raising the level of aristocratic competition in the city to new heights: both of these trends would have made it timely for owners of rural estates to maximize their income by means of intensive forms of agriculture. In revising the traditional model on these lines, the further investigation of the Italian countryside by means of archaeology, with the aim of sketching the varied implications for the different regions of Italy and a particular focus on the economic, political, and social structures of Rome's Italian allies (too frequently assumed to be similar or identical to those of Rome) will be of particular value and interest; likewise the further analysis of demographic patterns, which (as Lo Cascio, Morley, and Rosenstein have recently shown) are potentially of central importance to our understanding of Italy in this period (see also Chapter 27).[75]

Tota Italia

According to the *Res Gestae*, "all Italy of its own accord" swore an oath of allegiance to Octavian (*RG* 25.2). The Italy of Augustus was, however, strikingly different from the Italy of three centuries, or even one century, previously. Local languages, forms of funerary commemoration, and other traces of local identity were rapidly disappearing, swept away by decades of civil war, enforced military service, and the settlement of veterans. The peninsula now formed a unified political unit, divided up into *regiones* and *municipia*, which (notionally anyway) followed a standard model, though village settlement was in practice to prove more resilient in some areas. The Italian elites now looked to Rome, and more specifically to the *Princeps*, rather than to the Greek world, for models to follow in a new phase of urban embellishment. No longer could it be said that the Italians lacked a voice, however: the Augustan era was in many ways the golden age of the Italian elites, as the new *Princeps* was surrounded by ambitious and upwardly mobile Italians and the new regime was commemorated, honored, and satirized by poets and historians from all over the peninsula: Virgil from Mantua, Ovid from Sulmo, Horace from Venusia, Propertius from Asisium, and Livy from Patavium (see also Chapter 25).

Guide to Further Reading

The number of publications on the archaeology and history of Italy is massive, and as many of them appear in local journals or (increasingly) exhibition catalogs, it is difficult to keep up to date. See Curti, Dench, and Patterson 1996 for a recent attempt to review literature on some of the themes explored in this chapter. More general studies of Roman Italy are (for the early and mid-Republic) Cornell 1995, David 1996 (with a helpful bibliography in English compiled by T. J. Cornell), and (with a particular emphasis on the archaeological record) Potter 1987, while works on particular regions (in English) include Salmon 1967, Frederiksen 1984, Lomas 1993, Dench 1995, and Bradley 2000. The volumes in the *Guida Archeologica Laterza* series provide a good starting point for the study of the individual sites of Roman Italy. Important editions of collected papers include Gabba 1994b and Torelli 1999, and there are a series of valuable articles in Italy in the second edition of the *Cambridge Ancient History*, including Gabba 1989 and 1994a, Morel 1989, and Crawford 1996b. Lomas 1996 is a sourcebook which includes material on many aspects of the relationship between Rome and Italy. Among recent pieces of work Mouritsen 1998 and Rosenstein 2004 stand out, for their wide-ranging and radical reappraisal of central issues in the relationship of Rome and Italy in the mid- and late Republic.

Notes

1 De Juliis 1990; Crawford 1996b: 429–30, 987–9.
2 Harris 1979: 176–82; Keay and Terrenato 2001; see also Chapter 27 in this volume.
3 Sherwin-White 1973: 38–95, 119–33; Harris 1984b: 92–3; Cornell 1995: 348–52, 364–8.
4 Salmon 1969; Cassola et al.1988; Coarelli 1992; Gargola 1995.
5 Salmon 1969: 56–9; Coarelli 1988a.
6 Coarelli 1988a: 41–2; Laurence 1999: 13–21.
7 Laurence 1999: 39–42; Potter 1979: 101–20; Wiseman 1971: 28–30.
8 Centuriation: Museo civico archeologico-etnologico (Modena, Italy) 1983; Purcell 1990: 15–16.
9 Mertens 1991.
10 D'Andria 1990; Yntema 1993: 195–7.
11 Lomas 1993: 39–58.
12 De Ste Croix 1981: 519.
13 See esp. Morello 2002.
14 North 1981: 6–7; Cornell 1995: 364–8.
15 Lintott 1993: 70.
16 Toynbee 1965: 2.134–45; Harris 1984b: 97.
17 Coarelli 1994.
18 *CIL* I² 627–31 = *ILS* 21–21d = *ILLRP* 327–31, with *AE* 1973, 134 and Cic. *Orat.* 232; *Off.* 2.76.
19 Wilson 1966: 99–121.
20 Coarelli 1982; Rauh 1993: 289–341.
21 Crawford 1985: 178–9 with Appendix 46.
22 Gabba 1989: 224–5.
23 Morstein-Marx 2000.
24 See Brunt 1971a: 224–7 for the numbers involved.
25 Zevi 1976.
26 Manacorda 1994: 30.
27 Coarelli 1987.
28 La Regina 1976.
29 Beard, North, and Price 1998: 1.93–5; Mouritsen 1998: 49–57.
30 Gabba 1989: 225; Mouritsen 1998: 43.
31 Brunt 1971a: 677–86.
32 Salmon 1967: 307.
33 Coarelli and Monti 1998: 40; Mouritsen 1998: 118–19.
34 Gabba 1994a.
35 Brunt 1988c: 93–130.
36 Gabba 1976: 76–7.
37 Sherwin-White 1973: 134–49.
38 Mouritsen 1998, with the review by Bradley 2002.
39 Gabba 1994b: 74–96.
40 Zanker 1998: 62–72.
41 Gabba 1994b: 99–100.
42 Brunt 1971a: 285–7.
43 Brunt 1971a: 300–12.

44 Hobsbawm 1969: 30–40.

45 Stewart 1995.

46 Brunt 1971a: 285–93, 551–7.

47 E.g., Hopkins 1978: 3–98; Stockton 1979; Jongman 2003.

48 Toynbee 1965; Cornell 1996.

49 Morley 2001: 60–1; Jongman 2003: 111.

50 Ziolkowski 1986.

51 Oakley 1993; Rosenstein 2004: 7–12.

52 Brunt 1971a: 418–20.

53 Jongman 2003: 116.

54 Rosenstein 2004: 11.

55 See Livy 39.5.13–17, 39.7.1–5 for accounts of two such triumphs, M. Fulvius Nobilior's over the Aetolians and Cn. Manlius Vulso's over the Galatians, held within a period of three months in 187–186.

56 Gabba 1989: 197–207.

57 Rosenstein 2004: 26–62.

58 Morley 1996: 50–4; Broadhead 2000.

59 Rathbone 1981.

60 Foxhall 1990; Rosenstein 2004: 181–2.

61 De Neeve 1984b: 10–16; Carandini 1988: 339–57; Morley 1996: 55–82.

62 Laurence 1999: 95–122; Patterson 2004; Whittaker 1988.

63 Terrenato 2001b: 27.

64 Garnsey 1998: 110–11.

65 Frederiksen 1970–1.

66 Carandini 1994c: 168.

67 Carandini 1994c: 169–70; Carandini et al. 2002: 145–54; Arthur 1991a: 153–7; 1991b: 101–2.

68 Terrenato 2001a: 62; Liverani 1984: 48; Patterson, Di Giuseppe, and Witcher 2004.

69 Cornell 1996; Lo Cascio and Storchi Marino 2001.

70 Manacorda 1989: 446; Curti, Dench, and Patterson 1996: 176–7.

71 Jongman 2003: 113–14.

72 Brunt 1971a: 402–9; Gabba 1976: 1–19.

73 Rich 1983; Keppie 1984: 61–3, 69–70.

74 Cornell 1996: 97–8.

75 Lo Cascio 1999b: 166–71; Morley 2001; Rosenstein 2004.

CHAPTER 29

The Transformation of the Republic

Robert Morstein-Marx and Nathan Rosenstein

Defining the Problem

The "Fall of the Roman Republic" is the canonical English phrase – but a potentially misleading one. The Roman Republic did not "fall" in the way that the French Ancien Régime did, or the Third Reich, or the Soviet Union. Nor is just *when* it "fell" an objective, public fact: In 59 (Joseph. *AJ* 19.187), with the activation of the alliance between Caesar, Pompey, and Crassus that Varro called the "Three-Headed Monster"? In 49, when Caesar marched on Rome? In 48, 46, or 45, with each of Caesar's major victories in the Civil War? In 44, after Caesar's assassination? In 43, with the legal ratification of a kind of junta rule? In 42, on the funeral pyres of Philippi? In 31, with Octavian's defeat of Antony at Actium? In 28 and 27, when, paradoxically, public affairs were ostentatiously, and ostensibly, handed *back* to the Senate and People of Rome? In 23, when Augustus took the title of *Princeps* ("First Citizen") and assumed the complex of powers that would henceforth distinguish the ruling emperor? Or perhaps as late as AD 14, when Tiberius, the second Princeps, succeeded to his adoptive father's position in monarchic fashion and in effect abolished popular election to the magistracies?[1] One could construct a plausible argument for any one of these dates. The important point is that the end of the Republic was not something objectively and explicitly marked by some public fact in our evidence – the beheading of a king, the suicide of a dictator, the resignation of a General Secretary – but something that we must infer circumstantially from a variety of facts and factual changes over the course of several decades.

Consequently, in an objective sense the Republic *never* actually "fell" – an over-worked metaphor that anyway prejudices the issue in various ways: by prompting us to look for a single, catastrophic event; by insidiously suggesting that one side in the conflicts of the mid-first century represented the Republic, overcome by others seeking to destroy the Republic, or alternatively, that it "collapsed" of its own long-incubating illnesses. On the contrary, the *res publica* (usually best translated "state") to which Cicero devoted himself was transformed incrementally and for the most part imperceptibly into the *res publica* over which Augustus presided as Princeps. Contemporary Romans do not appear to have distinguished terminologic-ally between these phases in the life of their *res publica*. Use of that phrase to distinguish what we now call the Republic from the Principate is not unambiguously attested before Tacitus, writing toward the beginning of the second century AD; the most recent examination of the problem finds that, while consciousness of the special position of the Princeps *within* the *res publica* is of course manifest from the time of Augustus, the writings of the younger Seneca (mid-first century AD) are the first to betray a reasonably clear conceptualization of the Principate as monarchy, and thus as a fundamental change of the political system from the traditional Republic.[2]

The brilliant beginning of Tacitus' history of the post-Augustan Principate (*Ann.* 1.1–15) usefully highlights the problem of definition. "The names of officials remained the same. The younger men had been born after the victory at Actium, and most even of their elders, in the years of civil war. Few were left who had seen the Republic" (Tac. *Ann.* 1.3.7). Even when such a strong demarcation between Republic and Principate as this is imposed by an author looking back on this transformation from the distance of a century, "the Republic" still turns out to be something defined by experience and behavior, not the surface facts of political life. In these opening chapters of the *Annals*, the traditional Republic is conceptu-ally opposed to any personal domination, however cloaked by formal legitimization. However, republican norms had also been temporarily suspended in the past with-out thereby actually constituting the definitive end of the traditional state: Tacitus notes for the "early" Republic the dictatorship, the Decemvirate of 451–450 (see Chapter 11), and the period of military tribunes with consular imperium; for the "late" Republic, the personal dominance of Cinna, Sulla, and the so-called "First" and "Second" Triumvirates (*Ann.* 1.1.1). On this view, personal domination, if transitory, was not in fact inconsistent with the survival of the old Republic; and permanence is something that by its very nature is proven only to posterity. Before Tiberius assumed his predecessor's position in AD 14 it would have been possible even for a hypothetical contemporary Tacitus to see the entire "reign" of Augustus as an interruption, rather than the termination, of Rome's deeply embedded re-publican tradition.

But from the vantage point of history it *is* perfectly clear that something import-ant had changed over this considerable interval of time. If we are to dispense with the metaphor of the "Fall" of the Republic, how then *should* we describe the profound political change we see between the days of Cicero and those of Augustus? In essence, and irrespective of names and institutional formalities, a system directed by a relatively small and entrenched elite subject (to a greater or lesser extent) to popular approval became one apparently at least guided by a single man (cf. Tac. *Ann.* 4.33.2). The traditional diffusion of political power among leading senators (*principes civitatis*), the nobility, the Senate as a body, "knights" (*equites*), and the People, at least in part flowing along independent lines, was replaced by a much narrower concentration of power around *the* single Princeps and flowing directly from him.

Three Influential Modern Theories

Discussion of the end of the Republic has been dominated for a generation by the theories formulated by three of the great republican historians of our time – Peter Brunt, Erich Gruen, and Christian Meier – and published within a decade of each other in the late 1960s and early 1970s.

It would be fair to say that Peter Brunt's account of the end of the Republic became the orthodoxy in the English-speaking world; it therefore serves as the best point of departure for most readers of this volume. Brunt judges that the collapse of the Republic was the result of a shattering of political consensus as different sectors of Roman society in the late Republic developed irresolvably conflicting interests. The Senate, blinded by short-term self-interest, progressively eroded its own authority by its persistent failure to solve problems brought by Roman expansion through timely concessions to the Italians, "knights," urban plebs, peasantry, and soldiery. Thus eventually the state was left stripped of defenders and prey to powerful dynastic figures who could more effectively, if cynically, champion these interests. The process unfolded over many decades from at least the time of the Gracchi; but by the time that Caesar, the rebellious proconsul, was preparing to cross the Rubicon, all of these important sectors of Roman society were broadly alienated from senatorial governance and prepared either to stand aside or make common cause with the man who sought to destroy it.[3]

The theories of Christian Meier and Erich Gruen in effect rebut different aspects of this powerful and coherent thesis. Meier (to take him up first) did not dispute that the death of the Republic was directly caused by the rise of a sequence of excessively powerful individuals who could no longer be constrained in the traditional manner. His innovation lay rather in constructing a complex and challenging argument that despite the succession of grievous troubles into which the Late Republic sank, all contemporary stakeholders, from the political elite to the plebs, remained intellectually and psychologically in thrall to the traditional political system, and since they lacked an objective perspective upon the real causes of the institutional failure in which they found themselves, their responses were limited either to aporetic paralysis or clinging ever more tightly to the traditional, but now anachronistic system – which merely accelerated and worsened the crisis. None of those sectors of society that had a role in the system, from the ancient nobility down to the plebs and out to the newly enfranchised Italians, actually sought to destroy the Republic. On the contrary, this was, in Meier's coinage, a "Gefälligkeitsstaat," a neologism that is impossible to translate ("accommodation-state?"), but that attempts to describe a system in which the needs of those privileged elements of the citizenry that played a significant role were sufficiently accommodated to prevent any one of them from regarding the system as the problem rather than as an essential part of any solution. Thus there evolved a "crisis without alternative" ("Krise ohne Alternative"), in Meier's pithy but somewhat ambiguous formulation: that is, a crisis that was inevitably worsened and ultimately made irremediable by the inability of contemporaries to conceive realistically of, or at least to accept, an alternative to the failed Republic.[4]

One will note that this interesting theory is not so much an explanation for the end of the Republic as for the notable failure of contemporaries to diagnose and remedy the affliction besetting their state. It is also somewhat awkward that eventually – under Augustus – an "alternative" did in fact arguably emerge (though one acceptable largely because it could be presented not as an alternative, but as an improvement of the Republic). But the theory's major contribution is that it made a thought-provoking case for the seeming paradox that those who brought down the Republic, or were complicit with the leading agents in doing so, did not actually seek to destroy it but even arguably to save it (with the possible exception of Caesar). It followed that, in contrast to Brunt, it was unnecessary to show, or presume, that any of the major parties to the "Fall" had become deeply disillusioned with a traditional political system whose past glories gave it unparalleled prestige in the historical consciousness of all quarters of Roman society.[5]

It has seemed worthwhile to describe Meier's thesis at somewhat greater length than the others because, despite having enormous influence upon present-day German scholarship, it is unfortunately relatively little known and less read in the English-speaking world. Partly, no doubt, this is for merely linguistic reasons, but surely also because Meier's indulgence of sometimes murky abstraction and his pessimistic, almost tragic view of the gap between human cognition and historical process are both rather alien to the "Anglo-Saxon" empirical tradition of historical scholarship. That is a pity, for the richness of Meier's analysis can be easily measured by the lively and thoughtful debate it stimulated, and still stimulates, in German scholarship (see Chapter 1) on a subject about which the English tongue seems to have fallen strangely mute.

Erich Gruen targeted another premise of the traditional analysis.[6] Gruen was one with Meier in stressing that no one consciously sought the Republic's demise, but his even more provocative claim was that the state was suffering from no such terminal disease as scholars had long diagnosed. In his view, republican politics functioned in an essentially traditional fashion right down to the eve of the Caesarean civil war. The Senate showed, if anything, renewed vigor in its confrontation of continuing challenges after the death of Sulla. The recurring problems in the city and countryside, the association of great armies with powerful individuals, even the notorious "extraordinary" long-term commands such as that given Pompey against the pirates and then Mithridates in 67–62, or Caesar in Gaul ultimately from 58–49, which have so often been seen as crucial instruments of revolution – none of these were signs that the Republic was on its deathbed. Rather, "Civil war caused the fall of the Republic, not vice versa."[7] An unyielding proconsul dealt one grievous blow, his assassination another, and more than a decade of intermittent civil war finished the job. The view that by 49 the Republic was an empty shell ripe for toppling was, for Gruen, a product of the historian's professional vice of treating every result, no matter how undesired and paradoxical to contemporaries, as somehow inevitable in hindsight.

Despite their salient differences, it is clear that Meier and Gruen have together mounted a serious challenge to Brunt's central idea that the end of the Republic came because it (as represented by the Senate) had forfeited the allegiance of important sectors of its citizenry. This important divergence of ideas probably offers a promising opening for further progress in this debate.

Coming Unglued: The Loss of Elite Cohesion

Gruen's assault on historical hindsight is refreshing and illuminating. In the pages that follow will be heard many echoes of his powerful challenges to the conventional wisdom on the end of the Roman Republic. Yet it is hard to follow him too closely in his claim that the Caesarean Civil War was essentially an "accident" of human choices with world-historical consequences. While Gruen may well be right to draw our attention to the notable show of vigor with which in 52 the Senate and Pompey drew the Republic back from the chaos that had prevailed for more than half a decade, it is also hard to credit the suggestion that had the tribune Curio or Caesar himself only acted more diplomatically in 50–49 the Republic would have lasted very much longer (see also Chapter 9). Montesquieu had a point when he wrote: "If Caesar and Pompey had thought like Cato, others would have thought like Caesar and Pompey."[8] And it is not self-evidently obvious why the Republic could survive the damage wrought by Sulla, Marius, and Cinna in the 80s, complete with threefold military capture of the city itself and numerous bloodbaths of senators, "knights," and common citizens, but not the civil wars of the 40s – unless it was because the political system was in a much weakened state the second time around. This time there was to be no reconstituting the broader distribution of power that characterized the old Senate and People of Rome, and after a brief anarchic hiatus in 44–36 the process of concentration resumed until it yielded *the* single Princeps, Augustus.

Here our earlier definition of the phenomenon might usefully be invoked. The "Fall," "Collapse," or even simply "End of the Republic" are frequently useful shorthand phrases, but they tend to set us thinking about the phenomenon as if it were susceptible to the same kind of analysis we apply to a discrete historical event, that is, an examination of the motives and plans of individual historical actors within the context of the specific political, social, and economic factors that help to shape their decisions. These factors can never be considered entirely determinative, and thus events can never be regarded as entirely inevitable consequences of them. But if what we really mean by these phrases, as was argued above, is a long-term historical *process* (the "Transformation of the Republic") that cannot be encapsulated within any specific event – not even the Caesarean Civil War – then it cannot successfully be analyzed in these terms. An explanation of the transformation of the Republic cannot be reduced largely to an analysis of the motives, strategies, and results, intended or otherwise, of the chief political agents in the developing crisis of the year 50.

A broader perspective on the problem might start with the venerable and authoritative thesis that the Republic "fell" as a fairly direct result of acquiring its empire. Two of the founders of modern political theory, Niccolò Machiavelli (1469–1527) and Charles-Louis de Secondat, Baron de Montesquieu (1689–1755), meditated long on the history of the Roman Republic and the lessons it was thought to offer.

To account for the end of the Republic both perceived an ultimately fatal inconsistency between the Republic's institutions as a city-state and its administration of a great empire: great armies in far-flung places were entrusted for long periods to competitive aristocrats, to whom, as their commanders, the soldiers increasingly directed their loyalties rather than to the Senate and People.[9] If we call to mind the careers of Marius, Sulla, Pompey, and especially Caesar (see Chapters 8 and 9), their argument appears plausible, perhaps even self-evident. Yet underneath such apparently self-evident and traditionally recognized truths often lurk questionable, if generally unquestioned, assumptions. Until the twentieth century it still seemed as axiomatic as it had to Cassius Dio (44.2) in the third century AD that only monarchic governments could successfully govern large states; one may reasonably wonder whether this great lesson of history has not been "read into" the Roman example as much as deduced from it.[10] The assertion – often made but rarely, if ever, demonstrated in detail – that the Republic foundered on a fundamental contradiction between empire and the institutions of the city-state[11] is simply the modern version of this traditional critique. That does not, of course, make it wrong; but it certainly invites careful scrutiny.

In English-speaking scholarship of recent decades the most influential version of the argument that the crisis of the Republic was a consequence of its conquest of an overseas empire in the second and first centuries was formulated by Brunt in his seminal paper of 1962, "The Army and the Land in the Roman Revolution."[12] Conscription for continuous wars abroad, Brunt argued, ruined Italy's small farmers, while the profits from their victories flowed mainly into the purses of Rome's ruling class, who used them to buy up bankrupt farms and turn them into vast estates worked by the slaves whom these same victories had made cheap and abundant. The result transformed Italy's agrarian economy and created a large class of landless poor in the countryside, while overall the number of free inhabitants dwindled because their poverty prevented marriage and childrearing.[13] A series of reformers beginning with Tiberius Gracchus sought to alleviate their plight with various calls for land reform, but the event that made them an instrument of political change was Marius' decision to open the legions to these men by ignoring the customary property requirement for military service (see also Chapters 8 and 13). Subsequent generals followed suit, particularly during the crisis of the Social War, so that the legions of the late Republic contained a high proportion of landless men with no stake in the status quo. Not that they were bent on revolution; they simply wanted to better their lot in life. But that made them open to appeals for their loyalty and support from some of the politicians who commanded them, like Sulla and Caesar, who, finding themselves outmaneuvered in the political arena by their opponents, sought to continue the struggle "by other means" with the help of their armies in exchange for promises, explicit or tacit, of wealth and land.

Several elements within this reconstruction have come under fire in recent years. That the Republic's overseas wars in the second century would have ruined most or even many of the soldiers who fought them seems increasingly unlikely. Certainly, archaeological surveys in the countryside have failed to confirm a widespread decline in the numbers of small farms in Italy during this period, and recent studies have argued that scholars have greatly overestimated both the prevalence of large estates and the numbers of slaves working them. (For this and the remainder of this paragraph, see Chapters 14, 28, and 29.) It may be that, contrary to prior views, Roman manpower requirements for its wars abroad were not inconsistent with the traditional patterns of Italian agricultural life, so that the effects of these wars in the second century upon the Italian peasantry from which the armies were recruited were not nearly so negative, and far more complex, than have previously been thought.[14] Overall, the number of free inhabitants of Italy seems either to have held steady at around 4 million over the Republic's last two centuries or possibly even grown during that period at a healthy clip.[15] But if all this is so, then it invites an obvious and crucial question, that is: if the domestic consequences of the Republic's acquisition of an empire in the second century did not ruin Italy's rural population, then what caused the poverty and landlessness and resultant calls for land reform during the late Republic? Possibly population growth continued throughout the period, so that demographic pressures can be blamed. But a growing consensus views this as less likely than long-term stability in the numbers of free Italians. It may be that the rural poverty we see in this period arose from much shorter-term and more transient causes than usually thought, for example, the devastation and confiscations that attended both the Social War and the two civil wars of the 80s or the debt crises of the 80s to mid-60s.[16] Or perhaps there was much less poverty in the countryside than we have been led to believe by the powerful rhetoric and heightened passions that attended land reform proposals; perhaps these were actually aimed primarily at the urban population of Rome (which included recent migrants to the city), as the ancient sources sometimes claim[17] and an earlier generation of scholars accepted.

The special power of Brunt's thesis derived from the close link he forged between agitation for land in the late Republic and an erosion of the loyalty of the great late-republican armies to the republican political system. Yet this too proves, upon examination, to rest on little positive evidence. Key supports of that causal nexus were the hypotheses that the modest property-requirement to enjoy the status of an *assiduus* and thus be eligible for military service was steadily lowered in the late third and second centuries as the pool of non-destitute peasants dwindled, and that Marius decisively broke the link between wealth and military service by enrolling the property-less poor (*proletarii*) for his Jugurthan campaign of 107 (Sall. *Iug.* 86.2–3); this is supposed to have set the pattern thereafter and opened the way to the formation of armies conscripted largely from the very poor who served chiefly in the hope of material advancement and looked to their commanders rather than the Senate for satisfaction of this goal. The first claim – that regarding assiduate status – has, however, been shown to depend on circular argumentation, while the second – that Marius' precedent in 107 was followed more or less thereafter – seems to be a debatable extrapolation from a single known incident.[18] However that may be, on the third and most important point we simply do not know whether in fact the poor and landless constituted the bulk of the late Republic's legionaries.[19] Since the demographic and social consequences Brunt and others before him drew from the wars of the late third and second centuries no longer seem firmly founded, it no longer seems self-evidently true that a dwindling pool of *assidui* and a general resistance to conscription led recruiters to levy the poor, "the very class least able to secure exemption by bribes or favour."[20]

Moreover, Brunt himself, while contending against the common notion that the late-republican legions were essentially "client armies," acknowledged that it cannot be presumed as a rule that late-republican armies were simply disloyal to the Republic.[21] We would go further and note that, despite the prevalence of the idea of the late-republican "personal army," no single army that launches upon civil war can be shown to have entered upon its revolutionary course out of disaffection from the Republic or hopes to be rewarded with grants of land. Much cited in this connection is the motive Appian attributes to the army to which Sulla in 88 appealed to defend his *dignitas* by marching on Rome: "they were eager for the campaign against Mithridates because it was likely to be profitable, and they thought that Marius would recruit other soldiers for it in their place" (App. *B Civ.* 1.57). Observe that Appian says nothing here of the expectation of land-grants or of Sulla's potential capacity to obtain plots for his troops but refers instead to the expectation of rich plunder – a thoroughly traditional incentive to forceful military action noted at least as far back as the popular vote for war with Carthage in 264 (Polyb. 1.11.2).[22]

At times of deep crisis republican legitimacy itself was fragmented rather than directly denied, and it may well be that the soldiers who waged the struggles that ultimately established Caesar's and then Augustus' personal domination were motivated by their understanding of where that fragmented legitimacy predominated as much as by the material bounty that would come their way with victory.[23] This is fairly evident in the two notorious "Marches on Rome," by Sulla in 88 and by Caesar in 49. Scholars continue to be deeply shocked by Sulla's and Caesar's uninhibited citation of their wounded *dignitas* – "worthiness," thus roughly "honor" – as a justification for their (counter)-attacks upon those who had attempted to destroy it, and almost equally, by their armies' acceptance of that battle cry. Yet the respect and honor due from the community for personal *dignitas*, based upon achievements or the promise of achievements on behalf of the Commonwealth, lay at the very heart of the republican system.[24] An outright assault on high *dignitas*, such as the tribune P. Sulpicius' armed expulsion of both consuls from the city after deposing Sulla's colleague Q. Pompeius Rufus from his magistracy in a riotous assembly, was itself a gross violation of republican norms that had already thrown into doubt where legitimacy actually lay – quite apart from the outrage of Sulpicius' use of violence in the assembly, which had brought about the death of Pompeius' own son. Sulla's soldiers may well have felt that their own material interests coincided with those of the Republic, since they were after all defending the consuls of the Roman People (whom they had sworn in their military oath to obey), not rebelling against the Senate, cowed and intimidated as it was by "tyrants" (App. *B Civ.* 1.57; see also Chapter 8).[25] Much the same could be said of the reaction of Caesar's army to the virtual declaration of war passed on January 7, 49 by the Senate despite his extraordinary achievements (as they were seen) on behalf of the Republic.[26] The opening chapters of Caesar's *Civil Wars*, with their compelling picture of a craven Senate browbeaten by bullying enemies of Caesar, give a good sense of how the matter will have looked to his men: an attack by a vicious faction upon a popular and military hero whose services to Rome were second to none, exacerbated by a gross insult against the tribunate, was no merely personal quarrel.[27] If Brunt's observation that "without his army Caesar could neither have conquered Gaul nor overthrown the Republic" is self-evident, Gruen's reply seems equally true that "not even the soldiers of Julius Caesar marched into Italy with the intent or desire to bring down the Roman Republic."[28]

Perhaps, indeed, they marched to save it. The disputed US presidential election of 2000 is a salutary recent lesson in how rapidly what was once unthinkable can be contemplated, when each side in a political crisis feels that the other has violated the fundamental norms of the system and thus itself strives – out of *dedication* to its interpretation of that system rather than in disaffection – to "save" it by increasingly dubious methods. That calculation of personal interest can often coincide with such public-spirited reasons will surprise few. Sulla's and Caesar's armies may very well have expected to benefit materially by their actions, as soldiers whose victories had served the Republic had always done. There need have been no contradiction in their minds.

What emerges, then, is a process marked by the *fragmentation* of legitimacy, in which the Republic could no longer unreflectingly be associated with the contemporary Senate but might be seen as incorporated in persons – the odd proconsul and tribune – who were temporarily at least at odds with the Senate. But this is not the same thing as disaffection from the *Republic*. Indeed, just the reverse: the Senate's loss of a (near) monopoly of republican legitimacy was fully consistent with the continued monopoly status of the idea and traditions of the Republic as encoded in ancestral custom (*mos maiorum*). Adversaries of the Senate at any given time did not call for its abolition or overthrow but denounced the worthiness (and thus the moral legitimacy) *of its current leadership*, and called for a return to the paternalistic responsiveness of senatorial leadership to popular needs and demands that was a fundamental principle of the republican tradition.[29] The best evidence we possess for the political attitudes of the urban plebs – the speeches delivered to them in the Forum (*contiones*) – suggests that even they, who are often represented in modern accounts as the most disaffected of all, continued to embrace republican political traditions and favored those who most plausibly appeared to embody that tradition.[30] The power of this tradition, continually reinforced for the citizenry in mass oratory and civic rituals such as election, was such that no alternative model of state organization seen in recent history seems to have been realistically conceivable – certainly not the debased spectacle of late-Hellenistic monarchy.

The fragmentation of republican legitimacy doubtless had many causes and contributing factors which would reward careful analysis in future work and cannot be fully elaborated here. But we wish to stress one important point that seems to stand out fairly clearly. It was already in 133 that the astonishing cohesion of the senatorial order was blasted apart, first by Tiberius Gracchus' agrarian law and then even more by the circumstances of its passage; this explosion divided the elite and threw its parts back upon the two civic power-bases in Rome – Senate and People – and upon their corresponding, now often opposing legitimating principles. Thereafter, the Roman elite was frequently divided against itself in the face of major controversies, many or most of them precipitated in some way by imperial problems and responsibilities (the

Italians, Mithridates, land for veterans, the pirates, Gaul). However, the alternative source of power exploited by those individuals or factions who took up, or were forced into, a position in opposition to those who were able to work their will through the Senate was initially the People in their public meetings (*contiones*) and voting assemblies; the real exploitation of the military as an alternative source of power for its powerful commanders does not actually appear until more than four decades after Tiberius Gracchus in the 80s (Marius in 107–100 at most suggested the way). This observation casts further doubt on the traditional claim that the Republic "fell" because of the inability of a city-state to rein in its overweening provincial commanders – the still-popular core of the argument of Machiavelli and Montesquieu. This was a relatively late and secondary factor which raised the stakes enormously but was more consequence than cause of the division of the elite.

It is surely to the early and middle second century that we need to look more closely for the factors that heightened the potential for elite division to the inflammable level reached in 133. Notoriously, ancient writers put their finger on two underlying causes for what they persisted in viewing as essentially a moral collapse:[31] the enormous influx of wealth into Italy and Rome; and the removal of the last direct and plausible threat to Roman hegemonic domination of the Mediterranean basin. Although their analyses in detail sound quaintly moralizing to the modern ear, it would be hard to quarrel with the essential point that the victorious march of Roman arms from the Straits of Messana in 264 to the Carthaginian Byrsa in 146 produced a concentration of wealth and power in the hands of the Roman elite that could not but loosen or even spring the restraints that had long operated upon aristocratic behavior. What Roman historians like Sallust and Livy diagnosed in the language available to them as moral collapse, a modern historian of a sociological bent might describe as an increase of individualism and relaxation of the social constraint that earlier generations, faced repeatedly with military crises beginning in the fifth century and extending through the Hannibalic War, had imposed upon themselves in the face of the exigencies of self-preservation. A dangerous and threatening world forced the aristocracy to become not only aggressive and militaristic but extraordinarily disciplined as well (see also Chapters 6, 17, and 26). Although military crises did not cease with the destruction of Carthage in 146 – the invasion of the Cimbri and Teutones and the Social War being only the most urgent – the willingness of aristocrats to impose restraints upon themselves did, leading to a spiraling escalation of violence and transgression of the unwritten rules of the political game. Further, the *uneven* concentration of wealth and power across the elite, depending on access to armies and profitable military assignments, or public contracts, must in itself have further upset the equilibrium upon which social cohesion depends. The elite was not wholly unconscious of these tendencies, it seems, to judge from the appearance of sumptuary laws, age limits on office holding, extortion courts, and the various judicial battles over triumphs and misappropriation of plunder through the second century.[32] Yet the causes for the dissolution of elite cohesion are not to be found only among the elite. Unless one discounts altogether the role of the People in the Roman Republic one must acknowledge that urgent social, economic, and political discontents would tend to force themselves onto the consciousness of the political elite precisely because, in a highly competitive aristocracy, such problems offer opportunities for individual aristocrats prepared to part company with their peers to steal a march on their rivals by exploiting popular causes. Division among the elite was essentially a given during times of great sociopolitical stress (see also Chapter 18), as the period from at least 133 certainly was.

Still, it may be more fruitful, and indeed more consistent with historical patterns in the West, to turn the question of the "division among the elite" on its head. For the elite of the Roman Republic manifests a long-term strength, based on resilience and remarkable discipline, that seems unparalleled in European history. For 500-plus years men with the names Fabius, Claudius, Valerius, and so on supplied the state with generation after generation of consuls, priests, and censors. What is remarkable is not that this elite, whose competitive impulses were always, it seems, highly developed, eventually became chronically and sometimes violently polarized, but how such an artificial creation as a *cohesive* competitive elite had been created and was for so long sustained. In a discussion focusing on the end of the Republic it is reasonable to focus on the *loss* of cohesion, but we shall get the perspective right only if we understand that the survival of such a remarkable social construction was always tenuous, and that nothing would seem more natural than its dissolution through a kind of historical entropy.

Why, finally, did the gradual polarization and dissolution of a formerly cohesive elite entail concentration of power in the hands of one person, the defining step in the passage from Republic to Principate? Polybius, in his famous doctrine of the repetitive "cycle" (*anakyklosis*) of constitutions from monarchy to aristocracy to democracy and back again, had seemingly predicted some kind of democratic interlude (6.57.9), which, Tiberius and Gaius Gracchus (or Clodius) notwithstanding, never actually came about in Rome. A more plausible alternative, which emerges into plain sight after 43 with the War of Philippi and the unstable "Second" Triumvirate (with Sextus Pompeius thrown in for good measure), was a descent into warlordism. That this was averted through Octavian's and Marcus Agrippa's martial success at Naulochus in 36 and Actium in 31 may have been due to mere contingencies of personal decisions and chance, but it would be difficult to deny that the continuing power of the Roman political tradition and the continuing concentration of military power in Italy made it almost inevitable that if the unitary *imperium* was to survive, then the warlord who held on to Rome would ultimately possess it. The paradox that a process of deep fragmentation led ultimately to monarchy is therefore only apparent – although it remains a remarkable achievement that Augustus and his successors were able to sustain the monarchy he had created.

Guide to Further Reading

The best starting point in English is Brunt 1971b or the later, more profound analysis in Brunt 1988c: 1–92. For the current, vigorous debate about the validity of Brunt's premises in the areas of agrarian history, military manpower, and demography, see

Chapters 27 and 28 above; cf. Morley 2001, Rosenstein 2004, and Scheidel 2004. Gruen 1974: esp. 498–507 is bracingly revisionist; the 1995 edition contains an illuminating introduction. Somewhat heavy-handed criticism of Gruen may be found in Crawford 1976; Deininger 1980 includes a broad view of the historiography of the problem as well as a response to Gruen, whose central idea that the Republic was not on its deathbed has now been picked up in German by Girardet 1996 and Welwei 1996. Meier 1980 is tough going for those who are not native speakers of German (and perhaps for some who are); a brief sketch in English (without scholarly apparatus) of the theory of "crisis without alternative" may be found in Meier 1982: 349–63. (Some further references in Morstein-Marx 2004: 285 n.13.) An excellent critical review in English is Brunt 1968 (which Meier seeks to answer in the new introduction to Meier 1980: xv–xxxi); cf. also Badian 1990b. On Meier, see also Chapter 1 above. Recent debate has been carried forth almost exclusively by German scholars stimulated or provoked by Meier's views on the Roman Republic and on Caesar: see especially the works of Welwei and Girardet just cited, with the response by Deininger 1998. Alongside that debate, however, see also Bleicken 1995b and (in English) Eder 1996, the latter of whom emphasizes the breakdown of elite consensus and loss of the constitutional conventions that moderated the full exploitation of archaic institutions.

Notes

The first two sections of this chapter were drafted by RMM; responsibility for the final section is more or less equally shared by both authors.

1   Syme 1958: 369 (not his own view).
2   Cf. Meier 1980: 1; Sion-Jenkis 2000: 19–53.
3   Brunt 1971b, 1988c: 1–92.
4   Meier 1980 (first published 1966).
5   Brunt 1968 offers a rebuttal to Meier's "Gefälligkeitsstaat"; Meier 1980: xix–xxxi responds.
6   Gruen 1974.
7   Gruen 1974: 504.
8   Montesquieu, *Considerations on the Causes of the Greatness of the Romans and Their Decline*, ch. 11.
9   Machiavelli, *Discourses on the First Decade of Livy*, 3.24 (cf., however, 1.5, 1.37); stronger emphasis in Montesquieu, *Considerations*, esp. ch. 9.
10 Ungern-Sternberg 1998: 611–12. On the two sides of this issue, compare Welwei 1996: 485–7 with Deininger 1980, 1998: 133–4.
11 E.g., Bleicken 1995b: 102–3: a "fact now disputed by no one," dismissing Gruen 1974: 502–3. See however also Eder 1996: 441–7.
12 Updated in Brunt 1988c: 240–80.
13 See esp. Hopkins 1978: 1–98.
14 Rosenstein 2004.
15 See now also Scheidel 2004: 2–9, favoring the lower estimate.
16 Gruen 1974: 425–7; cf. Giovannini 1995.

17   Cic. *Leg. agr.* 2.70, *Att.* 1.19.4; Cass. Dio 38.1.3; cf. Morstein-Marx 2004: 129–30. See, however, App. *B Civ.* 1.13–14, 29–32 on the (earlier) land bills of Tiberius Gracchus and Saturninus.

18   Rich (1983: 328–30) accepts on general grounds that Marius' precedent was regularized in the time of the Social War. There seems to be no firm evidence.

19   See now Lo Cascio 2001: 126.

20   Brunt 1971a: 410.

21   Brunt 1988c: 257–9.

22   On which see Rosenstein 2004: 222 n.191.

23   Cf. de Blois 2000: 22, 29–30.

24   Good comments on this problem in Bleicken 1995b: 103–8. See, e.g., Cic. *Mil.* 82: "a thankful People should reward citizens who have earned the gratitude of the common-wealth (*bene meritos de re publica civis*)." *Dignitas*: Hellegouarc'h 1963: esp. 397–411; in elections, see Morstein-Marx 1998: 265–7.

25   Famously, all but one of Sulla's officers (*archontes*) deserted (App. *B Civ.* 1.57) – probably not, however, a good indicator of senatorial opinion, since the term may not include the senatorial legates, and in any case their replacements included members of established senatorial families (Levick 1982).

26   Cf. Cic. *Prov. cons.* 18–47; Caes. *B Civ.* 1.13.1; Suet. *Iul.* 30.4 (*tantis rebus gestis*, "despite such great achievements") with Plut. *Caes.* 46.1.

27   In his comprehensive study of the motives of the adversaries at the outbreak of the civil war, Raaflaub 1977 draws too sharp a line beween the "personal" and the "public."

28   Brunt 1968: 229; Gruen 1974: 384.

29   See, e.g., Cic. *Sest.* 137: "[Our ancestors] intended the Senate to protect and increase the freedom and privileges of the People;" cf. *Rep.* 1.52.5: "the People must not be made to think that their privileges are being neglected by the chief men" (an aristocratic principle that probably reflects Roman thinking).

30   Morstein-Marx 2004: esp. 279–87.

31   See Ungern-Sternberg 1982 and 1998 for an attempt to integrate ancient theories of moral collapse into a modern causal analysis.

32   Gruen 1992: 304–5; Gruen 1995: 60–73; Brennan 2000: 168–72, 235–6. On regulation of aristocratic competition in the middle Republic generally, see Rosenstein 1990.

Bibliography

Aberson, M. 1994. *Temples votifs et butin de guerre dans la Rome républicaine*. Rome.

Abrams, P. 1982. *Historical Sociology*. Ithaca.

Achard, G. (ed.) 1989. *Rhétorique à Herennius*. Paris.

Achard, G. (ed.) 1994. *Cicéron, de l'Invention*. Paris.

Adam, J. P. 1994. *Roman Building: Materials and Techniques*. Trans. A. Mathews. Blooming-ton.

Ager, S. 1996. *Interstate Arbitrations in the Greek World, 337–90 B.C.* Berkeley and Los Angeles.

Aldrete, G. 1999. *Gestures and Acclamations in Ancient Rome*. Baltimore.

Alessio, M., Bella, F., Cortesi, C., and Grasiadei, B. 1968. "University of Rome C-14 Dates VII." *Radiocarbon* 10, 350–64.

Alexander, M. 1982. "Repetition of Prosecution, and the Scope of Prosecutions, in the Standing Criminal Courts of the Late Republic." *ClAnt* 1, 141–66.

Alexander, M. 1985. "*Praemia* in the *Quaestiones* of the Late Republic." *CPh* 80, 20–32.

Alexander, M. 1990. *Trials in the late Roman Republic, 149 BC–50 BC*. Toronto.

Alexander, M. 2002. *The Case for the Prosecution in the Ciceronian Era*. Ann Arbor.

Alfaro Asíns, C., and Burnett, A. M. 2003. *A Survey of Numismatic Research, 1996–2001*. Madrid.

Alföldi, A. 1965. *Early Rome and the Latins*. Ann Arbor.

Alvarez, W. 1972. "The Treia Valley North of Rome: Volcanic Stratigraphy, Topographic Evolution and Geographical Influence on Human Settlement." *Geologia Romana* 11, 153–76.

Alvisi, G. 1970. *La viabilità romana della Daunia*. Bari.

Ameling, W. 1993. *Karthago: Militär, Staat und Gesellschaft*. Munich.

Ampolo, C. 1983. "La storiografia su Roma arcaica e i documenti," in E. Gabba (ed.), *Tria corda: scritti in onore di Arnaldo Momigliano*, 9–26. Como.

Ampolo, C. 1988a. "La città riformata e l'organizzazione centuriata. Lo spazio, il tempo, il sacro nella nuova realtà urbana," in Momigliano and Schiavone 1988: 1.203–39.

Ampolo, C. 1988b. "La nascita della città," in Momigliano and Schiavone 1988: 1.153–80.

Ampolo, C. 1990. "Aspetti dello sviluppo economico agl'inizi della repubblica romana," in Eder 1990: 482–93.

Anderson, E. 1999. *Code of the Street: Decency, Violence, and the Moral Life of the Inner City.* New York.

Anderson, J. C., Jr., 1997. *Roman Architecture and Society.* Baltimore and London.

Anderson, W. S. 1996. *Barbarian Play.* Toronto.

Ando, C. 2000. *Imperial Ideology and Provincial Loyalty in the Roman Empire.* Berkeley and Los Angeles.

Ando, C. (ed.) 2003. *Roman Religion.* Edinburgh.

Andreussi, M. 1996. "Murus Servii Tullii: mura repubblicane." *LTUR* 3, 319–24.

Appel, G. 1889. *De Romanorum precationibus.* Gießen.

Aron, R. 1973. *Peace and War: A Theory of International Relations.* New York.

Arthur, P. 1991a. "Territories, Wine and Wealth: Suessa Aurunca, Sinuessa, Minturnae and the Ager Falernus," in Barker and Lloyd 1991: 153–9.

Arthur, P. 1991b. *Romans in Northern Campania.* London.

Ashby, R. K. 1984. "The Poverty of Neorealism." *Int. Org.* 38, 225–86.

Assmann, J. 1992. *Das kulturelle Gedächtnis. Schrift, Erinnerung, und politische Identität in frühen Hochkulturen.* Munich.

Assmann, J. 2000. *Religion und kulturelles Gedächtnis. Zehn Studien.* Munich.

Assmann, J., and Hölscher, T. (eds.) 1988. *Kultur und Gedächtnis.* Frankfurt.

Astin, A. E. 1958. *The Lex Annalis before Sulla.* Brussels.

Astin, A. E. 1967. *Scipio Aemilianus.* Oxford.

Astin, A. E. 1978. *Cato the Censor.* Oxford.

Astin, A. E. 1989. "Roman Government and Politics, 200–134 BC," in Astin et al. 1989: 163–96.

Astin, A. E., Walbank, F. W., Frederiksen, M. W., and R. M. Ogilvie (eds.) 1989. *Rome and the Mediterranean to 133 B.C.* Vol. 8 of *The Cambridge Ancient History* [2]. Cambridge.

Atkinson, K. M. T. 1970. "The Education of the Lawyer in Ancient Rome." *The South African Law Journal* 87, 31–59.

Atkinson, M. 1984. *Our Masters' Voices: the Language and Body Language of Politics.* New York.

Atmore, A. E. 1984. "The Extra-European Foundations of British Imperialism: A Reassessment," in C. C. Eldridge (ed.), *British Imperialism in the Nineteenth Century,* 106–25. London and New York.

Attema, P. A. J., Delvigne, J., and Haagsma, B.-J. 1999. "Case Studies from the Pontine Region in Central Italy on Settlement and Environmental Change in the First Millennium BC," in P. Leveau, F. Trément, K. Walsh, and G. Barker (eds.), *Environmental Reconstruction in Mediterranean Landscape Archaeology,* 105–21. Oxford.

Attolini, I. et al. 1991. "Political Geography and Productive Geography between the Valleys of the Albegna and the Fiora in Northern Etruria," in Barker and Lloyd 1991: 142–52.

Aubert, J.-J. 1994. *Business Managers in Ancient Rome. A Social and Economic Study of Institores 200 BC–AD 250.* Leiden.

Auffarth, C., and Rüpke, J. (eds.) 2002. *Epitome tes oikoumenes: Studien zur römischen Religion in Antike und Neuzeit.* Stuttgart.

Austin, M. M. 1986. "Hellenistic Kings, War and the Economy." *CQ* 36, 450–66.

Backendorf, D. 1998. *Römische Münzschätze des zweiten und ersten Jahrhunderts.* Berlin.

Badian, E. 1954. "Lex Acilia Repetundarum." *AJPh* 75, 374–84.

Badian, E. 1955. "The Date of Pompey's First Triumph." *Hermes* 83, 107–18.

Badian, E. 1957. "Caepio and Norbanus: Notes on the Decade 100–90 B.C." *Historia* 6, 318–46 (= Badian 1964: 34–70).

Badian, E. 1958a. *Foreign Clientelae, 264–70 B.C.* Oxford.

Badian, E. 1958b. "Notes on Provincial Governors from the Social War down to Sulla's Victory." *PACA* 1, 1–18 (= Badian 1964: 71–104).

Badian, E. 1962a. *"Forschungsbericht*: From the Gracchi to Sulla." *Historia* 11, 197–245.

Badian, E. 1962b. "Waiting for Sulla." *JRS* 52, 47–61 (= Badian 1964: 206–34).

Badian, E. 1963–4. "Marius and the Nobles." *DUJ* 25, 141–54.

Badian, E. 1964. *Studies in Greek and Roman History.* Oxford.

Badian, E. 1968a. *Roman Imperialism in the Late Republic.*[2] Ithaca, NY.

Badian, E. 1968b. "The Early Historians," in T. A. Dorey (ed.), *The Latin Historians*, 1–38. London.

Badian, E. 1969. "Quaestiones Variae." *Historia* 18, 447–91.

Badian, E. 1970a. "Additional Notes on Roman Magistrates." *Athenaeum* 48, 3–14.

Badian, E. 1970b. *Lucius Sulla: The Deadly Reformer.* Sydney.

Badian, E. 1970–1. "Roman Politics and the Italians (133–91 B.C.)." *DArch* 4–5, 373–409.

Badian, E. 1972a. *Publicans and Sinners: Private Enterprise in the Service of the Roman Republic.* Ithaca.

Badian, E. 1972b. "Tiberius Gracchus and the Beginning of the Roman Revolution." *ANRW* 1.1, 668–731.

Badian, E. 1974. "The Attempt to Try Caesar," in J. A. S. Evans (ed.) *Polis and Imperium: Studies in Honour of Edward Togo Salmon*, 145–66. Toronto.

Badian, E. 1983a. "The Silence of Norbanus: A Note on Provincial Quaestors under the Republic." *AJPh* 104, 156–71.

Badian, E. 1983b. "Hegemony and Independence: Prolegomena to a Study of Rome and the Hellenistic States in the Second Century B.C." *Actes du VIIe Congrès de la F. I. E. C.*, 397–414. Budapest.

Badian, E. 1984. "The Death of Saturninus: Studies in Chronology and Prosopography." *Chiron* 14, 101–47.

Badian, E. 1990a. "The Consuls, 179 – 49 BC." *Chiron* 20, 371–413.

Badian, E. 1990b. Review of Meier 1982. *Gnomon* 62, 22–39.

Badian, E. 1996a. "Optimates, populares." *Oxford Classical Dictionary*[3]: 1070–1.

Badian, E. 1996b. *"Provincia/*Province." *Oxford Classical Dictionary*[3]: 1265–67.

Badian, E. 1996c. *"Tribuni plebis* and *Res Publica*," in Linderski 1996: 187–213.

Bain, D. 1979. "Plautus vortit barbare: Plautus, Bacchides 526–61 and Menander, Dis Exapaton 102–12," in D. West and A. J. Woodman (eds.), *Creative Imitation and Latin Literature*, 17–34. Cambridge.

Bakker, J. 1994. *Living and Working with the Gods: Studies of Evidence for Private Religion and its Material Environment in the City of Ostia (100–500 AD).* Amsterdam.

Baldwin, D. A. (ed.) 1993. *Neorealism and Neoliberalism: The Contemporary Debate.* New York.

Balsdon, J. P. V. D. 1938. "The History of the Extortion Court at Rome, 123–70 B.C." *PBSR* 14, 98–114 (= Seager 1969: 132–48).

Balsdon, J. P. V. D. 1939. "Consular Provinces under the Late Republic." *JRS* 29, 57–73, 167–83.

Balsdon, J. P. V. D. 1979. *Romans and Aliens.* Chapel Hill.

Barbet, A. 1985. *La peinture murale romaine. Les styles décoratifs pompéiens.* Paris.

Barchiesi, A., Rüpke, J., and Stephens, S. (eds.) 2004. *Rituals in Ink.* Stuttgart.

Bardon, H. 1950. "Q. Lutatius Catulus et son 'cercle littéraire'." *LEC* 18, 145–64.

Barker, G. 1989. "The Archaeology of the Italian Shepherd." *Transactions of the Cambridge Philosophical Society* 215, 1–19.

Barker, G. 1995. *A Mediterranean Valley. Landscape Archaeology and Annales History in the Biferno Valley.* Leicester.

Barker, G., and Grant, A. 1991. "Ancient and Modern Pastoralism in Central Italy: an Interdisciplinary Study in the Cicolano Mountains." *PBSR* 59, 15–88.

Barker, G., and Lloyd, J. (eds.) 1991. *Roman Landscapes: Archaeological Survey in the Mediterranean Region.* London.

Barker, G., and Rasmussen, T. 1998. *The Etruscans.* Oxford.

Barlow, J. 1998. "Noble Gauls and their Other in Caesar's Propaganda," in Welch and Powell 1998: 139–70.

Baronowski, D. W. 1993. "Roman Military Forces in 225 BC (Polybius 2.23–4)." *Historia* 42, 181–202.

Barsby, J. 1986. (ed. and trans.) *Plautus, Bacchides.* Warminster.

Barton, C. 1993. *The Sorrows of the Ancient Romans. The Gladiator and the Monster.* Princeton.

Barton, C. 2001. *Roman Honor. The Fire in the Bones.* Berkeley and Los Angeles.

Barwick, K. 1963. *Das rednerische Bildungsideal Ciceros.* Berlin.

Batstone, W. W. 1988. "The Antithesis of Virtue: Sallust's *Synkrisis* and the Crisis of the Late Republic." *ClAnt* 7, 1–29.

Batstone, W. W. 1990. "Intellectual Conflict and *Mimesis* in Sallust's *Bellum Catilinae*," in Allison, J. (ed.) *Conflict, Antithesis and the Ancient Historian*, 112–32. Columbus.

Batstone, W. W. 1993. "Rhetoric, Logic, and Poesis." *Helios* 20, 143–72.

Batstone, W. W. 1994. "Cicero's Construction of Consular *Ethos* in the *First Catilinarian*." *TAPhA* 124, 211–66.

Batstone, W. W. 2005. "Plautine Farce, Plautine Freedoms: An Essay on Metatheatre in Plautus," in W. W. Batstone and G. Tissol (eds.), *Defining Gender and Genre in Latin Poetry. Essays Presented to W. S. Anderson on his 75th Birthday.* New York.

Batty, R., 2000. "Mela's Phoenician Geography." *JRS* 90, 70–94.

Bauman, R. 1973a. "The Hostis-Declarations of 88 and 87 B.C." *Athenaeum* 51, 270–93.

Bauman, R. 1973b. "Roman Legal Writing: A Late Flowering of the Roman Literary Genius." *AClass* 16, 135–46.

Bauman, R. 1980. "The 'Leges iudiciorum publicorum' and their Interpretation in the Republic, Principate and Later Empire." *ANRW* 2.13, 103–233.

Bauman, R. 1983. *Lawyers in Roman Republican Politics: A study of the Roman jurists in their political setting, 316–82 BC.* Munich.

Bauman, R. 1985. *Lawyers in Roman Transitional Politics: A study of the Roman jurists in their political setting in the Late Republic and Triumvirate.* Munich.

Bauman, R. 1996. *Crime and Punishment in Ancient Rome.* London and New York.

Beacham, R. C., 1991. *The Roman Theater and Its Audience.* Cambridge.

Beagon, M. 1992. *Roman Nature. The Thought of Pliny the Elder.* Oxford.

Beard, M. 1986. "Cicero and Divination: The Formation of a Latin Discourse." *JRS* 76, 33–46.

Beard, M. 2003. "The Triumph of the Absurd: Roman Street Theatre," in Edwards and Woolf 2003: 21–43.

Beard, M., and Crawford, M. 1985. *Rome in the Late Republic: Problems and Interpretations.* (2nd ed. 1999.) London.

Beard, M., and Henderson, J. 2001. *Classical Art: from Greece to Rome.* Oxford.

Beard, M., and North, J. (eds.) 1990. *Pagan Priests: Religion and Power in the Ancient World.* London.

Beard, M., North, J., and Price, S. 1998. *Religions of Rome.* 2 vols. Cambridge.

Beck, H. 2000. "Quintus Fabius Maximus – Musterkarriere ohne Zögern," in K.-J. Hölkeskamp and E. Stein-Hölkeskamp (eds.), *Von Romulus zu Augustus. Große Gestalten der römischen Republik*, 79–91. Munich.

Beck, H. 2003. "'Den Ruhm nicht teilen wollen'. Fabius Pictor und die Anfänge des römischen Nobilitätsdiskurses," in Eigler, Gotter, Luraghi, and Walter 2003: 73–92.

Beck, H. 2005. *Karriere und Hierarchie. Die römischen Aristokratie und die Anfänge des cursus honorum in der mittleren Republik*. Cologne.

Beck, H., and Walter, U. 2001–4. *Die frühen römischen Historiker, herausgegeben, übersetzt und kommentiert*. 2 vols. Darmstadt.

Bederman, E. 2001. *International Law in Antiquity*. Oxford.

Belayche, N., Bendlin, A., Rüpke, J., et al. 2000. "Forschungsberichte Römische Religion 1990–1999." *Archiv für Religionsgeschichte* 2, 283–345.

Belayche, N., Bendlin, A., Rüpke, J., et al. 2003. "Forschungsberichte Römische Religion 1999–2002." *Archiv für Religionsgeschichte* 5, 297–371.

Bell, M. G., and Boardman, J. (eds) 1992. *Past and Present Soil Erosion: Archaeological and Geographical Perspectives*. Oxford.

Bell, M. J. V. 1965. "Tactical Reform in the Roman Republican Army." *Historia* 14, 404–22.

Beloch, K. J. 1886. *Die Bevölkerung der griechisch-römischen Welt*. Leipzig.

Bendlin, A. 1998. "Social Complexity and Religion at Rome in the Second and First Centuries BCE." Dissertation, University of Oxford.

Bendlin, A. 2001. "Rituals or Beliefs? 'Religion' and the Religious Life of Rome." *SCI* 20, 191–208.

Bennett, H. 1923. *Cinna and his Times. A Critical and Interpretative Study of Roman History During the Period 87–84 B.C.* Menasha.

Bérard, F. 2000. *Guide de l'épigraphiste*[3]. Paris.

Bergemann, J. 1990. *Römische Reiterstatuen. Ehrendenkmäler im öffentlichen Raum*. Mainz.

Bergmann, B. 1995. "Greek Masterpieces and Roman Recreative Fictions." *HSPh* 97, 79–120.

Bergmann, B. 2001. "House of cards." *JRA* 14, 56–7.

Bergmann, B., and Kondoleon, C. (eds.) 1999. *The Art of Ancient Spectacle*. Washington.

Bernhardt, R. 1998. *Rom und die Städte des hellenistischen Osten (3.–1. Jahrhundert v. Chr.). Literaturbericht*. Munich.

Bernstein, A. H. 1978. *Tiberius Sempronius Gracchus: Tradition and Apostasy*. Ithaca and London.

Bernstein, F. 1998. *Ludi publici: Untersuchungen zur Entstehung und Entwicklung der öffentlichen Spiele im republikanischen Rom*. Stuttgart.

Berrendonner, C. 2001. "La formation de la tradition sur M. Curius Dentatus et C. Fabricius Luscinus: un homme nouveau peut-il être un grand homme?" in Coudry and Späth 2001: 97–116.

Berry, D. 2003. "*Equester Ordo Tuus Est*: Did Cicero Win his Cases Because of his Support for the *Equites*?" *CQ* 53, 222–34.

Bertoletti, M., Cima, M., and Talamo, E. 1997. *Sculture di Roma Antica. Collezione dei Musei Capitolini alla Centrale Montemartini*. Milan.

Beston, P. 2000. "Hellenistic Military Leadership," in van Wees 2000: 315–35.

Bianchi Bandinelli, R. 1970. *Rome: The Center of Power*. Trans. P. Green. New York.

Bianchi Bandinelli, R. 1978. *Dall'ellenismo al medioevo*. Rome.

Bickermann, E. J. 1952. "*Origines Gentium*." *CPh* 47, 65–81.

Bieber, M. 1961. *History of the Greek and Roman Theater*[2]. Princeton.

Bieber, M. 1974. *Ancient Copies: Contributions to the History of Greek and Roman Art*. New York.

Biering, R. 1995. *Die Odysseefresken vom Esquilin.* Munich.

Bintliff, J. 1992. "Erosion in the Mediterranean Lands: A Reconsideration of Pattern, Process and Methodology," in Bell and Boardman 1992: 125–31.

Birley, E. 1953. "Senators in the Emperor's Service." *Proc. Brit. Acad.* 39, 197–214.

Bispham, E., and Smith, C. (eds.) 2000. *Religion in Archaic and Republican Rome and Italy: Evidence and Experience.* Edinburgh.

Blanckenhagen, P. H. von. 1963. "The Odyssey Frieze." *MRDI(R)* 70: 100–46.

Bleckmann, B. 2002. *Die römische Nobilität im Ersten Punischen Krieg: Untersuchungen zur aristokratischen Konkurrenz in der Republik.* Berlin.

Bleicken, J. 1955. *Das Volkstribunat der klassischen Republik.* Munich.

Bleicken, J. 1957. "Oberpontifex und Pontifikalkollegium. Eine Studie zur römischen Sakralverfassung." *Hermes* 85, 345–66.

Bleicken, J. 1975. *Lex publica: Gesetz und Recht in der römischen Republik.* Berlin and New York.

Bleicken, J. 1981. "Die Nobilität der römischen Republik." *Gymnasium* 88, 236–53.

Bleicken, J. 1990. "Tiberius Gracchus und die italischen Bundesgenossen", in W. Ax (ed.), *Memoria rerum veterum. Neue Beiträge zur antiken Historiographie und Alten Geschichte, Festschrift für Carl Joachim Classen zum 60. Geburtstag,* 101–31. Stuttgart.

Bleicken, J. 1995a. *Cicero und die Ritter.* Göttingen.

Bleicken, J. 1995b. *Gedanken zum Untergang der römischen Republik.* Stuttgart.

Bloch, M. 1977. "The Past and the Present in the Present." *Man,* n.s. 12, 278–92.

Bloch, R. S. 2002. *Antike Vorstellungen vom Judentum: Der Judenexkurs des Tacitus im Rahmen der griechisch-römischen Ethnographie.* Stuttgart.

Bloomer, M. W. 1993. *Valerius Maximus and the Rhetoric of the New Nobility.* London.

Blösel, W. 2003. "Die *memoria* der *gentes* als Rückgrat der kollektiven Erinnerung im republikanischen Rom," in Eigler et al. 2003: 53–72.

Bloy, D. 1998–9. "Greek Booty at Luna and the Aftermath of Manius Acilius Glabrio." *MAAR* 43/44, 49–61.

Bodel, J. 1994. *Graveyards and Groves: A Study of the Lex Lucerina.* Cambridge. (*AJAH* 11 (1986), 1–133.)

Bodel, J. 1997. "Monumental Villas and Villa Monuments." *JRA* 10, 5–35.

Bodel, J. 1999. "Death on Display: Looking at Roman Funerals," in Bergmann and Kondoleon 1999: 259–81.

Bodel, J. 2000. "Dealing with the Dead: Undertakers, Executioners and Potters' Fields in Ancient Rome," in Hope and Marshall 2000: 128–51.

Boëthius, A. 1978. *Etruscan and Early Roman Architecture²*. Harmondsworth and New York.

Boissevain, J. 1966. "Patronage in Sicily." *Man* 1, 18–33.

Boissevain, J. 1974. *Friends of Friends, Networks, Manipulators, and Coalitions.* Oxford.

Boissevain, J. 1977. "When the Saints Go Marching Out: Reflections on the Decline of Patronage in Malta," in Gellner and Waterbury 1977: 81–96.

Bol, P. C. 1972. *Die Skulpturen des Schiffsfundes von Antikythera.* Berlin.

Bömer, F. 1953. "Der Commentarius: zur Vorgeschichte und literarischen Form der Schriften Caesars." *Hermes* 81, 210–50.

Bonadonna, F. P., and Bigazzi, G. 1970. "Studi sul Pleistocene del Lazio VIII. Datazione di tufi intertirreniani della zona di Cerveteri (Roma) mediante il metodo delle tracce di fissione," *Bollettino della Società Geologica Italiana* 89, 463–73.

Bonatti, E. 1963. "Stratigrafia pollinica dei sedimenti postglaciali di Baccano, lago craterico del Lazio," *Atti della Società Toscana di Scienze Naturali (Serie A)* 70, 40–8.

Bonfante, L. 1994. "Etruscan Women," in E. Fantham, H. P. Foley, N. B. Kampen, S. B. Pomeroy, and H. A. Shapiro (eds.), *Women in the Classical World*, 243–59. New York and Oxford.

Bonifacio, R., 1997. *Ritratti romani da Pompei*. Rome.

Bonnefond-Coudry, M. 1989. *Le Sénat de la république romaine: de la guerre d'Hannibal à Auguste*. Rome.

Bonner, S. F. 1949. *Roman Declamation in the Late Republic and Early Empire*. Berkeley and Los Angeles.

Bonner, S. F. 1977. *Education in Ancient Rome*. London

Bordenache Battaglia, G. 1990. *Le Ciste prenestine*. Florence.

Boren, H. C. 1956–7. "Livius Drusus, t. p. 122, and His Anti-Gracchan Program." *CJ* 52, 27–36.

Boren, H. C. 1957–8. "The Urban Side of the Gracchan Economic Crisis." *AHR* 63, 890–902.

Boren, H. C. 1961. "Tiberius Gracchus: The Opposition View." *AJPh* 82, 358–69.

Boren, H. C. 1968. *The Gracchi*. New York.

Bourdieu, P. 1984. *Distinction: A Social Critique of the Judgement of Taste*. Trans. R. Nice. Cambridge, MA.

Bourdieu, P. 1990. *The Logic of Practice*. Trans. R. Nice. Stanford.

Bradley, G. 2000. *Ancient Umbria: State, Culture and Identity in Central Italy from the Iron Age to the Augustan Era*. Oxford.

Bradley, G. 2002. "The Romanisation of Italy in the 2nd c. B.C." *JRA* 15, 401–6.

Bradley, K. R. 1984. *Slaves and Masters in the Roman Empire: A Study in Social Control*. Brussels.

Bradley, K. R. 1989. *Slavery and Rebellion in the Roman World, 140 B.C.–70 B.C.* Bloomington.

Bradley, K. R. 1991. *Discovering the Roman Family: Studies in Roman Social History*. New York and Oxford.

Bradley, K. R. 1994. *Slavery and Society at Rome*. Cambridge.

Braudel, F. 1972. *The Mediterranean and the Mediterranean World in the Age of Philip II*. 2 vols. London.

Braudel, F. 1980. "History and the Social Sciences: The *Longue Durée*," in F. Braudel, *On History*, 25–54. Chicago.

Braun, M., Haltenhoff, A., and Mutschler, F.-H. (eds.) 2000. *Moribus antiquis res stat Romana. Römische Werte und römische Literatur im 3. und 2. Jh. v. Chr*. Munich.

Braund, D. 1984. *Rome and the Friendly King*. London.

Bremmer, J. 1987. "Romulus, Remus and the Foundation of Rome," in Bremmer and Horsfall 1987: 25–48.

Bremmer, J. 1991. "Walking, Standing, and Sitting in Ancient Greek Culture," in Bremmer and Roodenburg 1991: 15–35.

Bremmer, J., and Horsfall, N. (eds.). 1987. *Roman Myth and Mythography*. London.

Bremmer, J., and Roodenburg, H. (eds.). 1991. *A Cultural History of Gesture*. Ithaca.

Brendel, O. 1979. *Prolegomena to the Study of Roman Art*. New Haven.

Brennan, T. C. 1992. "Sulla's Career in the Nineties: Some Reconsiderations." *Chiron* 22, 103–58.

Brennan, T. C. 1993. "The Commanders in the First Sicilian Slave War." *RFIC* 121, 153–84.

Brennan, T. C. 2000. *The Praetorship in the Roman Republic*. 2 vols. Oxford.

Brilliant, R. 1963. *Gesture and Rank in Roman Art. The Use of Gestures to Denote Status in Roman Sculpture and Coinage*. New Haven.

Brilliant, R. 1998. "Some Reflections on the 'New Roman Art History'." *JRA* 11, 557–64.

Brilliant, R. 1999. "'Let the Trumpets Roar!' The Roman Triumph," in Bergmann and Kondoleon 1999: 221–9.

Bringmann, K. 1985. *Die Agrarreformen des Tiberius Gracchus. Legende und Wirklichkeit.* Stuttgart.

Briscoe, J. 1973. *A Commentary on Livy, Books XXXI–XXXIII.* Oxford.

Briscoe, J. 1981. *A Commentary on Livy, Books XXXIV–XXXVII.* Oxford.

Broadhead, W. 2000. "Migration and Transformation in North Italy in the 3rd–1st Centuries BC." *BICS* 44, 145–66.

Broughton, T. R. S. 1951–86. *The Magistrates of the Roman Republic.* 3 vols. New York and Atlanta.

Brouwer, H. H. J. 1989. *Bona Dea: The Sources and a Description of the Cult.* EPRO 110. Leiden.

Brown, A. G. 1997. *Alluvial Geoarchaeology: Floodplain Archaeology and Environmental Change.* Cambridge.

Brown, A. G., and Ellis, C. 1995. "People, Climate and Alluviation: Theory, Research Design and New Sedimentological and Stratigraphic Data from Etruria." *PBSR* 64, 45–74.

Brown, F. 1980. *Cosa. The Making of a Roman Town.* Ann Arbor.

Bruneau, P. 1983. *Guide de Délos.* Paris.

Bruneau, P. et al. 1970. *L'Îlot de la Maison des Comédiens.* Paris.

Bruno, V. J. 1985. *Hellenistic Painting. The Evidence of the Delos Fragments.* Leiden.

Bruno, V. J., and Scott, R. T. 1993. *Cosa IV: The Houses.* MAAR 38. University Park, PA.

Brunt, P. A. 1963. Review of D.C. Earl, *The Political Thought of Sallust. CR* 13, 74–5.

Brunt, P. A. 1966. "The Roman Mob." *P & P* 35, 3–27.

Brunt, P. A. 1968. Review of Meier 1980. *JRS* 58, 229–32.

Brunt, P. A. 1971a. *Italian Manpower, 225 B.C.–A.D. 14.* Oxford.

Brunt, P. A. 1971b. *Social Conflicts in the Roman Republic.* London.

Brunt, P. A. 1979. "Cicero and Historiography," in *Miscellanea di Studi Classici in Onore di Eugenio Manni,* Vol. 1. Rome, 3110–40 (= Brunt, P. A. 1988. *Studies in Greek History and Thought,* 181–209. Oxford).

Brunt, P. A. 1980a. "Free Labour and Public Works at Rome." *JRS* 70, 81–100.

Brunt, P. A. 1980b. "Patronage and Politics in the Verrines." *Chiron* 10, 273–89.

Brunt, P. A. 1980c. "On Historical Fragments and Epitomes." *CQ* 30, 477–94.

Brunt, P. A. 1982. "*Nobilitas* and *novitas.*" *JRS* 72, 1–17.

Brunt, P. A. 1988a. "*Clientela,*" in Brunt 1988c: 382–442.

Brunt, P. A. 1988b. "The Army and the Land in the Roman Revolution," in Brunt 1988c: 240–80.

Brunt, P. A. 1988c. *The Fall of the Roman Republic and Related Essays.* Oxford.

Bruun, C. (ed.) 2000. *The Roman Middle Republic: Politics, Religion, and Historiography c. 400–133 BC.* Rome.

Bucher, G. 1987. "The *Annales Maximi* in the Light of Roman Methods of Keeping Records." *AJAH* 12, 2–61.

Bulst, C. M. 1964. "'Cinnanum Tempus': A Reassessment of the 'Dominatio Cinnae'." *Historia* 13, 307–37.

Burckhardt, L. A. 1990. "The Political Elite of the Roman Republic: Comments on Recent Discussion of the Concepts of *Nobilitas* and *Homo Novus.*" *Historia* 39, 77–99.

Bürge, A. 1990. "Der mercennarius und die Lohnarbeit." *ZRG* 107, 80–135.

Burke, P. 1980. *Sociology and History.* London.

Burke, P. 1989. "History as Social Memory," in Butler, T. (ed.), *Memory: History, Culture and the Mind,* 97–113. Oxford.

Burkert, W. 1985. "Herodot über die Götter: Polytheismus als historisches Problem," *MH* 42, 121–32.

Burkert, W. 1987. *Ancient Mystery Cults.* Cambridge.

Burkert, W. 1995. "Lydia between East and West or How to Date the Trojan War: A Study in Herodotus," in J. B. Carter and S. P. Morris (eds.), *The Ages of Homer*, 139–48. Austin.

Burnett, A. M. 1977. "The Authority to Coin in the Late Republic and Early Empire." *NC* 17, 37–63.

Burnett, A. M. 1978. "The First Roman Silver Coins." *Quaderni Ticinesi* 7, 121–42.

Burnett, A. M. 1986. "The Iconography of Roman Coin Types in the Third Century BC." *NC* 146, 67–75.

Burnett, A. M. 1987. *Coinage in the Roman World.* London.

Burnett, A. M. 1989. "The Beginnings of Roman Coinage." *AIIN* 36, 33–64.

Burnett, A. M. 1998. "The Coinage of the Social War," in A. M. Burnett, U. Wartenburg, and R. Witschonke (eds.), *Coins of Macedonia and Rome: Essays in Honour of Charles Hersh*, 165–72. London.

Burnett, A. M., and Crawford, M. H. (eds.) 1987. *The Coinage of the Roman World in the Late Republic.* Oxford.

Burns, T. S. 2003. *Rome and the Barbarians, 100 B. C.–A. D. 400.* Baltimore.

Burroughs, W. J. 2001. *Climate Change. A Multidisciplinary Approach.* Cambridge.

Burton, P. J. 2003. "*Clientela* or *Amicitia?* Modeling Roman International Behavior in the Middle Republic (264–146 B.C.)." *Klio* 85, 333–69.

Cagnat, R. 1914. *Cours d'Épigraphie Latine*[4]. Paris.

Cagniart, P. F. 1989. "L. Cornelius Sulla's Quarrel with C. Marius at the Time of the Germanic Invasions (104–101 B.C.)." *Athenaeum* 67, 139–49.

Cagniart, P. F. 1991. "L. Cornelius Sulla in the Nineties: A Reassessment." *Latomus* 50, 285–304.

Calabi Limentani, I. 1982. "I fornices di Stertinio e di Scipione nel racconto di Livio." *CISA* 8, 123–35.

Calabi Limentani, I. 1991. *Epigrafia Latina*[4]. Milan.

Calboli, G. (ed.) 1978. *Marci Porci Catonis Oratio pro Rhodiensibus.* Bologna.

Calboli, G. 1982. "La retorica preciceroniana e la politica a Roma," in O. Reverdin and B. Grange (eds.), *Eloquence et Rhétorique chez Cicéron*, 41–108. Geneva.

Calboli, G. (ed.) 1993. *Cornifici Rhetorica ad C. Herennium.* Bologna.

Cambi, F. 2002. "La geografia," in Carandini, Cambi et al. 2002: 30–6.

Campbell, B. 2000. *The Writings of the Roman Land Surveyors.* London

Campbell, B. 2002. "Power Without Limit: 'The Romans Always Win,'" in A. Chaniotis and P. Ducrey (eds.), *Army and Power in the Ancient World*, 167–80. Stuttgart.

Canali de Rossi, F. 2001. *Il ruolo dei patroni nelle relazioni politiche fra il mondo greco e Roma in età repubblicana ed Augustea.* Leipzig.

Cancik, H. 1985/6. "Rome as a Sacral Landscape. Varro and the End of Republican Religion in Rome." *Visible Religion* 4/5, 250–65.

Carafa, P. 1998. *Il comizio di Roma dalle origini all'età di Augusto.* Rome.

Carandini, A. 1988a. "Domus e horrea in Palatio," in Carandini 1988c: 359–87.

Carandini, A. 1988b. "Orti e frutteti intorno a Roma," in Carandini 1988c: 339–57.

Carandini, A. 1988c. *Schiavi in Italia: gli strumenti pensanti dei Romani fra tarda repubblica e medio impero.* Rome.

Carandini, A. 1990a. "Domus aristocratiche sopra le mura e il pomerio del Palatino," in Cristofani 1990: 97–9.

Carandini, A. 1990b. "Palatino, pendici settentrionali. Campagne di scavo 1985–88." *Bollettino di Archeologia* 1–2, 159–65.

Carandini, A. 1994. "I paesaggi agrari dell'Italia romana visti a partire dall' Etruria," in *L'Italie d'Auguste à Dioclétien*, 167–74. Rome.

Carandini, A. 1997. *La nascita di Roma. Dèi, lari, eroi, e uomini all'alba di una civiltà.* (2nd ed. 2003.) Turin.

Carandini, A., Cambi, F., Celuzza, M., and Regoli, E. (eds.) 2002. *Paesaggi d'Etruria. Valle dell'Albegna, Valle d'Oro, Valle del Chiarone, Valle del Tafone.* Rome.

Carandini, A., and Carafa, P. 1995. *Palatium e Sacra Via I: prima delle mura, l'età delle mura e l'età delle case antiche, Bollettino di Archeologia* 31–3. Rome.

Carandini, A., and Ricci, A. 1985. *Settefinestre. Una villa schiavistica nell'Etruria romana.* Modena.

Caravaggi, L. 2002. "L'epoca moderna," in Carandini, Cambi et al. 2002: 287–341.

Carey, C. 2003. *Pliny's Catalogue of Culture. Art and Empire in the Natural History.* Oxford.

Carlsen, J. 1995. *Vilici and Estate Managers until AD 284.* Rome.

Carter, G. F. 1981a. "Die-Link Statistics for Crepusius Denarii and Calculations of the Total Number of Dies." *PACT* 5, 193–203.

Carter, G. F. 1981b. "Comparison of Methods for Calculating the Total Number of Dies from Die-Link Statistics." *PACT* 5, 204–13.

Carter, G. F. 1983. "A Simplified Method for Calculating the Original Number of Dies from Die-Link Statistics." *ANSMusN* 28, 195–206.

Cassola, F. 1962. *I gruppi politici romani nel III secolo a.C.* Trieste.

Cassola, F. et al. 1988. "La colonizzazione romana tra la guerra latina e la guerra annibalica." *DArch* 3rd s., 6.2. Rome.

Castner, C. J. 1988. *Prosopography of Roman Epicureans from the Second Century B.C. to the Second Century A.D.* Frankfurt.

Catalli, F. 2001. *La monetazione romana repubblicana.* Rome.

Celuzza, M., and Rendini, P. (eds.). 1991. *Relitti di Storia. Archeologia subacquea in Maremma.* Siena.

Champlin, E. 1991. *Final Judgments: Duty and Emotion in Roman Wills, 200 B.C.-A.D. 250.* Berkeley.

Chantraine, H. 1959. *Untersuchungen zur römischen Geschichte am Ende des 2. Jahrhunderts v. Chr.* Kallmünz.

Chaplin, J. D. 2000. *Livy's Exemplary History.* Oxford.

Charatzopoulou, C. 2000. "La peinture funéraire en Grèce du IVe au IIe s. av. J.-C. Un état de la recherché," in A. Barbet (ed.), *La peinture funéraire antique: IVe siècle av. J.-C. – IVe siècle ap. J.-C.*, 43–9. Paris.

Chassignet, M. (ed.) 1996–2004. *L'annalistique romaine.* 3 vols. Paris.

Chayanov, A. 1966. *The Theory of Peasant Economy,* ed. D. Thorner, B. Kerblay, and R. Smith. Homewood, IL.

Cherkauer, D. S. 1976. "Site K. The Stratigraphy and Chronology of the River Treia Alluvial Deposits," in T. W. Potter (ed.), *A Faliscan Town in South Etruria. Excavations at Narce 1966–71*, 106–26. London.

Cherry, D. 1993. "Hunger at Rome in the Late Republic." *EMC* 37, 433–50.

Ciacci, A. 1981. "L'ambiente naturale," in M. Cristofani (ed.), *Gli Etruschi in Maremma. Popolamento e attività produttive*, 9–28. Siena.

Ciancio Rossetto, P., and Pisani Sartorio, G. 1994. *Teatri, greci e romani: alle origine del linguaggio rappresentato.* Rome.

Cichorius, C. 1922. "Das Offizierskorps eines römischen Heeres aus dem Bundesgenossen-kriege," in C. Cichorius, *Römische Studien*, 130–85. Leipzig.

Cifani, G., 1997. "Le mura archaiche di Roma," in Carandini 1997: 623–7.

Cima, M., and La Rocca, E. 1998. *Horti Romani*. Rome.

Cimino, M. G., and Nota Santi, M. (eds.) 1998. *Corso Vittorio Emmanuele I: tra urbanistica e archeologia*. Naples.

Cimma, M. R. 1976. *Reges socii et amici populi Romani*. Milan.

Claridge, A. 1998. *Rome: An Oxford Archaeological Guide*. Oxford.

Clarke, J. R. 1991. *The Houses of Roman Italy 100 B.C.–A.D. 250*. Berkeley and Los Angeles.

Clarke, J. R. 1998. *Looking at Lovemaking: Constructions of Sexuality in Roman Art, 100 B.C.–A.D. 250*. Berkeley and Los Angeles.

Clarke, J. R. 2003. *Roman Sex 100 B.C.–A.D. 250*. New York.

Clarke, K. J. 1997. "In Search of the Author of Strabo's Geography." *JRS* 87, 92–110.

Clarke, K. J. 1999. *Between Geography and History. Hellenistic Constructions of the Roman World*. Oxford.

Clarke, M. L. 1951. "The Thesis in the Roman Rhetorical Schools of the Republic." *CQ* 1, 159–66.

Clarke, M. L. 1996. *Rhetoric at Rome: a Historical Survey*[3], revised by D. H. Berry. London.

Clavel-Lévêque, M. 1972. "Le syncrétisme gallo-romain: Structures et finalités," in F. Sartori (ed.), *Praelectiones Patavinae*, 91–134. Rome.

Cloud, D. 1994. "The Constitution and Public Criminal Law," in Crook, Lintott, and Rawson 1994: 491–530.

Coarelli, F. 1968. "La porta trionfale e la via dei trionfi." *DArch* 2, 55–102.

Coarelli, F. 1971–2. "Il complesso pompeiano del Campo Marzio e la sua decorazione scultorea." *RPAA* 44, 99–122.

Coarelli, F. 1972. "Il sepolcro degli Scipioni." *DArch* 6, 36–106.

Coarelli, F. 1973. "Frammento di affresco dall' Esquilino con scena storica," in *Roma medio-repubblicana. Aspetti culturali di Roma e del Lazio nei secoli IV e III a.C.*, 200–8. Rome.

Coarelli, F. 1977. "Public Building in Rome between the Second Punic War and Sulla." *PBSR* 45, 1–23.

Coarelli, F. 1978. *Studi su Praeneste*. Perugia.

Coarelli, F. 1982. "'L'agora des italiens' a Delo: il mercato degli schiavi?," in F. Coarelli, D. Musti, and H. Solin (eds.), *Delo e l'Italia*, 119–46. Rome.

Coarelli, F. 1983. "Il commercio delle opere d'arte in età tardo-repubblicana." *DArch* 3.1, 45–53.

Coarelli, F. 1983–5. *Il Foro Romano*, 2 vols. (2nd ed. of vol. 1, 1986). Rome.

Coarelli, F. 1987. *I santuari del Lazio in età repubblicana*. Rome.

Coarelli, F. 1988a. "Colonizzazione romana e viabilità." *DArch* 3.6, 35–48.

Coarelli, F. 1988b. "Demografia et territorio," in Momigliano and Schiavone 1988–: 318–39.

Coarelli, F. 1988c. *Il Foro Boario: dalle origini alla fine della repubblica*. Rome (2nd ed. 1992).

Coarelli, F. 1992. "Colonizzazione a municipalizzazione: tempi e modi." *DArch* 3.10, 21–30.

Coarelli, F. 1993. "Curia Hostilia." *LTUR* 1, 331–2.

Coarelli, F. 1994. "Due fregi da Fregellae: un documento storico della prima guerra siriaca?" *Ostraka* 3.1, 93–108.

Coarelli, F. 1996a. *Revixit ars: arte e ideologia a Roma dai modelli ellenistici alla tradizione repubblicana*. Rome.

Coarelli, F. 1996b. "Due rilievi fittili da Fregellae: un documento storico della prima guerra siriaca?," in Coarelli 1996a: 239–57.

Coarelli, F. 1996c. "Horrea Galbana." *LTUR* 3, 40–2.

Coarelli, F. 1997. *Il Campo Marzio: dalle origini alla fine della repubblica*. Rome.

Coarelli, F. 1998. "The Odyssey Frescoes of the Via Graziosa: A Proposed Context." *PBSR* 66, 21–37.

Coarelli, F. 1999a. "Porticus Aemilia." *LTUR* 4, 116–17.

Coarelli, F. 1999b. "Sepulcrum: M. Claudius Marcellus." *LTUR* 4, 279–80.

Coarelli, F. 1999c. "Sepulcrum: Ser. Sulpicius Galba." *LTUR* 4, 299.

Coarelli, F., and Monti, P. G. 1998. *Fregellae I: le fonti, la storia, il territorio*. Rome.

Coarelli, F., and Torelli, M. 1991. *Sicilia²*. Rome and Bari.

Coarelli, F. et al. 1981. *L'Area Sacra di Largo Argentina*. Vol. 1. Rome.

Cogrossi, C., 1979. "Preoccupazioni etniche nelle leggi di Augusto sulla 'manumissio servorum'?," in M. Sordi (ed.), *Conoscenze etniche e rapporti di convivenza nell' antichità*, 158–77. Milan.

Cohen, A. 1997. *The Alexander Mosaic: Stories of Victory and Defeat*. Cambridge and New York.

Cokayne, K. 2003. *Experiencing Old Age in Ancient Rome*. London.

Colamonico, C. 1960. *Memoria Illustrativa della Carta della Utilizzazione del Suolo della Puglia*. Rome.

Coleman, K., 2000. "Entertaining Rome," in Coulston and Dodge 2000: 210–58.

Colini, A. M., and Cozza, L. 1962. *Ludus Magnus*. Rome.

Comella, A. 1981. "Tipologia e diffusione dei complessi votivi in Italia in epoca medio- e tardo-repubblicana. Contributo alla storia dell'artigianato antico." *MEFRA* 93, 717–98.

Confino, A. 1997. "Collective Memory and Cultural History: Problems of Method." *AHR* 102, 1386–1403.

Copeland, D. C. 2000. *The Origins of Major Wars*. Ithaca.

Corbeill, A. 1996. *Controlling Laughter. Political Humor in the Late Roman Republic*. Princeton.

Corbeill, A. 2002. "Rhetorical Education in Cicero's Youth," in May 2002: 23–48.

Corbeill, A. 2004. *Nature Embodied. Gesture in Ancient Rome*. Princeton.

Corbeill, A. 2005. "Gesture in Early Roman Law: Empty Forms or Essential Formalities?," in D. Cairns (ed.), *Gesture and Non-Verbal Communication in the Classical World*, 159–76. Swansea.

Cornell, T. J. 1975. "Aeneas and the Twins: The Development of the Roman Foundation Legend." *PCPS* 201, 1–32.

Cornell, T. J. 1986a. "The Formation of the Historical Tradition of Early Rome," in I. S. Moxon, J. D. Smart, and A. J. Woodman (eds.), *Past Perspectives. Studies in Greek and Roman Historical Writing*, 67–86. Cambridge.

Cornell, T. J. 1986b. "The Value of the Literary Tradition concerning Archaic Rome," in Raaflaub 1986: 52–76.

Cornell, T. J. 1989. "Rome and Latium to 390 B.C.," "The Recovery of Rome," and "The Conquest of Italy," in Walbank et al. 1989: 243–308, 309–50, 351–419.

Cornell, T. J. 1991a. "Rome: The History of an Anachronism," in Molho, Raaflaub, and Emlen 1991: 53–69.

Cornell, T. J. 1991b. "The Tyranny of the Evidence: A Discussion of the Possible Uses of Literacy in Etruria and Latium in the Archaic Age," in J. H. Humphrey (ed.), *Literacy in the Roman World*, 7–33. Ann Arbor.

Cornell, T. J. 1993. "The End of Roman Imperial Expansion," in Rich and Shipley 1993: 139–70.

Cornell, T. J. 1995. *The Beginnings of Rome: Italy and Rome from the Bronze Age to the Punic Wars (c. 1000–264 BC)*. London.

Cornell, T. 1996. "Hannibal's Legacy: The Effects of the Hannibalic War on Italy," in T. J. Cornell, N. B. Rankov, and P. A. G. Sabin (eds.), *The Second Punic War: A Reappraisal*, 97–113. London.

Cornell, T. J. 2000a. "The City of Rome in the Middle Republic (400–100 BC)," in Coulston and Dodge 2000: 42–60.

Cornell, T. J. 2000b. "The Lex Ovinia and the Emancipation of the Senate," in Bruun 2000: 69–89.

Cornell, T. J., and Matthews, J. 1982. *Atlas of the Roman World*. Oxford.

Cotton, H. M. 1981. "Military Tribunates and the Exercise of Patronage." *Chiron* 2, 229–38.

Cotton, H. M. 1986a. "A Note on the Organisation of Tax-Farming in Asia Minor (Cicero, *Fam.* 13, 65)." *Latomus* 45, 367–73.

Cotton, H. M. 1986b. "The Role of Cicero's Letters of Recommendation: *iustitia* versus *gratia*?" *Hermes* 114, 443–60.

Coudry, M. 2001. "Camille: construction et fluctuations de la figure d'un grand homme," in Coudry and Späth 2001: 47–81.

Coudry, M., and Späth, T. (eds.) 2001. *L'invention des grands hommes de la Rome antique. Die Konstruktion der großen Männer Altroms*. Paris.

Coulston, J., and Dodge, H. (eds.) 2000. *Ancient Rome: the Archaeology of the Eternal City*. Oxford.

Crane, G. 1992. "Power, Prestige and the Corcyrean Affair in Thucydides 1." *ClAnt* 11, 1–27.

Crane, S. A. 1997. "Writing the Individual Back into Collective Memory." *AHR* 102, 1372–85.

Crawford, M. H. 1969. *Roman Republican Coin Hoards*. London.

Crawford, M. H. 1970. "Money and Exchange in the Roman World." *JRS* 60, 40–8.

Crawford, M. H. 1974. *Roman Republican Coinage*. Two vols. Cambridge.

Crawford, M. H. 1976. "Hamlet Without the Prince." *JRS* 66, 214–17.

Crawford, M. H. 1983a. "Numismatics," in Crawford 1983b: 185–233.

Crawford, M. H. (ed.) 1983b. *Sources for Ancient History*. Cambridge.

Crawford, M. H. 1985. *Coinage and Money under the Roman Republic*. London, Berkeley, and Los Angeles.

Crawford, M. H. 1996a. "Italy and Rome from Sulla to Augustus," in A. K. Bowman, E. Champlin, and A. Lintott (eds.), *The Augustan Empire, 43 B.C.–A.D. 69*, Vol. 10 of *The Cambridge Ancient History*[2], 414–33, 979–89. Cambridge.

Crawford, M. H. (ed.) 1996b. *Roman Statutes*. 2 vols. London.

Criniti, N. 1969. "M. Aimilius Q. f. M. n. Lepidus: 'ut ignis in stipula'." *MIL* 30, 319–460.

Criniti, N. 1970. *L'epigrafe di Asculum di Cn. Pompeo Strabone*. Milan.

Cristofani, M. (ed.) 1988. *Etruria e Lazio archaico*. Rome.

Cristofani, M. (ed.) 1990. *La grande Roma dei Tarquini*. Rome.

Crook, J. A. 1967. *Law and Life of Rome*. Ithaca.

Crook, J. A. 1994. "The Development of Roman Private Law," in Crook, Lintott, and Rawson 1994: 531–63.

Crook, J. A. 1995. *Legal Advocacy in the Roman World*. Ithaca.

Crook, J. A., A. Lintott, and E. Rawson (eds.) 1994. *The Last Age of the Roman Republic, 146–43 B.C*, Vol. 9 of *The Cambridge Ancient History*[2], Cambridge.

Curti, E., Dench, E., and Patterson, J. R. 1996. "The Archaeology of Central and Southern Roman Italy: Recent Trends and Approaches." *JRS* 86, 170–89.

D'Alessio, M. T., Ricci, G., and Carandini, A. 1997. "La villa dell'Auditorium dall'età arcaica all'età imperiale." *MDAI(R)* 104, 117–48.

Daly, G. 2002. *Cannae. The Experience of Battle in the Second Punic War*. London.

D'Ambra, E. 1998. *Roman Art*. Cambridge and New York.

D'Andria, F. 1990. *Archeologia dei Messapi: catalogo della mostra. Lecce, Museo provinciale 'Sigismondo Castromediano', 7 ottobre 1990–7 gennaio 1991*. Bari.

D'Angelo, S., and Oräzie Vallino, F. C. 1994. "La Sibaritide. Lineamenti geografico-ambientali ed insediamento umano," in R. Peroni and F. Trucco (eds.), *Enotri e Micenei nella Sibaritide. Vol. 2. Altri siti della Sibaritide*, 785–829. Taranto.

D'Arms, J. H. 1970. *Romans on the Bay of Naples: a Social and Cultural Study of the Villas and their Owners from 150 B. C. to A. D. 400*. Cambridge, MA.

Daube, D. 1961. "Texts and Interpretation in Roman and Jewish Law." *Jewish Journal of Sociology* 3, 3–28.

Dauge, Y. A. 1981. *Le Barbare: Recherches sur la conception romaine de la barbarie et de la civilisation*. Brussels.

David, J.-M., Demougin, S., Deniaux, E., Ferey, D., Flambard, J.-M., and Nicolet, C. 1973. "Le 'Commentariolum Petitionis' de Quintus Cicéron, État de la question et étude prosopographique." *ANRW* I.3, 239–77.

David, J.-M. 1979. "Promotion civique et droit à la parole. L. Licinius Crassus, les accusateurs et les rhéteurs latins." *MEFRA* 91, 135–81.

David, J.-M. 1980. "*Eloquentia popularis* et conduites symboliques des orateurs de la fin de la République: problèmes d'efficacité." *QS* 12, 171–211.

David, J.-M. 1983a. "L'action oratoire de C. Gracchus: l'image d'un modèle," in C. Nicolet and J.-L. Ferrary (eds.), *Demokratia et Aristokratia*. Paris.

David, J.-M. 1983b. "Les orateurs des municipes à Rome: intégration, réticences et snobismes," in *Les "bourgeoisies" municipales italiennes aux IIe et Ier siècles av. J.-C.*, 309–23. Paris and Naples.

David, J.-M. 1992a. *Le Patronat judiciaire au dernier siècle de la République romaine*. Rome.

David, J.-M. 1992b. "Compétence sociale et compétence oratoire à la fin de la République: apprendre à ressembler," in E. Frézouls (ed.), *La mobilité sociale dans le monde romain*, 7–19. Strasbourg.

David, J.-M. 1996. *The Roman Conquest of Italy*. Oxford.

David, J.-M. 1997. "La clientèle, d'une forme de l'analyse à l'autre," in *La fin de la République romaine, Un débat franco-allemand d'histoire et d'historiographie*. EFR 235, 195–210. Rome.

David, J.-M. 2000. *La République romaine de la deuxième guerre punique à la bataille d'Actium, 218–31: Crise d'une aristocratie*. Paris.

Davidson, J. 1991. "The Gaze in Polybius' Histories." *JRS* 81, 10–24.

De Blois, L. 2000. "Army and Society in the Late Roman Republic. Professionalism and the Role of the Military Middle Cadre," in G. Alföldy et al. (eds.), *Kaiser, Heer und Gesellschaft in der römischen Kaiserzeit*, 11–31. Stuttgart.

De Grummond, N. T., and Ridgway, B. S. (eds.) 1996. *From Pergamon to Sperlonga: Sculpture and Context*. Berkeley.

Deininger, J. 1980. "Explaining the Change from Republic to Principate in Rome." *Comparative Civilizations Review* 4, 77–101; 5, 96–9.

Deininger, J. 1998. "Zur Kontroverse über die Lebensfähigkeit der Republik in Rom," in P. Kneissl and V. Losemann (eds.), *Imperium Romanum. Festschrift für Karl Christ*, 123–36. Stuttgart.

De Jong, I., and Sullivan, J. P. 1994. *Modern Critical Theory and Classical Literature*. Leiden.

De Jorio, A. [1832] 2000. *Gesture in Naples and Gesture in Classical Antiquity* (*La mimica degli antichi investigata nel gestire napoletano*). Ed. and trans. A. Kendon. Bloomington.

De Juliis, E. M. 1990. *L'ipogeo dei Vimini di Canosa*. Bari.

DeLaine, J. 1995. "The Supply of Building Materials to the City of Rome," in N. Christie (ed.), *Settlement and Economy in Italy 1500 BC–AD 1500*, 555–62. Oxford.

DeLaine, J. 2000. "Building the Eternal City: The Construction Industry in Imperial Rome," in Coulston and Dodge 2000: 119–41.

Delano-Smith, C. 1979. *Western Mediterranean Europe. A Historical Geography of Italy, Spain and Southern France Since the Neolithic*. London.

de Ligt, L. 1993. *Fairs and Markets in the Roman Empire*. Amsterdam.

de Ligt, L. 1999. "Legal History and Economic History: The Case of the *actiones adiecticiae qualitatis*." *Tijdschrift voor Rechtsgeschiedenis* 67, 205–26.

de Ligt, L. 2000. "Studies in Legal and Agrarian History II: Tenancy under the Republic." *Athenaeum* 88, 377–91.

de Ligt, L. 2001. "Studies in Legal and Agrarian History III: Appian and the *Lex Thoria*." *Athenaeum* 89, 121–44.

de Ligt, L. 2002. "Restraining the Rich, Protecting the Poor. Symbolic Aspects of Roman Legislation," in W. Jongman and M. Kleijwegt (eds.), *After the Past: Essays in Ancient History in Honour of H. W. Pleket*, 1–45. Leiden.

de Ligt, L. 2003. *Bevolkingsontwikkeling en armoede in laat-Republikeins Italië*. Leiden.

de Ligt, L. 2004. "Poverty and Demography: The Case of the Gracchan Land Reforms." *Mnemosyne* 57, 725–57.

De Maria, S. 1988. *Gli archi onorari di Roma e dell'Italia romana*. Rome.

Demougeot, E. 1978. "L'invasion des Cimbres-Teutons-Ambrons et les Romains." *Latomus* 37, 910–38.

Dench, E. 1995. *From Barbarians to New Men: Greek, Roman, and Modern Perceptions of Peoples from the Central Apennines*. Oxford.

de Neeve, P. W. 1984a. *Colonus. Private Farm-Tenancy in Roman Italy During the Republic and the Early Principate*. Amsterdam.

de Neeve, P. W. 1984b. *Peasants in Peril: Location and Economy in Italy in the Second Century* BC. Amsterdam.

de Neeve, P. W. 1990. "A Roman Landowner and his Estates: Pliny the Younger." *Athenaeum* 78, 363–402.

Deniaux, E. 1973. "Un problème de clientèle: Marius et les Herennii." *Philologus* 117, 179–96.

Deniaux, E. 1987. "Les hôtes des Romains en Sicile," in F. Thelamon (ed.), *Sociabilité, pouvoirs et société*, 337–45. Rouen

Deniaux, E. 1993. *Clientèles et pouvoir à l'époque de Cicéron*. Rome.

Deniaux, E. 1994. "Le Cicéron et l'arrivée des blés de Sicile à Rome," in *Le ravitaillement en blé de Rome et des centres urbains des débuts de la République jusqu'au Haut Empire*, 243–53. Naples.

Deniaux, E. 1997. "La rue et l'opinion publique à Rome et en Italie (Ier siècle av. J-C)," in A. Lemémorel and A. Corbin (eds.), *La rue, lieu de sociabilité?*, 207–13. Rouen.

Deniaux, E., and Schmitt-Pantel, P. 1987–9. "La relation patron–client en Grèce et à Rome." *Opus*, 6–8, 147–63.

Denti, M. 1991. *Ellenismo e Romanizzazione nella X Regio: La Scultura delle élites locali dall'età repubblicana ai Giulio-Claudi*. Rome.

de Romilly, J. 1977. *The Rise and Fall of States According to Greek Authors*. Ann Arbor.

Derow, P. S. 1979. "Polybius, Rome, and the East." *JRS* 69, 1–15.

Derow, P. S. 1973. "Kleemporos." *Phoenix* 27, 118–34.

De Ruyt, C. 1983. *Macellum: marché alimentaire des romains*. Louvain-la-Neuve.

de Souza, P. 1999. *Piracy in the Graeco-Roman World*. London.

De Staebler, P. 2004. "How Romans Organized Greek Sculpture," unpublished paper presented to the Annual Conference of the College Art Association. Seattle.

de Ste. Croix, G. E. M. 1981. *The Class Struggle in the Ancient Greek World*. London.

Develin, R. 1987. "Sulla and the Senate." *AHB* 1, 130–4.

De Vos, A., and De Vos, M. 1982. *Pompei, Ercolano, Stabia*. Rome.

Di Bartolomeo, G. (ed.) 1976. *Carta della Montagna*. San Lorenzo.

Digest of Justinian 1985. Latin text ed. T. Mommsen and P. Krueger; English trans. ed. A. Watson. 4 vols. Philadelphia.

Digest of Justinian 1998. Revised English trans., ed. A. Watson. 2 vols. Philadelphia.

Dillon, S., and Welch, K. E. (eds.) forthcoming. *Representations of War in Ancient Rome*. Cambridge and New York.

Di Vito, M., and Luongo, G. 2003. "Bradyseism and Sea Variations in the Neopolitan Area over the Last 12,000 Years," in C. Albore Livadie and F. Ortolani (eds.), *Variazioni climatico-ambientali e impatto sull'uomo nell'area circum-mediterranea durante l'Olocene*, 13–22. Bari.

Dixon, S. 1986. "Family Finances: Terentia and Tullia," in B. Rawson (ed.), *The Family in Ancient Rome. New Perspectives*, 93–120. London and Sydney.

Dixon, S. 1992. *The Roman Family*. Baltimore.

Dixon, S. 2001. *Reading Roman Women*. London.

Dixon, S. 2003. "Sex and the Married Woman in Ancient Rome," in D. Balch and C. Osiek (eds.), *Early Christian Families in Context: an Interdisciplinary Dialogue*, 111–29. Grand Rapids.

Dodge, H. 2000. "'Greater than the Pyramids': The Water Supply of Ancient Rome," in Coulston and Dodge 2000: 166–209.

Doherty, L. 2001. *Gender and the Interpretation of Classical Myth*. London.

Donati, L. 2000. "Architettura civile, sacra e domestica," in Torelli 2000: 313–33.

Donnadieu, A. 1954. "La campagne de Marius dans la Gaule Narbonnaise (104–102 av. J.-C.): La bataille d'Aix-en-Provence (*Aquae Sextiae*) et ses deux épisodes." *REA* 56, 281–96.

Dörpfeld, W. 1896. *Das Griechische Theater*. Athens.

Dowling, M. B. 2000. "The Clemency of Sulla." *Historia* 49, 303–40.

Doyle, M. 1986. *Empires*. Ithaca.

Drummond, A. 1989. "Rome in the Fifth Century," in Walbank, Astin, Frederiksen, and Ogilvie 1989: 113–242.

Drummond, A. 1995. *Law, Politics and Power: Sallust and the Execution of the Catilinarian Conspirators*. Stuttgart.

Duckworth, G. E., 1955. "Plautus and the Basilica Aemilia," in P. de Jonge et al. (eds.), *Ut pictura poesis. Studia latina Petro Iohanni Enk septuagenario oblata*, 58–65. Leiden.

Dudley, D. R. 1967. *Urbs Roma: A Source Book of Classical Texts on the City and its Monuments*. London.

Dugan, J. 2001. "Preventing Ciceronianism: C. Licinius Calvus' Regimens for Sexual and Oratorical Self-Mastery." *CPh* 96, 400–28.

Dunbabin, K. M. D. 1999. *Mosaics of the Greek and Roman World*. Cambridge.

Duncan-Jones, R. 1982. *The Economy of the Roman Empire. Quantitative Studies*[2]. Cambridge.

Duncan-Jones, R. 1994. *Money and Government in the Roman Empire*. Cambridge.

Dupont, F. 1992. *Daily Life in Ancient Rome*. Oxford.

Dyck, A. 1996. *A Commentary on Cicero, De Officiis*. Ann Arbor.

Dyck, A. 2004. *A Commentary on Cicero, De legibus*. Ann Arbor.

Dyson, S. 1978. "Settlement Patterns in the Ager Cosanus: The Wesleyan University Survey, 1974–1976." *JFA* 5, 251–68.

Dyson, S. 1985. *The Creation of the Roman Frontier*. Princeton.

Earl, D. C. 1961. *The Political Thought of Sallust*. Cambridge.

Earl, D. C. 1963. *Tiberius Gracchus: A Study in Politics*. Brussels.

Earl, D. C. 1967. *The Moral and Political Tradition of Rome*. Ithaca.

Eckstein, A. M. 1980. "Polybius on the Rôle of the Senate in the Crisis of 264 B.C." *GRBS* 21, 175–90.

Eckstein, A. M. 1987. *Senate and General: Individual Decision-Making and Roman Foreign Relations, 264–194 B.C.* Berkeley and Los Angeles.

Eckstein, A. M. 1991. "Is There a 'Hobson–Lenin Thesis' on Late Nineteenth-Century Colonial Expansion?" *EHR* 44, 297–318.

Eckstein, A. M. 1994. "Polybius, Demetrius of Pharus, and the Origins of the Second Illyrian War." *CPh* 89, 46–59.

Eckstein, A. M. 1995. *Moral Vision in the 'Histories' of Polybios*. Berkeley.

Eckstein, A. M. 1997. "*Physis* and *Nomos*: Polybius, Rome, and Cato the Elder," in P. Cartledge, P. Garnsey, and E. Gruen (eds.), *Hellenistic Constructs: Essays in Culture, History, and Historiography*, 175–98. Berkeley.

Eckstein, A. M. 2000. "Brigands, Emperors, and Anarchy." *Int. Hist. Rev.* 22, 862–79.

Eder, W. 1969. *Das vorsullanische Repetundenverfahren*. Munich.

Eder, W. (ed.) 1990. *Staat und Staatlichkeit in der frühen römischen Republik*. Stuttgart.

Eder, W. 1991. "Who Rules? Power and Participation in Athens and Rome," in Molho, Raaflaub, and Emlen 1991: 169–96.

Eder, W. 1996. "Republicans and Sinners: The Decline of the Roman Republic and the End of a Provisional Arrangement," in Wallace and Harris 1996: 439–61.

Edmondson, J. C. 1999. "The Cultural Politics of Public Spectacle in Rome and the Greek East, 167–166 BCE," in Bergmann and Kondoleon 1999: 77–95.

Edwards, C. 1993. *The Politics of Immorality in Ancient Rome*. Cambridge.

Edwards, C. 1996. *Writing Rome. Textual Approaches to the City*. Cambridge.

Edwards, C. 1997. "Unspeakable Professions: Public Performance and Prostitution in Ancient Rome," in Hallett and Skinner 1997: 66–95.

Edwards, C. 2003. "Incorporating the Alien: The Art of Conquest," in Edwards and Woolf 2003: 44–70.

Edwards, C., and Woolf, G. (eds.) 2003. *Rome the Cosmopolis*. Cambridge.

Eigler, U., Gotter, U., Luraghi, N., and Walter, U. (eds.) 2003. *Formen römischer Geschichtsschreibung von den Anfängen bis Livius. Gattungen – Autoren – Kontexte*. Darmstadt.

Eilers, C. 2002. *Roman Patrons of Greek Cities*. Oxford.

Eisenstadt, S., and Roninger, L. 1980. "Patron–Client Relations as a Model of Structuring Social Exchange." *Comp. Stud. Soc. Hist.* 22, 42–77.

Eisenstadt, S., and Roninger, L. 1984. *Patrons, Clients and Friends, Interpersonal Relations and the Structure of Trust in Society*. Cambridge.

Elsner, J. 2004. "Some Recent Publications in Roman Art," *Art History* 27 (November), 806–14.

Endfield, G. H. 1997. "Myth, Manipulation and Myopia in the Study of Mediterranean Soil Erosion," in A. Sinclair, E. Slater, and J. Gowlett (eds.), *Archaeological Sciences 1995*.

Proceedings of a conference on the application of scientific techniques to the study of archaeology. Liverpool, July 1995, 241–8. Oxford.

Enea nel Lazio: Archeologia e mito. 1981. Rome.

Epstein, D. F. 1987. *Personal Enmity in Roman Politics, 218–43 BC.* London.

Erdkamp, P. 1995. "The Corn Supply of the Roman Armies during the Third and Second Centuries BC." *Historia* 44, 168–91.

Erdkamp, P. 1998. *Hunger and the Sword: Warfare and Food Supply in Roman Republican Wars (264–30 B.C.).* Amsterdam.

Erdkamp, P. 2000. "Feeding Rome, or Feeding Mars? A Long-Term Approach to C. Gracchus' *Lex Frumentaria.*" *AncSoc* 30, 53–70.

Erdkamp, P. 2001. "Beyond the Limits of the 'Consumer City'. A Model of the Urban and Rural Economy in the Roman World." *Historia* 50, 332–56.

Erskine, A., 2001. *Troy Between Greece and Rome.* Oxford.

Evans, E. 1969. *Physiognomics in the Ancient World.* Philadelphia.

Evans, J. D. 1992. *The Art of Persuasion: Political Propaganda from Aeneas to Brutus.* Ann Arbor.

Evans, J. K. 1988. "Resistance at Home: The Evasion of Military Service in Italy during the Second Century B.C," in T. Yuge and M. Doi (eds.), *Forms of Control and Subordination in Antiquity,* 121–40. Leiden.

Evans, J. K. 1991. *War, Women and Children in Ancient Rome.* London.

Evans, R. J. 1994. *Gaius Marius: A Political Biography.* Pretoria.

Evernden, J. F., and Curtis, G. H. 1965. "The Potassium-Argon dating of late Cenozoic rocks in East Africa and Italy." *Current Anthropology* 6, 343–64.

Fabre, G. 1981. *Libertus. Recherches sur les rapports patron-affranchi à la fin de la république romaine.* Paris.

Farrell, J. 2001. *Latin Language and Latin Culture.* Cambridge.

Fasolo, F., and Gullini, G., 1953. *Il santuario della Fortuna Primigenia a Palestrina.* Rome.

Favro, D. 1988. "The Roman Forum and Roman Memory." *Places* 5. 1, 17–24.

Favro, D. 1994. "The Street Triumphant: The Urban Impact of Roman Triumphal Parades," in Z. Çelik, D. Favro, and R. Ingersoll (eds.), *Streets: Critical Perspectives on Public Space,* 151–64. Berkeley.

Favro, D. 1996. *The Urban Image of Augustan Rome.* Cambridge.

Fears, J. R. 1981. "The Theology of Victory at Rome: Approaches and Problems." *ANRW* 2.17.2, 736–826.

Feeney, D. 1998. *Literature and Religion at Rome: Cultures, Contexts, and Beliefs.* Cambridge.

Fehrle, R. 1983. *Cato Uticensis.* Darmstadt.

Feig Vishnia, R. 1996. *State, Society and Popular Leaders in Mid-Republican Rome, 241–167 BC.* London.

Feldherr, A. 1998. *Spectacle and Society in Livy's History.* Berkeley.

Felmy, A. 2001. *Die Römische Republik im Geschichtsbild der Spätantike: Zum Umgang lateinischer Autoren des 4. und 5. Jahrhunderts n.Chr. mit den exempla maiorum.* Berlin.

Fentress, E. 2000. "Frank Brown, Cosa, and the Idea of a Roman City," in E. Fentress (ed.), *Romanization and the City: Creations, Transformations and Failures,* 9–24. Portsmouth, RI.

Fentress, E. (ed.) 2003. *Cosa V: an Intermittent Town, Excavations 1991–1997.* Ann Arbor.

Fentress, E., and Rabinowitz, A. 1996. "Excavations at Cosa 1995: Atrium Building V and a new Republican Temple." *MAAR* 41, 221–36.

Fentress, J., and Wickham, C. 1992. *Social Memory.* Oxford.

Ferrar, Jr., L. L. 1981. *Arrogance and Anxiety: The Ambivalence of German Power, 1848–1914.* Iowa City.

Ferrary, J.-L. 1977. "Recherches sur la législation de Saturninus et de Glaucia, I." *MEFRA* 89, 619–60.

Ferrary, J.-L. 1979. "Recherches sur la législation de Saturninus et de Glaucia, II." *MEFRA* 91, 85–134.

Ferrary, J.-L. 1983. "Les origines de la loi de majesté à Rome." *CRAI*, 556–72.

Ferrary, J-L. 1988. *Philhellénisme et impérialisme.* Rome.

Ferrary, J.-L. 1997. "De l'évergétisme hellénistique à l'évergétisme romain," in *Actes Xe Congrès international d'épigraphie grecque et latine*, 199–225. Paris.

Ferrea, L. 2002. *Gli dei di terracotta: la recomposizione del frontone da via S. Gregorio.* Milan.

Finley, M. I. 1965. "The Silent Women of Ancient Rome." *Horizon* 7, 57–64 (= M. I. Finley, 1977. *Aspects of Antiquity*, 129–42. London).

Finley, M. I. 1980. *Ancient Slavery and Modern Ideology.* London.

Finley, M. I. 1981. "The Ancient City from Fustel de Coulanges to Max Weber and Beyond," in B. Shaw and R. Saller (eds.), *Economy and Society in Ancient Greece*, 3–23. London.

Finley, M. I. 1983. *Politics in the Ancient World.* Cambridge.

Finley, M. I. 1985a. *The Ancient Economy*[2]. London.

Finley, M. I. 1985b. " 'How It Really Was'," in M. I. Finley, *Ancient History: Evidence and Models*, 47–66; 116–19. London.

Fittschen, K. 1976. "Zur Herkunft und Entstehung des 2. Stils-Probleme und Argumente," in Zanker 1976b: 539–59.

Fitzgerald, W. 1995. *Catullan Provocations: Lyric Poetry and the Drama of Position.* Berkeley.

Fitzgerald, W. 2000. *Slavery and the Roman Literary Imagination.* Cambridge.

Flach, D. 1990. *Römische Agrargeschichte.* Munich.

Flaig, E. 1995. "Entscheidung und Konsens: Zu den Feldern der politischen Kommunikation zwischen Aristokratie und plebs," in Jehne 1995c: 77–127.

Flaig, E. 2003. *Ritualisierte Politik. Zeichen, Gesten und Herrschaft im Alten Rom.* Göttingen.

Flemming, N. C. 1969. "Archaeological Evidence for Eustatic Change of Sea-Level and Earth Movements in the Western Mediterranean during the Last 2000 Years," *Geological Society of America Special Paper* 109.

Flower, H. 1995. "Fabulae Praetextae in Context: When Were Plays on Contemporary Subjects Performed in Republican Rome?" *CQ* 45, 170–90.

Flower, H. I. 1996. *Ancestor Masks and Aristocratic Power in Roman Culture.* Oxford.

Flower, H. I. 2003. " 'Memories' of Marcellus. History and Memory in Roman Republican Culture," in Eigler et al. 2003: 39–52.

Flower, H. I. 2004a. "Spectacle and Political Culture in the Roman Republic," in Flower 2004b: 322–43.

Flower, H. I. (ed.) 2004b. *The Cambridge Companion to the Roman Republic.* Cambridge.

Fögen, M. T. 2002. *Römische Rechtsgeschichten. Über Ursprung und Evolution eines sozialen Systems.* Göttingen.

Fontenrose, J. 1978. *The Delphic Oracle.* Berkeley.

Fornara, C. W. 1983. *The Nature of History in Ancient Greece and Rome.* Berkeley and Los Angeles.

Forsythe, G. 1994. *The Historian L. Calpurnius Piso Frugi and the Roman Annalistic Tradition.* Lanham.

Forsythe, G. 1999. *Livy and Early Rome: A Study in Historical Method and Judgment.* Stuttgart.

Forsythe, G. 2005. *A Critical History of Early Rome: From Prehistory to the First Punic War.* Berkeley and Los Angeles.

Fowler, D. P. 2000. *Roman Constructions: Readings in Postmodern Latin.* Oxford.

Fox, M. 1996. *Roman Historical Myths: The Regal Period in Augustan Literature.* Oxford.

Foxhall, L. 1990. "The Dependent Tenant: Land Leasing and Labour in Italy and Greece." *JRS* 80, 97–114.

Fraenkel, E. 1960. *Elementi Plautini in Plauto.* Florence.

Frank, A. H. E. 1969. "Pollen Stratigraphy of the Lake of Vico (Central Italy)." *Palaeogeography, Palaeoclimatology, Palaeoecology* 6, 67–85.

Frederiksen, M. 1966. "Caesar, Cicero and the Problem of Debt." *JRS* 56, 128–41.

Frederiksen, M. 1970–1. "The Contribution of Archaeology to the Agrarian Problem in the Gracchan Period." *DArch* 4–5, 330–57.

Frederiksen, M. 1984. *Campania.* ed. N. Purcell. London.

Fredrick, D. 2002a. "Mapping Penetrability," in Fredrick 2002b: 236–64.

Fredrick, D. (ed.) 2002b. *The Roman Gaze. Vision, Power, and the Body.* Baltimore.

Freyburger, G. 1986. *Fides.* Paris.

Frier, B. W. 1971. "Sulla's Propaganda and the Collapse of the Cinnan Republic." *AJPh* 92, 585–604.

Frier, B. W. 1980. *Landlords and Tenants in Imperial Rome.* Princeton.

Frier, B. W. 1983. "Urban Praetors and Rural Violence: The Legal Background of Cicero's *Pro Caecina*." *TAPhA* 113, 221–41.

Frier, B. W. 1985. *The Rise of the Roman Jurists: Studies in Cicero's pro Caecina.* Princeton.

Frier, B. W. 1989. *A Casebook on the Roman Law of Delict.* Atlanta.

Frier, B. W. 1999. (Reprint of 1979 ed. with new introduction.) *Libri Annales Pontificum Maximorum. The Origins of the Annalistic Tradition.* Rome and Ann Arbor.

Fuchs, H. 1938. *Der geistige Widerstand gegen Rom in der antiken Welt.* Berlin.

Fuchs, M. 1999. In hoc etiam genere Graeciae nihil cedamus: *Studien zur Romanisierung der späthellenistischen Kunst im 1. Jh. v. Chr.* Mainz.

Fuchs, W. 1963. *Der Schiffsfund von Mahdia.* Teubingen.

Fuhrmann, M. 1992. *Cicero and the Roman Republic.* Oxford.

Fullerton, M. 1998. "Atticism, Classicism, and the Origins of Neo-Attic Sculpture," in O. Palagia (ed.), *Regional Styles of Hellenistic Sculpture.* London.

Fustel de Coulanges, N. D. 1890. *Les origines du système féodal.* Paris.

Gabba, E. 1954. "Le origini della guerra sociale e la vita politica romana dopo l'88 a.C." *Athenaeum* 32, 41–114, 293–345 (= Gabba 1973: 193–345).

Gabba, E. 1956. *Appiano e la storia delle guerre civili.* Florence.

Gabba, E. 1958. *Appiani Bellorum civilium liber primus: Introduzione, testo critico e commento con traduzione e indici.* Florence.

Gabba, E. 1960. "Studi su Dionisio di Alicarnasso, I: La costituzione di Romolo." *Athenaeum* 38, 175–225.

Gabba, E. 1972. "Mario e Silla." *ANRW* 1.1, 765–805.

Gabba, E. 1973. *Esercito e società nella tarda repubblica romana.* Florence (= Gabba 1976).

Gabba, E. 1976. *Republican Rome: The Army and the Allies.* Trans. P. J. Cuff. Oxford (= Gabba 1973).

Gabba, E. 1982. "La storia di Roma arcaica di Dionigi d'Alicarnasso." *ANRW*, 2.30.1, 799–816.

Gabba, E. 1983. "Literature," in Crawford 1983b: 1–79.

Gabba, E. 1989. "Rome and Italy in the second century BC," in Astin et al. 1989: 197–243.

Gabba, E. 1991. *Dionysius and the History of Archaic Rome.* Berkeley and Los Angeles.

Gabba, E. 1994a. "Rome and Italy: The Social War," in Crook, Lintott, and Rawson 1994: 104–28.

Gabba, E. 1994b. *Italia romana.* Como.

Gabba, E. 1997. "Democrazia a Roma." *Athenaeum* 85, 266–71.

Gabba, E. 1998. "La Roma dei Tarquini." *Athenaeum* 86, 5–12.

Gabba, E., and Pasquinucci, M. 1979. *Strutture agrarie e allevamento transumante nell'Italia romana (III–I sec. a.C.).* Pisa.

Galinsky, K. 1996. *Augustan Culture.* Princeton.

Gallini, C. 1973. "Che cosa intendere per ellenizzazione. Problemi di metodo," *DArch* 7, 175–91.

Garbarino, G., 1973. *Roma e la filosofia greca dalle origini alla fine del II sec. a.C.* Turin.

Gardner, J. 1986. *Women in Roman Law and Society.* London and Sydney.

Gardner, J. 1993. *Being a Roman Citizen.* London.

Gardner, J. 1998. *Family and 'familia' in Roman Law and Life.* Oxford.

Gargola, D. J. 1989. "Aulus Gellius and the Property Qualifications of the *Proletarii* and the *Capite Censi.*" *CPh* 84, 231–4.

Gargola, D. J. 1995. *Lands, Laws, and Gods: Magistrates and Ceremony in the Regulation of Public Lands in Republican Rome.* Chapel Hill and London.

Gargola, D. J. 1997. "Appian and the Aftermath of the Gracchan Reform." *AJPh* 118, 555–81.

Garland, R. 1995. *The Eye of the Beholder. Deformity and Disability in the Graeco-Roman World.* Ithaca.

Garnsey, P. 1979. "Where Did Italian Peasants Live?" *PCPhS* 225, 1–25 (= Garnsey 1998: 107–33).

Garnsey, P. 1980. "Non-Slave Labour in the Roman World," in P. Garnsey (ed.), *Non-Slave Labour in the Greco-Roman World.* Cambridge, 34–47 (= Garnsey 1998: 134–50).

Garnsey, P. 1986. "Mountain Economies in Southern Europe: Thoughts on the Early History, Continuity and Individuality of Mediterranean Upland Pastoralism," in M. Mattmüller (ed.), *Wirtschaft und Gesellschaft in Berggebieten,* 1–25. Basel (= Garnsey 1998: 166–79).

Garnsey, P. 1988. *Famine and Food Supply in the Greco-Roman World: Responses to Risk and Crisis.* Cambridge.

Garnsey, P. 1996. *Ideas of Slavery from Aristotle to Augustine.* Cambridge.

Garnsey, P. 1998. *Cities, Peasants and Food in Classical Antiquity. Essays in Social and Economic History,* ed. W. Scheidel. Cambridge.

Garnsey, P., Gallant, T., and Rathbone, D. 1984. "Thessaly and the Grain Supply of Rome during the Second Century B.C." *JRS* 74, 30–44.

Garnsey, P., and Rathbone, D. 1985. "The Background to the Grain Law of Gaius Gracchus." *JRS* 75, 20–5.

Garnsey, P., and Saller, R. 1987. *The Roman Empire: Economy, Society and Culture.* London.

Gasperini, L. 1999. "Rinvenimenti e studi di epigrafia repubblicana in Italia nell'ultimo decennio," in *XI Congresso Internazionale di Epigrafia Greca e Latina. Roma, 18–24 settembre 1997,* 405–34. Rome.

Gazda, E. K. (ed.) 2002. *The Ancient Art of Emulation: Studies in Artistic Originality and Tradition from the Present to Classical Antiquity.* Ann Arbor.

Geller, D. S., and Singer, J. D. 1998. *Nations at War: A Scientific Study of International Conflict.* Cambridge.

Gellner, E., and Waterbury, J. 1977. *Patrons and Clients in Mediterranean Societies.* London.

Gelzer, M. 1959. *Pompeius*. Munich.

Gelzer, M. 1968. *Caesar: Politician and Statesman*. Trans. P. Needham. Oxford.

Gelzer, M. 1969. *The Roman Nobility*. Trans. R. Seager. Oxford. (Originally published 1912.)

George, M. (ed.) 2005. *The Roman Family in the Empire. Rome, Italy, and Beyond*. Oxford.

Giardina, A. and Schiavone, A. (eds.) 1981. *Società Romana e Produzione Schiavistica*. 3 vols. Rome.

Giovannini, A. 1983. *Consulare imperium*. Basel.

Giovannini, A. 1995. "Catilina et le problème des dettes," in Malkin and Rubinsohn 1995: 15–32.

Giovannini, A. 1998. "Les livres auguraux," in C. Moatti (ed.) *La mémoire perdue. Recherches sur l'administration romaine*, 103–22. Rome.

Giovannini, A. 1999. Review of A. Watson, *International Law in Archaic Rome. Gnomon 71*, 45–8.

Girardet, K. M. 1996. "Politische Verantwortung im Ernstfall. Cicero, die Diktatur und der Diktator Caesar," in E. Heitsch, L. Koenen, R. Merkelbach, and C. Zintzen (eds.), *Leniaka: Festschrift für Carl Werner Müller*, 217–51. Stuttgart and Leipzig.

Giuliani, L. 1986. *Bildnis und Botschaft: hermeneutische Untersuchungen zur Bildniskunst der römischen Republik*. Frankfurt.

Gladigow, B. 1983. "Strukturprobleme polytheistischer Religionen." *Saeculum 34*, 292–304.

Gladigow, B. 1998. "Polytheismus." *Handwörterbuch religionswissenschaftlicher Grundbegriffe 4*, 321–30.

Glaser, G. L. 1997. "The Security Dilemma Revisited." *World Politics 50*, 171–201.

Gleason, M. 1995. *Making Men: Sophists and Self-Presentation in Ancient Rome*. Princeton.

Glew, D. G. 1981. "Between the Wars: Mithridates Eupator and Rome, 85–73 B.C." *Chiron 11*, 109–30.

Goldberg, S. M. 1998. "Plautus on the Palatine." *JRS 88*, 1–20.

Goldmann, F. 2002. "*Nobilitas* als Status und Gruppe – Überlegungen zum Nobilitätsbegriff der römischen Republik," in Spielvogel 2002: 45–66.

Goldsworthy, A. 1996. *The Roman Army at War, 100 BC – AD 200*. Oxford.

Goldsworthy, A. 1998. " 'Instinctive Genius': The Depiction of Caesar as General," in Welch and Powell 1998: 193–212.

Goldsworthy, A. 2000a. *Roman Warfare*. London.

Goldsworthy, A. 2000b. *The Punic Wars*. London.

Goltz, A. 2000. "*Maiestas sine viribus* – Die Bedeutung der Lictoren für die Konfliktbewältigungsstrategien römischer Magistrate," in Linke and Stemmler 2000b: 237–67.

Gordon, A. E. 1983. *Illustrated Introduction to Latin Epigraphy*. Berkeley, Los Angeles, and London.

Gordon, P. 2002. "Some Unseen Monster: Rereading Lucretius on Sex," in Fredrick 2002b: 86–109.

Gordon, R. (with J. Reynolds). 2003. "Roman Inscriptions 1995–2000." *JRS 93*, 212–92.

Gotoff, H. C. 1993. *Cicero's Caesarian Speeches*. Chapel Hill.

Gowing, A. M. 1992. *The Triumviral Narratives of Appian and Cassius Dio*. Ann Arbor.

Graf, F. 1991. "Gestures and Conventions: The Gestures of Roman Actors and Orators," in Bremmer and Roodenburg 1991: 36–58.

Graf, F. (ed.) 1993. *Mythos in mythenloser Gesellschaft: Das Paradigma Roms*. Stuttgart.

Granatelli, R. 1990. "L'*in utramque partem disserendi exercitatio* nell'evoluzione del pensiero retorico e filosofico dell'Antichità." *Vichiana 1*, 165–81.

Grandazzi, A. 1997. *The Foundation of Rome: Myth and History*. Trans. J. M. Todd. Ithaca.

Grant, J. R. 1965. "A Note on the Tone of Greek Diplomacy." *CQ* 15, 261–6.

Gratwick, A. S. 1982a. "Ennius' *Annales*," in Kenney 1982: 60–76.

Gratwick, A. S. 1982b. "Drama," in Kenney 1982: 77–137.

Gratwick, A. S. 1982c. "Prose Literature," in Kenney 1982: 138–55.

Gratwick, A. S. 1982d. "The Satires of Ennius and Lucilius," in Kenney 1982: 156–71.

Great Britain, Hydrographic Department. 1978. *The Mediterranean Pilot* [10]. London.

Greenhalgh, P. A. L. 1980. *Pompey: The Roman Alexander.* London.

Greenidge, A. H. J. 1901. *The Legal Procedure of Cicero's Time.* London.

Greenidge, A. H. J., and Clay, M. 1986. *Sources for Roman History 133–70 B.C.*[2], revised by E. W. Gray. Oxford.

Griffin, M. T. 1973. "The 'Leges Iudiciariae' of the Pre-Sullan Era." *CQ* 23, 108–26.

Grimal, P. 1969. *Les jardins romains.* Paris.

Gros, P. 1973. "Hermodoros et Vitruve." *MEFRA* 85, 137–61.

Gros, P. 1976. *Aurea Templa: Recherches sur l'architecture religieuse de Rome à l'époque d'Auguste.* Rome.

Gros, P. 1978. *Architecture et société à Rome et en Italie méridionale aux derniers siècles de la République.* Brussels.

Gros, P. 1996–2001. *L'architecture romaine du début du IIIe siècle av. J.-C. à la fin du haut Empire: I. Les monuments publics; II. Maisons, palais, villas et tombeaux.* 2 vols. Paris.

Gros, P., Corso, A., and Romano, E. 1997. *De architectura/Vitruvio.* Turin.

Gros, P., and Torelli, M. 1991. *Storia dell'urbanistica. Il mondo romano.*[2] Rome and Bari.

Gruen, E. S. 1965. "The *Lex Varia*," *JRS* 55, 59–73.

Gruen, E. S. 1966a. "Political Prosecutions in the 90's B.C." *Historia* 15, 32–64.

Gruen, E. S. 1966b. "The Quaestorship of Norbanus." *CPh* 61, 105–7.

Gruen, E. S. 1968. *Roman Politics and the Criminal Courts, 149–78 B.C.* Cambridge.

Gruen, E. S. 1971. "Pompey, Metellus Pius, and the Trials of 70–69 B.C. The Perils of Schematism." *AJPh* 92, 1–16.

Gruen, E. S. 1974. *The Last Generation of the Roman Republic.* Berkeley and Los Angeles.

Gruen, E. S. 1982. "Macedonia and the Settlement of 167 B.C.," in W. L. Adams and E. N. Borza (eds.), *Philip II, Alexander the Great and the Macedonian Heritage,* 257–67. Lanham.

Gruen, E. S. 1984a. *The Hellenistic World and the Coming of Rome.* Berkeley.

Gruen, E. S. 1984b. "Material Rewards and the Drive for Empire," in Harris 1984c: 59–82.

Gruen, E. S. 1990a. "The Bacchanalian Affair," in Gruen 1990b: 34–78.

Gruen, E. S. 1990b. *Studies in Greek Culture and Roman Policy.* Leiden (repr. 1996, Berkeley and Los Angeles).

Gruen, E. S. 1991. "The Exercise of Power in the Roman Republic," in Molho, Raaflaub, and Emlen 1991: 251–67.

Gruen, E. S. 1992. *Culture and National Identity in Republican Rome.* Ithaca.

Gruen, E. S. 1995. "The 'Fall' of the Scipios," in Malkin and Rubinsohn 1995: 59–90.

Gruen, E. S. 1996. "The Roman Oligarchy: Image and Perception," in Linderski 1996: 215–34.

Gruen, E. S. 2002. *Diaspora: Jews amidst Greeks and Romans.* Cambridge, MA.

Guidoboni, E. 2003. "Les tremblements de terre méditerranéens de l'antiquité au XVe siècle: lignes méthodologiques et problèmes d'une récherche multidisciplinaire," in C. Albore Livadie and F. Ortolani (eds.), *Variazioni climatico-ambientali e impatto sull'uomo nell'area circum-mediterranea durante l'Olocene,* 141–53. Bari.

Gullini, G. 1956. *I Mosaici di Palestrina.* Rome.

Gullini, G., 1973. "La datazione e l'inquadramento stilistico del santuario della Fortuna Primigenia a Palestrina." *ANRW* I.4, 746–99.

Gunderson, E. 2000. *Staging Masculinity. The Rhetoric of Performance in the Roman World.* Ann Arbor.

Habicht, C. 1990. *Cicero the Politician.* Baltimore.

Habicht, C. 1997. *Athens from Alexander to Antony.* Cambridge.

Habinek, T. 1998. *The Politics of Latin Literature. Writing, Identity, and Empire in Ancient Rome.* Princeton.

Haehling, R. von. 1989. *Zeitbezüge des T. Livius in der ersten Dekade seines Geschichtswerkes.* Stuttgart.

Hall, J., and Bond, R. 2002. "Performative Elements in Cicero's Orations: an Experimental Approach." *Prudentia* 34, 187–228.

Hall, U. 1972. "Appian, Plutarch, and the Tribunician Elections of 123 B.C." *Athenaeum* 50, 3–35.

Hall, U. 1998. "*Species Libertatis*: Voting Procedure in the Late Roman Republic," in M. Austin, J. Harries, and C. Smith (eds.), *Modus Operandi: Essays in Honour of Geoffrey Rickman*, 15–30. London.

Hallett, C. H. 1995. "Kopienkritik and the Works of Polykleitos," in W. Moon (ed.), *Polykleitos, the Doryphoros, and Tradition*, 121–7. Madison.

Hallett, C. H. 2005. *The Roman Nude.* Oxford.

Hallett, J. 1989. "Women as 'Same' and 'Other' in Classical Roman Elite." *Helios* 16, 59–78.

Hallett, J. 1997. "Female Homoeroticism and the Denial of Reality in Latin Literature," in Hallett and Skinner 1997: 255–73.

Hallett, J., and Skinner, M. (eds.) 1997. *Roman Sexualities.* Princeton.

Handley, E. W. 1968. *Menander and Plautus: A Study in Comparison.* London.

Hands, A. R. 1965. "The Political Background of the 'lex Acilia de Repetundis'." *Latomus* 24, 225–37.

Hands, A. R. 1967. "Fulvius Flaccus, Caius Gracchus and the Italian Enfranchisement Question." *BICS* 14, 110.

Hands, A. R. 1972. "Livius Drusus and the Courts." *Phoenix* 26, 268–72.

Hands, A. R. 1976. "Land and Citizenship, 125–122 B.C." *Mnemosyne* 29, 176–80.

Hansen, G. C. 1985. "Das Datum der Schlacht bei Vercellae." *Klio* 67, 588.

Hanson, J. A. 1959. *Roman Theater Temples.* Princeton.

Hanson, V. D. (ed.) 1991. *Hoplites: The Classical Greek Battle Experience.* London.

Hanson, V. D. 2000. *The Western Way of War: Infantry Battle in Classical Greece.*[2] Berkeley.

Hantos, T. 1988. *Res publica constituta: Die Verfassung des Diktators Sulla.* Stuttgart.

Harmand, J. 1967. *L'armée et le soldat à Rome, de 107 à 50 avant notre ère.* Paris.

Harmand, L. 1957. *Un aspect social et politique du monde romain, le patronage sur les collectivités publiques des origines au Bas-Empire.* Paris.

Harries, J. 2002. "Cicero and the Defining of the *Ius Civile*," in G. Clark and T. Rajak (eds.), *Philosophy and Power in the Graeco-Roman World: Essays in Honour of Miriam Griffin*, 51–68. Oxford.

Harris, W. V. 1979. *War and Imperialism in Republican Rome, 327–70 B.C.* Oxford.

Harris, W. V. 1984a. "New Directions in the Study of Roman Imperialism," in Harris 1984c: 13–31.

Harris, W. V. 1984b. "The Italians and the Empire," in Harris 1984c: 89–109.

Harris, W. V. (ed.) 1984c. *The Imperialism of Mid-Republican Rome.* Rome.

Harris, W. V. 1989. *Ancient Literacy.* Cambridge.

Harris, W. V. 1990a. "Roman Warfare in the Economic and Social Context of the Fourth Century BC," in Eder 1990: 494–510.

Harris, W. V. 1990b. "On Defining the Political Culture of the Roman Republic: Some Comments on Rosenstein, Williamson and North." *CPh* 85, 288–94.

Harrison, S. J. (ed.) 2005. *The Blackwell Companion to Latin Literature.* Oxford.

Harward, V. J. 1982. "Greek Domestic Sculpture and the Origins of Private Patronage." Ph.D. dissertation, Harvard University.

Häuber, C. 1998. " 'Art as a Weapon' von Scipio Africanus Maior bis Lucullus: domus, horti, und Heiligtümer auf dem Esquilin," in Cima and La Rocca 1998: 83–112.

Haug, I. 1947. "Der römische Bundesgenossenkrieg 91–88 v. Chr. bei Titus Livius." *WJA* 2, 100–39, 201–58.

Hayne, L. 1972. "M. Lepidus (cos. 78): A Reappraisal." *Historia* 21, 661–8.

Heath, M. 2002. *Interpreting Classical Texts.* London.

Heckenbach, J. 1911. *De nuditate sacra sacrisque vinculis.* Giessen.

Hellegouarc'h, J. 1963. *Le vocabulaire latin des relations et des partis politiques sous la République* (2nd ed. 1972). Paris.

Hellenkemper Salies, G. (ed.), 1994. *Das Wrack. Der antike Schiffsfund von Mahdia.* Cologne.

Henrichs, A. 1995. "*Graecia Capta*: Roman Views of Greek Culture." *HSPh* 97, 243–61.

Hermon, E. 2001. *Habiter et partager les terres avant les Gracques.* Rome.

Hesberg, H. von. 1992. *Römische Grabbauten.* Darmstadt.

Hesberg, H. von. 1999. "The King on Stage," in Bergmann and Kondoleon 1999: 65–75.

Hesberg, H. von, and Zanker, P. 1987. *Römische Gräberstrassen: Selbstdarstellung, Status, Standard: Kolloquium in München vom 28. bis 30. Oktober 1985.* Munich.

Heurgon, J. 1973. *The Rise of Rome to 264 B.C.* Trans. J. Willis. Berkeley and Los Angeles.

Heurgon, J. 1976. "L'agronome carthaginois Magon et ses traducteurs en latin et en grec." *CRAI* 441–56.

Heuss, A. 1944. "Zur Entwicklung des Imperiums der römischen Oberbeamten." *ZRG* 64, 57–133.

Heuss, A. 1956. "Der Untergang der römischen Republik und das Problem der Revolution." *HZ* 182, 1–28.

Heuss, A. 1973. "Das Revolutionsproblem im Spiegel der antiken Geschichte." *HZ* 216, 1–72.

Heuss, A. 1988. "Theodor Mommsen als Geschichtsschreiber," in N. Hammerstein (ed.), *Deutsche Geschichtswissenschaft um 1900*, 37–95. Stuttgart.

Hickson, F. V. 1993. *Roman Prayer Language: Livy and the Aeneid of Vergil.* Stuttgart.

Hillard, T. 1989. "Republican Politics, Women, and the Evidence." *Helios* 16, 165–82.

Hillen, H. J. 2003. *Von Aeneas zu Romulus. Die Legenden von der Gründung Roms.* Düsseldorf.

Hillman, T. P. 1990. "Pompeius and the Senate: 77–71." *Hermes* 118, 444–54.

Hillman, T. P. 1992. "Plutarch and the First Consulship of Pompeius and Crassus." *Phoenix* 46, 124–37.

Himmelmann, N. 1989. *Herrscher und Athlet. Die Bronzen vom Quirinal.* Milan.

Hinard, F. 1985. *Les proscriptions de la Rome républicaine.* Paris and Rome.

Hind, J. G. F. 1994. "Mithridates," in Crook, Lintott, and Rawson 1994: 129–64.

Hobsbawm, E. P. 1969. *Bandits.* London.

Hobson, J. A. 1902. *Imperialism: A Study.* London.

Hoepfner, W., and Schwandner, E.-L. (eds.) 1990. *Hermogenes und die hochhellenistische Architektur.* Mainz.

Hofter, M. R. (ed.) 1988. *Kaiser Augustus und die verlorene Republik: eine Ausstellung im Martin-Gropius-Bau, Berlin, 7. Juni-14. August 1988.* Mainz.

Hölkeskamp, K.-J. 1987. *Die Entstehung der Nobilität.* Stuttgart.

Hölkeskamp, K.-J. 1993. "Conquest, Competition and Consensus: Roman Expansion in Italy and the Rise of the *Nobilitas.*" *Historia* 42, 12–39.

Hölkeskamp, K.-J. 1995. "*Oratoris maxima scaena*: Reden vor dem Volk in der politischen Kultur der Republik," in Jehne 1995c: 11–49.

Hölkeskamp, K.-J. 1996. "*Exempla* und *mos maiorum*: Überlegungen zum kollektiven Gedächtnis der Nobilität," in H.-J. Gehrke and A. Möller (eds.), *Vergangenheit und Lebenswelt. Soziale Kommunikation, Traditionsbildung und historisches Bewusstsein*, 301–38. Tübingen.

Hölkeskamp, K.-J. 1999. "Römische *gentes* und griechische Genealogien," in G. Vogt-Spira and B. Rommel (eds.), *Rezeption und Identität. Die kulturelle Auseinandersetzung Roms mit Griechenland als europäisches Paradigma*, 3–21. Stuttgart.

Hölkeskamp, K.-J. 2000a. "The Roman Republic: Government of the People, by the People, for the People?" *SCI* 19, 203–23.

Hölkeskamp, K.-J. 2000b. "*Fides-deditio in fidem-dextra data et accepta*: Recht, Religion und Ritual in Rom," in Bruun 2000: 223–49.

Hölkeskamp, K.-J. 2001a. "Capitol, Comitium und Forum. Öffentliche Räume, sakrale Topographie und Erinnerungslandschaften der römischen Republik," in St. Faller (ed.), *Studien zu antiken Identitäten*, 97–132. Würzburg.

Hölkeskamp, K.-J. 2001b. "Fact(ions) or Fiction? Friedrich Münzer and the Aristocracy of the Roman Republic – then and now." *IJCT* 8, 92–105.

Hölkeskamp, K.-J. 2004a. *Rekonstruktionen einer Republik. Die politische Kultur des antiken Rom und die Forschung der letzten Jahrzehnte.* Munich.

Hölkeskamp, K.-J. 2004b. *SENATVS POPVLVSQVE ROMANVS. Die politische Kultur der Republik – Dimensionen und Deutungen.* Stuttgart.

Hölkeskamp, K.-J. 2005. "Images of Power: Memory, Myth and Monuments in the Roman Republic." *SCI* 24, 249–71.

Holland, L. A. 1961. *Janus and the Bridge.* Rome.

Holliday, P. J. 2002. *The Origins of Roman Historical Commemoration in the Visual Arts.* Cambridge and New York.

Holloway, R. R. 1994. *The Archaeology of Early Rome and Latium.* London.

Hollstein, W. 2000a. "Die Stempelstellung – ein ungenutztes Interpretationskriterium für die Münzprägung der Römischen Republik," in B. Kluge and B. Weisser (eds.), *XII. Internationaler Numismatischer Kongress: Berlin 1997*, 487–91. Berlin.

Hollstein, W. 2000b. "Exkurs: Die Bedeutung der Stempelstellung für die Münzprägung der Römischen Republik," in W. Hollstein (ed.), *Metallanalytische Untersuchungen an Münzen der Römischen Republik*, 133–6. Berlin.

Hölscher, T. 1978. "Die Anfänge römischer Repräsentationskunst." *MDAI(R)* 85, 315–17.

Hölscher, T. 1980a. "Die Geschichtsauffassung in der römischen Repräsentationskunst." *JDAI* 95, 265–321.

Hölscher, T. 1980b. "Römische Siegesdenkmäler der späten Republik," in H. A. Cahn and E. Simon (eds.), *Tainia*, 351–71. Mainz.

Hölscher, T. 1982. "Die Bedeutung der Münzen für das Verständnis der politischen Repräsentationskunst der späten römischen Republik," in T. Hackens and R. Weiler (eds.), *Proceedings of the 9th International Congress of Numismatics, Berne 1979*, 269–82. Louvain.

Hölscher, T. 1984. *Staatsdenkmal und Publikum: vom Untergang der Republik bis zur Festigung des Kaisertums in Rom.* Constance.

Hölscher, T. 1990. "Römische Nobiles und hellenistische Herrscher," in *Akten des XIII. Internationalen Kongresses für Klassische Archäologie Berlin 1988*, 73–84. Mainz.

Hölscher, T. 1998. *Öffentliche Räume in frühen griechischen Städten.* Heidelberg.

Hölscher, T. 2001. "Das Alte vor Augen: Politische Denkmäler und öffentliches Gedächtnis im republikanischen Rom," in Melville 2001: 183–211.

Hölscher, T. 2004. *The Language of Images in Roman Art.* Trans. A. Snodgrass and A. Künzl-Snodgrass. Cambridge and New York.

Hölscher, T. forthcoming. "The Transformation of Victory into Power: From Event to Structure," in Dillon and Welch forthcoming.

Holsti, J. J. 1991. *Peace and War: Armed Conflicts and International Order, 1648–1989.* Cambridge.

Hong, S., Candelone, J.-P., Patterson, C., and Bouton, C. F. 1994. "Greenland Ice Evidence of Hemispheric Lead Pollution Two Millennia Ago by Greek and Roman Civilisations." *Science* 265, 1841–3.

Hope, V. M., and Marshall, E. (eds.) 2000. *Death and Disease in the Ancient City.* London.

Hopkins, K. 1966/7. "On the Probable Age Structure of the Roman Population." *Population Studies* 20, 245–64.

Hopkins, K. 1978. *Conquerors and Slaves.* Cambridge.

Hopkins, K. 1983a. *Death and Renewal.* Cambridge.

Hopkins, K. 1983b. "Models, Ships and Staples," in P. Garnsey and C. R. Whittaker (eds.), *Trade and Famine in Classical Antiquity*, 84–109. Cambridge.

Hopkins, K. 1991. "From Violence to Blessing: Symbols and Rituals in Ancient Rome," in Molho, Raaflaub, and Emlen 1991: 479–98.

Hopkins, K. 1993. "Novel Evidence for Roman Slavery," *P&P* 138, 3–27.

Hopkins, K. 2002. "Rome, Taxes, Rents and Trade," in W. Scheidel and S. von Reden (eds.), *The Ancient Economy*, 190–230. Edinburgh.

Hopkins, K., and Burton, G. 1983. "Political Succession in the Late Republic (249–50 BC)," in Hopkins 1983a: 31–120.

Horden, P., and Purcell, N. 2000. *The Corrupting Sea: A Study of Mediterranean History.* Oxford.

Hornblower, S., and Spawforth, A. (eds.) 1996. *Oxford Classical Dictionary.*[3] Oxford.

Horsfall, N. 2003. *The Culture of the Roman Plebs.* London.

Howgego, C. 1990. "Why Did Ancient States Strike Coins?" *NC* 150, 1–25.

Howgego, C. 1992. "The Supply and Use of Money in the Roman World 200 B.C. to A.D. 300." *JRS* 82, 1–31.

Howgego, C. 1994. "Coin Circulation and the Integration of the Roman Economy." *JRA* 7, 5–21.

Howgego, C. 1995. *Ancient History from Coins.* London and New York.

Hoyos, B. D. 1984. "Polybius' Roman οἱ πολλοί in 264 B.C." *LCM* 9, 88–93.

Hoyos, B. D. 1998. *Unplanned Wars: The Origins of the First and Second Punic Wars.* Berlin and New York.

Hughes, J. D. 1975. *Ecology in Ancient Civilizations.* Albuquerque.

Hughes, J. D., and Thirgood, J. V. 1982. "Deforestation in Ancient Greece and Rome: A Cause of Collapse." *The Ecologist* 12, 196–208.

Humbert, M. 1978. *Municipium et civitas sine suffragio. L'organisation de la conquête jusqu'à la guerre sociale.* Rome.

Hünemörder, C. 2002. "Wolf." *DNP* 12.2, 567–70.

Hunt, C. 1995. "The Natural Landscape and its Evolution," in Barker 1995: 62–83.

Hutchinson, G. O. 1998. *Cicero's Correspondence*. Oxford.

Hyam, R. 1999. "The Primacy of Geopolitics: The Dynamics of British Imperial Policy, 1763–1963," in R. D. King and R. W. Kilson (eds.), *The Statecraft of British Imperialism: Essays in Honour of Wm. Roger Louis*, 27–51. Ilford

Ikeguchi, M. 1999–2000. "A Comparative Study of Settlement Patterns and Agricultural Structures in Ancient Italy: A Methodology for Interpreting Field Survey Evidence." *Kodai* 10, 1–59.

Ioppolo, G. 1963–4. "Area sacra di S. Omobono. Esplorazione della fase repubblicana. Due monumenti repubblicani," *BCAR* 79, 68–90.

Isaac, B. 2004. *The Invention of Racism in Classical Antiquity*. Princeton.

Isager, J. 1991. *Pliny on Art and Society. The Elder Pliny's Chapter on the History of Art*. London and New York.

Jaeger, M. 1997. *Livy's Written Rome*. Ann Arbor.

James, L. 1997. *Raj: The Making and Unmaking of British India*. New York.

Janan, M. 1994. *"When the Lamp is Shattered": Desire and Narrative in Catullus*. Carbondale.

Jehne, M. 1993. "Geheime Abstimmung und Bindungswesen in der römischen Republik." *HZ* 257, 593–613.

Jehne, M. 1995a. "Einführung: Zur Debatte um die Rolle des Volkes in der römischen Politik," in Jehne 1995c: 1–9.

Jehne, M. 1995b. "Die Beeinflussung von Entscheidungen durch 'Bestechung': Zur Funktion des *ambitus* in der römischen Republik," in Jehne 1995c: 51–76.

Jehne, M. (ed.) 1995c. *Demokratie in Rom? Die Rolle des Volkes in der Politik der römischen Republik*. Stuttgart.

Jehne, M. 2000a. "Jovialität und Freiheit. Zur Institutionalität der Beziehungen zwischen Ober- und Unterschichten in der römischen Republik," in Linke and Stemmler 2000b: 207–35.

Jehne, M. 2000b. "Wirkungsweise und Bedeutung der *centuria praerogativa*." *Chiron* 30, 661–78.

Jehne, M. 2002. "Die Geltung der Provocation und die Konstruktion der römischen Republik als Freiheitsgemeinschaft," in G. Melville and H. Vorländer (eds.), *Geltungsgeschichten: Über die Stabilisierung und Legitimierung institutioneller Ordnungen*, 55–74. Cologne, Weimar and Vienna.

Jehne, M. 2003. "Integrationsrituale in der römischen Republik: Zur einbindenden Wirkung der Volksversammlungen," in K.-J. Hölkeskamp, J. Rüsen, E. Stein-Hölkeskamp, and H. Th. Grütter (eds.), *Sinn (in) der Antike: Orientierungssysteme, Leitbilder und Wertkonzepte im Altertum*, 279–97. Mainz.

Jehne, M., and Mutschler, F.-H. 2000. "Texte, Rituale und die Stabilität der römischen Republik." *AW* 31, 551–6.

Jervis, R. 1997. *System Effects: Complexity in Political and Social Life*. Princeton.

Jocelyn, H. D. 1977. "The Ruling Class of the Roman Republic and Greek Philosophers." *BRL* 59, 323–66.

Johnson, T., and Dandeker, C. 1989. "Patronage: Relation and System," in Wallace-Hadrill 1989b: 219–41.

Johnston, D. 1999. *Roman Law in Context*. Cambridge.

Jolowicz, H. F., and Nicholas, B. 1972. *Historical Introduction to the Study of Roman Law*.[3] Cambridge.

Jones, A. H. M. 1960. "(i) De tribunis plebis reficiendis; (ii) De legibus Iunia et Acilia repetundarum." *PCPhS* 6, 35–42.

Jones, A. H. M. 1972. *The Criminal Courts of the Roman Republic and Principate*. Oxford.

Jones, G. D. B. 1963. "Capena and the Ager Capenas. Part II." *PBSR* 31, 100–58.

Jones, M. W. J. 2000. *Principles of Roman Architecture*. New Haven.

Jongman, W. 1988. *The Economy and Society of Pompeii*. Amsterdam.

Jongman, W. 2003. "Slavery and the Growth of Rome. The Transformation of Italy in the Second and First Centuries BCE," in Edwards and Woolf 2003: 100–22.

Joshel, S. R. 1992. *Work, Identity, and Legal Status at Rome: A Study of the Occupational Inscriptions*. Norman and London.

Judson, S. 1963. "Erosion and Deposition of Italian Stream Valleys during Historic Time." *Science* 140, 898–9.

Judson, S. 1968. "Erosion Rates near Rome, Italy." *Science* 140, 1444–6.

Junkelmann, M. 2000. "Familia Gladiatoria: The Heroes of the Amphitheatre," in R. Jackson (ed.), *Caesars and Gladiators: the Power of Spectacle in Ancient Rome*, 39–80. Berkeley.

Kabus-Preisshofen, R. 1989. *Die hellenistische Plastik auf der Insel Kos*. Berlin.

Kähler, H. 1939. "Triumphbigen." *RE* 7A.1, 373–493.

Kähler, H. 1965. *Die Fries vom Reiterdenkmal des Aemilius Paullus in Delphi*. Berlin.

Kahler, M. 1997. "Inventing International Relations: International Relations Theory after 1945," in M. Doyle and G. I. Ikenberry (eds.), *New Thinking in International Relations Theory*, 20–53. Boulder.

Kahn, A. D. 1986. *The Education of Julius Caesar*. New York.

Kajanto, I. 1965. *The Latin Cognomina*. Helsinki.

Kallet-Marx, R. M. 1990. "The Trial of Rutilius Rufus." *Phoenix* 44, 122–39.

Kallet-Marx, R. M. 1995. *Hegemony to Empire: The Development of the Roman Imperium in the East from 148 to 62 B.C.* Berkeley and Los Angeles.

Kamermans, H. 1991. "Faulted Land: The Geology of the Agro Pontino," in A. Voorrips, S. H. Loving, and H. Kamermans (eds.), *The Agro Pontino Survey Project. Methods and Preliminary results*, 21–30. Amsterdam.

Kampen, N. 1981. *Image and Status: Roman Working Women in Ostia*. Berlin.

Kampen, N. 2003. "On Writing Histories of Roman Art." *Art Bulletin* 85 (June), 371–86.

Kaster, R. A. 1995. *Suetonius: De Grammaticis et Rhetoribus*. Oxford.

Katz, B. R. 1975. "The First Fruits of Sulla's March." *AC* 44, 100–25.

Katz, B. R. 1976a. "Studies on the Period of Cinna and Sulla." *AC* 45, 497–549.

Katz, B. R. 1976b. "The Siege of Rome in 87 B.C." *CPh* 71, 328–36.

Katz, B. R. 1977. "Caesar Strabo's Struggle for the Consulship – and More." *RhM* 120, 45–63.

Keaveney, A. 1978. "Pompeius Strabo's Second Consulship." *CQ* 28, 240–1.

Keaveney, A. 1979. "Sulla, Sulpicius and Caesar Strabo." *Latomus* 38, 451–60.

Keaveney, A. 1980. "Deux dates contestées dans la carrière de Sylla." *LEC* 48, 149–59.

Keaveney, A. 1982a. "Sulla and Italy." *CS* 19, 499–544.

Keaveney, A. 1982b. "Young Pompey: 106–79 B.C." *AC* 51, 111–39.

Keaveney, A. 1982c. *Sulla: The Last Republican*. London and Canberra.

Keaveney, A. 1983. "What Happened in 88?" *Eirene* 20, 53–86.

Keaveney, A. 1984. "Who Were the Sullani?" *Klio* 66, 114–50.

Keaveney, A. 1987. *Rome and the Unification of Italy*. London.

Keaveney, A. 1992. *Lucullus: A Life*. London and New York.

Keaveney, A., and Madden, J. A. 1982. "Phthiriasis and Its Victims." *SO* 57, 87–99.

Keay, S., and Terrenato, N. 2001. *Italy and the West: Comparative Issues in Romanization.* Oxford.

Keeley, L. H. 1996. *War Before Civilization: The Myth of the Peaceful Savage.* Oxford.

Kegley, C. W., Jr. 1995. *Controversies in International Relations Theory: Realism and the Neoliberal Challenge.* New York.

Kelly, J. M. 1966a. "The Growth-Pattern of the Praetor's Edict." *Irish Jurist* n.s.1, 341–55.

Kelly, J. M. 1966b. *Roman Litigation.* Oxford.

Kelly, M. G., and Huntley, B. 1991. "An 11,000-year record of vegetation and environment from Lago di Martignano, Latium, Italy." *Journal of Quaternary Science* 6, 209–24.

Kennedy, G. 1968. "The Rhetoric of Advocacy in Greece and Rome." *AJPh* 89, 419–36.

Kennedy, G. 1972. *The Art of Rhetoric in the Roman World.* Princeton.

Kenney, E. J. (ed.) 1982. *Latin Literature.* Cambridge.

Kent, J. P. C. 1978. *Roman Coins.* New York.

Keppie, L. 1983. *Colonization and Veteran Settlement in Italy, 47–14 BC.* London.

Keppie, L. 1984. *The Making of the Roman Army, From Republic to Empire.* London.

Keppie, L. 1991. *Understanding Roman Inscriptions.* London.

Kienast, D. 1975. "Die politische Emanzipation der Plebs und die Entwicklung des Heerwesens im frühen Rom." *BJ* 175, 83–112.

Kippenberg, H., and Stroumsa, G. (eds.) 1995. *Secrecy and Concealment: Studies in the History of Mediterranean and Near Eastern Religions.* Leiden.

Klar, L. forthcoming. "Re-Evaluating the Origins of the Roman Scaenae Frons: The Architecture of Triumphal Games in the Second Century BC," in Dillon and Welch forthcoming.

Kleiner, D. E. E. 1992. *Roman Sculpture.* New Haven.

Kleiner, F. S. 1985. *The Arch of Nero in Rome: A Study of the Roman Honorary Arch Before and Under Nero.* Rome.

Klose, E. 1982. *Die volkerrechtliche Ordnung der hellenistischen Staatenwelt in der Zeit von 289–168 v. Chr.* Munich.

Koch, C. 1937. *Der römische Juppiter.* Frankfurt.

Koch, C. 1986. *Giove Romano.* Rev. and trans. Luciano Arcella. Rome.

Koebner, R., and Schmidt, H. D. 1964. *Imperialism: The Story and Significance of a Political Word, 1840–1960.* Cambridge.

Kolb, F. 2002. *Rom. Die Geschichte der Stadt in der Antike.* Revised edition. Munich.

Konrad, C. F. 1987. "Some Friends of Sertorius." *AJPh* 108, 519–27.

Konrad, C. F. 1988. "Why Not Sallust On the Eighties?" *AHB* 2, 12–15.

Konrad, C. F. 1989. "Cotta Off Mellaria and the Identities of Fufidius." *CPh* 84, 119–29.

Konrad, C. F. 1994a. *Plutarch's Sertorius: A Historical Commentary.* Chapel Hill and London.

Konrad, C. F. 1994b. "Segovia and Segontia." *Historia* 43, 440–53.

Konrad, C. F. 1995. "A New Chronology of the Sertorian War." *Athenaeum* 83, 157–87.

Konrad, C. F. 1997. "Marius at Eryx (Sallust, P. Rylands 473.1)." *Historia* 46, 28–63.

Konstan, D. 1993. "Rhetoric and the Crisis of Legitimacy in Cicero's Catilinarian Orations," in T. Poulakos (ed.), *Rethinking the History of Rhetoric: Multidisciplinary Essays on the Rhetorical Tradition*, 11–30. Boulder.

Konstan, D. 1997. *Friendship in the Classical World.* Cambridge.

Kraus, C. S. 1994. *Livy Ab Urbe Condita VI.* Cambridge.

Kraus, C. S., and Woodman, A. J. 1997. *Latin Historians.* Oxford.

Kremer, B. 1994. *Das Bild der Kelten bis in augusteische Zeit.* Stuttgart.

Krostenko, B. 2001. *Cicero, Catullus, and the Language of Social Performance.* Chicago.

Kunkel, W. 1962. *Untersuchungen zur Entwicklungen des römischen Kriminalverfahrens in vorsullanischer Zeit.* Munich.

Kunkel, W. 1967. *Herkunft und Soziale Stellung der Römischen Juristen*[2]. Graz and Cologne.

Kunkel, W. 1973. *An Introduction to Roman Legal and Constitutional History.*[2] Trans. J. M. Kelley. Oxford.

Künzl, E. 1988. *Der römische Triumph. Siegesfeiern im anitken Rom.* Munich.

Kuttner, A. 1993. "Some New Grounds for Narrative. M. Antonius' Base (The Ara Domitii Ahenobarbi) and Republican Biographies," in P. J. Holliday (ed.), *Narrative and Event in Ancient Art*, 198–239. Cambridge and New York.

Kuttner, A. 1999. "Culture and History at Pompey's Museum." *TAPhA* 129, 343–73.

Kuttner, A. 2004. "Roman Art during the Republic," in Flower 2004b: 294–321, 391–3.

Labruna, L. 1976. *Il console sovversivo: Marco Emilio Lepido e la sua rivolta.* Naples.

Lacey, W. K. 1970. "*Boni atque improbi.*" *G&R* 17, 1–16.

Laffi, U. 1967. "Il mito di Silla." *Athenaeum* 45, 177–213, 255–77.

Laidlaw, A. 1985. *The First Style in Pompeii: Painting and Architecture.* Rome.

Laidlaw, A. 1993. "Excavations in the Casa di Sallustio at Pompeii: A Preliminary Assessment," in R. T. Scott and A. Reynolds Scott, *Eius Virtutis Studiosi: Classical and Postclassical Studies in Memory of Frank Edward Brown (1908–1988)*, 217–31. Washington, DC.

Lancel, S. 1995. *Carthage: A History.* Trans. A. Nevill. Oxford.

Laser, G. 1999. "Klientelen und Wahlkampf im Spiegel des commentariolum petitionis." *GFA* 2, 179–92.

La Regina, A. 1976. "Il Sannio," in Zanker 1976b: 219–54.

La Rocca, E. 1977. "Note sulle importazioni greche in territorio laziale nell'VIII secolo a.C." *PP* 32, 375–97.

Larsen, J. A. O. 1962. "Freedom and its Obstacles in Ancient Greece." *CPh* 57, 230–4.

Latte, K. 1960. *Römische Religionsgeschichte.* Munich.

Laurence, R. 1999. *The Roads of Roman Italy: Mobility and Social Change.* London.

Laurence, R. 2004. "The Economic Exploitation of Geological Resources in the Tiber Valley: Road Building," in H. Patterson (ed.), *Bridging the Tiber: Approaches to Regional Archaeology in the Middle Tiber Valley*, 285–95. London.

Laurence, R., and Wallace-Hadrill, A. (eds.) 1997. *Domestic Space in the Roman World.* Portsmouth, RI.

Lauter, H. 1976. "Die hellenistischen Theater der Samniter und Latiner in ihrer Beziehung zur Theaterarchitektur der Griechen," in Zanker 1976b: 413–30.

Lauter, H. 1998. "Hellenistische Vorläufer der Römischen Villa," in A. Fraser (ed.), *The Roman Villa. Villa Urbana*, 21–7. Philadelphia.

Lawrence, A. W. 1983. *Greek Architecture.*[3] Harmondsworth and Baltimore.

Lazenby, J. F. 1978. *Hannibal's War.* Warminster.

Lazenby, J. F. 1996. *The First Punic War: A Military History.* Stanford.

Lazenby, J. F., and Whitehead, D. 1996. "The Myth of the Hoplite's *hoplon.*" *CQ* 46, 27–33.

Leeman, A. D. 1963. Orationis ratio. *The Stylistic Theories and Practices of the Roman Orators, Historians and Philosophers*, 2 vols. Amsterdam.

Lehmann, P. W. 1979. "Lefkadia and the Second Style," in G. Kopce and M. B. Moore (eds.), *Studies in Classical Art and Archaeology: A Tribute to Peter Heinrich von Blanckenhagen*, 225–9. Locust Valley.

Leigh, M. 1995. "Wounding and Popular Rhetoric at Rome." *BICS* 40, 195–212.

Leigh, M. 2004. *Comedy and the Rise of Rome.* Oxford.

Lenin, V. I. 1920. *Imperialism: The Highest Stage of Capitalism.* Moscow.

Levene, D. S. 1992. "Sallust's *Jugurtha*: an 'Historical Fragment'?" *JRS* 82, 53–70.

Levene, D. S. 1993. *Religion in Livy.* Oxford.

Lévêque, P. 1968. "La guerre à l'époque hellénistique," in J.-P. Vernant (ed.), *Problèmes de la guerre en grèce ancienne,* 261–87. Paris.

Levick, B. 1982. "Sulla's March on Rome in 88 B.C." *Historia* 31, 503–8.

Lewis, R. G. 1974. "Catulus and the Cimbri, 102 B.C." *Hermes* 102, 90–109.

Lewis, R. G. 1991. "Sulla's Autobiography: Scope and Economy." *Athenaeum* 79, 509–19.

Libero, L. de. 1992. *Obstruktion: Politische Praktiken im Senat und in der Volksversammlung der ausgehenden römischen Republik (70–49 v.Chr.).* Stuttgart.

Libertini, G. 1926. *Centuripe.* Catania.

Liebeschuetz, J. H. W. G. 1979. *Continuity and Change in Roman Religion.* Oxford.

Lind, L. R. 1979. "The Tradition of Roman Moral Conservatism," in C. Deroux (ed.), *Studies in Latin Literature and Roman History* 1, 7–58.

Lind, L. R. 1986. "The Idea of the Republic and the Foundations of Roman Political Liberty," in C. Deroux (ed.), *Studies in Latin Literature and Roman History* 4, 44–108.

Linden, E. 1896. "De bello civili Sullano." Dissertation, University of Freiburg.

Linderski, J. 1966. "Were Pompeius and Crassus Elected in Absence to Their First Consulship?," in *Mélanges offerts à Kazimierz Michałowski,* 523–6. Warsaw.

Linderski, J. 1983. "A Witticism of Appuleius Saturninus." *RFIC* 111, 452–9.

Linderski, J. 1986. "The Augural Law." *ANRW* 2.16.3, 2146–312.

Linderski, J. 1990. "The Auspices and the Struggle of the Orders," in Eder 1990: 34–48.

Linderski, J. 1994. "*Si vis pacem, para bellum:* Concepts of Defensive Imperialism," in Harris 1984c, 133–64.

Linderski, J. 1995. *Roman Questions: Selected Papers.* Stuttgart.

Linderski, J. (ed.) 1996. *Imperium sine fine: T. Robert Broughton and the Roman Republic.* Stuttgart.

Ling, R. 1991. *Roman Painting.* Cambridge.

Linke, B., and Stemmler, M. 2000a. "Institutionalität und Geschichtlichkeit in der römischen Republik: Einleitende Bemerkungen zu den Forschungsperspektiven," in Linke and Stemmler 2000b: 1–23.

Linke, B., and Stemmler, M. (eds.) 2000b. *Mos maiorum: Untersuchungen zu den Formen der Identitätsstiftung und Stabilisierung in der römischen Republik.* Stuttgart.

Lintott, A. 1968. *Violence in Republican Rome* (2nd ed. 1999). Oxford.

Lintott, A. 1972a. "Imperial Expansion and Moral Decline in the Roman Republic." *Historia* 21, 626–38.

Lintott, A. 1972b. "Provocatio: From the Struggle of the Orders to the Principate." *ANRW* 1.2, 226–67.

Lintott, A. 1981. "What was the 'Imperium Romanum'?" *G&R* 28, 53–67.

Lintott, A. 1990. "Electoral Bribery in the Roman Republic." *JRS* 80, 1–16.

Lintott, A. 1992. *Judicial Reform and Land Reform in the Roman Republic: A New Edition, with Translation and Commentary, of the Laws from Urbino.* Cambridge.

Lintott, A. 1993. *Imperium Romanum: Politics and Administration.* London and New York.

Lintott, A. 1994a. "The Crisis of the Republic: Sources and Source-problems," in Crook, Lintott, and Rawson 1994: 1–15.

Lintott, A. 1994b. "The Roman Empire and Its Problems in the Late Second Century," in Crook, Lintott, and Rawson 1994: 16–39.

Lintott, A. 1994c. "Political History, 146–95 B.C.," in Crook, Lintott, and Rawson 1994: 40–103.

Lintott, A. 1997. "Dio Cassius and the History of the Late Roman Republic." *ANRW* 2.34.3, 2497–523.

Lintott, A. 1999a. *The Constitution of the Roman Republic.* Oxford.

Lintott, A. 1999b (= Lintott 1968).

Lippold, A. 1963. *Consules: Untersuchungen zur Geschichte des römischen Konsulates von 264 bis 201 v.Chr.* Bonn.

Liverani, P. 1984. "L'Ager Veientanus in età repubblicana." *PBSR* 52, 36–48.

Lo Cascio, E. 1994. "The Size of the Roman Population: Beloch and the Meaning of the Augustan Census Figures." *JRS* 84, 22–40.

Lo Cascio, E. 1999a. "Popolazione e risorse agricole nell'Italia del II secolo a.C.," in D. Vera (ed.), *Demografia, sistemi agrari, regimi alimentari nel mondo antico*, 217–40. Bari.

Lo Cascio, E. 1999b. "The Population of Roman Italy in Town and Country," in J. Bintliff and K. Sbonias (eds.), *Reconstructing Past Population Trends in Mediterranean Europe (3000 BC–AD 1800)*, 161–71. Oxford.

Lo Cascio, E. 2001. "Recruitment and the Size of the Roman Population from the Third to the First Century BCE," in Scheidel 2001c: 111–37.

Lo Cascio, E. 2003. "Il rapporto uomini-terra nel paesaggio dell'Italia romana." *Index* 32, 1–15.

Lo Cascio, E., and Storchi Marino, A. 2001. *Modalità insediative e strutture agrarie nell'Italia meridionale in età romana.* Bari.

Lomas, K. 1993. *Rome and the Western Greeks 350 BC – AD 200.* London.

Lomas, K. 1996. *Roman Italy, 338 BC–AD 200: A Sourcebook.* London.

Lomas, K. 2004. "Italy during the Roman Republic, 338–31 BC," in Flower 2004b: 199–224.

Long, A. A. 2003. "Roman Philosophy" in D. Sedley (ed.), *The Cambridge Companion to Greek and Roman Philosophy*, 184–210. Cambridge.

Losacco, U. 1944. "Il bacino postpliocenico del Val di Chiana." *L'Universo* 25, 45–73.

Louis, W. R. (ed.) 1976. *Imperialism: The Robinson–Gallagher Controversy.* New York.

Lovano, M. 2002. *The Age of Cinna: Crucible of Late Republican Rome.* Stuttgart.

Luce, T. J. 1977. *Livy: The Composition of His History.* Princeton.

Luce, T. J. (ed.) 1982. *Ancient Writers: Greece and Rome.* 2 vols. New York.

Lundestad, G. 1986. "Empire by Invitation? The United States and Western Europe, 1945–1952." *JPR* 23, 263–77.

Lundestad, G. 1990. *The American "Empire" and Other Studies of U.S. Foreign Policy in Comparative Perspective.* Oxford.

Ma, J. 2000. "Fighting Poleis of the Hellenistic World," in van Wees 2000: 337–76.

MacBain, B. 1982. *Prodigy and Expiation: A Study in Religion and Politics in Republican Rome.* Brussels.

Mack, D. 1937. *Senatsreden und Volksreden bei Cicero.* Hildesheim.

Mackay, C. S. 2000. "Sulla and the Monuments: Studies in his Public Persona," *Historia* 49, 161–210.

Mackie, N. 1992. "*Popularis* Ideology and Popular Politics at Rome in the First Century." *RhM* 135, 12–39.

MacMullen, R. 1974. *Roman Social Relations, 50 B.C. to A.D. 284.* New Haven.

MacMullen, R. 1980. "How Many Romans Voted?" *Athenaeum* 58, 454–7.

MacMullen, R. 1982a. "Roman Attitudes to Greek Love." *Historia* 31, 484–502.

MacMullen, R. 1982b. "The Epigraphic Habit in the Roman Empire." *AJPh* 103, 233–46.

MacMullen, R. 1991. "Hellenizing the Romans (2nd Century B.C.)." *Historia* 40, 419–38.

Magdelain, A. 1964. "Auspicia ad patres redeunt," in M. Renard and R. Schilling (eds.), *Hommages à Jean Bayet*, 427–73. Brussels.

Magdelain, A. 1978. *La loi à Rome: histoire d'un concept.* Paris.

Maier-Eichhorn, U. 1989. *Die Gestikulation in Quintilians Rhetorik.* Frankfurt.

Malaise, M. 1972. *Les conditions de pénetration et de diffusion des cultes égyptiens en Italie.* Leiden.

Malcovati, H. (ed.) 1967. *Oratorum Romanorum Fragmenta*[4]. Turin.

Malitz, J. 1983. *Die Historien des Poseidonios.* Munich.

Malkin, I., and Rubinsohn, Z. (eds.) 1995. *Leaders and Masses in the Roman World: Studies in Honor of Zvi Yavetz.* Leiden.

Malone, C., and Stoddart, S. (eds.) 1994. *Territory, Time and State. The Archaeological Development of the Gubbio Basin.* Cambridge.

Manacorda, D. 1989. "Le anfore dell'Italia repubblicana: aspetti economici e sociali," in *Amphores romaines et histoire économique: dix ans de recherche*, 443–67. Rome.

Manacorda, D. 1994. "Produzione agricola, produzione ceramica e proprietà delle terre nella Calabria romana tra repubblica e impero," in *Epigrafia della produzione e della distribuzione*, 3–59. Rome.

Mandell, S. 1989. "The Isthmian Declaration and the Early Stages of Roman Imperialism in the Near East." *CB* 65, 89–94.

Mandell, S. 1991. "Roman Dominion: Desire and Reality." *AW* 22, 37–42.

Manuwald, G. 2001. Fabulae praetextae: *Spuren einer literarischen Gattung der Römer.* Munich.

Marasco, G. 1986. "Interessi commerciali e fattori politici nella condotta romana in Illiria (230–219 A.C.)." *SCO* 36, 35–112.

Marcadé, J. 1969. *Au Musée de Délos: étude sur la sculpture hellénistique en rondebosse découverte dans l'île.* Paris.

Marcadé, J. 1983. "La sculpture hellénistique," in P. Bruneau and J. Ducat, *Guide de Délos*[3], 56–78. Paris.

Marcone, A. 2002. *Democrazie antiche. Istituzioni e pensiero politico.* Rome.

Marincola, J. M. 1997. *Authority and Tradition in Ancient Historiography.* Cambridge.

Marincola, J. M. 2001. *Greek Historians.* Oxford.

Marshall, A. J. 1984. "Symbols and Showmanship in Roman Public Life: The Fasces." *Phoenix* 38, 120–41.

Marshall, B. A. 1972. "The *Lex Plotia Agraria.*" *Antichthon* 6, 43–52.

Marshall, B. A. 1973. "Crassus and the Command against Spartacus." *Athenaeum* 51, 109–21.

Marshall, B. A. 1976. *Crassus: A Political Biography.* Amsterdam.

Marshall, B. A. 1985. *A Historical Commentary on Asconius.* Columbia, MO.

Marshall, B. A. 1997. "*Libertas populi*: The Introduction of Secret Ballot at Rome and its Depiction on Coinage." *Antichton* 31, 54–73.

Martelli, A. 2002. "Per una nuova lettura dell'iscrizione Vetter 61 nel contesto del santuario di Apollo a Pompei," *Eutopia* n.s. 2.2, 71–81.

Martin, H. G. 1987. *Römische Tempelkultbilder.* Rome.

Martin, J. 1965. "Die Popularen in der Geschichte der späten römischen Republik." Dissertation, University of Freiburg.

Martin, T. R. 1989. "Sulla, *Imperator Iterum*, the Samnites and Roman Republican Coin Propaganda." *Schweizerische Numismatische Rundschau* 68, 19–45.

Martindale, C. 1993. *Redeeming the Text: Latin Poetry and the Hermeneutics of Reception.* Cambridge.

Marvin, M. 1989. "Copying of Roman Sculpture: The Replica Series," in K. Preciado (ed.), *Retaining the Original: Multiple Originals, Copies, and Reproductions,* 29–45. Washington, DC and Hanover.

Mason, K. (ed.) 1944. *Italy.* Oxford.

Mattingly, D., and Aldrete, G. 2000. "The Feeding of Imperial Rome: The Mechanics of the Food Supply System," in Coulston and Dodge 2000: 142–65.

Mattingly, H. B. 1969. "The Two Republican Laws of the *Tabula Bembina.*" *JRS* 59, 129–43.

Maurach, G. 1988. *Der Poenulus des Plautus.* Heidelberg.

May, J. M. (ed.) 2002. *Brill's Companion to Cicero: Oratory and Rhetoric.* Leiden.

May, J. M., and Wisse, J. 2001. *Cicero: On the Ideal Orator (De Oratore).* Oxford.

Mazza, F. 1988. "The Phoenicians as Seen by the Ancient World," in S. Moscati (ed.), *The Phoenicians,* 548–67. New York.

Mazzanti, R., and Pasquinucci, M. 1983. "L'evoluzione del littorale lunense-pisano fino alla metà del XIX secolo." *Bollettino della Società Geografica Italiana* 10–12, 605–28.

McCall, J. B. 2002. *The Cavalry of the Roman Republic.* London.

McDonnell, M. 1990. "Virtus as a Social, Religious, and Political Concept in Republican Rome." Dissertation, Columbia University.

McDonnell, M. 2006. *Roman Manliness: Virtus and the Roman Republic.* Cambridge and New York.

McDonnell, M. forthcoming. "Roman Aesthetics and the Spoils of Syracuse," in Dillon and Welch forthcoming.

McGing, B. C. 1984. "The Date of the Outbreak of the Third Mithridatic War." *Phoenix* 38, 12–18.

McGing, B. C. 1986. *The Foreign Policy of Mithridates VI Eupator, King of Pontus.* Leiden.

McGinn, T. 1998. *Prostitution, Sexuality, and the Law in Ancient Rome.* New York and Oxford.

McGushin, P. 1977. *C. Sallustius Crispus. Bellum Catilinae. A Commentary.* Leiden.

McGushin, P. 1992–4. *Sallust: The Histories.* 2 vols. Oxford.

McIntosh, R. J., Tainter, J. A., and McIntosh, S. K. (eds.) 2000. *The Way the Wind Blows: Climate, History and Human Action.* New York.

McManus, B. 1997. *Classics and Feminism. Gendering the Classics.* New York.

Meadows, A., and Williams, J. H. C. 2001. "Moneta and the Monuments: Coinage and Politics in Republican Rome." *JRS* 91, 27–49.

Mearsheimer, J. J. 2001. *The Tragedy of Great Power Politics.* New York.

Médard, J.-F. 1976. "Le lien de clientèle: du phénomène social à l'analyse politique." *Revue française de Science Politique* 26, 103–31.

Meier, C. 1965. "*Populares.*" *RE* Supplement 10, 549–615.

Meier, C. 1966. Res publica amissa: *Eine Studie zu Verfassung und Geschichte der späten römischen Republik* (rev. ed. 1980). Wiesbaden.

Meier, C. 1978. "Fragen und Thesen zu einer Theorie historischer Prozesse," in K.-G. Faber and C. Meier (eds.), *Historische Prozesse,* 11–66. Munich.

Meier, C. 1980 (= Meier 1966).

Meier, C. 1982. *Caesar. A Biography.* Trans. D. McLintock. New York.

Meiggs, R. 1982. *Trees and Timber in the Ancient Mediterranean World.* Oxford.

Meinel, R. 1980. *Das Odeion. Untersuchungen an überdachten antiken Theatergebäuden.* Frankfurt and Berne.

Meister, K. 1998a. "Genealogie." *DNP* 4, 906–7.

Meister, K. 1998b. "Hellanikos." *DNP* 5, 295–6.

Mellor, R. 1975. *Thea Roma. The Worship of the Goddess Roma in the Greek World.* Göttingen.

Mellor, R. 1999. *The Roman Historians.* London.

Melville, G. (ed.) 2001. *Institutionalität und Symbolisierung. Verstetigungen kultureller Ordnungsmuster in Vergangenheit und Gegenwart.* Cologne.

Menichetti, M. 1995. *"Quoius forma virtutei parisuma fuit". Ciste prenestine e cultura di Roma medio-repubblicana.* Rome.

Merkelbach, R. 1990. "Hat der Bithynische Erbfolgekrieg im Jahre 74 oder 73 begonnen?" *ZPE* 81, 97–100.

Merla, G., Ercoli, A., and Torre, D. 1969. *Note illustrative della Carta geologica d'Italia alla scala 1:100,000.* Naples.

Mertens, J. 1991. "Alba Fucens: à l'aube d'une colonie romaine." *Journal of Ancient Topography* 1, 93–112.

Meyer, E. 1973. *Einführung in die lateinische Epigraphik.* Darmstadt.

Meyer, E. 1999. Review of K. Rigsby, *Asylia: Territorial Inviolability in the Hellenistic World.* *AJPh* 120, 460–1.

Michalowski, L. 1932. "Les portraits hellénistiques et romains," in Th. Homolle, M. Holleaux, G. Fougères, Ch. Picard, and R. Roussel (eds.), *Exploration archéologique de Délos faite par l'École française d'Athènes,* 13.1–63. Paris.

Michel, D. 1967. *Alexander als Vorbild für Pompeius, Caesar und Marcus Antonius.* Brussels.

Michels, A. K. 1967. *The Calendar of the Roman Republic* (repr. 1978). Princeton.

Midlarsky, M. I. 1988. *The Onset of World War.* Boston.

Mielsch, H. 1987. *Die römische Villa: Architektur und Lebensform.* Munich.

Miles, G. B. 1986. "The Cycle of Roman History in Livy's First Pentad." *AJPh* 107, 1–33.

Miles, G. B. 1988. *"Maiores, conditores* and Livy's Perspective on the Past." *TAPhA* 118, 185–208.

Miles, G. B. 1995. *Livy: Reconstructing Early Rome.* Ithaca and London.

Millar, F. 1964. *A Study of Cassius Dio.* Oxford.

Millar, F. 1984. "The Political Character of the Classical Roman Republic, 200–151 B.C." *JRS* 74, 1–19, (=Millar 2002b: 109–42).

Millar, F. 1986. "Politics, Persuasion and the People before the Social War (150–90 BC)." *JRS* 76, 1–11 (=Millar 2002b: 143–61).

Millar, F. 1988. "Cornelius Nepos, 'Atticus' and the Roman Revolution." *G&R* 35, 40–55 (=Millar 2002b: 183–99).

Millar, F. 1989. "Political Power in Mid-Republican Rome: Curia or Comitium?" *JRS* 79, 138–50, (=Millar 2002b: 85–108).

Millar, F. 1995. "Popular Politics at Rome in the Late Republic," in Malkin and Rubinsohn 1995: 91–113 (= Millar 2002b: 162–82).

Millar, F. 1998. *The Crowd in Rome in the Late Republic.* Ann Arbor.

Millar, F. 2002a. *The Roman Republic in Political Thought.* Hanover and London.

Millar, F. 2002b. *Rome, the Greek World, and the East, I: The Roman Republic and the Augustan Revolution,* ed. H. M. Cotton and G. M. Rogers. Chapel Hill and London.

Mitchell, R. E. 1986. "The Definition of *Patres* and *Plebs,*" in Raaflaub 1986: 130–74.

Mitchell, R. E. 1990. *Patricians and Plebeians: the Origin of the Roman State.* Ithaca.

Mitchell, T. N. 1975. "The *Volte-Face* of P. Sulpicius Rufus in 88 B.C." *CPh* 70, 197–204.

Mitchell, T. N. 1979. *Cicero: The Ascending Years.* New Haven.

Mitchell, T. N. 1991. *Cicero: The Senior Statesman.* New Haven.

Mitens, K. 1988. *Teatri Greci e Teatri Ispirati all' Achitettura Greca in Sicilia e nell' Italia Meridionale.* Rome.

Moatti, C. 1993. *Archives et partage de la terre dans le monde romain (IIe siècle avant – Ier siècle après J.-C.).* Rome.

Mocchegiani Carpano, C. 1995. "Emporium." *LTUR* 2, 221–3.

Moles, J. 1993. "Livy's Preface." *PCPhS* 39, 141–68.

Molho, A., Raaflaub, K., and Emlen, J. (eds.) 1991. *City States in Classical Antiquity and Medieval Italy.* Stuttgart and Ann Arbor.

Möller, C. 1993. "Die mercennarii in der römischen Arbeitswelt." *ZRG* 110, 296–330.

Momigliano, A. 1963. "An Interim Report on the Origins of Rome." *JRS* 53, 95–121.

Momigliano, A. 1975. *Alien Wisdom: The Limits of Hellenization.* Cambridge.

Momigliano, A. 1989. "The Origins of Rome," in Walbank et al. 1989: 52–112.

Momigliano, A. 1990. *The Classical Foundations of Modern Historiography.* Berkeley.

Momigliano, A., and Schiavone, A. (eds.) 1988–. *Storia di Roma.* Turin.

Mommsen, T. 1864. "Das römische Gastrecht und die römische Clientel," in *Römische Forschungen* 1.319–90. Berlin.

Mommsen, T. 1881–6. *Römische Geschichte*[7], 5 vols. (repr. 1976, Munich). Berlin.

Mommsen, T. 1887–8. *Römisches Staatsrecht*[3], 3 vols. Leipzig.

Mommsen, T. 1899. *Römisches Strafrecht.* Leipzig.

Mommsen, T. 1907 (= Mommsen 1881–6).

Mommsen, T. 1996 (Reprint of 1894 edition). *The History of Rome.* Trans. W. P. Dickson. 5 vols. London.

Mora, F. 1990. *Prosopografia Isiaca 2: Prosopografia storica e statistica del culto Isiaco.* Leiden.

Morel, J.-P. 1981. "La produzione della ceramica campana: aspetti economici e sociali," in Giardina and Schiavone 1981: 2.81–97.

Morel, J.-P. 1983. "Les producteurs de bien artisanaux à la fin de la république," in *Les "bourgeoisies" municipales italiennes aux II et I siècles av. J.-C.,* 21–39. Rome.

Morel, J.-P. 1989. "The Transformation of Italy, 300–133 BC: The Evidence of Archaeology", in Walbank et al. 1989: 477–516.

Morello, R. 2002. "Livy's Alexander Digression (9.17–19): counterfactuals and apologetics." *JRS* 92, 62–85.

Morgan, L. W. G. 1997. "*'Levi quidem de re . . .'*: Julius Caesar as Tyrant and Pedant." *JRS* 87, 23–40.

Morgan, M. G. 1990. "The Perils of Schematicism: Polybius, Antiochus Epiphanes, and the 'Day of Eleusis.'" *Historia* 39, 37–76.

Morgan, M. G., and Walsh, J. A. 1978. "Ti. Gracchus (tr. pl. 133 B.C.), the Numantine Affair, and the Deposition of M. Octavius." *CPh* 73, 200–20.

Morgenthau, H. J. 1973. *Politics Among Nations: The Struggle for Power and Peace.*[5] New York.

Morley, N. 1996. *Metropolis and Hinterland: The City of Rome and the Italian Economy.* Cambridge.

Morley, N. 2001. "The Transformation of Italy, 225–28 B.C." *JRS* 91, 50–62.

Morley, N. 2003. "Migration and the Metropolis," in Edwards and Woolf 2003: 147–57.

Morris, J. 1968. *Pax Britannia: The Climax of an Empire.* New York.

Morstein-Marx, R. 1998. "Publicity, Popularity and Patronage in the *Commentariolum Petitionis.*" *ClAnt* 17, 259–88.

Morstein-Marx, R. 2000. "The Alleged "Massacre" at Cirta and its Consequences (Sallust, *Bellum Iugurthinum* 26–7)." *CPh* 95, 468–76.

Morstein-Marx, R. 2004. *Mass Oratory and Political Power in the Late Roman Republic.* Cambridge.

Mouritsen, H. 1998. *Italian Unification: A Study in Ancient and Modern Historiography.* London.

Mouritsen, H. 2001. *Plebs and Politics in the Late Roman Republic.* Cambridge.

Münzer, F. 1910. "A. Gabinius (6–10)." *RE* 7.1, 423–4.

Münzer, F. 1999. *Roman Aristocratic Parties and Families.* Trans. T. Ridley. Baltimore and London (Originally published 1920).

Mura Sommella, A. 1997–8. "Le recenti scoperte sul Campidoglio e la fondazione del tempio di Giove Capitolino." *RPAA* 70, 57–79.

Mura Sommella, A. 2000. "'La grande Roma dei Tarquini.' Alterne vicende di una felice intuizione." *BCAR* 101, 7–26.

Mura Sommella, A. 2001. "Notizie preliminari sulle scoperte e sulle indagini archeologiche nel versante orientale del Capitolium." *BCAR* 102, 263–4.

Murphy, T. 2004. *Pliny The Elder's Natural Histories. The Empire in the Encyclopedia.* Oxford.

Murray, O. 1993. *Early Greece*[2]. Cambridge.

Museo civico archeologico-etnologico (Modena, Italy). 1983. *Misurare la terra: centuriazione e coloni nel mondo romano.* Modena.

Nappo, S. C. 1997. "Urban Transformation at Pompeii in the Late Third and Early Second Centuries B.C.," in Laurence and Wallace-Hadrill 1997: 91–120.

Narducci, E. 1989. *Modelli etici e società. Un'idea di Cicerone.* Pisa.

Narducci, E. 1997. *Cicerone e l'eloquenza romana: Retorica e progetto culturale.* Rome.

Nash, E. 1968. *Pictorial Dictionary of Ancient Rome*[2]. New York.

Neudecker, R. 1988. *Die Skulpturen-Ausstattung römischer Villen in Italien.* Mainz.

Neuhauser, W. 1958. *Patronus und orator.* Innsbruck.

Nicolet, C. 1966–74. *L'ordre équestre à l'époque républicaine (312–43 av. J.-C.)*, 2 vols. Paris.

Nicolet, C. 1975. "P. Terentius Hispo et la société de Bithynie." *AEHE* (IV sect.), 373–8.

Nicolet, C. 1977. *Rome et la conquête du monde méditerranéen, 1, Les structures de l'Italie romaine.* Paris.

Nicolet, C. 1980. *The World of the Citizen in Republican Rome.* Trans. P. S. Falla. Berkeley and Los Angeles.

Nicolet, C. 1994. "Economy and Society, 133–43 B.C.," in Crook, Lintott, and Rawson 1994: 599–643.

Nicolet, C., and Ferrary, J.-L. 1983. *Demokratia et Aristokratia.* Paris

Nielsen, I., and Poulsen, B. (eds.) 1992. *The Temple of Castor and Pollux.* Rome.

Niemeier, J.-P. 1985. *Kopien und Nachahmungen in Hellenismus.* Bonn.

Nippel, W. 1995. *Public Order in Ancient Rome.* Cambridge.

Nora, P. 1984. "Entre histoire et mémoire. La problématique des lieux," in P. Nora (ed.), *Les lieux de mémoire.* Vol. 1: *La République,* xv–xlii. Paris (= Nora 1996).

Nora, P. 1996. "Between Memory and History," in P. Nora (ed.), *Realms of Memory.* Trans. A. Goldhammer, 1–20. New York.

Nörr, D. 1991. *Die Fides in römische Völkerrecht.* Heidelberg.

North, J. 1979. "Religious Toleration in Republican Rome." *PCPhS* 25, 85–103.

North, J. 1981. "The Development of Roman Imperialism." *JRS* 71, 1–9.

North, J. 1990a. "Family Strategy and Priesthood in the Late Republic," in J. Andreau and H. Bruhns (eds.), *Parenté et stratégies familiales dans l'antiquité romaine,* 527–43. Rome.

North, J. 1990b. "Democratic Politics in Republican Rome." *P&P* 126, 3–21 (= R. Osborne (ed.) 2004. *Studies in Ancient Greek and Roman Society,* 140–58. Cambridge).

North, J. 1990c. "Politics and Aristocracy in the Roman Republic." *CPh* 85, 277–87.

North, J. 2000. *Roman Religion*. Oxford.

North, J. 2002. "Introduction: Pursuing Democracy," in A. K. Bowman, H. M. Cotton, M. Goodman, and S. Price (eds.), *Representations of Empire: Rome and the Mediterranean World*, 1–12. Oxford.

Northwood, S. J. forthcoming. "Cicero on Historiography; a Revised Interpretation." *Mnemosyne*.

Noy, D. 2000. *Foreigners at Rome: Citizens and Strangers*. London.

Nunnerich-Asmus, A. 1994. *Basilika und Portikus. Die Architektur der Säulenhallen als Ausdruck gewandelter Urbanität in später Republik und früher Kaiserzeit*. Weimar, Cologne, and Vienna.

Oakley, S. P. 1985. "Single Combat in the Roman Republic." *CQ* 35, 392–410.

Oakley, S. P. 1993. "The Roman Conquest of Italy," in Rich and Shipley 1993: 9–37.

Oakley, S. P. 1997–2004. *A Commentary on Livy, Books VI–X*. 3 vols. Oxford.

Offner, A. 1995. "Going to War in 1914: A Matter of Honor?" *Politics and Society* 23, 213–41.

Ogilvie, R. M. 1965. *A Commentary on Livy Books 1–5* (2nd ed. 1970), Oxford.

Olshausen, E. 1972. "Mithradates VI. und Rom." *ANRW* 1.1, 806–15.

Orlin, E. M. 1997. *Temples, Religion, and Politics in the Roman Republic*. Leiden.

Ortolani, F., and Pagliuca, S. 2003. *Variazioni climatiche cicliche e modificazioni ambientali nel periodo storico*, in C. Albore Livadie and F. Ortolani (eds.), *Variazioni climatico-ambientali e impatto sull'uomo nell'area circum-mediterranea durante l'Olocene*, 165–70. Bari.

Pailler, J.-M. 1988. *Bacchanalia: La répression de 186 av. J.-C. à Rome et en Italie: vestiges, images, tradition*. Rome.

Pairault Massa, F. H. 1992. *Iconologia e Politica nell'Italia Antica Roma, Lazio, Etruria dal VII al I secolo a. C.* Milan.

Pais, E. 1916. "I dodici Romani fatti dichiarare pubblici nemici da Silla nell'88 a.C." *AAN* 4.1, 67–72.

Pallottino, M. 1991. *A History of Earliest Italy*. Trans. M. Ryle and K. Soper. London.

Palmer, R. E. A. 1997. *Rome and Carthage at Peace*. Stuttgart.

Pani, M. 1997. *La politica in Roma antica: cultura e passi*. Rome.

Pape, M. 1975. *Griechische Kunstwerke aus Kriegsbeute und ihre öffentliche Aufstellung in Rom: von der Eroberung von Syrakus bis in augusteische Zeit*. Hamburg.

Parker, A. J. 1992. *Ancient Shipwrecks of the Mediterranean and the Roman Provinces*. Oxford.

Parker, H. 1997. "The Teratogenic Grid," in Hallett and Skinner 1997: 47–65.

Parkin, T. 1992. *Demography and Roman Society*. Baltimore and London.

Parkin, T. 2003. *Old Age in the Roman World. A Cultural and Social History*. Baltimore.

Parkins, H. M. (ed.) 1997a. *Roman Urbanism: Beyond the Consumer City*. London.

Parkins, H. M. 1997b. "The 'Consumer City' Domesticated? The Roman City in Elite Economic Strategies," in Parkins 1997a: 83–111.

Passerini, A. 1971. *Studi su Caio Mario*. Milan.

Patterson, H., Di Giuseppe, H., and Witcher, R. 2004. "Three South Etrurian 'Crises': First Results of the Tiber Valley Project." *PBSR* 72, 1–36.

Patterson, J. R. 1992a. "Patronage, *Collegia* and Burial in Imperial Rome," in S. Bassett (ed.), *Death in Towns: Urban Responses to the Dead and Dying, 100–1600*, 15–27. Leicester.

Patterson, J. R. 1992b. "The City of Rome: From Republic to Empire." *JRS* 82, 186–215.

Patterson, J. R. 1993. "Military Organization and Social Change in the Later Roman Republic," in Rich and Shipley 1993: 92–112.

Patterson, J. R. 1994. "The *Collegia* and the Transformation of the Towns of Italy in the Second Century AD," in *L'Italie d'Auguste à Dioclétien*, 227–38. Rome.

Patterson, J. R. 2000a. *Political Life in the City of Rome*. London.

Patterson, J. R. 2000b. "On the Margins of the City of Rome," in Hope and Marshall 2000: 85–103.

Patterson, J. R. 2000c. "Living and Dying in the City of Rome: Houses and Tombs," in Coulston and Dodge 2000: 259–89.

Patterson, J. R. 2004. "City, Territory and Metropolis: the Case of the Tiber Valley," in H. Patterson (ed.), *Bridging the Tiber. Approaches to Regional Archaeology in the Middle Tiber Valley*, 61–73. London.

Patterson, O. 1982. *Slavery and Social Death: A Comparative Study.* Cambridge.

Paul, G. M. 1984. *A Historical Commentary on Sallust's Bellum Jugurthinum*. Liverpool.

Pelling, C. B. R. (ed.) 1990a. *Characterization and Individuality in Greek Literature*. Oxford.

Pelling, C. B. R. 1990b. "Truth and Fiction in Plutarch's *Lives*," in D. A. Russell (ed.), *Antonine Literature*, 19–52. Oxford.

Perelli, L. 1993. *I Gracchi*. Rome.

Pesando, F. 1997. *Domus. Edilizia privata e società pompeiana fra III e I secolo a.C.* Rome.

Peter, H. (ed.) 1906–14. *Historicorum Romanorum Reliquiae²* (repr. 1967). Leipzig.

Petersen, L. H. 2003. "The Baker, His Tomb, His Wife, and Her Breadbasket: The Monument of Eurysaces in Rome." *Art Bulletin* 85, 230–57.

Petsas, Ph. M. 1966. *O Taphos ton Lefkadion*. Athens.

Piccirilli, L. 1973. *Gli arbitrati interstatali greci*. Pisa.

Pietilä-Castrén, L. 1987. *Magnificentia Publica. The Victory Monuments of the Roman Generals in the Era of the Punic Wars*. Helsinki.

Pina Polo, F. 1989. *Las contiones civiles y militares en Roma*. Zaragoza.

Pina Polo, F. 1996. *Contra arma verbis: Der Redner vor dem Volk in der späten römischen Republik*. Stuttgart.

Pirson, F. 1997. "Rented Accommodation at Pompeii: The Evidence of the Insula Arriana Polliana VI. 6," in Laurence and Wallace-Hadrill 1997: 165–81.

Pisani Sartorio, G. 1996. "Macellum." *LTUR* 3, 201–3.

Platner, S. B., and Ashby, T. 1929. *A Topographical Dictionary of Ancient Rome*. London.

Pobjoy, M. P. 1997. "A New Reading of the Mosaic Inscription in the Temple of Diana Tifatina." *PBSR* 65, 59–88.

Pobjoy, M. P. 1998. "The Decree of the Pagus Herculaneus and the Romanisation of 'Oscan' Capua." *Arctos* 32, 175–95.

Pobjoy, M. P. 2000a. "Building Inscriptions in Republican Italy: Euergetism, Responsibility, and Civic Virtue," in A. E. Cooley (ed.), *The Epigraphic Landscape of Roman Italy*, 77–92. London.

Pobjoy, M. P. 2000b. "The First *Italia*," in E. Herring and K. Lomas (eds.), *The Emergence of State Identities in Italy in the First Millennium BC*, 187–211. London.

Pollitt, J. J. 1966. *The Art of Rome c. 753 B.C.–337 A.D. Sources and Documents*. Englewood Cliffs.

Pollitt, J. J. 1978. "The Impact of Greek Art on Rome." *TAPhA* 108, 155–74.

Pollitt, J. J. 1986. *Art in the Hellenistic Age*. Cambridge.

Pomeroy, S. B. 1975. *Goddesses, Whores, Wives, and Slaves. Women in Classical Antiquity.* London.

Pontrandolfo, A., and Rouveret, A. 1992. *Le Tombe dipinte di Paestum*. Modena.

Porter, A. N. 1980. *The Origins of the South African War: Joseph Chamberlain and the Diplomacy of Imperialism, 1895–1899*. Manchester.

Potter, D. S. 1999. *Literary Texts and the Roman Historian*. London.

Potter, T. 1976. "Valleys and Settlement: Some New Evidence." *World Archaeology* 8, 207–19.

Potter, T. 1979. *The changing landscape of South Etruria*. London.

Potter, T. 1987. *Roman Italy*. London.

Potter, T. 1991. "Towns and Territories in Southern Etruria," in Rich and Wallace-Hadrill 1991: 191–209.

Poucet, J. 1985. *Les origines de Rome. Tradition et histoire*. Brussels.

Powell, A. 1998. "Julius Caesar and the Presentation of Massacre," in Welch and Powell 1998: 111–37.

Powell, J. G. F. 1990. "The Tribune Sulpicius." *Historia* 39, 446–60.

Powell, J. G. F., and North, J. A. 2001. *Cicero's Republic*. London.

Pozzi, E. 1913–14. "Studi sulla Guerra Civile Sillana." *AAT* 49, 641–79.

Prandi, L. 1979. "La 'fides punica' e il pregiudizio anticartaginese," in M. Sordi (ed.), *Conoscenze etniche e rapporti di convivenza nell' antichità*, 90–7. Milan.

Prayon, F. 2000. "L'architettura funeraria," in Torelli 2000: 335–43.

Preisshofen, F., and Zanker, P. 1970–1. "Reflex einer eklektischen Kunstanschauung beim Auctor ad Herennium." *DArch* 4–5, 100–19.

Premerstein, A. von. 1900. "Clientes." *RE* 4, 23–55.

Pritchett, W. K. 1974. *The Greek State at War*, 5 vols. Berkeley and Los Angeles.

Proietti, G. 1980. *Il Museo Nazionale Etrusco di Villa Giulia*. Rome.

Pugliese Carratelli, G. (ed.) 1990–. *Pompei, Pitture e Mosaici*. 11 vols. Rome.

Purcell, N. 1987. "Tomb and Suburb," in Hesberg and Zanker 1987: 25–41.

Purcell, N. 1990. "The Creation of Provincial Landscape: The Roman Impact on Cisalpine Gaul," in T. Blagg and M. Millett (eds.), *The Early Roman Empire in the West*, 7–29. Oxford.

Purcell, N. 1994. "The city of Rome and the *plebs urbana* in the late Republic," in Crook, Lintott, and Rawson 1994: 644–88.

Purcell, N. 1995. "Forum Romanum (the Republican Period)." *LTUR* 2, 325–36.

Quilici, L., and Quilici Gigli, S. 1995. "Un grande santuario fuori la porta occidentale di Tusculum." *Archeologia Laziale* 12, 509–34.

Raaflaub, K. 1977. *Dignitatis contentio. Studien zur Motivation und politischen Taktik im Bürgerkrieg zwischen Caesar und Pompeius*. Munich.

Raaflaub, K. (ed.) 1986. *Social Struggles in Archaic Rome: New Perspectives on the Struggle of the Orders*. Berkeley and Los Angeles (2nd ed., rev. 2005. Oxford).

Raaflaub, K. 1988. "Athenische Geschichte und mündliche Überlieferung," in Ungern-Sternberg and Reinau 1988: 197–225.

Raaflaub, K. 1990. "Expansion und Machtbildung in frühen Polis-Systemen," in Eder 1990: 511–45.

Raaflaub, K. 1991. "City-State, Territory, and Empire in Classical Antiquity," in Molho, Raaflaub, and Emlen 1991: 565–88.

Raaflaub, K. 1993. "Politics and Society in Fifth-Century Rome," in *Bilancio Critico su Roma arcaica fra monarchia e repubblica*, 129–57. Rome.

Raaflaub, K. 1996. "Born to be Wolves? Origins of Roman Imperialism," in Wallace and Harris 1996: 271–314.

Raaflaub, K. 2005 (= Raaflaub 1986).

Raaflaub, K. forthcoming a. "Romulus und die Wölfin: Roms Anfänge zwischen Mythos und Geschichte," in E. Stein-Hölkeskamp and K.-J. Hölkeskamp (eds.), *Erinnerungsorte der römischen Antike*. Munich.

Raaflaub, K. forthcoming b. "Epic and History," in J. M. Foley (ed.), *The Blackwell Companion to Ancient Epic*. Oxford.

Raaflaub, K., Richards, J. D., and Samons II, K. J. 1992. "Appius Claudius Caecus, Rome, and Italy before the Pyrrhic War," in T. Hackens, N. Holloway, R. Holloway, and G. Moucharte (eds.), *The Age of Pyrrhus*, 273–314. Louvain.

Raaflaub, K., and Rosenstein, N. (eds.) 1999. *War and Society in the Ancient and Medieval Worlds*. Washington, DC and Cambridge, MA.

Rajak, T., and Noy, D. 1993. "*Archisynagogoi*: Office, Title and Social Status in the Greco-Jewish Synagogue." *JRS* 83, 75–93.

Rasmussen, T. 1979. *Bucchero Pottery from Southern Etruria*. London.

Rasmussen, T. 1991. "Tuscania and its Territory," in Barker and Lloyd 1991: 106–14.

Rathbone, D. 1981. "The Development of Agriculture in the 'Ager Cosanus' during the Roman Republic: Problems of Evidence and Interpretation." *JRS* 71, 10–23.

Rathbone, D. 1983. "The Slave Mode of Production in Italy." *JRS* 73, 160–8.

Rathbone, D. 1993a. "The Census Qualifications of the *Assidui* and the *Prima Classis*," in Sancisi-Weerdenburg et al. 1993: 121–52.

Rathbone, D. 1993b. "The Italian Countryside and the Gracchan 'Crisis'." *JACT Review* 13, 18–20.

Rathbone, D. 2003. "The Control and Exploitation of *ager publicus* in Italy during the Roman Republic," in J.-J. Aubert (ed.), *Tâches publiques et enterprise privée dans le monde romain*, 135–8. Neuchâtel.

Rauh, N. K. 1993. *The Sacred Bonds of Commerce: Religion, Economy, and Trade Society at Hellenistic Roman Delos, 166–87 BC*. Amsterdam.

Rawlings, L. 1998. "Caesar's Portrayal of Gauls as Warriors," in Welch and Powell 1998: 171–92.

Rawlings, L. 1999. "Condottieri and Clansmen. Early Italian Warfare and the State," in K. Hopwood (ed.), *Organized Crime in the Ancient World*, 97–127. Swansea.

Rawson, B. 1989. "'Spurii' and the Roman View of Illegitimacy." *Antichthon* 23, 10–41.

Rawson, B. (ed.) 1991. *Marriage, Divorce and Children in Ancient Rome*. Oxford.

Rawson, B. 2003. *Children and Childhood in Roman Italy*. Oxford and New York.

Rawson, B., and Weaver, P. (eds.) 1997. *The Roman Family in Italy: Status, Sentiment, Space*. Oxford and New York.

Rawson, E. 1971a. "Prodigy Lists and the Use of the *Annales Maximi*." *CQ* 21, 158–69 (= Rawson 1991: 1–15).

Rawson, E. 1971b. "The Literary Sources for the Pre-Marian Army," *PBSR* 39, 13–31 (=Rawson 1991: 34–57).

Rawson, E. 1985. *Intellectual Life in the Late Roman Republic*. London and Baltimore.

Rawson, E. 1986. "The Expansion of Rome," in *The Oxford Illustrated History of the Roman World*, 39–59. Oxford.

Rawson, E. 1990. "The Antiquarian Tradition: Spoils and Representations of Foreign Armor," in Eder 1990: 158–73.

Rawson, E. 1991. *Roman Culture and Society: Collected Papers*. Oxford.

Rawson, E. 1994a. *Cicero: a Portrait*. Bristol.

Rawson, E. 1994b. "Caesar: Civil War and Dictatorship," in Crook, Lintott, and Rawson 1994: 424–67.

Rebenich, S. 2002. *Theodor Mommsen: Eine Biographie*. Munich.

Reinhold, M. 1984. *Classica Americana*. Detroit.

Reynolds, J. 1982. *Aphrodisias and Rome*. London.

Rich, J. 1976. *Declaring War in the Roman Republic in the Period of Transmarine Expansion.* Brussels.

Rich, J. 1983. "The Supposed Manpower Shortage of the Later Second Century B.C." *Historia* 32, 287–31.

Rich, J. 1989. "Patronage and International Relations in the Roman Republic," in Wallace-Hadrill 1989b: 117–35.

Rich, J. 1993. "Fear, Greed and Glory: The Causes of Roman War-Making in the Middle Republic," in Rich and Shipley 1993: 38–68.

Rich, J. 1996. "The Origins of the Second Punic War," in T. J. Cornell, N. B. Rankov, and P. A. G. Sabin (eds.), *The Second Punic War: A Reappraisal,* 1–37. London.

Rich, J. 1997. "Structuring Roman History: the Consular Year and the Roman Historical Tradition." *Histos* 1 (http://www.dur.ac.uk/Classics/histos/1997/rich1.html).

Rich, J. 1998. "Warfare in Early Rome," in M. Pearce and M. Tosi (eds.), *Papers from the EAA third annual meeting at Ravenna 1997,* 2.5–7. Oxford.

Rich, J., and Shipley, G. (eds.) 1993. *War and Society in the Roman World.* London.

Rich, J., and Wallace-Hadrill, A. (eds.) 1991. *City and Country in the Ancient World.* London.

Richard, C. J. 1994. *The Founders and the Classics.* Cambridge.

Richardson, E. H., and Richardson, L., Jr. 1966. "*Ad Cohibendum Bracchium Toga*: An Archaeological Examination of Cicero, *Pro Caelio* 5.11." *YClS* 19, 253–69.

Richardson, J. 1976. "The Spanish Mines and the Development of Provincial Taxation in the Second Century B.C." *JRS* 66, 139–52.

Richardson, J. 1979. "Polybius' View of the Roman Empire." *PBSR* 47, 1–11.

Richardson, J. 1980. "The Ownership of Italian Land: Tiberius Gracchus and the Italians." *JRS* 70, 1–11.

Richardson, J. 1986. *Hispaniae: Spain and the Development of Roman Imperialism, 218–82 BC.* Cambridge.

Richardson, J. 1987. "The Purpose of the *Lex Calpurnia de Repetundis*." *JRS* 77, 1–12.

Richardson, J. 1991. "*Imperium Romanum*: Empire and the Language of Power." *JRS* 81, 1–9.

Richardson, J. 1994. "The Administration of the Empire," in Crook, Lintott, and Rawson 1994: 564–98.

Richardson, J. 2000. *Appian. The Wars of the Romans in Iberia.* Warminster.

Richardson, L., Jr. 1988. *Pompeii: an Architectural History.* Baltimore.

Richardson, L., Jr. 1991. "Urban Development in Ancient Rome and the Impact of Empire," in Molho, Raaflaub, and Emlen 1991: 381–402.

Richardson, L., Jr. 1992. *A New Topographical Dictionary of Ancient Rome.* Baltimore.

Richlin, A. 1983. *The Garden of Priapus. Sexuality and Aggression in Roman Humor.* New Haven.

Richlin, A. 1993. "Not Before Homosexuality." *Journal of the History of Sexuality* 3, 523–73.

Richlin, A. 1997. "Gender and Rhetoric: Producing Manhood in the Schools," in W. Dominik (ed.), *Roman Eloquence. Rhetoric in Society and Literature,* 90–110. New York and London.

Richlin, A. 1999. "Cicero's Head," in J. I. Porter (ed.), *Constructions of the Classical Body,* 190–211. Ann Arbor.

Rickman, G. 1971. *Roman Granaries and Store Buildings.* Cambridge.

Rickman, G. 1980. *The Corn Supply of Ancient Rome.* Oxford.

Ridgway, B. 1984. *Roman Copies of Greek Sculpture. The Problem of the Originals.* Ann Arbor.

Ridgway, B. 1990–2002. *Hellenistic Sculpture,* 3 vols. Madison.

Ridley, R. T. 1986. "The Genesis of a Turning-Point: Gelzer's *Nobilität*." *Historia* 35, 474–502.

Riggsby, A. M. 1999. *Crime and Community in Ciceronian Rome.* Austin.

Rilinger, R. 1982. "Die Interpretation des Niedergangs der römischen Republik durch 'Revolution' und 'Krise ohne Alternative'." *AKG* 64, 279–306.

Rinkewitz, W. 1984. *Pastio Villatica. Untersuchungen zur intensiven Hoftierhaltung in der römischen Landwirtschaft.* Frankfurt.

Rizzo, G. E. 1936. *Monumenti della pittura antica III, Fasc. I: La Casa dei Grifi.* Rome.

Robinson, O. F. 1997. *The Sources of Roman Law: Problems and Methods for Ancient Historians.* London and New York.

Robinson, R. 1972. "Non-European Foundations of European Imperialism: Sketch for a Theory of Imperialism," in R. Owen and B. Sutcliffe, *Studies in the Theory of Imperialism,* 117–41.

Robinson, R., and Gallagher, J. 1961. *Africa and the Victorians: The Official Mind of Imperialism.* London.

Robinson, R., and Gallagher, J. 1962. "The Partition of Africa," in F. H. Hinsley (ed.), *The New Cambridge Modern History,* 9.593–640. Cambridge.

Roller, M. B. 2004. "Exemplarity in Roman Culture: The Cases of Horatius Cocles and Cloelia." *CPh* 99, 1–56.

Rosafio, P. 1993. "The emergence of tenancy and the *precarium*," in Sancisi-Weerdenburg et al. 1993: 164–76.

Rose, C. B. forthcoming. "Forging Identity in the Roman Republic: Veristic Portraiture and Trojan Ancestry," in *Role Models: Identity and Assimilation in the Roman World and in Early Modern Italy.* Ann Arbor.

Rosenberger, V. 1998. *Gezähmte Götter: Das Prodigienwesen der römischen Republik.* Stuttgart.

Rosenstein, N. 1990. *Imperatores Victi. Military Defeat and Aristocratic Competition in the Middle and Late Republic.* Berkeley and Los Angeles.

Rosenstein, N. 1992. "Nobilitas and The Political Implications of Military Defeat." *AHB* 6, 117–26.

Rosenstein, N. 1993. "Competition and Crisis in Mid-Republican Rome." *Phoenix* 47, 313–38.

Rosenstein, N. 1995. "Sorting Out the Lot in Republican Rome." *AJP* 115, 43–75.

Rosenstein, N. 1999. "Republican Rome," in Raaflaub and Rosenstein 1999: 193–216.

Rosenstein, N. 2002. "Marriage and Manpower in the Hannibalic War: *Assidui, proletarii* and Livy 24.14.7–8." *Historia* 51, 163–91.

Rosenstein, N. 2004. *Rome at War. Farms, Families, and Death in the Middle Republic.* Chapel Hill.

Rossi Doria, M. 1963. *Memoria Illustrativa della Carta della Utilizzazione del Suolo della Basilicata.* Rome.

Rostovtzeff, M. 1922. "International Relations in the Ancient World," in E. Walsh (ed.), *The History and Nature of International Relations.* London.

Roth, J. 1999. *The Logistics of the Roman Army at War (264 BC–AD 235).* Leiden.

Rouland, N. 1979. *Pouvoir politique et dépendance personnelle dans l'Antiquité romaine.* Brussels.

Rowland, R. J. 1983. "Rome's Earliest Imperialism." *Latomus* 42, 749–62.

Royo, M. 1999. *Domus Imperatoriae: topographie, formation et imaginaire des palais impériaux du Palatin.* Rome.

Ruocco, D. 1970. *Memoria Illustrativa della Carta della Utilizzazione del Suolo della Campania.* Rome.

Rüpke, J. 1990. *Domi militiae. Die religiöse Konstruktion des Krieges in Rom.* Stuttgart.

Rüpke, J. 1995a. "Fasti: Quellen oder Produkte römischer Geschichtsschreibung?" *Klio* 77, 184–202.

Rüpke, J. 1995b. *Kalender und Öffentlichkeit: Die Geschichte der Repräsentation und religiösen Qualifikation von Zeit in Rom.* Berlin.

Rüpke, J. 1996. "Charismatics or Professionals? Analyzing Religious Specialists." *Numen* 43, 241–62.

Rüpke, J. 2001a. "Kulturtransfer als Rekodierung: Überlegungen zum literaturgeschichtlichen und sozialen Ort der frühen römischen Epik," in J. Rüpke (ed.), *Von Menschen und Göttern erzählen: Formkonstanzen und Funktionswandel vormoderner Epik*, 42–64. Stuttgart.

Rüpke, J. 2001b. "Antike Religion als Kommunikation," in K. Brodersen (ed.), *Gebet und Fluch, Zeichen und Traum: Aspekte religiöser Kommunikation in der Antike*, 13–30. Münster.

Rüpke, J. 2001c. *Die Religion der Römer: Eine Einführung.* Munich (= J. Rüpke forthcoming. *The Religion of the Romans: An Introduction.* Trans. Richard Gordon).

Rüpke, J. 2005. *Fasti sacerdotum: die Mitglieder der Priesterschaften und das sakrale Funktions-personal römischer, griechischer, orientalischer und jüdisch-christlicher Kulte in der Stadt Rom von 300 v. Chr. bis 499 n. Chr.* 3 vols. Stuttgart.

Rüpke, J. forthcoming. "Triumphator and Ancestor Rituals between Symbolic Anthropology and Magic," in I. Gildenhard (ed.), *New Approaches to the Roman Republic.* Cambridge.

Rutter, K. (ed.) 2001. *Historia Numorum: Italy*³. London.

Ryan, F. X. 1998. *Rank and Participation in the Republican Senate.* Stuttgart.

Ryan, F. X. 2001. "Knappe Mehrheiten bei der Wahl zum Konsul." *Klio* 83, 402–24.

Ryan, F. X. 2002–3. "Abstand vom Ziel und Abstand zum Gegner bei der Wahl zum Konsul." *ACD* 18–19, 303–12.

Ryberg, I. S. 1955. *Rites of the Roman State Religion in Roman Art.* Rome.

Sabin, P. 2000. "The Face of Roman Battle." *JRS* 90, 1–17.

Sacks, K. S. 1990. *Diodorus Siculus and the First Century.* Princeton.

Säflund, G. 1932. *Le mura di Roma repubblicana.* Lund.

Salerno, F. 1999. *"Tacita libertas". L'introduzione del voto segreto nella Roma repubblicana.* Naples.

Sallares, R. 2002. *Malaria and Rome: A History of Malaria in Ancient Italy.* Oxford.

Saller, R. 1980. "Promotion and Patronage in Equestrian Careers." *JRS* 70, 44–59.

Saller, R. 1982. *Personal Patronage Under the Early Empire.* Cambridge.

Saller, R. 1989. "Patronage and Friendship in Early Imperial Rome: Drawing the Distinction," in Wallace-Hadrill 1989b: 49–62.

Saller, R. 1991. "Progress in Early Roman Historiography?" *JRS* 81, 157–63.

Saller, R. 1994. *Patriarchy, Property and Death in the Roman Family.* Cambridge.

Saller, R., and Shaw, B. 1984. "Tombstones and Roman Family Relations in the Principate: Civilians, Soldiers and Slaves." *JRS* 74, 124–56.

Salmon, E. T. 1967. *Samnium and the Samnites.* Cambridge.

Salmon, E. T. 1969. *Roman Colonization under the Republic.* London.

Sancisi-Weerdenburg, H., van der Spek, R. J., Teitler, H. C., and Wallinga, H. T. (eds.) 1993. *De agricultura. In memoriam Pieter Willem de Neeve (1945–1990).* Amsterdam.

Sandberg, K. 2001. *Magistrates and Assemblies: A Study of Legislative Practice in Republican Rome.* Rome.

Saulnier, C. 1980. *L'armée et la guerre dans le monde étrusco-romain, VIIIᵉ–IVᵉ siècles.* Paris.

Sauron, G. 1987. "Le complexe pompéien du Champ de Mars," in *L'Urbs. Espace urbain et histoire (Ier siècle av. J.-C.–IIIe siècle ap. J.-C.)*, 457–73. Rome.

Sauron, G. 1998. *La grande fresque de la villa des Mystères à Pompéi.* Paris.

Scanlon, T. F. 1980. *The Influence of Thucydides on Sallust.* Heidelberg.

Scanlon, T. F. 1987. *Spes Frustata. A Reading of Sallust.* Heidelberg.

Scanlon, T. F. 1988. "Textual Geography in Sallust's *The War With Jugurtha.*" *Ramus* 17, 138–75.

Schäfer, P. 1997. *Judeophobia: Attitudes toward the Jews in the Ancient World.* Cambridge, MA.

Schäfer, T. 1979. "Das Siegesdenkmal vom Kapitol," in H. G. Horn and C. B. Rüger (eds.), *Die Numider: Reiter und Könige nördlich der Sahara,* 243–50. Bonn.

Scheer, T. S. 2000. *Die Gottheit und ihr Bild: Untersuchungen zur Funktion griechischer Kultbilder in Religion und Politik.* Munich.

Schefold, K., 1962. *Vergessenes Pompeii.* Bern.

Scheid, J. 1987. "Polytheism Impossible or the Empty Gods: Reasons behind a Void in the History of Roman Religion." *History and Anthropology* 3, 303–25.

Scheid, J. 1995. "*Graeco Ritu*: A Typically Roman Way of Honoring the Gods." *HSPh* 97, 15–31.

Scheid, J. 2001. *Religion et piété à Rome*[2]. Paris.

Scheid, J. 2003. *An Introduction to Roman Religion.* Edinburgh.

Scheidel, W. 1994a. *Grundpacht und Lohnarbeit in der Landwirtschaft des römischen Italien.* Frankfurt.

Scheidel, W. 1994b. "Grain Cultivation in the Villa Economy of Roman Italy." in J. Carlsen, P. Orsted, and J. Skydsgaard (eds.), *Landuse in the Roman Empire,* 159–66. Rome.

Scheidel, W. 1994c. "Libitina's Bitter Gains: Seasonal Mortality and Endemic Disease in the Ancient City of Rome." *AncSoc* 25, 151–75.

Scheidel, W. 1996. *Measuring Sex, Age and Death in the Roman Empire. Explorations in Ancient Demography.* Ann Arbor.

Scheidel, W. 1997. "Quantifying the Sources of Slaves in the Early Roman Empire." *JRS* 87, 156–69.

Scheidel, W. 1999a. "Emperors, Aristocrats and the Grim Reaper: Towards a Demographic Profile of the Roman Élite." *CQ* 49, 254–81.

Scheidel, W. 1999b. "The Slave Population of Italy: Speculation and Constraints." *Topoi* 9, 129–44.

Scheidel, W. 2001a. "Progress and Problems in Roman Demography," in Scheidel 2001c: 1–82.

Scheidel, W. 2001b. "Roman Age Structure: Evidence and Models." *JRS* 91, 1–26.

Scheidel, W. (ed.) 2001c. *Debating Roman Demography.* Leiden.

Scheidel, W. 2003. "Germs for Rome," in Edwards and Woolf 2003: 158–76.

Scheidel, W. 2004. "Human Mobility in Roman Italy, I: The Free Population." *JRS* 94, 1–26.

Schiller, A. A. 1937–8. "Custom in Classical Roman Law." *Virginia Law Review* 24, 268–82 (= Schiller 1971: 41–55).

Schiller, A. A. 1941. "Roman Interpretatio and Anglo-American Interpretation and Construction." *Virginia Law Review* 27, 733–68 (= Schiller 1971: 56–91).

Schiller, A. A. 1958. "Jurists' Law." *Columbia Law Review* 58, 1226–38 (= Schiller 1971: 148–60).

Schiller, A. A. 1971. *An American Experience in Roman Law: Writings from Publications in the United States.* Göttingen.

Schiller, A. A. 1978. *Roman Law: Mechanisms of Development.* The Hague, Paris, and New York.

Schilling, R. 1954. *La religion romaine de Vénus, depuis les origines jusqu' au temps d'Auguste.* Paris.

Schmiedt, G., and Caputo, G. 1972. *Il antico livello del mar Tirenno: testimonianze dei resti archeologici.* Florence.

Schnegg-Köhler, B. 2002. *Die augusteischen Säkularspiele*. Munich.

Schulz, F. 1946. *History of Roman Legal Science*. Oxford.

Schumpeter, J. 1951. *The Sociology of Imperialisms*. New York.

Scobie, A. 1986. "Slums, Sanitation and Mortality in the Roman World." *Klio* 68, 399–433.

Scott, R. 2005. "The Contribution of Archaeology to Early Roman History," in Raaflaub 2005.

Scullard, H. H. 1973. *Roman Politics, 220–150 BC*[2]. Oxford.

Scullard, H. H. 1981. *Festivals and Ceremonies of the Roman Republic*. London.

Seager, R. 1964. "The First Catilinarian Conspiracy." *Historia* 13, 338–47.

Seager, R. 1967. "Lex Varia de Maiestate." *Historia* 16, 37–43.

Seager, R. (ed.) 1969. *The Crisis of the Roman Republic: Studies in Political and Social History.* Cambridge and New York.

Seager, R. 1973. "*Iusta Catilinae*." *Historia* 22, 240–8.

Seager, R. 1994a. "Sulla," in Crook, Lintott, and Rawson 1994: 165–207.

Seager, R. 1994b. "The Rise of Pompey," in Crook, Lintott, and Rawson 1994: 208–28.

Seager. R. 2002. *Pompey the Great: A Political Biography*[2]. London.

Sebesta, J. 1998. "Women's Costume and Feminine Civic Morality in Augustan Rome," in M. Wyke (ed.), *Gender and the Body in the Ancient Mediterranean*, 105–17. Oxford.

Sehlmeyer, M. 1999. *Stadtrömische Ehrenstatuen der republikanischen Zeit: Historizität und Kontext von Symbolen nobilitären Standesbewusstseins*. Stuttgart.

Sehlmeyer, M. 2000. "Die kommunikative Leistung römischer Ehrenstatuen," in Braun, Haltenhoff, and Mutschler 2000: 271–84.

Seiler, F. 1986. *Die griechische Tholos: Untersuchungen zur Entwicklung, Typologie und Funktion kunstmässiger Rundbauten*. Mainz.

Sestini, A. 1984. "The Apennines and Sicily," in C. Embleton (ed.), *Geomorphology of Europe*, 341–54. London.

Shackleton Bailey, D. R. 1965–8. *Cicero's Letters to Atticus*, 7 vols. Cambridge.

Shatzman, I. 1972. "The Roman General's Authority over Booty." *Historia* 21, 177–205.

Shatzman, I. 1975. *Senatorial Wealth and Roman Politics*. Brussels.

Shaw, B. 1987. "The Age of Roman Girls at Marriage: Some Reconsiderations." *JRS* 77, 30–46.

Shaw, B. 1996. " 'Seasons of Death': Aspects of Mortality in Ancient Rome." *JRS* 86, 100–38.

Sherk, R. K. 1969. *Roman Documents from the Greek East*. Baltimore.

Sherk, R. K. 1984. *Rome and the Greek East to the Death of Augustus*. Cambridge.

Sherwin-White, A. N. 1956. "Violence in Roman Politics." *JRS* 46, 1–9.

Sherwin-White, A. N. 1973. *The Roman Citizenship*[2]. Oxford.

Sherwin-White, A. N. 1980. "Rome the Aggressor?" *JRS* 70, 177–81.

Sherwin-White, A. N. 1982. "The *Lex Repetundarum* and the Political Ideas of Gaius Gracchus." *JRS* 72, 18–31.

Sherwin-White, A. N. 1984. *Roman Foreign Policy in the East 168 B.C. to A.D. 1*. London.

Siewert, P. 1978. "Die angebliche Übernahme solonischer Gezetze in die Zwölftafeln." *Chiron* 8, 331–44.

Sigurdsson, H. 2002. "Mount Vesuvius before the Disaster," in W. F. Jashemski and F. G. Meyer (eds.), *The Natural History of Pompeii*, 29–36. Cambridge.

Simon, C. 1988. "Gelzer's 'Nobilität der römischen Republik' als 'Wendepunkt': Anmerkungen zu einem Aufsatz von R. T. Ridley." *Historia* 37, 222–40.

Simon, H. 1962. *Roms Kriege in Spanien, 154–133 v. Chr.* Frankfurt.

Sion-Jenkis, K. 2000. *Von der Republik zum Prinzipat. Ursachen für den Verfassungswechsel in Rom im historischen Denken der Antike*. Stuttgart.

Sittl, C. 1890. *Die Gebärden der Griechen und Römer*. Leipzig.

Skinner, M. 1997. "*Ego mulier*: The Construction of Male Sexuality in Catullus," in Hallett and Skinner 1997: 129–50.

Skutsch, O. 1985. *The Annals of Q. Ennius*. Oxford.

Smith, C. 2000. "Early and Archaic Rome," in Coulston and Dodge 2000: 16–41.

Smith, I. M. 1995. *The Origins of the South African War*. London.

Smith, R. E. 1957. "The *Lex Plotia Agraria* and Pompey's Spanish Veterans." *CQ* 7, 82–5.

Smith, R. E. 1958. *Service in the Post-Marian Roman Army*. Manchester.

Smith, R. E. 1960. "Pompey's Conduct in 80 and 77 B.C." *Phoenix* 14, 1–13.

Smith, R. R. R. 1981. "Greeks, Foreigners, and Roman Republican Portraits." *JRS* 71, 24–38.

Smith, R. R. R. 1988. *Hellenistic Royal Portraits*. Oxford.

Smith, R. R. R. 1991. *Hellenistic Sculpture: A Handbook*. London.

Smith, R. R. R. 1994. "Spear-Won Land at Boscoreale: On the Royal Paintings of a Roman Villa." *JRA* 7, 100–28.

Snowden, F. M. 1970. *Blacks in Antiquity: Ethiopians in the Greco-Roman Experience*. Cambridge, MA.

Snowden, F. M. 1983. *Before Color Prejudice: The Ancient View of Blacks*. Cambridge, MA.

Solin, H. 1999. "Epigrafia repubblicana. Bilancio, novità, prospettive," in *XI Congresso Internazionale di Epigrafia Greca e Latina. Roma, 18–24 settembre 1997*, 379–404. Rome.

Solin, H., and Kajava, M. 1997. "Le iscrizioni aliene del Museo Irpino." *Epigraphica* 59, 311–51.

Sordi, M. 1988. "La decadenza della repubblica e il teatro del 154 a.C." *Invigilata Lucernis* 10, 327–41.

Spann, P. O. 1977. "M. Perperna and Pompey's Spanish Expedition." *HAnt* 7, 45–62.

Spann, P. O. 1984. "Saguntum vs. Segontia." *Historia* 33, 116–19.

Spann, P. O. 1986–7. "C., L. or M. Cotta and the 'Unspeakable' Fufidius: A Note on Sulla's *Res Publica Restituta*." *CJ* 82, 306–9.

Spann, P. O. 1987. *Quintus Sertorius and the Legacy of Sulla*. Fayetteville.

Spann, P. O. 1997. "The Lauro of the Sertorian War: Where Was It?" *Athenaeum* 85, 603–11.

Spano, G. 1950. "L'arco trionfale di P. Cornelio Scipione Africano." *MAL* 8, 173–205.

Späth, T. 2001. "Erzählt erfunden: Camillus. Literarische Konstruktion und soziale Normen," in Coudry and Späth 2001: 341–412.

Spielvogel, J. (ed.) 2002. *Res publica reperta: Zur Verfassung und Gesellschaft der römischen Republik und des frühen Prinzipats, Festschrift für J. Bleicken zum 75. Geburtstag*. Stuttgart.

Spirtas, M. 1996. "A House Divided: Tragedy and Evil in Realist Theory," in B. Frankel (ed.), *Realism: Restatements and Renewal*, 385–423. London and Portland, OR.

Spivey, N. J., and Stoddart, S. K. F. 1990. *Etruscan Italy*. London.

Spurr, S. 1986. *Arable Cultivation in Roman Italy, c. 200 B.C.–c. A.D. 100*. London.

Squires, S. 1990. *Asconius: Commentaries on Five Speeches of Cicero*. Bristol.

Stadter, P. 1972. "The Structure of Livy's History." *Historia* 21, 287–307.

Stambaugh, J. 1988. *The Ancient Roman City*. Baltimore.

Stein, P. 1966. Regulae Iuris: *From Juristic Rules to Legal Maxims*. Edinburgh.

Steinby, E. M. (ed.) 1993–2000. *Lexicon Topographicum Urbis Romae*, 6 vols. Rome.

Sterling, R. W. 1974. *Macropolitics: International Security in a Global Society*. New York.

Stevenson, D. 1997. *The Outbreak of the First World War: 1914 in Perspective*. New York.

Stewart, A. 1979. *Attika: Studies in Athenian Sculpture of the Hellenistic Age*. London.

Stewart, A. 1990. *Greek Sculpture: An Exploration*. New Haven and London.

Stewart, P. 2003. *Statues in Roman Society: Representation and Response*. Oxford and New York.

Stewart, P. 2004. *Roman Art*. Oxford.

Stewart, R. 1995. "Catiline and the Crisis of 63–60 BC: The Italian Perspective." *Latomus* 54, 62–78.

Stewart, R. 1998. *Public Office in Early Rome: Ritual Procedure and Political Practice*. Ann Arbor.

Stibbe, C. M., Colonna, G., De Simone, C., and Versnel, H.S. 1980. *Lapis Satricanus: Archaeological, Epigraphical, Linguistic and Historical Aspects of the New Inscription from Satricum*. The Hague.

Stockton, D. 1979. *The Gracchi*. Oxford.

Storey, G. R. 1997. "The Population of Ancient Rome." *Antiquity* 71, 966–78.

Strauss, B. 1997. "The Art of Alliance in the Peloponnesian War," in C. D. Hamilton and P. Krentz (eds.), *Polis and Polemos: Essays on Politics, War, and History in Ancient Greece in Honor of Donald Kagan*, 127–40. Claremont.

Strocka, M. 1996. "Pompeiani, Stili." *EAA Secondo Supplemento*. 4.414–25. Rome.

Strong, D. 1973. "Roman Museums," in D. Strong (ed.), *Archaeological Theory and Practice*. London.

Stroux, J. 1926. Summum ius summa iniuria: *Ein Kapitel aus der Geschichte der interpretatio iuris*. Leipzig and Berlin.

Stroux, J. 1949. *Römische Rechtswissenschaft und Rhetorik*. Potsdam.

Suerbaum, W. (ed.) 2002. *Die archaische Literatur von den Anfängen bis Sullas Tod: die vorliterarische Periode und die Zeit von 240 bis 78 v. Chr*. Munich.

Sumi, G. 1997. "Power and Ritual: The Crowd at Clodius' Funeral." *Historia* 46, 80–102.

Sumner, G. V. 1964. "Manius or Mamercus?" *JRS* 54, 41–8.

Sumner, G. V. 1970a. "The Truth about Velleius Paterculus: Prolegomena." *HShP* 74, 257–97.

Sumner, G. V. 1970b. "The Legion and the Centuriate Organization." *JRS* 60, 67–78.

Sumner, G. V. 1973. *The Orators in Cicero's Brutus: Prosopography and Chronology*. Toronto.

Syed, Y. 2005. "Romans and Others," in Harrison 2005: 360–71.

Syme, R. 1938. "The Allegiance of Labienus." *JRS* 28, 115–25.

Syme, R. 1939. *The Roman Revolution*. Oxford.

Syme, R. 1958. *Tacitus*. 2 vols. Oxford.

Syme, R. 1963. "Ten Tribunes." *JRS* 53, 55–60.

Syme, R. 1964. *Sallust*. Berkeley and Los Angeles.

Tainter, J. A. 2000. *Global Change, History and Sustainability*, in McIntosh, Tainter, and McIntosh 2000: 331–56.

Takács, S. A. 1995. *Isis and Serapis in the Roman World*. Leiden.

Tanner, J. 2000. "Portraits, Power, and Patronage in the Late Roman Republic." *JRS* 90, 18–50.

Taplin, O. P. (ed.) 2000. *Literature in the Roman World. A New Perspective*. Oxford.

Tassinari, S. 1993. *Il vasellame bronzeo di Pompei*, 2 vols. Rome.

Tatum, W. J. 1990. "The *Lex Clodia de Censoria Notione*." *CPh* 85, 34–43.

Tatum, W. J. 1991. "The Marriage of Pompey's Son to the Daughter of Appius Claudius Pulcher." *Klio* 73, 122–9.

Tatum, W. J. 1999. *The Patrician Tribune: Publius Clodius Pulcher*. Chapel Hill.

Tatum, W. J. 2004. "Elections in Rome," *CJ* 99, 203–16.

Taylor, L. R. 1949. *Party Politics in the Age of Caesar*. Berkeley and Los Angeles.

Taylor, L. R. 1960. *The Voting Districts of the Roman Republic*. Rome.

Taylor, L. R. 1962. "Forerunners of the Gracchi." *JRS* 52, 19–27.

Taylor, L. R. 1966a. *The Roman Voting Assemblies from the Hannibalic War to the Dictatorship of Caesar*. Ann Arbor.

Taylor, L. R. 1966b. "Appian and Plutarch on Tiberius Gracchus' Last Assembly." *Athenaeum* 44, 238–50.

Taylor, L. R., and Scott, R. T. 1969. "Seating Space in the Roman Senate and the *senatores pedarii.*" *TAPhA* 100, 529–82.

Taylor, R. 2003. *Roman Builders: A Study in Architectural Process.* Cambridge and New York.

Taylor, T. 1978. "Power Politics," in T. Taylor (ed.), *Approaches and Theory in International Politics.* London and New York.

Tellegen, J. 1983. "*Oratores, Iurisprudentes* and the '*Causa Curiana*'." *RIDA* 40, 293–311.

Terrenato, N. 1998. "*Tam firmum municipium.* The Romanization of Volaterrae and its Cultural Implications." *JRS* 88, 94–114.

Terrenato, N. 2001a. "A Tale of Three Cities: The Romanization of Northern Coastal Etruria," in Keay and Terrenato 2001: 54–67.

Terrenato, N. 2001b. "The Auditorium Site in Rome and the Origins of the Villa." *JRA* 14, 5–32.

Thomas, J. A. C. 1976. *Textbook of Roman Law.* Amsterdam, New York, and Oxford.

Thommen, L. 1989. *Das Volkstribunat der späten römischen Republik.* Stuttgart.

Thompson, L. A. 1989. *Romans and Blacks.* Norman.

Thompson, W. 1988. *On Global War: Historical-Structural Approaches to World Politics.* Columbia.

Thomsen, R. 1980. *King Servius Tullius: A Historical Synthesis.* Copenhagen.

Thornton, A. P. 1965. *Doctrines of Imperialism.* New York.

Thünen, J. H. von. 1966. *Isolated State; an English Edition of Der isolierte Staat.* Trans. C. M. Wartenberg, ed. P. Hall. Oxford and New York.

Tibiletti, G. 1953. "Le leggi *de iudiciis repetundarum* fino alla guerra sociale." *Athenaeum* 31, 5–100.

Torelli, M. 1980. "Innovazioni nelle tecniche edilizie romane tra il I sec.a.C. ed il I sec. d.C.," in *Tecnologia, economia e società nel mondo romano,* 139–61. Como.

Torelli, M. 1982. *Typology and Structure of Roman Historical Reliefs.* Ann Arbor.

Torelli, M. 1985. "Macedonia, Epiro e Magna Grecia. La pittura di età classica e protoellenistica," in *Magna Grecia, Epiro e Macedonia,* 379–98. Naples.

Torelli, M. 1986. "Tarquinia and its Emporion at Gravisca. A Case in Maritime Trade in the VIth Century B.C." *Thracia Pontica* 3, 46–53.

Torelli, M. 1988. "Paestum Romana," in *Poseidonia, Paestum,* 33–130. Taranto.

Torelli, M. 1989. "Archaic Rome between Latium and Etruria," in Walbank et al. 1989: 30–51.

Torelli, M. 1997. *Il rango, il rito e l'immagine. Alle origini della rappresentazione storica romana.* Milan.

Torelli, M. 1999. Tota Italia: *Essays in the Cultural Formation of Roman Italy.* Oxford.

Torelli, M. (ed.) 2000. *Gli Etruschi.* Milan (= Torelli 2001).

Torelli, M. (ed.) 2001. *The Etruscans.* New York (= Torelli 2000).

Torelli, M. 2003. "The Frescoes of the Great Hall of the Villa at Boscoreale: Iconography and Politics," in D. Braund and C. Gill (eds.), *Myth, History and Culture in Republican Rome. Studies in Honour of T.P. Wiseman,* 217–56. Exeter.

Torelli, M. 2004. "*Atrium Minervae.* Simbologia di un monumento e cerimonialità del congiarium." *ZRGG* 1 (2004) in press.

Toynbee, A. 1965. *Hannibal's Legacy. The Hannibalic War's Effects on Roman Life.* 2 vols. Oxford.

Toynbee, J. M. C. 1951. *Some Notes on Artists in the Roman World.* Brussels.

Toynbee, J. M. C. 1971. *Death and Burial in the Roman World.* Ithaca, NY.

Toynbee, J. M. C. 1978. *Roman Historical Portraits.* Ithaca, NY.

Treggiari, S. 1969. *Roman Freedmen During the Late Republic.* Oxford.

Treggiari, S. 1991. *Roman Marriage:* Iusti Coniuges *from the Time of Cicero to the Time of Ulpian.* Oxford and New York.

Twyman, B. L. 1976. "The Date of Sulla's Abdication and the Chronology of the First Book of Appian's *Civil Wars.*" *Athenaeum* 54, 77–97, 271–95.

Twyman, B. L. 1979. "The Date of Pompeius Magnus' First Triumph," in C. Deroux (ed.), *Studies in Latin Literature and Roman History,* 1.174–208. Brussels.

Tybout, R. 1989. Aedificiorum figurae. *Untersuchungen zu den Architekturdarstellungen des frühen zweiten Stils.* Amsterdam.

Tybout, R. 2001. "Roman Wall Painting and Social Significance." *JRA* 14, 33–56.

Udell, J. 2004. "The Pyramid of Gaius Cestius: A New Look at its Patron and Symbolic Function," an unpublished talk presented to the annual meeting of the Archaeological Institute of America. San Francisco.

Ungern-Sternberg, J. von 1970. *Untersuchungen zum spätrepublikanischen Notstandsrecht: Senatus consultum ultimum und hostis-Erklärung.* Munich.

Ungern-Sternberg, J. von 1982. "Weltreich und Krise: Äussere Bedingungen für den Niedergang der römischen Republik." *MH* 39, 254–71.

Ungern-Sternberg, J. von 1986. "The End of the Conflict of the Orders," in Raaflaub 1986: 353–77.

Ungern-Sternberg, J. von 1988. "Überlegungen zur frühen römischen Überlieferung im Lichte der Oral-Tradition-Forschung," in Ungern-Sternberg and Reinau 1988: 237–65.

Ungern-Sternberg, J. von 1990. "Die Wahrnehmung des 'Ständekampfes' in der römischen Geschichtsschreibung," in Eder 1990: 92–102.

Ungern-Sternberg, J. von 1993. "Romulus-Bilder: Die Begründung der Republik im Mythos," in Graf 1993: 88–108. Stuttgart.

Ungern-Sternberg, J. von 1998. "Die Legitimitätskrise der römischen Republik." *HZ* 266, 607–24.

Ungern-Sternberg, J. von, and Reinau, H. J. (eds.) 1988. *Vergangenheit in mündlicher Überlieferung.* Stuttgart.

Vaahtera, J. 2001. *Roman Augural Lore in Greek Historiography: A Study of the Theory and Terminology.* Stuttgart.

Valgiglio, E. 1975. "L'autobiografia di Silla nelle biografie di Plutarco." *StudUrb(B)* 49, 245–81.

Van Andringa, W. 2002. *La religion en Gaule romaine: Piété et politique (Ier-IIIe siècle apr. J.-C.).* Paris.

Vanderbroeck, P. 1987. *Popular Leadership and Collective Behaviour in the Late Roman Republic (ca. 80–50 BC).* Amsterdam.

van der Leeuw, S. E. 2000. "Land Degradation as Socio-Cultural Process," in McIntosh, Tainter, and McIntosh 2000: 357–83.

van der Mersch, C. 2001. "Aux sources du vin romain, dans le Latium et la Campania à l'époque médio-républicaine." *Ostraka* 10, 157–206.

Vanggaard, J. H. 1988. *The Flamen: A Study in the History and Sociology of Roman Religion.* Copenhagen.

Van Ooteghem, J. 1954. *Pompée le Grand, bâtisseur d'empire.* Brussels.

Van Ooteghem, J. 1959. *Lucius Licinius Lucullus.* Brussels.

Van Ooteghem, J. 1964. *Caius Marius.* Namur.

Van Ooteghem, J. 1967. *Les Caecilii Metelli de la république.* Namur.

Vansina, J. 1985. *Oral Tradition as History.* Madison.

van Straten, F. T. 1981. "Gifts for the Gods," in H. S. Versnel (ed.), *Faith, Hope and Worship: Aspects of Religious Mentality in the Ancient World*, 65–151. Leiden.

van Wees, H. (ed.) 2000. *War and Violence in Ancient Greece*. London.

Vasaly, A. 1993. *Representations: Images of the World in Ciceronian Oratory*. Berkeley, Los Angeles, and London.

Vaughn, J. W. 1985. "Law and Rhetoric in the *Causa Curiana*." *ClAnt* 4, 208–2.

Vecchio, G., Albore Livadie, C., and Castaldo, N. 2002. *Nola. Quattro mila anni fa. Il villaggio dell'età del Bronzo antico distrutto dal Vesuvio (Catalogo della mostra)*. Nola.

Versnel, H. S. 1970. *Triumphus: An Inquiry into the Origin, Development and Meaning of the Roman Triumph*. Leiden.

Vessberg, O. 1941. *Studien zur Kunstgeschichte der römischen Republik*. Lund.

Veyne, P. 1975. "Y a-t-il eu un impérialisme romaine?" *MEFRA* 85, 793–855.

Veyne, P. 1976. *Le pain et le cirque: sociologie historique d'un pluralisme politique*. Paris.

Veyne, P. 1990. *Bread and Circuses: Historical Sociology and Political Pluralism* (abridged translation of Veyne 1976). London.

Vigourt, A. 2001. "M'. Curius Dentatus et C. Fabricius Luscinus: les grands hommes ne sont pas exceptionels," in Coudry and Späth 2001: 97–116.

Virlouvet, C. 1987. "La topographie des distributions frumentaires avant la création de la Porticus Minucia Frumentaria," in *L'Urbs: espace urbain et histoire (Ier siècle av. J.-C.–IIIe siècle ap. J.-C.)*, 175–89. Rome.

Virlouvet, C. 1994. "Les lois frumentaires d'époque républicaine," in *Le ravitaillement en blé de Rome et des centres urbains des débuts de la République jusq'au Haut Empire*, 11–29. Naples and Rome.

Vishnia, R. F. 1996. *State, Society, and Popular Leaders in Mid-Republican Rome 241–167 BC*. London and New York.

von der Mühll, F. 1910. "A. Gabinius A. f. (11)," *RE* 7.1, 424–30.

Wagenvoort, H. 1947. *Roman Dynamism: Studies in Ancient Roman Thought, Language and Custom*. Oxford.

Walbank, F. W. 1957–79. *A Historical Commentary on Polybius*. 3 vols. Oxford.

Walbank, F. W. 1964. "Polybius and the Roman State." *GRBS* 5, 239–60.

Walbank, F. W. 1972. *Polybius*. Berkeley and Los Angeles.

Walbank, F. W. 1998. "A Greek Looks at Rome: Polybius VI Revisited." *SCI* 17, 45–59.

Walbank, F. W. 2002. *Polybius, Rome and the Hellenistic World*. Cambridge.

Walbank, F. W., Astin, A. E., Frederiksen, M. W., and Ogilvie, R. M. (eds.) 1989. *The Rise of Rome to 220 B.C.* Vol. 7, Part 2 of *The Cambridge Ancient History*[2]. Cambridge.

Walker, D. S. 1958. *A Geography of Italy*. London.

Walker, S, and Higgs, P. (eds.) 2001. *Cleopatra of Egypt: From Myth to History*. Princeton.

Wallace, R. W., and Harris, E. M. (eds.) 1996. *Transitions to Empire: Essays in Greco-Roman History, 360–146 B.C., in Honor of E. Badian*. Norman.

Wallace-Hadrill, A. 1989a. "Patronage in Roman Society: From Republic to Empire," in Wallace-Hadrill 1989b: 63–87.

Wallace-Hadrill, A. (ed.) 1989b. *Patronage in Ancient Society*. London

Wallace-Hadrill, A. 1990. "Greek Knowledge, Roman Power." *PCPhS* 36, 143–81.

Wallace-Hadrill, A. 1991. "Elites and Trade in the Roman Town," in Rich and Wallace-Hadrill 1991: 241–72.

Wallace-Hadrill, A. 1994. *Houses and Society in Pompeii and Herculaneum*. Cambridge and Princeton.

Wallace-Hadrill, A. 1997. "*Mutatio Morum*: The Idea of a Cultural Revolution," in T. Habinek and A. Schiesaro (eds.), *The Roman Cultural Revolution*, 3–22. Cambridge.

Wallace-Hadrill, A. 1998. "*Horti* and Hellenization," in Cima and La Rocca 1998: 13–22.

Wallace-Hadrill, A. 2001. "Emperors and Houses in Rome," in S. Dixon (ed.), *Childhood, Class and Kin in the Roman World*, 128–43. London.

Walsh, P. G. 1961. *Livy: His Historical Aims and Methods*. Cambridge.

Walt, S. 1997. *Der Historiker C. Licinius Macer*. Stuttgart.

Walter, U. 2000. "Marcus Furius Camillus – die schattenhafte Lichtgestalt," in K.-J. Hölkeskamp and E. Stein-Hölkeskamp (eds.), *Von Romulus zu Augustus. Große Gestalten der römischen Geschichte in 25 Porträts*, 58–68. Munich.

Walter, U. 2001. "Die Botschaft des Mediums. Überlegungen zum Sinnpotential von Historiographie im Kontext der römischen Geschichtskultur zur Zeit der Republik," in Melville 2001: 241–79.

Walter, U. 2002. "Der Historiker in seiner Zeit: Ronald Syme und die Revolution des Augustus," in Spielvogel 2002: 136–52.

Walter, U. 2003. "AHN MACHT SINN. Familientradition und Familienprofil im republikanischen Rom," in K.-J. Hölkeskamp, J. Rüsen, E. Stein-Hölkeskamp, and H. Th. Grütter (eds.), *Sinn (in) der Antike. Orientierungssysteme, Leitbilder und Wertkonzepte im Altertum*, 255–78. Mainz.

Walter, U. 2004. *Memoria und res publica. Zur Geschichtskultur der römischen Republik*. Frankfurt.

Walters, J. 1997. "Invading the Roman Body: Manliness and Impenetrability in Roman Thought," in Hallett and Skinner 1997: 29–46.

Waltz, K. N. 1959. *Man, the State and War: A Theoretical Analysis*. New York.

Waltz, K. N. 1979. *Theory of International Politics*. New York.

Waltz, K. N. 1988. "The Origins of War in Neorealist Theory." *JIH* 18, 615–28.

Waltz, K. N. 2000. "Structural Realism after the Cold War." *Int. Sec.* 25, 5–41.

Ward, A. M. 1977. *Marcus Crassus and the Late Roman Republic*. Columbia.

Wardle, D. 1998. *Valerius Maximus. Memorable Deeds and Sayings. Book 1*. Oxford.

Ward-Perkins, B., Mills, N., Gadd, D., and Delano-Smith, C. 1986. "Luni and the Ager Lunensis: The Rise and Fall of a Roman Town and its Territory." *PBSR* 54, 81–146.

Warrior, V. 1996. *The Initiation of the Second Macedonian War*. Stuttgart.

Warrior, V. 2002. *Roman Religion: A Sourcebook*. Newburyport.

Watkins, O. D. 1987. "*Caesar Solus*? Senatorial Support for the Lex Gabinia." *Historia* 36, 120–1.

Watson, A. 1971. *The Law of Succession in the Later Roman Republic*. Oxford.

Watson, A. 1973. "The Law of Actions and the Development of Substantive Law in the Early Roman Republic." *Law Quarterly Review* 89, 387–92.

Watson, A. 1974. *Law Making in the Later Roman Republic*. Oxford.

Watson, A. 1975. *Rome of the XII Tables. Persons and Property*. Princeton.

Watson, A. 1987. *Roman Slave Law*. Baltimore.

Waurick, G. 1975. "Kunstraub der Römer: Untersuchungen zu seinen Anfängen anhand der Inschriften." *JRGZM* 22, 1–46.

Weber, M. 1968. *Economy and Society: An Outline of Interpretive Sociology*. G. Roth and C. Wittich (eds.). 2 vols. Berkeley.

Welch, K., and Powell, A. (eds.) 1998. *Julius Caesar as Artful Reporter: the War Commentaries as Political Instrument*. London.

Welch, K. E. 1994. "The Roman Arena in Late Republican Italy: A New Interpretation." *JRA* 7, 59–80.

Welch, K. E. 1997. "L'origine del teatro romano antico: l'adattamento della tipologia greca al contesto romano." *Annali di Architettura: Rivista del Centro Internazionale di Studi di Architettura Andrea Palladio* 9, 7–16.

Welch, K. E. 2003. "A New View of the Origins of the Roman Basilica: the Atrium Regium, the Graecostasis, and Roman Diplomacy." *JRA* 17, 5–34.

Welch, K. E. forthcoming a. *The Roman Amphitheatre from its Origins to the Colosseum.* Cambridge and New York.

Welch, K. E. forthcoming b. "*Domi militiaeque*: Roman Domestic Aesthetics and War Booty in the Republic," in Dillon and Welch forthcoming.

Wells, C. M. 1972. *The German Policy of Augustus: An Examination of the Archaeological Record.* Oxford.

Welwei, K.-W. 1996. "Caesars Diktatur, der Prinzipat des Augustus und die Fiktion der historischen Notwendigkeit." *Gymnasium* 103, 477–97.

Welwei, K.-W. 2001. "Lucius Iunius Brutus: Zur Ausgestaltung und politischen Wirkung einer Legende." *Gymnasium* 108, 123–35.

Wendt, A. 1992. "Anarchy is What States Make It: the Social Construction of Power Politics." *Int. Org.* 46, 391–425.

Weynand, R. 1935. "Marius." *RE* supplement 6, 1363–425.

Wheeler, E. L. 1979. "The Legion as Phalanx." *Chiron* 9, 303–18.

White, H. 1973. *Metahistory.* Baltimore.

White, H. 1987. *The Content of the Form.* Baltimore and London.

Whittaker, C. R. 1988. *Pastoral Economies in Classical Antiquity.* Cambridge.

Whittaker, C. R. 1990. "The Consumer City Revisited: The *Vicus* and the City." *JRA* 3, 110–17.

Whittaker, C. R. 1993a. "The Poor," in A. Giardina (ed.), *The Romans*, 272–99. Chicago.

Whittaker, C.R. 1993b. "The Poor in the City of Rome," in *Land, City and Trade in the Roman Empire*, Chapter VII, 1–25. Aldershot and Brookfield, VT.

Whittaker, C. R. 1995. "Do Theories of the Ancient City Matter?," in T. Cornell and K. Lomas (eds.), *Urban Society in Roman Italy*, 1–20. London.

Wieacker, F. 1967. "The *Causa Curiana* and Contemporary Roman Jurisprudence." *Irish Jurist* 2, 151–64.

Wieacker, F. 1969. "Über das Verhältnis der römischen Fachjurisprudenz zur griechisch-hellenistischen Theorie." *Iura* 20, 448–77.

Wiedemann, T. 1994. *Cicero and the End of the Roman Republic.* London.

Wight, M. 1978. *Power Politics.* New York.

Wilkes, J. J. 1969. *Dalmatia.* London.

Will, E. 1984. "The Succession to Alexander," in F. W. Walbank, A. E. Astin, M. W. Frederiksen, and R. M. Ogilivie (eds.), *The Hellenistic World.* Vol. 7, Part 1 of *The Cambridge Ancient History*[2], 23–61. Cambridge

Willems, P. 1878–83. *Le sénat de la république romaine: Sa composition et ses attributions.* 2 vols. Louvain and Paris.

Williams, C. 1999. *Roman Homosexuality. Ideologies of Masculinity in Classical Antiquity.* New York and Oxford.

Williams, J. H. C. 2001. *Beyond the Rubicon: Romans and Gauls in Republican Italy.* Oxford.

Williams-Thorpe, O. 1988. "Provenancing and Archaeology of Roman Millstones from the Mediterranean Area." *Journal of Archaeological Science* 15, 253–305.

Wilson, A. J. N. 1966. *Emigration from Italy in the Republican Age of Rome.* Manchester.

Wirszubski, C. 1968. *Libertas as a Political Idea at Rome during the Late Republic and Early Principate.* Cambridge.

Wiseman, T. P. 1971. *New Men in the Roman Senate 139 BC–AD 14.* Oxford.

Wiseman, T. P. 1979. *Clio's Cosmetics. Three Studies in Graeco-Roman Literature.* Leicester.

Wiseman, T. P. 1984. *Catullus and His World: A Reappraisal.* Cambridge.

Wiseman, T. P. 1985. "Competition and Co-operation," in T. P. Wiseman (ed.), *Roman Political Life 90 BC–AD 69*, 3–19. Exeter.

Wiseman, T. P. 1987a. "*Conspicui postes tectaque digna deo*: The Public Image of Aristocratic and Imperial Houses in the Late Republic and Early Empire," in *L'Urbs: Espace urbain et histoire*, 393–413. Rome (= Wiseman 1994c: 98–115).

Wiseman, T. P. 1987b. *Roman Studies, Literary and Historical.* Liverpool.

Wiseman, T. P. 1989. "La Via Annia: dogma ed ipotesi," *Athenaeum* 67, 417–26.

Wiseman, T. P. 1994a. "The Senate and the Populares, 69–60 B.C.," in Crook, Lintott and Rawson 1994: 327–67.

Wiseman, T. P. 1994b. "Caesar, Pompey and Rome, 59–50 B.C.," in Crook, Lintott, and Rawson 1994: 368–423.

Wiseman, T. P. 1994c. *Historiography and Imagination: Eight Essays on Roman Culture.* Exeter.

Wiseman, T. P. 1995. *Remus. A Roman Myth.* Cambridge.

Wiseman, T. P. 1998. *Roman Drama and Roman History.* Exeter.

Wiseman, T. P. 2000. "Liber: Myth, Drama and Ideology in Republican Rome," in Bruun 2000: 265–99.

Wiseman, T. P. 2002. "Roman History and the Ideological Vacuum," in *Classics in Progress.* Oxford and New York.

Wiseman, T. P. 2004. *The Myths of Rome.* Oxford.

Wiseman, T. P., and Gill, C. (eds.) 1993. *Lies and Fiction in the Ancient World.* Exeter.

Wissowa, G. 1912. *Religion und Kultus der Römer*[2]. Berlin.

Witzmann, P. 2000. "Kommunikative Leistungen von Weih-, Ehren- und Grabinschriften: Wertbegriffe und Wertvorstellungen in Inschriften vorsullanischer Zeit," in Braun, Haltenhoff, and Mutschler 2000: 55–87.

Wohlforth, W. C. 2001. "The Russian-Soviet Empire: A Test of Neorealism." *Rev. Int. Stud.* 27, 43–63.

Wolff, H. J. 1951. *Roman Law: An Historical Introduction.* Norman.

Wood, E. M. 1995. *Democracy Against Capitalism: Renewing Historical Materialism.* Cambridge.

Woodman, A. J. 1975. "Questions of Date, Genre, and Style in Velleius: Some Literary Answers." *CQ* 25, 272–306.

Woodman, A. J. 1977. *Velleius Paterculus: the Tiberian Narrative.* Cambridge.

Woodman, A. J. 1983. *Velleius Paterculus: the Caesarian and Augustan Narrative.* Cambridge.

Woodman, A. J. 1988. *Rhetoric in Classical Historiography.* London.

Wuilleumier, P. 1939. *Tarente: des origines à la conquête romaine.* Paris.

Wünsche, R. 1972. "Der Jüngling vom Magdalenesberg: Studien zur römischen Idealplastik," in J. A. Schmoll gen. Eisenwerth, M. Restle and H. Weiermann (eds.), *Festschrift Luitpold Dussler*, 45–80. Munich.

Yakobson, A. 1992. "*Petitio et largitio*: Popular Participation in the Centuriate Assembly of the Late Republic." *JRS* 82, 32–52.

Yakobson, A. 1999. *Elections and Electioneering in Rome: A Study in the Political System of the Late Republic.* Stuttgart.

Yakobson, A. 2004. "The People's Voice and the Speakers' Platform: Popular Power, Persuasion and Manipulation in the Roman Forum." *SCI* 23, 201–12.

Yavetz, Z. 1958. "The Living Conditions of the Urban Plebs in Republican Rome." *Latomus* 17, 500–17.

Yavetz, Z. 1969. *Plebs and Princeps*. Oxford.

Yavetz, Z. 1983. *Julius Caesar and his Public Image*. Ithaca, NY.

Yntema, D. 1993. *In Search of an Ancient Countryside: The Amsterdam Free University Field Survey at Oria, Province of Brindisi, South Italy (1981–1983)*. Amsterdam.

Zanker, P. 1974. *Klassizistische Statuen: Studien zur Veränderung des Kunstgeschmacks in der römische Kaiserzeit*. Mainz.

Zanker, P. 1975. "Grabreliefs römischer Freigelassener." *JDAI* 90, 267–315.

Zanker, P. 1976a. "Zur Rezeption des hellenistischen Individualporträts in Rom und in den italischen Städten," in Zanker 1976b: 581–605.

Zanker, P. (ed.) 1976b. *Hellenismus in Mittelitalien: Kolloquium in Göttingen vom 5. bis 9. Juni 1974*. 2 vols. Göttingen.

Zanker. P. 1979. "Die Villa als Vorbild des späten pompejanischen Wohngeschmacks." *JDAI* 94, 460–523.

Zanker, P. 1988. *The Power of Images in the Age of Augustus*. Trans. A. Shapiro. Ann Arbor.

Zanker, P. 1992. "Bürgerliche Selbstdarstellung am Grab im römischen Kaiserreich," in H.-J. Schalles and H. von Hesberg (eds.), *Die römische Stadt im 2 Jh. N. Chr*, 339–58. Cologne and Bonn.

Zanker, P. 1995. "Individuum und Typus. Zur Bedeutung des realistischen Individualporträts der späten Republik." *AA* 110, 473–81.

Zanker, P. 1998. *Pompeii, Public and Private Life*. Trans. D. L. Schneider. Cambridge, MA.

Zennari, J. 1956. *I Vercelli dei Celti nella Valle Padana e l'invasione Cimbrica della Venezia*. Cremona.

Zennari, J. 1958. *La battaglia dei Vercelli o dei Campi Raudii (101 a.C.)*. Cremona.

Zevi, F. 1976. "Alatri," in Zanker 1976b: 1.84–96.

Zhmodikov, A. 2000. "Roman Republican Heavy Infantrymen in Battle (IV–II Centuries BC)." *Historia* 49, 67–78.

Zimmer, G. 1982. *Römische Berufsdarstellungen*. Berlin.

Ziolkowski, A. 1986. "The Plundering of Epirus in 167 BC: Economic Considerations." *PBSR* 54, 69–80.

Ziolkowski, A. 1992. *The Temples of Mid-Republican Rome and their Historical and Topographical Context*. Rome.

Ziolkowski, A. 1993. "*Urbs direpta*, or How the Romans Sacked Cities," in Rich and Shipley 1993: 69–91.

Index

Made in the USA
San Bernardino, CA
29 December 2018